The Corsini Encyclopedia of Psychology and Behavioral Science
Third Edition
VOLUME 4

Co-Editors

W. EDWARD CRAIGHEAD
University of Colorado
Boulder, CO

CHARLES B. NEMEROFF
Emory University School of Medicine
Atlanta, GA

Editorial Board

JOHN WILEY & SONS
New York • Chichester • Weinheim • Brisbane • Singapore • Toronto

ISBN 0-471-24096-6 (Volume 1)
ISBN 0-471-24097-4 (Volume 2)
ISBN 0-471-24098-2 (Volume 3)
ISBN 0-471-24099-0 (Volume 4)
ISBN 0-471-23949-6 (Four-volume set)

Printed in the United States of America
10 9 8 7 6 5 4 3 2 1

Preface

This revision of Raymond J. Corsini's successful *Encyclopedia of Psychology* is based on the need to update and expand the previous edition. Because of the advances in behavioral science and the relationship of those advances to psychology, this edition has been renamed to reflect the inclusion of those advances.

The major purpose of these volumes is to make the current knowledge in psychology and behavioral science available to the community at large. It is hoped that they will constitute a concise and handy reference for individuals interested in these topics. Each entry is designed to inform the reader on its particular topic; of necessity, however, an entry in an encyclopedia can be only a succinct summary of that topic. Cross-references are provided for the entries so that the reader can easily make his or her way to related topics for more detail.

In order to keep the encyclopedia to four volumes and still be inclusive of contemporary topics, several now-outdated topics were dropped from the prior edition. We updated about two-thirds of the prior edition, and replaced the remaining one-third with new topics. We have sought to keep the international flavor that Corsini had employed in the original encyclopedia; thus, we selected our contributors from an international list of scholars on the chosen topics.

Coordinating a publication of this magnitude is a formidable task, particularly when undertaken within the framework of one's regular job. Thus, we are extremely appreciative of those who have been so helpful in making this project possible. We are deeply grateful to the more than 1,000 authors who contributed to this encyclopedia; without them, these volumes would not have been. Our greatest appreciation is expressed to Alinne Barrera, Benjamin Page, and Fiona Vajk, who have served as managing editors for this project. We also express our gratitude to Nancy Grabowski (administrative assistant to W. Edward Craighead), who provided necessary support to the editors and managing editors. It is hard to imagine a better or more efficient working team than Kelly Franklin and Jennifer Simon at John Wiley & Sons. Even though many of us involved in this project have experienced numerous, and at times unbelievable, life events during the development and production of these volumes, the project has been brought to a successful and timely completion. We are happy and grateful to have been surrounded by such a fine group of wonderful and dedicated individuals.

In the final analysis, production of these volumes has allowed us to continue a warm friendship and professional collaboration begun about 15 years ago at Duke University Medical Center—a friendship and collaboration that have survived the selection, coordination, and editing of the contributions of well over 1,000 authors on more than 1,200 topics. We have treated patients together; we have conducted collaborative research; we have published together; we have presented together at professional meetings; and we have laughed and cried together in good times and bad. It has been a satisfying experience to edit these volumes together. We trust they will be useful to you, the reader.

W. Edward Craighead, PhD
Boulder, Colorado

Charles B. Nemeroff, MD, PhD
Atlanta, Georgia

Contributors List

NORMAN ABELES
Michigan State University

L. Y. ABRAMSON
University of Wisconsin

ROSEMARY C. ADAM-TEREM
Kapiolani Medical Center, Honolulu, HI

HOWARD S. ADELMAN
University of California, Los Angeles

BERNARD W. AGRANOFF
University of Michigan

LEWIS R. AIKEN
Pepperdine University

ICEK AJZEN
University of Massachusetts

GEORGE W. ALBEE
Florida Mental Health Institute

LYNN E. ALDEN
University of British Columbia

THERON ALEXANDER
Temple University

MARY J. ALLEN
California State College

LAUREN B. ALLOY
Temple University

G. HUGH ALLRED
Brigham Young University

NANCY S. ANDERSON
Emory School of Medicine

JOHN L. ADREASSI
City University of New York-Baruch College

J. E. ALCOCK
The Australian National University

L. B. AMES

RICHARD S. ANDRULIS
Andrulis Associates, West Chester, PA

HYMIE ANISMAN
Carleton University, Ottawa

H. L. ANSBACHER

RUBEN ARDILA
National University of Colombia

E. Ö. ARNARSON
University of Iceland

MARK ARONOFF
State University of New York, Albany

RICHARD M. ASHBROOK
Capital University

J. WILLIAM ASHER
Purdue University

J. A. ASTIN
University of Maryland School of Medicine

CAROL SHAW AUSTAD

ROBERT M. DAVISON AVILES
Bradley University

K. W. BACK

ALBERT BANDURA
Stanford University

DAVID H. BARLOW
Boston University

AUGUSTINE BARÓN, JR.
University of Texas, Austin

DANIEL BAR-TAL
Tel Aviv University

S. HOWARD BARTLEY
Memphis State University

VALENTINA BASSAREO
University of Cagliari, Italy

B. M. BAUGHAN
University of Colorado, Boulder

ANDREW SLATER BAUM
University of Pittsburgh Cancer Institute

ALAN A. BAUMEISTER
Louisiana State University

RAMÓN BAYÉS SOPENA
Universidad Autónoma de Barcelona

STEVEN BEACH
University of Georgia

AARON T. BECK
Beck Institute for Cognitive Therapy and Research

GARY S. BELKIN
Brown University

ALAN S. BELLACK
University of Maryland

JOEL B. BENNETT
Texas Christian University

THOMAS S. BENNETT
Brain Inquiry Recovery Program, Fort Collins, CO

HEATHER A. E. BENSON
University of Manitoba

P. G. BENSON
New Mexico State University

SHERI A. BERENBAUM
Southern Illinois University

S. BERENTSEN

LEONARD BERGER
Clemson University

JOANNE BERGER-SWEENEY
Wellesly College

GREGORY S. BERNS
Emory University

G. G. BERNTSON
Ohio State University

MICHAEL D. BERZONSKY
State University of New York, Cortland

SIDNEY W. BIJOU
University of Nevada

AIDA BILALBEGOVIC
Tufts University, Medford, MA

JEFFREY R. BINDER
Medical College Of Wisconsin

JERRY M. BINDER
Behavioral Health Consultant, Corona Del Mar

NIELS BIRMBAUER
University of Tübingen, Germany

D. W. BLACK
University of Iowa

THEODORE H. BLAU

BERNARD L. BLOOM
University of Colorado

MILTON S. BLOOMBAUM
Southern Oregon University

JODI L. BODDY
Simon Fraser University, British Columbia

C. ALAN BONEAU
George Mason University

EDWARD S. BORDIN
University of Michigan

EDGAR F. BORGATTA
University of Washington

P. BOSE
University of Florida

DALE E. BOWEN
Psychological Associates, Grand Junction, CO

A. D. BRANSTETTER

C. REGINALD BRASINGTON
University of South Carolina

MARGARET BRENMAN-GIBSON
Harvard Medical School

RONAL BRENNER
St. John's Episcopal Hospital, Far Rockaway, NY

WARRICK J. BREWER
The University of Melbourne & Mental Health Research Institute of Victoria

SARA K. BRIDGES
Humboldt State University

ARTHUR P. BRIEF
Tulane University

R. W. BRISLIN
University of Hawaii

GILBERTO N. O. BRITO
Instituto Fernendes Figueira, Brazil

DONALD E. BROADBENT
University of Oxford

J. D. BROOKE
Northwestern University

FREDERICK GRAMM BROWN
Iowa State University

ROBERT TINDALL BROWN
University of North Carolina, Wilmington

SHELDON S. BROWN
North Shore Community College

J. BROZEK

MARTIN BRÜNE
Ruhr University, Germany

B. R. BUGELSKI
State University of New York, Buffalo

GRAHAM D. BURROWS
University of Melbourne

JAMES M. BUTCHER
University of Minnesota, Minneaplois

ANN B. BUTLER
George Mason University

REBECCA M. BUTZ
Tulane University

J. T. CACIOPPO
University of Chicago

SHAWN P. CAHILL
University of Pennsylvania

JOHN B. CAMPBELL
Franklin & Marshall College

N. A. CAMPBELL
Brown University

TYRONE D. CANNON
University of California, Los Angeles

SAMUEL S. CARDONE
Illinois Department of Mental Health, Chicago

BERNARDO J. CARDUCCI
Shyness Research Institute, Indiana University Southeast

MARK CARICH
Adler School of Professional Psychology

PETER A. CARICH
University of Missouri

JOHN G. CARLSON
University of Hawaii, Honolulu

J. DOUGLAS CARROLL
Rutgers University

GIOVANNI CASINI
Tuscia University, Italy

T. CASOLI
I.N.R.C.A., Italy

LOUIS G. CASTONGUAY
Pennsylvania State University

CARL ANDREW CASTRO
Walter Reed Army Institute of Research

FAIRFID M. CAUDLE
College of Staten Island

JOSEPH R. CAUTELA

STEPHEN J. CECI
Cornell University

JAE-HO CHA
Seoul National University

PAUL F. CHAPMAN
University of Minnesota, Minneaplois

U. CHARPA
Cologne University, Germany

GORDON J. CHELUNE
The Cleveland Clinic Foundation

GLYN CHIDLOW
University of Oxford

IRVIN L. CHILD
Yale University

MARGARET M. CLIFFORD
University of Iowa

RICHARD WELTON COAN
Retired, University of Arizona

KIMBERLY PEELE COCKERHAM
Allegheny Ophthalmic and Orbital Associates, Pittsburgh

MARK S. COE
DePaul University

NORMAN J. COHEN
Baylor State University

P. COHEN-KETTENIS
Utrecht University, The Netherlands

RAYMOND J. COLELLO
Virginia Commonwealth University

GARY R. COLLINS
Trinity Evangelical Divinity School

MARY BETH CONNOLLY
University of Pennsylvania

M. J. CONSTANTINO
Pennsylvania State University

GERALD COOKE
Plymouth Meeting, PA

JEREMY D. COPLAND
Columbia University College of Physicians and Surgeons

STANLEY COREN
University of British Columbia

GERALD F. COREY
California State University, Fullerton

JOHN F. CORSO
State University of New York, Cortland

ERMINIO COSTA
University of Illinois, Chicago

JOSEPH T. COYLE
Harvard University

BENJAMIN H. CRAIGHEAD
Medical College of Virginia

W. EDWARD CRAIGHEAD
University of Colorado

PAUL CRITS-CHRISTOPH
University of Pennsylvania

ARNOLD E. DAHLKE
Los Angeles, CA

JOHN G. DARLEY
University of Minnesota, Minneaplois

WILLIAM S. DAVIDSON II
Michigan State University

EDWARD L. DECI
University of Rochester

CRISTINA MARTA DEL-BEN
Universidade de São Paulo, Brazil

H. A. DEMAREE
Kessler Medical Rehabilitation Research and Education Corporation

FLORENCE L. DENMARK
Pace University, New York

M. RAY DENNY
Michigan State University

DONALD R. DENVER
Quebec, Montreal, Canada

NORMAN K. DENZIN
University of Illinois, Urbana

SARAH E. DEROSSETT

FRANCINE DEUTSCH
San Diego State University

DAVID L. DEVRIES
Kaplan DeVries Institute

DONALD ALLEN DEWSBURY
University of Florida

ESTHER E. DIAMOND

MILTON DIAMOND
University of Hawaii, Honolulu

R. DIAZ-GUERRERO
University of Mexico

MANFRED DIEHL
University of Colorado

VOLKER DIETZ
University Hospital Balgrist, Zurich

R. DILLON

RAYMOND DINGLEDINE
Emory University School of Medicine

JOHN W. DONAHOE
University of Massachusetts

NICK DONNELLY
University of Southampton, UK

SYLVAIN DORÉ
Johns Hopkins University

MICHAEL G. DOW
University of South Florida

PETER W. DOWRICK
University of Hawaii, Manoa

JURIS G. DRAGUNS
Pennsylvania State University

CLIFFORD J. DREW
University of Utah

D. A. DROSSMAN
University of North Carolina

PHILIP H. DUBOIS

HUBERT C. J. DUIJKER
University of Amsterdam

BRUCE R. DUNN
The University of West Florida

M. O. A. DUROJAIYE
University of Lagos, Nigeria

TERRY M. DWYER
University of Mississippi School of Medicine

G. D'YDEWALLE
University of Leuven, Belgium

BARRY A. EDELSTEIN
West Virginia University

THOMAS E. EDGAR
Idaho State University

WILLIAM E. EDMONSTON, JR.
Colgate University

C. L. EHLERS
University of California, San Diego

HOWARD EICHENBAUM
Boston University

ROGER E. ENFIELD
West Central Georgia Regional Hospital, Columbus, GA

JOHN WILLIAM ENGEL
University of Hawaii, Honolulu

FRANZ R. EPTING
University of Florida

ANGELICA ESCALONA
Nova Southeastern University

DAVID RICHARD EVANS
University of Western Ontario

FREDERICK J. EVANS
Reading Hospital

ROBERT B. EWEN
Miami, FL

CORA E. EZZELL
Medical University of South Carolina

CLARA C. FAURA-GINER
Universidad Miguel Hernandez, Spain

HERMAN FEIFEL
Veterans Administration Outpatient Clinic, Los Angeles

LAURIE B. FELDMAN
State University of New York, Albany

EVA DREIKURS FERGUSON
Southern Illinois University

JOSEPH R. FERRARI
Depaul University

MICHAEL A. FIEDLER
University of Alabama, Birmingham

FRANK W. FINGER
University of Virginia

S. FINGER
Washington University

HAROLD KENNETH FINK
Honolulu, HI

NORMAN J. FINKEL
Georgetown University

CHET H. FISCHER
Radford University

DAVID A. FISHBAIN
University of Miami

DENNIS F. FISHER
U.S. Army Human Engineering Laboratory

DOUGLAS A. FITTS
University of Washington

REIKO MAKI FITZSIMONDS
Yale School of Medicine

DEBRA A. FLEISCHMAN
Rush-Presbyterian St. Luke's Medical Center

EDNA B. FOA
University of Pennsylvania

JAMES L. FOBES
Army Research Institute for the Behavioral Sciences

JOHN P. FOREYT
Baylor College of Medicine

BARBARA L. FORISHA-KOVACH
University of Michigan

GEORGE FOURIEZOS
University of Ottawa

MARCI GITTES FOX
Beck Institute for Cognitive Therapy and Research

NATHAN A. FOX
University of Maryland

J. FRANKENHEIM
National Institutes of Health

CALVIN J. FREDERICK
University of California, Los Angeles

MATS FREDERICKSON
Uppsala University, Sweden

C. R. FREEMAN
McGill University

W. O. FRIESEN
University of Virginia

ROBERT H. FRIIS
California State University, Long Beach

KARL J. FRISTON
Institute of Neurology, UK

BENJAMIN FRUCHTER
University of Texas, Austin

ISAO FUKUNISHI
Tokyo Institute of Psychiatry

TOMAS FURMARK
Uppsala University, Sweden

PAUL A. GADE
U. S. Army Research Institute

SOL L. GARFIELD
Washington University

G. GASKELL
University of York, UK

STEVEN J. GARLOW
Emory School of Medicine

TIMOTHY L. GASPERONI
University of California, Los Angeles

JEAN S. GEARON
University of Maryland

NORI GEARY
Weill Medical College of Cornell University

K. F. GEISINGER
Le Moyne College

MARK S. GEORGE
Medical University of South Carolina

T. D. GIARGIARI
University of Colorado, Boulder

KAREN M. GIL
University of North Carolina, Chapel Hill

RITA T. GIUBILATO
Thomas Jefferson University

THOMAS A. GLASS
Honolulu, HI

WILLIAM GLASSER
The William Glasser Institute, Chatsworth, CA

J. M. GLOZMAN
Moscow University

CHARLES J. GOLDEN
Nova Southeastern University

ROBERT N. GOLDEN
University of North Carolina School of Medicine

ARNOLD P. GOLDSTEIN
Syracuse University

JEFFREY L. GOODIE
West Virginia University

G. KEN GOODRICK
University of Houston

LEONARD D. GOODSTEIN
Washington, DC

BERNARD S. GORMAN
Nassau Community College

GILBERT GOTTLIEB
University of North Carolina, Chapel Hill

DONALD L. GRANT
Roswell, CTA

J. W. GRAU
Texas A & M University

MARTIN S. GREENBERG
University of Pittsburgh

W. A. GREENE
Eastern Washington University

SHELLY F. GREENFIELD
McLean Hospital, Belmont, MA

JAMES LYNN GREENSTONE
Southwestern Academy of Crisis Interveners, Dallas

WILLIAM EDGAR GREGORY
University of the Pacific

SEBASTIAN P. GROSSMAN
University of Chicago

AMANDA J. GRUBER
McLean Hospital, Belmont, MA

ROBERT M. GUION
Bowling Green State University

LAURA GULI
University of Texas, Austin

G. GUTTMANN
University of Vienna

RUSSELL A. HABER
University of South Carolina

HAROLD V. HALL
Honolulu, HI

KATHERINE A. HALMI
Cornell University Medical Center

MARK B. HAMNER
Medical University of South Carolina

GREGORY R. HANCOCK
University of Maryland

FOREST W. HANSEN
Lake Forest College

J. M. HARPER
Brigham Young University

JOSEPH T. HART
University of Colorado

ALISHA B. HART
Kupat Holim Klalit, Tel Aviv

E. I. HARTLEY

SCOTT HARTMAN
Center for Marital and Family Studies, University of Denver

DAVID B. HATFIELD
Eastern Washington University

ELAINE HATFIELD
University of Hawaii, Manoa

ROBERT P. HAWKINS
West Virginia University

STEPHEN N. HAYNES
University of Hawaii, Manoa

N. A. HAYNIE

DONALD A. HECK
Iowa State

S. R. HEIDEMANN
Michigan State University

J. HEIMAN
University of Washington

LYNNE M. HENDERSON
The Shyness Institute, Stanford

GREGG HENRIQUES
University of Pennsylvania

P. P. HEPPNER
University of Missouri, Columbia

GREGORY M. HEREK
University of California, Davis

EDWIN L. HERR
Pennsylvania State University

ALLEN K. HESS
Auburn University

ERNEST R. HILGARD
Stanford University

JEANNE SWICKARD HOFFMAN
Honolulu, HI

RALPH E. HOFFMAN
Yale School of Medicine

CHRISTINE HOHMANN
Morgan State University

P. Y. HONG
University of Kansas

B. HOPKINS
Seattle University

RONALD R. HOLDEN
Queen's University, Ontario

DAVID L. HOLMES
The Eden Institute, Princeton

DAVID SHERIDAN HOLMES
University of Kansas

WAYNE H. HOLTZMAN
University of Texas, Austin

BURT HOPKINS
Seattle University

J. HOSKOVEC

ARTHUR C. HOUTS
University of Memphis

ROBERT H. HOWLAND
University of Pittsburgh School of Medicine

C. H. HUBER
New Mexico State University

BRADLEY E. HUITEMA
Western Michigan University

LLOYD G. HUMPHRIES
University of Illinois, Champaign

MAX L. HUTT

G. W. HYNDE
University of Georgia

JAMES ROBERT IBERG
Chicago, IL

S. S. ILARDI
University of Kansas

DANIEL R. ILGEN
Michigan State University

Y. IWAMURA
Toho University, Japan

I. JACKSON
Brown University

L. JANOSI
Exponential Biotherapies, Inc.

ARTHUR R. JENSEN
University of California, Berkeley

QICHENG JING
Chinese Academy of Sciences, Beijing

DAVID W. JOHNSON
University of Minnesota, Minneaplois

JAMES H. JOHNSON
University of Florida

ORVAL G. JOHNSON
Centennial BOCES, La Salle, CO

ROGER T. JOHNSON
University of Minnesota, Minneaplois

EVE S. JONES
Los Angeles City College

LASZLO JANOSI
Exponential Biotherapies, Inc.

JON H. KAAS
Vanderbilt University

ROBERT B. KAISER
Kaplan DeVries Institute

AKIRA KAJI
Exponential Biotherapies, Inc.

JAMES W. KALAT
North Carolina State University

P. W. KALIVAS
Medical University of South Carolina

TOMOE KANAYA
Cornell

SAUL KANE
Queens College, City University of New York

BARRY H. KANTOWITZ
Battelle Institute, Seattle

RICHARD PAUL KAPPENBERG
Hawaii Professional Psychology Group, Honolulu

WERNER KARLE
Corona Del Mar, CA

NADINE KASLOW
Emory School of Medicine

A. J. KASTIN
University of New Orleans

BOJE KATZENELSON
University of Aarhus, Denmark

TERENCE M. KEANE
Boston University

A. J. KEARNEY
Behavior Therapy Institute

E. JAMES KEHOE
University of New South Wales

TIMOTHY KEITH-LUCAS
The University of the South

SALLY KELLER
Adelphi University

THOMAS M. KELLEY
Wayne State University

CAROLIN S. KEUTZER
University of Oregon

GREGORY A. KIMBLE
Duke University

JAMES E. KING
University of Arizona

BRENDA J. KING
University of Tennessee

DANIEL N. KLEIN
State University of New York

WALTER G. KLOPFER

MAX J. KOBBERT
Hochschule for Beildende Künste, Münster

ALBERT T. KONDO
University of Houston

S. J. KORCHIN

WILLIAM J. KOROTITSCH
University of North Carolina, Greensboro

SURESH KOTAGAL
Mayo Clinic

G. KOVACS
Dalhousie University

LEONARD KRASNER
Stanford University School of Medicine

DAVID R. KRATHWOHL
Syracuse University

ALAN G. KRAUT
American Psychological Society, Washington, DC

STEFAN KRUEGER
Yale School of Medicine

STANLEY KRIPPNER
Saybrook Graduate School, San Francisco

SAMUEL E. KRUG
MetriTech, Inc., Campaign, IL

CAROL LANDAU
Brown University Division of Medicine

PHILIPPE LANDREVILLE
Laval, Sainte-Foy, Quebec

TED LANDSMAN
University of Florida

CHRISTOPH J. G. LANG
University of Erlangen-Buremberg, Germany

GEORGE M. LANGFORD
Dartmouth College

KEITH LANGLEY
University of Strasbourg, France

E. K. LANPHIER
Pennsylvania State University

V. W. LARACH
Univerdidad de Chile

DAVID G. LAVOND
University of Southern California

ARNOLD A. LAZARUS
Center for Multimodal Psychological Services, Princeton

RICHARD S. LAZARUS
University of California, Berkeley

THOMAS H. LEAHEY
Virginia Commonwealth University

ROBERT A. LEARK
Pacific Christian College

ARTHUR LERNER
Los Angeles City College

RICHARD M. LERNER
Tufts University

L. S. LEUNG
University of Western Ontario

ALLAN LEVEY
Emory University

HARRY LEVINSON
The Levinson Institute

SHARON C. LEVITON
Southwestern Academy of Crisis Interveners, Dallas

EUGENE E. LEVITT
Indiana University School of Medicine

P. M. LEWINSOHN
Oregon Research Institute, Eugene

RONALD T. LEY
State University of New York, Albany

ANDRE L'HOURS
World Health Organization, Geneva

KAREN Z. H. LI
Max Planck Institute for Human Development

SHU-CHEN LI
Max Planck Institute for Human Development

P. E. LICHTENSTEIN

CAROL SCHNEIDER LIDZ
Touro College

SCOTT O. LILIENFELD
Emory University

G. LIN
National Institutes of Health

HENRY CLAY LINDGREN
San Francisco State University

RONALD LIPPITT

MARK W. LIPSEY
Vanderbilt University

A. LLOYD

JOHN E. LOCHMAN
University of Alabama, Tuscaloosa

JOHN C. LOEHLIN
University of Texas, Austin

JANE LOEVINGER
Washington University

DONALD N. LOMBARDI
Seton Hall University

WOLF-EKKEHARD LÖNNIG
*Max Planck Institut fur
  Züchtungsforschung, Köln, Germany*

JOSEPH LOPICCOLO
University of Missouri

JEFFREY P. LORBERBAUM
Medical University of South Carolina

O. IVAR LOVAAS
University of California, Los Angeles

ROBERT E. LUBOW
Tel Aviv University

J. O. LUGO
Fullerton, CA

K. LUKATELA
Brown University

ROBERT W. LUNDIN
Wheaton, IL

DAVID T. LYKKEN
University of Minnesota, Minneapolis

BRETT V. MACFARLANE
University of Queensland

ROBIN M. MACKAR
*National Institute on Drug Abuse, Bethesda,
  MD*

S. MADHUSOODANAN
*St. John's Episcopal Hospital, Far
  Rockaway, NY*

MICHAEL P. MALONEY
Pasadena, CA

HOWARD MARKMAN
*Center for Marital and Family Studies,
  University of Denver*

RONALD R. MARTIN
West Virginia University

C. MARTINDALE
University of Maine

P. MARUFF
La Trobe University, Australia

ROBERT C. MARVIT
Honolulu, HI

MELVIN H. MARX
N. Hutchinson Island, FL

JOSEPH D. MATARAZZO
Oregon Health Sciences University

BARBARA B. MATES
City College, NY

RYAN K. MAY
The University of Memphis

FAUZIA SIMJEE MCCLURE
University of California, San Diego

BARBARA S. MCCRADY
Rutgers University

JANET L. MCDONALD
Louis State University

JENNIFER J. MCGRATH
Bowling Green State University

JOHN PAUL MCKINNEY
Michigan State University

KATHLEEN MCKINNEY
University of Wisconsin

C. M. MCCLEOD
University of Toronto

JAMES H. MCMILLAN
Virginia Commonwealth University

PATRICK MCNAMARA
Boston University

NEIL MCNAUGHTON
University of Otago, New Zealand

JANICE MCPHEE
Florida Gulf Coast University

PAUL W. MCREYNOLDS
University of Nevada

HEATHER MEGGERS
University of Missouri

RICHARD MEILI
University of Bern, Switzerland

RONALD MELZACK
McGill University, Montreal

P. F. MERENDA
University of Rhode Island

STANLEY B. MESSER
Rutgers University

CINDY M. MESTON
University of Texas, Austin

JAMIE L. METSALA
University of Maryland

ANDREW W. MEYERS
The University of Memphis

K. D. MICHEVA
Stanford University

DAVID J. MIKLOWITZ
University of Colorado

STANLEY MILGRAM

MARK W. MILLER
Boston University

NEAL ELGAR MILLER
Yale University

RALPH R. MILLER
State University of New York, Binghamton

THEODORE MILLON
University of Miami

HENRYK MISIAK
Fordham University

AKIRA MIYAKE
University of Colorado

TAE-IM MOON

STEWART MOORE
University of Windsor, Ontario

JAMES A. MORONE
Brown University

DANIEL G. MORROW
University of New Hampshire

F. MUELLER
*Forschungszentrum Juelich GmbH,
  Germany*

K. L. MULLER
Rutgers University

R. MURISON
University of Bergen, Norway

FRANK B. MURRAY
University of Delaware

ANNE MYERS
St. Jerome Convent, Philadelphia

FRANCIS A. NEELON
Duke University

ROBERT A. NEIMEYER
University of Memphis

J. NEISEWANDER
Arizona State University

A. NELSON

ROSEMARY O. NELSON-GRAY
University of North Carolina, Greensboro

CORY F. NEWMAN

DAVID G. NICKINOVICH
University of Washington

PHILIP T. NINAN
Emory School of Medicine

J. T. NOGA
Emory University

TREVOR R. NORMAN
University of Melbourne

M. S. NYSTUL

WILLIAM H. O'BRIEN
Bowling Green State University

WALTER EDWARD O'CONNELL
Natural High Center, Bastrop, TX

W. O'DONOHUE

K. DANIEL O'LEARY
State University of New York, Stony Brook

G. A. OLSON
University of New Orleans

R. D. OLSON
University of New Orleans

MARLENE OSCAR-BERMAN
Boston University

THOMAS M. OSTROM
Ohio State University

J. BRUCE OVERMIER
University of Bergen, Norway

B. D. OZAKI
Honolulu Waldorf School

DANIEL J. OZER
University of California, Riverside

K. PACAK
National Institutes of Health

DAVID C. PALMER
Smith College

EDWARD L. PALMER
Davidson College

LOREN D. PANKRATZ
Oregon Health Sciences University

C. PANTELIS
University of Melbourne, Australia

WILLIAM M. PARDRIDGE
*University of California School of Medicine,
    Los Angeles*

ALAN J. PARKIN
University of Sussex, England

E. J. PARKINS
Nottingham University, England

H. MCILVANIE PARSONS
*Human Resources Research Organization,
    Alexandria, VA*

R. PATUZZI

PAUL PAULI
University of Tübingen, Germany

V. PEČJAK

PAUL PEDERSON
University of Alabama, Birmingham

T. M. PENIX

HAROLD BRENNER PEPINSKY
Ohio State University

KATHERINE L. PETERS
University of Alberta

C. PETERSON
University of Michigan

DONALD R. PETERSON
Rutgers University

CHARLES S. PEYSER
The University of the South

E. JERRY PHARES
Kansas State University

D. PHILIP
University of Florida

JESSICA M. PIERCE
Boston University

AARON L. PINCUS
Pennsylvania State University

LUIGI PIZZAMIGLIO
Universita Degli Studi di Roma, Italy

J. POIRIER
University of Washington

R. E. POLAND
University of California, Los Angeles

H. G. POPE, JR.
McLean Hospital, Belmont, MA

R. M. POST
National Institute of Mental Health

BRUNO POUCET
*Centre National de la Recherche
    Scientifique, France*

A. R. PRATKANIS
University of California, Santa Cruz

ANN B. PRATT
Capital University, Columbus, OH

ROBERT ALAN PRENTKY
Justice Resource Institute, Bridgewater, MA

AINA PUCE
*Swinburne University of Technology,
    Australia*

S. J. QUALLS
University of Colorado

MARK QUIGG
University of Virginia

KAREN S. QUIGLEY
Pennsylvania State University

RÉMI QUIRION
Douglas Hospital Research Center, Canada

ALBERT ISRAEL RABIN
Michigan State University

M. K. RAINA
Sri Aurobindo Marg, India

K. RAMAKRISHNA RAO
Duke University

U. RAO
University of California, Los Angeles

J. RAPPAPORT
University of Illinois, Chicago

MARK D. RAPPORT
University of Central Florida

RICHARD L. RAPSON
University of Hawaii, Manoa

NATHANIEL J. RASKIN
Northwestern University Medical School

R. L. RASMUSSON
Allegheny University of Health Sciences

A. RAVIV
Tel Aviv University

W. J. RAY
Pennsylvania State University

HERB REICH

ANTHONY H. REINHARDT-RUTLAND
University of Ulster

J. M. REINISCH
Indiana University

DANIEL REISBERG
Reed College

MAURICE REUCHLIN
*Institute Nationale D'Orientation
    Professionale, Paris*

MARY E. REUDER

G. R. REYES

CECIL R. REYNOLDS
Texas A&M University

GEORGE F. RHOADES, JR.
Ola Hou Clinic, Aiea, HI

ALEXANDER RICH
University of South Florida

DAVID C. S. RICHARD
Southwest Missouri State University

EDWARD J. RICKERT
University of Alabama, Birmingham

L. RIES

Y. RINGEL
University of North Carolina

ARTHUR J. RIOPELLE
Louisiana State University

CHRISTIE RIZZO
New York State Psychiatric Institute

DONALD ROBBINS
Fordham University

GARY JEROME ROBERTSON
Wide Range, Inc., Tampa

GEORGE H. ROBINSON
University of North Alabama

RONALD ROESCH
Simon Fraser University, British Columbia

MICHAEL J. ROHRBAUGH
University of Arizona

STEVEN PAUL ROOSE
Columbia University

R. ROSENBERG
Sleep Disorders Center, Evanston, IL

ROBERT ROSENTHAL
University of California, Riverside

SAUL ROSENZWEIG
Washington University

HELEN WARREN ROSS
San Diego State University

WILLIAM H. ROSS
University of Wisconsin

J. S. ROSSI
University of Rhode Island

B. O. ROTHBAUM
Emory University

DONALD K. ROUTH
University of Miami

PETER ROY-BYRNE
Harborview Medical Center, Seattle

MARK A. RUIZ
Pennsylvania State University

ROGER WOLCOTT RUSSELL
University of California, Irvine

J. J. RYAN
Central Missouri State University

DEBORAH SADOWSKI
Tufts University

W. S. SAHAKIAN

WILLIAM SAMUEL
University of California, San Diego

T. SAND
Norwegian University of Science and Technology

WILLIAM C. SANDERSON
Rutgers University

JEROME SANES
Brown University

LAWRENCE J. SANNA
Washington State University

C. SANTERRE
University of Arizona

JOHN WYNNE SANTROCK
University of Texas-Dallas, Richardson

EDWARD P. SARAFINO
The College of New Jersey, Ewing

WILLIAM IRVIN SAUSER, JR.
Auburn University

ALICE D. SCHEUER
University of Hawaii, Honolulu

K. SCHMIDTKE
University of Frieberg, Germany

DAVID A SCHULDBERG
University of Montana

ALEXANDER JULIAN SCHUT
Pennsylvania State University

JULIE B. SCHWEITZER
Emory School of Medicine

D. L. SEGAL
University of Colorado

SAUL B. SELLS
Texas Christian University

J. SHANTEAU

D. H. SHAPIRO
University of California, Irvine

KENNETH JOEL SHAPIRO
Psychologists for the Ethical Treatment of Animals

S. L. SHAPIRO
University of Arizona

J. A. SHARPE
University of Toronto

Y. SHAULY
Allegheny University of Health Sciences

ROBERT A. SHAW
Brown University

GLENN D. SHEAN
College of William and Mary

STEVEN D. SHERRETS
Maine Head Trauma Center, Bangor

EDWIN S. SHNEIDMAN
University of California School of Medicine, Los Angeles

VARDA SHOHAM
University of Arizona, Tucson

BERNARD H. SHULMAN
Northwestern University Medical School

JULIE A. SHUMACHER
State University of New York, Stony Brook

M. SIGUAN
Barcelona, Spain

ELSA A. SIIPOLA
Smith College

ALCINO J. SILVA
University of California, Los Angeles

HIRSCH LAZAAR SILVERMAN

L. SILVERN
University of Colorado, Boulder

HERBERT A. SIMON
Carnegie Mellon University

ALAN SIMPKINS
University of Hawaii, Honolulu

M. BREWSTER SMITH
University of California, Santa Cruz

WILLIAM PAUL SMITH
Vanderbilt University

DAWN SOMMER
University of Texas, Austin

SUBHASH R. SONNAD
Western Michigan University

PETER W. SORRENSEN
University of Minnesota, St. Paul

JANET TAYLOR SPENCE
University of Texas, Austin

DANTE S. SPETTER
New England Medical Center, Boston

ROBERT P. SPRAFKIN
Veterans Administration Medical Center, Syracuse

SCOTT STANLEY
Center for Marital and Family Studies, University of Denver

KEVIN D. STARK
University of Texas, Austin

STEPHEN STARK
University of Illinois, Champaign

TIMOTHY STEENBERGH
The University of Memphis

ROBERT A. STEER
University of Medicine and Dentistry of New Jersey

A. STEIGER
Max Plank Institute of Psychiatry, Germany

ROBERT M. STELMACK
University of Ottawa

ROBERT H. STENSRUD
University of Northern Iowa

R. J. STERNBERG
Yale University

GERALD L. STONE
University of Iowa

WILLIAM S. STONE
Harvard University

HUGH A. STORROW
University of Kentucky

EZRA STOTLAND
University of Washington

GEORGE STRICKER
Adelphi University

RICHARD B. STUART
Weight Watchers International

D. I. SUCHMAN
University of Florida

ARTHUR SULLIVAN
Memorial University, Newfoundland

S. W. SUMERALL
William Jewell College

NORMAN D. SUNDBERG
University of Oregon

J. T. SUPER

ROBERT J. SUTHERLAND
University of New Mexico

H. A. SWADLOW
Brown University

SUSAN SWEARER
University of Texas, Austin

JULIAN I. TABER
*Veterans Administration Medical Center,
   Reno*

ANA TABOADA
University of Maryland

YASUMASA TANAKA
Gakushuin University, Tokyo

JAMES T. TEDESCHI
State University of New York

J. A. TESTA
University of Oklahoma

ALEXANDER THOMAS
New York University School of Medicine

S. M. THOMPSON
University of Maryland

BEVERLY E. THORN
University of Alabama, Tuscaloosa

B. MICHAEL THORNE
Mississippi State University

DAVID F. TOLIN
University of Pennsylvania

ELEANOR REARDON TOLSON
University of Washington

JOE TOMAKA
University of Texas, El Paso

LOUIS G. TORNATZKY
*National Science Foundation, Washington,
   DC*

DANIEL TRANEL
University of Iowa

FREDERICK TRAVIS
*Maharishi University of Management,
   Fairfield, IA*

WILLIAM T. TSUSHIMA
Straub Clinic and Hospital, Inc., Honolulu

LEONARD P. ULLMANN
Incline Valley, Nevada

E. ULVESTAD

RHODA KESLER UNGER
Montclair State College

SUSANA PATRICIA URBINA
University of Northern Florida

T. BEDIRHAN ÜSTÜN
World Health Organization, Geneva

A. L. VACARINO
University of New Orleans

P. VALDERRAMA-ITURBE
Mexico

P. VANDEL
Hospital Saint-Jacques, Bensancon, France

R. D. VANDERPLOEG
University of South Florida

KIRSTEN M. VANMEENAN
University of Maryland

ANTHONY J. VATTANO
University of Illinois, Champaign

FRANCES E. VAUGHAN
*California Institute of Transpersonal
   Psychology, Menlo Park*

P. E. VERNON

WILLIAM F. VITULLI
University of Southern Alabama

N. J. WADE
University of Dundee, Scotland

REX ALVON WADHAM
Brigham Young University

E. E. WAGNER
Forest Institute of Professional Psychology

RICHARD D. WALK
George Washington University

ARLENE S. WALKER-ANDREWS
Rutgers University

PATRICIA M. WALLACE
University of Maryland

ROGER N. WALSH
University of California, Irvine

ZHONG-MING WANG
Zhejiang University, China

WILSE B. WEBB
University of Florida

JOEL LEE WEINBERGER
Adelphi University

ARNOLD D. WELL
University of Massachusetts

W. W. WENRICH
University of North Texas

MICHAEL WERTHEIMER
University of Colorado

DONALD L. WERTLIEB
Tufts University

IAN Q. WHISHAW
University of Lethbridge, Alberta

M. A. WHISMAN
University of Colorado, Boulder

SARAH WHITTON
*Center for Marital and Family Studies,
   University of Denver*

ERIKA WICK
St. John's University

DELOS N. WICKENS
Ohio State University

RICHARD E. WILCOX
University of Texas, Austin

SABINE WILHELM
*Massachusetts General Hospital,
   Charlestown*

DOUGLAS A. WILLIAMS
University of Winnipeg

RICHARD H. WILLIS
University of Pittsburgh

J. WILSON
University of Minnesota, Duluth

MARGARET T. T. WONG-RILEY
Medical College of Wisconsin

MICHAEL L. WOODRUFF
East Tennessee State University

D. S. WOODRUFF-PAK
Temple University

MARGARET P. WOODS

T. E. WOODS
University of Wisconsin School of Medicine

ROBERT L. WOOLFOLK
Rutgers University

ANTHONY WRIGHT
University of Manitoba

TRISTAM D. WYATT
University of Minnesota, St. Paul

R. C. WYLIE

LARRY J. YOUNG
Emory University

L. M. YOUNGBLADE
University of Colorado

ZAHRA ZAKERI
Queens College, City University of New York

O. L. ZANGWILL
Cambridge, England

JOHANNES M. ZANKER
The Australian National University

PATRICIA A. ZAPF
University of Alabama

W. ZHANG
New York Medical College

DANIEL J. ZIEGLER
Villanova University

PHILIP G. ZIMBAROO
Stanford University

M. ZUCKERMAN
University of Delaware

FIONA VAJK: MANAGING EDITOR
BENJAMIN PAGE: MANAGING EDITOR
ALINNE BARRERA: MANAGER EDITOR

The Corsini Encyclopedia of Psychology and Behavioral Science

Third Edition

Q

Q-SORT TECHNIQUE

The Q-sort technique is a general method for eliciting a detailed, subjective description of a stimulus. This description is quantitative and based on explicit, internal reference points. The letter "Q" was used by the inventor of the technique, W. Stephenson (1935, 1936), to indicate the affinity of the data provided by the technique for use in "Q-type" analyses (based on correlations between persons, in contrast to "R-type" analyses based on correlations between variables).

The Q-sort technique is used for two quite distinct purposes. First, as originally devised by Stephenson, the technique is a broadly applicable scaling method that can articulate, in great detail, the personal subjective understanding and experience of the respondent. Alternatively, when respondents describe the same stimulus, intersubjective agreement across descriptions provides a degree of validity for drawing inferences about the stimulus. In the former approach, the focus is on the perceiver; in the latter approach, the focus is on the perceived. The perceiver-focused approach is utilized most often in the study of social and political attitudes conducted in political science (see McKeown & Thomas, 1988, for a concise survey of this application of Q-technique). The second approach, predominant in psychology, follows Block's (1961) adaptation of the method for personality assessment. In this application, the stimulus is a target person who is typically described by multiple judges who are acquainted with the target.

Q-SORT PROCEDURE

The Q-sort method requires a set of items that might be used to describe any member of a class of stimuli. The respondent, or judge, sorts the items (typically words or phrases printed on separate cards) into ordered categories, ranging from extremely characteristic of the target stimulus to extremely uncharacteristic of the target. The number of items that may be placed in each category is fixed, and each category has a preassigned numerical label which becomes the score of the items placed in that category. A rank-ordering of items can be viewed as an example of the Q-sort method, where the number of items and the number of categories are equal in number. More typical is the California Adult Q-Set (Block, 1961) which contains 100 items to be sorted into 9 categories to form a quasinormal distribution (the number of items to be placed in categories 1 to 9, respectively, are 5, 8, 12, 16, 18, 16, 12, 8, and 5).

The fixed distribution of the Q-sort forces the judge to identify which items are most and least descriptive of the target person relative to the other items in the Q-set. Thus, if the Q-item is "friendly toward strangers", the judge compares the degree to which this item is an apt description of the target, compared to the other items. This is in marked contrast to the typical procedure, where judges are asked whether the target is "friendly toward strangers"

in comparison to other people. Ratings obtained using the explicit internal frame of reference created by the use of a fixed distribution were labeled "ipsative" by Cattell (1944) to distinguish them from the more usual "normative" ratings.

The ipsative character of the Q-sort is the source of both benefits and drawbacks of the method (Ozer, 1993). Among the benefits are encouraging the judge to apply considerable thought and effort to the numerous judgments; and removing judge differences in the distribution of ratings, thereby controlling for certain types of judge error and bias. Nonindependence among the item placements is the source of specific problems with Q-sort method. Item mean differences across groups, or in the same group over time, are difficult to interpret (Ozer & Gjerde, 1989). Ipsativity also presents difficulties for statistical procedures that assume independence among items (Clemans, 1966).

TYPES OF Q-SETS

In Stephenson's (1953) description of Q-methodology, Q-items were construed as members of a population, to be sampled for use in particular studies. Block (1961) argued against this view, noting both practical and scientific reasons to use one standard set of items to compose a particular Q-set. Numerous Q-sets have been developed for various purposes, but in general there are two broad types of item domains. Some Q-sets define a broad domain of item content and have relatively little redundancy among items. For example, Block's (1961) California Adult Q-Set provides near-comprehensive coverage of personality. Other Q-sets focus on a much narrower range of content and assess just a few, or even one primary construct. The Attachment Q-Set (Waters & Deane, 1985), which includes content clusters for particular attachment styles, is a well-known example of this second approach.

EVALUATION AND USE OF Q-SORT DATA

When judges' descriptions of target stimuli are used to make inferences about the target, it is important to establish that there is substantial judge agreement. Either the average item reliability or the average reliability of each target description is typically computed for this purpose (see Block, 1961; Ozer, 1993). The composite judge evaluations may be analyzed like any other rating data, but they also invite application of other sorts of analyses based on the correlation between persons, or the correlation between the description of the same person over multiple occasions. Such methods have been employed with some frequency in personality psychology, where correlations between the Q-sorts of different persons have been used to develop taxonomies of personality (e.g., Block, 1971); and correlations between different Q-sort descriptions of the same person at different ages have been used to assess personality consistency and change (e.g., Ozer & Gjerde, 1989).

REFERENCES

Block, J. (1961). *The Q-sort method in personality assessment and psychiatric research.* Springfield, IL: Thomas.

Block, J. (1971). *Lives through time.* Berkeley, CA: Bancroft.

Cattell, R. B. (1944). Psychological measurement: Normative, ipsative, interactive. *Psychological Review, 51,* 292-303.

Clemans, W. V. (1966). An analytical and empirical examination of some properties of ipsative measures. *Psychometric Monographs, 14.*

Stephenson, W. (1935). Correlating persons instead of tests. *Character and Personality, 6,* 17-24.

Stephenson, W. (1936). The foundations of psychometry: Four factor systems. *Psychometrika, 1,* 195-209.

Stephenson, W. (1953). *The study of behavior: Q-Technique and its methodology.* Chicago: The University of Chicago Press.

McKeown, B., & Thomas, D. (1988). *Q Methodology.* Newbury Park, CA: Sage.

Ozer, D. J. (1993). The Q-sort method and the study of personality development. In D. C. Funder, R. D. Parke, C. Tomlinson-Keasey, & K. Widaman (Eds.), *Studying lives through time: Personality and development* (pp. 147-168). Washington, DC: American Psychological Association.

Ozer, D. J., & Gjerde, P. F. (1989). Patterns of personality consistency and change from childhood through adolescence. *Journal of Personality, 57,* 483-507.

Waters, E., & Deane, K. E. (1985). Defining and assessing individual differences in attachment relationships: Q-methodology and the organization of behavior in infancy and early childhood. In I. Bretherton & E. Waters (Eds.), *Growing points of attachment theory and research* (pp. 41-65). Monographs of the Society for Research in Child Development, 50(1-2, Serial No. 209).

D. J. OZER
University of California, Riverside

PERSONALITY ASSESSMENT
TESTING METHODS

QUALITY OF LIFE

Quality of life has become a popular concept that is used by politicians, marketing executives, media and sports personalities, and members of the public. There is an extensive scientific literature of books, theoretical articles, and empirical studies on the subject by health practitioners, psychologists, sociologists, economists, geographers, social historians, and philosophers. Several millenia ago, scholars in ancient China and Greece were interested in quality of life, and renewed interest occurred in times of enlightenment in the centuries that followed. In more recent history, quality of life emerged as a political entity in the United States in the mid-1950s, and in Europe in the 1960s. United States presidents such as Eisenhower, Johnson, and Nixon popularized the term in presidential commissions and in their speeches. The focus on quality of life in the last half-century has increased along with the recognition that the health of countries must be judged in something more than gross economic factors, and that the health of individuals is something beyond the absence of illness.

The economic focus led to the development of social indicators directed at objectively measuring the quality of life of populations at large. In 1970 the Organization for Economic Cooperation and Development (OECD) encouraged member countries to develop and report measures of social well-being for their constituents. This resulted in a number of countries' reporting such social indicators as the number of schools per person, the number of hospital beds per person, and the number of health care professionals per person. It soon became apparent that while social indicators provided information about cultural entities (towns, states, countries) they provided little or no information about the quality of life of individuals within these entities. This led researchers in a number of countries, including the United States, Canada, Europe, and Australia, to assess the subjective or perceived quality of life of population samples within their countries. Perhaps the earliest such study was by Bradburn (1969), who surveyed two samples ($N = 2787$ and $N = 2163$) from several metropolitan areas in the United States. He employed as his measure the affect balance score, which was based on ratings of positive and negative affect and was assumed to be indicative of quality of life. A second landmark study in the United States was carried out by Campbell, Converse, and Rogers (1976), who sampled 2,160 individuals selected to be representative of the national population. Participants were asked to rate their satisfaction in a number of life domains and with their lives as a whole. Subsequent to these early cross-sectional studies, the methods of assessing quality of life in the population at large have become more complex, with an emphasis on longitudinal studies.

In 1947 the World Health Organization promulgated a definition of health that suggested that health was not just the absence of illness, but was also a state of physical, psychological, and social well-being. This definition provoked health professionals, particularly the researchers among them, to start to view the impact of interventions in a broader context than just symptom recovery. Thus, in the last two decades what have come to be known as Health Related Quality of Life (HRQOL) measures have proliferated. Perhaps the earliest HRQOL measure was the Karnofsky Index, which has been used in numerous studies since its development over 50 years ago (Karnofsky & Burchenal, 1949). Global and specific HRQOL measures have been developed in most branches of health care, including cardiology, oncology, epilepsy, urology, psychiatry, and general medicine, to name just a few. One of the most ambitious projects is that of the World Health Organization Quality of Life Group (1998), who are developing a global health measure of quality of life that can be employed with people from differing cultures world-wide.

Despite the popular and scientific interest in the subject, there is little agreement on what is meant by the term "quality of life." As Evans noted in 1994, "quality of life" has been used interchangeably with "well-being," "psychological well-being," "subjective well-being," "happiness," "life satisfaction," "positive and negative affect," and "the good life." There is in fact a high degree of similarity among many of these measures, and factor analyses with samples of the general population indicate that measures of life satisfaction, positive and negative affect, and quality of life are highly related to each other and form a single factor (Evans, 1997). Most researchers in the field believe that quality of life is a multidimensional concept and there is fair agreement as to the majority of subdomains within the construct; there is, however, some disagreement concerning the method by which measures in each of the subdomains should be aggregated to form an overall measure of quality of life.

The area of quality of life research, because of the way interest in the field has evolved, has an abundance of measures and a paucity of theoretical models. Two prominent models are the bottom-up and top-down models of quality of life. Proponents of the top-down model argue that one's general quality of life influences quality of life in the specific domains of his or her life; thus, the focus of research should be on these global measures. Those who advocate the bottom-up model propose that the quality of life in each life domain affects one's overall quality of life; thus the specific domains should be the focus of research.

Another current line of research is the identification of factors that influence an individual's quality of life. There is increasing evidence that personality dimensions such as self-esteem, locus of control, extraversion, neuroticism, and hardiness, to name but a few, influence an individual's quality of life. This network of relationships could form the basis for a more elegant theory in the field. Recent attempts to measure quality of life across the many cultures around the world has the potential to yield some of the parameters that would define a theory of quality of life. Emphasis in the future will be on the development of theoretical models of quality of life, and they in turn will impact the measurement issues available at present.

REFERENCES

Bradburn, N. M. (1969). *The structure of psychological well-being.* Chicago: Aldine.

Campbell, A., Converse, P. E., & Rogers, W. L. (1976). *The quality of American life.* New York: Russell Sage Foundation.

Evans, D. R. (1994). Enhancing quality of life in the population at large. *Social Indicators Research, 33,* 47-88.

Evans, D. R. (1997). Health promotion, wellness programs, quality of life and the marketing of psychology. *Canadian Psychology, 38,* 1-12.

Karnofsky, D. A., & Burchenal, J. H. (1949). The clinical evaluation of chemotherapeutic agents in cancer. In C. M. Macleod (Ed.), *Evaluation of chemotherapeutic agents* (pp. 191-205). New York: Columbia University Press.

The WHOQOL Group (1998). The World Health Organization Quality of Life Assessment (WHOQOL): Development and general psychometric properties. *Social Science and Medicine, 46,* 1569-1585.

D. R. EVANS
University of Western Ontario

ENVIRONMENTAL PSYCHOLOGY

QUAY, HERBERT C.

Herbert C. Quay was born in Portland, ME on August 27, 1927, son of George J. and Susannah Fay Quay. Six months later, his parents moved to Florida, carrying him on the back window ledge of a Model T Ford, thus engendering a lifelong love of cross-country auto travel.

He received his early education in the public schools of St. Petersburg, FL. After completing a year of junior college, he enlisted in the US Army in 1946, serving the majority of his term in General Headquarters, Far East Command, Tokyo, Japan.

He received his BS (1951) and MS (1952) from Florida State University. His interest in research was fostered by Sweetland, with whom he shared authorship on a paper on hypnotic dreams.

His first position as a masters-level clinician was at the Florida Industrial School for Boys, a state juvenile correctional institution. This early experience fostered a career-long interest in personality and behavioral dimensions in juvenile delinquents. He subsequently took a position as a clinical psychologist on the white female admission service at the Milledgeville, GA State Hospital, then the second largest mental hospital in the US. During his two-and-one-half year stay, he was sent by the hospital to a two week course on the Rorschach taught by Beck at the University of Chicago. While it was a wonderful experience, his Rorschach career was short as he cannot recall ever having administered one after leaving the hospital.

In 1955 he was accepted (barely) into the PhD program at the University of Illinois-Urbana. As a country boy from the South, he was naturally in awe of such famous figures as Osgood, Mowrer, Cattell, J. McV. Hunt, and Cronbach, among many others. At Illinois he had the opportunity to work closely with Peterson and Becker, and often benefited from the wise counsel of Hellmer, director of the Psychological Clinic. His dissertation was on the verbal reinforcement of the recall of early childhood memories, a cornerstone of psychoanalytic theory, and was the first study to show that personally meaningful material could be influenced by the minimal participation of the experimenter. The study was directed by J. Hunt who became a lifelong friend and mentor.

After receiving his degree in 1958, he joined the faculty at Vanderbilt University, moving in 1961 to Northwestern University as associate professor. While there he benefited from the counsel of W. A. Hunt, the ebullient chair of the department. While at Northwestern, he received his first NIMH grant to study, using factor analysis, dimensions of personality in juvenile delinquents housed in the National Training School for Boys, a facility of the Federal Bureau of Prisons in Washington, DC. As he recalls, the grant was for about $3,000 and provided summer salary and a part-time secretary as well as travel to DC.

In 1963 he returned to the University of Illinois as director of the to-be-built interdisciplinary research center on children's behavior disorders and mental retardation. While there he expanded his research interests to include the use of behavior modification to bring about behavior change and academic achievement in disruptive elementary age children in the public schools, publishing extensively in that area with colleagues Werry, Sprague, and Glavin. While coteaching a seminar on child psychopathology, he and Werry began work on their edited volume *Psychopathological Disorders of Childhood,* which was subsequently twice revised.

In 1968 he moved to Temple University as chairman of the Division of Educational Psychology in the College of Education. He continued his interest in the education of children with behavior disorders. A 1971 paper in that area, coauthored with Glavin (senior author) and Werry, was named a classic in the field of behavioral disorders in a study published in 1992. He also expanded his collaboration with the Federal Bureau of Prisons to help them develop differential treatments for juveniles who were grouped for intervention based on the results of his study at the National Training School. He also began studies investigating personality and behavioral dimensions in adult male offenders; this resulted in a four-subtype system of classification put to use by the Bureau as well as a number of state correctional systems. In 1972 he became the first editor of the *Journal of Abnormal Child Psychology,* a position which he held for the next 18 years.

In 1974 Florida beckoned an almost-native son and he accepted a position as director of the program in applied social sciences and professor of psychology at the University of Miami. He continued his research on both juvenile and adult offenders. He became chair of psychology in 1985, a position he retained until he retired in 1992. Also while at the University of Miami, he was chairman of the organizing committee of the International Society for Research in Child and Adolescent Psychopathology and served as its first president.

In the early 1980s, he discovered the writing and research of Gray, which led him to investigate the operations of Gray's behavioral inhibition and reward systems in childhood psychopathologies, principally undersocialized conduct disorder and attention deficit disorder. Bringing together findings from both behavioral and biochemical research, he and his students conducted a series of studies on the relevance of Gray's theory to childhood disorders. These studies have led other investigators to use Gray's work to formulate their own studies or interpret their data within his framework.

His honors and awards include the APA Division 12 Award for Distinguished Contributions to Clinical Psychology, the Section 1 of the Division 12 Distinguished Professional Contribution Award, and the Distinguished Professional Contribution Award of the American Association of Correctional Psychologists.

He considers his major research contributions to be his taxonomic work in both juvenile and adult offenders, his early work in the education of children with behavior disorders, and his more recent work in the experimental psychopathology of childhood and adolescent disorders. He would like to think that his coedited volumes with Werry set the tone for a more empirical approach to childhood disorders. He hopes his most recent volume, the *Handbook of Disruptive Behavior Disorders,* coedited with his wife Anne E. Hogan, will serve as a reference for years to come.

He is grateful for the many colleagues and friends he has had both in academia and the Federal Bureau of Prisons. His only regret is that 30 years of administration precluded his working with more graduate students who might have carried on in the empirical-experimental tradition which he hopes to have exemplified.

STAFF

QUESTIONNAIRES

Questionnaires are inventories used by researchers to gather various kinds of information from responding individuals. Questionnaires are typically self-administered, so-called "self-report" devices. As such, they are similar to interviews conducted face-to-face or over the telephone. In fact, frequently some or all of the individuals who do not choose to complete a survey are contacted and interviewed by a researcher so that their opinions and information may be made part of the study data. Among the advantages of questionnaires are their relatively low cost as a means of gathering data, a general freedom from bias on the part of an interviewer, the large number of individuals who may be asked to respond, the sense of anonymity that respondents may feel, the temporal flexibility afforded the respondent, the possibility of directly linking research questions and survey results, and the ease of data coding and analysis for interpretation of the results (Kidder, 1981). A major disadvantage of questionnaires relates to "return rates"; frequently only a small fraction of those originally provided with a questionnaire complete it. Also, respondents may not be honest or may permit subtle biases to influence their responses. Another disadvantage of questionnaires is that individuals may write answers which do not, in fact, adequately address a question; in an interview setting, a skilled interviewer may probe further to elicit the proper response. Furthermore, many Americans are still unable to read and write well enough to complete a questionnaire.

Questionnaires are used in both basic psychological research and applied research. They may be used in either experimental or correlational research. For example, many psychologists who investigate personality use survey questionnaires to gain insights about personal functioning. In applied research, questionnaires are often used in program evaluations, job analyses, needs assessments, and market research. They may also be used as dependent variables in experiments. Questionnaires should not generally be called tests in that the term *test* holds the connotation that there is a correct answer to a given question. Rather, most behaviors elicited by questionnaires are of the "typical behavior" variety (Tyler, 1965); these include personality variables, attitudes, values, beliefs, interests, and descriptions of past and present behavior. Furthermore, because most questionnaire research is correlational, causal attributions are, for the most part, inappropriate. However, it is the experimental design, rather than the nature of the variable per se, that dictates the ability to make causal statements.

TYPES OF QUESTIONNAIRES

Questionnaires are typically instruments that may be printed, photocopied, or mimeographed. Responses may either be placed on the survey itself or on a separate answer sheet; recent innovations involve the computerized administration of questionnaires where respondents enter their answers at a computer terminal. Most questionnaires are composed of numerous questions and statements. Statements are frequently used to determine the extent to which respondents agree or disagree—with a given thought, concept, or perspective. This "agree-disagree" format has become formalized and is often referred to as a Likert scale, after the industrial psychologist, R. Likert, who pioneered its use and analysis.

Questions may be of two general types: free response or response selection. Free response questions are often called open-ended questions; response selection questions are also known as close-ended or fixed-alternative questions. The chief advantage of response selection questions is that responses may be easily key-punched or transferred to computer files via optical scanners for data-analytic purposes. Answers to free response questions, on the other hand, must be first categorized, scored, and coded. Since this process often demands the knowledge and understanding of a professional, the process is inevitably time-consuming and expensive. Furthermore, respondents may find the work required of them to detail their answers in writing laborious and therefore may choose not to respond or to give short, largely inadequate responses.

CONSTRUCTING A QUESTIONNAIRE

There are a number of steps involved in performing a study involving a questionnaire. An example listing of these steps follows:

1. Specifying the objectives of the study.
2. Designing the questionnaire itself.
3. Drafting the questionnaire.
4. Editing the questionnaire.
5. Developing instructions for administering the questionnaire.
6. Pretesting the questionnaire.
7. Revising the questionnaire.
8. Developing a sampling plan for administering the questionnaire.
9. Executing the survey/data collection.
10. Data analysis.
11. Reporting the results.

For the sake of brevity, only the first seven of these steps are mentioned here. It is essential that goals of the study be carefully detailed; such work may lead to the elimination of unnecessary items from the questionnaire and result in a higher response rate. These objectives are then operationalized in an outline of the questionnaire. Once topics for questions are provided, decisions as to best item formats may be made (e.g., free response or response selection questions). Bouchard (1976) reported that while questionnaire construction is still primarily an art form, there are various "rules of thumb" based on both research and experience that may improve the decision-making at this stage. These suggestions include involving the respondent population in as many stages of the construction process as possible; avoiding ambiguity at all costs; limiting questions to a single idea, keeping items as short as possible; writing questions using a level of language appropriate for the respondent population; avoiding negatively worded sentences, and, even more, the use of double negatives; avoiding words with negative connotations; avoiding conditional clauses; using response selection questions rather than free response questions wherever possible; and implementing procedures to reduce the influence of social desirability (described below) and other response sets (such as agreeing with all items). Editing should be performed by specialists in questionnaire construction as well as members of the respondent population. Additionally, "readability" checks can insure that the wording is appropriate to the educational level of the respondents. The ordering of questions within the survey is important and must be performed with care.

Both introductions and instructions are advisable. Good introductions have been shown to increase the rate of returned questionnaires. Some researchers send postcards to potential respondents in advance of the survey advising them that it is coming. Cover letters which explain the purpose and importance of the questionnaire are strongly recommended. Instructions on the questionnaire should be clear and as simple as possible. If the survey is to be returned in the mail, a stamped, addressed envelope should be included.

Pretesting the questionnaire is essential. Interviews with or written comments from these respondents may highlight potential difficulties which may be avoided. Occasionally, when many respondents specify "other" responses to certain response selection questions, new options can be added.

Data-analytic issues cannot be detailed in a brief recitation such as this one. However, analyses used for other psychological measures (inter-item correlations or reliability and validity studies) are frequently appropriate for questionnaires.

There are two recurring problems in questionnaire research—response biases and nonrespondents. In many studies, respondents either avoid threatening questions or try to make themselves "look good"; this latter response style is known as social desirability. Bradburn, Sudman, and colleagues (1980) make a number of recommendations to reduce this effect. Long explanatory introductions to threatening questions help, as do promises of confidentiality. Permitting respondents to write sensitive answers rather than simply checking an answer is also beneficial. A potentially useful strategy is asking respondents to describe friends or "people like themselves" rather than themselves.

Increasingly, questionnaires are being used in cross-cultural research. In many such cases, more than one language becomes involved and the translation of a questionnaire from one language to another is required. Cautions need be involved in such instances, especially because language and culture must both be addressed (Geisinger, 1994).

Achieving an adequate and unbiased sample is perhaps the biggest problem in questionnaire research. The nonresponse problem is twofold. First, many individuals do not respond to surveys. Furthermore, these nonrespondents frequently differ from respondents. Strategies to increase return rates include appeals for help and offers of small rewards, for example. Another strategy is to interview a random sample of nonrespondents.

Because of their relative ease, low cost, and low intrusion value, questionnaires will certainly continue to be used frequently as data-collection devices in psychology. They are relatively new techniques compared with such methods as experimental procedures. Solutions to problems such as those mentioned in the previous paragraphs are likely to be sought. Even if good solutions are found, however, it is unlikely that experimental methodology will relinquish its preeminent status in psychology because causal relationships are more easily discerned with it. Nonetheless, questionnaire use is increasing and this growth will likely continue.

REFERENCES

Babbie, E. R. (1973). *Survey research methods.* Belmont, CA: Wadsworth.

Bouchard, T. J., Jr. (1976). Field research methods: Interviewing, questionnaires, participant observation, systematic observation, unobtrusive measures. In M. D. Dunnette (Ed.), *Handbook of industrial and organizational psychology* (pp. 363-413). Chicago: Rand McNally.

Bradburn, N. M., Sudman, S. O., Blair, E., Locander, W., Miles, C., Singer, E., & Stocking, C. (1980). *Improving interview method and questionnaire design.* San Francisco: Jossey-Bass.

Geisinger, K. F. (1994). Cross-cultural normative assessment: Translation and adaptation issues influencing normative interpretation of assessment instruments. *Psychological Assessment, 6,* 304-312.

Kidder, L. H. (1981). *Research methods in social relations* (4th ed.). New York: Holt, Rinehart and Winston.

Tyler, L. E. (1965). *The psychology of human differences* (3rd ed.). New York: Appleton-Century-Crofts.

K. F. GEISINGER
La Moyne College

LIKERT SCALE
RESEARCH METHODS
SELF-RATINGS AND SELF-REPORTS

R

RAIMY, VICTOR (1913–1987)

In a doctoral dissertation written at Ohio State University in 1943, Victor Raimy proposed that changes in the self-concept could be used to chart the course of psychotherapy as well as general changes in personality. Educated at Antioch College, Raimy became impressed with the ubiquity and influence of the self-concept. In his theory, the self-concept was seen as a guide or map that persons consult when faced with choices.

Always employed in an academic setting (University of Pittsburgh, Ohio State University, and the University of Colorado), Raimy conducted psychotherapy with both college students and hospitalized mental patients while exploring cognitive phenomena related to the self-concept. In 1975, he published a book explaining therapy in terms of cognitive principles—*Misunderstandings of the Self: Cognitive Psychotherapy and the Misconception Hypothesis.* Misconceptions about the self were proposed as disturbing aspects of the self-concept that account for much maladjustment and neurosis. Two major misconceptions that impede treatment are *phrenophobia,* the belief that one is losing one's mind, and the *Special Person misconception,* the spoiled child's refusal to come to terms with reality.

In addition to his interest in therapy, Raimy also participated in the postwar frenzy to train psychologists. In 1950, he compiled and wrote *Training in Clinical Psychology: The Report of the Boulder Conference on Graduate Education in Clinical Psychology,* which still serves as a major guideline for university psychology departments.

In 1978, Raimy retired to Honolulu, to part-time private practice.

STAFF

RAMON Y CAJAL, SANTIAGO (1832–1934)

Santiago Ramon y Cajal was forced by his father to study medicine instead of art, as he would have preferred. An uninspired student early in his career, he earned his first degree in medicine in 1873. After a short tour of service in the Spanish army and a case of malaria, he left the military and earned a doctorate in anatomy, in 1877. Ramon y Cajal held professorships in Valencia, Barcelona, and Madrid, and the chair in histology and pathology at Madrid from 1892 until his retirement in 1922. He shared the Nobel prize in medicine and physiology in 1906, and was elected a foreign member of the Royal Society in 1909.

A largely self-taught histologist, Ramon y Cajal made such important contributions to the understanding of the nervous system that he is called the father of present-day physiological psychology. His techniques for tracing neurons histologically, still a basic approach to physiological psychology, led him to demonstrate that the central nervous system is comprised of separate but communicating nerve cells. He described the basic structure and physiology of neurons, the direction of conduction of a neuron, and the means of regeneration of a severed cell. He also described the structure of the retina and provided a histological basis for cerebral localization of function.

Ramon y Cajal spent his entire career in Spain and insisted on publishing his research in Spanish. His publications were voluminous, but two stand out as central to his work. The first was his three-volume text on the nervous system (1899–1904); the other was his two-volume study of neural degeneration and regeneration (1913–1914).

T. KEITH-LUCAS
The University of the South

RANK, OTTO (1884–1939)

Of the distinguished followers of Freud, Otto Rank was the first whose professional formation was from the outset in a psychoanalytic framework. Viennese, and a graduate of a technical school, he was oriented toward becoming a novelist and poet when, at the age of 20, he discovered Freud's writings and drew on them in formulating an essay on artistic creativity. This essay made a great impression on Freud, who welcomed Rank into his inner circle and encouraged his university education. The essay was eventually published as a book in 1907 and was followed by a series of books interpreting mythic and literary themes (the anomalous birth of heroes, the incest theme, the stories of Lohengrin and of Don Juan, the theme of the "double"). His activities in the psychoanalytic movement expanded during these years into an important role as editor and as secretary of the small central group of leaders. After his return from war duties, he began, around 1920, to work also as a psychoanalytic therapist in Vienna.

Experience with patients led Rank to theoretical developments embodied in *The Trauma of Birth.* The idea that birth is the prototype of later anxiety had previously been advanced by Freud, and Rank felt his own elaboration to be a constructive advance in psychoanalytic theory. Rank considered dual anxiety about the birth process and about fantasies of return to uterine life the explanation for much that had been ascribed to sexual conflicts, including the Oedipus complex, and this replacement focused more attention on the child's relation to its mother rather than its father. Both of these elements disturbed Freud, and other members of the inner circle of psychoanalysis even more. The controversy initiated by this book led to Rank's expulsion from the inner circle and, eventually, to his contrasting his own approach to that of psychoanalysis.

During this period of controversy, and in the following years of work largely in Paris and New York, Rank continued his clinical practice and writing, and increasingly engaged also in teaching. He developed a highly innovative version of what he at times called "psychoanalysis of the ego structure," best represented in English by the double volume *Will Therapy* and *Truth and Reality.* After these technical works on therapeutic technique and personality theory, Rank wrote four books that were broader in character, at once psychological and philosophical. One centered on the concept of soul (Rank, 1931), one on education, and one—posthumously published—on social psychology (Rank, 1941); the other (Rank, 1932) was a more mature treatment of the topic of his first essay, artistic creativity. These considered the implications of his theory for a psychological interpretation of human history, for various problems of modern life, and for the sources of creative potential both in the artist and in all persons.

Rank was unusual among psychoanalytic writers in the extent to which he drew on historical and anthropological sources. This orientation was established in his early work in "applied psychoanalysis"—that is, the application of psychoanalytic theory to the interpretation of art, myth, and human culture generally. In that period, he had no clinical experience of his own to draw on. The same orientation remained strong in his later career, even though he now also had a fund of clinical experience and had abandoned much of the psychoanalytic theory with which he had previously been working. This orientation gives distinctive value to his work, particularly since it seems to have been a source of much that is most original in it. At the same time, it tends to alienate the modern reader, because it revolves around an early and outmoded anthropology. Like his predecessors (including Freud), he was very concerned with when and how various features of culture originated; he assumed the reality of a single course of development from primitive to civilized, and often treated almost as fact conjectures about the unknowable distant past. The tolerant reader, however, will find a wealth of ideas that can be easily transplanted to a setting of modern scientific thought.

Rank's mature thought was based on rejecting the aim, shared by Freud and most of academic psychology, of mechanistic explanation of human behavior or experience with a cause-effect paradigm. He sought to develop an alternative scientific approach built on the person as a voluntary interpreter of meaning and initiator of action. For example, his earlier conception of the birth trauma as a source of anxiety was largely replaced by a conception of womb and birth ideas as apt symbols used by an individual to express conflicting thoughts of moving on to risky new possibilities or stagnating comfortably in familiar routines, expressed metaphorically (and at times literally) as fear of life versus fear of death. Rank was thus a forerunner of tendencies that only later became conspicuous in orthodox psychoanalysis and academic psychology, and became the basis of such major developments as humanistic psychology.

I. L. CHILD
Yale University

RANKIAN PSYCHOLOGY

The influence of Otto Rank on psychological theory and professional practice has been institutionalized to a much lesser degree than has that of Freud, Jung, or even Adler. The *Journal of the Otto Rank Association,* published from 1965 to 1981, brought together many instances of Rank's influence on current thought, but these do not suggest that specifically Rankian training institutes are likely to arise. This lack of institutionalization seems consistent with the individualized and antidoctrinaire character of Rank's writings. Psychology with a Rankian flavor has long been evident, however, and in two ways: (a) Various significant developments in psychology have been clearly influenced by Rank's teaching and writing. (b) Additional important developments have a Rankian flavor that may arise only from his having been an intellectual forerunner but that is so marked as to have received extensive notice and comment.

DIRECT INFLUENCES

Rank regularly taught, in the 1930s, at the Pennsylvania School of Social Work, where he analyzed several of the faculty members, and he also lectured at two schools of social work in New York City. His ideas about therapeutic technique and psychological theory had a continuing influence in these schools, especially in Philadelphia, after his untimely death, and from there were widely diffused in the social work profession.

Carl Rogers, in the early years of his therapeutic work, was influenced by Rank and the Philadelphia social-work tradition Rank had helped form. His subsequent innovations in theory and practice, especially his reliance on brief therapy and his orientation toward growth and self-actualization, have been harmonious with the spirit of Rank's writings, and may be seen as a creative development out of the starting point provided by Rank.

Becker (1973) has presented an explicitly Rankian psychology of the ills of human society. It attempts to answer the question, "What unsatisfied needs are predominantly responsible for the widespread misery of human beings?" as did Freud's *Civilization and Its Discontents* (1930). Instead of Freud's implausible attribution of human suffering primarily to sexual repression demanded as a precondition of culture, Becker attributes it to the insatiable quest for symbols of immortality, arising from the universal fear of death.

ANTICIPATIONS

Rank's theory of personality and therapy, it has often been noted, bears marked similarity to psychoanalytic theory and treatment of narcissistic disturbances. These are largely new developments in psychoanalysis in the decades since Rank's death. Rank's acumen, and his long acquaintance with narcissistic problems in himself, thus enabled him to anticipate—perhaps, to some degree, to help bring about—substantial broadening and improvement of psychoanalytic theory (Stolorow & Atwood, 1979).

Rank's view of self-actualization as a dominant aim in a typical individual's life helped open the way for him to consider men and women with an attitude of complete equality. His own work thus avoided the male-dominated strain in Freudian thought. His account of psychological problems of women (Rank, 1941) is strikingly similar to many later feminist and humanistic discussions, though the similarity probably can be ascribed only to prescience and not to historical influence (Sward, 1980).

Rank's acceptance of and respect for irrationality, and his orientation of therapy more toward experiencing than toward explaining, show great resemblance to major aspects of transpersonal psychology (Amundson, 1981). Again, the relationship appears to be an instance of anticipation rather than direct historical connection.

MacKinnon (1965), in a personality study focused on creativity, studied three groups of architects—a least creative group, an intermediate group, and a most creative group. Toward the end of the study, he noticed that this grouping was similar to Rank's classification of personality types or stages of personal development, into an adapted or normal type, a conflicted or neurotic type, and an artistic or creative type. His findings about personal characteristics and life history of each group, moreover, closely paralleled Rank's theory. The plan and conclusions of the study were thoroughly Rankian, MacKinnon felt, yet he had not thought of Rank's theory while planning or conducting the study. Since he had read Rank's most relevant books some years previously, the question remains open whether this is only an anticipation by Rank of later developments, or also an instance of major influence not consciously recognized for lack of social support for detailed recall and recognition.

In sum, then, psychology, in various separate ways, has become more Rankian than it was in Rank's own time, but there is no isolated part of it that constitutes a Rankian psychology.

REFERENCES

Amundson, J. (1981). Will in the psychology of Otto Rank: A transpersonal perspective. *Journal of Transpersonal Psychology, 13,* 113–124.

Becker, E. (1973). *Escape from evil.* New York: Free Press.

Becker, E. (1973). *The denial of death.* New York: Free Press.

Freud, S. (1962/1930). *Civilization and its discontents.* New York: Norton.

MacKinnon, D. W. (1965). Personality and the realization of creative potential. *American Psychologist, 20,* 273–281.

Rank, O. (1958/1941). *Beyond psychology.* New York: Dover.

Stolorow, R. D., & Atwood, G. E. (1979). *Faces in a cloud: Subjectivity in personality theory.* New York: Aronson.

Sward, K. (1980). Self-actualization and women: Rank and Freud contrasted. *Journal of Humanistic Psychology, 20,* 5–26.

I. L. CHILD
Yale University

RAPID EYE MOVEMENT (REM) SLEEP

The two major phases of sleep are rapid eye movement (REM) sleep and nonrapid eye movement (NREM) sleep. REM sleep is often called dreaming (or D) sleep, because dreams are reported by about 70 to 80% of persons awakened during this period. It also has been referred to as paradoxical sleep, because the brain paradoxically seems to be in an activated state that is similar to, but not identical to, the waking state. For example, brain metabolism is normal or slightly increased during this period. REM sleep is characterized by an activated electroencephalogram (EEG) pattern (low-voltage, fast-frequency brain waves), loss of tone in the major antigravity muscles (i.e., muscular paralysis with the exception of diaphragmatic and ocular muscles), periodic bursts of rapid eye movements, and autonomic nervous system instability (e.g., variable blood pressure, heart rate, and respiration). In men, penile erections occur during REM sleep, which can be evaluated in sleep studies to distinguish organic from psychological causes of impotence. Finally, nightmares occur almost exclusively during REM sleep. By contrast, NREM sleep encompasses the other four stages of sleep, including the deepest state of sleep, in which the EEG pattern is less activated (high-voltage, slow-frequency brain waves), autonomic function is slower and steadier, brain metabolism is decreased, and both muscular paralysis and rapid eye movements are absent. Moreover, less than 30% of persons report dreaming during NREM sleep. For this reason, night terrors (which are qualitatively different than nightmares) occur during NREM sleep.

The time from falling sleep to the first onset of REM sleep is referred to as REM latency, which is normally about 70 to 100 minutes and progressively shortens in normal elderly persons to about 55 to 70 minutes. The amount of REM sleep also tends to decline with age. Approximately 50% of the sleep in babies is spent in REM sleep, which decreases to about 25% by age four, remains relatively constant throughout adult life, and then begins to decline again after age 60. The number of rapid eye movements during a REM period is referred to as REM density. REM and NREM sleep oscillate throughout the night with a cycle length of approximately 90 to 100 minutes. The relative proportion of time spent in REM sleep increases during the course of the night while NREM time decreases. Sleep deprivation is normally followed by several nights of increased REM sleep with shortened REM latency, referred to as REM rebound.

Although various brain regions are involved in the generation and regulation of sleep (e.g., the thalamus, hypothalamus, limbic system, and parts of the cerebral cortex), the major anatomical sites for control of REM sleep are in the brainstem. Neurons containing the neurotransmitters acetylcholine (cholinergic), serotonin (serotonergic), and norepinephrine (noradrenergic) originate in the brainstem and project to other parts of the brain. Cholinergic neurons primarily stimulate the onset of REM sleep and control the various characteristics of REM sleep described previously. For example, drugs that stimulate cholinergic neurons can increase REM sleep and shorten REM latency when given to normal subjects. When cholinergic neurons are active, serotonergic and noradrenergic neurons are inactive. Activation of serotonergic and noradrenergic neurons tends to stimulate NREM sleep and suppress REM sleep. Thus, there is a reciprocal inhibitory relationship among different neurotransmitter systems that regulate the REM-NREM sleep cycle. In addition, brainstem cholinergic neurons projecting to the spinal cord inhibit neuromuscular activity, accounting for the motor paralysis characteristic of REM sleep. When these specific neurons are destroyed in animals, they are not paralyzed during REM sleep, and these animals often demonstrate complex motor behaviors.

Sleep and dreaming has long been an area of clinical and scientific interest in psychology, psychiatry, and neuroscience. For example, the similarity between hallucinations and the often bizarre and strange content of most dreams naturally stimulated interest in studying REM sleep in patients with schizophrenia and other psychiatric disorders. Although such studies did not support the hypothesis that hallucinations represent waking dreams, further research in depression often found that REM latency is shortened to less than 60 minutes, REM density and the amount of REM sleep is increased, and the distribution of REM sleep is shifted to the earlier part of the night, compared to normal subjects. These findings had been considered a potential biological marker for depression, but shortened REM latency also has been found in some patients with other psychiatric disorders (e.g., schizophrenia, Obsessive-Compulsive Disorder, eating disorders, alcoholism, and Borderline Personality Disorder). Patients with schizophrenia and psychotic depression can have extremely short REM latencies, sometimes occurring immediately at the onset of sleep (sleep-onset REM). Increased REM sleep and shortened REM latency also occur in patients during the acute period of abrupt withdrawal from alcohol, benzodiazepines, and other sedative-hypnotic drugs. Patients with depression and schizophrenia, however, are more sensitive to the effects of cholinergic-stimulating drugs on REM sleep, compared to patients with other psychiatric disorders and to normal control subjects. Moreover, there is some evidence that shortened REM latency might be a genetic marker for depression within families, and many effective treatments for depression (including antidepressant drugs and electroconvulsive therapy) are associated with a decrease (or even suppression) of REM sleep and a lengthening of REM latency. Curiously, total sleep deprivation and even more selective sleep deprivation (e.g., waking patients during the onset of REM sleep throughout the night) has an antidepressant effect in many depressed patients, but this phenomenon is transient and depression usually returns again after a complete night of sleep.

REM sleep abnormalities have been described in two neurologic disorders. In narcolepsy, sleep-onset REM periods are very common. These patients abruptly fall asleep, and they often report hypnogogic hallucinations, which are vivid, dream-like states that are likely related to the rapid occurrence of sleep-onset REM periods. Patients with narcolepsy also develop cataplexy, which is the sudden brief loss of muscle tone during waking periods. This may be related to the muscular paralysis normally associated with REM sleep. These findings suggest that narcolepsy is characterized by dysregulated control of REM-NREM sleep. In REM behavior disorder, the normal paralysis of REM sleep is lost. These patients show complex vocal and motor behaviors during REM sleep, often appearing to enact dream content. This is similar to what is seen in animals with selective brainstem lesions, described previously.

Despite many decades of research, the precise function of sleep is not certain. Sleep studies in various animal species suggest that NREM sleep evolved earlier than REM sleep. These findings and other studies have suggested that NREM sleep might have a primary role in the conservation and restoration of energy, whereas REM sleep might be especially important to the development and maintenance of cognitive functioning. Long-term sleep deprivation, even selective REM sleep deprivation, is fatal in animals, suggesting a more complex relationship between REM and NREM sleep.

SUGGESTED READING

Benca, R. M., Obermeyer, W. H., Thisted, R. A., & Gillin, J. C. (1992). Sleep and psychiatric disorders: A meta-analysis. *Archives of General Psychiatry, 49,* 651–668.

Gillin, J. C., Zoltoski, R. K., & Salin-Pascual, R. (1995). Basic science of sleep. In H. I. Kaplan & B. J. Sadock (Eds.), *Comprehensive textbook of psychiatry* (6th ed., pp. 80–88). Baltimore: Williams & Wilkins.

Hobson, J. A. (1990). Sleep and dreaming. *Journal of Neuroscience, 10,* 371–382.

Howland, R. H. (1997). Sleep-onset rapid eye movement periods in neuropsychiatric disorders: Implications for the pathophysiology of psychosis. *Journal of Nervous and Mental Disease, 185,* 730–738.

Kelly, D. D. (1991). Sleep and dreaming. In E. R. Kandel, J. H. Schwartz, & T. M. Jessell (Eds.), *Principles of Neural Science* (3rd ed., pp. 792–804). Norwalk, CT: Appleton & Lange.

Kelly, D. D. (1991). Disorders of sleep and consciousness. In E. R. Kandel, J. H. Schwartz, & T. M. Jessell (Eds.), *Principles of Neural Science* (3rd ed., pp. 805–819). Norwalk, CT: Appleton & Lange.

Kupfer, D. J., & Ehlers, C. L. (1989). Two roads to rapid eye movement latency. *Archives of General Psychiatry, 46,* 945–948.

Lauer, C. J., Schreiber, W., Holsboer, F., & Krieg, J. C. (1995). In quest of identifying vulnerability markers for psychiatric disorders by all-night polysomnography. *Archives of General Psychiatry, 52,* 145–153.

Mahowald, M. W., & Schenck, C. H. (1992). Dissociated states of wakefulness and sleep. *Neurology, 42*(Suppl. 6), 44–52.

Steriade, M. (1992). Basic mechanisms of sleep generation. *Neurology, 42*(Suppl. 6), 9–18.

R. H. HOWLAND
University of Pittsburgh

NARCOLEPSY
SLEEP

RATING SCALES

In contrast to the items on a checklist, which require only a yes/no decision by the respondent, rating scale items require the respondent (rater) to make an evaluative judgment on some multicategory continuum. Rating scales are widely employed in business, industry, education, and other organizational contexts to evaluate various behavioral and personality characteristics. Ratings are usually made by another person (e.g., a teacher, supervisor, or peer), but individuals can also rate themselves. A comprehensive treatment of rating scales and checklists is given in Aiken (1996).

On a *numerical rating scale,* the rater assigns to the person being rated (the ratee) one of several numbers corresponding to particular descriptions of the characteristic to be rated. A simple numerical scale for rating a person on "friendliness," for example, might be one on which the rater assigns an integer from 0 to 4 to the person depending on how friendly that person is perceived as being. Also illustrative of a numerical rating scale is the *semantic differential technique,* which has been employed extensively in investigations of the connotative meanings of concepts. Each concept is rated on a 7-point, bipolar adjectival scale. As an example, the concept of "Mother" may be rated on the following three semantic differential scales, according to the concept's meaning to the respondent, in terms of the associated evaluation, potency, and activity dimensions.

                         MOTHER
BAD____:____:____:____:____:____:____GOOD
WEAK____:____:____:____:____:____:____STRONG
SLOW____:____:____:____:____:____:____FAST

Another widely-applied rating method is a *graphic rating scale,* such as the following:

Will lose control all of the time	Will lose control most of the time	Will retain control about half the time	Will retain control most of the time	Will retain control all of the time.

The rater checks the point on the line corresponding to the appropriate description of the ratee.

On a *standard rating scale,* the rater supplies, or is supplied with, a set of standards against which the ratees are to be compared. An example is the *man-to-man rating scale,* which was used for many years by the U.S. Army to rate officers on promotability. A man-to-man scale is constructed for rating individuals on a given trait, say, leadership ability, by instructing the rater to make judgments with respect to five people who fall at different points along a hypothetical continuum of leadership ability. The rater compares each ratee with the five individuals and indicates which of those people the ratee is most like in terms of leadership ability.

Three types of behavioral rating scales have been used extensively in industrial/organizational contexts to increase the objectivity of employee performance evaluations. The first of these is the *behaviorally-anchored rating scale* (BARS), which is constructed from behaviorally descriptive statements (critical incidents) determined from a consensus of expert judgments. On a BARS, evaluators rate employees on these behaviors. A variation of the BARS known as a *behavioral expectation scale* (BES) requires the respondent to rate a set of critical behaviors, not according to whether they have occurred but rather in terms of the respondent's perceived expectation of their occurrence. Also similar to a BARS, in that ratings are made with respect to critical behaviors on several performance dimensions, is a *behavioral observation scale* (BOS).

Ratings on a BOS concern the frequency (never, seldom, sometimes, generally, always) with which each behavior is observed during a specified time interval. Unfortunately, neither the BARS nor the BOS format has been found to be generally superior to a simple graphic or numerical rating scale.

On a *forced-choice rating scale,* raters are presented with two or more descriptions and asked to indicate which one best characterizes the ratee. If there are three or more descriptions, raters may also be told to indicate which is least characteristic of the ratee. An advantage of the forced-choice rating method is that it does a better job than other types of scales in controlling for certain errors in rating. Among these errors are giving ratings that are higher than justified (leniency error) or lower than justified (severity error). The forced-choice format is also promoted as controlling for certain response sets or styles, such as the tendency to answer an item in what the respondent perceives as the socially desirable direction. An example of a forced-choice format is the following tetrad item designed to rate the trait of "leadership ability":

____ Assumes responsibility easily.

____ Doesn't know how or when to delegate.

____ Has many constructive suggestions to offer.

____ Doesn't listen to others' suggestions.

Two of the statements are positive and two are negative, but only one statement in each pair is a critical (keyed) response. In a well designed forced-choice item, the statements in each pair are equal in social desirability so that the respondent cannot tell which is the keyed statement.

Leniency and severity are not the only types of rating errors. Other errors are checking the average (or middle) category too often (central tendency error); rating an individual highly on a certain characteristic or behavior simply because he or she rates highly in other areas (halo effect); rating a person more highly than justified merely because the previous ratee received a very low rating; or rating a person lower than justified because the previous ratee received a very high rating (contrast error). Related to the halo effect is the error of assigning similar ratings to characteristics that the rater views as logically related (logical error). Raters may also be prone to assigning similar ratings to items that are close together on the printed page (proximity error). All of these errors can affect the reliability and validity of ratings, so forced-choice ratings, which are generally less susceptible to such errors, are often considered preferable to other rating procedures. Unfortunately, raters sometimes find it difficult or unnatural to make forced-choice ratings, so the technique has not proved as advantageous as it may seem.

It is not easy to make reliable and valid ratings of people, especially when the behaviors or characteristics being considered are poorly defined or highly subjective. Not only are personal biases likely to affect ratings, but raters often have insufficient knowledge of the ratee to make accurate judgments. However, training in how to make objective ratings and what kinds of errors to be aware of can improve the accuracy of ratings. Familiarizing raters with the persons and characteristics to be rated and permitting them to omit items that they feel unqualified to judge can improve rating accuracy (Stamoulis & Hauenstein, 1993; Sulsky & Day, 1994). On the stimulus side, careful attention to the design of rating scales, especially to providing precise behavioral descriptions of the characteristics to be rated as well as descriptions of the points (anchors) on the rating scales, is important. On the response side, the use of multiple raters can assist in balancing the response biases of individual raters. Finally, an appropriate methodology (research design, sampling, statistical analysis) can help to eliminate or at least control for errors in rating and in interpretation of the results.

Although the majority of rating scales are ad hoc devices designed for use in a particular setting, many standardized scales are commercially available. In business and industry, standard rating scales are used in the selection and classification of personnel, in research on human factors in the work environment, and in analyzing consumer behavior. In educational contexts, standard rating scales are employed in the evaluation of performance by students, teachers, and administrators, and of other features of the educational environment. Standard rating scales are also used extensively in personality research and clinical diagnosis, and in assessing the effectiveness of treatment interventions. Finally, standard rating scales are used in social psychological and sociological studies to measure attitudes, values, and other sociopsychological constructs and behaviors.

REFERENCES

Aiken, L. R. (1996). *Rating scales and checklists.* New York: Wiley.

Stamoulis, D. T., & Hauenstein, N. M. A. (1993). Rater training and rating accuracy: Training for dimensional accuracy versus training for ratee differentiation. *Journal of Applied Psychology, 78,* 994–1003.

Sulsky, L. M., & Day, D. V. (1994). Effects of frame-of-reference training on rater accuracy under alternative time delays. *Journal of Applied Psychology, 79,* 515–543.

L. R. AIKEN
Pepperdine University

MEASUREMENT

RATIONAL EMOTIVE BEHAVIOR THERAPY

Rational Emotive Behavior Therapy (REBT; formerly Rational Emotive Therapy) is a theory of personality and a system of psychological treatment developed in the 1950s by Ellis, an American clinical psychologist. It emphasizes the role of unrealistic expectations and irrational beliefs in human misery. Emotions, Ellis asserted, largely follow from cognitions, not from events. The REBT "A-B-C theory" of personality holds that should an unfortunate event, such as a family quarrel, be followed by extreme anxiety or some other undesirable emotional consequence, inquiry will disclose that consequence C was caused not by activating event A but rather by some irrational belief or beliefs B about the nature or meaning of the quarrel, such as "I am an awful person" or "They are awful and should be punished" or "Without their approval, I cannot go on."

Ellis traces the origins of this discovery about the nature of human upset back nearly 2000 years to the writing of the later Stoic Epictetus and his disciple, Marcus Aurelius, Emperor of Rome, who wrote, "It is not this *thing* which disturbs you, but your own judgment about it" (AD 2nd century, p. 87). Take away the opinion and there is taken away the complaint (Aurelius, 1945, p. 35). However, REBT seeks not only to overcome disturbances caused by false beliefs but also to ameliorate the human predisposition toward crooked thinking that permits false beliefs to flourish. REBT theory, therefore, considers emotional disturbance in the light of human nature, which is viewed as having both biological and social aspects of great significance for theories of personality and treatment.

BIOLOGICAL ORIGINS OF PERSONALITY

The lowest organisms may show complex behavior in the apparent absence of learning because of genetic "preprogramming" or instinct. Such behaviors tend to be found in all members of a species and are performed in fixed stereotypical ways. Humans are largely lacking in fixed, instinctive behaviors, but instead possess a highly evolved capacity to acquire new behaviors through learning and to retain them through habit. What is "preprogrammed" in humans is the clear predisposition to learn and form habits. Thus what one learns to speak depends on culture, but that one learns to speak reflects a powerful predisposition to acquire language. Rational emotive behavior theory holds that such predispositions make some sorts of things more easily learned than others. Children easily learn the desire to be loved rather than hated and readily prefer satisfaction of a want to its frustration. The theory stresses that the capacity to learn includes the capacity to learn nonsense and that the predisposition to think is often the predisposition to think crookedly.

Among human predispositions with unfortunate consequences are tendencies to become overwhelmed by events, to acquire desires for obviously hurtful things, to shed even grotesquely inappropriate habits only with great difficulty, and to think in terms of absolutes that distort even relatively accurate beliefs into disturbingly inaccurate ones.

SOCIAL ORIGINS OF PERSONALITY

Ellis (1962) found many faulty cognitions that appear throughout Western culture. Among these are the beliefs that: to have value one must be loved or approved of by virtually everyone; that one must be perfectly competent and productive; and that it is a catastrophe when things go other than the way one wishes them to. In each instance, the irrational belief is absolutistic and establishes impossible expectations. Thus, while people tend by nature to be happiest when their interpersonal relationships are best, most emotional disturbances result from caring too much about the opinions of others and from holding catastrophic expectations about the consequences of breached relationships.

PERSONALITY AND DISTURBANCE

Rational emotive behavior theory regarding the biosocial origins of the predisposition to irrational thinking and emotional upsets holds that because we are human, it is easy to learn to disturb ourselves and very hard to stop. Accordingly, REBT devotes considerable attention to the mechanisms by which disturbance is perpetuated, because it is by disrupting these mechanisms that change might occur. If thoughts are the cause of emotional upsets, then thinking is the means by which disturbance is perpetuated. The theory holds that regardless of where an irrational belief comes from or how it was learned, it is maintained only by use. People disturb themselves and perpetuate their own misery through habitual internal verbalizations of their irrational beliefs. When confronted by an action or event that might fairly be called unfortunate, the person goes beyond an accurate, rational cognitive response to an exaggerated, absolutistic one that elicits emotional upsets and self-defeating behavior. The theory finds in the human tendency toward self-reindoctrination a significant access point into the self-defeating patterns of thought and action of its clients: Eliminate the irrational thought and the upset dissipates. Eliminate the irrational thinking and the problem will not recur. People tend to be happier and more effective when they are thinking and behaving rationally.

REBT APPROACHES TO TREATMENT

Although REBT therapists may employ a wide variety of specific techniques in therapy, the intent is to minimize or eradicate irrational beliefs and to foster a more rational lifestyle. The therapist seeks to reeducate the client, to break down old patterns and establish new ones, using logic, reason, confrontation, exhortation teaching, prescription, example, role-playing, behavioral assignments, and more. The central technique is disputation, a logicoempirical analysis through which irrational beliefs are identified and challenged.

The initial goal of therapy is to help the client achieve three insights in the course of therapy. Insight number one is that while self-defeating behaviors and emotional malfunctions have understandable origins in the past and provocations in the present, their current and proximal cause lies with one's irrational beliefs and not with one's parents, history, or circumstances. Insight number two is that these irrational, magical beliefs remain in force only in consequence of the continued mixed-up thinking and foolish behaviors that actively reinforce them. People remain disturbed because, and for only so long as, they continue to reindoctrinate themselves. Insight number three is that insights do not correct crooked thinking. Only hard work and practice can do this. Of the process of establishing these insights, Ellis has said that the essence of effective psychotherapy is "full tolerance of the client as an individual combined with a ruthless, hard headed campaign against his self-defeating ideas, traits, and performances" (Ellis, 1973, p. 169, emphasis in the original).

Fundamental to REBT is a broad campaign to push clients to work against their major irrational premises. This work is done on several fronts. Because humans can think about their thinking, it is possible to use cognitive methods to show clients the flawed nature of their expectations, demands, and beliefs, and to teach them to think more rationally. The REBT practitioner mainly relies on cognitive methods, but emotive procedures also may be used that, through role-playing and otherwise, may set the stage for the actual occurrence of irrational beliefs and their attendant upsets and behavioral tendencies, which can then be analyzed and corrected. They also may be used to counteract such beliefs at the level of demonstrations, as when the therapist, or perhaps the therapy group, accepts clients in spite of "unacceptable" traits or attributes. Emotive methods are also employed to evoke feelings and reactions leading directly to changes in attitudes or values. As an active, directive, educative approach, REBT also uses behavioral methods, both in the office and through homework assignments. Perfectionistic clients may be instructed to fail deliberately at some real task in order to observe the noncatastrophic nature of the consequences, or shy persons may be required to take progressively larger risks in social settings to learn that failure is neither inevitable nor intolerable. Once clients begin to behave in ways that challenge their major behavioral beliefs, they are encouraged to continue to do so, because actions may in fact speak louder than words in maintaining change. Ellis (1975) observed that "humans rarely change and keep disbelieving a profoundly self-defeating belief unless they act against it" (p. 20).

REBT has continuously evolved and grown since its inception in the 1950s. Along the way, Ellis has twice changed the name from its original designation as rational therapy (RT). In part, the name changes were educative, intended to identify first REBT's cognitive nature, and later to emphasize also the role of emotion in thinking and emotive methods to treatment. From 1961 through 1992, REBT was known by the now familiar title of rational emotive therapy. But REBT has also included a behavior emphasis from the beginning, which was incorporated into its current "full title." In part, the name change also reflects gradual changes in emphasis and methods.

Depending on clinical needs, REBT often incorporates cognitive, emotive, and behavioral elements within a single case, or even within a single complex intervention. Regardless of the methods used, the goal remains constant: to help clients to foster their "natural human tendencies to gain more individuality, freedom of choice and enjoyment," and to help them discipline themselves against their "natural human tendencies to be conforming, suggestible and unenjoying" (Ellis, 1973).

REFERENCES

Aurelius, Marcus. (1945). The meditations of Marcus Aurelius. In *Marcus Aurelius and his times.* New York: Black.

Ellis, A. (1962). *Reason and emotion in psychotherapy.* New York: Stuart.

Ellis, A. (1973). *Humanistic psychotherapy: A rational approach.* New York: Julian Press.

Ellis, A. (1973). Rational emotive behavior therapy. In R. J. Corsini (Ed.), *Current psychotherapies.* Itasca, IL: Peacock.

Ellis, A. (1975). The rational-emotive approach to sex therapy. *Counseling Psychologist, 5*(1), 14–22. (Reprinted, New York: Institute for Rational Living, 1975.)

R. E. ENFIELD

COGNITIVE BEHAVIOR THERAPY
PERSONALITY THEORY
PSYCHOTHERAPY

READING DISABILITIES

DEFINITION AND PREVALENCE ESTIMATES

A reading disability is one type of learning disability that has been identified in school age children. Public Law 94-142 defines a specific learning disability as

a disorder in one or more of the basic psychological processes involved in understanding or in using language, spoken or written, which may manifest itself in an imperfect ability to listen, speak, read, write, spell, or to do mathematical calculations. The term includes such conditions as perceptual handicaps, brain injury, minimal brain dysfunction, dyslexia, and developmental aphasia. The term does not include children who have learning disabilities which are primarily the result of visual, hearing, or motor handicaps, or mental retardation, or emotional disturbance, or of environmental, cultural, or economic disadvantage.

The term "reading disability" is often used interchangeably with the term "specific reading disability," and with the term "developmental dyslexia." While there is agreement that the major difficulty for children with such disabilities is at the level of written word recognition, there have been different approaches to defining reading disabilities. One approach has been to define a reading disability as a significant discrepancy between a child's potential ability (as measured by an IQ test) and his or her performance on a standardized reading test. Children who show this discrepancy have often been labeled as having a "specific reading disability," while children who show the same low reading performance without a discrepancy between their reading and IQ test scores have sometimes been classified as "garden variety" poor readers.

The merits of dividing poor readers into these two groups has fallen out of favor in much of the current literature on reading disabilities. Basic cognitive processes related to reading words do not appear to differ between these two groups of children (Stanovich & Siegel, 1994), and there is no evidence to suggest that the two groups would benefit differentially from remediation. One solution to this seemingly false dichotomy has been the operational definition of a reading disability often used in the research literature: A child who falls within the average range on an intelligence test and is performing worse than 75% of same-age peers on a standardized word recognition test is identified as reading-disabled (e.g., Metsala, 1997).

One popular misconception has been that a reading disability is

an entity in much the same way that a disease is an entity. It is more realistic, however, to characterize reading ability as a graded continuum, rather than a discrete category (Stanovich, 1989; Snow, Burns, & Griffin, 1998). At one end of the continuum are children with well-developed reading skills; at the other end are those whose reading development appears to have been arrested at a very early stage. The arbitrary nature of partitioning the reading ability continuum appears to preclude any concrete definition of reading disabilities. It is important to note that children who are close to a given cutoff criterion will show many similar cognitive characteristics to the group identified as disabled, and may need similar school support.

An estimate of the prevalence of reading disabilities varies with the criteria used to define the category. With large-scale epidemiological studies, these estimates range from 3.5 to 8% of school age children. It is believed that reading disabilities account for approximately 80% of the children classified in schools under the more general category of "learning disabled" (see Snow et al., 1998, for discussion).

READING PROFILE AND COGNITIVE PROCESSES IN READING DISABILITIES

Skilled readers recognize most words with such automaticity that conscious resources are available to focus at the level of comprehension (a multifaceted and complex skill). As young children learn to read, most letter patterns that make up written words are still unfamiliar to them. Children learn and use the individual correspondences between letters and sounds (phonemes) to read these unfamiliar words. Only a few successful trials of sounding out a word appear necessary before the letter pattern of a word is recognized accurately and quickly (Ehri, 1998). These words are often said to have become part of a child's sight-word vocabulary. Applying letter-sound correspondences to decode words plays a major role in the development of skilled reading (Share, 1995).

Children with reading disabilities are unable to read words accurately and/or quickly. The task of decoding words becomes so laborious that these children do not build up an adequate sight-word vocabulary, have little attention to focus on the meaning of a text, and become very discouraged with reading. There is consensus in the research that the task at which disabled readers fail is learning the letter-sound correspondences and applying these to read individual words, a process often referred to as phonological recoding. The argument that phonological recoding is the main task that arrests these children's reading development is supported by the robust finding that when compared to groups of younger children who recognize words at the same grade level, the reading-disabled group performs more poorly on recognizing pseudowords (Rack, Snowling, & Olson, 1992). Pseudowords (e.g., "blint") cannot be recognized as sight-words, but require a phonological recoding strategy to be read. Surprisingly, reading-disabled children do show the same advantage as normal readers for reading regular versus irregular words (Metsala, Stanovich, & Brown, 1998).

Disabled readers have been shown to have deficits at the level of processing the sound system of a language. These basic language deficits may, in part, explain the persistent difficulty with learning the letter-sound correspondences. One primary deficit for these children is in oral language tasks that require a child to recognize, isolate, and manipulate individual sounds (phonemes) within words. For example, reading-disabled children have difficulty counting the number of sounds in words (e.g., /ship/ has three individual sounds), or segmenting an orally presented word into its individual sounds (e.g., /cat/ is made up of each of the sounds, /c/ /a/ /t/). These tasks measure what is called phoneme awareness. Reading-disabled children show deficits in phoneme awareness even when compared to younger children who are reading at the same grade level as the disabled group. Facility with phoneme segments at an oral level facilitates learning grapheme-phoneme correspondences in normal reading development, and impairs this learning in the disabled reader.

The processes of phonological short-term memory and rapid access to phonological information have also been implicated as basic cognitive deficits of reading-disabled children. Torgesen, Morgan, and Davis (1992; for review see Torgesen & Burgess, 1998) have demonstrated that the processes of phoneme awareness, phonological short-term memory, and rapid automatic naming, form stable individual differences over the period of early childhood development and are therefore good candidates for proximal causes of reading disabilities.

NEUROLOGICAL BASES AND HERITABILITY OF READING DISABILITIES

From studies using technological methodologies such as positron emission topography (PET), computed tomography (CT), and functional magnetic resonance imaging (fMRI), it has been found that children and adults with reading disabilities have a higher incidence of cerebral symmetry or reverse asymmetry; this is different than the commonly found left-hemisphere asymmetry, found in normal readers linked to cerebral dominance for language functions (Riccio & Hynd, 1996). Studies using PET, MRI, and rCBF (regional cerebral blood flow) while subjects read words have shown that reading depends on neural activity in several brain regions in both right and left hemispheres. Differences have been found in the occipital and frontal lobe regions of dyslexics as compared to normal readers. For example, in single-word reading tasks, normal readers have demonstrated higher right than left prefrontal activity while dyslexic individuals had symmetric prefrontal activity. Auditory, phonological, and rhyming tasks have also evidenced less activation in left parietal and left-middle temporal areas for dyslexics than for normal controls (Rumsey et al., 1992; for review see Riccio & Hynd, 1996).

Olson and his colleagues (1989) have used behavior-genetic analyses to discriminate between heritable and environmental influences on two component processes in word recognition: phonological recoding and orthographic coding (ability to use word-specific knowledge). Their findings have suggested that phonological coding deficits are significantly heritable. These researchers suggest that an underlying causal factor of the phonological deficits in reading-disabled children is likely to be a heritable weakness in segmental language skills (Olson et al., 1989). Findings from both neurology and heritability studies are consistent with the cognitive research, which identifies language-based cognitive processes as underlying causes of reading disabilities.

RESEARCH ON TREATMENT AND REMEDIATION

Treatment programs that have been most successful with reading-disabled students have included explicit instruction in aspects of word recognition. Lovett, Ransby, and Barron (1988) have found that reading-disabled children provided with intense and systematic instruction in word decoding skills (segmenting and blending written words, written spelling, and rapid word recognition) improved in word recognition and spelling for trained words better than did children who were taught higher-order oral and written language skills. The positive results, however, did not transfer to new words.

Wise, Olson, Ring, and Johnson (1998; Olson, Wise, Ring, & Johnson, 1997) have used computer supported programs to help reading-disabled children to learn phonological recoding skills. Their results showed that the children with higher pretreatment levels of phonological awareness showed better gains in word recognition, and students receiving explicit instruction in phonological recoding showed greater improvement than did groups of children receiving computer support for word recognition, which was embedded in story contexts.

A consensus in the literature appears to be that for severely disabled readers, programs that contain an explicit and intense focus on phoneme awareness skills, followed by training in word decoding strategies, produce the best gains in generalizable word recognition skills (e.g., Lovett, 1997; Torgesen et al., 1992; Wise et al., 1998). To improve phoneme awareness in reading-disabled children, it may be necessary to provide intensive training in recognizing the articulatory gestures associated with each sound. This training, combined with instruction in grapheme-phoneme correspondences and practice on decontextualized word and pseudo-word reading, appears to have the most impact on the word recognition deficits in disabled readers.

REFERENCES

Ehri, L. C. (1998). Grapheme-phoneme knowledge is essential for learning to read words in English. In J. L. Metsala & L. C. Ehri (Eds.)., *Word recognition in beginning literacy* (pp. 3–40). Mahwah, NJ: Erlbaum.

Lovett, M. W. (1997). The effectiveness of remedial programs for reading disabled children of different ages: Does the benefit decrease for older children? *Learning Disability Quarterly, 20,* 189–207.

Lovett, M. W., Ransby, M. J., & Barron, R. W. (1988). Treatment, subtype, and word type effects in dyslexic children's response to remediation. *Brain and Language, 34,* 328–349.

Metsala, J. L. (1997). Spoken word recognition in reading disabled children. *Journal of Educational Psychology, 159–169.*

Metsala, J. L., Stanovich, K. E., & Brown, G. D. A. (1998). Regularity effects and the phonological deficit model of reading disabilities: A meta-analytic review. *Journal of Educational Psychology, 90,* 279–293.

Olson, R., Wise, B., Conners, F., Rack, J., & Fulker, D. (1989). Specific deficits in component reading and language skills: Genetic and environmental influences. *Journal of Learning Disabilities,* *22*(6), 339–347.

Olson, R. K., Wise, B. W., Ring, J., & Johnson, M. (1997). Computer-based remedial training in phoneme awareness and phonological decoding: Effects on post-training development of word recognition. *Scientific Studies of Reading, 1,* 235–253.

Rack, J., Snowling, M., & Olson, R. (1992). The nonword reading deficit in developmental dyslexia: A review. *Reading Research Quarterly, 27,* 28–53.

Riccio, C. A., & Hynd, G. W. (1996). Neuroanatomical and neurophysiological aspects of dyslexia. *Topics in Language Disorders,* *16*(2), 1–13.

Rumsey, J. M., Andreason, P., Zametkin, A. J., Aquino, T., King, A. C., Hamburger, S. D., Pikus, A., Rapoport, J. L., & Cohen, R. M. (1992). Failure to activate the left temporoparietal cortex in dyslexia. *Archives of Neurology, 49,* 527–534.

Share, D. L. (1995). Phonological recoding and self-teaching: Sine qua non of reading acquisition. *Cognition, 55,* 151–218.

Snow, C. E., Burns, M. S., & Griffin, P. (1998). *Preventing reading difficulties in young children.* Washington, DC: National Academy Press.

Stanovich, K. E. (1989). Various varying views on variation. *Journal of Learning Disabilities, 22,* 366–369.

Stanovich, K. E., & Siegel, L. S. (1994). The phenotypic performance profile of reading disabled children: A regression based test of the phonological-core variable-difference model. *Journal of Educational Psychology, 86,* 24–53.

Torgesen, J. K., & Burgess, S. R. (1998). Consistency of reading-related phonological processes throughout early childhood: Evidence from longitudinal-correlational and instructional studies. In J. L. Metsala & L. C. Ehri (Eds.), *Word recognition in beginning literacy* (pp. 161–188). Mahwah, NJ: Erlbaum.

Torgesen, J. K., Morgan, S. T., & Davis C. (1992). Effects of two types of phonological awareness training on word learning in kindergarten children. *Journal of Educational Psychology, 84,* 364–370.

Wise, B. W., Olson, R. K., Ring, J., & Johnson, M. (1998). Interactive computer support for improving phonological skills. In J. L. Metsala & L. C. Ehri (Eds.), *Word recognition in beginning literacy* (pp. 189–208). Mahwah, NJ: Erlbaum.

A. Taboada
J. L. Metsala
University of Maryland

LEARNING DISABILITIES

REALITY THERAPY

The concepts of reality therapy, developed by William Glasser, were first published in *Reality Therapy* in 1965. While the principles have remained the same, the original ideas have been continuously expanded and refined. The latest major expansion has been to relate the concepts to the way our brain works as an input control system, as described in Glasser's 1981 book, *Stations of the Mind.*

The theory of reality therapy holds that humans not only have the inherent need to survive, but are also driven by equally strong inherent needs to belong, compete, have fun, and be free. All those who need or seek psychotherapy suffer from their inability to control the world around them in a way in which these needs can be reasonably satisfied.

The task of the reality therapist is to gain enough rapport so that the client can face what it is he or she needs and then to get the client to evaluate the behaviors that the client is choosing to satisfy these needs. To do this, the therapist focuses upon present behavior by continually asking the question, "What are you doing?" The therapist then helps the client to assess strengths and to plan more need-fulfilling behavior to replace the behavior that the client judged inadequate.

When a satisfactory plan is worked out, the therapist asks that the client commit to the plan, accepts no excuses, and doggedly continues this plan until the client begins to fulfill needs in better ways. In the reality therapy casebook by Naomi Glasser entitled *What Are You Doing?*, 24 reality therapists tell in detail how this step-by-step process helps clients of all ages and in almost every conceivable psychological difficulty.

REALITY THERAPY THEORY

The theory of reality therapy is based upon Glasser's belief that all living creatures are driven by powerful needs that must be satisfied. Human beings, the most complex creatures evolution has produced, have the most complex needs: to survive, to become secure, to belong and love, to gain self-esteem and power, to have fun, and to be free. While these specific needs probably evolved from the basic survival need they are all equal in potency at this time in our evolution. For example, only humans will risk lives or commit suicide in efforts to fulfill needs. If they are able to satisfy them, humans behave in ways to maintain or increase the resulting pleasure. But if they are unable to satisfy these needs, pain occurs, and paradoxically, people may behave in ways to maintain, or even increase, the pain even though the ultimate purpose is to reduce suffering.

Reality therapy is a psychological system designed to help people to satisfy their needs in more efficient ways. Since all are driven by the same needs built into genetic structures, the main differences between people are the degrees of effectiveness by which they are able to satisfy these needs.

Reality therapists care little about standard psychological diagnoses and they generally describe people by the general behaviors chosen to attempt to satisfy their needs. People tend to choose similar behaviors in their constant struggle to satisfy these needs. Therefore, the few classification efforts in which reality therapists engage are an attempt to define similar behaviors but with full knowledge that differences between people are potentially so extreme that any system of classification will be fraught with error and will be, at best, inaccurate.

Essentially two broad classes of people defined by their similar behaviors are: (a) those who generally fulfill themselves and are successful and happy much of the time and (b) those unable to do so and who suffer much pain and failure. Those who fail are further divided into several groups. First are those who give up; for example, children who fail in school and seem to settle for this failure. Because of forces built into genetic structures, people who give up and stop trying temporarily begin compensatory behavior no matter how ineffective it may be. Second, some who attempt to give up find that they cannot do so. They then choose a wide variety of symptomatic behaviors, mostly painful and ineffective, but the best that they are capable of at the time. Examples are behaviors with powerful feeling components, such as anger, which lead to acting out, or depressed behaviors that lead to misery and apathy. In this general category are anxiety, headaches, and backaches, as well as phobic, obsessive, and compulsive behaviors. Even though humans are usually not aware of it, these behaviors are chosen as their best attempt to fulfill their needs.

Addictions are chosen behaviors, attempts to gain pleasure, and can be divided into two groups: *positive,* in which addicts become addicted to the pleasure of a repetitive strengthening behavior; and *negative,* in which they become dependent on the pleasure of chemicals such as alcohol or morphine even though the chemical is almost always eventually harmful. Finally, there are psychosomatic diseases in which real tissue damage occurs. Some people begin to behave in such creatively aberrant ways that they are judged insane. Neither psychosomatic disease nor psychosis is chosen in the same way as depressive behaviors or headaches are selected but both are products of an organism desperately trying to fulfill its needs, even if it leads to physiological self-destruction or denial of reality in this inexorable process. To fulfill needs, the human brain acts as a control system, continually acting on the world in an attempt to fulfill the needs built into it.

Reality therapy denies that behavior is primarily generated by forces outside the body and, therefore, all behaviorism (operant or not) that holds that people do not react to the world is viewed as essentially incorrect. Miserable as the struggles may be, humans always act to attempt to control the world; what is done is never primarily generated because of what is going on in the world. Simply stated, it only seems that a car stops because a light turns red. The real reason is that the driver wants to stay alive, and stopping a car is a sensible way to do this. Just as one stops at a red light to stay alive, people choose to be depressed to deal with painful situations, such as when a spouse has left. Humans use depression as a powerful cry for help. How this works is described in Glasser's *Stations of the Mind.*

Reality therapy is an attempt to help people take better or more effective control of what they choose to do with their lives—to choose better behaviors and, in doing so, better fulfill their innate needs.

REFERENCES

Glasser, W. (1965). *Reality therapy: A new approach to psychiatry.* New York: Harper & Row.

Glasser, W. (1981). *Stations of the mind.* New York: Harper & Row.

SUGGESTED READING

Glasser, W. (1972). *The identity society.* New York: Harper & Row.

Glasser, W. (1976). *Positive addiction.* New York: Harper & Row.

Powers, W. T. (1973). *Behavior: The control of perception.* Chicago: Aldine.

W. GLASSER
The William Glasser Institute

PSYCHOTHERAPY

RECIPROCAL INHIBITION

Animal central nervous systems (CNSs) together with peripheral reflex loops form the basis of all animal movements. It has long been recognized that the CNS is primarily responsible for generating the motor neuron firing patterns that underlie repetitive movements—that is, those that have a rhythmic expression (Delcomyn, 1980). An important aim in neurobiology is to identify the neuronal circuits underlying these rhythmic behaviors and to understand how the rhythmic motor patterns arise from neuronal connections and neuronal properties (Friesen & Stent, 1978).

The term "reciprocal inhibition" refers to a model or concept that was formulated at the beginning of this century by T. G. Brown (1911) to explain the neuronal origins of rhythmic walking movements. This first explanation for how a circuit of neurons can cause alternating limb movements was formulated long before specific neuronal circuits were identified. At that time, experiments by several researchers, including Brown, demonstrated that the stepping movements of animal limbs could be elicited even in deafferented mammalian preparations. That is, cats that had sensory axons severed to remove all possibility of sensory feedback from the periphery to the CNS could still perform at least the rudiments of stepping movements. These experiments led to the concept that a CNS oscillator exists within the vertebrate spinal cord to generate the neuronal impulse patterns that lead to repetitive animal movements. Brown's model for this central spinal oscillator envisioned two sets of neurons coupled by reciprocal (that is, mutually) inhibitory synapses (Fig. 1A) for each limb or even for each joint. Because of the synaptic inhibitory connections only one of the two inhibitory neurons (or perhaps pools of inhibitory neurons) can be active at any one time. Moreover, the activity of the two neurons alternates (Fig. 1B). With appropriate connections to motor neurons, output of these inhibitory neurons can control the activity of first flexor and then extensor motor neurons. Thus, the alternating neuronal patterns generated by the central circuit can drive the appropriate impulse patterns needed to command rhythmic flexion and extension, and hence to forward and backward movements of individual limbs (Brown, 1911).

Simple reciprocal inhibition alone cannot generate oscillations. Rather, additional dynamic (time-varying) properties are needed to ensure that mutually inhibitory neurons do not act as a simple, bistable switch (Friesen & Stent, 1978). Brown proposed two such dynamic properties: synaptic fatigue, a synaptic property; and postinhibitory rebound (PIR), a cellular property. If the strength of synaptic interactions is labile in a reciprocally inhibitory circuit, continuous excitation of either neuron will only transiently inhibit the other one (Fig. 1C1). If both neurons of the reciprocally in-

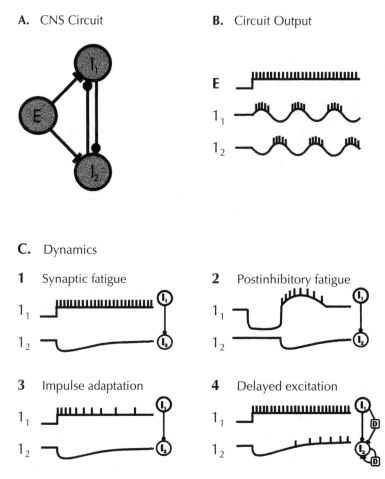

A. CNS Circuit

B. Circuit Output

C. Dynamics

1 Synaptic fatigue

2 Postinhibitory fatigue

3 Impulse adaptation

4 Delayed excitation

Figure 1. Model of a neuronal circuit that generates oscillations via reciprocal inhibition. A. Circuit diagram. Three neurons, one excitatory (E) and two inhibitory (I_1 and I_2) are interconnected by excitatory (—|) and inhibitory synapses (—•). The output of this circuit B. consists of antiphasic membrane potential oscillations and impulse bursts generated by the two inhibitory neurons when the excitatory cell is active. C. Dynamic properties associated with reciprocal inhibitory oscillator circuits. Insets at the right of the traces illustrate the synaptic interactions. The upper trace in each part of the figure shows the activity of a presynaptic neuron; the lower traces illustrate the effect of this activity on a postsynaptic cell. C1. Synaptic fatigue. Constant excitatory drive to I_1 generates an initially large, but then declining, hyperpolarization in I_2. C2. Postinhibitory rebound. When neuron I_1 is inhibited (hyperpolarized) briefly the termination of the inhibition is followed by an excitatory response with the membrane potential overshoots rest to generate a brief burst of impulses. This PIR causes transient inhibition of neuron I_2. C3. Impulse adaptation. Constant excitatory drive to neuron I_1 elicits a train of impulses whose frequency declines with time. The effect on neuron I_2 is a negative change in membrane potential (hyperpolarization) whose amplitude declines as the presynaptic impulse frequency declines. C4. Delayed excitation. "D" designates a delay factor for excitation that could be either synaptic or cellular.

hibitory pair receive continuous excitatory input, the result will be antiphasic oscillations, as demonstrated by the following consideration. If neuron 1 is activated first it will inhibit neuron 2 until the synapse fatigues. Once the synapse has weakened, neuron 2 will be relieved of inhibition and will be activated by the excitatory input, shutting off neuron 1. While neuron 2 is active, the synaptic terminal of the inhibited neuron recovers from fatigue and can once again inhibit neuron 2 when the synapse from neuron 2 to neuron 1 has weakened sufficiently for neuron 1 to become reactivated.

In neurons expressing the dynamic property PIR, the membrane potential overshoots the resting level at the termination of an inhibitory, hyperpolarizing input (Fig. 1C2). Also termed "paradoxical excitation," this property provides transient excitatory drive when inhibition ceases. Membrane properties that can generate PIR include inactivation of a sodium conductance, such as is associated with the nerve impulse, and activation of an excitatory,

inward current by membrane hyperpolarization (Calabrese & Arbas, 1989). As Brown realized, postinhibitory rebound in a circuit consisting of two reciprocally inhibitory neurons can suffice to generate stable, antiphasic oscillations (Perkel & Mulloney, 1974).

Two additional dynamic properties that can contribute to rhythmicity in neuronal circuits have been proposed. One cellular property is impulse adaptation, in which a continuously excited neuron emits a train of impulses with decreasing frequency (Fig. 1C3). The effect of adaptation, like that of synaptic fatigue, is to limit the duration of inhibition, again ensuring that a pair of mutually inhibitory neurons alternate activity rather than forming a bistable switch. A final dynamic effect is delayed excitation, which can arise either because of complex circuit properties in which the inhibitory interaction between cells is superceded in time by synaptic excitation, or because of hyperpolarization-induced excitatory currents. Rather than reducing the amplitude of the inhibitory interaction, these two cellular and circuit properties act as sources of delayed excitatory drive to overcome synaptic inhibition (Fig. 1C4).

Brown's neuronal model for rhythm generation is known either as reciprocal inhibition or as the half-center model. Although reciprocal inhibition served as the only important conceptual model for generating rhythmic movements for many years, it was first authenticated experimentally by the finding that reciprocal inhibition is one component of the rhythm-generating mechanism in the pyloric system of the lobster stomatogastric ganglion (Miller & Selverston, 1985). Since then, the model has been applied with success to a variety of neuronal circuits that generate animal behavior (Friesen, 1994). Examples include swimming movements in lamprey, tadpoles, the marine mollusks *Clione* and *Tritonia,* and the leech. The rhythmic contraction of leech heart tubes provides an especially well-described preparation in which reciprocal inhibition generates the oscillations (Calabrese & Arbas, 1989).

REFERENCES

Brown, T. G. (1911). The intrinsic factors in the act of progression in the mammal. *Proceedings of the Royal Society of London, 84,* 308–319.

Calabrese, R. L., & Arbas, E. A. (1989). Central and peripheral oscillators generating heartbeat in the leech *Hirudo medicinalis.* In J. W. Jacklet (Ed.), *Cellular and neuronal oscillators* (pp. 237–267). New York: Marcel Dekker.

Delcomyn, F. (1980). Neural basis of rhythmic behavior in animals. *Science, 210,* 492–498.

Friesen, W. O., & Stent, G. S. (1978). Neural circuits for generating rhythmic movements. *Annual Review of Biophysics & Bioengineering, 7,* 37–61.

Friesen, W. O. (1994). Reciprocal inhibition: A mechanism underlying oscillatory animal movements. *Neuroscience and Biobehavior Review, 18,* 547–553.

Miller, J. P., & Selverston, A. I. (1985). Neuronal mechanisms for the production of the lobster pyloric motor pattern. In A. I. Selverston (Ed.), *Model neural networks and behavior* (pp. 37–48). New York: Plenum.

Perkel, D. H., & Mulloney, B. (1974). Motor pattern production in reciprocally inhibitory neurons exhibiting postinhibitory rebound. *Science, 185,* 181–183.

W. O. FRIESEN
University of Virginia

REFLECTIVE LISTENING

RECOVERY OF FUNCTION

Everyone has had the experience of having had an injury, burning a finger, scraping an elbow, stubbing a toe, or perhaps cutting oneself or even breaking a bone. The universal feature of this experience is that, with care, treatment, and time, the injury heals and usually nothing more than a scar and a faded memory remain.

Such recovery is not common with an injury to the nervous system. One of the most important goals in the field of neuroscience is the issue of recovery of function following nerve, spinal cord, or brain injury. It is an unfortunate fact that injuries of the nervous system can produce profound deficits in quality of life. Sometimes these deficits are obvious, as when an injured nerve affects motor or sensory functioning. Sometimes there are profound deficits without obvious signs of injury, as when someone suffers from memory loss from developmental/aging effects, such as autism or Alzheimer's disease. In either case it is desirable to be able to restore functioning.

Sometimes, however, instances of considerable recovery of function following brain injury occur. Stroke patients who initially have profound language disorders, for example, may in the long term have restoration of much of their language function. Until recently, as found in the animal experimental literature, scientists have difficulty in localizing neural correlates of functioning because the effects of damage were only temporarily observed with significant amounts of recovery of function over time. Ideally, with enough understanding of the nervous system, we might be able to promote recovery of function. The study of brain-behavior relationships, of localization of function, and of recovery of function, are intimately associated themes.

THEORIES

The following are the four major theories that account for instances of recovery of function following brain injury. No one theory fully accounts for the spectrum of observed recovery, nor are the theories mutually exclusive—more than one factor may be involved in recovery. To a certain extent, these theories provide a heuristic outline of the factors that affect recovery. It is hoped that a better understanding of these factors will lead to more effective treatment of the injured.

Vicariation

Vicariation means "second-handed." Recovery by vicariation occurs when an injury damages the part of the nervous system that is actually responsible for a function, and a second neural structure that had never been involved in that function now takes over for the injured structure and performs the previously lost function. A key feature of vicariation is that the structure that takes over the function was never previously involved in the original behavior. This distinction is lost in some treatments.

The best example of vicariation is the observation that injuries in young individuals are said to be less deleterious than similar damage in adults. For example, damage to the left hemisphere in a stroke can cause profound loss of language functions in an adult. Children with left hemisphere damage, however, often do not show severe language deficits. This observation fits the idea of the plasticity of the developing organism.

This concept—that youngsters are less affected by brain injury—has been applied in laboratory experiments where it has generally been found that damage is less intrusive in young individuals. For example, damage to the frontal lobes does not produce delayed response deficits in young monkeys, and damage to the septal region does not produce social cohesiveness in young rats. However, it is not always true that an early lesion is beneficial. In these two examples, when the individual becomes an adult, delayed response deficits and increased social cohesiveness appear. Thus, the effects of the damage may not be obvious until the individual matures.

Of all the theories of recovery of function, the theory of vicariation is the least likely one to be true. This is because much of the recovery that has been attributed to vicariation is actually due to a region that already has some functioning. As a result, the following theories are more likely explanations, and thus more likely to cause recovery.

DIASCHESIS

Diaschesis refers to the effects of shock. Recovery by diaschesis occurs when a nervous system injury does not actually *damage* the tissue that is responsible for the lost function, but rather that the injury causes a shock effect that indirectly and deleteriously affects normal functioning, with function returning when the shock subsides. Shock can occur with temporary loss of the blood supply (loss of nutrients, including glucose and oxygen, or loss of functions that remove waste metabolic products), or with temporary loss of necessary modulating neural activity. The key feature is that when functioning returns it is mediated by the very same tissue that was responsible for the function in the first place, so that the recovered behavior is exactly the same as the original one. Thus, the idea of sparing is essential in the context of diaschesis.

Time appears to be the major manipulation to affect diaschesis. However, time itself is not a very profound or necessarily helpful explanation. The real question is what happens that takes time to dissipate the effects of shock, or more to the point, what can be done to diminish the effects of shock. Steroid drugs have been given to prevent the effects of swelling, for example, and have some effect in mitigating loss of function from some spinal cord injuries. To be effective the treatment must occur soon after the injury. Since the brain and spinal cord are enclosed within the cranium and spinal column, respectively, any swelling of the nervous system in these confined spaces can cause substantial damage that is secondary to the original injury. Thus, besides indirect effects of shock, any injury can cause additional damage.

One example of diaschesis from the laboratory is known as the Sprague effect. Damage to one superior colliculus in cats causes a visual neglect in the opposite visual field; that is, objects are ignored if they are presented in that visual field. Subsequent damage to the visual cortex on the same side immediately restores reactions in the affected visual field. This example represents diaschesis by loss of normal neural modulatory influences. Here, subcortical visual regions in the pretectal area receive two visual inputs, one from the eye through the optic nerve to the superior colliculus, the other through the visual cortex. Damaging the superior colliculus causes an imbalance in the pretectal region. By subsequently damaging the visual cortex, the balance in the pretectal region is restored. This illustrates one of the major ways of thinking about diaschesis, which is that it is a balance of modulation of neural sources.

Another example from the laboratory is the loss of a simple visual discrimination for brightness. Rats trained on a black-white discrimination will appear to have lost that memory when their visual cortices are removed. With subsequent training the rats reacquire the ability to discriminate black from white. Since it takes about as many trials to relearn as it did to originally learn, this appears to be a case of vicariation in which another part of the brain (presumably the remaining cortex) takes over functioning. If, however, subsequent training is creating a new memory, then it should not matter whether training after the brain injury is made with the black or white stimulus as the correct choice. But reversing the correct choice profoundly interferes with subsequent training. This shows that although the brain injury appears to have removed the original memory, in fact, the memory remains to interfere with reversal training.

A number of manipulations have been found to affect recovery through diaschesis, each associated with diminishing the effects of shock and enhancing the expression of the spared tissue: extensive preoperative training, interoperative retraining (serial lesions), extensive postoperative retraining, cross-modal training on similar problems (i.e., training using other sensory modalities), drugs that diminish shock (e.g., steroids), and drugs that enhance access to the spared tissue. As with strategies to improve performance on exams, a practical strategy to lessen the effects of future brain injury or the inevitable effects of aging would be to overlearn with multiple cues and learning methods.

Parkinson's disease provides an example from the clinical literature in which diminishing the effects of diaschesis prevents the initial appearance of symptoms. Parkinson's disease is a movement and thought disorder caused by progressive degeneration of cells in the substantia nigra that project dopamine to the basal ganglia. Its symptoms appear only when so many nigra cells die that only about 20% of the normal amount of dopamine remains in the basal ganglia. Until that point, it appears that the basal ganglia can compensate for the loss of dopamine (see supersensitivity, below). It is only when the dopamine projection to the basal ganglia falls below a critical point that the symptoms of Parkinson's show themselves. Presumably, slow progressive disorder does not produce the effects of shock that would be seen with one larger lesion.

Of the factors that account for recovery of function from brain injury, diaschesis is one of the most important.

Neural Reorganization

Neural reorganization generally refers to the body's own mechanisms for recognizing loss and for healing itself. However, man-made interventions can also be classified as reorganization. By far, neural reorganization receives the most attention of the four theories, although its practical usefulness has yet to be realized. Several means of effecting neural reorganization have been described. These mechanisms are adaptations of means that the nervous system has for normal development and growth rather than specialized adaptations that might have evolved solely for the purpose of a complex brain's ability to repair itself. That is, one questionable idea about brain organization in general is the idea that more complex brains, being more susceptible to injury of their delicate mechanisms, somehow developed a new method of dealing with brain injury. That seems not to be the case. The following is a brief review of the known mechanisms of reorganization.

Reactive Synaptogenesis   "Synaptogenesis" refers to new synapse formation. This mechanism is essential developmentally for correctly hooking up the nervous system (along with overproduction and selective cell death, as in programmed cell death or apoptosis). "Reactive" refers to an action in response to injury. New connections can be made by a number of activities, including new axonal growth (sprouting), new pre- and post-synaptic growth and terminal and dendrite formation, and new receptor formation and/or distribution, for example. Furthermore, injury to the visual cortex causes degeneration of its projections to subcortical visual areas, which leaves vacated synaptic space that is filled by sprouting of the optic nerve. In the previous example in which rats were trained on a black-white discrimination, sprouting in subcortical visual areas could account for the recovery of function. It is generally thought that sprouting should be beneficial and attempts have been made to promote sprouting. However, in the case of brightness discrimination, this idea is questionable since subsequent damage to the areas of sprouting has no permanent effect in preventing learning differences in brightness. In general, since rats with visual cortical damage do not recover perceptions of form and pattern, neural reorganization is not a significant factor for those functions.

Two examples illustrate where sprouting is actually less than helpful. First, spinal cord injuries cause sprouting that is accompanied by tremors. The tremors are alleviated when the sprouted connections are destroyed. Second, injury of one superior colliculus in hamsters causes sprouting to the opposite superior colliculus. The result is that the animals visually orient to the side away from the visual stimulus. Cutting the sprouted optic nerve to the remaining superior colliculus resolves the problem. Thus, in these two examples, blindly enhancing sprouting by generally giving nerve growth factors, for example, may not be such a good idea. The problem with sprouting is how to have control over where and what type of new growth takes place.

Neurogenesis   We learn that we are born with the total number of neurons that we are ever going to have, and that we continually lose neurons as we grow. The one celebrated exception to this rule is that certain birds that learn a new song each mating season show cell division and new neuron development as adults. Adult rats and, recently, adult humans have been shown to create new neurons in the hippocampus, a limbic system structure associated with certain kinds of memories. It remains to be determined whether there are sufficient numbers of new neurons and whether there are functional connections of these newly available neurons. Similarly, it is unknown whether these neurons have a role in repairing brain injury. However, on the face of it, this is an exciting development.

Transplants   Related to the idea of natural neural replacement (neurogenesis) is the idea that we can purposely implant neurons to replace the damaged ones. Transplants have been tried most often in patients with Parkinson's disease, where the transplant donor is either the patient (dopamine-producing cells from the patient's own adrenal glands) or an aborted fetus (dopamine-producing cells from the substantia nigra; this source is controversial). Initial results of such operations were mixed at best, with more recent limited successes. The ameliorating effects may not be due to the effects of dopamine or to neural connections formed by the implant, however. Nerve growth factors that are secreted by the implant are more likely candidates. Transplants themselves have been recently overshadowed by a return to surgical intervention with a procedure known as a pallidotomy, which is a lesion of the globus pallidus.

Supersensitivity   Synapses that are deprived of their normal expected amount of input activity can become supersensitive; that is, the synaptic transmission becomes unusually sensitive to small amounts of neurotransmitter. In Parkinson's disease the deleterious symptoms are delayed presumably because of the compensating supersensitivity of cells in the basal ganglia that are deprived of their usual amount of dopamine from degenerating neurons in the substantia nigra. It is only when there is too much loss of dopamine that the basal ganglia neurons cannot compensate and symptoms of Parkinson's appear. The actual mechanism of supersensitivity can involve increased sensitivity of the postsynaptic receptors, increased reactivity of postsynaptic receptors, increased number of postsynaptic receptors, changes in dendritic spines that reduce impedance (i.e., enhance transmission), increased transmitter release, and changes in intracellular events that enhance the signal.

Prostheses   Man-machine implants may be used to overcome deficits. For sensory loss, these involve a transduction device to convert an external stimulus into a neural-like signal and a neural stimulator. Currently, auditory implants into the cochlear nerve or nuclei are being tried to restore hearing. Visual implants using a primitive camera and stimulation of the visual cortex have a history of limited success in effecting primitive sensations. Not all prostheses are surgically placed into the brain. One alternative for visual problems is to place the pattern of visual stimuli onto a skin surface where the visual stimulus will now be interpreted as a tactile stimulus. Other approaches have not involved sensory transduction, but rather the replacement of the damaged element responsible for higher-level processing. In this regard a recent attempt has been made to implement functioning in a silicon chip that is used to replace a damaged hippocampus. For motor loss, electrodes have been implanted to stimulate muscles, coordinated by a computer, to effect walking. This requires sensors for proprioception and balance.

Unmasking   It is now well appreciated that the nervous system has multiple representations for each of the senses and motor functions. Moreover, it is becoming clear that representations may overlap each other, and that under normal circumstances some of the underlying representations may be suppressed. When a part of the main representation is damaged, the underlying map may begin to express itself, either preventing any deficit or causing an apparent recovery. Unmasking is generally found in instances in which the recovery occurs too quickly for sprouting or other types of reorganization to have been made.

Regeneration   Certain amphibians and lizards will grow a new limb to replace one that has been lost to a predator. Amphibians and lizards also have the ability to reestablish connections when a nerve is severed. This regeneration is also seen to varying degrees in the peripheral nervous system of mammals, aided by the supporting Schwann cells, which guide the reconnection. Although the capacity for regeneration persists in the central nervous system of mammals, regeneration is not a significant factor in recovery of function because central glial cells create scar tissue, which becomes a significant barrier to reconnection.

Substitution

Substitution refers to using an alternative means to achieve the same goal. If damage has actually removed that part of the brain responsible for a function (as opposed to diaschesis, for example) then substitution is the most likely means of recovery. When perusing the animal literature, one needs to be cognizant of factors like substitution; otherwise, false conclusions can be made about the nature of the recovery. Yet substitution is often ignored because it does not involve surgical or chemical intervention. There are three significant means of substitution; recovery by substitution occurs when another sense, motor act, or strategy can be used.

Sensory   A sensory stimulus or property of a stimulus can be used as a substitute for the original sensation. Damage to the visual cortex in rats makes them blind to form and pattern perception, yet they are still capable of detecting primitive visual experiences such as brightness and contour. As a result, such rats appear to be able to solve discriminations for orientation (for example, horizontal versus vertical black and white stripes) because they can make use of local brightness and contour cues to solve the problem. In extreme conditions in which the rats are prevented from using these local cues, they can no longer solve the orientation problem, and thus they are blind. The goal for a therapist would be to design conditions under which a problem can be solved in multiple ways. For example, persons who are red-green color blind can learn to drive by noting the position of the active light on a traffic signal.

Motor   One motor act can substitute for the original motor act. Cats with dorsal rhizotomies (denervation of the sensory roots of the spinal cord) for the hind limb initially have difficulty walking a thin railing. After a period of time, however, the cats negotiate the task very well and appear to be completely normal. However, upon close examination with high-speed photography, it has been shown that these cats adopt a motor strategy of shifting their weight to properly place the hind foot. Clearly, functional recovery does not imply neural recovery.

Another example from the older literature would be the rat that has been trained to run a maze. The same rat that has been trained to run can solve the very same maze when it is flooded and the rat has to swim. The same idea applies to conditions in which brain damage prevents the original behavior.

Strategy   After ruling out disruption of the senses and motor functions, the researcher might discover a problem with the implementation of a sequence of perceptions and actions. This higher-order activity can be referred to as a "strategy." For example, a woman with global (diffuse) brain damage was easily distracted, so much so that a telephone ring would be interruption enough that she would forget she was cooking. Or she would spend her whole day watching TV. Her strategy to overcome this deficit was to write a list of things to do, checking them off as she did them, and to have a timer set to go off every 15 minutes. At every alarm she would check her list to see what it was she was supposed to be doing.

From the animal literature comes another example. Rats with hippocampal brain damage have difficulty in alternately pressing one of two bars for a food reward. This task requires that the animals remember which bar was pressed last so that they can press the other bar the next time. Some clever rats figure out that if they hold onto the bar that they just pressed then they immediately know to press the other bar the next time.

FACTORS

The previous discussion identifies the major theories that can account for instances of recovery of function. Within this discussion we have identified a number of factors that can be used clinically and within the laboratory to promote recovery of function. It is reasonable at this time to simply list those factors, because although they were discussed in terms of theories, in truth, many of these factors apply to more than one theory. A listing of some factors that might enhance recovery of function includes: age at the time of injury; reduction in secondary effects of the injury (shock); the proficiency of pre-injury training; training on alternative stimuli, strategies, or acts; training between injuries (serial lesion effect); time after injury; amount of post-injury training on the same or similar tasks; and substitutions. It would be misleading to suggest that any or all of these factors will lead to recovery in all instances. It is a sad fact that injuries to the nervous system produce profound and lasting deficits. The hope for further research is to find new applications of these factors and to develop new methods of treatment.

IMPLICATIONS

Clinically, the importance of finding methods that enhance recovery of function is obvious. What is not so obvious is that the clinical and experimental literature about brain injury also give insight into the fundamental organization and operation of the brain and one's mental life. The mind-body problem—the relationship of our physical being to our mental experience—continues to be a fundamental interest in psychology. Both the clinical and experimental literature make fundamental contributions to each other. Newer methods of imaging the brain during cognitive activity (fMRI, PET, neuromagnetic methods, and the old standby, EEG) have, on the one hand, confirmed much of our understanding of the organization of the brain and what happens during injury, and have given insights and further directions on the other. The optimism of our times holds out great promise for sophisticated advances that may someday allow us to repair the damaged mind.

Importantly, we learn from the field of recovery of function the following lessons. First, localization of function is the norm in the nervous system. Second, the nervous system is hierarchically organized, with basic functions organized at low levels. Third, even low levels of the nervous system are capable of seemingly sophisticated functions, like learning and memory. Fourth, any one function is probably represented in only one place in the nervous system. However (fifth), similar functions can often accomplish the same goals.

FURTHER READING

Bach-y-Rita, P. (Ed.). (1980). *Recovery of function: Theoretical considerations for brain injury rehabilitation.* Baltimore: University Park Press.

Finger, S. (Ed.). (1978). *Recovery from brain damage.* New York: Plenum.

Finger, S., Levere, T. E., Almli, C. R., & Stein, D. (Eds.). (1988). *Brain injury and recovery: Theoretical and controversial issues.* New York: Plenum.

Johnson, J. A. (Ed.). (1990). *Occupational therapy approaches to traumatic brain injury.* Binghamton, NY: Haworth.

Levin, H. S., Benton, A. L., & Grossman, R. G. (1982). *Neurobehavioral consequences of closed head injury.* New York: Oxford University Press.

Montgomery, J. (Ed.). (1994). *Physical therapy for traumatic brain injury (clinics in physical therapy).* New York: Churchill Livingstone.

Scheff, S. W. (Ed.). (1984). *Aging and recovery of function in the central nervous system.* New York: Plenum.

Stein, D. G., Brailwsky, S., & Will, B. (1995). *Brain repair.* New York: Oxford University Press.

Stein, D. G., Rosen, J. J., & Butters, N. (Eds.). (1974). *Plasticity and recovery of function in the central nervous system.* New York: Academic.

Uzzell, B. P., & Stonnington, H. H. (Eds.). (1996). *Recovery after traumatic brain injury.* Hillsdale, NJ: Erlbaum.

D. G. LAVOND
University of Southern California

REFLECTIVE LISTENING

The term "reflective listening" refers to a way of responding to another person to communicate empathy. Empathy is widely believed to be an important element of psychotherapeutic interaction. Rogers (1957) postulated empathy to be one of the necessary and sufficient conditions for psychotherapy. In his 1975 article, "Empathic: An Unappreciated Way of Being", Rogers addressed what he believed to be a then-widespread lack of understanding of what he meant by empathy. There, he updated his definition as follows:

The way of being with another person which is termed empathic has several facets. It means entering the private perceptual world of the other and becoming thoroughly at home in it. It involves being sensitive, moment to mo-

ment, to the changing felt meanings which flow in this other person, to the fear or rage or tenderness or confusion or whatever, that he/she is experiencing. It means temporarily living in his/her life, moving about in it delicately without making judgments, sensing meanings of which he/she is scarcely aware, but not trying to uncover feelings of which the person is totally unaware, since this would be too threatening. It includes communicating your sensings of his/her world as you look with fresh and unfrightened eyes at elements of which the individual is fearful. It means frequently checking with him/her as to the accuracy of your sensings, and being guided by the responses you receive. You are a confident companion to the person in his/her inner world. By pointing to the possible meanings in the flow of his/her experiencing you help the person to focus on this useful type of referent, to experience the meanings more fully, and to move forward in the experiencing.

To be with another in this way means that for the time being you lay aside the views and values you hold for yourself in order to enter another's world without prejudice. In some sense it means that you lay aside your self and this can only be done by a person who is secure enough [to] not get lost in what may turn out to be the strange or bizarre world of the other, and [to] comfortably return to his[/her] own world when he[/she] wishes. Perhaps this description makes clear that being empathic is a complex, demanding, strong yet subtle and gentle way of being.

Thus, Rogers considered empathy a complicated way of perceiving, being with, and communicating with another person.

The importance of empathy and empathic listening has been written about in many approaches to and modalities of psychotherapy other than client-centered, including self-psychology, psychoanalysis, Gestalt, existential, focusing-oriented, pretherapy, child therapy, marital and couple therapy, disaster-recovery therapy, and clinical supervision. Some writers have emphasized the importance of nonverbal components of empathy (Corcoran, 1981; Hackney, 1978; Gendlin, 1996), which likely involve "nondominant" hemisphere brain functions as well as "dominant" hemisphere verbal cognitive functions. Schuster (1979) elucidated several similarities in the attitudes of empathy and those involved in some types of meditation. Rogers (1975) cited evidence that empathic ability is not associated with academic or diagnostic proficiency.

Reflective listening is one practical method for communicating empathy. First, it involves holding a distinct set of attitudes toward the person who is speaking. There is an acceptance of the content of the person's awareness. The listener trusts the resources of the speaker to evaluate, analyze, and decide about the situation, and therefore does not jump in with advice and suggestions about what to do or how to perceive things. When listening, one is nondiagnostic and nonevaluative. The aim of listening is to be in the other person's perceptual world, not to fit the other into the listener's perceptual world. Second, one communicates one's understanding of what the person is expressing. This is often best accomplished by staying close to the same language used by the person, to avoid possible connotations of different language that would not be correct for what the speaker is expressing. This does not mean limiting oneself to literally what was said in words. The listener can and should be sensing for and reflecting meanings not yet clear, some of which may not have even been mentioned in words, but that have been expressed nonverbally. Third, one communicates one's understanding a couple of times per minute, on average (Iberg, 1991, 1996), to stay in close contact, and give the speaker ample opportunities to correct misunderstandings or misstatements, or to revise what he or she says to articulate experiencing as it evolves.

This way of being with someone is expected to do something useful for him or her: In the process of being accurately and caringly understood, the person's feelings and ideas will change in a problem-solving, insight-producing, tension-releasing, responsibility-building, conflict-reducing way. In addition, the person gets the message that his or her experience makes sense, and that he or she is worthy of being taken seriously. It is paradoxical that this powerful way to foster change involves the listener studiously not pushing for change. The listener accepts what the speaker says without dispute, on the speaker's terms.

Gendlin's theories of personality change (1962, 1964, 1996) provide a theoretical basis for the expectation that change will ensue from the listening process. His work clarifies the "object" to which the listener listens, and the nature of the personality processes stimulated in this way. Gendlin (1981) defines the "bodily felt sense" as the basic stuff of personality. The bodily felt sense is more inclusive than what a person is clearly aware of consciously. It includes everything felt at the moment, even if only vaguely and subliminally. It often has opposing impulses present in it. The bodily felt sense is not a static object, but changes from moment to moment, as events proceed. The bodily felt sense of the speaker is the fluid object which the listener attempts to reflect.

Through research, Gendlin, Rogers, and others came to believe that certain attitudes, when directed toward the bodily felt sense, resulted in more positive personality change than other attitudes. Recent research has corroborated this:

Elliott and Lietaer have observed that clients who did well in therapy reported that their therapists' warmth, interest, involvement, support, empathy, respect, patience, and understanding were helpful to them. It is highly likely that these factors are related to therapists' empathic responsiveness to their clients. In contrast, when clients feel criticized, belittled, controlled, or neglected by their therapist they are unlikely to do well at the end of therapy. Thus empirical evidence would seem to confirm Rogers's view that the provision of an empathic climate is important to clients' well-being and progress in therapy. (Watson, Goldman, & Vanaerschot, 1998, p. 63–64).

Listening creates an interactional opportunity for the speaker to experience and have supported his or her own capacities for solving problems, for identifying the part he or she contributes to interpersonal difficulties, for building self-esteem, and for sorting out complicated personal concerns and motives. The common "helper" attitudes of evaluation, diagnosis, analysis, and advice seem to have the opposite effect, that of stopping this kind of process in favor of an attitude of dependence on (or resistance to) the guidance of external authority.

"Reflecting" is really a poor metaphor for what it is intended to describe, since the metaphor does not adequately convey the emergence of changed feeling and new meaning which results from good empathic listening. Empathic communication, when it occurs, is an intimate relationship event. The speaker experiences the calming, enlightening embrace of an affectionately indifferent, accepting attitude encompassing democratically all presently experienced feelings, thoughts, sensations, and images. This embrace, provided by the listener, enables the speaker to move toward unconditional acceptance and understanding of the subtle and complex experiencing of the self. Cornell (1996) refers to this intrapersonal attitude as the "radical acceptance of everything," which has a remarkable power to release a person's energy to move forward in constructive ways.

Reflective listening has been examined and taught in many fields beyond psychotherapy. Gordon (1970) recommends it to parents as a means of maintaining open and trusting relationships with their children, and to health care professionals for improving relations with patients (Gordon & Edwards, 1995). Teachers rated more empathic have been shown to achieve greater student involvement in educational settings (Aspy & Roebuck, 1975). Empathic listening has also been found helpful for school administrations in dealing with parents (Margolis, 1991). It plays a role in improving intimacy in spousal relationships (Siegel, 1992; Snyder, 1992; Sperry, 1999). Clinical and vocational supervision situations also benefit from this skill (Ricci, 1995). Many conflict management and mediation approaches use reflective listening as a core technique (Salem, 1993). Writings about building community emphasize the value of empathic listening techniques (Hampton & Norman, 1997; McGuire, 1981). Some philosophical writings (e.g., Sundararajan, 1995) cite this form of communication as a beneficial method.

Clark (1980) argued that empathy is a human capacity based on the most recently evolved part of the brain, and that it counterbalances egocentric power drives. He thus saw great social significance in empathy, believing it to be essential to collective solutions to resource allocation and peace. Perhaps the next decades will find the widely-valued method of reflective listening being taught as an essential social skill to more people as part of regular educational curriculums.

REFERENCES

Aspy, D., & Roebuck, F. M. (1975). From humane ideas to humane technology and back again, many times. *Education, 95,* 163–171.

Clark, K. (1980). Experiential empathy: A theory of a level experience. *Journal of Humanistic Psychology, 21,* 29–38.

Cornell, A. W. (1996). The power of focusing. Oakland, CA: New Harbinger.

Gendlin, E. T. (1962). Experiencing and the creation of meaning. New York: The Free Press of Glencoe.

Gendlin, E. T. (1964). A theory of personality change. In P. Worchel & D. Byrne (Eds.), *Personality change.* New York: Wiley. 101–148.

Gendlin, E. T. (1981). *Focusing* (2nd ed., rev.). New York: Bantam.

Gendlin, E. T. (1996). *Focusing-oriented psychotherapy: A manual of the experiential method.* New York: Guilford.

Gordon, T. (1970). *Parent effectiveness training.* New York: Wyden.

Gordon, T., & Edwards, W. S. (1995). *Making the patient your partner: Communication skills for doctors and other caregivers.* Westport, CT: Auburn House/Greenwood.

Hackney, H. (1978). The evolution of empathy. *Personnel and Guidance Journal, 57,* 35–38.

Hampton, M. R., & Norman, C. (1997). Community-building in a peer support center. *Journal of College Student Development, 38,* 357–364.

Iberg, J. R. (1991). Applying statistical control theory to bring together clinical supervision and psychotherapy research. *Journal of Consulting and Clinical Psychology, 59,* 575–586.

Iberg, J. R. (1996). Using statistical experiments with post-session client questionnaires as a student-centered approach to teaching the effects of therapist activities in psychotherapy. In R. Hutterer, G. Pawlowsky, P. F. Schmid, & R. Stipsits (Eds.), *Client-centered and experiential psychotherapy: A paradigm in motion,* (pp. 255–271). Frankfurtam Main: Peter Lang.

Margolis, H. (1991). Listening: The key to problem solving with angry parents. *School Psychology International, 12,* 329–347.

McGuire, K. (1981). *Building supportive community: Mutual self-help through peer counseling, training manual.* Eugene, OR: Focusing Northwest.

Ricci, W. F. (1995). Self and intersubjectivity in the supervisory process. *The Bulletin of the Menninger Clinic, 59,* 53–68.

Rogers, C. R. (1957). The necessary and sufficient conditions of therapeutic personality change. *Journal of Consulting Psychology, 21,* 95–103.

Rogers, C. R. (1975). Empathic: An unappreciated way of being. *The Counseling Psychologist, 5,* 2–10.

Salem, R. A. (1993). The Interim Guidelines need a broader perspective. *Negotiation Journal, 9,* 309–312.

Siegel, J. P. (1992). *Repairing intimacy: An object relations approach to couples therapy.* Northvale, NJ: Aronson.

Schuster, R. (1979). Empathy and mindfulness. *Journal of Humanistic Psychology, 19,* 71–77.

Snyder, M. (1992). A gender-informed model of couple and family therapy: Relationship enhancement therapy. *Contemporary Family Therapy: An International Journal, 14,* 15–31.

Sperry, L. (1999). Levels and styles of intimacy. In J. Carlson & L. Sperry (Eds.), *The intimate couple,* (pp. 33–40). Philadelphia: Brunner/Mazel.

Sundararajan, L. (1995). Echoes after Carl Rogers: Reflective listening revisited. *Humanistic Psychologist, 23,* 259–271.

Watson, J., Goldman, R., & Vanaerschot, G. (1998). Empathic: A postmodern way of being? In L. S. Greenberg, J. C. Watson, & G. Lietaer (Eds.), *Handbook of experiential psychotherapy.* New York: Guilford.

J. R. Iberg
Illinois School of Professional Psychology
Chicago, Illinois

CLIENT-CENTERED THERAPY
EMPATHY
EXPERIENTIAL PSYCHOTHERAPY

REFLEXES

A reflex is the central nervous system's least complex, shortest-latency motor response to sensory input. The expression of a reflex is an involuntary, stereotyped contraction of muscles determined by the locus and nature of the eliciting stimulus. Reflexes may be elicited by stimulation of any sensory modality. There are many reflexes; an exhaustive listing will not be provided here. Rather, the principles that apply to all reflexes will be described using a few examples.

The simplest reflex is the myotatic, or muscle stretch, reflex. This reflex can be elicited from any skeletal muscle, but the best known example is the patellar, or knee-jerk, reflex. The anatomical basis of the myotactic reflex is the monosynaptic (one synapse) connection between the sensory fibers that detect stretch on a muscle and the alpha (tr) motor neurons that supply nerve fibers to that same muscle. The sensory fibers have their cell bodies in the dorsal root ganglia. One end of the sensory fiber terminates in the sensory end-organ for muscle stretch, known as the muscle spindle. The other end of the nerve fiber enters the spinal cord through the dorsal root and dorsal horn and terminates in the ventral horn of the spinal cord on an a motor neuron.

Muscle spindles are embedded in the mass of each striated muscle. They are arranged in parallel with the extrafusal muscle fibers that contract when the motor nerves supplying them are stimulated. The central portion of the spindle is nonmuscular and receives the sensory nerve ending. When the central portion of the spindle is stretched, the sensory nerve increases its rate of production of action potentials. The axons that provide the input for the stretch reflex are the largest of the sensory nerve fibers and are called type Ia. Conduction is very rapid in these nerves. This fact, and the fact that they each make a monosynaptic contact with a motor neuron supplying the extrafusal muscle fibers, ensure that the reflex contraction of the whole muscle in response to stretch is very rapid. When the muscle contracts the muscle spindle shortens; the stimulus for sensory discharge is reduced, and the rate of action potential production in the sensory fibers decreases or stops.

In addition to a nonmuscular sensory middle, the muscle spindle has muscular tissue attached to each of its ends. These muscular endings of the muscle spindle are called intrafusal muscles and do not contribute to the contractile strength of the muscle. They are innervated by their own type of motor neuron called the gamma (γ) motor neuron. Motor areas in the brain, particularly in the reticular formation, send axons that influence the γ motor neurons and through this connection can modulate the stretch reflex by changing the tension on the nonmuscular central portion of the spindle.

The stretch reflex demonstrates the basic principles of all reflexes. A sensory, or afferent, limb is necessary. Severing the dorsal roots eliminates the stretch reflex. The eliciting stimulus is specific. The reflex is produced by stretch on the muscle, not by touch, pain, or some other stimulus. A motor, or efferent, limb is necessary. Severing the ventral roots eliminates the reflex. The efferent response is specific. Only the muscles that are stretched will reflexively contract. The reflex is graded. The greater the stretch, the greater the contraction.

More complex reflex arcs also exist. The anatomy of these reflexes includes the interposition of one or more interneurons between the afferent and efferent limbs of the reflex. These reflexes, therefore, have more than one synapse and are called polysynaptic. The Golgi tendon organ reflex provides an example of the simplest polysynaptic reflex. The sensory end-organ is found in the tendon; its cell body is in a dorsal root ganglion. Increased tension on the tendon, usually produced by contraction of the muscle to which it is attached, is the eliciting stimulus that increases activity in the tendon organ afferent fiber. The tendon organ afferent fiber synapses on an interneuron in the spinal cord. This interneuron inhibits as a motor neuron, thus decreasing activity in its efferent axon. Because this axon returns to the muscle to which the stretched tendon is attached, the muscle relaxes and the tension on the tendon is reduced.

The muscle stretch reflex and the Golgi tendon organ reflex work in concert to provide the basis for rapid regulation of the degree of contraction of the muscle. For example, these reflexes are useful for quick adjustments to change the position of the foot as a person hikes across uneven ground.

Other polysynaptic reflexes are involved in movement of whole limbs and the coordination of different limbs. These reflexes incorporate more interneurons. The divergent (from one neuron to several neurons) and convergent (from several neurons to one neuron) connections of the interneurons form the basis of these complex reflexes. An example is provided by a person who steps barefooted on a sharp object and reflexively withdraws the injured foot. The sensory input is pain. The pain afferents enter the dorsal horn of the spinal cord and continue to its ventral division, where they synapse on interneurons. Some of these interneurons excite motor neurons that cause the flexor muscles of the affected leg to contract to lift the foot, while other interneurons serve to inhibit the motor neurons that supply the extensor muscles of the same leg. This permits the leg to withdraw quickly and smoothly from the noxious stimulus. Other neurons receiving pain input send axons across the midline of the spinal cord and excite the motor neurons for extensors of the opposite leg and inhibit those that innervate that leg's flexors. This causes the leg to stiffen and provide support. Furthermore, interneurons relay information up and down the spinal cord to produce intersegmental reflexes that coordinate muscle contraction of the trunk and upper limbs. The entire reflex is known as the flexion–crossed extension reflex.

The spinal cord reflexes form the basis for maintenance and adjustment of posture. Brain motor systems influence spinal cord reflexes via input to interneurons and the γ motor neurons to produce normal movement and modulate reflexes. Changes in spinal cord reflexes may indicate pathology in the brain motor systems. For example, damage to the motor cortex or to axons originating in this part of the brain produces increased reflex response to muscle stretch.

Several optic reflexes exist. An example is the direct light reflex, which is the constriction of the pupil to light. It requires an intact retina, optic nerve, midbrain, and third cranial nerve, but not the lateral geniculate nucleus or visual cortex. If light is restricted to one eye only, a crossing pathway at the pretectal level of the midbrain produces constriction of the pupil opposite to the one into which the light is introduced; this is called the consensual light reflex. Several reflex changes (accommodation reflex) also occur when the eyes are directed toward a near object. These include convergence of the eyes as the medial recti contract; thickening of the lens; and pupillary constriction. Many components of the visual system are involved in this reflex, including the retina, optic nerve, occipital cortex, superior colliculus, lateral geniculate nucleus, and nuclei of the oculomotor nerve.

Reflexes can also be elicited from stimulation of sensory input from the viscera. The baroreceptor reflex is an example of such an autonomic reflex. An increase in blood pressure stretches receptors in large vessels near the heart. This increases afferent input to nucleus tractus solitarius of the medulla. Neurons in the nucleus tractus solitarius relay activity to the motor nucleus of the vagal nerve, as well as to the spinal cord automomic neurons, and heart rate and blood pressure decrease.

SUGGESTED READING

Goldberg, M. E., Eggers, H. M., & Gouras, P. (1991). The ocular motor system. In E. R. Kandel, J. H. Schwartz, & T. M. Jessell (Eds.), *Principles of neural science* (3rd ed., pp. 660–667). New York: Elsevier.

Gordon, J., & Ghez, C. (1991). Muscle receptors and spinal reflexes: The stretch reflex. In E. R. Kandel, J. H. Schwartz, & T. M. Jessell (Eds.), *Principles of neural science* (3rd ed., pp. 564–580). New York: Elsevier.

May, P. J., & Corbett, J. J. (1997). Visual motor system. In D. E. Haines (Ed.), *Fundamental neuroscience* (pp. 399–416). New York: Churchill Livingstone.

Mihailoff, G. A., & Haines, D. E. (1997). Motor system 1: Peripheral sensory, brainstem, and spinal influence on ventral horn cells. In D. E. Haines (Ed.), *Fundamental neuroscience* (pp. 335–346). New York: Churchill Livingstone.

Naftel, J. P., & Hardy, S. F. P. (1997). Visceral motor pathways. In D. E. Haines (Ed.), *Fundamental neuroscience* (pp. 418–429). New York: Churchill Livingstone.

Pearson, K. G. (1993). Common principles of motor control in vertebrates and invertebrates. *Annual Review of Neuroscience, 16*, 265–297.

M. L. WOODRUFF
East Tennessee State University

ACETYLCHOLINESTERASE
ENDORPHINS/ENKAPALINS
NEURAL NETWROK MODELS
NEUROTRANSMITTERS
SENSORIMOTOR PROCESS

REICH, WILHELM (1897–1957)

Wilhelm Reich's pursuits in various scientific realms constitute the body of work known as Orgonomy. Reich became a practicing analyst while still a medical undergraduate. He became interested in the outcome of analysis, particularly the bases for unsatisfactory results. He found that patients whose analyses were successful had all developed satisfactory genital functioning of a specific, and heretofore undescribed kind—a capacity he investigated and called *orgastic potency.*

Concurrently, in his analytic work, Reich began to attack resistances (in terms of behavioral traits). This new technique caused character structure to change, suggesting that not only were symptoms evidence of neurosis, but that character itself was neurotic. Reich called his new method *character analysis.* In successful analyses, Reich often elicited strong emotions, the expression of which he encouraged. After consistent, thorough release of affect, changes occurred in bodily attitudes, posture, and tonus. He became convinced that, concomitant with psychic character armor, there is a somatic muscular armor. This discovery led to an important innovation in technique, that of the possibility of attacking the neurosis somatically.

Reich parted from psychoanalysis as his pursuits led him into realms the analysts could not or would not follow. Emotions came to mean the manifestations of a tangible, demonstrable biological energy (*orgone,* as Reich called it, from "organism" and "orgasm")—the reality of the Freudian libido. Orgone therapy involves the therapeutic methodology evolved to bring the patient to a condition of health manifested by a state of orgastic potency. The function of the orgasm is to regulate the organism's energy, the further investigation of which became Reich's focus until his death.

A. NELSON

REIK, THEODOR (1888–1969)

Theodor Reik received the PhD degree at the University of Vienna in 1912. He became an early follower of Freud and was psychoanalyzed by Karl Abraham, an eminent psychoanalyst. Reik taught at the Berlin Psychoanalytical Institute and in 1938 came to the United States. His writings were intended for the intelligent lay person and were not specifically directed toward his professional colleagues.

He never received the MD degree but became one of the early lay analysts. Freud wrote *The Question of Lay Analysis* in defense of Reik's ability to practice psychoanalysis in the absence of medical training.

In *The Unknown Murderer,* Reik wrote of the criminal's unconscious desire to confess the crime. Criminals, he said, unconsciously betray themselves by bringing about their own self-punishment through a purposive act. In another book, *Listening with the Third Ear,* he described the ability of a good analyst to make use of intuitions, sensitivity, and subliminal cues to interpret clinical observations in individual and group psychotherapy. Actually the idea was first introduced by Friedrich Nietzsche and later applied by Reik to therapeutic situations.

Although a believer in many basic psychoanalytical concepts, Reik disagreed with Freud over certain matters of love and sex. Reik believed that true romantic love has little to do with sex, that it is felt most strongly when the loved one is absent. Further, he took issue with Freud's notion of primary narcissism (self-love), which he felt did not exist. He pointed out that normal sexual relations occur simply as a means of relieving the tensions of the sex drive. In falling in love, in a romantic way, one sees one's better self in someone else. For example, we show our dissatisfaction with ourselves by finding in another the qualities we lack. Another possible way to resolve our own dissatisfactions is by "falling in hate"—by having hostile feelings toward those who seem more satisfied with themselves than we are. Other possibilities include putting lesser demands on ourselves or doing something creative, which allows us to have a better opinion of ourselves.

Reik also wrote on primitive rituals, death rites, and religion as expressions of the fulfillment of unconscious desires.

R. W. LUNDIN
Wheaton, Illinois

REINFORCEMENT

Principles of learning play a major role in our understanding of behavior. Operant conditioning theory, in particular, stresses that the consequence of a given response determines that response's strength, that is, its rate, probability of occurrence, and so on. The term "reinforcement" refers to the specific learning process through which the strength of a response is increased as a result of its consequence. It differs from processes, such as punishment and extinction, that lead to a decrease of the strength of the relationship between a response and a consequence.

The roots of reinforcement theory can be traced back to laboratory research on learning conducted with animals. Thorndike is considered as a pioneer in this area. His early experiments consisted of observing cats placed inside a "puzzle box" that could only be opened from the inside by pulling a string. Food was delivered to the cat when it succeeded at opening the door and escaping the box. At first, the animal typically exhibited random behavior aimed at getting out of the box, such as scratching and biting. After a while, the animal accidently pulled the string and opened the door. Repetition of the procedure gradually led to a remarkable reduction in the time it took the cat to open the door. This observation led to the formulation of the "law of effect" (Thorndike, 1898), which basically states that stimulus-response (S-R) bonds are modified by the consequence of the response. The law of effect specifies that S-R connections are (a) strengthened by consequences that are satisfying to the organism, but (b) weakened by consequences that cause discomfort.

Two main forms of reinforcement, positive and negative, can be distinguished. Positive reinforcement occurs when the strength of a response is increased as a result of the presentation of a desired consequence. For example, a hungry rat placed in a cage in which food is delivered by pressing a bar may do so on the first occasion by chance or out of curiosity. Because food is a desirable consequence for the hungry animal, the bar-pressing behavior is reinforced or strengthened by this consequence. The same process may be observed in humans. A student aiming for good grades at school observes that he performs better at exams after spending a few hours studying rather than by relying on luck. Good grades, being desirable for this individual, serve to strengthen the studying behavior.

In negative reinforcement, the strength of the response is increased by the removal or avoidance of an undesirable consequence. This can be illustrated by a situation in which a young child is very interested in the family cat. Whenever he sees the cat, the infant calls his name and runs in his direction with his arms extended in front of him. From the animal's point of view, this behavior is perceived as threatening and, consequently, he always remains at least a few feet from the infant whenever they are both in the same room. In this situation, avoidance of direct contact with the child, which is perceived as undesirable by the cat, reinforces the animal's behavior of keeping at a safe distance. Human beings also present behaviors that are acquired in the same way. For example, using a detour rather than the direct way to get back home may be reinforced by avoidance of a dangerous neighborhood.

Applications of reinforcement theory can be found in a wide variety of domains. In applied gerontology, for example, reinforcement principles are useful in designing interventions to reduce agitation in older adults living in nursing homes. Both aggressive and verbally agitated behaviors have been successfully treated by manipulating reinforcing consequences of these behaviors (Landreville, Bordes, Dicaire, & Verreault, 1998). Other applications of reinforcement theory can be found in education, staff management, and clinical psychology.

REFERENCES

Landreville, P., Bordes, M., Dicaire, L., & Verreault, R. (1998). Behavioral approaches for reducing agitation in residents of long-term care facilities: Critical review and suggestions for future research. *International Psychogeriatrics, 10,* 397–419.

Thorndike, E. L. (1898). Animal intelligence: An experimental study in the associative processes in animals. *Psychological Review Monograph, 2,* 1–109.

P. LANDREVILLE
Laval University, Quebec

CLASSICAL CONDITIONING
OPERANT CONDITIONING

REINFORCEMENT SCHEDULES

In operant conditioning theory, a behavior is maintained by its consequences, that is, by the reinforcing or punishing events that follow the behavior. The relationship between a behavior and its consequences is called a contingency. While it is possible for a contingency to operate on a continuous basis, it is more common for contingencies to operate on an intermittent basis in which the behavior is sometimes followed by the reinforcing event, and sometimes is not. In other words, reinforcement generally operates on an intermittent schedule of some sort. In *The Behavior of Organisms,* Skinner pointed out that reinforcement may be scheduled in many ways, and demonstrated that subtle differences in scheduling can generate dramatic differences in behavior. Since the publication of that book in 1938, a number of reinforcement schedules have been defined and their effects on behavior studied.

Four basic schedules of reinforcement have been studied in detail. Two are ratio schedules, in which the presentation of a reinforcer is contingent on the number of responses emitted by the organism. In a fixed ratio (FR) schedule, every nth response is reinforced. In a variable schedule (VR), responses are reinforced on a certain average ratio, but the number of responses required for reinforcement varies unpredictably from reinforcement to reinforcement. The other two basic schedules are interval schedules, which are defined by the length of time that must elapse between reinforcements. The first response to occur after this time has elapsed is reinforced. In fixed interval (FI) schedules, this interval remains constant from reinforcement to reinforcement; in variable interval (VI) schedules, the intervals between reinforcements vary randomly about some mean interval.

In addition to these four basic schedules, there are a number of other schedules, such as differential reinforcement of low rates of response (DLR), differential reinforcement of other behaviors (DRO), and various complex and concurrent schedules, which are combinations of the four basic schedules.

Each schedule has a particular effect on behavior. Ratio schedules generally produce high rates of response, and interval schedules produce lower rates of response. Variable schedules, particularly variable interval schedules, produce a remarkably stable pattern of behavior. Behaviors maintained under variable schedules are also highly resistant to extinction, that is, the organism will continue to make many responses even after the reinforcement ceases altogether. This fact helps to explain why it is so difficult to extinguish undesirable behaviors, since most behaviors are maintained under variable schedules.

Reinforcement schedules also affect behaviors other than those directly involved in the reinforcement contingency. In studies with rats, particular schedules have been found to have an effect on such noninstrumental (i.e., nonreinforced) behaviors as polydipsia (excessive drinking of fluids), aggression, and wheel-running. These have been called schedule-induced behaviors (Christian et al., 1977). Intermittent reinforcement explains the persistence of gambling of addicted gamblers.

The reinforcement schedule is a fundamental element of the reinforcement contingency. The consequences that maintain behaviors always operate on a schedule of some sort, and this schedule exerts its characteristic influence over the behavior as strongly as the reinforcement itself. The study of schedules of reinforcement is an essential component of a complete analysis of behavior.

REFERENCES

Christian, W. P., Schaeffer, R. W., & King, G. D. (1977). *Schedule-induced behavior.* Montreal: Eden.

Skinner, B. F. (1938). *Behavior of organisms.* New York: Appleton-Century-Crofts.

SUGGESTED READING

Ferster, C. B., & Skinner, B. F. (1957). *Schedules of reinforcement.* New York: Appleton-Century-Crofts.

Schoenfeld, W. N. (Ed.). (1970). *The theory of reinforcement schedules.* New York: Appleton-Century-Crofts.

Zeiler, M. (1977). Schedules of reinforcement: The controlling variables. In W. K. Honig & J. E. R. Staddon (Eds.), *Handbook of operant behavior.* Englewood Cliffs, NJ: Prentice-Hall.

R. A. SHAW
Brown University

CLASSICAL CONDITIONING
LEARNING THEORIES
OPERANT CONDITIONING
PUNISHMENT
REINFORCEMENT
REWARDS AND INTRINSIC INTEREST
TOKEN ECONOMIES

RELATIONSHIP THERAPY

Relationship therapy refers to several forms of psychotherapy that invoke the relationship between the therapist and the client as the effective change mechanism. The two central theorists of relationship therapy are Harry Stack Sullivan (1953) and Martin Buber (1974), although Carl Rogers (1951) played an important role in the development of this style of psychotherapy.

Buber saw the essence of human living as the encounter in a direct experience between one person and another (I-Thou), rather than as the act of one person's seeing another (and being seen) as an object or through the barriers and filters of social roles (I-It). The humanizing influence one person's I-Thou experiencing of the other allows the other to feel fully human. Buber saw, rather than a static diagnostic entity to be treated, a human in relationship with another human who, as the therapist, is the expert in the human relationship. The I-Thou relationship provides the curative element of psychotherapy and serves more generally as the prophylactic and antidote to the oppression of a mechanical bureaucratic society that makes others into "its" rather than "thous." Buber's influence catapulted with the 1922 publication of *I and Thou,* reached a peak in the 1950s and 1960s and remains a force in pastoral and humanistic counseling today.

For Sullivan, personality developed as a function of the relationship. For example, an infant born to a teenage mother who consequently could not go to college would be viewed by that mother differently than would a baby who was born to a long-childless couple who desired a baby. The reactions of the parents constitute appraisals that are reflected back to the developing person either overtly, by verbal and other behavior, or covertly, by fa-

cial and emotional expressions and by vocal tone. The developing self contributes to personality or the "envelope of energy transformations." Abnormal behavior is the stereotyped response, or "parataxic distortion," to others for whom the response is not fitting. The psychotherapist begins the four stages of treatment with the "inception" or initial sizing-up of the patient and therapist of one another, and proceeds to the "reconnaissance," which is the more formal history-taking of the patient, ever mindful of the emotional tone from moment to moment in each session and for each topic covered. The problematic areas are scrutinized during the "detailed inquiry," and the progress is summed up in the "termination" phase. The anxieties or insecurities are revealed during the examination of the patient's life through various warps or strains in the relationship as seen in slips of the tongue, stuttering, misused words, silences, and gestures inconsistent with verbal statements or with the mood of the moment. These moods of the moment might be sensed by the therapist via Sullivan's "reciprocal emotions" or through the strains or "pulls" produced by the patient during the session. This sensing of the other may result in the therapist's responding in a way that the patient can use to examine, cognitively and emotionally, his or her experiencing and "unhook" or behave in a new way that is not condemned by the therapist. Sullivan's influence is strong but not generally acknowledged currently.

Rogers saw humans as motivated to grow when provided with the right conditions. These conditions could be supplied within the counseling or therapeutic context when the right relationship was presented. The basic ingredients include the therapist's unconditional positive regard, empathic understanding, and congruence of feelings that were communicated to the patient in the therapeutic relationship.

CONTEMPORARY DEVELOPMENTS

Recently, the traditional metaphors from the several dominant theoretical perspectives have grown brittle with age. The theoretical approaches have gravitated toward realizing the centrality of the role of the relationship as the force accounting for psychotherapy's effectiveness. Psychoanalytic approaches, through the concept of counter-transference, for example, have developed the idea of intersubjectivity as a way of including the role of the relationship between the psychoanalyst and the analysand as the change mechanism in therapy. Intersubjectivity denotes the interpersonal transactions in psychotherapy and the way by which corrective emotional experiences transpire. The corrective emotional experience might occur when the therapist responds in a different and an asocial fashion to a set of patient behaviors that, previously, have usually elicited a particular response. Thus a seduction by a patient in a session that does not elicit a sexual advance from the therapist might provoke the patient to experience him- or herself differently. The patient might now have to examine why he or she might be stuck in the role of using him- or herself as a sexual object in order to gain attention.

Behavioral approaches have increasingly employed notions such as the nonspecific therapist factors and the role of context in behavior change, rather than the more traditional use of behavior that is reinforced, as the central idea behind effective behavior therapy. The role of the therapist's personality in structuring the relationship and the use of the therapist-in-relationship are more realistic approaches to how behavior change works. The behavioral shift in theory and practice accords well with the therapy effectiveness research. Such research has found that the curative aspects of psychotherapy center on the nature of the relationship and the working-through of patient problems.

As psychadrnamic approaches shift from purely intrapsychic factors to interpersonal relationships and as behavioristics recognize that environmental effects mark the person's experiences and internal workings, the interpersonal or relationship is emerging as a dominant model of personality and of psychotherapy.

REFERENCES

Buber, M. (1974). *I and thou.* New York: Scribner's.

Rogers, C. R. (1951). *Client-centered therapy.* Boston: Houghton-Mifflin.

Sullivan, H. S. (1953). *The interpersonal theory of psychiatry.* New York: Norton.

A. K. HESS
Auburn University of Montgomery

SULLIVAN'S INTERPERSONAL THEORY

RELAXATION TRAINING

Although relaxation has been an integral part of meditative practices for centuries, especially in Eastern religions, its development and increasing popularity in the West in the twentieth century fall into three general phases: (a) Edmund Jacobson's pioneer work, beginning in 1908, and publication of his *Progressive Relaxation* in 1929; (b) Joseph Wolpe's use of relaxation in systematic desensitization therapy, outlined in his 1958 book, *Psychotherapy by Reciprocal Inhibition;* and (c) Herbert Benson's research into the common effective elements of relaxation/meditation techniques, and the physiological and psychological benefits from them, published in his 1975 book *The Relaxation Response.*

In an age of high-level stress and anxiety reactions, it may be difficult to see relaxation as a natural body state. It can be understood more readily if it is noted that stress activates the sympathetic nervous system and reactions of increased heart rate, higher blood pressure, and rapid breathing, the so-called fight-or-flight syndrome. This reaction has had evolutionary survival value, but is less appropriate in our age than it was in prehistoric eras. The body also has an opposite reaction to bring it back within normal limits: The parasympathetic nervous system slows the heart and reduces blood pressure, and the breathing rate decreases. Relaxation training helps the parasympathetic rebound to occur, and thus avoids chronic triggering and maintenance of high-level sympathetic arousal.

Highly useful and effective in itself as a corrective to the stress-induced anxiety of modern living, relaxation is also used in connection with various other techniques: hypnosis, yoga and Zen

Buddhism, meditation, biofeedback, autogenic training, and some modes of psychotherapy. Despite the need of many clients to relax, just telling them to relax, without proper instruction and supervision, may only increase their anxiety and sense of frustration and failure. A number of systems of relaxation are available, most of them evolving in some way from Jacobson's progressive relaxation system.

In accordance with its name, progressive relaxation starts with one muscle group and helps the client progress through the other groups. The client lies in a comfortable position on the back, eyes closed, first tensing and then relaxing one set of muscles at a time, noting the feeling of tension and of relaxation. The forearm, for example, is tensed by bending the hand back at the wrist; this feeling of tension is noted for several seconds, and then the arm is relaxed and the distinction noted between tension and no tension, or relaxation. Separate muscle groups are worked on before proceeding to other groups. Because of the extensive time necessary for this process, many therapists have altered and shortened Jacobson's method.

Several important findings are attributable to Jacobson's efforts: (a) tension and complete relaxation cannot exist together; (b) tension continues in muscles even when a person seems completely at rest (Jacobson identified this as residual tension); (c) clients must be able to distinguish clearly between tension and relaxation and then transfer this learning to the stress of their daily world, apart from therapy sessions; (d) internal states, such as imagination, affect muscle tension even when the muscles seem totally relaxed; and (e) training in relaxing the voluntary, skeletal muscles can be generalized to the involuntary, smooth muscles of the cardiovascular and gastrointestinal systems. Meditation and biofeedback are now demonstrating some of the implications of this early work of Jacobson.

Two other methods of relaxation training are autogenic training, a passive relaxation technique (compared with the more active tensing/relaxing alternating method of progressive relaxation), used in an auto-hypnotic way together with imagining feelings of heaviness and warmth; and Benson's relaxation response, described as "meditation" because of its meditative orientation.

Clients can be taught one of the many relaxation techniques during interview hours and can then practice on their own at home between interviews, thus making the most economical use of therapist interview time and reinforcing learning between sessions. A tape recording helps many clients; they play the tape and follow the instructions while relaxing. It is advisable for clients to go through their relaxation routines daily or twice daily as indicated, as free of distractions and interruptions as possible. They will not, however, always have the quiet place or the necessary time available to relax as completely as they can relax morning and evening in their own homes. The realities of the workaday world must be dealt with; relaxation is not just for practice during periods of withdrawal from the world.

THE PLACE ELEMENT

To be effective, relaxation must be applicable to the places where clients meet the stress of their work day. They cannot always sit down in a quiet room and close their eyes to relax. Through practice, they must first bring those places into their imagination while they relax at home; and then gradually bring the home-practiced relaxed state into the workplace. Thus the learning is transferred into coping with the real world.

THE TIME ELEMENT

Relaxation must be attainable within a reasonably short time to be effective in one's daily life. The actual practice periods can utilize 10 to 30 minutes to achieve a state of complete relaxation; but one must be able to relax under stress in the workplace within a matter of seconds, or else relaxation remains a means of resting upon withdrawal from the world rather than a means of coping with the stresses of the world. This time element is dealt with by practice in becoming fully aware of the deep state of relaxation achieved morning and evening at home, noting all the dimensions of it, and then transferring that deep state to the point of stress within a matter of a few seconds. It is not a simple accomplishment; it requires much practice.

Also, it helps to engage in a number of "mini" relaxation periods throughout the day, taking advantage of minutes wasted while waiting or riding or that are otherwise relatively unoccupied. Differential relaxation is another helpful device: One cannot relax the entire body while working or otherwise active, but those muscles not immediately used can be relaxed. While walking, we can relax our arms; while at a desk, we can relax our legs.

Relaxation training is not indicated for everyone, nor is it a cure-all. Bernstein and Borkovec in their manual *Progressive Relaxation Training* state that the most likely clients are those with high-stress responses that interfere with their lives. Insomniacs, clients with tension headaches, and those tense and tight with cases of "nerves" are among those who would qualify for consideration. Relaxation used within the interview situation may also aid a client in discussing emotion-laden material. Work on likely causes of the anxiety may proceed along with relaxation training, with the therapist helping the client to explore problem areas to determine whether the anxiety is a response to reality circumstances or is an irrational reaction. Relaxing in the face of certain intolerable situations may be an inappropriate response. Asserting oneself or working for realistic change may be indicated.

Rosen in *The Relaxation Book* advises individuals embarking on a self-help program of relaxation to structure appointments with themselves, just as they would with a therapist, to avoid losing interest or dropping out of training. Setting aside regular times and working at relaxation with good humor are important. Impatience for instant results is to be avoided; the goal is to relax. Rosen's illustrated manual has assessment forms, log sheets, and other aids for self-help training.

Most relaxation training programs, once the trainee has gained proficiency in both tensing and relaxing the muscles, dispense with the need for tensing, and allow the person to proceed directly into relaxing at each session. Another mark of the proficiency of the trainee is the ability to transfer the learning from the therapy milieu to his or her daily life of stressful situations: preparing and rehearsing before a potentially stressful event, then remaining relaxed during the period of stress, and, finally, reflecting upon the event while continuing to remain relaxed after its occurrence.

It is important that therapists become personally familiar with the program through experiencing the process and the benefits themselves, before they introduce their clients to relaxation training.

REFERENCES

Benson, H. (1975). *The relaxation response.* New York: Morrow.

Bernstein, D., & Borkovec, T. (1973). *Progressive relaxation training, a manual for the helping professions.* Champaign, IL: Research Press.

Jacobson, E. (1974/1929). *Progressive relaxation.* Chicago: University of Chicago Press.

Rosen, G. (1977). *The relaxation book: An illustrated self-help program.* Englewood Cliffs, NJ: Prentice-Hall.

Wolpe, J. (1954). Reciprocal inhibition as the main basis of psychotherapeutic effects. *Archives of neurology and psychiatry, 72,* 205–226.

SUGGESTED READING

Cautela, J. R., & Groden, J. (1978). *Relaxation: A comprehensive manual for adults, children, and children with special needs.* Champaign, IL: Research Press.

Edelman, R. (1970). Effects of progressive relaxation on autonomic processes. *Journal of Clinical Psychology, 26,* 421–425.

Jacobson, E. (1934). *You must relax.* New York: McGraw-Hill.

Jacobson, E. (1964). *Anxiety and tension control.* Philadelphia, PA: Lippincott.

Kahn, M., Baker, B., & Weiss, J. (1968). Treatment of insomnia by relaxation training. *Journal of Abnormal Psychology, 73,* 556–558.

Lader, M., & Mathews, A. (1970). Comparison of methods of relaxation using physiological measures. *Behavior Research and Therapy, 8,* 331–337.

Luthe, W. (1969). *Autogenic therapy.* New York: Grune & Stratton.

Schultz, J. & Luthe, W. (1959). *Autogenic training: A psychophysiologic approach in psychotherapy.* New York: Grune & Stratton.

Straughan, J., & Dufort, W. (1969). Task difficulty, relaxation, and anxiety level during verbal learning and recall. *Journal of Abnormal Psychology, 74,* 621–624.

White, J., & Fadiman, J. (1976). *Relax.* New York: Confucian Press.

S. MOORE
University of Windsor, Canada

BIOFEEDBACK
MEDITATION

RELIGION AND HEALTH

Religion and medicine have long been fused in response to illness and death. Premodern healers in most societies were religious figures. Sacrifice, pilgrimage, prayer, and spirit appeasement were common prescriptions for a host of physical maladies. A common idea across ancient cultures was that sickness was a result of violation of ethical or religious standards. In short, sickness was the result of sin (Kinsley, 1996). Today, the connections between religion and physical health may be muted, but they continue to exist. We are often urged to thank God for our good health or to pray for the sick and the dying. Indeed, many of our most prestigious medical schools and hospitals were founded by and receive support from established major religions. Of late, the question of a religion-health connection has enjoyed the scrutiny of scientific inquiry. Although methodological difficulties exist, the quality of research into the topic is improving; moving from anecdotal compilations to correlational reports and controlled studies.

RELIGION AND WELL-BEING

Exploratory studies designed to determine the paradigms for wellness across a person's lifespan consistently name religion as a characteristic necessary for optimal health (Frankel & Hewitt, 1994; Wilcock et al., 1999; Witmer & Sweeney, 1992). Ayele, Mulligan, Gheorghiu, and Reyes-Ortiz (1999) report that in their study of 155 men, intrinsic religious activity (e.g., prayer, Bible reading) was significantly positively correlated with life satisfaction. Positive associations between religion and general well-being are evident along the continuum of human aging. Holt and Jenkins (1992) emphasized the importance of religion to older persons and stressed the need for gerontologists to exhibit greater awareness of religion as a health enhancer. Other studies conclude that traditional Judeo-Christian beliefs and behaviors may be related to wellness in later life (Burbank, 1992; Koenig, 1991, 1993; Levin & Chatters, 1998). One study (Johnson, 1995) explored the significance for aging well by reviewing the importance of religion in the lives of older people and posits that religion provides added resources for the elderly when other sources begin to fade.

RELIGION AND MENTAL HEALTH

The associations between an individual's religiosity and their mental health have been reported across a variety of populations. Frequency of church attendance has been reported to be negatively related to depression, with frequent churchgoers being about half as likely to be depressed as nonchurchgoers (Koenig, Hays, George, & Blazer, 1997). Woods, Antoni, Ironson, and Kling (1999a, 1999b) report that greater use of religion as a coping mechanism resulted in fewer symptoms of depression and anxiety in two distinct samples of HIV-infected individuals. Another study (Mickley, Carson, & Soeken 1995) theorized that religion can have either a positive (e.g., encouraging social cohesiveness, helping establish meaning in life) or a negative (fostering excessive guilt or shame, using religion as an escape from dealing with life problems) impact on mental health. The same study reported that people who demonstrate high levels of intrinsic religiousness tend to have less depression, less anxiety, and less dysfunctional attention seeking. They

also display high levels of ego strength, empathy, and integrated social behavior. Payne, Bergin, Bielema, and Jenkins (1991), in their review of religion and mental health, reported positive influences of religiosity on mental health as relates to family variables, self-esteem, personal adjustment and social conduct. Furthermore, Gartner, Larson, and Allen (1991) determined that low levels of religiosity were most often associated with disorders related to undercontrol of impulse.

RELIGION AND PHYSICAL HEALTH

Religion may contribute to the preservation of physical health by enhancing the ability of individuals to maintain overall wellness, particularly among the elderly (Koenig, 1999; Witmer & Sweeney, 1992). One study reports that subjects describing themselves as "secular" had a significantly higher risk of myocardial infarction (MI) compared with subjects describing themselves as "religious", and this risk was independent of other, more traditional MI risk variables (Friedlander, Kark, & Stein, 1986). Another study reports that absence of strength and comfort from religion following elective open-heart surgery predicted greater mortality (Oxman, Freeman, & Manheimer, 1995).

MECHANISMS

The Immune System

The mechanism whereby religion contributes to the preservation of physical health may be the immune system. While studies examining the impact of religion on the immune system are few, they are methodologically sound and offer intriguing results. One study reports an inverse relationship between frequent attendance at religious services and interleukin-6, an inflammatory cytokine and putative immune system regulator (Koenig et al., 1997). Another study (Woods et al., 1999a) reports that subjects displaying high levels of religious behavior (e.g. attending religious services, praying) had significantly higher levels of T-helper inducer cell (CD4+) counts and higher CD4+ percentages.

Increased Social Support

Religion is often practiced in the fellowship of others. Frequent religious involvement may be associated with better health due to an expansion of the social support network. A long tradition of research in social epidemiology has demonstrated the salutary nature of social support (House, Landis, & Umberson, 1988) as well as social support's ability to exert a strong and positive influence over a person's ability to deal with and recover from serious illness (Cohen & Willis, 1985; Taylor, Falke, Shoptaw, & Lichtman, 1986).

Less Fear of Death

Most major religions speak to a continued and happy existence after life on earth is over. As such, another mechanism in the link between religion and health may be the lessened fear of death religious people tend to display. Modell and Guerra (1980) reported that fear of death led to significant postsurgical complications in 75% of the patients they studied. In a case review of older men undergoing treatment for advanced throat cancer, Pressman, Larson,

Lyons, and Humes (1992) found evidence suggesting that a lack of death anxiety explained as a belief in God played a more important role in mediating surgical anxiety than did other coping abilities.

Less Health-Risking Behaviors
Still another factor in the mechanism linking religion and health may be that religious behavior leads to less participation in those behaviors known to be in direct opposition to good health practices. Jarvis and Northcott (1987) reviewed the practices of members of nine major religious and found significant differences from nonpracticing controls in two main areas. They found that religion may reduce the risk of sickness or death by prescribing behavior which prevents illness or death or which assists in treatment of sickness or by proscribing behavior that is harmful to life or that would hinder treatment. Woods and Ironson (1999), in their examination of the role of religiosity/spirituality in medically ill patients, reported that those patients identifying themselves as religious were more apt to cite their religious beliefs as the reason they did not smoke, did not drink, and chose healthy diets than did those patients not identifying themselves as religious.

METHODOLOGICAL CONSIDERATIONS

While the examination of religion and spirituality's role as factors in physical and mental health has yielded consistently positive results, some methodological concerns exist. Primarily, the defining of the construct itself is necessary to operationalize the terms used and to assure validity and generalizability of any findings. For example, some studies define religion as the number of times one attends religious services, others use subject self-identification, and still others use belief in God as their definition of religion. Carefully defining the constructs would not only facilitate assessment, it would address the often confusing nature of what is being measured when one measures religion.

Another concern when studying religion's link to health relates to inadequate control for potentially moderating or mediating variables in most of the studies published to date. It is possible that what appears at first glance to be an association between religion and health may actually be mediated by social support, healthy diet, or any of a myriad of potentially confounding variables.

REFERENCES

Ayele, H., Mulligan, T., Gheorghiu, S., & Reyes-Ortiz, C. (1999). Religious activity improves life satisfaction for some physicians and older patients. *Journal of the American Geriatrics Society, 47*(4), 453–455.

Burbank, P. (1992). An exploratory study: Assessing the meaning in life among older adult clients. *Journal of Gerontological Nursing, 18*(9), 1123–1134.

Cohen, S., & Willis, T. (1985). Stress, social support, and the buffering hypothesis. *Psychological Bulletin, 98,* 310–357.

Frankel, G., & Hewitt, W. (1994). Religion and well-being among Canadian university students: The role of faith groups on campus. *Journal for the Scientific Study of Religion, 33*(1), 62–73.

Friedlander, Y., Kark, J., & Stein, Y. (1986). Religious orthodoxy and myocardial infarction in Jerusalem: A case control study. *International Journal of Cardiology, 10*(1), 62–73.

Gartner, J., Larson, D., & Allen, G. (1991). Religious commitment and mental health: A review of the empirical literature. *Journal of Psychology and Theology, 19,* 6–25.

Holt, M., & Jenkins, M. (1992). Research and implications for practice: Religion, well being/morale, and coping behavior in later life. *Journal of Applied Gerontology, 11*(1), 101–110.

House, J., Landis, N., & Umberson, D. (1988). Social relationships and health. *Science, 241,* 540–545.

Jarvis, G., & Northcott, H. (1987). Religion and differences in morbidity and mortality. *Social Science and Medicine, 25,* 813–824.

Johnson, T. (1995). The significance of religion for aging well. Special Issue: Aging well in contemporary society: I. Concepts and contexts. *American Behavioral Scientist, 39*(2), 186–208.

Kinsley, D. (1996). *Health, healing, and religion. A cross-cultural perspective.* Upper Saddle River, NJ: Prentice Hall.

Koenig, H. (1991). Religion and prevention of illness in later life. *Prevention in Human Services, 10*(1), 69–89.

Koenig, H. (1993). Religion and aging. *Reviews in Clinical Gerontology, 3*(2), 195–203.

Koenig, H., Cohen, H., George, L., Hays, J., Larson, D., & Blazer, D. (1997). Attendance at religious services, interleukin-6, and other biological parameters of immune function in older adults. *International Journal of Psychiatry Medicine, 27,* 233–250.

Koenig, H., Hays, J., George, L., & Blazer, D. (1997). Modeling the cross-sectional relationships between religion, physical health, social support, and depressive symptoms. *American Journal of Geriatric Psychiatry, 5,* 131–144.

Levin, J., & Chatters, L. (1998). Religion, health, and psychological well-being in older adults: Findings from three national surveys. *Journal of Aging and Health, 10*(4), 504–531.

Mickley, R., Carson, V., & Soeken, K. (1995). Religion and adult mental health: State of the science in nursing. *Issues in Mental Health in Nursing, 16*(4), 345–360.

Modell, J., & Guerra, F. (1980). Psychological problems in the surgical patient. In F. Guerra & J. A. Aldrete (Eds.), *Emotional and psychological responses to anesthesia and surgery.* New York: Grune & Stratton.

Oxman, T., Freeman, D., & Manheimer, E. (1995). Lack of social participation or religious strength and comfort as risk factors for death after cardiac surgery in the elderly. *Journal of Psychosomatic Medicine, 57*(1), 5–15.

Payne, I., Bergin, A., Bielema, K., & Jenkins, P. (1991). Review of religion and mental health: Prevention and the enhancement of psychosocial functioning. *Prevention in Human Services, 9*(2), 11–40.

Pressman, P., Larson, D., Lyons, J., & Humes, D. (1992). Religious belief, coping strategies, and psychological distress in seven elderly males with head and neck cancer. Unpublished manuscript.

Taylor, S., Falke, R., Shoptaw, S., & Lichtman, R. (1986). Social support, support groups, and the cancer patient. *Journal of Consulting and Clinical Psychology, 54,* 608–615.

Wilcock, A., van der Arend, H., Darling, K., Scholz, J., Siddall, R., Snigg, C., & Stephens, J. (1999). An exploratory study of people's perceptions and experiences of wellbeing. *British Journal of Occupation Therapy, 62*(2), 75–82.

Witmer, J., & Sweeney, T. (1992). A holistic model for wellness and prevention over the life span. *Journal of Counseling and Development, 71*(2), 140–148.

Woods, T., Antoni, M., Ironson, G., & Kling, D. (1999a). Religiosity is associated with affective and immune status in symptomatic HIV-infected gay men. *Journal of Psychosomatic Research, 46*(2), 165–176.

Woods, T., Antoni, M., Ironson, G., & Kling, D. (1999b). Religiosity is associated with affective status in symptomatic HIV-infected African-American women. *Journal of Health Psychology, 4*(3), 317–326.

Woods, T., & Ironson, G. (1999). Religion and spirituality in the face of illness: How cancer, cardiac, and HIV patients describe their spirituality/religiosity. *Journal of Health Psychology, 4*(3), 393–412.

T. E. WOODS
University of Wisconsin School of Medicine

RELIGION & PSYCHOLOGY
PHILOSOPHY & PSYCHOLOGY

RELIGION AND PSYCHOLOGY

Why are some people deeply religious whereas others have no belief in God and never attend religious services? Why do some people become Presbyterians while others are Episcopalians, Pentacostals, Roman Catholics, or Buddhists? Why do some believers have highly emotional religious experiences while others experience religion as a "dull habit"? Why are some people comforted and helped by their religious beliefs while others are plunged into overwhelming guilt and self-condemnation? What is the role of religion in mental health, psychotherapy, value clarification, and moral conduct?

These are some of the issues that concern psychologists who study religion. Although many have attempted to define *psychology of religion,* perhaps no definition is better than that of Cambridge professor Robert H. Thouless. He wrote, in *An Introduction to the Psychology of Religion,* that the psychological study of religion seeks "to understand religious behavior by applying to it the psychological principles derived from the study of non-religious behavior." Psychological methods are used in this field to study not only religious behavior, but also the attitudes, values, and experiences of people who believe in the existence and influences of a de-

ity or other supernatural forces. Although the psychology of religion sometimes studies parapsychological phenomena, the emphasis tends to focus on more traditional forms of religious experience, including prayer, conversion, mystical experiences, worship, and participation in religious communes and cults. Such study also raises issues of counseling, but the psychology of religion is more concerned with understanding religious behavior or experience and only minimally is there concern with pastoral counseling and other religious approaches to therapy.

Historically, the psychology of religion began with a great and productive burst of interest and enthusiasm near the beginning of this century, almost faded from existence during the 50 years following the birth of behaviorism, and more recently has reemerged as a legitimate and respectable field of study for psychologists. Division 36 of the American Psychological Association is a special-interest group for "psychologists interested in religious issues." Less than 10 years old, the division is growing rapidly, as increasing numbers of psychologists turn their attention to the understanding of religious behavior and thinking.

Although he described religion as an "illusion," a "universal neurosis," and a "narcotic" he hoped "mankind will overcome" (*The Future of an Illusion*), Freud nevertheless had a great interest in religious behavior and wrote several papers and three major books on the subject. Jung, Adler, and others in the early psychoanalytic movement continued the study of religion, often from a perspective that was less critical and more accepting of the psychological value of theological beliefs.

In the United States, the study of religion was considered an important branch of early general psychology. G. Stanley Hall, for example, was a brilliant educator, leader in child psychology, and first president of the American Psychological Association. He astutely applied scientific methods to the study of religion, founded the *Journal Of Religious Psychology,* and in 1917 published a book entitled *Jesus, the Christ, in the Light of Psychology.* Better known and much more influential were the Gifford lectures of William James. Published in 1902 under the title *Varieties of Religious Experience,* James's book has become perhaps the only classic psychological study of religion.

With the rise of behaviorism, the psychology of religion rapidly faded as a field of inquiry for psychologists. With its simple and appealing rationale, behaviorism lured psychology away from the study of such complex issues as the influence of beliefs, the development of moral or ethical standards, and the reasons for involvement in religious behavior. A few psychological writers (including Allport, Asch, Mowrer, Meehl, Maslow, Fromm, and Menninger) wrote books or articles about religious behavior. This kept interest in the field alive until its more recent reemergence as a serious subspecialty of psychology.

Any attempt to divide the psychology of religion into smaller areas of interest is certain to be arbitrary. Nevertheless, we could conclude that psychologists working in this field are concerned with a variety of issues, including methodology, the psychological origins of religion, religious development, religious experience, the dynamics of religious behavior, religion and social behavior, efforts to integrate psychology with theology, and psychological theories of religion.

SOME AREAS OF INTEREST

Methodology

The complexity of religious behavior and experience has led psychologists to use a diversity of measuring tools. These include the analysis of personal reports and introspections; clinical, natural, and participant observation; the use of surveys, questionnaires, and in-depth personal interviews; the analysis of documents such as diaries and autobiographies of religious people; the use of personality tests; examination of religious documents, including the Bible; and use of experimental techniques. The scientific study of religion is progressing, but such progress is slow and difficult because many religious phenomena (such as "faith," "belief," "conversion," and "commitment") are not easy to define or to measure with precision.

Psychological Origins of Religion

Religion is a widespread phenomenon (in that it extends to numerous cultures and influences people of every age, socioeconomic status, and educational level); it is long lasting and highly influential. Freud proposed that it began with primitive people struggling with guilt and sexual impulses. More recent psychologists have abandoned a search for the historical origins of religion and have concentrated, instead, on finding psychological roots for the origins and continuation of religion in modern individuals. Among these roots are social influences (including one's childhood experiences, contacts with religious people, and response to the power of suggestion); need satisfaction (the view that religion helps believers find such things as security, meaning in life and death, a reason for self-esteem, strength for times of stress or crisis, and a purpose for living); the influence of nature (which leads to a belief that God created beauty and order); and theological foundations (the idea that all people are drawn to the supernatural, perhaps even by supernatural forces).

Religious Development

As individuals pass through the life cycle, they change in their views of the world and in their perceptions of God. The child's faith is likely to be simple and magical. As one grows older, moral values, concepts of the supernatural, and involvement in religious practices all change. Psychologists of religion study these changes and have concluded, following writers such as Allport (*The Individual and His Religion*), that religion can be either mature or immature.

Religious Experience

This is a major area of interest for psychologists who study religion. William James analyzed the causes and influences of conversion, mystical experience, saintliness, and prayer. Later research has added studies of glossolalia (speaking in unknown "languages" as a result of religious arousal), religious content in dreams, the psychological nature of meditation, the influence of religious persuasion and ritual, faith healing, altered states of consciousness, the power of confession and forgiveness, the influence of occult and cult phenomena, the explanation of miracles, the use of drugs to stimulate religious experiences, and religious influences in psychopathology.

The Dynamics of Religious Behavior

In a pivotal volume, Paul Pruyser (*A Dynamic Psychology of Religion*) proposed that religion influences and is influenced by human perception, intellectual processes, thinking, linguistic functions, emotion, motor behavior, interpersonal relations, and relationships with things, ideas, and the self. Although it currently appears to occupy a minimal place in the psychology of religion, the study of the relationship of general psychology and religion holds interesting potential for future research.

Religion and Social Behavior

Social psychologists have a special interest in the social organization of churches and synagogues, the social structure and influence of religious bodies, the roles of religious leaders, and the nature of religious cults and study groups.

The Integration of Religion and Psychology

Working on assumptions such as the view that "all truth is God's truth" and that there cannot be internal conflict between different branches of truth, a number of writers have attempted to "integrate" psychology with theology. Currently, the most active work in this area appears to come from Protestant Christians of evangelical persuasion. Carter, Collins, Narramore, Fleck and others are leaders.

Psychological Theories of Religion

To date, there are few well-developed theories of the psychology of religion. Much of Freud's work was theoretical in nature, and so were some of the writings of Jung, Fromm, Maslow, Pruyser, and Allport. More modern writers appear to be waiting for the appearance of additional research before developing contemporary theories.

As an example of psychological studies of religion, it could be helpful to consider the issue of religious conversion. William James viewed conversion as a process that could be gradual or sudden, by which "a self hitherto divided, and consciously wrong, inferior and unhappy, becomes unified and consciously right, superior and happy" because of one's "former hold on religious realities."

A later writer, Leon Salzman, proposed that conversion could be both "progressive and maturational" for some individuals or "regressive and psychopathological" for others. Some writers have described different types of conversion, a variety of causes for conversion (such as social pressure, a response to fear, a desire for acceptance by God and other believers, the desire to find release from guilt or meaning to life), and both positive and negative results of conversion. William Sargant's controversial description of religious persuasion techniques (*Battle for the Mind*) has led to more recent studies of "deprogramming" and other ways in which people are persuaded to move away from their religious groups and beliefs. The effects of conversion have also been studied, along with evaluations of individual differences in the way people accept, reject, and are influenced by religious factors.

The psychology of religion concerns devoutly religious psychologists as well as atheists and agnostics. In a field undergoing a revival of interest, it is difficult to predict future trends. Perhaps there will be increasing interest in religious experience, the psychological needs and assumptions underlying religious beliefs and behavior, the social impact of religious organizations and politically oriented religious movements, and the religious implications of counseling. As the field develops, more empirical research is likely to arise, replacing some of the present tendency toward armchair observations.

REFERENCES

Freud, S. (1927). *The future of an illusion.* Garden City, NY: Doubleday.

Pruyser, P. W. (1968). *A dynamic psychology of religion.* New York: Harper & Row.

Sargant, W. (1957). *Battle for the mind.* New York: Doubleday.

Thouless, R. H. (1971). *An introduction to the psychology of religion* (3rd ed.). Cambridge, England: Cambridge University Press.

SUGGESTED READING

Fleck, J. R., & Carter, J. D. (Eds.). (1981). *Psychology and Christianity: Integrative readings.* Nashville, TN: Abingdon.

Fromm, E. (1950). *Psychoanalysis and religion.* New Haven, CT: Yale University Press.

James, W. (1914). *The varieties of religious experience: A study in human nature.* New York: Longmans, Green. (Original work published 1902)

Maslow, A. H. (1976/1970). *Religions, values, and peak experiences.* New York: Penguin Books.

G. R. COLLINS
Trinity Evangelical Divinity School

HUMANISTIC PSYCHOLOGY
RITUAL BEHAVIOR
SUPERSTITION

REPERTORY GRID TECHNIQUE

Developed within personal construct theory, repertory grid technique represents a widely used method for studying personal and interpersonal systems of meaning. Because of their flexibility, repertory grids (or repgrids) have been used in approximately 3,000 studies of a broad variety of topics, ranging from children's understanding of physical science principles and consumer preferences, to formal structures of self-reflection within cognitive science and the mutual validation of belief systems between friends. However, their most consistent area of application has probably been in the clinical domain, where grids have been used to assess the properties of meaning systems of different groups of individuals (e.g., those diagnosed as thought-disordered or agoraphobic), and how these change over the course of treatment.

The role construct repertory test (or reptest) was initially designed by George Kelly, the author of personal construct psychology (PCP), as a means of assessing the content of an individual's repertory of role constructs—the unique system of interconnected meanings that define his or her perceived relationships to others. In its simplest form, the reptest requires the respondent to compare and contrast successive sets of three significant people (e.g., my mother, my father, and myself), and formulate some important way in which two of the figures are alike, and different from the third. For example, if prompted with the above triad, a person might respond, "Well, my mother and I are very trusting of people, whereas my dad is always suspicious of their motives."

This basic dimension, trusting of people versus suspicious of their motives, would then be considered one of the significant themes or constructs that the person uses to organize, interpret, and approach the social world, and to define his or her role in it. By presenting the respondent with a large number of triads of varying elements (e.g., a previous romantic partner, best friend, a disliked person, one's ideal self), the reptest elicits a broad sampling of the personal constructs that constitute the person's outlook on life and perceived alternatives. These constructs can then be interpreted impressionistically, used as the basis for further interviewing of the respondent, or categorized using any of a number of reliable systems of content analysis, conducted either manually or using available computer programs.

While the results of the reptest are often revealing, most contemporary users prefer to extend the method beyond the simple elicitation of constructs, by prompting the respondent subsequently to rate or rank each of the elements (e.g., people) on the resulting construct dimensions. For example, using the triadic comparison method described above, a respondent might generate a set of 15 constructs (e.g., trusting vs. suspicious; moved by feelings vs. rational; ambitious vs. aimless; young vs. old), which might be arrayed in 15 rows on a sheet of paper. She might then be asked to assign a number to each of 10 elements (e.g., my mother, father, self, partner) arranged in columns going across the sheet, representing where each figure would fall on, say, a 7-point scale anchored by the poles of each construct. For instance, "mother" might be marked at 1 on trusting vs. suspicious, representing very trusting, whereas "father" might be placed at 5 on this same scale, representing moderately suspicious. The intersection of the 15 construct rows with the 10 element columns forms the grid, and the matrix of 150 specific ratings it contains is amenable to a wide range of analyses. In practice, repertory grids can be virtually any size, from 6 constructs and elements to literally hundreds of each for a given respondent. However, most research indicates that the amount of new information about the person's meaning system in a domain (e.g., perceptions of acquaintances) begins to peak with a sampling of approximately 15 to 20 constructs and a similar number of elements. Although the repgrid was originally devised as an interview-based or paper-and-pencil measure, most contemporary users rely on any of a number of computer programs for their elicitation and analysis, such as the popular *WebGrid II* program available via the Internet.

Although the specific element ratings on important constructs are often informative in themselves (e.g., seeing that a respondent views her father as suspicious and having no goals, but also as rational), it is typically more helpful to conduct a comprehensive analysis of the grid to discern larger patterns. This might involve correlating and factor analyzing the matrix of ratings to see at a glance which constructs go together for the respondent (e.g., everyone who is trusting may also be seen as moved by feelings), or to learn what people are most and least alike in the respondent's view. These linkages among constructs often suggest why people remain stuck in symptomatic patterns, as when a client resists reconstruing himself as happy instead of depressed, because the former is associated with being superficial as opposed to deep. Similarly, patterns of identification among elements in a grid can be clinically informative, with some of these (e.g., degree of correlation between actual self and ideal self) providing useful indices of progress in psychotherapy.

An interesting feature of grid technique is that it combines aspects of both idiographic assessment, which strives to reveal unique dimensions of a given respondent's outlook, and nomothetic research, which seeks general patterns across people. Thus, the format of the repgrid essentially guides the respondent in constructing his or her own questionnaire (by eliciting the individual's own constructs and relevant elements or figures to rate), while permitting comparisons across different people or groups. For example, depressed individuals, relative to others, tend to show not only distinctive themes in the content of their constructs (e.g., more self-references and more morally evaluative themes), but also distinctive overall structure (e.g., tighter intercorrelations among constructs, and more polarized or extreme perceptions). This blend of projective and objective testing has made grid technique useful to both clinicians and scientists seeking to understand how different persons and groups organize their views of themselves and the world.

Describing a few of the problems to which repgrids have been applied gives some idea about the range and flexibility of the method. Grids have been used to study the long-term adjustment of survivors of incest, who carry with them a sense of distance from other people decades after the sexual abuse. Grids have also been used to measure processes of identification with other clients and therapists within group therapy settings, and to predict who is most likely to benefit from this form of treatment. Grids have been applied to the study of the development and breakdown of romantic relationships and friendships, by looking at the degree of convergence between partners in the way they construe experiences at increasingly intimate levels. Other investigators have relied on grids to understand the distinctive differences between the knowledge structures of experts and novices in a given domain, and to refine the discriminations made by assembly-line workers in detecting product flaws. As the use of these methods continues to grow with the dissemination of ever more powerful computerized systems for their elicitation and analysis, it seems likely that repertory grids will become an increasingly popular tool for psychological assessment, consultation, and research.

SUGGESTED READING

Bell, R. C. (1990). Analytic issues in the use of repertory grid technique. In G. J. Neimeyer & R. A. Neimeyer (Eds.), *Advances in personal construct psychology* (Vol. 1, pp. 25–48). Greenwich, CT: JAI.

Bringmann, M. (1992). Computer-based methods for the analysis and interpretation of personal construct systems. In G. J.

Neimeyer & R. A. Neimeyer (Eds.), *Advances in personal construct psychology* (Vol. 2, pp. 57–90). Greenwich, CN: JAI.

Fransella, F., & Bannister, D. (1977). *A manual for repertory grid technique.* New York: Academic Press.

Neimeyer, R. A. (1993). Constructivist approaches to the measurement of meaning. In G. J. Neimeyer (Ed.), *Constructivist assessment: A casebook* (pp. 58–103). Newbury Park, CA: Sage.

R. A. NEIMEYER
University of Memphis

PERSONAL CONSTRUCT PSYCHOLOGY

RESCORLA, ROBERT A. (1940–   )

Robert A. Rescorla was born on May 9, 1940 in Pittsburgh, PA. He attended high school in Westfield, NJ, finishing third in a class of 300. His decision to enter Swarthmore College in 1958 profoundly affected the course of his life. He was suddenly immersed in an atmosphere that he characterizes as "uncompromisingly committed to ideas and intellectual excellence." At Swarthmore he found an unusually excellent psychology department. He took courses with Gleitman, Wallach, Asch, and Prentice. He was fortunate to participate in the honors program, majoring in psychology and minoring in philosophy and math. He graduated Phi Beta Kappa with highest honors in 1962. While at Swarthmore, he got his first taste of research, conducting perception experiments with Wallach, doing delayed response experiments on monkeys with Gleitman, and serving as Asch's research assistant doing human learning experiments.

Rescorla went directly to graduate work at the University of Pennsylvania, supported by an NSF fellowship. There he worked in the laboratory of Solomon. But he was also profoundly influenced by such eminent senior scientists as Luce, Green, Hurvich, Jameson, Nachmias, Irwin, Gleitman, and Teitlebaum. Solomon's laboratory was actively studying avoidance learning and Pavlovian emotional conditioning. During Rescorla's time in the laboratory, it contained many graduate students who would become influential in the study of learning: LoLordo, Maier, Overmier, and Seligman. In addition, postdoctoral fellows such as Church, Cohen, and Hammond worked in the laboratory. During his second year at Penn, Rescorla collaborated with LoLordo to begin a highly influential series of experiments on the modulation of instrumental behavior by Pavlovian elicitors and inhibitors of fear. This work was deeply influenced by the writings of Konorski, upon which Rescorla stumbled when he bought a used copy of *Conditioned Reflexes and Neuron Organization*. Rescorla went on to use these procedures to explore the importance of a CS's predicting a US, as distinct from its being paired with that US. This led to the development of the "truly random control" procedure, together with the contingency view of conditioning. During his last year at Penn, Rescorla collaborated with Solomon in the writing of their classic article on two-process learning theory.

In 1966 Rescorla received his PhD and took a position as an assistant professor of psychology at Yale University. With the help of funding from NSF, he pursued his studies of the conditions leading to Pavlovian excitatory and inhibitory conditioning. He entered into a highly fruitful collaboration with Wagner. In 1972, they published one of the most influential theories of elementary learning processes, the Rescorla-Wagner model. This theory integrated a wide variety of findings, including Rescorla's earlier work on contingency, Kamin's blocking experiments, Wagner's validity results, as well as the basic findings of conditioned inhibition. That theory continues to be one of the touchstones for thinking about Pavlovian conditioning. It is a version of an error-correction model, and serves as a forerunner to contemporary connectionist models which build upon the delta-rule.

In the later 1970s, Rescorla advocated the importance of studying the animal's learning about the events which enter into Pavlovian associations, the CS and US. He also began the study of Pavlovian second-order conditioning. He found this technique to be a highly effective tool for the analyzing of the contents of associative learning, and published a series of lectures in 1980 entitled *Pavlovian Second-Order Conditioning: Studies in Associative Learning.*

While at Yale, Rescorla benefited from the opportunity to interact with a broad range of prominent scholars, including Sheffield, Kessen, Tulving, Abelson, and Garner. He also pursued his interests in undergraduate education, serving as director of undergraduate studies in psychology and chair of the Yale Committee on Teaching in the Residential Colleges. He was a very popular undergraduate lecturer.

In 1981, Rescorla accepted a position at the University of Pennsylvania and in 1986 was appointed the James M. Skinner Professor of Science. At Penn, with the help of continuing NSF funding, he pursued his work on Pavlovian associations, analyzing the role of contextual stimuli and Gestalt perceptual processes. He also began the study of hierarchical Pavlovian relations, in which one stimulus provides information about the relation between two others. These studies of "occasion-setting" or "facilitation" have greatly broadened the domain of Pavlovian conditioning. He also entered into a fruitful collaboration with a postdoctoral fellow, Colwill. Together they developed techniques for the study of the associative structures in instrumental learning. These techniques have proven highly effective as analytic tools for the analysis of the contents of associative learning. They have provided some of the clearest evidence for the presence of associations between responses and outcomes in instrumental learning. These techniques have also allowed the focused measurement of associations before and after extinction, providing the ability to document the status of associations after such decremental manipulations as extinction. They have provided clear evidence that associations persist essentially untouched despite such operations.

At Penn, Rescorla has continued to pursue his interests in undergraduate education. Influenced by his own excellent experience at Swarthmore College, he has worked to provide broader research opportunities for undergraduates. He served both as director of undergraduate studies and as chair of the department of psychology. He also served as dean of the College of Arts and Sciences.

Rescorla's work has received recognition from a variety of sources. He was elected to the Society of Experimental Psycholo-

gists in 1975 and to the National Academy of Sciences in 1985. He received the Distinguished Scientific Contribution award of the American Psychological Association in 1986 and was elected a William James Fellow of the American Psychological Society in 1989. He received the Howard Crosby Warren Medal of the Society of Experimental Psychologists, 1991. One of his most prized honors is the Ira Abrams Distinguished Teaching Award of the School of Arts and Sciences at Penn, which he received in 1999.

Rescorla has been active in professional organizations, serving on the Governing Board and Publication Board of the Psychonomic Society, as president of the Eastern Psychological Association, president of the Division of Experimental Psychology of the American Psychological Association, and president of the Psychology Division of the American Association for the Advancement of Science. He has served as consultant editor on a variety of journals and as editor of *Animal Learning and Behavior.*

One theme which runs through Rescorla's empirical and theoretical work is the desire to retain continuity with the insights of past thinkers. He attributes many of his own ideas to his periodic rereading of a small set of classics: Kohler's *Gestalt Psychology,* Skinner's *Behavior of Organisms,* and Konorski's *Conditioned Reflexes and Neuron Organization.*

STAFF

RESEARCH METHODOLOGY

Research design methodology in psychology follows the principles of research methodology in the sciences as exemplified by Mill's method of difference. It states that if A is always followed by a, and *not-A* is always followed by *not-a,* then A is certainly the cause of a. In psychology, there are many special considerations in addition to this basic principle. Most of the variables are abstract and often have few direct referents to the biological or physical world. The very act of observing or measuring psychological variables can cause the subjects to react or change. In addition, actively placing persons into or excluding them from the "advantages" or "disadvantages" of receiving or not receiving a psychological treatment or condition may cause these subjects to differ from people in the day-to-day world. The consideration of scientific inquiry methods is the domain of research methodology in psychology.

As a start to understanding the problems of research methodology in psychology, an axiom and three basic facts are listed here. A general axiom of science is that there is no knowledge without comparison. That this is true can be seen from Mill's method of difference. Note that comparison is basic to understanding the observations under the conditions of A and *not-A.* Comparisons between pairs of several differing conditions are necessary for fuller understanding of a phenomenon.

The first fact is that measurement in psychology generally is rather imprecise and in reality never can be as precise as many typical measurements of variables in the physical and biological domains. (This is so because precision of psychological measurement is a direct function of test length or number of observers making a judgment.)

The second fact is that a relatively large number of variables are relatively independent, perhaps on the order of 400 or more. Some psychologists believe that there are many more; others believe there are a markedly fewer number of variables. Nevertheless, attempting to maintain control of or keep under observation even as few as 200 psychological variables presents a research methodology problem rather different from the limited number of basic variables in physics (time, space, mass, charge, and so on).

The third fact is that these dimensions of human behavior vary over time, some not as much (such as intelligence) as others which, by definition, are highly volatile (such as one's mood).

The purpose of psychology is to discover new psychological variables, to show the relationships among these new variables with already determined variables, and, of course, to discover new relationships among already known variables. The definition of a psychological variable is that it is a conceptual entity in the field of psychology. (Thus enters the creativity of the researchers. They are free to declare any organizing perception they see in the psychological world as a variable, which they must then show is indeed an entity to other researchers as well.)

It is in this context that research methodology is important. In science, the definition of a "fact" is the statement of the relationship between two variables. However, to have an understanding of the meaning of facts, researchers must have a context of comparative relationships in which to understand their data's scientific significance. It is the set of comparative relations, the context of the observations, that gives fuller meaning to the statements of relationship among variables. This context of comparative relationships is the domain of research methodology and design.

Since the purpose of most science is to understand why and how relationships occur, ultimately the strength, size, and causative direction statements (mutual cause, mutual effect, or reciprocal cause and effect) of these relationships must be determined. The quality of being able to infer a causal relationship is called the internal validity of the research design. In applied areas of psychology, such as industrial-organizational, school, and clinical psychology, these cause and effect relationships are immediately applicable because administrative and instructional decisions, recommendations, and application of therapies directly imply that certain effects are likely to ensue if certain decisions are made or certain treatments or therapies are imposed. Finally, these research relationships and cause and effect statements must be shown to generalize, to occur in the "real" world outside of the psychological laboratory or the somewhat controlled environment of a research study. These generalizations are called the external validity of the research design.

EXPERIMENTAL VERSUS PASSIVE OBSERVATIONAL RESEARCH DESIGNS

Research designs in psychology can be divided into two broad types: experimental research designs and passive observational designs. In the first type of design, variables are systematically imposed on or withheld from the subjects, either by the experimenter or by naturally forming conditions in society. Comparisons are then made on variables of interest among the groups of subjects that have had and have not had the imposed treatment variables or conditions. In the passive observational type of research design, the researcher merely observes participants under many natural conditions and records the participants' scores on a number of variables or describes their condition and surroundings. Later these scores and conditions under which the observations were made are interrelated. No attempt is made by the researcher to impose conditions or make systematic changes. Indeed, in a broad range of psychological research, it is difficult or impossible for the researcher to change the status of variables. Many of these variables are of great importance in psychology, such as age, gender, socioeconomic status, and intelligence.

True Experiments

Within the first broad type of research design, experimental designs, there are two major subtypes—true experiments and quasi-experiments. The classification "true experiments" contains just one type of research design, although that design can have many variations. In true experiments, the participants involved in the research are *randomly* allocated to experimental groups and control groups. This randomization process operates strictly by chance and is usually accomplished by using generated tables of random numbers, which by definition have no pattern, organization, or sequence that would occur more frequently than by chance. Because in the true experiment participants are assigned to the research groups on a chance basis (at random), it follows that the only differences among the research groups also would be those determined by chance alone. This statement holds true for all of the several hundred psychological variables (both defined and undefined) associated with the participants in the groups. Further statistical analysis theory can define with some precision the degree of differences expected on any variable. The research groups formed by allocation of participants to groups with the use of random numbers can be said to be not unequal on any variable except as expected by chance—and, as was indicated, the amount of expected differences can be determined with some precision. Rather than use the somewhat awkward phrase "not unequal," the simpler but not as precise term "equal groups" is used.

The Logic of Experiments in Psychology

This concept of the initial equality of groups is important because the basic cause-and-effect relationship logic (the internal validity) of experimental research in psychology follows the paradigm that equal groups, acted on by equal treatments, are still equal at the end of the research study (and for all time following). The opposite case is also true: Equal groups acted on by unequal treatments will be unequal on the after-treatment measures (the criteria). Thus, if researchers attempt to show that one learning method, A, is better than another, B, two groups of subjects can be formed "at random" for a true experiment. Method A is used by one group to learn, and method B is used by the other group. Since the groups are "equal" on all variables initially and would continue to be "equal" if treated equally (or not treated at all), then it follows that if both groups learned an equal amount, treatment methods A and B are not different; that is, they would be "equal." For the second case, if the amount learned under conditions A and B is unequal, then it can be inferred that one of the learning conditions, A or B, is superior to the other; that is, they are unequal. (This inference is called the inference of experimental logic, which is distinct from statistical inference. However, the determination of the differences between the amounts learned generally is made via statistical inference.)

Thus there are two basic inferences that can be made from the logic of a true experiment:

1. There are equal groups initially, equal results, and, therefore, the inference is made of equal treatments.

2. There are equal groups initially, unequal results, and, therefore, the inference is made of unequal treatments.

Note that there are always three parts in all experiments: (1) participants' groups, (2) experimental treatments, and (3) results (or criteria). In the true experiment, as the result of randomly assigning participants to groups, it can be assumed that all variables initially, and for all time to come, will be equal unless some systematically different treatments or conditions are applied. If, after seemingly different treatments are applied, it can be shown that a difference on any variable exists between groups, the primary inference is that the treatments or conditions *caused* that effect, and the treatments are indeed different. This is a very broad, strong statement and an important one in the development of an understanding of theory in psychology where cause-and-effect statements are ultimately necessary for full understanding of phenomena. For research where variables can be applied or withheld, the true experiment, with its initial random allocation of subjects to groups, is a powerful research design. Its internal validity is unsurpassed.

Quasi-experiments

Within the broad research design classification of experimental, there are two major types of research design: true experiments (just discussed) and quasi-experiments. Both types involve participant groups, the differential application of treatments, and the assessment of possible differences in criteria after the treatments have been applied. The difference is that in quasi-experiments no random allocation of participants to groups has been made. Quasi-experiment groups are formed naturally or via the intervention of others (but not at random), and the treatments or conditions imposed on these groups and criteria measures are described. Further, to be a quasi-experiment, pretreatment measures also must be available. (Note that for the true experiment this last condition is *not* necessary, although it is sometimes done.) A major difference in the quasi-experiment is that initial equality of groups *cannot* be assumed as it can be in the true experiment. In fact, often the groups clearly are unequal initially.

Initial status (equal groups or unequal groups) in quasi-experiments, then, must be determined by actual assessment. If the groups in a quasi-experiment can be demonstrated to be initially equivalent on one or more variables of interest to the researcher, then the research logic is nearly the same as it is in the true experiment. Groups demonstrated initially to be equal that are acted on by equal treatments will be equal on the criteria, and, of course, equal groups acted on by unequal treatments will produce differences among the groups on the criteria. However, many times in quasi-experiments, groups do differ initially. In these cases, the cause-and-effect research design logic takes a different form. After experimental treatment, they must be either more different or less different on the criteria than they were initially. Either way suggests that the treatment may cause the greater or lesser differences in the criteria.

There are three major types of research designs within the major category of quasi-experiments, and literally hundreds of variations within the three types. The three types can be labeled (1) *quasi-experiments* in which the initial measures show the groups to be equal; (2) *quasi-experiments* in which the groups are shown to be initially unequal; and (3) *interrupted time series designs.* The first two types of quasi-experiments generally emulate the cause-and-effect logic of true experiments rather well. Further, they are far more practical in the real world than true experiments, in which the researcher must have a major degree of ability to control the activities of those being studied and of those imposing the treatment conditions. In the true experiment, the researcher must be able to assign subjects to various experimental groups at random and to withhold treatments from some subjects. In quasi-experiments, the researcher can use naturally formed groups where some are in certain conditions, or are given differing treatments, and some are not. The researcher's task in developing a quasi-experiment is to obtain pretreatment measures and posttreatment measures, and to describe with care the conditions or treatments (or lack of them) that the several groups were given. Further, the researcher must hypothesize what would happen if no treatments were given.

The problem with quasi-experiments is that even in the ones where initial equality on several variables is established, it is difficult to determine that all prior conditions probably influencing the subjects were also equal, or even that all variables in the subjects' groups were equal prior to the application of the treatment. (All of these conditions can be assumed to be present in a true experiment.) Important unmeasured variables influencing the criteria may not be equal in the research groups. Variables may be changing in the groups. While they are equal when measured prior to the experimental treatment, they are moving to a status of inequality as the result of prior conditions or treatments in such a way that, in the future, observations will be unequal—*whether or not the experimental treatments were applied.* The research inference that the differing treatments caused the unequal status on the criteria would prove invalid.

At this point, two of the three basic facts will be applied to show problems in the research design validity of experiments. One fact is that psychological variables change over time. Another fact is imprecise measurement. These both suggest that one cannot ever be absolutely sure of experimental research findings—even in the true experiment. (If one has a need for certainty in a science, psychology will be an uncomfortable field.) Findings in any given experiment can occur by chance alone as the result of naturally occurring variability over time and by random fluctuations in measurement systems. This threat to internal validity, called instability, is controlled by statistical analysis.

In the quasi-experiment, these problems of inferring cause-and-effect relationships are compounded. Even in quasi-experiments where the groups are initially equal on the assessed variables, in addition to the instability of psychological variables within the time span of the experiment and the imprecise measurement of criteria, the researcher must also assume that all important variables operated in all groups equally and that all important prior conditions were the same. Both of these assumptions may be difficult to accept. In quasi-experiments where groups are known to be initially unequal, even more problems arise. As a direct consequence of the first fact stated (the inability to measure variables precisely), it is known that all observed scores on variables (except average scores) are biased. For highly precise measures and those in the group not too distant from the average score, the bias is small, but for many of the more typical measures commonly used in psychological research, when used to measure rather atypical subjects, the bias can be rather marked. The result is that for these latter subjects, when using rather imprecise measures, future observations are expected to change and to be nearer to the average—even when no treatments or unusual conditions intervene between the initial measurement and later measurements, such as those on a criterion after treatment in a quasi-experiment. This threat to internal validity is called regression-toward-the-mean.

In some quasi-experiments the participant groups differ initially on a pretreatment. Often, even if the experimental treatments have no effect, the observed differences on the criteria may well be less than the observed pretreatment differences. This naturally occurring change obviously complicates the cause-and-effect interpretation of experimental treatment or conditions and their possible influence on the criteria variables. In fact, it may be impossible to make any meaningful cause-and-effect relationship statements. However, increased differences on the criteria following treatment are not attributable to this regression-toward-the-mean problem and, therefore, are much more interpretable. Further, efforts to make these quasi-experiments into strong quasi-experiments by carefully selecting "equal" groups of participants from unequal groups of participants generally makes the problem of cause-and-effect interpretation worse. The selected participants' scores will regress toward the average of their original groups. Attempts to adjust the criteria scores to accommodate differences in the pretreatment scores in general cannot be done successfully. To use simple subtraction within groups using posttest minus pretest scores and then to compare gains (or losses) often yields a biased result. In addition, these difference scores are known to be very imprecise. Further, statistical adjustments in the great majority of cases are underadjustments because of the basic inability to measure with precision.

The conclusion is that while quasi-experiments are a common design in psychology, there can be interpretation difficulties. Their results must be viewed with some caution although generally the results of true and quasi-experiments are equivalent except where the premeasures are of attitudes and emotional variables.

The third major type of quasi-experiment is the interrupted time series design. It occurs when participants are observed periodically over time and a treatment is applied or a condition arises at some point or at several specified points in that time span. In essence, the participants serve as their own control in that they are observed before a treatment is given and then observed again after the treatment is given. While this research design model works rather well in the classical areas of the physical sciences and in those areas of biology where the phenomena are fairly stable, it is one of the three basic facts presented in the foregoing that psychological variables vary over time—even when no treatments are applied. Therefore, it is imperative that a number of observations be made both before and after the application of the treatment to assess the inherent stability (or lack of it) of the phenomenon being studied. These observations can help establish the natural variability of the phenomenon and aid in the determination of whether the treatment has effects beyond the naturally occurring changes. Systematic application and withdrawal of the treatment and consequent observation of the results aid in more firmly establishing the cause-and-effect relationship. As Mill's method states, when A is followed by a, and not-A is followed by not-a, then it is more likely that a is caused by A.

PASSIVE OBSERVATIONAL RESEARCH DESIGN

The second major classification of research designs is the passive observational—those that are not experimental and often involve intrinsic variables that cannot be applied and withheld, such as socioeconomic level, grade point average, and intelligence level. Cause-and-effect relationships are much more difficult to establish, and in fact may not be possible to determine. The analyses are typically in terms of strength of relationships among a number of variables, such as in path analysis. Treatment or condition variables may be difficult to distinguish from criteria variables. Often all observations are made at one interval in time, although the teasing out of the direction of effects is facilitated by observations made over time and in longitudinal studies where they are done over long developmental periods.

The passive observational types of studies can be categorized into four major types of research designs: prediction and classification, sampling and survey, quantitative descriptive, and qualitative descriptive. These last two categories especially encompass a very large number of variations and methods. All of the four major types typically involve anywhere from several variables to a large number of variables. Deliberate manipulation of variables and control groups as such usually is not present. A major key to the interpretation of the results of passive observational research is the development of elaborate theory about the nature of relationships among variables, and indeed which variables are important. Then all of these variables should be observed in the research, including variables suggested by alternative hypotheses about the cause of the behavior, so that they can be evaluated and accepted or rejected. In the passive observational studies, the three basic facts about psychological variables begin to play a major role in the interpretation of research data.

Prediction and Classification

These involve K variables, $K-1$ of which are used to predict the future (or even current) status, and the Kth variable is the predicted, or criterion, variable. In classification analyses, the Kth variable defines the classification categories such as college major or religious affiliation. The analytic method usually is statistical and involves multiple correlation and regression techniques or discriminant analysis. Prediction is also useful in selection processes when people are to be selected for entry into a program or for jobs, and the number of applicants is larger than the number to be accepted. It is known from Sawyer's 1966 study that all types of data available, test or observational, should be used in the selection process, but that the results of statistical regression procedures for prediction have never been surpassed. The major limitations of the method are that (1) descriptive prediction is not necessarily a cause-and-effect prediction, and (2) limits on the precision of measurement distinctly limit the degree of prediction possible. Conversely, if a prediction reaches these limits, then no other variable added to the prediction set of variables can increase the level of the prediction.

Sampling and Survey Studies

The purpose of this type of passive observational research design is to describe a large population of people usually on a relatively small number of variables. It is done by selecting a representative group, called the sample, from the population and making the descriptive observations. The averages and variability of these observations are then calculated and estimates are made for the larger population of the ranges within which the averages for these variables are likely to fall. Statistical methods have evolved to such elaborate degrees that costs, which are of prime interest in collecting the data, are minimized while the information gathered is maximized.

Quantitative Descriptive Design

This type of research design also includes a large number of variations. Typically the observations are made at or near one interval of time on a group or several groups of participants. All observations are quantified via the use of ratings, scales, test scores, and the like. The basic major analytical method used as a starting point in determining the degree of relationships between each pair of variables usually is correlational. Correlation is a statistical index that theoretically takes values from 0.00 (or no linear relationship) to ± 1.00, a perfect relationship between the two variables. All of these correlations can be organized into a square matrix. If there are K variables, then there are (K) times $(K-1)$ correlations in the K times K cells in the matrix (A with B, A with C, etc., as well as B with A and C with A, etc., but these B with A and C with A correlations are identical to the A with B and A with C, etc., correlations). Once this matrix of correlations is calculated, a number of multivariate analysis methods can be employed to test various hypotheses of strength and causal directions among the variables. Some of these are partial correlation, path analysis, and factor analysis. These multivariate procedures attempt to control some variables by reducing their correlational influence to zero, to test the conformity of the relationships among the variables to hypothesized strengths and directions, and to organize the set of correlational relationships into a lesser set of theorized major underlying variables that can account for the observed relationships among the K variables.

Strength of support of various hypotheses and alternative hypotheses are determined, and, it is hoped, theory is advanced. Problems from a research design standpoint are the basic facts of imprecise measurement and difficulty in the ability firmly to deter-mine cause-and-effect relationships. The basic fact of imprecise measurement distinctly limits the size of the correlations and the degree of imprecise measurement may change from variable to variable, making comparisons among the correlations difficult. Restrictions in the range of variables on the subjects, inability to measure the high or low levels of the variables with the instruments, short instruments or a small number of observers, and nonlinear relationships all serve to reduce the degree of observed relationships among the variables, often differentially, thus making comparisons difficult. However, the quantitative descriptive procedures are fundamental to the development of good-quality experimental research designs. Further, they are often the only design available where variables are intrinsic to the participants and cannot be manipulated, where it is unethical to manipulate variables, or where it is too expensive to manipulate variables. With well-developed theory, many measured variables adequate to test alternative hypotheses, a good knowledge of the effects of imprecise measures (measurement theory), and the effects of the various threats to internal validity, excellent research can be done using these quantitative descriptive designs.

Qualitative Descriptive Design

Qualitative research is a category of research method that has even more variations, approaches, and themes than quantitative descriptive research. Qualitative descriptive research includes much of basic research in which the aim is to discover new variables and new relationships among old and new variables. The method is limited only by the creativity and energy of psychologists in their quest for greater understanding of people. These observational procedures are typically incorporated into a theoretical system that suggests dimensions in the observational areas to be recorded. A clear objective is to conceptualize new dimensions of behavior, thought, feelings, and aspects of the inner and exterior environments that elicit them. Some of the methods and areas included in this broad natural observational category are case study, ecological, psychoanalytical, social, clinical, personality, abnormal, and comparative—almost the entire range of fields of psychology. It is of major use where only one or a small number of participants (or if group behavior is of interest, one or a small number of groups) are involved. Nor is the method independent of other types of research. It is almost inevitably a forerunner to all the other methods, because it is usually here that the new variables are discovered that are more fully developed in the quantitative descriptive method and later more rigorously studied in the experimental methods. In fact, in the experimental and quantitative descriptive methods, good researchers observe the participants in their experiments and testing sessions to see what new variables, other than those systematically examined, might aid in the explanation of phenomena. All methods helpful to understanding are useful. The results are typically lengthy narratives.

THREATS TO INTERNAL VALIDITY

"Threats to internal validity" is the phrase in research design that interpreters of data use to describe the set of questions they have about possible inaccuracies in interpretation of cause-and-effect relationships among research variables. Some of these threats already have been suggested, particularly in the description of quasi-experiments and quantitative descriptive methods. Recall that regression-toward-the-mean score was the phrase used to describe the effect of imprecise measurement on present and future observations, and it is a major threat to internal validity in research design in psychology.

Maturation is another threat because participants grow and develop on their own with the passage of time irrespective of what a researcher does to them. Adolescents gain social competence regardless of our organized activities for them—in fact, they might gain more without such activities. It is partly the result of this last hypothesis that control groups are used for comparisons with maturing subjects.

Mortality is another threat. The systematic reduction of groups of participants because of dropouts, absences, people moving away, unanswered criterion questionnaires, and so on can make those who do not do well, as the result of a treatment of influence, less visible. Thus, the more visible do better on the criteria, making the treatment influence look better.

The threat of selection works at the beginning of the researcher's time sequence. The systematic choosing or a passive choice (those who select themselves) of people for a treatment or condition may be different for some groups before the treatment. These groups would still be different from others after the treatment—*even if no treatment or condition had been imposed.* Again, the alternative hypothesis question (what the effects of no treatment or condition would be) must be asked and tested to develop strong internal validity (cause-and-effect statements) among variables. Children who originally were entered into Head Start programs were probably intellectually more able than children not entered—and thus would likely have done better in school even if they had not attended the Head Start programs, the experimental condition. Clearly, selection is a most important threat to cause-and-effect statements about treatments.

History is the threat to internal validity that involves changes in conditions surrounding the research such that those changes are intermixed with the research treatments. This confusion results in the inability to ascribe changes in participants to the research treatment or to the external changes. Running experimental groups in the summer and control groups in the winter might cause changes in mood that have little to do with the experimental treatments.

Instrumentation is a threat to internal validity that is somewhat unique to psychology because it involves changes in observers' standards over time or as the result of observational conditions. These changes result in different scores. Also, nonequated, differing forms of a criterion test may yield different scores. The problem is that these differences in measurement standards may be mistaken for changes resulting from treatments.

Testing is another threat to internal validity almost entirely unique to psychology. It involves the distinct effect of gains in participants' scores simply as the result of previously taking a test. It is a clearly existing, well-known phenomenon of some importance. Obviously in quasi-experiments, where by definition there must be measurement preceding the experimental treatment, gains will be noted. Fortunately, the gains will be in both the experimental and control groups so that valid comparisons of treatment effects can still be made. This is not true in all research designs.

Instability, as has been indicated, is the threat to internal validity that results from attempts to interpret the naturally occurring changes in participants and measurements both immediately or over longer periods of time. These changes follow from two of the basic facts of psychological research as stated, that measurement is imprecise and that participants' behavior changes over time. (It is interesting to note that this is the only threat to internal validity that statistical analysis controls.)

There are also four affective threats to internal validity: imitation, compensatory rivalry, compensatory equalization, and demoralization. These, too, are unique to the psychological sciences in that they result from emotional changes in subjects and administrators to adjust for the fact that they were not "favored" by receiving an experimental treatment.

EXTERNAL VALIDITY AND META-ANALYSIS

Finally, there is the concept of external validity, or the sum of the characteristics of research that allow the cause-and-effect statements made (as the result of good internal validity) to be generalized to participants' treatments and to criteria that were not used in the research, but are similar to those criteria.

Meta-analysis

The external validity of research findings is markedly enhanced when a number of studies of the same general treatment variable can be combined and summarized. This procedure is called meta-analysis. In meta-analysis, the strength of treatment effect and major conditions of the research on the criterion variables are determined. Essentially, the results of all true and quasi-experiments available in the literature are recorded in terms of differences of the experimental and control groups' average scores' effect size on the criteria variables, along with a quantification of many of the conditions under which the various studies took place. These conditions become variables, too, such as age or status of the participants, length of treatment, quality of research design (a true experiment, or quasi-experiment), training of the therapist, type of criteria assessment (test or clinical), and so on. These variables are developed as the result of the theoretical interests of the meta-analysis researcher. The set of relationships of most interest is the set of research condition variables and the criterion variable that is the research treatment effect size on the criteria variables. This effect size for each research study is determined simply by dividing the difference between the average scores on the criterion variable from the experimental control groups by a measure of individuals' variability within these groups. As the result of this analysis, numerous research condition variables may be shown to have no influence on a set of criteria, and therefore researchers can generalize the results from a number of studies *without* regard to these now-extraneous conditions.

Finally, the strength of each treatment variable and of all the condition variables can be determined with respect to their influence on the criteria. This is most important with regard to applied areas where simply saying that one variable influences another is not sufficient, but the size of that influence is. Finally, in basic research in psychology, understanding is a prime goal. In-depth understanding of the relationship of variables is hardly possible without knowledge of strength of relationships and cause-and-effect relationships. Thus the principles of internal validity, threats to internal validity, and external validity (via meta-analysis) are research methodology concerns in psychology and should be known by all who do research, interpret research, or apply psychological research findings.

REFERENCES

Vockell, E., & Asher, J. W. (1995). *Educational Research,* 2nd ed., Macmillan-Prentice Hall.

Cook, T. D., & Campbell, D. T. (1979, 1966). Quasi-experimentation: Design and analysis issues for field settings. Chicago: Rand-McNally.

Glass, G. V., McGaw, B., & Smith, M. L. (1981). Meta-analysis in social research. Beverly Hills, CA: Sage Publications.

Mill, J. S. (1973, 1993). A system of logic, ratiocinative and inductive. In J. M. Robson (Ed.) Collected works of John Stewart Mill, Vol. VIII. Toronto: University of Toronto Press.

Sawyer, J. (1966). Measurement and prediction, clinical, and statistical. *Psychological Bulletin,* 66(3), 178–200.

J. W. ASHER
Purdue University

CONTROL GROUPS
EXPERIMENTAL METHODS
HYPOTHESIS TESTING, POWER MEASUREMENT
STATISTICS IN PSYCHOLOGY

RESIDENTIAL ALTERNATIVES

Throughout the course of one's life, the need for residential care may arise. This need may be generated by a variety of reasons, such as a need for physical rehabilitation, or because of mental or physical illness, loss of shelter, or old age.

The current trend in residential alternatives is toward person-centered planning, in which individuals choose where and with whom they live (Braddock, Hemp, Bacfedler, & Fujina, 1995). This trend typically employs natural environments as the venue for such services. Natural environments might be the person's own home with supports, or another house or apartment where supports are shared.

Sometimes, however, a natural environment is not indicated for an individual, and there are many other specialized residential alternatives for people who require more care. Residential alternatives most often are thought to be institutions, emergency shelters, orphanages, and/or nursing homes. These, however, are but a few of the alternatives available for people in need of care. The following are some of the other residential alternatives.

A *boarding home* is one in which unrelated individuals reside with no supervision. Most boarding homes are privately operated and serve as a less expensive alternative to apartment/home living. The term "hospice" is often used interchangeably with boarding home.

Convalescent hospitals afford long-term residential care for those requiring extensive rehabilitation or nursing care, or who are terminally ill. Convalescent hospitals can be privately or publicly operated.

Foster homes are provided by families who open their houses to children who require shelter. Most children who receive foster care require such service because of the loss of parents or guardians. Foster care may be provided for developmentally disabled children who require specialized training outside of their natural homes. Foster parents are usually trained in effective parenting practices and are usually paid for their services by state or county social service agencies. Foster parents are not adoptive parents, since adoption results in a legal name change for the child, as well as legal guardianship of the child by the adoptive parent.

Group homes are provided by public and private agencies for children and adults who require supervised residential care. Unlike foster care programs, group homes generally have up to eight unrelated people residing with supervisory personnel. These supervisory personnel are identified as "teaching parents" by Dean Fixsen and colleagues (1973) and as "house parents/house couples" by Holmes (1998).

The very name *halfway house,* connotes a transition home. Generally, halfway houses are operated by public or private agencies for the express purpose of facilitating a person's movement from a highly supervised residential setting to independence in the community. Halfway houses also have been called transitional homes.

An *intermediate care facility* offers residential services to people with developmental disabilities. Unlike group homes, many intermediate care facilities are located on institutional grounds and follow a medical model, according to Thomas Stripling and Susan Ames (1977). Intermediate care facilities are sponsored by the federal government but administered by the states.

A *nursing home* is a private or publicly operated long-term care setting for the terminally ill, handicapped, or aged. Unlike convalescent hospitals, nursing homes do not have ready access to all the necessary life-support services that some long-term convalescent patients require.

An *orphanage* is a residential care center designed to offer shelter to homeless children. Unlike foster care settings, most orphanages are operated by religious organizations, but a few are sponsored by public and nonsectarian private agencies.

A *psychiatric hospital* is a residential hospital designed primarily for persons requiring psychiatric care. Unlike institutions for the mentally retarded and other developmentally disabled individuals, psychiatric hospitals specialize in offering services to the mentally ill. Most psychiatric hospitals are publicly operated.

A *residential school* is one in which the educational training programs are located on the same premises or under the same auspices as the residential program. Residential schools are available to children with or without special needs, in the form of preparatory schools. Residential schools can be either privately or publicly operated.

Respite care is a short-term residential service provided to individuals who require temporary shelter, primarily in cases of emergency, family crisis, family vacation, or trial separation. Respite care services can be found as a sub-unit in many private or public residential settings, or in centers designed solely for such services.

A *retirement home* is a residential alternative designed specifically for senior citizens. Retirement homes can follow many different models, including boarding homes, residential cottages, and apartments. Most retirement homes are privately operated.

A *sanitorium* is a residential alternative designed for the treatment of chronic disease and disorders, such as tuberculosis and various forms of mental illness. Sanitoriums generally follow a medical hospital model for service delivery. Most sanitoriums are publicly operated.

A *state school* is an institutional school for children with special needs. Not unlike many residential schools, state schools have residences and educational/training opportunities located on the same site. To a large extent, a cottage residence model is followed at state schools. State schools are publicly operated.

Supervised apartments are living alternatives for adults with special needs who are "capable of independent living" (Holmes, 1990) Supervised apartments can be found either in clusters or randomly located in an apartment complex. People residing in supervised apartments are regularly monitored by human services personnel to make certain that their personal and social needs are being met. Supervised apartments can be either privately or publicly sponsored.

REFERENCES

Braddock, D., Hemp, R., Bacfedler, L. & Fujina, G. (1995). *The state of the state in developmental disabilities.* Washington, DC: Association on American Mental Retardation.

Elitz, S. (1963). *Housing for the aged and disabled in Sweden.* Swedish Instistute for Cultural Relations with Foreign Countries, Stockholm, Sweden.

Fixsen, D. L., Wolf, M. M., & Phillips, E. L., (1973). Achievement Place: A teaching family model of community-based group homes for youth in trouble. In Hammerlynch et al. (Eds.), *Behavior Modifaction.* Champaign, IL: Research Press.

Fritz, M., Wofensburger, W., & Knowlton, M. (1971) *An apartment living plan to promote integration and normalization of mentally retarded adults.* Canadian Association for the Retarded, Ontario, Canada.

Holmes, D. L. (1998). *Autism through the life span: The Eden model.* Bethesda, MD: Woodbine House.

Holmes, D. L., (1990). Community based services for children and adults with autism. *Journal of Autism and Developmental Disorders, 20,* 339–351.

Jeffrey, D. A. (1943). A living environment for the physically disabled. *Rehabilitation Literature* (Vol. 4, pp. 97–103).

National Easter Seal Society for Crippled Children and Adults. *Housing — and handicapped persons: A resource guide of available publications from 1970 forward.*

Stripling, T., & Ames, S. (1977). Intermediate care facilities for the mentally retarded. *Federal Programs Information and Assistance Project, 54,* pp. 61180/6–02. Washington, DC.

Thompson, M. M. (1975) Congregate housing for older adults: Assisted residential living combining shelter and services. In *Report for Committee on Aging* Washington, DC: US Senate.

D. L. HOLMES
The Eden Institute

COMMUNITY PSYCHOLOGY
DAY HOSPITALS
HANDICAPPED, ATTITUDES TOWARD
HOSPICES

RETICULAR ACTIVATING SYSTEM

The ascending reticular activating system is the collection of anatomical and neurochemical systems proposed to underlie cortical electroencephalographic signs of arousal and the correlated behavioral activities of alerting and attention. The concept of the ascending reticular activating system (ARAS) was first formulated by Moruzzi and Magoun in 1949. Based on the effects of either stimulation or destruction of parts of the reticular formation of the brain stem, these authors concluded that "a background of maintained activity within this ascending brain stem activating system may account for wakefulness, while reduction of its activity either naturally, by barbiturates, or by experimental injury and disease, may respectively precipitate normal sleep, contribute to anesthesia, or produce pathological somnolence." While the accuracy of this prescient formulation has occasionally been challenged during the past 50 years, its general validity is still recognized and its underlying neural substrates have been described.

The anatomical basis of the ascending reticular activating system is the reticular formation. The reticular formation (RF) extends from the caudal medulla to the rostral midbrain. Its neurons form the core of the brain stem, in which are embedded the specific nuclear groups that supply the cranial nerves with axons. The ascending and descending long sensory and motor pathways of the brain stem pass through and around the reticular formation. Its neurons tend to have long axons with many branches. For example, a single RF neuron may have an axon that branches to reach the dorsal column nuclei, the spinal cord, and the hypothalamus. Because of such extensive branching, the neurons of the RF are capable of exerting profound effects on the general level of activity of the brain and spinal cord.

Projections from the RF to the diencephalon are involved in behavioral and electroencephalographic arousal and correspond to the ARAS. There are at least three aspects of arousal: (a) altering of consciousness to become more alert, often with increased concentration on selected stimuli; (b) appearance of orienting reactions if arousal is produced by introduction of a novel stimulus; and (c) desynchronization of the electroencephalogram (EEG).

The RF influences arousal through two anatomically distinct routes. One pathway extends from the RF through the hypothalamus, ventral thalamus, and basal forebrain to influence the cortex; this pathway is most probably involved in producing generalized arousal that makes the differences between sleep and waking. The second pathway extends from the RF to the reticular and intralaminar nuclei of the dorsal thalamus, and probably participates in alerting-reactions and alpha blocking.

In addition to having different pathways by which it influences different aspects of arousal, the RF can be divided into nuclear groupings according to anatomical and neurochemical criteria. The most convenient anatomical categorization is made along the medial-lateral dimension. The raphe nuclei are found in the midline of the RF. A large-celled region is found in the central core of the RF and a small-celled division is located in its lateral portion. These large, medial-lateral divisions may be subdivided along the rostral-caudal length of the RF. The nucleus gigantocellularis is the large-celled nucleus of the medulla. It gives rise to reticulospinal axons that influence movement. In the pons, the nuclei pontis caudalis and oralis take the place of the nucleus gigantocellularis, and also give rise to reticulospinal axons. However, these nuclei, especially the rostral-lying pontis-oralis, have many ascending projections and are involved in regulation of cortical arousal.

Some reticular nuclei may also be defined according to neurotransmitter content. Nuclei that contain norepinephrine have been identified in the medullary and pontine RF. The most extensively studied of these is the locus coeruleus. The ascending projections of this nucleus are involved in increasing wakefulness and in selective attention, and may be involved in alternating between non-REM (slow-wave) and REM sleep. Dopamine-containing neurons are found in several nuclei of the midbrain tegmental area. The best known of these nuclei is the substantia nigra. Loss of the dopaminergic neurons from the substantia nigra leads to Parkinsonism. There is some evidence that other dopaminergic nuclei participate in maintenance of waking, possibly by influencing the hypothalamus. Some nuclei within the rostral reticular formation utilize acetylcholine as a transmitter; their output forms the part of the ARAS that includes the ventral thalamus and basal forebrain. They may also influence other reticular formation regions to regulate REM sleep. Serotonin, the neurotransmitter produced by the raphe nuclei, has also been implicated in modulation of arousal. Lesions of the raphe or inhibition of serotonin synthesis produce insomnia. The insomnia induced by reduction in serotonin decreases with time after the insult, suggesting an alternative pathway for decreasing arousal. However, the marked initial effects of destruction of the raphe or permanent inhibition of serotonin synthesis, contrasted with the fact that enhancement of serotonin levels leads to decreased electrocortical arousal and slow-wave sleep, suggest an important role for this transmitter in regulation of arousal.

REFERENCE

Moruzzi, G., & Magoun, H. W. (1949). Brain stem reticular formation and activation of the EEG. *Electroencephalography and Clinical Neurophysiology, 1,* 455–473.

SUGGESTED READING

Role, L. W., & Kelly, J. P. (1991). The brain stem: Cranial nerve nuclei and the monoaminergic systems. In E. R. Kandel, J. H. Schwartz, & T. M. Jessell (Eds.), *Principles of neural science* (3rd ed., pp. 683–699). New York: Elsevier.

Steriade, M. (1996). Arousal: Reordering the reticular activating system. *Science, 272,* 225–226.

M. L. WOODRUFF
East Tennessee State University

BRAIN

RETROGRADE AMNESIA

Retrograde amnesia is defined as the loss of memories acquired before a brain injury or disease—a period usually termed the premorbid period. Less commonly, retrograde amnesia can also be a feature of memory disorders not associated with organic brain dysfunction. Clinically, retrograde amnesia can be assessed in a variety of ways, although, because of the wide variation in individuals' premorbid experience, there are very few standardized tests of retrograde amnesia. The deficit is usually reported by either the patient or relatives and is manifest in, for example, an inability to identify family members from old photographs or to recollect key personal events such as marriages, births, and deaths.

Retrograde amnesia can also be revealed using autobiographical cueing, in which the patient is required to generate personal memories from relatively shallow, single-word cues, such as "river". Patients with retrograde amnesia either fail to produce memories or provide rather lightweight, generic memories that have no event-specific detail. Recently there has been a tendency to contrast patients' retrograde amnesia for personal autobiographic memory with their personal semantic memory. Autobiographic memory refers to specific personal events, whereas personal semantic memory is general knowledge about oneself (e.g., schools attended). This division of assessment is justified because there is some evidence that the two forms of memory are dissociable.

More formally, patients with suspected retrograde amnesia can be given tests requiring the identification of famous people and events from the past. These tests are based on knowledge that most people should have. Application of these tests reveals a highly consistent feature of retrograde amnesia—a temporal gradient. Memories for the premorbid period are systematically more impaired for events immediately prior to the causative brain insult than for events earlier in life. This inverse relationship between the age of a memory and its vulnerability to retrograde loss is known as Ribot's Law. Until recently it was thought that language was immune to the effects of retrograde impairment, but studies have now shown that words acquired more recently in the premorbid period cannot be defined as easily as those learned earlier in life.

Retrograde amnesia is always present to some extent when a patient is presenting anterograde amnesia—hence the clinical maxim

"No AA without RA". However, the extent to which retrograde amnesia is present in any given case of anterograde amnesia is extremely variable, and the two forms of impairment are not correlated. The link with anterograde impairment results in the same range of pathologies' being responsible for retrograde memory impairment. Permanent retrograde amnesia is a characteristic feature of Wernicke-Korsakoff syndrome, closed head injury, carbon monoxide poisoning, encephalitic illnesses (most notably herpes simplex and varicella zoster encephalitis), temporal lobectomy, tumor, ischemic attack (both cortical and subcortical), ruptured aneurysms, and anoxic episodes induced by cardiac failure or specific interruption of the cerebrovascular system (e.g., failed hanging attempts). In addition, most dementing illnesses have retrograde amnesia as a prominent and early feature. Transient causes of retrograde amnesia include transient global amnesia, transient epileptic amnesia, and memory loss induced by electroconvulsive therapy. Marked retrograde amnesia is a principal feature of post-traumatic amnesia, the transient confusional state following a closed head injury. An interesting feature of transient retrograde amnesia is that there can be a pattern of recovery that reflects the temporal gradient—that is, the earlier a memory was formed, the more quickly it returns.

The neuropathology of retrograde amnesia is not particularly well understood. However, there is general agreement that retrograde impairment will be likely in patients who have extensive lesions of the temporal neocortex. This is borne out by cases of herpes simplex encephalitis, in which a characteristically dense and extensive retrograde impairment is seen in association with massive necrotic lesions of the temporal cortex. More puzzling are patients who present extensive retrograde loss with lesions that are so small it cannot be argued that there has been disruption to the storage sites of long-term memory. In these cases it has been reported that lesions restricted to the hippocampal formation can cause extensive retrograde loss, leading to the idea that the hippocampal formation continues to modulate long-term memory for many years after consolidation. Small lesions of the diencephalon have also resulted in severe retrograde deficits, and here it has been argued that some disconnection has occurred between memory storage areas and frontally-based structures mediating retrieval.

The origin of the temporal gradient remains an intriguing theoretical puzzle. One argument is that final consolidation is a very long-term process. However, not everyone is convinced by this, and there is also the problem of explaining dense retrograde loss associated with small diencephalic lesions. An alternative argument concerns redundancy in memory, and the idea that each use of a memory results in the formation of a new trace. Assuming that, on average, older memories have been used more, it follows that they have more representations and are thus less vulnerable to a brain insult affecting storage or the efficiency of retrieval mechanisms.

Recently, there has been discussion of a new disorder known as focal retrograde amnesia, in which the retrograde impairment appears more extensive than the anterograde impairment. A clear class of patients showing this phenomenon are those with temporal lobe damage centered on the anterior poles but with preserved hippocampal structures. However, the term has also been applied to a group of patients who show normal, or even superior, antero-grade memory performance but very extensive retrograde amnesia. Patients in this group typically have no significant brain injury and also exhibit features of malingering, and they should not be treated as having organic memory loss.

Retrograde amnesia is also a feature of psychogenic memory disturbance, such as hysterical amnesia, fugue, and multiple personality. Diagnosis of these disorders is fraught with difficulty and there is no evidence that the retrograde loss exhibited can be explained in the same framework used to account for organically-mediated retrograde impairment.

REFERENCE

Parkin, A. J. (1997). *Memory and amnesia: An introduction.* (2nd edition). Hove, UK: Psychology Press.

A. J. PARKIN
University of Sussex, England

ANTEROGRADE AMNESIA
MEMORY
FORGETTING

RETROGRADE SIGNALING

Dynamic bidirectional communication between presynaptic and postsynaptic neurons is essential in the establishment, maintenance, and activity-dependent modification of synaptic connections. In conventional anterograde synaptic transmission, arrival of an action potential to the presynaptic axon terminals results in the release of neurotransmitter and other modulatory factors which in turn act on postsynaptic receptors. Retrograde signals originating from the postsynaptic cell have immediate actions on presynaptic terminals, as well as long-term structural and metabolic effects affecting the survival, differentiation, and functioning of the presynaptic neuron.

RETROGRADE SIGNALING DURING SYNAPTOGENESIS

Upon arrival at appropriate target regions, growth cones begin to form synaptic connections with specific target cells. Local retrograde interactions regulate the development of synaptic connections, triggering the transformation of the motile growth cone to a stable and functional nerve terminal. Both positive and negative retrograde influences on synaptogenesis lead to highly specific cell-cell connections, allowing recognition and proper matching of axons with appropriate postsynaptic targets. Rapid changes in the properties of the presynaptic growth cone are induced by contact with the target, resulting in increased neurotransmitter secretion from the growth cone and increased intracellular Ca^{2+} levels within the presynaptic terminal. Evidence suggests surface cell adhesion molecules can underlie these early retrograde interactions during synaptogenesis.

Following the initial contact, retrograde signals influence the induction, maturation and modulation of transmitter secretion machinery in the presynaptic terminal. Maturation and stabilization of the axonal terminal involve formation of the active zone, the localization and assembly of transmitter secretion machinery, and clustering of synaptic vesicles at the site of contact with the target cell. The postsynaptic cell can influence the time-course of maturation of the neurotransmitter release machinery, the phenotype of the transmitter used by the presynaptic neuron, and the efficacy of neurotransmitter release from the presynaptic terminals. Long-range effects of retrograde signals can affect the growth and projection patterns of other processes of the presynaptic neuron, as well as afferent innervation of the presynaptic neuron by other neurons.

RETROGRADE SIGNALING IN ACTIVITY-DEPENDENT MODIFICATIONS OF SYNAPSES

Activity-dependent stabilization and elimination of nerve connections during the development of properly wired neural circuits involve synapse-specific strengthening or weakening mediated by target-derived factors. Similar retrograde mechanisms also play a role in the modulation of synaptic transmission in the mature nervous system. Synaptic efficacy is altered by activity, during successive activation of the presynaptic neuron (short-term plasticity) and following repetitive trains of low- and high-frequency stimuli (long-term plasticity). A number of studies have demonstrated that changes in the probability of neurotransmitter release from the presynaptic terminal underlie some forms of activity-dependent changes in efficacy. Both short- and long-term activity-dependent changes in efficacy of transmitter release can be influenced by the phenotype of the target cell or the level of activity detected by the postsynaptic cell.

Short-term depression or facilitation of postsynaptic responses depend on the postsynaptic target cell at many synapses. These include diverse neural synapses such as the crustacean neuromuscular junction, sensory synapses in the cricket, and rat cortical synapses in layer 2/3. Even different presynaptic terminals of a single presynaptic neuron can be differentially modulated in a target-dependent manner. Use of quantal analytic methods indicates underlying presynaptic mechanisms, suggesting a role for retrograde signals in the determination of presynaptic release properties. Rapid release of a retrograde substance could locally modify release to subsequent action potential arriving at the terminals. Alternatively, retrograde influences on the morphological structure of the presynaptic release sites, including regulation of the release machinery and vesicle pool, the number of Ca^{2+} channels, or the Ca^{2+} buffering capability of the terminal would give rise to synapse-specific modulation of short-term plasticity.

Repetitive synaptic activity at glutamatergic synapses throughout the brain can result in a persistent increase or decrease of synaptic efficacy, known as long-term potentiation (LTP) or long-term depression (LTD), respectively. As with short-term plasticity, the expression of long-term plasticity may depend on the phenotype of the target cell. Moreover, in some areas of the nervous system, while LTP and LTD are triggered by processes in the postsynaptic cell, the mechanisms for expression of LTP and LTD may involve persistent changes in the efficacy of presynaptic transmitter release. A presynaptic locus for the expression of LTP/D may

require retrograde signaling from the post- to presynaptic cell. The retrograde signal itself or second messenger molecules activated by the retrograde factor can rapidly affect transmitter release properties by their action on a large number of potential targets. These include presynaptic voltage-dependent ion channels (e.g., Ca^{2+} or K^+ channels), synaptic vesicle proteins, vesicle docking proteins, or cytosolic factors involved in regulating fusion of synaptic vesicles. In addition, either retrograde factors or their effector molecules can serve as instructive signals that exert long-range regulatory influences in the nucleus and trigger selective gene expression leading to maintenance of long-term changes in synaptic efficacy. Activity-dependent retrograde modulation of GABAergic synaptic transmission in the adult nervous system has also been identified.

MECHANISMS OF RETROGRADE SIGNALING

A number of target-derived membrane-permeable molecules and gases have been proposed as potential retrograde factors in LTP and LTD: arachidonic acid, platelet-activating factor, nitric oxide and carbon monoxide. These membrane-permeable factors are attractive candidates as intercellular messengers because they are extremely diffusible in both aqueous and lipid environments, allowing rapid transsynaptic spread of the signal, while the range of their action is limited by their concentration and short lifetime.

Activity-dependent vesicle-mediated secretion of factors from postsynaptic cells could also provide retrograde signals to the nerve terminal. Active back-propagation of action potentials into the dendrites following initiation in the postsynaptic cell body not only provides a retrograde signal of neuronal output to the dendritic tree of the postsynaptic cell, but may also provide a precisely timed trigger for dendritic exocytic release of a retrograde factor. The possibility of Ca^{2+}-regulated exocytosis of small classical neurotransmitters, neuropeptides and neurotrophins from dendrites is indicated by the existence of dendro-dendritic synapses and evidence for dendritic release of small classical neurotransmitters and neuropeptides. Recent evidence of acute effects of target-derived neurotrophic factors on synaptic efficacy, the interaction of their effects with synaptic activity, and the possibility of their regulated vesicle-mediated release from dendrites underscore their possible role as retrograde signals.

Finally, molecular activities initiated in the postsynaptic cytoplasm could be conveyed from the postsynaptic density and synaptic cleft to the presynaptic secretion machinery via changes in direct physical linkages between pre- and postsynaptic membranes. Structural changes such as the insertion of new postsynaptic receptors, or extracellular matrix components such as adhesion molecules, or conformational changes of existing postsynaptic components may signal and affect presynaptic release properties or stability. While an attractive hypothesis, however, there is no definitive evidence that transsynaptic physical linkage may play a role in retrograde signaling.

SUGGESTED READING

Alger, B., and Pitler, T. (1995). Retrograde signaling at GABA$_A$-receptor synapses in the mammalian CNS. *Trends in Neurosciences, 18,* 333–40.

Fitzsimonds, R. M., and Poo, M. M. (1998). Retrograde signaling in the development and modification of synapses. *Physiological Reviews, 78,* 143–70.

Landis, S. (1990). Target regulation of neurotransmitter phenotype. *Trends in Neurosciences, 13,* 344–350.

Landmesser, L. T. (1998). Synaptic plasticity: Keeping synapses under control. *Current Biology, 8,* R564–7.

Malenka, R. C. (1994). Synaptic plasticity in the hippocampus: LTP and LTD. *Cell, 78,* 535–538.

Reyes, A., Lujan, R., Rozov, A., Burnashev, N., Somogyi, P., Sakmann, B. (1998). Target-cell-specific facilitation and depression in neocortical circuits. *Nature Neuroscience, 1,* 279–285.

Stuart, G., Spruston, N., Sakmann, B., and Hausser, M. (1997). Action potential initiation and back-propagation in neurons of the mammalian CNS. *Trends in Neurosciences, 20,* 125–31.

Thoenen, H. (1995.) Neurotrophins and neuronal plasticity. *Science, 270,* 593–598.

R. M. Fitzsimonds
Yale School of Medicine

ACTION POTENTIAL

RETT SYNDROME

Rett Syndrome (RS) is a disorder that initially appears as a deterioration of apparently normal development in infancy or early childhood. It involves a slowdown in normal development, deceleration of head growth, disinterest in the environment, deterioration of motor functioning, loss of hand use and subsequently locomotion, hand stereotypies (typically hand wringing or clapping), loss of expressive language, autistic and self-abusive behavior, and eventual severe to profound mental retardation. Prevalence estimates of classic RS vary, but are in the 1:10,000 to 1:15,000 range (Hagberg, 1995b). Cases occur in all parts of the world and in all ethnic groups (e.g., Naidu, 1997). First described by Andreas Rett in 1966, it initially came to the world's attention largely through the work of Hagberg and his associates (Hagberg, Aicardi, Dias, & Ramos, 1983). A summary of Rett's contributions is in Hagberg (1995b).

Unique to RS is apparently normal initial development followed by rapid mental and physical deterioration followed by stabilization or even reduction in some symptoms (e.g., Hagberg, 1995b). Unusual in other ways, RS (1) apparently affects only women, whereas most gender-specific disorders affect only men; (2) is manifested in part through loss of acquired function, but is apparently neurodevelopmental and not neurogenerative (e.g., Glaze & Schultz, 1997); and (3) occurs in a set of behavioral symptoms that has consistent developmental trends. Although the subject of hundreds of articles, it is still relatively unknown in comparison to many other developmental disorders of comparable prevalence. As described below, its X-chromosome has recently been described. RS is associated with numerous neuroanatomical and neurochemical disturbances, summaries of which can be found in Brown and Hoadley (1999), and Percy (1996).

DIAGNOSTIC SYMPTOMS: CLASSIC RS AND RS VARIANT

Necessary for diagnosis of classic RS is apparently normal pre-, peri-, and early postnatal development followed in infancy or early childhood by sudden deceleration of head growth and loss of acquired skills, including hand use and language (Rett Syndrome Diagnostic Criteria Work Group, 1988). Also required is evidence of mental retardation and intense and persistent hand stereotypies: "The almost continuous repetitive wringing, twisting or clapping hand automatisms during wakefulness constitute the hallmark of the condition" (Hagberg, 1995b, p. 973). Girls who had developed walking must show gait abnormalities; some never develop walking. EEG abnormalities, seizure disorder, spasticity, marked scoliosis, and overall growth retardation are also typical. A number of other behaviors may also be shown, including episodic hyperventilation and breath-holding, bloating owing to air swallowing, bruxism, hypoplastic cold red-blue feet, scoliosis, and night laughing (Hagberg, 1995a).

The RS variant model was developed owing to the realization that females with RS are much more heterogeneous than originally thought (Hagberg, 1995a, 1995b). Diagnosis of RS variant should be made only in girls of ten years or older when a subset of the symptoms for classic RS have been met. These behaviors may appear throughout childhood. Typically, girls who meet the criteria for RS variant show less severe symptoms than those associated with classic RS. Both gross and fine motor control may be more spared and mental retardation is less severe. RS variant girls may retain some language, although it tends to be abnormal and telegraphic. Those with language tend to have had a later and milder regression period.

For both parents and therapists, diagnosis should be made as early as possible. Some physicians may be reluctant to diagnose RS early owing to the eventual severity of the disorder, but many parents are frustrated by the lack of a diagnosis that fits their children's behaviors or has implications for treatment and care (Brown & Hoadley, 1999). For that reason, the term "potential RS" (Hagberg, 1995b) has been suggested for use with young cases. RS may be confused with a number of other disorders, particularly autism, so careful diagnosis is necessary.

DEVELOPMENTAL TREND

Most girls with classic RS develop through a predictable four-stage sequence of behavioral and physical changes first described by Hagberg and Witt-Engerström (1986). Age of onset, duration of each stage, and transition from one stage to another are highly variable, however. Except as specifically referenced, information in this section comes from Brown and Hoodley (1999), Hagberg (1995b), Hagberg and Witt-Engerström (1986), and Naidu (1997). Development appears essentially normal until at least five to six months of age. Early motor skills appear, including reaching for objects, self-feeding, weaning onto solid foods, and frequently walking, but often with an unusual gait. However, appearance of many infant developmental milestones is delayed or absent. Some slowing of brain growth may be seen in unusually low occipito frontal circumference as early as two months of age. Many girls develop single-word communication and a few use short phrases.

Stage 1: Early Onset Stagnation

The first stage begins from six to 18 months of age and may last from weeks to months. The infant appears to hit a developmental wall: Many aspects of cognitive development cease. A deceleration of head growth leads to head circumference generally below average by the end of the second year of life. Hypotonia, disinterest in play and the environment, and loss of acquired hand functions and random hand movements are typical. No obvious pattern of abnormalities is apparent, however.

Stage 2: Rapid Developmental Regression

Between one and three or four years of age, functioning begins to deteriorate so generally and rapidly that the onset may be taken for a toxic or encephalitic state (Hagberg & Witt-Engerström, 1986). General cognitive functioning, purposeful hand use, and expressive language deteriorate. The classic hand stereotypies (including hand wringing), washing, and mouthing typically appear and may be continuous during waking hours. Walking may deteriorate or not develop. Gait abnormalities, particularly a spread-legged stance, are generally evident in girls who can walk. Hyperventilation and breath-holding are common, as are behaviors characteristic of autism. Seizures and vacant spells resembling seizures may occur, and virtually all RS girls have abnormal EEGs.

Stage 3: Pseudostationary

Stage 3 has a highly variable age of onset, occurring at the end of the rapid deterioration, and lasts until about ten years of age. Hand stereotypies continue, and mobility may further deteriorate. Mental retardation in the severe to profound range is characteristic. On the other hand, autistic symptoms may diminish, and social interactions, hand use, communication, alertness, and self-initiated behavior may increase. Tremulousness, ataxia, bruxism, hyperventilation or breath-holding, and seizures are common. Overall rigidity is likely to increase and scoliosis to appear. Nonverbal communication through eye pointing may improve.

Stage 4: Late Motor Deterioration

After about ten years of age, motor function decreases further with increased rigidity, scoliosis, and muscle wasting. Mobility continues to decrease; many girls will be wheelchair-bound. Hands may be held in the mouth for long periods. Expressive language, if previously present, generally disappears, and receptive language decreased. Eye pointing as communication may continue. Chewing and swallowing may be lost, necessitating artificial feeding. However, the final phenotypic characteristics of classic RS cases vary widely. Life span varies, but overall longevity is shorter than normal (Naidu, 1997).

OVERALL INTELLECTUAL CHARACTERISTICS

Formal assessments indicate that RS girls function at a severe to profound level of mental retardation, but their actual cognitive functioning may be difficult to assess owing to motor and language impairments. For a group of RS girls with a mean age of 9.4 years, Perry, Sarlo-McGarvey, and Haddad (1991) reported Vineland Adaptive Behavior Scale (VABS) scores at about the 18-to-25 month level. Mean mental age on the Cattell Infant Intelligence was 3.0 months. Most girls attended to visual and auditory stimuli, were interested in toys, and anticipated being fed. Only one appeared to have object permanence, and none succeeded on items requiring language or fine motor skills. The girls attended when spoken to, showed some understanding, but most did not speak or have any other communication system. Most could feed themselves, some with their fingers, and some could use a cup. Most were in diapers, and did not perform other self-care tasks. They showed some interest in other people and could discriminate among them, but showed virtually no play behaviors.

OVERALL EMOTIONAL CHARACTERISTICS

RS girls show a variety of emotional and behavioral problems. The following information is from a survey of parents by Sansom, Krishnan, Corbett, and Kerr (1993) when the girls' mean age was 10.6 years. Over 75% showed anxiety, particularly in response to external situations. Most episodes were brief, and consisted of screaming, hyperventilation, self-injury, frightened expression, and general distress. Precipitating events included novel situations and people, sudden noises, some music, change of routine, and high activity by others close to the child. Low mood, reflected partly in crying, occurred in 70%. Almost 50% showed self-injurious behaviors. Most were relatively mild, such as biting fingers or hands, but more serious chewing of fingers, head banging, and hair pulling also occurred. Epilepsy was reported in 63%. Although most slept well, early wakening and nighttime laughing, crying, and screaming were common.

GENETIC BASIS

From the outset of its description as occurring only in girls, RS was presumed to have a genetic basis. Its almost complete concordance in monozygotic twins and disconcordance in dizygotic twins further supported a genetic basis, as did the finding of occasional familial cases. Additionally, many Swedish cases of RS were been traced back to a small number of eighteenth-century homesites in which consanguineous marriages were common. Several authors suggested that the appearance of RS solely in females owed to the X-chromosome defect being lethal prenatally to males, who would be unlikely to have a counterpart gene on the Y chromosome. Recently, a progression of RS symptoms has been described in a boy with Klinefelter syndrome karyotype (47,XXY). He showed normal development until eight months with some single word utterances. Deterioration began at about 11 months of age initially, with loss of language and purposeful hand movements and subsequent development of bruxism, constipation, stereotyped hand movements, and mental retardation (Schwartzman et al., 1999).

The sporadic appearance of the disorder and relatively few familial cases impeded discovery of the specific genetic basis. However, in 1999, the apparent genetic basis was discovered (Amir, Van den Veyver, Wan, Tran, Francke, & Zoghbi, 1999). The X-chromosome gene is normally involved in development of a switch that stops production of specific proteins. The mutated gene fails to perform its function, perhaps leading to overproduction of these proteins and resulting central nervous system failure.

TREATMENT AND MANAGEMENT

No completely effective treatment regime is available, and the symptoms appear to follow an inexorable course. However, active intervention may delay the appearance of some symptoms and alleviate others. More details about, and primary references for, successful and unsuccessful intervention programs are in Brown and Hoadley (1999) and Glaze and Schultz (1997). RS girls typically have very long latencies to respond to directions, an important consideration in all aspects of therapy. Delay to respond may be as long as a minute. Accurate diagnosis is important both to ensure appropriate treatment and to avoid ineffective treatment. For example, behavior modification programs that are effective with disorders such as autism may be ineffective with RS girls. Individual differences in the degree of various impairments and responsiveness to, as well as tolerance of, various interventions necessitate individualized treatment programs. Owing to the multiplicity and diversity of problems associated with RS, a team approach is indicated.

Specialized behavior modification programs have been successful on a variety of behaviors in RS girls of different ages. Techniques such as shaping, graduated guidance, and hand regulation may increase self-feeding and ambulation in RS girls. Use of mechanical and computer-based adaptive devices may also modify RS girls' behavior, enabling them to communicate and discriminate between such things as favored and nonfavored foods (e.g., Van Acker & Grant, 1995). One caution must be expressed, however, about the routine implementation of some of these programs, particularly by parents. Much effort, persistence, and tolerance for frustration are required, since improvement can be slow and even difficult to see without detailed response records.

As apraxia is one of the main effects of RS, physical therapy is critical. It helps RS girls to maintain or reacquire ambulation and to develop or maintain transitional behaviors needed to stand up from sitting or lying positions. The stereotypic hand movements are involuntary, so behavior modification techniques designed to reduce them will likely not only be ineffective, but may actually increase the movements by increasing anxiety. Several techniques, including restraints that prevent hand-to-mouth movements or simply holding the girl's hand, may be effective. Generally, whirlpool baths may be helpful. Some of the stereotyped hand clasping and other movements may be reduced by allowing the girl to hold a favored toy (Hanks, 1990).

Most RS girls begin to develop scoliosis before age eight, and many also show kyphosis (hunchback). The disorders are basically neurogenic but are exacerbated by other factors such as loss of transitional motor skills and spatial perceptual orientation, postural misalignment, and rigidity. Physical therapy and careful positioning in seated positions may help slow the development of scoliosis, but corrective surgery is often required.

Although showing strong appetites, most RS girls show serious growth retardation to the point of meeting criteria for moderate to severe malnutrition. Chewing and swallowing problems, as well as gastroesophageal reflux and digestive problems, contribute to the retardation. Speech therapy may be helpful not so much for retaining language as for facilitating chewing and swallowing. Supplementary tube feedings may be necessary to help increase growth (Glaze & Schultz, 1997). Further complicating feeding issues, constipation is common in RS. Although generally controllable through diet, laxatives or enemas may be necessary in some cases.

Seizures occur in most RS girls, and their control is an important aspect of primary care. Seizures occur most commonly in Stage III (Glaze & Schultz, 1997). Most seizures can be controlled with antiseizure medication, most frequently carbamazepine or valproic acid. Occasionally, in otherwise intractable cases, the ketogenic diet may be used, although it presents its own management problems.

Agitation, screaming, and tantrums are frequently reported. The rapid neurologic and physical changes associated with the onset of the disease may understandably provoke emotional outbursts. RS girls frequently respond negatively to stimulus or routine change, so transitions from one setting or pattern to another should be gradual and accompanied by a parent if possible. Agitation or screaming may also reflect pain or irritation from a physical condition that, in the absence of language or gestures, RS individuals may have no other way to signal. Since the girls go through puberty, caretakers need to be sensitive to their menstrual cycles. Some agitation in older individuals may reflect premenstrual discomfort or some other gynecologic disorder which may be easily treatable. A variety of treatment approaches have been used; behavior modification may be helpful.

Owing to the life-long impact of the disorder on parents and other family members, ranging from home care issues to decisions about educational and other placement, counseling for them will be particularly important. Training of the parents in behavior modification may be helpful in managing some aspects of their RS daughter's behavior, including tantrums. Given the degree of care that RS adults may require and their relative longevity, parents will eventually need to face the issue of lifelong care and make financial arrangements for care of the woman after their death.

Two of many useful websites are *http://www.ncbi.nlm.nih.gov/entrez/query.fcgi?db=PubMed&term=rett+syndrome* and *http://www.rettsyndrome.org* (International Rett Syndrome Association).

REFERENCES

Amir, R. E., Van den Veyver, I. B., Wan, M., Tran, C. Q., Francke, U., & Zoghbi, H. Y. (1999). Rett syndrome is caused by mutations in X-linked MECP2, encoding methyl-CpG-binding protein 2. *Nature Genetics, 23,* 185–188.

Brown, R. T., & Hoadley, S. L. (1999). Rett syndrome. In S. Goldstein & C. R. Reynolds (Eds.), *Handbook of Neurodevelopmental and Genetic Disorders of Children* (pp. 459–477). New York: Guilford.

Glaze, D. G., & Schultz, R. J. (1997). Rett syndrome: Meeting the challenge of this gender-specific neurodevelopmental disorder. *Medscape Women's Health, 2*(1), 1–9, online journal: http://

www.medscape.com/medscape/WomensHealth/journal/1997/ v02.n01/w223.glaze/w223.glaze.html.

Hagberg, B. (1995a). Clinical delineation of Rett syndrome variants. *Neuropediatrics, 26,* 62.

Hagberg, B. (1995b). Rett syndrome: Clinical peculiarities and biological mysteries. *Acta Paediatrica, 84,* 971–976.

Hagberg, B., Aicardi, J., Dias, K., & Ramos, O. (1983). A progressive syndrome of autism, dementia, ataxia, and loss of purposeful hand use in girls. Rett's syndrome: Report of 35 cases. *Annals of Neurology, 14,* 471–479.

Hagberg, B., & Witt-Engerström, I. (1986). Rett syndrome: A suggested staging system for describing impairment profile with increasing age toward adolescence. *American Journal of Medical Genetics, 24* (Suppl. 1), 47–59.

Hanks, S. (1990). Motor disabilities in the Rett syndrome and physical therapy strategies. *Brain and Development, 12,* 157–161.

Naidu, S. (1997). Rett syndrome: A disorder affecting early brain growth. *Annals of Neurology, 42,* 3–10.

Percy, A. K. (1996). Rett syndrome: The evolving picture of a disorder of brain development. *Developmental Brain Dysfunction, 9,* 180–196.

Perry, A., Sarlo-McGarvey, & Haddad, C. (1991). Brief reports. Cognitive and adaptive functioning in 28 girls with Rett syndrome. *Journal of Autism and Developmental Disabilities, 21,* 551–556.

Rett Syndrome Diagnostic Criteria Work Group (1988). Diagnostic criteria for Rett syndrome. *Annals of Neurology, 23,* 425–428.

Sansom, D., Krishnan, V. H. R., Corbett, J., & Kerr, A. (1993). Emotional and behavioural aspects of Rett syndrome. *Developmental Medicine and Child Neurology, 35,* 340–345.

Schwartzman, J. S., Zatz, M., Vasquez, L. R., Gomes, R. R., Koiffmann, C. P., Fridman, C., & Otto, P. G. (1999). Rett syndrome in a boy with a 47,XXY karyotype. *American Journal of Human Genetics, 64,* 1781–1785.

Van Acker, R., & Grant, S. H. (1995). An effective computer-based requesting system for persons with Rett syndrome. *Journal of Childhood Communication Disorders, 16,* 31–38.

R. T. Brown
University of North Carolina, Wilmington

REWARDS AND INTRINSIC INTEREST

It is usually assumed that giving rewards for performing a task increases future motivation for and engagement in that task activity. A large body of research supports this assumption (Baldwin & Baldwin, 1998, Sarafino, 1996). In the early 1970s, however, studies began to find that under certain conditions the opposite effect seemed to occur: External rewards for performing an intrinsically interesting activity undermined subsequent interest in and performance of that task.

DEMONSTRATING AND EXPLAINING AN UNDERMINING EFFECT OF REWARDS

The procedure that has generally been used to demonstrate this undermining effect is illustrated by the research of Lepper, Greene, and Nisbett (1973). Preschool children who pretested as being interested in the target activity of drawing with Magic Markers were assigned to reward and control conditions. The former group of children were shown a Good Player Award that they would get for drawing pictures, but the control subjects were not. After drawing the pictures, the children who expected the reward received it, and the controls did not. Later, all the children were secretly observed while the drawing materials and other activities were freely available, with no prizes offered to anyone. The children who had previously expected and received rewards for drawing spent less time playing with the drawing materials than those who had not received a reward. This undermining effect was soon demonstrated with older children and college students, using a variety of tasks and material rewards (deCharms & Muir, 1978; Lepper & Greene, 1976).

The explanation given by Lepper and his colleagues (1973; Lepper & Greene, 1976) for the undermining effect of rewards is called the "overjustification" hypothesis. If an external reward is offered and then provided for engaging in an initially enjoyable task, individuals perceive the target activity as overjustified because a reward is not necessary. They infer that engaging in the activity was "basically motivated by the external contingencies of the situation, rather than by any intrinsic interest in the activity itself" (Lepper et al., 1973, p. 130). Another theory proposes that rewards can reduce feelings of self-determination (Deci & Ryan, 1985).

CURRENT STATUS OF THE UNDERMINING EFFECT

On the face of it, the idea that rewards reduce people's interest in activities they enjoy seems to contradict common sense and observation. After all, many people get paid for work they enjoy and continue to work hard despite receiving paychecks. Research since the 1970s has produced mixed findings, with many studies reporting no decrease in interest after people got rewards for performing enjoyable activities (Dickinson, 1989; Flora, 1990; Cameron & Pierce, 1994). The undermining effects of rewards seem to occur only under limited conditions (Eisenberger & Cameron, 1996; cf. Lepper, Keavney, & Drake, 1996; Ryan & Deci, 1996). Rewards may undermine motivation under three conditions.

1. *High initial interest.* Rewards can undermine very high interest, but enhance motivation when there is less initial interest (Calder & Staw, 1975; Sarafino & DiMattia, 1978).

2. *Tangible and salient rewards.* Tangible rewards, such as candy or money, sometimes undermine interest in a task, especially if the reward is salient, such as when a child focuses attention on it (Sarafino, 1984). But praise as a reward usually enhances motivation for the task (Dollinger & Thelen, 1978; Eisenberger & Cameron, 1996).

3. *The norm is for no reward.* If a person believes that people are not normally given a reward for the activity, being given a reward can undermine interest. But if the person believes it is

normal and appropriate to receive a reward for the activity, the reward increases motivation (Staw, Calder, Hess, & Sandelands, 1980).

When reduced interest does occur, these decrements are usually minor; transient, if the person continues to perform the task following the reward; and unlikely at all, if performance meets or exceeds stated standards or receives repeated rewards (Dickinson, 1989; Eisenberger & Cameron, 1996). In summary, it appears that rewards can undermine people's interest in enjoyable activities under limited conditions, but the likelihood, strength, and durability of these effects are slight.

REFERENCES

Baldwin, J. D., & Baldwin, J. I. (1998). *Behavior principles in everyday life* (3rd ed.). Upper Saddle River, NJ: Prentice Hall.

Calder, B. J., & Staw, B. M. (1975). Self-perception of intrinsic and extrinsic motivation. *Journal of Personality and Social Psychology, 31,* 599–605.

Cameron, J., & Pierce, W. D. (1994). Reinforcement, reward, and intrinsic motivation. A meta-analysis. *Review of Educational Research, 64,* 363–423.

deCharms, R., & Muir, M. S. (1978). Motivation: Social approaches. *Annual Review of Psychology, 29,* 91–113.

Deci, E. L., & Ryan, R. M. (1985). *Intrinsic motivation and self-determination in human behavior.* New York: Plenum Press.

Dickinson, A. M. (1989). The detrimental effects of extrinsic reinforcement on "intrinsic motivation." *Behavior Analyst, 12,* 1–15.

Dollinger, S. J., & Thelen, M. H. (1978). Overjustification and children's intrinsic motivation: Comparative effects of four rewards. *Journal of Personality and Social Psychology, 36,* 1259–1269.

Eisenberger, R., & Cameron, J. (1996). Detrimental effects of reward: Reality or myth? *American Psychologist, 51,* 1153–1166.

Flora, S. R. (1990). Undermining intrinsic interest from the standpoint of a behaviorist. *Psychological Record, 40,* 323–346.

Lepper, M. R., & Greene, D. (1976). On understanding "overjustification": A reply to Reiss and Sushinsky. *Journal of Personality and Social Psychology, 33,* 25–35.

Lepper, M. R., Greene, D., & Nisbett, R. E. (1973). Undermining children's intrinsic interest with extrinsic reward: A test of the "overjustification hypothesis." *Journal of Personality and Social Psychology, 28,* 129–137.

Lepper, M. R., Keavney, M., & Drake, M. (1996). Intrinsic motivation and extrinsic rewards: A commentary on Cameron and Pierce's meta-analysis. *Review of Educational Research, 66,* 5–32.

Ryan, R. M., & Deci, E. L. (1996). When paradigms clash. Comments on Cameron and Pierce's claim that rewards do not undermine intrinsic motivation. *Review of Educational Research, 66,* 33–38.

Sarafino, E. P. (1984). Intrinsic motivation and delay of gratification in preschoolers: The variables of reward salience and length of expected delay. *British Journal of Developmental Psychology, 1,* 149–156.

Sarafino, E. P. (1996). *Principles of behavior change: Understanding behavior modification techniques.* New York: Wiley.

Sarafino, E. P., & DiMattia, P. A. (1978). Does grading undermine intrinsic interest in a college course? *Journal of Educational Psychology, 70,* 916–921.

Staw, B. M., Calder, B. J., Hess, R. K., & Sandelands, L. E. (1980). Intrinsic motivation and norms about payment. *Journal of Personality, 48,* 1–14.

E. P. SARAFINO
The College of New Jersey

INTRINSIC MOTIVATION
MOTIVATION
REINFORCEMENT
REWARDS

RHINE, JOSEPH BANKS (1895–1980)

Joseph Banks Rhine, considered the father of experimental parapsychology, spent over 50 years in active research that brought psychic research from closed séance rooms of mediums into open laboratories of scientists. Born into a farming family he was originally headed for a career in the ministry. But Rhine soon became disenchanted with religious studies because of their lack of objectivity, and turned to science, eventually earning the PhD degree in plant physiology at the University of Chicago in 1925. In 1920, he married another botanist, Louisa Ella Weckesser, who remained his partner at home and work until his death.

Begun in 1927 under the sponsorship of William McDougall at Duke University, Rhine's work soon provided strong evidence for extrasensory perception (ESP), the ability to acquire information shielded from the senses. The results of his early studies were published in 1934 in his *Extrasensory Perception,* a book "of such a scope and of such promise as to revolutionize psychical research and to make its title literally a household phrase" (Mauskopf & McVaugh, 1980). The book received worldwide attention and became the focus of controversy that was to continue for many years. In *Extrasensory Perception after Sixty Years,* which he wrote in 1940 with a number of his colleagues, Rhine dealt meticulously with all of the objections raised against his and similar work. Rhine's research results also provided evidence for the existence of psychokinesis (PK), the ability to influence external systems shielded from normal energetic sources, and for the relative independence of ESP and PK from space-time constraints. Nontechnical and more popular accounts of his work and its implications are contained in his *New Frontiers of the Mind, The Reach of the Mind,* and *New World of the Mind.*

For almost a half century, Rhine was the undisputed leader in the field of parapsychology. He gave it its concepts and methods, defined its scope, mapped out its territory, and provided the instrumentalities necessary for its professionalization, including the establishment of the *Journal of Parapsychology* and the founding of the Parapsychological Association. Yet he felt that his work was far from complete. In some of his unpublished notes, he briefly indicated what he considered to be the main challenge of parapsychology—the great elusiveness of the phenomena. "It has functions wide and lawful enough," he wrote. "Yet it evades most of the controlled applications all the known sensorimotor abilities permit."

Though he pursued psi research with total devotion, parapsychology for Rhine was not an end in itself. It was the implications of the existence of psi that fascinated him most. "Like many of the founders of parapsychology," he once said, "I am searching for light on man's nature with respect to the physical order. I had found it hard to hold on to a religious view that rested on the supernatural." The science of parapsychology, he hoped, would answer questions about "man's transcendent nature."

During all his professional life, Rhine waged a battle to gain academic acceptance for parapsychology, a battle that he did not quite win. But he stirred up a significant number of academics who are continuing the work.

K. R. RAO
Duke University

RIBOSOME

The prokaryotic ribosome represented by the E. coli ribosome has a molecular mass of 2.5 million daltons, and a volume of 3 million cubic Ås (Yonath & Franceschi, 1998), and is designated a 70S particle. The 70S ribosome has three tRNA binding sites: the acceptor (A) site, the peptidyl (P), exit (E) site. It is made up of dissociable subunits, a 30S subunit (0.8 million) and a 50S subunit (1.7 million). The 30S subunit is a complex of one large RNA strand (16S RNA, 1,542 bases long) and 21 proteins (denoted S1 to S21). The 50S subunit is a complex of two RNA strands (23S rRNA, 2,904 bases long; 5S RNA, 120 bases long) and at least 33 proteins (denoted L1 to L34; there is no L8). X-ray crystallography and nuclear magnetic resonance (NMR) have been applied to determine the high resolution structure of a number of ribosomal proteins and limited regions of RNA and of protein RNA complexes. Thanks to the progress in the crystallography of ribosomes, reasonably accurate structural models for the subunits and for one or two complexes of 70S ribosomes are available (Ban et al., 1998; Moore, 1998; Yonath, private communication, 1998). The relative spatial arrangements of each ribosomal component are now understood (resolution approximately 7–10 Å). In addition, cryoelectron microscopy elucidated the structure of the 70S ribosome and complexed ligands such as tRNA, mRNA, EF-G, and EF-Tu at 7- to 10-Å resolution. Other approaches helping us to understand the structure of ribosomes include neutron scattering, immunoelectron microscopy, fluorescence energy transfer, cross-linking, and chemical footprinting. On the basis of the information obtained by these studies, computer-based, three-dimensional models of ribosomes have been built.

The most extensive studies on eukaryotic ribosomes were conducted on rat ribosomes (Wool, Chan, & Gluck, 1996). Although these eukaryotic ribosomes are in principle similar to their prokaryotic counterparts, important differences do exist. Mammalian ribosomes (80S particles) are composed of 40S and 60S subunits. The 40S subunit has 18S RNA and 33 proteins, while the 60S subunit has three RNAs—5S, 5.8S, and 26S—and 47 proteins. Mammalian ribosomal proteins have an average molecular weight of 18,500 and contain 165 amino acids. They are very basic, with an average isoelectric point of 11.05. A common feature of mammalian ribosomal proteins is the repetition of short amino acid sequences, generally of three to eight. The number of genes encoding the ribosomal protein is 12, but there is no evidence that more than one gene is functional. Ribosomal proteins from all eukaryotic species are closely related and appear to be derived from a common ancestral gene.

FUNCTION OF RIBOSOMES

The function of ribosomes is to synthesize protein from aminoacyl tRNA according to the information in the messenger RNA (mRNA) with the help of soluble protein factors. Protein synthesis can be divided into four steps: translation initiation, peptide chain elongation, translation termination (release of the completed chain), and disassembly of the posttermination complex for the recycling of the translational machinery.

Translation Initiation

During the protein synthesis initiation process, the small ribosomal subunit binds to the mRNA and positions the initiation codon of the mRNA into the ribosomal decoding center at the P- (peptidyl-) site. The second codon on the mRNA is at the ribosomal A- (acceptor-) site. The charged initiator tRNA is bound at the ribosomal P-site. The resulting ribosome:mRNA:initiator-tRNA complex is called the initiation complex. Bacteria and organelles (mitochondria and chloroplasts) of eukaryotes form the initiation complex in much the same way. The analogous process in the cytoplasm of the eukaryotes differs from that of prokaryotes in several respects, and the prokaryotic and eukaryotic translation initiations will be separately described.

Prokaryotic Translation Initiation   Three soluble factors, IF1, IF2, and IF3, are involved in this process. The first event of the initiation process is the dissociation of the released free 70S ribosome into its large and small subunits via one of the two known functions of IF3 (Gualerzi & Pon, 1990). IF3 also prevents subunit reassociation and helps the 30S subunit to bind to the initiation site of mRNA. The initiator fMet-tRNA^{fMet} and mRNA, with appropriate initiation signals, bind the 30S subunit. This process takes place in random order (Wu, Iyengar, & RajBhandary, 1996). The initiation site of mRNA usually has the ribosome binding sequence (Shine-Dalgarno [SD] sequence), a few nucleotides (optimally 3–9) upstream of the initiation codon (AUG > GUG > UUG > AUU). Base pairing between this SD sequence and a few nucleotides at the

3' end of the 16S rRNA is important for the selection of the translational start site of mRNA by the 30S subunit (Hui & De Boer, 1987; Jacob, Santer, & Dahlberg, 1987).

In some cases translation may occur from mRNAs lacking an SD sequence; alternative mechanisms therefore exist (Sprengart & Porter, 1997)—for example, bridging the mRNA to the ribosome by the S1 ribosomal protein, which recognizes U-rich stretches in the 5' untranslated region. Base pairing with 16S rRNA nucleotides 1082 to 1093 and 1343 to 1355 with the 5' untranslated sequence of mRNAs plays a role in this case. Other mechanisms include base pairing with 16S rRNA nucleotides 1469 to 1483, with mRNA sequences downstream from the initiation codon.

In all cases, the interaction between the 16S rRNA and the mRNA is such that the initiation codon is positioned at the decoding center of the ribosome in the 1400/1500 nucleotide region of the 3' end of the 16S rRNA. Association of the 30S subunit and mRNA, and the concomitant translation initiation, may occur at several different initiation points along the bacterial polycistronic mRNA.

IF2, the largest of the three initiation factors, promotes the binding and correct positioning of fMet-tRNA^{fMet} to the P-site of the ribosome and prevents the participation of elongator aminoacyl-tRNA in the initiation process. This is achieved by specific recognition of the blocked (formylated) amino group of initiator fMet-tRNA^{fMet} by IF2 (Hartz, McPheeters, & Gold, 1989; Wu & RajBhandary, 1997). IF2 functions as a carrier of fMet-tRNA^{fMet} to the 30S ribosomal P-site in much the same way as EF-Tu functions as a carrier of aminoacyl-tRNAs to the A-site of 70S ribosomes (see the section Peptide Chain Elongation). The sites of fMet-tRNA^{fMet} contacting IF2 have been studied by footprinting experiments and were found primarily within the T loop and the minor groove of the T stem. The footprints of IF2 on fMet-tRNA^{fMet} in the binary fMet-tRNA^{fMet}·IF2 complex and in the 30S·IF2·fMet-tRNA^{fMet}·AUG complex are similar. This suggests that the interactions between IF2 and either the isolated fMet-tRNA^{fMet} or the P-site–bound fMet-tRNA^{fMet} are essentially the same (Wakao et al., 1989). In addition, IF2 interacts with the 3' end of the initiator tRNA and protects the ester linkage in fMet-tRNA^{fMet} from deacylation (Petersen, Roll, Grunberg-Manago, & Clark, 1979). No effect of IF2 on the reactivity pattern of the 16S rRNA in the protection assays was seen, suggesting that this factor interacts primarily through protein-protein interactions with the ribosome in the initiation complex (Moazed, Samaha, Gualerzi, & Noller, 1995).

IF3, bound to the 30S subunit, recognizes the anticodon stem of the initiator tRNA and helps to prevent the binding of elongator tRNAs to the 30S initiation complex (Hartz et al., 1989). Furthermore, IF3-dependent protection of 16S rRNA from chemical modification is found in the vicinity of a region that is also protected by P-site–bound tRNA. This indicates that the IF3 may also interact with the anticodon domain of fMet-tRNA^{fMet} or influence the properties of the 30S P-site during initiation (Moazed et al., 1995). The placement of IF3 by cryoelectron microscopy on the 30S subunit allows an understanding in structural terms of the biochemical functions of this initiation factor (McCutcheon et al., 1999).

IF1 is the smallest of the three initiation factors. It stimulates the activity of IF2 and IF3 on formation of the 30S initiation complex. The affinity of IF2 to the ribosome is increased in the presence of IF1 (Gualerzi & Pon, 1990). Footprinting revealed that the binding of IF1 to the 30S ribosomal subunit protects the same nucleotides in 16S rRNA from modification as the EF-Tu–dependent binding of aminoacyl-tRNA to the ribosomal A-site (Moazed et al., 1995). This suggests that during initiation, IF1 binds to the ribosomal A-site at the same position as the anticodon domain of the aminoacyl-tRNA during elongation. Thus, the function of IF1 may be to prevent the premature binding of elongator aminoacyl-tRNA to the A-site during the initiation process, and a complex of IF1 and IF2 interact with the ribosomal A-site, mimicking the structure of the elongation factor G (Brock, Szkaradkiewicz, & Sprinzl, 1998). As these initiation factors and EF-G fulfill a similar function in placing a tRNA to the ribosomal P-site, structural similarities between them may indicate similar molecular mechanisms of action.

The 30S initiation complex forms the 70S initiation complex by association with the 50S ribosomal subunit. Concomitant with this process, IF1 and IF3 are ejected. The process is stimulated by IF2, whose GTPase activity is activated, and IF2 is released upon hydrolysis of GTP. At this stage, the fMet-tRNA^{fMet} is located in the ribosomal P-site, ready to form the first peptide bond. The mechanism of initiation in bacteria has been extensively reviewed (Hartz et al., 1989; Gualerzi & Pon, 1990; RajBhandary & Chow, 1995).

Initiation in the Cytoplasm of Eukaryotic Cells One peculiar feature of eukaryotic mRNAs is that the 5' end of most of them has a structure called a cap. This is a structure involving methylated guanine triphospho nucleotide, ^{7}mGpppN, where N denotes any base. Many factors are involved in the eukaryotic initiation process and are designated as eIFs. A cap-dependent mechanism accounts for the translation of the vast majority of cellular mRNAs. An alternative cap-independent initiation mechanism is responsible for translation of a small number of mRNAs (Gray & Wickens, 1998). The process of initiation is similar in germ line cells and during embryogenesis as well (Jackson & Wickens, 1997).

In both the cap-dependent and the cap-independent pathways, the initiation proceeds via formation of a 43S preinitiation complex consisting of the 40S ribosomal subunit, a ternary complex of eIF2·GTP·Met-tRNA$_i^{Met}$ (the initiator tRNA in eukaryotes is not formylated in contrast to its prokaryotic counterpart), and eIF3. Ribosomes at physiological Mg^{2+} concentration (>1 mM) predominantly exist as 80S monosomes. The equilibrium between 80S monosomes and dissociated subunits is shifted toward dissociation by eIF3, eIF1A (alternative name eIF-4C), and eIF3A (alternative name eIF6). EIF3 and eIF1A bind to the 40S subunit, while eIF3A binds to the 60S subunit, making 40S subunits available for initiation (Hershey, 1991; Merrick, 1992; Pain, 1996). EIF1A is a single subunit factor with basic N-terminus and acidic C-terminus.

eIF-3 consists of at least 8 polypeptides in mammalian cells and *S. cerevisiae,* and 10 polypeptides in wheat germ cells. This initiation factor remains bound to the 40S subunit and is necessary for the stable binding of the eIF2·GTP·Met-tRNA$_i^{Met}$ ternary complex (Gray & Wickens, 1998; Merrick & Hershey, 1996; Merrick, 1992) to the small subunit. eIF3A (one of the proteins of eIF3 complex), which remains bound to the 60S subunit, is a single subunit protein (Merrick, 1992).

eIF2 consists of three subunits: γ, β, and α. The γ-subunit possesses the GTP-binding elements. In the absence of GTP, eIF2 is not able to bind to initiator tRNA. Based on cross-linking studies, both the γ- and the β-subunits bind to Met-tRNA$_i^{Met}$ (Gaspar et al., 1994). The main known function of the α-subunit is to link translation to regulatory circuits via the presence of a conserved phosphorylation site (Ser51 in mammalian cells) present in its sequence. When the α-subunit is phosphorylated, eIF2 loses its ability to replace its spent GDP with GTP. In addition, the phosphorylated α-subunit segregates the nucleotide exchange factor eIF2B from the rest of eIF2 by tightly binding to it. This makes eIF2B less available for replacing the GDP with GTP on the eIF2·GDP binary complex. As a consequence, availability of the eIF2·GTP·Met-tRNA$_i^{Met}$ ternary complex for the initiation decreases, fewer 43S preinitiation complexes are formed, and translation decreases (Gray & Wickens, 1998; Pain, 1996).

In the cap-dependent pathway, this 43S preinitiation complex is then recruited at the 5′ end of the mRNA, involving the ^{7}mGpppN cap structure on the 5′ end with the association of eIF4 group initiation factors, including 4F and B. The complex is frequently called the 48S preinitiation complex.

The eIF4F consists of three subunits with distinctive functions: eIF4E, eIF4A, and eIF4G. eIF4E is a cap-binding protein; eIF4A has an ATP-dependent RNA helicase activity; and eIF4G has affinity in its N-terminal third to eIF4E (Lamphear, Kirchweger, Skern, & Rhoads, 1995; Mader, Lee, Pause, & Sonenberg, 1995), while its C-terminal two-thirds has affinity to both eIF3 and eIF4A (Lamphear et al., 1995). Therefore, eIF4G bridges the cap structure of the mRNA (via eIF4E), the 40S subunit of the ribosome (via eIF3), and eIF4A (Hentze, 1997; Jackson & Wickens, 1997). Both eIF4E and eIF4G have been shown to participate in regulatory circuits affecting translation in the initiation step (Gray & Wickens, 1998; Jackson & Wickens, 1997; Hentze, 1997).

It has been shown in *S. cerevisiae* that the poly(A) tail–stimulated translation is mediated by a protein, Pab1p, which binds to a stretch of 10 A nucleotides at the 3′-ends of mRNAs. Pab1p acts synergistically with the cap structure, but also can work in its absence and exerts its stimulatory effect via binding to the eIF4G.

There is also growing evidence that some signal transduction/phosphorylation systems positively regulate translation via the involvement of eIF4E. Thus, the eIF4E binding protein 1 (4E-BP1) strongly binds eIF4E and sequesters it from entering the eIF4F initiation complex. Phosphorylation of 4E-BP1, elicited, for instance, by insulin, makes eIF4E available for eIF4G binding and hence increases 48S preinitiation complex formation.

Another eIF4 group factor (but not part of eIF4F), eIF4B joins the 48S preinitiation complex and stimulates the unwinding of the secondary structures in the 5′ untranslated region of the mRNA via eIF4A (Lawson et al., 1989; Rozen et al., 1990). EIF4B also interacts with eIF3; this ability may aid in binding the 43S preinitiation complex to the mRNA (Merrick, 1992).

The 40S ribosomal subunit, with the associated initiation factors, has to relocate from the cap through the 5′-untranslated region (5′-UTR) of the mRNA to the site of initiation, which is generally 100 to 150 nucleotides downstream along the mRNA. This process is termed "scanning" (Kozak, 1978) or "shunting" (Gray & Wickens, 1998). In the scanning model, the preinitiation complex migrates along the mRNA in a continuous manner from the 5′-UTR to the initiation site. In the shunting model, scanning toward the initiation site is discontinuous; the preinitiation complex hops over secondary mRNA structures, which in themselves are inhibitory for the scanning. The scanning is an ATP-dependent process, and is dependent on eIF1 and eIF1A (Pestova et al., 1998).

The scanning preinitiation complex selects the site of initiation generally at the location of the first initiation codon, overwhelmingly AUG, but occasionally GUG or CUG (Kozak, 1989, 1994). Sometimes it is not the first initiation codon, mainly when the ORF is preceded by short ORFs (sORFs), and the ORF is not translated when translation of sORF is prevented (Hinnebush, 1996). RNA:RNA interactions may play a role in positioning the initiation codon in the decoding center of the 40S ribosomal subunit, although it is not so apparent as in prokaryotes (Sprengart & Porter, 1997). There is a consensus sequence of approximately 10 nucleotides for the initiation site (Kozak, 1994). The most important positions are a purine, at –3 position, and a G, at +4 position, where A of the initiator AUG codon is position +1. The fidelity of interaction between the codon and the complementary anticodon loop of the initiator tRNA is controlled by both eIF3 (Naranda, MacMillan, Donahue, & Hershey, 1996), and eIF2 (Pain, 1996).

In the alternative cap-independent initiation pathway, a *cis*-acting mRNA element (the internal ribosome entry segment [IRES]) promotes direct access of the 43S preinitiation complex to the initiation codon and can even allow several cycles of translation of a covalently closed circular mRNA (Chen & Sarnow, 1995). Although IRES is similar in strictly operational terms to the Shine and Dalgarno sequence of prokaryotic mRNAs (Pestova, Shatsky et al., 1998), IRES is much larger. Internal entry was first discovered with picornavirus RNA, and evidence for its existence has widened since then (Jackson & Kaminski, 1995; Bernstein, Shefler, & Elroy-Stein, 1995; Gan & Rhoads, 1996). Internal initiation of viral mRNA allows some viruses whose mRNAs do not have a cap structure to shut down the translation of most of the cellular mRNAs during viral infection via cleavage of eIF4G. This gives the advantage to the virus, which will then use all cellular protein synthesis machinery for its own replication. The cleavage separates eIF4G into an amino-terminal one-third portion that binds the cap-binding initiation factor eIF4E, and a carboxy-terminal two-thirds fragment that binds eIF3 and the helicase eIF4A.

After the initiation site is selected by the 40S subunits, the 60S ribosomal subunit associates with the complex forming of the 80S ribosome. This step requires eIF5 and the energy of hydrolysis of the GTP bound to eIF2 in the preinitiation complex. The hydrolysis is catalyzed by eIF5, which has GTPase motifs in its sequence (Das, Chevesich & Maitra, 1993; Chakravarti & Maitra, 1993). Upon association of the large subunit, initiation factors are released and the 80S ribosome is ready to enter the elongation cycle.

Peptide Chain Elongation

For catalyzing peptide chain elongation, the ribosome has three tRNA binding sites: the acceptor (A) site, the peptidyl (P) site, and the exit (E) site (Agrawal & Frank, 1999; Nyborg & Liljas, 1998;

Moore, 1998, 1997; Frank, 1997). The ribosomal A-, P-, and E-sites are situated in the cavity between the large and small subunit interface, with the E-site positioned toward the L1 arm side of the large subunit, the A-site positioned toward the L7/L12 arm on the opposite side of the large subunit, and the P-site in between the other two sites. The A- and P-sites span the large and the small subunit, whereas the E-site is localized to the large subunit only.

Peptide chain elongation takes place in the absence of soluble factors, though very slowly, (Wilson & Noller, 1998). Under physiological conditions, the prokaryotic ribosome requires elongation factors EF-Tu, EF-Ts, and EF-G. These factors are single-subunit proteins, except for EF-Ts, which forms a dimer (Czworkowski & Moore, 1996; Green & Noller, 1997). In eukaryotes, three factors function for peptide chain elongation: EF-1α (a monomeric protein) corresponds to EF-Tu; eEF-1βγ (composed of two subunits) corresponds to EF-Ts; and eEF-2 (a monomeric protein) corresponds to the prokaryotic EF-G (Merrick, 1992; Hershey, 1991). An additional factor, eEF-3, which stimulates the translation 5- to 30-fold, has been identified only in yeast and fungi (Merrick, 1992). This factor is necessary for the removal of the deacylated tRNA from the E-site, which has a stronger affinity for tRNA in eukaryotes (especially in fungi) than in prokaryotes (Spahn & Nierhaus, 1998).

The repetitive elongation cycle proceeds in three consecutive steps: aminoacyl-tRNA binding to the ribosomal A-site, peptide bond formation, and translocation of the ribosome one codon towards the 3'-end on the mRNA with concomitant translocation of the deacylated tRNA from the P-site to the E-site, and the peptidyl-tRNA from the A-site to the P-site together with the mRNA movement.

In the first step of chain elongation, the elongator aminoacyl-tRNA is brought to the ribosomal A-site as a ternary complex: aminoacyl-tRNA·EF-Tu (EF-1α in the cytoplasm of eukaryotic cells)·GTP (Pape, Wintermeyer, & Rodnina, 1998; Rodnina, Pape, Fricke, Kuhn, & Wintermeyer, 1996; Rodnina, Fricke, Kuhn, & Wintermeyer, 1995; Rodnina, Pape, Fricke, & Wintermeyer, 1995). The initial rapid and reversible phase is a codon-independent complex formation between the ribosome and the ternary complex. With the cognate aminoacyl tRNA, the subsequent event, inducing the GTPase conformation of EF-Tu and the ribosome-induced GTP hydrolysis, proceeds at a rate four orders of magnitude higher than in the case of binding a noncognate ternary complex. The affinity of the cognate aminoacyl tRNA to the A-site is greatly influenced by whether the E-site is occupied with deacylated tRNA according to the allosteric model (described below), because the configuration of ribosomes are greatly influenced by tRNA on the E-site (Spahn & Nierhaus, 1998).

During the binding process, the anticodon end of the aminoacyl tRNA binds to the A-site of the 30S subunit. The opposite end of the complex contacts the L7/L12 region of the 50S subunit, and the amino acid on the acceptor end of the tRNA is held by the elongation factor so that it is not yet accessible for the peptidyl transferase center on the 50S subunit (Stark et al., 1997; Nyborg & Liljas, 1998; Krab & Parmeggiani, 1998). When the GTP of the ternary complex is hydrolyzed by the GTPase activity of the elongation factor, EF-Tu undergoes a second conformational change, which leads to the release of the aminoacyl-tRNA from the ternary

complex. Subsequently, in a rotational movement, the acceptor end of the aminoacyl-tRNA becomes positioned into the large subunit part of the A-site and becomes accessible for the peptidyl transferase center on the 50S subunit (accommodation step; Stark et al., 1997; Nyborg & Liljas, 1998). In the eukaryotic system, the binding of aminoacyl tRNA proceeds in a similar way with EF-1α (corresponding to EF-Tu). Because both the prokaryotic EF-Tu and the eukaryotic EF-1α bind GDP with high affinity, an additional elongation factor, EF-Ts in prokaryotes and EF-1βγ in eukaryotes, helps to regenerate the GTP form of these factors.

The next step is the peptide bond formation. The peptidyl transferase activity is an inherent property of the ribosomes. Peptide bond formation is catalyzed by the large ribosomal subunit (Maden, Traut, & Monro, 1968; Nierhaus, Stuhrmann, & Svergun, 1998; Green & Noller, 1997). The peptidyl-transferase is located at the interface side of the subunit below the central protuberance of the 50S subunit. In vitro ribosome reconstitution experiments, and the recent finding that the peptidyl transferase activity of *Thermus aquaticus* ribosomes is very resistant to protein extraction procedures, point to the ribosomal proteins L2, L3, and the 23S rRNA as prime candidates for exerting the activity.

The next step is translocation; but before a discussion of translocation, the two models of the ribosomal tRNA binding site must be introduced. They are the hybrid site (Moazed & Noller, 1989) and the allosteric α-ε–site models (Nierhaus, 1990; Dabrowski, Spahn, Schafer, Patzke, & Nierhaus, 1998; Spahn & Nierhaus, 1998; Burkhardt, Junemann, Spahn, & Nierhaus, 1998; Nierhaus et al., 1998; Wilson & Noller, 1998; Green & Noller, 1997; Czworkowski & Moore, 1996; Merrick, 1992; Hershey, 1991).

In the hybrid site model, the main feature is that one portion of tRNA (3' end) bound to the large subunit moves independently of the other portion (anticodon part) during peptide chain elongation. Loading of the aminoacyl-tRNA occurs in two well defined steps: In the first step, the aminoacyl-tRNA occupies only the small subunit portion of the A-site; the second step leads to the full occupation of the A-site. Before peptidyl transfer, the peptidyl-tRNA is in the P-site and the aminoacyl tRNA is in the A-site. After the peptidyl transfer (peptide bond synthesis), the peptidyl-tRNA is bound to the A-site of the 30S subunit at the anticodon portion while the acceptor portion of the peptidyl-tRNA with peptide group is bound to the P-site of the large subunit. At the same time, the anticodon portion of the deacylated tRNA (formed as a result of the peptide bond formation) remains at the P-site of the 30S subunit, while the CCA end (the acceptor end) of the tRNA moves to the E-site of the large subunit. Translocation moves the anticodon portion of the deacylated tRNA, together with the mRNA, to the E-site so that the deacylated tRNA fully occupies the E-site. On the other hand, the anticodon portion of the newly elongated peptidyl-tRNA moves, together with the mRNA, to the P-site of the 30S subunit. Thus, the peptidyl-tRNA is now fully situated in the P-site.

The allosteric α-ε model stems from the finding that the ribosomal binding domains of the A-site and of the P-site–bound tRNAs in the pre-translocation state ribosome do not change significantly when these tRNAs are translocated to the P- and E-sites respectively. This suggests that the microenvironment for the tRNAs remains very similar in both states, although there are considerable conformational changes in the ribosome itself. Therefore, the ribosome behaves as if it had a movable block preserving the contact sites for the tRNAs during translocation. The α part of the ribosome preferentially binds an acylated tRNA (aminoacyl or peptidyl tRNA) and covers the A- or P-site. The ε part of the ribosome preferentially binds a deacylated tRNA and covers the P- or E-site. At the pre-translocation step, the α part is found only at the A-site; after translocation, the ε part is located exclusively at the E-site. In the post-translocational state, two high-affinity sites (P and E) exist. It is known that aminoacyl tRNA can bind to the post-translocational state ribosomes (Triana-Alonso, Chakraburtty, Nierhaus, 1995) at the A-site. Therefore, the α-ε model postulates the third nonmovable decoding site, ∂. The affinity of the ∂-site is increased when the E-site is emptied due to the allosteric effect of the E-site on the affinity and fidelity of the A-site. The ∂-site is separated from the α-ε domain in the post-state but overlaps with the α domain at the prestate.

Translocation is the movement of the mRNA, tRNA, and ribosome complex by one codon length toward the 3' end for about 12Å (Wadzack et al., 1997). Two tRNAs are relocated from the A- and P-sites to the P- and E-sites, respectively. The role of EF-G·GTP (eEF-2·GTP in eukaryotes) in this process is mainly to reduce the activation energy barrier between the pre- and the post-translocational states, which is about 90 kJ/mol under physiological conditions (Schilling-Bartetzko, Nierhaus, 1992). In support of this concept is the fact that, in the absence of the elongation factors, translocation is still possible at a reduced speed (Bergemann & Nierhaus, 1983; Schilling-Bartetzko et al., 1992). During the translocation step, the GTP of the elongation factor is hydrolyzed. The EF-G·GDP (eEF-2·GDP in eukaryotes) complex loses its affinity for the ribosome and is released. A striking similarity in the overall shape of the EF-G·GDP (Czworkowski, Wang, Steitz, & Moore, 1994) and the aminoacyl-tRNA·EF-Tu·GTP (Nissen et al., 1995) complexes were found recently. This leads to the speculation that the two macromolecules may share common ribosomal structures for their binding and some kind of common mechanism in their function (Wilson & Noller, 1998).

The elongation cycle is the most energy-requiring process in protein biosynthesis. It essentially takes two high-energy phosphates brought about by elongation factor·GTP complexes and two high-energy phosphates used to generate each aminoacyl-tRNA (ATP + AA + tRNA → AMP + PP$_i$ + AA-tRNA). Thus, the formation of each peptide bond costs four high-energy phosphates for the cell.

Translation Termination

When the prokaryotic ribosomes engaged in the peptide chain elongation come to the end of the open reading frame, the termination codon, UAA, UAG, or UGA, is placed in the A-site (acceptor site) of the ribosomes. The release of completed chain takes place at this point with the help of certain factors. With most of the prokaryotes, except for *M. genitalium*, the smallest free-living organism, three soluble factors RFs (release factors) 1, 2, and 3 are involved. RF1 functions with UAA and UAG, while RF2 functions with UAA and UGA (Scolnick, Tompkins, Caskey, Nirenberg, 1968). Regions in helix 34 and 44 of the 16S RNA (Goringer, Hi-

jazi, Murgola, & Dahlberg, 1991; Brown & Tate, 1994) have been implicated in the recognition of the stop codon. RF1 and RF2 are composed of two domains, one responsible for recognition of the stop codon and the other responsible for hydrolysis of the ester linkage between 3' OH of tRNA and COOH of amino acid (Moffat & Tate, 1994; Brown & Tate, 1994). The function of RF3 is to promote the recycling of RF1 (Grentzmann, 1998; Freistroffer et al., 1997). As for the relationship between RF2 and RF3, RF3 either stimulates recycling of RF2 (Freistroffer et al., 1997) or simply promotes the binding of RF2 to the termination complex (Grentzmann et al., 1998). The differential effect of RF3 on RF1 and RF2 is supported by the in vivo experiment in which RF3 was shown to act preferentially on RF2 (Grentzmann et al., 1995). During the action of RF3 in vitro, GTP is required (Grentzmann et al., 1998); this is understandable because RF3 has the GTPase motif (Grentzmann et al., 1994) and ribosome-dependent GTPase activity (Grentzmann et al., 1998).

The process of the completed peptide chain release in eukaryotes is similar but somewhat different. Only two factors, eRF1 and eRF3, are involved. eRF1 functions for recognition of all three termination codons (Frolova et al., 1994), and eRF3 functions as GTPase only in the presence of eRF1 and ribosomes (Frolova et al., 1996). ERF3 is essential for cell survival (Ter-Avanesyan et al., 1993). The human eRF3 is 138 amino acids long (Jean-Jean, LeGoff, & Philippe, et al., 1996) and therefore much shorter than prokaryotic RF3. In yeast, eRF3 was first recognized as *SUP35* (Stansfield & Tuite, 1994; Kushnirov et al., 1988), the omnipotent suppresor if damaged by mutation. In a similar manner, the yeast eRF1 was first recognized as SUP45 (Stansfield et al., 1995), which was later identified as RF1 by sequence homology with mammalian RF1 (Frolova et al., 1994).

eRF3 of yeast (Sup35 protein) is capable of propagating a specific conformation that gives rise to the [psi+] nonsense suppressor determinant (Wickner, 1994). This is due to the fact that eRF3 of yeast with [psi+] phenotype has prion-like characteristics. Sup35 protein (yeast eRF3) molecules interact with each other through their N-terminal domain in [psi+] but not in [psi–] cells (Patino, Liu, Glover, & Lindquist, 1996; Paushkin, Kushnirov, Smirnov, & Ter-Avanesyan, 1996). Thus, cells containing this form of eRF3 (Sup35p) show a depletion in the levels of soluble functional eRF3 that is sequestered in high–molecular weight, prion-like fibers. Though isogenic [psi+] and [psi–] strains show no difference in growth rates under normal laboratory conditions, [psi+] strains exhibit enhanced tolerance to heat and chemical stress, compared to [psi–] strains. Thus, the prion-like determinant [psi+] is able to regulate translation termination efficiency in response to environmental stress.

Ribosome Recycling

The termination step described in the preceding section leaves behind the ribosomal post-termination complex; the next step is disassembly of that complex. In *E. coli,* this process is catalyzed by two factors: elongation factor G (EF-G; Hirashima & Kaji, 1972, 1973) or RF3 (Grentzmann et al., 1998), and ribosome recycling factor (RRF, originally called ribosome releasing factor; Janosi, Shimizu, & Kaji, 1994). In addition to disassembly of the post-termination complex, RRF appears to help maintain translational fidelity during chain elongation (Janosi, Ricker, & Kaji, 1996). Discovered in 1970 (Hirashima & Kaji, 1970), RRF is present in every organism (Janosi, Hara, Zhang, & Kaji, 1996; Janosi, Ricker, & Kaji, 1996) and is essential (Janosi et al., 1994) for maintenance of life in all bacteria except archaebacteria (Archaea; Bult et al., 1996). *M. genitalium,* being the smallest free-living organism, with only 500 genes, manages without RF2 and RF3 (Fraser et al., 1995), but it retains RRF, suggesting the importance of RRF.

When RRF was omitted in the in vitro translation system, ribosomes remaining on the mRNA reinitiated unscheduled translation from the triplet next to the termination codon (Ryoji, Berland, & Kaji, 1981). Upon inactivation of RRF in vivo, a ribosome may frame-shift into all possible frames and may slide downstream as many as 10 to 45 nucleotides before it randomly starts translation of the mRNA (Janosi et al., 1998).

Eukaryotic RRF is an organelle protein (e.g., in chloroplasts or mitochondria) that is involved in protein synthesis within the organelles in much the same way bacterial RRF functions (Rolland et al., 1999). This conclusion is further supported by the fact that translation in chloroplasts is similar to that in prokaryotes (Harris, Boynton, & Gillham, 1994; Danon, 1997) and the fact that yeast (Kanai et al., 1998) and human (Zhang & Spremulli, 1998) RRF may be a mitochondrial protein. It should be noted that none of the Archeons contains RRF. Archeons, in between eukaryotes and prokaryotes in their phylogenetic development, have a protein synthesis system similar to that of eukaryotic cytoplasm. This suggests that the eukaryotic homologues of RRF are involved in the organelle protein synthesis but not in the cytoplasmic protein synthesis. This raises a question as to the factors responsible for the disassembly of the post-termination complex involved in the cytoplasmic protein synthesis in eukaryotes. This is an important question, which should be answered in near future. Four review articles on RRF have been published (Janosi, Hara, Zhang, & Kaji, 1996; Janosi, Ricker, & Kaji, 1996; Kaji, Teyssier, & Hirokawa, 1998; Kaji & Hirokawa, 1999).

REFERENCES

Agrawal, R. K., & Frank, J. (1999). Structural studies of the translational apparatus. *Current Opinion in Structural Biology, 9,* 215–221.

Ban, N., Freeborn, B., Nissen, P., Penczek, P., Grassucci, R. A., Sweet, R., Frank, J., Moore, P. B., & Steitz, T. A. (1998). A 9 Å resolution X-ray crystallographic map of the large ribosomal subunit. *Cell, 93,* 1105–1115.

Bergemann, K., & Nierhaus, K. H. (1983). Spontaneous, elongation factor G independent translocation of *Escherichia coli* ribosomes. *Journal of Biological Chemistry, 258,* 15105–15113.

Bernstein, J., Shefler, I., & Elroy-Stein, O. (1995). The translational repression mediated by the platelet-derived growth factor 2/c-sis mRNA leader is relieved during megakaryocytic differentiation. *Journal of Biological Chemistry, 270,* 10559–10565.

Brock, S., Szkaradkiewicz, K., & Sprinzl, M. (1998). Initiation factors of protein biosynthesis in bacteria and their structural relationship to elongation and termination factors. *Molecular Microbiology, 29,* 409–417.

Brown, C. M., & Tate, W. P. (1994). Direct recognition of mRNA stop signals by *Escherichia coli* polypeptide chain release factor two. *Journal of Biological Chemistry, 269,* 33164–33170.

Bult, C. J., White, O., Olsen, G. J., Zhou, L., Fleischmann, R. D., Sutton, G. G., Blake, J. A., Fitzgerald, L. M., Clayton, R. A., Gocayne, J. D., Kerlavage, A. R., Dougherty, B. A., Tomb, J.-F., Adams, M. D., Reich, C. T., Overbeek, R., Kirkness, E. F., Weinstock, K. G., Merrick, J. M., Glodek, A., Scott, J. L., Geoghagen, N. S. M., Weidman, J. F., Fuhrmann, J. L., Nguyen, D., Utterback, T. R., Kelley, J. M., Peterson, J. D., Sadow, P. W., Hanna, M. C., Cotton, M. D., Roberts, K. M., Hurst, M. A., Kaine, B. P., Borodovsky, M., Klenk, H.-P., Fraser, C. M., Smith, H. O., Woese, C. R., & Venter, J. C. (1996). Complete genome sequence of the methanogenic archaeon, *Methanococcus jannaschii. Science, 273,* 1058–1073.

Burkhardt, N., Junemann, R., Spahn, C. M. T., & Nierhaus, K. H. (1998). Ribosomal tRNA binding sites: Three-site models of translation. *Critical Reviews in Biochemistry and Molecular Biology, 33,* 95–149.

Chakravarti, D., & Maitra, U. (1993). Eukaryotic translation initiation factor 5 from *Saccharomyces cerevisiae:* Cloning, characterization, and expression of the gene encoding the 45,346-Da protein. *Journal of Biological Chemistry, 268,* 10524–10533.

Chen, C.-Y., & Sarnow, P. (1995). Initiation of protein synthesis by the eukaryotic translational apparatus on circular RNAs. *Science, 268,* 415–417.

Czworkowski, J., & Moore, P. B. (1996). The elongation phase of protein synthesis. *Progress in Nucleic Acids Research and Molecular Biology, 54,* 293–332.

Czworkowski, J., Wang, J., Steitz, T. A., & Moore, P. B. (1994). The crystal structure of elongation factor G complexed with GDP, at 2.7 Å resolution. *EMBO Journal, 13,* 3661–3668.

Dabrowski, M., Spahn, C. M. T., Schafer, M. A., Patzke, S., & Nierhaus, K. H. (1998). Protection patterns of tRNAs do not change during ribosomal translocation. *Journal of Biological Chemistry, 273,* 32793–32800.

Danon, A. (1997). Translational regulation in the chloroplast. *Plant Physiology, 115,* 1293–1298.

Das, K., Chevesich, J., & Maitra, U. (1993). Molecular cloning and expression of cDNA for mammalian translation initiation factor 5. *Proceedings of the National Academy of Sciences, U.S.A., 90,* 3058–3062.

Frank, J. (1997). The ribosome at higher resolution: The donut takes shape. *Current Opinion in Structural Biology, 7,* 266–272.

Fraser, C. M., Gocayne, J. D., White, O., Adams, M. D., Clayton, R. A., Fleischmann, R. D., Bult, C. J., Kerlavage, A. R., Sutton, G., Kelley, J. M., Fritchman, J. L., Weidman, J. F., Small, K. V., Sandusky, M., Fuhrmann, J., Nguyen, D., Utterback, T. R., Saudek, D. M., Phillips, C. A., Merrick, J. M., Tomb, J.-F., Dougherty, B. A., Bott, K. F., Hu, P.-C., Lucier, T. S., Peterson, S. N., Smith, H. O., Hutchinson, C. A., III, & Venter, J. C.

(1995). The minimal gene complement of *Mycoplasma genitalium*. *Science, 270,* 397–403.

Freistroffer, D. V., Pavlov, M. Y., MacDougall, J., Buckingham, R. H., & Ehrenberg, M. (1997). Release factor RF3 in *E. coli* accelerates the dissociation of release factors RF1 and RF2 from the ribosome in a GTP-dependent manner. *EMBO Journal, 16,* 4126–4133.

Frolova, L., LeGoff, X., Rasmussen, H. H., Cheperegin, S., Drugeon, G., Kress, M., Arman, I., Haenni, A. L., Celis, J. E., Philippe, M., Justesen, J., & Kisselev, L. (1994). A highly conserved eukaryotic protein family possessing properties of polypeptide chain release factor. *Nature, 372,* 701–703.

Frolova, L., LeGoff, X., Zhouravleva, G., Davydova, E., Philippe, M., & Kisselev, L. (1996). Eukaryotic polypeptide chain release factor eRF3 is an eRF1- and ribosome-dependent guanosine triphosphatase. *RNA, 2,* 334–341.

Gan, W., & Rhoads, R. E. (1996). Internal initiation of translation directed by the 5′-untranslated region of the mRNA for eIF4G, a factor involved in the picornavirus-induced switch from cap-dependent to internal initiation. *Journal of Biological Chemistry, 271,* 623–626.

Gaspar, N. J., Kinzy, T. G., Scherer, B. J., Humbelin, M., Hershey, J. W., & Merrick, W. C. (1994). Translation initiation factor eIF-2. Cloning and expression of the human cDNA encoding the gamma-subunit. *Journal of Biological Chemistry, 269,* 3415–3422.

Goringer, H. U., Hijazi, K. A., Murgola, E. J., & Dahlberg, A. E. (1991). Mutations in 16S rRNA that affect UGA (stop codon)-directed translation termination. *Proceedings of the National Academy of Sciences, U.S.A., 88,* 6603–6607.

Gray, N. K., & Wickens, M. (1998). Control of translation initiation in animals. *Annual Review of Cellular Development and Biology, 14,* 399–458.

Green, R., & Noller, H. F. (1997). Ribosomes and translation. *Annual Review of Biochemistry, 66,* 679–716.

Grentzmann, G., Brechemier-Baey, D., Heurgué, V., Mora, L., & Buckingham, R. H. (1994). Localization and characterization of the gene encoding release factor RF3 in *Escherichia coli*. *Proceedings of the National Academy of Sciences, U.S.A., 91,* 5848–5852.

Grentzmann, G., Brechemier-Baey, D., Heurgué-Hamard, V., & Buckingham, R. H. (1995). Function of polypeptide chain release factor RF-3 in *Escherichia coli:* RF-3 action in termination is predominantly at UGA-containing stop signals. *Journal of Biological Chemistry, 270,* 10595–10600.

Grentzmann, G., Kelly, P. J., Laalami, S., Shuda, M., Firpo, M. A., Cenatiempo, Y., & Kaji, A. (1998). Release factor RF-3 GTPase activity acts in disassembly of the ribosome termination complex. *RNA, 4,* 973–983.

Gualerzi, C. O., & Pon, C. L. (1990). Initiation of mRNA translation in prokaryotes. *Biochemistry, 29,* 5881–5889.

Harris, E. H., Boynton, J. E., & Gillham, N. W. (1994). Chloroplast ribosomes and protein synthesis. *Microbiology Review, 58,* 700–754.

Hartz, D., McPheeters, D. S., & Gold, L. (1989). Selection of the initiator t-RNA by *Escherichia coli* initiation-factors. *Genes & Development, 3,* 1899–1912.

Hentze, M. W. (1997). eIF4G: A multipurpose ribosome adapter? *Science, 275,* 500–501.

Hershey, J. W. B. (1991). Translational control in mammalian cells. *Annual Review of Biochemistry, 60,* 717–755.

Hinnebush, A. G. (1996). Translational control of GCN4: Gene specific regulation by phosphorylation of eIF2. In J. W. B. Hershey, M. B. Mathews, & N. Sonenberg (Eds.), *Translational control* (pp. 199–244). Cold Spring Harbor, NY: Cold Springs Harbor Laboratory Press.

Hirashima, A., & Kaji, A. (1970). Factor dependent breakdown of polysomes. *Biochemistry and Biophysics Research Communications, 41,* 877–883.

Hirashima, A., & Kaji, A. (1972). Purification and properties of ribosome-releasing factor. *Biochemistry, 11,* 4037–4044.

Hirashima, A., & Kaji, A. (1973). Role of elongation factor G and a protein factor on the release of ribosomes from messenger ribonucleic acid. *Journal of Biological Chemistry, 248,* 7580–7587.

Hui, A., & De Boer, H. A. (1987). Specialized ribosome system: Preferential translation of a single mRNA species by a subpopulation of mutated ribosomes in *Escherichia coli*. *Proceedings of the National Academy of Sciences, U.S.A., 84,* 4762–4766.

Jackson, R. J., & Kaminski, A. (1995). Internal initiation of translation in eukaryotes: The picornavirus paradigm and beyond. *RNA, 1,* 985–1000.

Jackson, R. J., & Wickens, M. (1997). Translational controls impinging on the 5′-untranslated region and initiation factor proteins. *Current Opinion in Genetic Development, 7,* 233–241.

Jacob, W. F., Santer, M., & Dahlberg, A. E. (1987). A single base change in the Shine-Dalgarno region of 16S rRNA of *Escherichia coli* affects translation of many proteins. *Proceedings of the National Academy of Sciences, U.S.A., 84,* 4757–4761.

Janosi, L., Hara, H., Zhang, S., & Kaji, A. (1996). Ribosome recycling by ribosome recycling factor (RRF): An important but overlooked step of protein biosynthesis. *Advances in Biophysics, 32,* 121–201.

Janosi, L., Mottagui-Tabar, S., Isaksson, L. A., Sekine, Y., Ohtsubo, E., Zhang, S., Goon, S., Nelken, S., Shuda, M., & Kaji, A. (1998). Evidence for *in vivo* ribosome recycling, the fourth step in protein biosynthesis. *EMBO Journal, 17,* 1141–1151.

Janosi, L., Ricker, R., & Kaji, A. (1996). Dual functions of ribosome recycling factor in protein biosynthesis: Disassembling the termination complex and preventing translational errors. *Biochimie, 78,* 959–969.

Janosi, L., Shimizu, I., & Kaji, A. (1994). Ribosome recycling factor (ribosome releasing factor) is essential for bacterial growth.

Proceedings of the National Academy of Sciences, U.S.A., 91, 4249–4253.

Jean-Jean, O., Le Goff, X., & Philippe, M. (1996). Is there a human [psi]? *Comptes Rendus de l'Academie des Sciences, 319,* 487–492.

Kaji, A., & Hirokawa, G. (1999). *The ribosome: Structure, function antibiotics and cellular interactions: Disassembly of post termination complex by RRF (ribosome recycling factor), a possible new target for antimicrobial agents.* Washington, DC: American Society of Microbiology.

Kaji, A., Teyssier, E., & Hirokawa, G. (1998). Disassembly of the post-termination complex and reduction of translational error by ribosome recycling factor (RRF): A possible new target for antibacterial agents. *Biochemical and Biophysical Research Communications, 250,* 1–4.

Kanai, T., Takeshita, S., Atomi, H., Umemura, K., Ueda, M., & Tanaka, A. (1998). A regulatory factor, Fe1lp, involved in depression of the isocitrate lyase gene in *Saccharomyces cerevisiae:* A possible mitochondrial protein necessary for protein synthesis in mitochondria. *European Journal of Biochemistry, 256,* 212–220.

Kozak, M. (1978). How do eukaryotic ribosomes select initiation regions in messenger RNA? *Cell, 15,* 1109–1123.

Kozak, M. (1989). Context effects and inefficient initiation at non-AUG codons in eucaryotic cell-free translation systems. *Molecular and Cellular Biology, 9,* 5073–5080.

Kozak, M. (1994). Determinants of translational fidelity and efficiency in vertebrate mRNAs. *Biochimie, 76,* 815–821.

Krab, I. M., & Parmeggiani, A. (1998). EF-Tu, a GTPase odyssey. *Biochimica et Biophysica Acta, 1443,* 1–22.

Kushnirov, V. V., Ter-Avanesyan, M. D., Telckov, M. V., Surguchov, A. P., Smirnov, V. N., & Inge-Vechtomov, S. G. (1988). Nucleotide sequence of the *SUP2 (SUP35)* gene of *Saccharomyces cerevisiae. Gene, 66,* 45–54.

Lamphear, B. J., Kirchweger, R., Skern, T., & Rhoads, R. E. (1995). Mapping of functional domains in eukaryotic protein synthesis initiation factor 4G (eIF4G) with picornaviral proteases: Implications for cap-dependent and cap-independent translational initiation. *Journal of Biological Chemistry, 270,* 21975–21983.

Lawson, T. G., Lee, K. A., Maimone, M. M., Abramson, R. D., Dever, T. E., Merrick, W. C., & Thach, R. E. (1989). Dissociation of double-stranded polynucleotide helical structures by eukaryotic initiation factors, as revealed by a novel assay. *Biochemistry, 28,* 4729–4734.

Maden, B. E. H., Traut, R. R., & Monro, R. E. (1968). Ribosome-catalysed peptidyl transfer: The plophenylalanine system. *Journal of Molecular Biology, 35,* 333–345.

Mader, S., Lee, H., Pause, A., & Sonenberg, N. (1995). The translation initiation factor eIF-4E binds to a common motif shared by the translation factor eIF-4 gamma and the translational repressors 4E-binding proteins. *Molecular and Cellular Biology, 15,* 4990–4997.

McCutcheon, J. P., Agrawal, R. K., Philips, S. M., Grassucci, R. A., Gerchman, S. E., Clemons, W. M., Jr., Ramakrishnan, V., & Frank, J. (1999). Location of translational initiation factor IF3 on the small ribosomal subunit. *Proceedings of the National Academy of Sciences, U.S.A., 96,* 4301–4306.

Merrick, W. (1992). Mechanism and regulation of eukaryotic protein synthesis. *Microbiology Review, 56,* 291–315.

Merrick, W. C., & Hershey, J. W. B. (1996). The pathway and mechanism of eukaryotic protein synthesis. In J. W. B. Hershey, M. B. Mathews, & N. Sonenberg (Eds.), *Translational Control* (pp. 31–69). Cold Spring Harbor, NY: Cold Spring Harbor Laboratory Press.

Moazed, D., & Noller, H. F. (1989). Intermediate states in the movement of transfer RNA in the ribosome. *Nature, 342,* 142–148.

Moazed, D., Samaha, R. R., Gualerzi, C., & Noller, H. F. (1995). Specific protection of 16S rRNA by translational initiation factors. *Journal of Molecular Biology, 248,* 207–210.

Moffat, J. G., & Tate, W. P. (1994). A single proteolytic cleavage in release factor 2 stabilizes ribosome binding and abolishes peptidyl-tRNA hydrolysis activity. *Journal of Biological Chemistry, 269,* 18899–18903.

Moore, P. B. (1997). Ribosomes: Protein synthesis in slow motion. *Current Biology, 7,* R179–R181.

Moore, P. B. (1998). The three-dimensional structure of the ribosome and its components. *Annual Review of Biophysics and Biomolecular Structure, 27,* 35–58.

Naranda, T., MacMillan, S. E., & Donahue, T. F., & Hershey, J. W. (1996). SUI1/p16 is required for the activity of eukaryotic translation initiation Factor 3 in *Saccharomyces cerevisiae. Molecular and Cellular Biology, 16,* 2307–2313.

Nierhaus, K. H. (1990). The allosteric three-site model for the ribosomal elongation cycle: Features and future. *Biochemistry, 29,* 4997–5008.

Nierhaus, K. H., Stuhrmann, H. B., & Svergun, D. (1998). The ribosomal elongation cycle and movement of tRNAs across the ribosome. *Progress in Nucleic Acids Research and Molecular Biology, 59,* 177–204.

Nissen, P., Kjeldgaard, M., Thirup, S., Polekhina, G., Reshetnikova, L., Clark, B. F. C., & Nyborg, J. (1995). Crystal structure of the ternary complex of Phe-tRNA^{Phe}, EF-Tu and a GTP analog. *Science, 270,* 1464–1472.

Nyborg, J., & Liljas, A. (1998). Protein biosynthesis: Structural studies of the elongation cycle. *FEBS Letters, 430,* 95–99.

Pain, V. M. (1996). Initiation of protein synthesis in eukaryotic cells. *European Journal of Biochemistry, 236,* 747–771.

Pape, T., Wintermeyer, W., & Rodnina, M. V. (1998). Complete kinetic mechanism of elongation factor Tu-dependent binding of aminoacyl-tRNA to the A-site of the *E. coli* ribosome. *EMBO Journal, 17,* 7490–7497.

Patino, M. M., Liu, J. J., Glover, J. R., & Lindquist, S. (1996). Support for the prion hypothesis for inheritance of a phenotypic trait in yeast. *Science, 273,* 622–626.

Paushkin, S. V., Kushnirov, V. V., Smirnov, V. N., & Ter-Avanesyan, M. D. (1996). Propagation of the yeast prion-like [psi(+)] determinant is mediated by oligomerization of the *SUP35*-encoded polypeptide chain release factor. *EMBO Journal, 15,* 3127–3134.

Pestova, T. V., Borukhov, S. I., & Hellen, C. U. (1998). Eukaryotic ribosomes require initiation factors 1 and 1A to locate initiation codons. *Nature, 394,* 854–859.

Pestova, T. V., Shatsky, I. N., Fletcher, S. P., Jackson, R. J., & Hellen, C. U. (1998). A prokaryotic-like mode of cytoplasmic eukaryotic ribosome binding to the initiation codon during internal translation initiation of hepatitis C and classical swine fever virus RNAs. *Genes and Development, 12,* 67–83.

Petersen, H. U., Roll, T., Grunberg-Manago, M., & Clark, B. F. (1979). Specific interaction of initiation factor IF2 of *E. coli* with formylmethionyl-tRNA f Met. *Biochemical and Biophysical Research Communications, 91,* 1068–1074.

RajBhandary, U. L., & Chow, C. M. (1995). Initiator tRNAs and initiation of protein synthesis. In *tRNA: Structure, biosynthesis and function* (pp. 511–527). Soll, D. & RajBhandary, U. (eds.). Washington, DC: American Society of Microbiology.

Rodnina, M. V., Fricke, R., Kuhn, L., & Wintermeyer, W. (1995). Codon-dependent conformational change of elongation factor TU preceding GTP hydrolysis on the ribosome. *EMBO Journal, 14,* 2613–2619.

Rodnina, M. V., Pape, T., Fricke, R., Kuhn, L., & Wintermeyer, W. (1996). Initial binding of the elongation factor Tu·GTP·aminoacyl-tRNA complex preceding codon recognition on the ribosome. *Journal of Biological Chemistry, 271,* 646–652.

Rodnina, M. V., Pape, T., Fricke, R., & Wintermeyer, W. (1995). Elongation factor Tu, a GTPase triggered by codon recognition on the ribosome: Mechanism and GTP consumption. *Biochemistry & Cell Biology, 73,* 1221–1227.

Rolland, N., Janosi, L., Block, M. A., Shuda, A., Teyssier, E., Miege, C., Cheniclet, C., Carde, J. -P., Kaji, A., & Joyard, J. (1999). Plant ribosome recycling factor homologue is a chloroplastic protein and is bactericidal in *Escherichia coli* carrying temperature-sensitive ribosome recycling factor. *Proceedings of the National Academy of Sciences, U.S.A., 96,* 5464–5469.

Rozen, F., Edery, I., Meerovitch, K., Dever, T. E., Merrick, W. C., & Sonenberg, N. (1990). Bidirectional RNA helicase activity of eukaryotic translation initiation factors 4A and 4F. *Molecular and Cellular Biology, 10,* 1134–1144.

Ryoji, M., Berland, R., & Kaji, A. (1981). Reinitiation of translation from the triplet next to the amber termination codon in the absence of ribosome-releasing factor. *Proceedings of the National Academy of Sciences, U.S.A., 78,* 5973–5977.

Schilling-Bartetzko, S., Bartetzko, A., & Nierhaus, K. H. (1992). Kinetic and thermodynamic parameters for tRNA binding to the ribosome and for the translocation reaction. *Journal of Biological Chemistry, 267,* 4703–4712.

Scolnick, E., Tompkins, R., Caskey, T., & Nirenberg, M. (1968). Release factors differing in specificity for terminator codons. *Proceedings of the National Academy of Sciences, U.S.A., 61,* 768–774.

Spahn, C. M. T., & Nierhaus, K. H. (1998). Models of the elongation cycle: An evaluation. *Biological Chemistry, 379,* 753–772.

Sprengart, M. L., & Porter, A. G. (1997). Functional importance of RNA interactions in selection of translation initiation codons. *Molecular Microbiology, 24,* 19–28.

Stansfield, I., & Tuite, M. F. (1994). Polypeptide chain termination in *Saccharomyces cerevisiae. Current Genetics, 25,* 385–395.

Stansfield, I., Jones, K. M., Kushnirov, V. V., Dagkesamanskaya, A. R., Poznyakovski, A. I., Paushkin, S. V., Nierras, C. R., Cox, B. S., Ter-Avanesyan, M. D., & Tuite, M. F. (1995). The products of the *SUP45* (eRF1) and *SUP35* genes interact to mediate translation termination in *Saccharomyces cerevisiae. EMBO Journal, 14,* 4365–4373.

Stark, H., Rodnina, M. V., Rinke-Appel, J., Brimacombe, R., Wintermeyer, W., & van Heel, M. (1997). Visualization of elongation factor Tu on the *Escherichia coli* ribosome. *Nature, 389,* 403–406.

Ter-Avanesyan, M. D., Kushnirov, V. V., Dagkesamanskaya, A. R., Didichenko, S. A., Chernoff, Y. O., Inge-Vechtomov, S. G., & Smirnov, V. N. (1993). Deletion analysis of the *SUP35* gene of the yeast *Saccharomyces cerevisiae* reveals two nonoverlapping functional regions in the encoded protein. *Molecular Microbiology, 7,* 683–692.

Triana-Alonso, F. J., Chakraburtty, K., & Nierhaus, K. H. (1995). The elongation factor 3 unique in higher fungi and essential for protein biosynthesis is an E-site factor. *Journal of Biological Chemistry, 270,* 20473–20478.

Wadzack, J., Burkhardt, N., Junemann, R., Diedrich, G., Nierhaus, K. H., Frank, J., Penczek, P., Meerwinck, W., Schmitt, M., Willumeit, R., & Stuhrmann, H. B. (1997). Direct localization of the tRNAs within the elongating ribosome by means of neutron scattering (proton-spin contrast-variation). *Journal of Molecular Biology, 266,* 343–356.

Wakao, H., Romby, P., Westhof, E., Laalami, S., Grunberg-Manago, M., Ebel, J. P., Ehresmann, C., & Ehresmann, B. (1989). The solution structure of the *Escherichia coli* initiator tRNA and its interactions with initiation factor 2 and the ribosomal 30S subunit. *Journal of Biological Chemistry, 264,* 20363–20371.

Wickner, R. B. (1994). [URE3] as an altered Ure2 protein: Evidence for a prion analog in *Saccharomyces cerevisiae. Science, 264,* 566–569.

Wilson, K. S., & Noller, H. F. (1998). Molecular movement inside the translational engine. *Cell, 92,* 337–349.

Wool, I. G., Chan, Y.-L., & Gluck, A. (1996). Mammalian ribosomes: The structure and the evolution of the proteins. In J. W. B. Hershey, M. B. Mathews, & N. Sonenberg (Eds.),

Translational control (pp. 685–711). Cold Spring Harbor: Cold Spring Harbor Laboratory Press.

Wu, X. Q., Iyengar, P., & RajBhandary, U. L. (1996). Ribosome-initiator tRNA complex as an intermediate in translation initiation in *Escherichia coli* revealed by use of mutant initiator tRNAs and specialized ribosomes. *EMBO Journal, 15,* 4734–4739.

Wu, X. Q., & RajBhandary, U. L. (1997). Effect of the amino acid attached to *Escherichia coli* initiator tRNA on its affinity for the initiation factor IF2 and on the IF2 dependence of its binding to the ribosome. *Journal of Biological Chemistry, 272,* 1891–1895.

Yonath, A., & Franceschi, F. (1998). Functional universality and evolutionary diversity: Insights from the structure of the ribosome. *Structure, 6,* 679–684.

Zhang, Y., & Spremulli, L. L. (1998). Identification and cloning of human mitochondrial translational release factor 1 and the ribosome recycling factor. *Biochimica Et Biophysica Acta, 1443,* 245–250.

A. KAJI
L. JANOSI
Exponential Biotherapies, Inc.
ljanosi.e6i@erols.com

RIGIDITY

Although the term "rigidity" has no precise definition, one offered by Chown (1959) in a review article, "Rigidity—A flexible concept," comes closest to a working definition. Chown stated that rigidity "has been used to describe behaviors characterized by the inability to change habits, sets, attitudes, and discriminations." Moreover, it can be said that rigidity is especially apparent when a person's behavior fails to change even when the demands of new situations require different behaviors.

Many terms in psychology refer to rigidity, including "perseveration," "conservatism," "dogmatism," "anality," "intolerance of ambiguity," and "compulsiveness." Terms such as "flexibility," "lability," "tolerance of ambiguity," and, to some degree, "creativity," have served as labels for tendencies contrasted with rigidity. As Chown stated, these terms have been used rather loosely. Therefore, it is highly unlikely that rigidity is a single psychological construct or personality factor. It is, however, valuable to examine some specific subtypes of rigidity in order to seek some common relationships among them.

RIGIDITY AS PERSEVERATION

In *The Abilities of Man,* Spearman (1927/1970) presented a "law of inertia" that stated that cognitive processes are slow both to start and to finish, and then questioned whether there could be individual differences in inertia. Along these lines, Cattell (1935) isolated two factors of trait rigidity—one labeled "inertia," in which the person is unable to switch between two well-established skills, and the other labeled "dispositional rigidity," which refers to the inability to apply an old skill to a new but different situation.

In his studies of neurological patients, Goldstein (1934/1959) noted that it was common to see patients who were unable to shift from one task to another. In addition, when faced with difficult tasks involving abstract thought, some patients would blurt out immediate but incorrect answers. In the 1940s, Goldstein and Scheerer (1941) developed a test battery that contained a variety of sorting and classification tasks. They found that brain-damaged individuals could often sort a group of objects according to one classification scheme (e.g., by color) but would be unable to shift to another scheme (e.g., by shape).

Goldstein believed that, under ordinary circumstances, the healthy person functions as a whole system with well-integrated and articulated subsystems. However, in brain damage, the integrity of the system is destroyed and the person is unable to handle the complexity required by abstract problems. Goldstein stated that the rigid, concrete behavior shown by brain-damaged patients was not a simple deficit, but rather was an attempt to reduce complexity and to make a potentially overwhelming situation more manageable. Thus, Goldstein was able to link perseveration, brain injury, and concreteness into one pattern (Goldstein & Scheerer, 1941).

Laboratory studies conducted by Luchins (1942) and Maltzman and Morrisett (1953) indicated that when subjects were repeatedly presented with a problem-solving task that, at first, had a fixed solution formula, they often rigidly continued to use the same solution formula for subsequent problems, even though these new tasks could be solved in a variety of ways. Although these authors attributed rigidity to task variables, other researchers were inspired to find individual differences in problem-solving perseveration by using these tasks and attempting to find correlations with measures of other ability and personality traits.

INTOLERANCE OF AMBIGUITY

A number of researchers and theoreticians, including Adorno, Frenkel-Brunswick, and Levinson (1950), Rokeach (1960), Fromm (1941/1965), Shapiro (1965, 1981, 1994), Breskin (1968), Primavera and Higgins (1973), and Gorman and Breskin (1969) have noted a fairly consistent constellation of traits that includes strict obedience to authority figures, intolerance of opposing opinions, prejudice, a tendency to construct an oversimplified view of the world, a tendency to employ sharply polarized, black and white cognitive constructs, and a cynical view of human nature. Numerous studies have indicated that this constellation is not limited to rigid social and political beliefs alone, but extends to many laboratory tasks as well.

The development of such authoritarian and dogmatic personality patterns has been attributed to socialization practices that include blind, unquestioning obedience to parents and other authority figures, and discipline practices that emphasize power and coercion, rather than reasoning, induction, and explanations of personal moral choices. Therefore, the rigid person has been constantly exposed to situations in which they are told that there are absolute rules to be followed and that deviations from such rules will be met with severe punishment.

Discussions of rigid, authoritarian, and dogmatic belief systems have been extended to psychopathology. Clinically, highly dogmatic and rigid behaviors can be observed in obsessive-compulsive and paranoid patients. Such patients' thoughts and actions are replete with examples of logical contradictions, rigid and overselective constructions of situations, and complaints of being driven to perform certain actions.

In *Neurotic Styles* (1965) and *Autonomy and Rigid Character* (1981), Shapiro explored a paradox in these disorders: namely, that although patients claim to be rigidly following and driven by principles seen as alien to their selves, they consciously plan and execute behaviors instrumental in supporting these beliefs. Shapiro reconciled this paradox by noting that the mandated "shoulds" and "oughts" are the beliefs of important authority figures. Although the rigid person does not desire to carry out these demands, he or she feels powerless to disobey them. For example, an obsessive patient may know that it is useless to worry, but also believes that to display conscientiousness to others is the proper thing to do. Thus, the person is placed in a conflict between beliefs about his or her own lack of personal efficiency and the presumed power of others over the self.

AN INTEGRATION OF APPROACHES

How can observations that rigid people display perseveration, concreteness, intolerance of ambiguity, and avowals of authority-centered beliefs be subsumed under a single term? Perhaps an explanation may be found using Jean Piaget's theory of cognitive development.

Throughout his many writings, Piaget showed how new cognitive schemes develop through the clash of two opposite adaptive tendencies: assimilation (the tendency to fit new knowledge into existing schemes) and accommodation (the tendency to modify behavior according to the demands of the situation). Either tendency alone could be properly considered to be rigidity. However, through situations in which assimilation is checked by accommodation, and vice versa, new and more flexible equilibrated schemes are formed (Piaget, 1968).

Piaget showed how early thought is characterized by overassimilation and overaccommodation, and cogently demonstrated that young children and retarded adults employ one-dimensional, rigid, centered cognitive strategies in comparison with the multidimensional, flexible, decentered strategies employed by older children and normal adults. According to Piaget, affective and moral development is inseparable from cognitive development. Therefore, the rigid behaviors found in intellectual tasks have their parallels in the lack of autonomy, the perseveration, and the rigid constructions of personal and interpersonal values found in social behaviors.

It may be that rigidity, in both the intellectual and affective domains, is a manifestation of unbalanced schemes in which either accommodation or assimilation predominates. As many factors, including cognitive immaturity, neurological damage, and authority-oriented child-rearing practices, may hinder the development of adequately equilibrated schemes, rigidity may stem from many different roots.

REFERENCES

Adorno, T. W., Frenkel-Brunswik, E., Levinson, D. J., & Sanford R. N. (1950). *The authoritarian personality.* New York: Harpers.

Breskin, S. (1968). Measurement of rigidity: A non-verbal test. *Perceptual & Motor Skills, 27,* 1203–1206.

Chown, S. M. (1959). Rigidity—A flexible construct. *Psychological Bulletin, 56,* 195–233.

Cattell, R. B. (1935). On the measurement of perseveration. *British Journal of Educational Psychology, 5,* 76–92.

Fromm, E. (1965). *Escape from freedom.* New York: Avon Books. (Original work published 1941)

Goldstein, K. (1959). *The organism: A holistic approach to biology derived from psychological data in man.* New York: American Book. (Original work published 1934)

Goldstein, K., & Scheerer, M. (1941). Abstract and concrete behavior: An experimental study with special tests. *Psychological Monographs, 53* (239).

Gorman, B. S., & Breskin, S. (1969). Non-verbal rigidity, creativity, and problem solving. *Perceptual & Motor Skills, 29,* 715–718.

Luchins, A. S. (1942). Mechanization in problem solving: The effect of *Einstellung. Psychological Monographs, 54* (48).

Maltzman, I., & Morrisett, L., Jr. (1953). Different strengths of set in the solution of anagrams. *Journal of Experimental Psychology, 45,* 351–354.

Piaget, J. (1968). *Six psychological studies.* New York: Vintage.

Piaget, J. (1981). *Intelligence and affectivity: Their relationship during child development.* Palo Alto, CA: Annual Reviews. (Original work published 1953)

Primavera, L. H., & Higgins, M. (1973). Nonverbal rigidity and its relationship to dogmatism and Machiavellianism. *Perceptual & Motor Skills, 36,* 356–358.

Rokeach, M. (1960). *The open and closed mind.* New York: Basic Books.

Shapiro, D. (1965). *Neurotic styles.* New York: Basic Books.

Shapiro, D. (1981). *Autonomy and rigid character.* New York: Basic Books.

Spearman, C. E. (1970). *The abilities of man: Their nature and measurement.* New York: AMS Press. (Original work published 1927)

SUGGESTED READING

Lewin, K. (1935) *A dynamic theory of personality: Selected papers of Kurt Lewin.* New York: McGraw-Hill.

B. S. GORMAN
Nassau Community College

AUTISM
LEARNED HELPLESSNESS
OBSESSIVE-CONVULSIVE PERSONALITY
PERSONALITY DISORDERS

RITUAL BEHAVIOR

Ritual is a conventionalized joint activity that is given to ceremony, involves two or more persons, is endowed with special emotion and often sacred meaning, is focused around a clearly defined set of social objects, and when performed, confers upon its participants a special sense of the sacred and the out-of-the-ordinary (Denzin, 1974, p. 272). When a ritual is performed, ritual participants through their actions convey their respect to themselves to "some object of ultimate value . . . or to its stand-in" (Goffman, 1971, p. 62). A ritual consists of interrelated activities and acts, termed "rites," and is performed within sacred or special interactional situations, termed "ritual settings." Ritual performances legitimitize the selves of the ritual performers and solidify their standing within a social relationship's or a social order's hierarchy of morality. Ritual may grow out of any sector of group life, including sexual, economic, political, religious, legal, and interpersonal arenas of discourse and interaction (Douglas, 1975, pp. 60–61). Rituals permit few variations and are subject to the pressures of interactional normalization. They have the features of drama and involve the reenactment of cultural and world views held to be salient and central by human groups (Geertz, 1973; Harrison, 1912). Modifying Bateson (1972) slightly, one may say that "ritual" is the name of a frame for action, and within the frame of ritual, individuals act ritualistically.

Durkheim (1912) divided ritual into two categories: positive and negative, or sacred and profane. Positive rituals bring interactants together in ways that support their social relationship and permit offerings of various kinds, including the giving of gifts and greetings (Goffman, 1971). Negative or avoidance rituals, commonly termed taboos, protect the individuals and their properties from the intrusions of others.

Religious rituals, in contrast to interpersonal rituals, are the rules of conduct that prescribe how a person should comport him- or herself "in the presence of . . . sacred objects" (Durkheim, 1912, p. 41). Interpersonal rituals are "brief rituals one individual performs for and to another, attesting to civility and good will on the performer's part and to the recipient's possession of a small patrimony of sacredness" (Goffman, 1971, p. 63). According to many observers, including Goffman, interpersonal rituals have replaced sacred rituals in contemporary western societies. A confusion over interpersonal, religious, and cultural rituals characterizes many of the developing nations of the world today (Geertz, 1973).

Rituals may be performed, as Malinowski (1913), Radcliffe-Brown (1922), Frazer (1890), Smith (1889), Durkheim (1912), Levi-Strauss (1962), van Gennep (1909), and Warner (1962) have argued, for purely magical, mystical, or religious reasons; so as to mark or gain some control over the uncontrollable, often occur-

rences in the natural world; transgressions of the group's moral code; or the existential certainties of birth, death, and the life cycle transitions from status position to status position within the group's social structure (e.g., child to adult, male to husband and father, female to wife and mother, etc.). Rituals are also enacted for the emotional effects the performance bestows upon individuals. Participation may be voluntary or obligatory, large or small in numbers of participants, and negative or positive in tone, and often will be connected to sacred (religious) and secular (political and interpersonal) calendars (Warner, 1962).

Ritual performances require the organization and focusing of ritual acts around stand-in objects whose presence is required for the ritual to be accomplished. These objects include, at a minimum, actors (performers and audiences), settings or stages for the ritual performance, a class of previously selected objects to be acted on during the occasion of ritual display, and a script, or prearranged interactional text, that will be followed, spoken, and enacted. Stand-in objects may include wedding rings, hymns, music, food, drink, and talk. The meanings of the ritual derive from the actions that persons direct toward these stand-in objects and toward themselves.

Serial ritual display characterizes ritual performances. In no sense can a ritual be accomplished all at once—it must proceed through phases, which are scheduled, interconnected, and made up of sequences of small ritual acts or rites. Ritual meals (Douglas, 1975) display this feature of serial ritual display. The social organization of ritual activities, in terms of serial ritual display, reveals the underlying power and control hierarchies in a group's social structure (Leach, 1968).

SOCIAL RELATIONSHIPS AND RITUAL

Social anthropologists, sociologists, and social psychologists "claim that their special field is the study of social relationships" (Leach, 1968, p. 524). While social relationships cannot be studied directly, the interactions that occur between individuals can be, and to the extent that these interactions are ritualized and conventionalized, ritual becomes a principal means for studying social relationships. Goffman's (1971) analysis of supportive and remedial interchanges, rituals of ratification, access, and departure in interpersonal rituals suggests that rituals serve to separate and join persons simultaneously. Greetings, for instance, maintain distance between persons, while joining them, if only momentarily, in a shared interactional exchange.

Perhaps more important than this joining and separating feature of rituals in social relationships is the fact that they have meaning only within the context of social relationships. That is, in social relationships, persons find and confirm their identities, and in these relationships, they join their actions to the ongoing fabric of the social life of their group. Rituals become one of several avenues (others include routines and problematic acts) for bridging the gap between persons and the social order, and provide a salient bond for connecting persons to one another.

At a deeper relational level, it can be argued that persons are connected to their societies through ritual ties. Thus ceremonies such as the coronation of the queen in England are seen by Shils and Young (1953) as instances of national communion in which ordinary, everyday individuals are drawn together into the moral fabric of their society. The queen and her coronation ritually embody all that being English entails and means. Participation in the ritual by members of the audience symbolically accomplishes a joining of the person with the society. It is a paradox that the rituals that stand nearest to the core of a society (coronations, inaugurations, etc.) are most typically at the society's most distant, peripheral interpersonal edges. Thus, core interpersonal rituals of the person and the group often stand in contradistinction to the core, sacred values and rituals of society at large (Shils, 1976).

RITUAL AS INTERACTION

Ritual must be understood as interaction, and not in static, strictly structural terms. While rituals do, in the abstract, stand outside and above persons, their lived meaning resides in the world of face-to-face interaction wherein they are acted on, defined, produced, and interpreted. When a number of persons join hands around a table and begin reciting the Lord's Prayer in unison, they are interactionally, collectively, and conjointly engaging in a shared ritual activity. With eyes closed, left hand clasping the extended right hand of the person to the left, right hand clasping the left hand of the person to the right, they, individually and interactionally, join and offer their presence to the collective presence of the group. Their voices are embodiments of their physical presence and participation in the ritual. Each individual is a part of the ritual, just as the ritual becomes a part of each person. The interactional accomplishment of a ritual requires individual and collective participation; but most importantly, it requires interaction. Ritual, then, is symbolic interaction, and should be studied as such (see Blumer, 1969).

ALTERNATIVE VIEWS OF RITUAL

The foregoing suggests that the meaning of ritual lies in interaction, not in rituals per se or in abstract structures. There are, however, alternative ways of formulating ritual. Rituals may be studied semiotically and structurally, in terms of the binary oppositions that constitute the inner or primary text of the ritual (Barthes, 1967; Levi-Strauss, 1962, 1963). Thus, paired oppositions within rituals and myths (male-female, life-death, near-far, old-young, etc.) may be examined and fitted together within a structural totality.

Rituals may be studied dramaturgically and their symbolic and cultural contents may be given special attention. Rituals may be studied in terms of the power they are intended to produce, just as they may be conceptualized as beliefs in illusion or in myth, magic, or religion. However, when ritual action transforms people's relationships to themselves, to others, and to their environment, more than the belief in an illusion is involved. Rituals and the actions they entail are real and consequential in their interactional implications, especially when the meanings of the ritual carry over into other sectors of the group's and the individuals' lives.

CONCLUSIONS

The import of ritual in everyday life may be summarized in terms of the following three assertions:

1. That which a group takes to be problematic will be subjected to pressures to make those problematic objects, acts, and events predictable and routine. This is necessary if orderly actions are to be taken toward them.

2. Groups and relationships display constant negotiated struggles over what is problematic, routine, and predictable.

3. At the heart of organized group life lies a complex network of rituals—interpersonal, positive, negative, sacred, and secular—that are communicated to newcomers to the group and that, when taught and successfully performed, lead to systematic ways of making everyday group life predictable, ordinary, and taken for granted.

An understanding of the everyday, taken-for-granted features of group life requires the systematic study of ritual. The understanding of how persons are connected to others and to the society at large demands similar study. Rituals stand at the intersection of the individual and society and require detailed examination by the disciplines of social anthropology, sociology, social psychology, psychology, religion, and philosophy. Indeed, Rosaldo (1993) suggests that ritual is best viewed as a busy intersection, as a place where a number of distinct and important cultural processes intersect. The notion of ritual as a busy intersection anticipates the more contemporary view of culture as a complex, ongoing process. In this view culture is not a self-contained whole made up of coherent, stable, unchanging patterns and rituals (Rosaldo, 1993).

REFERENCES

Bateson, G. (1972). *Steps to an ecology of mind.* New York: Ballantine.

Durkheim, E. (1912). *The elementary forms of religious life.* London: Allen & Unwin.

Goffman, E. (1971). *Relations in public.* New York: Basic Books.

N. K. DENZIN
University of Illinois

COMMUNICATION PROCESS
CONFORMITY
CROSS-CULTURAL PSYCHOLOGY

ROGERS, CARL RANSOM (1902–1987)

As Carl Ransom Rogers pointed out, both hard work and a commitment to Protestant Christianity were equally stressed in his youth. Certainly, both are implicit in his theories. He received the BA degree from the University of Wisconsin and then attended the Union Theological Seminary in New York City. He received the PhD in 1931 from Teacher's College of Columbia University. He began his career at the Institute for Child Guidance there and later accepted a position in the child study department of the Society for the Prevention of Cruelty to Children in Rochester, New York, where he soon became the director. In 1939 he accepted a post at the Rochester Guidance Center. The following year he moved to Ohio State University, where he began to develop a new system of psychotherapy known first as nondirective, then client-centered, and more recently, person-centered therapy. It began to gain attention with the publication of his first book, *Counseling and Psychotherapy.* Some considered it to be an affront to Freudian psychoanalysis, because interpretations were not given. In 1945, he went to the University of Chicago serving as executive of their counseling center. After Chicago, he returned to his alma mater, Wisconsin, as professor. During the next decade he published *Client-Centered Therapy* and probably his most popular book, *On Becoming a Person.*

In the therapeutic process, the individual (designated as a client not a patient) enters with the therapist into a relationship in which the client becomes increasingly aware of his or her own feelings and experiences. In the process, the therapist reflects the feelings of the client. Their relationship becomes warm and friendly. The therapist may never make any critical or punishing statement.

Rogers also became renowned for helping to develop the prevailing trend of humanistic psychology, following in the footsteps of Abraham Maslow. The theory gradually evolved stressing the final inherent goal of self-actualization. In Rogers's therapy, the client, not the therapist decides each move. Everyone, of course, does not reach self-actualization. Furthermore, he believed the technique could be applied to other areas outside psychology such as pastoral counseling, teaching, and nursing. In his last fifteen years Rogers applied his methods to training policymakers, leaders, and groups in conflict.

His theories were very much at odds with the behaviorist B. F. Skinner. Rogers was concerned with inner feelings and experiences, whereas Skinner emphasized only external behavior. On several occasions the two engaged in friendly debates at various universities. Neither ever won, as the listener has the distinct impression that the two really were not communicating.

Even when Rogers was in his 80s, he was active at the Center for the Study of the Person at La Jolla, of which he had been a cofounder. His many distinctions included the presidency of the American Psychological Association and the Distinguished Contribution Award of the same organization.

R. W. LUNDIN
Wheaton, Illinois

ROKEACH, MILTON (1918–1988)

What people believe, why they believe, and what difference it makes are the recurring themes that have preoccupied Milton Rokeach in his research career. His earliest work in the late 1940s moved away from conceptualizations about rightist forms of au-

thoritarianism and intolerance to more general formulations: the study of ideology and cognitive functioning, the organization and measurement of belief systems and ideological dogmatism, the effects of race versus belief as determinants of racial and ethnic discrimination. These investigations were followed by detailed accounts of the closed belief systems of three paranoid schizophrenics claiming to be Christ, and by observations of the cognitive and behavioral effects of confrontations among them over the issue of identity.

A decade of continuing focus on belief systems led him back to the classical issue of social attitudes and their relation to behavior, the effects of attitude change on behavioral change, and theories of cognitive interaction. His work in the 1970s moved from a concern with the nature of attitudes to the nature of human values, their measurement, their distribution, and their changes within U.S. society, as well as their functional relation to attitudes and behavior, the conditions under which they will undergo change, and the effects of long-term value change on attitude and behavioral change. In demonstrating such long-term effects—in the laboratory, in the classroom, and, most recently, through television in the natural context—Rokeach has provided a theory of cognitive and behavioral change.

His work in the 1980s moved beyond earlier formulations of G. W. Allport to the view that there are really three central concepts in social psychology—the self, values, and attitudes—in that order of importance, and to the view that theories of cognitive change in social psychology must become reunified with theories of cognitive stability, thus overcoming the present compartmentalization of the fields of personality and social psychology.

STAFF

ROLE PLAYING

Although terminology in the area of role analysis (role theory) is nonstandardized, *role playing* most often refers to enactment; what individuals say and do insofar as such behaviors are expected and evaluated by others qualifies as role enactment, as opposed to the process of *role taking* where an individual imaginatively constructs the role of self or other so as to provide directives for ongoing behavior. Walter Coutu in Roleplaying vs. Roletaking clearly distinguished these concepts and further distinguished between two different types of enactment, employing the term *role playing* to refer to enactments of roles in which an individual is the true incumbent, and the term *playing at a role* to refer to enactments of roles only temporarily assigned to an individual, as in children's play or on the legitimate theater stage. An actor playing the role of Brutus in Shakespeare's *Julius Caesar* simultaneously enacts his real-life occupational role—in this case, that of actor—while enacting Brutus's role onstage as written and directed. This distinction may be observed in subsequent critical reviews of the performance when some comments are directed to the skill with which the actor performed, while other comments are directed to the issue of the manner in which Brutus's part was intimately interwoven with that of Mark Antony.

Moreno and Zeleny (1958) summarize the role drama (psychodrama, sociodrama, axiodrama) as introduced and developed by Moreno; although his interests were largely in the growth and development of the human personality, much has also been done in the area of personality assessment as exemplified by the U.S. Office of Strategic Services Assessment Staff's *Assessment of Men,* where careful selection of men during World War II for work behind enemy lines utilized role dramas. In addition, role dramas have been successfully employed in providing social laboratories where research into human interaction has been possible. Using this technique, Borgatta (1961) showed that certain personality traits are stably associated with the amount of interactive behavior.

There is a rich literature in which the psychodrama especially has been explored in terms of its usefulness in psychotherapy, education, and reeducation. Most typically, the increased adequacy or improved functioning of individuals in their own roles is viewed as the primary aim. Greenberg assembled a representative collection in this regard in *Psychodrama: Theory and Therapy.* Sociodramas have been employed to a greater extent in educational settings, while axiodramas as contexts for developing and understanding ethical considerations have not received the same amount of interest as have psycho- or sociodramas.

The concept of role playing insofar as it may be part of an ongoing subfield of inquiry must be viewed as part of the larger conceptual structure called role theory or role analysis. Although the overall development of the conceptual structure has been largely on the basis of theoretical rather than empirical work, there remains strong belief among many theorists that the explanatory power of role theory is substantial, and that the empirical operations that precede confirmation will appear in time. When and if that happens, it is also likely that a more standard set of terms will be adopted.

REFERENCES

Borgatta, E. F. (1961). Roleplaying specification, personality and performance. *Sociometry, 24,* 218–233.

Coutu, W. (1951). Roleplaying vs. roletaking. *American Sociological Review, 16,* 180–187.

Greenberg, I. A. (Ed.). (1974). *Psychodrama: theory and therapy.* New York: Behavioral Publications.

Moreno, J. L., & Zeleny, L. D. (1958). Role theory and sociodrama. In J. S. Roucek (Ed.), *Contemporary sociology.* New York: Philosophical Library.

SUGGESTED READING

Biddle, B. J., & Thomas, E. J. (1966). *Role theory: Concepts and research.* New York: Wiley.

Goffman, E. (1959). *The presentation of self in everyday life.* New York: Doubleday.

Goffman, E. (1961). *Encounters.* Indianapolis, IN: Bobbs Merrill.

Gross, N., Mason, W. S., & McEachern, A. W. (1957). *Explorations in role analysis.* New York: Wiley.

Heiss, J. (1981). Social roles. In M. Rosenberg, & R. H. Turner (Eds.), *Social psychology.* New York: Basic Books.

McDavid, J. W., & Harari, H. (1968). *Social psychology: Individuals, groups, societies.* New York: Harper & Row.

Nye, F. I. (1976). *Role structure and analysis of the family.* Beverly Hills, CA: Sage.

Secord, P. F., & Backman, C. W. (1964). *Social psychology.* New York: McGraw-Hill.

Turner, R. H. (1956). Role-taking, role standpoint, and reference-group behavior. *American Journal of Sociology, 61,* 316–328.

Turner, R. H. (1962). Roletaking: Process versus conformity. In A. M. Rose (Ed.), *Human behavior and social processes: An interactionist approach.* Boston: Houghton Mifflin.

Turner, R. H. (1978). The role and the person. *American Journal of Sociology, 84,* 1–23.

M. S. BLOOMBAUM
Southern Oregon University

PSYCHOTHERAPY

RORSCHACH, HERMANN (1884–1922)

Hermann Rorschach received his degree from Zürich in 1912 with a dissertation concerning hallucinations that was supervised by Bleuler. Except for a year on the staff of a sanitorium near Moscow, his career was spent in posts at Swiss mental hospitals. Heavily influenced by Freud, he was a promoter of psychoanalysis among Swiss psychiatrists.

In 1896, Binet and Henri had suggested the use of standardized inkblots to measure imagination. Rorschach was also familiar with Jung's verbal free association testing technique. Putting these two notions together, he extended the inkblot technique to the measurement of the entire personality, but especially unconscious emotions.

Rorschach developed the 10 bilaterally symmetrical cards we know today from a very large number administered to a variety of psychiatric groups beginning in 1911. After supplementary testing with normals, retardates, and other special groups, he issued the first German edition in 1921. Intended for use from preschool to adult (although his data were mostly from adults), the test was scored primarily for the ratio of color to movement responses. His somewhat typological scoring system was based upon a combination of the observable and clinical insight or intuition.

With the development of a statistically based scoring system by Samuel Beck during the 1930s and by Bruno Klopfer in the early 1940s, the technique became popular in the United States. Both the Beck and Klopfer systems have declined in popularity, being replaced either by the Exner method of scoring the Rorschach or by the more empirically based Holtzman Inkblot Technique.

C. S. PEYSER
The University of the South

RORSCHACH TECHNIQUE

The Rorschach technique was launched by the publication in 1921 of Hermann Rorschach's *Psychodiagnostik.* Rorschach had done some related research in 1916. He viewed mental disorders as disease entities and liked to speak of the faculties of the organism such as will, emotions, intellect, and imagination. He was primarily a Jungian analyst and his original purpose in experimenting with inkblots was to discover a means of predicting whether patients would be introversive or extratensive. By comparing the number of human movement responses that the subject perceives on the inkblots with the number of times that color was used to determine concepts, he discovered he could predict whether the subject's behavior would be characterized more by introversion (innerdirectedness) or by extratension (outer-directedness).

By 1929, there were 30 titles relating to the Rorschach technique. This rose to about 230 by 1939, and after that there were thousands. The Rorschach became popular during the time in the history of clinical psychology when the psychoanalytic view was preeminent, when inner processes and the unconscious were the assessment target for clinical psychologists. Readers were impressed by studies such as the one by Fosberg, "Rorschach reactions under varied instructions." He purported to have demonstrated that the Rorschach was a "foolproof" X-ray of the personality not subject to situational set. Twenty-two years later a review, "The influence of situational and interpersonal variables in projective testing," by Masling, demonstrated that, on the contrary, situational and interpersonal variables did have a significant impact. The early emphasis on "signs" in the Rorschach tended to disappear when it was discovered that signs were overlapping and nondiscrete, having little value in making differential diagnosis between borderline conditions. Style and structure proved to be of less value than other aspects of Rorschach performance, and in the later literature there was more focus on content, special scales, variations in administration, and the like.

In the recent literature, many different views concerning the present status of the Rorschach have been aired. Its demise has been predicted but it continues to be a popular instrument in wide use. A reasonable position is one enunciated by Rabin who, in Buros' *Seventh Mental Measurement Yearbook,* wrote: "The Rorschach is a field of study in research which permits workers to investigate such diverse concepts as body image, primary process thinking, hypnotizability, orality, and ego strength. Not unlike a good deal of the general psychological literature many Rorschach studies deal with trivialities, are inconsistent and not replicated and are inconclusive."

The Rorschach is no longer considered a magical instrument with a mysterious capacity for probing beyond the immediate, mystically revealing the inner essence. Part of this is due to the fact that one's inner essence is no longer sought after in the same manner as before. Rather, most clinicians currently are interested in predicting behavior under specified conditions. That the Rorschach can be influenced by transient and situational variables may be considered hopeful rather than discouraging. Potkay, in *The Rorschach Clinician,* has suggested an appropriate way of determining how clinicians actually make judgments using the Rorschach. Exner, after reviewing various Rorschach interpreta-

tion systems and culling the valuable essence of each, composed a comprehensive system that has begun to create more uniformity in the administration, scoring, and research use of the test (Exner, 1974).

The most distinct contribution that the Rorschach test continues to make is in revealing aspects of motivation and personality that do not fit neatly into either the self-concept or behavioral categories. Creative capacities, hidden resources, and potentialities currently not in use are personality aspects that emerge when persons respond to the inkblots. Many a child or adult has been encouraged as a result of enthusiasm aroused by a psychologist who has seen untapped potential in individuals via this fascinating projective method.

REFERENCES

Exner, J. E. (1974). *The Rorschach: A comprehensive system.* New York: Wiley Interscience.

Fosberg, I. A. (1938). Rorschach reactions under varied instructions. *Rorschach Research Exchange, 3,* 12–31.

Masling, J. (1960). The influence of situational and interpersonal variables in projective testing. *Psychological Bulletin, 57,* 65–85.

Potkay, C. C. (1971). *The Rorschach clinician.* New York: Grune & Stratton.

Rabin, A. I. (1972). Rorschach. In O. K. Buros (Ed.), *Seventh mental measurements yearbook* (Vol. I). Highland Park, NJ: Gryphon.

Rorschach, H. (1949/1921). *Psychodiagnostics.* New York: Grune & Stratton.

SUGGESTED READING

Klopfer, W. G. (1973). The short history of projective techniques. *Journal of the History of the Behavioral Sciences, 9*(1), 60–65.

Klopfer, W. G., & Taulbee, E. S. (1976). Projective tests. *Annual Review of Psychology, 27,* 543–569.

W. G. KLOPFER

CLINICAL ASSESSMENT
PROJECTIVE TECHNIQUES
THEMATIC APPERCEPTION TESTS

ROSENZWEIG PICTURE-FRUSTRATION (P-F) STUDY

The Rosenzweig Picture-Frustration (P-F) Study is a semiprojective technique of personality diagnosis that has been successfully used for the past half-century both as a clinical device and as an investigative procedure. It was developed as a "method for exploring concepts of frustration theory and examining some dimensions of projective methodology" (Rosenzweig, 1945). Based on earlier experiments on psychodynamic concepts, including frustration, repression, and directions and types of aggression, an Adult form appeared in 1948. A Children's form for ages 4 to 13 was published 4 years later, and in 1964 a form for Adolescents was added.

The P-F is a semi-projective technique consisting of a series of 24 cartoon-like pictures, each depicting two persons involved in mildly frustrating situations of common occurrence. Facial features and other expressions of emotion are deliberately omitted from the pictures. The figure at the left is always shown saying certain words that help to describe the frustration of the other individual. In the blank caption box above the frustrated figure on the right, the subject is asked to write the first reply that enters his or her mind.

It is assumed as a basis for P-F scoring that the examinee unconsciously or consciously identifies with the frustrated individual in each picture and projects his or her own bias into the responses given. To define this bias, scores are assigned to each response under two main dimensions: direction of aggression and type of aggression. Direction of aggression includes extraggression (EA), in which aggression is turned onto the environment; intraggression (IA), in which it is turned by the subject onto him- or herself; and imaggression (MA), in which aggression is evaded in an attempt to gloss over the frustration. It is as if extraggressiveness turns aggression *out*, intraggressiveness turns it *in*, and imaggressiveness turns it *off*. Type of aggression includes obstacle-dominance (OD), in which the barrier occasioning the frustration stands out in the response; ego (etho) defence (ED), in which the ego of the subject predominates to defend itself; and need-persistence (NP), in which the solution of the frustrating problem is emphasized by pursuing the goal despite the obstacle. From the combination of these six categories, there result for each item nine possible scoring factors.

It is essential to observe that aggression in the P-F and in the construct on which it is based is not necessarily negative in implication. In the context of the P-F, aggression is generically defined as assertiveness, which may be either affirmative or negative in character. Need-persistence represents a constructive (sometimes creative) form of aggression, whereas ego (etho) defense is frequently destructive (of others or of oneself) in import. This point is particularly noteworthy because in many technical theories of aggression this distinction is overlooked and aggression is thought to be practically synonymous with hostility or destructiveness. Common parlance, when not contaminated by psychoanalytic or other psychological conceptualizations comes close to the broader usage of the term "aggression," which the P-F Study employs.

Although the scoring of the P-F is always phenotypic (according to the explicit wording used in the response), interpretation is genotypic, involving three kinds of norms: universal (nomothetic), group (demographic), and individual (idiodynamic). Statistical data used in interpretation refer to group norms, that is, the extent to which the individual performs vis-à-vis the group to which he or she belongs (based on age, sex, etc.). Individual (idiodynamic) norms, which derive from the unique wording of the responses and in interrelation of the scored factors in the protocol, complement the group norms. Universal (nomothetic) norms are represented by the constructs on which the instrument is based, and these underlie both group and individual norms. A Group Conformity Rating (GCR) measures the subject's tendency to agree with the modal responses of a normal population sample.

Interscorer reliability has been found to be 85% for the adult form. The results of a retest reliability, with some variations, have been demonstrated to be high. The various scoring categories selectively showed significant reliability as determined by the split-half method, but by the retest method the major scoring dimensions of the P-F have been demonstrated to agree with significant reliability.

The P-F has been studied for both construct (criterion-related) and pragmatic validity with significantly positive results. In addition to the clinical purposes for which the Study was originally intended, it has been used as a screening or selection device in business, industry, and schools, and for research on cultural differences. In particular, the GCR has proved to be of value. The categories "etho-defense" and "need-persistence" also have been shown to have differentiating potential, and some positive results have been obtained for obstacle-dominance. The results of P-F in hospital and clinic settings have proved useful, but an exclusive reliance on the P-F as a symptom-differentiating tool in such contexts is not recommended. Used in conjunction with other tests or as part of a configuration index, the technique has significant potential.

The published evidence for P-F reliability and validity are summarized in the *Basic Manual* (Rosenzweig) and discussed in detail in the book *Aggressive Behavior and the Rosenzweig Picture-Frustration (P-F) Study* (Rosenzweig, 1978a).

It is important to observe that the P-F Study is one of the few projective methods that directly applies a systematic theory of behavior, in this case, of aggression. Moreover, by employing in its scoring the three types of norms (nomothetic, demographic, and idiodynamic) the instrument is compatible with the general theory of personality known as idiodynamics.

The P-F has been translated and adapted, with standardization, in nearly all the countries of the Americas, Europe, and Asia, and thus has become a natural tool for cross-cultural investigation. It is particularly noteworthy that the Japanese have intensively pursued the relationship between the constructs of frustration theory and the standpoint of idiodynamics. A book on that topic by Hayashi and Ichitani is planned for publication in the year 2000.

SUGGESTED READING

Clarke, H. J., Fleming, E. E., & Rosenzweig, S. (1947). The reliability of the scoring of the Rosenzweig Picture-Frustration Study. *Journal of Clinical Psychology, 3,* 364–370.

Pareek, U. N. (1958). Reliability of the Indian adaptation of the Rosenzweig P-F Study (Children's Form). *Journal of Psychological Researches, 2,* 18–23.

Pichot, P., & Danjon, S. (1955). La fidelite du Test de Frustration de Rosenzweig. *Revue de Psychologie Appliquee, 5,* 1–11.

Rauchfleisch, U. (1978). *Handbuch zum Rosenzweig Picture-Frustration Test (PFT)* (Vols. 1–2). Bern, Switzerland: Hans Huber.

Rosenzweig, S. (1944) An outline of frustration theory. In J. McV. Hunt (Ed.), *Personality and the behavior disorders* (Vol. 1., pp. 379–388). New York: Ronald Press.

Rosenzweig, S. (1945). The picture-association method and its application in a study of reactions to frustration. *Journal of Personality, 14,* 3–23.

Rosenzweig, S. (1945). Frustration tolerance and the picture-frustration study. *Psychological Service Center Journal, 2,* 109–115.

Rosenzweig, S. (1951). Idiodynamics in personality theory with special reference to projective methods. *Psychological Review, 58,* 213–223.

Rosenzweig, S. (1960). The Rosenzweig Picture-Frustration Study, Children's Form. In A. I. Rabin & M. Haworth (Eds.), *Projective techniques with children* (pp. 149–176). New York: Grune & Stratton.

Rosenzweig, S. (1970). Sex differences in reaction to frustration among adolescents. In J. Zubin & A. Freedman (Eds.), *Psychopathology of adolescence* (pp. 90–107). New York: Grune & Stratton.

Rosenzweig, S. (1977). Outline of a denotative definition of aggression. *Aggressive Behavior, 3,* 379–383.

Rosenzweig, S. (1978a) Aggressive behavior and the Rosenzweig Picture-Frustration Study. New York: Praeger.

Rosenzweig, S. (1978). An investigation of the reliability of the Rosenzweig Picture Frustration (P-F) Study, Children's Form. *Journal of Personality Assessment, 42,* 483–488.

Rosenzweig, S., & Adelman, S. (1977). Construct validity of the Rosenzweig PictureFrustration Study. *Journal of Personality Assessment, 41,* 578–588.

Rosenzweig, S., Ludwig, D. J., & Adelman, S. (1975). Retest reliability of the Rosenzweig Picture-Frustration Study and similar semiprojective techniques. *Journal of Personality Assessment, 39,* 3–12.

Rosenzweig, S., & Rosenzweig, L. (1952). Aggression in problem children and normals as evaluated by the Rosenzweig P-F Study. *Journal of Abnormal & Social Psychology, 47,* 683–687.

Rosenzweig, S., & Sarason, S. (1942). An experimental study of the triadic hypothesis: Reaction to frustration, ego-defense and hypnotizability: I. Correlational approach. *Character & Personality, 11,* 1–19.

Rosenzweig, S. (1978). *Basic manual for the Rosenzweig Picture-Frustration (P-F) Study.* St. Louis: Rana House. (Distributed by Psychological Assessment Resources, Odessa, FL)

S. ROSENZWEIG
Washington University

CLINICAL ASSESSMENT
IDIODYNAMICS IN RE PERSONALITY THEORY
PERSONALITY ASSESSMENT
PROJECTIVE TECHNIQUE

ROTTER, JULIAN B. (1916–   )

Julian B. Rotter received the BA from Brooklyn College, the MA from the University of Iowa, and the PhD (1914) from Indiana University. He interned at Worcester State Hospital in 1938–1939. In 1941, Rotter went to Norwich State Hospital for 1 year. He then went into the army as a personnel consultant in the armored force and later as an aviation psychologist in the air force. He left the army in 1946 to teach at Ohio State University, where he directed the clinical psychology training program from 1951 to 1959 and in 1962 to 1963. In 1963, he went to the University of Connecticut as director of the Clinical Psychology Training Program, retiring in 1987.

Rotter has been a frequent instructor of APA- and NSF-sponsored postdoctoral courses and a visiting professor at the universities of Colorado, Minnesota, California, and Pennsylvania. He also served as a consultant for the Veterans Administration, Surgeon General's Office, and Peace Corps. He served in numerous positions in APA, including two terms on the Education and Training Board and the APA Council and as president of the Division of Social Personality and the Division of Clinical Psychology. He was president of the Eastern Psychological Association, and his honors include awards for Distinguished Contribution to the Science and Profession of Clinical Psychology, Distinguished Scientific Contribution (APA), and Award for Contributions to Clinical Psychology Training (Council of University Directors of Clinical Training). He has received an honorary DSci degree from Ohio State University. He is best known for his social learning theory and for several personality tests.

STAFF

SEXUAL DEVIATIONS

RUSH, JOHN A.

For nearly 30 years, John A. Rush has conducted clinical investigations that span both biological and psychosocial issues in mood disorders in adults, children, and adolescents. He has promoted the application of clinical research findings to clinical practice in order to improve diagnosis and treatment for these patients. His publications include over 250 journal articles and book chapters, and eight books.

Rush is a graduate of Princeton (BA, biochemistry, 1964); Columbia University College of Physicians and Surgeons (MD, 1968); Northwestern University (internship in internal medicine, 1969); and the University of Pennsylvania (psychiatric residency, 1972–1975). He served in the U.S. Army (1969–1971) as a general medical officer and in the Special Action Office for Drug Abuse Prevention in Washington, D.C. (1971–1972).

Rush is a fellow of the American Psychiatric Association, the American College of Neuropsychopharmacology, the American College of Psychiatry, and the Benjamin Rush Society, and a member of the Alpha Omega Alpha Medical Society. He has served as president of the Society of Psychotherapy Research, and of the Society of Biological Psychiatry. He chaired the *DSM-IV* Workgroup on Mood Disorders; he also chaired the Panel on Practice Guidelines for Depression in Primary Care for the Agency for Health Care Policy and Research. He has served on National Institute of Mental Health (NIMH) and Veterans Administration merit review committees. He is an editorial board member or reviewer for over a dozen psychiatric journals.

Rush's most recent honors include the Award for Research in Mood Disorders from the American College of Psychiatrists and the Paul Hoch Award from the American Psychopathological Association (1999). He was named Exemplary Psychiatrist by the Dallas Alliance for the Mentally Ill (1996 and 1997) and the Outstanding Psychiatrist of the Year by the Texas Society of Psychiatric Physicians (1995). He is a recipient of the Gerald L. Klerman Lifetime Research Award of the National Depressive and Manic Depressive Association (1994), and Professional of the Year Award from the Dallas Alliance for the Mentally Ill (1994). He has received the Strecker Award (Institute of Pennsylvania Hospital) and the Charles C. Burlingame Award (Institute of Living) in recognition of his research, teaching, and clinical work.

Major contributions of Rush's research efforts include, in the area of psychotherapy, the development, specification, and prospective evaluation of cognitive therapy for depressed adults (with A. T. Beck); the adaptation of cognitive therapy to depressed adolescents (with C. Wilkes); and the adaptation of cognitive therapy for patients with bipolar disorder (with M. Basco).

In the area of clinical management of depressed patients, Rush has contributed to the development and evaluation of both a clinician- and a patient-rated depression rating scale (the Inventory of Depressive Symptomatology [IDS]); the development of practice guidelines for managing depressed patients; the development of consensus algorithms to assist in the implementation of practice guidelines; and the conduct of trials to determine the clinical and economic costs and benefits of implementing guidelines versus treatment-as-usual.

His contributions in the area of psychopharmacology include the establishment of fluoxetine as an effective antidepressant in children and adolescents (with G. Emslie); the establishment of sodium divalproex as an effective antimanic agent (with C. Bowden); the establishment of clozapine as an effective treatment for patients with treatment-resistant bipolar disorder (with T. Suppes); the establishment of nefazadone in combination with a special form of cognitive behavioral therapy as a more effective treatment than either alone for chronic depression (with M. Keller, J. McCullough, and others); the preliminary data to suggest that vagus nerve stimulation may well be an effective treatment for patients with treatment-resistant depression (with H. Sackeim, M. George, and others).

Finally, Rush's contributions in the area of neurobiological characterization of mood disorders include the recognition that selected parameters of the sleep EEG appear to be trait-like (with R. Armitage and H. Roffwarg); the development of preliminary data to suggest that selected sleep EEG parameters appear abnormal in those at risk for but not yet ill from depression; and the characterization of the relationships between neuroendocrine and sleep physiobiological parameters in depressed patients.

STAFF

S

SACCADIC EYE MOVEMENTS

Saccades are the rapid eye movements that quickly redirect the eyes so that the image of an object is brought to the fovea of the retina, where it can be seen optimally. The term "saccade" is derived from the French "saquer," meaning "to pull" (referring to the jerking of a horse's head by a tug on the reins or to the flicking of a sail in a gust of wind; Sharpe, 1998). Saccades occur simultaneously in both eyes and in the same direction (i.e., conjugately). They include both voluntary and visually-guided changes of fixation position; the quick phases of vestibular and optokinetic nystagmus; and the fast eye movements that occur during REM sleep. The visual stimulus for a saccade is usually the image of an object of interest seen in the visual periphery. Prenuclear circuits in the brainstem generate the motoneuron innervation that is shared by all of the fast eye movements. Saccades are identified by their velocities and durations.

SACCADIC VELOCITY, AMPLITUDE, AND WAVEFORM

Saccades show a relatively invariant relationship between peak velocity and size of movement. The larger the eye movement, the higher its top speed. This amplitude–peak velocity relationship has been called the main sequence and can be used to identify saccades as such. Peak velocities of saccades vary from 30 to 700°/s, and their duration varies from 30 to 100 ms for movements from 0.5 to 40 degrees in amplitude (Bahill, Clark, & Stark, 1975; Sharp, Troost, Dell'Osso, & Daroff, 1975). The peak velocity saturates for large amplitude saccades; this relationship is the same for vertical and horizontal saccades and changes little with age 30 to 100 degrees/s (Sharpe & Zackson, 1987; Huaman & Sharpe, 1993). Although saccadic velocities cannot be voluntarily controlled, they are very slightly reduced by decreased alertness or inattention, and are higher when directed to unpredictable visual target locations than to predictable targets, or when in darkness (Fletcher & Sharpe, 1986; Schmidt, Abel, Dell'Osso, & Daroff, 1979) they are not reduced by neuromuscular fatigue (Fuchs & Binder, 1983; Barton, Huaman, & Sharpe, 1994). Saccades are about 10% slower in complete darkness than in the light (Bahill et al., 1975; Becker & Fuchs, 1969).

For a typical saccade, the eye accelerates rapidly, reaching its peak velocity between 1/3 and 1/2 of the way through the movement (Figure 1). The eye then decelerates, and usually stops relatively abruptly. Occasionally the eye drifts for a few hundred milliseconds after the initial rapid portion of the horizontal saccade is finished. Such postsaccadic drifts have been called glissades (Weber & Daroff, 1972) and may represent a mismatch between the sizes of the phasic pulse and tonic step of motoneuron innervation that produce saccades.

At the end of a saccade, the eye occasionally makes an immediate, oppositely-directed, small saccade of about 1/4 to 1/2 degree before coming to rest. This small saccade is called dynamic overshoot (Sharpe, 1998) and is thought to be caused by a brief reversal of the central saccadic command, or by elastic restoring force in the eye muscle. Dynamic overshoot is more frequent after small saccades and is often monocular, in the abducting eye. Microsaccades (about 1/5 degree), which occur during normal fixation, often consist of a pair of to-and-fro saccades of almost equal size separated by an interval, so that the eyes come to rest almost where they began. Microsaccades can be suppressed voluntarily (Kowler & Steinman, 1980), and have no known visual function.

SACCADIC LATENCY (INITIATION TIME) AND ACCURACY

The interval between the appearance of a target of interest and the onset of a saccade is normally about 150 to 250 ms. If a fixation target is extinguished for several hundred ms, creating a gap in fixation before a new peripheral target appears, the latency of the saccade is reduced to about 100 ms; these short-latency saccades are called express saccades (Fischer et al., 1989; Kalesnykas & Hallett, 1987). Conversely, if the original fixation target remains active while a saccade is made to a new target, the overlap target condition (Figure 2) delays the saccade onset by more than 200 to 250 ms. These gap and overlap conditions illustrate the effects of fixation and attention on the timing of saccades to new visual targets.

Ideally, the amplitude of a saccade would be such that the target

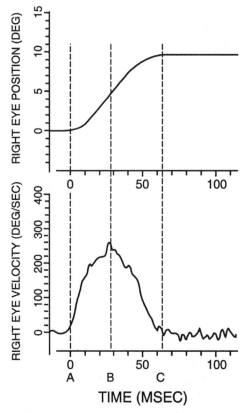

Figure 1: Position (top) and velocity (lower) of the right eye during a rightward saccade. A. saccade onset; B. time of peak velocity; C. end of saccade.

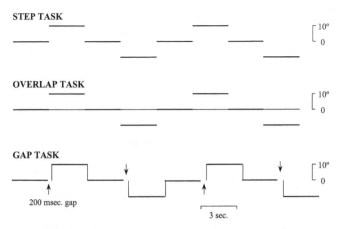

STEP TASK

OVERLAP TASK

GAP TASK

200 msec. gap

3 sec.

Figure 2. Overlap, step and gap tasks, for eliciting saccades. The overlap task (A) delays saccade initiation since fixation is not readily disengaged when a target is continuously present. The target step task (B) reduces saccade latency. If target steps are unpredictable in timing, direction and amplitude, reflexive visually evoked saccades occur. If target steps are predictable, the saccades are both voluntary and visually elicited, but not reflexive. When target steps are preceded by turning off the fixation target for about 200 msec (C), a gap task, saccadic mean latencies are further reduced. When the target steps after the gap are predictable, saccades often begin in response to target offset at the beginning of the gap. When target steps after the gap are not predictable, *express saccades* occur in response to the target step, at mean latencies of about 100 msec. (From Johnston JL, Sharpe JA and Morrow MJ. Spasm of fixation: a quantitative study. *J Neurological Sciences* 107: 166–171, 1992).

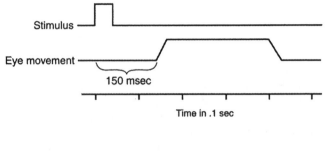

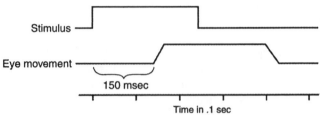

Figure 3. A, in response to a double target jump, there is a 150 msec latency period before the eye moves. The eye then moves to where the target was after its initial movement, stays in this location for a set period of time, and then moves back to the new (original) location of the target. B, even when the target jumps to a new location and then moves back to its original location following the eye movement, the eye remains in its new position for the same amount of time as in A before moving back to the original target position. (Redrawn from Westheimer, *G. Arch. Ophthalmol.* 52:932–941, 1954).

image is brought to the fovea with a single eye movement. In fact, many normal individuals show small degrees of both conjugate and disconjugate saccadic dysmetria: slight undershooting (hypometria), or infrequently, slight overshooting (hypermetria). The degree of dysmetria is usually small, about 10% of the amplitude of the saccade (Weber & Daroff, 1972). Although saccades may be made to imagined targets in darkness, such saccades are quite inaccurate.

Normally, after an individual makes a hypometric saccade, he or she makes a corrective saccade usually after a latency of only 100 to 130 ms—considerably less than the normal saccadic reaction time. A corrective saccade may occur even if the target is extinguished before the initial saccade is completed. Therefore, a nonvisual or extraretinal signal may provide information about whether the first movement is accurate, so that a corrective saccade can be triggered if necessary. This nonvisual information is not proprioceptive, using afferent signals from the extraocular muscles, but is based upon the monitoring of efferent ocular motor commands, called efference copy or corollary discharge. Vision is certainly important, however, since both the probability and the accuracy of a corrective saccade increase if visual information about a retinal error (the distance of the image of an object from the fovea) is available at the end of the initial saccade (Prablanc, Masse, & Echallier, 1978).

QUICK PHASES OF NYSTAGMUS

The fast eye movements of vestibular and optokinetic nystagmus, which comprise one phase of jerk nystagmus, are usually termed "quick phases" rather than saccades, although they have the same amplitude-duration and amplitude–peak velocity relationships as voluntary saccades (Bahill et al., 1975). Quick phases are generated

through the vestibulo-ocular and optokinetic systems (Chun & Robinson, 1977), and move the eyes in the anticompensatory direction (i.e., the direction opposite that of the slow phase) during vestibular or optokinetic stimulation (Lau, Honrubia, & Baloh, 1978).

PROCESSING OF VISUAL INFORMATION FOR SACCADIC EYE MOVEMENTS

If a target suddenly jumps to a new position and then rapidly returns to its initial location before a subject begins a saccade to the new position, the subject still makes a complete saccade toward the new (transient) target location (Figure 3). Then, after a fairly constant interval of about 150 to 200 ms, the subject makes a corrective saccade back to the original target position. The interval between saccades is relatively independent of the interval between the changes in target position (Westheimer, 1954). The saccadic system can acquire and use visual information continuously up to about 70 ms before the saccade begins. This is about the time it takes visual information to traverse the retina and central visual pathways and reach the brainstem ocular motor structures. Under certain conditions, two saccades may occur back to back with virtually no intersaccadic interval; there is no obligatory refractory period between saccades (Becker & Jürgens, 1979). Rather, the central nervous system can process information in parallel in order to program more than one saccade at a time (Robinson, 1973). However, because of their high speed, once a saccade has begun, there is usually not enough time to process the new visual information required to modify the saccade before it has finished.

Visual information may be acquired even during a saccade and used to influence the time of occurrence, size, and direction of subsequent saccades. When a target is briefly flashed directly onto the fovea during a saccade, a subsequent saccade may be produced that takes the eye to the actual location of the target even though no retinal error ever existed (since the target was flashed on the fovea) and the target is no longer visible (Hallett & Lightstone, 1976). Thus, the saccadic system calculates the position of the target relative to the head using a combination of: (a) knowledge of the position of the eye in the orbit during the saccade at the instant the target was flashed, and (b) knowledge that the retinal error was zero (in this case). Thus the saccadic system can program a movement using a head-coordinate as well as a retinal-coordinate scheme.

Although the visual world sweeps rapidly across the retina during a saccade, there is no sense of a blurred image. We do not seem to see during saccadic eye movements. This phenomenon has been called saccadic omission (Campbell & Wurtz, 1978) and is caused by two factors. First, the threshold for detecting a brief flash of light during a saccade is slightly elevated (saccadic suppression). Saccadic suppression plays only a minor role in saccadic omission. A more important factor is visual masking, a process by which the presence of a stationary, highly contoured visual background before (forward masking) or after (backward masking) a saccade eliminates the perception of the blurred visual image during the saccade. Visual masking probably happens independently of eye movement, since it also occurs if a pattern is briefly moved across a stationary retina at the speed of a saccade (Martin, 1974; Mitrani, Mateef, & Yamikoff, 1971). Visual interactions in both the striate cortex and the superficial layers of the superior colliculus appear to reduce the response of many neurons to visual stimulation during saccadic eye movements, and may be responsible for both saccadic omission and saccadic suppression (Judge, Wurtz, & Richmond, 1980; Wurtz, Richmond, & Judge, 1980).

Constancy of spatial relations is also maintained during and after saccades. Despite the fact that the visual scene shifts with each saccade, we maintain our sense of where straight-ahead is; this spatial constancy is probably accomplished by signals of the eye movement commands (efference copy) that are sent as corollary discharges to perceptual areas that register retinal input with motor commands (Ilg, Bridgeman, & Hoffman, 1989).

NEUROPHYSIOLOGY OF SACCADES

Mechanical properties of the orbital tissues must be overcome to move the eyes and, once the eyes are in position, to hold them in place. For fast eye movements a powerful phasic burst of contraction of the extraocular muscles is necessary to overcome viscous drag against the eyeball. The very high frequency burst required to drive the eyes at saccadic speeds is called a pulse of innervation (Robinson, 1970). Once the eyes have been brought to a new position, they must be held there against orbital elastic forces that tend to rotate the globe toward the primary position. In order to prevent this centripetal drift, a sustained, tonic contraction of the extraocular muscles must follow the phasic contraction produced by the pulse of innervation. This sustained contraction is called a step of neural activity (Figure 4). For each position of the eye there are a specific step discharge rate of agonist motor units and a reciprocally lower step discharge rate for their antagonist motor units.

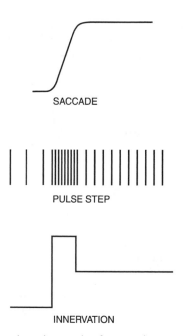

Figure 4. Pulse and step innervation for saccades.

Thus, because of the viscous and elastic forces in the orbit, the ocular motor control signal for a saccadic eye movement is a pulse and a step of innervation (Robinson, 1975). The saccadic pulse and step are phasic eye velocity and tonic eye position commands.

Saccades are initiated by supranuclear trigger signals that inhibit pause neurons located in the midline pontine tegmentum. Inhibition of pause cells releases the discharge of excitatory burst neurons (BNs), and the duration of their firing determines the amplitude of the saccades. A command signal of desired eye position (for example, retinal target error), which is independent of the trigger signal, determines how long the burst cells fire. Collaterals of excitatory BNs excite inhibitory BNs, which in turn inhibit the pause cells during the saccade (Horn, Buttner-Ennever, & Buttner, 1996). The burst output is the saccades' velocity command (the pulse) and is also integrated in a network called the neural integrator (NI). The output of the NI is the new eye position command (the step). The step of discharge also provides a feedback signal of eye position, which inhibits the BNs (Figure 5). Once the actual eye position matches the desired eye position, the burst cells cease firing, the pause cells resume activity, and the saccade stops (Scudder, 1988). Burst neurons for horizontal saccades are located in the paramedian reticular formation of the pons, whereas BNs for vertical and torsional saccades reside in the rostral interstitial nucleus of the medial longitudinal fasciculus, located in the upper midbrain (Horn et al., 1996). The nucleus prepositus hypoglossi and vestibular nucleus are the site of the NI for horizontal saccades (Kaneko, 1997), and the interstitial nucleus of Cajal together with the vestibular nucleus constitute the NI for upward, downward, and torsional saccades (Helmchen, Rambold, Fuhry, & Buttner, 1998).

The cerebral hemispheres serve as what we might call the commanders-in-chief of voluntary and visually-evoked eye movements. They deliver trigger, retinal error, and intended eye position commands to the superior colliculus and to brainstem BNs and pause cells in order to begin saccades and guide them to their targets. Dif-

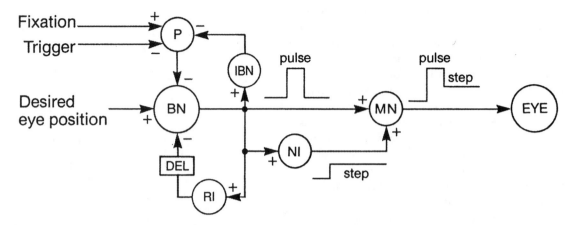

Figure 5. Model for generation of saccades. Fixation maintains activity of omnipause pause neurons (P) until a trigger signal inhibits them, releasing excitatory medium lead burst neurons (BN). BN excite inhibitory burst neurons (IBN) which stop pause cell activity and also inhibit motor neurons of antagonist muscles. The burst neurons send a velocity command (the pulse) to motoneurons (MN) and to the neural integrator (NI) which creates a position command (the step) for the eye. Anolther integrator, resettable after each saccade (RI), creates a negative freedback signal of eye position, BN cease firing, pause cells are disinhibited and the saccade stops. (From Sharpe JA. Neural Control of Ocular Motor Systems. In Walsh and Hoyt's Clinical Neuro-ophthalmology. Miller NR, Neuman NJ (eds). Williams and Wilkins, Baltimore, Volume 1, 1998: 1101–1167, page 1114.

ferent cortical areas share roles in governing saccades (Sharpe, 1998; Sweeney et al., 1996). The parietal eye field (PEF) programs visually guide reflexive saccades; the frontal eye field (FEF) processes both reflexive saccades to visual targets and volitional saccades. While the FEF is involved mainly in intentional saccades to visual targets, the PEF is involved more in reflexive visual exploration. The supplementary eye field in the parasagittal cortex of the frontal lobe participates in sequences of voluntary saccades to specific orbital positions. The dorsolateral prefrontal cortex contributes to advanced planning of environmental scanning, using memory of target location.

REFERENCES

Bahill, A. T., Clark, M. R., & Stark, L. (1975). The main sequence: A tool for studying human eye movements. *Mathematics and Bioscience, 24,* 191–204.

Barton, J. J. S., Huaman, A. G., & Sharpe, J. A. (1994). Effects of edrophonium on saccadic velocity in normal subjects, myasthenic and non-myasthenic ocular palsies. *Annals of Neurology, 36,* 585–594.

Becker, W., & Fuchs, A. F. (1969). Further properties of the human saccadic system: Eye movements and correction saccades with and without visual fixation points. *Vision Research, 9,* 1247–1258.

Becker, W., & Jürgens, R. (1979). An analysis of the saccadic system by means of double step stimuli. *Vision Research, 19,* 967–983.

Campbell, F. W., & Wurtz, R. H. (1978). Saccadic omission: Why we do not see a grey out during saccadic eye movement. *Vision Research, 18,* 1297–1303.

Chun, K. S., & Robinson, D. A. (1977). A model of quick phase generation in the vestibuloocular reflex. *Biological Cybernetics, 28,* 209–221.

Fischer, B., Weber, H., Biscaldi, M., Aiple, F., Otto, P., & Stuhr, B. (1989). Separate populations of visually guided saccades in humans: Reaction times and amplitudes. *Experiments in Brain Research, 92,* 528–541.

Fletcher, W. A., & Sharpe, J. A. (1986). Saccadic eye movement dysfunction in Alzheimer's disease. *Annals of Neurology, 20,* 464–471.

Fuchs, A. F., & Binder, M. D. (1983). Fatigue resistance of human extraocular muscles. *Journal of Neurophysiology, 49,* 28–34.

Hallett, P. E., & Lightstone, A. D. (1976). Saccadic eye movements to flashed targets. *Vision Research, 16,* 107–114.

Helmchen, C., Rambold, H., Fuhry, L., & Buttner, U. (1998). Deficits in vertical and torsional eye movements after uni- and bilateral muscimol inactivation of the interstitial nucleus of Cajal of the alert monkey. *Experiments in Brain Research, 119*(4), 436–452.

Horn, A. K. E., Buttner-Ennever, J. A., & Buttner, U. (1996). Saccadic premotor neurons in the brainstem: Functional neuroanatomy and clinical implications. *Neuro-ophthalmology, 16,* 229–240.

Huaman, A., & Sharpe, J. A. (1993). Vertical saccades in senescence. *Investigations in Ophthalmology and Visual Sciences, 34,* 2588–2595.

Ilg, U. J., Bridgeman, B., & Hoffmann, K. P. (1989). An influence of mechanical disturbance on oculomotor behavior. *Vision Research, 29,* 545–551.

Judge, S. J., Wurtz, R. H., & Richmond, B. J. (1980). Vision during saccadic eye movements: I. Visual interactions in striate cortex. *Journal of Neurophysiology, 43,* 1133–1155.

Kalesnykas, R. P., & Hallet, P. E. (1987). The differentiation of visually guided and anticipatory saccades in gap and overlap paradigms. *Experiments in Brain Research, 68,* 115–121.

Kaneko, C. R. (1997). Eye movement deficits after ibotenic acid lesions of the nucleus prepositus hypoglossi in monkeys: I. Saccades and fixation. *Journal of Neurophysiology, 78*(4), 1753–1768.

Kowler, E., & Steinman, R. M. (1980). Small saccades serve no useful purpose: Reply to a letter by R. W. Ditchburn. *Vision Research, 20,* 273–276.

Lau, C. Y., Honrubia, V., & Baloh, R. W. (1978). The pattern of eye movement trajectories during physiological nystagmus in humans. In J. D. Hood (Ed.), *Vestibular mechanisms in health and disease* (pp. 37–44). London: Academic Press.

Matin, E. (1974). Saccadic suppression: A review and an analysis. *Psychological Bulletin, 81,* 899–917.

Mitrani, L., Mateeff, S., & Yakimoff, N. (1971). Is saccadic suppression really saccadic? *Vision Research, 11,* 1157–1161.

Prablanc, C., Masse, D., & Echallier, J. F. (1978). Error-correcting mechanisms in large saccades. *Vision Research, 18,* 557–560.

Robinson, D. A. (1970). Oculomotor unit behavior in the monkey. *Journal of Neurophysiology, 33,* 393–404.

Robinson, D. A. (1973). Models of the saccadic eye movement control system. *Kybernetik, 14,* 71–83.

Robinson, D. A. (1975). Oculomotor control signals. In G. Lennerstrand & P. Bach-y-Rita (Eds.), *Basic mechanisms of ocular motility and their clinical implications* (pp. 337–374). Oxford: Pergamon.

Schmidt, D., Abel, L. A., Dell'Osso, L. F., & Daroff, R. B. (1979). Saccadic velocity characteristics: Intrinsic variability and fatigue. *Aviation, Space, and Environmental Medicine, 50,* 393–395.

Scudder, C. A. (1988). A new local feedback model of the saccadic burst generator. *Journal of Neurophysiology, 59,* 1455–1475.

Sharpe, J. A. (1998). Neural control of ocular motor systems. In N. R. Miller & N. J. Newman (Eds.), *Neuro-ophthalmology* (Vol. 1, pp. 1101–1167). Baltimore: Williams and Wilkins.

Sharpe, J. A., Troost, B. T., Dell'Osso, L. F., & Daroff, R. B. (1975). Comparative velocities of different types of fast eye movements in man. *Investigations in Ophthalmology, 14,* 689–692.

Sharpe, J. A., & Zackon, D. H. (1987). Senescent saccades: Effects of aging on their accuracy, latency and velocity. *Acta Otolaryngologica, 104,* 422–428.

Sweeney, J. A., Mintun, M. A., Kwee, S., Wiseman, M. B., Brown, D. L., Rosenberg, D. R., & Carl, J. R. (1996). Positron emission tomography study of voluntary saccadic eye movements and spatial working memory. *Journal of Neurophysiology, 75,* 454–468.

Weber, R. B., & Daroff, R. B. (1972). Corrective movements following refixation saccades: Type and control system analysis. *Vision Research, 12,* 467–475.

Westheimer, G. (1954). Eye movement responses to a horizontally moving visual stimulus. *Archives of Ophthalmology, 52,* 932–941.

Wurtz, R. H., Richmond, B. J., & Judge, S. J. (1980). Vision during saccadic eye movements: III. Visual interactions in monkey superior colliculus. *Journal of Neurophysiology, 43,* 1168–1181.

J. A. SHARPE
University of Toronto

EYE

SADISTIC RITUAL ABUSE

Sadistic Ritual Abuse (SRA) (Goodwin, 1992), also known as Satanic Ritual Abuse or Ritual Abuse, has been defined as:

a brutal form of abuse of children, adolescents, and adults, consisting of physical, sexual, and psychological abuse, and involving their rituals. Ritual does not necessarily mean satanic. However, most survivors state that they were ritual abused as part of satanic worship for the purpose of indoctrinating them into satanic beliefs and practices. Ritual abuse rarely consists of a single episode. It usually involves repeated abuse over an extended period of time (Report of the Ritual Abuse Task Force, Los Angeles County Commission for Women, 1991, p. 1)

LEVELS/SYMBOLS OF SATANISM

Satanism has been defined in four levels (Simandl, 1997)

1. *The experimental-dabbler,* typically a teenager (male and female, age range between 10 and 20), who exhibits ritual behaviors but does not have family involvement.

2. *Nontraditional, self-styled satanists* are described as "individuals with psychotic personality disorders . . . obsessed with satanic themes . . . who may practice their gruesome rituals alone or in small groups" (Pulling, 1989, p. 32). Hicks (1991) sees these satanists as "social isolates" who "invented ideologies to affirm their behavior" (p. 49).

3. *Organized traditional satanists* are organized religious groups worshiping Satan, and are protected by religious freedom under American law. The Church of Satan and The Temple of Set are typical examples of organized traditional satanists and reportedly are not linked to ritualistic crime (Gallant, cited in Kahaner, 1988). The Process Church of the Final Judgement has been reportedly linked to both Charles Manson and the "Son of Sam" (Terry, 1987).

4. *Occultic networking or transgenerational cults* (Ryder, 1992) are described as groups "perpetuated through family generations" (p. 14). This level of satanism, often identified as SRA, will be the focus of this article.

Commonly reported satanic symbols (Pulling, 1989) include the pentagram, inverted pentagram, hexagram (Star of David), cross of Nero (peace symbol or broken cross), swastika, anarchy, thaumaturgic triangle, udjat (all-seeing eye), scarab, lightning bolts, 666, ankh, inverted cross, black mass indicator, an emblem of Baphomet, the symbol of the Church of Satan in San Francisco, and the cross of confusion.

THE SRA CONTROVERSY

The Satan Seller (Warnke, 1972) and *Michelle Remembers* (Smith & Pazder, 1980) introduced SRA to public awareness. The FBI first received reports of possible SRA activity in 1983 (Lanning, 1991). The initial explosion of interest in and controversy surrounding SRA in Christian (Passantino & Passantino, 1992) professional (Mulhern, 1992; Putnam, 1991), and law enforcement circles (Hicks, 1991; Lanning, 1989) was soon supplanted by the controversy over "recovered memory" and the "backlash" (Myers, 1992) against reported survivors of sexual abuse and their therapists. In 1998, the potential legal suits against mental health professionals were estimated from 1000 to several thousand (Brown, Scheflin, & Hammond, 1998).

More books than journal articles have been written on SRA, with an "extreme polarization of opinion" by the authors and professional community (Ross, 1995, p. viii). Book authors have included reported survivors (Ryder, 1992), a parent accused of sexual abuse (Pendergrast, 1995), journalists (Nathan & Snedeker, 1995), researchers (Loftus & Ketcham, 1994), and therapists (Fraser, 1997; Ross, 1995; Sakheim & Devine, 1992; Yapko, 1994). In addition, fictionalized accounts of SRA (James, 1994) and children's books have been published (Sanford, 1990).

The basic controversy is over whether such cults exist, and if they do exist, how they are organized, and how they conspire to abuse people (Sakheim & Devine, 1992). Greaves (1992) identified four groups or positions regarding SCSs [satanic cult survivors]. The *nihilists* have alternative explanations of possible SRA allegations and see presentations of SCSs as untrue. *Apologists* tend to view SCS presentations as "could be true" and "must be true," respectively. *Heuristics,* uncommitted to the veracity of the SRA claims, have found that treating "their SCS patients' reports in a confirming manner has resulted in favorable outcomes in treatment" (Greaves, 1992, p. 47). *Methodologists* scientifically investigate SRA.

Lanning (1991) has noted that there is little to no evidence of "large-scale baby breeding, human sacrifice and organized satanic conspiracies" (p. 173). Lanning's (1992) possible alternatives for SRA allegations include pathological distortion, errors in processing reality due to mental disorders; traumatic memory, in which fear and severe trauma may cause distortion of reality and confusion in relating painful events; normal childhood fears and fantasy; misperception, confusion, and trickery by perpetrators; overzealous interveners (Ganaway, 1992) such as parents, family, doctors, therapists, social workers, law-enforcement officers, and prosecutors; and urban legends.

Other possible alternative explanations for SRA included contaminating effects from the media (Ganaway, 1989), social contagion or contamination between parents and professionals (Jones, 1991), a social delusion (Mulhern, 1994), a moral panic (Victor, 1998), and SRA training seminars (Mulhern, 1992). Coons (1994) noted that the pseudomemories could possibly be accounted for by "suggestion, social contagion, hypnosis, misdiagnosis, and the misapplication of hypnosis, dreamwork, or regressive therapies" (p. 1377).

Leavitt and Labott (1998) adapted the Word Association Test (WAT) to assess experience with satanic abuse. Their results suggested that "an experience base is shared by individuals reporting SRA that is not found in individuals who do not report satanic abuse (even if they do report sexual abuse)." Further research with the WAT (Leavitt, 1998) and the Rorschach (Leavitt & Labott, in press) revealed that the increased production of satanic word associations was not found to be associated with high hospital or media exposure.

The SRA controversy was broadened with the "recovered memory" debate, the formation of the False Memory Syndrome Foundation (Goldstein, 1992), and the characterization that the proliferation of sexual abuse and SRA allegations was the "Salem witch trials revisited" (Gardner, 1991). A number of states amended their statutes of limitations to grant "delayed discovery," wherein adult survivors of childhood sexual abuse could sue their reported abusers (Crnich & Crnich, 1992). Five states (Louisiana, Missouri, Texas, Idaho, and Illinois) have passed laws addressing the ritual abuse of children (Simandl, 1997). Ritual abuse prosecutions (Tate, 1994) and research by therapists (Jonker & Jonker-Bakker, 1991; van der Hart, Boon, & Jansen, 1997) in Europe have shown that SRA is not just a North American phenomenon.

RITUAL ABUSE OF CHILDREN

Snow and Sorensen (1990) conducted a study of ritualistic child abuse in five separate neighborhood settings. They discovered that in four out of the five neighborhoods, three distinct components of the sexual abuse appeared: incest, juvenile perpetration, and the adult ritual sex ring.

Finkelhor and Williams (1988) conducted a study of sexual abuse in daycare centers in America. Over a 3-year period, they identified 270 day care centers with a total of 1639 victims of sexual abuse. They noted that 13% of the cases involved ritualistic abuse. Kelly (1989) examined the effects of sexual and of ritualistic abuse in daycare centers. Compared with the victims of sexual abuse, ritualistically abused children "experienced significantly more types of sexual abuse" (p. 508), more severe physical abuse, and along with the sexual abuse group was "extremely frightened by threats made by the offenders" (p. 508). Kelly found that there were significantly more victims per daycare center and more offenders per child when ritualistic abuse was involved. "The children were also threatened with threats that supernatural powers such as Satan would always know where they were and what they were doing" (p. 509).

CHILD THERAPEUTIC ISSUES

Gould (1992) noted three reasons why ritually abused children seldom spontaneously disclose their abuse. First, these children are often drugged before the abuse. Second, hypnosis is often used to implant posthypnotic suggestions that they would not remember the abuse, and if they should, that the children would have to harm or kill themselves. Third, the abuse is so intolerable that dissociation usually occurs. These three factors combined in the ritualistic abuse of children before the age of six often create "amnesic barriers," making spontaneous disclosure unlikely.

Gould (1992) developed a checklist for signs and symptoms of ritualistic abuse in children that includes twelve categories: (1) sexual behavior and beliefs; (2) toileting and the bathroom; (3) supernatural, rituals, occult symbols, religion; (4) small spaces or being tied up; (5) death; (6) the doctor's office; (7) certain colors; (8) eating; (9) emotional problems, including speech, sleep, and learning problems; (10) family relationships; (11) play and peer relations; and (12) other fears, references, disclosures and strange beliefs. The recommended form of therapy (Gould, 1992) includes "a combination of play therapy and the disclosure [by the child] of the abuse to the therapist and the parents (when the abuse is extrafamilial)" (p. 247). The therapist is to be active in the treatment in structuring the therapeutic activities and providing motivation to the child to address issues that the child may otherwise avoid. Play therapy can be adapted to address possible multiplicity and "mind-control" programs (Gould & Cozolino, 1992) that may have resulted from the ritual abuse. Treatment is typically done in three stages (Herman, 1992), such as Engagement, The Trauma Work, and Resolution (Waters & Silberg, 1996), addressing the five domains (Silberg, 1996) of cognitive, affective, physical, interpersonal, and spiritual.

RITUAL ABUSE OF ADOLESCENTS

Tennant-Clark, Fritz, and Beauvais (1989) focused on the impact of occult participation on adolescent development. They noted a psychosocial profile of occult participants: chemical substance abuse, low self-esteem, negative feelings about school, poor self-concept, low desire to be considered a good person, negative feelings about religion, high tolerance for deviance, negative feelings about the future, low social sanctions against drug use, and feeling blamed (p. 768).

Simandl (1997) noted the following common behaviors of teen dabblers, involved in ritual practices:

1. Suicide/attempted suicide
2. Undue fascination with death, torture and suicide
3. Violent and aggressive behavior directed toward parents, siblings, and authority figures
4. Obnoxious antisocial behavior
5. Alienation from family and religion
6. Self-mutilation and tattooing
7. Fascination for edged weapons
8. Bizarre cruelty
9. Drug and alcohol abuse
10. Drastic change in grades
11. High truancy rate
12. Leaving home at unusual hours
13. New peer group
14. Compulsive interest in occult material, fantasy role games, and films and videos (all with themes of death, torture, and suicide) (pp. 216–217).

ADULT SURVIVORS OF CHILDHOOD RITUAL ABUSE

Young, Sachs, Braun, and Watkins (1991) reported a study of 37 adult dissociative disorder patients who reported ritual abuse as children. All reported abusive rituals during Satanic worship. The types of abuses reported were, in order of decreasing percents: sexual abuse, witnessing and receiving physical pain or torture, witnessing animal mutilation or killings, death threats, forced drug usage, witnessing and forced participation in human adult and infant sacrifice, forced cannibalism, marriage to Satan, buried alive in coffins or graves, forced impregnation, and sacrifice of own child. The marriage to Satan and forced impregnation percentages were based on 33 female patients.

ADULT THERAPEUTIC CONSIDERATIONS

Young and Young (1997) noted the following clinical symptoms for reported SRA survivors: "dissociative symptoms [Leavitt, 1994], posttraumatic stress disorder (PTSD) symptoms, cult-related phenomena, bizarre self-abuse, and unremitting eating, sleep, and anxiety disorders" (p. 69). These symptoms often lead to early recognition of possible SRA in patients. Treatment for SRA patients with dissociative symptoms should thus involve principles and techniques that have been found to be effective with PTSD and dissociative disorders (van der Kolk, 1987; van der Kolk, McFarlane, & Weisaeth, 1996; Kluft, 1985, Putnam, 1989, 1997; Silberg, 1996; Whitfield, 1995).

The phases of treatment (Young, 1992) involve (1) developing a therapeutic alliance, (2) evaluation and assessment, (3) clarifying the dissociative system, (4) discovering repressed information and dissolving dissociative barriers, (5) reconstructing memory and reframing beliefs, (6) countering indoctrinated beliefs, (7) desensitizing triggers and cues (programming), and (8) coming to terms with the past and finding new meaning and purpose in life. Young discusses different modes of treatment, including abreaction; hypnosis; expressive therapies such as journaling, art, and sand tray; medication; and hospitalization, including voluntary restraints. Shaffer and Cozolino (1992) also reported the benefit of twelve-step groups as an adjunct to therapy.

It is common for SRA survivors to become depressed and suicidal subsequent to uncovering traumatic memories (Shaffer & Cozolino, 1992). It is important to establish and then to maintain safety and stability before and while working on the patient's reported trauma. Therapists are also encouraged to take precautions to help prevent false memory allegations (Rhoades, 1995a, 1995b, 1995c) and should approach therapy with a "humane willingness to join empathically in the patient's experience without aligning with the pathology" (Young, 1997).

REFERENCES

Brown, D., Scheflin, A. W., & Hammond, D. C. (1998). *Memory, trauma treatment, and the law.* New York: W. W. Norton.

Coons, P. M. (1994). Reports of satanic ritual abuse: Further implications about pseudomemories. *Perceptual and Motor Skills, 78,* 1376–1378.

Crnich, J. E., & Crnich, K. A. (1992). *Shifting the burden of truth: Suing child sexual abusers—A legal guide for survivors and their supporters.* Lake Oswego: Recollex Publishing.

Finkelhor, D., & Williams, L. M., with Burns, N. (1988). *Nursery crimes: Sexual abuse in day care.* Newbury Park, CA: Sage.

Fraser, G. A. (Ed.). (1997). *The dilemma of ritual abuse: Cautions and guides for therapists.* Washington, D.C.: American Psychiatric Press.

Ganaway, G. (1989). Historical truth verses narrative truth: Clarifying the role of exogenous trauma in the etiology of multiple personality and its variants. *Dissociation, 21*(4), 205–220.

Ganaway, G. (1992). Some additional questions: A response to Shaffer & Cozolino, to Gould and Cozolino and to Friesen. *Journal of Psychology and Theology, 20*(3), 201–203.

Gardner, R. A. (1991). *Sex abuse hysteria. Salem witch trials revisited.* Cresskill: Creative Therapeutics.

Goldstein, E., with Farmer, K. (1992). *Confabulations: Creating false memories—destroying families.* Boca Raton, FL: SIRS Books.

Goodwin, J. (1992, November). *Pre-conference workshop: Sadistic ritual abuse issues in the 1990s.* Comments made at the Ninth International Conference on Multiple Personality Dissociative States, Chicago.

Gould, C. (1992). Diagnosis and treatment of ritually abused children. In D. K. Sakheim & S. E. Devine (Eds.), *Out of darkness.* New York: Lexington.

Gould, C., & Cozolino, L. (1992). Ritual abuse, multiplicity, and mind-control. *Journal of Psychology and Theology, 20*(3), 194–196.

Greaves, G. B. (1992). Alternative hypotheses regarding claims of satanic cult activity: A critical analysis. In D. K. Sakheim & S. E. Devine (Eds.), *Out of darkness.* New York: Lexington.

Herman, J. L. (1992). *Trauma and recovery.* New York: Basic.

Hicks, R. (1991). *In pursuit of Satan: The police and the occult.* New York: Prometheus.

James, S. (1994). *Dabblings: A journey of horror and hope.* Gresham: Vision House.

Jones, D. (1991). Ritualism and child sexual abuse. *Child Abuse and Neglect, 15,* 163–170.

Jonker, F., & Jonker-Bakker, I. (1991). Experiences with ritualistic child sexual abuse: A case study from the Netherlands. *Child Abuse and Neglect, 15,* 191–196.

Kahaner, L. (1988). *Cults that kill.* New York: Warner.

Kluft, R. P. (Ed.). (1985). *Childhood antecedents of multiple personality.* Washington, D.C.: American Psychiatric Press.

Kelly, S. (1989). Stress responses of children to sexual abuse and ritualistic abuse in day care centers. *Journal of Interpersonal Violence, 4*(4), 502–513.

Lanning, K. (1989, October). Satanic, occult, ritualistic crime: A law enforcement perspective. *The Police Chief, 62*–83.

Lanning, K. (1991). Ritual abuse: A law enforcement view or perspective. *Child Abuse and Neglect, 15,* 171–173.

Lanning, K. (1992). A law-enforcement perspective on allegations of ritual abuse. In D. K. Sakheim & S. E. Devine (Eds.), *Out of darkness.* New York: Lexington.

Leavitt, F. (1994). Clinical correlates of alleged satanic abuse and less controversial molestation. *Child Abuse and Neglect, 18*(4), 387–392.

Leavitt, F. (1998). Measuring the impact of media exposure and hospital treatment on patients alleging satanic ritual abuse. *Treating Abuse Today, 8*(4), 7–13.

Leavitt, F., & Labott, S. M. (1998). Revision of the Word Association Test for assessing associations of patients reporting satanic ritual abuse in childhood. *Journal of Clinical Psychology, 54*(7), 933–943.

Leavitt, F., & Labott, S. M. (in press). The role of media and hospital exposure on Rorschach response patterns shared by patients reporting satanic ritual abuse. *American Journal of Forensic Psychology.*

Loftus, E., & Ketcham, K. (1994). *The myth of repressed memory.* New York: St. Martin's.

Mulhern, S. (1992). Ritual abuse: Defining a syndrome versus defending a belief. *Journal of Psychology and Theology, 20*(3), 230–232.

Mulhern, S. (1994). Satanism, ritual abuse, and multiple personality disorder: A sociohistorical perspective. *The International Journal of Clinical and Experimental Hypnosis, 42*(4), October, 265–288.

Myers, J. E. B. (Ed.). (1992). *The backlash: Child protection under fire.* Thousand Oaks, CA: Sage.

Nathan, D., & Snedeker, M. (1995). *Satan's silence: Ritual abuse and the making of a modern American witch hunt.* New York: Basic.

Passantino, B., & Passantino, G. (1992). The hard facts about satanic ritual abuse. *Christian Research Journal, 14*(3), Winter, 20–27.

Pendergrast, M. (1995). *Victims of memory: Incest accusations and shattered lives.* Hinesburg: Upper Access, Inc.

Pulling, P. (1989). *The Devil's web.* Louisiana: Huntington House.

Putnam, F. W. (1989). *Diagnosis & treatment of multiple personality disorder.* New York: Guilford.

Putnam, F. W. (1991). The satanic ritual abuse controversy. *Child Abuse & Neglect, 15,* 175–179.

Putnam, F. W. (1997). *Dissociation in children and adolescents: A developmental perspective.* New York: Guilford.

Ritual Abuse Task Force (1991). Los Angeles County Commission For Women. *Ritual abuse: Definitions, glossary, the use of mind control.* September 15.

Rhoades, G. F. (1995). *Traumatic Memory* (Three Cassette Tapes). Pearl City: Maxwell.

Ross, C. A. (1995). *Satanic ritual abuse: Principles of treatment.* Toronto: University of Toronto Press.

Ryder, D. (1992). *Breaking the circle of satanic ritual abuse.* Minneapolis: CompCare.

Sakheim, D. K., & Devine, S. E. (1992). Introduction: The phenomenon of satanic ritual abuse. In D. K. Sakheim & S. E. Devine (Eds.), *Out of darkness.* New York: Lexington.

Sanford, D. (1990). *Don't make me go back mommy: A child's book about satanic ritual abuse.* Portland, OR: Multnomah.

Shaffer, R., & Cozolino, L. (1992). Adults who report childhood ritualistic abuse. *Journal of Psychology and Theology, 20*(3), 188–193.

Silberg, J., (Ed.). (1996). The five-domain crises model: Therapeutic tasks and techniques for dissociative children. In J. Silberg (Ed.), *The dissociative child: Diagnosis, treatment, and management.* Lutherville: Sidran.

Simandl, R. J. (1997). Teen involvement in the occult. In G. A. Fraser (Ed.). *The dilemma of ritual abuse: Cautions and guides for therapists.* Washington, D.C.: American Psychiatric Press.

Smith, M., & Pazder, L. (1980). *Michelle remembers.* New York: Congdon and Lattes.

Snow, B., & Sorensen, T. (1990). Ritualistic child abuse in a neighborhood setting. *Journal of Interpersonal Violence, 5*(4), December, 474–487.

Tate, T. (1994). Press, politics and paedophilia: A practitioner's guide to the media. In V. Sinason (Ed.), *Treating survivors of satanist abuse.* London: Routledge.

Tennant-Clark, C., Fritz, J., & Beauvais, F. (1989). Occult participation: Its impact on adolescent development. *Adolescence, 24*(96), Winter, 757–772.

Terry, M. (1987). *The ultimate evil: An investigation into a dangerous satanic cult.* New York: Bantam.

van der Hart, O., Boon, S., & Jansen, O. H., (1997). Ritual abuse in European countries: A clinician's perspective. In G. A. Fraser (Ed.), *The dilemma of ritual abuse: Cautions and guides for therapists.* Washington, D.C.: American Psychiatric Press.

van der Kolk, B. A. (Ed.). (1987). *Psychological trauma.* Washington, D.C.: American Psychiatric Press.

van der Kolk, B. A., McFarlane, A. C., & Weisaeth, L., (Eds.) (1996). *Traumatic stress: The effects of overwhelming experience on mind, body, and society.* New York: Guilford.

Victor, J. (1998). Moral panics and the social construction of deviant behavior: A theory and application to the case of ritual child abuse. *Sociological Perspectives, 41*(3), 541–565.

Warnke, M. (1972). *The Satan seller.* Plainfield, NJ: Logos International.

Waters, F., & Silberg, J. (1996). Therapeutic phases in the treatment of dissociative children. In J. Silberg (Ed.), *The dissociative child: Diagnosis, treatment, and management.* Lutherville: Sidran.

Whitfield, C. L. (1995). *Memory and abuse: Remembering and healing the effects of trauma.* Deerfield Beach: Health Communications.

Yapko, M. D. (1994). *Suggestions of abuse: True and false memories of childhood sexual trauma.* New York: Simon & Schuster.

Young, W., Sachs, R., Braun, B., & Watkins, R. (1991). Patients reporting ritual abuse in childhood: A clinical syndrome. *International Journal of Child Abuse and Neglect,* 2nd Quarter.

Young, W. C. (1992). Recognition and treatment of survivors reporting ritual abuse. In D. K. Sakheim & S. E. Devine (Eds.), *Out of darkness.* New York: Lexington.

Young, W. C., & Young, L. J. (1997). Recognition and special treatment issues in patients reporting childhood sadistic ritual abuse. In G. A. Fraser (Ed.), *The dilemma of ritual abuse: Cautions and guides for therapists.* Washington, D.C.: American Psychiatric Press.

G. F. RHOADES, JR.
Ola Hou Clinic, Aiea, Hawaii

CHILD ABUSE
EXORCISM
LIFE EVENTS
SADOMASOCHISM
SEXUAL DEVIATIONS

SADOMASOCHISM

Etymologically, the term *sadomasochism* is a composite of the words *sadism* and *masochism.* An individual who derives direct pleasure from inflicting pain on other organisms is described as sadistic. When the object of the sadistic behavior is human, the inflicted pain can also be psychological. Like masochism, sadism has a sexual connotation. It is generally accepted among experts in sexology that the pleasurable aspect of sadism is that it is usually sexually arousing to the sadist.

The reason for the composite term *sadomasochism* is that most individuals who have sadistic inclinations also harbor masochistic desires. Exclusive sadists are rare. Hans Toch in *Violent Men* reported that the large majority of the men he studied obtained no *direct* gratification from the use of force. It was simply a mechanism by which various desires were gratified and different purposes fulfilled. Less than 6% obtained direct satisfaction from the employment of violence.

According to a survey conducted by Charles A. Moser, "An exploratory-descriptive study of a self-defined S/M (sadomasochistic) sample," less than 9% of men inclined to sadomasochism prefer the dominant (sadistic) role exclusively, and less than 8% prefer the submissive (masochistic) role exclusively. The data for women were somewhat different, with less than 7% preferring the dominant role but more than 17% preferring the submissive role. However, for both sexes, a large majority preferred some of both behaviors.

REFERENCES

Moser, C. A. (1965). *An exploratory-descriptive study of a self-defined S/M (sadomasochistic) sample.* Unpublished doctoral dissertation, Institute for the Advanced Study of Human Sexuality, 1979.

Toch, H. (1969). *Violent men.* Chicago: Aldine.

SUGGESTED READING

Ellis, A., & Abarbanel, A. (Eds.). (1973/1960). *Encyclopedia of sexual behavior.* New York: Hawthorn.

E. E. LEVITT
Indiana University School of Medicine

SEXUAL DEVIATIONS

SAMPLING

Sampling procedures are ways of selecting a small number of units from a population to enable researchers to infer the nature of that population from the sample. Sampling is used in public opinion and consumer polling to make inferences from the responses of the sample as to how the population will vote on election day or how consumers will react to a new product or television program. Sampling is also used in experiments, for example, to infer from a sample of subjects trained to do speed reading with a broad range of magazine articles whether individuals in general could be taught to increase their overall magazine reading speed. In this example, sampling procedures are involved both in the selection of subjects and in the selection of magazine articles used for training material. To judge the success of the training, a sample of magazine reading would be used. Sampling as a concept is pervasive not only in experimental research, but in daily life, as when we judge a new supermarket by our first shopping visit there, or decide that the whole roast is underdone from the portion on our plate.

PRINCIPLES OF SAMPLING

We intuitively use sampling principles all the time. We remember, as children, reaching into a cookie jar too high on a shelf to see into. If we were smart, we did not take the top cookie, but reached in, mixed them up, and then drew our sample of cookies (the principle underlying random sampling). We understood that if the first cookie was stale, and also the second, and the third—in other words, the larger the sample—the more sure we were that it contained only stale cookies (the principle underlying sample size determination). But if the first three included two stale ones and one fresh one, we knew there was such variability that we had to take more cookies to determine, on the average, how fresh or stale the cookies were. With little variability in freshness, a small sample would suffice to represent the rest—greater variability requires larger samples (the principle underlying stratified samples). Since it was hard to reach into the bottom of the crock, once the cookies were well mixed, we could just as easily make our judgment from those in the top layer that were easier to reach (the principle underlying cluster sampling). We typically kept drawing new samples until we were sure enough to make up our mind about freshness (an example of sequential sampling). If we knew the jar contained chocolate chip, oatmeal, and raisin cookies, to determine the freshness of each kind, we would continue pulling out and putting back cookies until we had sampled a reasonable number, say five cookies, of each kind (an example of quota sampling).

As these examples illustrate, the various common sampling procedures named are based on simple and intuitively convincing principles.

PROBABILITY AND NONPROBABILITY SAMPLES

Sampling procedures are divided into those yielding probability samples that involve random sampling and, therefore, probability theory, and those yielding nonprobability samples that do not involve random sampling. Types of probability sampling, in addition to simple random sampling, are systematic, stratified, and cluster sampling. By using the mathematical theory of probability, one is able to infer the characteristics of the population from a probability sample within a determinable margin of error. Further, one can set that margin of error at any level of precision or certainty desired (e.g., odds of 20:1, 100:1, or 1000:1 that the population value lies within a specified range). More certainty requires larger samples, more complex designs, or both.

Quota, panel, and convenience samples (using whatever cases are handy) are nonprobability samples. Nonprobability samplers also make estimates of population values, but since they do not involve random sampling, their estimates do not have the same convincing probability theory base and are viewed with suspicion by those committed to probability sampling. Yet nonprobability samples are widely used because of their comparative convenience and economy. Those using them commercially believe that, with experience, their results are sufficiently valid and more cost effective.

BASIC SAMPLING CONCEPTS

Basic to sampling procedures is an understanding of the nature of the population and its relation to the sampling frame, the unit of sampling, and sample size.

The Population or Universe and the Sampling Frame

A first decision is to determine the population or universe to which one wishes to generalize. Ideally it should be identical with the sampling frame, which is the complete list of units in the universe from which the sample will be drawn. When one wishes to poll the membership of the American Psychological Association on their satisfaction with the current governance structure, the membership list is the sampling frame as well as the population about which one wants information.

In the case of the earlier speed reading example, the intent was to generalize to magazine reading. It would be difficult to get a sample of all possible magazines, but it probably would be acceptable to use as the universe those popular magazines that are likely to be read by persons in the population in which one was interested. In this case, the universe and frame, though not identical, are a close enough match. In still other instances, however, the population and frame may not be identical, either because the listing is incomplete or because it cannot be complete as the units to be sampled are not available. As an example of the latter, one may sample children in a national day care program to determine its effectiveness, but the population to which one wishes to generalize is too young to be part of that sample—indeed, most are not yet born.

As Deming (1966) and others have pointed out, sampling probability theory works only in the inference from sample to frame; the inference from frame to universe is a judgment based on knowledge of how closely the frame represents the universe. In the day care program example, the judgment to be made is how well the sample of currently enrolled children matches in essential characteristics the population that is the future clientele for the program. One can argue that sampling is irrelevant if we are seeking to validate a universal program applying to *all* 3- and 4-year-olds. But nearly all our "universals" turn out to have boundaries of some sort—culture, age, sex, heredity, and so forth—so that it is rare that the relation of sample frame to population is irrelevant.

Unit of Analysis

In studying school problems, one might sample school districts, school buildings, classrooms, or pupils. The level about which one wishes to draw conclusions determines the unit to be sampled. If it is about pupils, one samples pupils. But if it is about teaching methods, the unit to be sampled is classrooms. The number of classrooms sampled determines the effective sample size, not the number of pupils.

Confusing the level of analysis with the unit sampled, or the lowest level enumerated, is a common error. The unit of analysis is the smallest unit where the treatment is completely and uniformly administered. For example, suppose four classes of 20 students each are chosen for the day care program study. If all the students in a class experience a common program, then the unit is the classroom, and there are four cases per treatment, not 80.

Size of Sample

It may seem that the larger the sample, the better—but this is not necessarily true. One may get more precision than is needed, and thus waste resources. In many instances, resources concentrated on carefully gathering data from a sample will yield better data than a census that could not be as thorough or as carefully controlled. If one has prior information about the variability of the characteristic being studied, one can estimate the size of the sample required for any desired level of precision. (Herman Burstein gives tables in *Attribute Sampling* for this purpose.) If the study is an experiment and the size of the effect likely to be produced by the experimental variable can be estimated from prior research or pilot studies, one also can determine the needed sample size for a given precision. Most advanced statistics texts give the formulas. For example, see William Hays's *Statistics for the Social Sciences* (1973, p. 419–424).

The size of the population bears no relation to the required sample size. A randomly sampled cup of beans would permit one to infer the average bean size with the same precision whether the sample were taken from a bushel basket or from a whole train load of such well-mixed beans. The mixing of the beans provides, on the average, a representative sample in either case. The problem of representation relates to the breadth of variability in bean size to be represented rather than the size of the population as such. If the beans were all much the same size, a cupful might permit a precise estimate—if they were highly varied, it would not. Rather than actually mixing the beans, typically we allow random numbers to provide the "mixing."

SAMPLING PROCEDURES

Following is a brief description of the most commonly used sampling procedures and their advantages and drawbacks. The choice of an appropriate procedure requires one to balance such considerations as level of desired certainty, availability of complete sampling frame list, geographical dispersion if interviews are involved, and available resources. Because of this complexity, specialists are often consulted regarding the design of sampling plans and procedures.

Simple Random Sampling

In simple random sampling, every unit must have an equal chance of being drawn in each selection, and each selection must be made independently of the others. Selection is usually done by using random numbers either from a table (e.g., Rand Corporation, 1955) or

from a computer's random number generator to select from an enumerated sampling frame.

Although the requirement that every unit have an equal chance of being drawn every time requires putting each case back after it is drawn (sampling with replacement), this is important only for small universes and there is a correction for drawing without replacement. The correction is very small for large populations.

Simple random sampling requires only an enumeration of the complete sampling frame. It is easy to analyze the data and compute error sizes. Contacting the sampled units can be very expensive if the population is geographically dispersed, hence cluster sampling is used. Further, although the sample will be representative, on the average, this is little consolation if the sample drawn happens to be atypical with respect to one or more important characteristics, and hence we have stratified sampling.

Systematic Sampling

The drawing of every *nth* person from the frame is a simple way of getting a random sample if there is no periodicity to the list. Picking every *nth* name from a list of apartment dwellers arranged by room number however, might give all corner apartments that are normally the most expensive and desirable, and, therefore, hardly a representative sample.

On the other hand, if the list is ordered with respect to a pertinent property, it ensures representativeness with respect to that characteristic. For example, a systematic sample of a club membership list arranged in order of annual income would ensure that all levels of income were represented in a dues increase poll. Further, it gives a stratification effect that yields increased precision for the same size sample.

Stratified Random Sampling

Stratifying requires breaking the frame into two or more parts on the basis of some characteristic which, if not properly represented in the sample, might bias our inferences. Consider, for example, determination of the level of educational achievement in a given school. We could take a random sample of the students in that school, but, since grade level is very important to achievement, we would want to be sure that each grade was properly represented in the sample in accordance with its proportion in the school as a whole. Thus we might break the sample into strata, one for each grade, and then randomly sample within each stratum. The number taken from any one stratum is determined by the stratum's size in relation to the school as a whole.

How would this increase the precision of sampling? Since the range of achievement within each grade level would be much less than the variation in achievement over the school as a whole, each grade is more homogeneous and therefore can be adequately represented by fewer cases. We can take fewer from each stratum, thus reducing the size of the sample as a whole, and still maintain the original precision of estimation. Alternatively, we can maintain the planned sample size and, by stratification, increase the precision of our estimates.

Stratified sampling requires that, in addition to correct enumeration of the frame, there be both information correctly allocating units to strata and correct information on the proportion each stratum is of the whole. If systematic sampling is used to extract cases from within strata, the problem of determining correct strata proportions is eliminated, since by taking every *nth* case, the strata are correctly represented.

If we wish to maximize the information gained from a given size of sample, there is still a better strategy than proportional stratified sampling. Consider the school case again. Since poor students build on a poor foundation of previous learning, they tend to lag farther and farther behind the better students from first grade on. Thus the spread of achievement in the upper grades will be much greater than that in the lower ones. Therefore, to adequately represent the spread of achievement at each grade level, more cases will be required in upper than in lower grades. In general, the most efficient use of a sample of a given size is made by varying the proportion of the sample assigned to any given stratum in relation to that stratum's homogeneity or variability in comparison with the other strata—the more variability, the larger proportion of the cases are taken from it. This is called optimum allocation sampling. It requires knowledge of the variability of each stratum on the stratifying characteristic.

One may stratify on more than one characteristic at the same time. For example, in sampling the school, since girls appear to do better in reading and languages, and boys in mathematics and science, it might be important to assure balanced representation of the sexes. Thus one could stratify not only by grade, but also by sex. One would randomly sample the boys of the first grade, the girls of that grade, the boys of the second grade, and so on. Stratifying on too many variables, however, gains little and wastes resources unless each variable is largely independent of the other. One must be wary of stratifying on more than one from a cluster of interrelated variables. A common such cluster is education, income, housing, or socioeconomic class.

Cluster and Multistage Sampling

Particularly for interview studies of a widely dispersed population, simple and stratified random sampling can require considerable travel and be quite expensive. Cluster sampling reduces this cost considerably by geographically clustering the cases. It involves placing a grid over the geographic area of the population, randomly selecting squares (clusters) from the grid to represent it, and then using the cases in each cluster for the study. Because there may be more cases in a cluster than needed, cluster sampling is often used as the first stage of a multistage procedure. It might be followed by simple, systematic, or stratified sampling as a second stage to choose cases within each cluster. Alternatively, as a second stage, one might drop a grid on the selected clusters, do a second cluster selection, and then use simple, systematic, or stratified sampling as a third stage in each of the second-stage cluster selections.

Since housing choice, zoning laws, and land-use plans are likely to produce patterns that give a special nonrepresentative character to particular clusters, it is often important to stratify the clusters with respect to such characteristics, and use a combination of cluster and stratified sampling for the first stage. This is especially true if the clusters are based on natural groupings rather than on the groupings of an arbitrary grid, which is less likely to divide along social pattern lines.

Since one needs complete lists only in the clusters selected, there are savings beyond those of travel. The data from each cluster can be independently analyzed and clusters based on natural groupings are usually of special interest. Cluster sampling is likely to have somewhat less precision for the same sample size than other methods. If the number of clusters is small, it may be difficult to properly represent all strata.

Sequential Sampling

If the characteristics or opinions being studied will not change over the time the study is being done, and if it is easy and efficient to return to the field to gather additional data, sequential sampling has advantages. It permits use of any of the foregoing sampling plans. Each successive sample is added to the previous samples until stability of estimates within the desired range of precision is attained. This method has been of increased interest for telephone surveys. The interviewees' responses are entered directly into a computer keyboard by the researcher as they are guided through the interview by questions that appear on the screen. Responses are coded according to directions after each question so that keyboard entries are already coded. The computer output can provide continuous tabulation of results, or tabulation in small batches, so that estimates of precision as well as indications as to when stability is attained can be read as the results come in and interviewing can be terminated when the desired level is reached.

Quota Sampling and Panels

Quota sampling and panels are nonprobability samples. Their goal is basically to establish a replica of the population to be sampled. Thus quotas are established for the important features of the population likely to affect the characteristic being studied. Characteristics commonly used are sex, education, socioeconomic status, ethnicity, and residence location. Interviewers might be told to select men and women equally, with a certain age distribution, and certain social class characteristics. Since some of these characteristics can be determined only during the interview, adjustments are made during the analysis for characteristics above or below quota by weighting responses. Therefore, in quota sampling, the important characteristics and their level of representation in the population must be known. It is more important that enough cases are gathered to represent each stratum so that appropriate adjustments may be made in the analysis, than that the quotas as such be met exactly. This makes the choice of subjects easier than generally realized.

Quota samples are really sophisticated convenience or accidental samples, and are heavily dependent on the conscientiousness of the interviewers. Interviewers must avoid picking people because they know them, because subjects are better dressed, because they are available on the street (versus those who never leave home), and so forth.

Panels and purposive samples, like quota sampling, are hand-picked to create a replica of the population that can then be observed over time or returned to from time to time with new surveys. They require the same information about the population as quota sampling and one has the additional problem of keeping the character of the panel stable and representative as persons move away, fall ill and are unable to participate, and so on.

Sometimes nonprobability sampling designs are combined with probability designs. For example, a political poll uses a cluster sample procedure to select neighborhoods and then a quota sample to assure representation of age, sex, and political party affiliation within the neighborhood.

Snowball Sampling

Snowball sampling is a nonprobability sampling procedure used to define a social group, or those in a network of communication. Once a few members of the group are identified, they are asked for names of others in that group (e.g., "Who are the most influential persons in this community?"). That same question is then asked of the persons newly identified, and the process continues until few new names are received and the group or community appears to be identified.

REFERENCES

Burstein, H. (1971). *Attribute sampling: Tables and explanations.* New York: McGraw-Hill.

Deming, W. E. (1966). *Some theory of sampling.* New York: Dover.

Hays, W. L. (1981/1973). *Statistics for the social sciences.* (2nd ed.). New York: Holt, Rinehart & Winston.

SUGGESTED READING

Cochran, W. G. (1977). *Sampling techniques.* (3rd ed.). New York: Wiley.

Kish, L. (1965). *Survey sampling.* New York: Wiley.

Yates, F. (1981). *Sample methods for censuses and surveys* (4th ed.). New York: Macmillan.

D. R. KRATHWOHL

MEASUREMENT

STATISTICS IN PSYCHOLOGY

SAPOLSKY, ROBERT (1957–   )

Robert Sapolsky is professor of biological sciences at Stanford University, of neurology at Stanford University School of Medicine, and a research associate at the Institute of Primate Research, National Museums of Kenya. He was born in New York City in 1957, and was educated at Harvard University (biological anthropology) and the Rockefeller University (neuroendocrinology). After a post-doctoral fellowship at the Salk Institute, he joined the Stanford faculty. Sapolsky's work is in four broad areas of psychology and neuroscience.

GLUCOCORTICOIDS AND HIPPOCAMPAL DAMAGE

Glucocorticoids (GCs) are the adrenal steroid hormones secreted during stress, and while such secretion is critical for surviving an acute physical stressor (such as a sprint across a savanna), pro-longed stress and prolonged GC secretion can have various adverse consequences. Sapolsky was one of the individuals first demonstrating that excessive GCs can damage the hippocampus, a primary GC target site in the brain. Much of his work has examined the cellular and molecular mechanisms underlying GC-induced hippocampal neurotoxicity, its relevance to hippocampal damage during aging, and to the ability of the hippocampus to withstand other neurological insults. Recent studies, prompted by Sapolsky's work, suggests that the same may occur in humans, in that hippocampal atrophy is observed in a number of neuropsychiatric disorders associated with an excess of stress or GCs.

THE HIPPOCAMPUS AS A NEGATIVE FEEDBACK REGULATOR OF GC SECRETION

Early work by Sapolsky, along with others, indicated that the hippocampus is one of the sites in the brain that inhibits GC secretion, such that hippocampal damage leads to an excess of GCs. Sapolsky posited that the damaging effects of GCs on the hippocampus, coupled with the subsequent hypersecretion of GCs thanks to such hippocampal damage, form a degenerative feedforward cascade of damage that can occur during aging.

GENE THERAPY FOR NEUROLOGICAL INSULTS TO THE HIPPOCAMPUS

Sapolsky's more recent work has focused on developing gene transfer techniques for saving hippocampal neurons from neurological insults, and from the adverse effects of GCs themselves.

PSYCHOENDOCRINE STUDIES OF WILD BABOONS

For more than twenty years, Sapolsky has also maintained a parallel line of research, carried out annually in the Serengeti of East Africa. He has studied the same troop of baboons, examining relationships among social rank, personality, and patterns of stress-related disease; to date, these remain the only ones of this kind carried out with a population of primates living in the wild. His work has indicated that, in a stable dominance hierarchy, it is the socially subordinate animals who are most prone towards stress-related disease. However, he has also found that the relationship is just the opposite during periods of instability. Moreover, he has found that personality can be an even more powerful predictor than are either rank or the sort of hierarchy in which the rank occurs. Thus, particularly salutary physiological profiles are found among animals with the highest degrees of social affiliation, and who are the most adept at differentiating between threatening and neutral interactions with rivals.

In addition to his technical writing (approximately 250 papers and one monograph) Sapolsky writes regularly for nonscientists. These works have been published in *Scientific American, Discover, Natural History, The New Yorker, Harper's, The Sciences,* and *USA Today.* In addition, he has published two books for nonscientists, *Why Zebras Don't Get Ulcers: A Guide to Stress, Stress-Related Diseases and Coping* and a collection of his essays, entitled, *The Trouble With Testosterone and Other Essays on the Biology of the Human Predicament.*

Sapolsky is a recipient of a MacArthur Fellowship (1987), the

Lindsley Prize of the Society for Neuroscience (1985), and Young Investigator of the Year awards from the Society of Biological Psychiatry (1990), the International Society of Psychoneuroendocrinology (1990), and the Society for Neuroscience (1992). He lives in San Francisco with his wife Lisa, a clinical neuropsychologist, and their two children, Benjamin and Rachel.

STAFF

SAVANT SYNDROME

Hinsie and Campbell, in their *Psychiatric Dictionary* (1974) noted that in early times "idiot referred to any person who lived as a recluse in a private world" (p. 377). The French term "savant," means a person of knowledge (Hill, 1978). Rimland (1978), who coined the term "autistic savant," described an idiot savant or autistic savant as "an individual who can perform various mental feats at a level far beyond the capacity of any normal person, but whose general intellectual level is very low."

Those believing that subnormal intelligence is due to mental retardation have traditionally referred to such an individual as an idiot savant. Those who believe, as Rimland does, that subnormal intellectual functioning results from autism, refer to the individual as an autistic savant. Treffert (1988), who has performed an extensive investigation, prefers the term "savant syndrome."

Savant syndrome is very rare, with estimates of fewer than 0.5% of the developmentally disabled population presenting its symptoms. In addition, there appear to be more males with the disorder than females (6:1).

Whether the person is labeled an idiot savant, autistic savant, or as having the more inclusive savant syndrome, the presenting behavior is the same: general subnormal intelligence combined with superior intellectual abilities in one or more of the following areas: music, memory, art, pseudoverbal, mathematics, geography, motor coordination, calendar, and extrasensory perception (Sasks, 1995)

REFERENCES

Hill, A. L. (1978) Savants: Mentally retarded individuals with special skills. In N. Ellis (Ed.), *International Review of Research in Mental Retardation* (Vol. 9). New York: Academic.

Rimland, B. (1978). *Infantile autism: The syndrome and its implications for a neural theory of behavior.* Englewood Cliffs, NJ: Prentice Hall.

Sacks, O. (1998). *An Anthropologist on Mars.* New York: Alfred A. Knopp.

Treffert, D. A. (1988). The idiot savant: a review of the syndrome. *American Journal of Psychiatry, 145,* 563–572.

Hinsie, L., & Campbell, R. (1974). *Psychiatric Dictionary* (p. 377). London: Oxford University Press.

D. L. HOLMES
The Eden Institute, Princeton

AUTISM
HUMAN INTELLIGENCE

SCAPEGOATING

Scapegoating is the process by which one finds a substitute victim on which to vent anger. The term comes from the Old Testament (Leviticus 16:8, 10, 26) and refers to the goat driven into the desert on the Day of Atonement to carry away the sins of Israel. It was a way of canceling the sins of individual Israelites, so they were "wiped off the books." It has since come to mean any substitute recipient of anger or rejection. By condemning the "scapegoat," one is able to vent one's feelings without attacking the real subject of one's ire or blaming oneself. In the Old Testament sense, it was a deliberate means of wiping the slate clean each Day of Atonement, but in the modern psychological sense it is apt to be an unconscious projection. One blames a helpless minority for the problems of the overall economy, for instance. Or one blames the labor unions for the decline in the auto industry. More obviously, the worker blames the tool. It is a faulty tool, or even a malicious one, seeking to thwart the worker's aims.

The most obvious case of scapegoating in the modern world is that of Nazi Germany. Here the overwhelming defeat of Germany in 1918, the collapse of the monarchy, the disastrous inflation, and so forth were all blamed on an international conspiracy manipulated by the Jews. The holocaust, "Germany's permanent solution of the Jewish problem," was the consequence. Of course, the Jews were not the only scapegoats. The Nazis projected their problems onto all alien peoples—Slavs, Latins, Orientals, and so on.

While the most dramatic examples of scapegoating are in intergroup relations, its most frequent use is probably individual, such as students blaming their "unreasonable" professors or the peer who kept them from studying, or the child blaming a brother or sister ("She made me do it").

W. E. GREGORY
University of the Pacific

AGGRESSION
ATTITUDES
MALINGERING

SCHACHTER, STANLEY (1922–1997)

The social psychologist Stanley Schachter obtained the bachelors and masters degrees from Yale University before leaving for the University of Michigan to work for the PhD degree, which he received in 1950. Most of Schachter's career was spent at Columbia University, where he was a professor in the Psychology Department since 1960. Before that, he was a Fulbright professor at the University of Amsterdam in the early 1950s and later served for some years with the Organization of Comparative Social Research. For his accomplishments, the American Psychological Association bestowed on him its Distinguished Scientific Award in 1969.

Schachter developed a cognitive theory of emotion in which he established that people cannot discriminate one emotion from another unless they have some cognitive indication as to what their feelings relate. Schachter's is a psychobiological theory of emotion, claiming that physiological arousal is insufficient to induce emotion, as cognition also must be present.

Schachter's other research interests included obesity, smoking, stress, hunger, and the need for affiliation. This last subject was discussed in detail in *The Psychology of Affiliation.* Other subjects are found in his *Emotion, Obesity and Crime.*

STAFF

SCHAIE, K. WARNER (1928–   )

K. Warner Schaie was born on February 1, 1928, in Stettin, Germany (now in Poland). He emigrated to Shanghai, China, in 1939, then to the United States in 1947. He received an AA degree in 1951 at City College of San Francisco; a BA in psychology in 1952 at the University of California at Berkeley; and an MS (1953) and a PhD (1956) in psychology at the University of Washington.

Schaie held a post-doctoral fellowship in medical psychology at Washington University from 1956 to 1957. Since then he has been assistant and associate professor of psychology at the University of Nebraska (1957–1964); associate professor and then professor of psychology (as well as department chair) at West Virginia University (1964–1973); professor of psychology and director of the Gerontology Research Institute, Andrus Gerontology Center, University of Southern California (1973–1981); professor of human development and psychology at Pennsylvania State University (1981–1985); then Evan Pugh Professor of Human Development and Psychology and director of the Gerontology Center, at the same university (1985–present). He has been an affiliate professor of psychiatry and behavioral sciences at the University of Washington since 1992, and has been a visiting professor at the University of Missouri (1960); University of the Saar (Germany; 1961, 1962); University of Washington (1963–1964); University of Bern (Switzerland; 1970–1971); McQuarrie University (Australia; 1976); University of Trier (Germany; 1979–1980, 1984); and University of Michigan (1987). He has also been a visiting research scientist at the University of California at Berkeley (1988); Center for Advanced Studies in the Behavioral Sciences at Stanford University (1990–1991); and the Lund Gerontology Center (Sweden; 1995).

Schaie's honors and awards include the Kleemeier Award of the Gerontological Society of America (1981); Distinguished Scientific Contributions Award of the American Psychological Association (APA; 1993); Distinguished Mentor Award, Behavioral and Social Sciences Section, Gerontological Society of America (1996); and an honorary doctorate at the Friedrich Schiller University of Jena (1997). He was elected in 1998 as a member of the Akademie gemeinnühtziger Wissenschaften zu Erfurt (Erfurt Academy of Sciences in the Public Interest, in Germany).

Schaie is an APA fellow (Divisions 5, 7, & 20) and a past president of Division 20 (1973–1974). He has been a member of the APA Council of Representatives (1976–1979, 1983–1986) and the Board of Social and Ethical Responsibilities (1990), as well as a fellow of the Gerontological Society of America. He also has been a member of the Expert Panel on Commercial Airline Pilot Retirement (National Institutes of Health [NIH]; 1981); and Developmental Behavioral Sciences Study Section (NIH; 1970–1972; chair, 1972–1974). He has chaired the Human Development and Aging–2 Study Section (NIH; 1979–1984), and has been a member of the NIH Data and Safety Board, Systolic Hypertension in the Elderly Project (1984–1991); the Advisory Committee on Interdisciplinary Aging Research (Ministry of Science and Technology, Federal Republic of Germany; 1989–1991); the board of trustees for the German Center for Aging Research (University of Heidelberg; 1996–present); and the International Expert Group on Longitudinal Studies, Swedish Social Sciences and Planning Councils (1997, 1999–present). He has served as editor of the *Journal of Gerontology: Psychological Sciences* (1988–1991).

Schaie's published books include *Color and Personality* (with R. Heiss, 1964); *Theories and Methods of Research on Aging* (1968); *Life-span Developmental Psychology: Personality and Socialization* (with P. B. Baltes, 1973); *Developmental Human Behavior Genetics: Nature-nurture Redefined* (with V. E. Anderson, G. E. McClearn, & J. Money, 1975); *Handbook of the Psychology of Aging* (with J. E. Birren, 1977, 1985, 1991, 1996); *Developmental Psychology: A Life-span Approach* (with Birren, D. Kinney, & D. S. Woodruff, 1981); *Adult Development and Aging* (with S. L. Willis, 1982, 1986, 1992, 1996); *Longitudinal Studies of Adult Psychological Development* (1983); *Cognitive Functioning and Social Structure over the Life Course* (with Schooler, 1987); *Methodological Issues in Aging Research* (with R. T. Campbell, W. M. Meredith, & S. C. Rawlings, 1988); *Social Structure and Aging: Psychological Processes* (with C. Schooler, 1989); *Age Structuring in Comparative Perspective* (with D. Kertzer, 1989); *Self-directedness: Cause and Effects throughout the Life Course* (with J. Rodin & Schooler, 1990); *Aging, Health Behavior and Health Outcomes* (with D. Blazer & J. House, 1992); *Societal Impact on Aging: Historical Perspectives* (with W. A. Achenbaum, 1993); *Adult Intergenerational Relations: Effects of Societal Change* (with V. L. Bengtson & L. M. Burton, 1995); *Intellectual Development in Adulthood: The Seattle Longitudinal Study* (1996); *Older Adults' Decision-making and the Law* (with M. A. Smyer & M. Kapp, 1996); *Societal Competence in Old Age* (with Willis & M. Hayward, 1997); *Impact of the Work Place on Older Persons* (with Schooler, 1998); *Handbook of Theories of Aging* (with Bengtson, 1999); and *Aging and Mobility* (with M. Pietrucha, 2000). Schaie is also the author of over 250 journal articles and book chapters.

Schaie's work has focused primarily on the study of cognitive development from young adulthood to advanced old age, as exemplified by the ongoing Seattle Longitudinal Study, which he has conducted since 1956. In that study he has investigated health, personality, and environmental factors that contribute to individual differences in successful cognitive aging. This study has also investigated family similarities in cognition, environmental factors, and health behaviors, and has included the long-term follow-up of cognitive training effects in older adults. Schaie has also contributed to developmental methodology by introducing the age-cohort-period model to psychology, and he was one of the first authors to apply event-history (survival analysis) methods to issues of cognitive development in adulthood. He contributed to the testing literature by publishing the Test of Behavioral Rigidity (1975) and the Schaie-Thurstone Test of Adult Mental Abilities (1985). Earlier in Schaie's career he investigated the relationship between color and personality.

STAFF

SCHIZOID PERSONALITY DISORDER

The Schizoid Personality Disorder is described by Kaplan and Saddock (1995) as an illness that, beginning by early adulthood and exhibited in various contexts, is characterized by a restricted range of emotional expression in interpersonal situations and a pervasive pattern of detachment from social relationships. Thus, schizoid personalities tend to be socially withdrawn and shy and only minimally engaged in day-to-day interactions. Individuals with this personality have a particularly difficult time expressing their dissatisfaction or hostility. These emotions may become pent-up and nurtured, thereby reinforcing the schizoid person's sense of detachment and isolation. Schizoid types, however, have often achieved an ego-syntonic view of their socially inappropriate behavior and so may feel somewhat comfortable with themselves.

The Schizoid Personality Disorder is placed on Axis II of the classification system described in the *Diagnostic and Statistical Manual of Mental Disorders,* or *DSM-IV* (APA, 1994). In *DSM-IV,* the terms used to describe this disorder include shyness, oversensitivity, seclusiveness, eccentricity, and avoidance of any close or competitive relationships. These individuals are likely to have few friends and to occupy themselves with tasks and hobbies that can be performed alone. The seclusiveness seems to develop from an extreme sensitivity to the evaluative reactions of others. As a defense, the schizoid individual may retreat into excessive daydreaming and assume a masklike social façade that reveals as little as possible of his or her internal emotional life. At the same time, the person appears relatively insensitive to the nonverbal cues—gestures, expressions, intonation, eye contact, and so forth—used by others to communicate how they are feeling. The ability to express either humor or hostility is often notably lacking in schizoid types. Acquaintances describe them as "in a fog," "in another world," or "not really there." Although inadequate interpersonal relations are indicative of several types of personality disorders, Schizoid Personality Disorder is somewhat unique in that affected individuals do not care about their poor social relations and are usually not concerned with seeking treatment.

Schizoid Personality Disorder in an adult individual is often preceded by schizoid behavior in childhood or adolescence. These children have few close friends, and any friend they do have is likely to be another social isolate. Team sports, clubs, and dances are avoided. The schizoid adolescent displays an unstable cycle of excessive inhibition and impulsiveness and may become hostile and aggressive if pressured to conform to accepted standards of social

behavior. While often of above-average intelligence, this individual is an underachiever in school, especially in mathematics. He or she is strongly attracted to television or movie plots with violent or supernatural themes. Less generally, schizoid adolescents may be distinguished from peers by an inordinate preoccupation with listening to music or by an avid interest in books on philosophy, psychology, religion, or the occult. These individuals rarely share their inner feelings with anyone or express any emotion. Schizoid males often remain single. Schizoid females, pursued by normal males, seem to have a better chance of marrying. In considering occupations, the schizoid individual does best when limited interaction with others is required. Others report feeling uncomfortable when working around them. They exhibit little motivation to advance or excel in their position, and often make mistakes. Usually they have held many jobs, being unable to keep one for any acceptable length of time.

Many schizophrenic patients will have displayed a schizoid personality prior to their psychotic break with reality, but it does not seem to be the case that most persons displaying a schizoid personality at a young age will progress to Schizophrenia in adulthood. One study followed up 54 children thought by their child guidance center to be schizoid types (Morris, Soroker, & Burruss, 1954). Between 16 and 27 years later, only two of these children did not appear to have made a reasonably normal social adjustment, though one of the two was formally diagnosed as schizophrenic. *DSM-IV* notes that withdrawal and self-absorption may either increase following the appearance of a schizoid personality during childhood or may become moderated over time and replaced with role-appropriate social skills. The factors promoting progression or remission of the condition are not well understood. A schizoid personality is more common among boys than girls.

Some researchers have explored possible genetic sources for this personality disorder (Heston, 1970). At the same time, Kaplan and Saddock (1995) have reviewed much evidence for environmental influences on the long-term expression of schizoid traits. For example, these individuals sometimes have a history of extremely cold and neglectful parenting, beginning early in childhood, which may result in an expectation of poor and unfulfilling relationships with others.

The estimated prevalence of Schizoid Personality Disorder ranges from 0.5 to 7 percent in the general population. Research on inpatients and outpatients shows that although clinicians rarely give this diagnosis, about 10 percent of patients meet criteria for this condition (Kaplan & Saddock, 1995). Though one must be wary of making a diagnosis based on a second-hand description of another's behavior, the *Time* magazine account of two adolescent boys who committed a horrific massacre and suicide at Columbine High School near Denver, Colorado, in April of 1999 revealed that the boys held a bizarre and socially detached belief system highly suggestive of Schizoid Personality Disorder (Gibbs & Roche, 1999). In this case, schizoid thinking was carried to a rare and hyperviolent extreme, but the incident serves to alert us to the need for better detection of and therapeutic intervention for this disorder. As noted above, however, most schizoid children probably achieve a fairly normal social adjustment by adulthood, even without treatment.

REFERENCES

American Psychiatric Association. (1994). *Diagnostic and statistical manual of mental disorders (DSM-IV)*. Washington DC: Author.

Gibbs, N., & Roche, T. (1999). Special report/The Columbine tapes. *Time, 154*(25), 24 ff.

Heston, L. L. (1970). The genetics of schizophrenia and schizoid disease. *Science, 167*, 249–256.

Kaplan, H. I., & Saddock, B. J. (Eds.). (1995). *Comprehensive textbook of psychiatry, 6th ed*, Vol. 2. (pp. 451–455 & 1444–1446). Baltimore, Md: Williams & Wilkins.

Morris, D., Soroker, E., & Burruss, G. (1954). Follow-up studies of shy, withdrawn children: I. Evaluation of later adjustment. *American Journal of Orthopsychiatry, 24*, 743–754.

W. SAMUEL
F. SIMJEE
University of California, San Diego

AVOIDANT PERSONALITY
PERSONALITY DISORDERS
SCHIZOPHRENIA
SCHIZOTYPAL PERSONALITY

SCHIZOPHRENIA

Schizophrenia is a lifelong psychotic illness typically striking during young adulthood. Its treatment requires continuous medication and periodic hospitalization for acute exacerbations of the illness. Treatment is often incomplete, failing to eradicate psychotic symptoms such as delusions and hallucinations and negative symptoms such as apathy and blunted affect. Furthermore, treatment is frequently accompanied by prominent side effects. The human tragedy of the illness cannot be overemphasized, as many people with schizophrenia are unable to care for themselves, work, or develop lasting and meaningful relationships. This article first pulls together information concerning the nature of schizophrenia and then focuses on the etiology of the disorder.

DEFINITION OF THE DISORDER

Schizophrenia is marked by a variety of positive and negative symptoms that manifest themselves similarly across cultures, even though the expression and pattern of these symptoms can vary widely among individuals. Most individuals with schizophrenia predominately express one of three symptom clusters: (a) hallucinations (sensory experiences not based on real stimuli) and delusions (beliefs that are unreasonable, illogical, or absurd); (b) disturbances in form of thought (tangentiality or loosening of associations) and bizarre behavior; or (c) negative symptoms (apathy, lack of interest or pleasure, deficits in attention, poverty of speech or content, and affective flattening) (Carpenter, Buchanan, Kirkpatrick, 1993). The primary expression of one symptom cluster, however, does not preclude lesser manifestations of either of the other two symptom clusters.

As there is no gold standard or biological test by which to identify the illness and few people with schizophrenia exhibit all the characteristic symptoms, the diagnostic criteria defining the disorder must be derived by expert consensus. The most widely accepted definition in the United States appears in the *Diagnostic and Statistical Manual of Mental Disorders*–Fourth Edition (*DSM-IV;* American Psychiatric Association, 1994). This definition requires that acute symptoms persist for at least one month and that continuous signs of the illness (e.g., a prodrome) be present for at least six months before a diagnosis can be made.

PREVALENCE AND COURSE

Epidemiological Catchment Area (ECA) research estimates the lifetime prevalence rate of schizophrenia to be 1.3% of the population, or approximately 1.5 million people (Rosenstein, Milazzo-Sayre, & Manderscheid, 1989). A precipitous drop in social functioning during the first several years after onset characterizes the course of schizophrenia. Following these often devastating and tumultuous early years, however, is a relatively flat or stable course of illness (Tamminga, 1997). In later years (in individuals over 50 years old), significant improvement is often evident in symptoms and function.

While the lifetime prevalence rates are equal for women and men, women tend to experience a more benign course of illness as evidenced by a later age of onset, higher premorbid functioning, fewer psychiatric hospitalizations, and less debilitating psychiatric symptoms (Goldstein, 1988).

THE HETEROGENEITY OF SCHIZOPHRENIA

The heterogeneity of the symptom pattern of schizophrenia has prompted the search for specific subtypes of the disorder. Two of the most prominently regarded and researched distinctions are (1) positive versus negative schizophrenia, and (2) deficit and nondeficit schizophrenia.

Crow (1985) posited two dimensions of pathology underlying schizophrenia: Type I (characterized by positive symptoms) and Type II (characterized by negative symptoms). Positive-symptom schizophrenia is hypothesized to reflect a neurotransmitter (dopaminergic) disturbance that is responsive to neuroleptic treatment. Negative-symptom schizophrenia is hypothesized to reflect neuroanatomical changes (such as enlarged ventricles) that, because of the structural anomalies involved, are not amenable to neuroleptic treatment. These two subtypes are not conceptualized as independent, but rather as overlapping constellations of symptoms. Research, however, on the validity of these subtype distinctions is at best mixed (Bellack, Gearon, & Blanchard, in press).

Wagman, Heinrichs, and Carpenter (1987) have argued that the effort to use negative symptoms to define a putative subtype of schizophrenia has failed because no clear distinction has been made between the primary, enduring negative symptoms (labeled "deficit symptoms") and the more transient negative symptoms secondary to other factors such as depression and side effects of medication. Consequently, they have proposed a deficit and nondeficit distinction of schizophrenia. Diagnostic criteria include *DSM-IV* criteria for schizophrenia, and two of the following negative symptoms must have been present for the preceding 12 months and during periods of clinical stability or recovery from psychotic exacerbation: (a) affective flattening; (b) alogia; and/or (c) avolition. Initial validity research examining this subtype of schizophrenia is promising and indicates that deficit syndrome patients have neuropsychological and eye-tracking impairments that distinguish them from other chronic schizophrenic patients (Thacker, Buchanan, Kirkpatrick, & Tamminga, 1988).

THE ETIOLOGY OF SCHIZOPHRENIA

In recent years, many significant advances that have been made through biological and psychosocial studies of schizophrenia offer promising insights about the etiology of schizophrenia. The three most accepted etiological models of schizophrenia are the neurobiological, genetic, and environmental models.

Neurobiological

The availability of computed tomography (CT), magnetic resonance imaging (MRI), and positron emission tomography (PET) has enabled scientists to study the neuroanatomy and psychobiology of people with schizophrenia. CT and MRI brain scanning along with post mortem brain tissue studies have revealed lateral ventricle enlargement in people with schizophrenia, suggesting either a degenerative change, possibly occurring as part of an abnormal brain development during adolescence or over the early course of the illness, or early-life periventricular pathology (Sweeney, Haas, & Nimgaonkar, in press). The degree of ventricle enlargement has been shown to have a moderate relationship to the severity of cognitive and behavioral deficits in schizophrenia patients. PET scan studies have revealed reduced metabolism in the prefrontal cortex. This decreased frontal activity, commonly referred to as hypofrontality, has been linked with negative symptoms (Sweeney, Haas, & Nimgaonkar, in press).

The most widely accepted biochemical theory of schizophrenia has been coined "the dopamine hypothesis." Driving this theory is the notion that increased activity in dopaminergic neurons is associated with acute psychosis. This theory has had a remarkable survival in a rapidly changing bioscience environment because the most effective drugs used to treat schizophrenia block dopamine receptors, and agents that make schizophrenia worse—such as PCP, crack, and amphetamines—increase dopamine levels (Gottsman, 1991).

Genetic Factors

Family and twin studies have provided compelling evidence for a genetic link to schizophrenia. Approximately 15 to 25% of schizophrenia patients have a first- or second-degree relative with a history of schizophrenia (Kendler et al., 1993). Family members of schizophrenia patients are also more likely to demonstrate other psychiatric illnesses such as schizoaffective, schizotypal, schizoid, and paranoid personality disorders. Furthermore, unaffected relatives of people with schizophrenia are more likely than controls to express specific neurobehavioral abnormalities, such as deficits in smooth-pursuit eye movements, attention, and other soft neuro-

logical signs. Finally, twin studies provide evidence of a genetic link as they demonstrate concordance rates for monozygotic (MZ) and dizogotic (DZ) twins to be 48% and 17%, respectively. The fact that concordance rates for MZ twins (who share virtually all their genetic characteristics) are not 100% suggests that environmental factors play a significant role (Sweeney, Haas, & Nimgaonkar, in press).

Environmental Factors

Environmental factors potentially contribute to the etiology of schizophrenia in three ways: as *triggers* precipitating the onset of familial forms of the disorder, as *causal agents* producing a pathophysiologic abnormality causing nonfamilial forms of schizophrenia, or as *moderating factors,* modulating the severity or phenotypic expression of the illness. Environmental factors themselves can be placed broadly into two categories, physical and psychosocial. Physical factors include those that can alter the course of normal brain development, such as biochemical toxins, psychoactive chemicals, viruses, season of birth, obstetric complications, and cerebral infections. Psychosocial factors include sociocultural conditions, stressful life events, or family communication patterns that may modulate the expression of the disorder or possibly potentiate the onset of illness in a genetically predisposed individual. For more detail regarding research in these areas, the reader is referred to Sweeney, Haas, & Nimgaonkar (in press) or Gottsman (1991).

The Stress-Vulnerability Model

While the neurobiologic, genetic, and environmental models of schizophrenia have each enjoyed empirical successes, they have also failed to provide a full understanding of the phenomenon of schizophrenia. In response to this failure, researchers have sought to study the interaction of these two models within one superordinate model encompassing both: the stress-vulnerability model (Bellack, Gearon, & Blanchard, in press). This model posits that an individual's vulnerability to schizophrenia is either inborn (i.e., genetically linked) or acquired (e.g., by sociodevelopmental events, prenatal or perinatal trauma, toxins, or disease). An individual's degree of vulnerability will interact with stressors to determine the ultimate risk of exceeding some threshold and moving from normal functioning to the onset or relapse of illness. Although this model remains heuristic, it provides great promise for the integration of various scientific disciplines in the study of this devastating disorder. As more is learned about the nature and etiology of the illness, clinicians will be able to intervene effectively and help improve the quality of their patients' lives.

REFERENCES

American Psychiatric Association. (1994). *Diagnostic and statistical manual of mental disorders* (4th ed.). Washington, DC: Author.

Bellack, A. S., Gearon, J. S., & Blanchard, J. J. (in press). Schizophrenia: Psychopathology. In A. S. Bellack & M. Hersen, *Psychopathology in adulthood* (2nd ed.). Boston: Allyn and Bacon.

Carpenter, W. T., Buchanan, R. W., & Kirkpatrick, B. (1993). Strong inference, theory testing, and the neuroanatomy of schizophrenia. *Archives of General Psychiatry, 50,* 825–831.

Crow, T. J. (1985). The two-syndrome concept: Origins and current status. *Schizophrenia Bulletin, 10,* 204–232.

Goldstein, J. M. (1988). Gender differences in the course of schizophrenia. *American Journal of Psychiatry, 145,* 684–689.

Gottsman, I. (1991). *Schizophrenia Genesis: The Origins of Madness.* Freeman and Company. New York.

Kendler, K. S., McGuire, M., Gruenberg, A. M., O'Hare, A., Spellman, M., & Walsh, D. (1993). The Roscommen family study. III. Schizophrenia-related personality disorder in relatives. *Archives of General Psychiatry, 50*(10), 781–8.

Rosenstein, M. J., Milazzo-Sayre, L. J., & Manderscheid, R. W. (1989). Care of persons with schizophrenia. A statistical profile. *Schizophrenia Bulletin, 15,* 45–58.

Sweeney, J., Haas, G., & Nimgaonkar, V. (in press). Schizophrenia: Etiology. In A. S. Bellack & M. Hersen, *Psychopathology in adulthood* (2nd ed.). Boston: Allyn and Bacon.

Tamminga, C. A. (1997). Gender and schizophrenia. *Journal of Clinical Psychiatry, 58,* 33–37.

Thacker, G., Buchanan, R., Kirkpatrick, B., & Tamminga, C. (1988). Eye movements in schizophrenia: Clinical and neurobiological correlates. *Society for Neuroscience Abstracts, 14,* 339.

Wagman, A. M. I., Heinrichs, D. W., & Carpenter, W. T. (1987). Deficit and nondeficit forms of schizophrenia: Neuropsychological evaluation. *Psychiatry Research, 22,* 319–330.

J. S. GEARON
A. S. BELLACK
University of Maryland

ANTIPSYCHOTIC DRUGS
HALLUCINATIONS

SCHIZOTYPAL PERSONALITY

Coined as a syndromal designation in the 1950s by Sandor Rado, the schizoptypal trait constellation had been described under a variety of other terms for several prior decades. According to the 1980 revision of the *Diagnostic and Statistical Manual of Mental Disorders, Third Edition* (*DSM-III*), where the label was assigned official status, the prime characteristics of the disorder include various eccentricities in behavior, thought, speech, and perception. Although not invariable, periodic and marked social detachment may be notable, often associated with either flat affect or severe interpersonal anxiety. There is a tendency to follow a meaningless, idle, and ineffectual life, drifting aimlessly and remaining on the periphery of normal societal relationships. Some possess significant affective and cognitive deficiencies, appearing listless, bland, unmotivated, and obscure, and only minimally connected to the external world. Others are dysphoric, tense, and withdrawn, fearful and intentionally seclusive, inclined to damp down hypersensitivities and to disconnect from anticipated external threats. Notable also are their social attainment deficits, their repeated failure to maintain durable, satisfactory, and secure roles consonant with age. Many have experienced several brief and reversible periods in which either bizarre behaviors, extreme moods, irrational impulses, or delusional thoughts were exhibited. To many clinicians, the schizophrenic disorder is a syndromal prototype of which the schizotypal personality is a dilute and nonpsychotic variant.

Although not labeled as such, the early history of the schizotypal concept may be traced in allusions found in the literature to dementia praecox and schizophrenia. A more recent parallel may be seen in the designation *ambulatory schizophrenics,* a term employed by Zilboorg in 1941 to represent patients who "seldom reach the point at which hospitalization appears necessary . . . although they remain inefficient, peregrinatory, (and) casual in their ties to things and people." A similar formulation was presented in 1948 by Schafer in his depiction of what he termed the *schizophrenic character.* In 1949, Hoch and Polatin proposed another variant in their conception of *pseudoneurotic schizophrenia.* A major pathognomonic sign they noted was "the lack of inhibition in displaying certain emotions that is especially striking in otherwise markedly inhibited persons." To Rado (1956), who coined the schizotypal label, the primary defect is an "integrative pleasure deficiency," evident in the patient's lack of joy, love, self-confidence, and the capacity to engage in the "affectionate give and take in human relationships." Elaborating on Rado's formulation, Meehl presented an inventive neurologic-social learning thesis in 1962, seeking to elucidate the developmental origins of the schizotypal pattern. Along similar lines, Millon utilized the biosocial–learning theory in his 1969 *Modern Psychopathology* text as a basis for the following diagnostic criteria:

1. Social detachment (e.g., prefers life of isolation with minimal personal attachments and obligations; over time, has drifted into increasingly peripheral social and vocational roles).

2. Behavioral eccentricity (e.g., exhibits peculiar habits frequently; is perceived by others as unobtrusively strange or different).

3. Nondelusional autistic thinking (e.g., mixes social communication with personal irrelevancies, obscurities, and tangential asides; appears self-absorbed and lost in daydreams with occasional blurring of fantasy and reality).

4. Either (a) anxious wariness (e.g., reports being hypersensitive and apprehensively ill at ease, particularly in social encounters; is guarded, suspicious of others, and secretive in behavior); or (b) emotional flatness (e.g., manifests a drab, sluggish, joyless, and spiritless appearance; reveals marked deficiencies in activation and affect).

5. Disquieting estrangement (e.g., reports periods of depersonalization, derealization, and dissociation; experiences anxious feelings of emptiness and meaninglessness).

REFERENCES

American Psychiatric Association. (1980). *Diagnostic and statistical manual of mental disorders* (*DSM-III*). Washington, DC: American Psychiatric Association.

Hoch, P. H., & Polatin, P. (1949). Pseudoneurotic form of schizophrenia. *Psychiatric Quarterly, 23,* 248–276.

Millon, T. (1969). *Modern psychopathology: A biosocial approach to maladaptive learning and functioning.* Philadelphia: Saunders.

Rado, S. (1956). Schizotypal organization: Preliminary report on a clinical study of schizophrenia. In S. Rado & G. E. Daniels (Eds.), *Changing concepts of psychoanalytic medicine.* New York: Grune & Stratton.

Schafer, R. (1948). *The clinical application of psychological tests.* New York: International Universities Press.

Zilboorg, G. (1941). Ambulatory schizophrenia. *Psychiatry, 4,* 149–155.

T. MILLON
University of Miami

AUTISM
DIAGNOSTIC AND STATISTICAL MANUAL
PERSONALITY DISORDERS
SCHIZOID PERSONALITY
SCHIZOTYPAL PERSONALITY

SCHOLASTIC APTITUDE TEST (SAT)

The SAT is a three-hour multiple-choice test that measures verbal and mathematical abilities important for success in college. All operational forms of the SAT in use at any one time are secure; administration is carefully controlled and takes place only at approved centers. Currently more than one million high school students take the SAT each year. A typical form of the SAT contains 85 verbal items (opposites, analogies, sentence completion, reading comprehension) in two 30-minute sections and 60 mathematics items (mathematics problems, quantitative comparison) in two 30-minute sections. In addition, there is a 30-minute Test of Standard Written English and a 30-minute section used to try out new items for future use (College Entrance Examination Board, 1982).

Separate scores are reported for the Verbal and Mathematical sections on a scale ranging from 200 to 800. Each form of the SAT is equated to this basic reference scale based on the performance of all candidates tested in April 1941. Current percentile rank norms for general high school students and college-bound students are available (Angoff, 1971).

The first SAT, administered in 1926 to 8040 candidates, consisted of nine separate subtests containing 312 items. The various SAT forms used from 1926 to 1941 were constructed by Princeton University psychologist Carl Brigham; since 1948, all forms have been constructed by the Educational Testing Service. Evolution of the test has been carefully documented (Angoff, 1971), and the procedures used in its development are rigorous and exacting. The SAT scores are typically used in conjunction with high school grade average to predict success in college. A special form of the SAT—the Preliminary Scholastic Aptitude Test/National Merit Scholarship Qualifying Test (PSAT/NMSQT)—is administered to secondary school juniors annually in October for guidance purposes and to name semifinalists in the National Merit Scholarship competition.

REFERENCES

Angoff, W. H. (Ed.). (1971). *The College Board Admissions Testing Program: A technical report on research and development activities relating to the Scholastic Aptitude Test and achievement tests.* New York: College Entrance Examination Board.

College Entrance Examination Board. (1982). *Admissions testing program guide for high schools and colleges, 1982–83.* New York: College Entrance Examination Board.

SUGGESTED READING

College Entrance Examination Board. (1981). *An SAT: Test and technical data for the Scholastic Aptitude Test administered in April 1981.* New York: College Entrance Examination Board.

College Entrance Examination Board. (1981). *Five SATs.* New York: College Entrance Examination Board.

G. J. ROBERTSON
Wide Range, Inc.

MILLER ANALOGIES TEST

SCHOOL ADJUSTMENT

School adjustment is a multi-domain, dynamic construct composed of school interest/motivation, academic achievement, behavioral and social-emotional adjustment (including negotiating interpersonal relationships with peers and school personnel), and knowledge of classroom and school systems. A child's school adjustment depends on the match between his or her skills in these domains and expectations or demands of the educational environment. A child's school adjustment may fluctuate across years or classrooms, or across different domains within the same year.

School adjustment is impacted by both past and ongoing events or experiences. Children who attended preschool have experience with the tasks of separating from parents, accepting teachers' authority, and interacting within the peer group, and therefore may show better kindergarten adjustment. Events that concurrently impact children's school adjustment include stressful life events, peer victimization, parent involvement, and the family-school relationship.

Markers of school adjustment include achievement and grade information, competence and problem behaviors, frequency of school absence, comfort and/or involvement with the school environment, anxiety or avoidance behaviors, and negative attitudes about school. Chronic poor school adjustment can lead to low achievement, school dropout, and delinquency. Because adjustment in the early primary grades is related to later school adjustment, it is important to prevent poor school adjustment early in children's school careers. Interventions designed to reduce poor school adjustment target the mismatch between the child's skills and the demands of the educational environment by addressing child skills, environmental demands, or both.

SUGGESTED READING

Perry, K. E., & Weinstein, R. S. (1998). The social context of early schooling and children's school adjustment. *Educational Psychologist, 33*(4), 177–194.

E. K. LANPHIER
Pennsylvania State University

SCHOOL LEARNING

As with learning in other contexts, school learning is both formal and informal. Formal school learning is associated primarily with the instructional processes and curricular content applied by the teaching staff. Less directly, formal learning also stems from school-wide socialization processes, such as exposure to established institutional standards and their enforcement. Informal learning at school, sometimes called the hidden curriculum, is associated with experiences of success and failure and with modeling and social persuasion.

DETERMINANTS OF SCHOOL LEARNING

A reciprocal determinist view of behavior emphasizes the transactions between person and environment (Bandura, 1978; Lewin, 1951; Walsh, Craik, & Price, 1992). From this perspective, school learning is the product of the reciprocal interplay among student and school variables. Each student brings to any schooling-related activity adaptive assimilated schemata consisting of capacities and attitudes accumulated over time, as well as current states of being and behaving. These variables transact with each other and also with those transacting variables encountered at school and in coping with school requirements outside the school setting (Adelman & Taylor, 1994).

Key variables related to formal school learning encompass not only instructional processes and content, but also the physical and social contexts in which instruction and related practice are the primary focus. Informal learning is the product of the many variables impinging on a student during times when instruction and related practice are not the agenda, and occurs in various settings, such as the playing field, eating areas, and hallways, as well as in classrooms and homework situations.

TYPES OF SCHOOL LEARNING

The impact of transacting variables can lead to four types of learning (Adelman & Taylor, 1993):

- *Desired learning*—changes and expansion of capacities and attitudes in keeping with the school's goals

- *Deviant learning*—changes and expansion of capacities and attitudes not in keeping with the school's goals

- *Disrupted learning*—interference with learning functions, including possible confusion that distorts attitudes and decreases capacities

- *Delayed and arrested learning*—little change or possibly a decay in capacities and attitudes

School learning outcomes are accompanied by concomitant shifts in current states of being and behaving. Any specific outcome may primarily reflect the contribution of person variables, environmental variables, or both.

PERSON-ENVIRONMENT MATCH

Many bodies of research have relevance for understanding school learning. These range from basic research on learning and social learning to applied research on teaching and schooling. The theoretical underpinnings are rooted in the paradigm of person-environment match or fit (Hunt & Sullivan, 1974; Hunt, 1961; Piaget, 1952; Vygotsky, Vygotsky, & John-Steiner, 1980). For example, with respect to formal school learning, the paradigm broadly proposes that the better the match, the more likely it is that instruction will lead to desired learning outcomes. Conversely, the poorer the match, the less likely it is that desired outcomes will be achieved. Concern about quality of the match arises at the outset of instruction and remains throughout.

The problem of creating a good match in teaching is viewed broadly as that of establishing an appropriate challenge to the adaptive assimilated schemata of a student. In theory, some degree of appropriate match is always feasible—assuming availability and sound use of resources.

The concept of the match can be operationalized using observer or actor viewpoints or both. For example, the psychological perspective of the teacher may be the sole referent in deciding which student characteristics are considered, which instructional processes and content are used, and whether an appropriate match is established. In contrast, some teachers decide how to proceed and judge quality of fit based on student perspectives.

MATCHING MOTIVATION AND DEVELOPED CAPABILITY

Efforts to optimize the person-environment match focus on both motivation and development. Cognitive-affective theories underscore the necessity of addressing individual differences in motivation as a primary concern in creating an optimal match for learning what is formally taught at school. The focus is on four broad considerations.

First, motivation is considered a key antecedent condition—a prerequisite to school learning. For example, poor motivational readiness may be either a cause of inadequate and problem functioning, or a factor that maintains such problems, or both. Thus, strategies are called for that can result in a high level of motivational readiness (including reduction of avoidance motivation and reactance) so that a student is mobilized to participate and learn.

Second, motivation is a key ongoing process concern; processes must elicit, enhance, and maintain motivation so that the student stays mobilized. For instance, a student may value a certain outcome but may not be motivated to pursue certain processes for obtaining it, and many students who are motivated at the beginning of an instructional activity do not maintain that motivation.

Third, it is necessary to avoid or at least minimize conditions likely to produce avoidance and reactance. Of particular concern are activities that students perceive as unchallenging/uninteresting, overdemanding, or overwhelming, and procedures that seriously limit a student's range of options or that are experienced as overcontrolling and coercive.

Finally, development of intrinsic motivation is an outcome concern (Deci & Ryan, 1985). This requires strategies to enhance stable, positive intrinsic attitudes that mobilize a student's ongoing pursuit of desirable ends outside the school context and after graduation.

Matching a student's level of developed capability is another primary consideration in facilitating school learning. Variations in functional capacity stem from differences related to sensory, perceptual, motor, cognitive, language, social, and emotional development. To facilitate an appropriate match, functional differences are accommodated through modifying instructional processes and curricular content. This encompasses accounting for areas in which development is lagging and in which development meets or surpasses expectations.

In general practice, overall patterns are considered in designing instruction to fit groups of students, with the observed patterns reflecting both accumulated capacities and attitudes. Such patterns may be described in terms of differences, diversity, assets, deficits, and/or disabilities observed among students in a given classroom and school. Researchers and practitioners interested in patterns of differences in functioning find it useful for observation and measurement purposes to stress four key performance dimensions: (a) rate (the pace of performance), (b) style (preferences with regard to ways of proceeding), (c) amount (the quantity of produced outcomes), and (d) quality (care, mastery, and aesthetic features demonstrated in performance) (Gagne, 1985).

ENVIRONMENTAL FACTORS

Facilitating school learning by focusing on the environmental side of the person-environment match has two facets: (a) directly enhancing facilitative factors, and (b) minimizing extrinsic factors that are barriers to learning. Research of relevance to these matters comes from ecological and environmental psychology, systems theory and organizational research, and the study of social and community interventions. Examples of key variables include setting and context characteristics associated with school learning; characteristics of the persons in the setting and its context; and task, process, and outcome characteristics. With specific respect to barriers to learning, the focus is on factors that are insufficient to stimulate learning, exceed the student's capacity for accommodative modification, or are so intrusive/hostile that they lead to cognitions and affect that disrupt learning.

Because teachers can affect only a relatively small segment of the physical environment and social context in which school learning is to occur, increasing attention is being given to analyses of school-wide factors and combinations of school, home, and community variables.

REFERENCES

Adelman, H. S., & Taylor, L. (1993). *Learning problems and learning disabilities: Moving forward.* Pacific Grove, CA: Brooks/Cole.

Adelman, H. S., & Taylor, L. (1994). *On understanding intervention in psychology and education.* Westport, CT: Prager.

Bandura, A. (1978). The self system in reciprocal determinism. *American Psychologist, 33,* 344–58.

Deci, E. L., & Ryan, R. M. (1985). *Intrinsic motivation and self-determination in human behavior.* New York: Plenum Press.

Gagne, R. M. (1985). *The conditions of learning and theory of instruction* (4th ed.). Fort Worth, TX: Holt, Rinehart & Winston.

Lewin, K. (1951). *Field theory and social sciences.* New York: Harper & Row.

Hunt, D. E., & Sullivan, E. V. (1974). *Between psychology and education.* Chicago: Dryden Press.

Hunt, J. McV. (1961). *Intelligence and experience.* New York: Ronald Press.

Piaget, J. (1952). *The origins of intelligence in children.* New York: International Universities Press.

Vygotsky, L. S., Vygotsky, S., & John-Steiner, V. (Eds.). (1980). *Minds in society: The development of higher psychological processes.* Cambridge, MA: Harvard University Press.

Walsh, W. B., Craik, K. C., & Price, R. H. (Eds.). (1992). *Person-environment psychology: Models and perspectives.* Hillsdale, NJ: Erlbaum.

H. S. ADELMAN
University of California, Los Angeles

EDUCATIONAL PSYCHOLOGY

SCHOOLS OF PROFESSIONAL PSYCHOLOGY

Most psychologists are educated in academic departments of psychology. Even those entering such professional fields as clinical or counseling psychology usually pursue their graduate studies in departmental programs comparable in size and administrative structure to programs in experimental, developmental, or social psychology. Increasing numbers of psychologists preparing for careers in practice, however, are educated in schools of professional psychology administratively comparable to schools of law, medicine, engineering, or business. The earliest schools of professional psychology were free-standing institutions, unaffiliated with universities. Currently, many of the schools are situated in universities, though many others continue to operate independently.

Schools of professional psychology are distinguished by several characteristics. First, their explicit mission is to prepare students for careers in practice. Second, their organizational structure is that of a school or college rather than of a departmental program. This status carries several consequences. The chief administrator is usually a dean. The academic unit is accorded a high degree of autonomy in defining its curriculum, selecting faculty, admitting students, and other matters of policy and procedure. Administrative resources and controls are relatively direct, usually through officers of the central administration in university-based schools and through boards of directors in free-standing schools. Enrollments are typically much larger than in departmental programs.

A third characteristic of professional schools is that the curriculum is specifically designed to prepare people for professional work. Supervised experience in psychological practice is therefore emphasized throughout graduate study as well as in an internship. A dissertation is required in the programs of nearly all professional schools, but the inquiry is conceived as a form of practice, not as an end in itself. Fourth, the faculties include large numbers of practitioners, and all faculty members are ordinarily expected to maintain some involvement in professional activity. Finally, the degree awarded upon completion of graduate study is in nearly all cases the Doctor of Psychology (PsyD) degree rather than the Doctor of Philosophy (PhD).

The forerunner of contemporary schools of professional psychology was the program in clinical psychology at Adelphi University. When the Adelphi program was approved by the American Psychological Association Committee on Accreditation in 1957, it became the first accredited program whose primary objective was to educate clinicians for practice, instead of to educate them as scientists or scientist-practitioners. Prior to that time, all of the clinical and counseling programs in the United States and Canada had followed the Boulder model of education that was defined in a conference on the training of clinical psychologists in Boulder, Colorado, in 1949. The conference held that clinical psychologists were to be trained in academic psychology departments, prepared to conduct research as well as to practice psychology, and awarded the PhD degree upon completion of graduate studies. The early Adelphi program preserved the administrative structure that was common to other departmental programs, changed the curriculum mainly by introducing more supervised clinical experience than usual, and retained the PhD as the terminal degree. It differed fundamentally from all other programs at the time, however, by affirming the legitimacy of direct education for psychological practice, with or without the promise of contributory research.

The first institution administratively organized as a school for practitioners of psychology was the Graduate School of Psychology in the Fuller Theological Seminary. Psychologists were initially brought into the seminary faculty to train clergy in pastoral counseling, but in time they expanded their activities to form a comprehensive doctoral program combining clinical psychology with theological studies. The Fuller school was established in 1965.

Large-scale development of schools of professional psychology did not begin, however, until the California School of Professional Psychology was founded in 1969. Overwhelmed by demands for psychological services in an increasingly populous state and frustrated by repeated refusals of academic psychologists to increase the size and implicitly change the emphases of their tiny, research-oriented clinical programs, a group of practitioners resolved to create their own professional school that would be independent of any university. Faculty were to be practicing professionals, teaching on a part-time basis. The curriculum duplicated the Adelphi pattern and, as at Adelphi, the PhD degree was to be awarded to graduates. Capital funds were obtained from several private benefactors. For the first year, the founding group offered their time as administrators and faculty free of charge as an operational endowment. The plan was approved in 1969, and in 1970 the California School of Professional Psychology admitted students to its first two campuses, in San Francisco and Los Angeles. Additional campuses were opened in San Diego and Fresno over the next two years.

In 1973, another conference on professional training in psychology was held in Vail, Colorado. The conference concluded that psychology had matured sufficiently to justify creation of explicit professional programs, in addition to those for scientists and scientist-professionals. Professional schools were recognized as appropriate settings for training, and the PsyD degree was endorsed as the credential of choice upon completion of graduate requirements in practitioner programs. Over the following years, schools of professional psychology were established in many locations throughout the United States. Some were in universities and some were in free-standing institutions. Some awarded the PhD; others awarded the PsyD degree. The Graduate School of Applied and Professional Psychology, established at Rugers University in 1974, was the first university-based professional school to offer the PsyD. At Rutgers, as in the Illinois PsyD program that preceded it, a scientist-practitioner program leading to the PhD was maintained for students interested primarily in research. This pattern—a relatively large school of professional psychology designed expressly to train practitioners and awarding the PsyD degree alongside a smaller PhD program to prepare students for research careers—has since been adopted by several other universities and independent professional schools. Toward the end of the 20th century, more than 35 professional schools were in operation, approximately half in universities and half as free-standing institutions. During this period, nearly one-third of students receiving doctorates in clinical psychology were graduated from professional schools.

As the schools have evolved, they have changed in several ways. Early faculties in free-standing schools were employed almost entirely on a part-time basis. Proportions of full-time faculty in the independent schools have increased over the years, and professional schools in universities employed large proportions of full-time faculty from the beginning. Psychological centers, analogous to the teaching hospitals of medical schools, are now an integral part of nearly all professional schools, and provide the controlled settings in which faculty and students offer public services, students are trained, and research is conducted. Dissertation requirements, which were eliminated completely in some of the early schools, are now an essential part of nearly every program, though the emphasis on direct education for practice and the view of systematic investigation as a form of professional service has been retained. The PsyD degree has replaced the PhD degree in almost all of the professional schools in operation at this time.

In 1976, the National Council of Professional Schools was established to provide a forum for exchange of information among professional schools, to develop standards for the education and training of professional psychologists, and to improve in every way possible the educational process so that graduates would serve public needs most effectively. Later, the name of the organization was changed to the National Council of Schools and Programs of Professional Psychology, to acknowledge the inclusion of some 20 programs that share the fundamental aims, curricula, and degree-granting practices of professional schools but differ in their smaller enrollments and departmental administrative structures. Through a series of conferences and reports, the council has conducted self-studies, defined curricula, and established means for quality assurance among its member organizations. Along with the Council of Graduate Departments of Psychology and the Councils of University Directors of Clinical, Counseling, and School Psychology, the National Council of Schools and Programs of Professional Psychology is an influential participant in shaping educational policy in American psychology.

SUGGESTED READING

Peterson, R. L., Peterson, D. R., Abrams, J. C., & Stricker, G. (1997). The National Council of Schools and Programs of Professional Psychology educational model. *Professional Psychology: Research and Practice, 28,* 373–386.

Stricker, G., & Cummings, N. A. (1992). The professional school movement. In D. K. Freedheim (Ed.), *History of psychotherapy: A century of change.* Washington, DC: APA Books.

D. R. PETERSON
Rutgers University

AMERICAN PSYCHOLOGICAL ASSOCIATION
AMERICAN PSYCHOLOGICAL SOCIETY
DOCTOR OF PSYCHOLOGY DEGREE
PSYCHOTHERAPY TRAINING

SCHOOL PSYCHOLOGISTS

The applications of psychological assessment, consultation, and intervention within public school settings are the primary responsibility of school psychologists. The dual relationship of education and psychology is reflected in the diversity of academic curricula offered by colleges and universities and in the requirements for certification as a school psychologist adopted by state departments of education, in addition to the range of professional responsibilities and activities of school psychologists.

School psychology programs are usually located within an institution's college of education (guidance and counseling or special education department) or college of arts and sciences (psychology department). Of the approximately 230 higher education institutions offering graduate training leading to school psychologist certification, over 60% are at the specialist's level or require a master's degree plus 30 quarter hours.

Over 40 states designate specific criteria for certification as a school psychologist; most include a supervised internship in addition to prescribed academic coursework. Academic programs are typically related to the state certification guidelines, although there is considerable variation among states in the proportionate balance of required psychology and education courses. A majority of school psychologists have teaching certificates and have pursued graduate training after one or more years of teaching experience. Some states permit nonteacher certified individuals to pursue training in school psychology if their baccalaureate is in the behavioral sciences; generally additional coursework and classroom observation are then required.

A 1982 study conducted by the National Association of School Psychologists estimates that there are between 20,000 and 23,000 certified school psychologists, university-affiliated trainers of school psychologists, and students. Most school psychologists work within public educational settings, although some may be employed by community mental health agencies or by private schools, or may be in private practice. Some states have established specific criteria for "school psychology" licensure, although most states offer a generic "psychology" license for eligible school psychologists.

Twenty-nine states have consultants for school psychology within the state department of education, usually attached to the division of special education or the division of pupil personnel. The state consultant maintains a liaison between the department of education and the field school psychologist, provides leadership in interpreting psychological interventions and strategies, as well as state standards within the educational bureaucracy, and provides opportunities for in-service and continuing professional development.

The responsibilities of school psychologists vary within states as much as between them; the differing academic and certification requirements parallel the diversity in role and function expectations by local school systems. Most school psychologists are integrally involved with extensive psychoeducational evaluation and educational programming for students with perceived learning, behavioral, or emotional problems. The primary role of school psychologists is to ferret out the circumstances hindering optimum school performance for referred children and to assist the school system in the provision of educational plans for these children. This role relies on a knowledge of learning theories, psychometric assessment, child development, and family systems, in addition to a functional understanding of classroom analysis, school organization, and curriculum.

Individual child study begins with referral from a teacher, parent, school administrator, or community agency. Written parental permission is usually secured prior to any psychological evaluation or service. A comprehensive assessment is based on the school psychologist's consultation with parents, teachers, and administrators; observations of the student's behavior; and the administration of tests of general intelligence, perception, specific abilities, personality, and educational achievement. Available health, developmental, and sociocultural information is also incorporated into the comprehensive assessment. This information may be gathered through formal and informal assessment, interviews with significant individuals involved with the child, and reviews of school records. Additional school personnel, such as a school nurse, speech therapist, or learning disabilities specialist, may be asked to gather further information.

An individual child study generally culminates in a conference with parents, teachers, and/or school administrators, at which time the results of the evaluation are reviewed and recommendations are made regarding appropriate educational programming. Recommendations may include one or more of the following: teacher strategies to employ within the classroom, special class placement, remedial techniques, referral to community or mental health agencies, counseling within the school setting, retention, acceleration of grade, and the like.

In addition to individualized student evaluations, a variety of other services may be provided by a school psychologist, depending on the school system's priorities and the personality and competencies of the psychologist. Psychological services may also include group appraisal of school children, coordination with community (child-serving) agencies, counseling and psychotherapy, coordination with other pupil personnel workers, preventative mental health consultation on programs for the gifted, participation on curriculum committees, research, provision of in-service training, collection and calculation of local normative data, and numerous other areas. Since school psychologists generally have the most formal training in child development, research, and individual assessment in public education systems, consultation in these areas of expertise is often a major responsibility.

Since the passage of the Education for all Handicapped Children Act of 1975 (Public Law 94-142), the diverse nature of many school psychologists' functioning has decreased. This legislation mandates that each school system provide an appropriate educational program for all handicapped children in the least restrictive setting and requires specific assessment techniques (multifactored, nondiscriminatory) and adherence to due process procedures in the course of identification, assessment, and provision of educational programming for children with suspected or identified handicaps. The law also provides for each identified handicapped child to receive a comprehensive evaluation every three years. Approximately 10% of school-age children are currently enrolled in special educational programs for identified handicapping conditions.

Ensuring compliance with Public Law 94-142 has resulted in a large proportion of time devoted to special education screening and assessment. Since its enactment, many school psychologists have less time for involvement in preventative mental health and other consultative functions. Despite these existent pressures toward a narrowing of role functioning, there has been expansion of specialization within the field to include the areas of preschool education, vocational school psychology, urban and rural school psychology, and psychoneurological assessment as it relates to school-age children. The blending of psychological applications within an educational setting directly or indirectly to promote optimum learning for students is the purpose of school psychology.

SUGGESTED READING

Abromowitz, E. A. (1981). School psychology: A historical perspective. *School Psychology Review, 10*(2), 121–126.

Bardon, J. I. (1976). The state of the art (and science) of school psychology. *American Psychologist, 31*(12), 785–796.

Brown, D. T., & Minke, K. (1982). *Directory of school psychology training programs in the United States.* Washington, DC: National Association of School Psychologists.

Grimes, J. (1981). Shaping the future of school psychology. *School Psychology Review, 10*(2), 206–231.

Peterson, D. (1982). *Status of professional standards in school psychology.* Washington, DC: National Association of School Psychologists.

Ramage, J. C. (1979). National survey of school psychologists: Update. *School Psychology Digest, 8,* 153–161.

Tractman, G. (1981). On such a full sea. *School Psychology Review, 10*(2), 138–181.

A. THOMAS
New York University School of Medicine

EDUCATIONAL MAINSTREAMING AND INCLUSION

SCHOOL READINESS

The concept of school readiness is applicable to learning throughout the school years, although it is usually associated with the primary grades—kindergarten through third grade. It can be defined as the ability of the child successfully to meet the cognitive, social, physical, and emotional expectations that accompany school attendance.

In the United States, children typically enter kindergarten or first grade by 6 years of age, although the exact birth-date requirements vary among states. Every industrialized society has specific age requirements for the beginning of formal schooling, normally between ages 5 and 7.

School readiness is determined by assessing the developmental level of children in such areas as listening comprehension, visual perceptual and fine motor skills, expressive and receptive vocabulary, and experiential knowledge. Readiness in these varied areas is generally considered to be the necessary foundation upon which to base more diverse and complex learning skills. Many school districts have preschool clinics, conducted by multidisciplinary school personnel, to evaluate children's readiness. Those children who are relatively lacking in one or more of these areas are considered less ready and at risk unless some type of educational or family intervention is provided. Controlling for other factors, the chronologically older child from a higher socioeconomic background will typically achieve more during the initial school years. Depending on the ability and the resourcefulness of schools to acknowledge and adapt to the individual special needs of their students, the influence of these age and socioeconomic status differences in school readiness can be minimized.

For many children, initial school attendance marks the first time that the home is replaced as the primary source of instruction. Children who successfully meet school expectations continue to more complex learning activities. Children who are unable to meet these indices of successful performance are often deemed failures and may develop associated negative and defeatist attitudes toward learning in general and schooling in particular. The readiness of children to comply with these norms is crucial in developing and promoting a positive attitude toward learning, there being a staggering loss of potential that may be attributed to the frustrations caused by early school failure.

Research supports the finding that up to 20% of primary grade children are seen as not ready for their educational programs. The most common method of dealing with perceived lack of instructional readiness during the first years of school is retention in grade, or, for initial kindergarten attendance, requesting that the child remain home for an additional year. Attempts to raise the school entrance age have not resulted in a corresponding lowered retention rate.

In addition to retention or delayed entry, school systems have attempted to accommodate differing levels of school readiness by providing differential curricula based on student assessment. Such attempts have included the provision of separate classrooms, frequently called transition or readiness rooms, the homogeneous grouping of classes by ability, the subgrouping of children within a regular classroom, and individual tutoring.

The concept of school readiness is a factor throughout the school years and has been recognized as an important instructional consideration by most leading educational and developmental theorists. School readiness is not only a function of children's characteristics, but also of the expectations held by the school as an institution.

SUGGESTED READING

Childers, P. R., & Matusiak, I. (1972). Social-emotional maturity correlates of achievement and adjustment in kindergarten and first grade. *Psychology in the Schools, 9,* 396–403.

Di Pasquale, G. W., Moule, A. D., & Flewelling, R. W. (1980). The birthdate effect. *Journal of Learning Disabilities, 13,* 4–8.

Donofrio, A. F. (1977). Grade repetition: Therapy of choice. *Journal of Learning Disabilities, 10,* 346–351.

Gredler, G. R. (1978). A look at some important factors in assessing readiness for school. *Journal of Learning Disabilities, 11,* 284–290.

Jinks, P. C. (1964). An investigation into the effect of date of birth on subsequent school performance. *Educational Research, 6,* 220–225.

May, C. R., & Campbell, R. (1981). Readiness for learning: Assumptions and realities. *Theory Into Practice, 20,* 130–134.

Wendt, R. N. (1979). Prekindergarten screening: Point-counterpoint. *Viewpoints in Teaching and Learning, 55,* 18–24.

A. Thomas
New York University School of Medicine

ACADEMIC UNDERACHIEVERS
LEARNING DISABILITIES
SCHOOL ADJUSTMENT

SCHOOL TRUANCY

In its strictest sense, school truancy has been defined as students' absence from school without parents' knowledge or approval. In accordance with more common usage, truancy has referred to student absenteeism for unacceptable reasons, irrespective of whether it is known, or approved by, the parents. Porwoll (1977), in a report prepared for the Educational Research Service, identified truancy as being consistently listed by school principals as one of the major problems in the daily administration of the schools. Truancy was seen as influencing the entire school spectrum, from students whose education is affected to teachers whose instruction is disrupted, principals who must account for empty desks, superintendents who must rely on attendance for government aid, home-school counselors and law enforcement officials who must contact the parents and locate truant students, judges who occasionally rule on truancy cases, and merchants who complain of daytime financial losses attributable to adolescent loitering and misbehavior.

Research findings have been fairly consistent with regard to family factors associated with school truancy. Lower social class, higher than average family size, poverty, and poor housing conditions have all been significantly associated with school truancy. In general, the school behavior of truant students has been characterized by academic and behavioral failure, dislike for school, feelings of frustration, and frequent absenteeism beginning in the early school years. These same findings have been reached by a number of investigators, including Elliot and Voss (1974), Finlayson and Loughran (1978), Glueck and Glueck (1974), and Kvaraceus (1966). Zieman and Benson (1980) proposed that truancy is a coping mechanism maintained by short-term reduction of frustration and discomfort with little regard for long-term consequences. These researchers discovered that many of the truant students they sampled desired good grades, a sense of belonging, to be liked by teachers, and not to be labeled as problem students—however, they felt blocked in achieving these goals. Dreikurs' (1962, 1968) theory of delinquency has been used as a focal point from which to establish remedial efforts regarding truancy, given the "coping mechanism" conceptualization. It states that problem behavior stems from feelings of inferiority and acting out behavior is a maladaptive attempt to compensate for lack of success in school. Supporting Dreikurs' postulates, Zieman and Benson (1980, 1981) and Reynolds and Birch (1977), among others, have suggested that school failure precedes truancy problems and academic success appears to diminish these problems.

REFERENCES

Dreikurs, R. (1962). *Prevention and correction of juvenile delinquency.* Chicago: Alfred Adler Institute.

Dreikurs, R. (1968/1957). *Psychology in the classroom.* New York: Harper & Row.

Elliott, D. S., & Voss, H. L. (1974). *Delinquency and dropout.* Lexington, MA: Heath.

Finlayson, D. S., & Loughran, J. L. (1978). Pupils' perceptions in high and low delinquency schools. *Educational Research, 18,* 138–145.

Glueck, S., & Glueck, E. (1974). *Of delinquency and crime: A panorama of years of search and research.* Springfield, IL: Thomas.

Kvaraceus, W. C. (1966). *Anxious youth: Dynamics of delinquency.* Columbus, OH: Merrill.

Porwoll, P. J. (1977). *ERS report: School absenteeism.* Arlington, VA: Educational Research Service.

Reynolds, M., & Birch, J. (1977). *Teaching exceptional children in all America's schools: A first course for teachers and principals.* Reston, VA: Council for Exceptional Children.

Zieman, G. L., & Benson, G. P. (1980). School perceptions of truant adolescent boys. *Behavioral Disorders, 5,* 212–222.

Zieman, G. L., & Benson, G. P. (1981). School perceptions of truant adolescent girls. *Behavioral Disorders, 6,* 197–205.

SUGGESTED READING

Hershov, L., & Berg, I. (Eds.). (1980). *Out of school: Modern perspectives in truancy and school refusal.* New York: Wiley.

Turner, B. (1974). *Truancy.* London: Word Lock Educational.

C. H. HUBER
New Mexico State University

SCHOOL ADJUSTMENT

SCIENTIFIC FRAUD

Scientific fraud (also scientific misconduct) is a particular form of transgression against the principles of good scientific practice. It takes place when researchers deceive their colleagues about the nature and results of their work or their personal achievement.

IDENTIFYING SCIENTIFIC FRAUD

In accordance with the normal view of fraud, it is assumed that the scientific defraudor acts against his better knowledge with the intention of deceiving others. As the distinction between fraud and error depends on the particular mental circumstances of the perpetrator, it is pointless to examine a suspected fraud directly. Even a confession is insufficient, as it could also be based on an error or on an intention to deceive. It therefore seems reasonable, as in everyday life or in court, to speak of fraud when the supposition of a fraudulent intention represents the best explanation for questionable actions. However, the actions objected to are also past occurrences which have to be reconstructed using witnesses' statements, laboratory records, and other sources. Frequently the sources do not provide unambiguous evidence. For example, in the case of the so-called cold fusion, the reports are so vague that it is impossible to decide whether error or fraud is involved (Huizenga, 1992). A further problem is drawing a link between fraud and defrauder when several persons are involved. The unspecified presentation of research results in a multiauthored article suggests collective responsibility, but it seems insupportable to accuse an individual of fraud when no personal culpability is involved.

FORMS OF SCIENTIFIC FRAUD

Consideration of scientific fraud focuses on falsification, fabrication, and plagiarism (National Academy of Sciences, 1992; Office of Science and Technology Policy, 1999). In its simplest form, falsification occurs when a person who has established *a* claims to have established not *a*, but *b*. Fabrication takes place when a person claims to have established *a*, without in fact having established anything of the kind. A person is guilty of plagiarism when he claims to have established something himself, although this has been done by other people.

In a specific case the circumstances may be very complex. The fraud may, for example, lie in the suppression of a variable, or it may result from an inappropriate mathematical model, so that data which in themselves are correct are misleadingly presented. An interesting relationship exists between false claims of authorship and the falsification or fabrication of factual material. Plagiarism does not affect the integrity of the relevant research, but attributes it incorrectly to one or more persons. Thus, the *better* the research a person falsely attributes to himself, the more worthwhile plagiarism becomes.

EXTENT AND EFFECTS OF SCIENTIFIC FRAUD

In several spectacular cases fraud has been demonstrated, or the suspicion of fraud has been widely discussed. It is generally agreed, for example, that Burt fabricated data on the inheritability of intelligence (Broad & Wade, 1983). The so-called Baltimore case (Kevles, 1998) not only received extensive media attention, but has also been more precisely investigated than any of the outstanding research achievements of the twentieth century, although only of marginal importance in scientific terms.

In contrast to the wide interest in the topic, statistics (e.g., those provided by the HHS Office of Research Integrity) suggest that fraud is very rare and can only be measured in cases per thousand. On the other hand, evidence from the history of science suggests that questionable research practices are widespread. It has been demonstrated, for example, that Mendel, Newton, Millikan, and many other famous scientists have at least massaged their data (Broad & Wade, 1983). The possibility has also been raised that to some extent every scientific presentation, when closely examined, over glamourizes and transgresses against the principle of honesty. In terms of the number of researchers involved, the most significant fraud in scientific history was that associated with the biochemist Aberhalden. In this case a scientist of the highest rank, by using skillful maneuvers involving hundreds of other researchers, succeeded in defending a fabricated phenomenon (the supposed formation of defense enzymes) against questioning for more than half a century (Deichmann & Müller-Hill, 1998). The archives of the World Wide Web have increased opportunities for scientific fraud, especially of plagiarism. In addition, protection against fraud in this area requires specific techniques which are not available to all researchers.

With reference to the standards of good epistemic practice,

fraud has several undesirable results. It increases the number of reliable conceptions and reduces the number of unreliable ones. It decreases the speed and efficiency with which knowledge is gained, in that time and working capacity are wasted when people are deceived by fraud or have to correct the results. In addition, the recruitment of reliable research personnel is affected when the dishonest gain an advantage over the honest.

Fraud is regarded as having only a minor effect as long as one works on the assumption that research is conducted by cognitively independent individuals who are always in a position to assess claims made by others. The associated idea of the self-correcting power of science (Peirce, Popper) renders the distinction between error and fraud meaningless. But if one considers the division of labor and the mutual dependency within the research community, trust in the reliability of other people becomes a fundamental factor (Hardwig, 1991; Thagard, 1997). Every case of fraud means it becomes less rational to trust the work of colleagues.

INTENTIONS AND REASONS OF DEFRAUDERS

The common conception sees scientific fraud as a means to an end; for example, improving career opportunities, or preventing loss of face after an overeager announcement of positive results. The intentions of defrauders need not always be wholly despicable. A possible explanation for the minor cheating of Newton and Mendel, for example, might be that they were (rightly) so convinced of the value of their views that they did not want to see them endangered by unfavorable data. Preferred social goals can also displace the motive of scientific integrity: the desire, for example, to retain jobs at an institution by claiming a success. Psychological experiments like that based on the Good Samaritan parable (Darley & Batson, 1973) can be interpreted as suggesting that external circumstances like shortage of time both hinder rational calculation and reduce the weight of ethical considerations. This thesis is supported by the statements of exposed perpetrators (Summerlin, 1983).

FRAUD AND RESEARCH ETHICS

Research ethics (Resnik, 1998) offers different approaches to scientific fraud. According to deontological theories, scientific fraud is an infringement of categorical rules. It is rejected because it cannot be made into a general rule. This view forms the basis for context-free catalogues of forbidden actions, formulated on analogy with legal regulations.

Consequentialism concerns itself with calculating the amount of damage caused by or to be expected from fraud. In this view, for example, Newton's irregularities on behalf of a good theory would be perceived as ethical behavior. With plagiarism the question arises of whether it may not be useful if well-known researchers plagiarize the work of less well-known colleagues and thus ensure it greater attention. But if one applies consequentialism to the benefits and adverse effects of rules instead of individual actions, then fraud itself is regarded as an unethical action, just as in duty ethics.

For virtue, ethics fraud represents a depraved action which is committed or avoided according to the personal characteristics of the researcher. This view, in contrast to an orientation towards du-

ties or utilitarian rules, more closely matches the common assumption that researchers are not conformists who follow rules, but individuals whose actions are based on personal motivation.

STRATEGIES AGAINST SCIENTIFIC FRAUD

If one assumes, in accordance with an individualistic theory of knowledge, that in the long term science corrects itself (Peirce, Popper), no particular weapons are needed against fraud. In this view misconduct cannot persist. With falsified or fabricated data, unsuccessful attempts to repeat the observation, experiment, or exploration should force correction of the bad practice. But every attempt at repetition involves human and material variables, so that only an approximation of the original conditions is possible. And in any case, in the light of the competition between researchers and institutions, the idea of repeating research that has already been carried out is not very attractive. Only a small proportion of scientific claims attracts sufficient attention to warrant critical investigation. Even then, scientists are interested first and foremost in independent variations of a procedure. Attempts at repetition in the narrow sense only play a significant role in the training of students and are confined to a limited number of well-known examples. And, further, it is conceivable that the repetition of standard experiments in training leads to an uncritical attitude. In the case of plagiarism the exposure of fraud might be achieved by detective like activities, stylistic analysis, or similar techniques, which do not belong to scientific practice.

Peer review is often seen as ensuring good scientific practice. But it is concerned above all with factors like correct argument, the plausibility of the experimental setup, the potential significance and originality of the results. Referees usually focus their attention only on the presentation and not on claims relating to the underlying practice. They do not investigate laboratory notes or examine witnesses. In addition, the refereeing process involves the danger of plagiarism. Attempting to avoid this by setting short deadlines may in turn affect the effectiveness of the check.

While the exposure of fraud is regarded as a matter for science itself, its prevention is a matter of broad scientific policy. In various countries, institutions like the Office of Research Integrity have come into being, which provide support when there is a suspicion of fraud, and which have laid down rules for procedures in suspected cases of fraud. US institutions which apply for federal research grants under the aegis of the NIH must conform to these rules. The process starts with an informal inquiry, which is followed by a formal investigation. These are the responsibility of the relevant research institution. Nonuniversity bodies are informed during a formal investigation if financial support has been received from the NIH or NSF. After fraudulent activity has been established sanctions are imposed, on the part of the institution, for example, by revoking the right to make applications.

The prerequisite for the exposure of fraud is the readiness of researchers to voice suspicions of fraud. If one assumes that science is self-correcting, the whistle-blower has little importance, as fraud is no more damaging than error. By contrast, from the perspective of collaborative knowledge, the whistle-blower has a very important function in maintaining the network of trust within the scientific community. Accordingly, not only is institutionalized protection desirable, but also a general strengthening of the position of the whistle-blower. It would make sense to combine this with the effort to avoid error and misconduct on the part of the accuser. It is desirable to establish whistle-blowing as a reliable process in which sensible decisions are made as early as possible and moral research standards (carefulness, etc.) are observed.

Hope of avoiding difficult situations like a confrontation between a whistle-blower and a researcher accused of fraud is placed in such things as ethics courses and other efforts towards the moral cultivation of research institutions.

REFERENCES

Broad, W., & Wade, N. (1983). *Betrayers of the truth: Fraud and deceit in the halls of science.* New York: Simon & Schuster.

Darley, J. M., & Batson, C. D. (1973). From Jersualem to Jericho: A study of situational and dispositional variables in helping behavior. *Journal of Personality and Social Psychology, 27,* 100–108.

Deichmann, U., & Müller-Hill, B. (1998). The fraud of Abderhalden's enzymes, *Nature, 393,* 109–111.

Hardwig, J. (1991). The role of trust in knowledge. *Journal of Philosophy, 88,* 693–708.

Huizenga, J. R. (1992). *Cold fusion: The scientific fiasco of the century.* Rochester, NY: University of Rochester Press.

Kevles, D. J. (1998). *The Baltimore case: A trial of politics, science, and character.* New York: Norton.

National Academy of Sciences. (1992). *Responsible science: Ensuring the integrity of the research process* (Vol. 1). Washington, DC: National Academy Press.

Office of Science and Technology Policy. (1999). Proposed federal policy on research misconduct to protect the integrity of the research record. *Federal Register,* October 14, Vol. 64. Nr. 198, 55722–5.

Resnik, D. (1998). *The ethics of science: An introduction.* London: Routledge.

Thagard, P. (1997). Collaborativek knowledge. *Nous, 31,* 242–61.

U. Charpa
Cologne University

SCIENTIFIC METHOD

Psychology, as a science, uses the scientific method, which is a set of procedures designed to establish general laws through evaluating theories that attempt to describe, explain, and predict phenomena. The scientific method involves explicitly stated theories. Hypotheses are made from such theories; the hypotheses are evaluated using objective, controlled, empirical investigations; and conclusions are open to public scrutiny, analysis, and replication.

Conclusions about reality can be made in at least four different ways: on faith ("I believe that God created heaven and earth"), on common sense or intuition ("I feel that women have a maternal drive"), on logic ("I think, therefore I am"), or on the analysis of empirical data (the scientific method).

The scientific approach is analytical. Complex events are analyzed into relevant variables, relationships among these variables are investigated, and theories consistent with the empirical results are created and critically evaluated. For example, if disease is more common among the poor, the scientist may postulate a set of variables that are the cause of this phenomenon, such as differences in diet, education, medical availability, environmental factors, and genetic susceptibility. Then empirical data are collected to analyze the effect of such variables on disease, so that a general theory can be constructed and tested by other scientists.

The scientific method involves a critical approach to data analysis and interpretation. Issues of observer bias (the researcher who sees or emphasizes only those results that are consistent with a theory), subject bias (the subject who cooperates with the researcher by conforming to the experimenter's expectations), and confounding or extraneous variables (alternative variables that could explain the observed phenomena) receive serious attention as scientists interpret the results of their studies.

The scientific method involves a broad array of alternative procedures ranging from carefully observing the variables as they naturally occur to collecting data under controlled situations with subjects randomly assigned to conditions. Scientific research design can be grouped into three major categories. Studies can be designed to describe events, to describe correlational relationships among events, or to establish cause-and-effect relationships between events. Descriptive and correlational studies can be used to provide information for theory construction and hypothesis testing. Causal research allows the researcher to establish the direct effect of one variable on another, rather than simply to establish that two variables may correlate.

An important maxim to remember is that "correlation does not imply causation." Two variables may correlate with each other, although neither causes the other. For example, literacy rates and levels of air pollution may correlate across countries. Literacy does not cause air pollution and air pollution does not cause literacy; both variables may be caused by the demands of an industrialized society. To establish a cause-and-effect relationship, the researcher must demonstrate that by manipulating or controlling the causal variable, a change in the affected variable systematically occurs. This is a scientific experiment. Sometimes, however, this is impossible. For example, to see if being orphaned causes personality disorders, the researcher would have to randomly select a sample of children and make them into orphans. Since this clearly is unethical, psychologists sometimes must rely on correlational evidence and cannot provide scientific evidence for some cause-and-effect theories.

Scientists construct theories out of a collection of building blocks, with research studies and their results providing these blocks. Theories for which the cumulative evidence does not support their construction fall, and theories built on a solid foundation of supporting evidence survive. A single study, by itself, rarely is considered a sufficient basis on which to accept or discard a theory. Replication (producing duplicate studies) and cross-validation (conducting studies by defining variables in different ways or using different types of samples) are necessary for the scientific community to accept the validity of a scientific theory. They also provide evidence for refining theories—that is, more carefully delimiting conditions under which a theory holds true.

Probably one of the easiest research methodologies is the archival method, which involves seeking information from public and private records, such as newspapers or diaries. For example, research on sexism in the media could be based upon content analyses of randomly selected newspapers, magazines, and radio and television programs. While such research avoids some problems of subject bias, experimenter bias must be carefully controlled. Archival data are only as accurate as the original recorders; subjective judgments by these recorders may undermine the validity of the data.

Another type of scientific method involves a case study of a particular individual in depth. Clinical psychologists may examine a patient to learn how the patient's symptoms relate to various factors in the environment or to treatment strategies. Retrospective data about the patient's childhood and currently observed data about the patient's behaviors and environment are systematically collected, described, and analyzed. Although case studies can be used to evaluate hypotheses derived from theories about the etiology or the environmental influences on the patient, results from a single case may not be generalizable to other cases, so that the need for cross-validation is particularly important when single-case studies are interpreted.

The systematic observation method can be extended from the case study of an individual to the study of entire groups. If the researcher does nothing intentionally to affect the group being observed, this technique generally is called the method of naturalistic observation. Naturalistic observations might be made of children as they play in a school yard, of senior citizens as they interact on holidays, or of wild animals as they roam their natural habitats. Naturalistic observations can lead to theories (for example, how dominance hierarchies are established in animals) or can be used to test hypotheses based on theories (for example, a theory may lead to the hypothesis that senior citizens are more sociable on holidays).

Interpreters of data gathered through naturalistic observations must weigh the possibility that observer bias or subject bias affected the results. The very fact that an observer is present may alter the environment and thus induce atypical behaviors. Observer bias may lead to misperceptions and misinterpretations. For example, an observer who believes that boys are more aggressive than girls may consider any male-initiated ruckus as aggression (although the boy simply may be calling to a distant friend) and may ignore such behaviors in girls. Similarly, the presence of an adult observer on a playground may induce an abnormal amount of aggression among a few boys who want to show off for the observer, behaviors that would not have occurred if the observer were absent.

Naturalistic observations may be obtained in a number of ways, each of which provides a systematic data-gathering strategy. First, the researcher must clarify which aspects of behavior are to be noted. This involves creating operational definitions of the variables to be studied, that is, definitions that maximize objectivity. For example, a researcher could operationally define physical aggression as deliberately striking another person with a hand, foot, or object. This operational definition allows the researcher to make rapid, relatively objective records of the observations. However, when observing complex scenes such as playgrounds full of active children, the researcher may not be able to keep up with all of the activities, so a sampling strategy must be employed. Sampling can be based on time or some other unit. A time-sampling strategy involves recording only those events that occur during predetermined intervals, for example, 30-second intervals with one-minute pauses for recording. An alternative is to sample by unit; for example, the observer would randomly select one child at a time for observation and ignore the behaviors of other children. If more than one variable is to be measured, the researcher may elect to measure only one variable at a time, with time-sampling or unit-sampling strategies, or may choose to attempt to record all targeted behaviors simultaneously. Alternative data-recording strategies generally are tested before the actual research begins, so that optimum data can be attained.

Naturalistic observation data collected in real-life settings generally are less artificial than data collected under carefully controlled laboratory settings, so that generalized results may be more valid. However, the data are of a descriptive or correlational nature only, so that cause-and-effect conclusions cannot be made.

Because the presence of an observer can affect the behaviors of subjects, researchers must attempt to reduce this effect. Sometimes observations can be made less obtrusively by acclimating the subjects to the observer (the researcher spends enough time in the setting before the research begins, so that subjects learn to ignore the researcher's presence) or by hiding the observer (behind barriers or one-way mirrors). An alternative approach is the participant-observer research strategy, in which the researcher directly interacts with the subjects, as if the researcher were a member of the community being observed. For example, Rosenhan's (1973) classic study of mental hospitals was conducted by researchers who simulated psychiatric problems so that they could serve as participant-observer mental patients. Staff, unaware of the researchers' ruse, treated them as they treated any other patients, thus allowing Rosenhan's researchers to gather data without subject bias and, perhaps, to understand better what it feels like to be a mental patient.

There are serious ethical problems with participant-observer strategies. Most psychologists agree that participation as a research subject generally should be voluntary and informed. If Rosehan had received permission to collect his data before he began, the ethical problem would have been resolved, but the subject bias problem would have occurred. Further, participant-observation strategies magnify the problems of experimenter bias, since, as a participant, the researcher might actively initiate events that might not occur naturally, and might influence the group's reaction to these and other events.

Another modification of the naturalistic observation approach is to structure it by creating a common standard condition under which observations are recorded. For example, a study of bystander intervention may have research confederates simulate heart attacks in public places to see how people respond. Like the participant-observer strategy, subject bias is reduced, but experimenter bias and ethical issues are raised. This method also can be used in a laboratory setting. A study of how children respond to strange rooms might be done as a structured observation, with children brought to a laboratory and left there. Observers would record each child's behavior. This example is not a true experiment, since the type of room is not a variable; all children are observed under the same condition.

An alternative research strategy is the use of surveys, questionnaires, and structured interviews. Subjects knowingly participate as research participants and provide the data in response to specific questions. The questions can be presented in writing (such as an attitude survey or personality test) or orally (such as an individual IQ test or public opinion poll). The quality of the data depends upon the cooperation and honesty of the subjects, as well as the quality of the questions asked. Survey techniques allow for the collection of large amounts of data under fairly standardized conditions.

Construction of valid instruments for the survey method is complex, since the questions must be unbiased, unambiguous, and at a vocabulary level appropriate for the population to be examined. For example, "Do you believe that evil, lugubrious widows should receive their fair share of the estate?" is biased (the word "evil"), is ambiguous (what is a "fair share"?), and involves vocabulary beyond the comprehension of most people ("lugubrious"). Pilot testing of the instrument (trying it out on a sample of subjects and/or professional researchers) can help to refine the tool before it is used for actual research.

While the survey method can provide large amounts of data inexpensively and allows subjects to volunteer to participate while their confidentiality is protected, it also has limitations. First, self-report data sometimes are of questionable validity. Social desirability response sets (the tendency to give the more socially accepted answers) may invalidate the data. For example, people who have cheated on exams or who have racial prejudice may not be willing to admit to these characteristics, even on an anonymous questionnaire. This problem would be more severe for interview data, especially if the interviewer is perceived as someone who would form judgments based upon the responses. Since participation is voluntary, specific subgroups of the population may be over- or under-represented in the sample. For example, respondents who are willing to be interviewed on their sexual habits may be substantially different from people who refuse such an interview, so that generalization of results may be questionable.

All of these methods provide data for descriptive or correlational studies. Only an experiment in which the researcher manipulates the causal variable (the independent variable) and observes the effect on the affected variable (the dependent variable) can lead to conclusions about causality. It is crucial that all other variables that may affect the dependent variable (extraneous or nuisance variables) be controlled for, so that results can be unambiguously interpreted. It is also important that the operational definitions of the variables be reasonable, so that results can be generalized.

SUGGESTED READING

Allen, M. J. (1995). *Introduction to psychological research*. Itasca, IL: Peacock.

Babbie, E. (1995). *The practice of social research* (7th ed.). San Francisco: Wadsworth.

Rosenhan, D. (1973). On being sane in insane places. *Science, 179*, 250–258.

M. J. ALLEN
California State University, Bakersfield

EXPERIMENTAL METHODS
HYPOTHESIS TESTING
RESEARCH METHODOLOGY

SCOTT, WALTER DILL (1869–1955)

Walter Dill Scott, regarded as the founder of industrial psychology, was largely self-taught relative to his early education. As a farm boy, he studied in the fields at 10-minute intervals while his horses rested from plowing. His undergraduate work was at Northwestern University. Later he became a student of Wilhelm Wundt. After earning the PhD in psychology from the University of Leipzig in 1900, Scott returned to the United States to study laboratory techniques under Edward B. Titchener and to accept a faculty position at Northwestern University. He was hired to teach laboratory psychology, but without a laboratory. At Northwestern, he made his mark as an innovative teacher and a caring person.

Scott sought to transfer his psychological insights into the world of work. With the publication of *The Theory and Practice of Advertising* followed by *The Psychology of Advertising* and other books, he introduced the business uses of psychology into advertising, selling, and consumer behavior. Thus he created a new field—industrial psychology, which has been combined into industrial-organizational psychology. He also was an advertising consultant and conducted market surveys. He eventually became head of a firm of business and industry consultants. In recognition of his contributions to the field of advertising, Scott was elected to the Advertising Hall of Fame.

In 1918, his colleagues chose him to be the president of the American Psychological Association. At the same time he was appointed as the world's first professor of applied psychology, and lectured at the Carnegie Institute of Technology where he established the Bureau of Salesmanship Research.

Scott contributed to military psychology by spearheading a system for classifying and promoting army personnel during World War I. His efforts were rewarded with the Distinguished Service Medal in 1919. In the same year, Northwestern University recalled its notable alumnus to serve as president, and for nearly two decades Scott built the institution academically and structurally into one of America's leading universities.

S. S. BROWN
North Shore Community College

SEARS, ROBERT R. (1908–1989)

Robert R. Sears received the AB degree from Stanford University and the PhD degree from Yale University in 1932. His initial interests in physiological psychology shifted to personality and motivation in his first appointment at the University of Illinois. During the next decade, he performed a number of verification studies on psychoanalytic concepts, culminating in the publication of his *Survey of Objective Studies of Psychoanalytic Concepts* (1943). At Yale, between 1936 and 1942, he participated in research and theory building in the Institute of Human Relations, and was a coauthor of *Frustration and Aggression* (Dollard et al.). This was the first major attempt to bring Freud's psychoanalytic theory and Hull's behavior theory together.

Sears turned to the developmental study of personality in 1942, when he became director of the Iowa Child Welfare Research Station. Working with preschool children, he and a research team (V. Nowlis, J. Whiting, P. S. Sears) investigated the child-rearing antecedents of dependency and aggression. A major finding was the influence of punishment as an inducer of aggression. At Iowa, also, the two Sears published the first research on the effects of father absence. In 1949, Sears established another laboratory at the Harvard Graduate School of Education, from which came the multiauthored *Patterns of Child Rearing*. He continued research on early childhood when he went to Stanford as department head in 1953, publishing *Identification and Child Rearing* in 1965, but much of his time was devoted to university administration after he became dean of the School of Humanities and Sciences in 1961. In later years, he has continued the Terman Gifted Children longitudinal research and has published psychobiographical papers on Mark Twain.

STAFF

SEASHORE, CARL EMIL (1866–1949)

Carl Emil Seashore received the PhD degree at Yale University in 1895, and subsequently worked in the Yale psychological laboratory under Edward Scripture. He then transferred to the University of Iowa, and for many years devoted his experimental efforts there to the study of the psychology of music. He is considered the leading pioneer in this area. In 1919, he published the first set of tests to measure various aspects of musical talent. Seashore's thesis was that musical talent consisted of many different capacities. His initial tests measured the ability to discriminate various aspects of tone, including pitch, loudness, time, rhythm, consonance, and tonal memory. In 1939, the tests were revised—the test of consonance was dropped and one for timbre discrimination was added.

Seashore maintained that these talents or capacities were strictly inherited and were not necessarily related to each other, but the person who scored well on all in the ability to make fine discriminations in these areas would be in the best possible position to take up the study of a musical instrument. *The Psychology of Music* by Seashore remains a classic in the field. In it he related the various aspects of musical discriminations to the sound wave.

Besides attempting to predict musical success through his tests, he devised experimental techniques for measuring musical performance on the piano, violin, and voice. In his studies of the vibrato, using an apparatus he invented called the tonoscope, he measured the degree in fluctuation in the production of a musical sound. In the book *In Search of Beauty in Music,* he set forth his theory of musical aesthetics. He believed that aesthetic experience is closely related to how a person reacts emotionally to the music heard.

R. W. LUNDIN
Wheaton, Illinois

SECONDARY GAIN

DEFINITIONS OF PRIMARY AND SECONDARY GAIN

Gain is a psychoanalytic concept first noted and defined by Freud (1959). He described two types of gains from illness, primary and secondary. To Freud, primary gain was a decrease in anxiety brought about through a defensive operation that had resulted in the production of the symptom of the illness. Primary gain was therefore an intrapsychic phenomenon. An example of primary gain would be the patient who shoots his wife using his right hand. He is guilty and conflicted over this action. The right arm then becomes paralyzed via a conversion mechanism. He is therefore punished. This results in decreased guilt and a reduction in intrapsychic conflict and decreased anxiety (i.e., primary gain). Freud went on to define secondary gain as an interpersonal or social advantage attained by the patient as a consequence of the illness.

Since Freud's time, the psychiatric definitions for primary and secondary gain have remained essentially the same. Barsky and Klerman (1983) defined secondary gain as "acceptable or legitimate interpersonal advantages that result when one has the symptom of a physical disease." The *DSM-III-R* defined primary gain as the gain achieved from generating a conversion symptom that results in keeping an internal conflict need out of awareness. The generated symptom has symbolic value to the underlying conflict. Secondary gain is defined as the gain achieved from the conversion symptom in avoiding a particular activity that was noxious to the patient or enabled the patient to get support from the environment that might not otherwise be forthcoming, or both. It should be noted that the Freud and Barsky definitions relate to illness in general, while the *DSM-III-R* definitions relate specifically to conversion disorder. However, secondary gain is not a diagnosis in the *DSM-III-R*. Finally, both primary and secondary gains are thought to occur by unconscious mechanisms (Barsky & Klerman, 1983). A large number of "interpersonal advantages" or secondary gains have been described in the literature. These are presented in Table 1.

DEFINITION OF TERTIARY GAIN

Tertiary gains were first described and defined by Dansak (1973). These were gains sought or attained from a patient's illness by someone other than the patient, usually a family member. Since then, this type of gain has been noted in chronic pain patients (Bokan, Ries, & Katon, 1981) and cancer cases. The types of tertiary gains described in the literature are presented in Table 2. Authors have not commented on whether the wish for these gains by

Table 1.   Types of Secondary Gain

1. Gratification of preexisting unresolved dependent strivings (Ross, 1982)
2. Gratification of preexisting unresolved revengeful strivings (e.g., getting paid for not working in a setting where the employee felt unappreciated or was engaged in a risky job, revenge at insurance carriers or adjusters who gave patient a hard time; Ross, 1982)
3. Attachment behavior, an attempt to elicit caretaking (Bokan, Ries, & Katon, 1981)
4. Oversolicitousness and overprotectiveness by significant others (Bokan, Ries, & Katon, 1981)
5. Family antagonism (anger) because of disability may increase patient resentment and determination to get his or her due to prove entitlement (Modlin, 1986)
6. Preferential or less hazardous work conditions (Finneson, 1976) or means of avoiding work
7. Sympathy and concern of family and friends (Finneson, 1976)
8. Ability to withdraw from an unpleasant or unsatisfactory life role or activity (Connors, 1985; Finneson, 1976)
9. Sick role allows the patient to communicate and relate to others in a new, socially sanctioned manner (Engel, 1970)
10. Financial rewards associated with disability (Bokan, Ries, & Katon, 1981; Finneson, 1976, Long & Webb, 1980)
11. Drugs (Colbach, 1987)
12. Holding the spouse in a marriage (Bokan, Ries, & Katon, 1981)
13. Maintenance of status in family (Overholser, 1990)
14. Maintenance of family love (Overholser, 1990)
15. Domination of family (Bokan, Ries, & Katon, 1981; Overholser, 1990)
16. Being freed from the socioemotional role (Connors, 1985)
17. Means of contraception (Connors, 1985)

Table 2.   Types of Tertiary Gains

1. Collusion on the part of the significant other, to maintain focus on partner's somatic complaints, in order to divert attention from existential issues (cancer/death), thus providing attainable medical goals (Wright & Nekemkis, 1984)
2. Significant other may enjoy changes in roles that result from the illness or chronic pain (i.e., family role conflicts are solved) (Bokan, Ries, & Katon, 1981)
3. Financial gain (Bokan, Ries, & Katon, 1981; Dansak, 1973)
4. Sympathy from social network over the family member with pain (Bokan, Ries, & Katon, 1981)
5. Decrease family tension and keep family together (Hughes, Medley, Turner, & Bond, 1987)
6. Resolve marital difficulties (Hughes, Medley, Turner, & Bond, 1987)

Table 3.   Alleged Reinforcers for Pain Behaviors (Fordyce, 1976)

1. Rest
2. Relief from pain
3. Change in mood after medication
4. Avoiding responsibility
5. Money (compensation)
6. Avoiding sexual demands
7. Attention and concern of others (e.g., spouse)
8. Avoiding situations that expose inadequacies
9. PRN pain medication scheduled
10. Exercise to tolerance levels
11. Approval from doctor
12. Pending litigation
13. Hostility toward or dependency on other family members
14. Prestige at being the sick family member
15. Little job satisfaction before injury
16. Stressful job before injury
17. Poor relationship with employer before injury

rists such as Fordyce and colleagues (1968) to explain the maintenance of pain behavior. Some alleged reinforcers for pain behavior are presented in Table 3.

The relationship between the secondary gain concept and reinforcers has never been clearly spelled out in the literature. When comparing the types of reinforcers (Table 3) to the secondary gains (Table 1), it appears that some gains could operationally be akin to reinforcers. However, Fordyce (1976) has made it clear that he believes that although reinforcers can maintain pain behavior, they need not have necessarily produced that behavior. Fordyce and colleagues (1968) further state that reinforcers have nothing to do with whether pain is real or not real. They believe that labels such as "secondary gain" reflect application of the medical and disease model and refer to presumed underlying psychic processes for the generation of pain. Although the literature has not made a clear distinction between secondary gains and reinforcers, one can conclude the following: (a) operationally, some are the same; (b) the gain is the reinforcement; and (c) secondary gains are the more unconscious motivation for the observed behaviors.

WHY IS THE CONCEPT OF SECONDARY GAIN IMPORTANT?

The psychiatric nomenclature has identified a number of psychiatric diagnoses which as a group are termed the "Abnormal Illness-Affirming States" (Pilowsky, 1990). Specifically, these are the following *DSM-IV* diagnoses: Somatoform Disorders (conversion disorder, hypochondriasis, somatization disorder, pain disorder); Factitious Disorders (including Munchausen's Syndrome); and malingering (not a *DSM-IV* diagnosis). In all these diagnoses or conditions, secondary gain is thought to be responsible for the production of some or all of the patients' signs and symptoms. These diagnoses and conditions are also often found in patients involved in some form of litigation after a compensable injury. As such, clinicians are often asked if the patient's symptoms or signs are related to secondary gain. Thus, there is intense medicolegal interest in this concept (Fishbain, Rosomoff, Cutler, & Steele Rosomoff, 1995).

the family members occurs at a conscious or unconscious level. However, there is no reason to believe that this psychic operation should be different than for secondary gain.

IS THERE A DIFFERENCE BETWEEN REINFORCERS AND SECONDARY GAIN?

An operant is a response that operates on the environment. The operant conditioning model states that these responses or operants are influenced by consequences that can reinforce the operant or response (Fordyce, 1976; Fordyce, Fowler, Lehman, & DeLateur, 1968). Thus, reinforcers can then be thought of as rewards for operant behaviors. Reinforcers have been utilized by behavior theo-

Table 4.   Described Secondary Losses

1. Economic loss (Thompson, 1991)
2. Loss of meaningfully relating to society through work
3. Family life (Thompson, 1991)
4. Recreational activities (Thompson, 1991)
5. New role not comfortable and not well-defined
6. Loss of respect and attention from those in the helping roles (Munn & Baker, 1987)
7. Loss of community approval
8. Social stigma of being chronically disabled
9. Guilt over disability (Katz, Shurka, & Florian, 1978)
10. Communications of distress are now unclear
11. Negative sanctions from family
12. Loss of support social network (Freeman, 1993)

IS THERE SCIENTIFIC EVIDENCE THAT ALLEGED SECONDARY GAINS CHANGE BEHAVIOR?

To answer this question, Fishbain and colleagues (1995) performed a structured review in which 38 studies were reviewed in detail. It was concluded that the receipt of disability benefits does change patient behavior. This, however, does not necessarily mean that preinjury or postinjury patients consciously act in ways to obtain these benefits.

SECONDARY LOSSES

Biernoff (1946) was the first to point out that if a patient allegedly responds to secondary gains, the consequences of this behavior generally result in secondary losses. These are losses occurring from disabilities related to secondary gain (Munn & Baker, 1987). The secondary losses previously described in the literature are presented in Table 4. The patients appear to act in spite of these losses. Often the secondary losses appear to far outweigh the secondary gains. This problem with the economy of secondary gains and losses is a direct challenge to the integrity of the secondary gain concept.

DIFFICULTIES WITH AND ABUSE OF THE SECONDARY GAIN CONCEPT

A number of authors have noted difficulties with, and abuse of, the secondary gain concept. These difficulties and abuses occur in all areas of medicine, including pain treatment, and often relate to the treating and legal professional. First, the presence of secondary gain factors is usually equated with malingering (Finneson, 1976). This is incorrect and a basic misunderstanding of the secondary gain concept. Second, in the chronic pain and rehabilitation literature, secondary gain, as a term, "has developed increasing use and has generally referred to the financial rewards associated with disability" (Finneson, 1976). The presence of potential financial rewards is usually then equated with malingering (Finneson, 1976). Consequently, the mere presence of litigation or disability benefits, or both, is recognized as a secondary gain issue that in turn is translated into the malingering paradigm. Third, because the presence of secondary gain issue is usually equated with malingering, the resultant suspicion of the patient interferes with treatment and development of empathy (Naftulin, 1970). The secondary gain issues are then often used as an excuse for treatment failure (Munn & Baker, 1987). Fourth, little has been written about secondary losses

and treating professionals appear to ignore the concept of secondary loss and only focus on secondary gain. Fifth, if all patients in a medical facility were examined for alleged secondary gains, most would be noted to have one or more secondary gains. Finally, the identification of an alleged secondary gain does not necessary mean that the secondary gain has had an etiological or reinforcing effect on the illness.

REFERENCES

Barsky, A. J., & Klerman, G. L. (1983). Overview: Hypochondriasis bodily complaints and somatic styles. *American Journal of Psychiatry, 140*(3), 273–282.

Biernoff, J. (1946). Traumatic neurosis of industry. *Industrial Medicine and Surgery, 15,* 109–112.

Bokan, J. A., Ries, R. K., & Katon, W. J. (1981). Tertiary gain and chronic pain. *Pain, 10,* 331–335.

Dansak, D. (1973). On the tertiary gain of illness. *Comprehensive Psychiatry, 14,* 523–534.

Engel, G. (1970). Conversion symptoms. In C. M. MacBryde & R. S. Blacklow (Eds.), *Signs and symptoms.* Philadelphia: J. B. Lippincott.

Finneson, B. E. (1976). Modulating effect of secondary gain on the low back pain syndrome. *Advances in Pain Research and Therapy, 1,* 949–952.

Fishbain, D. A., Rosomoff, H. L., Cutler, R. B., & Steele Rosomoff, R. (1995). Secondary gain concept: A review of the scientific evidence. *Clinical Journal of Pain, 11,* 6–21.

Fordyce, W. E. (1976). *Behavioral methods for chronic pain and illness.* St. Louis: Mosby.

Fordyce, W. E., Fowler, R. S., Lehmann, J. F., & DeLateur, B. J. (1968). Some implications of learning in problems of chronic pain. *Journal of Chronic Disease, 21,* 179–190.

Freeman, D. W. (1993). Sick role dynamics and chronic back pain in the injured worker. *Seventh World Congress on Pain* [Abstract 315], Paris, France, 109.

Freud, S. (1959). *Introductory lectures on psychoanalysis.* London: Hogarth.

Hughes, A. M., Medley, I., Turner, G. N., & Bond, M. R. (1987). Psychogenic pain: A study of marital adjustment. *Acta Psychiatrica Scandinavia, 7*(2), 166–170.

Katz, S., Shurka, E., & Florian, V. (1978). The relationship between physical disability, social perception, and psychological stress. *Scientific Journal of Rehabilitative Medicine, 10*(3), 109–113.

Munn, J. S., & Baker, W. H. (1987). Recurrent sympathetic dystrophy: Successful treatment by contralateral sympathectomy. *Surgery, 102*(1), 102–105.

Naftulin, D. H. (1970). The psychological effects of litigation on the industrially injured patient: A research plea. *Industrial Medicine, 39*(4), 167–170.

Pilowsky, I. (1990). The concept of abnormal illness behavior. *Psychosomatics, 31*(2), 207–213.

Ross, D. W. (1982). Differentiating compensation factors from traumatic factors. In J. J. Leedy (Ed.), *Compensation in psychiatric disability and rehabilitation* (p. 31). Springfield, IL: Thomas.

Wright, M. H., & Nekemkis, A. M. (1984). Functional use of secondary cancer symptomatology. *International Journal of Psychiatry Medicine, 13*(4), 267–275.

D. FISHBAIN
University of Miami
School of Medicine

PSYCHOANALYSIS

SECOND-SIGNAL SYSTEM

The second-signal system refers to human verbal or inferential capabilities and denotes the ability to engage in abstraction from concrete objects and acts. Coined by Pavlov, "the second-signal system is contrasted with the first-signal system, which has to do with the concrete effect of objects and actions on the living animal organism. While both humans and other animals respond—react to—concrete objects, only the human consistently responds to the verbal or linguistic representation of the object in a manner similar to that in which the human responds to the object itself. Abstract thought is achieved because the image of objects and actions expressed in words and ideas replaces their concrete effect on the organism" (Platonov, 1959, p. 16). Both animals and people may salivate to an actual piece of food, but only people salivate to the word "food." The ability of abstract notations (words) to call forth the concrete effect of the object or action named is achieved through conditioned reflex bonds, connecting the word with the first-signal system response (the concrete response). These connections are made in the cerebral cortex, and thus the dichotomy of first- and second-signal systems parallels the anatomical distinction of subcortical and cortical, in the same way that it parallels the dichotomies of concrete–abstract and nonverbal–verbal.

The second-signal system was the foundation of Pavlov's theory of hypnosis and the distinction he made between animal (first-signal system) and human (second-signal system) hypnosis. It is through the second-signal system and its conditioned bonding with first-signal system responses that the verbal instructions during hypnosis are effective.

REFERENCES

Platonov, K. (1959). *The word as a physiological and therapeutic factor.* Moscow: Foreign Languages Publishing House.

SUGGESTED READING

Edmonston, W. E. (1981). *Hypnosis and relaxation.* New York: Wiley.

W. E. EDMONSTON, JR.
Colgate University

CLASSICAL CONDITIONING
COMMUNICATION PROCESSES
INFORMATION PROCESSING
SHORT-TERM MEMORY
STIMULUS GENERALIZATION

SELECTIVE ATTENTION

Within the field of cognitive psychology, "selective attention" refers to the differential processing of simultaneous sources of information. Perhaps the best-known real life example of selective attention is one in which a person is capable of listening to a single voice in a room full of people talking at the same time, while apparently being oblivious to all other conversations. This instance of auditory selective attention was described by Cherry (1953) when he noted that while a person may appear to be selectively attending to only his or her own conversation while ignoring all other voices, that person sometimes notices important stimuli, such as his or her own name. Cherry referred to this so-called cocktail-party phenomenon when he framed many of his principal questions about selective attention.

One of the main questions about selective attention concerns what factors make it easy or difficult. Much of the research on this question in auditory selective attention makes use of a dichotic listening task, in which two different auditory messages are presented simultaneously, one to each ear, via the use of headphones. Participants are instructed to selectively attend to one of the messages and repeat, or "shadow," this relevant message as quickly and accurately as possible. In general, participants have little difficulty shadowing the relevant message; that is, they can quickly and accurately repeat the relevant message in the attended ear while repeating very little, if any, of the irrelevant message in the unattended ear. Findings from modified dichotic listening task studies seem to indicate that selectivity occurs on the basis of the spatial location of the messages, as well as on the basis of frequency differences between the relevant and irrelevant messages. For example, if each of the two messages is played simultaneously at equal intensity in both ears (eliminating differences in spatial location as determined by variances in interaural intensity) using the same voice (eliminating differences in frequency), selectivity of just one message becomes considerably more difficult (Cherry, 1953). Selectivity improves, however, if the voices of the two messages differ in pitch; that is, the ease of shadowing increases when the irrelevant message is delivered by a different gender (Cherry, 1953). Shadowing is also improved when spatial localization is produced by introducing even moderate differences in interaural intensity between the two messages (Treisman, 1964).

What factors affect the ease of selective attention has also been an issue with respect to the visual modality. That is, what factors make it easier or more difficult for a person to attend selectively to a particular visual stimulus while excluding others? Visual selective attention is often studied using a visual filtering task, in which participants are asked to selectively attend to one visual stimulus embedded within an array of visual distracter items. Other tasks involve superimposing two different videotaped events onto a single video. Participants are instructed to selectively attend to one visual scene and press a button whenever an unusual event occurs in the relevant scene. Results seem to suggest that the ease with which participants can selectively attend to the relevant visual stimulus depends on the degree to which the relevant and irrelevant stimuli differ in terms of simple physical attributes, such as location, color, size, and brightness (Pashler, 1998).

Since Cherry first drew attention to the topic of selective attention in the early 1950s, two primary types of structural models of selective attention have been proposed. So-called early selection models of Broadbent (1958) and Treisman (1964) viewed selective attention in the context of an information processing model in which incoming stimuli are successively transformed from basic sensory attributes into more complex semantic representations. Selective attention was seen as a type of filter or bottleneck that restricted the flow of information through the system. According to Broadbent and Treisman, this bottleneck occurred early in the information processing system, such that only low-level perceptual characteristics could be perceived prior to attentional selection. Thus, early-selection theories suggest that higher-level semantic characteristics cannot be perceived early in processing. In contrast, late-selection theories hold that the bottleneck occurs later in the information processing system, such that higher-level, abstract processing of meaning can occur before attentional selection takes place (Deutsch & Deutsch, 1963). Despite the fact that several decades have passed since the articulation of this issue, the question of whether selection occurs early or late has remained largely unresolved.

This question of whether selective attention takes place early in stimulus processing, before semantic analysis of any stimulus, or whether it takes place later in processing, after semantic analysis of all stimuli, has preoccupied researchers for many years. Research on this question also makes use of the dichotic listening task. Results from these types of studies show that participants can remember almost nothing about the content of the irrelevant message, but are able to note if the gender of the speaker of that message is switched or if the irrelevant message is replaced with a tone (Cherry, 1953). These results seem to indicate that selection takes place before the stimulus has been analyzed on the basis of its meaning. However, other studies have shown that participants are able to notice the insertion of their own names into the irrelevant message (Moray, 1959) and that they sometimes shift their shadowing from the relevant message to the irrelevant message when midway through a shadowing task, messages are switched between ears (Treisman, 1960).

In visual modality studies, evidence for semantic processing of unattended stimuli is also somewhat mixed. Experiments reported by Underwood (1981) involved presentation of central (relevant) and right (irrelevant) parafoveal word stimuli, in order to determine whether semantic attributes of the irrelevant word would influence processing of the relevant word. Following presentation of the word stimuli, participants were asked to respond by naming the category to which the relevant word belonged. It was found that the latency of the category-naming response was influenced by the semantic relationship between the relevant and irrelevant words. However, in several other studies of a similar nature, no semantic biasing or priming effects were observed (Inhoff & Rayner, 1980; Paap & Newsome, 1981).

In summary, the totality of research seems to indicate that while selection on the basis of physical sensory cues is usually superior to selection on the basis of semantic cues, stimuli in the irrelevant message do sometimes undergo semantic analysis (Johnston & Dark, 1986). It seems clear that the basic versions of both the early and late selection theories cannot provide an adequate account of all the data, and that the relationship between selectivity and stages of processing will continue to be a long-running controversy within attentional theory.

REFERENCES

Broadbent, D. E. (1958). *Perception and communiation.* New York: Pergamon.

Cherry, C. (1953). Some experiments on the recognition of speech with one and two ears. *Journal of the Acoustical Society of America, 25,* 975–979.

Deutsch, J. A., & Deutsch, D. (1963). Attention: Some theoretical considerations. *Psychological Review, 70,* 80–90.

Inhoff, A. W., & Rayner, K. (1980). Parafoveal word perception: A case against semantic preprocessing. *Perception and Psychophysics, 27,* 457–464.

Moray, N. (1959). Attention in dichotic listenings: Affective cues and the influence of instructions. *Quarterly Journal of Experimental Psychology, 11,* 56–60.

Johnston, W. A., & Dark, V. J. (1986). Selective Attention. *Annual Review of Psychology, 37,* 43–75.

Paap, K. R., & Newsome, S. L. (1981). Parafoveal information is not sufficient to produce semantic or visual priming. *Perception and Psychophysics, 29,* 457–466.

Pashler, H. E (1998). *The psychology of attention.* Cambridge, MA: MIT Press.

Treismann, A. M. (1960). Contextual cues in selective listening. *Quarterly Journal of Experimental Psychology, 12,* 242–248.

Treisman, A. M. (1964). The effect of irrelevant material on the efficiency of selective listening. *American Journal of Psychology, 77,* 533–546.

Underwood, G. (1981). Lexical recognition of embedded unattended words: Some implications for reading processes. *Acta Psychologica, 47,* 267–283.

J. E. McPhee
Florida Gulf Coast University

ATTENTION
COCKTAIL PARTY PHENOMENON
COMMUNICATION PROCESS

SELF: LOOKING-GLASS CONCEPT

The looking-glass concept of self is commonly attributed to Charles Horton Cooley (1902), who, in elaborating on William

James' (1890) discussion of the social self, suggested that a reflected self arises when individuals appropriate a self-feeling on the basis of how they think they appear in the eyes of other individuals. Cooley stated: "A social self of this sort might be called the reflected or looking-glass self: *Each to each a looking-glass / Reflects the other that doth pass*" (1902, p. 184).

While Cooley is credited with the looking-glass metaphor, its appearance in literature can actually be traced to the works of Adam Smith, who, in *The Theory of Moral Sentiments,* stated: "We examine our persons limb by limb, and by placing ourselves before a looking-glass, or by some expedient, endeavor as much as possible to view ourselves at the distance and with the eyes of other people" (1892, p. 162). Society, he suggested, provides the mirror in which individuals can see themselves as spectators of their own behavior. "This is the only looking-glass by which we can, in some measure, with the eyes of other people, scrutinize the propriety of our own conduct" (1892, p. 164).

The metaphor of the looking glass carries a double meaning in Smith's and Cooley's formulations. In everyday life, individuals see their faces, figures, and dress in the glass and "are interested in them because they are ours, and pleased or otherwise with them according as they do or do not answer to what we should like them to be" (Cooley, 1902, p. 184). In interactions with others, it is necessary for one to imagine how he or she appears in the eyes of the other. The other becomes the mirror, and forms his or her interpretation of the individual given that individual's gestures, facial expressions, and statements. Anselm Strauss has captured this relationship with the other in the title of his essay on identity, "Mirrors and Masks" (1958).

The self-idea that incorporates self-feeling, according to Smith and Cooley, has two principal components—the imagination of the other's judgment of that appearance, and some sort of "self-feeling, such as pride or mortification" (Cooley, 1902, p. 184). The self-feeling is appropriated on the basis of the imagined judgment of the other. This imputed sentiment, taken from the other, and directed inward, to the self, moves the individual. The evaluation of the other, in whose mind the person sees the self, determines this self-feeling. Cooley states: "We are ashamed to seem evasive in the presence of a straightforward man, cowardly in the presence of a brave one, gross in the eyes of a refined one, and so on" (1902, p. 184).

The basic structure of self-feeling is threefold, involving (a) a feeling for one's self, (b) a feeling of this feeling, and (c) a revealing of the self through this feeling (Heidegger, 1982). The other directly enters into this process, imaginatively, for it is the other's presence that provides the grounds against which self-feeling is judged and felt. The feeling person feels the self in emotion. Self-feeling is central to an understanding of the empirical social self (James, 1890).

Cooley elaborated the looking-glass self-concept in a brief comment in "On a remark of Dr. Holmes," that "six persons take part in every conversation between John and Thomas" (1927, p. 200). There is a real John, John's ideal John (never the real John), and Thomas' ideal John, and there are three parallel Thomases. The matter then becomes more complicated; in everyday life, 12 persons participate in every interaction, six on each side. For example, Alice, who has a new hat, meets Angela, who has a new dress. In

this situation, there is the real Alice, Alice's idea of herself in her new hat, her idea of Angela's judgment of her new hat, and her idea of what Angela thinks she thinks of herself in her new hat. Also, there is Angela's actual idea of Alice, Angela's idea of what Alice thinks of herself, and six analogous phases of Angela and her dress (Cooley, 1927).

Self-feelings move through these imputed and imagined reactions of each interactant to the other's real and imagined judgments of their social selves. Every interaction is peopled by many selves, with always more persons present in a situation than there are real bodies (Stone, 1981; Strauss, 1958; Maines, 1978). The strength of Cooley's formulation lies in its emphasis on the multiplicity of definitions, feelings, and meanings that arise in any situation in which two persons come together for interaction. Multiple awareness contexts of interaction characterize such situations (Glaser & Strauss, 1967).

The looking-glass self-concept is basic to the symbolic interactionist theory of interaction, and remains central to current social psychological theorizing on the social self and on emotion. The centrality of the self and of self-processes in the study of emotional feeling and emotional expression is pivotal in current neuropsychological formulations of emotion (Pribram, 1981). Cooley's concepts of self-feeling and the looking-glass self warrant reexamination in light of this fact.

Cooley's arguments are quite compatible with more contemporary theories of the self that stress its gendered, semiotic, and performative character (see Wiley, 1994; Dunn, 1998; Butler, 1997).

REFERENCES

Butler, J. (1997). *Excitable speech: A politics of the performative.* London: Routledge.

Dunn, R. G. (1998). *Identity crises: A social critique of postmodernity.* Minneapolis: University of Minnesota Press.

Wiley, N. (1994). *The semiotic self.* Cambridge, England: Polity Press.

N. K. DENZIN
University of Illionois

DEINDIVIDUATION
INTERPRESONAL PERCEPTION

SELF-ACTUALIZATION

Self-actualization pertains to the human need for self-fulfillment. It implies that individuals require, and will work toward, becoming everything they possibly can become (Maslow, 1970/1954). As a need, self-actualization is not a personal preference or inclination, but a biological and psychological imperative.

Most of the studies that pertain to self-actualization derive from the work of Abraham Maslow on the hierarchy of human needs. According to Maslow, there are five levels of human needs: basic physiological needs, safety needs, belongingness needs, esteem needs, and self-actualization needs. Roberts (1978) drew on the later writings of Maslow to suggest that there exists implicitly a sixth level of need—the need for self-transcendence.

Maslow credited Kurt Goldstein with first using the term self-actualization in his work *The Organism* (1939). Maslow's writing in *Motivation and Personality* (1970/1954) and in *Toward a Psychology of Being* (1968/1962) has most influenced the study of self-actualization as a psychological construct. Maslow first presented his theory of motivation in a 1943 article, of which *Motivation and Personality* essentially was an expansion. In that article, Maslow argued that the organism responded to the environment as an organized whole. The organism responded intentionally and in an integrated manner toward the satisfaction of its needs. These needs were arranged hierarchically so that basic needs had to be satisfied before higher needs emerged. The situation or field within which the organism existed contributed to the organism's responses to need deficiencies but only as a moderator variable. The perceptual processes of the organism were the primary factors determining its behavior.

The self-actualization need was an exigency that shaped the perceptions and behaviors of the organism. What people perceive as a *possibility,* they tend to consider a *necessity.* People tend not to be content with being "normal," but strive toward being exceptional. To the extent that this striving is satisfied, people can be considered self-actualizing. Self-actualizing individuals tend to have a genuine desire to help the human race; they behave more kindly and less self-consciously, and have closer interpersonal relationships than do non-self-actualizers. Self-actualizers demonstrate a strong belief in democratic principles while remaining highly discriminating in their friendships. While they choose to associate with people with similar tastes and personalities, self-actualizers behave in accordance with their democratic values in all relationships.

Self-actualizers tend to be more creative than other people. Maslow (1970/1954) described their creativity as a "naive creativity" in that these people are able to look at the world with fresh perceptions. This capacity also makes self-actualizers capable of resisting enculturation. Such people transcend the culture within which they live and are part of a world culture practicing universal values.

In another work, Maslow described self-actualization as the consequence of a peak experience (1968/1962). In this sense, self-actualization is not a static state but a dynamic experience that occurs when people are performing at their optimal capacity.

In a later work, Maslow took these findings further and differentiated between nontranscending self-actualizers and transcending self-actualizers (1971). To Maslow, the transcending self-actualizers perceived the peak experience as more precious, were more comfortable talking about transcendent experiences, were more responsive to beauty and love, and had transcended their own egos and, therefore, were more "global" or "holistic" in their thinking. While all self-actualizers Maslow studied were exceptional, the transcending self-actualizers were even more so.

A major limitation of Maslow's work was that he sought out specific subjects rather than random members of the general population. Also, his research approach was phenomenological. Such

an approach gave tremendously rich data, but the generalizability of his findings has been questioned.

To use a more commonly accepted research paradigm in the study of self-actualization, Schultz (1958) designed a self-actualization questionnaire. This instrument was not widely accepted and Shostrom (1962) later designed the Personal Orientation Inventory (POI). Shostrom's standardized questionnaire has become the most widely used instrument in the assessment of self-actualization. The Personal Orientation Inventory consists of 12 subscales: time competence, inner directedness, self-actualizing value, existentiality, feeling reactivity, spontaneity, self-regard, self-acceptance, nature of man, synergy, acceptance of aggression, and capacity for intimate contact. All subscales were derived from the writings of Maslow pertaining to self-actualizing individuals. Shostrom (1964) reported a test–retest reliability for this inventory of between 0.91 and 0.93. Other studies, however, reported lower reliabilities (Klavetter & Mogar, 1967; Ilardi & May, 1968; Tosi & Hoffman, 1972). Shostrom reported high construct validity for all of the subscales (1964) and much subsequent research has studied the predictive validity of the instrument.

The Personal Orientation Inventory has been examined in hundreds of studies. Although not all research has confirmed its effectiveness in studying topics related to self-actualization, it seems this instrument at least adds an important dimension to the concept of self-actualization. Critics have suggested that it is open to faked responses (Forest & Sicz, 1981), but others have found that this is not the case (Grater, 1968). A comprehensive review of literature pertaining to self-actualization and the Personal Orientation Inventory has yet to be published. With the conflicting findings that presently exist, the lack of such a review precludes a critique of self-actualization theory since Maslow's seminal work. Maslow's writings remain the best source of information on self-actualization.

REFERENCES

Forest, J., & Sicz, G. (1981). Pseudo-self-actualization. *Journal of Humanistic Psychology, 21,* 77–83.

Goldstein, K. (1959/1934). *The organism. A holistic approach to biology derived from pathological data in man.* New York: American Book.

Grater, M. (1968). *Effects of knowledge of characteristics of self-actualization and faking of a self-actualized response on Shostrom's Personal Orientation Inventory.* Unpublished master's thesis, University of Toledo, Toledo, Ohio.

Ilardi, R., & May, W. (1968). A reliability study of Shostrom's Personal Orientation Inventory. *Journal of Humanistic Psychology, 8,* 68–73.

Klavetter, R. E., & Mogar, R. E. (1967). Peak experiences: Investigation of their relationship to psychedelic therapy and self-actualization. *Journal of Humanistic Psychology, 7,* 171–177.

Klavetter, R. E., & Mogar, R. E. (1967). Stability and internal consistency of a measure of self-actualization. *Psychological Reports, 21,* 422–424.

Maslow, A. H. (1943). A theory of human motivation. *Psychological Review, 50,* 370–396.

Maslow, A. H. (1968/1962). *Toward a psychology of being.* New York: Van Nostrand Reinhold.

Maslow, A. H. (1970/1954). *Motivation and personality* (2nd ed.). New York: Harper & Row.

Maslow, A. H. (1971). *The farther reaches of human nature.* New York: Viking.

Roberts, T. (1978). Beyond self-actualization. *Re-Vision, 1,* 42–46.

Schultz, K. (1958). The psychologically healthy person: A study in identification and prediction. *Journal of Clinical Psychology, 14,* 112–117.

Shostrom, E. (1964). An inventory for the measurement of self-actualization. *Educational and Psychological Measurement, 24,* 207–218.

Tosi, D., & Hoffman, S. (1972). A factor analysis of the personal orientation inventory. *Journal of Humanistic Psychology, 12,* 86–93.

R. H. STENSRUD
University of Northern Iowa

AVOIDANT PERSONALITY
OPTIMAL FUNCTIONING

SELF-CONCEPT

For centuries, theologists, philosophers, and lay persons have agreed that the origins and effects of self-conceptions merit serious attention. For example, Socrates' famous dictum, "Know thyself," stemmed from his belief that such knowledge was important for the attainment of virtue. Hume's notion that "self" was a bundle of associated impressions was his attempt to bring this topic within a skeptical, empirical philosophy of knowledge. Descartes's idea that the concept of self is inborn, and hence must be placed in our minds by God, was part of his attempt to reconcile doubt and faith. Some modern thinkers' unquestioning supposition that only human beings can experience self-conceptions is part of the long-standing theological/philosophical attempt to find some aspect of psychological functioning unique to our species. As far as lay persons' thoughts are concerned, every day brings confident assertions in conversation and in the media about how our self-conceptions are affected by yet another social or educational influence or advertised product or activity.

Some of the propositions taken for granted by numerous contemporary psychologists, social workers, psychiatrists, and educators sound quite similar to many of these lay assertions. However, there have been few attempts to define self-conception terms rigorously enough to evaluate the extent to which philosophical, lay, and professional/scientific thinkers may all be considering the same idea(s).

Between the late nineteenth and mid-twentieth centuries, professional ideas concerning self-conceptions were kept alive and developed in an essentially abstract or theoretical way by a few psy-chologists, sociologists, and psychiatrists. The rarity of attempts at measurement and research during this period seems to be attributable to at least three factors: (a) the personal disinclinations toward scientific work on the parts of almost all those thinkers who considered self-concepts to be important; (b) the necessarily great difficulty anyone must encounter in attempting scientific research in this area; and (c) the extremely negative reactions of popular and respected behaviorists who dominated mainstream U.S. psychology during the period, and who did not want to admit any fuzzy hypothetical constructs (internal, nonobservable processes or characteristics) into their systematic thinking and research.

At the beginning of this period, the most famous nineteenth century treatment of the topic of self by a psychologist was presented by William James (1890), who based his statements on astute, uncontrolled, everyday observations, including his own perceptive brand of introspecting on his conscious processes. Mary Calkins (1915) attempted to bring the study of self-conceptions into the psychological laboratory, using the highly artificial and controlled method of introspection then popular in certain laboratories. This line of work soon languished as the usefulness of the technique to study any psychological topic was increasingly discredited by its failure to yield agreed-upon results. By 1935, Kurt Koffka, from Germany, was including the self as an important topic to be addressed by Gestalt psychologists, who used so-called phenomenological introspection in which observers reported their conscious experiences without the artificial restraints or analyses used by Calkins.

Meanwhile sociologists such as Cooley (1902) and Mead (1934) were arguing for the importance of social interactions in shaping individuals' self-conceptions, which in turn were assumed to be crucial determinants of their social behavior. However, these discussions were based on personal observations, not research.

Concurrently, a long line of clinicians in Europe and the United States (e.g., Adler, 1912; Freud, 1933; Fromm, 1939; Horney, 1937; Jung, 1928; Lecky, 1945; Sullivan, 1938) were keeping alive various versions of the idea that self-conceptions are important in attaining a clinical understanding of individuals, and in making the general statements that comprised their respective theories of personality. On the whole, however, their ideas, based almost entirely on uncontrolled clinical observations of single cases, seemed to lack rigor and testability, or even sometimes to repudiate the assumptions of scientific determinism. Accordingly their views were excluded for several decades from the mainstream of U.S. research psychology. This occurred even though experimentalists themselves were recognizing that such self-referent variables as ego involvement played a role in their subjects' laboratory behaviors, and the German Gestalt psychologists' ideas about the methods and usefulness of phenomenological introspections were attaining some acceptance by U.S. experimentalists concerned with perception, learning, and motivation.

Throughout the period, limitations of the generally accepted thinking and research in psychology were gradually becoming apparent. Therefore, by the time Hilgard, an experimentalist, delivered his 1949 presidential address to the American Psychological Association, many psychologists were ready to agree with his argument that the time was ripe for psychologists generally to increase their attention to self-referent constructs to attain a more plausible and complete theoretical account of human conduct.

In the ensuing three decades, self-conception variables were accorded importance in an increasing number and variety of research-oriented theories, as shown by the following examples.

Child psychologists began to explore the development of social cognition—knowing about others and one's self in relation to others (Shantz, 1975). This included such questions as whether qualitatively different developmental stages in social cognition may occur (Piaget, 1980; Selman, 1980), and whether developmental trends in acquisition of ordinary language are associated with developing conceptions of self and others (Bromley, 1977). Additionally, the issue of the influence of parental characteristics and behaviors on self-conceptions was raised (Coopersmith, 1967), and theory and research on moral development were obviously relevant to the acquisition of self-concept and ideals for self (Kohlberg, 1969).

Social psychologists accorded importance to self-conception variables in their theories about interpersonal attraction, about humans' persuasibility and conformity behaviors, and about cognitive dissonance (the alleged tendency of persons to try to reconcile inconsistencies among their beliefs and cognitions, and also between these, on the one hand, and their behaviors on the other) (Wylie, 1979). Self-conception variables also figured in attribution theory—which considers the conditions under which persons assign causal influences to themselves, to others, or to impersonal factors (Gorlitz, 1980). Also, social psychologists have joined sociologists in considering the effects of such variables as age, class, race, and gender on self-conceptions (Wylie, 1979).

Social learning theorists developed arguments about such variables as locus of control and learned helplessness, both of which are concerned (as is attribution theory) with the conditions under which a person sees his or her own characteristics or behavior as important factors in determining outcomes (Lefcourt, 1976; Garber & Seligman, 1980).

Psychologists interested in accounting for vocational choice and performance accorded theoretical importance to such ideas as the guiding role of prechoice self-conceptions and the eventual development of a vocational self-concept (Super et al., 1963).

And in personality theory, interest in self-conception continued and expanded, for example, in arguing for parallels between ordinary persons' uses of self-conceptions in guiding everyday behavior and the scientist's uses of hypotheses and theories in guiding research behaviors (Kelly, 1955; Epstein, 1973).

At the beginning of this period of rapidly spreading interest, psychologists were little closer than lay persons to being able to define terms specifically enough to facilitate communication, theorizing, and research. Then, in 1951, Rogers, the first clinician to attempt extensive research on self-conceptions, offered the following definition (Rogers, 1951, p. 136):

The self-concept or self-structure may be thought of as an organized configuration of perceptions of the self which are admissible to awareness. It is composed of such elements as the perceptions of one's characteristics and abilities; the percepts and concepts of self in relation to others and the environment; the value qualities which are perceived as associated with experiences and objects; and goals and ideas which are perceived as having positive or negative valence.

As exemplified in this statement, theorists and researchers thus far have considered almost entirely the *phenomenal or conscious self-concept,* not the so-called unconscious self-concept (a theoretically possible aspect of personality that has been almost ignored in modern work, perhaps because of formidable difficulties in measuring it).

In analyzing Rogers' complex statement, and examining hundreds of more recent writings about self-conceptions, one can discern a number of aspects of the phenomenal or conscious self-concept, as enumerated in the following. Unfortunately, many of these refinements have thus far received scant attention:

1. *Personal self-concept.* This is one's descriptive attributes or behavioral characteristics as seen from one's personal perspective. These characteristics may range from rather specific (e.g.: "I have brown eyes." "I'm a boy." "I'm a senior citizen." "I roller skate well.") to quite broad (e.g.: "I'm intelligent." "I feel shy around others." "I am an inefficient worker."). Note that the personal self-concept includes not only physical, behavioral, and internal characteristics, but also such aspects as gender identity (one's recognition of one's status as male or female), racial/ethnic identity, socioeconomic class identity, age identity, and a sense of self-continuity as being, in some respects, the same individual through time.

Although most psychological writing about personal self-concept characteristics implies their generality across situations, persons, and times, an individual may more typically have a qualified view regarding many of them. In other words, a person may feel that an attribute is self-descriptive only under certain circumstances, and/or in relation to certain other persons at certain times (Bromley, 1977). For example, one could say, "I'm a patient father except when I have headaches." Such qualifications could be a crucially important part of a verbal report of self-concept, but they are rarely elicited or analyzed by researchers, who have mostly required the subject to use adjective check lists, simple ratings scales, or simple general sentences requiring "yes" or "no" answers. Thus research coverage to date has been severely narrowed. (The reader should note that the complications and qualifications introduced in this paragraph also apply to items 2 through 6.)

2. *Social self-concepts.* These are self-descriptive attributes or behavioral characteristics as one thinks they are seen by others. As James (1890) noted, one has a number of different social self-concepts respectively applicable to the various individuals and groups with whom one interacts.

These characteristics, too, range from rather specific to quite broad, and they may or may not agree with the attributes one sees as characterizing one's self from one's personal viewpoint. That is, the social self-concepts may or may not agree with the personal self-concept. For example, one might say, "I believe others [too] think I'm intelligent; I believe others think I'm usually outgoing [whereas I think of myself as being shy]."

3. *Self-ideals regarding one's personal self-concept.* These are conceptions of what one would personally wish to be like. Again, these may range from rather specific to general. For example, "I'd like to have blue eyes." Or: "I want to be a lawyer." "I'd like to act intelligently." Or: "I'd like to be an outgoing person."

4. *Self-ideals regarding one's social self-concepts.* These are conceptions of how one would like others to see one. It follows from item 2 that one may have a number of different self-ideals regarding one's social self-concepts, respectively applicable to the different individuals and to the groups with whom one interacts. Again, these characteristics range from rather specific to quite broad.

5. *Evaluations of descriptive personal self-conceptions in relation to the ideals for self regarding those attributes.* These refer to evaluations of item 1 in relation to item 3. For example, one might say: "I'm quite dissatisfied with my brown eyes." Or: "I'm happy that I'm intelligent." Or: "It's rather unimportant to me that I roller skate well." Or: "My status as a black person is a source of pride."

6. *Evaluations of descriptive social self-concepts in relation to the ideals for one's social self-concepts.* These refer to evaluations of item 2 in relation to item 4. For example, one might say: "It's important to me that others think I'm intelligent." Or: "I'm glad they feel I'm outgoing [whether or not I see myself as accurately described in that way]."

SELF-ESTEEM

This term has been used to refer to some hypothetical overall or global level of self-evaluation or self-regard. The common assumption may or may not be true that global self-esteem is comprised of or based upon a combination of self-evaluations referring to aspects of both the personal self-concept and the social self-concepts. Important unanswered questions include: (a) Is it true that self-esteem represents some combination of self-evaluations on various behaviors and attributes? (b) If the answer to this question is yes, what is the role of the independently measured salience or importance of each respective attribute in determining self-esteem? (c) To what extent is the construct "chronic" self-esteem (dispositional, stable self-esteem) the same as or different from the construct "acute" self-esteem (momentary level of self-esteem as experimentally or naturally manipulated)? (Wylie, 1979, pp. 559–561).

Most theoretical writing and research in the self-concept area concerns "self-esteem." The term *self-acceptance* also has been much used in the self-concept literature to refer to liking or respecting one's self while acknowledging one's shortcomings. In practice, there is so much overlap between purported self-esteem measures and purported self-acceptance measures that no clear operational distinction between the two has been demonstrated (e.g., Wylie, 1974, pp. 155–156). Therefore, no attempt is made here to consider these constructs separately.

What is to be done to incorporate all the self-concept variables into scientifically and practically useful theories? As is true in any scientific work, measurement of the variables that are to be related

is a central problem that must be addressed before undertaking substantive research.

First, one must decide what kinds of observations could be appropriate indexes of one's constructs. Regarding conscious self-conceptions, it appears that, despite their obvious shortcomings, verbal reports, taken under proper conditions, are almost always the most appropriate indexes (Wylie, 1974). [Some intriguing nonverbal techniques have been used to show that chimpanzees and children reared with access to mirrors develop clear behavioral signs of self-recognition (Gallup, 1979; Lewis & Brooks, 1975)].

Although considerable agreement has been reached on the general idea of what to measure, progress in the measurement area has been slowed by (a) the intractable complexity of the set of variables involved; (b) the failure to attempt to disentangle the separate strands in self-conception, and to develop respectively suitable measures; and (c) the neglect of acceptable procedures for establishing suitable reliability and construct validity of one's measures before using them in substantive research. (Reliability refers to the repeatability of the measure, and construct validity to the degree to which the measure reflects the underlying characteristic, e.g., self-esteem, which supposedly is being measured.)

Thus far, only a few instruments, mostly purporting to measure only one of the many self-conception variables (chronic or stable self-esteem levels), have been subjected to reasonably extensive psychometric development and analysis. In the majority of studies, unfortunately, the reliability and validity of the measuring instruments, whether of self-esteem or one of the other kinds of variables listed, are unknown or inadequate. Of course, this greatly weakens the conclusiveness of the research.

Beyond the measurement problems, one needs to specify what relationship one expects (a) among the measured self-conception variables, and (b) between the self-conception variables and other variables that one supposes are related to self-conceptions. Then one needs to test those postulated relationships under suitably controlled research conditions.

Traditionally, workers in this area have been concerned with the following model:

| Antecedents of self-conceptions | → | Self-conceptions | → | Behavioral outcomes of self-conceptions |

For example, one might guess that rejection by parents leads to poor self-esteem, which in turn leads to poor academic performance. However, it has often been impossible to specify, even theoretically, such clear-cut sequences. For example, poor self-esteem could cause poor academic performance, but the reverse could also be true. Accordingly, researchers have most frequently contented themselves with predicting and reporting only correlations between variables rather than the cause-and-effect relationships suggested in the foregoing.

McGuire (1973) and Bandura (1978), among others, have taken more systematic account of these difficulties, and have proposed welcome extensions and modifications of the foregoing model. The following scheme by Bandura is compatible with his view of the place of self-referent constructs in social learning theory:

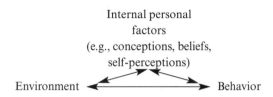

Internal personal
factors
(e.g., conceptions, beliefs,
self-perceptions)

Environment ⟷   ⟶ Behavior

According to this diagram, environment can affect behavior, but behavior can also affect environment. Of even greater relevance here is the idea that environmental and internal personal factors can reciprocally influence each other, as is the case with behavior and internal personal factors as well. Thus far, virtually no research has attempted to take into account such plausible complexities.

Wicklund (1979) has made the additional suggestion that the observable relationships between self-conceptions and respectively corresponding behaviors are stronger when the person is in a "self-aware" state. This state may be induced by working in the presence of a mirror or a tape recording of one's own voice, or it may be a generally characteristic state for some persons as compared with others.

Partly because hundreds of factors have been thought to be related to self-conceptions, the several thousand published research studies tend to be widely and thinly scattered across substantive areas (Wylie, 1979). On the side of self-conception variables included in the foregoing schema (and elaborated in items 1 through 7), the most frequent focus of published research studies has been on persons' characteristic levels of overall self-esteem or self-acceptance. The next most frequent focus has been on self-conceptions of relatively stable ability levels. Almost everything remains to be done with the more particularized and qualified self-conception variables and with the ideal self-conception variables involved in our earlier definitions.

Regarding factors that researchers have tried to relate to self-conception variables, the greatest concentration of studies has been on achievement, ability, and creativity; age and developmental level; authoritarianism and dogmatism; family variables; gender; interpersonal attraction; psychotherapy; racial/ethnic status; and socioeconomic status (Wylie, 1979).

It is most striking that zero or weak associations have been repeatedly obtained between self-esteem and each of several variables to which both theory and conventional wisdom confidently assumed self-esteem would be strongly related, for example, age, race, sex, socioeconomic level, psychotherapy, creativity, and persuasibility. This resounding lack of support occurs despite the fact that great individual variations in stable self-esteem are repeatedly obtained. Therefore, although problems do exist in both measurement and research design, one cannot preserve one's original idea about the importance of these influences simply by claiming that the self-esteem reports are unreliable or invalid. In fact, the origins of these stable individual differences in self-esteem need to be addressed from other perspectives. It seems likely that a more sophisticated reformulation of theory could lead to more useful and in-

teresting findings. For example, more attention should be paid to the problems raised here with respect to examining (a) the components of self-esteem; (b) the way(s) in which separate aspects of self-conception achieve differential salience in determining self-esteem (probably differing from individual to individual); and (c) the likelihood that neither children nor adults compare themselves with the very broad, generalized reference groups implicitly assumed to be important by researchers who look for sex, race, or class influences on self-esteem (Rosenberg & Simmons, 1972). In addition, explorations of the types of reciprocal determinism suggested by Bandura's scheme could play a part in yielding more interpretable findings.

Also emerging from current research is the suggestion that positive findings are more likely to occur when one examines much more restricted and qualified aspects of self-concept in relation to more specifically relevant variables, such as self-conceptions of scholastic ability versus academic achievement measures.

All things considered, it seems clear that lay persons and behavioral scientists (both theoretical and applied) will continue to accord importance to self-conceptions, but that refinements of both theory and method will be required to evaluate adequately the usefulness of these concepts in both theoretical and applied work.

REFERENCES

Adler, A. (1974/1912). *The neurotic constitution.* New York: Arno Press.

Bandura, A. (1978). The self-system in reciprocal determinism. *American Psychologist, 33,* 344–358.

Bromley, D. B. (1977). Natural language and the development of the self. In H. E. Howe, Jr. (Ed.), *Nebraska Symposium on Motivation* (Vol. 25). Lincoln, NE: University of Nebraska Press.

Calkins, M. W. (1915). The self in scientific psychology. *American Journal of Psychology, 26,* 495–524.

Cooley, C. H. (1956/1902). *Human nature and the social order.* Glencoe, IL: Free Press.

Coopersmith, S. (1967). *The antecedents of self-esteem.* San Francisco: Freeman.

Epstein, S. (1973). The self-concept revisited or a theory of a theory. *American Psychologist, 28,* 404–416.

Freud, S. (1933). The psychology of women. In *New introductory lectures on psychoanalysis.* New York: Norton.

Fromm, E. (1939). Selfishness and self-love. *Psychiatry, 2,* 507–523.

Gallup, G. G., Jr. (1979). Self-awareness in primates. *American Scientist, 67,* 417–421.

Garber, J., & Seligman, M. E. P. (1980). *Human helplessness: Theory and applications.* New York: Academic.

Gorlitz, D. (Ed.). (1980). *Perspectives in attribution and theory.* Cambridge, MA: Ballinger.

Horney, K. (1937). *The neurotic personality of our times.* New York: Norton.

Jung, C. G. (1928). *Contributions to analytical psychology.* (C. F. and H. G. Baynes trans.) New York: Harcourt Brace. London: Kegan Paul.

Kelly, E. L. (1955). Consistency of the adult personality. *American Psychologist, 10,* 659–681.

Kohlberg, L. (1969). Stage and sequence: The cognitive-developmental approach to socialization. In D. A. Goslin (Ed.), *Handbook of socialization theory and research.* Chicago: Rand-McNally.

Lecky, P. (1969/1945). *Self-consistency: A theory of personality.* Garden City, NY: Doubleday/Anchor.

Lefcourt, H. M. (1982/1976). *Locus of control: Current trends in theory and research.* Hillsdale, NJ: Erlbaum.

Lewis, M., & Brooks, J. (1975). Infants' social perception: A constructivist view. In L. Cohen & S. Salapatek (Eds.), *Infant perception: From sensation to cognition* (Vol. 2). New York: Academic.

McGuire, W. J. (1973). The yin and yang of progress in social psychology: Seven koan. *Journal of Personality and Social Psychology, 26,* 446–456.

Mead, G. H. (1934). *Mind, self, and society: From the standpoint of a social behaviorist.* Chicago: University of Chicago Press.

Rogers, C. R. (1951). *Client-centered therapy.* Boston: Houghton Mifflin.

Rosenberg, M., & Simmons, R. G. (1972). *Black and white self-esteem: The urban school child.* Washington, DC: American Sociological Association.

Selman, R. L. (1980). *The growth of interpersonal understanding: Developmental and clinical analyses.* New York: Academic.

Shantz, C. U. (1975). The development of social cognition. In E. M. Hetherington (Ed.), *Review of child development research* (Vol. 5). Chicago: University of Chicago Press.

Sullivan, H. S. (1938). Psychiatry: Introduction to the study of interpersonal relations. *Psychiatry, 1,* 121–134.

Super, D. E., Starishevsky, R., Matlin, N., & Jordaan, J. P. (1963). *Career development: Self-concept theory.* New York: College Entrance Examination Board.

Wicklund, R. A. (1979). The influence of self-awareness on human behavior. *American Scientist, 67,* 187–193.

Wylie, R. C. (1974). *The self-concept* (Rev. ed.) (Vol. 1). *Review of methodological considerations and measuring instruments.* Lincoln, NE: University of Nebraska Press.

Wylie, R. C. (1979). *The self-concept* (Rev. ed.) (Vol. 2). *Theory and research on selected topics.* Lincoln, NE: University of Nebraska Press.

R. C. WYLIE

BODY IMAGE

SELF-DETERMINATION

The science of psychology was built on the assumption that behavior is lawful. This led behaviorists to propose that behavior is controlled by associative bonds that develop through reinforcement processes (Hull, 1943; Skinner, 1953). From that perspective, behavior is beyond the individual's control; in other words, it cannot be self-determined.

Beginning in the 1950s, cognitive concepts such as expectations, goals, and decisions began to replace associative bonds to describe the processes underlying behavioral regulation (Lewin, 1951; Tolman, 1959). From this perspective, people behave in order to attain goals, outcomes, or reinforcements. Thus, their behavior is not controlled by past reinforcements, but is regulated by their decisions to pursue future reinforcements. As Nobel laureate Roger Sperry (1977) stated, people do have some capacity to choose their own behaviors based on their thoughts and feelings.

This change in focus from past reinforcements to expectations about future reinforcements was a dramatic shift, and social learning theorists such as Bandura (1989) argued that people's pursuit of outcomes they feel able to attain represents the paradigm of self-motivation. It is, he said, the essence of human agency. Implicit in that view is the assumption that there is only one type of motivation, that motivation varies only in amount, and that to be motivated is to be agentic. The amount of an individual's motivation, and thus his or her agency, depends on the expectation that behavior will lead to reinforcements and on his or her feeling competent to do the behavior.

Other theorists have identified serious problems with that reasoning, however (Deci & Ryan, 1991). Even casual reflection reveals different kinds of motivation. In other words, motivation varies not only in *level* (the amount of motivation), but also in *orientation* (the type of motivation). Sometimes people behave with a full sense of willingness, with a sense of freedom and excitement, finding the task quite enjoyable. Other times they behave while feeling coerced, with the sense that they have to do the behavior even if they do not want to. In both cases they are motivated, and they might even have equal amounts of motivation, but the type or orientation of motivation is clearly very different, and the consequences of the two types of motivation will be different.

For example, think of an employee who is highly motivated to produce a product because he or she is paid a certain amount for each unit produced. The employee would probably feel pressured to keep producing and might even feel a sense of alienation from the job itself. After all, the job is just an instrument for obtaining money. In contrast, think of an employee who is motivated because he or she has the desire to perform well and finds the job interesting and important. This employee, too, might have a very high level of motivation but, unlike the other, would be working with a sense of commitment and enjoyment. The job itself is important to him or her.

These two examples convey the distinction between *intrinsic motivation,* which refers to doing something because it is inherently satisfying, and *extrinsic motivation,* which refers to doing something because it leads to a separate outcome. Intrinsically motivated behaviors do not require reinforcements and thus do not operate by the same expectancy principles as extrinsic motivation. In fact, intrinsic motivation is the prototype of self-determination and agency, whereas extrinsic motivation that involves feeling co-erced by reinforcement contingencies does not constitute self-determination. In short, in spite of the social-learning perspective, only some motivated behaviors are truly self-determined, voli-tional, and agentic.

Self-determination involves experiencing a sense of choice about what one is doing, and research has now shown that while in-trinsic motivation is the model of self-determination, extrinsically motivated behavior can also become self-determined. This occurs through the processes of internalization and integration of behav-ioral regulations (Deci & Ryan, 1985). Internalization involves tak-ing in a regulation, and integration involves fully transforming it into one's own. Thus, there are different forms of extrinsic motiva-tion: one in which the regulation is external to the person; one in which the regulation has been internalized but not integrated; and one in which the regulation has been fully integrated. Although the latter two both represent internal motivation, only integration re-sults in a full sense of volition and personal commitment.

Together, intrinsic motivation and fully integrated extrinsic motivation are the bases for self-determination. More than three decades of research has shown that the quality of experience and performance vary as a function of the degree to which a behavior is self-determined. Those behaviors that are more self-determined are associated with a stronger sense of personal commitment, greater persistence, more positive feelings and self-perceptions, better quality performance, and better mental health (Deci & Ryan, 1991). Thus, given the relation of self-determination to both personal experience and performance outcomes, a critical ques-tion concerns how to promote self-determination.

Studies have shown that one factor affecting the degree to which people will be self-determined in performing behaviors is whether the behaviors are valued by others to whom they feel con-nected. This suggests that the starting point for facilitating self-determination in others relating to them in an authentic way. Further, people must feel competent in performing the target be-haviors in order to be self-determined in carrying them out. People will, for example, be more likely to internalize and integrate a goal if they have the relevant skills and understanding to succeed at it. Thus, supporting competence by offering optimal challenges and providing effectance-relevant feedback will also facilitate self-determination. Finally, for people to become self-determined with respect to a behavior, they must grasp its meaning to themselves, have their own perspectives acknowledged, and feel a sense of choice about doing the behaviors. In other words, facilitating self-determination in others requires providing them with these sup-ports for autonomy (Deci, Eghrari, Patrick, & Leone, 1994).

In sum, self-determination, which is based in intrinsic motiva-tion and integrated extrinsic motivation, has been associated with a variety of positive performance and affective outcomes in the ar-eas of education, parenting, work, health-care, and sport, and has been found to depend on interpersonal supports for relatedness, competence, and autonomy (Ryan & Deci, 2000).

REFERENCES

Bandura, A. (1989). Human agency in social cognitive theory. *American Psychologist, 44,* 1175–1184.

Deci, E. L., Eghrari, H., Patrick, B. C., & Leone, D. R. (1994). Fa-cilitating internalization: The self-determination theory per-spective. *Journal of Personality, 62,* 119–142.

Deci, E. L., & Ryan, R. M. (1985). *Intrinsic motivation and self-determination in human behavior.* New York: Plenum.

Deci, E. L., & Ryan, R. M. (1991). A motivational approach to self: Integration in personality. In R. Dienstbier (Ed.), *Nebraska symposium on motivation: Vol. 38. Perspectives on motivation* (pp. 237–288). Lincoln, NE: University of Nebraska Press.

Hull, C. L. (1943). *Principles of behavior.* New York: Appleton-Century-Crofts.

Lewin, K. (1951). Intention, will, and need. In D. Rapaport (Ed.), *Organization and pathology of thought* (pp. 95–153). New York: Columbia University Press.

Ryan, R. M., & Deci, E. L. (2000). Self-determination theory and the facilitation of intrinsic motivation, social development, and well-being. *American Psychologist, 55,* 68–78.

Skinner, B. F. (1953). *Science and human behavior.* New York: Macmillan.

Sperry, R. W. (1977). Bridging science and values: A unifying view of mind and brain. *American Psychologist, 32,* 237–245.

Tolman, E. C. (1959). Principles of purposive behavior. In S. Koch (Ed.), *Psychology: A study of a science* (Vol. 2, pp. 92–157). New York: McGraw-Hill.

E. L. DECI
University of Rochester

FREE WILL
INTRINSIC MOTIVATION

SELF-EFFICACY

People contribute to their own functioning and well-being through mechanisms of personal agency. Among the mechanisms of per-sonal agency, none is more central or pervasive than people's be-liefs in their capability to exercise control over their own function-ing and over environmental events (Bandura, 1997). Efficacy beliefs are the foundation of human agency. Unless people believe that they can produce desired results by their actions, they have little incentive to act or to persevere in the face of difficulties. That self-efficacy beliefs play an influential role in human adaptation and change is amply documented by meta-analyses which combine the findings of numerous studies in different spheres of functioning (Holden, 1991, Holden, Moncher, Schinke, & Barker, 1990, Mul-ton, Brown, & Lent, 1991, Stajkovic & Luthans, 1998).

SOURCES OF SELF-EFFICACY

People's beliefs about their efficacy are constructed from four prin-cipal sources of information. The most effective way of instilling a strong sense of efficacy is through mastery experiences. Successes build a robust belief in one's personal efficacy. Failures undermine it, especially if frequent failures occur in early phases in the development of competencies. Development of resilient self-efficacy requires experiences in overcoming obstacles through perseverant effort. The second method is by social modeling. Models serve as sources of competencies and motivation. Seeing people similar to oneself succeed by perseverant effort raises observers' beliefs in their own capabilities. Social persuasion is the third mode of influence. Realistic boosts in efficacy can lead people to exert greater effort, which increases their chances of success. People also rely partly on their physiological and mood states in judging their capabilities. The fourth way of altering self-efficacy beliefs is to enhance physical states, reduce stress and depression, and correct misinterpretations of somatic states.

EFFICACY-ACTIVATED PROCESSES

Self-efficacy beliefs regulate human functioning through four major processes. They include cognitive, motivational, emotional, and selection processes.

Cognitive Processes

The effects of self-efficacy beliefs on cognitive processes take various forms. Much human behavior, being purposive, is regulated by forethought embodying cognized goals. Personal goal-setting is influenced by self-appraisal of capabilities. The stronger the perceived self-efficacy, the higher the goal challenges people set themselves, and the firmer their commitment to meeting them.

Most courses of behavior are initially shaped in thought. People's beliefs about their efficacy influence the types of anticipatory scenarios they construct and rehearse. Those who have a high sense of efficacy visualize success scenarios that provide positive guides for performance. Those who judge themselves as inefficacious are more inclined to visualize failure scenarios, which undermine performance by dwelling on personal deficiencies and on how things will go wrong. A major function of thought is to enable people to predict the occurrence of events and to create the means for exercising control over those that affect their daily lives. It requires a high sense of efficacy to stick with the laborious cognitive activity needed to extract predictive and operational knowledge from information that contains many ambiguities, redundancies, and uncertainties. The stronger the perceived self-efficacy, the more effective people are in their analytic thinking and in constructing successful courses of action.

Motivational Processes

Beliefs of personal efficacy play a central role in the self-regulation of motivation. Most human motivation is cognitively generated. In cognitive motivation, people motivate themselves and guide their actions anticipatorily through the exercise of forethought. They form beliefs about what they can do, they anticipate likely outcomes of prospective actions, and they set goals for themselves and plan courses of action designed to realize valued futures. Different theories—attribution theory, expectancy-value theory and goal theory—have been built around these various forms of cognitive motivators.

Perceived self-efficacy operates as a central factor in each of these forms of cognitive motivation (Bandura, 1986, 1991). Effi-

cacy beliefs bias the extent to which people attribute their successes and failures to personal capabilities or to external factors. People act on their beliefs about what they can do, as well as their beliefs about the likely outcomes of various actions. The effects of outcome expectancies on performance motivation are, therefore, partly governed by self-beliefs of efficacy. There are many activities which, if done well, guarantee valued outcomes, but they are not pursued by people who doubt they can do what it takes to succeed. Perceived self-efficacy also contributes in several ways to motivation through goal systems (Bandura, 1991; Locke & Latham, 1990). It is partly on the basis of efficacy beliefs that people choose what challenges to undertake, how much effort to expend in the endeavor, and how long to persevere in the face of obstacles and failures.

Human attainments and positive well-being require an optimistic sense of personal efficacy (Bandura, 1986, 1997). This is because ordinary social realities are strewn with difficulties. In a world full of impediments, failures, adversities, setbacks, frustrations, and inequities, people must have a robust sense of personal efficacy to sustain the perseverant effort needed to succeed.

Affective Processes

People's beliefs in their coping capabilities also play a pivotal role in the self-regulation of affective states (Bandura, 1997). There are four principal ways in which self-efficacy beliefs affect the nature and intensity of emotional experiences. Such beliefs create attentional biases and influence how potentially aversive life events are construed and cognitively represented; they affect the exercise of control over perturbing thought patterns, and they sponsor courses of action that transform distressing and threatening environments into more benign ones (Williams, 1992). These alternative paths of affective influence are amply documented in the self-regulation of anxiety arousal and depressive mood.

People who believe they can exercise control over potential threats do not conjure up apprehensive cognitions and, hence, are not distressed by them. But those who believe they cannot manage potential threats experience high levels of anxiety arousal. They dwell on their coping deficiencies, view many aspects of their environment as fraught with danger, magnify the severity of possible threats, and worry about perils that rarely, if ever, happen. Through such inefficacious thought they distress themselves and constrain and impair their levels of functioning. It is not the sheer frequency of perturbing cognitions, but the perceived inefficacy to turn them off that is the major source of distress.

In addition, people with a high sense of efficacy to manage unpleasant emotional states by palliative means can get themselves to relax, direct their attention to favorable things, calm themselves, and seek support from friends, family, and others. For those who believe they can get relief in these ways, anxiety and sadness are easier to tolerate.

A low sense of efficacy to gain and maintain what one values highly contributes to depression in at least three ways. One route is through unfulfilled aspiration. People who impose on themselves standards of self-worth which they judge unattainable drive themselves to bouts of depression. A second efficacy route to depression is through a low sense of social efficacy to develop social relationships that bring satisfaction to one's life and cushion the adverse effects of chronic stressors. A low sense of social efficacy contributes to depression both directly and by curtailing development of socially supportive relationships. The third route to depression is through thought control efficacy. People live in a psychic environment largely of their own making. Much human depression is cognitively generated by dejecting, ruminative thought. A low sense of efficacy to exercise control over ruminative thought contributes to the occurrence, duration, and recurrence of depressive episodes.

Selection Processes

The final way in which self-beliefs of efficacy contribute to human adaptation and change concerns selection processes (Bandura, 1995). Beliefs of personal efficacy shape the courses of lives by influencing selection of activities and environments. People tend to avoid activities and situations they believe exceed their coping capabilities, but they readily undertake challenging activities and pick social environments they judge themselves capable of handling. Any factor that influences choice behavior can profoundly affect the direction of personal development. This is because the social influences operating in selected environments continue to promote certain competencies, values, and interests long after the decisional determinant has rendered its inaugurating effect. Career choice and development is but one example of the power of self-efficacy beliefs to affect the course of life paths through choice-related processes (Lent, Brown, & Hackett, 1994).

People with a low sense of efficacy in a given domain of functioning shy away from difficult tasks, which they tend to perceive as personal threats have low aspirations and weak commitment to the goals they choose; turn inward on their self-doubts instead of thinking about how to perform successfully; dwell on obstacles, the consequences of failure, and their personal deficiencies when faced with difficulties; attribute failures to deficient capability; slacken their efforts or give up quickly in the face of difficulties; are slow to recover their sense of efficacy after failures or setbacks; and are prone to stress and depression. People who have a strong sense of efficacy, by contrast, approach difficult tasks as challenges to be mastered rather than as threats to be avoided; set challenging goals and sustain strong commitment to their goals; concentrate on how to perform successfully rather than on disruptive personal concerns in the face of problems; attribute failures to insufficient effort or deficient knowledge and skills which are remediable; redouble their effort in the face of obstacles quickly recover their sense of efficacy after failures or setbacks; and display low vulnerability to stress and depression.

REFERENCES

Bandura, A. (1986). *Social foundations of thought and action: A social cognitive theory.* Englewood Cliffs, NJ: Prentice Hall.

Bandura, A. (1991). Self-regulation of motivation through anticipatory and self-regulatory mechanisms. In R. A. Dienstbier (Ed.), *Perspectives on motivation. Nebraska symposium on motivation* (Vol. 38, pp. 69–164). Lincoln: University of Nebraska Press.

Bandura, A. (Ed.). (1995). *Self-efficacy in changing societies.* New York: Cambridge University Press.

Bandura, A. (1997). *Self-efficacy: The exercise of control.* New York: Freeman.

Holden, G. (1991). The relationship of self-efficacy appraisals to subsequent health related outcomes. A meta-analysis. *Social Work in Health Care, 16,* 53–93.

Holden, G., Moncher, M. S., Schinke, S. P., & Barker, K. M. (1990). Self-efficacy of children and adolescents. A meta-analysis. *Psychological Reports, 66,* 1044–1046.

Lent, R. W., Brown, S. D., & Hackett, G. (1994). Toward a unifying social cognitive theory of career and academic interest, choice, and performance. *Journal of Vocational Behavior, 45,* 79–122.

Locke, E. A., & Latham, G. P. (1990). *A theory of goal setting and task performance.* Englewood Cliffs, NJ: Prentice Hall.

Multon, K. D., Brown, S. D., & Lent, R. W. (1991). Relation of self-efficacy beliefs to academic outcomes. A meta-analytic investigation. *Journal of Counseling Psychology, 38,* 30–38.

Schwarzer, R. (Ed.). (1992). *Self-efficacy: Thought control of action.* Washington, DC: Hemisphere.

Stajkovic, A. D., & Luthans, F. (1998). Self-efficacy and work-related performance. A meta-analysis. *Psychological Bulletin, 124,* 240–261.

Williams, S. L. (1992). Perceived self-efficacy and phobic disability. In R. Schwarzer (Ed.), *Self-efficacy: Thought control of action* (pp. 149–176). Washington, DC: Hemisphere.

A. BANDURA
Stanford University

BEHAVIORAL INHIBITION
MOTIVATION

SELF-FULFILLING PROPHECY

Prophets and prophecies have been a part of the three major religious traditions—Jewish, Christian, and Islamic—with the greatest number of prophets being recorded in the Old Testament. The prophets arose mostly during times of social unrest or crisis and the prophecies were related to the major problems facing them. Once the authenticity of the prophets or the source of the prophecy was confirmed or acknowledged, the prophecy was accepted, repeated, and awaited. It was then expected that the prophecies would be duly fulfilled, and actually, the prophecies became the touchstones to test whether social occurrences of individual claims met the conditions laid out in the prophecy. Another example would be the prophecies of the oracles in ancient Greece. Prophets and prophecies in the traditional meaning are now suspect, though social expectations often affect social reality. During 1998 and 1999, there was an anticipation of world wide disruptions due to the Y2K problem. The consequent reaction of individuals to the problem was an example of social beliefs controlling social facts. The term "self-fulfilling prophecy" is used to describe such phenomena.

DESCRIPTION OF THE PHENOMENON

The term "self-fulfilling prophecy" is associated with Robert K. Merton (1968), whose conception of self-fulfilling prophecy was based on the idea posited by Thomas and now often referred to as the Thomas theorem. The basic premise of the Thomas theorem was that, "If men define these situations as real, they are real in their consequences" (Janowitz 1966, p. 301). The idea, however, was not new and many famous individuals in the past, including Shakespeare, Pirandello, and Freud, had made use of that idea in one form or another. The idea had been forwarded by others such as Moll, a hypnotist, who stated that prophecy caused its own fulfillment in the case of his subjects. For example, a run on a bank could result in the closure of that bank in spite of its financial solvency because of rumors about financial risks associated with that particular bank. This was most likely during the 1930s, when many banks failed.

Merton put forth the idea of self-fulfilling prophecy in 1948 as a phenomenon with wider social applications than had been envisioned by others. He had raised the issue of self-defeating predictions earlier. The concept addressed the general relationship between social beliefs/expectations and social reality. According to Merton, the self-fulfilling prophecy is, in the beginning, a *false* definition of the situation evoking a new behavior that makes the originally false conception come *true* (Merton, 1968). The concept has since been refined or modified, and incorporated in many areas such as education, military, industry and production, health practices, and sociological theories.

Today, the concept has been diffused, many synonyms have been substituted, and a number of other definitions of self-fulfilling prophecy are being used. A self-fulfilling prophecy can take place at an individual, group, or organizational level. An individual may have self-imposed expectations of himself or herself, and therefore the prophecy is personal or private. Or, these expectations could be generated from external sources, by one or more individuals, and therefore be interpersonal and of social relevance. For example, youngsters who feel that they are personally responsible for their success tend to be more successful because they are likely to strive harder. The concept can also be used to illustrate prejudices, supposedly based on facts, by small or large groups towards minorities around the world.

The phenomenon of self-fulfilling prophecy has also been noticed in the field of psychology, but it was operationalized as expectancy effect or perceived expectancy research. It is generally agreed by psychologists, who have also tried to understand the process for the last 50 years (Fleming & Manning, 1994), that beliefs and expectations can create social reality. Allport, for example, suggested in 1950 that suspicion of hostile intentions by two countries could trigger a conflict between the two nations. The phenomenon of expectancy fulfillment and demand characteristics of experimental situations were known to many researchers. Rosenthal demonstrated experimentally the subtle but measurable effects of researcher expectations in experimental situations (Rosenthal, 1966). Human relations theorists had also realized the potential of the concept, such as the possible impact of the manager's expectations of the subordinates (Likert, 1961), but the idea was not pursued vigorously as it was not the main focus of their theories. Psy-

chologists have often extended their research in this area to nonverbal behavior and less formal types of interaction among individuals and small groups. They have also studied the effects of labeling inside and outside such organizations as mental institutions. Psychologists have generally tried to provide the dynamics of the process, the sequence and combination of motives, and the attitudes and goals necessary to effect self-fulfilling prophecy and the constraints and conditions under which it works.

APPLICATION AND TESTING

The concepts of labeling and secondary deviance in sociology incorporate the idea of self-fulfilling prophecies. Labeling theory asserts that deviance results in what people do and in the response of others to the deviant acts. A deviant behavior from an individual provokes a reaction from others, and the individual is given a label because of his or her acts of primacy deviance. Because of the labeling and the stigma attached to it, primary deviance is likely to develop into secondary deviance. Thus, the reaction of others based on that label may push or force the individual into further deviant acts, and thus the individual takes on the identity of deviant. The development of secondary deviance can thus be viewed as another illustration of self-fulfilling prophecy, because deviant behavior is associated with the reaction of others. Similarly, many psychiatrists have criticized the label of mental illness.

The idea of self-fulfilling prophecy has been more actively tested in the educational context than in any other discipline. In the field of education, the term Pygmalion effect has been widely used to describe the self-fulfilling prophecy. Pygmalion is a figure from Greek mythology. He was a sculptor who carved a statue of a perfect woman, and fell in love with the statue. Aphorodite, the goddess of love, who had watched his anguish over the statue of Galatea, endowed it with life. Thus, the sculptor's wish was fulfilled.

The research issue in the field of education is whether, and to what extent, the positive and negative expectations for students by their teachers are fulfilled. The research has indicated that the teachers' expectations come to be shared by the students, often resulting in changes in the direction of the prior anticipations of the teachers (Rosenthal, 1966; Jones, 1977; Tauber, 1997). The process of self-fulfilling prophecy has also been explored by educational researchers. A model by Good and Brophy suggested five steps (Good & Brophy, 1978) in the process: (a) the teacher forms expectations; (b) the teacher acts differently because of those expectations; (c) the treatments convey what is expected to the students; (d) given consistency over a period of time, and lack of resistance by the students involved, it affects the behavior and achievement of the students; and (e) the achievement and behavior of the students will conform more closely to the expectations. This may also hold in the case of nonverbal communication. Though there is criticism of the self-fulfilling prophecy in the field of education that it is self-fulfillment of the self-fulfilling prophecy (Wineburg, 1987), teacher expectation bias effects are generally acknowledged in that field.

The placebo effect in the relief of pain or healing has been very widely documented since the 1940s in the medical literature, from the treatment of warts to the healing of damaged tissues. The placebo has been used in a number of situations in conventional, traditional, and alternative medicines. The curative and destructive power of Voodoo, including death, can be viewed as a placebo effect. Cures have been achieved through inert or inactive placebo as well as through active placebo materials.

An observation that has been made about the nature of prophecy—that the ultimate function of prophecy is not to tell the future but to make it—seems applicable to business and industry. Self-fulfilling prophecy has been applied in business and industry in order to increase productivity, better sales, and performance. Studies conducted with defense personnel in Israel and the U.S. Navy are generally supportive of increased performance when it is expected by the superior officers. The changes in performance are affected by the gender of the participants and the level of increased expectations. Corporations hold workshops to exploit the concept of self-fulfilling prophecy in order to develop leaders, to outperform the competition, or to increase sales of their products by communicating to the employees that they are capable of meeting the increased expectations. The model based on self-fulfilling prophecy states that increased expectancies lead to new behavior based on changed self-expectancies, resulting in the prophecy's (expectation's) being fulfilled, thus further reinforcing the validity of the prophecy or expectation (Eden, 1990).

What happens when prophecy fails? A book by the same title gives an account of a direct prophecy gone wrong (Festinger, Riecken, & Shachter, 1956). The failure of a self-fulfilling prophecy is different in nature from the failure of a direct prophecy. A self-fulfilling prophecy does not have the same type of stigma attached, nor the same level of accountability to others. A teacher's private expectations of a student may go wrong, and the teacher may face some disappointment, but may not have to justify the expectations to anyone else. Philosophers and psychologists use the concept of confirmation or confirmatory bias to account for the acceptance of a statement that was only partially confirmed and partially proved to be false. Confirmatory bias refers to the act of accounting for only the phenomenon that came to pass, ignoring all the other aspects or events that were in contradiction of expectations.

Of course, many prophecies are neither self-fulfilling nor inevitable. All prophecies are subject to change, failure, or defeat. In addition to the concept of the Pygmalion effect, many variations of the theme—such as the Galatea effect, which involved directly raising expectations of the employees, and the Golem effect, which is intended to denote negative consequences—have been used to indicate different types of procedures and impacts. In addition to the self-fulfilling and self-defeating themes suggested by Merton, many other variations of the theme have appeared in the literature, variously called self-destroying prophecies, self-frustrating predictions, and self-confirming predictions (Sztompka, 1986, p. 234). Merton has addressed the problems of changing both the self-fulfilling prophecy and the self-defeating prophecy in his work. He pointed out that the initial definition of the situation needs to be abandoned and that only then can the self-fulfilling prophecy be broken because the cycle is broken. The dire predictions about Y2K were self-defeating because deliberate institutional controls were established to attack the problem, and billions of dollars were spent in rewriting the old programs.

The research literature has indicated the wide scope of application of the phenomenon of self-fulfilling prophecy, as well as process and limitations. For example, labeling is often effective for minor deviant acts but not for major offenses, such as murder. Research in this area indicates that a self-sustaining prophecy is harder to achieve. Often there is no single prophecy but many different scenarios, as in the case of Y2K, and the effect of such inconsistencies is not known. The predictions have been modified and changed already, and those in charge have made a concerted effort to avoid the serious problems and defeat the prophecy. Still, the beliefs and behaviors of many were altered different degrees. Some installed electric generators in their homes, some decided not to travel on the eve of the year 2000, and some withdrew money from the bank. Year 2000 prophecies will continue to provide an interesting set of case studies, as they include the possibilities and problems involved in understanding the process, power, and limitations of the phenomenon of self-fulfilling prophecy, a double-edged sword.

REFERENCES

Eden, D. (1990). *Pygmalion in management: Productivity as a self-fulfilling prophecy.* Lexington: Lexington Books.

Festinger, L., Riecken, H. W., and Schacter, S. (1956). *When prophecy fails.* Minneapolis: University of Minnesota Press.

Fleming, J. H., and Manning, D. J. (1994). Self-fulfilling prophecies. In V. S. Ramachandran (Ed.), *Encyclopedia of human behavior* (Vol. 4, pp. 89–97). San Diego: Academic Press.

Good, T. L., and Brophy, J. E. (1978). *Looking in classrooms* (2nd ed.). New York: Harper & Row.

Janowitz, M. (Ed.). (1966). *W. I. Thomas on social organization and social personality.* Chicago: University of Chicago Press.

Jones, R. A. (1977). *Self-fulfilling prophecies: Social, psychological, and physiological effects of expectancies.* Hillsdale: Lawrence Erlbaum Associates.

Likert, R. (1961). *New patterns of management.* New York: McGraw-Hill.

Merton, R. K. (1968). *Social theory and social structure* (enlarged ed.). New York: The Free Press.

Rosenthal, R. (1966). *Experimenter effects in behavioral research.* New York: Appleton-Century Crofts.

Tauber, R. T. (1997). *Self-fulfilling prophecy: A practical guide to its use in education.* Westport: Praeger.

Sztompka, P. (1986). *Robert K. Merton: An intellectual profile.* New York: St Martin's Press.

Wineburg, S. S. (1987). The self-fulfillment of the self-fulfilling prophecy. *Educational Researcher, 16*(9), 28–37.

SUGGESTED READING

Rosenthal, R., & Jacobson, L. (1968). *Pygmalion in the classroom: Teacher expectation and pupils' intellectual development.* New York: Holt, Rinehart, & Winston.

Wineburg, S. S., and Shulman, L. S. (1980). The self-fulfilling prophecy: Its genesis and development in American education. In J. Clark, C. Modgil, and S. Modgil (Eds.), *Robert K. Merton, concensus and controversy.* London: The Falmer Press.

S. R. SONNAD
Western Michigan University

PYGMALION EFFECT

SELF-HELP GROUPS

Self-help groups are more or less formal organizations of people working (usually without professional assistance) toward a common goal to benefit each member of the group, whether by attaining greater control of their behavior or alleviating their painful or unhappy conditions. They are sometimes referred to as "mutual aid" or "mutual help" groups. Some so-called self-help groups are oriented mainly toward social or political advocacy or action (e.g., to improve housing, food purchases, education, energy use); they are not considered here. The discussion centers, instead, on groups whose primary goal is to achieve psychological or behavioral gains for their members, who typically address a single problem or condition, and who are committed to two principles: that people who are coping or have coped effectively with a personal problem are better helpers than professionals who do not have firsthand experience, and that such people help themselves by helping each other. A common theme is "only I can change my condition, but I cannot do it alone." The discussion includes what are sometimes called "support groups," although so-called "support groups" often rely on a degree of professional facilitation and focus more on mutual support and comfort than on active change.

ORIGINS AND PRESENT STATUS

Various strains of ancestry have been cited for self-help groups: a long tradition of mutual support by family, community, church, and ethnic group members; the Friendly Societies that originated in seventeenth-century England; trade unions and cooperatives; Christian group-confessional religious practices; and the American (USA) tradition of individual and small group self-reliance. Whatever their antecedents, contemporary self-help groups have evolved at least partly to meet therapeutic needs that often are not, or not adequately, dealt with by existing social institutions.

Alcoholics Anonymous (AA) is the oldest, largest, and best-known ongoing therapeutic self-help group. Founded in 1935 by Bill W. and Dr. Bob, it is an organization of, by, and for alcoholics (with offshoots Al-Anon and Al-Ateen for relatives and friends). Although its program was described in the 1937 publication *Alcoholics Anonymous,* the general public knew little about AA until a 1944 article in the Saturday Evening Post. It now has well over a million members in 100 countries. Its twelve-step program has been adopted by dozens of other self-help groups, including Gamblers Anonymous, Overeaters Anonymous, Schizophrenics Anonymous, Narcotics Anonymous, Debtors Anonymous, and (more recently) Cocaine Anonymous. Other early and well-known self-help organizations are Recovery, Inc., founded in 1937 by psychiatrist Abraham Low for former patients of mental health institutions, and Synanon, founded in the 1950s by Charles Dederich for drug addicts (and, later, ex-convicts).

Self-help groups grew in number in the late 1950s and early 1960s. One directory listed 265 such groups in 1963; after that, they proliferated. In 1976 both the *Journal of Applied Behavior Science* and *Social Policy* had special issues on self-help. The Directory of *Self-Help Mutual Aid Groups—Chicago Metropolitan Area 1981–82,* edited by Pasquale, listed 650 local chapters from 120 different self-help organizations in the Chicago area alone. Katz (1993) estimated that at the time of his writing there were perhaps 750,000 self-help groups in the United States with 10 to 15 million members.

Especially since the mid-1970s, the growth of self-help groups has been seen by some as a major movement in psychotherapy, a "fourth force" following the "third force" of humanistic psychotherapy. Self-help has become a subject of conferences, of formal presentations at annual conventions of the American Psychological Association, and of a slowly growing body of scholarly research. A national workshop on self-help and public health was organized by United States Surgeon General C. Everett Koop in 1987. Besides several national self-help "clearinghouses," there are such centers of information in at least 25 states; and although the movement is American in its origin and major growth, there are self-help clearinghouses in Canada, Australia, Israel, Japan, and a dozen European countries.

In addition to their growth and claims of efficacy, self-help groups can be seen as meeting a need that cannot possibly be met, simply in terms of increasing psychological, physical, and financial burdens, by traditional human services systems. Instead of being consumers of mental health services, self-help groups can be dispensers of such services (Riessman and Carroll, 1995). The self-help trend also perhaps both influences and is influenced by recent interest in alternative and preventive medicine.

TYPES OF GROUPS

While a number of typologies of self-help groups have been made, including the simple demarcation into twelve-step (modelled on AA) and non-twelve-step groups by Katz (1993) and others, Levy's (1976) four types continue to illuminate those with a therapeutic orientation.

Type I groups aim primarily at behavioral control or change, especially for addicts and people with other compulsions. Examples of such groups are AA, Gamblers Anonymous, TOPS (Take Off Pounds Sensibly), and Parents Anonymous (for those coping with child-abuse tendencies).

Levy's Type II groups, whose members have in common a stressful status or condition, could be further divided into subtypes. Some organize around particular physical health problems; for example, Mended Hearts (for those who have had heart surgery), Make Today Count (for cancer patients and their families and friends), and Reach to Recovery (for women who have had mastectomies). Reissman and Carroll (1995) claim that there is now a self-help group for every major illness listed by the World Health Organization. Other groups have members coping with a mental illness; affective and anxiety disorders and even schizophrenia (e.g., Schizophrenics Anonymous) are represented. Still other Type II groups focus on such crises as rape, murder of one's child, and coping with a suicide. Another category deals with what might be called life transitions (Geriatric Rap, Widow-to-Widow, Parents Without Partners) or transitions toward normality (for former mental patients, ex-convicts, Viet Nam war veterans). Many Type II groups work mainly on coping with rather than changing the status of members.

Type III groups are composed of people felt to be discriminated against because of sex, race, class, or sexual orientation.

Finally, Type IV groups share no particular common problem but work toward general self-actualization and enhanced effectiveness. Levy includes Mowrer's Integrity Groups (1972) under this classification, and it covers many consciousness-raising and sensitivity self-help groups.

Not all groups fit neatly into just one of these types, just as not all restrict their goals simply to changes within their members rather than in social institutions. In addition, there are many groups for people without a primary disability but involved as a family member, caretaker, or friend of the affected person (e.g., Children of Aging Parents).

THERAPEUTIC FACTORS IN SELF-HELP GROUPS

In spite of the great diversity of organizations already noted, one can distinguish a number of generally common therapeutic features or processes that help members of self-help groups make attitudinal or behavioral changes.

1. *Shared experience.* For most self-help groups, a particular kind of shared experience or situation is the basis and rationale for membership. People thereby tend to feel immediately understood and thus not psychologically alone. The commonality tends also to reduce defensiveness and encourage self-revelation, with its usual cathartic utility and reduction of shame.

2. *Helping others.* The "helper therapy principle" of self-help groups, first enunciated by Riessman in 1965, posits that the more group members help others, the more they are helped themselves. A variety of writers have analyzed ways in which this works: Helpers feel greater competence, make learning gains, receive social approval, gain in self-confidence, practice and thereby self-reinforce desirable role behavior, and achieve a greater measure of objectivity concerning their particular problem.

3. *Ongoing support network.* Members of self-help groups often receive supportive compliments or praise at their meetings. But typically the support extends virtually around the clock, with members on call. The support network becomes something like a concerned extended family.

4. *Information sharing.* A good deal of benefit comes from receiving information, whether technical or part of folk wisdom:

everything from explaining medical jargon to advice about child rearing. Some groups are especially adept at keeping up on the latest research and treatment modalities in their area of concern.

5. *Finding models.* Membership in a self-help group provides opportunities to observe how others cope effectively and to use them as models.

6. *Gaining feedback.* In the openness and honesty that typify self-help groups, members' behaviors tend to be accurately observed and commented on. Such directness, in a supportive atmosphere, helps people "find their way."

7. *Learning special methods.* With some self-help groups such as AA and other twelve-step programs, Recovery, and Synanon, successful coping is closely linked to following special procedures or techniques. Members are trained to learn and perpetuate them, and the pattern provides a structure that many find valuable.

8. *Other cognitive processes.* Much of the helpful impact of self-help group processes seems related to other principles of cognitive therapy such as raising self-image, increasing self-understanding, expanding perceived alternatives, making useful discriminations, and redefining norms.

SELF-HELP VERSUS PROFESSIONAL PSYCHOTHERAPY

The relationship between self-help groups and professional and institutional helpers has varied from close cooperation to antagonism. Professional group psychotherapy typically differs from the self-help group process in a number of ways. The professional obviously has formal training and credentialing, and therefore some kind of expertise; professional help is paid for and time-limited to arranged appointments; the professional does not expect emotional support in return; the professional operates from an explicit theoretical base which claims empirical support; and so on. For some self-help groups, independence from the authority, methods, and funding of professionals is a matter of principle (and sometimes of antiprofessional rhetoric).

But even strong self-help advocates make increasing acknowledgement of important ways in which professionals have started, advised, and legitimized some such groups. Among professional therapists who have founded self-help groups are Low (Recovery, Inc.), Mowrer (Integrity Groups), and Silverman (Widow-to-Widow). Research suggests that about a third of self-help groups started with at least the assistance of professional helpers. Especially in many groups related to physical health, there is much interaction between professionals and lay persons. Organizations such as AA are often strongly endorsed by psychiatrists and clinical psychologists. The National Institute of Mental Health has sponsored studies of self-help groups and of their interactions with professional workers and institutions. In recent years cooperation between self-help groups and professional psychologists and psychotherapists seems to be increasing, with growing recognition of ways in which they can be of service to each other.

Comparatively little of the literature about self-help groups is negatively critical. But evidence of their effectiveness is largely anecdotal, and research on the effectiveness of many groups is difficult by their very nature (e.g., anonymity, transient membership, lack of record-keeping). Quite aside from such pragmatic issues, challenges to some groups might be raised about questionable founding premises and pressures toward conformity. Good empirical research on the effectiveness of self-help groups is limited (Powell, 1993; Kurtz, 1990). On the other hand, the continued growth of self-help groups and the increasing and respectful attention paid them by professional psychologists recommend giving credence to many of their principles and wider application to many of their methods. Reissman and Carroll (1995) put this in a larger psychosociopolitical context: "A major reason for the current resonance of the self-help approach relates to the significant world problems to which a self-help model is potentially responsive, including widespread feelings of powerlessness and alienation . . . and of isolation; widespread addictions; . . . the tremendous expansion of chronic illnesses," and, a host of other social, political, and even professional problems and limitations.

REFERENCES

Alcoholics Anonymous. (1976/1937). *Alcoholics anonymous.* New York: A. A. World Services.

Gartner, A., & Reissman, F. (Eds.). (1984). *The self-help revolution.* New York: Human Services.

Goodman, G., & Jacobs, M. (1994). The self-help, mutual-support group. In A. Fuhriman & G. Burlingame (Eds.), *Handbook of group psychology.* New York: Wiley.

Journal of Applied Behavior Science. (1976). Special issue on self-help groups. *12*(3).

Katz, A. H. (1993). *Self-help in America: A social movement perspective.* New York: Twayne.

Katz, A. H., & Bender, E. I. (1990). *Helping one another: Self-help groups in a changing world.* Oakland, CA: Third Party.

Katz, A. H., et al. (Eds.). (1991). *Self-help: Concepts and applications.* Philadelphia: Charles.

Kurtz, L. F. (1990). The self-help movement: Review of the past decade of research. *Social Work with Groups, 13,* 101–115.

Kurtz, L. F. (1997). *Self-help and support groups: A handbook for practitioners.* Thousand Oaks, CA: Sage.

Levy, L. H. (1976). Self-help groups: Types and psychological processes. *Journal of Applied Behavioral Science, 12,* 310–322.

Mowrer, O. H. (1972). Integrity groups: Basic principles and procedures. *The Counseling Psychologist, 3,* 7–33.

Pasquale, F. (Ed.). (1981). *Directory of self-help mutual aid groups—Chicago metropolitan area, 1981–1982.* Evanston, IL: Self-Help Center.

Powell, T. J. (1993). Self-help research and policy issues. *Journal of Applied Behavioral Science, 29*(2), 151–165.

Riessman, F. (1965). The "helper" therapy principle. *Social Work, 10,* 27–32.

Riessman, F., & Carroll, D. (1995). *Redefining self-help: Policy and practice.* San Francisco: Jossey-Bass.

Self-help sourcebook. (1988). Denville, NJ: Self-Help Clearinghouse.

Social Policy. (1976). Special double issue on self-help.

Watkins, T. R., & Callicutt, J. W. (1997). Self-help and advocacy groups in mental health. In T. R. Watkins & J. W. Callicutt (Eds.), *Mental health policy and practice today.* Thousand Oaks, CA: Sage.

F. W. HANSEN
Lake Forest College

SELF-MONITORING

Self-monitoring refers to a procedure in which individuals are asked to notice and document instances of particular target thoughts, feelings, and behaviors as they occur in natural settings. Self-monitoring is considered to be one of the most direct forms of behavioral assessment (Cone, 1978), and is widely used in clinical psychology (Elliot, Miltenberger, Kaster-Bundgaard, & Lumley, 1996). An alternative means of direct measurement by the use of trained observers is frequently impractical due to time constraints, reactivity, cost factors, and/or the unavailability of observers. Self-monitoring is more practical, and is also the only available direct measure when target responses are private by nature (e.g., thoughts and feelings), or by convention (e.g., sexual behavior). Rather than asking persons to recall each occurrence of a target behavior some time later (e.g., during an interview), in self-monitoring, information is recorded as the target behavior occurs. Self-monitoring can therefore provide important information not only concerning the occurrence and frequency of a target behavior, but also about the context or circumstances in which it occurs. Events that follow a target behavior that might be important consequences influencing its occurrence are also recorded. With this information in hand, important situational patterns or consequences may then be identified. For example, a person might learn that he or she eats more in social situations than at home. Many important factors influencing behavior may not be recalled later, and are best assessed at the time the target behavior occurs.

There are several ways that self-monitoring can be implemented. If a target behavior is fairly low in frequency, it is often feasible to ask that each occurrence be recorded. This provides an ongoing frequency count of the target behavior. Other situational information, such as time of day or features of the setting, might also be recorded. Frequency counts may be burdensome for the self-recorder if a target behavior occurs very often. When this is the case, the individual may be asked to record within particular blocks of time (e.g., two mornings out of a week), or to record at intervals (e.g., recording every two hours), whether or how frequently the target behavior occurred. These latter approaches are less direct and information is likely to be lost; however, they may produce greater compliance than daily frequency counts.

It is often important to measure the duration of a target behavior. For instance, if the target behavior is studying, the amount of time spent on this activity is an important variable. In these cases, the self-recorder is asked to record the duration of the target behavior each time it occurs. This information is probably more precise for responses, like studying, that have a more salient onset and ending. Other activities, such as worrying or nail-biting, may begin without as much notice. The self-recorder may be asked to estimate the starting time when he or she engaged in this type of target activity.

Particularly in the early stages of clinical assessment, specific target behaviors to measure and change can be difficult to identify. For example, an individual might have the goal of being less angry, but may not be able to specify all the responses that would be candidates for change. Even when target behaviors are readily identified, it is often desirable to collect as much information as possible concerning the circumstances and potential consequences associated with these behaviors. In these cases, diary formats may be preferred. Diary formats allow the self-recorder to supply more elaborate and narrative descriptions of his or her behavior and the environment in which it occurs. Clinical assessment often begins with this broader approach, then moves to more specific target behaviors and more structured self-recording forms as initial information helps to focus assessment on particular difficulties.

Aside from its value as an assessment tool, self-monitoring carries an additional advantage when used with clinical populations. Research has consistently demonstrated that the frequency of self-monitored behaviors changes when individuals begin self-monitoring. This phenomenon is termed reactivity (Nelson, 1977). Reactivity poses problems when the primary goal is to collect accurate data, because the data collection procedure may actually change the frequency of the behavior being measured. However, one advantage of reactivity is that the behavior change is generally in a desirable direction. When unwanted behaviors are self-monitored, their frequency tends to decrease, while the frequency of desirable self-monitored behaviors tends to increase. Reactive effects are typically small and short-lived; however, they are relatively immediate, and may be beneficial and encouraging to persons beginning to pursue behavior change.

While there are several advantages to self-monitoring, there are several factors that can detract from the accuracy and utility of the resulting data. As noted above, the procedure involves two separate responses. The self-recorder must first notice the occurrence of the behavior, then must record that occurrence. Both responses must take place for consistent and accurate information to be collected, and problems may arise that interfere with one or both. For example, self-monitors may have difficulty noticing behaviors that are not clearly defined. For instance, aggressive behavior may be defined as including only physical aggression toward people or destruction of property; however, verbal aggression such as yelling, or impulses to engage in aggressive acts might also be included. Alternatively, some clearly defined target behaviors may be difficult to notice. For example, a person might be asked to self-record instances when he or she has the thought, "I'm a failure." While the thought may be clear, it may be so fleeting or ego-syntonic that the person does not notice each instance. In either case, information may be lost. Other factors can influence whether a noticed behavior is actually recorded. For example, failure to record might occur when forms are not readily available, when target behaviors are socially unacceptable, or when the act of recording is awkward in so-

cial situations. Alternatively, recordings can occur in the absence of noticed behaviors. For example, highly desirable behaviors or behaviors the self-recorder feels pressured to increase might be overly recorded. Self-recorders who have difficulty completing or complying with the procedure might complete forms all at once just before returning them to the assessor rather than collecting data in an ongoing fashion.

Many of these difficulties can be alleviated by implementing procedures that have been shown to influence the accuracy of self-monitored data. These include (a) clearly defining target behaviors; (b) requiring that recordings be made immediately after the target behavior occurs; (c) providing training to self-monitors; (d) emphasizing the importance of accurate data collection and providing reinforcement for accurate data collection; (e) minimizing the number of target behaviors being monitored at one time; and (f) regularly checking the accuracy of self-monitored data and informing self-monitors that their accuracy will be checked (see Korotitsch & Nelson-Gray, in press, for a review).

While there is no perfect measure of behavior that can be compared to self-monitored data, the accuracy of self-recordings can sometimes be checked through comparison with data collected by observers. For example, a spouse might occasionally collect observations to compare with the self-recordings of an insomniac. For some target behaviors, other measurements can corroborate self-monitored data. For instance, regularly collected measurements of weight might be compared to self-monitored food intake in a weight reduction program.

In conclusion, self-monitoring is a widely used assessment device because of its convenience, the accuracy of data collected under the conditions specified previously, and the initial therapeutic benefits due to reactivity.

REFERENCES

Cone, J. D. (1978). The Behavioral Assessment Grid (BAG): A conceptual framework and a taxonomy. *Behavior Therapy, 9,* 882–888.

Elliot, A. J., Miltenberger, R. G., Kaster-Bundgaard, J., & Lumley, V. (1996). A national survey of assessment and therapy used by behavior therapists. *Cognitive and Behavioral Practice, 3,* 107–125.

Korotitsch, W. J., & Nelson-Gray, R. O. (in press). An overview of self-monitoring research in assessment and treatment. *Psychological Assessment.*

Nelson, R. O. (1977). Methodological issues in assessment via self-monitoring. In J. D. Cone & R. P. Hawkins (Eds.), *Behavioral assessment: New directions in clinical psychology.* New York: Brunner/Mazel.

W. J. KOROTITSCH
R. O. NELSON-GRAY
University of North Carolina, Greensboro

CLINICAL ASSESSMENT
SOCIAL INFLUENCE

SELF-REPORT AND SELF-RATINGS

Within the category of self-report are assessment methods in which individuals are asked to describe their behaviors and experiences in a summative fashion, and/or to report this information retrospectively. The distinction between self-report and self-monitoring is somewhat arbitrary, with the latter referring to a procedure in which behaviors are observed and recorded at the time of their occurrence, rather than summarized or reported retrospectively. Self-report measures include interviews, questionnaires/surveys, self-ratings, and cognitive assessment methods such as think-aloud procedures (verbalizing one's thoughts as they occur in a particular situation). In each of these cases, rather than directly observing or measuring the behavior of interest, the individual is asked to report, recall, and/or summarize this information. For this reason, self-report is considered to be the most indirect method for assessing behavior. However, in many cases, more direct measurement is not feasible. For instance, thoughts and feelings cannot be measured more directly by any means other than by asking persons to verbalize or report them. For these phenomena, self-report may be considered one of the most direct assessment methods available.

Interviews, questionnaires, and rating scales are the most widely used psychological assessment methods. Interviews vary in the degree to which they are structured (confined to particular areas of inquiry) and standardized (with uniform procedures for administration and scoring). In unstructured interviews, the information collected follows no predetermined order and varies widely depending on the responses or concerns of the interviewee, and the specific training and preferences of the interviewer. This open-ended approach is often a useful starting point in clinical assessment. The interview generally becomes more focused as problem areas are identified and assessed. In contrast, structured interviews contain standard questions, in a set sequence, with specific phrasing specified within the interview. These interviews are generally designed for nonprofessionals to administer and are frequently used to establish diagnostic status of multiple individuals for research purposes. A more common approach, frequently used to conduct diagnostic evaluation for clinical and research purposes, is the semi-structured interview. Similar to structured interviews, the general content of these interviews is outlined, and questions are suggested. However, these interviews are designed for professionals to administer and allow much more flexibility, while providing sufficient structure to allow for comparison of interview results across administrations and clinicians.

Questionnaires are frequently used to obtain information in the absence of face-to-face inquiry. They have the major advantage of being easy to administer and are therefore highly cost- and time-efficient. They are also face valid assessment tools, thus increasing the client's compliance. Questionnaires can generally be divided into broad and specific types (Korotitsch & Nelson-Gray, 1999). Broad questionnaires assess general functioning in multiple life areas, multiple diagnostic categories, or general psychological constructs such as traits. Personality inventories would fall within this category. Specific or brief questionnaires focus on particular behaviors or areas of functioning. For example, one brief questionnaire might assess recent symptoms of depression, while another might assess thoughts and beliefs associated with depression.

Broad questionnaires have the advantage of providing comprehensive assessment of multiple life areas. However, they require more time and resources to administer, score, and interpret. Due to the more general content and breadth of broad questionnaires, they tend to be less sensitive to small or specific changes in behavior over time or as a result of treatment. For these reasons, broad questionnaires are usually administered infrequently, such as before and after treatment. Specific questionnaires are more often suitable for frequent measurement of ongoing behavior change.

Questionnaires carry the potential advantage of having norms. These measures can be administered to very large groups of people, with responses quantified into numerical scores. The average score for a population therefore can be determined, and particular scores can be identified as falling far above or below that average. Norms can be used to estimate the clinical magnitude of behavior change. For example, a person might initially score much higher than average on a depression questionnaire, but may score closer to the average as he or she progresses in treatment. If the questionnaire or set of rating scales is brief, this information can be collected frequently and used to assess the person's progress in treatment.

Self-ratings are also brief and economical assessment measures. Respondents are asked to provide a numerical summary of the responses being assessed. For example, rather than reporting the symptoms of depression, that person might be asked to rate his or her feelings of sadness on a scale of 1 to 7. Rating scales can be constructed for virtually any phenomenon an assessor is interested in measuring and are useful when no appropriate specific questionnaires are available. Guidelines for constructing individualized self-rating scales are offered by Bloom, Fischer, and Orme (1995).

Cognitive assessment methods are infrequently-used forms of self-report in which individuals are asked to verbalize their thoughts in a particular situation. For instance, a phobic might be asked to verbalize his thoughts while approaching an airplane. Persons might be asked to verbalize all their thoughts continually (think-aloud), to report their most recent thought when given a cue (thought-sampling), or to report thoughts they recall immediately after the situation (thought-listing). These approaches have the advantage of providing information about thoughts and experiences as they occur. Their major disadvantage is that responses are difficult to quantify or compare across individuals.

There are several disadvantages to consider when using self-report methods. Most are related to the more indirect and summative nature of self-reports. The accuracy of self-report may be impossible to determine and may be vulnerable to several factors. Data may be omitted, added, or otherwise distorted because of natural errors and imperfections in memory. They may also reflect the respondent's own beliefs or personal theories concerning the nature, causes, and stability of his or her behavior (Ross, 1989), rather than more objective observations. Self-reported information can also be modified, withheld, or minimized, particularly when assessing socially unacceptable behaviors, attitudes, beliefs, and so on. Similarly, more desirable or socially accepted responses may be too frequently given, as may undesirable behaviors or difficulties, depending on the situation.

Self-report can also be influenced by response biases, for example, a tendency toward answering "true" to questions regardless of their content or toward choosing the extreme high, extreme low, or exact middle rating on a scale. Many broad questionnaires include scales that assess response bias and the tendency to distort or provide inaccurate information. However, many brief scales cannot assess these biases. A final concern is that self-report measures must be designed with careful attention to the level of sophistication and the clarity of questions. Inaccurate information can often be traced to misleading, confusing, overly sophisticated, or ambiguous questions.

Despite their disadvantages, self-report measures are widely used in psychology, since they have the advantages of being economical, quantifiable, and easy to administer. More importantly, many self-report measures have published norms to aid in interpretations of a given score. They also provide a means for assessing subjective or private phenomena that cannot be observed directly. There has been rapid proliferation of specific questionnaires over the past 20 years (Froyd, Lambert, & Froyd, 1996). Choosing a given questionnaire from among these options can be daunting. An excellent resource for clinicians is provided by Fischer and Corcoran (1994). These authors have compiled and published a large collection of specific questionnaires, with summaries and descriptions of each questionnaire's development, available norms, and psychometric properties.

REFERENCES

Bloom, M., Fischer, J., & Orme, J. (1995). *Evaluating practice: Guidelines for the accountable professional.* Englewood Cliffs, NJ: Prentice Hall.

Fischer, J., & Corcoran, K. (1994). *Measures for clinical practice: A sourcebook* (2nd ed., Vols. 1–2). New York: Macmillan.

Froyd, J. E., Lambert, M. J., & Froyd, J. D. (1996). A review of practices of psychotherapy outcome measurement. *Journal of Mental Health, 5,* 11–15.

Korotitsch, W. J., & Nelson-Gray, R. O. (1999). Self-report and physiological measures. In S. C. Hayes, D. H. Barlow, & R. O. Nelson-Gray (Eds.), *The scientist-practitioner: Research and accountability in the age of managed care* (2nd ed., pp. 320–352). New York: Allyn & Bacon.

Ross, M. (1989). Relation of implicit theories to the construction of personal histories. *Psychological Review, 96,* 341–357.

W. J. KOROTITSCH
R. O. NELSON-GRAY
University of North Carolina, Greensboro

MEASUREMENT
QUESTIONAIRES
RATING SCALES

SELIGMAN, MARTIN E. P.

Martin E. P. Seligman works on learned helplessness, depression, and the subject of optimism and pessimism. He is currently Fox Leadership Professor of Psychology in the Department of Psychology at the University of Pennsylvania. He is well known in academic and clinical circles and is a best-selling author.

His bibliography includes 15 books and 150 articles on motivation and personality. Among his better-known works are *Learned Optimism* (Knopf, 1991), *What You Can Change & What You Can't* (Knopf, 1993), *The Optimistic Child* (Houghton Mifflin, 1995), *Helplessness* (Freeman, 1975, 1993), and *Abnormal Psychology* (Norton, 1982, 1988, 1995, with David Rosenhan). He is the recipient of two Distinguished Scientific Contribution awards from the American Psychological Association (APA), the Laurel Award of the American Association for Applied and Preventive Psychology, and the Lifetime Achievement Award of the Society for Research in Psychopathology. He holds an honorary Ph.D. from Uppsala, Sweden, and a Doctor of Humane Letters from the Massachusetts School of Professional Psychology. Seligman received both the American Psychological Society's William James Fellow Award (for contribution to basic science) and the James McKeen Cattell Fellow Award (for the application of psychological knowledge).

Seligman's research and writing have been broadly supported by a number of institutions, including the National Institute of Mental Health (NIMH, continuously since 1969), the National Institute on Aging, the National Science Foundation (NSF), the Guggenheim Foundation, and the John D. and Catherine T. MacArthur Foundation. His research on preventing depression received the MERIT Award of NIMH in 1991. He is the network director of the Positive Psychology Network and scientific director of the Telos Project of the Mayerson Foundation.

For 14 years, Seligman was director of the clinical training program of the psychology department at the University of Pennsylvania. He was named a Distinguished Practitioner by the National Academies of Practice, and in 1995 received the Pennsylvania Psychological Association's award for Distinguished Contributions to Science and Practice. He is a past president of the Division of Clinical Psychology of APA, and served as the leading consultant to *Consumer Reports* for its pioneering article, which documented the effectiveness of long-term psychotherapy. He is scientific director of Foresight, Inc., a testing company, which predicts success in various walks of life.

His books have been translated into more than a dozen languages and have been best-sellers both in America and abroad. His work has been featured on the front page of the *New York Times, Time, Newsweek, U.S. News and World Report, Reader's Digest, Redbook, Parents, Fortune, Family Circle,* and many other popular magazines. He has been a spokesman for the science and practice of psychology on numerous television and radio shows and has written columns on such far-ranging topics as education, violence, and therapy. He has lectured around the world to educators, industry, parents, and mental health professionals.

In 1996 Seligman was elected president of APA by the largest vote in recent memory. His primary aim as APA president was to join practice and science together so both might flourish, a goal that has dominated his own life as a psychologist. His major initiatives concerned the prevention of ethnopolitical warfare and the study of positive psychology.

STAFF

SELYE, HANS (1907–1982)

Hans Selye has become internationally known as the father of the stress concept. He studied in Prague, Paris, and Rome, receiving both the MD and PhD from the German University at Prague and then the DSci from McGill University in Montreal, Canada. As a medical student he became aware of what he called the syndrome of "just being sick." This led to the development of his stress concept. The whole nature of stress that is so widely discussed today led him to realize that many degenerative diseases including coronary thrombosis, kidney failure, arthritis, peptic ulcer, hypertension, and possibly cancer can result from the poor handling of stress.

The mechanisms, of course, are biological. Fairly early in his career he identified the general adaptation syndrome (GAS) to refer to the various stressors in life and our general reaction to them. He identified three stages of GAS: (a) the alarm reaction; (b) resistance; and (c) exhaustion. What are commonly called psychosomatic symptoms occur and persist in the body's defense system as reactions to prolonged stress. These biological findings led Selye to investigate in more detail both the psychological and philosophical implications of stress. He believed in what he called altruistic egoism. This is interpreted as gaining the respect and goodwill of others.

He served as professor and director of the Institute of Experimental Medicine and Surgery at the University of Montreal and as president of the International Institute of Stress. He was the author of 18 books and hundreds of articles. His best-known books include *The Psychology and Pathology of Exposure to Stress, The Stress of Life, Selye's Guide to Stress Research,* and *Stress Without Distress.*

R. W. LUNDIN
Wheaton, Illinois

SENSATION SEEKING

Sensation seeking is a personality trait behaviorally expressed in the generalized tendency to seek varied, novel, complex, and intense sensations and experiences and to take physical risks for the sake of such experiences (Zuckerman, 1979, 1983, 1994). Others have used different terms to describe what is essentially the same trait (e.g., monotony avoidance, venturesomeness, thrill seeking, and arousal seeking).

The construct and the first form of the Sensation Seeking Scale (SSS) were developed as part of an experimental program in sensory deprivation conducted in the 1960s (Zuckerman, 1969, 1979), and the scale was first used to predict responses to sensory deprivation. High sensation-seekers tended to become more restless in sensory deprivation and responded more strongly than low sensation-seekers in working for visual or kinesthetic stimulation.

TEST DEVELOPMENT

Initially, the SSS consisted of only a general scale, but subsequent factor analyses of items yielded four subscales:

1. *Thrill and Adventure Seeking (TAS).* Items reflect a desire to engage in activities or sports providing some unusual sensations and involving risk.

2. *Experience Seeking (ES).* Items indicate an openness to new kinds of sensations and experiences through travel, art, music, drugs, and an unconventional lifestyle.

3. *Disinhibition (Dis).* Items describe the seeking of exciting sensations and experiences in social situations such as wild parties, social drinking, and sexual activity.

4. *Boredom Susceptibility (BS).* Items reflect an intolerance for repetious and predictable kinds of experiences in routine work or with dull people, and a restlessness when the individual cannot escape from routine or sameness of stimulation.

Form V is currently the most widely used form of the SSS and may be scored for each of the previous four factors, along with a total score based on the sum of the factors (Zuckerman, Eysenck, & Eysenck, 1978). A form VI, limited to TAS and Dis scales, has been developed and is divided into two parts: The first part consists of reported experiences in TA or Dis areas; The second part contains intention scales for activities an individual would like to do in the future, regardless of past experiences (Zuckerman, 1994). A broad factor that combines sensation seeking with impulsivity has been incorporated as one of the five basic personality traits in a new questionnaire (Zuckerman et al., 1993). Another version of the SSS has been developed for children 7 to 12 years of age (Russo et al., 1991).

DEMOGRAPHICS

Men generally score higher than women on the total score and on all the SSS subscales except ES. Sensation Seeking Scale scores increase during childhood, peak in the late teens or early twenties, and thereafter decrease steadily with age (Russo et al., 1991; Zuckerman, 1979; Zuckerman & Nee, 1980). Divorced males score higher than single and married males, and divorced and single females score higher on the SSS than married females. Education and intelligence are positively (but weakly) related to sensation seeking, and socioeconomic status of self and family are weakly related to sensation seeking (females only). Atheists and agnostics are higher sensation-seekers than are those who practice one of the conventional religions, and among the latter, church attendance is inversely related to sensation seeking.

PHENOMENAL EXPRESSIONS OF SENSATION SEEKING

Sports

High sensation-seekers are more likely than lows to engage in sports providing novel sensations (e.g., parachute jumping, hang gliding, scuba diving, cave exploring, and mountain climbing), speed and excitement (e.g., auto racing and skiing), or physical contact (e.g., football and rugby; Zuckerman, 1979a, 1983b). Low sensation-seekers are more likely than highs to persist in sports or physical activities that demand endurance and training (e.g., long-distance running or aerobic exercises) but do not provide much intense excitement or exhilaration. Those who engage in sensation-seeking sports generally score higher on more than the one most relevant scale, TAS.

Sexual Attitudes and Behavior

Sensation seekers have permissive attitudes toward sexual behavior; young, single college students who score high on sensation seeking tend to have had more varied types of sexual experiences with more partners than low sensation-seekers have had (Zuckerman, Tushup, & Finner, 1976). There seems to be no difference in sensation seeking between heterosexual and homosexual males in the same population (Zuckerman & Myers, 1983).

Social, Love, and Marital Relationships

In casual social contacts, high sensation-seekers are more inclined to engage in interactions with frequent eye gazing, vocalization, smiles, laughter, and self-disclosure (Cappella & Green, 1984; Franken, Gibson, & Mohan, 1990). They are likely to dominate in a group situation. High sensation-seekers are more likely to regard love as a game, and their lack of commitment tends to lead to their having many more relationships. Despite their inconstancy, there is a mutual attraction based on sensation seeking in unmarried and married couples; their sensation-seeking scores tend to be positively correlated (Ficher, Zuckerman, & Neeb, 1981; Thomquist, Zuckerman, & Exline, 1991). There is a much lower correlation between sensation-seeking scores in couples requiring marital therapy (Ficher et al., 1981).

Drug and Alcohol Use

Sensation seeking is highly related to the use both of illegal drugs and of tobacco and alcohol in college and non-college populations (Zuckerman, 1983c, 1987; Zuckerman, Ball, & Black, 1990). Sensation seeking is related to the variety of drugs used rather than to the specific class of drugs preferred. Users of illegal drugs score higher on sensation seeking than those who use only alcohol, and those who use drugs stronger than marijuana score even higher on the trait. Sensation seeking predicts drug and alcohol use from adolescence to young adulthood through its relationship with general deviance of behavior over time, as well as through certain specific links between SSS subscales and use of legal or illicit drugs (Newcomb & McGee, 1991).

Food Preferences and Eating Habits

High sensation-seekers like to try novel foods and prefer spicy foods in both American and Japanese societies (Logue & Smith, 1986; Kish & Donnetiwerth, 1972; Terasak & Imada, 1988). Low sensation-seekers tend to like foods that are familiar, bland, and sweet. Binge eating in bulimics is not related to sensation seeking. Sensation seekers tend to be gourmets rather than gourmands. Vegetarians tend to be low sensation-seekers.

Psychopathology

Sensation-seeking scores are elevated in antisocial personalities compared with the scores of non-antisocial criminals (Zuckerman, 1979a; Zuckerman & Neeb, 1979), and in manic depressives (individuals with Bipolar Disorder) even when they are not in the manic state (Cronin & Zuckerman, 1992; Zuckerman, 1985). Sensation seeking is elevated even in the children of those with Bipolar Dis-

order, indicating a probable genetic connection (Nurnberger et al., 1988). There are several biological markers that sensation seeking and Bipolar Disorder have in common, including augmenting of the cortical evoked potential and low levels of the enzyme monoamine oxidase (MAO). The evidence on unipolar major depressive disorders is inconsistent, but a recent study suggests they are low on sensation seeking, even after recovery from a depressive episode (Carton, Jouvent, Bungener, & Widlocher, 1992). Schizophrenics, particularly those who tend to be inactive or catatonic, tend to be low sensation-seekers (Kish, 1970).

Media, Art, and Music Preferences

High sensation-seekers prefer designs that are novel, complex, and asymmetrical, while lows prefer familiar, simple, and symmetrical designs (Zuckerman, 1979a, 1988). High sensation-seekers prefer art that is impressionistic or expressionistic with high tension levels (Zuckerman, Ulrich, & McLaughlin, 1993); lows prefer realistic, low-tension art. High sensation-seekers like films with explicit sex and violence; lows avoid such themes in any form (Zuckerman & Litle, 1986). High sensation-seekers watch television less often than do lows, but when they do watch, they tend to be channel-switchers. Highs prefer loud and complex rock or jazz music; lows prefer quieter popular or background music (Litic & Zuckerman, 1996).

Vocational Preferences

High sensation-seekers enjoy risky or even periodically stressful vocations such as piloting aircraft, air-traffic control, and hospital emergency-room work, or occupations providing a great deal of varied social contacts (Zuckerman, 1979). Low sensation-seekers are relatively more attracted to solitary business or clerical occupations. Female high sensation-seekers tend to be interested in nontraditional occupations for women, such as the practice of law, while female low sensation-seekers prefer more traditionally feminine occupations, such as elementary-school teaching and housekeeping. Job satisfaction was found to be inversely related to sensation seeking in an industrial setting, and when these workers were put on a simulated job that was very monotonous, their negative affect and satisfaction states were related to their sensation-seeking trait levels (Perone, DeWaard, & Baron, 1979).

Risk Taking

Many, but not all, of the activities and substances preferred by high sensation-seekers are risky. This does not mean that risk is the point of their activities, because most tend to minimize the risk to derive maximal enjoyment from the activity. Antisocial personalities and pathological gamblers may be exceptions to this generalization; for both of these, the risk adds a significant arousal factor essential to the enjoyment of the activity (Anderson & Brown, 1984). Appraisal of risk varies inversely with sensation seeking and engaging in risky behaviors in most areas of risk taking (Horvath & Zuckerman, 1993; Zuckerman, 1979b). The inclination or disinclination to engage in risky activities is the outcome of an approach-avoidance conflict in which the expected pleasure from the activity motivates the approach, and the expected fear or harm constitutes the avoidance motive. High sensation-seekers have steeper approach gradients and flatter avoidance gradients than do low sensation-seekers (Zuckerman, 1979b). The theory explains why high sensation-seekers are more likely than lows to volunteer for experiments perceived as risky but that promise some kind of novel experience.

Cognitive Styles and Attention

Despite a low, positive correlation between intelligence and sensation seeking, high sensation-seekers often do not do well in conventional academic learning situations, presumably because of their competing interests in noncognitive experiences (Zuckerman, 1979a). Cognitive curiosity is not related to sensation seeking, although sensation seekers tend to be more open to experience and more creative in open-ended problem-solving. Sensation-seekers tend toward broad cognitive generalizations and a tendency to use more complex cognitive categories. They are more accepting of unusual beliefs such as paranormal phenomena. Low sensation-seekers tend to be more narrow and dogmatic in cognitive judgments. High sensation-seekers have a strong capacity for focused attention on a stimulus or task even with competing stimuli or task distractions (Ball & Zuckerman, 1992); this strong attention may be reflected in their stronger orienting reactions to novel stimuli compared to the reactions of low sensation-seekers (Zuckerman, 1990).

BIOLOGICAL CORRELATES AND POSSIBLE BASES OF SENSATION SEEKING

Zuckerman (1991) has proposed a psychobiological model for personality consisting of a top-down approach that examines the relationships among personality traits and their biological substrates from psychophysiology to genetics. Sensation seeking is probably the most thoroughly studied trait across all of these levels. Psychobiological models for sensation seeking have been proposed to incorporate these data (Zuckerman, 1979a, 1983a, 1984b). Sensation seeking is suggested to be the outcome of strong biological approach mechanisms and a weakness in inhibitory mechanisms (disinhibition).

Psychophysiology

High sensation-seekers have a strong orienting reaction to novel stimuli, particularly as measured by heart rate deceleration, while low sensation-seekers tend to respond with defensive reactions (heart rate acceleration) when encountering novel stimuli of moderate intensity. However, the differences between high and low sensation-seekers in orienting and defensive reactions tend to disappear when stimuli are repeated, unless the stimuli are of special interest to the high sensation-seekers. Thus it is primarily reaction to novel stimuli that is related to sensation seeking. The strong orienting tendency may represent part of the biological approach mechanism underlying sensation seeking (Zuckerman, 1990; Zuckerman, Buchsbaum, & Murphy, 1980).

Another difference between high and low sensation-seekers lies in the capacity of the cortex to respond to intense stimulation. High sensation-seekers tend to show augmented cortical evoked potentials in direct relationship to the intensity of visual or auditory stimuli. Low sensation-seekers tend to show little augmentation, and often show a reduction of cortical response in reaction to high-intensity stimuli. There is a direct relationship between this kind of cortical inhibition and behavioral inhibition in situations of uncertainty or overstimulation both in humans and in other species.

Psychopharmacology

Information about psychopharmacology can be found in Zuckerman (1979, 1983, 1984) and Zuckerman et al. (1980).

Hormones High sensation-seeking males, particularly as defined by the disinhibition subscale, have high levels of plasma testosterone and estradiol compared with the average levels found in low sensation-seekers. Testosterone also correlates with sociability, impulsivity, and extent of heterosexual experience in the same males. Cortisol in the cerebrospinal fluid (CSF) correlates negatively with sensation seeking, particularly that of the disinhibitory type, suggesting it may be a factor in the lack of behavioral inhibition in these sensation-seekers.

Enzymes and Neurotransmitters Monoamine oxidase (MAO) regulates levels of MAO neurotransmitters in the brain by catabolic reduction of the neurotransmitters in the presynaptic neurons or in the synaptic cleft. The type B MAO in blood platelets is the type in dopaminergic neurons in the brain. Platelet MAO is negatively related to sensation seeking in many studies. Although the relationship is not strong (median r is about -0.25), it is usually significant when a sufficient number of cases is used. Monoamine oxidase shows many relationships that also are characteristic of the sensation-seeking trait: it is lower in men than in women; it rises with age; it is related to activity in newborn infants, to criminal behavior, and to drug and alcohol use and abuse in young adults; and it is low in those with Bipolar Disorder. Monoamine oxidase is also linked to augmentation or reduction of the cortical evoked potential; augmentors have lower MAO levels than reducers. Similar behavioral correlations have been found in monkeys living in a social colony; low MAO monkeys are more sociable, playful, aggressive, and sexually active than high MAO monkeys.

The findings of the relationship between sensation seeking and MAO led to a broad study of the relationships among the trait, monoamines, and their enzymes and metabolites, found in CSF, plasma, and urine (Ballenger et al., 1983). The only monoamine or monoamine metabolite showing a significant relationship to sensation seeking was norepinephrine in the CSF, which correlated negatively with sensation seeking. Despite the failure of the dopamine metabolite (homovanillic acid) to correlate with sensation seeking, data from an experimental study support the theory (Zuckerman, 1979a) that high sensation-seekers have strongly active or reactive dopaminergic systems. Netter and Rammsayer (1991) gave the dopamine precursor L-dopa and the dopamine antagonist haloperidol to normals and observed the effects of these drugs on the performance and mood of high and low sensation-seekers. Given the dopamine blocker, the low sensation-seekers decreased in performance and felt less relaxed, while the highs increased or remained constant in performance and felt more relaxed. The results were opposite for the dopamine agonist L-dopa. The findings suggest that the high sensation-seekers are already at or above an optimal level of dopamine system activity and benefit most from a dopamine blocker, whereas the lows are underreactive or below an optimal level of dopamine activity and, therefore, benefit more from a dopamine stimulant.

Genetics of Sensation Seeking

Comparisons of identical and fraternal twins on the SSS yielded an uncorrected heritability of 58%, near the upper limit of heritability values found for personality traits (Fulker, Eysenck, & Zuckerman, 1980). Recent data from the Minnesota twins study showed correlations of 0.54 between identical twins, and 0.32 between fraternal twins separated at or shortly after birth and raised in different families (Lykken, 1992, personal communication). The first figure is a direct measure of heritability: 54%. The correlation between separated fraternal twins must be doubled to obtain the heritability, and thus yields a heritability of 64%. Averaging the two estimates yields a heritability estimate of 59%, almost identical to that obtained in the Futker et al. (1980) study of twins reared together. The effects of shared environment were negligible in both studies. The implication is that the environmental influences affecting sensation seeking are specific ones that are likely to exist outside the family, such as differential peer experience. Although one has no choice in selecting his or her parents or siblings, the genotype is likely to influence one's selection of friends. As with other personality traits, genes may affect the development of personality not only by how they govern the construction of the nervous system but in indirect ways through two-way phenotype-environment influences.

SUGGESTED READINGS

Zuckerman, M. (1979). *Sensation seeking: Beyond the optimal level of arousal.* Hillsdale, NJ: Erlbaum.

Zuckerman, M. (1983). A biological theory of sensation seeking. In M. Zuckerman (Ed.), *Biological bases of sensation seeking, impulsivity, and anxiety* (pp. 37–76). Hillsdale, NJ: Erlbaum.

Zuckerman, M. (1984). Sensation seeking: A comparative approach to a human trait. *Behavioral and Brain Sciences, 7,* 413–471.

Zuckerman, M. (1990). The psychophysiology of sensation seeking. *Journal of Personality, 58,* 313–345.

Zuckerman, M. (1994). *Behavioral expressions and biosocial bases of sensation seeking.* New York: Cambridge University Press.

M. ZUCKERMAN
University of Delaware

BOREDOM
INTRINSIC MOTIVATION
PERSONALITY TYPES

SENSORIMOTOR PROCESSES

The control of human movement is located within the central nervous system (CNS), which consists of the brain and the spinal cord. With the exception of very simple reflex movements, neural impulses that initiate movements originate within the cortex of the brain. The area of the cortex from which the neural impulses originate is called the sensorimotor area and is primarily located within the two convolutions (elevations known as gyri) on either side of the central fissure, the groove that marks the dividing line between the front and the back of the cortex of the brain. The sensorimotor area of the right hemisphere of the brain controls the left half of the body and that of the left hemisphere controls the right side of the body.

The anterior portion of the sensorimotor strip is primarily responsible for sending motor impulses. The posterior portion is primarily responsible for receiving sensory feedback. Since neither function alone is sufficient to produce purposeful movement, they are combined in the sensorimotor strip to work in harmony with each other. When the motor portion of the sensorimotor strip has been damaged, movement is not initiated and paralysis occurs. When the sensory portion of the sensorimotor strip has been damaged, movements cannot be executed correctly and ataxic or spastic movement results.

There are two distinct neural pathways that carry impulses to and from the sensorimotor strip. The descending, or efferent, pathways carry neural impulses from the motor area to the muscles responsible for executing a particular movement. The ascending, or afferent, pathways carry neural impulses from receptors in the joints, muscles, and skin to the sensory area of the sensorimotor strip. After an impulse has been sent from the motor portion of the sensorimotor strip, the movement is constantly monitored by sensory receptors and information from them is received by the sensory area of the sensorimotor strip. Through this process of constant feedback, corrections of the intended movements are made as soon as any minute deviations occur and smooth, purposeful movements are made possible.

SUGGESTED READING

Clark, R. G. (1975). *Manter and Gatz's essentials of clinical neuroanatomy and neurophysiology.* Philadelphia: Davis.

Gardner, E. (1975/1963). *Fundamentals of neurology.* Philadelphia, London: Saunders.

Kandel, E. R., Schwartz, J. H., & Jessell, T. M. (1991). *Principles of neural science* (3rd ed.). New York: Elsevier.

Netter, F. H. (1977/1974). *The CIBA collection of medical illustrations illustrations* (Vol. I). *The nervous system.* Rochester, NY: Case-Hoyt.

D. E. BOWEN
Psychological Associates

CENTRAL NERVOUS SYSTEM
NEUROCHEMISTRY

SENSORY DEPRIVATION

Sensory deprivation is an experimental procedure in which an attempt is made to remove or restrict sensory stimuli with human subjects. Such experiments were initiated by Donald Hebb and colleagues. The original situation required that subjects lie on a bed in a cubicle 24 hours a day for as long as possible, with time out only for meals and going to the toilet. Translucent plastic visors transmitted diffuse light but prevented pattern vision. Cotton gloves and cardboard cuffs extending beyond the finger tips restricted touch, and auditory stimulation was reduced by a U-shaped pillow fitted around the head and a continuous hum of air-conditioning equipment.

Tests, including simple arithmetic, anagrams, and word associations, given after 12, 24, and 48 hours of isolation, showed increasingly impaired performance in this monotonous environment. After awhile, subjects had difficulty concentrating on any one topic and became increasingly irritable. A striking effect was the report of hallucinations involving scenes of people, animals, and geometric patterns. The hallucinations were not limited to visual experiences, but included auditory ones, such as voices and music, and tactile ones, such as being hit by pellets and receiving electric shocks. Brain-wave recordings obtained during the isolation period showed a marked slowing as compared with preisolation recordings. Upon emerging from isolation, subjects frequently reported perceptual distortions and it took several hours for brain-wave patterns to return to normal. Studies of sensory deprivation suggest that a changing sensory environment is essential for normal human perceptual functioning. Monotonous situations, with their repetitions of the same stimuli, are not conducive to efficient performance, and severe sensory restrictions have serious psychological and physical effects (Schiffman, 1976).

REFERENCES

Schiffman, H. R. (1982/1976). *Sensation and perception. An integrated approach* (2nd ed.). New York: Wiley.

J. L. ANDREASSI
City University of New York, Baruch College

ADAPTATION
AUDITORY DISORDERS
HABITUATION

SENTENCE COMPLETION TEST

The sentence completion test was first applied to personality assessment in 1928 by H. F. Payne. Since that time, such tests have become a regular part of most clinical test batteries and are commonly used in industrial and military personnel selection. The method consists of a set of uncompleted sentences (stems) that the subject is to complete, for example, "I wish _____" or "My mother is _____." Sentence completion tests are simple to design and can be adapted to many purposes. This flexibility, along with their economical group administration, has resulted in a proliferation of unstandardized as well as standardized completion forms to meet specific clinical and research

purposes. The better known tests are those by Holsopple and Miale, Sacks and Levy, Rohde, Stein, Forer, and Rotter.

The Rotter Incomplete Sentences Blank (ISB) is the most rigorously standardized, and so is described here at considerable length. Designed for the specific purpose of assessing the personality adjustment of college students, it contains 40 short stems, mostly in the first person. A manual by Rotter and Rafferty (1950) provides scoring instructions, sample responses, and normative data on college students. The scoring consists of classifying the responses in three categories—conflict, neutral, and positive—and assigning them weighted scores. For example, to the stem "My mother _____," the response "hates me" is given a high score on *conflict* whereas the response "is wonderful" rates a high score on *positive*. The scores on the 40 stems are summed to obtain an overall adjustment total. Interscorer reliability is high.

Interpretation of the ISB is based upon these total scores obtained for the content analysis. A cutting score of 135 correctly identified over 68% of the maladjusted students and over 80% of the well-adjusted students in a study by Rotter and colleagues (1949). Although impressionistic or objective content analysis is the typical method of interpretation, formal analyses of the length of completions, use of personal pronouns, verb-adjective ratios, and so forth are sometimes used.

Goldberg (1965) has summarized the results of 50 studies of validity using 26 different forms of the sentence completion test, including 15 validity studies of the ISB. Of the latter, a clear majority showed significant relationships to the validation criteria, which consisted of case histories, interviews, adjustment ratings, and the presence of psychiatric complaints. The best validities occurred when standardized scoring systems such as Rotter's were used. The most consistent success has been in assessing the psychological adjustment of adults and the severity of psychiatric disturbance. The success of the ISB can be attributed to its single-minded purpose. It was planned and scored to measure the adjustment of college students and was validated by behavioral data related to adjustment in college.

There has been considerable research on the many variables that influence the nature of sentence completions. Goldberg provides an extensive review of this research on such variables as the effects of instructions and sets, variations of the sentence stem and stem structure, and type of person reference.

There is little agreement on the important issue of what level of the personality is revealed by the subject's sentence completions. Do they reveal conscious, preconscious, or unconscious aspects of the psyche? Goldberg also reviews this issue at length and observes that the lack of agreement may be related to differences in the instructional set given the subject by the various forms of the test. Some clinicians and forms (e.g., Stein, 1947; Forer, 1950) stress speed and immediacy of responding while others (e.g., Holsopple & Miale, 1954; Rotter & Rafferty, 1950) allow freedom from time pressure. The latter consider sentence completion to represent a conscious level of responding controlled by the subject, whereas the former assume the inclusion of deeper levels of responding. This observation is supported by the research of Siipola (1968). She found a direct relation between the amount of ego-alien content elicited by a sentence completion test and the amount of time pressure imposed. Despite the lack of agreement on the exact level of awareness at which the sentence completion test should be positioned, most clinicians agree that the bulk of the material elicited is closer to conscious control than that obtained in the TAT and Rorschach.

REFERENCES

Forer, R. B. (1950). A structured sentence completion test. *Journal of Projective Techniques, 14,* 15–29.

Goldberg, P. A. (1965). A review of sentence completion methods in personality assessment. *Journal of Projective Techniques and Personality Assessment, 29,* 12–45.

Holsopple, J., & Miale, F. R. (1954). *Sentence completion: A projective method for the study of personality.* Springfield, IL: Thomas.

Payne, A. F. (1928). *Sentence completions.* New York: New York Guidance Clinic.

Rotter, J. B., Rafferty, E., & Schachtitz, E. (1949). Validation of the Rotter Incomplete Sentences Blank for college screening. *Journal of Consulting Psychology, 13,* 345–356.

Rotter, J. B., & Rafferty, J. E. (1950). *The Rotter Incomplete Sentences Blank manual: College form.* New York: Psychological Corp.

Siipola, E. M. (1968). Incongruence of sentence completions under time pressure and freedom. *Journal of Projective Techniques and Personality Assessment, 32,* 562–571.

Stein, M. I. (1947). The use of a sentence completion test for the diagnosis of personality. *Journal of Clinical Psychology, 3,* 46–56.

SUGGESTED READING

Churchill, R., & Crandall, V. T. (1955). The reliability and validity of the Rotter incomplete sentences test. *Journal of Consulting Psychology, 19,* 345–350.

Hanfmann, E., & Getzels, J. W. (1953). Studies of the sentence completion test. *Journal of Projective Techniques, 17,* 280–294.

E. M. SIIPOLA
Smith College

CLINICAL ASSESSMENT
PROJECTIVE TECHNIQUES

SEPARATION ANXIETY

Attachment is a cross-species phenomenon in which both animals and humans display a characteristic set of behaviors upon separation from the primary caregiver. Ethologists explain the evolutionary significance of these behaviors as aiding in survival by increasing the probability of maintaining close proximity to the caregiver,

and therefore protection from predation. Attachment behaviors include displays of distress such as crying and, at later ages, approaching or following the attachment figure. Hofer (1987) demonstrated that young rats display anxious reactions to separation from their mothers and companions. Furthermore, attachment in primate research has centered upon a physical separation of rhesus macaques from their mothers in the first six months (Suomi, Collins, Harlow, & Ruppenthal, 1976) and have involved fear-producing situations that elicit attachment behavior analogous to human infant research studies of separation anxiety (Harlow, 1967). Similar patterns of behavior have been found across cultures in humans despite great variation in child-rearing practices. Fox (1977) found similar separation behaviors in a study of kibbutz infants, where children have multiple caretakers, as has been found in Western cultures. These findings are important in that they elucidate general patterns of attachment across the human species.

Anxiety resulting from separation from an attachment figure has been accepted as an attribute of normal development since the early part of this century (Bowlby, 1973; Freud, 1909/1955). It was not until the 1980's, however, that separation anxiety was considered a discrete clinical diagnostic category. The *Diagnostic and Statistical Manual of Mental Disorders* (3rd ed.) (*DSM-III*), published in 1980, designated Separation Anxiety Disorder (SAD) as one of the three Anxiety Disorders of Childhood and Adolescence (American Psychiatric Association, 1980). Current diagnostic criteria of SAD include excessive anxiety with respect to separation from an attachment figure (most commonly the mother or primary caregiver) or separation from familiar surroundings, such as home (Black, 1995).

Children experiencing SAD may exhibit both behavioral and physiological symptoms, such as extreme distress, terror, hyperventilation, or heart palpitations, when anticipating separation. (For a complete listing see American Psychiatric Association, 1994, p. 113.) Children with SAD seek to avoid separation from attachment figures and, not surprisingly, are most commonly referred to clinicians as a result of a hesitancy or unwillingness to attend school. Similarly, both refusals to sleep and sleep disturbances are also characteristic of SAD.

In normal development, separation anxiety begins to appear between the ages of 7 and 12 months and peaks around the ages of 15 to 18 months (when anxiety of strangers begins to develop), before it begins to decline. Anxiety or distress pertaining to separation from an attachment figure is a common occurrence in young children and is even considered a normal part of the development of attachment relationships. However, "separation anxiety" (crying or clinging to the mother upon separation) and "separation distress" (apprehension of separation) (Stayton, Ainsworth, & Main, 1973) may become extreme or maladaptive and may be associated with other dysfunctional behaviors. Studies that examine comorbidity of psychiatric disorders indicate that children and adolescents with SAD are commonly diagnosed with other disorders as well. One-half of children with SAD are also diagnosed with other anxiety disorders (Bell-Dolan & Brazeal, 1993), and one-third are diagnosed with depression (Last, Strauss, & Francis, 1987). It has been suggested that children with SAD may have become overly dependent upon the attachment figure, often after a stressful life event such as illness or the loss of a loved one (Erickson, 1998). SAD occurs in approximately 2 to 4 percent of children and adolescents, and a diagnosis of SAD may lead to increased risk for psychopathology in adulthood (Ollendick & Huntzinger, 1990). Current treatment approaches to SAD include behavioral interventions, psychotherapy, and family interventions, as well as psychopharmacological treatments.

Freud (1959) first conceived of the concept of anxiety neurosis in 1895 and suggested that anxiety was a symptomatic consequence of a repressed libido. Only later, in 1926, did he begin to take note of separation anxiety. The psychoanalytic perspective viewed separation anxiety as a tendency for adults to experience apprehension with the loss of a significant other (Freud, 1926). Freud's later studies led him to conclude that anxiety was an emotion that resulted from the experience of traumatic events. Since that time, separation anxiety has been studied in a variety of contexts, and importantly, in the attachment literature.

Studies of attachment and separation anxiety have revealed that children have a tendency to exhibit similar attachment behaviors with a mother or a father (Fox, Kimmerly, & Schaeffer, 1991). These finding suggest that attachment may not be relationship-specific, but rather, that there is temperamental contribution involved. The literature on childhood anxiety, therefore, has emphasized the important influence of temperament factors (Kagan, 1984) in this area of study. It has been found that the incidence of childhood anxiety disorders is greater in children who exhibit the temperamental characteristic of behavioral inhibition (Biederman et al., 1990). This characteristic, described as withdrawal from novelty, is thought to be related to childhood anxiety. As a result, this temperamental model suggests that childhood anxiety is inherited as a physiological predisposition to display inhibition (Kagan et al., 1984). The developmental literature also reveals that separation distress is also reported to be the result of cognitive apprehension. Kagan (1972) suggests that this behavior may result from the infant's inability to interpret the event. This literature implies that protest at separation may have a closer link to the child's cognitive understanding of the separation than to the child's affective relationship to the attachment figure.

Psychophysiological research also suggests a relationship between separation response in infants and cerebral asymmetry. Davidson and Fox (1989) report a pattern of greater right frontal EEG (electroencephalogram) activation associated with a temperamental disposition to cry in response to maternal separation, and similar findings by Fox, Bell, and Jones (1992) suggest modest stability of frontal asymmetry over time. These findings suggest that patterns of right frontal EEG asymmetry may serve as a marker of an underlying temperamental disposition to express negative emotions.

In summary, the attachment literature in both humans and animals has enhanced our understanding of separation anxiety as a normative phenomenon. It has also elucidated the possible etiology of non-normative behaviors that lead to the occurrence of the psychiatric disorder of childhood and adolescence known as Separation Anxiety Disorder (SAD). More specifically, the attachment literature has provided a sound model for the examination of separation anxiety across the life span.

REFERENCES

American Psychiatric Association. (1980). *Diagnostic and statistical manual of mental disorders* (3rd ed.). Washington, DC: Author.

American Psychiatric Association. (1994). *Diagnostic and statistical manual of mental disorders* (4th ed.). Washington, DC: Author.

Bell-Dolan, D., & Brazeal, T. J. (1993). Separation anxiety disorder, overanxious disorder, and school refusal. *Child and Adolescent Psychiatric Clinics of North America, 2,* 563–580.

Biederman, J., Rosenbaum, J. F., Hirshfield, D. R., Faraone, S. V., Bolduc, E. A., Gersten, M., Meminger, S. R., Kagan, J., Snidman, N., & Resnick, J. S. (1990). Psychiatric correlates of behavioral inhibition in young children of parents with and without psychiatric disorders. *Archives of General Psychiatry, 47,* 21–16.

Black, B. (1995). Separation Anxiety Disorder and Panic Disorder. In J. S. March (Ed.), *Anxiety disorders in children and adolescence* (pp. 212–228). New York: Guilford.

Bowlby, J. (1973). *Separation, anxiety and anger. Attachment and loss:* Vol. 2. New York: Basic Books.

Davidson, R. J., & Fox, N. A. (1989). Frontal brain asymmetry predicts infants' response to maternal separation. *Journal of Abnormal Psychology, 98,* 127–131.

Erickson, M. T. (1998). *Behavior disorders of children and adolescents: Assessment, etiology, and intervention.* New Jersey: Prentice Hall.

Fox, N. A. (1977). Attachment of kibbutz infants to mother and metapelet. *Child Development, 48,* 1228–1239.

Fox, N. A., Bell, M. A., & Jones, N. A. (1992). Individual differences in response to stress and cerebral asymmetry. *Developmental Neuropsychology, 8,* 161–184.

Fox, N. A., Kimmerly, N. L., & Schaeffer, W. D. (1991). Attachment to mother/attachment to father: A meta-analysis. *Child Development, 62,* 210–225.

Freud, S. (1926). Inhibitions, symptoms and anxiety. In *The standard edition of the complete psychological works of Sigmund Freud.* London: Hogarth.

Freud, S. (1955). Analysis of a phobia in a five-year-old boy. In J. Strachey (Ed.), *The standard edition of the complete psychological works of Sigmund Freud* (Vol. 10, pp. 1–149). London: Hogarth. (Original work published 1909)

Freud, S. (1959). On the grounds for detaching a particular syndrome from neurasthenia under the description "anxiety neurosis." In J. Strachey (Ed.), *The standard edition of the complete psychological works of Sigmund Freud* (Vol. 3, pp. 87–116). London: Hogarth. (Original work published 1895)

Harlow, H. F. (1967). Love in infant monkeys. In J. L. McGaugh, N. M. Weinberger, & R. E. Whalen (Eds.), *Psychobiology: The biological bases of behavior* (pp. 100–106). San Francisco: Freeman.

Hofer, M. A. (1987). Early social relationships: A psychobiologist's view. *Child Development, 58,* 633–647.

Kagan, J. (1972). Do infants think? *Scientific American, 226,* 74–82.

Kagan, J., Resnick, J. S., Clarke, C., Snidman, N., & Garcia-Coll, C. (1984). Behavioral inhibition to the unfamiliar. *Child Development, 55,* 2212–2225.

Kotelchuck, M., Zelazo, P. R., Kagan, J., & Spelke, E. (1975). Infant reaction to parental separations when left with familiar and unfamiliar adults. *The Journal of Genetic Psychology, 126,* 255–262.

Last, C. G., Strauss, C. C., & Francis, G. (1987). Comorbidity among childhood anxiety disorders. *Journal of Nervous and Mental Disease, 175,* 726–730.

Ollendick, T. H., & Huntzinger, R. M. (1990). Separation anxiety disorder in childhood. In M. Herson & C. G. Last (Eds.), *Handbook of child and adult psychopathology: A longitudinal perspective* (pp. 133–149). New York: Pergamon.

Stayton, D. J., Ainsworth, M. D. S., & Main, M. B. (1973). Development of separation behavior in the first year of life: Protest, following, and greeting. *Developmental Psychology, 9,* 213–225.

Suomi, S. J., Collins, M. L., Harlow, H. F., & Ruppenthal, G. C. (1976). Effects of maternal and peer separations on young monkeys. *Journal of Child Psychology and Psychiatry, 17,* 101–112.

KIRSTEN M. VANMEENEN
NATHAN A. FOX
University of Maryland

ANXIETY
APPROACH-AVOIDANCE CONFLICT
ATTACHMENT STYLES
SEPERATION DISTRESS/ANXIETY

SEPARATION DISTRESS/ANXIETY

Distress resulting from separation from an attachment figure has been accepted as an attribute of normal infant development since the early part of this century (Bowlby, 1973; Freud, 1909/1955). Bowlby interpreted the distress that infants displayed to maternal separation as reflecting the child's anxiety at being left alone. Indeed, he saw fear of being left alone as the root cause of generalized human anxiety (Bowlby, 1973). In normal development, distress due to separation appears between the ages of 7 and 12 months and peaks around the ages of 15 to 18 months of age. This inverted U–shaped curve to the onset, peak, and diminution of distress to separation has been found across various cultures among which the pattern of rearing has varied considerably. For example, Fox (1977) found this pattern to occur among infants raised on the Israeli kibbutz (where infants slept separately from their mothers and were cared for by a primary caregiver other than the mother). Barr,

Konner, Bakeman, and Adamson (1991) report a similar developmental function for infants raised among the !Kung bushmen in the Kalari Desert, as has Kagan (1973) for infants raised in rural Guatemala. The common development change in separation distress across cultures most probably reflects universal changes in the infant's abilities to understand and represent its mother's disappearance from view. Thus, this behavior should not be considered as maladaptive but rather as a normative part of early development.

There are reports of individual differences in the tendency to display distress to separation. Davidson and Fox (1989), for example, report a pattern of greater right frontal electroencephalogram (EEG) activation associated with a temperamental disposition to cry in response to maternal separation. Similar findings by Fox, Bell, and Jones (1992) suggest modest stability of frontal asymmetry over time.

While normative changes in distress to separation find it diminishing around 18 to 24 months of age, instances of continued distress response to separation from mother have been described in the child clinical literature. These instances were described under the heading of separation anxiety. Freud (1895/1959) first conceived of the concept of anxiety neurosis in 1895 and suggested that anxiety was a symptomatic consequence of a repressed libido. Only later, in 1926, did he begin to take note of separation anxiety. The psychoanalytic perspective viewed separation anxiety as a tendency for adults to experience apprehension after the loss of a significant other (Freud, 1926). Freud's later studies led him to conclude that anxiety was an emotion that resulted from the experience of traumatic events. Since that time, separation anxiety has been studied in a variety of contexts, including the attachment literature. It is not until the 1980s that separation anxiety was considered a discrete clinical diagnostic category. The *Diagnostic and Statistical Manual of Mental Disorders* (3rd ed., or *DSM-III*) designated Separation Anxiety Disorder (SAD) as one of the three anxiety disorders of childhood and adolescence (American Psychiatric Association, 1980). Current diagnostic criteria of SAD include excessive anxiety with respect to separation from an attachment figure (most commonly the mother or primary caregiver) or separation from familiar surroundings such as home.

Children experiencing SAD may exhibit both behavioral and physiological symptoms such as extreme distress, terror, hyperventilation, or heat palpitations when anticipating separation. Children with SAD seek to avoid separation from attachment figures and, not surprisingly, are most commonly referred to clinicians as a result of a hesitancy or unwillingness to attend school. Similarly, both sleep disturbances and refusals to sleep are also characteristic of SAD.

Studies that examine comorbidity of psychiatric disorders indicate that children and adolescents with SAD are commonly diagnosed with other disorders as well. One-half of children with SAD are diagnosed with other anxiety disorders, while one-third are diagnosed with depression. It has been suggested that children with SAD may have become overly dependent upon the attachment figure, often after a stressful life event such as the illness or loss of a loved one (Erickson, 1998). SAD occurs in approximately 2 to 4% of children and adolescents, and those with this disorder may be at increased risk for psychopathology in adulthood. Current treatment approaches to SAD include behavioral interventions, psychotherapy, and family interventions, as well as psychopharmacological treatments.

The literature on childhood anxiety has recently emphasized the important influence of temperament factors (Kagan, 1894) in this area. It has been found that the incidence of childhood anxiety disorders is greater in children who exhibit the temperamental characteristic of behavioral inhibition (Biederman et al., 1990). This characteristic, described as the tendency to withdraw from novel or social situations, may be related to separation anxiety.

Separation distress is a normative response, across different caregiving and cultural contexts, for infants to display distress upon separation from the caregiver. This behavioral response appears during the second half of the first year of life and is no longer present by the beginning of the third year of life. This behavioral pattern is distinct and apparently unrelated to the phenomenon known as separation anxiety. Little is known currently about the etiology of separation anxiety in young children. Current research suggests that there may be a temperamental basis to withdraw from discrepancy or novelty. Such a bias may in some instances lead to the behavioral pattern known as separation anxiety in children.

REFERENCES

American Psychiatric Association. (1980). *Diagnostic and statistical manual of mental disorders* (3rd ed.). Washington, DC: Author.

Barr, R. G., Konner, M., Bakeman, R., & Adamson, L. (1991). Crying in !Kung San infants: Test of the cultural specificity hypothesis. *Developmental Medicine and Child Neurology, 33,* 601–610.

Biederman, J., Rosenbaum, J. F., Hirshfield, D. R., Faraone, S. V., Bolduc, E. A., Gersten, M., Meminger, S. R., Kagan, J., Snidman, N., & Resnick, J. S. (1990). Psychiatric correlates of behavioral inhibition in young children of parents with and without psychiatric disorders. *Archives of General Psychiatry, 47,* 21–26.

Bowlby, J. (1973). *Separation, anxiety and anger: Vol. 2 Attachment and Loss.* New York: Basic Books.

Davidson, R. J., & Fox, N. A. (1989). Frontal brain asymmetry predicts infants'response to maternal separation. *Journal of Abnormal Psychology, 98,* 127–131.

Erickson, M. T. (1998). *Behavior disorders of children and adolescents: Assessment, etiology, and intervention.* New Jersey: Prentice Hall.

Fox, N. A. (1977). Attachment of kibbutz infants to mother and metapelet. *Child Development, 48,* 1228–1239.

Fox, N. A., Bell, M. A., & Jones, N. A. (1992). Individual differences in response to stress and cerebral asymmetry. *Developmental Neuropsychology, 8,* 161–184.

Fox, N. A., Kimmerly, N. L., & Schaeffer, W. D. (1991). Attachment to mother/attachment to father: A meta-analysis. *Child Development, 62,* 210–225.

Freud, S. (1926). Inhibitions, symptoms and anxiety. In J. Strachey (Ed.), *The standard edition of the complete psychological works of Sigmund Freud.* London: Hogarth.

Freud, S. (1955). Analysis of a phobia in a five-year-old boy. In J. Strachey (Ed.), *The standard edition of the complete psychological works of Sigmund Freud* (Vol. 10, pp. 1–149). London: Hogarth. (Original work published 1909)

Freud, S. (1959). On the grounds for detaching a particular syndrome from neurasthenia under the description "anxiety neurosis." In J. Strachey (Ed.), *The standard edition of the complete psychological works of Sigmund Freud* (Vol. 3, pp. 87–116). London: Hogarth. (Original work published 1895)

Kagan, J., & Klein, R. E. (1973). Cross-cultural perspectives on early development. *American Psychologist, 28,* 947–961.

Kagan, J., Resnick, J. S., Clarke, C., Snidman, N., & Garcia-Coll, C. (1984) Behavioral inhibition to the unfamiliar. *Child Development, 55,* 2212–2225.

K. M. VanMeenen
N. A. Fox
Istitute for Child Study, University of Maryland

SEROTONERGIC NEURONS

The serotonergic neurons are one of the diffusely organized projection systems in the central nervous system (CNS). Although Page and his collaborators (Rapport and Green) succeeded in the isolation and identification of serotonin (5-HT) more than four decades ago (1948) (Sjoerdsma & Palfreyman, 1990), the distribution of these neurons and their cell bodies in the CNS became possible only with the availability of fluorescent histochemistry and immunocytochemical methods. The distribution of serotonergic neurons and their cell bodies in the CNS was originally identified using fluorescent histochemistry (Dahlstrom & Fuxe, 1964; Ungerstedt, 1971), and subsequently by more sensitive immunocytochemical methods (Steinbusch, 1981).

In the CNS, serotonergic neurons are limited to a group of brain stem reticular formation nuclei, the raphe nuclei. Dahlstrom and Fuxe (1964) have originally described nine serotonergic cell groups, which they named B1-B9. Most of these groups are associated with the raphe nuclei and the reticular region of the lower brain stem from which they project rostro-caudally, and thus virtually all areas of the CNS receive serotonergic inputs. Serotonergic neurons in the midbrain and pontine dorsal and median raphe project to higher brain centers: cerebral cortex, cerebellum, hippocampus, thalamus, hypothalamus, and basal ganglia. In contrast, serotonergic cell bodies in the ventral medulla, caudal pons and pontomesencephalic reticular formation provide long descending projections to the spinal cord.

Considerable research carried out over the past 40 years has clearly established the serotonergic system as a major neurotransmitter system subserving a number of important physiological and psychological functions. The origins of the serotonergic projections to the dorsal horn are the neurons of the raphe magnus and adjacent reticular formation (Bowker, Westland, Sullivan, & Coulter, 1982). They travel to the spinal cord in the dorsolateral fasciculus between the tip of the dorsal horn and the surface of the spinal cord (Basbaum, Clarta, 7 Fields, 1978), and are mainly involved in pain sensation. The serotonergic neurons that terminate in the ventral horn arise primarily from the raphe obscurus and raphe pallidus nuclei (Bowker et al., 1982) and facilitate motor activity. The preganglionic sympathetic neurons of the intermediolateral column in the thoracic cord also receive serotonergic input, mostly from the ventrolateral medulla (Loewy & McKellar, 1981) and are involved in blood pressure regulation and perhaps other autonomic functions. The pathways from the midbrain raphe to the prefrontal cortex may mediate depressive and cognitive effects of serotonin. The pathway from the midbrain raphe to basal ganglia hypothetically underlies the role of serotonin in the pathophysiology of related to Obsessive-Compulsive Disorder. This pathway is also thought to be related to the regulatory action of serotonin on locomotion. The regulatory functions of serotonin on emotions, anxiety, and memory are thought to be related to the pathway from the raphe to the limbic cortex. The pathway from midbrain raphe to hypothalamus might mediate the effects of serotonin on appetitive behaviors. Sexual function mediated by serotonin might be related to the descending pathways from the raphe to the spinal cord.

Although a small amount of 5-HT is present in the cytoplasm of serotonergic cell bodies and nerve terminals, most of the neurotransmitter is stored in the vesicles. Serotonin is produced from the aromatic amino acid natural substrate L-tryptophan into the serotonin neuron. First, tryptophan is converted into 5-hydroxytryptophan (5-HTP) by the enzyme tryptophan hydroxylase. Finally, 5-HTP is converted into 5-HT by the enzyme L-aromatic amino acid decarboxylase and stored in synaptic vesicles until released by a neuronal impulse. Although studies with humans, dogs, rats and numerous other animals indicate that serotonin is widely distributed in the blood, intestinal tract, and different organ systems, a discussion of their roles in these tissues is beyond the scope of this article. After release from the synaptic vesicle, much of the serotonin is reused through a high-affinity, energy-dependent uptake system. Serotonin can be metabolized in the brain and periphery to yield important active and inactive products. The principal metabolite of serotonin is 5-hydroxyindole acetic acid (5-HIAA) and is produced by the action of the enzyme monoamine oxidase (MAO). The level of 5-HIAA in cerebrospinal fluid is the index of serotonin turnover in the CNS. It is also metabolized to the hormone melatonin (5-methoxy-N-acetyltryptamine) in the pineal gland; melatonin is thought to play an important role in both sexual behavior and sleep. Quinolinic acid and kynurenic acid are the two major tryptophan metabolites that may have clinical importance in trauma and stroke (Stone, 1993). Quinolinic acid is a potent agonist at N-methyl-D-aspartate (NMDA) receptors and results in convulsions and neurotoxicity. In contrast, kynurenic acid is an antagonist at NMDA receptors. The roles of tryptophan metabolites in neurological disorders have yet to be established.

It has been suggested that serotonin plays a key role in a number of behaviors which have been mentioned partly earlier, including sleep, feeding, reward, locomotion, and mood. The action of serotonergic neurons, as a whole, is complex and it is difficult to understand how specific changes in serotonin neurotransmission affect specific behaviors or neurological functions. This issue becomes even more challenging by the molecular cloning of more than 14 serotonin receptor subtypes, each with its own expression pattern, coupling mechanism, and pharmacological profile. Thus, the physiological response to serotonergic innervation reflects the nature of the postsynaptic receptors. The serotonin receptors thus far identified include 5-HT_{1A}, 5-HT_{1B}, 5-HT_{1C}, 5-HT_{1D}, 5-HT_2, 5-HT_{2A}, 5-HT_{2B}, 5-HT_{2C}, 5-HT_3, 5-HT_4, 5-HT_5, 5-HT_6, 5-HT_7, and 5-HT_X. The 5-HT_{1B} and 5-HT_{1D} receptors are autoreceptors and they regulate further release of 5-HT through inhibition of adenyl cyclase. These receptors are both somatodendritic and presynaptic autoreceptors. The somatodendritic autoreceptors suppress cell firing and are believed to play a role in collateral inhibition among serotonergic neurons. These autoreceptors also lead to reductions in serotonin synthesis and release in the areas to which the cells project by inhibiting neuronal activity. On the other hand, presynaptic autoreceptors are not believed to influence cell firing, but instead, inhibit serotonin release, and possibly also synthesis from the nerve terminals. Most serotonergic synapses are inhibitory, though some are excitatory.

Serotonergic nerve terminals may contain other neurotransmitters, such as acetylcholine (ACh), noradrenaline (NE), substance-P (SP), enkephalins, thyrotropin-releasing hormone (TRH), calcitonin gene-related peptide (CGRP) and postraglandins. The serotonergic nerve terminals have two types of vesicles: small clear vesicles containing serotonin and large dense-core vesicles containing other neurotransmitters. Thus, in the spinal cord, dense-core vesicles contain serotonin, SP, and TRH. The involvement of the serotonergic system in motor function in vertebrates was indicated initially by its dense axon terminal innervation of motoneurons in both the brain stem and spinal cord. Secondary motor structures, such as the basal ganglia, substantia nigra, and habenula, also receive significant serotonergic input as mentioned before. Administrations of serotonergic agonists produce a motor syndrome in rats: head shakes, hyperreactivity, tremor, hindlimb abduction, lateral head weaving, and reciprocal forepaw treading. Extracellular recordings in conjunction with microiontophoresis of serotonin onto motoneurons in the rat facial motor nucleus or in the spinal cord ventral horn showed that when serotonin interacts with excitatory influences on motoneurons it produces a strong facilitation of neuronal activity (via 5-HT_2 receptors, Jacobs & Vanhoutte, 1993). Administration of serotonergic agonists directly into the trigeminal nerve in cats produced an increase in the amplitude of the electromyography (EMG) of both the masseter muscle and of an externally elicited jaw-closure reflex (Jacobs et al., 1993).

Recent immunohistochemical studies documented that immunoreactive (IR)-neuronal fibers that contain serotonin sprouted in the cervical ventral horn of the motoneuron disease model "Wobbler" mouse by presymptomatic postnatal day 7 (Bose & Vacca-Galloway, 1999). Surprisingly, IR-CGRP-containing motoneurons undergo significant losses after postnatal day 14 and by the time symptoms are expressed at Stage 1 of this diseased (around postnatal day 21) mouse. These results suggest that the neural substance (serotonin) contained within the presumed early sprouts might have excitotoxic effects on motoneurons, and thus be causal to the loss of motoneurons in the Wobbler mouse. Alternatively, the sprouting may occur subsequent to the hypothetical disturbance of Cilliary and Brain derived neurotrophic factors (CNTF and BDNF) in this motoneuron disease mouse model.

Studies of serotonin function over the last few decades have brought clinical evidence which suggests that altered serotonin function is involved in the pathophysiology of depression, anxiety, and Obsessive-Compulsive Disorder (OCD). The strongest support for these comes from studies demonstrating that a variety of serotonergic drugs, especially those that block the reuptake of synaptically released serotonin into the presynaptic terminal, are frequently effective in treating depression, anxiety, and OCD. Moreover, recent studies suggest that antiserotonergic drugs, such as the combined 5-HT_{2A}- and 5-HT_{2C}-receptor antagonist, clozapine, can alleviate some of the symptoms (especially negative symptoms) of schizophrenia, and that aberrant function of the serotonergic system may indeed be a major component of the disease. Moreover, alterations in serotonin uptake have been demonstrated in postmortem tissue studies in limbic system of schizophrenic patients. Recent evidence suggests that there may be a strong genetic component underlying Anorexia Nervosa, though it was originally thought a purely psychological disorder. However, there is some evidence to suggest that there may be serotonergic dysfunction in at least some Anorexia Nervosa patients (Kaye, Gwirtsman, George, & Ebert, 1991). Moreover, serotonin has been implicated in the regulation of circadian rhythms through its actions on the suprachiasmatic nucleus (SCN). Recent data suggests that along with excitatory amino acids, serotonin may be important in the neural pathway that mediates the transmission of photic information to the circadian system. Recently, it has been demonstrated that the serotonergic system has a link to neuroadaptive changes that occur in substance dependence. For example, extracellular serotonin levels decreased dramatically during cocaine withdrawal (Parson, Koob, & Weiss, 1995).

REFERENCES

Basbaum, A. I., Clanton, C. H., & Fields, H. L. (1978). Three bulbospinal pathways from the rostral medulla of the cat: An autoradiographic study of pain modulation systems. *Journal of Comparative Neurology, 178,* 209–224.

Bose, P., & Vacca-Galloway, L. L. (1999). Increase in fiber density for immunoreactive serotonin, substance P, enkephalin and thyrotropin-releasing hormone occurs during the early presymptomatic period of motoneuron disease in Wobbler mouse spinal cord ventral horn. *Neuroscience Letters, 260*(3), 196–200.

Bowker, R. M., Westlund, K. N., Sullivan, M. C., & Coulter, J. D. (1982). Organization of descending serotonergic projections to the spinal cord. *Progress in Brain Research, 57,* 239–265.

Dahlstrom, A., & Fuxe, K. (1964). Evidence for the existence of monoamine-containing neurons in the central nervous system. *Acta Physiologica Sacadinavia, 232*(Suppl.), 1–55.

Erspamer, V. (1963). 5-hydroxytryptamine. In U. S. von Euler & H. Heller (Eds.), *Comparative Endocrinology,* (Vol. 2, pp. 159–181). New York.

Jacobs, B. L., Vanhoutte, P. M. (Eds.). (1993). *Serotonin,* 231–237. Armstardam, Netherlands: Kluwer Academic Publishers and Fondazione Giovanni Lorenzini.

Kaye, W. H., Gwirtsman, H. E., George, D. T., & Ebert, M. H. (1991). Altered serotonin activity in anorexia nervosa after long-term weight restoration. *Archives of General Psychiatry, 48,* 556–562.

Loewy, A. D., & McKellar, S. (1981). Serotonergic projections from the ventral medulla to the intermediolateral cell column in the rat. *Brain Research, 211,* 146–152.

Page, I. H. (1968). *Serotonin.* Chicago: Year Book Medical Publishers, Inc.

Page, I. H. (1976). The discovery of serotonin. *Perspective in Biology and Medicine, 20,* 1–8.

Parson, L. H., Koob, G. F., & Weiss, F. (1995). Serotonin dysfunction in the nucleus accumbens of rats during withdrawal after unlimited access to intravenous cocaine. *Journal of Pharmacological Experimental Therapeutic, 274,* 1182–1191.

Sjoerdsma, A., & Palfreyman, M. G. (1990). History of serotonin and serotonin disorders. *Annals of the New York Academy of Sciences, 600,* 1–8.

Steinbusch, H. W. M. (1981). Distribution of serotonin-immunoreactivity in the central nervous system of the rat. *Neuroscience, 4,* 557–618.

Stone, T. W. (1993). Neuropharmacology of quinolinic and kynurenic acids. *Pharmacology Review, 45,* 309–379.

Twarog, B. M. (1988). Serotonin: History of a discovery. *Comparative Biochemistry and Physiology, 91,* 21–24.

Ungerstedt, U. (1971). Steriotaxic mapping of the monoamine pathways in the rat brain. *Acta Physiologica Sacadinavia, 367* (Suppl.), 1–48.

P. BOSE
University of Florida College of Medicine and Brain Institute

CENTRAL NERVOUS SYSTEM
NEUROTRANSMITTERS
SEROTONIN

SEROTONIN

Serotonin (5-hydroxytryptamine, or 5-HT) is an indoleamine neurotransmitter and hormone that has many actions in the central nervous system and in the periphery. Serotonin was initially described as hormonal activity in the serum from clotted blood that caused vasoconstriction, hence the term "serum tonic factor," or "serotonin." Serotonin was purified from blood and identified as 5-HT in 1949. In 1953, serotonin was first detected in the central nervous system (CNS). The first serotonin receptors, termed "D" and "M" types, were characterized in guinea pig intestinal smooth muscle in 1957 (Gaddum & Picarelli, 1957). The D type caused smooth muscle relaxation in response to dibenzyline (D), and the M type mediated depolarization of enteric cholinergic neurons in response to morphine (M), but this classification schema has been superceded and is no longer in use. Serotonin achieved the status of neurotransmitter in 1963, when it was specifically identified in neurons of the raphe nuclei. The first serotonin receptors in the CNS, the serotonin-1 and serotonin-2 receptors, were described in 1979, triggering an explosion of investigation and discovery in the serotonergic system that continues unabated to the present (Peroutka & Snyder, 1979). The gene that encodes the 5-HT$_{1A}$ receptor was the first serotonin receptor gene cloned and sequenced (1986), which rapidly led to the identification of many new and unexpected serotonin receptor types (Kobilka et al., 1987). By 1998 there were at least 15 distinct serotonin receptor variants cloned, sequenced, and grouped into seven broad families by DNA sequence homology, effector coupling, and pharmacological characteristics. Knowledge of the serotonergic system is increasing at an exponential rate as measured by the total number of scientific publications: There are over 40,000 citations in Med-Line identified with the keyword "serotonin," with the numbers of citations doubling in each 5-year segment of the Med-Line database.

Serotonin is an evolutionarily old neurotransmitter. All metazoan species with organized nervous systems appear to use serotonin as a neurotransmitter. Serotonergic neurons and receptors, and serotonin mediated behaviors, have been described in the nematode *C. elegans,* the fruitly *D. melanogaster,* and the crayfish, mouse, rat, cat, pig, chimpanzee, and human, among others. Serotonin has been shown to participate in many different behaviors, including feeding and satiety behaviors, mating and copulatory behaviors, nociception, circadian rhythmicity, arousal, sleep and REM sleep production, perception, temperature regulation, aggression, and seizure vulnerability. The serotonergic system has also been implicated in a variety of psychopathological conditions, including mood and anxiety disorders, psychotic disorders, aggressive and violent behaviors, and substance use disorders.

In primates, serotonin exists in two distinct compartments, the CNS and the periphery. In humans, approximately 90% of total body serotonin is in the gastrointestinal (GI) tract, approximately 8% in the platelets, and approximately 1 to 2% in the CNS. All of the serotonin in the body, in both peripheral and central compartments, is synthesized de novo, as dietary serotonin is rapidly degraded in the GI tract. The biosynthetic pathway for the production of serotonin is identical in the GI tract and CNS. The amino acid tryptophan is the precursor from which serotonin is produced (Figure 1). Tryptophan is converted to 5-hydroxytryptophan (5-HTP) by tryptophan hydroxylase. This is the rate-limiting step in the synthesis of serotonin and is dependent on the concentration of tryptophan. The 5-HTP is rapidly converted to 5-HT (serotonin) by aromatic amino acid decarboxylase. All of the serotonin in the GI tract and CNS is synthesized in those compartments. Despite having high intracellular concentrations, serotonin is not synthesized in platelets. The serotonin in platelets is pumped into the cells from the serum. The serotonin in serum is synthesized and secreted

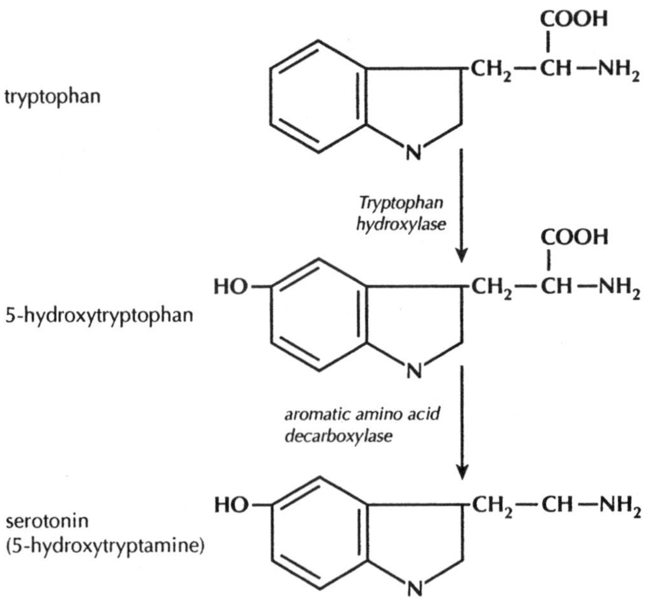

Figure 1

by cells in the GI tract and subsequently concentrated in the platelets. Platelets have high concentrations of serotonin transporters on their surfaces that pump the serotonin into the cells, where it is subsequently packaged into secretory granules.

The amount of serotonin synthesized in the CNS is controlled by the serum concentration of tryptophan (Maes et al., 1990). The serum concentration of tryptophan determines the amount of tryptophan that crosses the blood-brain barrier, which in turn controls the amount of serotonin synthesized in the CNS (Carpenter et al., 1998). The ratio of the serum concentration of tryptophan to the concentration of other large neutral amino acids that use the same transport mechanism controls the amount of tryptophan that enters CNS. Because the serum concentration of tryptophan controls the amount of serotonin synthesized in the CNS, dietary manipulation of tryptophan and other amino acids that compete for the transporter (phenylalanine, tyrosine) can alter the concentration of serotonin in the CNS. Serotonin in the periphery, either from platelets or in the serum, does not appear to enter the CNS.

In the periphery, serotonin has several important actions. Serotonin participates in platelet activation and clot formation. There are significant species differences in the role serotonin plays in platelet reactivity. In cats, serotonin can trigger the clotting process, while in humans, serotonin does not activate platelets. In humans, serotonin acts as an amplifier or accelerator of clot formation once the platelets have entered the clotting cascade by another activation pathway. There are serotonin receptors on many types of peripheral smooth muscle cells, including gastrointestinal, vascular, and uterine types. In the GI tract, serotonin participates in peristalsis by causing intestinal smooth muscle contraction and relaxation. Serotonin causes vasoconstriction via the serotonin receptors on the vascular smooth muscle. Serotonin produces a number of responses in uterine smooth muscle, including contraction, but it also causes synthesis and secretion of collagenase and possibly other enzymes. There are serotonin receptors on many other peripheral cell types, including cells in the immune system. In many peripheral cell types, there is evidence that serotonin acts as a growth factor, promoting cell division and proliferation. In these peripheral cell types, serotonin also causes complex changes in gene expression and may regulate the synthesis and secretion of a variety of substances (enzymes, growth factors, hormones, cytokines, etc.) from these cells.

Serotonin behaves like a classical neurotransmitter in the CNS. Serotonin is synthesized in neurons of the raphe nuclei in the brainstem, packaged in synaptic vesicles in the axon terminals, and released into the synapse in response to membrane depolarization caused by passing action potentials. All of the serotonin in the brain is synthesized in the cells of the raphe nuclei. The serotonergic cells of the raphe nuclei have axons that project widely throughout the CNS. The rostral raphe nuclei supply ascending serotonergic axons that innervate cortical and limbic structures, while the caudal raphe nuclei have descending axons that innervate the spinal column. The serotonergic axons also project recurrently back onto the serotonergic cell bodies in the raphe. In this way the serotonergic cells can regulate their firing rate and the amount of serotonin synthesized and available for synaptic release. The anatomical structure of the serotonergic system, with all of the transmitter being synthesized in a relatively small number of cells (which, in turn, project widely throughout the brain), is the reason that serotonin is able to modulate so many different neurobehavioral and cognitive processes.

Neurotransmission in the serotonergic system obeys the rules of classical neurotransmission. Depolarization of the membrane of the axon terminal causes serotonin to be released into the synapse from synaptic vesicles. The serotonin diffuses across the synapse and binds to postsynaptic serotonin receptors. There is a serotonin receptor, the 5-HT_{1B} type on the presynaptic membrane (terminal autoreceptor), that regulates the firing rate of individual serotonergic synapses. Transmission is terminated by the actions of the serotonin transporter (SERT) that pumps the serotonin back into the presynaptic neuron. The SERT is a member of the 12 transmembrane transport molecule family, with homology to the norepinephrine and dopamine transporters (Blakely et al., 1991). In the CNS, the SERT is exclusively on the axon terminals of presynaptic serotonergic neurons. The SERT on platelets is identical to the SERT on serotonergic neurons in the CNS (Lesch, Wolozin, Murphy, & Riederer, 1993). The SERT is the site of action of many different types of antidepressants, including the selective serotonin reuptake inhibitors (SSRIs). The SERT is also the site of action of certain drugs of abuse, including cocaine and MDMA (Ecstasy).

There have been at least 15 different serotonin receptors identified. These receptors are grouped into families according to molecular and pharmacological homology. The 5-HT_3 type is a pentameric, ligand gated ion channel receptor similar in structure to the nicotinic cholinergic receptor. The other serotonin receptors are 7-transmembrane, G-protein coupled receptors. The 5-HT_{1A} type is the serotonin receptor on the serotonergic cells in the raphe and therefore is referred to as the somatodendritic autoreceptor. Serotonin binding to the 5-HT_{1A} receptor on serotonergic neurons decreases the firing rate of these neurons. As mentioned previously, the 5-HT_{1B} type is on the presynaptic face in serotonergic synapses, and is referred to as the terminal autoreceptor. Serotonin binding

to this receptor regulates the amount of serotonin released into the synapse. Several of the serotonin receptors have been implicated in the pathophysiology of major mental illnesses. The 5-HT_{2A} type has been implicated in the biology of depression and schizophrenia. This receptor is the site of action of some antidepressants (trazodone, nefazodone), the site of action of atypical antipsychotics (clozapine, olanzapine, etc.), and is one of the sites of action of LSD and other hallucinogenic drugs. The advent of molecular biology has revealed that there are many more serotonin receptors than initially posited and that this system is much more complex than previously anticipated. The actual biological functions of most of the newly discovered serotonin receptors have yet to be clearly determined, as have the roles that these receptors play in psychopathology and response to therapeutic agents.

The serotonergic system has been hypothesized to participate in the pathophysiology of major mental illnesses including major depression, schizophrenia, anxiety disorders, impulse control disorders, and substance use disorders. There has been a large and concerted research effort devoted to studying the role of the serotonergic system in major depression and schizophrenia (Meltzer & Lowy, 1987; Maes & Meltzer, 1995). The evidence that connects the serotonergic system to these different syndromes comes from direct observation of serotonergic function and from the actions of various pharmacological agents. Measurement of serotonin or its principal metabolite 5-hydroxy indole acetic acid (5-HIAA) has provided equivocal evidence of serotonergic hypofunction in major depression (Garlow, Musselman, & Nemeroff, 1998). The most consistent observation of low serotonin (low 5-HIAA in cerebrospinal fluid) is in subjects who are impulsively and violently suicidal or are prone to other acts of impulsive aggression or violence, independent of psychiatric diagnosis (Traskman, Asberg, Bertilsson, & Sjostrand, 1981; Van Praag, 1982). But transiently lowering central serotonin levels via dietary manipulation of tryptophan can provoke depressive symptoms (Young, Smith, Pihl, & Ervin, 1985; Delgado, Charney, Price, Landis, & Henninger, 1990). In patients who have been successfully treated for depression, dietary tryptophan depletion can cause a frank relapse into major depression (Heninger, Delgado, Charney, Price, & Aghajanian, 1992; Smith, Fairburn, & Cowen, 1997). Curiously, tryptophan depletion of untreated depressed subjects does not cause worsening of depressive symptoms. Increasing serotonergic transmission, via drugs that block serotonin reuptake, clearly treats major depression. Many antidepressants block serotonin reuptake as part of their mechanism of action, and this is central to the activity of the SSRI class of agents (Prozac, Paxil, Zoloft, Celexa, Luvox). One of the principal pharmacological actions of the new generation of atypical antipsychotics is blocking the 5-HT_{2A} type of serotonin receptor (Meltzer, Matsubara, & Lee, 1989). All of these agents (clozapine, olanzapine, risperidone, quetiapine, etc.) are potent 5-HT_{2A} antagonists, which differentiates this class from the older types of antipsychotics that are potent dopamine antagonists with little action on the serotonin receptors.

Clearly the serotonin system in the CNS is highly complex and subtly nuanced. Serotonin participates in the regulation of many different neurobehavioral and cognitive processes. Dysfunction of the serotonergic system appears to play a role in the pathophysiology of major mental illnesses, in particular the major mood and psychotic disorders. Drugs that modify serotonergic function can be both psychotherapeutic (antidepressants, antipsychotics, anxiolytics) or agents of abuse (MDMA, cocaine, LSD, etc.). Knowledge of the structure and function of the serotonergic system is in its infancy, but is currently in a period of exponential expansion, with new discoveries reported with astonishing regularity.

REFERENCES

Blakely, R. D., Berson, H. E., Fremeau, R. T., Caron, M. G., Peek, M. M., Prince, H. K., & Bradley, C. C. (1991). Cloning and expression of a functional serotonin transporter from rat brain. *Nature, 354,* 66–70.

Carpenter, L. L., Anderson, G. M., Pelton, G. H., Gudin, J. A., Kirwin, P. D., Price, L. H., Heninger, G. R., & McDougle, C. J. (1998). Tryptophan depletion during continuous CSF sampling in healthy human subjects. *Neuropsychopharmacology, 19*(1), 26–35.

Delgado, P. L., Charney, D. S., Price, L. H., Landis, H., & Heninger, G. R. (1990). Neuroendocrine and behavioral effects of dietary tryptophan restriction in healthy subjects. *Life Sciences, 45,* 2323–2332.

Gaddum, J. H., & Picarelli, Z. P. (1957). Two kinds of tryptamine receptor. *British Journal of Pharmacology & Chemotherapy, 12,* 323–328.

Garlow, S. J., Musselman, D. L., & Nemeroff, C. B. (1998). The neurochemistry of mood disorders: Clinical Studies. In D. S. Charney, E. J. Nestler, & B. S. Bunney (Eds.), *The neurobiology of mental illness* (pp. 348–364). New York: Oxford.

Heninger, G. R., Delgado, P. L., Charney, D. S., Price, L. H., & Aghajanian, G. K. (1992). Tryptophan-deficient diet and amino acid drink deplete plasma tryptophan and induce a relapse of depression in susceptible patients. *Journal of Chemical Neuroanatomy, 5,* 347–348.

Kobilka, B. K., Frielle, T., Collins, S., Yang-Feng, T., Kobilka, T. S., Franke, U., Lefkowitz, R. J., & Caron, M. G. (1987). An intronless gene encoding a potential member of the family of receptors coupled to guanine nucleotide regulatory proteins. *Nature, 329,* 75–79.

Lesch, K. P., Wolozin, B. L., Murphy, D. L., & Riederer, P. (1993). Primary structure of the human platelet serotonin uptake site: Identity with the brain serotonin transporter. *Journal of Neurochemistry, 60,* 2319–2322.

Maes, M., Jacobs, M.-P., Suy, E., Minner, B., Leclercq, C., Christiaens, F., & Raus, J. (1990). Suppressant effects of dexamethasone on the availability of plasma L-tryptophan and tyrosine in healthy controls and depressed patients. *Acta Psychiatrica Scandinavica, 81,* 19–23.

Maes, M., & Meltzer, H. Y. (1995). The serotonin hypothesis of major depression. In E. Bloom J. Kupfer (Eds.), *Psychopharmacology: The fourth generation of progress* (pp. 933–944). New York: Raven.

Meltzer, H. Y., & Lowy, M. T. (1987). The serotonin hypothesis of depression. In H. Y. Meltzer (Ed.), *Psychopharmacology: The third generation of progress* (pp. 513–526). New York: Raven.

Meltzer, H. Y., Matsubara, S., & Lee, J.-C. (1989). Classification of typical and atypical antipsychotic drugs on the basis of dopamine D-1, D-2 and Serotonin 2 pKi values. *Journal of Pharmacology & Experimental Therapy, 251*(1), 238–246.

Peroutka, S. J., & Snyder, S. H. (1979). Multiple serotonin receptors: Differential binding of [³H]-serotonin, [³H]-lysergic acid diethylamide and [³H]-spiroperidol. *Molecular Pharmacology, 16,* 687–699.

Smith, K. A., Fairburn, C. G., & Cowen, P. J. (1997). Relapse of depression after rapid depletion of tryptophan. *Lancet, 349,* 915–919.

Traskman, L. M., Asberg, L., Bertilsson, L., & Sjostrand, L. (1981). Monoamine metabolites in CSF and suicidal behavior. *Archives of General Psychiatry, 38*(6), 631–636.

Van Praag, H. M. (1982). Depression, suicide, and the metabolites of serotonin in the brain. *Journal of Affective Disorders, 4,* 21–29.

Young, S. N., Smith, S. E., Pihl, R., & Ervin, F. R. (1985). Tryptophan depletion causes a rapid lowering of mood in normal males. *Psychopharmacology, 87,* 173–177.

S. J. GARLOW
Emory University

NEUROTRANSMITTERS

SEVERITY OF PSYCHOSOCIAL STRESSORS SCALE

The Severity of Psychosocial Stressors Scale was developed for Axis IV of the *DSM-III* and *DSM-III-R*. The scale assessed precipitating stress in mental disorders and formed part of the multiaxial system of modern diagnosis, designed to improve the view of patients' background, symptoms, and functioning. The Severity Scale was founded upon research on stressors that took place in the 1960s and 1970s, particularly the Holmes-Rahe Scale that rated stressful life events along a hierarchy of severity.

The scale was described in the *DSM-III-R* as follows:

Axis IV provides a scale, the Severity of Psychosocial Stressors Scale . . . for coding the overall severity of a psychosocial stressor or multiple psychosocial stressors that have occurred in the year preceding the current evaluation and that may have contributed to any of the following:

(1) development of a new mental disorder
(2) recurrence of a prior mental disorder
(3) exacerbation of an already existing disorder

(American Psychiatric Association, 1987, p. 18)

The scale was also able to measure for Post-Traumatic Stress Disorder which may be precipitated by stressors prior to the one-year period.

The scale was divided into six categories of stress severity that ranged from no stress to catastrophic stress. Some examples of stressors given in the scale are school graduation (mild), job loss (moderate), unemployment (severe), serious chronic illness (extreme) or death of a child (catastrophic). The *DSM-III-R* maintained that:

The rating of the severity of the stressor should be based on the clinician's assessment of the stress an "average" person in similar circumstances and with similar sociocultural values would experience from the particular psychosocial stressor(s).

(American Psychiatric Association, 1987, p. 19)

Research has distinguished the impact of time-limited events from that of more deleterious chronic stressors. For example, years of unemployment will likely be more stressful than a recent job loss; years of incarceration will likely be more harmful than an arrest; and long-term spouse abuse will likely be more deleterious than divorce. Consequently, the Severity Scale in the *DSM-III-R* was rated for either acute events lasting less than six months (e.g., death in the family) or enduring conditions lasting more than six months (e.g., chronic illness). In addition, separate scales were provided for assessing stressors in adults (e.g., marital problems) and in adolescents or children (e.g., rejection by parents).

The Severity of Psychosocial Stressors Scale was intended to help clinicians plan treatment, better understand etiology, and predict course and outcome. For treatment, information on specific stressors helps clinicians plan interventions to cope with the stress.

In terms of etiology, research on most mental disorders suggests that many factors may be involved as influences or causes. These factors may include social (external) events in combination with biologic or genetic (internal) dispositions. According to current diathesis-stress or vulnerability models of pathology, an inherent or biological vulnerability (diathesis) in an individual may be triggered by a stressful life event. Biological, social, and psychological etiologic factors vary widely in their type and effect on a disorder. Similar models have been used to elucidate the causes and outcome of medical illnesses such as diabetes or coronary heart disease.

In terms of prognosis, theorists have suggested that acute symptoms precipitated by specific stressors that are external to the disorder may have a better prognosis than symptoms whose onset is gradual and less related to stress. For example, outcome research has distinguished good-prognosis, reactive schizophrenia (with acute onset and precipitating stress) from poor-prognosis, process schizophrenia (with gradual onset and no precipitating stress). Similar dichotomies and prognoses have been noted for mood disorders and alcoholism.

However, a review of the research (Skodol, 1991) reported several difficulties with the Severity of Psychosocial Stressors Scale and with assessing stress in general. The scale did not seem to be widely used by clinicians. The reliability and validity of the scale were also questioned. Reliability ratings were generally low, in part due to the difficulties of rating stress. Validity was also moderate to poor for various disorders. Precipitating stress was a poor predictor of illness course in the psychotic disorders such as schizophrenia; the most positive predictive results occurred in depression—but not on a uniform basis. Yet significant results were generally in the hypothesized direction, with severe stressors associated with better outcomes. In addition, the prevalence of stressors varied by diagnosis: They were more likely to be found in several disorders such as major depression and anxiety disorders than in schizophrenia (Skodol, 1991).

Explanations for problems with the Severity Scale included:

1. The stressors reported by clients were retrospective and subject to memory distortions. Clients may repress the memory of important stresses.

2. The rating was often subjective and reflected what clinicians thought was stressful. Some clinicians focused on stressors ignored by other clinicians.

3. The background for assessment was average functioning rather than the distinct impact of the event on the individual. Critics suggest that the same stressor may have different effects on different clients.

4. The impact of multiple stressors, which often occurs, was difficult to assess. For example, a recently widowed person may also experience financial problems and social isolation.

5. The impact of continuous daily "hassles" (rather than single, major events) could not be accurately assessed. For example, the concept of expressed emotions, in which emotional overinvolvement or hostile, critical comments within families have been found to significantly impact relapse in several mental disorders, is difficult to assess by the Severity Scale.

Another major criticism was that only risk factors or negative stressors, but not protective factors such as social supports and personal resources, were assessed. Increasingly, research has suggested that positive events, personal strengths, and social attachments may be of more import than deficits, symptoms, or negative events in predicting outcome. Positive, protective factors such as social networks often mitigate the impact of stressful events. For example, financially secure, caring parents may provide a supportive environment for recovery from mental illness.

Most importantly, some theorists suggest that the illness process itself may decide the protective or risk factors experienced by the individual. In other words, stressful events may be the result of the illness rather than the cause. For example, prospective, longitudinal research findings have shown that depressed individuals are more vulnerable to experiencing negative events than are nondepressed individuals (Cui & Vaillant, 1997). Individuals with severe mental disorders are more likely than others to be unemployed or divorced, or to experience other negative life events as a consequence of the illness, and these events may in turn exacerbate the illness. Conversely, some mentally healthy individuals actually seek some types of stressors (such as job changes) as challenges or opportunities for creativity. To a great extent, internal and external risk and protective factors are involved in complex, developmental interactions across the life span, and it is quite difficult to unravel the causes and consequences of a mental disorder.

Because of these myriad problems, the Severity Scale was dropped and replaced with a new Axis IV in the *DSM-IV:* Psychosocial and Environmental Problems. The new Axis IV is a simple notation of problems in nine possible areas: such as "educational problems" or "economic problems." (American Psychiatric Association, 1994). There are no restrictions on the number of stressors that clinicians can note, and severity ratings are not made. The new Axis IV scale in the *DSM-IV* is simpler than the Severity of Psychosocial Stressors Scale. It is hoped that the new scale will be more widely used and informative to clinicians planning treatment.

REFERENCES

American Psychiatric Association (1987). *Diagnostic and statistical manual of mental disorders* (3rd ed., rev.). Washington, DC: Author.

American Psychiatric Association. (1994) *Diagnostic and statistical manual of mental disorders* (4th ed.). Washington, DC: Author.

Cui, X., & Vaillant, G. E. (1997). Does depression generate negative life events? *Journal of Nervous and Mental Disease, 185*(3), 145–150.

Skodol, A. E. (1991). Axis IV: A reliable and valid measure of psychosocial stressors? *Comprehensive Psychiatry, 32*(6), 503–515.

J. F. WESTERMEYER
Adler School of Professional Psychology

CLINICAL ASSESSMENT
DIAGNOSIS
QUESTIONAIRES
RATING SCALES
STRESS

SEX CHROMOSOME DISORDERS

Normal sexual differentiation into genetic and phenotypic male and female takes place prenatally, and in various orderly stages. The first stage occurs at the time of conception; contribution of the XX or XY chromosomes determines genetic sex. In the second embryonic month, the gonads begin differentiation into ovaries or testes. During the third month of gestation, hormonal secretions by the testes (androgens) signal differentiation of internal and external male sexual organs. The absence of androgens, as in most genetic females, results in female internal and external differentiation. Occasionally genetic or hormonal disorders result in ambiguous differentiation and may cause confusion as to the sex of the child at birth. Behavioral observation of these individuals by John Money and his associates (1972) provides evidence that environment (i.e., whether one is reared and treated as a male or fe-

male) influences gender role and identity much more than do genetic or morphologic sex.

Disorders of the sex chromosomes can occur during meiosis (cell division producing gametes, cells with only half of the chromosomes complement) or during mitosis (division of all cells past the gamete stage). Genetic errors during meiosis yield organisms with too few or too many sex chromosomes; mosaicism (combinations of more than one chromosomal pattern in the same individual) is caused by errors during mitosis. Breakage rather than total absence of sex chromosomes may also occur, resulting in a variety of gonadal and sex organ abnormalities. Missing or additional sex chromosomes are the most distinct sex chromosome disorders.

The only viable condition of sex chromosome loss is the occurrence of an X without a partner sex chromosome. The male counterpart of this syndrome (YO) is always lethal. Turner's syndrome (genetic karyotype 45/X0, indicating 45 total chromosomes with only one sex chromosome) occurs in one out of 7,000 newborns, but is much higher in spontaneously aborted fetuses. Of Turner's syndrome females, about half are the "pure" genetic karyotype 45/XO; the other half have a variety of sex chromosome constitutions, usually caused by a defect in the second chromosome. Primary signs of this disorder are gonadal dysgenesis (undeveloped ovaries) and infertility. Phenotypically, internal and external sexual organs remain infantile, no menstruation occurs at puberty, and only with estrogen therapy can secondary sexual characteristics develop. These females also exhibit a distinctive cluster of congenital abnormalities, including short stature, webbed neck, and widely spaced nipples, giving their chests a shield-like appearance. Turner's syndrome females are assigned the sex role of female and reared as girls with stereotypically female gender role and identity.

Individuals with Klinefelter's syndrome, a disorder in which at least one X chromosome is added to the normal 46/XY karyotype (most commonly 47/XXY), are phenotypically male with a small to average penis size, extremely small nonfunctional testes, rounded hips, and some breast development. A high incidence of chronic medical disorders, including pulmonary and liver diseases and decreased intelligence, is common. A higher than normal incidence of psychopathology has been documented, and variations in sexual preference have been noted, although these individuals have a lowered sex drive, perhaps because of the lack of testosterone secretion. An increased frequency of this disorder is found in mental and penal institutions. Individuals with genetic karyotypes of more than one additional X (e.g., 49/XXXXY) have greater retardation, more severe genital immaturity, and other physical abnormalities. Incidence of Klinefelter's syndrome is one in 400 live-born males, and combinations of genetic abnormalities (mosaics) are not uncommon.

In the 47/XYY karyotype condition (referred to as "supermale"), there is also at least one extra sex chromosome. The phenotype is male. The extra Y results in increased height, but does not influence the expression of any other qualities that might be termed "super"-male. These males are often infertile and mentally retarded, and exhibit delinquent behavior, characterized by impulsive acting out and poor long-term planning. Though an increased incidence of this disorder is found in penal institutions, it is probably not accurate to conclude that a 47/XYY karyotype is a genetic marker for criminal activity. Its side effects of mental retardation, impulsivity, and physical stature (increasing visibility, and perhaps the perception of fearsomeness) may increase the likelihood of incarceration.

Just as an additional Y in an XY male does not make a supermale, addition of X chromosomes in XX females does not enhance femaleness. The 47/XXX females (called "superfemales") exhibit no definite physical stigmata, although IQ may be slightly lower. These females have stereotypic gender role/identity. Although fertile, they report greater than average menstrual problems and early menopause; their fertility increases the probability of producing XXY or XXX offspring. Additional X's result in progressively more severe retardation, possibly linking chromosomal excesses of any kind with decreased intelligence.

REFERENCES

Money, J., & Ehrhardt, A. (1972). *Man and woman, boy and girl: The differentiation and dimorphism of gender identity from conception to maturity.* Baltimore: Johns Hopkins University Press.

SUGGESTED READING

Federman, D. D. (1967). *Abnormal sexual development: A genetic and endocrine approach to differential diagnosis.* Philadelphia: Saunders.

B. E. Thorn
University of Alabama

CHROMOSOME DISORDERS
GENETIC DOMINANCE AND RECESSIVENESS

SEX DIFFERENCES

The study of sex differences derives from the field of differential psychology, introduced by Sir Francis Galton in the year 1883, in his book *Inquiries into Human Faculty and its Development.* As part of his study of individual differences, Galton measured, quantified, and compared various physical and mental traits in men and women. Two classic textbooks in the area of individual differences, each written by a former president of the American Psychological Association, continued in this vein. *Differential Psychology* by Anne Anastasi and *The Psychology of Human Differences* by Leona Tyler each devoted a chapter to sex differences in such areas as mental abilities, personality, motivation, and interests.

The field of sex differences received new impetus from a major study by Maccoby and Jacklin (1974), in which they reviewed the psychological literature in over 50 content areas encompassing more than 1,600 studies to determine what sex differences actually existed. Using a "box score" approach in their survey, they categorized studies in terms of their specific content and counted the total number of studies in a given area that showed that males scored higher than females, females scored higher than males, or no dif-

ference was reported. They concluded that a sex difference existed only when a predominant number of studies in an area showed consistent effects in favor of one sex. Using this approach, they concluded that consistent sex differences could be found only in four areas: girls have greater verbal ability than boys; boys excel in visual-spatial ability; boys show greater mathematical ability than girls; and males are more aggressive than females. Suggestive, but ambiguous, evidence of sex differences was found in the following areas: girls have greater tactile sensitivity; males are more active, especially in the company of others; girls are more likely or more willing to report fear, timidity, or anxious behavior; males are more competitive; males are more dominant; and girls tend to be more compliant. They failed to find consistent evidence of sex differences in other traditional areas of investigation.

A statistical technique called meta-analysis has been used to analyze the results of numerous independent studies in a single area. Meta-analyses of the literature on sex differences in influenceability by Eagly and Carli (1981) and in cognitive areas such as verbal, quantitative, and visual-spatial abilities by Hyde (1981) suggest that the variability accounted for by sex differences is typically very small. It has been estimated that approximately 1% of the variance in influenceability is accounted for by sex. Even in the area with the largest sex difference—spatial ability—Hyde reports that sex accounts for only about 5% of the variability found.

In addition to questions about the number of sex differences that actually exist and the importance of those that do exist, one of the most problematic aspects of the study of sex differences is the question of their origin. Explanations of the same sex difference may range from biological factors, such as chromosomes or genes, differences in neural structure, or hormonal influences before or after birth, to environmental factors, such as differential parental reinforcement based on sex, preferred sex role, or labeling based on anatomical structures and the need for behavioral consistency (Wittig & Petersen, 1978).

The area of sex differences is one in which the nature–nurture arguments still persist. Although most students of the area regard sex differences as the product of biological–environmental interaction, in practice, researchers tend to concentrate on either biological or environmental variables. Moreover, a number of different interactions are possible in a given area, which may generate quite different research and policy decisions (Newcombe, 1980). The area is a particularly controversial one because of the potential impact of findings in terms of social policies in areas such as education and employment.

Criticism of biologically based theories of sex differences has been particularly evident in the newly emerging area of the psychology of women. Critics have focused on the effect of the sex of the experimenter or other evaluator of the person's performance in the production of sex differences (Harris, 1971; Pedersen et al., 1968; Rumenik et al., 1977). Effects may be produced either by differences in the demand characteristics of different sex researchers (Eagly & Carli, 1981) or by sex differences in the probability with which researchers ask questions about sex differences (Signorella et al., 1981). Other criticisms note that sex biases exist in the choice of what content area to study with what sex subject (McKenna & Kessler, 1977) and in the selection of methodologies by which the "same" characteristic is evaluated in females and males. For example, pencil-and-paper measures have been found to be used more frequently to measure aggression in females whereas more active measures, such as the willingness to inflict electric shock on another person, are more frequently used in studies of aggression in males (Frodi et al., 1977).

Criticism of sex difference research may be conceptual as well as methodological. For example, no general theoretical framework exists to determine when a given sex difference should be examined or what it means if it is found. Therefore, findings on sex differences have tended to be scattered throughout the research literature. Since such findings also tend to be inconsistent and small in size, generalizations about sex differences have tended to be based either on arbitrary decision making or on stereotypic assumptions about what should be true. Few researchers have attempted to provide theoretical or empirical explanations for the sex differences they describe. Descriptions involving sex, however, tend to be treated as explanations because biological processes are inferred whether or not explanatory mechanisms have been provided by the researcher (Unger, 1979).

The area of sex differences provides a case study of an area in intellectual ferment. It provides a dilemma for researchers because of the need for a data base even when the methods used to accumulate those data are suspect. The area is also problematic because the extent to which one can generalize about individual performance based on group averages is a particularly critical issue (Wittig, 1976). Since there are no separate but equal categories in most discussions of male versus female abilities, it is important to stress that explorations in this area should proceed cautiously.

REFERENCES

Anastasi, A. (1958/1949/1937). *Differential psychology* (3rd ed.). New York: Macmillan. (translations: German, Italian, Portuguese, Spanish)

Eagly, A. H., & Carli, L. L. (1981). Sex of researchers and sex-typed communications as determinants of sex differences in influenceability: A meta-analysis of social influence studies. *Psychological Bulletin, 90,* 1–20.

Frodi, A., Macaulay, J., & Thome, P. R. (1977). Are women always less aggressive than men? A review of the experimental literature. *Psychological Bulletin, 84,* 634–660.

Galton, F. (1883). *Inquiries into human faculty and its development.* London: Macmillan.

Harris, S. (1971). Influence of subject and experimenter sex in psychological research. *Journal of Consulting and Clinical Psychology, 37,* 291–294.

Hyde, J. S. (1981). How large are cognitive gender differences? A meta-analysis using ω^2 and *d. American Psychologist, 36,* 892–901.

Maccoby, E. E., & Jacklin, C. N. (1974). *The psychology of sex differences.* Stanford, CA: Stanford University Press.

McKenna, W., & Kessler, S. J. (1977). Experimenter design as a source of sex bias in social psychology. *Sex Roles, 3,* 117–128.

Newcombe, N. (1980). Beyond nature and nurture. *Contemporary Psychology, 25,* 807–808.

Pedersen, D. M., Shinedling, M. M., & Johnson, D. L. (1968). Effects of sex of examiner and subject on children's quantitative test performance. *Journal of Personality and Social Psychology, 10,* 251–254.

Rumenik, D. K., Capasso, D. R., & Hendrick, C. (1977). Experimenter sex effects in behavioral research. *Psychological Bulletin, 84,* 852–877.

Tyler, L. E. (1965/1947). *The psychology of human differences* (3rd ed.). New York: Appleton-Century-Crofts.

Unger, R. K. (1979). *Female and male: Psychological perspectives.* New York: Harper & Row.

Unger, R. K. (1979). Toward a redefinition of sex and gender. *American Psychologist, 34,* 1085–1094.

Wittig, M. A. (1976). Sex differences in intellectual functioning: How much of a difference do genes make? *Sex Roles, 2,* 63–74.

SUGGESTED READING

Benbow, C. P., & Stanley, J. C. (1980). Sex differences in mathematical ability: Fact or artifact? *Science, 210,* 1262–1264.

Block, J. H. (1976). Debatable conclusions about sex differences (Review of *The psychology of sex differences* by E. E. Maccoby & C. N. Jacklin). *Contemporary Psychology, 21,* 517–522.

Buss, A. R. (1976). Galton and sex differences: An historical note. *Journal of the History of the Behavioral Sciences, 12,* 283–285.

Eagly, A. H. (1978). Sex differences in influenceability. *Psychological Bulletin, 85,* 86–116.

Gould, S. J. (1981). *The mismeasure of man.* New York: Norton.

McHugh, M. C., Koeske, R. D., & Frieze, I. H. (1981, December). *Guidelines for nonsexist research.* Report of the Task Force of Division 35 of APA.

Parsons, J. E. (Ed.). (1980). *The psychobiology of sex differences and sex roles.* New York: McGraw-Hill.

Sherman, J. A. (1978). *Sex-related cognitive differences: An essay on theory and evidence.* Springfield, IL: Thomas.

Shields, S. A. (1975). Functionalism, Darwinism, and the psychology of women: A study of social myth. *American Psychologist, 30,* 739–754.

Unger, R. K. (1982). Through the looking glass: No Wonderland yet! *Psychology of Women Quarterly, 7.*

R. K. UNGER
Montclair State College

ANDROGYNY
COPING
OPTIMAL FUNCTIONING
SELF-FULFILLING PROPHECY
SEX DIFFERENCES
SEXISM

SEX ROLES

Although a large number of books and articles have the term *sex roles* as part of their title, there is remarkably little consistency in the definition of this term. At the most general level, a sex role may be defined as "the set of behaviors and characteristics widely viewed as typical of women or men (sex role stereotypes) and desirable for women and men (sex role norms)" (Pleck, 1981, p. 10). Characteristics that have been considered to be encompassed within one's sex role include personality traits, values, abilities, interests, and behaviors performed within the framework of familial or occupational roles.

The contents of sex roles are usually both descriptive and prescriptive in nature. Sex-role stereotypes are widely shared descriptive beliefs about what the sexes actually *are.* They are obtained by asking individuals to rate each sex as a group according to a standardized list of terms. Sex-role norms are widely shared prescriptive beliefs about what the sexes *should be,* obtained by asking people to rate each sex for "ideal" characteristics. Both stereotypes and norms are the product of a group consensus—determined by a substantial level of agreement among the surveyed individuals.

While sex-role stereotypes and norms represent beliefs about males and females as social groups, the term *sex typing* refers to the characteristics of a particular individual with respect to sex-related dimensions. It is measured by the way one rates one's own characteristics rather than those of others. Degree of sex typing is estimated by comparing the number and/or level of sex-related characteristics a person rates himself or herself to possess in relation to the ratings of other individuals of the same sex.

Beginning in the 1930s masculinity–femininity scales were designed to assess how individuals ranked on a hypothetical continuum ranging from typically and appropriately male to typically and appropriately female. Sex typing as measured by various standardized tests may be regarded as the operationalization of the concept of sex-role identification (Pleck, 1981). Early scales such as the Attitudes-Interests Test developed by Terman and Miles (1936) and the fe scale developed by Gough (1952) conceptualized sex-role identity as a single overall dimension of the personality. These tests were standardized using a known group method; for example, items were rated as either masculine or feminine depending on whether a statistically significant larger number of males or females responded in a particular direction. The more consistently an individual responded in terms of the statistical norms for individuals of the same sex, the more sex-typed he or she was considered to be.

In the 1940s and 1950s, psychoanalytic influences led theorists to make a distinction between conscious and nonconscious aspects of sex typing. The term most directly derived from psychoanalytic theory is sex-role identification. This concept relates to the extent to which an individual has internalized the traits and behaviors considered appropriate to an individual of one's own sex. The most frequently used scale designed to measure the more unconscious aspects of sex-role identification was the It Scale for Children (Brown, 1956). Subjects were requested to rate which of two sex-typed items would be preferred by an ambiguous stick figure—the It.

Early critics of the concept of sex-role identification (Lynn, 1959) noted that a child might prefer certain sex-typed characteristics of the opposite sex, but still identify with the child's own sex. Lynn distinguished between sex-role preference (perceiving the characteristics of one sex as preferable to or more desirable than the other) and sex-role adoption (practicing aspects of behavior regarded as appropriate for individuals of a particular sex without necessarily identifying with other aspects of the role). For example, a female may like to participate in team sports or wear pants or other items of male apparel without wishing to be a male.

More recent theories about sex roles have involved the conception of masculinity and femininity as two independent psychological dimensions (Constantinople, 1973). Two important instruments designed to measure sex roles in terms of this multidimensional formulation are the BSRI (Bem, 1974) and the PAQ (Spence et al., 1974). Originally both formulations viewed the simultaneous possession of high numbers and/or levels of traits stereotypically considered masculine and feminine (androgyny) as the ideal sex-role identity in terms of mental health. Other new theories view sex roles in terms of developmental stages (Block, 1973; Rebecca et al., 1976). These theories conceive sex roles as developing from a relatively undifferentiated stage through a phase of acceptance of traditional stereotypic sex roles to a state in which the individual reorganizes social norms in terms of his or her individual characteristics and needs. Rebecca and her associates (1976) have termed this stage *sex-role transcendence.*

SEX-ROLE SOCIALIZATION

Theories also differ in terms of how sex roles are acquired and on the differential implication of sex roles for males and females. The earliest treatment of sex-role socialization is that of Freud (1930, 1948), a theory largely based on unconscious, instinctual, or maturational processes due to the possession of differential anatomical equipment by males and females. Possession of a particular kind of genital anatomy is believed to determine the different psychosexual development of males and females.

Another important theoretical framework is based on social learning theory (Bandura, 1969; Mischel, 1970). This theory stresses the physical and social properties of the parent and the nature of reinforcement processes in children's acquisition of sex roles. Children are assumed to use the same-sex parent as a model because of his or her similarity to themselves. Parents are also utilized as models because of their availability, nurturant qualities, and power over resources. Parents and other salient individuals in the child's environment reinforce the modeled behavior when it is considered sex appropriate and ignore or punish it when it is not.

Cognitive development theory (Kohlberg, 1966, 1969) stresses the role of the child's own behavior in the reinforcement of appropriate sex roles. This theory stresses the important role of self-categorization as a "boy" or "girl" rather than the passive acquisition of a behavioral repertoire via the reinforcement processes of others. Once the child has acquired a gender label (which appears to occur no later than the second year of life), he or she comes to value positively behaviors, objects, and attitudes consistent with that label. Thus the child selects actively from the available environment to receive input that is consistent with maintenance of the appropriate identity.

Both social learning and aspects of cognitive development appear to operate in the acquisition of sex-appropriate roles. For example, there is considerable cross-cultural evidence that there are consistent and persistent differences in the ways in which mothers and fathers treat their sons and daughters to enhance autonomy in the former and affective relationships in the latter (Block, 1978). Nevertheless, parental behaviors may be inconsistent with reference to individuals. The impact of parental socialization practices may be modified by such variables as the physical characteristics of the child, his or her birth position, and the sex of siblings. Racial, ethnic, and social-class differences in parental behaviors have also been found, as well as differences in terms of the task investigated and the context in which it is studied (Unger, 1979).

Empirical studies find that children acquire various aspects of gender understanding in a rather invariant sequence (Eaton & Von Bargen, 1981; Thompson, 1975). A given level of attainment is achieved first when the self is the referent, next when a same-sex other is the referent, and last when an opposite-sex other is the referent. No sex differences in the acquisition of these sex-role concepts have been found among the preschool children studied. Studies of somewhat older children (4 to 6 years of age) divided into those who had achieved a high level of gender constancy and those who had not (based on the number of questions about sex roles answered correctly) found that only high-gender constant children were influenced by the sight of an opposite-sex child playing with a toy on a television commercial. As compared with low-gender constant children of the same age, these children avoided a toy when it had been played with by a child of the opposite sex and stated verbally that it was not appropriate for them to play with it (Ruble et al., 1981). These findings demonstrate a connection between the child's developmental level and the impact of sex-role-related information.

A major issue not resolved by social learning or cognitive development theory is the differential impact of sex-role socialization on girls and boys in our society. Although girls and boys may acquire concepts related to their own gender identity at about the same early age, throughout childhood many more girls than boys show a preference for aspects of the role of the opposite sex (Hyde et al., 1977; Nash, 1975). There are several possible explanations for this sex asymmetry. One is that masculine characteristics are considered more useful and desirable to society as a whole. It would not be surprising, therefore, if females preferred characteristics and behaviors productive of more social esteem than accrues to the usual feminine role. Spence and colleagues (1975) have found that high self-esteem is associated with high masculinity scores on the PAQ for both males and females, irrespective of scores on the femininity component of their scale.

Females do not appear to be penalized as much as males for deviating from their traditional sex role. The differential penalties for deviation by males as compared with females may be attributable to the higher status of the male role (Feinman, 1981; Unger, 1976, 1978). Thus a female who deviates from normative role expectations may balance any negative consequences by acquiring a second set of positively valued traits. Males who adopt cross-sex characteristics confront status expectations as well as role pre-

scriptions. These considerations suggest that changes in intrapsychic sex roles in the direction of greater androgyny cannot be evaluated without taking into account societal norms.

RECENT DEVELOPMENTS IN THE STUDY OF SEX ROLES

The concept of sex role as it has been used in psychology appears to be too global in nature. Spence and Helmreich (1978) have suggested replacing the term with four distinct categories: gender identity (awareness of one's invariant biological sex, which is nonproblematic except for a few statistically rare transsexuals); sexual orientation; sex-role attitudes and behaviors; and personality characteristics. Sex or gender identity (there is some disagreement about which term should be used) appears to be an important factor in the processing of information about the self and others. The physical characteristics of that self and those of others are important indicators in the assessment of sex role (Spence & Sawin, in press). Various elements of sex role, however, may remain relatively independent of each other.

Attention has also been focused on situational factors and their interaction with personal variables. Sex and gender roles belong to situations and the social structure; however, a person is not a role, but occupies or plays out a role (Sherif, 1982). Advances in our understanding of the sex roles have been facilitated by person–situational analyses in such areas as aggression, influenceability, and helping (O'Leary et al., in press).

A particularly intriguing area of study is the influence of self-fulfilling prophecies on the production of stereotypically appropriate sex-related behaviors. For example, Zanna and Pack (1975) found that female subjects who expected to meet an attractive, desirable male portrayed themselves as more "feminine" and performed less intelligently on a bogus IQ test when they thought the male held conventional rather than nonconventional views about women. A subsequent study (von Baeyer et al., 1981) found that, apparently without being fully aware of it, female applicants for a job presented themselves in a more traditionally "feminine" manner when they believed that the interviewer held traditional views of women. The women who thought that they were meeting a traditional employer wore significantly more makeup and clothing accessories such as earrings and scarves and gave more traditional answers to questions relating to children and career plans.

An overwhelming body of evidence indicates that sex labeling performs important cognitive functions in our society. Infants' personal characteristics undergo perceptual reorganization when they are labeled "male" or "female" (Seavey et al., 1975). Parents select sex-appropriate toys for their sons and daughters even when they express a belief in a sex-egalitarian ideology (Rheingold & Cook, 1975). Peers appear to be particularly important in the regulation of conformity to sex roles during early adolescence (Unger, 1979). Sex roles may be maintained during adulthood by situational factors and by the differential distribution of males and females into occupational and domestic contexts. It is clear that exploration of the intrapsychic nature of sex roles must wait until the far-reaching implications of their regulatory aspects have been further explored.

REFERENCES

Bandura, A. (1969). Social-learning theory of identificatory processes. In A. D. Goslin (Ed.), *Handbook of socialization theory and research.* Chicago: Rand-McNally.

Bem, S. L. (1974). The measurement of psychological androgyny. *Journal of Consulting and Clinical Psychology, 42,* 155–162.

Block, J. H. (1973). Conceptions of sex role: Some cross-cultural and longitudinal perspectives. *American Psychologist, 28,* 512–526.

Block, J. H. (1978). Another look at sex differentiation in the socialization behaviors of mothers and fathers. In J. Sherman & F. Denmark (Eds.), *Psychology of women: Future directions of research.* New York: Psychological Dimensions.

Brown, D. (1956). Sex-role preference in young children. *Psychological Monographs, 70*(No. 421).

Constantinople, A. (1973). Masculinity–femininity: An exception to a famous dictum? *Psychological Bulletin, 80,* 389–407.

Eaton, W. O., & Von Bargen, D. (1981). Asynchronous development of gender understanding in preschool children. *Child Development, 52,* 1020–1027.

Feinman, S. (1981). Why is cross-sex role behavior more approved for girls than for boys? A status characteristic approach. *Sex Roles, 7,* 289–300.

Gough, H. G. (1952). Identifying psychological femininity. *Educational and Psychological Measurement, 12,* 427–439.

Hyde, J. S., Rosenberg, B. G., & Behrman, J. (1977). Tomboyism. *Psychology of Women Quarterly, 2,* 73–75.

Kohlberg, L. (1966). A cognitive-developmental analysis of children's sex-role concepts and attitudes. In E. E. Maccoby (Ed.), *The development of sex differences.* Stanford, CA: Stanford University Press.

Kohlberg, L. (1969). Stage and sequence: The cognitive-developmental approach to socialization. In D. A. Goslin (Ed.), *Handbook of socialization theory and research.* Chicago: Rand-McNally.

Lynn, D. B. (1959). A note on sex differences in the development of masculine and feminine identification. *Psychological Review, 66,* 126–135.

Mischel, W. (1970). Sex-typing and socialization. In P. H. Mussen (Ed.), *Carmichael's manual of child psychology.* New York: Wiley.

Nash, S. C. (1975). The relationship among sex-role stereotyping, sex-role preference, and the sex difference in spatial visualization. *Sex Roles, 1,* 15–32.

O'Leary, V. E., Unger, R. K., & Wallston, B. S. (in press.) *Women, gender, and social psychology.* Hillsdale, NJ: Erlbaum.

Pleck, J. H. (1981). *The myth of masculinity.* Cambridge, MA: MIT Press.

Rebecca, M., Hefner, R., & Oleshansky, B. (1976). A model of sex-role transcendence. *Journal of Social Issues, 32,* 197–206.

Rheingold, H. L., & Cook, K. V. (1975). The contents of boys' and girls' rooms as an index of parents' behavior. *Child Development, 46,* 459–463.

Ruble, D. N., Balaban, T., & Cooper, J. (1981). Gender constancy and the effects of sex-typed televised toy commercials. *Child Development, 52,* 667–673.

Seavey, C. A., Katz, P. A., & Zalk, S. R. (1975). Baby X: The effect of gender labels on adult responses to infants. *Sex Roles, 1,* 103–110.

Sherif, C. W. (1982). Needed concepts in the study of gender identity. *Psychology of Women Quarterly, 6.*

Spence, J. T., & Helmreich, R. L. (1978). *Masculinity and femininity: Their psychological dimensions, correlates, and antecedents.* Austin, TX: University of Texas Press.

Spence, J. T., Helmreich, R. L., & Stapp, J. (1974). The Personal Attributes Questionnaire: A measure of sex-role stereotypes and masculinity-femininity. *JSAS Catalog of Selected Documents in Psychology, 4,* 127.

Spence, J. T. Helmreich, R. L., & Stapp, J. (1975). Ratings of self and peers on sex-role attributes and their relation to self-esteem and conceptions of masculinity and femininity. *Journal of Personality and Social Psychology, 32,* 29–39.

Spence, J. T., & Sawin, L. L. (in press). Images of masculinity and femininity: A reconceptualization. In V. E. O'Leary, R. K. Unger, & B. S. Wallston (Eds.), *Women, gender, and social psychology.* Hillsdale, NJ: Erlbaum.

Terman, L., & Miles, C. (1936). *Sex and personality.* New York: McGraw-Hill.

Thompson, S. K. (1975). Gender labels and early sex role development. *Child Development, 46,* 339–347.

Unger, R. K. (1976). Male is greater than female: The socialization of status inequality. *The Counseling Psychologist, 6,* 2–9.

Unger, R. K. (1978). The politics of gender: A review of relevant literature. In J. Sherman & F. Denmark (Eds.), *Psychology of women: Future directions of research.* New York: Psychological Dimensions.

Zanna, M. P., & Pack, S. J. (1975). On the self-fulfilling nature of apparent sex differences in behavior. *Journal of Experimental Social Psychology, 11,* 583–591.

SUGGESTED READING

Snyder, M., Tanke, E. D., & Berscheid, E. (1977). Social perception and interpersonal behavior: On the self-fulfilling nature of social stereotypes. *Journal of Personality and Social Psychology, 35,* 656–666.

Spence, J. T., Deaux, K., & Helmreich, R. L. (in press). Sex roles in contemporary American society. In G. Lindzey & E. Aronson

(Eds.), *Handbook of social psychology* (3rd ed.). Reading, MA: Addison-Wesley.

Storms, M. (1980). Theories of sex-role identity. *Journal of Personality and Social Psychology, 38,* 783–792.

R. K. UNGER
Montclair State College

ANDROGYNY
OPTIMAL FUNCTIONING
SELF-FULFILLING PROPHECIES
SEXISM

SEXISM

Sexism is defined by David Stang and Lawrence Wrightsman in their *Dictionary of Social Behavior and Social Research Methods* as "any attitude, action, or institutional structure that bases a response to a person on the fact of his or her sex when sex should be irrelevant to the decision. Sexism usually is reflected in discrimination against women purely because of their sex." Personal sexism that reflects individual differences in negative attitudes toward women should be distinguished from societal or institutional sexism that reflects customary attitudes or behaviors that may not stem from an individual's personal biases.

PERSONAL SEXISM

Personal sexism is usually measured by attitude scales. The scale most frequently used currently is the Attitudes Toward Women Scale (AWS) developed by Janet Spence and Robert Helmreich in 1972 and discussed in their book *Masculinity and Femininity.* Some items in the scale derive from the earliest instrument used to measure sexist attitudes published in 1936 by Kirkpatrick. The present brief version of the AWS contains 15 items (reduced from the original 55) and measures attitudes concerning the political, economic, and social equality of women and men.

Researchers have found that women score as more profeminist than men, and that college students of either sex score as more profeminist than their same-sex parent (Spence & Helmreich 1972). Some characteristics associated with negative attitudes toward women have been enumerated by Rhoda Unger in *Female and Male.* First-year female college students have less liberal attitudes than college seniors; women students in business and education are more conservative than those in other fields; self-esteem is lower in males who hold strongly antifeminist views; and so on. Goldberg (1968) notes that negative attitudes toward females seem to exist in males almost universally. However, Brannon (1978) points out that measures of sex prejudice share with measures of race prejudice little evidence of behavioral validity.

Nonverbal behaviors may be more indicative of personal sexism than are more reactive verbal indicators. Henley (1977) enumerates nonverbal behaviors used to connote power and status differences between the sexes, including eye contact, body orientation and interpersonal distance, and touching. Further research reported by Mayo and Henley (1981) indicates that women are more nonverbally adaptive than men and often change their nonverbal behaviors to the level of dominance of their male partner.

SOCIETAL SEXISM

Studies designed to determine that negative attitudes toward women exist as part of a general social reality have been more successful than those attempting to evaluate individual degrees of sexism. Goldberg (1968) showed that women evaluated an identical essay more poorly if a female name was associated with it. Other researchers have demonstrated similar negative biases in the evaluation of works of art, poetry, and professional attainments. Deaux (1976) extensively documents the existence of such biases.

Numerous studies of sex stereotypes indicate that perceptions of males and females can be distinguished by two major clusters of traits. Broverman and her associates (1972) found that typical male traits as perceived by both sexes comprise independence, logic, objectivity, worldliness, and ability in mathematics, science, and business. Typical female traits include awareness of others' feelings, gentleness, and tact. Mental health experts perceived that the characteristics of the mentally healthy male and mentally healthy adult (sex unspecified) were similar, but that the mentally healthy female was more emotional and less mature than the mentally healthy adult. Such sex stereotypes appear to have created a double bind for women—they can be feminine or mature, but not both. Perceptions about males do not involve such contradictory trait prescriptions.

Sources of sex stereotypes appear to be universal. Busby (1975) provides data on more than 100 such studies. Differences found include a larger proportion of males than females in most books and television programs as well as a greater variety of roles available to males. In children's textbooks, boys are portrayed as displaying more aggression, physical exertion, and problem-solving ability than girls (Saario et al., 1973). Subtle forms of sexism may be present even when females are featured. Thus Sternglanz and Serbin (1974) noted that in children's television programs, the female major characters are portrayed as having magical powers of some sort and getting their way by means of indirect methods in contrast to male characters who engage in more direct confrontations.

Sexism in language has been extensively documented. A particularly good resource is that by Thorne and Henley (1975). Studies presented in this book indicate that the English language demeans women by trivializing female gender forms, by labeling female exceptions in occupations or behaviors defined as being in the male domain, and by excluding females, as in the generic use of masculine pronouns when both sexes are included.

Much of the content of differential perceptions about males and females involves competence and achievement. Rosen and Jerdee (1974) find women less likely to be seen as suitable for executive and managerial positions than men with identical qualifications.

It has been estimated by Treiman and Terrell (1975) that most of the difference in the wages between the sexes can be accounted for by sex discrimination. Even when women hold positions equivalent to those of men, they may receive less reward for comparable achievements. Rossi and Calderwood (1973) show that promotions are less closely tied to publications for women in academia than for men.

In sum, sexism exists in a number of forms: as individual attitudes that may be measured either by self-reports or nonverbally; as nonconscious societally based perceptions and attributions that are usually examined as stereotypes, but that actually may take the form of a social reality agreed upon by individuals of both sexes; and as institutionalized practices that stem from differential evaluation of the attainments of women and men and that lead to the occupational segregation of women and their cumulative disadvantage.

REFERENCES

Brannon, R. (1978). Measuring attitudes toward women (and otherwise): A methodological critique. In J. Sherman & F. Denmark (Eds.), *The psychology of women: Future directions of research.* New York: Psychological Dimensions.

Broverman, I. K., Vogel, S. R., Broverman, D. M., Clarkson, F. E., & Rosenkrantz, P. S. (1972). Sex-role stereotypes: A current appraisal. *Journal of Social Issues, 28,* 59–78.

Busby, L. J. (1975 Autumn). Sex-role research on the mass media. *Journal of Communication,* 107–131.

Deaux, K. (1976). *The behavior of women and men.* Monterey, CA: Brooks/Cole.

Goldberg, P. A. (1968, April). Are women prejudiced against women? *Transaction,* 28–30.

Henley, N. M. (1977). *Body politics.* Englewood Cliffs, NJ: Prentice-Hall.

Kirkpatrick, C. (1936). The construction of a belief pattern scale for measuring attitudes toward feminism. *Journal of Social Psychology, 7,* 421–437.

Mayo, C., & Henley, N. M. (Eds.). (1981). *Gender and nonverbal behavior.* New York: Springer-Verlag.

Rosen, B., & Jetdee, T. H. (1974). Influence of sex role stereotypes on personnel decisions. *Journal of Applied Psychology, 59,* 9–14.

Rossi, A. S., & Calderwood, A. (Eds.). (1973). *Academic women on the move.* New York: Russell Sage Foundation.

Saario, T. N., Jacklin, C. N., & Tittle, C. K. (1973). Sex-role stereotyping in the public schools. *Harvard Educational Review, 43,* 386–416.

Spence, J. T., & Helmreich, R. L. (1972). The Attitudes Toward Women Scale: An objective instrument to measure attitudes toward the rights and roles of women in contemporary society. *JSAS Catalog of Selected Documents in Psychology, 2,* 66.

Stang, D. J., & Wrightsman, L. S. (1981). *Dictionary of social behavior and social research methods.* Monterey, CA: Brooks/Cole.

Sternglanz, S. H., & Serbia, L. A. (1974). Sex role stereotyping in children's television programs. *Developmental Psychology, 10,* 710–715.

Thorne, B., & Henley, N. (Eds.). (1975). *Language and sex: Difference and dominance.* Rowley, MA: Newbury House.

Treiman, D. J., & Terrell, K. (1975). Sex and the process of status attainment: A comparison of working women and men. *American Sociological Review, 40,* 174–200.

SUGGESTED READING

Basow, S. A. (1980). *Sex-role stereotypes: Traditions and alternatives.* Monterey, CA: Brooks/Cole.

Brannon, R. (1981). Current methodological issues in paper-and-pencil measuring instruments. *Psychology of Women Quarterly, 5,* 618–627.

Cherry, F., & Deaux, K. (1978). Fear of success versus fear of gender-inappropriate behavior. *Sex Roles, 4,* 97–101.

Lakoff, R. (1975). *Language and woman's place.* New York: Harper Colophon Books.

Laws, J. L. (1975). The psychology of tokenism: An analysis. *Sex Roles, 1,* 51–67.

Laws, J. L. (1978). Work motivation and work behavior of women: New perspectives. In J. Sherman & F. Denmark (Eds.), *The psychology of women: New directions of research.* New York: Psychological Dimensions.

Mednick, M. T. S., Tangri, S. S., & Hoffman, L. W. (Eds.). (1975). *Women and achievement: Social and motivational analysis.* Washington, DC: Hemisphere.

Moulton, J., Robinson, G. M., & Elias, C. (1978). Sex bias in language use: Neutral pronouns that aren't. *American Psychologist, 33,* 1032–1036.

O'Leary, V. E. (1974). Some attitudinal barriers to occupational aspirations in women. *Psychological Bulletin, 81,* 809–826.

Unger, R. K. (1981). Sex as a social reality: Field and laboratory research. *Psychology of Women Quarterly, 5,* 645–653.

Wallston, B. S., & O'Leary, V. E. (1981). Sex and gender make a difference: The differential perceptions of women and men. In L. Wheeler (Ed.), *Review of personality and social psychology* (Vol. 2.) Beverly Hills, CA: Sage.

Weitz, S. (1976). Sex differences in nonverbal communication. *Sex Roles, 2,* 175–184.

R. K. Unger
Montclair State College

ANDROGYNY
PREJUDICE AND DISCRIMINATION

SEXUAL DESIRE

Sexual desire is commonly defined as a wish, need, or drive to seek out or respond to sexual activities, or the pleasurable anticipation of such activities in the future. It is an appetitive state distinct from physiological or subjective genital arousal and sexual activity. The mechanisms underlying sexual desire are not well-known, though it is frequently believed to have both biological and psychological components.

A number of biological factors are likely to play a role in sexual desire, including testosterone, serotonin, dopamine, and the catecholamines. In humans, testosterone is the most widely studied of these to date. It has been repeatedly shown that testosterone supplementation administered to hypogonadal men can restore sexual desire to normal levels. However, testosterone supplementation in nonhypogonadal men has not been consistently shown to increase desire, and the majority of studies assessing women with low desire have not shown testosterone supplementation to be efficacious. Dopamine and serotonin have generally been shown to play a role in the sexual motivation of animals, but very little research in this area has yet been conducted in humans.

It is believed that the psychological components of sexual desire stem from both intrapsychic and interpersonal factors. Social influences also play a role in the expression and experience of sexual desire. The interactions of these elements on the development and manifestation of sexual desire are not clearly understood.

There are currently two disorders associated with sexual desire: Hypoactive Sexual Desire Disorder (HSDD) and Sexual Aversion Disorder (SAD). HSDD is defined as persistently or recurrently deficient or absent sexual fantasies and desire for sexual activity, taking into account factors that affect sexual functioning, such as age and the context of a person's life. To meet HSDD diagnostic criteria, such an absence or deficiency must cause marked distress or interpersonal difficulty. SAD, in contrast, is characterized by persistent or recurrent extreme aversion to, and avoidance of, all (or almost all) genital sexual contact with a sexual partner. As with HSDD, the aversion or avoidance must cause marked distress or interpersonal difficulty. Interestingly, no diagnoses are associated with excessive, or hyperactive, sexual desire.

Current estimates suggest an annual prevalence of disorders of desire of approximately 23 percent in the U.S. (Laumann, Paik, & Rosen, 1999), though some studies indicate that this figure may be significantly higher. The occurrence of desire disorders is believed to be on the rise, and dysfunctions of sexual desire are now the most common presenting problem at sex therapy clinics, occurring in over 50 percent of couples seeking sex therapy (Schover & LoPiccolo, 1982). In the early phase of research in this area, it was estimated that women experienced desire disorders at twice the rate of men, but there is increasing evidence that these rates are equalizing across genders (Kaplan, 1995; Schover & LoPiccolo, 1982), with rates in men rapidly approaching those in women.

Although very little research has been done on disorders of desire in general, the vast majority of research to date has focused on HSDD rather than SAD. HSDD, however, is the subject of much disagreement among researchers, including issues of prevalence, diagnostic criteria, etiology, and treatment methods. Indeed, there are those who argue that the diagnosis itself is merely the pathologization of normal human variation in desire levels (i.e., low desire only becomes a problem when one's partner has a higher level of desire). Such areas of disagreement are exacerbated by the difficulty in accurately measuring levels of sexual desire. In the absence

of a consensus of what constitutes the most salient and measurable aspects of sexual desire (e.g., frequency of sexual behavior, frequency of sexual fantasy, intensity of sexual urges, etc.), researchers frequently are in disagreement as to what aspects of sexual desire are actually being studied.

Nevertheless, research to date indicates that HSDD responds less favorably to treatment than dysfunctions of orgasm or arousal and requires more treatment sessions to achieve positive results. This finding is complicated by the high concurrent prevalence (41%) of other comorbid sexual dysfunctions in patients with HSDD (Segraves & Segraves, 1991). Indeed, in many recurring cases of orgasm or arousal dysfunction, relapse may be due to an underlying desire disorder that was not successfully treated.

Major factors contributing to the development of HSDD are marital conflict, current or past depression, religious orthodoxy, and use of oral contraceptives. A number of commonly used medications (e.g., antidepressants, anticonvulsants, and antihypertensive agents) are also associated with a decrease in sexual desire (for a more complete listing of medications associated with decreased desire, see Finger, Lund, & Slagle, 1997).

A number of psychological treatments for low sexual desire have been proposed and evaluated to date. Such treatments include modified versions of standard sex therapy (e.g., Masters and Johnson's sensate focus treatment), marital therapy, cognitive-behavioral therapy, and orgasm consistency training. All of these treatments have shown some degree of success, though the characteristics likely to predict who will respond to which treatment have not been fully explored, and overall response in several of these studies is lower than for many other disorders. In addition, a number of medications have been evaluated in the treatment of low sexual desire, including testosterone, bupropion, diazepam, and yohimbine. Of these, only testosterone has been evaluated in multiple studies, and, as noted above, has only been shown to be clearly efficacious in improving desire in hypogonadal men. The sole study evaluating bupropion in the treatment of low sexual desire showed promising results (Crenshaw, Goldberg, & Stern, 1987), but the studies evaluating yohimbine (Piletz et al., 1998) and diazepam (Carney, Bancroft, & Mathews, 1978) did not. Future research is expected to expand the range of pharmacological and psychological options available for the treatment of disorders of desire.

REFERENCES

Carney, A., Bancroft, J., & Mathews, A. (1978). Combination of hormonal and psychological treatment for female sexual unresponsiveness: A comparative study. *British Journal of Psychiatry, 133,* 339–346.

Crenshaw, T. L., Goldberg, J. P., & Stern, W. C. (1987). Pharmacologic modification of psychosexual dysfunction. *Journal of Sex & Marital Therapy, 13,* 239–252.

Finger, W. W., Lund, M., & Slagle, M. A. (1997). Medications that may contribute to sexual disorders: A guide to assessment and treatment in family practice. *Journal of Family Practice, 44,* 33–43.

Kaplan, H. S. (1995). *The sexual desire disorders: Dysfunctional regulation of sexual motivation.* New York: Brunner/Mazel.

Laumann, E. O., Paik, A., & Rosen, R. C. (1999). Sexual dysfunction in the United States: Prevalence and predictors. *JAMA: The Journal of the American Medical Association, 281,* 537–544.

Piletz, J. E., Segraves, K. B., Feng, Y. Z., MacGuire, E., Dunger, B., & Halaris, A. (1998). Plasma MHPG response to yohimbine treatment in women with hypoactive sexual desire. *Journal of Sex & Marital Therapy, 24,* 43–54.

Schover, L. R., & LoPiccolo, J. (1982). Treatment effectiveness for dysfunctions of sexual desire. *Journal of Sex & Marital Therapy, 8,* 179–197.

Segraves, K. B., & Segraves, R. T. (1991). Hypoactive sexual desire disorder: Prevalence and comorbidity in 906 subjects. *Journal of Sex & Marital Therapy, 17,* 55–58.

SUGGESTED READING

Beck, J. G. (1995). Hypoactive sexual desire disorder: An overview. *Journal of Consulting and Clinical Psychology, 63,* 919–927.

Leiblum, S. R., & Rosen, R. C. (Eds.). (1988). *Sexual desire disorders.* New York: Guilford.

T. D. GIARGIARI
University of Colorado, Boulder

SEXUAL DEVELOPMENT

According to Sigmund Freud's psychoanalytic theory of personality, sexuality begins in infancy (Freud, 1920/1969). The development of sexuality is a major part of the development of personality. According to Freud, the individual passes through several psychosexual stages that include oral, anal, phallic, latency, and genital. These stages reflect the primary areas of focus for the developing child. For instance, in the early stages of infancy (the oral stage), the newborn receives much stimulation orally from the mouth in feeding. During the anal stage, the child derives pleasure from the expulsion and retention of feces, thus learning control/autonomy. The phallic stage, the name of which reveals Freud's gender bias, is the period in which the child's emerging awareness of his or her sexuality focuses on the genitals. The latency stage of development (roughly between 5 and 12 years of age) reflects a resting period in which the child focuses much attention on peers of the same sex. The genital stage of development occurs with the child's full sexual potential, the onset of puberty.

Behaviorally, puberty marks the onset of human genital sexuality. Puberty begins between approximately 10 and 14 years of age for females and 12 and 16 years of age for males. Hypothalamic stimulation of the pituitary gland causes secretion of pituitary hormones, including those directed to the gonads (gonadotropic) and to the adrenal glands (adrenocorticotropic). These glands, in turn, secrete the hormones responsible for the physical changes at puberty: a rapid increase in growth, the development of secondary sex characteristics, and the development of the reproductive capacity. In addition, the individual experiences an increase in sexual awareness and a heightening of sexual drives. Sexual activity (including kissing, petting, and even intercourse) is a frequent component of the adolescent experience.

Although intercourse is most often considered in the context of marriage, the incidence of premarital coitus has increased over the years. In fact, by 1982 almost two-thirds of women and three-fourths of men approved of sexual intercourse if there is affection for the other partner in a committed relationship (Walsh, Ganza, & Finefield, 1983). Recent reports concerning frequency of sex in adulthood have revealed that the pattern of having sex a few times per month among adults is similar for those who are cohabiting (36% of men, 35% of women) and for those who are married (43% of men, 47% of women) (Michael, Gagnon, Laumann, & Kolata, 1994). Although one's sexual development is individual, the choice to have sex with a partner is guided by our culture. In fact, it has been shown that sexual practices are embedded in a social context where religion, education, age, and racial/ethnic backgrounds strongly influence one's choice of a partner (Laumann, Gagnon, Michael, & Michaels, 1994). Therefore, sexual development, like other areas of human development, cannot be understood outside the social world.

REFERENCES

Freud, S. (1969). *A general introduction to psychoanalysis.* New York: Pocket Books. (Original work published in 1920).

Laumann, E. O., Gagnon, J. H., Michael, R. T., & Michaels, S. (1994). *The social organization of sexuality: Sexual practices in the United States.* Chicago: The University of Chicago Press.

Michael, R. T., Gagnon, J. H., Laumann, E. O., & Kolata, G. (1994). *Sex in America: A definitive study.* Boston: Little, Brown.

Walsh, R., Ganza, W., & Finefield, T. (1983, April). *A fifteen year study about sexual permissiveness.* Paper presented at the meeting of the Midwest Sociological Society, Kansas City, MO.

J. P. MCKINNEY
*Professor emeritus, Dept. of Psychology,
Michigan State University*

K. MCKINNEY
*Asst. Professor, Health Promotion and Human Development,
University of Wisconsin–Stevens Point*

SEXUAL DEVIATIONS

Sexual deviations, or *paraphilias,* are psychosexual disorders characterized by sexual arousal in response to objects or situations that are not part of normative sexual arousal-activity patterns and that in varying degrees may interfere with capacity for reciprocal affectionate sexual activity (*Diagnostic and Statistical Manual of Mental Disorders*). In former nosologies, these disorders were termed "sexual deviations," but with the 1980 publication of the third edition of the American Psychiatric Association's *Diagnostic and Sta-*

tistical Manual of Mental Disorders (DSM-III), the term paraphilia was introduced to cover these disorders. This term simply emphasizes that the deviation (para) is in that to which the individual is attracted (philia). It encompasses a number and variety of sexual behaviors which, at this time, are sufficiently discrepant from society's norms and standards concerning sexually acceptable behavior as to be judged "deviant."

In the DSM-III classification, paraphilias are of several types: (a) preference for use of a nonhuman object for sexual arousal (e.g., fetishism, in which the person may become sexually excited by the thought of or by handling female underclothing); and (b) repetitive sexual activity with persons involving real or simulated suffering or humiliation (e.g., sexual sadism, in which the individual is sexually excited by inflicting suffering upon the partner); and (c) repetitive sexual activity with nonconsenting partners (e.g., voyeurism, in which a man derives sexual satisfaction from looking at unsuspecting women who are either naked, undressing, or engaging in sexual activity).

Traces of paraphilias are commonly found in the realm of normal sexuality. For example, many a man derives sexual pleasure from gazing upon the naked body of his female sexual partner. But such men do not necessarily qualify as voyeurs. In paraphilias, the activity in question (e.g., in this case, looking or peeping) moves from a peripheral to a central role in producing sexual excitement and satisfaction. That is, in voyeurism, the act of looking at the woman displaces direct sexual activity with the woman herself as the focal point of sexual satisfaction. Thus the many individuals who may be somewhat aroused by female underclothing, occasionally entertain mild sadistic fantasies, or derive pleasure from looking at nude women are by no means paraphiliacs. It is only when such activities become the focal point of sexual gratification, and thereby displace direct sexual behavior with a consenting adult partner, that paraphilias may be said to exist.

The causes of paraphilias are seen as psychogenic rather than biogenic, and hence depend very much upon the paradigm one adopts within psychopathology. For example, within the psychoanalytic paradigm, these disorders are viewed as a consequence of aberrations occurring during psychosexual development in early childhood; in the behavioristic paradigm, they are seen as unadaptive sexual behavior resulting from learning and conditioning experiences; in the humanistic paradigm, they presumably represent particular outgrowths of each individual's unique, albeit distorted, subjective world of experience.

TYPES OF PARAPHILIAS

What follows is a brief description of each recognized paraphilia, following closely the DSM-III categorization and description system (see Table 1 for a brief overview).

Fetishism

Fetishism is essentially characterized by the use of nonliving objects or, less frequently, parts of the human body as the preferred or exclusive method of producing sexual excitement. These objects or body parts (called fetishes) are essential for sexual satisfaction in the fetishist and constitute the focal point of sexual arousal.

Table 1   The Paraphilias and Their Defining Characteristics

Paraphilia	Defining Characteristics
Fetishism	Use of nonliving objects or parts of the body as the preferred or exclusive method of producing sexual excitement.
Transvestism	Recurrent and persistent cross-dressing by a heterosexual male for the purpose of his own sexual arousal.
Zoophilia	Use of animals as a repeatedly preferred or exclusive method of achieving one's own sexual excitement.
Pedophilia	Preference for repetitive sexual activity with children.
Exhibitionism	Repetitive acts of exposing one's genitals to an unsuspecting stranger for the purpose of producing one's own sexual excitement.
Voyeurism	Repetitive seeking out of situations in which one looks ("peeps") at unsuspecting women who are either naked, undressing, or engaging in sexual activity.
Sexual sadism	Infliction of physical or psychological suffering on another person as a method of stimulating one's own sexual excitement and orgasm.
Sexual masochism	Production of sexual excitement through one's own suffering.
Atypical paraphilia	Paraphilias that cannot be classified in any of the other categories.

Fetishists are almost always males, and fetishistic objects exclude any that may be sexually stimulating because of their physical properties, such as vibrators. The objects involved in fetishism can be quite varied and commonly include women's underpants, shoes, stockings, and gloves; parts of the body that typically become fetishes include breasts, hair, ears, hands, and feet.

Transvestism

In the psychosexual disorder of transvestism, there is recurrent and persistent cross-dressing by a heterosexual male for the purposes of his own sexual arousal. That is, the man achieves sexual satisfaction simply by putting on women's clothing, although masturbation (and heterosexual intercourse) is often engaged in once the individual is attired in female garb. The gamut of transvestism extends from secretive, solitary wearing of female clothes, through sexually relating to one's spouse while so attired, to appearing in public cross-dressed and accompanied by extensive involvement in a like-minded subgroup.

Zoophilia

Zoophilia is marked by the use of animals as the repeatedly preferred or exclusive method of achieving sexual excitement. The animal may serve as the object of sexual intercourse or may be trained sexually to excite the paraphiliac by means of licking or rubbing. Typically, the preferred animal is one with which the person had contact during childhood years, such as a household pet or farm animal. In this disorder, the animal is preferred regardless of other available sexual outlets.

Pedophilia

Pedophilia (from the Greek, meaning "love of children") is essentially characterized by a preference for repetitive sexual activity with children. Such activity may vary in intensity, and includes stroking the child's hair, holding the child close while covertly masturbating, manipulating the child's genitals, encouraging the child to manipulate his, and, less frequently, attempting intromission. Any age youngster up to puberty may be the object of pedophiliac attention, with force being seldom employed.

Exhibitionism

Exhibitionism is characterized by repetitive acts of exposing one's genitals to an unsuspecting stranger for the purpose of producing one's own sexual excitement. In a typical instance, the exhibitionist (virtually always a male) drives or walks in front of a passing woman and exposes his genitals, sometimes accompanied by masturbatory or other suggestive gestures. Usually, but not always, he has an erection and, typically, as soon as the woman has seen him and registered a reaction, he flees the scene. Normally no further contact with the woman is sought.

Voyeurism

Voyeurism is fundamentally characterized by the repetitive seeking out of situations in which the individual looks ("peeps") at unsuspecting women who are either naked, undressing, or engaging in sexual activity. Voyeurs (popularly known as "peeping Toms") are almost always males and derive intense sexual excitement from their peeping behavior. They usually either masturbate to orgasm during the voyeuristic activity or immediately afterward in response to the scene they have witnessed. Further sexual contact with the observed woman (usually a stranger) is rarely sought, and most voyeurs, like exhibitionists, are not physically dangerous.

Sexual Sadism

The widely used term *sadism* derives from the infamous Marquis de Sade (1740–1814), who, for erotic purposes, perpetrated such cruelty on his victims that he eventually was committed as insane. Today the term is practically synonymous with cruelty in general. In a more restricted sense, however, sexual sadism refers to a disorder essentially characterized by the infliction of physical or psychological suffering on another person as a method of stimulating one's own sexual excitement and orgasm. Moreover, persistent sexually stimulating fantasies of this nature are also experienced by the individual. In some instances, the sadistic activities function as stimulants in building up to sexual relations, while in others the sadistic practices alone are sufficient for complete sexual gratification. While the partners of sadists may be consenting or nonconsenting, the majority of sadistic behavior seems to occur in a relationship with a willing partner.

Sexual Masochism

The essential feature of sexual masochism is sexual excitement produced in an individual by his or her own suffering. That is, in this disorder, the preferred or exclusive means of achieving sexual gratification is being humiliated, bound, beaten, whipped, or otherwise made to suffer. Such situations may be sufficient in themselves for full sexual gratification or they may be a necessary prelude to direct sexual behavior, such as intercourse. Like sadism, then, masochism essentially involves suffering; unlike sadism, the suffering here is inflicted upon oneself rather than on others. And also like sadism, masochism derives its name from a historical figure—Leopold V. Sacher-Masoch (1826–1895), an Austrian novelist whose characters were greatly preoccupied with the sexual pleasure of pain.

Atypical Paraphilia

In *DSM-III,* atypical paraphilia is a residual category for individuals with paraphilias that cannot be classified in any of the other categories. These disorders include coprophilia (feces), frotteurism (rubbing), kiismaphilia (enema), mysophilia (filth), necrophilia (corpse), telephone scatologia (lewdness), and urophilia (urine).

D. J. ZIEGLER
Villanova University

CHILD ABUSE
PEDOPHILIA
SEXUAL DEVELOPMENT

SEXUAL INTERCOURSE, HUMAN

Human sexual intercourse, or coitus, is one of the most common sexual outlets among adults. While it is usually considered in the context of marriage, premarital and extramarital intercourse are also widely practiced. Adolescents appear to be engaging in sexual intercourse more frequently than was true in the past. Although cultures differ widely in their acceptance of premarital intercourse, traditionally U.S. customs have been more restrictive than most.

Sexual intercourse generally refers to penile penetration of the vagina, the most common opposite-gendered partnered sexual expression practiced in the United States. In a large national survey study of over three thousand participants, Laumann, Gagnon, Michael, and Michaels (1994) found that 95 percent of men and 97 percent of women report that they have experienced vaginal intercourse. Other sexual techniques with opposite-gender partners include both anal intercourse and oral sex, both cunnilingus (male mouth on female genitalia) and fellatio (female mouth on male genitalia). These sexual expressions are far less common, however, than vaginal intercourse both in terms of life incidence and most recent experience.

In practice, North American sexual customs have changed from a double standard in which sexual intercourse was permissible for males but not for females, to a standard of permissiveness with affection. Many adolescents and adults, however, still adhere to a standard of abstinence until marriage as an ideal. Despite that, the age at first intercourse has steadily declined over the past forty years, according to Laumann, Gagnon, Michael, and Michaels (1994).

Cultures differ, too, in the preferred manner of experiencing intercourse. While American partners prefer a face-to-face man-above position, this practice is by no means a universal preference. In *Human Sexuality* (1967), McCary noted that while 70 percent of

American males had never copulated in any other manner, this technique was relatively rare in other cultures. As do many authors of texts and manuals on human sexuality, McCary describes alternative patterns with their respective physiological and psychological advantages.

REFERENCES

Laumann, E. O., Gagnon, J. H., Michael, R. T., & Michaels, S. (1994). *The social organzation of sexuality: Sexual practices in the United States.* Chicago: University of Chicago Press.

McCary, J. L. (1973/1967). *Human sexuality.* New York: Van Nostrand.

J. P. MᴄKɪɴɴᴇʏ
Michigan State University

SEX ROLE DEVELOPMENT

SEXUALITY: ORIENTATION AND IDENTITY

DEFINITIONS

Sexual orientation refers to the erotic/love/affectional partners a person prefers. The terms *heterosexual, homosexual,* and *bisexual* are better used as adjectives, not nouns, and are better applied to behaviors, not people. In lay usage, however, one often speaks of a person as a homosexual or heterosexual, and indeed people often refer to themselves the same way. Such causal usage often links together those whose regular sexual partners are of the same sex with those whose same-sex encounters are rare in comparison with heterosexual contacts. The term *homosexual* is best reserved for those whose sexual activities are exclusively or almost exclusively with members of the same sex, the term *heterosexual* for those whose erotic companions are always or almost always with the opposite sex, and the term *bisexual* for those with more or less regular sexual activities with members of either sex.

Lately Diamond encourages the terms *androphilic, gynecophilic,* and *ambiphilic* be used to describe the sexual/erotic partners one prefers (andro = male; gyneco = female; ambi = both; philic = to love). The use of such terms obviates the need to define specifically the sex of the subject and focuses on the sex of the desired partner. This usage is particularly advantageous when discussing transsexuals or intersexed individuals (see below). These latter terms also do not carry the social weight of the former ones.

Sexual identity refers to the way one views one's self as a male or female. This inner conviction of identification may or may not mirror the outward physical appearance, the gender role society imposes, or the role one develops and prefers. These distinctions are crucial particularly in regard to transsexualism and the intersexed. In the real world, the *transsexual,* as are others, is identified in terms of overt sexual anatomy. Transsexuals are reared as society views them. Nevertheless, the self-image of transsexuals is of the opposite sex. Their physical realities are in conflict with their

mind's image (Benjamin, 1966; Docter, 1990). An *intersexed* individual is one born with physical characteristics that are both male and female (e.g., an individual can be XX in chromosomal configuration but have a male-like phallus; another individual might be XY in chromosomal makeup and have a vagina). Intersexed individuals might identify as female, male, or intersexed (Diamond, 1999).

One's sexual identity is an aspect of life tangentially related to their sexual orientation. Any individual even if transsexual or intersexed may be androphilic, gynecophilic, or ambiphilic in inclination. In everyday terms, anybody may "identify" themselves as homosexual or see their "identity" as heterosexual. This use of the terms is an affiliative sense: It is as if one might identify as an American or a Unitarian.

One's *gender, gender pattern,* or *gender role* is different, although related, to the concept of orientation and identity. Gender and gender role refer to society's idea of how boys and girls or men and women are expected to behave and should be treated. A *sex role* is the acting out of one's biological predisposition or the manifestation of society's imposition. The terms *boys* and *girls* and *men* and *women* are social terms; the terms *male* and *female* are biological terms. Gender has everything to do with the society in which one lives and may or may not have much to do with biology (Gagnon & Simon, 1973). Males, for instance, may live as women and females may live as men: A male may be reared as a boy but grow to live as a woman and vice-versa. For most people their identity, orientation, and gender are in concert. The typical male sees himself as such, has masculine behavior patterns (a combination of biologically and socially determined behaviors), is treated as a male by society, and prefers to have sexual interactions with females. The typical female sees herself as such, has feminine behavior patterns (also a combination of biologically and socially determined behaviors), is treated as a female by society, and prefers to have sexual interactions with males. Variations occur when an individual prefers erotic relations with one of the same sex or when a male sees himself as a female (male transsexual), a female sees herself as a male (female transsexual), or an intersexed individual elects to follow aspects of both male and female life.

It is thus obvious that one's sexual profile as a male or female or man or woman is more than how one "identifies" or acts in public. At least five components are needed to adequately describe a person in sex and gender. The mnemonic for recalling these is PRIMO: gender *P*atterns, *O*rientation, and *I*dentity have been discussed. *M*echanisms are inherent physiological factors that structure significant features of erotic life. Well-known and sexually obvious mechanisms are male penile erection and female lubrication as functions of erotic arousal. Male ejaculation is another obvious distinctive mechanism. *R*eproduction, both in its basic physiology and all its social and cultural features, is another main component of sexuality to be considered.

A typical heterosexual male sees himself as a male, lives as a male, enjoys his penis, and prefers erotic relations with a female. A homosexual male also sees himself as a male, lives as a male, and also enjoys his penis, but prefers to have erotic relations with another male. In contrast, the usual male transsexual sees himself as a female, prefers to live as a woman, wants to have his penis removed and replaced with a vulva and vagina, and wants to have breasts. Usually, but not always, he will be androphilic and view this as a heterosexual encounter because he sees himself as a female. No male homosexual would want to have his penis removed and replaced with a vagina: This, however, is the frequent desire of the male transsexual. For a female transsexual the converse is true. Although due to surgical or other difficulties she may not always opt to have a penis and scrotum constructed to replace her vagina and labia, she usually wants her breasts removed and her periods to cease, because they are constant and visible reminders of what she thinks she is not. Intersexed individuals are of such great variety that no consistent description would hold for all.

Transvestitism is a related phenomenon. People who enjoy dressing in the clothing of the opposite sex are broadly termed transvestites or cross-dressers (TVs or CDs). The large majority of transvestites are male and heterosexual. If they are androphilic they are usually called drag queens. The motivation behind such cross-dressing behavior is varied. For some there is erotic satisfaction; for others cross-dressing is an expression of a personality component comfortable in the clothes of the opposite sex. For some it is a response to a compulsion neither they nor science understand. The majority of homosexuals do not enjoy cross-dressing. Transsexuals cross-dress because it is in keeping with movement toward living in the sex they feel is them. Individuals that are primarily transvestites often express feelings of temporarily exchanging gender identity when cross-dressed (Docter, 1990).

To this lexicon a relatively new term has come into use: *transgender*. A transgendered individual is one that sees gender as being either constructed or inborn but nevertheless open in manifestation. Many transgendered persons eschew any strict male-female dichotomy and, in their own lives, mix characteristics that are most often considered both male and female.

These complexities are much more common than generally believed because most such individuals tend to live in "private closets." There is probably more variation in sexual ideas and actions than in any other set of human behaviors. Because these combinations are usually private they arouse neither comment nor criticism. When these combinations appear in public they often provoke social concern or curiosity.

NUMBERS

The prevalence of all these behaviors or types is in dispute. Transsexualism is accepted as rare with rough estimates of 1 in 25,000 to 50,000 (Docter, 1990), with male to female transsexuals outnumbering 2 to 1 to 5 to 1 those who go from female to male. Intersexed individuals are much more common, perhaps numbering some 1 in 100 to 200 with those born with ambiguous genitalia numbering about 1 in 1,000 to 2,000. While their numbers are larger, intersexed individuals are much more hidden in society. Most cultures recognize that it is more advantageous in status, economics, and other ways to be a man and, therefore, more readily accept a desire to change from female to male. People do not as easily understand the reverse: males wanting to be female or having individuals choose to live as intersexed or transgendered.

Contention surrounds estimates of the population of homosex-

ually active individuals. References to 10% of any country's males as homosexual are common and frequent. They are, however, not accurate (Diamond, 1993). This percentage is a rough extrapolation from the original work of Kinsey and colleagues (Kinsey, Pomeroy, & Martin, 1948; Kinsey, Pomeroy, Martin, & Gebhard, 1953). Unfortunately, these studies were not based on random samples. Later, more representative samples from the United States, Britain, the Netherlands, France, Japan, Thailand, and elsewhere became available. Considering consistent patterns of sexual activity based only on erotic attraction, 5% is a closer approximation to the proportion of males exclusively or nearly exclusively homosexual. Ambisexual males seem to account for no more than an additional 3% to 4% of the general population. For females these figures, in turn, are to be halved (Diamond, 1993).

Kinsey, to describe accurately people's actions, devised a 7-point scale (0 to 6). Individuals whose behaviors were exclusively homosexual were classified as 6 or nearly so as 5. Those exclusively heterosexual were classified as 0 and those nearly so 1. Intergrades were rated accordingly so that an individual with the same proportion of same-sex and opposite-sex encounters would be listed as a 3 (Kinsey et al., 1948). Recognizing that people may wish one thing and do another, he simultaneously recorded people's orientation within their fantasies. A married woman exclusively having sex with her husband might be imagining she is with a female. A prisoner can have a homosexual encounter while fantasizing a heterosexual event. Kinsey and colleagues would average behavior and fantasy scores. Transsexual (Benjamin, 1966) and transvestite (Docter, 1990) behaviors also have been graded to reflect better the many types of individuals linked under these broad categories.

This discussion of population percentages and sexual activities, while of scientific import, also has sociopolitical implications. Some gay activists and homophobes assume that anyone who has engaged in any homosexual activity ought be counted as homosexual. Bisexuals are often seen as fence-sitters who, for different reasons, would prefer not being identified as homosexual. Groups on both sides of this fence see the numbers as politically meaningful, abhorring the gray areas. These percentages have epidemiological and political implications. They affect the laws societies will enforce; social or medical issues like AIDS research and treatment; and whether openly gay individuals will be accepted in politics or the military.

SUBCULTURES

The term homosexual refers to private behavior; the term *gay* refers to public behavior and association with a subculture. Many homosexually oriented individuals are open about their sexual preferences and often are identified by various mannerisms and activities. These observable traits may be effeminate ones by males or masculine ones by females. These may be natural expressions of self or part of highly formalized codes that signal group identity. Many of the social cues used to signal erotic interest are the same for homosexuals and heterosexuals (e.g., eye contact; use of double entendres). Yet, for male and female homosexuals moving in a primarily heterosexual (straight) world, certain codes are useful: subtle uses of voice tone, stance, mannerisms, and code words, and frequenting known contact places such as gay bars, bath houses, or park areas.

The visibility and social acceptance of homosexual activity has varied with time and place. There was probably more visibility and acceptance of a gay lifestyle and homosexuality in the West in the 1990s than ever before. There is no evidence, however, that same-sex behavior is any more or less prevalent than in the past. Transsexuality became more visible as surgical techniques become increasingly available; transsexual people could turn wish to reality. Intersexuality has only in the last half dozen years or so opened up as a publically recognized phenomenon.

Ambisexual behavior too has come to be more openly discussed in the 1990s than in the past. There is again no evidence that it is any more prevalent than at any other prior era. Bisexuals more often congregate with homosexuals than heterosexuals but see themselves, and might well be considered, in a category of their own. As lesbians have done before them, they call for recognition as separate from homosexuals in general, with particular group needs and interests.

Women who prefer same-sex erotic and love activities exclusively or occasionally used to be called "romantic friends" in Victorian times. Even more so than males, they were a secret minority in the West whose visibility only became public after World War II. Into the 1960s they were lumped with males as "female homosexuals" or "female gays." Later, for political reasons they preferred to be called lesbians, because it gave them identity as a group. While many common needs exist among male and female homosexuals, lesbians have some special needs. In particular, they feel most strongly about not being stereotyped. As with individuals of any other orientation or identity, they can be feminine or macho, conservative or liberal, devout or atheist, uninterested in orgasm or orgasm-driven, promiscuous or monogamous, in the closet or out of it, and attractive or plain. Their motivations or reasons for identifying with the lesbian community are often broader than those for male homosexuals. Some women will engage in same-sex activity for (feminist) political reasons, while comparable activity is nonexistent among males.

In any culture, clothes are symbols of maleness or femaleness and mark affiliation or separateness. Clothes serve in obvious ways to keep the genders distinct and readily identifiable. There is demonstrably a great deal of psychic and social investment in clothing and many people are disturbed that others do not keep inviolate the clothes, and thus group identity, that society prefers. For children younger than six, or somewhat older, it is often clothing (or hair style or occupation) rather than genitals which determines their understanding of gender and serves as their means of identifying man from woman (Goldman & Goldman, 1982).

ROOTS OF SEXUAL BEHAVIOR

The interacting forces that lead to any type of behavior are not always clear. Why do some find it easy to follow social standards and indoctrinations while others find it difficult? No one is certain why a majority of individuals are heterosexual and a minority are homosexual. Most clues, however, point to genetic and endocrine forces interacting with social training. These biological factors set

a bias, a predisposition, with which the individual meets society. This, as with an individual's body characteristics, in turn has an effect on sexual orientation, identity, and sexual behavior (Diamond, 1965, 1976, 1979). Not everyone, however, sees biology as playing so strong a role (Gagnon & Simon, 1973; Reiss, 1986).

The strongest evidence that sexual orientation has a genetic bias, until recently, comes from studies of human families and twins. The classical studies in this area were done in the 1950s by Kallmann working with 40 monozygotic and 45 dizygotic male twin pairs in which at least one of the twins in each pair, at the onset of the study, admitted to homosexual behavior. Among these twins Kallmann found, without exception, that if one of the identical (monozygotic) twins was homosexual so too was his brother. Among the nonidentical (dizygotic) brothers, on the other hand, the twins were essentially similar to the general male population relative to sexual preference. Kallmann also found that if one member of a monozygotic twin pair of brothers rated a five or six on the Kinsey scale, then the chance that his brother also rated five or six was better than 90%. Kallmann reported that if the brothers differed in rating it was usually only within one or two points on the Kinsey scale.

Kallmann's work was not easily accepted. The mood of the 1950s and 1960s preferred to view human behavior as a matter of social construction or free will rather than biological predisposition. Furthermore, the timing of Kallmann's work competed with that of Kinsey, who thought sexual orientation a product of upbringing or social situation. The fact that Kallmann's numbers seemed to come out so cleanly also encouraged skepticism. A slew of studies soon followed that reported monozygotic twins not concordant for homosexuality (Puterbaugh, 1990), and theories that held to a genetic component to homosexuality lost support. Masters and Johnson also argued that homosexuality was of social rather than biologic origin.

This situation essentially lasted until the 1980s. Subsequent studies, however, strongly support a major biological component to sexual orientation. In one set of studies, Pillard and colleagues examined 186 families in which at least one member was openly homosexual. A set of heterosexual "index" individuals were controls. The investigators then inquired of the sexual orientation of all siblings. Their basic finding was that if a family contained one son who was homosexual, 20% to 25% of his brothers would also be homosexual. If an index brother was heterosexual, the chance of other brothers being homosexual was only 4% to 6%. Eckert and colleagues reported similar findings among six pairs of monozygotic twins reared apart in which at least one member of each pair was homosexually active. A newer report by Bailey and Pillard most strongly supported their original findings. This study of 110 pairs of twins found that 52% of identical twin brothers of self-identified homosexual men were also homosexual, compared with 22% of fraternal twins, compared with 11% of unrelated adoptive brothers. Findings of Whitam, Diamond, and Martin found similarly among 61 sets of twins a concordance of approximately 65% for identical male twins and 30% for fraternal twins. Although the figures do not match those of Bailey and Pillard, they indicate that genetic makeup is a large component of sexual orientation. There also was a high concordance for homosexuality among female respondents. When the twins were discordant, however, the divergence in Kinsey-scale score was usually large. One might be a Kinsey-six while the other was a Kinsey-zero. The reasons for the difference in identical twins, who share the same set of genes and upbringing, are not yet understood. Other interacting factors must be involved.

A new avenue of family studies is being followed by Blanchard and colleagues. This research basically finds a definite birth order effect relative to male homosexuality. Younger brothers are much more likely to be androphilic than older brothers. Some type of immune response within the mother during pregnancy with later male children, as with an Rh phenomenon, has been hypothesized (Blanchard, 1997). The (1994) work of Hall and Kimura also deserves mention. These investigators found that fingerprint patterns significantly differ between populations of androphilic and gynecophilic males. Since these patterns are formed before birth, social forces are not involved. Other genetic immune system and pheromonal processes are also seen as possibly influencing sexual orientation (Diamond, Binstock, & Kohl, 1996).

A great deal of attention has turned to brain and gene studies. Several research reports from the Netherlands and the United States indicate certain brain structures differ between heterosexuals and homosexuals. The Dutch researchers Swaab and Hofman, in 1990, found that a region of the brain called the suprachiasmatic nucleus is much larger in androphilic than gynecophilic males, and LeVay in the United States found a region of the hypothalamus (interstitial nucleus of the anterior hypothalamus #3) smaller in androphilic males and women than in gynecophilic males (LeVay, 1991, 1993). Similar male-female differences have been found in the work of Byne and colleagues. The brains of lesbians are yet to be examined. Others also (Collaer & Hines, 1995) have found different areas of the brain differ between men and women and that these differences are associated with nonreproductive as well as reproductive functions. Such structural differences may yet be found to differ among heterosexual and homosexual individuals.

Critics of such sex research say scientists seldom look for causes or unique features of heterosexuality. For most researchers, however, homosexuality and heterosexuality are two sides of the same coin; to learn the developmental forces of one set of behaviors helps understanding of the other. The following studies document instances in which biological biases for heterosexuality and maleness override the social conditioning of rearing males as girls.

In one spectacular case now known worldwide in the scientific literature as the John/Joan case, a male infant whose penis had been accidentally burned off was raised as a girl (pseudonym Joan) from the age of 17 months on. Despite all efforts by family and therapists to have Joan adjust to this situation, she rebelled. As soon as this child (David Reimer) was able, he switched to living as a male (pseudonym John) and sought reconstructive surgery to remove his breasts—induced by physician-administered estrogen—and fashion a penis. Subsequently John identified and developed as a gynecophilic male with strong manly mannerisms and attitudes. He now lives as a married male with adopted children (Colapinto, 2000; Diamond & Sigmundson, 1997).

The work of Imperato-McGinley and colleagues also is instructive in this regard (Imperato-McGinley, Peterson, Gautier, &

Sturla, 1979). Among a group of natives in the Dominican Republic it was found, due to a genetic quirk (an enzyme deficiency), that some males were born without penises. Their parents thought these offspring to be girls and raised them accordingly. However, this same genetic condition resulted in the penis and scrotum developing by puberty. Despite having been raised as females from birth, 17 of 18 of these teenagers then switched to life as heterosexual males. Upbringing as girls destined to marry males had little influence on their adult orientation or sexual identity. Rösler and colleagues (Rösler, 1992) found similarly with male individuals born in Gaza and raised as females; and Diamond has found similarly. Other investigators (e.g., Mendez in Mexico; Mendonca in Brazil) found somewhat the same with males born with female phenotype and reared as such. These cases add grist to the argument that sexual orientation and identity are more likely matters of prenatally induced predisposition than social upbringing alone. For these latter cases, some argue that the parents of these children knew in advance they would be switching their children's gender so these subjects do not constitute a true test of the nature–nurture issue. This is certainly true for some of the latter cases studied, but it does not hold for the early cases before their association with modern medicine.

SOCIAL AND LEGAL INFLUENCES

Actually, what is evidenced is not a nature–nurture dichotomy but rather an interaction of both sets of forces. The rules, codes, traditions, and ideals of any society—the environment—also interact to structure an individual's behavior. These influences modify and work with or against any inherent behavioral bias. It is probably safe to say that acceptance of the idea of interaction effects is now generally the case among the scientific community world wide (Diamond, 1965, 1979, 1993a; Diamond, Binstock, & Kohl, 1996; Ellis & Ebertz, 1997, 1998; Unger & Crawford, 1992).

A fundamental question arises. If rearing has only minor influence in structuring a person's identity, how do individuals come to "know" who and what they are? Diamond contends they do so by comparing themselves with others. All children have in common that they compare themselves with others as they grow up (Goldman & Goldman, 1982). In doing so, they consciously and unconsciously analyze their inner feelings and behavior preferences in comparison with those of their peers. One of the most crucial analyses everyone makes is that of "who am I like and who am I unlike." Consider three different scenarios: typical development; development of a transsexual individual; development of an intersexed person. Typical children see themselves as like other boys or girls; their interests and overall behaviors are similar; and they easily come to accept their appropriate gender labels. They have no cause to question their identities. Their behaviors and interests have nothing to do with their genitals. Children may be aware of genital differences but usually do not understand that they are crucial for classification of gender: Hair length, clothing, and behaviors are the child's typical clues to who is a male and who female (Goldman & Goldman, 1982).

The transsexual male similarly compares himself with others and assesses himself to be different from other boys. At first this is puzzling, but at a basic level he comes to recognize that his interests are not like those of male peers. Without understanding where or how these feelings develop, he knows he is unlike other boys and sees himself as a "non-boy"; some sort of unique freak or alien. With time he sees himself as more like those called "girls," but the presence of his genitals is puzzling and confusing to him. Parents and others he trusts call him a "boy," and he wants to believe them or at least not disappoint them. The discord between what he is and what he thinks he truly is or wants to be doesn't allow him to easily consider another option other than continuing to live as a boy. With much mental struggle and great trepidation, however, the transsexual male begins thinking: "My feelings of being a girl and wanting to live as a woman are overwhelming. I must attempt to live and be the woman I believe I am and should be." He then attempts to live as a female would. At first this may be just in dress. Eventually he looks forward to developing into a woman with the removal of his genitals and fabrication of breasts, a vulva, and a vagina. While this epiphany of condition usually occurs by puberty, actual transformation typically occurs much later when conditions are more favorable. The female transsexual essentially experiences a development which is the mirror image of the male transsexual.

The intersexed individual undergoes a somewhat different developmental sequence. But, since there are so many types of intersex the process is highly variable. With growth, the intersexed child compares himself or herself with others and recognizes differences. With a degree of flexibility unavailable to either the typical child or the transsexual one, the intersexed child attempts to adjust and "fit in." Frequently, however, this is a difficult process, and body and mind are in conflict, particularly if his or her genitals are not in concert with the child's understanding of self. The individual strives to achieve resolution. Eventually, often with much pain and difficulty, the intersexed person integrates himself or herself with society identifying as a man, woman, or intersex. For every individual, the five PRIMO components of the person's sexual profile are evaluated to best integrate personal needs with abilities. This typically is a compromise which melds genetic-endocrine forces with social and cultural conditions and interpersonal relationships (Diamond, 1979, 1995, 1999). Many intersexed individuals raised in one sex revert to the other sex, or live with aspects of both.

Legal restrictions, which are generally a reflection of social attitudes, are also strong modifiers of preferred behavior. It takes a strong-willed individual or one with a compulsive drive to display openly homosexual, transgendered, or any divergent sexual behavior if the sanctions against the activity are strong enough. Stringent prohibitions against any overt sexual expression, even against public kissing or women displaying parts of their arms or legs, are seen, for instance, in some Islamic societies. For such minor offenses the punishment may be caning or flogging. For homosexual behaviors, the punishment can be as severe as capital punishment or long-term imprisonment. Algerian and Pakistani liberals, for instance, fight against the death sentence for homosexuality and adultery. Homosexuality and transsexuality will be rarely seen openly in these countries because the overt display of such behaviors is life-threatening. Unfortunately, due to ignorance and prejudice, this is occasionally also so in our own culture.

Laws regarding such activities vary widely. In the United King-dom, consenting sexual activity between two males has only recently been changed so that it is legal if both men are over 18; it had been 21. In contrast, heterosexual activity is legal after 16, the age of consent for females. In the UK lesbianism is not seen as worthy of note by the courts. In the United States every state has its own laws on homosexual behaviors; these range from being illegal and punishable by imprisonment to being legal and of no concern to the government.

In the former USSR homosexuality was both illegal and politically incorrect; it was castigated as a product of capitalistic society. Among the regimes of the former USSR, homosexual behaviors are now visible and not being prosecuted. In the People's Republic of China, although homosexuality is not illegal by statute, a strong homophobic attitude exists, and persons displaying homosexual behaviors are often charged with hooliganism or some other catch-all crime. Homosexual activities nevertheless exist in a furtive underground.

There is no known culture where adult–adult homosexual behavior is encouraged or is a preferred mode of behavior. There are, however, societies in which adult–child same-sex activities are fostered. Although these are same-sex activities, they are not a preferred type of sexual outlet; the behaviors are with nonerotic motives. For example, among the Kaluli of New Guinea, Schiefenhövel has reported that all boys are the recipients of anal intercourse by the men. Among the Sambia of New Guinea, Herdt and Davidson have reported that all boys fellate the adult men to obtain their semen. In these cultures it is believed such practices allow for the transmission of maleness from man to boy. When these boys attain manhood, despite years of same-sex "training," they switch to heterosexual erotic behaviors. Many cultures exhibit behaviors that would be considered sexual in the West but are not considered erotic within the society in question.

In some traditions, homosexual and or transvestic activities were accepted with equanimity and even seen as practices of the gods. In the *Mahabharata,* the classical Hindu epic poem about good and evil, the god Krishna is viewed as bisexual; in one episode he dresses as a woman and gives himself as the first sex experience to the firstborn son of Artun, the great warrior. Other gods in the Hindu pantheon are openly gay. In the days of precontact Hawaii, several of the island chiefs are known to have proudly had both same and opposite sex lovers.

COMING OUT AND OUTING

Among the more difficult processes of being different sexually is *coming out*. The precise meaning of the term keeps shifting, but it essentially means admitting to oneself that one is homosexually oriented, a transsexual, transvestite, or intersexed; and then coming out of the denial or secrecy "closet." After admitting this to oneself, coming out means revealing this sexual difference to others. But much of society, even among the most tolerant people, contains hidden minefields that not everyone wants to change. For this reason, not everyone come out. For many that do, it is usually a continuing, slow, and difficult process. Depending on how far one wants to go, others at work, sports, and the medical clinic will be informed. Friends are usually the first to know, and family (parents in particular) are usually the last. No accurate estimates are available for that proportion of homosexual, transgendered, or intersexed individuals that are out. Most activists in these subcultures believe that as more people come out, it will be more difficult for society to remain homophobic, heterosexist, and discriminatory. In the United States and elsewhere, national coming out days have been instituted to support this effort. One road block to coming out is that, while individuals recognize their private homosexual activities, they don't accept, manifest, or identify with what they perceive are public aspects of a gay lifestyle.

Outing is a much more controversial phenomenon started in the 1990s. Seemingly born of frustration by society's slow acceptance of gays, this is the practice of gay activists divulging the (alleged or actual) homosexual or transgendered behaviors of politicians, sports or media stars, and others. Activists and other groups have taken up the practice. The argument is that doing so provides a host of role models for those ashamed of their own situation. It also reduces the power of those who would use secrecy to mask sexophobic activities they might use to hide their own behaviors. On the other side, the process has been called philosophical rape, psychic violence, and ethical blackmail. Outing can certainly damage careers or lives.

THE MEANING OF BEING DIFFERENT

For some people, being different is a conscious decision. For others it is not a choice. They are different by birth or from events over which they have little control, and societies reject or accept them according to cultural myths, beliefs, and codes. From a world view, there are many similarities and dramatic differences within cultures' reactions to sexual difference. It is not a matter of right versus wrong: just *different*. Within any society there may be a neutral response, a reaction to a perceived threat, or a view that the behavior is a gift from God that deserves special thanks.

REFERENCES & SUGGESTED READINGS

Benjamin, H. (1966). *The transsexual phenomenon.* New York: Julian.

Blanchard, R. (1997). Birth order and sibling sex ratio in homosexual versus heterosexual males and females. *Annual Review of Sex Research, 8*(4), 27–67.

Colapinto, J. (2000). *As nature made him: The boy who was raised as a girl.* New York: Harper Collings.

Collaer, M. L., & Hines, M. (1995). Human behavioral sex differences: A role for gonadal hormones during early development. *Psychological Bulletin, 118*(1), 55–107.

Crawford, M. & Unger, R. K. (2000). *Women & gender: A feminist psychology* (3rd ed.). New York: McGraw-Hill.

Diamond, M. (1965). A critical evaluation of the ontogeny of human sexual behavior. *Quarterly Review of Biology, 40,* 147–175.

Diamond, M. (1976). Human sexual development: Biological foundation for social development. In F. A. Beach (Ed.), *Human sexuality in four perspectives* (pp. 22–61). Baltimore, MD: The John Hopkins Press.

Diamond, M. (1979). Sexual identity and sex roles. In V. Bullough (Ed.), *The frontiers of sex research* (pp. 33–56). Buffalo, NY: Prometheus.

Diamond, M. (1993). Homosexuality and bisexuality in different populations. *Archives of Sexual Behavior, 22,* 291–311.

Diamond, M. (1995). Biological aspects of sexual orientation and identity. In L. Diamant & R. McAnulty (Eds.), *The psychology of sexual orientation, behavior and identity: A handbook* (pp. 45–80). Westport, CT: Greenwood.

Diamond, M. (1997). Sexual identity and sexual orientation in children With traumatized or ambiguous genitalia. *Journal of Sex Research, 34,* 199–222.

Diamond, M. (1999). Pediatric management of ambiguous genitalia and traumatized genitalia. *Journal of Urology,* (162), 1021–1028.

Diamond, M., Binstock, T., & Kohl, J. V. (1996). From fertilization to adult sexual behavior. Nonhormonal influences on sexual behavior. *Hormones and Behavior, 30*(December), 333–353.

Diamond, M., & Sigmundson, H. K. (1997). Sex reassignment at birth: Long term review and clinical implications. *Archives of Pediatrics and Adolescent Medicine, 151*(March), 298–304.

Docter, R. F. (1990). *Transvestites and transsexuals: Toward a theory of cross-gender behavior.* New York: Plenum.

Ellis, L., & Ebertz, L. (1997). *Sexual Orientation.* Westport, CT: Praeger.

Ellis, L., & Ebertz, L. (1998). *Males, Females, and Behavior.* Westport, CT: Praeger.

Gagnon, J. H., & Simon, W. (1973). *Sexual conduct: The social origins of human sexuality.* Chicago: Aldine.

Goldman, R., & Goldman, J. (1982). *Children's sexual thinking: A comparative study of children aged 5 to 15 years in Australia, North America, Britain, and Sweden.* London: Routledge & Kegan Paul.

Haug, M., Whalen, R. E., Aron, C., & Olsen, K. (1993). *The Development of Sex Differences and Similarities in Behavior.* Dordrecht: Kluwer Academic.

Imperato-McGinley, J., Peterson, R. E., Gautier, T., & Sturla, E. (1979). Male pseudohermaphroditism secondary to 5 alpha-reductase deficiency—A model for the role of androgens in both the development of the male phenotype and the evolution of a male gender identity. *Journal of Steroid Biochemistry, 11*(1B), 637–645.

Kinsey, A. C., Pomeroy, W. B., & Martin, C. E. (1948). *Sexual behavior in the human male.* Philadelphia and London: W. B. Saunders.

Kinsey, A. C., Pomeroy, W. B., Martin, C. E., & Gebhard, P. H. (1953). *Sexual behavior in the human female.* Philadelphia and London: W. B. Saunders.

Laumann, E. O., Gagnon, J. H., Michael, R. T., & Stuart, M. (1994). *The social organization of sexuality: Sexual practices in the United States.* Chicago: The University of Chicago Press.

LeVay, S. (1993). *The sexual brain.* Boston: MIT Press.

Puterbaugh, G. (1990). *Twins and Homosexuality: A Casebook.* New York: Garland.

Reiss, I. L. (1986). *Journey into sexuality: An exploratory voyage.* Englewood Cliffs, NJ: Prentice Hall.

Rösler, A. (1992). Steroid 17B-hydroxysteroid dehydrogenase deficiency in man: An inherited form of male pseudohermaphroditism. *Journal of Steroid Biochemistry and Molecular Biology, 43*(8), 989–1002.

M. DIAMOND
University of Hawaii

SHAKOW, DAVID (1901–1982)

David Shakow received the undergraduate and graduate degrees from Harvard University. He worked for several years as a psychologist in mental hospitals, including the McLean Hospital, Worcester State Hospital, and Boston Psychopathic Hospital. Next he became affiliated with the Worcester Child Guidance Clinic. In 1946, he became professor of psychology at the University of Illinois College of Medicine. He served as consultant to many commissions and committees and in 1967 became senior research psychologist with the National Institute of Mental Health.

Shakow was the recipient of many honors and awards for his contributions to clinical psychology. He was the coauthor of *The Influence of Freud on American Psychology* (1963) and author of *Clinical Psychology as Science and Profession: A Forty-Year Odyssey* (1969).

P. E. LICHTENSTEIN

SHAM RAGE

There has been much research in the area of "sham rage," which has been characterized as an affective and pathological aggressive state (Heilman, Bowers, & Valenstein, 1993). Unfortunately, attempts to better understand the anatomical substrate associated with sham rage, using primarily stimulation and ablation procedures throughout the entire limbic system, have produced somewhat confusing results. Sham rage research has often yielded con-

tradictory data, perhaps because of the diffuse interconnections between the limbic system and other brain areas which, themselves, may be partly responsible for the complex emotional and motoric behavior associated with "pathological" aggression. Moreover, the use of different species in the investigation of sham rage has produced varied results, further muddling our understanding of this behavioral and emotional phenomenon. This chapter will outline the most consistent neurological findings of sham rage in both animals and humans. The major connections from the limbic system, and the amygdala in particular, to other brain regions will then be elucidated. In conclusion, a general model of hostility and sham rage will be presented.

One of the primary findings in the study of animal rage is that temporal lobe ablation produces placidity, whereas temporal lobe arousal generally yields hostility. One of the earliest experiments to produce data supporting this notion was performed by Kluver and Bucy (1937), who found that bilateral fronto-temporal ablation tamed previously aggressive rhesus monkeys. Woods (1956), too, found that the ablation of the amygdaloid bodies (within the temporal lobe) promoted pacification in the Norway rat. Ursin (1960), on the other hand, was one of the first researchers to demonstrate that temporal lobe stimulation produced a rage-like response in conjunction with the intensification of negative affective behaviors. It has been generally accepted that the amygdaloid bodies (within the temporal lobe) play a particularly important role in the production of hostile behavior (see Demaree & Harrison, 1997a, 1997b).

Animal research also indicates that septal arousal, as opposed to amygdaloid body arousal, may play an integral role in producing emotional calming and placidity. Some of the earliest research demonstrated that septal lesions caused sham rage (Brady & Nauta, 1955), whereas septal stimulation yielded an apparently pleasant state (Olds, 1958). Septum stimulation in the Olds (1958) experiment apparently was rewarding, as animals continuously pressed a lever to stimulate their own septal regions.

Researchers generally support the notion that humans experience similar emotional and behavioral sequalae as animals from septal and amygdaloid dysfunction. For example, using noninvasive procedures, amygdaloid lesions in humans were found to produce a placid response (Poeck, 1969). Moreover, partial complex seizures within the temporal lobes have been documented to cause nonpurposeful violence (Ashford, Schulz, & Walsh, 1980) and, although hotly contested (see Stevens & Hermann, 1981), perhaps purposefully directed rage (Mark & Ervin, 1970; Pincus, 1980). Irrespective of a temporal lobe seizure's sequelae, stereotactic amygdaloidectomy has been found to decrease rage behavior in highly aggressive patients who have a seizure disorder (Mark, Sween, & Ervin, 1972). Last, like animals, human septal dysfunction (from tumor) has been associated with irritability and rage (Zeman & King, 1958; Poeck & Pilleri, 1961).

Given the extensive interconnections of the amygdala with other brain structures which promote the "fight or flight" response (from Kandel, Schwartz, & Jessell, 1995), it is easy to understand the amygdala's role in sham rage. Specifically, amygdaloid activation promotes arousal (and behavioral output) of the lateral hypothalamus (producing tachycardia, galvanic skin response increase, pupil dilation, and blood pressure elevation), parabrachial nucleus (panting, respiratory distress), ventral tegmental area, locus coeruleus, dorsal lateral tegmental nucleus (behavioral electroencephalographic arousal, increased vigilance), and periventricular nucleus (corticosteroid release for the "stress response"). Thus, amygdaloid hyperactivation may not produce sham rage itself. Rather, it starts a chain of neuroanatomical events which produce their own cognitive, emotional, and behavioral features. When summated, these features equate to sham rage. Similarly, amygdaloid body lesion produces the reverse pattern of behavior (placidity).

Both data and theory have supported the notion that the hypothalamus is integral to rage production. The septum and amygdala are both extensively interconnected with the hypothalamus, thus providing neuroanatomical support for the hypothalamic role in rage. Indeed, lesion studies with cats (e.g., Decsi & Nagy, 1974; Lu, Shaikh, & Siegal, 1982) and case studies with humans (Flynn, Cummings, & Tomayasu, 1988; Tonkonogy & Geller, 1992) support the hypothalamic role in rage production. It is thus proposed that the hypothalamus acts to balance the septum and amygdaloid regions to promote "normal" levels of hostility (MacLean, 1952), and that prefrontal and temporal regions also interact (via the inhibitory uncinate tract) to yield stable aggression levels (Heilman et al., 1993). Given these theories, it would then be expected that lesion of the septum or hypothalamus or stimulation of the amygdaloid bodies may produce sham rage.

REFERENCES

Ashford, J. W., Schulz, C., & Walsh, G. O. (1980). Violent automatism in a partial complex seizure: Report of a case. *Archives of Neurology, 37,* 120–122.

Brady, J. V., & Nauta, W. J. (1955). Subcortical mechanisms in control of behavior. *Journal of Comparative Physiology and Psychology, 48,* 412–420.

Decsi, L., & Nagy, J. (1974). Chemical stimulation of the amygdala with special regard to the influence on the hypothalamus. *Neuropharmacology, 7,* 201–207.

Demaree, H. A., & Harrison, D. W. (1997a). Physiological and neuropsychological correlates of hostility. *Neuropsychologia, 35,* 1405–1411.

Demaree, H. A., & Harrison, D. W. (1997b). A neuropsychological model relating self-awareness to hostility. *Neuropsychology Review, 7,* 171–185.

Flynn, F. G., Cummings, J. L., & Tomayasu, U. (1988). Altered behavior associated with damage to the ventromedial hypothalamus: A distinctive syndrome. *Behavioral Neurology, 1,* 49–58.

Heilman, K. M., Bowers, D., & Valenstein, E. (1993). Emotional disorders characterized with neurological diseases. In K. M. Heilman & E. Valenstein (Eds.), *Clinical neuropsychology* (3rd ed.). New York: Oxford University Press.

Kandel, E. R., Schwartz, J. H., & Jessell, T. M. (1995). *Essentials of neural science and behavior.* Norwalk, CT: Appleton and Lange.

Kluver, H., & Bucy, P. C. (1937). "Psychic blindness" and other symptoms following bilateral temporal lobe lobectomy in rhesus monkeys. *American Journal of Physiology, 119,* 352–353.

Lu, C., Shaikh, M. B., & Siegal, A. (1982). Role of NMDA receptors in hypothalamic facilitation of feline defensive rage elicited from the midbrain periaqueductal gray. *Brain Research, 581,* 123–132.

Mark, V. H., & Ervin, F. R. (1970). *Violence and the brain.* New York: Harper and Row.

Mark, V. H., Sween, W. H., & Ervin, F. R. (1972). The effect of amygdalectomy on violent behavior in patients with temporal lobe epilepsy. In E. Hitchcock, L. Laitinen, & K. Vernet (Eds.), *Psychosurgery.* Springfield, IL: Thomas.

Olds, J. (1958). Self-stimulation of the brain. *Science, 127,* 315–324.

Pincus, J. H. (1980). Can violence be a manifestation of epilepsy? *Neurology, 30,* 304–307.

Poeck, K. (1969). Pathophysiology of emotional disorders associated with brain damage. In P. J. Vinken & G. W. Bruyn (Eds.), *Handbook of neurology,* (vol. 3). New York: Elsevier.

Poeck, K., & Pilleri, G. (1961). Wutverhalten and pathologischer Schlaf bei Tumor dervorderen Mitellinie. *Arch. Psychiatr. Nervenkr., 201,* 593–604.

Stevens, J. R., & Hermann, B. P. (1981). Temporal lobe epilepsy, psychopathology and violence: The state of evidence. *Neurology, 31,* 1127–1132.

Tonkonogy, J. M., & Geller, J. L. (1992). Hypothalamic lesions and intermittent explosive disorder. *Journal of Neuropsychiatry and Clinical Neurosciences, 4,* 45–50.

Ursin, H. (1960). The temporal lobe substrate of fear and anger. *Acta Psychiatrica Scandinavia, 35,* 378–396.

Woods, J. W. (1956). Taming of the wild in Norway rat by rhinocephalic lesions. *Nature, 170,* 869.

Zeman, W., & King, F. A. (1958). Tumors of the septum pellucidum and adjacent structures with abnormal affective behavior: An anterior midline structure syndrome. *Journal of Nervous and Mental Diseases, 127,* 490–502.

H. A. DEMAREE
Kessler Medical Rehabilitation
Research and Education Corporation

SHARING BELIEFS IN GROUPS

Many of an individual's beliefs are shared by a few individuals, by members of a small group, by members of a society, or even by the majority of human beings. Shared beliefs are usually acquired from external sources, after having been disseminated through interpersonal communication networks or via societal mechanisms of communication. Moreover, certain societal institutions, such as the mass media or schools, are established in order to propagate shared beliefs. The most salient categories of disseminated shared beliefs are common beliefs which pertain to general knowledge and scientific knowledge, spread widely among people in different parts of the world. Such beliefs facilitate common understanding and communication among people.

Of special importance for group life are those shared beliefs which play a determining role in the development of social identity, solidarity, interdependence, unity and coordination of group activity—all necessary conditions for the functioning of social systems. These beliefs are formed on the basis of common experiences of group members and exposure to the same channels of communication. Groups, further, not only form these shared beliefs, but also make a special effort to disseminate them among group members and maintain them.

From the perspective of a century, it can be noted that although the interest in shared beliefs is as long as the history of modern psychology, it has never been a major thrust of study, except at the beginning of the emerging discipline. Distinguished early psychologists were interested in how groups think, how they form common mental products, and the natures of the shared thoughts. Durkheim (1898) discussed collectively shared cognitive products labeled as collective representations, which consist of the totality of beliefs and sentiments common to average members of the same society. LeBon (1968) focused on the collective mind of a crowd which guides contagious and common behaviors. Wundt (1916), in his classic work on folk psychology, suggested that each group, whether a local community, tribe, or nation, develops through reciprocal activity collective mental products, the folk souls. McDougall (1920), who is considered one of the first professed social psychologists, introduced the controversial concept of group mind, referring to the continuity of shared thoughts, sentiments, and tradition despite the turnover of group members. Within the realm of early psychology should also be noted the work of Vygotsky, the renowned Soviet social developmental psychologist. Vygotsky argued that thinking and reasoning are always products of social activity molded by society. This social activity allows the transmission of common symbolic tools that are internalized through the mediation of language and used in joint action (Vygotsky, 1962).

After the first wave of psychologists who were preoccupied with collective mental products, the interest in this topic somewhat faded away until it reappeared in the work of the three founding fathers of modern social psychology: Sherif, Lewin, and Asch. All three were interested in group behavior and recognized that group membership affects individuals' perceptions of their world. Sherif (1936) demonstrated in a series of experiments how individuals in a group form a joint norm (i.e., shared belief) and how it becomes part of their repertoire, affecting their perception and judgment. Lewin focused on the study of psychological forces which influence the group at any given moment (Lewin, 1948) and assumed that any prediction of group behavior has to take into account group goals, group standards, group values, and the way a group "sees" its own situation and that of other groups. Asch (1951), in turn, spoke about a mutually shared field for group members, which enables them to understand the viewpoints of others and form shared actions, feelings, or ideas.

The work of Moscovici on social representation is the most extensive elaboration of shared beliefs in the recent work of social psychology (Moscovici, 1988). Based on Durkheim's conception of collective representation, he focused on the plurality and diversity of representations within a group or society and their continuous evolvement through communication.

Recently, a new interest in shared beliefs has emerged from several different directions. This new line of research does not necessarily use the term "shared beliefs," but takes from social cognitive tradition the term "shared cognition" (e.g., Resnick, Levine, & Teasley, 1991). The work by Bar-Tal (1990, 2000) and by Fraser and Gaskell (1990) analyzes shared group and societal beliefs, which play important functions in the formation and maintenance of social identities and in guiding social behaviors. Bar-Tal (1990) introduced the concept of group beliefs, which denotes convictions that group members are aware of sharing and consider as defining their "groupness." In this conception, group beliefs affect such group processes as schism, mergence, subgrouping, or disintegration. Another direction of investigating shared beliefs has emerged in the study of small groups, with the assumption that they play a determinative function in group formation and functioning (e.g., Hinsz, Tindale, & Vollrath, 1997; Nye & Brower, 1996). According to this line of study, group members can interdependently act only when they form an understanding of goals, norms, and procedures. The development for such understanding is a condition for small groups successful and efficient performance.

In all groups and societies, however, shared beliefs have significant social, political, and cultural functions. First of all, shared beliefs have an important influence on group behavior. Coordinated behaviors of group members always have an epistemic basis. Group members, in the majority of cases, need rationale and justification for their social behaviors in addition to common understanding, in order to take part in coordinated activities. In this role, shared beliefs in a group are often used as a rationale for social behaviors, because group members share them and often consider them to be true.

The acquired shared beliefs play a further role in the formation of new shared knowledge, since there is continuous reciprocal interaction between the shared beliefs and new experiences of the society. On one hand, the new experiences serve as a source for the formation of new shared beliefs of a group; and on the other hand, the already accumulated shared beliefs serve as a prism through which the new experiences are understood and new beliefs are formed. Shared beliefs in a group allow a firm construction of group reality in spite of the fact that their contents often concern ambiguous social events, abstract concepts, and information which in most cases is not observed or experienced firsthand. The study of shared beliefs in groups, thus, opens new avenues for understanding the world of groups as well as of individuals.

REFERENCES

Bar-Tal, D. (1990). *Group beliefs: A conception for analyzing group structure, processes, and behavior.* New York: Springer-Verlag.

Bar-Tal, D. (2000). *Shared beliefs in a society: A social psychological analysis.* Thousand Oaks, CA: Sage.

Durkheim, E. (1898). Representations individuelles et representations collectives. *Rev. de metaphysique, 6,* 274–302. (Transl.

D. F. Pocock, *Sociology and philosophy.* New York: Free Press, 1953).

Fraser, C., & Gaskell, G. (Eds.). (1990). *The social psychology of widespread beliefs.* Oxford: Clarendon.

Hinsz, V. B., Tindale, R. S., & Vollrath, D. A. (1997). The emerging conceptualization of groups as information processors. *Psychological Bulletin, 121,* 43–64.

Le Bon, G. (1968). *The crowd: A study of the popular mind* (2nd ed.). Dunwoody, GA: Berg. Originally published in 1895.

Lewin, K. (1948). *Resolving social conflicts.* New York: Harper & Row.

McDougall, W. (1920). *The group mind.* New York: G. P. Putnam's Sons.

Moscovici, S. (1988). Notes towards a description of social representations. *European Journal of Social Psychology, 18,* 211–250.

Nye, J. L., & Brower, A. M. (Eds.). (1996). *What's social about social cognition? Research on socially shared cognition in small groups.* Thousand Oaks, CA: Sage.

Sherif, M. (1936). *The psychology of social norms.* New York: Harper.

Vygotsky, L. S. (1962). *Thought and language.* Cambridge, MA: MIT Press.

Wundt, W. (1916). *Elements of folk psychology.* London: Allen & Unwin.

D. BAR-TAL
Tel Aviv University

PEER INFLUENCES
SOCIAL INFLUENCE

SHERIF, MUZAFER (1906–1988)

Muzafer Sherif received the BA degree from Izmir International College and the MA degree from Istambual University. He came to the United States in 1929, where he entered Harvard University and earned a second MA degree in 1932. He returned to Turkey where he began to work on norm formulation that eventually resulted in his doctoral dissertation. In 1935 he received the PhD degree from Columbia University. He returned to Turkey for a second time but found himself in conflict with the Turkish government and some officials at Ankara University over certain of their pro-Nazi attitudes. He was imprisoned and put in solitary confinement, but he was eventually released through the efforts of the U.S. State Department and of a number of influential American psychologists with whom he had been associated at Columbia. He spent the next 2 years at Princeton University, where he collaborated with Hadly Cantril on *The Psychology of Ego-Involvement.*

His collaboration with Carl Hovland on the anchoring effects of social judgment resulted in the book *Social Judgment, Assimilation and Contrast Effects in Communication and Cultural Change.* For the next 16 years he taught at the University of Oklahoma,

where he published his best-known works: *Intergroup Conflict and Cooperation* and the *Introduction to Social Psychology* (with Carolyn Wood). In 1966, he and Wood joined the faculty at the Pennsylvania State University: she in psychology and he in sociology.

In 1967 he received the APA's Distinguished Contribution Award and the first Cooley-Mead Award for contributions to social psychology from the American Sociological Association. His efforts mark him as one of the scientific pioneers in social psychology.

R. W. LUNDIN
Wheaton, Illinois

SHORT-TERM MEMORY

With the increased interest in information-processing models for learning, memory, and perception in the late 1950s, there rose a great deal of inquiry into the sequencing characteristics from intake to retention to retrieval of the information. Most information-processing approaches propose an iconic storage or sensory register as the initial stage, a short-term-memory intermediate stage, and then a long-term-memory stage in learning. Within and between these stages, attention and linguistic factors can intervene. Retrieval of information can be accessed from either the short-term- or long-term-memory phases. During the 15-year period from 1958 to 1973, 1,500 research reports appeared that delineated the various characteristics of short-term memory.

Basically, short-term memory is a fleeting or transient, limited-capacity (five to nine items) memory storage. Its duration ranges between 20 seconds and 1 minute. The transfer of information from short-term to the more permanent long-term memory is by the process of rehearsal or memorial repetition. Here verbal material and selected aspects of the pictorial material are repeated, grouped, and summarized to facilitate storage. Short-term memory is very vulnerable. The memory trace has been shown to decay rapidly with *time* and *interference* from competitive acoustic (similar sounds) or semantic (similar meaning) information.

Common laboratory tasks, used to study short-term memory, involved the presentation of numerical, alphabetic, or word lists followed by the counting of the number of correctly remembered items. These included *distractor tasks,* where presentation of a list of items is followed by forcing the subject to count backward by threes; *continuous or probe tasks,* where within a sequence of items, one of the items is repeated and the subject is required to remember the item that appeared after it first appeared; and *paired associates,* where one member of matched pairs of lists of items had to be remembered after one viewing of the pairs and then subsequent viewing of one member. Depending on the temporal or spatial parameters used in the experiment—for example, items presented in rapid succession can be seen to disrupt rehearsal more than slower rates—these tasks contributed to either the decay of trace or interference notions.

Although short-term memory has limited capacity, researchers have found that this capacity can be enhanced through chunking. That is, each of six or seven items that can be remembered can serve as superordinate categories for six or seven other kinds of items or members of that superordinate category. For example, letters, numbers, and symbols might serve as superordinate labels to facilitate memory of the sequence A, G, M, P, Q, 3, 7, 11, 14, 21, plus, minus, triangle, square, heart. Short-term-memory chunking, however, was found to be much more volatile than the long-term-memory superordinate categorization, probably because of the limited time available for rehearsal.

Although stimulus characteristics such as item similarity and meaningfulness can cause interference, so can the sequential placement of items. *Proactive* interference causes information from previously learned material to reduce memory for new items, while *retroactive* interference causes poor recall of previously learned material because of the information recently learned. The effects of item interference can be seen in recall of lists of items. Here the performance curve of position of item recalled resembles a "U." The serial position curve is high for beginning (primacy) and ending (recency) items and quite low for items toward the middle. The middle items seem to be the object of greatest interference, while the beginning list items have received much rehearsal and the ending items are still "fresh" in memory, so recall is enhanced.

Along with the quantitative assessments of short-term memory came the qualitative assessments of the information-processing sequence. Questions of whether short-term memory and long-term memory are independent processes or continuous processes were vigorously argued in the literature. Arthur Melton led the fight for a continuous process model and drew many parallels between the two systems, primarily as to the qualitative nature of interference. Many others opted for an independent process approach. Some saw short-term memory as the optimal way station. It was here where less important information was utilized and then abandoned, whereas more important information, as judged by the operator, was subsequently rehearsed and placed in long-term memory.

D. F. FISHER
Churchville, MD

ATTENTION
MEMORY

SHYNESS

DEFINED AND CATEGORIZED
Shyness may be defined experientially as excessive self-focus characterized by negative self-evaluation that creates discomfort or inhibition in social situations and interferes with pursuing one's interpersonal or professional goals. The experience of shyness can occur at any or all of the following levels: cognitive (e.g., excessive negative self-evaluation), affective (e.g., heightened feelings of anxiety), physiological (e.g., racing heart), and behavioral (e.g., failure to respond appropriately) and may be triggered by a wide variety of situational cues. Among the most typical situations are interactions with authorities and strangers, one-on-one opposite sex in-

teractions, and unstructured social settings. Subcategories of shyness reflect the degree (i.e., mild social awkwardness to totally inhibiting social phobia) and frequency of experienced shyness, and include chronic shyness (self-labeling as shy and the experience of shyness in numerous social situations), situational shyness (the experience of shyness in specific social situations), and shy extroverts (experience anxiety and negative self-evaluation but are publicly outgoing). Although similar in its overt expression, introversion is not a subcategory of shyness. Introverts, like extroverts, do not fear social situations, but simply prefer solitary activities. Shy individuals would prefer to be with others but are restrained by the experience of shyness.

PREVALENCE AND DIAGNOSIS
The percentage of adults in the United States reporting that they are chronically shy has increased from 40 percent (+/–3%) since the early 1970s to 48 percent (+/–2%) within the last decade. Another 40 percent indicated that they had considered themselves as shy previously but no longer, 15 percent as being shy in some situations, and only about 5 percent believed they were never shy. Most clinical referrals for shyness meet the criteria for generalized social phobia (i.e., difficulty in initiating and maintaining social interactions) and many meet criteria for avoidant personality disorder (i.e., excessively sensitive to rejection). Other frequent comorbid diagnoses are dysthymia, generalized anxiety disorder, specific phobias, dependent personality disorder, schizoid personality disorder, and, in some extreme cases, obsessive-compulsive and paranoid personality.

THE CONSEQUENCES OF SHYNESS
A common observation in virtually all shyness research is that the consequences of shyness are deeply troubling. Shy individuals don't take advantage of social situations, date less, are less expressive verbally and nonverbally, and experience more loneliness than nonshys. Shy men have been found to marry and have children later, have less stable marriages, delay establishing careers, and exhibit lower levels of career achievement than their nonshy peers. Shy people have been found to use alcohol in an effort to relax socially, which may lead to impaired social performance and substance abuse. A perceived inability to socialize by shy individuals, along with a pessimistic outlook for social interactions, becomes an excuse for anticipated failure and a self-handicapping strategy (e.g., "I can't do it because I am shy"). Finally, severe shyness that continues into the later years of life can result in chronic social isolation that leads to increasingly severe loneliness and related psychopathology, and even to chronic illness and a shorter lifespan.

GENETICS AND THE INTERACTIONIST INTERPRETATION OF SHYNESS
Research suggesting a genetic contribution to the origins of shyness is the finding that approximately 15 percent to 20 percent of newborns exhibit an inhibited temperament characterized by high reactivity (e.g., excessive crying and vigorous movement of head and limbs) to novel stimulation, along with elevated *in utero* heart rates. In early childhood, such infants tend to exhibit more behav-

ior defined operationally as timid or shy (e.g., playing near primary caretaker) and have close relatives who reported more childhood shyness than uninhibited children. Supporting an interactionist interpretation to shyness suggests that being born with the easily aroused inhibited temperament may lead to social withdrawal in childhood and adolescence from parents, siblings, and peers, thus promoting a shy response style. Other environmental factors fostering such withdrawal include being teased or bullied, dominating older siblings, family conflict, and overprotective parenting. Finally, the development of shyness in adulthood is usually due to experiences of rejection and self-blame for failure in social domains.

NEUROLOGICAL BASES OF SHYNESS

The neurological foundation of the social fear/anxiety component of shyness is found in the action of the amygdala and hippocampus. The amygdala appears to be implicated in the association of specific stimuli with fear. The more general pervasive conditioning of background factors related to the conditioning stimuli is known as contextual conditioning. This diffuse contextual conditioning occurs more slowly and lasts longer than most traditional CS-US classical conditioning. It is experienced as anxiety and general apprehension in situations that become associated with fear cues, such as classrooms and parties, for shy people. Contextual conditioning involves the hippocampus, crucial in spatial learning and memory, as well as the amygdala. The bed nucleus of the striate terminalis (BNST) is also involved in emotional-behavioral arousal and extends to the hypothalamus and the brain stem. The hypothalamus triggers the sympathetic nervous system and the physiological symptoms of shyness, among them trembling, increased heart rate, and muscle tension.

SHYNESS AND CULTURE

Cross-cultural research indicates a universality of shyness. A large proportion of participants in all cultures reported experiencing shyness to a considerable degree—from a low of 31 percent in Israel to a high of 57 percent in Japan and 55 percent in Taiwan. In Mexico, Germany, India, and Canada, shyness was more similar to the 40 percent reported in the US. Explanations of cultural differences in shyness have focused on the distinction between collectivistic cultures, which promote the esteem of the group over that of the individual, thus fostering emotional control and inhibition, and individualistic cultures, which promote the esteem of the individual, thus fostering self-expression and concern about public scrutiny of oneself.

TREATMENT

Existing treatments generally include a comprehensive initial assessment session (e.g., structured clinical interview, shyness inventory, fear of negative evaluation scale, depression inventory) and exposure to a hierarchy of feared situations, usually simulated in treatment sessions or in-vivo, and some kind of cognitive modification, anxiety management, or social skills training. A promising new treatment program that includes many of these elements is the 26-week Social Fitness Training Model (SFTM) provided

at the Stanford/Palo Alto Shyness Clinic. Unique features of the SFTM, which contribute to its ecological validity, are the in-group simulated exposures of feared situations, using both other group members and outside "confederates"; between-session in-vivo exposures (e.g., making conversation with coworkers) called "behavioral homework"; and skills tool kit (like tennis drills or calisthenics) that includes education and training in positive social behavior, including skills to build trust and intimacy, exercises to convert maladaptive thoughts (including attributions and self-concept distortions to more adaptive cognitive patterns), and training in effective communication skills, including assertiveness and negotiation. As exemplified by the SFTM, any successful treatment program for shyness must consider the cognitive, behavioral, physiological, and emotional components that constitute each individual's unique experience of shyness.

SUGGESTED READING

Carducci, B. J. (1999). *Shyness: A bold new approach.* New York: HarperCollins.

Henderson, L., & Zimbardo, P. (in press-a). Shyness as a clinical condition: The Stanford Model. In L. Alden & R. Crozier (Eds.), *International Handbook of Social Anxiety.* Sussex, England: John Wiley & Sons.

Henderson, L., & Zimbardo, P. (in press-b). Shyness, relationship to social anxiety and social phobia. In S. Hofmann & P. di Bartolo (Eds.), *Social phobia.* New York: Allyn & Bacon.

Zimbardo, P. G. (1977/1990). *Shyness: What it is, what to do about it.* Reading, MA: Addison-Wesley.

L. M. HENDERSON
The Shyness Institute

P. G. ZIMBARDO
Stanford University

B. J. CARDUCCI
Shyness Research Institute

ANXIETY
AVOIDANT PERSONALITY

SIBLING RELATIONSHIPS

The sibling group consists of brothers and sisters in one's own nuclear family and is a nonvoluntary relationship. An individual's sequential position among siblings, known as birth order or sibling status, has been important in deciding the distribution of familial property, and primogeniture refers to the practice of assigning all such rights to the firstborn male, while other siblings receive nothing.

SIBLING RIVALRY

Since the days of Cain and Abel, primogeniture has promoted a belief in sibling rivalry; has formed the basis for untold numbers of fairy tales, plays, and novels; and became the major focus of the study of siblings highlighted by Adler's (1928) theory of sibling relationships in the early 1920s. Adler, a physician and disciple of Sigmund Freud, maintained that feelings of competition, jealousy, and hostility would be prevalent when the first child was "dethroned." Over the years, however, empirical research has shown that such rivalry is not as pervasive as was once thought. Rivalry among brothers and sisters is displayed among less than half of all firstborns; is reported as most intense only among same-gender siblings who are close in age (1½ to 3 years apart); and is found primarily among children whose parents practice inconsistent discipline practices regardless of the form (Sutton-Smith & Rosenberg, 1960). It seems that children's personalities, especially their ability to adapt to the new, whether people, places, or things, contribute to reduced sibling rivalry (Chess et al., 1965). Moreover, parental behaviors can intensify a child's feelings of displacement, promote rivalry, and also interact with the child's personality to produce differing rates of sibling adjustment. For example, mothers who showed less playful attention, were less sensitive to interests, and generally ordered, demanded, and confronted their firstborns more after the birth of their second child, had firstborns who displayed intense rivalry toward their siblings. However, those who were "initiators," that is, persisted to gain attention from mother, while other firstborns withdrew such attempts, appeared to adjust more quickly to their new sibling than did the latter. Also, children's adjustment appears to be facilitated by fathers who devote more time and attention to them than prior to the birth (Lamb, 1978).

Besides parental behavior and children's personalities having an impact on sibling dynamics, especially militating against rivalry, social factors also have an influence. Firstborns who tend to assume dominant roles toward younger brothers or sisters exhibit less competition (Sutton-Smith & Rosenberg, 1960) and in many cases their influence has a greater impact than that of parents. For example, in studies (Cicirelli, 1976a, 1976b, 1978) that compared differences between siblings and unrelated children who were closely and widely spaced in age, girls were identified as better teachers of their own younger siblings than boys, and siblings of gender similar to their older brother or sister responded most favorably to tutoring. Interaction styles differed for boys and girls. Girls used deductive reasoning—describing, explaining, and demonstrating—while boys used inductive reasoning—illustrating and letting the learner abstract the concept. Also, boys were less patient than girls. Gender-typing differences based on early socialization experiences are offered as interpretations for these data.

It seems that main effects of birth order or gender must be viewed with care because the dynamics of sibling interactions are affected by age spacing and parental behavior. Eldest children (those 9 months to 3 years old) tend to be bossier, and more likely to interfere or ignore and to bribe or physically attack younger siblings, as contrasted with second borns with younger siblings or those whose spacing is farther apart. On the other hand, younger siblings are likely to be more tolerant of the behavior of their older sisters. And when the age spacing is four or more years, their acceptance of sibling behaviors seems to extend to brothers as well. These findings however, are mediated by the behavior of mothers.

Mothers who encourage children to assume aspects of parental roles toward younger siblings are instrumental in promoting a higher quantity and better quality of sibling interactions in the family. Data also show that mothers with firstborn sons tend to explain and communicate more with their children in general than those with first-born daughters, and their propensity seems imitated by older children in their relations with younger brothers and sisters (Cicirelli, 1976a, 1976b, 1978). In some cases, older children even serve as attachment figures more so than parents for their younger siblings.

According to one investigator (Zajonc, 1976), the oldest child, regardless of gender, has an advantage over younger children because of sharing a home with two adults for a period of time. Most forms of stimulation, especially intellectual, appear to be geared to an adult level in families with only one child. When a sibling arrives, these children also benefit from serving as teachers of younger siblings. Again, reported effects are magnified when age spacing is greater than three years.

In addition, family size influences sibling dynamics. While parents who expect and plan for large families often generate a warm accepting climate for all their children to model, those who do not exude resentment, hostility, and anger. In fact, parents of large families, in general, tend to resort to authoritarian child-rearing techniques, and these in turn are displayed by older children toward younger siblings (Bossard & Boll, 1966). In addition to the issue of a lack of pregnancy or adoption planning having a negative impact on the family and sibling relationships is the issue of family system disruption. Crises such as death of a family member, especially a parent, or unemployment, can adversely interrupt the family in terms of parent-child relationships, sibling interactions, or spousal relations (Freedman & Coombs, 1966).

BIRTH-ORDER PORTRAITS

During the late 1800s, Sir Francis Galton observed that an exceptionally large number of prominent British scientists were firstborns. Since Galton's time, numerous studies of siblings (Booth, 1981; Falbo, 1977; Hawke & Knox, 1978; Segal & Yahres, 1979; Snow, 1981; Sutton-Smith & Rosenberg, 1960; Zajonc & Marcus, 1975) have been conducted and composite portrayals of birth positions represented. Initially differences between firstborns and later borns were documented, but more recently researchers (Deutsch, 1975; McGurk & Lewis, 1972) stressed the importance of differentiating among only children, firstborns, middle children, and last borns. Only children are the most dependent and achievement-oriented compared with children in the other positions. Their parents often make excessive demands on them, and the children view themselves as misunderstood and unfairly treated. They often seek the company of adults, have difficulty in relating to peers, and are less mature, partially because they missed the interactive learning involved in tutoring a younger sibling. Firstborns also have parents who expect much of them, and they receive and emit more behaviors than other children. They tend to be highly motivated, have high goals, adhere to rules, and are generally more likely to need social contacts and praise. They, however, are fearful, sensitive to pain, and seem less able to cope with anxiety compared with their birth-order counterparts. They tend to be conservative and cautious, are quite dependent on parents, and are often uncertain about their roles. Although middle borns may feel unloved and imposed on, they often turn to endeavors in which they can excel, and show less anxiety and are more easy going. They also are more likely to attempt new tasks, activities, and behaviors, such as talking to strangers. More likely to support unconventional ideas, one study (Sulloway, 1972) found that over 90% of the scientists who initially supported Charles Darwin's evolutionary ideas during the 19th century were middle children. Last borns resemble firstborns in that they tend to be spoiled and are the focus of parental attention. They, however, remain quite babyish, are less likely to develop feelings of independence, and become discouraged with achievements or the lack of them. They are prone to high anxiety and personal problems that relate to their constant need to negotiate, accommodate, and tolerate. They also seldom have opportunities for assuming responsibility.

Since each of these birth-order patterns can be modulated by many factors—family size, age spacing, parental attitudes, economic conditions, and so on—they only represent composite averages. In addition, investigations tend to concentrate on middle class families, are cross-sectional rather than longitudinal, and rely on self-report retrospective data. While portraits need cautious interpretation because of these methodological weaknesses, they provide information showing the importance of sibling relationships in terms of their impact on individuals and their duration of effects. Even with poor sibling relationships, brothers and sisters seem to rally in times of crisis, usually their own or that of their parents. Perhaps this is one reason why the expression "blood is thicker than water" persists.

SIBLING RELATIONSHIPS ACROSS THE LIFE SPAN
Very few studies have been conducted to understand better sibling relationships during adulthood, middle age, and old age. Siblings often are not geographically available for interactions—especially in metropolitan families (Peterson, 1970). Sibling ties tend to decrease with age, but often become strong during a family crisis or when there is an aged parent to provide a focus of common concern or interest. However, siblings are of primary importance in their unmarried, childless, or widowed brothers' and sisters' lives. Upon a disruption of a marriage, they also tend to reunite for support for varying periods of time (Shanas, 1967, 1968, 1973). Some researchers (Toman & Gray, 1961) assert that the closer marital relationships resemble those of an individual's sibling childhood, the more successful they will be. Thus a firstborn would be encouraged to marry an individual who is a second born, and so on. Brothers with younger sisters who married sisters with older brothers were found to have more satisfactory marital relationships than other sibling pairs. In fact, opposite-gender sibling pairs should have a greater chance for later marital success than same-gender siblings. Findings, however, are equivocal, again warranting cautious interpretations.

It can be concluded that some children may benefit from having brothers or sisters, while others may not. For the most part, sisters are the ones who form stronger ties to each other across their life spans than do brothers, and there is some evidence that cross-gender ties are the next strongest sibling bond that persists over time (Adams, 1968).

Most of the sibling literature focuses on relationship differences due to birth order with the older child identified as having the most influence over younger brothers and sisters. Although evidence shows that parents do not pay as much attention to later borns, there is a lack of information on ways parents influence their younger children and how these children affect each other. For siblings of various ages and birth-order positions, the effects of family composition, parental behavior, and attitudes, and even the influence of outside systems such as school and peers, not only can interpenetrate parent-child relationships, but can also influence sibling dynamics. Thus the sibling data can be read to provide support for those of a behaviorist persuasion who tend to consider human development in terms of early determinancy and constancy of effects, or support for those with a proclivity toward organismic theory who see individuals as an open system undergoing various transformations in the course of development.

REFERENCES
Adams, B. (1968). *Kinship in an urban setting.* Chicago: Markham.

Adler, A. (1928). Characteristics of the 1st, 2nd, and 3rd child. *Children, 14*(5).

Booth, C. L. (1981, April). *Contingent responsiveness and mutuality in mother-infant interaction: Birth-order and sex difference?* Presented at the Society for Research in Child Development, Boston.

Bossard, J. H. S., & Boll, E. S. (1966). *The sociology of child development* (4th ed.). New York: Harper & Row.

Chess, S., Thomas, A., & Birch, G. H. (1965). *Your child is a person.* New York: Viking (Compass Books).

Cicirelli, V. G. (1976a). Family structure and interactions: Sibling effects on socialization. In M. F. McMillan & S. Henao (Eds.), *Child psychiatry: Treatment and research.* New York: Brunner/Mazel.

Cicirelli, V. G. (1976b). Siblings teaching siblings. In V. L. Allen (Ed.), *Children as teachers: Theory and research on tutoring.* New York: Academic.

Cicirelli, V. G. (1978). Effect of sibling presence on mother-child interaction. *Developmental Psychology, 14*(3), 315–316.

Deutsch, F. (1975). Birth order effects on measures of social activities for lower-class preschoolers. *Journal of Genetic Psychology, 127,* 325–326.

Falbo, T. (1977). The only child: A review. *Journal of Individual Psychology, 33,* 47–61.

Freedman, R., & Coombs, L. (1966). Child spacing and family economic position. *American Sociological Review, 31,* 631–648.

Hawke, S., & Knox, D. (1978). The one-child family: A new lifestyle. *The Family Coordinator, 27*(3), 215–219.

Lamb, M. E. (1978). The development of sibling relationships in infancy: A short-term longitudinal study. *Child Development, 49,* 1189–1196.

McGurk, H., & Lewis, M. (1972). Birth order: A phenomenon in search of an explanation. *Developmental Psychology, 7,* 366.

Peterson, J. A. (1970). A developmental view of the aging family. In J. E. Birren (Ed.), *Contemporary gerontology: Concepts and issues.* Los Angeles: University of Southern California Gerontology Center.

Segal, J., & Yahraes, H. (1979). *A child's journey: Forces that shape the lives of our young.* New York: McGraw-Hill.

Shanas, E. (1967). Family help patterns and social class in three countries. *Journal of Marriage and the Family, 29,* 257–266.

Shanas, E. (1968). The family and social class. In E. Shanas, P. Townsend, D. Wedderbarn, H. Frus, P. Milkoj, & J. Stehouwer (Eds.), *Old people in three industrial societies.* New York: Atherton.

Shanas, E. (1973). Family-kin networks and aging in cross-cultural perspective. *Journal of Marriage and the Family, 35,* 505–511.

Snow, M. E. (1981, April). *Birth and differences in young children's intentions with mother, father, and peer.* Presented at the Society for Research in Child Development, Boston.

Sulloway, F. R. (1972). *The role of cognitive flexibility in science.* Unpublished paper, Harvard University.

Sutton-Smith, B., & Rosenberg, B. G. (1968). Sibling consensus on power tactics. *Journal of Genetic Psychology, 112,* 63–72.

Toman, W., & Gray, B. (1961). Family constellations of "normal" and "disturbed" marriages: An empirical study. *Journal of Individual Psychology, 17,* 93–95.

Zajonc, R. B. (1976). Family configuration and intelligence: Variations in scholastic aptitude scores parallel trends in family size and the spacing of children. *Science, 192,* 227–236.

Zajonc, R. B., & Markus, G. B. (1975). Birth order and intellectual development. *Psychological Review, 82,* 74–88.

F. Deutsch
San Diego State University

BIRTH ORDER
PEER INFLUENCES

SIMON, HERBERT A. (1916–   )

Herbert A. Simon was born on June 15, 1916, in a predominately German neighborhood of Milwaukee, Wisconsin. His father was an electrical engineer who emigrated to the United States in 1903, and his mother was a third-generation descendant of German immigrants from Prague. In addition to Simon's strong precollege education in the Milwaukee public schools, he was also an avid reader who spent hours in the local public library and museum exploring topics central to the social sciences, biology, and physics. He entered the University of Chicago in 1933 well prepared for a life of scholarship. Since his excellent high school training went a long way toward preparing him for his second-year examinations, he soon began to audit upper-division and graduate-level courses. Simon sampled the rich array of faculty teaching at Chicago during this time, including study with mathematical biophysicist Nicolas Rashevsky, econometrician Henry Schultz, and logician Rudolph Carnap, as well as the wonderful faculty that Charles Merriam had brought together in the political science department, including Harold Gosnell, Harold Lasswell, and Merriam himself. At age 21, Simon had his first publication, with Ridley in the serialized version of "Measuring Municipal Activities" that was published in *Public Management.* This work led to an appointment at Berkeley (1939–1942) to direct a program of studies of local government in California. He wrote his PhD exams while in California and returned to Chicago for his orals, receiving his PhD in political science from the University of Chicago in 1943. His dissertation, *Administrative Behavior* (1947), would become one of the most influential books of this century on the theory of organizations, in particular, and on the theory of human rationality (bounded rationality, according to Simon) in general.

Simon's first teaching appointment was at Illinois Institute of Technology in Chicago, where he stayed for seven years. His work *Public Administration* (with Don Smithburg and Victor Thompson) has influenced many generations of students in administrative theory. When the new Graduate School of Industrial Administration at the Carnegie Institute of Technology was in the planning stages, Simon served as a key adviser. He was then asked to become a full professor of administration in the new school, as well as chairman of the Department of Industrial Management. In view of the generous resources that had just been given to the Carnegie Institute by the Mellon family, Simon made the decision to move to what was to become his academic home for the rest of his life. Not only did he help to build the Department of Industrial Management, but Simon and his colleagues turned their energies into building a new kind of business school, one based on rigorous social science research and empirical findings.

At Carnegie, Simon continued his extensive research on human decision-making. In the early years he drew on the work of cognitive psychologists during an era when their work was ignored by behaviorists, who reigned supreme. Throughout his career he drew on the work of mathematicians, logicians, economists, political scientists, philosophers, computer scientists, and psychologists, as well as on that of the early contributors to what was to become the cybernetic revolution in the social sciences. In the early 1950s he joined forces with Allen Newell and Cliff Shaw, then at the RAND Corporation, in an undertaking that attained its first successes in 1956: to use the new electronic computers as instruments for modeling the processes of human thinking, so that computer programs, like the Logic Theorist, the General Problem Solver, and the Elementary Perceiver and Memorizer became basic formal theories of major cognitive processes. This work with Allen Newell and their faculty colleagues and graduate students, continued in the succeeding years at Carnegie Mellon University to have major impact on the understanding of human thinking.

Although Simon's research since the 1960s consisted mainly of modeling and experimenting on cognitive processes, the resultant general theory of rationality that is bounded by limits of human knowledge and computational ability has also been increasingly influential in redirecting economics and political science toward more realistic views of human reason. According to Simon, individuals satisfice when they have not the wits to optimize, and choose their problem solutions by highly selective heuristic search, guided by patterns made familiar by experience.

The thread of continuity through all Simon's work has been his interest in human decision-making and problem-solving processes, and the implications of these processes for social institutions. For more than 40 years, he has been making extensive use of the computer as a tool both for simulating human thinking and for augmenting it with artificial intelligence.

Simon's books include *Administrative Behavior; Human Problem Solving,* written jointly with Allen Newell; *The Sciences of the Artificial; Scientific Discovery,* with Pat Langley, Gary Bradshaw, and Jan Zytkow; and *Models of My Life* (autobiography).

Simon is Richard King Mellon University Professor of Computer Science and Psychology. In 1978, he received the Alfred Nobel Memorial Prize in Economic Sciences, and in 1986 the National Medal of Science.

STAFF

SIMULTANEOUS CONDITIONING

Dual-task methodology involves assessing performance when individuals perform two tasks simultaneously, and in cognitive neuroscience the dual-task approach is a means to test hypotheses about shared brain substrates of behavioral processes. Simultaneous conditioning uses the dual-task design and is part of a long tradition of psychological research (see Pashler, 1994, for a review). A general model for use in localization of behavioral functions is called the "functional cerebral space" model (Kinsbourne & Hicks, 1978). In this model, performance of an ongoing behavior is predicted to activate regions in the brain that are the substrates for that behavior. In a dual-task paradigm in which two behaviors are performed simultaneously, a second region of activation associated with the second task also occurs. The closer in the brain the regions activated by the two tasks are to each other, the greater the chance that there will be interference between them due to overflow of activation from one to the other.

Using the functional cerebral space approach, experiments are designed to compare simultaneous task performance under two conditions: (a) conditions in which the tasks are hypothesized to involve a common neural system; and (b) conditions in which the tasks are hypothesized to involve separable neural systems. Interference should be obtained when the tasks share a common neural substrate, but there should not be interference when the tasks use separate neural systems. Eyeblink classical conditioning is a form of associative learning for which the essential brain circuitry has been almost entirely identified (Thompson, 1986). Simultaneous conditioning or the application of the dual-task approach using eyeblink classical conditioning and other behaviors is a way to test hypotheses about shared brain substrates with classical conditioning.

In the delay eyeblink classical conditioning procedure, the conditioned stimulus (CS), a tone, is presented first and followed after a delay (in most studies with humans the delay is about half a second) by a corneal air puff unconditioned stimulus (US), and the CS and US end together. Early in the conditioning process when the first paired CS-US presentations are made, participants respond by producing a reflexive eyeblink unconditioned response (UR) to the US. After an average of 40 paired presentations of the CS and US, young adult participants produce conditioned responses (CRs) by blinking before the onset of the US. The well-learned response or CR is an eyeblink to the tone occurring just before the onset of the air puff US. Although the response is timed precisely, the participant typically has little awareness of blinking to the tone CS. This absence of awareness that learning is occurring coupled with the fact that medial temporal-lobe circuits are not essential for acquisition qualifies delay eyeblink conditioning as a nondeclarative form of learning.

The neural circuitry for this form of learning has been documented in nonhuman mammals using a variety of techniques (see Steinmetz, 1996; Thompson & Krupa, 1994, for reviews) and extended to humans in studies of neurological patients (Woodruff-Pak, 1997) and in brain imaging studies in normal human adults (e.g., Logan & Grafton, 1995). The neural pathways for eyeblink classical conditioning involve sensory pathways for the CS and US that converge in the cerebellum on the same side (ipsilateral) as the eye that receives the air puff. The association between the tone CS and airpuff US occurs at two loci within the cerebellum: the interpositus nucleus in nonhuman mammals (globose nucleus in humans) and cerebellar cortex. Using this clear delineation of the eyeblink classical conditioning circuitry, we can undertake behavioral dual-task studies to examine whether tasks interfere with one another and draw implications about the locus of activation of these tasks.

Papka, Ivry, and Woodruff-Pak (1995) conducted a dual-task study to test the hypothesis that timed-interval tapping and eyeblink classical conditioning are both dependent upon cerebellar cortical substrates. Eyeblink conditioning was assessed with a 400-ms delay paradigm, and concurrent with conditioning, separate groups of subjects were tested on a timed-interval tapping task, an explicit memory recognition task, a choice reaction-time task, or, for a baseline control, video-watching. The hypothesis was that simultaneous conditioning and timed-interval tapping performance would produce interference, whereas simultaneous conditioning and memory recognition, choice reaction-time, or video-watching would not produce interference. This hypothesis was supported, and Papka et al. (1995) reported selective interference between eyeblink conditioning and timed-interval tapping but not during any of the other simultaneous conditioning situations.

A task developed to test motor learning is rotary pursuit, in which the participant holds a stylus on a rotating circular disk. With practice, the time that the participant is able to keep the stylus on target increases and errors of going off the target decrease. Simultaneous conditioning with rotary pursuit produced little or no interference suggesting separate neural substrates for the two tasks (Green & Woodruff-Pak, 1997). Word-stem completion priming is a form of learning in which previous experience with a word makes it more likely to be cued by a word stem. Additional work in our laboratory indicated that simultaneous conditioning with word-stem completion priming produced no interference with either task, supporting the contention that these two forms of learning have separate neural substrates (Green, Small, Downey-Lamb, & Woodruff-Pak, in press).

A stronger test of the separability of these two nondeclarative forms of learning and memory was carried out in my laboratory by testing young and older adults on simultaneous conditioning and word-stem completion. The fact that older adults tend to perform more poorly as the complexity of the task is increased is interpreted as an indicator of limited processing resources. The perspective of a diminution of processing capacity in older adulthood is long-standing (e.g., Birren, 1964; Welford, 1958), and contemporary research addressing issues such as aging and working memory continue to reinforce this position. From the perspective that older adults have a diminished processing capacity, it follows that older adults might be impaired in simultaneous conditioning and word-stem completion priming even though younger adults are not impaired in this dual-task situation. Comparing groups of younger and older adults on simultaneous conditioning and priming and comparing their performance to conditioning and priming as single tasks, Downey-Lamb (1999) found no evidence of interference in the simultaneous condition for the young or older adults. Thus, simultaneous conditioning studies demonstrate tasks that do not share the same neural substrate as well as tasks that share cerebellar substrates.

REFERENCES

Birren, J. E. (1964). *The psychology of aging.* Englewood Cliffs, NJ: Prentice Hall.

Downey-Lamb, M. M. (1999). Dual task performance in younger and older adults: Evidence for brain structures engaged during nondeclarative tasks. Unpublished doctoral dissertation, Temple University.

Green, J. T., Small, E. M., Downey-Lamb, M. M., & Woodruff-Pak, D. S. (in press). Dual task performance of eyeblink classical conditioning and visual repetition priming: Separate brain memory systems. *Neuropsychology.*

Green, J. T., & Woodruff-Pak, D. S. (1997). Concurrent eyeblink classical conditioning and rotary pursuit performance: Implications for independent nondeclarative systems. *Neuropsychology, 11,* 474–487.

Kinsbourne, M., & Hicks, R. E. (1978). Functional cerebral space: A model for overflow, transfer and interference effects in human performance: A tutorial review. In J. Requin (Ed.), *Attention and Performance VII* (pp. 345–362). Hillsdale, NJ: Erlbaum.

Logan, C. G., & Grafton, S. T. (1995). Functional anatomy of human eyeblink conditioning determined with regional cerebral glucose metabolism and positron-emission tomography. *Proceedings of the National Academy of Sciences (USA), 92,* 7500–7504.

Papka, M., Ivry, R. B., & Woodruff-Pak, D. S. (1995). Selective disruption of eyeblink classical conditioning by concurrent tapping. *Neuroreport, 6,* 1493–1497.

Pashler, H. (1994). Dual-task interference in simple tasks: Data and theory. *Psychological Bulletin, 116,* 220–244.

Steinmetz, J. E. (1996). The brain substrates of classical eyeblink conditioning in rabbits. In J. R. Bloedel, T. J. Ebner, & S. P. Wise (Eds.), *The acquisition of motor behavior in vertebrates* (pp. 89–114). Cambridge, MA: MIT Press.

Thompson, R. F. (1986). The neurobiology of learning and memory. *Science, 233,* 941–947.

Thompson, R. F., & Krupa, D. J. (1994). Organization of memory traces in the mammalian brain. *Annual Review of Neuroscience, 17,* 519–549.

Welford, A. T. (1958). *Ageing and human skill.* London: Oxford University Press.

Woodruff-Pak, D. S. (1997). Classical conditioning. In R. J. Bradley, R. A. Harris, & P. Jenner (Series Eds.), *International Review of Neurobiology* (Vol. 41); J. D. Schmahmann (Ed.), *The cerebellum and cognition* (pp. 341–366). San Diego: Academic.

D. S. WOODRUFF-PAK
Temple University

COGNITIVE NEUROSCIENCE OF LEARNING AND MEMORY EYELID CLASSICAL CONDITIONING

SINGLE PARENTHOOD

The number of single-parent families in the United States maintained by women increased by 131% between 1960 and 1978 (Miller, 1980). This resulted in one in five children becoming a member of a single-parent family. The single-parenthood phenomenon is not restricted to the United States. For example, in 1976 there were 160,000 single parents in Australia raising 282,000 children (Social Welfare Commission, 1976). Perhaps, the most comprehensive international report on single-parent families was released by Finer in 1974. The report noted that single-parent families were faced with such problems as social isolation and loneliness, financial hardships, and pressure on children to be responsible for domestic duties that were beyond their capabilities.

The nature of the problems facing single-parent families has been investigated by several researchers. The studies can be divided into two areas—impact on children and impact on parents.

IMPACT ON CHILDREN

A review of the literature suggests that single-parent children have a tendency to become poorly socialized, be cognitively deficient, and experience poor parent-child interactions (Hetherington et al., 1975; Wallerstein & Kelly, 1975). Hetherington and colleagues (1978) also found that during the first year following divorce, children are more aggressive, oppositional, distractible, and demanding than children from intact families. Several other studies support these findings (Felner et al., 1975; Tuckman & Reagan, 1966; Wallerstein & Kelly, 1975).

Crossman and Adams (1980) described two social psychological theories that can be used to understand the potential negative effects of divorce on children. Crisis theory suggests that divorce is an undesirable and stressful event that can have undesirable consequences for a family member. The theory suggests that some children may be more sensitive and vulnerable to the stresses associated with divorce. These children, therefore, would experience more negative effects.

Zajonc (1976) describes a second theory that emphasizes the importance of the amount of time that the parent and child spend interacting. The theory argues that a certain amount of time for the parent and child to interact is critical to the child's social and cognitive development, an assumption supported by research (Shinn, 1978). Zajonc's theory suggests that single parents tend to have less time to spend with their children because of additional role demands. The children's social and cognitive development thus tends to suffer because they do not have enough time to interact with their parent.

IMPACT ON PARENT

The most common initial reaction to single parenthood by a parent is depression. Often the parent feels victimized, alone, and angry. They tend to worry about unpredictable income, poor housing, and feelings of inadequacy (Miller, 1980). Other emotional reactions experienced by single parents include guilt or a sense of failure about a marriage breakdown, grief, fear, anxiety, confusion, and, in some cases, relief (Burgess & Nystul, 1977). The advent of single parenthood may also result in increased strain on the single parent's time, energy, emotions, and ability to work (Burgess & Nystul, 1977).

There has been a limited amount of research on the factors associated with "successful single-parent families." Barry (1979) has identified tasks for the adjustment period and tasks for the new family period that promote a positive single-parenthood experience.

Tasks for the Adjustment Period

1. It must be realized that changes have occurred within the family and that they will affect each member.

2. It must be realized that it will take time for each family member to experience the full impact of these changes.

3. Each family member needs to be allowed to mourn the loss of the parent who has left the family.

4. The limits and opportunities of the new situation must be assessed realistically.

5. The parent should try to understand, and to be accepting and supportive of, the children's attempts to react and adjust to the situation.

6. Parents should seek professional help for themselves and children if progress on these tasks is blocked.

Tasks for the New Family Period

1. The role of the parent who has left the family must be clarified in a manner that maximizes the parent's contribution to self and children.

2. Problem-solving and decision-making skills should be used to cope with such practical concerns as financial planning.

3. Communication and leadership skills should be used to readjust family roles for parents and children.

4. Realistic goals should be established for each family member.

5. Social networks should be established that support the personal goals set.

6. Positive parenting principles should be practiced.

7. Short- and long-term family goals with the children should be established and continually worked on.

REFERENCES

Barry, A. (1979). A research project on successful single-parent families. *American Journal of Family Therapy, 7,* 65–73.

Burgess, P., & Nystul, M. S. (1977). The single-parent family: A review of the literature. *Australian Child and Family Welfare, 8,* 19–26.

Crossman, S. M., & Adams, G. R. (1980). Divorce, single-parenting, and child development. *The Journal of Psychology, 106,* 205–217.

Felner, R., Stolberg, A., & Cowen, E. (1975). Crises events and school mental health referral patterns of young children. *Journal of Counsulting and Clinical Psychology, 43,* 305–310.

Hetherington, D. M., Cox, M., & Cox, R. (1975, April). Beyond father absence: Conceptualization of effects of divorce. Presented at the meeting of the Society for Research in Child Development, Denver, CO.

Hetherington, D. M., Cox, M., & Cox, R. (1978, May). Family interaction and the social, emotional, and cognitive development of children following divorce. Presented at the Symposium on the Family: Setting Priorities, sponsored by the Institute for Pediatric Service of Johnson and Johnson, Washington, DC.

Miller, J. R. (1980). Problems of single-parent families. *Journal of New York State Nurses Association, 11,* 5–8.

Shinn, M. (1978). Father absence and children's cognitive development. *Psychological Bulletin, 85,* 295–324.

Social Welfare Commission. (1976). *Needs of lone parent families in Australia.* Canberra, Australia: Department of Social Security.

Tuckman, J., & Reagan, R. A. (1966). Intactness of the home and behavioral problems in children. *Journal of Child Psychology and Psychiatry, 7,* 225–233.

Wallerstein, J. S., & Kelly, J. B. (1975). The effects of parental divorce: Experiences of the preschool child. *Journal of American Academy of Child Psychiatry, 14,* 600–616.

Zajonc, R. B. (1976). Family configuration and intelligence: Variations in scholastic aptitude scores parallel trends in family size and the spacing of children. *Science, 192,* 227–236.

M. S. NYSTUL

SINGLE-SUBJECT RESEARCH DESIGNS

Single-subject research designs involve the intensive study of one organism continuously or repeatedly across time. The organism may be a person or a single molar unit such as an industrial organization or a political unit. As with conventional group designs based on reasonably large samples of subjects, single-subject designs are employed to determine whether different variables are related or whether a treatment or intervention causes some effect on relevant response measures. There are situations in which it is more meaningful, more convenient, more ethical, or less expensive to study one or very few subjects intensively than to study many subjects. A basic difference between group and single-subject designs is that one or very few observations are generally obtained from each subject in group designs, whereas many observations are obtained from one or very few subjects across time in the case of single-subject designs. The design categories of correlational, quasi-experimental, and experimental are used frequently to classify different types of group designs; and they can also be used to classify various single-subject designs.

CORRELATIONAL DESIGNS

Single-subject correlational designs involve a collection of scores obtained across time (a time-series) on some dependent variable of interest. In addition, either a series of scores on some other variable collected at the same time points (the concomitant series), or a log of events that occur during the time-series is obtained. An analysis is then carried out to determine whether changes in the dependent variable time-series are associated with changes in the concomitant series or the occurrence of events that have been recorded. If an association is identified (through visual or statistical analysis), this may lead to the hypothesis that variability in the dependent variable series has been caused by a concomitant variable. It may be possible to test such a hypothesis using a quasi-experiment or an experiment. Unlike the single-subject quasi-experimental designs, the correlational design is not characterized by the experimental manipulation of some independent variable. Quasi-experiments and experiments differ in the extent to which the experimenter can rule out explanations for change other than the independent variable, but both design types employ manipulation of an independent variable that is under the control of the experimenter.

QUASI-EXPERIMENTAL DESIGN

The quasi-experimental AB design consists of two phases: the baseline (A phase) and the intervention (B phase). Data are collected during the A phase to describe the behavior before the treatment is introduced. The amount of baseline data collected depends on the type of behavior studied, the type of subject, the situational variables, and other aspects of the study. A useful guideline is to have sufficient baseline data to obtain a clear picture of the stability of the behavior. After the baseline data are collected, the experimenter introduces an intervention, and data continue to be collected during the B phase. The intervention may be applied throughout this phase or only briefly at the beginning of the phase, depending on the nature of the intervention, the dependent variable, and the purpose of the study. The intervention should be in-

troduced when other variables surrounding the experiment that can be expected to affect the dependent variable are stable. If conditions other than the intervention change at the time the intervention is introduced, the change on the dependent variable from the A to the B phase will be confounded. A major weakness of the AB design is that it is often difficult to know if some condition other than the intervention has changed between the A and B phases. Since the logic of the design is that behavior during the A phase is predictive of behavior during the B phase in the absence of an intervention, it is desirable to have baseline behavior that is reasonably stable and unaffected by conditions other than the intervention. It is not unusual, however, to have little or no control over conditions that may change at the same time the intervention is introduced. Stronger experimental designs are required to cope with this problem.

EXPERIMENTAL DESIGNS

Several single-subject experimental designs are described here; others exist but they are slight variants of these basic designs. Each of these designs provides greater certainty that a planned intervention is responsible for a change observed in time-series data than is provided by the AB quasi-experiment.

Reversal Designs

The direct extensions of the AB design are the ABA (baseline-intervention-baseline) and ABAB (baseline-intervention-baseline-intervention) designs. The ABAB design is often referred to as a "reversal" design in the behavior modification literature because the intervention condition is said to be reversed (or more appropriately, withdrawn) after it is first applied. The advantage of these designs is that there is repeated demonstration of the effect of changing conditions that are manipulated by the experimenter. These designs help rule out the interpretation that some event other than the intervention may be responsible for change on the dependent variable. If the level of behavior during the second A phase in an ABA experiment returns to a level similar to that observed during the original A phase, the argument is strengthened that the intervention has caused a change. The argument is further strengthened if the intervention condition is introduced again after the second A phase; this collection of phases yields the ABAB design. If the behavior is consistent within the two baseline conditions, consistent within the two intervention conditions, but clearly different between baseline and intervention conditions, a convincing case can be made that the intervention is effective and that the effect has been replicated within the subject. There are, however, many logical, ethical, and practical problems with these designs.

Many interventions are one-shot treatments such as surgical ablation or teaching a skill (e.g., how to ride a bicycle). Once these treatments are applied, it may be illogical to expect the behavior of the subject to revert to a preintervention level. Thus, these designs are appropriate only if the dependent variable is a behavior that can be expected to return to the level observed during the baseline phase when the intervention is withdrawn. Sometimes behavior is expected to revert to the baseline level but does not do so because conditions other than the intervention not present during the baseline phase maintain the behavior. In other situations, ethical arguments are incompatible with the design requirements; for example, an intervention may change a behavior that is harmful to the subject and consequently should not be withdrawn.

Irrespective of ethical issues, few psychotherapists are inclined to cooperate with a researcher who suggests returning to a baseline condition once an intervention appears to be effective in reducing the severity of a problem. These and related problems greatly reduce the number of situations in which ABA and ABAB designs are appropriate. Other single-subject designs can solve these problems.

Multiple Baseline Designs

Most of the difficulties associated with reversal designs can be solved with some version of the multiple baseline design. This design is useful in a wide variety of basic and applied research settings. In a sense, this design is a collection of AB designs. Data are collected on two or more baseline series and an intervention is applied to the first one. If the intervention appears to shift the time-series to which it is applied but does not shift the other baseline series, it is then applied to the second series. If the application of the intervention to the second series has an effect on this series but not on the other series, the next series is then exposed to the intervention. Hence each available baseline series is exposed to the intervention, but the intervention is never initiated on more than one series at a time. Because the intervention is introduced in a staggered manner to the various baselines, it is implausible that some event unrelated to the intervention is the cause of the apparent effect on each series.

There are essentially three versions of the multiple baseline design; each version is identified by the nature of the baselines observed. The multiple baselines may be based on data collected across several different behaviors (dependent variables) from one subject in one setting, several different situations on one behavior on one subject, or several different subjects on one behavior in one setting. In the case of multiple baselines across subjects, the design no longer qualifies as "single-subject," but the rationale for all versions is similar. A problem with the versions involving multiple baselines across behaviors is that the behaviors may be highly correlated and, as a result, will not provide independent sources of information on the intervention effects. In this case, if the intervention is applied to and has an effect on the first baseline, it will also shift other correlated behaviors even though the intervention has not been directly applied to these behaviors. Although such an outcome supports the generality of the shift in behavior across several measures, the reason for the shift then becomes suspect because the nontreated behaviors are not useful controls in this case.

Similar problems can occur with multiple baselines across situations or subjects, but the latter version is not as vulnerable to these problems because different subjects can often be isolated from each other. In general, multiple baseline designs avoid the ethical problem of withdrawing an effective intervention, are useful with interventions and behaviors that are either reversible or nonreversible, and are practical to implement in a wide variety of research settings.

Single-Subject Randomized Experiment

Unlike the previously described designs, the single-subject randomized experiment does not employ a different condition throughout each of a small number of phases. Instead, the order of two (or more) different conditions is randomly assigned to the subject. Random assignment allows greater confidence that the difference in behavior between conditions is caused by the experimental manipulation than is the case with designs having only two or three nonrandom phases. The reason for this high level of confidence is that each condition is introduced and withdrawn many times during the experiment. A disadvantage of this approach is that the logic of the design dictates the use of treatments having very rapid effects that will not carry over long enough to contaminate the other treatments.

Alternating Treatments Design

The differential effects of two or more treatments can be examined through the alternating treatments design. This design combines aspects of conventional multiple baseline designs with the single-subject randomized experiment. Multiple baseline data on one dependent variable (e.g., amount of pain experienced) are repeatedly collected from one subject in two or more situations (e.g., at home and at school) during the first phase. In the second phase, one treatment is applied in the first situation, and then another treatment is applied in another situation. The treatments are alternated or presented in random order for each situation across time for the duration of the second phase. If one of the treatments is identified as most effective during the second phase, this treatment alone may be applied in all situations during a third phase to confirm the effect across situations. Advantages of this design over the reversal design are that several treatments can be studied within a short period of time, it is not necessary to withhold all treatments after baseline data are collected, and generality of results across situations is established. Carryover effects and multiple-treatment interference, however, are possible interpretation issues. Other versions of this design involve the study of a single treatment, multiple dependent variables, or more complex arrangements in which multiple treatments, multiple dependent variables, or multiple subjects are employed.

COMPARISON OF SINGLE-SUBJECT AND GROUP DESIGNS

Single-subject and group designs differ in terms of several important characteristics, including data collection problems, the nature of question answered, and data analysis.

Data Collection Problems

Although it may be desirable to proceed from the use of single-subject designs for treatment refinement to group designs for outcome estimation, the realities of the research environment and the nature of the variables of interest usually dictate the design choice. Some internally valid single-subject design is feasible if the subject is available repeatedly across a reasonable amount of time and is willing to participate, if treatment manipulation is under the control of the experimenter, if the environmental context in which the subject is observed and treated is reasonably constant across the duration of the experiment, and if the dependent variable is a measure that can be obtained repeatedly or continuously. There are many variables (both independent and dependent) that are not easily (or at reasonable cost) employed repeatedly. This aspect of single-subject designs is perhaps the most limiting. If the experimenter is not able to treat and measure repeatedly (for logical, practical, or political reasons), a group design may be the only choice.

Group designs, however, are associated with other limitations. Randomized group designs, for example, are often impossible to carry out because random assignment of subjects to conditions may not be possible or there may be very few subjects available for the experiment. If continuous treatment and measurement are not possible but data from several treatment and measurement periods can be collected on a few subjects, repeated measurement group designs are appropriate.

Question Answered

At a general level, both single-subject and group experimental designs provide an answer to the question of whether there is a treatment effect. They differ in terms of how the "effect" is defined and studied. The typical between-group approach is to compare two or more groups at one or very few points in time on means and variances. If the groups are equal before the treatment is applied (as a result of random assignment), the differences between means and variances are viewed as descriptions of the treatment "effects." In the case of a two-group randomized experiment in which one group is a control and the other receives a treatment, the difference between the sample means can be interpreted as an unbiased estimate of the number of units the treatment causes the population mean to increase (or decrease). The mean difference is often measured at one time point after the treatment administration.

The ABAB single-subject design, for example, also involves a comparison of behavior under two conditions, but the process of change is recorded across time. The comparison of the A and B phases can illustrate the difference in performance associated with a behavior repeatedly measured under two conditions, but the difference is not a mean difference between treated and untreated subjects and should not be interpreted as an estimate of the effect the treatment would have on a population of untreated subjects. The ABAB design provides important information on the form of change across time (both within and between phases) for a single subject, whereas the between-groups design provides an estimate of the intervention magnitude (generally at one time point) for a specified population of subjects. The usefulness of the information obtained from each design depends on the type of external validity of greatest relevance.

If the major issue is the identification of a treatment that will be effective for a particular patient, a comparison of treatment and control means from a group comparison experiment may be of little value. If the purpose of the research is to estimate the effectiveness of a treatment for patients as a whole, the single-subject experiment may be of little value. The adequacy of both group designs for making treatment decisions regarding the individual and single-subject designs for estimating treatment effects for patients as a whole depend upon the same thing: variance of treatment ef-

fects across patients. Thus it is necessary to study the efficacy of treatments across many subjects if the generality of results is to be established. But this is not an argument for the use of group rather than single-subject designs. The two types of design can be integrated.

A strong argument can be made that the nature of the treatment process should be investigated first with single-subject designs. An advantage of this approach is the ease with which various aspects of the intervention can be fine-tuned in response to the feedback provided by continuously recorded behavior. An effective intervention may be developed through the intensive study of one or a few subjects. The hypothesis can be tested on other subjects by using the same intervention with them. This is often called "direct replication" if the intervention, experimenter, setting, and dependent variable are unchanged from the original experiment. If the outcome of several direct replications confirms the findings of the original experiment, generality of results is established across subjects.

Direct replications are often followed with "systematic replications" in which the intervention is applied by different experimenters, in different settings, with different types of subjects on a variety of measures. In group design terminology, the purpose of systematic replication is to establish the external validity of the experiment; that is, to provide evidence for the generality of the intervention across settings, experimenters, and measures as well as across subjects. After an intervention or treatment package is developed using single-subject designs, it is often convincing subsequently to employ the treatment in a group design outcome study.

The advantage of the group design is that it can provide answers to questions concerning the magnitude of the expected effect with a population of untreated and unmeasured subjects having specified characteristics. Estimates of the mean effect and the proportion of subjects who improve after a specified period under treatment and control conditions are essential in many applied situations.

Data Analysis

Historically, group designs have been associated with the use of statistical inference as the major form of data analysis, whereas single-subject designs in most areas of psychology have usually been analyzed using only visual analysis of graphed data. Formal statistical methods are now available for the statistical analysis of various single-subject designs. Some of these methods are based on minor modifications of conventional regression methods; others employ recently developed computer-intensive approaches.

SUGGESTED READING

Barlow, D. H., & Hersen, M. (1984). *Single case experimental designs: Strategies for studying behavior change.* New York: Pergamon.

Guyatt, G. H., Heyting, A., Jaeschke, R., Keller, J., Adachi, J. D., & Roberts, R. S. (1990). N of 1 randomized trials for investigating new drugs. *Controlled Clinical Trials, 11,* 88–100.

Hayes, S. C. (1992). Single-case experimental design and empirical clinical practice. In A. E. Kazdin (Ed.), *Methodological issues &*

strategies in clinical research (pp. 491–521). Washington, DC: American Psychological Association.

Johnston, J. M., & Pennypacker, H. S. (1993). *Strategies and tactics of behavioral research* (2nd ed.). Hillsdale, NJ: Erlbaum.

Johnston, J. M., & Pennypacker, H. S. (1993). *Readings for strategies and tactics of behavioral research* (2nd ed.). Hillsdale, NJ: Erlbaum.

Kazdin, A. E. (1982). *Single-case research designs.* New York: Oxford University Press.

B. E. Huitema
Western Michigan University

EXPERIMENTAL DESIGN
RESEARCH METHODOLOGY

THE SIXTEEN PERSONALITY FACTOR QUESTIONNAIRE

The Sixteen Personality Factor Questionnaire (16PF) is one of the most widely used, theory-based instruments for assessing normal-range personality characteristics in adults. Since the time of its first US publication in 1949, the test has been translated into nearly 50 languages. The test is used worldwide to evaluate a set of 16 reasonably independent personality characteristics that predict a wide range of socially significant criteria. Adaptations of the original questionnaire have been developed for assessing personality in younger populations, effectively extending the age range of the test down to six years old.

The test was developed by Cattell and a series of coauthors over a period of many decades after extensive research intended to clarify the basic organization of human personality. Cattell, who was born in England and emigrated to the United States during the 1930s, was interested primarily in identifying a relatively small set of "source traits" that could be used to explain variations in the much larger set of "surface" characteristics observable in behavior and recorded in language.

Cattell looked primarily to language to begin his search, because he was convinced that "all aspects of human personality which are or have been of importance, interest, or utility have already become recorded in the substance of language" (Cattell, 1943). Whether or not it is true that language exhaustively delimited the field of study, it is certainly true that language extensively described the field of study. At about the time Cattell began his studies, Allport and Odbert (1936) had identified about 18,000 words in the English dictionary alone that described distinctive aspects of human behavior. When he eliminated terms that were essentially evaluative (e.g., adorable, evil), metaphorical (e.g. alive, prolific), or that described temporary states (e.g., rejoicing, frantic), 4,504 terms still remained. Cattell began with that list and conducted a series of reductive analyses to eliminate overlap among them. His analyses encompassed a variety of perspectives (e.g., peer ratings, self-reports), populations (e.g., undergraduates, mili-

tary personnel, working adults), and methodologies (e.g., cluster analysis, factor analysis). By beginning his search with the entire universe of trait names and conducting the reduction systematically, Cattell reasoned that the set finally remaining must be judged to be "source traits." His undergraduate training as a chemist undoubtedly influenced Cattell's argument. In the same way that water, for example, could be conceptualized as a weighted combination of elementary molecules (two parts hydrogen, one part oxygen), Cattell believed that human characteristics such as creativity or depression could be conceptualized as weighted combinations of the small set of source traits that survived his analyses.

The first publication of the 16PF did not occur until more than a decade after Cattell began his studies. Since then the test has undergone several major and more numerous minor revisions. The most recent, in 1993, was the last Cattell completed before his death in 1998.

The current test contains 185 items, requires 35 to 50 minutes to complete, and has a fifth grade reading level. The test can be scored by hand, but computerized scoring and an extensive array of interpretive reports are also available. Many of the items in the test are statements (e.g., "I get embarrassed if I suddenly become the center of attention in a social group") to which the examinee responds by choosing from three options (true, uncertain, false). Others present a set of contrasted choices (e.g., "If I could, I would rather exercise by (a) fencing or dancing, (b) uncertain, (c) wrestling or baseball"). The test provides scores for 16 "primary" scales and five "global" factors. The global factors (called "second-order" factors in earlier test editions) result from factor analyses of the 16 primary scales and are conceptualized as major organizing influences behind the primary scales. The average primary scale test-retest scale reliability coefficient is .83 after a few weeks and .72 over a period of two months. Corresponding values for the global scales are slightly higher. Internal consistency reliabilities of the primary scales average .75.

The primary scales of the test, which are designated by alphanumeric symbols, are as follows: A–Warmth, B–Reasoning, C–Emotional Stability, E–Dominance, F–Liveliness, G–Rule-Consciousness, H–Social Boldness, I–Sensitivity, L–Vigilance, M–Abstractedness, N–Privateness, O–Apprehension, Q_1–Openness to Change, Q_2–Self-reliance, Q_3–Perfectionism, Q_4–Tension. The five global factors (Extroversion, Anxiety, Tough-mindedness, Independence, Self-control) assess features similar to those described as the "big five" in contemporary personality research. Besides the primary scales and global factors, the 16PF can be scored for approximately 100 criteria that derive from years of research on 16PF applications in clinical, counseling, and organizational psychology.

Besides the substantive scales just described, the 16PF provides three response style indicators: Impression Management, Infrequency, and Acquiescence. These scales are helpful in identifying unusual response patterns that may affect the validity of the profile. The Impression Management scale correlates with social desirability of the alternatives selected. Because elevated scores on the Infrequency scale reflect overuse of the middle ("uncertain") response category, elevations on this scale suggest attempts to dissimulate by failing to reveal information about oneself. The Acquiescence scale assesses tendency to agree without regard to the content of the item. Elevations on this scale could reflect a high need for approval; they might also signify a thoughtless, random response pattern.

Interpretation of the 16PF is enhanced by the extensive body of research findings related to its use that have accumulated over time. A great deal is known, for example, about how test scores relate to career preference, job performance, academic achievement, creativity, interpersonal relationships, and marital satisfaction. Although the 16PF was not specifically designed for use with clinical populations, clinical research suggests that the test can be useful in understanding the dynamics of adjustment and personality disorders, addiction, and spousal abuse. Carefully-conducted longitudinal studies have also identified physical health correlates among the primary scales. For example, test scores have been shown to be predictive of subsequent heart attacks in symptom-free adults.

The 16PF is primarily used to provide an objective determination of what a person is like and, therefore, tell what the person is likely to do in various situations. For example, will the person function effectively in jobs that require a strong technical orientation? Can he or she be counted on to finish things he or she starts? Will he or she be an effective leader? Are these the kinds of people who are likely to handle high-stress situations well? Applications of the test in the area of relationship counseling stem from the test's ability to predict likely patterns of social interaction.

The 16PF's content overlaps with that of other omnibus instruments designed to assess normal-range personality, like the California Psychological Inventory, the NEO Personality Inventory, and the Personality Research Form. Correlational studies show that relationships among individual scales of these inventories are often quite high (Conn & Riecke, 1994). However, the multivariate model that underlies the 16PF is quite distinct from those on which these other instruments are built, and the 16PF is embedded within a broader theoretical framework that Cattell developed to address individual differences in learning and human development (Cattell, 1979, 1980).

Over 50 years, the 16PF has developed into a widely-used instrument for assessing adult personality. A long history of empirical research with the test by Cattell and others and an origin within a well-established theory provide a rich source of interpretation for test users.

REFERENCES

Allport, G. W., & Odbert, H. S. (1936). Trait-names, a psycholexical study. *Psychological Monographs, 47.*

Cattell, R. B. (1943). The description of personality: Basic traits resolved into clusters. *Journal of Abnormal and Social Psychology, 38,* 476–506.

Cattell, R. B. (1979). Personality and learning theory (Volume 1): The structure of personality in its environment. New York: Springer.

Cattell, R. B. (1980). Personality and learning theory (Volume 2): A systems theory of maturation and structured learning. New York: Springer.

Conn, S. R., & Riecke, M. L. (1994). *The 16PF fifth edition technical manual.* Champaign, IL: Institute for Personality and Ability Testing.

S. E. KRUG
MetriTech, Inc.

MEASUREMENT
PERSONALITY ASSESSMENT
QUESTIONNAIRES

SKINNER, BURHUS FREDRICK (1904–1990)

Burhus Fredrick Skinner is judged by many as one of a half dozen most important psychologists of the 20th century. However, like anyone who takes a strong position, he had throughout his career many critics. He will be regarded as a great teacher, experimental psychologist, behavior theorist, and never-ending promoter of a strictly objective psychology.

Skinner received the AB from Hamilton College, where he majored in English and the classics. He received the MA and PhD (1931) from Harvard University. After a period of postdoctoral research, he went to the University of Minnesota (1931–1943), Indiana University (1943–1948), and then returned to Harvard for the remainder of his teaching career.

During the 1930s his experimental research efforts were devoted to developing a set of learning principles using white rats as his subjects. When he went to Indiana, he began to use pigeons instead. His research with the rats resulted in the publication of his first book, *The Behavior of Organisms*. Perhaps his most important contribution to experimental psychology was the invention of the operant-conditioning chamber, commonly referred to as the Skinner box. In the original version with rats, the animals pressed a lever on the side of the cage to receive what Skinner called a reinforcement (usually a pellet of food). Later, Skinner and others adapted the apparatus for pigeons, monkeys, humans, and a variety of other organisms. This apparatus has been used for thousands of experiments to test various principles of learning. The rate of responding is measured by a cumulative recorder, also invented by Skinner.

As the period of the 1960s approached, Skinner became appalled by the inefficiency of American education, and he put his efforts to developing a teaching machine and programmed learning. In this process the subject is allowed to proceed at his or her own rate in very small steps until a body of knowledge has been mastered. Subjects are given immediate feedback as to the correctness of their answers. Over the years programmed learning never was adopted by most educators, perhaps because they were afraid that the machine would take over their jobs. However, it has been and is being used in business, industry, and other aspects of human endeavor.

In 1953, Skinner applied his ideas to human behavior, which resulted in the book *Science and Human Behavior*. Earlier, in 1948, he tried his hand at writing a novel (*Walden two*), a book that was used more in psychology classes than in English assignments. It presented a psychological utopia. In 1957 Skinner collaborated with Charles Ferster in a large research project that culminated in the publication of *Schedules of Reinforcement*, which showed that reinforcements need not be delivered after every response but could be programmed as to time and ratio. In the same year, he published *Verbal Behavior*, an analysis of language applying principles of learning developed in the laboratory to human speech. His book *Beyond Freedom and Dignity* hit the best-seller list, but it generally received poor reviews from the literary press. In it he dealt with social issues, freedom, dignity, value, and control. Basically, his reviewers, not being psychologists, probably did not understand what he was trying to say. In the late 1970s, he wrote a three-volume autobiography: *Particulars of My Life, The Shaping of a Behaviorist*, and *A Matter of Consequences*. Up until the night before his death, he continued to write and lecture.

Skinner received many awards and honors, including APA's Distinguished Contribution Award, the National Medal of Science Award, and the Gold Medal Award from the American Psychological Foundation. Shortly before his death, he received a special award from the American Psychological Association for a lifetime of distinguished service to psychology, the first ever to be given.

Besides the establishment of a division of the American Psychological Association (Division 25) devoted to his brand of psychology, several journals are devoted to experiments and theorizing of his position, the most important being *The Journal of the Experimental Analysis of Behavior*. Like the founder of behaviorism, John B. Watson, Skinner's ideas have been controversial. He remained a radical behaviorist to the end. Those who are sympathetic to his position believe he did more to promote psychology as a science than anyone else of the time. He fostered a completely objective approach and opposed the mentalism of psychoanalysis, humanistic, and cognitive psychologies.

R. W. LUNDIN
Wheaton, Illinois

SLEEP

Sleep is both commonplace and mysterious. Like other natural functions such as breathing and walking, sleep is a continuing and usual aspect of our lives. When we consider sleep, however, we are aware of its mysterious nature. Before its presence, all behavior bows down and consciousness of ourselves and our surrounding moves from its accustomed place. Contemporary research has done much to inform us about sleep's dark kingdom.

THE BACKGROUND OF SLEEP RESEARCH

Formal speculations about sleep extend back to the Grecian times (Aristotle wrote a chapter on sleep), and research findings about sleep emerged as a part of the development of life science research in the 19th century. As findings about the circulatory system and the central nervous system (CNS) were developed, descriptions of the changes in these systems associated with sleep would be noted and often translated into theories of sleep. Three landmark books

cumulated these emerging findings: Manaciene's *Sleep: Its Physiology, Pathology, Hygiene and Psychology* in 1899 (English edition), Pieron's *Le Problème Physiologique de Sommeil* in 1913, and Kleitman's *Sleep and Wakefulness* in 1939.

A major technological development took place in 1937. The electroencephalogram (EEG), which measures brain waves, showed distinct and systematic pattern changes with the onset of and throughout sleep. For the first time, sleep could be measured objectively and continuously and could be viewed as an active process.

A second major breakthrough occurred in 1953 when Kleitman and his student Eugene Aserinsky discovered a regularly reoccurring "stage" of sleep characterized by rapid eye movements (REMs) and an active "awake" EEG pattern. This pattern, appearing spontaneously about every 90 minutes, was found to "index" the presence of the dream in human subjects.

This finding, in combination with rapid advances in CNS research and the discovery of the "activated" sleep analog in animals, dates the beginning of the explosive development of sleep research. Prior to the late 1950s, there were some 100 to 200 sleep research papers a year. By the 1980s, the number exceeded 2,000 annually.

Sleep research is an interdisciplinary effort of central interest to no single discipline but of pertinence to many. The researchers include biochemists, biologists, endocrinologists, neuroscientists, pediatricians, physiologists, psychiatrists, and psychologists. The particular studies range from single nerve cell activity to dream interpretation; the subjects include the entire phyla of organisms, infants, the elderly, and a full range of pathological states.

The early research of this period was primarily laboratory research that concentrated on explicating the REM sleep period. Some 40 to 50% of the studies focused on the CNS. There has been increasing emphasis on the clinical aspects of sleep disorders.

THE DIMENSIONS OF SLEEP

There are three measurement domains: sleep structure, sleep patterns, and subjective responses. Sleep structure refers to the dimensions of the ongoing sleep process; sleep patterns describe the amounts and placements of sleep within the 24 hours; subjective responses include evaluative statements about sleep and dream recall.

Sleep structure is conventionally indexed by the EEG. In the young human adult, there are four "stages" of sleep (1–4) that are roughly related to sleep depth and the 1–REM (stage 1 plus REMs).

Figure 1 shows a typical night of sleep of a young adult indexed by stages. Each night all humans will approximate this record: 50% (±5%) stage 2; 25% (±4%) 1–REM; 15% (±3%) Stage 4; 7% (±2%) stage 3; and 3% (±2%) stage 1. The first REM period will occur after about 90 to 100 minutes and at intervals of 90 to 100 minutes thereafter with increases in the lengths of the bursts. Most of stages 3 and 4 will occur in the early third of the night. There may be a few spontaneous awakenings. Stages occur in sequence with REM emerging from stage 2. This is the organized, inherent pattern of sleep from night to night, from person to person, among young adults. There are no discernible sex, race, or status differences.

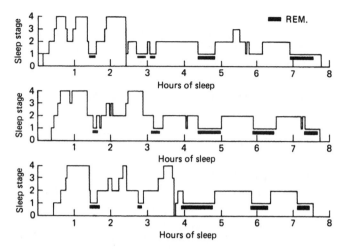

Figure 1. The sleep of a young adult described in stages. Stages 1 through 4 are indicated vertically and stage 1–REM is indicated by the black bars. The horizontal indicates the passage of time across eight hours. From Webb, *Sleep, the gentle tyrant* (New York: Prentice-Hall, 1975).

Sleep patterns primarily index total sleep time, sleep onset, and termination times, and the placement and number of episodes. In young adult sleep, this is typically a major nocturnal period with interjected naps. Of particular note is the large between-subject difference in average total sleep. The mean in widely different geographical and social samples is between seven and eight hours. The standard deviation approximates one hour. Thus the range of "normal" sleep amounts ranges from 4½ to 10½ hours. Naps show high responsitivity to environmental and cultural contexts.

Subjective responses may range from simple awareness of the time to get to sleep or within-sleep awakenings, through evaluative terms such as "light" and "deep" or "refreshing" sleep to more global statements such as "good" and "bad" sleep. Only limited research has been done on these responses, but that research has indicated a general looseness of the relationship between these responses and the objective measures of sleep. This is particularly true among persons who are expressing sleep complaints.

These measured properties of sleep may be viewed as dependent or independent variables, that is, we may ask what determines the variations in these measures or we may ask what the consequences are of variations in the measures.

Determinants of Sleep

A major determinant of sleep structure and patterns is species differences. The sleep of animals varies widely. Humans and primates have similar sleep structure, that is, four stages of sleep plus REM or "activated" sleep. However, the sleep of other species generally is comprised of two stages of sleep: slow-wave sleep, which resembles stages 3 and 4 of humans, and "activated" sleep, which involves cyclical episodes of brain activation within sleep equivalent to human 1–REM or dreaming sleep. The percentage and cycling vary. Birds have some 2 to 4%, while opposums, for example, have 30% activated sleep. The intervals between episodes are short in smaller animals, for example, about seven minutes in the rat. Major differences are seen in total sleep amounts, number of episodes,

and placement. Grazing animals such as cattle tend to sleep only two to four hours each 24 hours while smaller rodents sleep more than 12 hours per day. Primates generally have a long major sleep period, whereas most animals have frequent and limited sleep periods. Of course, some animals sleep during the day while others sleep at night. The varied sleep of animals is most useful in attempts to construct theories about the functions of sleep.

A second major determinant of sleep variations is age. In the human, age is associated with the largest changes in our lifetime. The stages of sleep develop quite rapidly and are intact by about 6 months of age. The major change is seen in 1–REM, which constitutes about 50% of newborns' sleep and diminishes exponentially to approximately 25% by the end of the first decade. From this point, the distribution of stages remains remarkably constant into the sixth and seventh decades. The most dramatic changes are seen in the systematic developmental change in sleep patterns. The neonate averages about 16 hours of sleep in about six episodes equally distributed across the 24 hours. Within a few days, there begins a systematic consolidation of sleep into a major night period and a reduction of sleep within the waking period. This reduction occurs by consolidation into two nap periods (morning and afternoon), the elimination first of the morning nap and then the elimination of the afternoon nap in the fourth or fifth year. The nighttime sleep amount remains relatively stable. Thus the average amount of sleep decreases from some 16 hours to about 12 hours for the 4-year-old with little change in night sleep amounts. With aging, in the fourth and fifth decade and beyond, the primary change in sleep is an increasing inability to sustain sleep, that is, awakening during the night and early sleep termination. There is some evidence to suggest that the primary change in total sleep time of older subjects is an increase in the standard deviation between subjects, that is, some subjects sleep more and some sleep less.

Another major determinant of the sleep dimensions is variations in time schedules resulting from voluntary or involuntary factors. Simply, sleep may be delayed, terminated after a limited period of time, or displaced in time such as with shift work schedules. All of these result in changes in sleep patterns *per se*—less total sleep, variations in the time of sleep, and length and number of sleep episodes.

Changes in sleep patterns have predictable effects on sleep structures. Because sleep stages are asymmetrically ordered in time, reducing nighttime sleep, for example, by one-fourth has little effect on stages 3 and 4 and disproportionally reduces 1–REM sleep. Displacing sleep from, say, 11 P.M. to 8 A.M. to 8 A.M. to 4 P.M. markedly affects the temporal order of the sleep structure. The latency of the first 1–REM period is sharply reduced and may occur on sleep onset. Further, frequent awakenings and early sleep terminations are increased.

These variables act in generalized ways and we have cited average figures. What must be emphasized is the wide range of individual differences under controlled conditions and in response to the variables cited. We noted that in a common age group of young human adults total sleep time will vary by 6 hours between subjects. With regard to aging, different developmental rates are superimposed on these basal differences so that at any particular age in the young and the old, individual differences are manifest. When one considers time schedule variations that, in humans, reflect highly individual choices and circumstances, the role of individual differences is enhanced.

Sleep is a behavioral response system, and is at least partially determined by external stimulus conditions and psychological states. Simply, sleep onset and termination are affected by such variables as noise, heat, and other physical conditions, as well as by the presence of incompatible continuing response tendencies. In very general terms, the determinants primarily affect sleep patterns and subjective responses with limited effects on sleep structure. Second, sleep is also mediated by the CNS, and variations imposed on that system by hypnotics, stimulants, or permanent alterations modulate the sleep response. Indeed, none-too-successful attempts to control sleep by sleeping pills is a major industry.

When sleep is considered as an independent variable, research has focused on the effects of sleep loss and on modified sleep structures, particularly variations in 1–REM sleep.

It is very clear that sleep loss results in increased sleepiness. There is a linear log relationship between sleep onset latency and the amount of prior wakefulness and latencies approach zero after some 60 hours of wakefulness. The exception to this rule is that sleep tendencies are modulated by a 24-hour effect. In extended deprivation, sleepiness is less during the day period than during the regular sleep period. There are a few established physiological effects from even prolonged sleep deprivation of up to 10 days in humans. The performance effects are highly task dependent. Short-term highly motivated responding is remarkably resistant to sleep deprivation; long-term and monotonous tasks are highly sensitive. The general picture is one of an inability to sustain performance rather than a loss of the capacity to respond.

Hundreds of experiments have experimentally reduced or eliminated 1–REM or activated sleep in humans and animals. These experiments have affirmed the development of a state "pressure," that is, 1–REM or activated sleep is increasingly difficult to eliminate and there is a "rebound" in amounts in recovery sleep. However, behavioral effects are less certain. Substantial cognitive or personality effects have not been clearly demonstrated. Correlational studies relating extant sleep stage differences to postsleep measures (including subjective evaluations) have established only limited relationships.

There has been an increasing and significant interaction between sleep research and biological rhythm research. Experiments with environments without time cues, modified time schedules such as 90 minutes (1 hour awake–30 minutes asleep) or nine hours (6 hours awake–3 hours asleep), and displacement designs in which the time of sleep is shifted have established the fact that sleep is organized in a systematic circadian pattern. In short, sleep is a biological rhythm. Thus the methodology and conceptualizing that have been developed by biological rhythm research have become substantial aspects of sleep research.

REFERENCES

Manaceine, M. (1899/1897). *Sleep: Its physiology, pathology, hygiene and psychology.* New York: Scribners.

Piéron, H. (1913). *Le probléme physiologique du sommeil.* Paris: Masson.

Webb, W. B. (1975). *Sleep, the gentle tyrant.* New York: Prentice-Hall.

SUGGESTED READING

Chase, M. H., Kripke, D. F., & Walter, P. L. (Eds.). (1972–1981). *Sleep research* (Vols. 1–10). Los Angeles: Brain Information Service, Brain Research Institute.

Kleitman, N. (1963). *Sleep and wakefulness* (2nd ed.). Chicago: University of Chicago Press.

Webb, W. B. (Ed.). (1973). *Sleep: An active process.* Glenview, IL: Scott, Foresman.

W. B. WEBB
University of Florida

CIRCADIAN RHYTHM
DREAMS
RELAXATION TRAINING

SLEEP CYCLE

Sleep, in mammals including humans and birds, has a cyclic structure. Polygraphic recordings (sleep electroencephalogram or EEG) reveal the alternating occurrence of periods of nonrapid eye-movement (nonREM) and rapid eye-movement (REM) sleep. One sleep cycle consists of one nonREM and one REM period. Normal adult humans have 3 to 5 sleep cycles per night (see Figure 1).

In young adults the major portion of slow-wave sleep (SWS), the sleep stages 3 and 4, is found during the first nonREM period, whereas less SWS occurs during the second half of the night. Then, during nonREM periods, stage 2 sleep dominates. Correspondingly, EEG spectral analysis reveals the highest amount of EEG

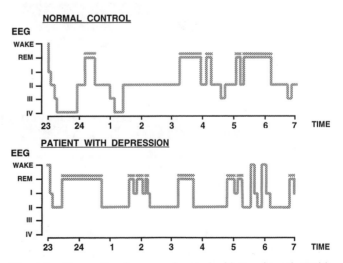

Figure 1.   Sleep pattern in a normal control subject and a patient with depression. REM-rapid-eye-movement-sleep. I to IV means stages of nonREM sleep.

delta power (slow wave activity or SWA) during the first nonREM period. In normal subjects in all sleep cycles, the duration of the nonREM period is longer than of the REM period. However, the nonREM/REM ratio changes across the sleep cycles with an increasing duration of REM periods throughout the night. Similarly, REM density (the amount of rapid eye movements during REM periods) increases throughout the night. Correspondingly, in young healthy adults the first REM period is relatively short with a relatively low REM density, whereas the last REM period is the longest with the highest REM density. The mean duration of sleep cycles in human adults is widely constant between individuals ranging from about 85 minutes to 115 minutes. The average duration of the first sleep cycle is about 70 to 100 minutes, and the average length of the subsequent cycles is approximately 90 to 120 minutes.

The duration of the sleep cycle in a certain species is correlated to the ratio of the body volume/body surface. Therefore, the duration of a sleep cycle is in mice about 7 minutes, in rats about 13 minutes, in cats about 25 minutes, in rhesus monkeys about 40 minutes, and in elephants about 180 minutes.

The duration and the composition of sleep cycles is affected by age, illness, psychiatric disorders, and drugs, particularly antidepressants. Maturation and aging affect sleep cycles throughout the life span. The cyclic alternation of nonREM and REM sleep exists already in the newborn, with a shorter period (about 50 to 60 minutes) than in adults. Babies spend the major portion of the day asleep. They sleep polyphasically, and they have the highest amount of REM sleep (about 50% of sleep time). The amount of REM sleep decreases during childhood and adolescence, and then remains stable for several decades. During senescence, the time

spent in REM sleep may decrease. SWS, however, shows a sharp decrease during adolescence and the third decade, followed by a progressive decline. As a result, SWS is often absent in subjects above 60 years. It is thought that the shortening of REM latency is due to the decrease of SWS.

During depression, changes in sleep EEG and the sleep cycles similar to age-related change are found. These include disturbed sleep continuity, decrease of SWS, and disinhibition of REM sleep. The latter results in a shortened REM latency (e.g., the interval between sleep onset and the occurrence of the first REM period), a prolonged first REM period and an enhanced REM density (measure for rapid eye movements during REM sleep; see Figure 2). Prominent differences between patients with depression and age-matched normal controls may be restricted to the first sleep cycle with a shorter REM latency and a decreased amount of SWS in the patients (Lauer, Krieg, Garcia-Borreguero, Özdagalai, & Holsboer, 1992). Due to synergism of depression and aging, elderly depressed patients show the most distinct sleep EEG changes. Sleep onset REM periods (SOREMPs), defined by a REM latency between 0 and 10 minutes, may occur during depression. In healthy subjects SOREMPs seldom occur. In addition to patients with affective disorders, patients with narcolepsy frequently show SOREMPs. In young patients with depression, a shift of the major portion of SWS from the first to the second sleep cycle is a robust finding. Severe disruption of the sleep-wake cycle is one of the symptoms of Alzheimer's dementia and is one of the major nursing problems in these patients.

A common effect of most antidepressant drugs is the suppression of REM sleep. Antidepressants of various classes (tricyclics, irreversible and reversible selective monoamine oxidase inhibitors,

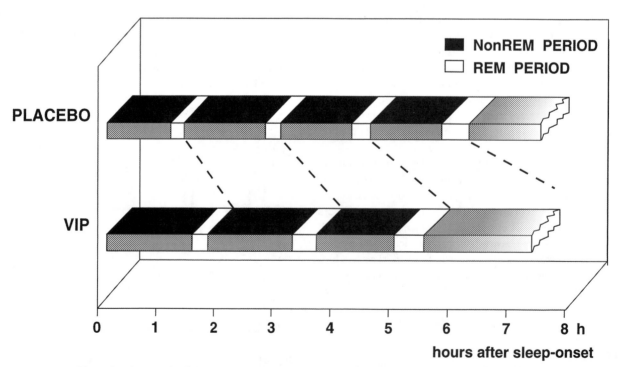

Figure 2.   Summarized sleep cycles in normal controls under placebo (*A*) and 4 × 50 μg VIP (*B*); *n* = 10. Open bar, nonREM period; solid bar, REM period (from Murck et al. 1996).

Table 1. Effects of VIP (4 × 50 μg) on sleep electroencephalogram (total night)

	Placebo	VIP (4 × 50 μg)
SPT, min	449.9 ± 14.0	449.9 ± 12.3
Time in each sleep stage, min		
SWS	53.7 ± 20.6	54.4 ± 22.7
REM	76.4 ± 18.4	84.0 ± 10.7
Awake	24.0 ± 13.2	36.2 ± 31.6
Stage I	40.3 ± 14.4	35.5 ± 18.0
Stage II	250.9 ± 20.4	234.9 ± 22.0
Stage III	38.0 ± 13.7	39.2 ± 17.9
Stage IV	15.7 ± 14.1	15.3 ± 14.5
REM latency, min	66.1 ± 17.8	87.8 ± 36.9
REM density	2.2 ± 0.5	1.9 ± 0.5

Values are means ±SD; $n = 10$. VIP, vasoactive intestinal peptide; SPT, sleep period time; SWS, slow-wave sleep duration; REM, rapid eye movement sleep duration. P values for VIP (4 × 50 μg) were not significantly different from those with placebo by Wilcoxon paired-rank test.

serotonin reuptake inhibitors, and noradrenaline reuptake inhibitors) suppress REM sleep. REM suppression is linked to the prolongation of the first nonREM period, or alternatively an increase in REM latency. Various substances differ in their potency to suppress REM sleep. Furthermore, this effect depends on the dosage. Substances which are weak REM suppressors (e.g., trazodone, moclobemide) induce only a prolongation of the REM latency, whereas potent suppressors like tranylcypromine and clomipramine may abolish REM sleep totally. Cessation of these drugs is followed by a REM rebound lasting several days. During REM rebound, REM latency is decreased, and the duration of REM periods and REM density increase. It has been hypothesized that REM suppression is the mechanism of action of antidepressants (Vogel, Thurmond, Gibbons, Sloan, & Walker, 1975). This theory is contradicted, however, by the fact that a few substances (e.g., trimipramine, nefazodone) are effective antidepressants, but they do not diminish REM sleep. Trimipramine even enhances REM sleep in patients with depression (Sonntag, Rothe, Guldner, Yassouridis, Holsboer, & Steiger, 1996).

There are interactions between the sleep cycle and various other ultradian rhythms. The most distinct ties to the nonREM-REM cycle are documented for nocturnal penile tumescence (NPT) in healthy males and for the secretion of renin. In males, spontaneous erections (NPT) occur in a rather strict association with REM periods. Simultaneous recordings of sleep EEG and NPT are used as diagnostic tools for sexual impotence. In normal young men, a dissociation of REM sleep and NPT was observed when individuals took antidepressants without cholinergic properties. Under these drugs the nocturnal NPT pattern persisted, whereas REM sleep was suppressed (Steiger, Holsboer, & Benkert, 1987). Renin is the key enzyme of the renin-angiotensin-aldosterone system regulating water and salt metabolism. Plasma renin activity (PRA) shows oscillations of about 90-minute periods strongly linked to the nonREM-REM sleep cycles. PRA increases in nonREM sleep and decreases in REM sleep. It was demonstrated that the increases of SWA and PRA are connected (Brandenberger et al., 1994).

The sleep cycle underlies a complex regulation. "REM-on" and "REM-off" neurons of the brainstem are thought to trigger the alternations of nonREM and REM episodes. Cholinergic neurons of the junction of the pons and the midbrain begin to discharge before the onset of REM sleep. EEG activation is promoted via cholinergic projections to the thalamus, and projections to the reticular formation enhance excitability and discharge activity in these effector regions for REM phenomena. In turn, these mesopontine cholinergic neurons are modulated by REM-suppressing norepinephrinergic locus coeruleus and sertoninergic dorsal raphe projections (McCarley, Greene, Rainnie, & Portas, 1995). Furthermore, various neuropeptides acting as neurotransmitters and neuromodulators participate in sleep regulation. A reciprocal interaction of growth hormone-releasing hormone (GHRH) and corticotropin-releasing hormone (CRH) influences the amount of SWS and sleep-related hormone secretion. GHRH promotes SWS and growth hormone release and inhibits cortisol, whereas CRH promotes opposite effects. Changes of the GHRH/CRH ratio probably contribute to changes of sleep-endocrine activity during aging (decline of GHRH activity) and depression (CRH overactivity; Steiger & Holsboer, 1997). Administration of vasoactive intestinal polypeptide (VIP), which is found in marked concentrations in the suprachiasmatic nucleus (SCN), decelerated in young men the nonREM-REM cycle (Figure 2) and advanced the occurrence of the cortisol rise (Murck et al., 1996).

REFERENCES

Brandenberger, G., Follenius, M., Goichot, B., Saini, J., Spiegel, K., Ehrhart, J., & Simon, C. (1994). Twenty-four-hour profiles of plasma renin activity in relation to the sleep-wake cycle. *Journal of Hypertension, 12,* 277–283.

Lauer, C. J., Krieg, J. C., Garcia-Borreguero, D., Özdaglai, A., & Holsboer, F. (1992). Panic disorder and major depression: A comparative electroencephalographic sleep study. *Psychiatry Research, 44,* 41–54.

McCarley, R. W., Greene, R. W., Rainnie, D., & Portas, C. M. (1995). Brainstem neuromodulation and REM sleep. *The Neurosciences, 7,* 341–354.

Murck, H., Guldner, J., Colla-Müller, M., Frieboes, R. M., Schier, T., Wiedemann, K., Holsboer, F., & Steiger, A. (1996). VIP decelerates non-REM-REM cycles and modulates hormone secretion during sleep in men. *American Journal of Physiology, 271,* R905–R911.

Sonntag, A., Rothe, B., Guldner, J., Yassouridis, A., Holsboer, F., & Steiger, A. (1996). Trimipramine and imipramine exert different effects on the sleep EEG and on nocturnal hormone secretion during treatment of major depression. *Depression, 4,* 1–13.

Steiger, A., & Holsboer, F. (1997). Neuropeptides and human sleep. *Sleep, 20,* 1038–1052.

Steiger, A., Holsboer, F., & Benkert, O. (1987). Dissociation of REM sleep and nocturnal penile tumescence in volunteers treated with brofaremine. *Psychiatry Research, 20,* 177–179.

Vogel, G. W., Thurmond, A., Gibbons, P., Sloan, K., & Walker, M. (1975). REM sleep reduction effects on depression syndromes. *Archives of General Psychiatry, 32,* 765–777.

A. STEIGER
Max Planck Institute of Psychiatry
Munich, Germany

RAPID EYE MOVEMENT (REM) SLEEP

SLEEP

SLEEP DISORDERS

The field of sleep medicine has grown to comprise a broad spectrum of syndromes, disorders, and diseases. The predominance of psychology and psychiatry in the field has given way to increasing neurology and pulmonary medicine involvement, with most centers preferring a multidisciplinary approach. Comprehensive sleep disorders centers, accredited by the American Sleep Disorders Association (ASDA), provide clinical assessment, polysomnography, and treatment for patients. The ASDA has developed a diagnostic and classification manual for sleep disorders, standards of practice, and standards for accreditation of sleep disorders centers. Increasing awareness of sleep disorders and the development of effective treatments has led to remarkable growth in the number of sleep disorders centers.

Sleep-related breathing disorders are currently the most common diagnoses that are made in sleep centers. Based on a random sample of 602 employed people between 30 and 60 years of age, Young and colleagues estimated that 4 percent of men and 2 percent of women meet diagnostic criteria for sleep apnea syndrome. Obesity, large neck circumference, and hypertension are associated with sleep apnea. Most patients are loud snorers and are sleepy during the day, although these complaints often come from spouses or other family members rather than the patients themselves.

The polysomnogram provides objective evidence of sleep apnea. Airflow, chest and abdominal movement, and oxygen saturation are monitored continuously during the night. Sleep stages are identified by recording the electroencephalogram, eye movements, and chin muscle tone. Initially breathing was assessed by counting the number of episodes of complete cessation of airflow lasting more than 10 seconds. More recently, decreases of airflow and arousals related to diminished breathing have been recognized as clinically significant as well. Treatment decisions are based on a respiratory distress index that combines all sleep-related breathing events, oxygen desaturations, cardiac arrhythmia, and the severity of symptoms.

The cause of sleep apnea appears to be the susceptibility of the upper airway to collapse during inspiration when muscle tone decreases with sleep onset. Tracheotomy cures obstructive sleep apnea by bypassing the site of obstruction, but is poorly tolerated and rarely used at present. The most common treatment for sleep-related breathing disorders is continuous positive airway pressure (CPAP) delivered by a mask over the nose. Patients are titrated during polysomnography for the minimum pressure that resolves apnea, eliminates snoring, and improves sleep pattern. Regular use of CPAP usually resolves daytime sleepiness, improves blood pressure control, and is easily tolerated. Some treatment alternatives have been developed for patients unable to tolerate CPAP, including upper airway surgery, oral appliances, and nasal dilators. These treatments are not as reliable as CPAP in their control of sleep apnea.

Restless legs syndrome and periodic limb movement disorder are associated with prolonged latency to sleep onset and daytime sleepiness. Patients complain of crawling sensations or involuntary jerking of the legs, particularly during the evening or when sitting for prolonged periods. Sensors detect muscle contractions or overt movements of the legs during sleep, recurring at regular intervals of about 30 seconds. The movements may cause a brief burst of waking electroencephalographic activity or an increase in heart rate. The clinical significance of these movements is debated, but most experienced clinicians have heard patients describe gratifying responses with adequate treatment. Patients report resolution of the restless legs symptoms, improved concentration during the day, and decreased daytime sleepiness.

Insomnia may arise from a variety of causes, and a variety of treatments is available. Sleep onset insomnia may arise from anxiety disorders or "jet lag" and be perpetuated by psychophysiological conditioning. The anxiety component may respond to cognitive behavioral therapy or relaxation techniques. A stimulus deconditioning protocol specific to patients with insomnia has been developed and demonstrated to be effective. Some patients complaining of onset insomnia may have restless legs syndrome or sleep apnea. Patient complaints may lead the clinician to suspect these diagnoses, or a polysomnogram may be necessary after other treatments fail.

Sleep maintenance insomnia and early morning awakening are hallmarks of depression. Patients with depression who undergo polysomnography frequently have a shortened latency to REM sleep. This biological marker of depression may appear before a clinical depression is present, and may persist despite adequate symptomatic treatment. Tricyclic antidepressants usually have a beneficial effect on sleep maintenance insomnia, reducing the number of awakenings and increasing total sleep time. REM sleep latency may also be normalized. Serotonin reuptake inhibitors also suppress REM sleep, but may increase the number of awakenings during the night.

Narcolepsy typically presents at about age 18 with excessive daytime sleepiness. Classically, patients have irresistible sleep attacks, which are followed by brief refractory periods. Several accessory symptoms are associated with narcolepsy, including cataplexy (a sudden loss of muscle tone with strong emotion or surprise), sleep paralysis (an inability to move for several minutes on awakening or at sleep onset), hypnagogic hallucinations (visual, tactile, or auditory sensations, often occurring in association with sleep paralysis) and automatic behaviors. There is a strong association with an Human Leukocyte Antigen (HLA), and probably a genetic susceptibility to narcolepsy. However, blood tests are neither sensitive nor specific in the diagnosis of narcolepsy. Current practice for establishing a diagnosis includes a polysomnogram to evaluate breathing and leg movements during sleep, followed by a Multiple Sleep Latency Test (MSLT). The MSLT provides an objective measure of sleepiness, as defined by the tendency to fall asleep during the day. In addition, patients with narcolepsy often have extremely short latencies to REM sleep at night and during naps. The presence of REM sleep during two or more of the 20-minute naps on the MSLT is considered consistent with a diagnosis of narcolepsy.

Narcolepsy often responds to treatment with stimulants. Methylphenidate and pemoline have been used for many years; modafinil has recently been introduced in the United States. Amphetamines are usually reserved for patients that fail other therapies due to the potential for tolerance and elevation of blood pressure. However, most narcoleptics reach a stable dose of stimulant and do not require frequent increases in dosage. Most patients are able to find a dose of stimulant that they feel adequately controls their symptoms, but this dose may not normalize sleep latency on the MSLT. Cataplexy reaches a level requiring treatment in some patients. Antidepressants, either tricyclics or serotonin reuptake inhibitors, are effective in controlling cataplexy.

Parasomnias comprise a small portion of patients diagnosed at sleep disorders centers, but are of theoretical interest as they may represent dissociation of aspects of sleep stages. Intrusions of waking behaviors in nonREM sleep include sleepwalking, night terrors, episodic nocturnal walking, and nocturnal eating disorders. Although extremely common and usually benign in adolescents, parasomnias in adults may be accompanied by violence to the self or others. The diagnosis of violent sleepwalking has been successfully used as a defense in murder trials. REM behavior disorder is a failure of the normal muscle paralysis that prevents movement during REM sleep, thus representing an intrusion of wakefulness during REM sleep. Patients with this disorder "act out their dreams," occasionally causing significant injuries. This disorder has been associated with several neurological disorders, especially Parkinsonism.

With increasing awareness of available treatment and improved treatment efficacy, the frequency of diagnosis of sleep disorders has increased markedly. Research efforts are underway to determine whether treatment of sleep-related breathing disorders decreases the risk of heart attack and stroke. The impact of treatment of other sleep disorders is only recently being recognized. Daytime sleepiness contributes to automobile accidents, employee absenteeism, and mood disorders, among other significant consequences. Sleep disorders centers provide a focus for diagnosis and treatment, as well as a resource for research and teaching.

SUGGESTED READING

American Sleep Disorders Association (1997). *ICSD—International classification of sleep disorders, revised: Diagnostic and Coding Manual.* Rochester, MN: Author.

Young, T., Palta, M., Dempsey, J., Skatrud, J., Weber, S., & Badr, S. (1993). The occurrence of sleep-disordered breathing among middle-aged adults. *New England Journal of Medicine, 328,* 1230–1235.

Chokroverty, S. (Ed.). (1999). *Sleep disorders medicine: Basic science, technical considerations, and clinical aspects, 2nd edition.* Boston: Butterworth, Heinemann.

Hauri, P. J. (Ed.). (1991). *Case studies in insomnia.* New York: Plenum.

Kryger, M. H., Roth, T., & Dement, W. C. (Eds.). (1994). *Principles and practice of sleep medicine.* Philadelphia: Saunders.

R. ROSENBERG
Sleep Disorders Center
Evanston Hospital

SLEEP
SLEEP TREATMENT

SLEEP TREATMENT

The specialized field of sleep treatment includes the application of pharmacology, psychotherapy, educational methods, and electrosleep. Electrosleep methods have been widespread in Soviet countries, and have gained increased attention in the United States since the mid-1970s. In *Sleep,* Gay Gaer Luce and Julius Segal describe how electrosleep treatment has been used by the Soviets for a wide range of ailments, including psychiatric and psychosomatic problems. It has even been used in relaxation training with cosmonauts, and as an anesthesia.

A somewhat different approach has developed in the United States and Canada. Sleep researchers and clinicians see the possibilities of the electrosleep method and are continuing such investigations as those reviewed by Templer (1975). However, they tend to focus more on the development of sleep treatment methods that emphasize a combination of pharmacological, psychotherapeutic, and educational approaches. Kales and colleagues (1974) emphasize that the patient is best cared for when the sleep specialist is working to assist the primary physician and thus becomes part of the treatment team. While Soviet sleep clinics have tended to treat *many* ailments, their U.S. counterparts have turned their focus to sleep disorders first and other disorders secondarily.

Perhaps the major sleep disorder encountered is insomnia. The insomniac has difficulty in falling and/or remaining asleep and thus lacks sufficient sleep. Severity varies, but as summarized by Weitzman (1974), insomniacs usually show an elevated MMPI depression scale and are more often middle-aged and female. Pharmacological treatments include hypnotic and psychotropic drugs. The most effective psychotherapy interventions are active and direct rather than psychodynamic. Usdin reports (1973) that a combination of both approaches is recommended for severe cases.

Narcolepsy and hypersomnia are conditions of excessive sleep. Guilleminault and colleagues (1976) noted that narcolepsy is associated with rapid-eye-movement (REM) disturbances and has a substantial genetic factor. Antidepressants and dietary considerations are recommended for both disorders. Psychotherapy may also be of benefit since there is evidence of stress-related narcoleptic attacks.

Bruxism refers to teeth grinding during sleep. It can damage dental structures, is seen more frequently in females, can occur in response to life stress, and is associated with stage 2 sleep. Hypnosis, electromyograph biofeedback, and a variety of behavioral interventions are used in treatment. Drug treatment is secondary and emphasizes muscle relaxants (Goldberg, 1973).

Sleep apnea is a potentially dangerous respiratory disturbance that involves a blockage of the upper airway and is frequently due to a loss of tonus of the pharyngeal constrictors with a resulting tendency of the tongue to relapse. It has been described in detail by Weitzman (1974). The most extreme cases occur during REM sleep. Treatments include pharmacological and mechanical methods designed to regulate oxygen usage. An interesting approach has been described by Cartwright and colleagues (1980), in which the sleeper wears a mouth guard device that pulls and holds the tongue forward by suction.

Webb and Cartwright (1978) have listed an entire class of sleep disorders that are often associated with childhood and show clear developmental peaks. They include sleepwalking, night terrors, nightmares, and enuresis. These disorders are usually outgrown, but some may persist into adulthood. They are associated with slow-wave sleep, and enuresis and sleepwalking are seen more in males. Treatment includes waiting for the individual to outgrow them. Of course, the sleepwalker must be protected from injury if necessary. When a disorder is severe, stage 4 suppressant drugs are used. Supportive psychotherapy can also benefit the child with enuresis as well as the parents. Parents are counseled to be tolerant and the child is helped with guilt feelings. Sleep treatment methods have also enjoyed success in the adjunctive treatment of psychiatric and neurological disorders as reported by Chase (1972), internal medicine conditions reviewed by Kales and Tan (1969), and other pathological conditions as discussed by Webb (1973).

REFERENCES

Cartwright, R., Samelson, C. F., Weber, S., Gordon, L., Krusnow, R., Paul, L., & Stephenson, K. (1980). A mechanical treatment for obstructive sleep apnea: The tongue retaining device (TRD). In M. H. Chase, D. F. Kripke, & P. L. Walter (Eds.), *Sleep research* (Vol. 9). Los Angeles: BIS/BRS.

Chase, M. H. (Ed.). (1972). *The sleeping brain.* Los Angeles: BIS/BRS.

Goldberg, G. (1973). The psychological, physiological and hypnotic approach to bruxism in the treatment of periodontal disease. *Journal of the American Society of Psychosomatic Dentistry and Medicine, 20*(3), 75–91.

Guilleminault, C., Passouant, P., & Dement, W. C. (1976). *Narcolepsy.* New York: Spectrum.

Kales, A., Bixler, E. O., & Kales, J. D. (1974). Role of the sleep research and treatment facility: Diagnosis, treatment and education. In E. D. Weitzman (Ed.), *Advances in sleep research* (Vol. 1). New York: Spectrum.

Kales, A., & Tan, T. L. (1969). Sleep alterations associated with medical illness. In A. Kales (Ed.), *Sleep: physiology and pathology.* Philadelphia: Lippincott.

Luce, G. G., & Segal, J. (1966). *Sleep.* New York: Coward-McCann.

Templer, D. I. (1975). The efficacy of electrosleep therapy. *Canadian Psychiatric Association Journal, 20*(8), 607–613.

Usdin, G. (Ed.). (1973). *Sleep research and clinical practice.* New York: Brunner/Mazel.

Webb, W. B. (Ed.). (1973). *Sleep: An active process.* Glenview, IL: Scott, Foresman.

Weitzman, E. D. (Ed.). (1974). *Advances in sleep research* (Vol. 1). New York: Spectrum.

SUGGESTED READING

Casa, J. M., Beemsterboer, P., & Clark, G. T. (1982). A comparison of stress reduction behavioral counseling and contingent nocturnal EMG feedback for the treatment of bruxism. *Behavior Research and Therapy, 20*(1), 9–15.

Von Richthofen, C. L., & Mellor, C. S. (1979). Cerebral electrotherapy: Methodological problems in assessing its therapeutic effectiveness. *Psychological Bulletin, 86*(6), 1264–1271.

W. KARLE
Corona Del Mar, California

J. R. BINDER
Medical College of Wisconsin, Milwaukee

ANTIANXIETY DRUGS
BRAIN WAVES
CIRCADIAN RHYTHM
PSYCHOPHARMACOLOGY
SLEEP

SLEEPER EFFECT

A sleeper effect in persuasion is a delayed increase in the impact of a persuasive message. In other words, a sleeper effect occurs when a communication shows no immediate persuasive effects, but, after a period of time, the recipient of the communication becomes more favorable toward the position advocated by the message. As a pattern of data, the sleeper effect is opposite to the typical finding that experimentally induced opinion change dissipates over time (Cook & Flay, 1978). As such, the sleeper effect is an "interesting quirk" that has attracted much research and textbook attention.

The first documented sleeper effects—although not termed as such at the time—were obtained by Peterson and Thurstone (1933) and by Lewin (1947). Peterson and Thurstone found that a film entitled *Four Sons* proved to be more effective in promoting pro-German attitudes after a six-month delay than immediately after being shown to Genoa, IL high school students. They speculated that since Genoa did not have a movie theater at the time, the experiment created considerable discussion, which was responsible for the delayed opinion change. In the Lewin study, housewives were led in a discussion of the importance of serving nutritional but undesirable foodstuffs (liver, kidneys, and other sweetbreads) as part of the war effort. The results showed that more housewives served these foods four weeks compared to two weeks after the discussion.

The term "sleeper effect" was first used by Hovland, Lumsdaine, and Sheffield (1949) to describe opinion change produced by the US Army's training film, *The Battle of Britain,* used during World War II. Specifically, Hovland and colleagues found that recruits' confidence in the fighting ability of their British allies was stronger nine weeks after the film was shown compared to an earlier assessment.

Although Hovland and colleagues proposed four explanations for their sleeper effect, it was their source forgetting—or what later was termed the dissociation discounting cue hypothesis—that set the stage for future research. According to this dissociation hypothesis, a sleeper effect occurs when a persuasive message is presented with a discounting cue (such as a low credible source or a counterargument). Just after receiving the message, the recipient recalls both message and discounting cue, resulting in little or no opinion change. After a delay, as the association between message and discounting cue weakens, the recipient may "remember what was said without thinking about who said it" (Hovland, Janis, & Kelley, 1953, p. 259). In other words, a sleeper effect occurs because of a spontaneous dissociation of a message and discounting cue over time.

Hovland and Weiss (1951) provided the first direct test of the dissociation hypothesis. In their study, subjects received persuasive messages attributed to either a trustworthy (e.g., Robert J. Oppenheimer on atomic submarines) or an untrustworthy (e.g., the Soviet news agency Pravda on atomic submarines) source. The results showed an increase in the percentage of people agreeing with the message given by the untrustworthy source four weeks after the presentation compared to immediately after the message was received. The Hovland and Weiss study (1951; with others reviewed in Hovland et al., 1953) gave the sleeper effect scientific status as a replicable phenomenon and gave the dissociation discounting cue hypothesis credibility as the explanation for this phenomenon. The sleeper effect was discussed in almost every social psychology textbook of the time, appeared in related literatures (such as marketing, communications, public opinion, and sociology), and even obtained some popular notoriety as a lay idiom.

However, in 1974, Gillig and Greenwald published a series of seven studies that would prove to be disconcerting for believers in the sleeper effect. In their studies, over 600 subjects received messages that were attributed to a low-credibility source. Unlike the Hovland and Weiss study, the results revealed no indication that a sleeper effect had occurred. Other studies also have failed to produce a sleeper effect even though they paired a discounting cue with an effective message (Chaiken, 1980; Hennigan, Cook, & Gruder, 1982; Maddux & Rogers, 1980; Whittaker & Meade, 1968).

The Gillig and Greenwald study raises an important question: "Is the sleeper effect a reliable phenomenon?" Two sets of studies by Gruder and colleagues (1978) and by Pratkanis, Greenwald, Leippe, and Baumgardner (1988) have answered "yes" to this question and have specified one set of empirical conditions needed for producing a sleeper effect. In both studies, reliable sleeper effects were obtained when (a) message recipients were induced to pay attention to message content by noting the important arguments in the message, (b) the discounting cue came after the message, and (c) message recipients rated the credibility of the message source immediately after receiving the message and cue. For example, in a study conducted by Gruder and colleagues and replicated by Pratkanis and colleagues, subjects read a message arguing against the four-day work week. As they read the message, subjects underlined the important arguments. After reading the message, subjects received a discounting cue stating that the previous message was false and then rated the trustworthiness of the source of the message. This set of procedures resulted in a sleeper effect—subjects were more opposed to the four-day work week six weeks after (compared to immediately after) receiving the message.

The procedures developed by Gruder and Pratkanis and their colleagues for reliably producing a sleeper effect are sufficiently different from earlier studies to warrant a new interpretation of the sleeper effect. As a replacement for the dissociation hypothesis, the Pratkanis study proposed a differential decay interpretation. According to this hypothesis, a sleeper effect occurs when (a) the impact of the message decays more slowly than the impact of the discounting cue and (b) the information from the message and from the discounting cue is not immediately integrated to form an attitude (and thus the discounting cue is already dissociated from message content). The procedures employed in both studies are likely to produce these conditions; underlining important arguments, for example, strengthens the persistence of impact of the message, while presenting the discounting cue after the message limits the message recipient's ability to think about the materials and integrate the content of message and discounting cue.

Ironically, although the earliest sleeper effects were obtained in field settings, the set of procedures for obtaining a sleeper effect identified by the Gruder and Pratkanis studies are not likely to occur with high frequency in everyday life. This does not diminish the theoretical importance of this research, yet it does raise the question, "Are there other ways of obtaining sleeper effects?" Researchers have suggested the following techniques for producing sleeper effects: (a) delayed reaction to a fear-arousing message (Insko, Arkoff, & Insko, 1965), (b) delayed insight into the implications of a message (McGuire, 1960), (c) leveling and sharpening of a persuasive message over time (Papageorgis, 1963), (d) dissipation of the effects of forewarning of persuasive intent (Watts & Holt, 1979, but see Leve & Pratkanis, 1990), (e) group discussion of a message after a delay (Festinger, 1955; Peterson & Thurstone, 1933), (f) the dissipation of reactance induced by a message (Brehm & Mann, 1975), (g) delayed internalization of the values of a message (Rokeach, 1973), (h) wearing-off of initial annoyance with a negative or tedious message (Crandall, Harrison, & Zajonc, 1976; Moore & Hutchinson, 1985), (i) delayed acceptance of an ego-attacking message (Stotland, Katz, & Patchen, 1959; Stotland & Patchen, 1961), and (j) delayed impact of minority influence (Mugny & Perez, 1991). Although these other procedures for obtaining a sleeper effect have been less well-researched (and thus we can be less sure of their reliability), they may indeed be more common in everyday life than sleeper effects based on the well-documented differential decay hypothesis.

REFERENCES

Brehm, J. W., & Mann, M. (1975). Effect of importance of freedom and attraction to group members on influence produced by group pressure. *Journal of Personality and Social Psychology, 31,* 816–824.

Chaiken, S. (1980). Heuristic versus systematic information processing and the use of source versus message cues in persuasion. *Journal of Personality and Social Psychology, 39,* 752–766.

Cook, T. D., & Flay, B. R. (1978). The persistence of experimentally induced attitude change. In L. Berkowitz (Ed.), *Advances in experimental social psychology* (Vol. 11, pp. 1–57). New York: Academic.

Crandall, R., Harrison, A. A., & Zajonc, R. B. (1976). The permanence of positive and negative effects of stimulus exposure: A sleeper effect. Unpublished manuscript. University of Michigan.

Festinger, L. J. (1955). Social psychology and group processes. In C. P. Stone & Q. McNemar (Eds.), *Annual review of psychology* (Vol. 6, pp. 187–216). Stanford, CA: Annual Reviews.

Gillig, P. M., & Greenwald, A. G. (1974). Is it time to lay the sleeper effect to rest? *Journal of Personality and Social Psychology, 29,* 132–139.

Gruder, C. L., Cook, T. D., Hennigan, K. M., Flay, B. R., Alessis, C., & Halamaj, J. (1978). Empirical tests of the absolute sleeper effect predicted from the discounting cue hypothesis. *Journal of Personality and Social Psychology, 36,* 1061–1074.

Hennigan, K. M., Cook, T. D., & Gruder, C. L. (1982). Cognitive tuning set, source credibility, and attitude change. *Journal of Personality and Social Psychology, 42,* 412–425.

Hovland, C. I., Janis, I. L., & Kelley, H. H. (1953). *Communication and persuasion: Psychological studies of opinion change.* New Haven, CT: Yale University Press.

Hovland, C. I., Lumsdaine, A. A., & Sheffield, F. D. (1949). *Experiments on mass communications.* Princeton, NJ: Princeton University Press.

Hovland, C. I., & Weiss, W. (1951). The influence of source credibility on communication effectiveness. *Public Opinion Quarterly, 15,* 635–650.

Insko, C. A., Arkoff, A., & Insko, V. M. (1965). Effects of high and low fear-arousing communications upon opinions toward smoking. *Journal of Experimental Social Psychology, 1,* 256–266.

Leve, C., & Pratkanis, A. R. (1990, April). *Where is the forewarning sleeper effect?* Western Psychological Association, Los Angeles, CA.

Lewin, K. (1947). Group decision and change. In T. M. Newcomb & E. L. Hartley (Eds.), *Readings in social psychology* (pp. 330–334). New York: Holt.

Maddux, J. E., & Rogers, R. W. (1980). Effects of source expertise, physical attractiveness, and supporting arguments on persuasion: A case of brains over beauty. *Journal of Personality and Social Psychology, 39,* 235–244.

McGuire, W. J. (1960). A syllogistic analysis of cognitive relationships. In M. J. Rosenberg, C. I. Hovland, W. J. McGuire, R. P. Abelson, & J. W. Brehm (Eds.), *Attitude organization and change: An analysis of consistency among attitude components* (pp. 65–111). New Haven, CT: Yale University Press.

Moore, D. L., & Hutchinson, J. W. (1985). The influence of affective reactions to advertising: Direct and indirect mechanisms of attitude change. In L. F. Alwitt & A. A. Mitchell (Eds.), *Psychological processes and advertising effects* (pp. 65–87). Hillsdale, NJ: Erlbaum.

Mugny, G., & Perez, J. A. (1991). *The social psychology of minority influence.* New York: Cambridge University Press.

Papageorgis, D. (1963). Bartlett effect and the persistence of induced opinion change. *Journal of Abnormal and Social Psychology, 67,* 61–67.

Peterson, R. C., & Thurstone, L. L. (1933). *Motion pictures and the social attitudes of children.* New York: MacMillan.

Pratkanis, A. R., Greenwald, A. G., Leippe, M. R., & Baumgardner, M. H. (1988). In search of reliable persuasion effects: III. The sleeper effect is dead. Long live the sleeper effect. *Journal of Personality and Social Psychology, 54,* 203–218.

Rokeach, M. J. (1973). *The nature of human values.* New York: Free Press.

Stotland, E., Katz, D., & Patchen, M. (1959). Reduction of prejudice through arousal of insight. *Journal of Personality, 27,* 507–531.

Stotland, E., & Patchen, M. (1961). Identification and change in prejudice and authoritarianism. *Journal of Abnormal and Social Psychology, 62,* 265–274.

Watts, W. A., & Holt, L. E. (1979). Persistence of opinion change induced under conditions of forewarning and distraction. *Journal of Personality and Social Psychology, 37,* 778–789.

Whittaker, J. O., & Meade, R. D. (1968). Retention of opinion change as a function of differential source credibility: A cross-cultural study. *International Journal of Psychology, 3,* 103–108.

A. R. PRATKANIS
University of California, Santa Cruz

FORGETTING
IMPLICIT LEARNING

SMALL-SAMPLE STATISTICS

The notion of small-sample or "small-*n*" statistics was first developed by W. S. Gosset, who was then a statistician working at the Guinness Brewery in the United Kingdom. One of his duties was to analyze successive samples of freshly brewed stout. Due to the inherent variability in the nature of the brewing process and the length of time required to test samples, Gosset experimented with the idea of substantially reducing the number of samplings to be taken from the very large number of available barrels. He found that the sampling distribution for small samples differed markedly from the normal distribution. Further, the distribution changed depending on the size of the sample, giving rise to a whole family of distributions. The results of his experiments with small samples led to the development of the t distribution in 1908. Because the brewery did not permit him to use his own name, Gosset published his results anonymously, using the pseudonym Student. In addition to being the first paper to explicitly recognize and deal with the problem of small samples, it was also the first attempt to combine experimental design with statistical testing—probably also the first to suggest anything like the .05 level as a reasonable criterion for rejecting the null hypothesis. Although not immediately recognized as such, Gosset's work on the t distribution with small samples was a critical breakthrough in the history of statistics, leading to the development of a number of other procedures, including the analysis of variance.

THE t DISTRIBUTION

The t distribution, like the normal (z) distribution, applies to the testing of the null hypothesis that two samples have been randomly selected from the same population; therefore, the calculated statistics (mean and standard deviation) are unbiased estimates of the population parameters. However, unlike the z, the t distribution for small samples does not require prior knowledge or precise estimates of the population mean and standard deviation. Furthermore, whereas testing the mean difference between two large samples for statistical significance requires the underlying assumption that the population measures are normally distributed, the t distribution theory does not require assumptions regarding parameters.

Normally distributed measures follow a single curve, the Gaussian curve, that satisfies the following equation:

$$y = \frac{N}{\sigma\sqrt{n\pi}} e^{-1/2z^2}$$

The t distribution utilizes a whole family of curves, represented by the following equation:

$$y = \frac{\Gamma\left(\dfrac{n+1}{2}\right)}{\Gamma\left(\dfrac{n}{2}\right)\sqrt{n\pi}} \left(1 + \frac{t^2}{n}\right)^{-(n+1)/2}$$

A different curve satisfies the equation as n varies, resulting in a family of curves.

DEGREES OF FREEDOM

In the equation above for t, n signifies the degrees of freedom (df) involved in the estimate of the population variance (σ^2). The concept of the degrees of freedom of a statistical distribution or of a statistical test refers to how many observations in the analysis are free to vary. In the t distribution, one of the deviations from the sample mean is always fixed because the sum of all deviations from

the sample mean must equal zero. This has an effect on the calculation of the sample variance as an unbiased estimate of the parameter σ^2. For the t distribution, df is equal to the number of observations (N) minus one for each sample. Hence, in the development of the formulas and procedures for calculating the t test for the difference between two means, there are $N - 2$ degrees of freedom.

THE F DISTRIBUTION

The t test is used to test the null hypothesis that two samples are drawn at random from the same population or from two different populations with the same variance. But what if more than two groups are involved in the analysis? This question began to be answered after Gosset's work on the t distribution by two of the most prominent statisticians of the 20th century. One was the great British statistician Sir R. A. Fisher, who proposed the first theoretical formulations that led to the development of the analysis of variance and the F distribution, and whose works on small-sample theory, following Gosset, were published around 1925. The other was G. W. Snedecor, one of the first American statisticians, who developed the ratio of two variance estimates as a means of comparing two independent samples of any size. He named this ratio the F ratio, in honor of Fisher. Fisher himself never used the term F ratio, which is still sometimes referred to as Snedecor's F to honor both Fisher and Snedecor.

Based on the work of these individuals and others, there followed the postulation of the F distribution as a distribution of the ratio of two χ^2 statistics, each in regard to their respective degrees of freedom:

$$F = (\chi_1^2/\mathrm{df}_1) / (\chi_2^2/\mathrm{df}_2)$$

From this emerged the classic works of Fisher on the analysis of variance, an explicitly small-sample statistical methodology.

The sampling distribution of F, with its dual $n = \mathrm{df}$ equations, is as follows:

$$y = \frac{\Gamma\left(\dfrac{n_1 + n_2}{2}\right)^{n_1 n_1/2 n_2 n_2/2}}{\Gamma\left(\dfrac{n_1}{2}\right)\left(\dfrac{n_2}{2}\right)} \times \frac{F^{(n_1-2)/2}}{(n_1 F + n_2)^{(n_1+n_2)/2}}$$

As in the case of t, there is a family of distributions that satisfies the equation for F. In this case, however, there are two separate degrees of freedom involved in the F ratio, one for the numerator (between-groups) and one for the denominator (within-groups or error).

TABLES FOR EVALUATING THE t AND F STATISTICS

For large-sample statistics, normally only one table is necessary for reference in testing the null hypothesis. That table is the one involving the normal deviate, z, and showing the area under the normal curve between any two z points. Tables for the t and F distributions, however, are necessarily more complex, because these tables are based on multiple distributions that result from the varying degrees of freedom. While t and F are both frequency distributions, as is the normal distribution, they differ with respect to the four moments that describe them. The *t* distribution, for example, is symmetrical (note the t^2 in its equation) for all degrees of freedom, but becomes increasingly platykurtic as sample size decreases. Platykurtic curves tend to be less asymptotic (that is, heavier in the tails) than mesokurtic curves such as the normal curve. This difference leads to marked discrepancies between *t* and *z* points on the abscissa, especially for small sample sizes. For example, a *t* of 2.57 with df = 5 is required for a *p* value of .05 (two-tailed), whereas for the normal distribution, a *z* score of only 1.96 is required for *p* = .05. Hence, a *t* value of 2.57 with 5 degrees of freedom indicates statistical significance at the 5% level; but for the normal curve, a *z* of 2.57 would indicate statistical significance at the 1% level. Similar comparisons may be made with the *F* distribution.

WHAT CONSTITUTES A "SMALL" SAMPLE?

Not infrequently, the question is raised as to what size a sample must be to be considered small. There cannot be a definitive answer to this question. However, it is conventionally accepted that the cutoff between a small and a large sample is set at df = 30. The reason for this somewhat arbitrary judgment stems from the comparison between the *t* and normal distributions. As noted previously, the discrepancies between *t* and *z* tend to increase as df decreases, but decrease as df increases. In fact, *t* begins to approach *z* quite closely, long before it reaches its limit at df = infinity when *t* = *z*. Inspection of tabled *t* values suggests that the approximation becomes rather rapid at and beyond df = 30. For example, for df = 30, the comparative values for *t* and *z* are, respectively: 2.042 and 1.960 for *p* = .05; 2.750 and 2.576 for *p* = .01; and 3.646 and 3.291 for *p* = .001.

OTHER SMALL SAMPLE STATISTICS

The *t* test and the analysis of variance (ANOVA) *F* test procedures are explicitly designed for use with small samples, although they are valid for large samples as well. There are, however, many other statistical methods applicable to small samples. Chief among these are the nonparametric, or distribution-free methods. These statistics were designed primarily for use with data that do not fit the definition of either ratio or interval levels of measurement, but rather are either ordinal (rank) or nominal measures. For nonparametric statistics, no assumptions are made regarding parameters, especially relating to variance estimates. For this reason, nonparametric methods are sometimes used for ratio and interval scale measures when sample sizes are small and it is likely that some of the underlying assumptions on which parametric statistics are based are being violated. Among the procedures that have been used in such situations are Fisher's exact probability test, Friedman's ANOVA for ranked data, Kendall's tau correlation method for ranked data, Kendall's coefficient (W) of concordance method, the Kruskal-Wallis *H*-test for ranked data in single-group ANOVA, the Mann-Whitney *U*-test, the median test, the sign test, Spearman's rho correlation method for ranks, and Wilcoxin's *t*-test. However, it should be noted that parametric procedures have been shown to be quite robust to violations of many of their underlying

assumptions and that use of nonparametric procedures in such cases may lead to decreased statistical power.

A relatively new approach to small sample statistical analysis is time-series analysis (TSA). This procedure is appropriate for repeated and equally spaced observations on single units or even single subjects, making it the ultimate in small-sample statistical procedures. Because TSA involves repeated observations, serial dependency (autocorrelation) in the data is an important issue. Identification of an appropriate underlying statistical model is necessary to evaluate and remove serial dependency from the data. This is typically accomplished using one of several alternative ARIMA (autoregressive integrated moving average) models. The most widely used procedures in the social and behavioral sciences involve interrupted TSA. These techniques have broad utility in applied research because of their ability to estimate intervention (interruption) effects and to identify patterns in the data such as trend effects, cyclical (seasonal) variation, and patterns of serial dependency. Pooled TSA procedures are also available to combine data from several different individuals or observational units.

J. S. Rossi
P. F. Merenda
University of Rhode Island

PROBABILITY
STATISTICS IN PSYCHOLOGY

SNYDER, SOLOMON H. (1938–   )

Constantly "bubbling forth with new ideas," in the words of one of his colleagues, and never afraid to risk being wrong, Solomon H. Snyder made headlines in 1973, when he and neuropharmacology graduate student Candace Pert announced that they had identified opiate receptors in the brain—an achievement for which Snyder shared the 1978 Albert Lasker Award for Basic Medical Research, one of the most prestigious prizes in medical science. Their discovery opened the door to vastly increased understanding of the mechanisms of cell-to-cell communication within the brain, of the actions of such neuroactive drugs as painkillers, and of the dynamics of narcotic addiction, in addition to many other advances in molecular neuroscience. Moreover, their research method offered a means of screening potential neuroactive drugs that was far faster and less expensive than any other existing testing system, primarily because, unlike those systems, it did not require the use of laboratory animals. The method has since led to the formulation of many widely-prescribed pharmaceuticals.

In the 1980s, in another scientific first, Snyder and his coworkers coaxed adult brain cells to reproduce in the laboratory. He later demonstrated that nitric oxide is an integral part of the brain's communication system and revealed carbon monoxide to be another probable message carrier, thus establishing gases as a new class of neurotransmitters. By identifying, isolating, and synthesizing the so-called odorant binding protein, Snyder has helped to unravel mysteries surrounding the way animals detect odors. Yet another of his far-reaching contributions has been his guidance of graduate students at the Johns Hopkins University School of Medicine, many of whom have become accomplished scientists in their own right. A faculty member at Johns Hopkins since 1966, Snyder is currently Distinguished Service Professor of neuroscience, pharmacology, and psychiatry, and is the director of the Department of Neuroscience. He has written or cowritten more than 800 journal articles, and he is the author, coauthor, or editor of 13 books. At the conclusion of *Brainstorming: The Science and Politics of Opiate Research* (1989), which is largely autobiographical, he wrote, "I often wonder at my good fortune, being paid a salary to pursue my favorite hobby."

The second of the five children of Samuel Simon Snyder and Patricia (Yakerson) Snyder, Solomon Halbert Snyder grew up in Washington, DC, where he was born on December 26, 1938. His accomplished siblings include a scientific illustrator with the Smithsonian Institution, a psychiatric nurse, a social worker, and a National Endowment for the Arts administrator. The Snyder children's father worked for the National Security Agency, where, as an expert in cryptanalysis, he helped to break enemy codes during World War II and, after the war, pioneered the use of computers in code-breaking. "[My father is] quiet and modest and has always regarded good science as the most important thing," the younger Snyder said in a 1981 interview. His mother was a real-estate broker and a highly successful game show contestant.

When Snyder was nine his father taught him how to write computer programs. In adolescence he began studying classical guitar; he practiced 4 hours daily, and in his teens began giving guitar lessons and performing in public. As a high school student, he enjoyed reading philosophy and writing, and had little interest in science. "I don't enjoy memorizing books and learning lots of details," he said in a 1991 interview. Abandoning philosophy by his senior year because "in philosophy you [are] not dealing with anything substantive," he settled instead on medicine as a profession, both because he wanted to be like his friends, all of whom planned to become doctors, and because he was attracted to psychiatry, which, through his extensive reading of works by Sigmund Freud, he had come to regard as "a practical form of philosophy."

After graduating high school in 1955, Snyder enrolled in the premed program at Georgetown College in Washington, DC; he was admitted directly to Georgetown Medical School at the end of his junior year, in 1958, without his having received a bachelor's degree. He earned an MD (cum laude) from Georgetown in 1962, then spent a year as an intern at the Kaiser Foundation Hospital in San Francisco. On one of his days off, in what interviewer M. Holloway, described as a "personal experiment," he ingested the hallucinogen LSD. His experience while under its influence, he said, made him "realize that there is more to awareness than ordinary awareness and that there are incredible things going on in the brain."

Starting in 1963, Snyder took a 2-year break in his medical training to serve as a research associate in neuroscience at the National Institute of Mental Health (NIMH). (Since his actual employer was the quasi-military U.S. Public Health Service, he thereby fulfilled his military obligation.) He worked in the laboratory of the biochemist and pharmacologist Julius Axelrod, whom

Snyder had met in 1958 and who, in 1970, won the Nobel Prize for physiology or medicine. Axelrod had a profound effect on Snyder's development as a scientist, helping him realize "that real science is as creative as any of the arts," and, as Snyder wrote in *Brainstorming,* that "the important element in grown-up research is not technical virtuosity but original ideas." Axelrod also transmitted his conviction that experiments must be elegant—that is, scientifically precise, simple, and efficient—and designed to generate results quickly. His guiding principle, Snyder said, was that "if you can do an experiment in one day, then in 10 days you can test 10 ideas, and maybe one of the 10 will be right. Then you've got it made."

From 1965 to 1968, Snyder was an assistant resident in the Department of Psychiatry at the Johns Hopkins Hospital in Baltimore. In recalling his few experiences as a therapist, he has said that he "like[d] doing psychotherapy a lot, but you're exposed to all kinds of heavy things, and it is stressful." Meanwhile, in 1966, Snyder, having already gained a reputation for the quality of his research, joined the faculty of the Johns Hopkins University School of Medicine as an assistant professor of pharmacology and experimental therapeutics—an unusually high rank for a medical resident. When he completed his residency, he was promoted to associate professor, and he also became an associate professor of psychiatry. He rose to full professor in both disciplines in 1970, at the age of 31; in 1977, he was named Distinguished Service Professor of pharmacology and psychiatry, and since 1980 he has held the title of Distinguished Service Professor of neuroscience, pharmacology, and psychiatry, and has served as the director of the Department of Neuroscience.

Snyder's first published research paper, "A Mechanism of Schizophrenia," reflected his growing fascination with physiological and chemical factors in mental illness and his desire to combine clinical psychiatry with basic research in his professional life. Some three dozen articles with his name as primary author or coauthor emerged from his affiliation with Axelrod, including several on histamine, a compound related to the essential amino acid histidine. Snyder soon became known as an authority on histamine and on hallucinogens. Named the Maryland Academy of Sciences Outstanding Young Scientist in 1969, in 1970 Snyder won both the John Jacob Abel Award from the American Society for Pharmacology and Experimental Therapeutics and the A. E. Bennett Award from the Society for Biological Psychiatry.

Snyder's first book, *Uses of Marijuana,* was published by Oxford University Press in 1971. That same year President Richard Nixon declared a "war on drugs," and Congress allocated $2 million for research into heroin addiction. Partly through Snyder's efforts, six federally funded drug research centers were established, one of them at Johns Hopkins. As he admitted in *Brainstorming,* at that time Snyder "hardly knew heroin from horseradish," but he was determined to seize what he saw as an excellent opportunity to secure support for basic research. After several months of intensive study of the scientific literature, he concluded that locating the receptors for heroin and other opiates on brain cells was critical to the understanding of addiction. The existence of such receptors had been assumed for some time among scientists but had never been established. Like other cellular receptors, the opiate receptors were believed to be, in effect, molecular locks. The opiates would then be the keys to those locks; a precise fit of key into lock would trigger the chain of events that results in say, a feeling of euphoria, or a decrease in pain or stress.

Snyder's collaborator in his search was Candace Pert (mentioned earlier). Adapting for their purposes a technique called reversible ligand binding, Snyder and Pert mixed whipped tissue from the brains of mice, rats, and guinea pigs with measured quantities of heroin, morphine, and other opiates that had been combined with a radioactive tracer, then washed the mixture over filter paper. The brain membranes and whatever opiates had bound to them remained on the paper, while unbound opiates passed through it. By tracing the radioactivity in the remaining cell-opiate mixture, Snyder and Pert were able to pinpoint the precise locations of opiate receptors in particular areas of the brain. Moreover, through what Snyder dubbed their grind-and-bind method, they demonstrated that the relative potencies of drugs in binding to brain tissue at receptor sites correlated with the potency of the drugs in humans. The researchers also showed that drugs chemically unrelated to opiates did not bind at all, and that narcotic antagonists—drugs that render narcotics impotent—did bind but produced no effect.

Heroin, morphine, and codeine are derivatives of opium, which is obtained from the unripe seed pods of opium poppies. If the human body wasn't born with opium in it, why, Snyder asked, did neurons contain receptors for it? Proceeding on the assumption that "nature did not put opiate receptors in the brain solely to interact with narcotics," Snyder and another student collaborator, Rabi Simantov, began a search for opiate-like neurotransmitters produced naturally by the body. Knowing that such a discovery would be a scientific plum, other researchers threw their energies into a similar undertaking, and in 1975, shortly before Snyder and Simantov reached their goal, Kosterlitz and Hughes (University of Aberdeen, Scotland) scooped them by announcing their identification of two naturally occurring opiates, which they named the enkephalins. Snyder, meanwhile, had begun extending the use of reversible ligand binding to all the major neurotransmitter receptors in the brain. By illuminating the biochemical properties and dynamics of receptors, he also shed light on the mechanisms of action of dopamine and other neurotransmitters and of major neuroactive drugs. For his pioneering work in identifying the opiate receptors and demonstrating their relation to the enkephalins, Snyder shared with Kosterlitz and Hughes the 1978 Albert Lasker Award for basic medical research.

In the mid-1980s, stirred by the ideas of graduate student Jeffrey Nye, Snyder challenged the then-universally held conviction that brain cells (except fetal brain cells) cannot reproduce. In 1987, doctors at Johns Hopkins Hospital removed one cerebral hemisphere from a toddler with a rare brain disorder in an attempt to save her life, and Nye was given a tiny portion of the excised tissue. Snyder and Nye, with the help of Lynda Hester & Gabriele Ronnett, concocted a growth medium in which some of the brain cells not only survived but also began to proliferate—though they did not, at first, display all the characteristics of normal brain cells. After more than 2 years, Snyder and his collaborators were able to announce that they were maintaining a colony of true neurons that were not only functioning normally (e.g., producing known neuro-

transmitters) but also multiplying. Since then Snyder has sent to scientists at more than 200 other laboratories around the world samples from the colony for use in their own research.

Snyder devotes as much time as he can to reading and thinking; in particular, he reads about research in a wide array of disciplines, even when it seems unrelated to his own work, because as he told interviewer M. Holloway, "some of the finest advances come from jumping fields. . . . When I read something about the heart, I think 'Does that fit into the brain?' When I read something about cancer genes, I think, 'Do they fit into the brain?'" In another interview, he pointed out that since "nature uses certain principles," a mechanism at work in, say, the digestive system may very well be operating in the brain, too. In one such intuitive leap (as a colleague termed it) Snyder launched an investigation into the possible presence of nitric oxide in the brain after learning from scientific journal articles that nitric oxide had been found to play a role in the relaxation of blood vessels (and thus in regulating blood pressure) and in processes connected with inflammation. "This is too nice not to be in the brain," he thought. In collaboration with student David S. Bredt, he ascertained, through a simple, ingeniously designed assay, that nitric oxide is indeed in the brain, and that nitric oxide synthase, the enzyme that produces it, is more abundant in cerebral tissue than anywhere else in the body. "It appears likely that virtually every neuron in the brain receives input from [nitric oxide]-releasing neurons," Snyder reported in the *Encyclopedia Britannica Yearbook* (1995). He also discovered that nitric oxide is a culprit in strokes caused by blood clots: Although some brain cells die as a direct result of blockage of blood vessels, far more die in the cloud of nitric oxide that is subsequently unleashed, an event triggered by a chemical called glutamate. Intriguingly, the cells that release the nitric oxide survive. Snyder and colleagues also identified "the gene for the protein that brain cells use to make nitric oxide," and for the past few years, they have accumulated evidence that carbon monoxide is also a neurotransmitter, diffusing from one nerve cell to another to relay messages within the brain.

On another occasion, having read about the ability of the immunosuppressive drug FK-506 to bind with receptors in white blood cells, Snyder initiated research that led to the discoveries in his laboratory that receptors for FK-506, called immunophilins, are up to 50 times more abundant in the brain than in white blood cells. By neutralizing the action of glutamate, drugs such as FK-506, which bind to the immunophilins, can inhibit the production of nitric oxide in the brain. Snyder and his coworkers have been trying to determine whether administering FK-506 to stroke victims would be beneficial. In the 1980s, Snyder contributed many suggestions for potential drugs of various kinds to researchers at Nova Pharmaceutical Corporation, which he cofounded with David Blech and Isaac Blech in 1982 and which subsequently merged with the Scios Corporation.

Snyder's books include *Madness and the Brain* (1974), *Opiate Receptor Mechanisms* (written with S. Matthysse; 1975), *The Troubled Mind* (1976), *Biological Aspects of Mental Disorder* (1980), and *Drugs and the Brain* (1986). He is a fellow of the American Academy of Arts and Sciences, the Institute of Medicine of the United States National Academy of Sciences, and the American Philosophical Society. Among his many honors are four honorary doctoral degrees, four dozen honorary lectureships, and 29 scientific prizes, among them the Hofheimer Award (1972) and the Distinguished Service Award (1989) from the American Psychiatric Association; the Research Pacesetter Award from the National Institute on Drug Abuse (1977); the Scientific Achievement Award from the American Medical Association (1985); and the Bower Award from the Franklin Institute (1992), which is the largest monetary award given in the United States for scientific achievement and which recognizes distinguished scientists who embody the "practical, entrepreneurial, and humanitarian spirit" of Benjamin Franklin.

Snyder and his wife, psychotherapist Elaine (Borko) Snyder, have been married since 1962 and are the parents of two daughters, one a psychiatrist and one a playwright and internet consultant.

STAFF

SOCIAL CASEWORK

Social casework is the counseling method employed by the social work profession to assist individuals and families troubled by biopsychosocial problems. Casework consists of strategies for social reform and techniques of clinical practice. This method originated in charity organization societies of England and the United States during the late 1870s. The charity organization movement was dedicated to applying the scientific method to eliminate poverty, crime, and disease. Thus the exciting new developments that took place in medicine, law, and psychology at the turn of the century influenced the work done by "friendly visitors" from the societies. Academicians, including G. Stanley Hall, were associated with the movement, and their ideas contributed to a new scientific philanthropy.

DEVELOPMENT OF THE CASEWORK METHOD

Richmond's book *Social Diagnosis,* published in 1917, reflected the spirit of the times by incorporating many concepts from the medical model. This influential text emphasized the need for social reform, along with the systematic collection of data on people's behavior and the assessment of facts to uncover the causes of social ills and their treatment. These developments took place during the period of World War I when Smith College established a training school for psychiatric social workers to assist the emotional casualties of the war and their families. Shortly afterward, medical social work was developed at the Massachusetts General Hospital. These events provided the impetus for specialized social work practice, and the extension of casework services to clients who were not necessarily poor.

The infusion of Freudian psychoanalytic concepts into casework theory and practice in the 1920s and 1930s directed caseworkers' attentions to individual processes and behavior within a framework of study, diagnosis, and treatment. This event diluted social work's traditional concern with environmental issues and social action.

Social casework was further influenced by various writings during the 1940s and 1950s. Hamilton's *Theory and Practice of Social Casework* focused on the connections between individual behavior and social situations, providing a psychosocial perspective. Another major theme was the active involvement of the client in the change process. In a somewhat different mode, writers from the University of Pennsylvania School of Social Work based their practice on the concepts of Otto Rank, emphasizing the characteristics of the client–worker relationship, the use of agency function, and the time dimension in providing service.

In 1957, Perlman attempted to "put the social back in social work" while retaining features of the psychosocial model and the Pennsylvania "school." Her book *Casework: A Problem-solving Process* presented a model of practice that gave prominence to client social roles, and the stages of the problem-solving process, based on the work of John Dewey. Casework practice, therefore, increasingly blended social reform with contributions from social science and concepts from psychoanalytic theory. Meanwhile this theory had moved from a psychology of the id to an ego psychology. Casework's dual but uneven concern with psychological and social processes was strengthened by publication of Hollis's *Casework: A Psychosocial Therapy* in 1964. This book developed a classification scheme for clinical and environmental treatment procedures, with major emphasis on the former.

CASEWORK AS A PROFESSIONAL DESIGNATION

The renewed concern with poverty and environmental issues during the 1960s and 1970s raised serious questions about casework's relevance and effectiveness. Fischer (1973) analyzed a series of casework outcome studies, using the methodology from Eysenck's (1952) research on the effectiveness of psychotherapy. Fischer's disputed conclusion that casework was ineffective precipitated a major self-examination within the social work profession that resulted in a reconceptualization of casework as a professional rather than a methodological designation. The separation of casework from a particular theoretical orientation opened the way for employment of a variety of approaches to helping people, and a search for those most effective.

Current approaches to casework, while differing in many respects, are based on a similar view of social work practice which prizes the worth and dignity of the individual; is committed to reduce the dehumanizing forces of society by means of social action and change; and recognizes that individualized services are essential to diminish human suffering, especially for those who are discriminated against or stigmatized.

CURRENT APPROACHES TO CASEWORK

Most contemporary caseworkers integrate the functions of clinician, environmental change agent, and broker/advocate. The clinician role is often most prominent. The majority pattern their practice on one or more of the following approaches.

Psychosocial Treatment

This view emphasizes assessment, diagnosis, and treatment based on Freudian psychoanalytic theory, augmented by newer concepts related to communications and systems theory, family therapy, crisis intervention, and planned short-term treatment. The major contribution to this approach comes from Hollis's research at Columbia University on classifying direct (clinical) and indirect (environmental) treatment procedures (see Hollis & Woods, 1981).

Family Therapy

Working with families is an important part of a caseworker's activity. Interventions are directed at bringing about change in the total family. Family therapy developed around a synthesis of ideas from psychoanalysis and theoretical constructs about communication, homeostasis, social systems, and roles. Many different models of family therapy are utilized, including experientially structural and behavioral approaches.

Crisis Intervention

Caseworkers often encounter clients in crisis who require short-term assistance. Crisis intervention is derived from studies of people in natural and human-generated disasters. A state of crisis is not viewed as an illness or pathology, but as an opportunity to promote growth in the client. This approach employs strategies and techniques from traditional and newer models of casework. However, the distinctive aspect is the focus on limited goals rather than attempts at deep personality change or other time-consuming activity.

The Behavioral Approach

Social workers have adopted behavioral methods and procedures from psychology in response to the need for an empirically based approach to practice. Edwin Thomas of the University of Michigan introduced behavior modification to social work in 1968. Educators and practitioners have applied behavioral techniques in a variety of practice settings. The use of single-subject research designs and cognitive procedures have been of particular interest to the profession.

Task-Centered Practice

Closely related to the behavioral model, task-centered practice was developed by Reid and Epstein (1972). Based on casework research that established the greater effectiveness of short-term treatment, this approach was originally viewed as an overall structure that could employ procedures from a number of casework models. However, major features, such as specifying client tasks to be accomplished and the careful attention to outcome, are compatible with the behavioral approach. Therefore, task-centered practice increasingly employs the methods and procedures of behavior modification while retaining its separate identity.

Eclectic Casework

After proclaiming the ineffectiveness of the traditional model of practice, Fischer designed what he termed the eclectic approach to casework in 1978. Fischer's basic view is that "if it can be objectively shown to work, use it." Therefore, his approach utilizes principles and procedures demonstrated by empirical evidence to lead to successful outcomes for clients. The four major components of eclectic casework are as follows: (a) structured procedures, such as the use of contracts, setting time limits, and planning and setting goals; (b) behavior modification techniques, including modeling, reinforcement, and systematic desensitization; (c) cognitive procedures aimed at correcting "faulty" thinking; and (d) core conditions of helping—therapist empathy, warmth, and genuineness. Fischer's textbook (1978) has done much to temper the earlier criticism directed at him for "attacking" casework.

The Life Model of Social Work Practice

The most recent addition to casework is the life model based on an ecological perspective. Germain and Gitterman (1980) developed this approach to be more suited to the broad purpose of social work rather than the more clinically oriented models. Their ecological perspective emphasizes the reciprocal relationship between organisms and their surroundings, as well as the ecosystem. The life model is directed to strengthening people's adaptive capacities and influencing their social settings. Professional intervention is focused on the "interface" between person and environment. The goal is to enhance the individual's coping abilities and to increase environmental responsiveness. This model provides the most comprehensive view to date of the person and environment as an integrated system. However, no original techniques have been developed to implement the particular perspective of the life model.

The rapid development of new casework approaches in recent years supports the view that significant change is taking place in social work. The major feature of this revolution is the adoption of scientifically based approaches to practice.

REFERENCES

Eysenck, H. J. (1952). The effects of psychotherapy: An evaluation. *Journal of Consulting Psychology, 16*, 319–324.

Fischer, J. (1973). Is casework effective? A review. *Social Work, 18*, 5–20.

Germain, C. B., & Gitterman, A. (1980). *The life model of social work practice.* New York: Columbia University Press.

Hamilton, G. (1951/1940). *Theory and practice of social casework* (Rev. ed.). New York: Columbia University Press.

Hollis, F., & Woods, M. E. (1981/1964). *Casework: A psychosocial therapy* (3rd ed.). New York: Random House.

Perlman, H. H. (1957). *Social casework: A problem-solving process.* Chicago: University of Chicago Press.

Reid, W. J., & Epstein, L. (1972). *Task-centered casework.* New York: Columbia University Press.

Richmond, M. (1917). *Social diagnosis.* New York: Columbia University Press.

SUGGESTED READING

Fischer, J. (1981). The social work revolution. *Social Work, 26*, 199–207.

Germain, C. (1970). Casework and science: A historical encounter. In W. Roberts & H. Nee (Eds.), *Theories of social casework.* Chicago: University of Chicago Press.

Golan, N. (1978). *Treatment in crisis situations.* New York: Free Press.

Schwartz, A., & Goldiamond, L. (1975). *Social casework: A behavioral approach.* New York: Columbia University Press.

Taber, M. A., & Vattano, A. J. (1970). Clinical and social orientations in social work: An empirical study. *Social Service Review, 44,* 34–43.

A. J. VATTANO
University of Illinois

CRISIS INTERVENTION
PSYCHIATRIC SOCIAL WORK

SOCIAL CLIMATE RESEARCH

Social climate (psychological climate, social context) is typically defined as the perceptions of a social environment that tend to be shared by a group of people. Climate is rooted in perception ("how I see the way things are done or how people treat each other around here"). Culture refers more to the beliefs, values, and norms that comprise the interdependent experiences and practices of larger collectives ("what we—as a group—should do and why and how we do it") (Denison, 1996; Schneider, 1990). Like meteorological or atmospheric climate, social climate is relatively distinctive across groups (as the Tropics differ from the Himalayas); dynamic or changeable within groups (like the seasons); and can influence behavior (like an individual's choice of clothing). Social climate research has grown considerably since White and Lippitt's (1960) early experiments comparing democratic, autocratic, and laissez-faire leadership in small groups of children. The concept and measurement of social climate have since been applied across widely diverse disciplines both within and outside the field of psychology.

Such diversity, and its parallel with atmospheric climate, can be demonstrated through a random sampling of recent research. Regarding distinctiveness, separate studies suggest that climates differ between support and therapy groups (Toro, Rappaport, & Seidman, 1987), between hospital units (Johnson, Rosenheck, & Fontana, 1997), and between multi-user Internet groups and face-to-face groups (Sempsey, 1998). Changes in the prevailing social climate have been seen as important in attitude assessment, such as in changing attitudes towards women (Twenge, 1997), and important to clinicians who modify services to fit social trends (Lyth, 1990). Studies of climate change have ranged in subjects from animal behavior (e.g., lizard aggression; Klukowski & Nelson, 1998) to organizations (e.g., small colleges; Oakley, 1997). A positive work climate has also been shown to relate to behavior or productivity (Brown & Leigh, 1996).

Researchers have developed questionnaires assessing social climate in diverse settings and content areas. These include, but are not limited to, family settings (see Knight & Simpson, 1999), adolescent peer groups (Simpson & McBride, 1992), organizational wellness (Bennett & Lehman, 1997), university teaching environments (Mateo & Fernandez, 1995), organizational learning (cf. transfer of training climate; Bennett & Lehman, 1999a), among the institutionalized elderly (Fernandez-Ballesteros, Montorio, & Fernandez de Troconiz, 1998), work-group use of alcohol (Bennett & Lehman, 1998), and hospital wards (Moos & Lemke, 1996). Perhaps the most studied aspect of climate is social cohesiveness (group pride and interdependence; Mullen & Copper, 1994).

DIMENSIONS OF SOCIAL CLIMATE RESEARCH

Given this diversity, it helps to identify the important dimensions of social climate research. Moreover, recent emphasis on self-report measures is often not based on strong theory or methodology. Theory, measurement, and the new direction of research in social climate can benefit from some taxonomy. Six different dimensions are used here (Figure 1). These are: (a) level of analysis issues (whether method/theory is sensitive to multi-level effects); (b) temporality (sensitivity to change and developmental processes); (c) type of setting (whether climate applies to one or many settings); (d) the dimension or domain studied; (e) consideration of social health; and (f) homogeneity (e.g., agreement, diversity, or multicultural processes).

Levels of Analysis

As described by Dansereau and Alutto (1990) and by Klein, Dansereau, and Hall (1994), the measurement of climate may be based on individual perceptions often referred to as "psychological climate" (level 1). These perceptions may be aggregated by summing or averaging scores, such as across members of a work group or classroom (level 2). Multiple groups can be combined into collectives such as work departments or schools (level 3). These may be aggregated into micro-societal entities such as organizations or school districts (level 4), which may then be combined into higher-level or macro-societal entities—for example, the state of an industry, profession, educational system (level 5). Researchers have focused on level 1 measurement, but recent efforts have used multi-level statistical techniques (e.g., hierarchical linear modeling; Bryk & Raudenbush, 1992). Examples include group-level cohesiveness, which predicts courteous behaviors (Kidwell, Mossholder, & Bennett, 1997), and neighborhood cohesiveness/social integration, which predicts taking safety precautions against crime (Rountree & Land, 1996). Levels of analysis are critical for assessing such things as cross-level congruence and co-determination, and bottom-up versus top-down processes (see Kozlowski & Salas, 1997).

Temporality

Group facilitators and coaches use models of group development that anticipate and guide shifts in social climate (e.g., forming, storming, norming, and performing; Tuckman, 1965). Organizational psychologists are increasingly being called upon to improve the climate of a business or workplace (e.g., Schneider, 1990). Despite strong interest in application of ideas of climate change, little has been written about the temporal qualities of climate. For example, how do the boundaries and shape of social climate change over time? Which dimensions are changeable and at what rate? Answers to such questions may come from related studies of time in work groups (McGrath, 1990) and dynamic systems in social psychology (Vallacher & Nowak, 1994).

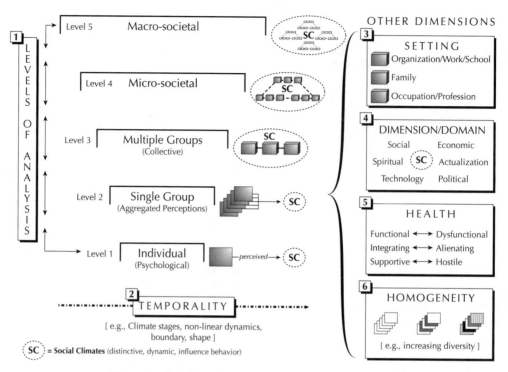

Figure 1.   Six Dimensions of Research into Social Climates.

Setting

As seen in the above review, researchers examine social climate within diverse settings. Thus, measures are often developed for specific rather than universal application. Predominantly, these have been in organizations (e.g., service, safety, and team climate), schools (e.g., social order, study climate), family settings (e.g., affective involvement, conflict), and some specific occupations or professions (e.g., academic and healthcare).

Dimensions and Domains

Most studies of social climate view it as multidimensional, with anywhere from three to ten different factors. Factor analysis is often used to support multidimensionality. Kopelman, Brief, and Guzzo (1990) view all work climates as having five core dimensions: goal emphasis, means emphasis, reward orientation, task support, and socioemotional support. Denison (1996) also derives five dimensions found across both culture and climate research: structure, support, risk, identity, and standards. It should be noted that social climate overlaps with group-level perceptions in a variety of domain and event areas. Domains include spiritual (church, prayer group), socio-technical (Internet, shared equipment), economic (distress due to job scarcity), actualization/leisure (self-help groups, shared hobbies), and political (common leaders, partisan loyalty). Researchers have also examined the climate of events or occasions within domains (e.g., holiday seasons, trade shows, business meetings, competitive events, conventions).

Social Health and Safety

Social support/health is a dimension found or implied in nearly all climate measures, and many climate researchers explore the degree to which a group is healthy or unhealthy. For example, studies ex-

amine the degree to which the social climate supports substance use (e.g., smoking in adolescents [Byrne & Reinhart, 1998]; drinking at work [Bennett & Lehman, 1999b]). Studies of social integration (vs. alienation), social health, and workplace safety (Cox, 1998) also examine social climate.

Homogeneity and Heterogeneity

Recent research suggests that climate may not always be perceived in the same way by the people who comprise the social group. From a methodological standpoint, researchers have yet to determine how much within-group variability is due to error variance, to actual disagreement, or to some other critical factor such as cultural or gender diversity. Here, the study of social climate borrows from studies of perception within groups (Gigone & Hastie, 1997), measurement of agreement (James, Demaree, & Wolf, 1984), and the field of relational demography (Harrison, Price, & Bell, 1998).

REFERENCES

Bennett, J. B., & Lehman, W. E. K. (1997). Employee views of organizational wellness and the EAP: Influence on substance use, drinking climates, and policy attitudes. *Employee Assistance Quarterly, 13*(1), 55–71.

Bennett, J. B., & Lehman, W. E. K. (1998). Workplace drinking climate, stress, and problem indicators: Assessing the influence of teamwork (group cohesion). *Journal of Studies on Alcohol, 59*(5), 608–618.

Bennett, J. B., & Lehman, W. E. K. (1999a). Change, transfer climate, and customer orientation: A contextual model and analysis of change-drive training. *Group and Organizational Management, 24*(2), 188–216.

Bennett, J. B., & Lehman, W. E. K. (1999b). Employee exposure to coworker substance use and negative consequences: The moderating effects of work group membership. *Journal of Health and Social Behavior, 40,* 307–322.

Brown, S. P., & Leigh, T. W. (1996). A new look at psychological climate and its relationship to job involvement, effort and performance. *Journal of Applied Psychology, 81*(4), 358–368.

Bryk, A. S., & Raudenbush, S. W. (1992). *Hierarchical linear models: Applications and data analysis methods.* Newbury Park, CA: Sage.

Byrne, D. G., & Reinhart, M. I. (1998). Psychological determinants of adolescent smoking behaviour: A prospective study. *Australian Journal of Psychology, 50*(1), 29–34.

Cox, T. R. (Ed.). (1998). The study of safety climate and safety culture [Special section]. *Work & Stress, 12* (3).

Dansereau, F., & Alutto, J. A. (1990). Level-of-analysis issues in climate and culture research. In B. Schneider (Ed.), *Organizational climate and culture* (pp. 193–236). San Francisco: Jossey-Bass.

Denison, D. R. (1996). What is the difference between organizational culture and organizational climate? A native's point of view on a decade of paradigm wars. *Academy of Management Review, 21*(3), 619–654.

Fernandez-Ballesteros, R., Montorio, I., & Fernandez de Troconiz, M. (1998). Personal and environmental relationships among the elderly living in residential settings. *Archives of Gerontology and Geriatrics, 26*(2), 185–198.

Gigone, D., & Hastie, R. (1997). Proper analysis of the accuracy of group judgments. *Psychological Bulletin, 121*(1), 149–167.

Harrison, D. A., Price, K. H., & Bell, M. P. (1998). Beyond relational demography: Time and the effects of surface- and deep-level diversity on work group cohesion. *Academy of Management Journal, 41*(1), 96–107.

James, L. R., Demaree, R. G., & Wolf, G. (1984). Estimating within-group interrater reliability with and without response bias. *Journal of Applied Psychology, 69,* 85–98.

Johnson, D. R., Rosenheck, R., & Fontana, A. (1997). Assessing the structure, content, and perceived social climate of residential posttraumatic stress disorder treatment programs. *Journal of Traumatic Stress, 10*(3), 361–376.

Kidwell, R. E., Jr., Mossholder, K. W., & Bennett, N. (1997). Cohesiveness and organizational citizenship behavior: A multilevel analysis using work groups and individuals. *Journal of Management, 23*(6), 775–793.

Klein, K. J., Dansereau, F., & Hall, R. J. (1994). Levels issues in theory development, data collection, and analysis. *Academy of Management Review, 19*(2), 195–229.

Klukowski, M., & Nelson, C. E. (1998). The challenge hypothesis and seasonal changes in aggression and steroids in male northern fence lizards (Sceloporus undulatus hyacinthinus). *Hormones and Behavior, 33*(3), 197–204.

Knight, D. K., & Simpson, D. D. (1999). Family assessment. In P. J. Ott, R. E. Tarter, & R. T. Ammerman (Eds.), *Sourcebook on substance abuse: Etiology, epidemiology, assessment, and treatment* (pp. 236–247). Boston: Allyn and Bacon.

Kopelman, R. E., Brief, A. P., & Guzzo, R. A. (1990). The role of climate and culture in productivity. In B. Schneider (Ed.), *Organizational climate and culture* (pp. 282–318). San Francisco: Jossey-Bass.

Kozlowski, S. W., & Salas, E. (1997). An organizational systems approach for the implementation and transfer of training. In K. Ford, (Ed.), *Improving training effectiveness in work organizations* (pp. 247–290). Hillsdale, NJ: Erlbaum.

Lyth, I. M. (1990). A psychoanalytical perspective on social institutions. In E. Trist, H. Murray, & B. Trist (Eds.), *The social engagement of social science: A Tavistock anthology: Vol. 1. The socio-psychological perspective* (pp. 463–475). Philadelphia: The University of Pennsylvania Press.

Mateo, M. A., & Fernandez, J. (1995). Evaluation of the setting in which university faculty carry out their teaching and research functions: The ASEQ. *Educational and Psychological Measurement, 55,* 329–334.

McGrath, J. E. (1990). Time matters in groups. In J. Galegher, R. E. Kraut, & C. Egido (Eds.), *Intellectual teamwork: Social and technological foundations of cooperative work* (pp. 23–61). Hillsdale, NJ: Erlbaum.

Moos, R. H., & Lemke, S. (1996). *Evaluating residential facilities: The multiphasic environmental assessment procedure.* Thousand Oaks, CA: Sage.

Mullen, B., & Copper, C. (1994). The relation between group cohesiveness and performance: An integration. *Psychological Bulletin, 115*(2), 210–227.

Oakley, K. L. (1997). Different destinies: Organizational transformation at two Midwestern Catholic women's colleges, 1965–1990. *Dissertation Abstracts International, 57*(11-A), 4615.

Rountree, P. W., & Land, K. C. (1996). Burglary victimization, perceptions of crime risk, and routine activities: A multilevel analysis across Seattle neighborhoods and census tracts. *Journal of Research in Crime and Delinquency, 33*(2), 147–180.

Schneider, B. (Ed.). (1990). *Organizational climate and culture.* San Francisco: Jossey-Bass.

Sempsey, J. J. (1998). A comparative analysis of the social climates found among face to face and Internet-based groups within multi-user dimensions. *Dissertation Abstracts International, 59* (3-B), 1414.

Simpson, D. D., & McBride, A. A. (1992). Family, friends, and self (FFS) assessment scales for Mexican American youth. *Hispanic Journal of Behavioral Sciences, 14*(3), 327–340.

Toro, P. A., Rappaport, J., & Seidman, E. (1987). Social climate comparison of mutual help and psychotherapy groups. *Journal of Consulting and Clinical Psychology, 55*(3), 430–431.

Tuckman, B. W. (1965). Developmental sequences in small groups. *Psychological Bulletin, 63,* 384–399.

Twenge, J. M. (1997). Attitudes toward women, 1970–1995: A meta-analysis. *Psychology of Women Quarterly, 21*(1), 35–51.

Vallacher, R. R., & Nowak, A. (Eds.). (1994). *Dynamical systems in social psychology.* San Diego: Academic Press.

White, R. K., & Lippitt, R. (1960). *Autocracy and democracy: An experimental inquiry.* New York: Harper.

J. B. Bennett
Texas Christian University

**GROUP DYNAMICS
LEADERSHIP STYLES**

SOCIAL COGNITION

The field of social cognition is concerned with the cognitive activity that mediates and accompanies social behavior. It provides an analysis of how stimulus information is initially encoded, organized (and transformed) in memory, and drawn upon as the person moves through the social world.

Social cognition, which is neither a single theory nor a narrow empirical domain, refers instead to a particular conceptual level of analysis used in the joint explanation of human thought and social behavior. It is explicitly mentalistic in orientation, focusing on the nature of cognitive activity and its role in determining human inferences, judgments, choices, and decisions. The level of analysis is molecular rather than molar. Theorists working within this orientation utilize "mental" constructs at the level of individual thoughts, categories, and concepts. These constructs are abstract enough to encompass a wide range of content domains (such as thoughts about people, traits, situations, animals, and works of art). Most researchers in this field, although mentalistic, do not restrict themselves to the study of "conscious" thought. The mental constructs are usually defined so as to leave open the question of consciousness.

Social cognition is a blending of interests in social processes and cognitive processes. A variety of areas of psychology have an abiding interest in social processes. In the middle to late 1970s, researchers in several of these branches became explicitly concerned with the information-processing theories of cognitive psychology. This trend could be seen clearly in developmental, social, and personality psychology, and to a lesser extent in clinical, counseling, and industrial-organizational psychology.

Basic research in human cognition took a form in the early 1970s that made it relevant to the work of "social process" researchers. Workers in the fields of cognitive psychology, psycholinguistics, and artificial intelligence became preoccupied with higher order cognitive processes, and interested in explaining complex types of human information-processing, such as the comprehension and retention of stories, action sequences, and other thematically coherent stimulus ensembles. Cognitive researchers began using stories and facts about people as stimulus items in their research. The relevance of such research (and its accompanying level of analysis) soon became apparent to those fields of psychology explicitly concerned with social processes.

The concept of a "schema" provided the initial meeting ground for the social and cognitive research groups. The elements of our cognitive world do not exist in some random, unrelated array. Rather, they are interassociated into higher order structures. When we think of a physician, a number of associated thoughts come to mind. Some may be definitional in character (e.g., has earned a medical degree) and others may be more ideosyncratic (e.g., rich, plays golf).

The schema concept was quite congenial to social psychologists because they already had been using a number of schema-like concepts. These included such terms as stereotype, norm, value, attitude, and implicit personality theory. Some workers in social cognition have developed taxonomies of schemas to aid in establishing conceptual similarities across different topics. Some of the categories proposed are person, role, event, trait, pictorial (or visual), and social group. Taxonomies have also been developed from the cognitive process point of view that classify schemas in terms of their conceptual properties. For example, one can distinguish between central tendency (representing a "typical" instance), template (providing a filing system for incoming information), and procedural (organizing experience and providing a pattern for subsequent action) schemas.

INFORMATION-PROCESSING PERSPECTIVE

The social cognition approach views the human mind as an information-processing system. Information is received from the stimulus world, processed through the cognitive system, and drawn upon when engaging in social behavior. Theorists strive for a detailed conceptualization of this mediating cognitive activity. In doing so, they have tended to ignore the perceptual systems that transform physical stimulation into some form of elementary cognitive representation, and the motoric systems that transform implicit cognitive activity into observable responses.

One stage of information-processing deals with the problems of encoding and organization. The concern here is with the initial interpretation of information and how it becomes related to preexisting knowledge structures. The main issue is to understand why mental representations of stimuli differ so much from the initiating stimulus ensemble. There is rarely (if ever) a one-to-one correspondence between the stimulus field and its cognitive representation. Schemas are viewed as introducing two kinds of distortions. They tend to screen out information that is schema-irrelevant and they tend to supplement the representation with schema-congruent, but unencountered, "facts."

A second information-processing topic area deals with the problem of cognitive retrieval. What determines the flow of thought, and how do we access prior information and inferences when engaging in social behavior? Sometimes we actively search our memory for specific facts and observations (as when eyewitnesses are quizzed by police). Other times our memory search is less focused and more leisurely (as when reminiscing with old friends).

There is also the problem of implicit retrieval that occurs in the case of more or less spontaneous social responses. People rarely (if ever) undertake a fully exhaustive search of the relevant information stored in their memory when making judgments and decisions. A search for previously acquired information can be bypassed when a behaviorally relevant schema is available.

A third category of issues has to do with information integration. People often face situations for which they have no adequate schemas. They have to make a judgment or reach a decision, but the information available does not coincide with any previously encountered and meaningfully organized patterns. Especially when people anticipate encountering such situations often in the future, it is in their interest to develop a new schema to deal with the kinds of variations found in this setting. It has been found, in the case of person impressions, that people sometimes resort to an algebraic summary of the information as a way of "integrating" the information.

A fourth topic area is response selection. How do people survey their response alternatives, tacitly select one, and behaviorally implement it? A particular thought can be communicated in many ways, including both verbal and nonverbal modes. Communication context and knowledge of the audience's point of view can affect how and when cognitive responses are transmitted.

Little work, unfortunately, has been done on the problem of response generation and selection. This is so because most cognitively oriented researchers provide their subjects with a small number of fixed-response alternatives. Such a methodology bypasses any need for research subjects creatively to seek out new action solutions.

Several lines of research have shown that the correspondence between a subjective judgment and the overt response is not perfect. Since many responses are made in social contexts, factors such as social desirability, audience involvement, and frame of reference will influence the correspondence.

UNRESOLVED ISSUES

Social cognition researchers have generally avoided the issue of how cognitive systems are energized. Schemas are like sewing machines with all the electrical wiring removed. By careful examination, one can understand how the machine works once an energy source is applied to the drive shaft, but there is no clue as to what the energy source is and how it is connected to the machinery.

An allied concern is the role of cognitive systems in regulating motivational energies. It is clear that many schemas are directly connected to affective systems (as in the case of romances and prejudices). Higher order cognitive structures must be linked to motivational systems since observable responses have both directional and intensity components. The nature of this linkage is not yet well understood.

It is unparsimonious to allow the schema concept to proliferate without bound. It becomes scientifically meaningless if a new schema is invented for every episode in a person's life. One approach to this problem is to assume that there are building blocks that can be incorporated into a variety of higher order structures.

Social environments are exceedingly complex. The amount and diversity of information contained in a social interaction are enormous. This is true of even a brief five-minute conversation among two or three friends in a cocktail lounge. From the point of view of any one of those present, there is a seemingly limitless number of ways cognitively to represent and organize this information. For example, the information can be organized by person, by conversation topic, by race or gender subgroups, by temporal sequence, and by trait. How does the person arrive at a particular organizational mode? Does the mode fluctuate from one point in the conversation to another, and is it possible to encode (and/or store) the information in two or more ways simultaneously?

These are the kinds of questions that become salient when adopting the level of analysis characteristic of the social cognition perspective. One measure of the field's success will be the extent to which it can provide answers.

SUGGESTED READING

Fiske, S. T., & Taylor, S. E. (in press). *Social cognition.* Reading, MA: Addison-Wesley.

Forgas, J. E. (Ed.). (1981). *Social cognition: Perspectives on everyday understanding.* New York: Academic.

Hastie, R., Ostrom, T. M., Hamilton, D. L., Ebbesen, E., Wyer, R. S., & Carlston, D. (Eds.). (1980). *Person memory: The cognitive basis of social perception.* Hillsdale, NJ: Erlbaum.

Higgins, E. T., Herman, C. P., & Zanna, M. P. (Eds.). (1981). *Social cognition: The Ontario symposium* (Vol. 1). Hillsdale, NJ: Erlbaum.

Isen, A. M., & Hastorf, A. H. (1982). Some perspectives on cognitive social psychology. In A. Hastoff & A. Isen (Eds.), *Cognitive social psychology.* New York: Elsevier/North-Holland.

Schank, R. C., & Abelson, R. P. (1977). *Scripts, plans, goals and understanding: An inquiry into human knowledge structures.* Hillsdale, NJ: Earlbaum.

Wyer, R. S. (1981). An information-processing perspective on social attribution. In J. Harvey, W. Ickes, & R. Kidd (Eds.), *New directions in attribution research* (Vol. 3). Hillsdale, NJ: Erlbaum.

T. Ostrom
Ohio State University

ATTENTION
IMPRESSION FORMATION
INFORMATION PROCESSING
SOCIAL INFLUENCE

SOCIAL COMPETENCE

Social competence is a term that is used broadly to reflect the full range of skills, abilities, and cognitive processes that are involved in effective social interaction. Social competence facilitates the development of relationships. It is related to the amount of positive reinforcement received from others, and is an important predictor of occupational and personal success. Social and interpersonal difficulties are the focus of many psychological treatment procedures, and are relevant to many psychological disorders. Thus, social competence is an important and influential megaconstruct in psychology.

Social competence may be contrasted with other terms, such as assertiveness, social skill, social perception, interpersonal attraction, or social phobia, which are used to describe specific aspects of the social interchange with typically less emphasis on the social-ethological function of developing social relationships, sharing resources, and promoting survival. Assertive skills, for example, are not socially competent if used in a situation that brings about personal dislike and future avoidance—even if the immediate instrumental goal is accomplished.

Social competence does not refer to a singular process or set of behaviors, but to a general class of behavior and cognitive processes. Moreover, the resources and skills required for effective functioning will differ with specific situations and major developmental tasks of the life span; the same person could be socially competent in one situation and incompetent in another. Likewise, social competence is not an endpoint or an outcome, but a process of social interaction. It is best understood within a multicausal, transactional framework. Social competence in any given situation is the result of many factors, including genetics, maturation, learning, reinforcement, social support, and environmental conditions. Successful interpersonal transactions require a balance between personal needs and desires and those of other people—resulting in satisfying close relationships and participation in social networks.

COMPONENTS OF SOCIAL COMPETENCE

Social competence involves cognitive and emotional intelligence, self-regulation and arousal, social skills, and self-efficacy beliefs. In most situations, social competence is associated with reduced reactivity to stress; greater self-control of attention, emotion, and behavior; better interpersonal problem-solving; and the capacity to express positive emotions in a reciprocal manner. Socially effective individuals are able to perceive and understand the goals, needs, and behaviors of other people. In contrast, individuals who react strongly to stress and have poor self-regulation may have difficulty negotiating social goals and tasks. Those who have difficulty with social problem-solving may have deficits in perspective-taking, empathy, alternative and means-ends thinking, and the ability to judge the social consequences of their actions. Social skill deficits may include difficulty approaching others, keeping a conversation going, asking questions, showing interest, and maintaining positive affect.

SOCIAL COMPETENCE ACROSS THE LIFE SPAN

Each stage of development presents new tasks or challenges. In infancy and early childhood, the development of basic motor skills and language are important for effective functioning. Secure attachment and support from proficient role models provides a context that enables young children to achieve socially expected goals. During middle childhood, the developmental tasks of achieving academically, making friends, and developing prosocial rules of conduct present significant challenges. During this stage, the self-regulation of attention, emotion, and behavior is of utmost importance. Adolescence brings new challenges—learning complex academic subjects, participating in extracurricular activities, developing close friendships with same- and opposite-sex peers, and forming a cohesive self-identity. During the early phase of adulthood, selecting a partner and developing a family network, establishing a career, and cultivating social ties are important. Child-rearing, career advancement, and the development of financial security characterize the middle phase. The latter part of prime adulthood brings tasks of maintaining life style, parenting older children, and caring for elderly parents. Balancing individual needs against the perceived needs of others is crucial for the successful negotiation of these tasks. Finally, the stage of late adulthood brings with it the challenges of developing alternative activities after retirement, adapting to reduced functioning, and the loss of loved ones. In this stage, the ability to recognize changes in need state, develop new friendships, select an appropriate living environment, and reach out for support are all crucial.

Developmental trajectories concerning social competence are not predictable in any simple, linear, and causal way from earlier stages of development. Instead, significant social problems can occur or remit at any point in the life span.

SOCIAL COMPETENCE AND PSYCHOPATHOLOGY

Deficits in social competence increase the risk for developing psychopathology and influence the course and prognosis of mental disorders. In particular, social and interpersonal problems have been associated with depression, schizophrenia, anxiety, phobias, behavioral and attention deficit disorders, substance use, and marital discord. Although the functional relevance and manifestation of social difficulties may vary for different individuals within the same diagnostic classification, research has attempted to isolate the most common problems associated with the various disorders. Two examples, depression and schizophrenia, can be illustrative. Research has shown that depressed individuals have relatively strict self-evaluations of social competence, which may limit social approach. There is also behavioral evidence that observers rate depressed individuals as less skillful than normal controls. However, few reliable specific conversational skill differences have been identified—depressed people speak less and have a greater latency to speak. They report relatively few friendships. It appears that reduced social interaction contributes to decreased mood and promotes extinction of social behavior. In addition, poor social problem-solving appears to be a vulnerability factor that increases the risk of depression. Although there is limited relevant research concerning bipolar depression, it is noteworthy that these individuals report a particularly high rate of divorce—suggesting a need for improved social problem solving, self-regulation, conflict resolution, and family education.

Persons with schizophrenia are less likely to have an established intimate relationship, and they often have negative symptoms such as social withdrawal and flat affect. Family interaction difficulties may also play a role in triggering relapse—high rates of critical comments or overinvolvement is an established risk factor. Poor activities of daily living (ADL) skills and difficulty with social problem-solving, grooming, and hygiene are also relevant. Vigilant overarousal or the failure to monitor the reactions of others are sometimes present. Reduced social competence is an important risk factor for relapse or need for intensive treatment.

TREATMENT APPROACHES

The most common treatment approaches have involved skills training (instruction, modeling, role-playing, feedback, encouragement, and homework), deconditioning (exposure, relaxation, systematic desensitization), and cognitive interventions (self-statement retraining, problem-solving, cognitive restructuring). Individual, group, and dyadic (marital) treatments have been developed. Treatment outcome research has shown improved functioning, although generalizability and maintenance of results appears somewhat limited. Thus, it is important to match treatment procedures to the specific types of social problems that each individual experiences. For individuals with extensive deficits, ongoing treatment or periodic booster sessions may be necessary.

Finally, those who study social competence are not only interested in the prevention and reduction of social difficulties, but also in the continued development of human potential and well-being. This positive mental health approach strives to improve the competence of all individuals. Multiply directed strategies are needed that focus on individual capabilities and environmental contexts (education, reform, or the opening of opportunities), with the goal of encouraging and supporting prosocial relationships.

SUGGESTED READING

Beelmann, A., Pfingsten, U., & Losel, F. (1994). Effects of training social competence in children: A meta-analysis of recent evaluation studies. *Journal of Clinical Child Psychology, 23,* 260–271.

Penn, D. L., Mueser, K. T., Spaulding, W., Hope, D. A., & Reed, D. (1995). Information processing and social competence in chronic schizophrenia. *Schizophrenia Bulletin, 21,* 269–281.

Pushkar, D., Bukowski, W. M., Schwartzman, A. E., Stack, D. M., & White, D. R. (1998). *Improving competence across the lifespan: Building interventions based on theory and research.* New York: Plenum.

Rose-Krasnor, L. (1997). The nature of social competence: A theoretical review. *Social Development, 6,* 111–135.

M. G. Dow
A. Rich
University of South Florida

SOCIAL SKILLS TRAINING

SOCIAL DESIRABILITY

Social desirability is the tendency for individuals to portray themselves in a generally favorable fashion. Within the field of psychological testing in general, and personality assessment in particular, the concept of social desirability has fueled heated debates for decades. Arguments have focused on the definition of social desirability, its pervasiveness, problems it presents for the interpretation of psychological tests, and methods for its control.

Social desirability has variously been defined as the tendency to give culturally sanctioned and approved responses (Crowne & Marlowe, 1960), to provide socially desirable responses to statements in self-description (Edwards, 1957), or to describe oneself in terms judged as desirable and to present oneself favorably (Jackson, 1984). Noted here is that the emphasis is on a style of responding irrespective of the specific personality content dimension to be measured by a psychological test. Consequently, a potential problem for a self-report personality test is whether an elevated score represents a high score on the test's content dimension or a greater tendency to present oneself favorably. For example, does a high score on a particular self-report scale of ambitiousness reflect a test-taker's true level of ambitiousness or the respondent's tendency to answer test items in terms of desirability? The possible existence of such ambiguous interpretations has produced a great deal of debate and research.

Research on scales of social desirability has led to the finding that there are two facets of social desirability (Holden & Fekken, 1989; Paulhus, 1984; Paulhus & John, 1998). The first aspect concerns the self and a belief in one's own ability. Terms used to label this facet include "sense of own general capability" and "egoistic bias." The second component focuses on an orientation toward others, and its labels have included "interpersonal sensitivity" and "moralistic bias." It should be noted that individual scales designed to assess social desirability may measure either one or both of these facets.

Some assessment experts believe that self-report tests that have been developed without explicit attempts to minimize the influence of social desirability will be saturated with this stylistic influence. Consequently, any interpretations from such tests are ambiguous and suspect. In contrast to this perspective is the belief that social desirability is itself a personality variable that may be a legitimate component of individual differences. For example, it might be argued that a strong belief in one's own abilities (i.e., social desirability) is a legitimate aspect of the concept of ambitiousness. This, however, then presents a problem: If social desirability is a feature of many different constructs of personality (e.g., ambitiousness, friendliness, neatness, etc.) and social undesirability (i.e., negative social desirability) is a component of various facets of psychopathology (e.g., depression, hostility, alienation), then these constructs are not truly and legitimately independent and should not be theorized, measured, or reported as such.

Various methods have been proposed for coping with social desirability in self-report tests. First, a forced-choice response format could be used for a test. Response options for any test item would then be matched for social desirability. Second, test items could be selected for a scale based on those items being more strongly representative of the psychological concept of interest than social desirability. This would involve a test construction strategy that used some form of item selection from an initial larger pool of test stimuli in which items had somehow been measured for appropriate content and inappropriate response bias (e.g., social desirability).

Third, test instructions could be tailored to reduce the likelihood that test-takers will respond in terms of social desirability. For example, a statement to test-takers indicating that the test contains an index for monitoring inaccurate responses could serve to reduce socially desirable responding. Fourth, social desirability could be statistically removed from the score generated on the test. This would require the use of a social desirability scale, the score of which would then be used to adjust the initially obtained score for the psychological concept of interest.

Despite the fact that the rancorous debates of the 1960s concerning social desirability have mellowed into the polite disagreements of present times, test developers and users are well advised to be aware of the issues. To construct tests of personality and psychopathology without due consideration of noncentral influences on test responding (such as social desirability) is to flirt with theoretical and practical disaster.

REFERENCES

Edwards, A. E. (1957). *The social desirability variable in personality assessment and research.* New York: Dryden.

Holden, R. R., & Fekken, G. C. (1989). Three common social desirability scales: Friends, acquaintances, or strangers? *Journal of Research in Personality, 23,* 180–191.

Jackson, D. N. (1984). *Personality Research Form manual* (3rd ed.). Port Huron, MI: Sigma Assessment Systems.

Paulhus, D. L. (1984). Two-component models of socially desirable responding. *Journal of Personality and Social Psychology, 46,* 598–609.

Paulhus, D. L., & John, O. P. (1998). Egoistic and moralistic biases in self-perception: The interplay of self-deceptive styles with basic traits and motives. *Journal of Personality, 66,* 1025–1060.

R. R. Holden
Queen's University

PERSONALITY ASSESSMENT
SELF-CONCEPT
TESTING METHODS

SOCIAL EXCHANGE THEORY

Social exchange theory is based on the assumption that human beings will form and sustain relationships if they believe that rewards they derive from such relationships will exceed costs. In developing a theory of social exchange, Homans (1961) attempted to explain behavior as the outcome of interaction in which individuals trade or exchange resources broadly defined. Although Homans derived his statement of modern exchange theory from behavioral psychology and microeconomics, analogous theories also are found in anthropology (Levi-Strauss, 1949; Mauss, 1954) and political science (Elster, 1986). While social exchange theory best explains interactions between two persons, the theory has also been extended

to intergroup processes (Blalock & Wilken 1979), organizational structures (Blau, 1964), and exchange networks (Cook et al., 1983; Marsden, 1982). It has been applied to dyadic behaviors, such as friendship and marriage (Hatfield et al., 1979; Waller, 1937) and, more recently, to more complex interactions such as game theory (Taylor, 1987) and collective action (Coleman, 1975). Recognition of the ubiquitous inequalities inherent in the exchange process has led to the development of a more general theory of equity (Adams, 1965).

The five basic propositions of modern exchange theory were formally stated by Homans (1961). He attempted to explain social behavior using basic notions of behavior originally developed by behavioral psychologists and neoclassic economists. The behaviorists' model of operant conditioning is based on the utilitarian principle that individuals will seek to maximize their pleasure and to avoid or minimize their pain. Individuals are expected to respond in predictable ways to rewards and punishments. Each interaction is an opportunity to exchange resources from which each participant attempts to receive resources of higher value than he or she has contributed or foregone. Generally speaking, social psychologists refer to things exchanged as resources. While resources can be anything tangible or intangible, Foa and Foa (1974) have identified six classes of exchange resources: love, status, information, money, goods, and services. They further state that any resource falling into one of these six classes can be described with respect to one of two dimensions: particularism and concreteness. The particularism of resources is the extent to which its value depends on the particular person involved in the exchange. For example, an exchange of affection holds more value to a loved one than to a total stranger while an exchange of money holds a more universal value. The second dimension, concreteness, refers to the degree to which the resource is tangible such as a raise in salary as opposed to an increase in one's occupational status. From additional research, Foa and Foa found that particularistic resources tend to be exchanged for resources in the same class (e.g., love for love rather than love for money) but that less particularistic resources are commonly exchanged for resources in different classes. For example, money is often exchanged for goods or services.

Homans (1974) developed five general propositions concerning social behavior and the exchange of resources. Three of these propositions reflect the behavioral psychologists' model. The first proposition, directly derived from the model of operant conditioning, states that "for all actions taken by persons, the more often a particular action of a person is rewarded, the more likely the person is to perform that action" (Homans, 1974, p. 16). The second proposition acknowledges past learning: "If in the past the occurrence of a particular stimulus, or set of stimuli, has been the occasion on which a person's action has been rewarded, and the more similar the present stimuli are to the past ones, the more likely the person is to perform the action, or some similar action now" (Homans, 1974, p. 22). On the other hand, the third proposition states that "when a person's action does not receive the reward he expected, or receives punishment he did not expect, he will be angry and he becomes likely to perform aggressive behavior" (Homans, 1974, p. 43).

The last two propositions are more closely linked to economic theory. Microeconomic theory also is rooted in utilitarian traditions. One underlying assumption is that in the process of maximizing pleasure and avoiding pain, humans are utility maximizers. That is, "for each person each state of the world has a particular utility level, where utility is that which the person seeks to maximize through his actions" (Coleman, 1975, p. 81). As such, the fourth proposition states that "the greater the profit a person receives as a result of his actions, the more likely he is to perform the action" (Homans, 1974, p. 31). In Homans's terms profit is the net result of the benefits or rewards of an interaction less the costs associated with it.

The final proposition reflects the economic notion of declining marginal utility. Homans (1974) states that "the more often in the recent past a person has received a particular reward the less valuable any further unit of that reward becomes for him" (p. 29). The idea is that one can become satiated with any given good such that additional units are no longer desired or hold the same value as they did initially.

Although Homans refers to individual's interactional inputs and outcomes as "costs, investment, rewards, and profits," his theory is purely social, not economic. Rather than to attempt to explain all social behavior, Homans excludes from explanation behaviors that result from coercive actions or as a response to social customs, norms, or internalized behavior (Heath, 1976). "People do things for fear of other men or for fear of God or for fear of their conscience, and nothing is gained by trying to force such action into a conceptual framework of exchange" (Blau, 1964, p. 89).

Social exchange and economic exchange are further differentiated by the terms of the interaction. Whereas economic exchanges maintain explicit terms of the costs and benefits for each party involved, social exchanges are never explicit. In addition, the terms of the contract for an economic exchange are discussable, negotiable, and enforceable by law. On the other hand, for social exchanges, it would be considered in bad taste to attempt to negotiate a more profitable exchange and the terms of the exchange do not constitute an enforceable contract, creates feelings of personal obligation, and has intrinsic significance for the participants. Social exchanges, it is said, entail unspecified obligations. "One person does another a favor, and while there is a general expectation of some future return, its exact nature is definitely not stipulated in advance" (Blau, 1964, p. 93).

Although Homans has gone a long way to provide powerful propositions to explain why an individual takes one course of action or maintains some relationships while dissolving others, he does not provide an explanation of what constitutes a benefit to one individual and a cost to another. Resources received are not necessarily valuable in the abstract but are valued in relation to anticipations given past association, current expectations, and comparisons to what others receive in similar interactions. Thibaut and Kelley (1959) present a description of preference hierarchies that takes into account individuals' histories and social comparisons.

DEVELOPMENT OF A PREFERENCE HIERARCHY

Social exchange theory can be seen as a theory of choice behavior. In choosing among alternatives, individuals need some standard or baseline by which to judge the relative reward of the alternatives. Individuals choose between alternatives "by evaluating the experiences or expected experiences with each in terms of a preference ranking and then selecting the best alternative" (Blau, 1964, p. 18). Thibaut and Kelley (1959) have addressed the issue of preference ranking in their theory of small group interaction. They suggest that individuals develop a scale of preferences against which they compare alternative choices. The midpoint of this scale is referred to as the comparison level (CL). Thibaut and Kelley (1959) state that individuals develop a CL that is:

a standard by which the person evaluates the rewards and costs of a given relationship in terms of what he feels he "deserves." Relationships, the outcomes of which fall above the CL would be relatively "satisfying" and attractive to the member; those entailing outcomes that fall below the CL would be relatively "unsatisfying" and unattractive. The location of the CL on the person's scale of outcomes will be influenced by all of the outcomes known to the member, either by direct experience or symbolically. (p. 21)

The actual level of outcomes that yields this midpoint on the satisfaction–dissatisfaction scale will depend on the level of recently experienced outcomes or those outcomes for which the individual had major causal responsibility. They will be satisfied if they get more than they anticipate and dissatisfied if they get less.

While each individual has a set CL for any resource, he or she also has a comparison level for alternative resources or exchange partners (CLalt). The value of a particular resource from one's exchange partner depends, to some degree, on the availability of alternative exchange partners or substitute resources. For example, if person A offers person B $10 to do a job, it is necessary to know if $10 for that job falls below or above the CL for person B and if person B has an alternative offer (CLalt) before it is possible to predict his or her response.

It is the conception of CLalt that leads to a discussion of power in social exchange relationships. To the extent that one exchange partner controls the access to scarce or desired resources, he or she has power over the other partner. In this case, there is no alternative exchange partner or the alternatives provide less desirable outcomes. Whichever person in a relationship has outcomes closer to his or her CLalt will have more power over the other. It is also assumed that the person least interested in maintaining the relationship for whatever reason, has the power to dominate that relationship. This is referred to as the principle of least interest and leads to the conclusion that "power resides implicitly in the other's dependency" (Emerson, 1962, p. 32). Emerson developed a theory of power-dependence relations based on the notion that because exchanges involve at least two parties, each is dependent on the other to some degree for interaction to occur. In a unilateral monopoly, person A can only obtain resources from person B. In terms of that resource, person B has ultimate power over A. And the more different kinds of resources A gets from B, the more A is dependent on B, hence the more power B has over A. This work has been extended to the study of coalition formation, power networks, and organizational linkages.

The recognition of power-dependence relations leads individuals to either cooperation or competition. In the context of social exchange theory, cooperation and competition reflect the opposite ends of a continuum of actions ranging from those acts favoring all involved (cooperation) to those acts favoring one participant at the expense of all others (competition). Much research on cooperation and competition has used a payoff matrix as suggested by Thibaut and Kelley (1959). The matrix, in its simplest form, describes an exchange between two parties for which two choices of behavior exist: either to cooperate or to compete with the other. The outcomes of any possible exchange combination can easily be determined from the matrix.

It is from different combinations of payoff matrices that game theory and social exchange theory overlap. A mixed-motive game is one in which the highest outcome for one party also poses the most risk, and each party's gain will be the other's loss. They are called mixed-motive games because motives to trust and cooperate exist simultaneously with motives to be suspicious of the other and compete. A second type of payoff matrix creates what is called a zero-sum game. Here the payoff combinations are such that a positive outcome for one party necessarily means a negative outcome for the other party—the winner takes all.

Even though subjects in research using payoff matrices are fully aware of the advantages of mutual cooperation, they tend to favor competitive choices (McClintock & McNeal, 1966; Messick & Thorngate, 1967). It appears that subjects are more interested in maximizing the differences between themselves and their game partners than maximizing their own rewards. Exceptions to this finding appear under conditions in which communication between the players was available or when the two players shared a close personal relationship. In both cases there is a basis for mutual trust thus fostering cooperative strategies.

An additional source of power in social exchange relationships comes when one exchange partner can influence the other's outcomes through his or her own actions. Thibaut and Kelley (1959) have argued that an individual can control the other's actions or behaviors by his or her own choice in two different ways. The first type of influential control or power is called *fate control*. "If, by varying his behavior, A can affect B's outcomes regardless of what B does, A has fate control over B" (Thibaut & Kelley, 1959, p. 102). By initiating this type of control, one individual has narrowed the responses available to the other—B's fate depends on A's actions.

The second type of influential control is referred to as *behavior control*. "If, by varying his behavior, A can make it desirable for B to vary his behavior too, then A has behavior control over B" (Thibaut & Kelley, 1959, p. 103). This is likely to occur when A can initiate a choice in behavior that increases the outcomes for B for a specific response or increases the costs of an alternative response from B. While B still has a choice of behavior, A has the capacity to have a great deal of influence over B's outcomes and, as a result, a great deal of influence in B's behavior.

EXTENSIONS OF EXCHANGE THEORY

While the discussion of a theory of social exchange within a dyadic relationship has benefited from the simplicity it afforded, it is widely recognized that extensions need to be made to more complex social interactions. One extension has been the development

of equity theory that suggests that the successes of other people will enter into the calculation of satisfaction with one's own success. One views their outcomes in relation to how others have done in addition to their own investments. Distributions of rewards, it is suggested, should be on the basis of individual effort and investment leading to the development of theories of distributive justice (Rawls, 1971).

Exchange networks and the power of resource control has been another expansion of social exchange theory. As Thibaut and Kelley's (1959) discussion of fate and behavior control would suggest, one individual with control over a scarce resource maintains a source of power over others in exchange network.

Social exchange theory has also been considered an important development in linking microprocesses with macrostructures. Blau (1964) initiated this work, which continues to gain attention. As was earlier noted, much of this interest crosses disciplinary boundaries with all forms of the social sciences exploring derivations of social exchange theory.

REFERENCES

Adams, J. S. (1965). Inequity in social exchange. In L. Berkowitz (Ed.), *Advances in experimental social psychology* (Vol. 2). New York: Academic.

Blalock, H. M., Jr., & Wilken, P. (1979). *Intergroup processes: A micro-macro perspective.* New York: Free Press.

Blau, P. M. (1964). *Exchange and power in social life.* New York: Wiley.

Coleman, J. (1975). *The mathematics of collective action.* London: Heinemann.

Cook, K., Emerson, R., Gillmore, M., & Yamagishi, T. (1983). The distribution of power in exchange networks. *American Journal of Sociology, 89,* 275–305.

Elster, J. (Ed.). (1986). *Rational choice.* Oxford, UK: Blackwell.

Emerson, R. (1962). Power-dependency relations. *American Sociological Review, 27,* 31–41.

Foa, U. G., & Foa, E. B. (1974). *Societal structures of the mind.* Springfield, IL: Thomas.

Hatfield, E., Utne, M. K., & Traupmann, H. (1979). Equity theory and intimate relationships. In R. L. Burgess & T. L. Huston (Eds.), *Social exchange in developing relationships.* New York: Academic.

Heath, A. (1976). *Rational choice and social exchange: A critique of exchange theory.* Cambridge, UK: Cambridge University Press.

Homans, G. C. (1974/1961). *Social behavior: Its elementary forms.* New York: Harcourt, Brace & World.

Levi-Strauss, C. (1969). *The elementary structures of kinship.* Boston: Beacon. (Original work published 1949)

Marsden, P. V. (1982). Brokerage behavior in restricted exchange networks. In P. V. Marsden & N. Lin (Eds.), *Social structure and network analysis* (pp. 201–218). Beverly Hills, CA: Sage.

Mauss, M. (1954). *The gift: Forms and functions of exchange in archaic societies.* Glencoe, IL: Free Press.

McClintock, C. G., & McNeel, S. P. (1966). Reward and score feedback as determinants of cooperative and competitive game behavior. *Journal of Personality and Social Psychology, 4*(6), 606–613.

Messick, D. M., & Thorngate, W. B. (1967). Relative gain maximization in experimental games. *Journal of Experimental Social Psychology, 3*(1), 85–101.

Rawls, J. (1971). *A theory of justice,* Cambridge, MA: Harvard University Press.

Taylor, M. (1987). *The possibility of cooperation.* Cambridge, UK: University of Cambridge Press.

Thibaut, J. W., & Kelley, H. H. (1959). *The social psychology of groups.* New York: Wiley.

Waller, W. (1937). The rating and dating complex. *American Sociological Review, 2,* 727–734.

L. RIES

OPERANT BEHAVIOR
REWARDS AND INTRINSIC INTEREST
SOCIAL PSYCHOLOGY

SOCIAL FACILITATION

The question of social facilitation research is how the presence of another person affects performance. If you play a musical instrument alone or in front of an audience, is your performance typically better or worse? If you type with no one around, with someone else merely working in the background, or with an audience observing you and evaluating you, how do these conditions affect both the speed and accuracy of your typing?

Allport (1924) first used the term "social facilitation" for "an increase in response merely from the sight or sound of others making the same movement" (p. 262), although it now refers to either an increase or a decrease in response from a person who might not be making the same movement. Vaughan and Guerin (1997) argued that an earlier experiment by Triplett (1898), commonly said to be the first in social facilitation, was not actually related.

The factors affecting performance in the presence of another person were comprehensively delineated by Allport (1924) and Dashiell (1935), and include competition (rivalry), modeling, encouragement or social reinforcement, arousal, monitorability, imitation, group membership, distraction, and evaluation (Guerin, 1993). There is solid evidence for each of these and they each have a separate research literature.

Social facilitation research has probably held together as a distinct topic only because of the work of Zajonc (1965). The first important feature of Zajonc (1965) was his hypothesis that new or poorly learned actions would be inhibited or made worse by the presence of another person, whereas well-learned actions would be facilitated. For example, an accomplished flute player would perform better with other people present whereas a poor or beginner flute player would do worse. This formed a simple 2 × 2 experi-

mental design with participants performing alone or with someone else present, and performing either a well-learned or a new behavior. At least 15 theories for this were proposed between 1965 and 1993, and at least 100 tests were based upon this simple design (Guerin, 1993).

The second important feature of Zajonc (1965) was his suggestion that apart from the factors mentioned earlier, there still might be effects from just the "mere presence" of another person, a term first used by Burnham (1910, p. 766). This negative definition led researchers to attempt to control for all the other factors while measuring performance changes. However, it was difficult to control for so many other factors, and only 91 out of 313 studies had suitable controls (Guerin, 1993). The most common fault was to have an experimenter present in the "Alone" condition.

It has been argued that this whole research endeavor was unsuccessful not only because all the factors could not easily be controlled but also because a single performance measure was typically used as evidence for both social facilitation and the proposed alternative theory (Guerin, 1993). Theories were needed of what mere presence *was* rather than what it was not, so that independent measurements could be made of performance and the theoretical mechanism. Links to other areas such as social loafing have been fruitful (Harkins, 1987). Researchers also extrapolated to applied settings, forgetting that factors like the excluded factors of competition, intergroup rivalry, social reinforcement, and modeling are probably far more powerful in real life than are "mere presence" effects.

Of the reliable effects that have been found using the simple designs and single measures, there seem to be two that are prevalent. First, when someone else is present, people tend to behave in accordance with socially expected standards of performance. This leads to conformity with what they think the experimenter wants them to do, which is usually to try harder at their performance and to do well, but only when they believe that they can be monitored (when there can be consequences) by the experimenter. The second main effect found is an increase in alertness or attention. That is, people are more attentive to what is going on, more rule-governed or verbally governed in their behavior, when someone is present than when they are alone. This impacts their performance in different ways: If the task is difficult or new, they will do worse if they are paying attention elsewhere (Sanders, 1984); if the task is easy, they might be more aroused if they have time to watch what people are doing around them and so do better (Guerin, 1993).

There is also a large social facilitation research literature with nonhuman animals. The findings seem to reflect species differences that depend upon what the species normally does alone or in groups (Guerin, 1993). Normally solitary animals, such as cats, will become fearful if put in the presence of another animal, and will therefore reduce feeding but increase other aggressive or defensive behaviors. When animals that normally live in groups are put together, what they do depends again upon the species and the wider social context. The evidence is that rats will tend to interact socially and therefore eat less (which is typically the measure of "social facilitation") but play more. Chicks put together in groups become less fearful but do not interact and are therefore found to eat more than when alone.

The problem, then, is similar to the one suggested for the human studies. If only a single measure is used, such as the facilitation or inhibition of feeding, then there are contradictory findings—rats eat less in groups but chicks eat more. If the whole context or social ecology is measured, the contradictions disappear—the rats use their time together to groom and play and therefore stop eating, whereas the chicks reduce their fear activities when in groups and spend the extra time eating. The problems of social facilitation research with humans also come down to this—that too much reliance has been made of simple designs and sparse measures. It is not enough to know that people type less when someone else is present with them. Like the animal studies, we need to measure what they are doing instead. Multiple measures will help us solve the problems of this area, because we already know that there are multiple conditions for someone playing a flute in front of an audience and that there are multiple consequences of doing so. Measuring "number of correct notes" alone will not explain the social behavior.

REFERENCES

Allport, F. (1924). *Social psychology.* New York: Houghton Mifflin.

Burnham, W. H. (1910). The group as a stimulus to mental activity. *Science, 31,* 761–766.

Dashiell, J. F. (1935). Experimental studies of the influence of social situations on the behavior of individual adults. In C. Murchison (Ed.), *A handbook of social psychology* (pp. 1097–1158). Worcester, MA: Clark University Press.

Guerin, B. (1993). *Social facilitation.* Cambridge: Cambridge University Press.

Harkins, S. G. (1987). Social loafing and social facilitation. *Journal of Experimental Social Psychology, 23,* 1–18.

Sanders, G. S. (1984). Self-presentation and drive in social facilitation. *Journal of Experimental Social Psychology, 20,* 312–322.

Triplett, N. (1898). The dynamogenic factors in pacemaking and competition. *American Journal of Psychology, 9,* 507–533.

Vaughan, G. M., & Guerin, B. (1997). A neglected innovator in sports psychology: Norman Triplett and the early history of competitive performance. *International Journal of the History of Sport, 14,* 82–99.

Zajonc, R. B. (1965). Social facilitation. *Science, 149,* 269–274.

B. GUERIN
University of Waikato

SOCIAL INFLUENCE

All human interaction involves power and influence. Individuals must be skillful in influencing others and must take responsibility for such influence. There are three different perspectives on social influence: the trait-factor, the dynamic-interdependence, and the bases of power.

TRAIT-FACTOR PERSPECTIVE

The trait-factor approach to social influence may be traced to Aristotle, whose rhetoric dealt at some length with the characteristics of an effective influencer and gave detailed advice on the techniques of persuasion (Johnson, 2000; Johnson & Johnson, 2000). From the trait-factor point of view, social influence is a function of the characteristics of (a) the person exerting the influence, (b) the person receiving the influence, and (c) the influence attempt itself. This view is based on two assumptions. First, a person's traits, not circumstances, fortune, or opportunities, explain the person's behavior (certain people are born influencers and others are not). Second, people are rational in the way they process information and are motivated to attend to a message, learn its contents, and incorporate it into their attitudes. The major post–World War II application of the trait-factor approach to social influence was the Yale Attitude Change Program headed by Carl Hovland (Hovland et al., 1949). Most of the research in this program focused on the area in which the trait-factor view is strongest—the effects of a single attempt to influence an audience delivered through the mass media. In situations in which a politician is giving a speech to an audience, an announcer is delivering a television commercial, or a health official is warning the public about a health danger, the findings from the Yale Program are quite useful. In each of these situations, the contact between the communicator and the receiver of the communication is brief and is not repeated. Moreover, the communication is one-way; there is no interaction between the two parties. Because single instances of one-way communication are essentially static, a trait-oriented theory is quite helpful in analyzing them.

Much of the post–World War II research on social influence stemmed from Hovland's wartime studies of propaganda and was organized around the theme question, "Who says what to whom with what effect?" Investigators have usually broken this question down into variables relating to the source (the characteristics of the communicator), the message (the characteristics of the communication), and the receiver (the characteristics of the person receiving the message). Social influence occurs when a credible and attractive communicator delivers an effectively organized message to a vulnerable or influenceable audience.

The two most researched aspects of communicators are credibility and attractiveness. The credibility of communicators depends on their perceived ability to know valid information and on their perceived motivation to communicate this knowledge without bias. More specifically, credibility depends on objective indicators of relevant expertise, perceived reliability as an information source, a lack of self-interest in the issue, warmth and friendliness, a confident and forceful delivery of the message, and considerable social support from others. The attractiveness of communicators depends on their facilitation of the receiver's goal accomplishment, physical appearance, perceived similarity, perceived competence, warmth, and familiarity.

Messages that inspire fear with specific instructions for action, messages that acknowledge opposing viewpoints, and the size of the discrepancy between the content of the message and the receiver's position all promote social influence. Influence attempts are aimed at a receiver. The receiver's self-esteem, present attitudes, forewarning of the intention to influence, practice in defending a position, and intelligence all affect the success of an influence attempt. Actively role-playing a previously unacceptable position, furthermore, increases its acceptability to the receiver.

The trait-factor approach to social influence is weak both logically and empirically in situations in which two or more individuals are constantly interacting.

DYNAMIC-INTERDEPENDENCE PERSPECTIVE

The term "dynamic" means in a constant state of change; "interdependence" means that each member's actions affect the outcomes of other members. The dynamic-interdependence view of social influence posits that who is influencing whom to what degree changes constantly as individuals strive to achieve mutual goals (Johnson, 2000; Johnson & Johnson, 2000). Influence exists in relationships, not in individuals. A person cannot be an influencer if there is no influencee. Furthermore, for influence to be constructive, it has to occur in a cooperative (not competitive) context. In a cooperative context, influence is used to maximize joint benefits and promote the achievement of mutual goals. In a competitive context, influence is used to gain advantage and promote one's own success at the expense of others. Influence attempts in a competitive context result in resistance. Resistance is the psychological force aroused in an individual that keeps him or her from accepting influence.

When individuals work together to achieve mutual goals, social influence is inevitable. They must influence and be influenced by each other, each modifying and adjusting his or her behavior to respond to what the other person is doing. The speed of conversation, the attitudes expressed, and the phrasing of messages are all influenced by the others with whom one is interacting. The use of influence is essential to all aspects of relationships. Goals cannot be established, communication cannot take place, leadership cannot exist, decisions cannot be made, and conflicts cannot be resolved unless there is mutual influence. The degree of influence is dynamic in that it constantly changes as the individuals make progress in obtaining their goals, as their costs (in energy, emotion, time, etc.) of working collaboratively vary, and as other relationships become available in which the goals might be better achieved. If the individuals make progress toward achieving the goals, the costs of working together are low, and no other relationships are as rewarding, then the ability of the individuals involved to influence each other increases.

BASES OF INFLUENCE PERSPECTIVE

According to social exchange theory, influence is based on the control of valued resources. The more an individual wants a specific resource, the more power the people who control the resource have over him or her. Different types of influence can be specified based on what types of resources are under a person's control (Raven, 1992). There are six possible bases for a person's social influence: one's ability to reward and to coerce; one's legal position; one's capacity as a referent with whom others wish to identify; one's expertise; and one's information. Each of these sources (reward, coercion, legitimacy, referent capacity, expertise, information) enables one to influence others.

CONFLICT AND SOCIAL INFLUENCE

The French social psychologist Serge Moscovici (1985) proposed an intergroup conflict model of social influence in which power defines whether a group is a majority or a minority. He assumes that both majorities and minorities are sources and targets of influence attempts. Majorities tend to use their power to force minorities to yield and conform to the majorities' expectations. Minorities tend to convert majorities to the minorities' position. A power majority is the group with the most control over the way important resources are distributed (they may be the numerical minority). A power minority is a group that has little control over the distribution of important resources (they may be a numerical majority). In the United States and Europe, for example, white males (a numerical minority) have traditionally controlled the distribution of the top posts in government and industry (they have been the power majority), while Asians and others are part of the power minorities. In Japan, however, so-called pure Japanese are the power majority and white Europeans are a power minority.

REFERENCES

Johnson, D. W. (2000). *Reaching out: Interpersonal effectiveness and self-actualization* (7th ed.). Boston: Allyn & Bacon.

Johnson, D. W., & Johnson, F. (2000). *Joining together: Group theory and group skills.* Boston: Allyn & Bacon.

Moscovici, S. (1985). Innovation and minority influence. In S. Moscovici, G. Mugny, & E. Van Avennaet (Eds.), *Perspectives on minority influence* (pp. 9–51). Cambridge: Cambridge University Press.

Raven, B. (1992). A power/interaction model of interpersonal influence: French and Raven thirty years later. *Journal of Social Behavior and Personality, 7,* 217–244.

D. W. JOHNSON
R. T. JOHNSON
University of Minnesota

ADVERTISING
COMMUNICATION PROCESSES
FACIAL EXPRESSIONS
PERCEPTUAL TRANSACTIONALISM
PROPAGANDA
SYMBOLIC INTERACTION

SOCIAL ISOLATION

Social interaction is integral to mental health across development. Lack of social interaction, or social isolation, not only is a painful experience but can negatively impact child development. For infants and young children, lack of interaction with a primary caretaker can lead to marked delays in cognitive, socio-emotional, linguistic, and motoric domains. For school age children and adolescents, peer interaction becomes an increasingly important socializing agent that provides them with opportunities for social, emotional, and cognitive development. Through interpersonal interaction, children develop the skills of collaboration, perspective taking, empathy, and social competence, which help to promote prosocial behavior and decrease aggressive behavior. Social isolation can lead to feelings of low self-esteem; negative self-concept or powerlessness; increased shyness; decreased creativity; childhood depression and maladjustment; social and academic difficulties; and, in some cases, delinquent behavior. Although early developmental research suggested that many withdrawn children outgrow their isolate behaviors, recent studies have found that for some children, social isolation is an enduring experience. For these children, the negative effects of social isolation may persist beyond early childhood, leading both to internalizing problems in middle childhood and to adult maladjustment.

Socially isolated children seldom initiate contact with others or respond to the invitations of others. These children are often not actively disliked by their peers, but rather are ignored and neglected due to their lack of a conspicuous presence. Identification and treatment of social isolation often occurs within academic settings where teachers become aware of withdrawn children's social difficulties. Socially isolated children can be identified through observation or sociometric measures.

As a treatment for social isolation, social skills training targets social skills performance-deficiencies, such as the abilities to correctly interpret social situations and to competently seek entry into a peer group. Such training helps socially withdrawn children learn skills for developing gratifying relationships with others. An added component to social skills training interventions may include pairing socially withdrawn children with socially competent peers. Within such pairings, socially withdrawn children have an opportunity to imitate positive social behavior.

SUGGESTED READING

Rubin, K. H., & Asendorpf, J. B. (Eds.). (1993). *Social withdrawal, inhibition, and shyness in childhood.* Hillsdale, NJ: Erlbaum.

E. K. LANPHIER
Pennsylvania State University

PEER RELATIONS
SOCIAL ADJUSTMENT
SOCIAL ANXIETY
SOCIAL WITHDRAWAL

SOCIAL LEARNING THEORIES

Social learning theories of personality are first and foremost *learning* theories. As such, they follow from the traditions established by Ivan Pavlov, John Watson, Clark Hull, and B. F. Skinner. Such theorists particularly emphasized the role of reinforcement in learning and the careful identification of the stimuli present in learning situations. However, much of this older theory was based on laboratory research with rats, pigeons, and other lower organisms. But the complexity of human beings seemed to defy explanations drawn from such simple organisms and often equally simple laboratory settings. Consequently many personologists either clung steadfastly to psychoanalytic theory or else stubbornly persisted in trying to twist human behavioral complexity into a simple form that could be accommodated by the animal–laboratory model.

In 1950, a major development in the history of social learning theory took place: John Dollard and Neal Miller published their classic work, *Personality and Psychotherapy.* They described personality from a learning vantage point and in so doing blended the concepts of Hull and Freud. While some critics dismissed their work as a mere translation of Freudian concepts into the language of learning, this seems a harsh judgment. Their translation opened up entirely new horizons for personality research and conceptualization. They showed that social-personality events could be described and explained with the more objective and reliable constructs of learning theory. Thus behavior could be analyzed by recourse to notions such as drive, cue, response, and reward. The psychic warfare among id, ego, and superego yielded to an analysis by means of a conflict model. Repression lost its aura of mystery as they analyzed it merely as "a stopping thinking response" that could be reinforced in the same way as any other response. The significance of the work of Dollard and Miller is now largely historical. But their influence on clinical psychology, personality theory and development, and personality assessment and structure has been great.

Social learning theory was spawned by the foregoing events and thus heavily emphasized reinforcement ideas. But modern social learning theory has assumed a distinctly cognitive cast. The importance of reinforcement has been integrated with concepts that depict a thinking, knowing person who has expectations and beliefs. Thus the roots of modern social learning theory can be traced to theorists such as Kurt Lewin and Edward Tolman. From a social, interpersonal standpoint, the work of George Herbert Mead and Harry Stack Sullivan is probably also germane. Indeed, it has been said that had Sullivan been trained as a psychologist instead of a psychiatrist, he might have become the world's first social learning theorist.

Currently the major social learning theorists are considered to be Julian Rotter, Albert Bandura, and Walter Mischel. However, the social behaviorism of Arthur Staats bears some notable similarities to Bandura's work. Some would even include Hans Eysenck and Joseph Wolpe as social learning theorists because of the nature of their therapy methods, which follow a learning model.

ROTTER'S SOCIAL LEARNING THEORY

While Dollard and Miller were among the first to employ the term *social learning,* it is probably fair to say that Rotter's was the first comprehensive social learning *theory* to appear on the scene. Rotter has been the major architect of this social learning theory of personality. He usually refers to it as *a* social learning theory to signify that there are other social learning approaches as well. The theory began to assume its present shape in the late 1940s and early 1950s, and this early period was capped by the 1954 publication of Rotter's basic work, *Social Learning and Clinical Psychology*. The 1960s represented a period in which the applications of the theory were explored. This period culminated in the publication in 1972 of the book *Applications of a Social Learning Theory of Personality* by Rotter in collaboration with June Chance and Jerry Phares. In the 1970s, the significance of Rotter's 1966 monograph on internal versus external control (I-E) was recognized. This ushered in a period in which the theory came to grips with generalized personality variables such as I-E and interpersonal trust.

Several prime features characterize Rotter's theory. First, he adopts a construct point of view. This means that he is interested not in reconstructing reality via his theory but in developing a series of concepts that provide predictive utility. Second, he is concerned with the language of description. He sought to develop concepts free of vagueness or ambiguity and ones whose meaning did not overlap much with that of other concepts in the system. He also tried to include only those terms absolutely necessary for prediction. Third, he made a strong effort to employ operational definitions that specified the actual measurement operations for each concept.

Rotter's use of the term *social learning* was a calculated one. He believed that much human behavior is acquired or learned. What is more, it takes place in a meaningful environment that is rife with social interactions with other people. As he put it: "It is a *social* learning theory because it stresses the fact that the major or basic modes of behaving are learned in social situations and are inextricably fused with needs requiring for their satisfaction the mediation of other people" (Rotter, 1954, p. 84).

A major feature of the theory is the employment of both motivational (reinforcement) and cognitive (expectancy) variables. Where other theories sometimes seem to flounder in encompassing human social behavior because they rely exclusively on *either* reinforcement variables *or* cognitive ones, Rotter integrates both into a comprehensive framework. The theory is also distinctive in its utilization of an empirical law of effect. To avoid the pitfalls inherent in defining reinforcement in terms of drive reduction, Rotter defines a reinforcement in terms of its effects on the direction of behavior. Anything is a reinforcement if it results in movement toward or away from a goal.

Finally, the emphasis of this theory is on performance rather than on the acquisition of behavior. It does not provide a precise account of how behavior is learned. Rather, it focuses on the prediction of which behavior (once learned) in the person's repertoire of behaviors will occur in a specific situation or class of situations. Some might wish to argue, therefore, that the theory really should be called a "social performance theory."

Basic Concepts

Rotter's theory requires four concepts or variables to predict an individual's behavior. First, there is behavior potential (BP). This refers to the potential for any given behavior to occur in a specific

situation in connection with the pursuit of a specific reinforcement or set of reinforcements. Behavior here is defined broadly and includes motor acts, cognitive activity, verbalizations, emotional reactions, and so on.

The second major variable is expectancy (E). This is the probability held by an individual that a particular reinforcement will occur as a function of a specific behavior executed in a specific situation. Expectancies are subjective and do not necessarily coincide with any actuarial probability calculated objectively on the basis of prior reinforcement. One's perceptions are the crucial element. Rotter discusses two kinds of expectancies: those specific to one situation (E′) and those expectancies generalized from related situations (GE). For example, one might have an expectancy for success in a specific chemistry course (E′) or a generalized expectancy (GE) for success in academic situations generally.

The third major concept is reinforcement value (RV). This is defined as the degree of preference for any reinforcement to occur if the possibilities of their occurring were all equal. Individuals will differ in the degree to which they value various reinforcements, although on a cultural basis there is a considerable amount of homogeneity regarding preferences for certain classes of reinforcements.

Finally, there is the psychological situation, which, according to social learning theory, is an important predictive element. It is necessary to understand the psychological relevance of a given situation in affecting both reinforcement values and expectancies accurately to predict behavior in that situation.

In summarizing the specific relationships among the four variables, Rotter (1967, p. 490) employs the following formula:

$$BP_{X,s1,Ra} = f(E_{x,Ra,s1} \ \& \ RV_{a,s1}).$$

This formula may be read as follows: The potential for behavior X to occur in situation 1 in relation to reinforcement a is a function of the expectancy of the occurrence of reinforcement a following behavior x in situation 1 and the value of reinforcement a in situation 1.

The foregoing formula is often not a very practical one for personologists or clinicians. They are typically not interested in predicting very specific behavior in equally specific situations. More often, their interest is in dealing with broad classes of behaviors and goals. For example, what is the likelihood that a man will respond aggressively when his needs for masculinity are threatened? Thus the issue becomes one of the potential for *any* one of a class of specific aggressive behaviors to occur as a function of the individual's mean expectancy for the occurrence of a set of related goals. The analog of the previous formula becomes:

$$NP = f(FM \ \& \ NV).$$

Here we have: Need potential is a function of freedom of movement and need value. The situational construct is implicit in the formula. Clearly, then, behavior is determined by one's needs and the expectation that the behavior in question will lead to their satisfaction. In terms of content, Rotter has described six needs. These are recognition–status, dominance, independence, protection–

dependency, love and affection, and physical comfort. What is more, he states that when need value is strong and the freedom of movement or expectancy of satisfying that need is low, the door is opened to defensive, maladjusted, and irreal behaviors.

Problem-Solving Expectancies

In recent years, a great deal of research has been devoted to problem-solving generalized expectancies. These cognitive variables are akin to attitudes, beliefs, or mental sets about how problem situations should be construed to facilitate their solution. Individuals differ widely in terms of these cognitions. Two generalized expectancies have been the focus of this research. They are internal versus external control of reinforcement (locus of control) and interpersonal trust. In the first instance, people differ in their beliefs about whether what happens to them is determined by their own behavior and attributes (internal) or is caused by luck, fate, chance, or powerful others (external). People will behave quite differently depending on which generalized expectancy they hold. In the case of interpersonal trust, some individuals expect that others can be relied upon to tell the truth while others believe to the contrary. Again, which belief is held will be a powerful determinant of how people approach solutions to the problems they face.

BANDURA'S OBSERVATIONAL LEARNING

The social learning approach of Bandura complements the social learning theory of Rotter. It is hardly a theory at all in the sense of providing a well-integrated set of concepts that will account for the behavioral choices that people make. But it does exactly what Rotter's theory fails to do. It accounts for the ways in which people acquire a variety of complex behaviors in social settings.

Bandura has been the recipient of numerous honors in the field of psychology, including the presidency of the American Psychological Association. He has published a heavy volume of high-quality research papers over the years. This research output has been as responsible as anything for the prominence enjoyed by his social learning approach. He has written extensively on many topics, including social learning, behavior modification, aggression, and, more recently, self-efficacy. Some of his better known works are *Social Learning and Personality Development,* published in collaboration with Richard Walters in 1963; *Principles of Behavior Modification,* published in 1969; *Aggression: A Social Learning Analysis,* which appeared in 1973; and *Social Learning Theory,* a 1977 publication.

A basic notion of Bandura's is that of observational learning, a concept that can be traced to Mead's work on imitation and vocal gestures. The subsequent analysis of imitation by Miller and Dollard in their book *Social Learning and Imitation* provided an important springboard for Bandura. The work of O. Hobart Mowrer on sign learning and reward learning was also influential. It was the unique capacity of Bandura to see in all of this work the opportunity to follow novel paths of research on learning.

Basic Concepts

Most traditional views of social behavior have often suggested that person variables and environmental variables operate independently to produce behavior. Instead, Bandura argues for a reciprocal relationship among behavior, person variables, and environmental variables. We are not simply driven by inner forces, nor are we pawns of some set of environmental contingencies. We are influenced, but we also exert influence.

Bandura asserts that an enormous amount of human learning involves modeling, observation, and imitation. Consequently he does not view the creation of a complex behavior as an additive product of tiny elements of conditioning. Animals may indeed be trained to produce complicated acts by "shaping" their behavior. That is, the animal is rewarded for successively approximating the behavior in which we are ultimately interested. But this is such a slow, painstaking process that it is doubtful that we could survive as a species if this were our only method of producing complex behavior.

In effect, Bandura is asserting that much human learning transpires without the customary reinforcement that operant and classical conditioning principles require. People can learn in the absence of both reward and punishment. This does not mean however, that reinforcement is irrelevant. Indeed, once a behavior is learned, reinforcement is quite important in determining whether the behavior will occur. Furthermore, observational learning is neither inevitable nor automatic. Many factors influence whether or not such learning takes place in a given situation. Such factors include the model's age and competence. The person's level of motivation may also enhance or retard modeling, imitation, and observation. Finally, Bandura does not restrict imitation and observational learning to motor acts alone or to ones that are quite molecular. A variety of social responses, such as aggression, sex-typed behavior, and emotional reactivity, among many others, are observed and hence learned.

A Cognitive Emphasis

To account for observational learning phenomena, Bandura believes that we employ symbolic representations of environmental events. Without such symbolic activity, it is hard to explain the tremendous flexibility in human behavior. It is his thesis that behavioral changes that occur through classical and instrumental conditioning, as well as through extinction and punishment, are actively mediated by cognitions. Also critical in human behavior are self-regulatory processes. People regulate their behavior by visualizing the consequences of that behavior. Thus relationships between stimulus and response are affected by these self-control processes.

Walter Mischel has continued this cognitive emphasis in his analysis of several cognitive social learning person variables. His 1973 paper "Toward a cognitive social learning reconceptualization of personality" drew on concepts from Rotter's theory, Bandura's general approach, and elsewhere. He asserts that people differ with respect to certain person variables, and it is these differences that give rise to the enormous range of personality characteristics we observe in others. First, there are competencies. These are repertoires of abilities that influence our thoughts and actions. Second, people differ in their encoding strategies in the sense that they represent or symbolize environmental stimulation in different ways. Third, there are expectancies or learned probabilities, which refer to the likelihood that certain behaviors or events will lead to certain outcomes. A fourth variable, subjective values, indicates that people differ in the values they attach to various outcomes. Last, there are self-regulatory systems and plans. Here, we regulate our behavior by self-imposed standards.

Behavioral Change

Bandura's work has been highly important in the development of new approaches to therapeutic intervention. In particular, the acquisition of new cognitive and behavioral competencies through modeling has been prominent. Through modeling and guided participation, patients can be taught new skills and can learn also to deal with debilitating fears. In a classical series of studies, Bandura demonstrated, for example, how children could be induced, by observing live and filmed models, to approach previously feared objects and situations.

More recently, Bandura has contended that the therapeutic reduction of fear and avoidance by observation of models occurs through feelings of enhanced self-efficacy. The individual develops a heightened perception of the ability to cope with specific situations. This, in turn, reduces debilitating expectancies that have promoted anxiety and fear and that have led to defensiveness and neurotic behavior.

Bandura's work has had an important impact on both learning and personality as well as on the treatment of clinical problems. In no small measure this has been the result of the large volume of carefully executed research stimulated by his theoretical approach. In addition, however, that research has focused on important human activities. Bandura has certainly not been loathe to alter his theoretical stance as new evidence develops or as alternative concepts are suggested by other theorists. This gives the theory a vital, open quality. On the other hand, Bandura's social learning approach is not a particularly systematic or comprehensive behavioral theory. Formerly, many of his notions were criticized as being more descriptive than explanatory. Others were less than satisfied with his theoretical account of observational learning. Still others have been disappointed over his lack of attention to developmental and maturational issues. But the fact remains that his approach has been a seminal one that has stimulated a variety of practical applications.

REFERENCES

Dollard, J., & Miller, N. E. (1950). *Personality and psychotherapy: An analysis in terms of learning, thinking, and culture.* New York: McGraw-Hill.

Rotter, J. B. (1967). Personality theory. In H. Helson & W. Bevan (Eds.), *Contemporary approaches to psychology.* New York: Van Nostrand.

Rotter, J. B. (1980/1973/1954). *Social learning and clinical psychology.* New York: Johnson Reprint.

Rotter, J. B., Chance, J. E., & Phares, E. J. (Eds.). (1972). *Applications of a social learning theory of personality.* New York: Holt, Rinehart & Winston.

SUGGESTED READING

Bandura, A. (1968). A social learning interpretation of psychological dysfunctions. In P. London & D. Rosenhan (Eds.), *Foundations of abnormal psychology.* New York: Holt, Rinehart & Winston.

Bandura, A. (1971). Psychotherapy based upon modeling principles. In A. E. Bergin & S. L. Garfield (Eds.), *Handbook of psychotherapy and behavior change: An empirical analysis.* New York: Wiley.

Bandura, A. (1978). The self-system in reciprocal determinism. *American Psychologist, 33,* 344–358.

Bandura, A. (1982). Self-efficacy mechanism in human agency. *American Psychologist, 37,* 122–147.

Bandura, A., Adams, N. E., & Beyer, J. (1977). Cognitive processes mediating behavioral change. *Journal of Personality and Social Psychology, 35,* 125–139.

Holland, C. J., & Kobasigawa, A. (1980). Observational learning: Bandura. In G. M. Gazda & R. J. Corsini (Eds.), *Theories of learning: A comparative approach.* Itasca, IL: Peacock.

Lefcourt, H. M. (1982/1976). *Locus of control: Current trends in theory and research.* Hillsdale, NJ: Erlbaum.

Mischel, W. (1974). Processes in delay of gratification. In L. Berkowitz (Ed.), *Advances in experimental social psychology* (Vol. 7). New York: Academic.

Mischel, W., & Mischel, H. N. (1976). A cognitive social learning approach to morality and self-regulation. In T. Lickona (Ed.), *Moral development and behavior: Theory, research, and social issues.* New York: Holt, Rinehart & Winston.

Mowrer, O. H. (1960). *Learning theory and symbolic processes.* New York: Wiley.

Phares, E. J. (1976). *Locus of control in personality.* Morristown, NJ: General Learning Press.

Phares, E. J. (1980). Rotter's social learning theory. In G. M. Gazda & R. J. Corsini (Eds.), *Theories of learning: A comparative approach.* Itasca, IL: Peacock.

Reck, A. (Ed.). (1964). *Selected writings: George Herbert Mead.* New York: Bobbs-Merrill, 1964.

Rotter, J. B. (1966). Generalized expectancies for internal versus external control of reinforcement. *Psychological Monographs, 80*(1, Entire No. 609), 1–28.

Rotter, J. B. (1971). Generalized expectancies for interpersonal trust. *American Psychologist, 26,* 443–452.

Rotter, J. B. (1978). Generalized expectancies for problem solving and psychotherapy. *Cognitive Therapy and Research, 2,* 1–10.

Staats, A. W. (1975). *Social behaviorism.* Homewood, IL: Dorsey.

E. J. PHARES
Kansas State University

IMITATIVE LEARNING
SOCIAL COGNITION

SOCIAL NEUROSCIENCE

Social neuroscience refers to the study of the relationship between neural and social processes. Despite the early recognition that molecular processes and mechanisms bear on molar social psychological processes and vice versa, the early identification of biology with innate mechanisms and the identification of social psychology with self-report data contributed to an antipathy that endured long after each field became more sophisticated. Accordingly, neuroscientific analyses tended to be limited to the behavioral phenomena occurring within an organism (e.g., attention, learning, memory), whereas social psychological analyses traditionally eschewed biological data in favor of self-report and behavioral data.

The 1990s were declared by the U.S. Congress to be the "decade of the brain," reflecting the interest in and importance of the neurosciences in theory of and research on cognition, emotion, behavior, and health. The decade led to a realization that a comprehensive understanding of the brain cannot be achieved by a focus on neural mechanisms alone. The human brain—the organ of the mind—is a fundamental component of a social species. Indeed, humans are such social animals that a basic need to belong has been posited (Gardner, Gabriel, & Diekman, in press). People form associations and connections with others from the moment they are born. The very survival of newborns depends on their attachment to and nurturance by others over an extended period of time. Accordingly, evolution has sculpted the human genome to be sensitive to and succoring of contact and relationships with others. For instance, caregiving and attachment have hormonal and neurophysiological substrates (Carter, Lederhendler, & Kirkpatrick, 1997). Communication, the bedrock of complex social interaction, is universal and ubiquitous in humans. In the rare instances in which human language is not modeled or taught, language develops nevertheless (Goldin-Meadow & Mylander, 1983).

The reciprocal influences between social and biological levels of organization do not stop at infancy. Affiliation and nurturant social relationships, for instance, are essential for physical and psychological well-being across the lifespan. Disruptions of social connections, whether through ridicule, separation, divorce, or bereavement, are among the most stressful events an individual must endure (Gardner et al., in press). Berkman and Syme (1979) operationalized social connections as marriage, contacts with friends and extended family members, church membership, and other group affiliations. They found that adults with fewer social connections suffered higher rates of mortality over the succeeding 9 years even after accounting for self-reports of physical health, socioeconomic status, smoking, alcohol consumption, obesity, race, life satisfaction, physical activity, and preventive health service–usage. In their review of five prospective studies, House, Landis, and Umberson (1988) concluded that social isolation was a major risk factor for morbidity and mortality from widely varying causes. This relationship was evident even after statistically controlling for known biological risk factors, social status, and baseline measures of health. The negative health consequences of social isolation were particularly strong among some of the fastest growing segments of the population: the elderly, the poor, and minorities such as African Americans. Astonishingly, the strength of social isolation as a risk factor was found to be comparable to high blood pressure, obesity, and sedentary lifestyles. Social isolation and loneliness are associated with poorer mental and physical well-being (e.g., Cacioppo et al., in press).

Initially, studies of the neural structures and processes associated with psychological and social events were limited to animal models, post-mortem examinations, multiply determined peripheral assessments, and observations of the occasional unfortunate individual who suffered trauma to or disorders of localized areas of the brain. Developments in electrophysiological recording, functional brain imaging, neurochemical techniques, neuroimmunologic measures, and ambulatory recording procedures have increasingly made it possible to investigate the role of neural systems and processes in intact humans. These developments fostered multilevel integrative analyses of the relationship between neural and social processes. Cacioppo and Berntson (1992) coined the term "social neuroscience" to refer to the study of the relationship between neural and social processes, and they outlined several principles for spanning molar and molecular levels of organization.

Recent research has provided growing evidence that multilevel analyses spanning neural and social perspectives can foster more comprehensive accounts of cognition, emotion, behavior, and health (Anderson, 1998). First, important inroads to the logic of social processes have come from theory and research in the neurosciences (Clark & Squire, 1998). Second, the study of social processes has challenged existing theories in the neurosciences, resulting in refinements, extensions, or complete revolutions in neuroscientific theory and research (Glaser & Kiecolt-Glaser, 1994). Third, reciprocal benefits and more general psychological theories have been achieved by considering or jointly pursuing macrolevel and microlevel analyses of psychological phenomena. (Berntson, Boysen, & Cacioppo, 1993). Fourth, the social environment shapes neural structures and processes and vice versa (Liu et al., 1997). Finally, deciphering the structure and function of the brain is fostered by sophisticated social psychological theories in which the elementary operations underlying complex social behaviors are explicated, and by experimental paradigms that allow these social psychological operations to be studied in isolation using neuroscientific methods (Sarter, Berntson, & Cacioppo, 1996).

Why is a social neuroscience perspective productive in our attempt to understand human cognition, emotion, and behavior? Three principles help answer this question. The principle of multiple determinism specifies that a target event at one level of organization, but particularly at molar (e.g., social) levels of organization, can have multiple antecedents within or across levels of organization. On the biological level, for instance, researchers identified the contribution of individual differences in the susceptibility of the endogenous opioid receptor system, while on the social level investigators have noted the important role of social context. Both operate, and our understanding of drug abuse is incomplete if either perspective is excluded.

The principle of nonadditive determinism specifies that properties of the whole are not always readily predictable from the properties of the parts. In an illustrative study, the behaviors of nonhuman primates were examined following the administration of amphetamine or placebo (Haber & Barchas, 1983). No clear pattern emerged until each primate's position in the social hierarchy was considered. When this social factor was taken into account, amphetamine was found to increase dominant behavior in primates high in the social hierarchy and to increase submissive behavior in primates low in the social hierarchy. A strictly physiological (or social) analysis, regardless of the sophistication of the measurement technology, may not have unraveled the orderly relationship that existed.

Finally, the principle of reciprocal determinism specifies that there can be mutual influences between microscopic (i.e., biological) and macroscopic (i.e., social) factors in determining behavior. For example, not only has the level of testosterone in nonhuman male primates been shown to promote sexual behavior, but the availability of receptive females influences the level of testosterone in nonhuman primates (Berntstein, Gordon, & Rose, 1983). Accordingly, comprehensive accounts of human behaviors cannot be achieved if either the biological or the social level of organization is considered unnecessary or irrelevant.

REFERENCES

Anderson, N. B. (1998). Levels of analysis in health science: A framework for integrating sociobehavioral and biomedical research. *Annals of the New York Academy of Sciences, 840,* 563–576.

Berkman, L. F., & Syme, S. L. (1979). Social networks, host resistance, and mortality: A nine-year follow-up study of Alameda County residents. *American Journal of Epidemiology, 109,* 186–204.

Berntson, G. G., Boysen, S. T., & Cacioppo, J. T. (1993). Neurobehavioral organization and the cardinal principle of evaluative bivalence. *Annals of the New York Academy of Sciences, 702,* 75–102.

Berntstein, I. S., Gordon, T. P., & Rose, R. M. (1983). The interaction of hormones, behavior, and social context in nonhuman primates. In B. B. Svare (Ed.), *Hormones and aggressive behavior* (pp. 535–561). New York: Plenum.

Cacioppo, J. T., & Berntson, G. G. (1992). Social psychological contributions to the decade of the brain: The doctrine of multilevel analysis. *American Psychologist, 47,* 1019–1028.

Cacioppo, J. T., Ernst, J. M., Burleson, M. H., McClintock, M. K., Malarkey, W. B., Hawkley, L. C., Kowalewski, R. B., Paulsen, A., Hobson, J. A., Hugdahl, K., Spiegel, D., & Berntson, G. G. (in press). Lonely traits and concomitant physiological processes: The MacArthur Social Neuroscience Studies. *International Journal of Psychophysiology.*

Carter, C. S., Lederhendler, I. I., & Kirkpatrick, B. (1997). *The integrative neurobiology of affiliation.* New York: New York Academy of Sciences.

Clark, R. E., & Squire, L. R. (1998). Classical conditioning and brain systems: The role of awareness. *Science, 280,* 77–81.

Gardner, W. L., Gabriel, S., & Diekman, A. B. (2000). Interpersonal processes. In J. T. Cacioppo, L. G. Tassinary, & G. G. Berntson (Eds.), *Handbook of psychophysiology* (pp. 643–664). New York: Cambridge University Press.

Glaser, R., & Kiecolt-Glaser, J. K. (1994). Handbook of human stress and immunity. San Diego: Academic Press.

Goldin-Meadow, S., & Mylander, C. (1983). Gestural communication in deaf children: Noneffect of parental input on language development. *Science, 221,* 372–374.

Haber, S. N., & Barchas, P. R. (1983). The regulatory effect of social rank on behavior after amphetamine administration. In P. R. Barchas (Ed.), *Social hierarchies: Essays toward a sociophysiological perspective* (pp. 119–132). Westport, CT: Greenwood.

House, J. S., Landis, K. R., & Umberson, D. (1988). Social relationships and health. *Science, 241,* 540–545.

Liu, D., Diorio, J., Tannenbaum, B., Caldji, C., Francis, D., Freedman, A., Sharma, S., Pearson, D., Plotsky, P. M., & Meaney, M. J. (1997). Maternal care, hippocampal glucocorticoid receptors, and hypothalamic-pituitary-adrenal responses to stress. *Science, 277,* 1659–1662.

Sarter, M., Berntson, G. G., & Cacioppo, J. T. (1996). Brain imaging and cognitive neuroscience: Towards strong inference in attributing function to structure. *American Psychologist, 51,* 13–21.

J. T. CACIOPPO
The University of Chicago

G. G. BERNTSON
Ohio State University

SOCIAL PHOBIA

Social phobia was first officially recognized diagnostically with the publication of *Diagnostic and Statistical Manual of Mental Disorders* (Third Edition, Revised) in 1980, when the disorder was included within the classification of anxiety disorders. In *DSM-III-R* (American Psychiatric Association [APA], 1987), the diagnostic criteria describe social phobia as "a persistent fear of one or more situations (the social phobic situations) in which a person is exposed to possible scrutiny by others and fears that he or she may do something or act in a way that will be humiliating or embarrassing" (p. 243). In social phobia, a person fears one or a few distinct situations. In generalized social phobia, the person avoids most social situations. Examples of social phobia provided in the *DSM-III-R* criteria include an inability to continue talking in public-speaking situations, choking on food when eating with others, or saying foolish things in social situations. Other criteria include: (a) an invariable "immediate anxiety response" when exposed to the specific phobic stimulus; (b) avoidance (or endurance with intense anxiety) of the phobic situation; (c) usually some interference with social activities and relationships, including one's job; and (d) a recognition that the fear is "excessive or unreasonable." A social phobia is diagnosed only if criterion 3 applies or if there is "marked distress about having the fear." The disorder usually appears in late childhood or early adolescence (APA, 1987); an average age of onset of about 16 has been repeatedly reported, with a mean age of those with the disorder at about 30 (Turner & Beidel, 1989). Social phobia appears with about the same frequency in both sexes.

Avoidant personality may coexist with social phobia. In the personality disorder the person will avoid "social or occupational activities that involve significant interpersonal contact" (APA, 1987, p. 351), whereas in social phobia the individual mainly avoids certain situations. Others have suggested that the distinction may be one of degree—avoidant personality disturbances being the more severe and pervasive of the two disorders (Turner & Beidel, 1989) and presumably the more generally debilitating. In addition, the social phobic desires to be able to function in the feared social situation and may even suffer the consequences of voluntarily repeated exposure, whereas the individual displaying avoidant personality more commonly adopts avoidance of interpersonal interactions as a general strategy (Heimberg, Dodge, & Becker, 1987).

There is a high likelihood that social phobia will coexist with other anxiety disorders, but not as often with depression (Stein, Tancer, Gelernter, Vittone, & Uhde, 1990). In a recent study of 71 social phobic patients (Turner, Beidel, Borden, Stanley, & Jacob, 1991), the secondary *DSM-III-R* Axis I disorders most commonly diagnosed along with social phobia were generalized anxiety disorder (33.3% of the patients), and simple phobia (11.1%). Although social phobics may report panic attacks in certain social situations, a fact that can lead to misdiagnosis, the individual afflicted with panic disorder appears to be more greatly concerned with losing control over bodily functions or becoming disabled psychologically. By contrast, the social phobic mainly fears negative evaluations by others, an important difference between this disorder and the social-related anxieties that appear in a wide variety of other anxiety disorders (Turner & Beidel, 1989). In short, it is specifically *what* is feared that provides the most obvious basis for the distinction.

ASSESSMENT

Reviews of both cognitive and behavioral methods for the assessment of social phobia are available (Arnkoff & Glass, 1989; Glass & Arnkoff, 1989). Among broad fear surveys, the Fear Survey Schedule (FSS), a general survey of fears seen in clinics, contains selected items relevant to social anxiety in various versions. This portion of the survey has been related to treatment outcome for social skills training (Curran, 1975) and to other indicators of anxiety (e.g., Borkovec, Stone, O'Brien, & Kaloupek, 1974), providing some demonstrations of the validity of the scale for use in the assessment of social phobia. The Fear Questionnaire (FQ) measures social phobia on a subscale that assesses avoidance of five social settings (Marks & Mathews, 1979). The FQ inventory has been shown to differentiate successfully effects of cognitive and behavioral interventions for social phobia.

Among the variety of questionnaires specifically directed at social anxiety, two that appear to be cited most often in clinical research are the Social Avoidance and Distress (SAD) scale and the Fear of Negative Evaluation (FNE) scale, both developed by Watson and Friend (1969). A number of recent treatment outcome studies have documented the usefulness of both of these scales in

assessing change in social phobics due to clinical interventions (e.g., Heimberg, Dodge, Hope, Kennedy, Zollo, & Becker, 1990).

The Anxiety Disorders Interview Schedule (ADIS) is among the most widely used behavioral interview methods for assessment of anxiety and phobias (DiNardo, O'Brien, Barlow, Waddell, & Blanchard, 1983). A revision by DiNardo, Barlow, Cerny, Vermilyea, Vermilyea, Himadi, and Waddell (1985), the ADIS-R, also is in use, which has been shown to have high reliability among raters of social phobia.

The most common method for assessing the client in actual phobic situations is via self-monitoring. The self-monitoring instrument ideally provides information regarding the type of social interaction, degree of anxiety experienced, antecedents and consequences of specific behaviors, duration of interactions, who was involved, and other aspects of the social phobic's problem situations (Glass & Arnkoff, 1989).

Since social phobia is classified as an anxiety disorder, there are good reasons to suppose that there would be a variety of somatic and autonomic indicators for the condition. In some research, efforts have been made to assess one or more physiological indicators to document differences between social phobia and other disorders. Heimberg and colleagues (1987) found that generalized social phobics manifested significantly *lower* heart rate responses in behavioral simulations of the phobic situation than did subjects diagnosed as public speaking phobics. More systematic have been questionnaire studies aimed at reports of physiological manifestations of social phobia. Cameron, Thyer, and Nesse (1986) determined that skin conductance responding (sweating) was more frequently mentioned by social phobics than by subjects diagnosed with panic or generalized anxiety disorders. On the other hand, heart palpitations were less often reported in social phobics than in these other groups. In another more extensive comparison among subjects with diagnoses of social phobia, panic disorder, and generalized anxiety disorder, Reich, Noyes, and Yates (1988) found that more than half of the social phobics characterized themselves as manifesting sweating and flushing, a dry mouth, and persistent "nervousness." What is clearly lacking in this area of assessment are studies aimed at direct psychophysiological assessment of a variety of somatic and autonomic indicators of social phobia.

TREATMENT

In his overall review of 17 studies on the treatment of social phobia, Heimberg (1989) observed that all studies yielded positive treatment outcomes irrespective of the form of intervention. The wide variety of manipulations hamper further conclusions about relative effectiveness of procedures. Forms of treatment have included social skills training, systematic desensitization, self-control desensitization, in vivo and imaginal exposure (flooding), anxiety management training, and several types of cognitive restructuring. While exposure to phobic events is considered a fundamental feature of phobia treatment (e.g., Barlow, 1988), the addition of cognitive–behavioral techniques (especially cognitive restructuring) may enhance the effectiveness of treatments of social phobia using exposure. However, there have been few studies assessing exposure alone as a comparison procedure, so this conclusion is tentative. Butler (1989) pointed out that it is often difficult to assess the effects of exposure on social phobics owing to the variety of potential phobic social situations and the relative uncontrollability of the nature of the cues, a difficulty not so characteristic of other types of phobic events. Even more tentative, relaxation training, either alone or in combination with other methods, has not been adequately assessed, and the outcomes of several studies were contradictory. Other problems in the treatment outcome research on social phobia are cited by Heimberg (1989).

In two treatment outcome studies (Mersch, Emmelkamp, Bögels, & van der Sleen, 1989; Mersch, Emmelkamp, & Lips, 1991), both social skills training (SST) and rational emotive therapy (RET) were found to be effective in treating social phobia, although there seemed to be a slight (nonsignificant) advantage for the former on some dimensions. Moreover, SST was no more effective for subjects classified as "behavioral reactors" than for those classified as "cognitive reactors"; nor was RET differentially effective for the two groups. Like all of the previous treatment outcome studies conducted with social phobics, these also showed that "there is not one treatment strategy that is superior to all others" (Mersch et al., 1989, p. 422).

Wlazlo, Schroeder-Hartwig, Hand, Kaiser, and Münchau (1990) also looked at effects on social phobia obtained with social skills training, but in this case by comparison with two forms of exposure treatment—individualized exposure and group exposure. All three methods produced decreases in all three categories of assessment. The group exposure technique appeared to be more effective with those patients manifesting social skills deficits, but those patients with more purely phobic difficulties showed no differentiation with respect to type of training. It was argued by Wlazlo and colleagues that the advantage of the exposure training may owe to the opportunity for direct application of acquired skills in a phobic situation.

Drug interventions with social phobia have been reviewed by Levin, Schneier, and Liebowitz (1989). Positive effects have been obtained with β blockers, such as propranolol, but the evidence as to effectiveness appears to be mixed. More generally positive have been reports of the use of monoamine oxidase inhibitors such as phenelzine, which appear to impact significantly both the anxiety and avoidance components of social phobia (studies cited in Levin et al., 1989).

REFERENCES

American Psychiatric Association. (1987). *Diagnostic and statistical manual of mental disorders* (3rd ed., rev.). Washington, DC: Author.

Arnkoff, D. B., & Glass, C. R. (1989). Cognitive assessment in social anxiety and social phobia. *Clinical Psychology Review, 9,* 61–74.

Barlow, D. H. (1988). *Anxiety and its disorders.* New York: Guilford.

Borkovec, T. D., Stone, N. M., O'Brien, G. T., & Kaloupek, D. G. (1974). Evaluation of a clinically relevant target behavior for analog outcome research. *Behavior Therapy, 5,* 503–513.

Cameron, O. G., Thyer, B. A., Nesse, R. M., & Curtis, G. C. (1986). Symptom profiles of patients with *DSM-III* anxiety disorders. *American Journal of Psychiatry, 141,* 572–575.

Curran, J. P. (1975). Social skills training and systematic desensitization in reducing dating anxiety. *Behaviour Research and Therapy, 13,* 65–68.

DiNardo, P. A., Barlow, D. H., Cerny, J., Vermilyea, B. B., Vermilyea, J. A., Himadi, W., & Waddell, M. T. (1985). *Anxiety Disorders Interview Schedule–Revised (ADIS-R).* Albany: State University of New York, Phobia and Anxiety Disorders Clinic.

DiNardo, P. A., O'Brien, G. T., Barlow, D. H., Waddell, M. T., & Blanchard, E. B. (1983). Reliability of *DSM-III* anxiety disorder categories using a new structured interview. *Archives of General Psychiatry, 40,* 1070–1074.

Glass, C. R., & Arnkoff, D. B. (1989). Behavioral assessment of social anxiety and social phobia. *Clinical Psychology Review, 9,* 75–90.

Heimberg, R. G. (1989). Cognitive and behavioral treatments for social phobia: A critical analysis. *Clinical Psychology Review, 9,* 107–128.

Heimberg, R. G., Dodge, C. S., & Becker, R. E. (1987). Social phobia. In L. Michelson & M. Ascher (Eds.), *Cognitive behavioral assessment and treatment of anxiety disorders.* New York: Plenum.

Heimberg, R. G., Dodge, C. S., Hope, D. A., Kennedy, C. R., Zollo, L. J., & Becker, R. E. (1990). Cognitive behavioral group treatment for social phobia: Comparison with a credible placebo control. *Cognitive Therapy and Research, 11,* 1–23.

Levin, A. P., Schneier, F. R., & Liebowitz, M. R. (1989). Social phobia: Biology and pharmacology. *Clinical Psychology Review, 9,* 129–140.

Marks, I. M., & Mathews, A. M. (1979). Brief standard self-rating for phobic patients. *Behaviour Research and Therapy, 17,* 263–267.

Mersch, P. P. A., Emmelkamp, P. M. G., & Lips, C. (1991). Social phobia: Individual response patterns and the long-term effects of behavioral and cognitive interventions. A follow-up study. *Behaviour Research and Therapy, 29,* 357–362.

Mersch, P. P. A., Emmelkamp, P. M. G., Bögels, S. M., & van der Sleen, J. (1989). Social phobia: Individual response patterns and the effects of behavioral and cognitive interventions. *Behaviour Research and Therapy, 27,* 421–434.

Reich, J., Noyes, R., & Yates, W. (1988). Anxiety symptoms distinguishing social phobia from panic and generalized anxiety disorders. *The Journal of Nervous and Mental Disease,* 510–513.

Stein, M. B., Tancer, M. E., Gelemter, C. S., Vittone, B. J., & Uhde, T. W. (1990). Major depression in patients with social phobia. *American Journal of Psychiatry, 147,* 637–639.

Turner, S. M., & Beidel, D. C. (1989). Social phobia: Clinical syndrome, diagnosis, and comorbidity. *Clinical Psychology Review, 9,* 3–18.

Turner, S. M., Beidel, D. C., Borden, J. W., Stanley, M. A., & Jacob, R. G. (1991). Social phobia: Axis I and II correlates. *Journal of Abnormal Psychology, 100,* 102–106.

Watson, D., & Friend, R. (1969). Measurement of social-evaluative anxiety. *Journal of Consulting and Clinical Psychology, 33,* 448–457.

Wlazlo, Z., Schroeder-Hartwig, K., Hand, I., Kaiser, G., & Munchau, N. (1990). Exposure *in vivo* vs social skills training for social phobia: Long-term outcome and differential effects. *Behaviour Research and Therapy, 28,* 181–193.

J. G. CARLSON
University of Hawaii

ANTIANXIETY DRUGS
COPING
FACTITIOUS DISORDERS
FEAR
PHOBIAS
SOCIAL SKILLS TRAINING

SOCIAL PSYCHOLOGY

Social psychology bridges the interest of psychology, with its emphasis on the individual, with sociology, with its emphasis on social structures. As a field, it is as old as the two disciplines from which it draws, but it did not have a well-structured identity until the beginning of the 20th century. A substantial number of quite different works became the basis for social psychology. Gabriel Tarde (1895, 1898), who possibly first used the words *social psychology* as a part of a title of a book, had written extensively on the concept of imitation as basic to the formulation of and maintenance of the social fabric. James M. Baldwin (1897) used the concept of imitation centrally for his interpretation of the development of the child, and for all practical purposes laid much of the groundwork for what subsequently became the fields of child development and socialization. Baldwin's work is particularly modern in terms of how social psychologists have subsequently modeled social behavior and social learning.

Another thrust well developed by the turn of the century was concern with collective behavior, particularly the concept of the crowd (LeBon, 1896; Sighele, 1897, 1903). In these writings, concepts of suggestion and association of ideas dominate, and emphasis is on analyzing irrational and ill-considered behavior. Behavior in crowds was seen as departing from the process of social development with a return to essentially baser motives and behavior. These works subsequently became organized under the concept of social control, which has been associated with sociological writings (Ross, 1901).

Compte (1830) partitioned the social sciences, with sociology at top, but indicated its necessary relationship with "psychic" sciences. Attention to the content of social psychology was more visible in the general writings, such as the landmark text by James (1890), which covered, albeit lightly, some of the issues involved in dealing with social factors determining individual behavior.

The first volume with the title *Social Psychology* actually tended to be a moral consideration and barely touched on topics that today would be considered central to the subject (Orano, 1902). On the other hand, the first volume that actually was a general social psychology text used the more descriptive title of *Human Nature and the Social Order* (Cooley, 1902). Cooley's work was notable for several reasons, including the fact that he was an influential teacher. His writings were based on what now would be described as armchair speculation and direct observation of persons in one's own environment, including his children; but, based on a scholarship that was both broad and eclectic, his writings were exceptionally clean from the point of view of older theories. Thus it is virtually impossible to find traces in his writings of instinct psychology, racism, phrenology, or other similar theories found in the works of most of his contemporaries.

The blossoming of the field of social psychology is usually associated with the joint appearance of two textbooks under that title, one by Ross (1908) and the other by McDougall (1908). Ross's work reflected his prior involvement in the analyses of collective behavior, and did not emphasize the individual in the social context. By contrast, McDougall emphasized individual behavior, and dealt extensively with mechanisms and tendencies to behave. His presentation involved analysis of hierarchical ordering of motives, and narrow reading of his work suggests a commitment to instinct explanations of social behavior. Broader interpretation of his writings would place them as behavioral with some attention to social influence processes.

Another thrust in this early period was in "formal" sociology, with the main exponent being Simmel (1896, 1902, 1950). Although Simmel dealt with many aspects of group analysis and the structure of interaction, possibly the logical basis for his analysis was the most important reason for appearing to be *the* sociologist of the time. Simmel in many ways laid the groundwork for the subsequent massive development of interest in dominance and submission in group behavior, but more particularly of the systematic analysis of group structure and its impact on participants. While his work was in no way associated with experimental procedures, most theory that subsequently became important in the experimental analysis of groups is to be found in Simmel. In many ways, Simmel's work is seen as the major inspiration for later efforts involving group dynamics and small-group research.

Many of the developments of the early period tended to be relatively isolated in impact. For example, Wundt (1910) wrote extensively in the area that became known as culture and personality, but it did not attract development by other psychologists. Similarly, Terman (1904) did early comprehensive research on factors of leadership in group behavior, clearly anticipating many subsequent developments in social psychology, but additional work did not follow on the part of other investigators.

In the post-World War II period, the field experienced virtually an explosion of growth reflected in the hundreds of journals devoted to social psychology and subspecialties, and in the array of books and monographs too numerous for a private library. Additionally, the expansion was accompanied by developments that have broken down disciplinary barriers, so that political scientists and economists, to name two disciplines, have become interested in bringing social psychological analysis and interpretation to their professions. More pointedly, in the modern period, there has also been a great move toward applied science, and social psychology has been critically involved. This has ranged from concern with questions of analysis of social, ethnic, racial, sex, and other factors in intragroup and intergroup relations to more explicit studies with regard to policies in the private and public sectors under the rubric of evaluation research. In colleges and universities, social psychology is taught primarily in psychology departments, but social psychology is the single most frequently named substantive specialty among sociologists. Textbooks tend to be dominated by authors who are psychologists by training, but the array of orientations represented includes highly interpretive phenomenological approaches to "hard-nosed" essentially behavioristic and experimentally based treatises.

Notable advances in social psychology were lacking until the 1930s. One exception was the work of Allport (1920, 1924), who studied the effects of group participation on performance. The seminal period in the postdepression (1929–1939) years included the work of Lewin (Lewin, 1948, 1951; Lewin & Lippitt, 1938) and his students that emphasized field theory and group dynamics. Moreno (1934), and his associate Jennings (1950), in this period advanced the utilization of sociometric analysis, and with this a complex of additional procedures that included role playing and psychodrama. The more analytic materials stemming from child development were interpreted through such scholars as Mead (1934). Freudian theoretical interests were also beginning to enter social psychology through academic interpreters, and the works of Fromm (1941), for example, were read by sociologists quite widely. Public opinion polls had come on the scene with both good and disastrous results in prediction, and the academic basis of opinion and attitude research was becoming a strong basis for research, as reflected in the post-World War II publication by Stouffer and colleagues (1949) of the *American Soldier*. Possibly a landmark in the transition to the post-World War II period was a publication by Murphy and colleagues (1937), which summarized much of the basic research of the period and established clearly that, as an experimental field based on systematic research, social psychology had a fundamental core and a body with reasonable appendages.

The relationship between psychology and sociology has sometimes been described as the difference between an experimental approach and a general descriptive approach. Such a distinction possibly overstates differences among investigators, since most persons will see the virtues of both approaches. When the approaches are viewed singly, however, their limitations can be seen quite pointedly. Since much of sociological and psychological research may be described as activity without progress, the limitations need to be kept in the forefront for those who wish to advance their sciences. On the one hand, sociologists who have been concerned with observation in "natural" settings have often been unaware of the limitations of their generalizations as a result of the lack of variation of significant and important variables. Since the subject matter usually involves many variables in a system that can be described as multiply determined, that is, with many relationships among the variables and feedback or interaction among the variables, decomposing the relationship among the variables in such a complex situation is difficult, and sometimes impossible. Drawing inferences about causation is even more risky, and even with the development in recent times of causal models applicable to such descriptive data, awareness of the limitations of generalization has become acute. In addition, sociologists, often using survey and other procedures, have frequently not profited sufficiently from the knowledge accumulated in other fields, such as with regard to measurement and the need to develop well-defined systems of variables.

By contrast, psychologists often are concerned with more limited theories, and their approach frequently involves the manipulation in experimental procedures of one or a few variables. The experimental procedure is appropriate where theories are well defined and specified, which is the case in much of physical science but not in the social psychological arena. Thus limitations in the experimental approach can be many, and have been outlined by Campbell and Stanley (1966). Obviously, however, the limitations that apply to the experimental procedures apply equally to the rules of evidence in inferring from natural situations. Failings, in addition to those outlined by Campbell and Stanley, sometimes are ignored. For example, a theory can be incomplete with regard to the specification of variables, in which case the inferences drawn may be appropriate for the limited system, but not for the general system, that is, the behavior of the person or persons. The most serious criticism, however, is that the interpretation of experiments frequently is misstated as demonstrating that a relationship has been found between two variables. Actually, the more conservative and appropriate statement to describe most experiments in social psychology is that situations can be found in which a manipulation is of sufficient strength to make a difference in the dependent variables. Such a conclusion is remote from a more general statement that a particular relationship exists between two variables in a system of variables.

From the point of view of accumulation of findings and their integration into theory, social psychology suffers, as most of the social and psychological sciences do. Progress has been meager in spite of a substantial amount of activity, especially in the post-World War II period. At the same time, the availability of computers, acknowledgment of the limitations of relatively small-scale experiments and observation, and the growth of a more general fabric of communication among the disciplines suggests that social psychology provides both an opportunity and potential for scientific progress.

REFERENCES

Allport, F. H. (1920). The influence of the group upon association and thought. *Journal of Experimental Psychology, 3,* 159–182.

Allport, F. H. (1924). *Social psychology.* Boston: Houghton Mifflin.

Baldwin, J. M. (1973). *Social and ethical interpretations in mental development: A study in social psychology.* New York: Arno Press. (Original work published 1897)

Campbell, D. T., & Stanley, J. C. (1966). *Experimental and quasi-experimental designs for research.* Chicago: Rand-McNally.

Cooley, C. H. (1956/1902). *Human nature and the social order.* Glencoe, IL: Free Press.

Fromm, E. (1965/1941). *Escape from freedom.* New York: Avon Books.

James, W. (1890). *The principles of psychology.* New York: Henry Holt.

Jennings, H. H. (1950). *Leadership and isolation.* New York: Longman, Green.

Le Bon, G. (1896). *The crowd. A study of the popular mind.* London: Benn.

Lewin, K. (1948). *Resolving social conflicts.* New York: Harper.

Lewin, K. (1951). *Field theory in social science.* New York: Harper.

Lewin, K., & Lippitt, R. (1938). An experimental approach to the study of autocracy and democracy. *Sociometry, 1,* 292–300.

McDougall, W. (1926/1908). *An introduction to social psychology.* Boston: Luce.

Mead, G. H. (1934). *Mind, self, and society: From the standpoint of a social behaviorist.* Chicago: University of Chicago Press.

Moreno, J. L. (1953/1934). *Who shall survive?* New York: Beacon House.

Murphy, G., Murphy, L. B., & Newcomb, T. M. (1937). *Experimental social psychology.* New York: Harper.

Orano, P. (1902). *Psicologia sociale.* Bari, Italy: Laterza.

Ross, E. A. (1901). *Social control.* New York: Macmillan.

Ross, E. A. (1908). *Social psychology.* New York: Macmillan.

Sighele, D. (1903). *L'intelligenza della folla.* Turin, Italy: Bocca.

Sighele, S. (1897). *La coppia criminale.* Turin, Italy: Bocca.

Simmel, G. (1896). Superiority and subordination as subject-matter of sociology. *American Journal of Sociology, 2,* 167–189, 392–415.

Simmel, G. (1902). The number of members as determining the sociological form of the group. *American Journal of Sociology, 8,* 1–46, 158–196.

Simmel, G. (1950). *The sociology of George Simmel.* New York: Glencoe Press.

Stouffer, S. A., Lumsdahe, A. A., Lumsdaine, M. H., Williams, R. M., Jr., Smith, M. B., Janis, I. L., Star, S. A., & Cottrell, L. S., Jr. (1949). *The American soldier: Combat and its aftermath.* Princeton, NJ: Princeton University Press.

Tarde, G. (1895). *Les lois de l'imitation.* Paris: Alcan.

Tarde, G. (1898). *Etudes de psychologie sociale.* Paris: Giard & Briere.

Terman, L. M. (1904). A preliminary study of the psychology and pedagogy of leadership. *Pedagogical Seminary, 11,* 413–451.

Wundt, W. (1916). *Volkerpsychologie.* Leipzig: Engelmann. 1910. Translated as *Elements of folk psychology.* New York: Macmillan.

E. F. BORGATTA
University of Washington

OBSERVATIONAL METHODS
PEER INFLUENCES
QUALITY OF LIFE
RITUAL BEHAVIOR
STEREOTYPING

SOCIAL SKILLS TRAINING

Recent interest in social skills training, dating from the early 1970s, has a long past but a short history (to paraphrase Ebbinghaus' often cited quote). Concern about social competencies had long been secondary to other social and educational endeavors. It was generally assumed that one learned appropriate interpersonal skills "naturally," through the traditional socializing institutions—home, school, church, and workplace. When social inadequacies were noted, they were attributed to faulty socialization: poor breeding, poor schooling, or poor religious and moral training. Even traditional mental health concepts viewed interpersonal inadequacies as symptomatic of more basic, underlying conflicts or psychopathologies.

Changes in social institutions effect changes in their traditional functions, including the teaching and nurturance of social competencies. By the early 1970s, a number of such changes were evident. Family structure had been modified, with a rapid rise in single-parent families, as well as families in which both mothers and fathers worked outside the home. Religious institutions no longer held the central position or support they once had. Schools were called upon to educate a more heterogeneous group of youngsters, coming from divergent backgrounds and value systems and displaying a wider range of in-school behaviors. And the impact of a new socializing agent, television, began to be noted, often with alarm. These various societal changes created a *Zeitgeist* ripe for the direct teaching of social skills.

The two major fields particularly receptive to social skills training were education and psychology. Indeed, social skills training is historically descended from these parent disciplines. Throughout the history of education, the teaching of interpersonal, social, and moral behaviors and values sometimes has been an explicit goal, but almost always an implicit goal. When made explicit, as with the Character Education movement in the 1920s, didactic educational methods were applied to teaching leadership skills, decision making, and ethical interpersonal behaviors.

Psychology's involvement in social skills training can be traced through the emergence of the behavior modification movement in the 1950s. Many psychologists trained in academic psychology's traditional concern with understanding and enhancing the learning process began to focus their attention on therapeutics. From that perspective, treatment efforts were reconceptualized in learning theory terms, with problematic behaviors viewed as examples of inadequate or faulty learning. Treatment typically emphasized laboratory-derived procedures, specified treatment goals, with the change agent frequently functioning as a teacher, trainer, or facilitator of new or more adequate behaviors.

A favorite target population for the early behavior modifiers was institutionalized psychiatric patients. Prior to 1955, the year in which antipsychotic medications were introduced on a broad scale in U.S. psychiatric hospitals, there were over 550,000 psychiatric inpatients. Since then, the psychiatric inpatient population has been reduced to less than one-third of the original number. Many of the first behavior modification efforts were directed toward eliminating the bizarre, disturbed, and disturbing behaviors that often characterized patients, and teaching skills necessary for adequate outside functioning. There was little disagreement that these chronic patients were deficient in social skills. Whether their deficiencies were primarily attributable to the lack of opportunity to use such skills within the institution, or whether they had never adequately learned appropriate social skills (e.g., Zigler & Phillips, 1961; Phillips, 1978) is still a matter of debate.

Most such training efforts espouse the rationale that the individual is deficient in important interpersonal competencies, having never learned them adequately in the past. However, some (e.g., Wolpe, 1969) believe that the relevant skills may have been acquired, but their appropriate usage is inhibited by conditioned anxiety. Still other researchers emphasize cognitive factors, such as negative expectations and self-appraisals, as causal (e.g., Meichenbaum, 1977). This view parallels the broader introduction and acceptance of cognitive factors into more traditional behavioral approaches to treatment, emerging under the rubric of "cognitive-behavior modification" (Meichenbaum, 1977).

Initial behavior modification efforts in institutions were often aimed at controlling, diminishing, or extinguishing undesirable or bizarre behaviors. Once accomplished, however, the patient/trainee did not necessarily behave in a socially competent manner. Hence coping skills needed to be taught.

Individual training is sometimes used as a supplement to group training. Those who view it as a preferred treatment emphasize the desirability of tailoring the training to the trainee without the potential for interference, distractions, and negative feedback from other trainees (Lazarus, 1971). Group training is often touted as more economical as well as offering the potential advantage of positive feedback and support from peers (Field & Test, 1975).

COMPONENTS

While not all social skills training programs are alike, there are many commonalities. Programs differ in the relative emphasis placed upon particular components, as well as their presentation, sequence, and utilization. Components most frequently included in training programs are: (a) rationale presentation; (b) modeling; (c) role playing; (d) feedback; and (e) homework/transfer of training.

Rationale

An overview of the skills to be taught generally precedes training proper. The meaning of the terminology used and the relevance of the skill(s) to trainees' lives are often dealt with. With some skills, the rationale and relevance have become embedded in the cultural context, so that an elaborate description is unnecessary. Examples include "assertiveness" and "dating."

Terminology used in describing various social skills is not uniform across training programs. Assertiveness in one training program may be treated as dating behavior in another. Actual behaviors taught in a given session might be addressed at the level of "eye contact," "stating an opinion," and the like. No standard taxonomy of social skills and their behavioral referents yet exists.

Modeling

A clear presentation of the behaviors to be learned is a part of most training programs regardless of whether the theoretical basis is skill deficit or conditioned anxiety. Modeling displays are presented in written form, on film, or on video- or audiotape. Many modeling presentations include cognitive behaviors (self-verbalizations) as well as overt behaviors. Most modeling displays present examples of the skills to be taught. Some, however, demonstrate poor or inadequate behaviors as well, so that trainees can learn to discriminate the ineffective responses (Thalen et al., 1976).

Role Playing

After trainees have been exposed to modeled examples they are given opportunities to practice the behaviors. Trainees may role-play both overt and covert responses, with the expectation that individualized practice will increase adequate skills in real-life situations. Since most social skills involve interpersonal situations, other trainees and/or the trainer usually serve as co-actors, enacting the roles of significant others in the trainee's life. Some programs involve outside people as co-actors.

Trainers often serve as "stage directors" during roleplays to ensure that practice attempts will be successful. They frequently coach, prompt, and shape, so that behavioral rehearsals can successively approximate the target behaviors.

Feedback

An integral component of virtually all social skills training programs is feedback and social reinforcement. Feedback may be in the form of approval, praise, or encouragement, or it may be corrective in nature, with concrete suggestions for improved performance. Suggestions are likely to be followed by additional practice. Some programs, particularly those with young children or chronic psychiatric patients, may also use tangible reinforcement such as money, food, candy, or tokens (Doty, 1975).

Some social skills programs utilize self-reinforcement techniques. In a forthright effort at shifting the locus of evaluation from external to internal, attempts are made to teach self-monitoring, self-evaluation, and self-reward as an important aspect of skill acquisition and generalization (Goldstein et al., 1980).

Homework/Transfer of Training

A most neglected area is transfer of training. Psychotherapists and educators tend to devote most of their effort and attention to the clinic or classroom, with relatively little attention paid to the vital task of transferring gains to real-life applications.

Some social skills training programs acknowledge and deal with the transfer problem directly (Goldstein et al., 1976; Curran & Gilbert, 1975; Twentyman & Zimering, 1979). The most frequently used technique for facilitating transfer is homework, which usually takes the form of a contractual agreement with the trainer for trainees to use the skills learned at some predetermined later time.

Another major approach to facilitating successful generalization is the incorporation of "transfer enhancers" (Goldstein et al., 1976). Transfer enhancers are those training ingredients that increase the likelihood that transfer of training will occur. Goldstein and colleagues (1976) present five transfer enhancers: (a) provision of general principles, or presenting trainees with appropriate concepts, rules, or strategies for proper skill use; (b) identical elements, or making the training setting, both physically and interpersonally, as much like the real-life application setting as possible; (c) overlearning, or providing repeated practice of successful skill enactment in the training session; (d) stimulus variability, or presenting trainees with opportunities to practice their newly learned social skills in a variety of physical and interpersonal settings; and (e) real-life reinforcement, or maximizing the likelihood that trainees will receive adequate (external) social reinforcement and/or (internal) self-reinforcement as they use their skills successfully in their real-life environment.

SUMMARY

A specific definition of social skills has been offered because, as Curran states, "Everyone seems to know what good and poor social skills are but no one can define them adequately" (Curran, 1979, p. 321). The most useful definitions of social skills are still most likely to emerge in the context of the specific skills being taught, since precision is not possible at a more global level.

The other major topic not addressed here is that of assessment. Curran and Mariotto (1980) agree with Hersen and Bellack's (1977) earlier conclusion that no "best" device or technique for assessing social skills yet exists. This state of affairs is related directly to the definitional issues, since one cannot very well assess that which is not defined. Most assessment approaches use some combination of questionnaire/self-report measures of behaviors, cognitions and/or affective responses, naturalistic observations, and role-play simulations. Traditional psychological tests have typically not been used. Since neither a standardized nomenclature of skills nor a uniform assessment package yet exists, it is not possible specifically to compare training effectiveness across training programs, although a recent study by Curran and colleagues (1982) offers encouraging possibilities for such comparisons.

REFERENCES

Curran, J. P. (1979). Social skills: Methodological issues and further directions. In A. S. Bellack & M. Hersen (Eds.), *Research and practice in social skills training.* New York: Plenum.

Curran, J. P., & Gilbert, F. J. (1975). A test of the relative effectiveness of a systematic desensitization program and an interpersonal skill training program with date anxious subjects. *Behavior Therapy, 6,* 510–521.

Curran, J. P., & Mariotto, M. J. (1980). A conceptual structure for the assessment of social skills. In M. Hersen, R. M. Eisler, & P. M. Miller (Eds.), *Progress in behavior modification* (Vol. 10). New York: Academic.

Curran, J. P., Wessberg, H. W., Farrell, A. D., Monti, P. M., Corriveau, D. P., & Coyne, N. A. (1982). Social skills and social anxiety: Are different laboratories measuring the same constructs? *Journal of Consulting and Clinical Psychology, 50,* 396–406.

Doty, D. W. (1975). Role playing and incentives in the modification of the social interaction of chronic psychiatric patients. *Journal of Consulting and Clinical Psychology, 43,* 676–682.

Field, G. D., & Test, M. A. (1975). Group assertive training for severely disturbed patients. *Journal of Behavior Therapy and Experimental Psychiatry, 6,* 129–134.

Goldstein, A. P., Sprafkin, R. P., & Gershaw, N. J. (1976). *Skill training for community living.* New York: Pergamon.

Goldstein, A. P., Sprafkin, R. P., Gershaw, N. J., & Klein, P. (1980). *Skillstreaming the adolescent.* Champaign, IL: Research Press.

Hersen, M., & Bellack, A. A. (1977). Assessment of social skills. In A. R. Ciminero, K. S. Calhoun, & H. E. Adams (Eds.), *Handbook of behavioral assessment.* New York: Wiley.

Lazarus, A. A. (1971). *Behavior therapy and beyond.* New York: McGraw-Hill.

Meichenbaum, D. (1977). *Cognitive behavior modification: An integrative approach.* New York: Plenum.

Phillips, E. L. (1978). *The social skills basis of psychopathology.* New York: Grune & Stratton.

Thalen, M. A., Fry, R. A., Dollinger, S. J., & Paul, S. C. (1976). Use of videotaped models to improve the interpersonal adjustment of adolescents. *Journal of Consulting and Clinical Psychology, 44,* 492.

Twentyman, C. T., & Zimering, R. T. (1979). Behavioral training of social skills: A critical review. In M. Hersen, R. M. Eisler, & P. M. Miller (Eds.), *Progress in behavior modification* (Vol. 7). New York: Academic.

Wolpe, J. (1982/1969). *The practice of behavior therapy.* New York: Pergamon.

Zigler, E., & Phillips, L. (1961). Social competence and outcome in psychiatric disorder. *Journal of Abnormal and Social Psychology, 63,* 264–271.

SUGGESTED READING

Arkowitz, H., Lichtenstein, E., McGovern, K., & Hines, P. (1975). The behavioral assessment of social competence in males. *Behavior Therapy, 6,* 3–13.

Bellack, A. S., & Hersen, M. (Eds.). (1979). *Research and practice in social skills training.* New York: Plenum.

Cartledge, G., & Milburn, J. F. (Eds.). (1980). *Teaching social skills to children.* New York: Pergamon.

Eisler, R. M., & Frederiksen, L. W. (1980). *Perfecting social skills.* New York: Plenum.

Goldsmith, J. B., & McFall, R. M. (1975). Development and evaluation of an interpersonal skill-training program for psychiatric inpatients. *Journal of Abnormal Psychology, 84,* 51–58.

Goldstein, A. P. (1981). *Psychological skills training.* New York: Pergamon.

Hersen, M., & Bellack, A. S. (Eds.). (1976). *Behavioral assessment: A practical handbook.* New York: Pergamon.

Liberman, R. P., King, L. W., DeRisi, W. J., & McCann, M. (1975). *Personal effectiveness.* Champaign, IL: Research Press.

Libet, J. M., & Lewinsohn, P. M. (1973). The concept of social skills with special reference to the behavior of depressed persons. *Journal of Consulting and Clinical Psychology, 40,* 304–312.

Singleton, W. T., Spurgeon, P., & Stammers, R. B. (1980). *The analysis of social skill.* New York: Plenum.

Troyer, P., Bryant, B., Argyle, M., & Marzillier, J. (1978). *Social skills and mental health.* Pittsburgh, PA: University of Pittsburgh Press.

R. P. SPRAFKIN
Veterans Administration Medical Center, Syracuse

ASSERTIVENESS TRAINING
BEHAVIOR THERAPY
COGNITIVE BEHAVIOR THERAPY
GROUP PSYCHOTHERAPY

SOCIAL SUPPORT

The term "social support" refers to supportive relationships that arise with oneself and friends, family members, and other persons (Friis & Sellers, 1999). The social support concept embodies material and emotional resources that accrue through our relationships with others (Friis & Taff, 1986). Social support results in the feeling that one is cared for and loved, esteemed and valued, or is part of a network of mutual interpersonal commitments (Cobb, 1976). In addition, social contact, received emotional support, and anticipated support are interrelated. Increased social contact is associated with increased emotional support and perceptions of support availability. Persons who have high levels of social support are thought to confront stressful or adverse conditions more successfully than those who lack social support. Conversely, those who have inadequate levels of social support may be at risk of experiencing deleterious consequences for their own mental and physical health.

MECHANISMS OF SOCIAL SUPPORT

The protective effects of social support against stressful occurrences are thought to arise from several mechanisms. One is from the encouragement (e.g., kind words from a close confidant) that one may receive when faced with adverse circumstances. The other is the availability of material aid and resources for dealing with challenges or adversity. For example, when one is confronted with the need to move to a new house, the availability of many friends to help with the move is indeed reassuring. Thus, social support enhances the individual's ability to cope with changes and crises, which are inevitable in life (Cobb, 1976).

SOCIAL SUPPORT VERSUS SOCIAL NETWORK TIES

A distinction exists between supportive relationships and the total number of social ties that the individual has. Social support denotes perceived emotional support that one receives from or the value that one attributes to social relationships. In contrast, the term "social network ties" is a more quantitative concept that embraces the number, structure, or pattern of ties that one has with other people or organizations. The mere existence of social ties is neither a necessary nor a sufficient condition for social support, nor is the absolute number of ties strongly correlated with social support. In fact, some types of social ties may be intrusive, stressful, or at best, perfunctory. Close friendships and relationships with partners, spouses, or family members that are perceived as valuable or helpful engender social support. Social relationships, including those with family members and significant others, may be at best a mixed blessing—many of the stresses that we experience evolve from our interactions with others. These stresses may arise from interactions with our very own family members who may experience different intensities and outcomes of stress. In support of this argument, several studies have demonstrated the differential effects of spousal ties upon men and women, the former being more likely to receive positive, protective effects from the marital relationship.

THE BUFFERING MODEL OF SOCIAL SUPPORT

A considerable body of research studies has focused on the stress-buffering effects of social support and social network ties. The term "buffering" (sometimes called "moderating") suggests that the impacts of noxious stimuli or stresses are attenuated by the availability of social support; absence of support, according to the buffering hypothesis, is linked to experience of the full consequences of stressful situations (Cobb, 1976; LaRocco, House, & French, 1980; Kaplan, Cassel, & Gore, 1977). The stress-buffering effect is more likely to occur when the social network is perceived as ready to provide assistance. The buffering model has also been extended to social network ties by specifying that they may lessen the adverse psychologic consequences of stress (Friis & Nanjundappa, 1989). The buffering role of social support is attractive to practitioners, because it is often more feasible to change social relationships than to change the conditions wherein adversity arises. Theorists posit that social support buffers some stressors more effectively than others, depending on the nature of the stressor. For example, a person who experiences a socially acceptable stress (such as personal illness) may be more likely to seek assistance from social support resources than one who is confronted with a less socially acceptable stress, such as substance abuse (Mitchell, Billings, & Moos, 1982).

SOURCES OF SOCIAL SUPPORT

There is evidence that variations in the effects of support are related to the source of support—and that these effects may be conditioned by marital status, age, and gender. For example, support from spouses or friends may be more important than support from other network ties. Marital status, found to be salient in the social support process, causes married older adults to have more contact with family members than with friends and to receive more emotional support than unmarried older adults. An apparent paradox arises when comparing gender differences in social support. Some data suggest that women, in comparison to men, give and receive more support and tend to have higher rates of psychological distress (Fuhrer, Stansfield, Chemali, & Shipley, 1999).

SOCIAL SUPPORT AND HEALTH-RELATED OUTCOMES

Investigators have examined the association among stress, social support, and mental and physical health outcomes. Not only have researchers examined the role of social support in mental disorders, but they have also studied outcomes such as complications of pregnancy, all-cause mortality, chronic disease, and immune status. For example, immune status as a function of social support was studied among the spouses of cancer patients (assumed to be experiencing severe, chronic life stresses); in comparison to those with low levels of support, spouses with higher levels of social support had better indices of immune function.

Although researchers hypothesize that social support is generally associated with both physical and mental well-being, a substantial body of literature concerns the role of stressors and social support in the etiology of mental disorders. Noting that individuals vary considerably in their vulnerabilities to stressors, some authorities believe that social support may help to explain why some individuals who face high levels of stress do not develop psychiatric disorders (Lin & Dean, 1984). Absence of social support may be linked to psychiatric symptomatology, especially depressive symptoms. Studies of patients who were suffering from depression reported that they had significantly fewer social supports than control patients. Not only do some researchers believe that the presence of social support plays a crucial role in the positive functioning of psychiatric patients, lack of social support has also been associated with re-hospitalization for depression.

REFERENCES

Cobb, S. (1976). Social support as a moderator of life stress. *Psychosomatic Medicine, 38,* 300–314.

Friis, R. H., & Nanjundappa, G. (1989). Life events, social network ties, and depression among diabetic patients. In *Human Stress: Current Selected Research* (Vol. 3). New York: AMS.

Friis, R. H., & Sellers, T. A. (1999). *Epidemiology for public health practice* (2nd ed.). Gaithersburg, MD: Aspen.

Friis, R. H., & Taff, G. A. (1986). Social support and social networks, and coronary heart disease and rehabilitation. *Journal of Cardiopulmonary Rehabilitation, 6,* 132–147.

Fuhrer, R., Stansfeld, S. A., Chemali, J., & Shipley, M. J. (1999). Gender, social relations and mental health: Prospective findings from an occupational cohort. *Social Science and Medicine, 48,* 77–87.

Kaplan, B. H., Cassel, J. C., & Gore, S. (1977). Social support and health. *Medical Care, 15,* 47–58.

LaRocco, J. M., House, J. S., & French, J. R. P. (1980). Social support, occupational stress, and health. *Journal of Health and Social Behavior, 21,* 202–218.

Lin, N., & Dean, A. (1984). Social support and depression: A panel study. *Social Psychiatry, 19,* 83–91.

Mitchell, R. E., Billings, A. G., & Moos, R. H. (1982). Social support and well-being: Implications for prevention programs. *Journal of Primary Prevention, 3,* 77–98.

Thoits, P. A. (1982). Conceptual, methodological, and theoretical problems in studying social support as a buffer against life stress. *Journal of Health and Social Behavior, 23,* 145–159.

R. H. FRIIS
California State University, Long Beach

COPING
SOCIAL ISOLATION

SOCIALIZATION

SOCIALIZATION AND AGENTS OF SOCIALIZATION

Socialization is the process of becoming a social being. During this process of development, individuals acquire ways of learning, communicating, thinking, acting, interacting, and feeling that enable them to familiarize themselves with the culture and participate in the social process. Socialization provides a social and psychological identity to each individual participating in the process. The importance and significance of socialization is best demonstrated through known cases of inadequate socialization of human children.

The main agents of socialization typically include parents/family, peers, schools, media, and religion. Family has traditionally been considered the primary agent of socialization, especially during the early formative years. In recent years, there has been increasing attention paid to the roles of peers and the media. The rise in dual-income and single-parent families results in peer groups gaining more importance in the lives of children and adolescents. Schools are important in teaching individuals what is expected of them in the larger society—both in terms of skills and abilities and also in terms of appropriate behaviors and characteristics. Along with the influence of the family, religion can play an important role in an individual's sense of distinguishing right from wrong and having an awareness of social responsibility. In addition, the television often takes on some of the roles of a surrogate parent or a babysitter.

There are at least two commonly used approaches to the study of socialization. The first approach emphasizes the individual and the development of the individual in the context of the culture and society. Psychologists have typically emphasized the development involved in the process of socialization. Studies from the field focus on topics such as stages involved in cognitive development, life stages, and personality development. The second approach is a social perspective that emphasizes the development of the social self and the process of social and cultural transmission between generations. This is the major focus of socialization research among sociologists and cultural anthropologists. The two approaches, however, should be viewed as supplementary and complementary to each other. The work of many psychologists and sociologists traverses the different approaches to socialization, including sociobiological and feminist perspectives. Moral development studies, for example, can be approached from any one or a combination of these different perspectives.

Theories of Socialization

With regard to cognitive development of the individual, the works of Piaget and Kohlberg are important. Piaget identified four stages of cognitive development: sensorimotor, preoperational, concrete operational, and formal operational. The child's thought advances from the simple to the complex. Important at each stage is one's functioning in relation to the environment. This is accomplished in two ways: assimilation that involves modifying the environment in order to fit with an existing cognitive scheme, and accommodation that entails modifying oneself in response to environmental demands. Both processes are reflective of the view Piaget had of the individual as active. Kohlberg extended Piaget's theory by adding the dimension of emotional development, which parallels cognitive development. In addition, social development is described by Kohlberg in terms of changes that occur in the self-concept as the child compares himself or herself with others and acquires more and more information about his niche in the social environment.

An important expected outcome of child and adolescent socialization is moral development. Freud's psychoanalytic theory emphasizes the affective component of morality. Children are viewed as motivated to act in accordance with their ethical principles in order to experience positive affects such as pride, and to avoid negative moral emotions such as guilt and shame. Cognitive-developmental theory emphasizes the cognitive aspects of moral reasoning; the way the individual conceptualizes right and wrong and makes decisions about how to behave. The most basic assumption of this approach is that moral development depends heavily on cognitive development.

For Piaget, the moral judgment of young children is characterized by an emphasis on abiding by the rules. The child has a strong respect for the rules and believes that they must be obeyed at all times. The child is likely to judge the naughtiness of an act by its objective consequences rather than the actor's intent. The moral judgment of the older child, however, is characterized by the individual viewing rules as arbitrary agreements that can be challenged. Judgments of right and wrong are dependent more on the actor's intent to deceive or to violate social rules than on the objective consequences of the act itself. According to Piaget, moving from an authoritarian moral code to one based more on autonomy requires both cognitive maturation and social experience. The kind of social experience that Piaget considered especially important was equal-status contact with peers. When conflicts arise during play, children learn to integrate their points of view with those of their peers in order for the play to continue and thus, grow in their personal understanding. According to Kohlberg, moral judgment is the most important factor in moral behavior. Other factors that are necessary for moral judgment to become moral action include the situation and its pressures, motives and emotions, and a general sense of will or purpose. Thus, Kohlberg considered both personality and situational variables. It was Kohlberg's contention that a moral choice involves choosing between two or more universal values as they conflict (e.g., concerns of affection and truth).

The approaches to development of the social self are represented here by Cooley and Mead. Cooley's concept of the "Looking Glass Self" suggests the importance of others in the development of one's self. The individual imagines how his behavior appears to others and, based upon his perceptions of others' judgments, the self develops. According to Mead, the idea of the self emerges as one acquires language and interacts with others. The self is a gift to the individual from the society.

The age-old nature–nurture debate is relevant in the consideration of the socialization processes. While sociobiologists provide explanations of human behavior from an evolutionary perspective, the work of social scientists most heavily emphasizes the role of nurture (or social and cultural environment) in shaping human behavior. The nature–nurture controversy continues to be discussed in spite of the fact that the issue is improperly presented in a dichotomous or hierarchical sense. It is generally agreed that both nature and nurture are necessary to the development of an individual. These findings have been substantiated not only in the research on human species, but primate studies as well. Primarily, studies of identical human twins have been considered ideal in the study of the impact of nature and nurture in human beings. It is really not yet possible to apportion accurately the extent of impact of one factor after eliminating or holding constant the effects of the other factor.

The theoretical emphasis in the field has shifted from a functional or deterministic model, where the children were considered to be passive recipients, to a constructivist model of an active child. Psychologists like Piaget view children as being active participants who construct the environment from their own perspective.

Process and Types of Socialization

Though the socialization process is most evident during childhood and adolescence, it covers the entire course of the life span. Erickson's eight stages illustrate the enduring process of socialization. The term "resocialization" emphasizes socialization as a process that never ends. A clear example of resocialization is what happens when someone joins a branch of the armed services. The uniforms, the regulations, and the regimen require the new recruit to learn new behaviors and attitudes appropriate to the new role. Any new role requires some amount of resocialization. Going away to college, getting a new job, and beginning retirement will mean the learning of something new. The term "anticipatory socialization" is used to explain this process. When one is aware of a social role that he or she is expected to play at some time in the future, he or she engages in anticipatory socialization, which involves anticipation and preparation for what will be expected of him or her in that new role.

Socialization is not simply a one-way process. While it is often taken for granted that parents and other adults socialize children, what is often not considered is the extent to which children socialize their parents. In the case of immigrants, for example, it is typically the children who teach their parents how to speak the dominant language. Reciprocal socialization is also evident in the area of fashion or, more generally, popular culture and use of technology. Children, for example, may suggest to their parents what to wear for certain occasions, or may introduce them to music and games that interest them.

Recent Issues

A number of issues are being more widely discussed in the literature in recent years. They include peer groups, family socialization, feminist perspectives, failure of socialization, gender role socialization and multigroup diversity. The significance of peer groups in the socialization process has been widely studied since the 1950s, but has recently become one of the topics that is gaining more attention in the literature. Harlow's studies reported that peer groups could contribute to the socialization process of baby rhesus monkeys without a mother. Peer group pressure has been cited as one of the reasons for the use of tobacco, alcohol, and other drugs among adolescents in the US. Even in the concentration camps of Germany during World War II, groups of adolescents helped each other, and many children are believed to have survived as a result of such peer bonding. Similarly, countries as diverse as Brazil, Kenya, and Egypt have adolescents living with other adolescents in groups in order to survive. The significance of siblings and peer groups in the caring and socialization of children in Cameroon and India, for example, has also drawn attention to the contribution of peer groups in the socialization process among comparative researchers.

The family system has been subjected to crucial and significant changes that include single-parent child rearing, stepparent socialization, multiple parent siblings, and fragmentation of family roles and responsibilities. The recognition of major differences among siblings within a single family has resulted in a closer look at the family socialization and birth order. These findings have extended the study of family as a more complex system.

The contribution of feminist perspectives in different areas of study has resulted in a shift in the emphasis directed to socialization, especially since the contributions of Chodrow and Gilligan. Chodrow utilized a psychoanalytic perspective to build on Freud's work, and suggested that the sense of mothering in women was not biological, and that it was a result of an ongoing relationship between mother and child. Gilligan's perspective on morality is marked by its recognition that men and women do not have identical patterns of moral development. She is critical of the major approaches of Piaget, Erikson, and Kohlberg because their findings may apply only to men and thus disadvantage women. Her research shows that concerns about justice and care are both represented in moral dilemmas, but males are more likely to have an abstract justice focus, and women are more likely to have a care focus due to the differential socialization process undergone by men and women.

One explanation for deviant behavior, especially among youth, is that those individuals engaging in deviant acts have not been socialized properly. Deviant subcultures often provide a means for individuals to establish identity, even if it is a negative identity. Recent tragic events like school shootings in various areas throughout the United States are often explained, at least in part, by alluding to a failure in socialization. The media, with their emphasis on violent acts, are also targeted. It is important, however, not to mistake correlation for causation. Many other variables are involved in attempting to understand these recent violent events.

During the early stages of socialization, the child develops an awareness of himself or herself as male or female. Sex-appropriate behavior is emphasized whenever it is transgressed. Parents may have differential expectations about their children's behaviors, attitudes, and appearance based on sex. In school, differing expectations of performance, different activities, and divergent career plans might be emphasized. In peer groups, nontraditional behavior is apt to be punished. This is especially the case for boys. Children will be rewarded, then, when they act in a way that is consistent and appropriate for their sex. Conversely, the choices in sexual orientations are being more openly pursued. These include bisexuality, heterosexuality, and homosexuality.

Though social class and ethnic distinctions in socialization have not been neglected in the past, the introduction of multicultural perspectives in socialization is gaining more attention. Multicultural perspectives include issues of class, race, language, and other ethnic viewpoints. The goals of socialization and the process of socialization vary significantly by social class, race, and ethnicity. For example, the exercise of discipline, values, attitudes, and belief systems may vary from group to group within the same culture.

In addition, topics within areas of socialization, such as child development, adolescence, and family socialization studies, have become specialties in their own right, and thus many more topics such as processes of learning, hostility, deviance, and emotions are being addressed in the context of socialization.

SUGGESTED READING

Chodorow, N. (1978). *The reproduction of mothering: Psychoanalysis and the sociology of gender.* Berkeley: University of California Press.

Cooley, C. H. (1964). *Human nature and the social order.* New York: Schocken Books. (Original work published 1902)

Erikson, E. H. (1980). *Identity and the life cycle.* New York: Norton.

Gilligan, C. (1982). *In a different voice: Psychological theory and women's development.* Cambridge, MA: Harvard University Press.

Ginsburg, H., & Opper, S. (1969). *Piaget's theory of intellectual development.* Englewood Cliffs, NJ: Prentice-Hall.

Harlow, H. F., & Harlow, M. K. (1962). Social deprivation in monkeys. *Scientific American, 207*(5), 136–146.

Kohlberg, L. (1981). *The psychology of moral development: The nature and validity of moral stages.* New York: Harper & Row.

Mead, G. H. (1962). Mind, self and society from the perspective of a social behaviorist. In C. W. Morris (Ed.), *Mind, self, and society.* Chicago: University of Chicago Press. (Original work published 1934)

Piaget, J. (1932). *The moral judgement of the child.* London: Routledge & Kegan.

Piaget, J., & Inhelder, B. (1969). *The psychology of the child.* (Translated by Helen Weaver). New York: Basic Books.

J. WILSON
University of Minnesota, Duluth

S. SONNAD
Western Michigan University

MORAL DEVELOPMENT
SOCIAL INFLUENCE

SOCIOBIOLOGY

Sociobiology studies relationships between biological environments and social behavior in animals and humans. It is an integration of numerous fields, including sociology, biology, ethnology, evolution, and ethology. Its origins can be traced to the earliest discussions of the mind—body controversy. Its growth has proceeded along parallel paths within various scientific and social science areas. No single event, date, or founder can be solely credited with its inception and development as a special area of study and research. Edward Wilson has helped to shape some basic sociobiological principles. His books *Insect Societies* (1971), *Sociobiology: The New Synthesis* (1975), and *On Human Nature* (1978) have created a conceptual framework for the field and controversy over its existence.

Some social scientists have taken the position that human behavior (and to a lesser degree, animal behavior) is infinitely malleable, depending upon environmental alterations. Some biologists have taken an equally extreme position that the environment has little effect upon behavior, which is largely a function of heredity. Sociobiology argues that a growing body of research appears to demonstrate that the two factors always interact.

Sociobiology not only attempts to predict and explain behavior of individuals, but also seeks to explain and predict evolutionary changes in social and cultural behavior of groups. Sociobiology heavily relies upon an extension of Darwin's genetic theory. Each organism has a behavioral genotype (genetic code) that offers a biological substrate or hereditary instructions that can affect later behavior. Development that actually takes place is the phenotype, the genetically orchestrated behavior and physical appearance produced within a particular environment. This basic theory is stated to be true of all species. The ultimate goal is for reproductive success through environmental adaptation so that the genetic codes can be preserved and carried on through future life.

Sociobiologists vary in the degree to which they place an emphasis on the social or biological part of their theorizing. Most believe that human beings are extremely adaptable to a wide variety of environments and that the genetic endowment, even when less than ideal for achieving adaptation, is of less importance than the environment. While it is impossible to control the two factors, most sociobiologists place primary emphasis upon the environment as the primary shaper of behavior, particularly in the case of humans. Generally this concept has been more acceptable relative to the behavior of social animals than to humans. Wilson, in his earliest work (1971), focused upon the behavior of social insects and proposed that the same principles of population biology and comparative zoology could apply to humans. He asserted that biological principles acceptable in understanding animal behavior could be extended to human social sciences.

Common core principles of sociobiology include the belief in a natural order of development of social behavior, a multilevel explanation of behavior, purposefulness of behavior (which is to achieve adaptation and subsequently continuation of the gene pool), and a biological substrate to the behavior that follows predictable patterns. Beyond these common core principles, sociobiological theories vary considerably in terms of proposed mechanisms of action and the relative contributions that the environment provides. Altruistic behavior in humans was a particularly difficult problem for Darwinian genetics. From a genetic standpoint, it did not appear to make sense for an individual to engage in behavior that could even result in death, and subsequently the death of genetic material that the person was carrying. However, such altruistic behavior has frequently been observed in social insects such as worker bees who fulfill labor tasks for the bee colony even though they themselves are sterile. An understanding of this puzzle of altruism came from Hammilton's work (1964) on the concept of "inclusive fitness," which explains altruistic behavior in social insects as an act that, while jeopardizing the genetic material of the individual, assures the likelihood of survival of genetically related social partners. The closer the genetic resemblance between the sacrificed individual and the benefactors, the greater is the likelihood that such behavior will result in preservation of the related gene pool. This has been referred to as "reciprocal altruism"—aiding others with an expectation of return.

Critics of sociobiological theories have been numerous, and in some cases quite vocal. Among the concerns voiced are those reflecting potential social-economic and political costs of the theory, and the impossibility of validating it, a biological reductionism and deterministic view that negates the role of the environment. Many authors have argued that the complexity of human behavior is such that any attempt at reductionism is impossible. The complexity of any individual theory of sociobiology, however, determines whether or not it is a reductionistic theory. Some theories place more emphasis on the environment, while other, more complex, well-integrated theories take into account what is known of biology and the environment and couples such knowledge together in a reciprocal fashion. Such theories cannot be considered reductionistic.

It appears impossible, from either an ethical or a methodological standpoint, to validate the theories through anything other than largely implicit research with numerous conflicting and confounding explanations for the results. Some individuals have argued that the theory has been getting too much attention in the absence of the ability empirically to validate it. One major concern is that attention is being taken away from environmental theories, which can be validated to a greater degree. This shift in emphasis can be deliberately or inadvertently used to create a system that justifies racial and sexual prejudices. Some sociobiologists would, for example, argue that racial or sexual differences are not simply a function of the way the environment has treated an individual, but more accurately reflect actual biological differences that exist between individuals. That theory may then be taken to validate the inappropriate treatment for a few selected groups of individuals within society. It also runs the risk of producing an implicit conflict between the "biological determinism" and an individual's genotype with society's legal, moral, or religious and ethical directives.

REFERENCES

Hamilton, W. D. (1964). The genetical theory of social behavior: I and II. *Journal of Theoretical Biology, 7,* 1–52.

Wilson, E. O. (1971). *The insect societies.* Cambridge, MA: Harvard University Press.

Wilson, E. O. (1975). *Sociobiology: The new synthesis.* Cambridge, MA: Harvard University Press.

Wilson, E. O. (1978). *On human nature.* Cambridge, MA: Harvard University Press.

SUGGESTED READING

Barash, D. (1977). *Sociobiology and behavior.* New York: Elsevier/North Holland.

Caplan, A. (1978). *The sociobiology debate: Readings on ethical and scientific issues.* New York: Harper & Row.

Clutton, B., & Harvey, P. (1978). *Readings in sociobiology.* San Francisco: Freeman.

Dawkins, R. (1976). *The selfish gene.* New York: Oxford University Press.

Harris, M. (1979). *Cultural materialism: The struggle for a science of culture.* New York: Vintage Press.

Ruse, M. (1979). *Sociobiology: Sense or nonsense.* Boston: Reidel.

Sahlins, M. (1976). *The use and abuse of biology: An anthropological critique of sociobiology.* Ann Arbor, MI: University of Michigan Press.

S. D. SHERRETS
Maine Head Trauma Center, Bangor

ACCULTURATION
ALTRUISM
COMPARATIVE PSYCHOLOGY
ETHOLOGY
EVOLUTION
GENETIC DOMINANCE AND RECESSIVENESS
HERITABILITY OF PERSONALITY
INSTINCT
MIND/BODY PROBLEM
NATURE–NURTURE CONTROVERSY

SODIUM-POTASSIUM PUMP

Three families of membrane proteins hydrolyze ATP to obtain the energy needed for the transport of ions against their electrochemical gradients: V-type ATPases (for instance, transporters of hydrogen ions into lysosomal vacuoles and synaptic vesicles), F-type ATPases (for instance, the ATP synthase of the mitochondrial inner membrane), and P-type ATPases (which share a common asp~P reactive site, and include the calcium ATPase of the cell membranes and the sarcoplasmic reticulum, the H-K ATPase of the stomach and elsewhere, and the sodium-potassium ATPase found on almost every animal cell membrane). The sodium-potassium ATPase (Na-K ATPase) pumps sodium out of the cell in exchange for potassium. This process consumes a quarter of the basal metabolic rate and has profound consequences on the cell volume, ionic composition, and membrane potential, as well as on fluid transport across epithelial surfaces (DeWeer, 1985).

FUNCTIONAL PROPERTIES OF THE SODIUM-POTASSIUM PUMP

Maintenance of Cell Volume

The Na-K ATPase is a powerful tool to counter the tendency of extracellular water to enter the cell, driven by the oncotic pressure of cell proteins. One immediate consequence of pump activity is that potassium becomes concentrated within the cell. Because cells are relatively permeable to potassium, chemical forces will tend to favor the loss of this excess potassium from the cell (cells are relatively impermeant to sodium at rest, so there will be little movement of that ion). Efflux of potassium, an osmotically active cation, will in turn obligate the movement of water and chloride, a permeant anion, out of the cell. Thus, because osmotic forces move water and potassium at a ratio of approximately 50:1, the Na-K ATPase is a particularly efficient water pump (Dwyer, 1998).

Establishment of a Membrane Potential

As the Na-K ATPase continues to operate, potassium will accumulate, and cell chloride will deplete, each establishing chemical gradients across the cell membrane. Consequently, electrical diffusion potentials develop that are negative for both ions. When steady state is reached, the electrical forces on the cell's permeant ions just counter their chemical gradients, and the resting cell membrane potential is established (Hille, 1992).

Transport of Fluid Across Epithelial Surfaces

The existence of a sodium gradient allows the cell to use other transport proteins to move a wide variety of solutes, nutrients, and waste products into and out of the cell, a process termed "secondary transport." Both electrical forces (the negative resting membrane potential) and chemical forces (the sodium concentration gradient) provide energy to couple the uphill transport of one molecule to the energetically favorable movement of sodium. Thus it is possible to absorb large quantities of fluid from the intestinal lumen by the cotransport of sodium and sugars or amino acids into epithelial cells lining the small intestine. While most epithelia locate the Na-K ATPase on the basolateral aspect, neuroepithelia such as the choroid plexus and pigmented epithelia of the retina place the Na-K ATPase on the apical surface in order to better regulate potassium and bicarbonate concentrations in the brain (Rizzolo, 1999).

Electrogenic Property of the Na-K ATPase

Three sodium ions move out of the cell for every two potassium transported into the cell, generating a small electrical current. When the membrane surface area to cell volume ratio is high, such as in nerve processes, the pump current is sufficient to hyperpolarize the membrane by up to 11 milivolts, potentially altering the electrical excitability of the nerve (DeWeer, 1985).

Metabolic Control of Pump Activity

The pump rate depends on intracellular sodium and extracellular potassium, with half-maximal stimulation at 10 to 20 mM sodium and 1.5 to 2.5 mM potassium. Minute-to-minute control of pump activity is modulated by a variety of protein kinases and phosphatases, with the identity of the Na-K ATPase subunit and the kinase or phosphatase determining whether the final result is stimulatory or inhibitory. Dopamine, for instance, inhibits the pump by an indirect cAMP-mediated inhibition of protein phosphatase 1. In the long term, pump activity is controlled by changing the number or type of the Na-K ATPase subunit present in the cell membrane. (Blanco & Mercer, 1998).

STRUCTURE OF THE SODIUM-POTASSIUM PUMP

Molecular Structure

The Na-K ATPase is a heterotrimeric protein integral to the cell membrane. The 112 kDa α-subunit contains the site where ATP is hydrolyzed, as well as the ouabain/digitalis inhibitory binding site, the sodium- and much of the potassium-binding site. The 40 to 60 kDa β-subunit shepherds the α-subunit to the cell surface, participates in the binding of potassium, and contains a very large, highly glycosylated extracellular domain that can act as an adhesion molecule, for instance, on glial cells. The 8 to 14 kDa γ subunit is a hydrophobic polypeptide of uncertain function.

Various isoforms of both the α- and the β-subunits are found in human cells, with the α_1- and β_1-subunits being the most common dimer. Identifiable nerve cells contain characteristic combinations of α_1, α_2, and α_3 subunits; for instance, in the eye, amacrine cells express α_2 subunits, bipolar cells express α_3, horizontal cells express α_1 and α_3, and ganglia cells express all three α isoforms. Glial cells can express α_2 or α_3 isoforms. The functional consequence of the highly specific tissue distribution of a multiplicity of subunit combinations may lie in differences in kinetic or thermodynamic parameters of the specific heterotrimers or in a differential sensitivity to metabolic control (Blanco & Mercer, 1998).

A Molecular Cycle of the Pump

The sodium-potassium pump is perfectly reversible—capable of consuming ATP to pump sodium out and potassium into the cell, as well as generating ATP by the movement of sodium into the cell and potassium out. The function of the pump molecule is determined solely by the concentration of extracellular potassium and intracellular sodium, ADP and ATP; under physiological conditions, the cycle always consumes ATP to remove sodium from the cell. To be able to perform this pump cycle, the Na-K ATPase exists in two structural conformations, one that has a high affinity for sodium (termed E_1) and a second that has a high affinity for potassium (E_2). The $E_2\sim P$ form can either bind ouabain or digitalis and become inactive, or bind two potassium ions and transport them towards the interior of the cell membrane, initiating a pump cycle. At this point, the protein releases the phosphate, gains an ATP molecule and changes to the E_1 conformation, losing its affinity for potassium. With the subsequent loss of the potassium ions, the protein gains three sodium ions, which are then brought towards the interior of the membrane, and an aspartate in the α-subunit is phosphorylated. Next, one sodium is released from this complex, generating the electrogenic current, and then the remaining two sodium ions are delivered to the cell surface regenerating $E_2\sim P$, the

starting form. Thus, if the cell has sufficient ATP, the pump cycle will continue to cycle in the forward direction, extruding sodium and sequestering potassium (Blanco & Mercer, 1998).

REFERENCES

Blanco, G., & Mercer, R. (1998). Isozymes of the Na-K ATPase: Heterogeneity in structure, diversity in function. *American Journal of Physiology, 275,* F633–F650.

DeWeer, P. (1985). Cellular sodium-potassium transport. In D. W. Seldin & G. Giebisch (Eds.), *The Kidney: Physiology and pathophysiology.* New York: Raven.

Dwyer, T. M. (1998). Osmotically active particles and the cell. Available online: http://phys-main.umsmed.edu

Hille, B. (1992). *Ionic channels of excitable membranes* (2nd ed.). Sunderland, MA: Sinauer.

Rizzolo, L. J. (1999). Polarization of the Na-K ATPase in epithelia derived from the neuroepithelium. *International Review of Cytology, 185,* 195–235.

T. M. DWYER
University of Mississippi Medical Center

EXCITATORY AND INHIBITORY SYNAPSIS
VOLTAGE-GATED SODIUM AND POTASSIUM CHANNELS

SOFT DETERMINISM

A soft determinist takes an intermediate position between strict causality and complete indeterminism. This position was accepted by Alfred Adler (1964) in his personalistic, subjective, and phenomenological psychology, although he never used the term in his writings. Soft determinism means that behavior is not capricious or random, but rather is orderly, lawful, and predictable, but within the limits of individual creativity. The idea that all behavior is completely determined by prior events is the position taken by the strict determinist. The idea that any individual has full freedom is the position of the strict indeterminist.

A soft determinist holds that behavior is mainly controlled by the individual in terms of future purposes, the teleological position in science. Goals and purposes are subject to change, and consequently any individual's behavior will change accordingly in relation to that person's private, subjective, phenomenological views. This subjectivistic phenomenological stance placed Adler at odds with the rest of academic and professional psychology in the period of his activity, dominated then by the deterministic depth psychology of psychoanalysis, on the one hand, and by deterministic behaviorism, on the other.

Adler's psychology held the creative self to be a central construct. In the dispute between Freud and his followers and Adler and his colleagues, this theme became a central battleground. In this regard, Allport noted (Allport, 1955, p. 22):

Hence the individuality of man extends infinitely beyond the puny individuality of plants and animals, who are primarily or exclusively creatures of tropism or instinct. . . . Man talks, laughs, feels bored, develops a culture, prays, has a foreknowledge of death, studies theology and strives for the improvement of his own personality.

Given that Allport's speculation is accurate, then Adler (1964) was one of those theorists who was a "voice in the wilderness" of the pre-World War I days, crying that the self or soul must remain the focal point if psychology is to provide satisfactory explanations.

In proposing the creative self as a major theoretical construct in his theory, Adler introduced a sort of principle of indeterminancy similar to the Heisenberg principle in physics. Adler (1970, p. 414) claimed that the environment and heredity acting together on the child provided only probabilities at most:

Consequently the views of those who believe in the causative influence of heredity on the one hand, or environment on the other are as complete explanations of his personality, made untenable by the assumption of the creative power of the child. The drive (to move toward mastery, perfection) is without direction until it has been incorporated into the movement toward the goal which he creates in response to his environment. This response is not simply a passive reaction but a manifestation of creative activity on the part of the individual. It is futile to attempt to establish psychology on the basis of drives alone without taking into consideration the creative power of the child which directs the drive, molds it into form, and supplies it with a meaningful goal.

For large numbers of persons born under similar environmental conditions and with similar genetic inheritance, rather accurate probability predictions may be made. As an example, for a large number of slum children in a certain ghetto, all of whom are black and who come from divided homes, one may predict accurately that 80% will not complete high school. But for any one child selected from that larger group, accurate predictions based on heredity and environment simply cannot be made.

One must consider, when trying to predict for one child, the creative power of *that* child. The behavior of the child is certainly influenced by both heredity and environmental conditions. Children (and adults) do tend to draw similar conclusions from similar circumstances. But the one who wishes to predict the future of an individual must know what use that individual has made of his or her experience. Environment and heredity provide the brick and mortar, but we must consider how the individual uses these materials if we are to understand that person.

As Adler (1964, pp. 176–177) declared:

We concede that every child is born with potentialities different from those of any other child. Our objection to the teachings of the hereditarians and every other tendency to overstress the significance of constitutional disposition is that the important thing is not what one is born with, but what use one makes of that equipment. We must ask ourselves: "Who uses it?" . . . To understand this fact we find it necessary to assume the existence of still another force, the creative power of the individual. We have been impelled to attribute to the child a creative power, which casts into movement all the influences upon him and all his potentialities, a movement toward the overcoming of an obstacle.

This addition of the creative self to Adler's psychology is one of the major reasons why his point of view had gained so little acceptance by academic psychologists prior to World War II. The early psychologists were intent upon being "scientific," upon discovering the laws determining human behavior, of modeling psychology upon the "real" sciences such as chemistry and/or physics. With the concept of the creative self firmly in place, Adler's psychology clearly rejected the fundamental assumption of the scientific psychologists that behavior is caused by a complex array of external and potentially understandable and measurable factors.

Adler repeatedly returned to the creative self (or to human creativity) as he continued to develop his point of view. Perhaps one of the clearest statements of his beliefs concerning creativity and the style of life is the following (Adler, 1964, p. 187):

We cannot know in advance what the child will make of all the influences and the experience of his organs. Here the child works in the realm of freedom with his own creative power. Probabilities abound. I have always endeavored to point them out and at the same time to deny that they are causally determining. . . . Here [in heredity and environment] there are thousands of possibilities in the realm of freedom and of error. Everyone will form an error, because no one can get hold of the absolute truth.

Adler, in placing the creative power of the individual in a central position in his psychology, allied himself with the emerging "third force" in psychology.

REFERENCES

Adler, A. (1964/1956). *The individual psychology of Alfred Adler: A systematic presentation in selections from his writings.* New York: Harper & Row.

Adler, A. (1970). *Superiority and social interest, a collection of later writings.* Evanston, IL: Northwestern University Press.

Allport, F. H. (1955). *Theories of perception and the concept of structure.* New York: Wiley.

T. E. EDGAR
Idaho State University

ADLERIAN PSYCHOTHERAPY
BEHAVIORISM

SOLOMON, RICHARD LESTER (1919–1992)

Richard Lester Solomon received all three of his academic degrees from Brown University (AB, MS, PhD, 1947). During World War II, he served as Research Psychologist for the Office of Scientific Research and Development. He has taught at Brown and Harvard, and also at the University of Pennsylvania, where he was director of a research program involving the effects of Pavlovian conditioning on instrumental learned behavior. In 1966, he received the Distinguished Scientific Contribution Award from the American Psychological Association.

His research has involved many areas of experimental psychology, with both human and animal subjects. He has studied problems in sensory discrimination, word recognition thresholds, and Pavlovian and instrumental conditioning in lower animals. Of particular importance have been his many studies of traumatic avoidance learning in dogs. In these studies, he explored many parameters of the problem. For example, he found that the avoidance of electric shock can be quickly learned in a matter of a few trials, and once the behavior has been acquired, the animals will continue to avoid the shock for hundreds of trials when a buzzer is pressed as a warning signal.

STAFF

SOMATOPSYCHICS

DEFINITION

The term somatopsychics is derived from the Greek terms *soma,* meaning body and *psyche,* which has become an English term as well. Somatopsychics refers to psychological effects engendered by somatic conditions. Such psychological states range from normal, mild mood alterations, (like irritability due to low blood sugar) to major psychiatric conditions.

Somatopsychics needs to be contrasted with psychosomatics. Psychosomatic mechanisms are operating when psychological conditions produce physical symptoms, such as dry mouth and nervous sweating as a result of stress. The distinction between psychosomatic and somatopsychic is clear, in most cases and in theory, but in reality, when phenomena of both kinds become intertwined and feed on each other, causes and effects are difficult to disentangle.

When somatic and psychological causes successively bring about effects that begin to serve as the cause for the next level of effects, an etiological spiral evolves, making it difficult to identify the degrees to which psychosomatic or somatopsychic factors contributed to the final outcome. For example: Stress leads to tachycardia (psychosomatic effect) which in turn causes uneasiness and anxiety (somatopsychic outcome), resulting in a headache (psychosomatic effect) which may trigger irritability (somatopsychic effect).

HISTORY

Neither the concept nor the term somatopsychics is new, but not all contributions to somatopsychics have been labeled accordingly. Sometimes descriptors like, "of somatic origin", are substituted. The scientific literature further reveals that many researchers have used the popular term "psychosomatic" in lieu of somatopsychic, whenever they referred to a body mind connection, regardless of the direction in which the cause and effect arrow pointed.

Linguistics offers proof for the recognition of somatopsychic connections. Examples are thymus gland and hysteria. The thymus gland, considered to be the seat of emotions, was named after the Greek word *thymos,* meaning mood. Hysteria, formerly believed to be related to the uterus, and therefore only diagnosable in women, was labeled after the Greek term for uterus, *hyster.*

Somatopsychic connections were understood by Hippocrates, Aristotle and Galen. Later, from the 18th to 20th century, magnetists as well as geo-and cosmo-psychologists (Anschütz, 1953) promoted the notion that external physical influences affect body and psyche. The term "lunacy" stems from the belief that heavenly bodies affect human beings. Notably the moon, *luna* in Latin, was considered powerful enough to influence body and mind, capable of precipitating mental illness, in some individuals, or at least, cause intermittent insanity or noctambulism (Sadger, 1914) generally related to full moon phases.

In the 1700s Lammetrie's "L' homme machine" functioned on a somatopsychic basis and Cabanis declared the mind to be a mere function of the brain. Priestley equating brain and psyche shared some common ground with Comte who connected emotions, character and intellect to the 3 anatomical parts of the brain that he discerned. Lavater's physiognomic research alleged a connection between facial characteristics and personality features. Gall developed phrenology, which Lombroso later connected to his findings about "the criminal mind."

The theory of "psycho-physical parallelism" developed by Fechner (1860) asserted that every physical event has a psychological correlate and vice versa. Lotze's work on the physiology of the psyche, affirmed that all mental states emanate from physical processes. Ribot emphasized the role of genetics and viewed mental disorders as physiologically based. Sir Francis Galton, Darwin's cousin, studied genetics arriving at the result that mental traits as well as genius are inherited. In the second half of the 19th and at the beginning of the 20th century, many researchers were devoted to finding the causes of mental illness. While strictly psychological theories had their proponents, somatopsychic explanations of psychological and psychiatric phenomena had their advocates as well. Among prominent promoters of somatic hypotheses were Broca (localization of brain functions), Taine (nerve reflexes), Müller, Weber, Wundt, Jakobi, Griesinger, Westphal, Meynert, Kraepelin, Bleuler, Wernicke, who actually used the term "somatopsychic", and many others. Meynert, for example, not only argued for an etiology of mental illness rooted in brain pathology, but he also supported it with specific observations concerning destruction of fibers, blood flow to the brain, and so on. Kretschmer, a psychiatrist, studied the correlation between body build and personality and a corresponding somatically based affinity towards a specific mental illness. Sheldon later expanded on Kretschmer's work. Around 1900 Pavlov established scientific proof for four personality types based on distinguishable patterns of nervous system reactivity.

In 1913 Karl Jaspers presented several etiologies of mental illness, among them the somatopsychic etiology which is divided into three parts: 1. brain pathology (trauma, tumors, infection, vascular system related pathology, genetic deficits, deterioration due to aging, etc.), 2. physical illness producing symptomatic psychoses (infectious diseases, endocrine disorders, uremia, etc.) and 3. effects of toxic substances (morphine, cocaine, carbon monoxide, alcohol, etc.) (1965).

With the rapid expansion of biomedical research in the 20th

century evidence for a somatic basis of many psychological disturbances mounted and lent credence to orthomolecular psychiatry. The theories of Pauling (1974), Kety (1972), Rimland (1974), Pfeiffer (1976), Hoffer (1962), Osmond (1973), Cott (1973), and Hawkins (with Pauling, 1973) identified specific mental disorders as somatopsychic effects of biological etiology. They countered adverse genetic, biochemical, nutritional and environmental conditions with megavitamin and/or mineral therapy to treat and prevent mental illness.

Richard W. C. Hall's 1980 landmark book moved the concept of somatopsychics into focus. With his colleagues he documented and catalogued psychological presentations of physical illness as well as psychological side-effects of pharmacological agents. Additional somatopsychic outcomes were reported to be related to genetic factors, normal physical changes such as hormonally induced biorhythms or life phase changes, but also to toxic substances, including gases and to ambient environmental conditions.

New millennium research into the somatic etiology of mental disorders is growing rapidly, forecasting a more accurate understanding of mental illness and leading to a new, largely somatopsychically based systematization and to new codification.

SOMATOPSYCHICS OF EVERYDAY LIFE

Everyday life is full of experiences illustrating etiology and effects of somatopsychic mechanisms. Parents are familiar with the mood changes that occur in children when they are hot, tired or hungry. They may, however, fail to recognize that they are equally irritable, because low blood sugar, heat and fatigue affect people of all ages. Effects of sensory overload, like noise or heat, many forms of sensory extremes, including sensory deprivation are reflected in psychological sequelae. Total sensory deprivation as used in some prisons can lead to psychotic states and hallucinations. On the other hand, enjoyable sensations trigger psychological effects as well. Scents can evoke pleasant feelings which may include seductive messages. Music can be stimulating or calming, depending on tone, volume and rhythm.

Diminished alertness and reactivity are well documented in fatigued drivers of motor vehicles. Fatigue is a generally recognized factor in diminished capacity to function mentally, particularly in learning. In fact, one of the earliest psychological tests was developed by Ebbinghaus (1897) to study fatigue in school children along with finding the best arrangements for children's working hours (Heidbreder 1933). Limitations of reasoning ability are easily accepted as an effect of a not yet matured brain in young children, but create concern when it is the result of a deteriorating brain in an aging person.

Hormones are known to cause emotional changes in adolescence, in pregnancy and menopause, and are related to mood swings in premenstrual syndrome (PMS). Post partum depression, "Baby blues" are attributed to the birth-related sudden disruption of the hormone levels accompanying pregnancy.

Somatopsychic effects of "common use" substances are well recognized: the stimulating effects of caffeine and nicotine, as well as the initially relaxing but later depressing and judgment impairing effects of alcohol. Many toxic substances have more than a somatic

impact. Lawsuits alleging lead poisoning cite outcomes of learning disabilities, lethargy, and so forth. Carbon monoxide exposure, as from a car exhaust, can lead to memory deficits, apathy, and depression. Brain trauma due to insults from various causes like forceps birth, domestic abuse, accidents or brain surgery may result in mental deficiencies, adverse emotional reactions and personality changes. In rare cases trauma has caused a state of euphoria.

Sports related somatopsychic phenomena include the "runner's high", attributed to endorphins (Masters, 1992) and the SCUBA divers' "rapture of the deep", a state of nitrogen narcosis which expresses itself in a euphoric, drunk-like state, accompanied by cognitive impairment, and poor judgement. High altitude exposure affects mountain climbers, skiers along with inactive sightseers. Apart from physical distress it may cause irritability, impaired judgement, and in extreme cases panic attacks, delirium and hallucinations (Brugger, Regard, Landis, & Oelz, 1999; Morrison, 1997).

Light availability affects mood. Diminished presence of daylight in the northern and southern regions, as in Alaska and Scandinavia cause depression in many people. "Wetterfühligkeit", more readily acknowledged in Europe, refers to weather sensitivity. It implies that a person's vascular system is affected by weather conditions, particularly highs and lows in barometric pressure, which triggers emotional highs and lows paralleling mostly the pronounced pressure highs and lows. The Föhn, oppressive warm alpine winds are blamed for migraine headaches as well as for bringing on depression and even suicides, in susceptible individuals.

Disruption of circadian rhythm, especially when resulting in sleep deprivation, reduces optimal physical and mental performance and also appears to play a major role in depression. Leading causes are jet lag, shift work, particularly, when shift cycles alternate as soon as the body has begun to adjust.

MEDICAL ILLNESS PRODUCING PSYCHOLOGICAL/PSYCHIATRIC SYMPTOMS

The Diagnostic and Statistical Manual of Mental Disorders, Fourth Edition, (DSM IV; American Psychiatric Association [APA], 1994) recognizes the existence of somatopsychic conditions as long as the "Mental Disorder (is) Due to a General Medical Condition" (p. 165). While the causal connection between the somatic base for these psychiatric results is recognized, the term "somatopsychic" is not applied. Psychiatric conditions that are neither due to a recognized general medical condition nor substance-induced are classified as "primary mental disorders."

Medical disorders, recognized by DSM IV as medical conditions likely to generate psychological or psychiatric effects include brain tumors, head trauma, neoplasms, neurological, endocrine and cardiovascular conditions, specific infections, autoimmune disorders, hepatic and renal disease, fluid or electrolyte imbalance (APA, 1994).

Specific somatic effects with origins in various illnesses were detailed by Hall (1980), Morrison (1997), Antonowicz (1998), and others. Their works raise awareness of the prevalence of those psychiatric symptoms which although they are substance or illness related side effects, will frequently lead to a misdiagnosis of mental illness. Antonowicz, addresses the occurrence of "missed diagnoses" related to brain tumors. He paired specific tumors with their corresponding psychiatric symptoms. Cancer of the frontal lobe leads to personality, affective and cognitive changes; temporal lobe tumors may manifest themselves in altered perceptions, hallucinations, anxiety and depression; parietal lobe cancer is likely to be accompanied by cognitive disturbances, tactile hallucinations and depression while visual hallucinations and affective changes can be triggered by occipital lobe tumors. Misdiagnosis prevents early intervention.

SUBSTANCE RELATED SOMATOPSYCHICS

Somatopsychic effects may be related to a substance of abuse or to withdrawal from it. They also occur when a person incurs a deficit or accumulates a toxic amount of a needed substance, like a vitamin or mineral. Psychotic, mood and anxiety disorders, for instance, may be associated with intoxication with and/or withdrawal from many substances, including alcohol, amphetamines, cannabis, cocaine, hallucinogens, phencyclidine (PCP), lysergic acid diethylamide (LSD), opioids, and others. PCP, for instance, causes a sense of emotional numbing, detachment and isolation and change in body and spatial images. If it triggers a psychotic episode, the symptoms may be indistinguishable from those of schizophrenia; LSD may, in addition, precipitate "flashbacks" to states of intoxication, which can take place unexpectedly, years later (Taylor, 1988; DSM IV, 1994).

Common use substances like alcohol, caffeine and nicotine have their somatopsychic effects: Caffeine increases energy and alertness, acts as a mood elevator, but anxiety, fatigue and depression are bound to follow at abstinence. Side-effects of alcohol consumption vary with individuals. They take many forms from elevated mood, impaired judgement to anger, rage and violence. Others respond with extreme fatigue. Memory deficits are common after heavy drinking. Dysphoria and depression are recognized after-effects of alcohol. Excessive, long term use, can lead to amnestic disorder, dementia and delirium (Taylor, 1988; APA, 1994). Nicotine use increases arousal, vigilance and concentration and reduces stress and irritability. Severe irritability accompanies nicotine withdrawal (Sommese & Patterson, 1995).

Somatopsychic effects due to nutritional deficiencies, although present in the general population, have prominently been noted in the elderly due to both insufficient intake and diminished absorption capacity. Incorrect diagnoses of organic brain syndrome, paranoia or depression have been made in patients suffering from nutritional deficits (Kendall & Wisocki, 1991). Vitamin and mineral deficiencies can lead to irritability, mental deterioration, dementia, confusion, disorientation, delusions, disorientation, hallucinations, apathy, depression, anxiety and so on. Accumulation of toxic amounts of vitamins and minerals can generate similar outcomes. Toxic levels of copper, may even mimic psychosis indistinguishable from bipolar disorder or schizophrenia (Fredericks, 1981; Hall, 1980; Beckwith & Botros, 1998).

Major somatopsychic effects related to malnutrition of any kind, be it due to poverty, food refusal by anorexics, fad diets or other reasons, alter emotional reactivity and cognitive efficacy and impair normal development. This may explain the impossible task of convincing anorexics to eat. After starvation has affected reasoning ability, patients would first need to get well, in order to mentally and emotionally comprehend the need to eat.

SOMATOPSYCHICS OF MENTAL DISORDERS AND OTHER PSYCHOLOGICAL CONDITIONS

Some mental conditions are exclusively of somatic etiology. Most types of mental retardation and autism fit this category. Not as clear cut are the etiologies of schizophrenia, mood and anxiety disorders. These disorders, depending on type and/or severity are believed to arise from psychogenic and/or somatogenic conditions. Stress can interact with genetic predisposition. In addition, psychological factors can precipitate a psychosomatic outcome. Depending on the resulting somatic condition, it may become the somatic basis for a mental disorder. A selection of recognized etiologies follows. The samples provided are not intended to be all-inclusive.

1. Mental Retardation (MR)

Most cases of MR are somatically based. According to the American Association on Mental Retardation (1992) MR can originate in the pre-, peri- or postnatal phase.

a. Prenatal period. Conditions implicated in the etiology of MR include chromosomal disorders, which includes Down syndrome; various syndrome disorders (such as muscular, skeletal, etc.), inborn errors of metabolism (phenylketonuria, etc.); further disorders of the urea cycle, copper metabolism and so forth. Familiar are developmental disorders of brain formation like hydro- and micro-cephalus. Damaging effects from substances such as alcohol and Thalidomide, toxins and teratogens are well recognized, as are those from conditions affecting the mother's health and/or the placenta. Prominent among them are maternal malnutrition or addiction, chicken pox, German measles, diabetes and so forth.

b. Perinatal phase. A healthy fetus can become a retarded child due to unfavorable birth related events. Reasons may be abnormal labor and delivery, prematurity of baby, maternal sepsis, also birth delays, umbilical cord accidents, head trauma (forceps delivery), or oxygen deficiency, but also problems related to or multiple gestation conditions. Neonatal disorders or consequences of them, like infections, seizures, or intracranial hemorrhage can equally be responsible for MR.

c. Postnatal phase. Severe malnutrition is a leading cause of MR. Other damaging factors are head injuries, lead and mercury poisoning, along with the Aspirin related Reye syndrome. Childhood onset of metabolic disorders can result in MR, as can infections, particularly encephalitis, postimmunization disorders, parasitic infestations as in malaria, demyelinating disorders, seizure disorders etc. Psychosocial neglect is not merely a psychological factor. Lack of stimulation affects brain development. Results range from physical and mental retardation (failure to thrive) all the way to death.

2. Autism

Delong (1999) distinguished between two types of autism. One is related to bilateral brain damage in early life, the second type, the idiopathic (familial) form, is presumed to have genetic roots. Other recognized etiologies name neurochemical and immunological factors, deficient oxygen delivery to the brain, in utero insults and so forth.

3. Schizophrenia

The causes of schizophrenia (SCH) "are still not completely understood" (Carlson, 1998 p. 513). While the evidence for somatic etiologies of SCH is increasing, a patient's psychological environment is, in many cases, still believed to be a contributing factor. No singular somatic cause of SCH has been identified. This suggests that either the identified range of schizophrenic symptoms may arise from differing etiologies, or that the different presentations of SCH, still labeled by DSM IV as one disorder, are actually a complex collection of symptoms generated by a variety of etiological conditions (Kane, 1999), which have been forced together under the single umbrella of the SCH classification. The broad variety of etiologies of SCH calls for a somatopsychically based reinterpretation of SCH. Renaming conditions according to their etiologies might permit the term "schizophrenia" to be retired as the label for a single disease.

The following are some of the more widely recognized somatopsychic etiologies of SCH. They center on: a. genetic factors (Kety 1972; Rutter, Silberberg, O'Connor & Siminoff, 1999); b. environmental factors, including maternal malnutrition, effects of infectious agents or antibodies operating prenatally (Andreasen 1990); c. lipid dysfunction (Swain & Pradhan 1999); d. abnormal brain lateralization and/or abnormal hemispheric communications, (Crow, Ball, Bloom, Brown, Bruton, Colter, Frith, Johnstone, Owens, & Roberts, 1989); brain damage occurring as a result of abnormal prenatal brain development, head-injury and hypoxia (van Kammen, Petty, Kelley, Kramer, Barry, Yao, Gurklis, & Peters, 1998) and so forth; e. neurodevelopmental errors and neurological malfunction; f. extreme prematurity at birth.

4. Depression

Somatopsychic etiology of depression has been related to genetics, biorhythms, and environmental and biochemical factors. Rosenthal (1971) found that close relatives of people with depression are ten times more likely to develop the disorder than those with no afflicted family members. Twin studies (Gershon, Bunney, Leckman, Van Eerdewegh, & DeBauche, 1976) have shown that monozygotic twins had a concordance rate for the affliction nearly four times higher than that of dizygotic twins.

Environmental and biological cycles, especially circadian rhythms, appear to play a role in depression. Seasonal affective disorder is related to diminished hours of sunlight in winter. Lack of optimal hours of sleep and REM sleep abnormalities have been related to depression (Giles, Roffwarg, & Rush 1987; Weibel, Follenius & Brandenberger, 1999). The monoamine hypothesis has suggested that depression is related to "insufficient activity of monoaminergic neurons" (Carlson, 1998, p. 529). The roles of diminished norepinephrine and serotonin activity (Guyton & Hall, 1996; Anand & Charney, 1997), dopamine deficiency (Depue & Iacono, 1989), and the reuptake of norepinephrine, serotonin and dopamine have shown themselves to be promising areas of research. Among other hypotheses that support a somatopsychic etiology of depression are immune changes reflective of increased plasma glucocorticoids (Leonard & Song, 1996); hypersecretion of cytokines associated with hyperactivity of the hypothalamic-pituitary-adrenal axis (Connor & Leonard, 1998); and a dysregulation of the stress response involving its central effectors, (O'Connor, O'Halloran, & Shanahan, 2000). Increased activity of thyrotropin-releasing hormone (TRH) has been implicated in depression as well. In women, hormone related depression has been associated with premenstrual syndrome, pregnancy, the post partum period and menopause.

5. Mania

In addition to genetics, mania has been related to various somatic etiologies, such as excess epinephrine and serotonin production (Guyton & Hall, 1996), cerebral trauma (Mitrovic, Misic-Pavkov, Ivanovic, Dickov, 1997), left hemisphere injury (Lim, 1996), sleep disruption, CD4 count in HIV infected patients (Lyketsos, Schwartz, Fishman, & Treisman, 1997). Herpes simplex encephalitis can give rise to hypomanic symptoms (Fisher, 1996).

6. Anxiety

a. Panic Disorder: According to Crowe, Noyes, Wilson, Elston & Ward, (1987) a single dominant gene causes a predisposition to panic disorder (PD). A panic experience can take effect when the autonomic nervous system is activated by agents like caffeine, yohimbine, lactic acid, increased CO_2 inhalation, and so on. Sodium lactate has also been found to cause PD in patients with multiple chemical sensitivity syndrome (Stenn & Binkley, 1998). Roth (1992) hypothesized that patients with panic disorder may chronically be in a higher state of arousal.

b. Obsessive Compulsive Disorder (OCD): OCD, classified as an anxiety disorder, is increasingly recognized as a somatopsychic disorder. Research suggests a number of possible somatic etiologies. OCD may be related to genetics (Rasmussen & Tsuang, 1986), abnormal brain structures (Rapoport & Wise, 1988; Baxter, Schwartz & Guze, 1991) and/or a dysfunction of the serotonergic system (Liebowitz & Hollander, 1991) and is amenable to treatment with Selective Serotonin Reuptake Inhibitors (SSRI) (PDR, 1998; Schwartz, 1997).

OUTLOOK

The rapidly expanding body of scientific findings has broadened the knowledge about the role of somatic factors in the etiology of psychological and psychiatric presentations. Unless a condition is strictly psychogenic, symptoms are less significant in defining a disorder than is its somatic origin, particularly, since identical presentations of psychopathology can result from vastly different somatic origins. This situation calls for a reassessment of the historically evolved understanding of mental illness, which is largely phenomenologically based. Sullivan, Coplan, & Gorman (1998), among others, challenged the old symptom-enumerating categorization which neglects demonstrated "biologic abnormalities that cut across DSM IV diagnostic categories" (p. 397) and thus permits disorders of different somatic origins to be classified as the same, identical mental disorder, simply because they express themselves in matching symptoms.

Unfortunately, etiology is not necessarily reciprocally related to symptoms. There are fewer recognized psychiatric/psychological symptoms than there are etiological causes for them. On this premise it becomes compelling to investigate etiologies rather than symptoms, in order to develop a reasonably precise diagnostic grid. As many of the old categories cannot adequately accommodate disorders defined by new and different standards and diagnosed with innovative methods of investigation, old stigmatizing terminology should be abandoned, making room for 21st century nosology.

With psychiatric disorders redefined according to the somatic categories they fall into, corresponding terminology, based on etiology can be developed. Such terminology portraying mental illness largely as a side-effect of somatic conditions would remove stigmatization of mental patients and would encourage them to seek timely treatment. More accurate diagnoses invite more precisely targeted interventions which will improve the efficacy of treatment.

REFERENCES

American Psychiatric Association. (1994). *Diagnostic and statistical manual of mental disorders* (4th ed.). Washington, DC: Author.

Anand, A., & Charney, D. S. (1997). Catecholamines in depression. In A. Honig, H. M. van Praag, et al. (Eds.). *Depression: Neurobiological psychopathological and therapeutic advances,* (pp. 147–178). Chichester, UK: Wiley.

Andreasen, N., Ehrhardt, J., Swayze, V., Alliger, R., Wuh, T., Cohen, G., & Ziebell, S. (1990). Magnetic resonance imaging of the brain in schizophrenia. *Archives of General Psychiatry, 47,* 35–44.

Anschütz, G. (1953). *Psychologie: Grundlagen, Ergebnisse und Probleme der Forschung.* [Psychology: basis and results of and problems in research]. Hamburg: Meiner Verlag.

Antonowicz, J. L. (1998). Missed diagnoses in consultation liaison psychiatry. *The Psychiatric Clinics of North America, 21,* 705–714.

Baxter, L. R., Schwartz, J. M., & Guze, B. H. (1991). Brain imagery: Toward a neuroanatomy of OCD. In J. Zohar, T. Insel, & S. Rasmussen (Eds.), *The psychobiology of obsessive-compulsive disorder.* New York: Springer.

Beckwith, M. C. & Botros, L. R. (1998). Clinical implications of hypomagnesemia. *Journal of Pharmaceutical Care in Pain and in Symptom Control, 6,* 65–77.

Brugger, P., Regard, M., Landis, T., & Oelz, O. (1999). Hallucinatory experiences in extreme-altitude climbers. *Neuropsychiatry, Neurobiology and Behavioral Neurology, 12,* 67–71.

Carlson, N. (1998). *Physiology of Behavior.* (6th ed.) Needham Heights, MA: Allyn and Bacon.

Connor, T. J., & Leonard, B. E. (1998). Depression, stress and immunological activation: The role of cytokines in depressive disorders. *Life Sciences, 62,* 583–606.

Cott, A. (1973). Medical orthodoxy and orthomolecular psychiatry. *Psychiatric Opinion, 10,* 12–15.

Crow, T. J., Ball, J., Bloom, S. R., Brown, R., Bruton, C. J., Colter, N., Frith, C. D., Johnstone, E. C., Owens, D. G., & Roberts, G. W. (1989). Schizophrenia as an anomaly of development of cerebral asymmetry. A postmortem study and a proposal concerning the generic basis of the disease. *Archives of General Psychiatry, 46,* 1145–1150.

Crowe, R. R., Noyes, R., Wilson, A. F., Elston, R. C., & Ward, L. J. (1987). A linkage study of panic disorder. *Archives of General Psychiatry, 44,* 933–937.

DeLong, G. R. (1999). Autism: New data suggest a new hypothesis. *Neurology, 52,* 911–916.

Depue, R. A., & Iacono, W. G. (1989). Neurobehavioral aspects of affective disorders. *Annual Review of Psychology, 40,* 457–492.

Diagnostic and Statistical Manual of Mental Disorders, (1994, 4th ed.) Washington, DC: American Psychiatric Association.

Fisher, C. M. (1996). Hypomanic symptoms caused by herpes simplex encephalitis. *Neurology, 47,* 1374–1378.

Fredericks, C. (1981). *Psycho-nutrition.* New York: Grosset & Dunlap.

Gershon, E. S., Bunney, W. E., Leckman, J., Van Eerdewegh, M., & DeBauche, B. (1976). The inheritance of affective disorders: A review of data and hypotheses. *Behavior Genetics, 6,* 227–261.

Giles, D. E., Roffwarg, H. P., and Rush, A. (1987). REM latency concordance in depressed family members. *Biological Psychiatry, 22,* 910–924.

Guyton, A. C. & Hall, J. E. (1996). *Textbook of medical physiology.* (9th ed.) Philadelphia: Saunders.

Hall, R. C. W. (1980). *Psychiatric presentations of medical illness: somatopsychic disorders.* New York: Spectrum.

Hawkins, D. & Pauling, L. (1973). *Orthomolecular psychiatry—treatment of schizophrenia.* San Francisco: Freeman.

Heidbreder, E. (1933). Seven psychologies. New York: Appleton-Century.

Hoffer, A. (1962). *Niacin therapy in psychiatry.* Springfield, IL: Thomas.

Jaspers, K. (1965). *Allgemeine Psychopathologie.* [General psychopathology] (8th ed.). Berlin: Springer Verlag. (1st Edition 1913).

Kendall, K. E., Wisocki, P. A. & Pers, D. B. (1991). Nutritional factors in aging. In P. A. Wisocki (Ed.), *Handbook of clinical behavior therapy with the elderly client* (pp. 73–95). New York: Plenum Press.

Kety, S. (1972). Toward hypotheses for a biochemical component in the vulnerability to schizophrenia. *Seminars in Psychiatry, 4,* 233–258.

Leonard, B. E. & Song, C. (1996). Stress and the immune system in the etiology of anxiety and depression. *Pharmacology, Biochemistry and Behavior, 54,* 299–303.

Liebowitz, M. R., & Hollander, E. (1991). Obsessive-compulsive disorder: Psychobiological integration. In J. Zobar, T. Insel, & S. Rasmussen. (Eds.), *The psychobiology of Obsessive-Compulsive Disorder.* New York: Springer.

Lim, L. C. (1996). Mania following left hemisphere injury. *Singapore Medical Journal, 37,* 448–450.

Lyketsos, C. G., Schwartz, J., Fishman, M., & Treisman, G. (1997). AIDS Mania. *Journal of Neuropsychiatry and Clinical Neuroscience, 9,* 277–279.

Masters, K. S. (1992). Hypnotic susceptibility, cognitive dissociation and runner's high in a sample of marathon runners. *American Journal of Clinical Hypnosis, 34,* 193–201.

Mitrovic, D., Misic-Pavkov, G., Ivanovic, S., Dickov, A. (1997). A manic syndrome after cerebral trauma: case report. *Medicinski Pregled, 50,* 391–393.

Morrison, J. (1997). *When psychological problems mask medical disorders: A guide for psychotherapists.* New York: Guilford Press.

O'Connor, T. M., O'Holloran, D. J., & Shanahan, F. (2000). The stress response and the hypothalamic-pituitary-adrenal axis: From molecule to melancholia. *QJM, 93,* 323–333.

Osmond, H. (1973). Come home psychiatry! The megavitamin treatment and the medical model. *Psychiatric Opinion, 10,* 14–23.

Pauling, L. (1974). On the orthomolecular environment of the mind: Orthomolecular theory. *American Journal of Psychiatry, 131,* 1251–1257.

Pfeiffer, C. C. (1976). Psychiatric hospital versus brain biocenter. *Journal of Orthomolecular Psychiatry, 5,* 28–34.

Physicians' Desk Reference to Pharmaceutical Specialties and Biologicals. (1998). Montvale, NJ: Medical Economics.

Rapoport, J. L., & Wise, S. P. (1988). Obsessive-compulsive disorder: Evidence for basal ganglia dysfunction. *Psychopharmacology Bulletin, 24,* 380–384.

Rasmussen, S. A., & Tsuang, M. T. (1986). Clinical characteristics and family history in DSM-III obsessive-compulsive disorder. *American Journal of Psychiatry, 143,* 317–322.

Rimland, R. (1974). Infantile autism. Status of research. *Canadian Psychiatric Association Journal, 19,* 130–133.

Rosenthal, D. (1971). A program of research on heredity in schizophrenia. *Behavioral Science, 16,* 191–201.

Roth, W. T., Margraf, J., Ehlers, A., Taylor, C. B., Maddock, R. J., Davies, S., and Agras, W. S. (1992). Stress test reactivity in panic disorder. *Archives of General Psychiatry, 49,* 301–310.

Rutter, M., Silberg, J., O'Connor, T., & Siminoff, E. (1999). Genetics in child psychiatry: II. Empirical research findings. *Journal of Child Psychology and Psychiatry and Allied Disciplines, 40,* 19–55.

Sadger, J. (1914). *Ueber Nachtwandeln und Mondsucht.* Leipzig: Deuticke.

Schwartz, J. M. (1997). *Brain lock.* New York: Harper Collins.

Sommese, T., & Patterson, J. (1995). Acute effects of cigarette smoking: A review of the literature. *Aviation, Space and Environmental Medicine, 66,* (2), 164–167.

Stenn, P. G., & Binkley, K. (1998). Multiple chemical sensitivity. *Psychosomatics, 39,* 393–394.

Sullivan, G. M., Coplan, J. D., & Gorman, J. M. (1998). Psychoneuro-endocrinology of anxiety disorders. *Psychiatric Clinics of North America, 21,* 397–412.

Swain, S., & Pradhan, C. (1999). Lipids and schizophrenia. *British Journal of Psychiatry, 175,* 88–89.

Taylor, P., Jr. (1988). *Substance Abuse: Pharmacologic and Developmental Perspectives.* Springfield, IL: Thomas.

van Kammen, D. P., Petty, F., Kelley, M. E., Kramer, G. L., Barry, E. J., Yao, J. K., Gurklis, J. A., & Peters, J. L. (1998). GABA and brain abnormalities in schizophrenia. *Psychiatric Research: Neuroimaging, 82,* 25–35.

Weibel, L., Follenius, M., & Brandenberger, G. (1999). Les rhythmes biologiques: leur alteration chez les travailleurs de nuit. [Biological rhythms: their alterations in night workers.] *La presse medicale, 28,* 252–258.

E. WICK
St. John's University

PSYCHOENDOCRINOLOGY
PSYCHOPHARMACOLOGY

SOMATOSENSORY FUNCTION

Somatosensory function is the ability to interpret bodily sensation. Sensation takes a number of different forms, including touch, pressure, vibration, temperature, itch, tickle and pain. The somatosensory system allows one to interpret sensory messages one receives from the body, and consists of sensory receptors located in the skin, tissues, and joints; the nerve cell tracts in the body and spinal cord; and the brain centers that process the incoming sensory information (Figure 1).

Sensory information is first detected in at least six specialized sense organs in the skin, categorized by their rapid or slow response characteristics. Rapid responses occur in hair-follicle receptors, which detect the movement of hairs on hair-covered skin. Hairless skin contains receptors called Meissner's corpuscles that respond rapidly to sudden displacements of skin and to low-frequency vibration of up to 80 Hz. Another rapid sense receptor, found in both hairy and hairless skin, is the Pacinian corpuscle, which responds to sudden displacements of the skin and to high-frequency vibration, and can sense signals at 30 to 800 Hz. These rapid sense receptors detect movement across the skin, as well as vibration and fast but subtle changes in pressure. Sense receptors with slower responses include Merkel's disks, which respond predominantly to skin indentation, Ruffini endings, which respond to skin stretch,

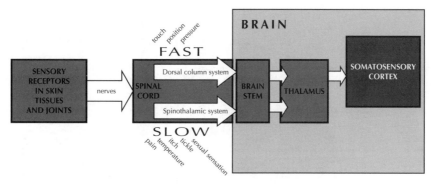

Figure 1.

and free nerve endings, which detect touch, pressure, pain, and thermal sensations. These slower receptors are all found in both hairy and hairless skin. Free nerve endings are also found in arterial walls and joint surfaces. Various types of nerve endings in joints, tendons, and muscles provide input for kinesthesis—the knowledge of the position and movement of one's body parts. Visceral sensation comes largely from the nerve endings in the muscles that surround the viscera, which themselves are fairly insensitive to touch, temperature, and pain.

The sensory receptors send their information to the spinal cord through peripheral afferent nerves in the arms, legs, body, and head. A total of 31 pairs of nerves[1] enter the spinal cord from the body, and 4 so-called cranial nerves supply sensory information from the head, including such structures as the tongue and pharynx. As the nerves enter the spinal cord, they make a number of connections, or synapses, within the cord tissue, and then the sensory information travels to the brain via two major pathways.

The two pathways that convey sensory information from the spinal cord to the brain serve largely different functions. The first is known as the dorsal column-lemniscal system, and transmits mainly touch and pressure information. It consists of large and fast nerve fibers that transmit signals at rates of 30 to 110 m/s. The fast information flow in this system enables sensations of movement across the skin to be detected, as well as rapidly repetitive signals to be ultimately sensed as vibratory sensations. In addition, this pathway transmits information with high spatial resolution. Touch sensations are localized with a high degree of accuracy, and fine discriminations in intensity can be made. These processes are due to a key characteristic of this system: rapid adaptation, in which a response to a persistent stimulus dies away quickly.

The second system is the spinothalamic system. This slower, low-resolution pathway transmits mainly information relating to pain, temperature, tickle, itch, and sexual sensations. Typical signal transmission rates range from 8 to 40 m/s, and are generally slow because the information is sent down smaller nerves than in the dorsal column system. Thus, the ability to transmit rapidly repetitive signals is poor. The spatial resolution for this pathway is also fairly crude; in addition, the spinothalamic system does not adapt quickly. This is important, because a persistent sensation of hot,

cold, or pain will stimulate the individual to remove the affected body part from a noxious and potentially damaging stimulus.

When fibers from the dorsal column and spinothalamic systems enter the spinal cord the nature of the connections they make are quite different. Fibers from the dorsal column system take two directions: the so-called lateral and medial branches. Fibers from the lateral branch make a number of synapses in the spinal cord that ultimately produce spinal cord reflexes, and a pathway connecting the spinal cord and the brain's cerebellar hemispheres, structures that play a key role in motor control. Fibers from the medial branch travel to the brain stem in a structure known as the medulla. Here the fibers decussate, or cross from one side of the body over to the other side. From the medulla the tactile information flows through the medial lemniscus to the thalamus of the brain.

By contrast, in the spinothalamic system some fibers synapse and then decussate locally in the spinal cord. The spinothalamic system sends its information forward via two major routes. First, crossed fibers travel to two regions of the thalamus: One set goes to the same thalamic region as do the dorsal column fibers, whereas the other travels to another part of the thalamus. Second, crossed and uncrossed fibers are sent to the reticular nuclei in the brain stem and the thalamus. These latter connections are important for the perception of chronic pain. The increased arousal that these signals produce explains why it is difficult to sleep when one is in pain.

The thalamus is the brain's relay station for all sensory input, including vision and hearing. From the thalamus, the tactile information travels to a brain region called the somatosensory cortex (Figure 1). The somatosensory cortex is the primary brain region dealing with sensation. It lies in a region of the brain known as the parietal lobe, namely on a surface and fold of brain known as the post-central gyrus and the central sulcus, respectively. The central sulcus separates the sensory cortex from the motor cortex (Figure 2).

Each side of the body's surface is mapped to the somatosensory cortex of the contralateral, or opposite, side of the brain. Sensation in the pharynx, tongue, and teeth is located below that in the face and hands, which sensations in turn are located in regions below

---

[1]For a given nerve pair, one member of each pair comes from each side of the body.

[2]The arrangement of the motor cortex follows a similar topographical organization. Hence, injuries to these brain regions can be localized from observed impairments in sensory and motor functions of various parts of the body.

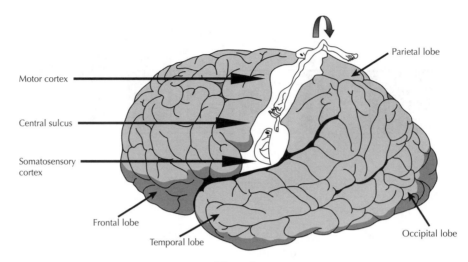

Figure 2.

those for the trunk and the legs (Figure 2). Sensation in the feet and genitalia are located in the cortex that lies between the two hemispheres of the brain.[2] The spatial map of the somatosensory cortex is not a precise representation of the body. The hands, face, and especially the lips take up a disproportionately large part of the somatosensory map. These regions of the body typically are the most sensitive and hence supply the most information about a contacting stimulus relative to other areas on the body, such as the back. The distorted somatosensory map of the body's surface is often known as the sensory homunculus, and is illustrated schematically in Figure 2.

The secondary somatosensory cortex, located slightly below and behind the primary somatosensory cortex in each hemisphere, also deals with sensory information. It receives its input from two thalamic regions predominantly via the spinothalamic system, in addition to receiving input from the primary somatosensory cortex.

The analysis of tactile information in the brain does not stop at the somatosensory cortices. We can recognize objects when our eyes are closed by running our fingers over them or by moving them around in our hands. This is possible because the somatosensory (and the motor) cortices also send information to other brain regions that perform these sophisticated functions.

A. PUCE
Swinburne University of Technology, Australia

BRAIN SPECIALIZATION

SOMATOTYPES

The basic notion behind the idea of a somatotype is that behavior or personality is determined by physical body characteristics. The process of somatotyping is the method by which physical aspects of a body are described. This process of somatotyping has been highly systematized in the work of William Sheldon.

HISTORICAL ANTECEDENTS OF SOMATOTYPE THEORY

The suggestion that a relation exists between body characteristics and behavior dates at least as far back as the Greek physician Hippocrates (c. 460–370 B.C.). Hippocrates proposed a typology in which people could be divided into four basic temperamental types—choleric, phlegmatic, sanguine, and melancholic—depending on which of four liquid substances ("humours") in the body was predominant. Although there were others after Hippocrates who related body factors to temperament, not until the work of Ernst Kretschmer, beginning in the 1920s, was the modern stage set for somatotyping. Kretschmer devised an elaborate check list representing the major parts of the body. The check list was filled out with the subject standing naked in front of the investigator. Kretschmer arrived at a schema for classifying human physique as *pyknic* (plump), *athletic* (muscular), or *asthenic* (frail and linear). A fourth category, *dysplastic,* described individuals who deviated greatly from any of the basic categories. Based on a study of 260 psychotic patients, Kretschmer concluded that there was a clear relationship between manic-depressive psychosis and the pyknic body build, and a similar association between schizophrenia and the asthenic, athletic, and certain dysplastic body builds.

Influenced by Kretschmer's views, but finding his theoretical approach inadequate, Sheldon, in the 1940s and 1950s, proposed a somatotype theory that associated body structure and temperament in a new way. Based upon a careful examination of thousands of photographs of the naked male body, Sheldon (1942) identified three basic dimensions for assessing physical structure. These were described as endomorphy, mesomorphy, and ectomorphy. The corresponding temperamental dimensions are viscerotonia, somatotonia, and cerebrotonia. When *endomorphy* predominates, there is a soft roundness throughout the various regions of the body and the digestive viscera are massive and tend to dominate. *Mesomorphy* refers to the relative predominance of muscle, bone, and connective tissue. The mesomorphic physique is normally heavy, hard, and rectangular with a predominance of muscle and bone. *Ectomorphy* refers to long, slender, poorly muscled extremities. Relative to mass, the ectomorph has the largest brain. In Sheldon's technique of somatotyping, each individual is ranked in terms of the extent to which each of the primary physical dimensions is present in the person's physique. Subjects are assigned a score from 1 to 7 according to the strength of each component, with 7 representing a high degree of a particular dimension and 1 a low degree. Thus, in Sheldon's scheme, a 7–1–1 would be an extreme endomorph with a negligible development of mesomorphic or ectomorphic trends. The first digit always refers to degree of endomorphy, the second to mesomorphy, and the third to ectomorphy. Sheldon considers that in the normal population there is a normal distribution of endomorphy, mesomorphy, and ectomorphy, but that certain combinations of these appropriately may be called somatotypes.

Parallel to the three basic physical components, Sheldon postulates three temperamental components. Extreme *viscerotonia* is characterized by love of comfort, gluttony, sociability, and affection. *Somatotonia,* when predominant, indicates a craving for muscular activity and is generally associated with a lust for power, a certain callous ruthlessness, and a love of risk and chance. *Cerebrotonia,* in extreme form, means excessive restraint, inhibition, and shrinking from social contact. Sheldon has developed temperament scales by which an average score is computed for each component. Hence an individual with an index of 1–1–7 would be low in viscerotonia, low in somatotonia, and extremely high in cerebrotonia (Sheldon, 1942). Most of Sheldon's research revolves around the question of how much association exists between his components of physique and components of temperament. In one of his initial studies, extending over a period of five years, Sheldon reports some very high statistical correlations between his somatotypes and temperamental components. Thus Sheldon's findings suggest that there is a close correspondence between temperament, as measured by observer ratings, and physique, as derived from measures taken from somatotype photographs. Sheldon reports that while the somatotype and the temperamental type do not always agree perfectly, the instances of any reversal of order of dominance in the three components are rare. Sheldon has also done somatotyping of female bodies.

In general, it may be said that U.S. psychologists have not taken too favorable a view of Sheldon's theory, perhaps unjustifiably. While there has generally been support from other investigators of Sheldon's empirical findings, the relationships between the somatotypes and temperament ratings have not been nearly as high as those reported by Sheldon. In this theoretical approach, Sheldon has reminded psychologists that an important aspect of a person should not be overlooked in their considerations of factors that determine personality. Whether one is inclined to accept Sheldon's formulations or not, it must be admitted that the way in which a person interacts with others and with environmental events is in some way determined by physique.

REFERENCES

Sheldon, W. H., & Stevens, S. S. (1942). *Varieties of human temperament: A psychology of constitutional differences.* New York: Harper.

J. L. ANDREASSI
City University of New York, Baruch College

PERSONALITY TYPES
SOCIOBIOLOGY
TEMPERAMENTS

SPAIN, PSYCHOLOGY IN

Despite the fact that the history of Spanish psychology shows a marked lack of continuity, it is possible to pinpoint a number of outstanding figures whose work achieved international dimensions. Ullman and Krasner (1975) in *A Psychological Approach to Abnormal Behavior,* point out that Vives (1492–1540), born in Valencia in the year in which Columbus first set foot on American soil, attempted to focus his contemporaries' attentions on the direct observation of human behavior rather than on such indefinable concepts as the soul or the mind. Vives, whose thinking would later have an influence on the English empiricists, constantly stressed the need for making the most of direct experience as the most reliable source of knowledge. Foster Watson, in 1915, called Vives the "father of modern psychology."

Another Spanish name worth mentioning is that of Huarte de San Juan (1529–1589), whose book *Examen de Ingenios para las Ciencias* (1575) presents an ingenious theory about the relationship between psychology and physiology, explaining how good vocational guidance can be built upon this relationship. Because of the suspicion with which the Spanish Inquisition looked upon all scientific innovations, the book had a wider circulation elsewhere than it did in Spain and several translations were issued (there is an English edition dated 1594). Apart from its interest as a pioneer attempt in the field of applied psychology, the book is also worth mentioning for some other specific features: its determinist stand, its incipient evolutionism, and the importance it places on the influence of environmental factors on biological makeup.

Eminent Contributors to Psychology by Robert L. Watson, published in 1976 includes biographical accounts of two other Spaniards. Ramón y Cajal (1852–1934), who was awarded the Nobel Prize in 1906, is credited with theories and discoveries on nerve cells and synapses that paved the way for a considerable amount of research work in psychophysiology. Mira y López (1896–1964) was to have been president of the 12th International Congress of Psychology in Madrid in 1936, which was canceled because of the outbreak of the Spanish Civil War (1936–1939). A prolific writer, Mira y López was probably the first Spanish-speaking psychologist to show an interest in behaviorism, and he was one of the first to study the work of Sigmund Freud. His published writings include works on psychoanalysis, legal psychology, psychiatry, evolutive psychology, vocational guidance, and experimental psychology. His best known contribution is a personality test, which he called "Myokinetic Psychodiagnosis" (MKP). The book was presented to the Royal Society of Medicine in 1939, and later published as a book in French, Spanish, English, and German. At the end of the Spanish Civil War, Mira y López went into exile and died in Brazil after living in several countries.

Another name that should be mentioned is that of Turró (1854–1926). He undertook the forceful defense of the experimental method, personifying the spirit of Bernard in the mentalist scene that prevailed in Spain at the turn of the century. A great admirer of Pavlov (who, coincidentally, revealed the results of his research on conditioned reflexes in Madrid, in 1903), Turró pursued some interesting experiments with newly-born animals to determine how they learn their first specific responses as a basis for all later knowledge. Despite the fact that Pavlov's influence is obvious in all his work, Turró's standpoint on many subjects was truly original. Had he had followers, the psychological dimensions of his work would probably have had broad repercussions.

International psychological trends found their way into Spain and were welcome there, but with different degrees of success. In same year in which Wundt published his *Physiological Psychology,* Giner de los Ríos (1840–1915)—a follower of the Spanish philosopher Sanz del Río (1814–1869), himself a student in Heidelberg when Wundt was an assistant to Helmholtz—published a small handbook entitled *Lecciones Sumarias de Psicología.* In its second edition, in 1877, the handbook mentions Fechner, Helmholtz, Wundt, and several others (cfr. Lafuente, 1982). Thus Spain became aware of Wundt's thinking, and although his work never had much influence in the field of empirical research, it was highly appreciated on a theoretical level, at least up until the Spanish Civil War.

Despite not having written much, one of the key figures in introducing scientific psychology into Spain was Simarro (1851–1921). Simarro, like Sanz del Río and Giner de los Ríos, was a member of the Institución Libre de Enseñanza, a movement that attempted the political and social renewal of Spain through the renewal of its educational system. In 1902, after studying physiology and psychiatry in Paris, Simarro was appointed professor of experimental psychology in Madrid's faculty of sciences, probably the first faculty of sciences in the world to have such a professor. Unfortunately, after his death, both his chair and his laboratory remained without successors.

The phenomenology and Gestalt movements found their way into Spain a little later, thanks to people such as Ortega y Gasset (1851–1955), who tried to open the country to the trends in psychology and philosophy that appeared in Europe after Wundt. About the same time, the "Geneva School" also started to show its influence in the country, an influence still noticeable today. Claparéde and Piaget gave lectures and were well-known and appreciated in Spain. Some Spaniards—such as Rodrigo, Mallart, and Roselló, who became director of the International Education Service created by the League of Nations—moved to Switzerland. In the early 1930s, all of Piaget's books to that date had been translated into Spanish.

In 1917, following ideas advanced in Germany by Munsterberg in 1911, an Instituto de Orientación Professional (Institute for Vocational Guidance) was established in Barcelona. This was one of the first centers of applied psychology in the world. The institute organized two International Conferences of Psychotechnics in Barcelona, in 1922 and in 1930. In 1931, Mira y López was elected to head the institute.

During the 1920s, another Instituto de Orientación Professional was established in Madrid. The team in charge included Mallart, Melián, and Rodrigo, and was led by Germain. Germain had studied with Claparéde in Geneva, with Köhler in Berlin, and with Janet in Paris. After the Civil War, he was of key importance in helping to bridge the gap between the postwar generations and the scientific psychology that was trying to become established in Spain in the early 1930s.

The year 1946 saw the publication of the first issue of *Revista de Psicología General y Aplicada (Journal of General and Applied Psychology),* the first psychological magazine to be published after the Civil War. In 1948, the Consejo Superior de Investigaciones Científicas (Higher Council of Scientific Research) founded the Department of Experimental Psychology with Germain as principal. Among those who worked for the department were Pinillos, Siguán, and Yela. Some years later, they were to be the first professors of psychology in Spanish universities, in charge of establishing the systematical study of this field in the country. The Sociedad Española de Psicología (Spanish Psychological Society) was established in 1952.

In 1953, the Escuela de Psicología y Psicotecnia de la Universidad de Madrid (Madrid University's School of Psychology and Psychotechnics) was inaugurated. The first attempt to establish university studies of a purely psychological nature, this school was open only to postgraduate students. In 1964, a similar center was set up in Barcelona. Eventually, in1968 the universities of Madrid and Barcelona began to offer five-year courses in psychology for undergraduates. Their example was soon followed by the remaining Spanish universities.

From 1969 onward, several new journals started publication: *Anuario de Psicología* (1969), *Anuario de Sociología y Psicología Jurídicas* (1974), *Analisis y Modificación de Conducta* (1975), *Cuadernos de Psicología* (1975), *Revista de Historia de la Psicología* (1980), *Estudios de Psicología* (1980), *Psicología* (1980), and so on.

During the 1970s in particular, thanks to the efforts of various Spanish and Latin American publishers, essential works by such important figures as Cattell, Eysenck, Kantor, Luria, Pavlov, Schoenfeld, Sechenov, Sidman, and Skinner were translated into Spanish. Spanish psychologists who saw their own work in print include Amón, Anguera, Arnau, Bayés, Caparrós, Carpintero, Carrobles, Cerdá, Coll, Cruz-Hernández, Del Val, Doménech, Fernádez-Ballesteros, Fernandez-Trespalacios, Genovard, Munné, Peiró, Pelechano, Pinillos, Seoane, Siguán, Toro, and Yela. Spanish lecturers went abroad for further training, while foreign psychologists were asked to lecture in Spain—among them Brengelmann, Cautela, Eysenck, Fraisse, Gormezano, Kanfer, Liberman, Mahoney, Meichenbaum, Mussen, Richelle, Stambach, and Wolpe.

At the beginning of the 1980s, many topics were being pursued by Spanish psychologists. Pinillos and Seoane were working on theoretical and epistemological aspects of psychology. Siguán was involved with problems arising from bilingualism. Genovard was interested in highly gifted children. Amón, Doménech, Riba, Yela, and Jáñez were trying to establish the foundations of mathematical psychology. Pelechano was the driving force behind much work on the so-called psychology of intervention. Fernández-Ballesteros dealt with problems arising from assessment, and Arnau did the same with experimental design. Carpintero and Peiró systematically used bibliometric technics. Fernández-Trespalacios and García-Hoz were carrying out research on conditioning. Morgado used intracranial electric stimulation in research, following techniques mainly developed by Rodríguez-Delgado. Burillo, Torregrosa, Ridruego, Ibañez, and Munné were trying to define the field of social psychology. And Bayés, Toro, and Penzo were working on health psychology.

The last fifteen years of the twentieth century have been marked by a considerable expansion in Spanish psychology. Degrees in psychology are offered by more than twenty universities, most of them public universities, with many PhD programs in psychology. As a result, by the end of the century there will be more than 30,000 licensed psychologists in the country. In 1980, there were only five full professors in psychology at the Spanish universities; twenty years later this figure exceeds one hundred.

The dominant behaviorist influence in the seventies and earlier eighties was followed by a dominance of cognitive psychology (Delclaux, De Vega, Mayor, Riviere, Seoane, Tudela). Recently, an important sector of psychologists—basic and applied—are increasing the importance of the field of emotions (Páez, Moltó, Vila).

The fields of research and application have expanded from health psychology (Carrobles, Costa, Echeburua, Labrador, Rodríguez Marín, Saldaña) and sport psychology (Buceta, Capdevila, Cruz, Riera, Roca) to forensic psychology (Garrido, Munné, Redondo) and traffic psychology (Montoro, Tortosa). Interdisciplinary areas, such as psycho-oncology (Blasco, Die-Trill, Font, lbañez) and psychoneuroimmunology (Borrás) are also developing and, in a growing number of hospitals, psychologists are included in the palliative care teams (Comas, Schröder). Spanish psychologists are now working on topics such as adherence to the new AIDS antiretroviric drugs (Ferrer, Tuldá), anorexia and bulimia (Cervera, Raich, Toro), addictive behaviors (Becoña, Gil Roales-Nieto, Marín, Salvador), counseling (Arranz, Bimbela, García-Huete, Martorell), burnout (Cano, Fernández, González-Barrón, Tobal), death coping (Barbero, Barreto, Bayés, Limonero), risk behaviors (Blanco, Páez, Portell), and so on.

In 1992, the Spanish journal *Evaluacion Psicología* became *The European Journal of Psychological Assessment* and, before 1996, some important English and American assessment instruments in health psychology were adapted to Spanish populations and edited by Badía, Salamero, Alonso, and Ollé.

REFERENCES

Applied Psychology: An International Review. (1994). Monograph number on contemporary psychology in Spain. *Autor, 43*(2).

Badía, X., Salamero. M., Alonso, J., & Ollé, A. (1996). *La medida de la salud. Guia de escalas de medicion en espanol.* Barcelona: Promociones y Publicaciones Universitarias.

Huarte de San Juan, J. (1991). *Examen de ingenios para las ciencias.* Madrid: Espasa-Calpe. (Original work published 1575)

Lafuente, G. (1982). La psicología de Giner de los Ríos y sus fundamentos krausistas. *Revista de Historia de la Psicología, 3* (3), 247–269.

Prieto, J. M., Fernández-Ballesteros, R., & Carpintero, H. (1994). Contemporary psychology in Spain. *Annual Review of Psychology, 45,* 51–78.

Ullmann, L. P., & Krasner, L. (1975). A *psychological approach to abnormal behavior* (2nd ed.). Englewood Cliffs, NJ: Prentice-Hall.

Watson, F. (1915). The father of psychology. *Psychological Review, 22,* 333–353.

Watson, R. I. (1974–76). *Eminent contributors to psychology* (Vol. I and II). New York: Springer.

Wundt, W. (1874). *Grudzüge der physiologischen psychologie.* Leipzig: Engelman.

R. BAYÉS SOPENA
Universidad Autónoma de Barcelona

SPATIAL MEMORY

One of the most challenging questions for contemporary neuroscience is to understand the mechanisms by which the brain processes, encodes, and stores information. In this respect, our understanding of memory has considerably improved in the last two decades. Although such progress is largely due to our increased ability to obtain accurate functional images of the human brain, it has also greatly benefited from the use of animal models. Animal models allow us not only to tackle the problem of memory from a comparative perspective, but also to raise empirical issues which cannot be addressed in humans.

Spatial memory is a model of memory that is currently very popular. One reason is that spatial memory is ubiquitous. Almost every action takes place in space and requires some form of spatial memory. Another reason is that it can easily be studied in animals which often have outstanding spatial capabilities. Consider, for instance, the memory capabilities of food-storing birds. During autumn, many birds store seeds that they retrieve later on (often several months after the storing episode) when the environment does not provide the necessary amount of fresh food. An individual bird will store hundreds of food items in numerous caches scattered throughout its home range. Retrieving these food caches will depend at least partly on the bird's memory for their locations. For example, laboratory experiments show that Clark's nutcrackers show excellent retention of many spatial locations over time periods greater than nine months. Other observations suggest that scrub jays remember more than just spatial locations. They also remember what type of food has been cached and whether or not it is perishable (see Clayton, 1998 for a review).

Such capabilities are not unique to birds since they are found in many rodents as well. For example, laboratory rats perform very well on the radial maze, a memory task in which they have to gather food at the end of the arms of a radial maze. As arms depleted of food are not refilled with bait, rats learn to avoid locations that have already been visited. To do so, they form a memory of depleted arms, based on a representation of the food locations relative to the configuration of visual cues within the testing environment (Roitblat, 1987). Rats are also very proficient at another spatial task, the water maze navigation task, in which they must find a safe platform in a pool filled with water. As the start position is changed from trial to trial and the platform is not visible, the animal cannot apply rigid solutions to the problem. Instead, it must rely on the visual cues located outside the swimming pool so as to infer the platform location. Rats quickly learn to swim directly towards the platform, even when novel start points are used. Thus, they learn the platform location relative to the environment and are able to plan direct paths, whatever their current location.

Other studies suggest that the rat's spatial memory is not limited to single locations but encompasses the general structure of space. Such "cognitive maps" allow rats to use efficient novel paths when the circumstances require it: for example, they can make detours when previously available paths are blocked (Poucet, 1993). Although cognitive maps contain much information, they do not provide an exact copy of the real environment. Metric relationships are often distorted and some studies show that the stored information is specific to certain classes of spatial relationships. In general, overall geometry is privileged over the absolute position of objects (Gallistel, 1990).

Since rats remember various aspects of their spatial environment, it seems natural to look for the brain processes that underlie this ability. One locus which has received much attention in the recent years is the hippocampal formation, a structure which lies below the cortex in mammals.

Damage to the hippocampal formation induces dramatic and permanent deficits in a wide variety of spatial abilities. For instance, rats with such lesions are impaired in the water maze navigation task and have an impaired spatial memory in the radial maze. Their spatial patterns of exploration are also strongly altered following hippocampal damage, and they fail to detect spatial changes in a familiar environment (see Poucet & Benhamou, 1997 for a review). However, the critical evidence for the spatial function of the hippocampal formation is the existence of cells that carry a spatial signal. Such cells can be classified as "place cells" and "head direction cells." Place cells are found in the hippocampus proper. A place cell fires rapidly when the rat is in a restricted portion of the environment independent of the animal's heading, and is usually silent elsewhere (O'Keefe, 1976). Each place cell has its own specific firing location. Head direction cells are primarily found in the postsubiculum, an area closely related to the hippocampus. The firing pattern of head direction cells depends only on the heading of the animal, independent of its location (Taube, 1998). Each head direction cell has its own specific preferred firing direction. Both head direction cells and place cells share many properties, including being under the control of visual and idiothetic (motor-related) inputs. Thus, the two types of cells have access to the same information, and form a tightly connected functional neural network which provides the animal with information about both its location and its heading. Their cooperative function is hypothesized to allow the rat to navigate efficiently in its current environment.

Interestingly, cells that carry somewhat similar spatial signals have been found in the hippocampus of nonhuman primates, suggesting a comparable function in higher species (Ono, Nakamura, Nishüo, Eifuku, 1993). In addition, recent evidence, based on functional neuroimaging of brain activity during navigation in familiar yet complex virtual reality environments, suggests that the human hippocampus also plays a special role in spatial navigation.

Activation of the right hippocampus is strongly associated with knowing accurately where places are located and navigating between them (Maguire et al., 1998). This finding bears a direct relation to animal studies and supports the hypothesis that the role of the hippocampal formation in spatial memory should be extended to other mammal species including humans. Further work will be necessary, however, to understand how the hippocampal formation interacts with other structures which are important for the representation of spatial information such as the posterior parietal cortex (Thinus-Blanc, 1996).

REFERENCES

Clayton, N. S. (1998). Memory and the hippocampus in food-storing birds: A comparative approach. *Neuropharmacology, 37,* 441–452.

Gallistel, C. R. (1990). *The organization of learning.* Cambridge: MIT Press.

Maguire, E. A., Burgess, N., Donnett, J. G., Frackowiak, R. S. J., Frith, & C. D., & O'Keefe, J. (1998). Knowing where and getting there: A human navigation network. *Science, 280,* 921–924.

O'Keefe, J. (1976). Place units in the hippocampus of the freely moving rat. *Experimental Neurology, 51,* 78–109.

Ono, T., Nakamura, K., Nishijo, H., & Eifuku, S. (1993). Monkey hippocampal neurons related to spatial and nonspatial functions. *Journal of Neurophysiology, 70,* 1516–1529.

Poucet, B. (1993). Spatial cognitive maps in animals: New hypotheses on their structure and neural mechanisms. *Psychological Review, 100,* 163–182.

Poucet, B., & Benhamou, S. (1997). The neuropsychology of spatial cognition in the rat. *Critical Reviews in Neurobiology, 11,* 101–120.

Roitblat, H. L. (1987). *Introduction to comparative cognition.* New York: Freeman.

Taube, J. S. (1998). Head direction cells and the neurophysiological basis for a sense of direction. *Progress in Neurobiology, 55,* 225–256.

Thinus-Blanc, C. (1996). *Animal spatial cognition: Behavioral and neural approaches.* Singapore: World Scientific.

B. POUCET
Centre National de la Recherche Scientifique, Marseille

HIPPOCAMPUS
MEMORY
NEURAL MECHANISMS OF LEARNING

SPEARMAN, CHARLES EDWARD (1863–1945)

Charles Edward Spearman came to psychology relatively late in life. As a youth, he entered a career in the military service, which he referred to many years later as "the mistake of my life . . . for these almost wasted years I have since mourned as bitterly as ever Tiberius did for his lost legions" (Spearman, 1930, p. 300). Having attained the rank of major, he retired from the British army at the age of 34, and thenceforth devoted himself completely to academic studies, except for a brief return to service during the Boer War. His first love, philosophy, along with his scientific and mathematical bent, led him to psychology, in which he earned the PhD degree at Leipzig, under Wilhelm Wundt. After further study of psychology in Germany, under Kulpe and Müller, Spearman, at the age of 40 returned to London. There, on the recommendation of William McDougall, he was appointed reader in psychology at the University of London. Soon after, when McDougall moved to Oxford, Spearman succeeded him as professor of psychology at London; he held that chair for 25 years, and was succeeded by Sir Cyril Burt.

Spearman claimed Wundt and Galton as the major influences and inspiration for his psychological research. The importance of his own contributions to cognitive and differential psychology and psychometrics can hardly be exaggerated. His first important article on "General intelligence" (1904) is a landmark in the psychology of human abilities. He had discovered that individual differences on all tests of mental abilities, however diverse the knowledge and skills they call upon, are positively intercorrelated in representative samples of the general population. Spearman's predecessors had failed to make this important discovery, although they had tried, because they did not take into account the effect of measurement error (i.e., unreliability) on the correlation between tests. To solve this problem, Spearman invented the method for correcting the correlation coefficient for attenuation (i.e., weakening of the correlation because of unreliability of the correlated measurements). His discovery of consistently positive intercorrelations among diverse tests of mental abilities inspired his well-known two-factor theory: Every mental test measures a general ability, g, common to all tests, and a specific ability, s, peculiar to each test. Spearman developed a mathematical procedure, factor analysis, that permitted a rigorous test of the two-factor theory and, more important, made it possible to estimate precisely the correlation (or "factor loading") of each test in a battery of tests with the g factor. Spearman regarded g as the *sine qua non* of intelligence tests. He characterized the g factor as a capacity for grasping relationships ("the eduction of relations and correlates") and abstraction. Further empirical studies eventually forced Spearman to recognize that his two-factor theory was too simple and that other abilities ("group factors") besides g could be found in batteries of diverse tests. He conceived of g theoretically as the overall level of "mental energy" that a person could bring to bear in performing a cognitive task; other abilities were viewed as independent specialized "engines" for the performance of certain types of tasks. The theory is most fully explicated in Spearman's most famous work, *The abilities of man*, which ranks among the classics of psychology. But the development of factor analysis, aside from any theoretical interpretation of the factors themselves, is now generally recognized as Spearman's greatest contribution. His other enduring contributions to psychometric methodology are the correction of correlation for attenuation, the rank-order correlation coefficient, and the exact formulation of the relationship of test reliability to the length of the test (known as the Spearman–Brown prophesy formula).

Spearman himself valued his first book on the *Nature of Intelligence* the most highly of all his efforts. It established him as the first major cognitive theorist. In it, he expressed his faith that: "Cognitive events do, like those of physics, admit throughout of being reduced to a small number of definitely formulatable principles in the sense of ultimate laws" (Spearman, 1923, p. 341). The three basic "noegenetic" laws of cognition propounded by Spearman concern the apprehension of experience and the education of relations and correlates. Although these principles are closely linked to Spearman's theory of intelligence, the most enduring aspect of his theory is the g factor in all cognitive tests. As g is a large source of individual differences that cannot be described in terms of any particular knowledge or skills required by the diverse tests that reflect g, its theoretical explanation continues to challenge present-day cognitive psychologists.

A. R. JENSEN
University of California, Berkeley

SPECIES-SPECIFIC BEHAVIOR

Many behavioral patterns of nonhuman animals are characteristic of all appropriate members of the species and develop in the absence of specific learning experiences. These patterns are sometimes referred to as species-specific behavior. However, there are various conceptual traps when dealing with species-specific behavioral patterns, so some sharpening of definitions and explorations of their implications are appropriate.

The term may be used in a broad or narrow sense. In the broad sense, species-specific behavior refers to the behavior displayed by all or most members of a species when reared and tested under appropriate conditions. Some researchers, however, use the term in a narrower sense, restricting it to patterns that characterize a particular species and no other. Such behavioral patterns are *specific* to the species in the much more real sense that they are exclusive to the species. An example would be the songs of many species of birds that provide us with reliable cues as to their species identity. Some researchers would use the terms *species-characteristic* or *species-typical* when referring to behavior that is species-specific in the broader sense (i.e., characteristic of the species under study but perhaps of other species as well).

DEVELOPMENT

One of the conceptual traps related to species-specific behavior relates to its development. The term often has been used as an alternative to innate or instinctive. The European ethologists often referred to such patterns as fixed-action patterns. All of these terms have excess meaning with respect to the nature of the factors important in the development of the behavior. They may suggest to the reader that the environment is unimportant in the development of the behavior. *Species-specific* is more neutral and sometimes has been preferred for that reason.

According to contemporary views, development entails epigenetic processes, suggesting that all behavior is the product of the continuous and dynamic interaction of the developing organism, its genotype, and the environment. The environment is as important for the development of the organism and its species-specific behavior as for any other behavioral patterns. What is unusual about many species-specific behavioral patterns is that they do not require specific input for the behavioral pattern that will develop.

An example may help clarify the last point. In the breeding season, male sticklebacks, small fish that breed in brackish water, develop a red belly. Males defend a territory against other males that intrude into it. By contrast, they display courtship behavior toward approaching females, whose distended undersides suggest that they are gravid. The red belly and distended underside are key stimuli used by the resident male in directing the appropriate behavior at intruders of various types. The development of these patterns is critically dependent on the environment. The organism and its genes interact with the environment as the animal matures. Visual input may be necessary for proper functioning of the visual system, critical to the behavior. Exercise may be critical for the proper development of the muscles used in the behavior. The animal and its behavior are products of both genes and environment. However, what is remarkable about the development of many species-specific behavioral patterns is that the animal does not require specific experience. The male stickleback that develops in an appropriate environment reacts appropriately to intruders with red versus distended bellies the first time he encounters them. He does not have to learn these characteristics. It is in this sense that the behavior develops as the product of dynamic interaction between genes and environment but is not dependent on specific input.

Another example is provided by the patterns of copulatory behavior in different species of rodents. These patterns differ among related species with respect to fairly stable characteristics (Dewsbury, 1975). For example, the pattern of a grasshopper mouse, *Onychomys leucogaster,* is different from that of a deer mouse, *Peromyscus maniculatus.* There are many environmental manipulations that can affect both whether or not an animal mates, and if so, the timing and frequency of various events in the sequences of the two species. However, there is no known manipulation that qualitatively alters the species-specific pattern: of those male grasshopper mice that mate, all mate like grasshopper mice and all deer mice mate like deer mice.

Some researchers believe that to call a behavioral pattern innate or instinctive suggests that it is preformed and need only unfold according to some predetermined plan, rather than developing via dynamic organism–gene–environment interactions. It is for these reasons that they prefer the term species-specific.

SPECIES

Another conceptual trap surrounding the concept of species-specific behavior concerns what is meant by *species.* If the concept of species-specific is to be clear, so must be the concept of species. Our common-sense conception of species is both typological and morphological. Members of a species are often thought of as all being of some ideal type, and the type is thought of structurally. Thus one distinguishes between cardinals and bluejays on the basis of their appearance and thinks of them as representations of

ideal type specimens. A more biological concept defines a species as a group of animals capable of interbreeding among themselves under natural conditions but reproductively isolated from individuals that belong to different species. Thus species are conceptualized in relation to the possibility of reproduction in nature, rather than structure. It is important that this refers only to natural conditions; lions and tigers can produce ligers and tiglons in zoos, but they would not do so if placed together in nature. The most critical aspect of this conception is that members of a species may look very different but still belong to the same species, if they are part of a potentially unified reproductive group. In some species, the males and females may look so different that they were previously classified as belonging to different species. In others, developmental stages, such as metamorphosis, may render them unrecognizable as members of the same species unless individuals are followed longitudinally. All are members of the species; there is no ideal type.

Application of the biological species concept to the problem of species-specific behavior enables one to make further refinements. Species-specific behavior is characteristic of all *appropriate* members of the species. Some species-specific patterns may be characteristic only of males or females. This is true of territorial defense in sticklebacks. Other patterns may appear only under particular conditions. Behavior may be different during the breeding season from behavior at other times of the year. Behavior may be changed radically as animals metamorphose through different developmental stages. All of these kinds of behavioral patterns may be regarded as species-specific characteristics, as long as one remembers that they are displayed only by the appropriate animals and only under the appropriate conditions.

TAXONOMY

Although species are defined in relation to reproductive activities, individuals usually are classified on the basis of structure. Species-specific behavioral patterns can be so characteristic of a species as to be useful in determining the appropriate relationships among closely related species. Characteristics are said to be homologous when they constitute a resemblance between two species that can be explained by descent from a common ancestor possessing the character in which they are similar to each other. Thus the wings of all species of bats are homologous to those of all other bat species, but are not homologous with the wings of birds or insects, which evolved in different lineages.

In general, species that are more closely related evolutionarily have more homologous characteristics, including species-specific behavioral patterns. These can be useful in classifying species that are difficult to classify using morphological criteria. For example, some species of fireflies cannot be told apart on the basis of appearance, but display different courtship patterns and are reproductively isolated from each other. They are thus good, biological species, but can be classified only on the basis of their species-specific behavior. Ethologist Konrad Lorenz (1941) developed a taxonomy of the Anatidae, ducks and geese, based on shared behavioral patterns. Because the resulting diagram resembled an old-fashioned shaving brush, it sometimes is referred to as the shaving-brush model.

By classifying and comparing the motor patterns used by different species of snakes when applying constrictive coils to prey, Greene and Burghardt (1978) showed these patterns to fit a consistent pattern through the evolution of closely related species. A single pattern was displayed by members of 48 species in four different primitive families, suggesting that the pattern evolved no later than the early Paleocene. Such findings provide support for more traditional systems of classification and reveal the precise structure of the pattern found in the evolution of behavioral patterns. They also reveal how specific species-specific behavior can be.

SOME EXAMPLES

Two more examples may help to sharpen these ideas. The songs of many species of birds are species-specific, even in the narrow sense of the term. The ontogeny of birds' songs, however, differs greatly among different species. The songs of some of the more primitive, or suboscine, species, appear to be innate, in the sense that no specific input is required for the development of normal song. Thus willow flycatchers and alder flycatchers taken from the nest at a very early age and isolated in the laboratory come to sing normal, species-characteristic songs (Kroodsma, 1984). By contrast, in the more advanced oscine songbird species there is a more complex interplay between nature and nurture. Thus if a young male white-crowned sparrow is to learn its song from a tape recording played to it, it must hear the song during a critical period that occurs between about 10 and 50 days of age (Marler, 1970). The song must resemble the species-specific song or else it will be without effect. The young sparrow does not sing at this age. When it does begin to sing, 2 to 6 months later, it need not hear other birds sing, but it must hear itself. There is thus a dynamic interaction among genes, environment, and organism in song learning and specific input must be present for the development of normal song. The period for learning is greatly extended if a live, rather than taped, tutor is used.

Another example is provided by so-called species-specific defense reactions (SSDRs) (Bolles, 1970). Psychologists have long been interested in how animals learn to avoid noxious stimuli. The idea behind SSDRs is that such "learning" does not occur gradually and incrementally, as often has been thought. Rather the test situation triggers the release of a set of SSDRs that the species has evolved for use in such situations. If the demands of the task are compatible with the species' SSDRs, improved performance will occur quickly. If not, however, it may take a very long time for the animal to learn the task. Faced with dangerous situations in nature, an animal does not have hundreds of trials in which to learn an appropriate response, as are required in many laboratory tasks. Its species-specific behavioral patterns allow it to respond quickly and to survive.

CONCLUSIONS

Many behavioral patterns are characteristic of all appropriate members of a species. Some are so specific as to be characteristic only of members of that species. The latter clearly are species-specific. The former may be referred to as species-specific, species-

characteristic, or species-typical depending on one's definitions. It is important to remember, however, that even though these behavioral patterns are common in virtually all appropriate members of a species, they have complex ontogenetic patterns that are the result of dynamic developmental relationships.

REFERENCES

Bolles, R. C. (1970). Species-specific defense reactions and avoidance learning. *Psychological Review, 77,* 32–48.

Dewsbury, D. A. (1975). Diversity and adaptation in rodent copulatory behavior. *Science, 190,* 947–954.

Greene, H. W., & Burghardt, G. M. (1978). Behavior and phylogeny: Constriction in ancient and modern snakes. *Science, 200,* 74–77.

Kroodsma, D. E. (1984). Songs of the alder flycatcher (*Empidonax alnorum*) and willow flycatcher (*Empidonax trailii*) are innate. *The Auk, 101,* 13–34.

Lorenz, K. Z. (1941). Vergleichende Bewegungsstudien an Anatinen. *Supplement, Journal of Ornithology, 89,* 194–294.

Marler, P. (1970). A comparative approach to vocal learning: Song development in white-crowned sparrows. *Journal of Comparative and Physiological Psychology Monograph, 71*(2), 1–25.

SUGGESTED READING

Dewsbury, D. A. (1978). *Comparative animal behavior.* New York: McGraw-Hill.

Mayr, E. (1963). *Animal species and evolution.* Cambridge, MA: Harvard University Press.

Tinbergen, N. (1951). *The study of instinct.* New York: Oxford University Press.

D. A. Dewsbury
University of Florida

ADAPTATION
EVOLUTION
INSTINCT
RITUAL BEHAVIOR

SPECIFIC HUNGERS

A specific hunger is an increased preference for foods that contain a specific nutrient, such as a mineral or a vitamin, generally as a result of increased need for that nutrient. It is distinguished from pica, which is a preference for ingesting something useless or harmful, such as clay.

Specific hungers were first documented by Richter (1943), who found that rats would adaptively modify their intake of carbohydrates, fats, proteins, sodium, calcium, the B vitamins, vitamin E, and others. For example, adrenalectomized rats increase their intake of sodium chloride (NaCI). Parathyroidectomized rats increase their calcium intake. Pregnant and nursing rats increase their intake of proteins and calcium. Later researchers have demonstrated that rats also increase their preference for high-protein diets after a period of protein deficiency (DiBattista & Holder, 1998).

The specific hunger for sodium chloride, unlike other known specific hungers, apparently depends on an innately programmed mechanism that can be triggered by need. When a rat becomes deficient in NaCl, it immediately shows an enhanced preference for foods and liquids containing NaCl or the similar-tasting, but toxic, LiCl (Nachman, 1962). This preference depends on changes in the taste of the salt solution (Scott, 1992) and is greatly weakened after damage to the chorda tympani, the nerve responsible for taste from the anterior tongue (Frankmann, Sollars, & Bernstein, 1996). Anecdotal evidence suggests that humans have similar mechanisms for sodium hunger (Wilkins & Richter, 1940). Thus, the salt craving reported by athletes after extensive sweating or by women after heavy menstrual bleeding probably has a biological basis.

In contrast, other specific hungers develop by trial-and-error learning, and largely by process of elimination (Rozin & Kalat, 1971). For example, if a calcium- or thiamine- (vitamin B_1) deficient rat is offered several foods, one of which contains the needed nutrient, it shows no immediate preference but gradually learns an aversion to the deficient foods and thus a preference for the food containing the nutrient. Similarly, rats on a diet deficient in certain amino acids learn an aversion to that diet, and therefore prefer a new and potentially better diet by a process of elimination (Wang, Cummings, & Gietzen, 1996).

Under some conditions, an animal may develop a preference for a "recovery" food that elevates it above other "safe" foods that did not cause deficiency (Zahorik, 1977). Animals also imitate the food preferences of other animals, which presumably learned adaptive preferences from their own experiences (Galef, 1996).

REFERENCES

DiBattista, D., & Holder, M. D. (1998). Enhanced preference for a protein-containing diet in response to dietary protein restriction. *Appetite, 30,* 237–254.

Frankmann, S. P., Sollars, S. I., & Bernstein, I. L. (1996). Sodium appetite in the sham-drinking rat after chorda tympani nerve transection. *American Journal of Physiology, 40,* R339–R345.

Galef, B. G. (1996). Food selection: Problems in understanding how we choose foods to eat. *Neuroscience and Biobehavioral Reviews, 20,* 67–73.

Nachman, M. (1962). Taste preferences for sodium salts by adrenalectomized rats. *Journal of Comparative and Physiological Psychology, 55,*1124–1129.

Richter, C. P. (1943). The self-selection of diets. In *Essays in biology in honor of Herbert M. Evans* (pp. 501–505). Berkeley, CA: University of California Press.

Rozin, P., & Kalat, J. W. (1971). Specific hungers and poison avoidance as adaptive specializations of learning. *Psychological Review, 78,* 459–486.

Scott, T. R. (1992). Taste: The neural basis of body wisdom. In A. P. Simopoulos (Ed.), *Nutritional triggers for health and in disease* (pp. 1–39). Basel: Karger.

Wang, Y., Cummings, S. L., & Gietzen, D. W. (1996). Temporal-spatial pattern of c-Fos expression in the rat brain in response to indispensable amino acid deficiency: 2. The learned taste aversion. *Molecular Brain Research, 40,* 35–41.

Wilkins, L., & Richter, C. P. (1940). A great craving for salt by a child with cortico-adrenal insufficiency. *Journal of the American Medical Association, 114,* 866–868.

Zahorik, D. M. (1977). Associative and non-associative factors in learned food preferences. In L. M. Barker, M. Best, & M. Domjan (Eds.), *Learning mechanisms in food selection* (pp. 181–199). Waco, TX: Baylor University Press.

J. W. KALAT
North Carolina State University

SPEECH AND HEARING MEASURES

Clinical, industrial, forensic, and research purposes are among those served by speech and hearing measurement. The nature of the tests and procedures used depends upon the purposes of the testing.

SPEECH-LANGUAGE MEASUREMENT

Speech Communication Systems

For purposes such as development of telephone fidelity, speech may be measured by experimental psychologists or engineers in terms of sound wave properties such as frequency, amplitude, and sound waveform. The amount of power given off by a speaker and the distribution of that power over time may also be measured. Licklider (1951) and Miller (1951) have mentioned graphical methods, which use mathematical Fourier analysis of the waveform for analyzing speech into its component frequencies. They have also described the use of electrical methods, such as the sound spectrograph, which notes the changes in intensity-frequency pattern as a function of time. Visual patterns (spectrograms) may be obtained and compared for various words or phrases. The efficacy of speech communication systems may be measured by use of laboratory articulation testing methods. These patterns may be applied by forensic investigators and others for voiceprints, which are unique to each individual. Speech and hearing scientists also use such methods in research.

Physiological Function

Physiological aspects of speech and voice production may be studied by such methods as electrophysiological and cinefluorographic methods. Studies of respiration may be tied to voice production, which requires a flow of air between the vocal bands. With development of more recent technology, magnetic resonance imaging

(MRI), positron emission tomography (PET) scans, and computerized axial tomography (CAT) scans may be used for studies of brain function of various aspects of both normally functioning and disordered speech and hearing activities.

Language

Assessment of language disorders has been discussed by Owens (1995), among others. Some experimental approaches to the measurement of various aspects of verbal context of speech are discussed by Miller (1951), who cites reviews of experimental techniques for a number of other areas of speech and language. Interdisciplinary approaches to child language have been noted by Abrahamsen (1977).

Clinical Assessment of Speech-Language

Evaluation of speech-language function for clinical purposes entails assessment of one or more of a number of sub-areas of speech and language. These sub-areas may include auditory perception for speech and language function; articulation, or phonology (the production of speech sounds); voice, or phonation, and resonance; language perception, processing, and production; and fluency (which includes stuttering). Language and speech recall, memory, and sequencing functions as well as phonological awareness for reading and writing may also be assessed.

Personnel qualified to administer clinical evaluations include certified speech-language pathologists and certified audiologists who have received the Certificate of Clinical Competence (CCC) in speech-language or in audiology from the American Speech-Language-Hearing Association (ASHA).* State licensure may be alternate evidence of qualification. When determining etiology and planning treatment of voice and hearing problems, medical evaluation should always be considered in the assessment plan. Although numerous standardized tests have continued to be developed, because of the variability of cultural and regional norms, speech-language evaluation frequently includes informal assessment by qualified professionals. Clinical assessment of bilingual speakers is a growing area of need, also requiring the services of certified and/or licensed bilingual professionals. Standard texts and assessment manuals in speech-language pathology, such as those by Shipley and McAfee (1998) and Golper (1998), address these matters in detail.

HEARING MEASUREMENT

Measurement of hearing for research purposes has been discussed by Licklider (1951). Electrical responses from the central auditory system yield information that may be of both experimental and clinical interest (Davis & Silverman, 1960). Clinically, standard texts and reference books in audiology, such as those edited by Northern and Downs (1991) and Katz (1994), provide assessment details. Pure-tone audiometers generate vibrations that may be adjusted to vary the intensity (loudness) of tones ranging from low to high frequency (pitches). By indicating when each tone is heard, an individual may be assessed for the threshold of hearing throughout the audible range of frequencies. An audiogram is used to graph the results of the test. Hearing loss, in decibels, is recorded for frequencies tested. The type of hearing loss may then be determined by evaluating the data obtained from audiometric and other clinical tests.

Technological Influences on Applications

Technological development has led to more direct translation of audiogram data into hearing aid design and adjustment to meet individual needs of hard-of-hearing people. Digital, reprogrammable hearing aids have also been developed. Cochlear implants may be used for infants and older individuals in specific cases of extreme deafness. Such implants do not restore hearing but may transmit impulses from certain audible frequencies that, with therapeutic training, may provide assistance in identifying common sounds such as ringing telephones and doorbells. Cochlear implants may also be helpful in teaching oral speech recognition and production to profoundly deaf individuals.

REFERENCES

Abrahamsen, A. A. (1977). *Child language: An interdisciplinary guide to theory and research.* Baltimore: University Park Press.

Davis, H., & Silverman, S. R. (Eds.). (1960). *Hearing and deafness* (Rev. ed.). New York: Holt, Rinehart & Winston.

Golper, L. A. (1998). *Sourcebook for medical speech pathology* (2nd ed.). San Diego: Singular Publishing Group.

Katz, J. (Ed.). (1994). *Handbook of clinical audiology* (4th ed.). Baltimore: Williams & Wilkins.

Licklider, J. C. R. (1951). Basic correlates of the auditory stimulus. In S. S. Stevens (Ed.), *Handbook of experimental psychology.* New York: Wiley.

Miller, G. A. (1951). Speech and language. In S. S. Stevens (Ed.), *Handbook of experimental psychology.* New York: Wiley.

Northern, J. L., & Downs, M. (Eds.). (1991). *Hearing disorders in children* (4th ed.). Baltimore: Williams & Wilkins.

Owens, R. E. (1995). *Language disorders: A functional approach to assessment and intervention* (2nd ed.). Needham, MA: Allyn & Bacon.

Shipley, K. G., & McAfee, J. G. (1998). *Assessment in speech-language pathology: A resource manual* (2nd ed.). San Diego: Singular.

B. B. MATES
City College of New York, City University of New York

---

*American Speech-Language Hearing Association (ASHA), 10801 Rockville Pike, Rockville, MD, 20852–3279; telephone (301) 897–5700; Internet: http://www.asha.org

MEASUREMENT
PSYCHOPHYSICS

SPEECH DEVELOPMENT

Until the 1960s, most students of speech–language development viewed the child as a relatively passive learner, hearing and absorbing the language patterns of older speech emitters. Two "insights" (Dale, 1972) have changed this viewpoint. The first is that children speak their own languages, with their own sets of rules and patterns. A child's speech is *not* merely a garbled simplification of the language of adults. Second, children must be their own linguists, listening to the speech of others and hypothesizing the rules of language. They then test those hypotheses by using them to try to understand the speech of others and to formulate their own speech. This hypothesis formulation and testing is evident when a child says, "We buyed ice cream." The hypothesis here is that all past tenses are formed by the addition of *ed.* The hypothesis is then likely to be disconfirmed by a reaction the child gets from someone (probably an adult or older child) who hears the statement.

The acquisition of language, occurring as it does to a great extent as an unplanned and unorganized process (Falk, 1973), seems so natural that it is not commonly thought of as unusual or remarkably complex. Yet the rapidity of speech and language learning is unmatched by the acquisition rate for other kinds of cognitive learning, despite the complexity and abstractness of linguistic structure. According to McNeill (1966), "Grammatical speech does not begin before one-and-one-half years of age; yet, as far as we can tell, the basic process is complete by three-and-one-half years. Thus a basis for the rich and intricate competence of adult grammar must emerge in the short span of twenty-four months."

STAGES OF DEVELOPMENT

The development of speech in young children typically follows a sequential pattern. What varies is the *rate* at which each child progresses through the various stages. Occasionally children move so quickly through a stage that they appear to have skipped it altogether. The *prelanguage* stage extends through the first year of life, and encompasses the cooing and babbling periods. Usually during the third month of life, the child moves out of the crying-noises-only stage into the cooing stage. By the fifth month, most children are at the babbling stage, producing an increased variety of sounds. There is no convincing evidence that cooing and babbling are in any way essential to subsequent speech development. In the later months of the babbling stage, the child's linguistic environment begins to assert itself, so the babbling slowly takes on some of the intonational characteristics of the language to which the child is exposed.

The child's first words normally appear around the beginning of the second year of life. This begins the *holophrastic* stage, when the child uses single words, usually meant to convey the meaning of a whole (if short) sentence. "Mommy" means variously "Take me, Mommy," "Where is Mommy?"—or almost anything else related to the mother.

At age 18 to 20 months, the child begins to put words together. New combinations appear with increasing frequency, and the repertory burgeons. These early efforts to communicate by combining words result in *telegraphic speech,* which is effective despite the lack of articles, prepositions, affixes, and other formative aspects of language. Of that period when children first begin to combine words, Dale (1972) says, "In the sense that language is essentially a means for expressing an unlimited number of ideas with a limited system, this is the true beginning of language." Wood (1976) notes that while acquisition of syntax begins at about 18 months, the syntax learning process continues through elementary school, and she delineates six stages in that process.

THEORETICAL CONSIDERATIONS

Researchers, theorists, and students of speech and language development have tended to divide into two basic camps in the search for answers to some vexing fundamental questions. The division follows the lines of the durable nature–nurture issue. On the one side are the empiricists, generally committed to the concept of language as a learned skill. The behaviorists among them maintain essentially that children are reinforced for certain behaviors and that their speech is patterned accordingly. The paradigm is that children respond to some stimulus and adults selectively reinforce their responses. Another empiricist viewpoint is that language is learned as children imitate the speech models to which they are exposed. Some empiricists believe that contextual generalization is the basis for language learning. Thus a child may hear "Go home," "Go potty," and so on, and then use other nouns in this context.

Contrasted with this is the rationalist position, which assumes some innate knowledge of the basic structure of language. The rationalists maintain that the ease and speed with which children progress in language development can come about only through some genetic bioprogramming. Thus each child is born with a basic linguistic system according to this viewpoint, and it causes language to develop much more quickly and thoroughly than it could in the absence of that facilitating genetic mechanism. Bickerton (1982) supports the general rationalist position on the basis of conclusions from his studies of Creole languages.

REFERENCES

Bickerton, D. (1982). *Roots of language.* Ann Arbor, MI: Karoma.

Dale, P. S. (1976/1972). *Language development: Structure and function* (2nd ed.). New York: Holt.

Falk, J. S. (1973). *Linguistics and language.* Lexington, MA: Xerox.

McNeill, D. A. (1966). Developmental psycholinguistics. In F. Smith & G. A. Miller (Eds.), *The genesis of language: A psycholinguistic approach.* Cambridge, MA: MIT Press.

Wood, B. S. (1976). *Children and communication.* Englewood Cliffs, NJ: Prentice-Hall.

SUGGESTED READING

Chomsky, N. (1965). *Aspects of the theory of syntax.* Cambridge, MA: MIT Press.

Chomsky, N. (1968). *Language and the mind.* New York: Harcourt, Brace & World.

MacGinitie, W. M. (1969). Language development. In R. L. Ebel (Ed.), *Encyclopedia of educational research.* New York: Macmillan.

McCarthy, D. (1954). Language development in children. In L. Carmichael (Ed.), *Manual of child psychology.* New York: Wiley.

Skinner, B. F. (1957). *Verbal behavior.* New York: Appleton-Century-Crofts.

O. G. JOHNSON
Centennial BOCES, La Salle, Colorado

ACCULTURATION
COMMUNICATION PROCESS
COMMUNICATION SKILLS TRAINING
EARLY CHILDHOOD DEVELOPMENT
HUMAN DEVELOPMENT

SPEECH DISORDERS

Speech is disordered when it interferes with communication, creates a problem for the listener, or causes maladjustment in the speaker. Mistakes occur in the speech of all persons, but the frequency and intensity of these errors do not exceed normal speech patterns in such a way as to be included in the foregoing definition.

Speech disorders are classified into four broad symptom types: (a) rhythm; (b) phonation; (c) articulation; and (d) symbolization (Van Riper, 1947). *Disorders of rhythm* essentially comprise various types of stuttering (stammering). Most modern speech pathologists make no distinction between stuttering and stammering. In this disorder, the flow of speech is interrupted by difficulty encountered at the initial part of a word or by sudden breaks and spasms once the sound begins. Children often begin to stutter at around 3 years of age or when entering school. The pattern usually occurs in the form of repetitions and prolongations of the initial part of the word, although blocks may occur in the middle of longer words. Without undue pressure to speak, the problem ordinarily abates and disappears. When attention is called to children's malfunctioning speech or they are labeled as stutterers, generally then secondary symptoms of avoidance, struggling, and grimacing develop. The speech of cerebral palsied persons often presents itself as a rhythmical disorder of phrasing and lack of air, since speech is produced with great effort.

In disorders of rhythm, anxiety plays a prominent role. Some persons use the symptom to bind anxiety similar to that found in psychophysiological (psychosomatic) disturbances, while in others the anxiety is unbound or free floating, increasing directly with a heightening of blocks or spasms. The relearning and deconditioning of feared situations can be of value in treating the psychological aspects of the problem while reducing the intensity and frequency of stuttering spasms. Many distraction devices and procedures have been employed, including feedback gadgets, but these are apt to supply only temporary relief because the stutterer has not been deconditioned to stressful conflict situations by the use of his or her own resources. Disorders of rhythm are largely psychological in nature, but on occasion they can result from cerebral vascular accidents or neurophysiological disturbances.

Phonation disorders are characterized by disturbances in timbre, intensity, and pitch. Stereotyped inflections, hypernasal sounds, falsettoes, guttural speech, marked foreign accents, and cleft-palate speech all comprise examples of disturbances in phonation. These disorders lend themselves to treatment by a speech correctionist, whereas stuttering, with its highly charged emotional conflicts, may require the services of a professional psychologist knowledgeable in speech pathology or of other individuals with similar training and expertise.

Articulatory disturbances involve patterns where distortion, omission, substitution, and addition of speech sounds are evident. Characteristic illustrations are delayed speech, where a paucity of sounds or unintelligibility prevails; lalling, where sluggish use of the tongue tip occurs; lisping of all varieties (frontal, lingual, lateral, and occluded), when sibilant sounds and the *t* or *d* letters are involved; and baby talk, where infantile letters and sounds continue past the age of 2 to 3 years.

Disorders of symbolization occur largely in aphasia or dysphasia. Expressive problems predominate, although sensory disturbances often influence aphasic speech as well. Words that symbolize others are substituted during the effort to communicate, for example, *hair* may be uttered instead of *comb.* Anatomical physical insults and organic brain disorders may operate in combination with psychological problems, or as an initial cause in and of themselves, to produce symbolic disorders. Aphasia, in particular, is the result of organic brain impairment, most frequently resulting from a cerebral vascular accident.

REFERENCES

Van Riper, C. (1947). *Speech correction.* New York: Prentice-Hall.

SUGGESTED READING

Frederick, C. J. (1982). *Learning theory and stuttering behavior.* Unpublished manuscript.

Sheehan, J. G. (1954). An integration of psychotherapy and speech therapy through a conflict theory of stuttering. *Journal of Speech and Hearing Disorders, 19,* 474–482.

C. J. FREDERICK
University of California, Los Angeles

BIOLOGICAL RHYTHMS
COMMUNICATION PROCESS
EARLY CHILDHOOD DEVELOPMENT

SPENCE, JANET TAYLOR

After receiving her undergraduate degree from Oberlin College in 1945, Janet Taylor entered the graduate program at Yale University with the intent of entering the field of clinical psychology. The following year, she joined the New York State Rotating Internship Program, an experience that showed her that her interests lay in research and other academic pursuits. She then went to the University of Iowa and completed her PhD in 1949. In her doctoral dissertation, supervised by Kenneth Spence, she developed a theory, based on the Hull-Spence behavior theory, in which she proposed that anxiety, as a personality variable, had motivational (drive) properties and that its effects on performance were either facilitating or detrimental, depending on the complexity of the task. She continued this work on the implications of drive theory, which at the time attracted a good deal of attention in the literature, as a member of the psychology faculty at Northwestern University. Although learning theory was supplanted by more cognitively oriented theories in the early 1960s, the empirical phenomena this research revealed remain. Also surviving is the Taylor Manifest Anxiety Scale (TMAS), the measure she developed for her dissertation to assess anxiety as a stable personality characteristic.

After marrying Kenneth Spence and moving with him to the University of Texas at Austin, Janet Taylor Spence expanded her interests to include the motivational and information properties of tangible and symbolic reinforcers in both children and adults. Hers were the first studies to demonstrate that, contrary to the then-common contention that rewards lead to better performance, rewards are complex events and often have detrimental effects.

In the late 1960s, largely in response to the emerging women's movement, Spence, along with her colleague Robert Helmreich, became involved in research related to gender, an involvement that quickly escalated into a second research career. These studies were aimed at investigating a number of conventional beliefs about the differences between men and women, and led in multiple directions: sex-role attitudes, personality differences in agentic and communal characteristics, achievement-related motives, and so forth. Each of these areas of investigation generated a self-report measure (the Spence-Helmreich Attitudes towards Women Scale, the Personality Attributes Questionnaire, and the Work and Family Orientation Questionnaire) that has become highly popular and has taken on a life of its own. One of her abiding interests has been in the ill-defined but pervasive concepts of masculinity and femininity that have long dominated both psychologists' thinking and popular beliefs—namely, that masculinity and femininity represent end-points of a single underlying dimension along which individual men and women can be placed by assessing the degree to which they exhibit specific, gender-stereotypic attributes and behaviors. Her research demonstrated, however, that these sets of gender-differentiating characteristics contribute to many factors, a multidimensional view that is now widely accepted. Based on the concept of gender identity, Spence has offered an alternative view of masculinity and femininity as fundamental phenomenological senses. She has also proposed a theory of their emergence and maintenance throughout the life span that takes into account the fact that males and females differ widely in the constellations of gender-related attributes they display and fail to display.

Spence has also contributed to professional affairs, among other things, serving on the governing boards of the American Psychological Association (APA), the Psychonomic Society, and the American Psychological Society (APS) (of which she was one of the founders). She served as president of APA in 1985, and as president of APS in 1988. She has also been heavily involved in editorial responsibilities, having served as chair of the publication committees of APA and the Psychonomic Society, as a member of editorial boards of a number of journals, and as associate and then editor of *Contemporary Psychology* and as editor of the *Annual Review of Psychology*. For these services, she was given a National Academy of Sciences Award for Scientific Reviewing. Her honors also include honorary doctorates from Oberlin College, the University of Toledo, and Ohio State University. She is also a member of the American Academy of Arts and Sciences.

Spence retired from the University of Texas at Austin in 1997 and in the spring of that year, was honored by a festschrift. The proceedings of the conferences were published in 1998 in the volume *Gender and Gender Roles: The Gender Psychology of Janet Taylor Spence,* published by APA.

STAFF

SPENCE, KENNETH W. (1907–1967)

Over the course of his career, Kenneth W. Spence gained eminence as a theorist, experimentalist, and methodologist, distinctions that resulted in his election to the National Academy of Sciences. He was raised in Montreal, Canada, and received the BA and MA degrees from McGill University. In 1933, he was awarded the PhD degree by Yale University, where he did his dissertation with Robert Yerkes. After appointments at the Yale Laboratories of Primate Biology and the University of Virginia, he moved in 1938 to the University of Iowa, where he remained until 1964. At the time of his death, he was on the faculty at the University of Texas at Austin.

Spence's name was linked throughout his career to that of Clark L. Hull, since his theoretical and experimental contributions represented elaborations and extensions of Hull's general theory of learning and behavior. Although Spence's approach and theoretical views differed from Hull's in significant ways, such as his greater emphasis on motivational processes, both were committed to the development of an objective theory of behavior based on classical and instrumental conditioning.

In collaboration with the philosopher Gustav Bergmann, Spence sought in the philosophy of science and the tenets of logical empiricism the bases on which psychology could proceed as an objective, empirical science. His brand of pragmatic, methodological behaviorism has its roots in the early, rather than later, radical behaviorism of John B. Watson, or, more contemporaneously, of B. F. Skinner. Spence's methodological and metatheoretical interests led him to write several penetrating analyses of competing theories of behavior, in which he sought to discern the similarities as well as the more apparent differences.

His publications include *Behavior Theory and Conditioning,* a book outlining Hull–Spence theory that was based on the Silliman Lectures at Yale, delivered in 1955, and *Behavior Theory and Learning.*

J. T. SPENCE
University of Texas at Austin

SPIELBERGER, CHARLES D.

Charles D. Spielberger is distinguished research professor of psychology, and director of the Center for Research in Behavioral Medicine and Health Psychology at the University of South Florida (USF), where he has been a faculty member since 1972. He previously directed the USF doctoral program in clinical psychology, and was a tenured faculty member at Duke University (1955–1962), Vanderbilt University (1962–1966), and Florida State University (1967–1972), where he was also director of clinical training. A Diplomate in Clinical Psychology of the American Board of Professional Psychology and Distinguished Practitioner of the U.S. National Academies of Practice. He also served as training specialist in psychology at the National Institute of Mental Health (NIMH, 1965–1967) and was a research fellow (1979–1980 and 1985–1986) at The Netherlands Institute for Advanced Study.

Author, co-author, or editor of more than 400 professional publications, Spielberger's current research focuses on anxiety; curiosity; depression; the experience, expression, and control of anger; behavioral medicine and health psychology; job stress and stress management; and the effects of stress, emotions, and lifestyle factors on the etiology of hypertension, cardiovascular disorders, and cancer. His books include *Anxiety and Behavior* (1966); *Contributions to General Psychology* (1968); *Anxiety and Educational Achievement* (1971); *Anxiety: Current Trends in Theory and Research* (1972); *Cognitive and Affective Learning Strategies* (1979); *Police Selection and Evaluation* (1979); *Understanding Stress and Anxiety* (1979); *Anxiety in Sports* (1988); *Cross-Cultural Anxiety* (Volumes 1–4, 1976–1990, with R. Diaz-Guerrero); *Personality Assessment in America* (1992); *Test Anxiety: Theory, Assessment and Treatment* (1995); and the continuing 16-volume research series on *Stress and Emotion* (1975–1996, with I. Sarason).

Spielberger's *State-Trait Anxiety Inventory* (1970, 1983), with translations in 58 languages and dialects, has become a standard international measure of anxiety. He is also author of the State-Trait Anxiety Inventory for Children (1973), the Test Anxiety Inventory (1980), the State-Trait Anger Expression Inventory (1988, 1999), and the Job Stress Survey (1995, 1999). His research contributions have been recognized in the awards he has received from the American Psychological Association (APA; 1993); the APA Divisions of Community Psychology (1982) and Clinical Psychology (1989); the Florida Psychological Association (1977, 1988); the Society for Personality Assessment (1990); and the STAR Lifetime Achievement Award of the International Stress and Anxiety Research Society (1998). He founded the *American Journal of Community Psychology* in 1971, serving as its editor for seven years, and currently serves as associate editor of the *Journal of Occupational Health Psychology, Personality and Individual Differences,* and the *International Journal of Stress Management.* He is also editor of the LEA series *Advances in Personality Assessment* (Volumes 1–10, 1982–1995, with J. Butcher), and two continuing book series, *Clinical and Behavioral and Community Psychology* (with I. Sarason) and *Health Psychology and Behavioral Medicine.*

During 1991 and 1992, Spielberger served as the 100th president of APA. He was APA national treasurer from 1987 to 1990, a member of the APA board of directors from 1987 to 1993, and council representative for three terms (1985–1987; 1993–1998) of

the APA Division of Clinical Psychology. He is currently president of the International Association of Applied Psychology (1998–2002) and the International Stress Management Association (1993–2000); chair of the National Academy of Science's International Psychology Committee (1996–2000); and a member of the APA Policy and Planning Board. He has chaired five APA national committees (Accreditation, Budget, Finance, Elections, International Relations), and served on both the APA Board of Scientific Affairs and Publications and the APA Communications Board. He previously served as chair of the National Council of Scientific Society Presidents and as president of the Society for Personality Assessment, the Society for Test Anxiety Research, the International Council of Psychologists, the APA Divisions of Clinical and Community Psychology, the Southeastern Psychological Association, and Psi Chi (the national honor society in psychology). He is a fellow of Sigma XI, the American Academy of Arts and Sciences, the Society for Behavioral Medicine, the Society for Personality Assessment, and 14 APA Divisions (1, 3, 5, 8, 12, 13, 17, 26, 27, 38, 42, 46, 47, 52). Spielberger is also a member of the Academy of Behavioral Medicine Research, the Psychonomic Society, the Society for Psychophysiological Research, and the New York Academy of Sciences.

STAFF

SPLIT-BRAIN RESEARCH

Systematic split-brain research was initiated by Roger Sperry. A "split-brain" patient or experimental animal is produced when the main connecting link of millions of nerve fibers between the two halves of the cerebral cortex of the brain is severed. This most prominent connecting link is called the corpus callosum. Observations of human patients and experimental animals who had undergone this type of hemispheric disconnection led to little noticeable disruption of brain function. But experiments by Sperry and his associates revealed that the split brain is not entirely normal in its function. For example, it was found in experimental animals that when the corpus callosum was cut, information learned by one side of the brain was not transferred to the other hemisphere. Subsequent studies using visual and touch discriminations and motor learning supported this basic finding (Sperry, 1968).

Sperry and others later studied patients who underwent sectioning of the corpus callosum to prevent the spread of epileptic seizure activity from one hemisphere to another. After this type of brain surgery, split-brain patients seem normal in most aspects of daily life. Their temperament, personality, and general intelligence are seemingly unaffected. However, experiments show that if a picture of an object is presented to the left hemisphere, the patient can find the object with the right hand when it is grouped with several other objects, but not with the left hand. This occurs because the left, or language, hemisphere, which verbally labeled the object (say, as a knife), also controls the right hand. Conversely, left-hand movements are controlled by the nonverbal right hemisphere—hence the difficulty in selecting the unlabeled correct object. The right hemisphere, while lacking language capacity, has proved superior in certain tasks, such as drawing and copying figures and arranging blocks to form geometric designs, and in other nonverbal activities involving musical and artistic abilities (Gazzaniga et al., 1979). Thus there is evidence that the right hemisphere is generally superior to the left in spatial, motor, and other nonverbal activities. Evidence has also accumulated to support the conclusion that the left hemisphere of most human brains is concerned with numerical and analytic as well as the aforementioned linguistic activities. Split-brain research, and other research on hemispheric differences in normal individuals, continues to reveal fascinating new information about functions of the two hemispheres of the brain.

REFERENCES

Gazzaniga, M. S., Steen, D., & Volpe, B. T. (1979). *Functional neuroscience.* New York: Harper & Row.

Sperry, R. W. (1968). Hemisphere deconnection and unity in conscious awareness. *American Psychologist, 23,* 723–733.

J. L. ANDREASSI
City University of New York, Baruch College

BRAIN LATERALITY
LATERAL DOMINANCE
NEUROPSYCHOLOGY

SPORT PSYCHOLOGY

The discipline of sport psychology is dedicated to the investigation of the relationship between psychological factors and sport and exercise. Sport scientists and sport psychologists use physical activity settings to examine issues of competition, performance enhancement, skill acquisition, children's development through sport, team interaction, and the maintenance of physical and mental health.

HISTORY OF SPORT PSYCHOLOGY

In 1897 Triplett, a psychologist and bicycle enthusiast from Indiana University, conducted what is generally considered to be the first empirical sport psychology experiment. He examined the effects of competition on motor performance by observing cyclists performing against the clock, against a standard goal, or against other cyclists in competition. Triplett found that cyclists in competition performed best.

Coleman Griffith is considered the father of North American sport psychology. Griffith is often credited with the founding of the first sport psychology laboratory in 1925 at the University of Illinois. He was known for his rigorous empirical work in psychomotor skill development, learning theory applied to sport, and the role of personality in athletic performance. In addition, he conducted interviews and field observations with elite athletes. In the 1930s he joined the Chicago Cubs professional baseball organization, becoming the first psychologist in professional sports.

Development in the field of sport psychology proceeded slowly until the 1960s, when Ogilvie and Tutko (1966) attempted to integrate psychological assessment and personality theory into sport psychology. They concentrated on the development of a personality test that they hoped would allow them to predict the performance of athletes. While conflicting claims have been made, the effort to predict athletic performance from personality tests has yielded little of value (Whelan, Mahoney, & Meyers, 1991).

While Ogilvie and Tutko were pursuing their personality test work, other researchers (e.g. Richardson, 1967) were exploring imagery or "mental practice" interventions for performance enhancement. However, it was not until 1972 that Suinn brought sport psychology into contact with contemporary clinical psychology. Suinn applied cognitive-behavioral interventions, typically used with clients working to manage stress more effectively, to athletes in an attempt to improve sport performance. He reported that training elite skiers in relaxation and imagery skills, combined with a behavioral rehearsal technique, improved race performance. Based on Suinn's work, "mental practice" interventions for performance enhancement became more intricate, and began to resemble the growing body of cognitively oriented clinical interventions.

CURRENT RESEARCH AND APPLICATIONS

Perhaps the most visible domain of research and application in sport psychology is the use of cognitive and behavioral psychology strategies for athletic performance enhancement. In addition to the use of imagery and mental rehearsal, modern sport psychology encompasses a broad range of interventions directed at improving individual performance.

A major focus of performance enhancement efforts has been on athletes' abilities to manage arousal and anxiety. Many performance enhancement interventions include an anxiety management component intended to allow athletes to increase or decrease their arousal to match the demands of their competitive task. These interventions mirror the anxiety reduction, stress management, and motivational work prevalent with clients experiencing anxiety or depression in the clinical psychology literature.

Sport psychologists are also interested in goal-setting and its effects on performance. This work has largely been taken from industrial-organizational psychology (e.g., Locke & Latham, 1990), where the use of goal-setting strategies has become a reliable behavior change technique. Locke and Latham suggested that goal-setting may enhance the motivation for involvement, and promote more positive self-evaluation of training and competitive performance. These changes may facilitate task performance and therefore lead to performance change.

Kirschenbaum (Kirschenbaum & Bale, 1980) has proposed that an individual's athletic skill development can be viewed as a self-regulatory process, and that athletic performance is a test of the athlete's skill in self-directed cognition and action. Sport psychologists use interventions such as self-monitoring and self-instruction to teach athletes to successfully execute a physical skill, monitor their performance, evaluate their performance against some standard or goal, and alter the execution of physical skills. Such self-regulation processes are intended to enable the athlete to transfer his or her performance improvement skills to other tasks and settings.

Although these performance enhancement intervention strategies should be relevant to athletes of all ages and skill levels, most controlled evaluations of these interventions occur with nonelite athletes and recreational sport participants. A quantitative review of such studies found that these athletic performance enhancement interventions are more effective than control conditions (Whelan, Meyers, & Donovan, 1995).

While performance enhancement is the most visible component of sport psychology, the field is much broader. Another major area of research is that of sport and exercise behavior across the life span. Sport psychologists are interested in physical skill acquisition and development, focusing on such areas as modeling of skills, attention in skill acquisition and performance, and decision-making. Sport psychologists are also interested in children's psychological development through sport, including such areas as children's motivation for participation in sport, why children discontinue participation in sport, stress and burnout, and effective coaching practices in youth sport.

Much of sport and exercise takes place in a group or team context. Thus, sport psychologists are also interested in the dynamics of such groups. Attention in sport psychology is given to examining issues such as what makes a group successful, the development and characteristics of leaders of successful groups, and the development and deterioration of group cohesion.

It is a generally accepted fact that regular participation in sport and exercise enhances an individual's physical health. Sport psychologists also attempt to understand how participating in physical activity affects an individual's psychological well-being. Research in the field has indicated that aerobic exercise is associated with acute, and in many instances, long-term reductions in the exerciser's levels of anxiety and depression. In addition, exercise has shown positive effects on other aspects of emotional life, including increasing feelings of control, improving self-confidence, and improving mental functioning. The psychological and physiological benefits associated with exercise throughout the life span support the increasing importance of exercise as one ages.

A BURGEONING SCIENCE

Exposure at the 1984 Los Angeles Olympic Games brought a dramatic increase in attention to the field of sport psychology. With this attention to sport psychology also came an increase in the professional growth of the field. Several journals dedicated to disseminating information on research and applied activities in the area of sport and exercise psychology were introduced. These journals include *The Journal of Applied Sport Psychology, The Journal of Sport and Exercise Psychology,* and *The Sport Psychologist.*

Several professional organizations are dedicated to the advancement of sport and exercise psychology. The North American sport and exercise psychology organizations include the Association for the Advancement of Applied Sport Psychology, Division 47 of the American Psychological Association, and the North American Society for the Psychology of Sport and Physical Activity. Members of these organizations include psychologists interested in sport and exercise and sport scientists who study psychological influences on sport and physical activity. These organizations provide a professional forum for individuals committed to both empirical and applied components of sport psychology through the dissemination of new and relevant knowledge about research in sport psychology. These organizations are committed to establishing and upholding professional standards for the competent and ethical practice of sport psychology.

CONCLUSION

In his book *Men at Work,* Will (1990) related that, "The day Custer lost at Little Big Horn, the Chicago White Sox beat the Cincinnati Red Legs, 3–2." Will's observation highlights the significant and continuing impact sport has on our culture. Although it has been over a century since the initial empirical investigation of psychological influences on sport behavior, the science and profession of sport psychology are broad and vibrant. Performance enhancement may be the most visible domain of sport psychology, but the field includes the study of children and the elderly, teams and leaders, and physical as well as emotional health. With sport and exercise continuing to play a meaningful role in our culture, the study of these behaviors will continue to have a place in the science and practice of psychology.

REFERENCES

Kirschenbaum, D. S., & Bale, R. M. (1980). Cognitive-behavioral skills in golf: Brain power golf. In R. M. Suinn (Ed.), *Psychology in sports: Methods and application* (pp. 334–343). Minneapolis: Burgess.

Locke, E. A., & Latham, G. P. (1990). *A theory of goal setting and task performance.* Englewood Cliffs, NJ: Prentice Hall.

Ogilvie, B. C. & Tutko, T. A. (1966). *Problem athletes and how to handle them.* London: Pelham.

Richardson, A. (1967). Mental practice: A review and discussion (Part 1). *Research Quarterly, 38,* 95–107.

Triplett, N. (1897). The dyamogenic factors in pacemaking and competition. *American Journal of Psychology, 9,* 507–553.

Suinn, R. M. (1972). Behavioral rehearsal training for ski racers. *Behavior Therapy, 3,* 519–520.

Whelan, J. P., Meyers, A. W., & Donovan, C. (1995). Competitive recreational athletes: A multisystemic model. In S. M. Murphy (Ed.), *Sport psychology interventions* (pp. 71–116). Champaign, IL: Human Kinetics.

Whelan, J. P., Mahoney, M. J., & Meyers, A. W. (1991). Performance enhancement in sport: A cognitive behavioral domain. *Behavior Therapy, 22,* 307–327.

Will, G. F. (1990). *Men at work.* New York: Macmillan.

R. K. MAY
A. W. MEYERS
University of Memphis

HEALTH PSYCHOLOGY

SPOUSE ABUSE

Gelles and Straus (1979) report that between 20 and 40% of all murders in the United States involve domestic relationships. Police reports indicate that the majority of calls for help are from spouses involved in domestic disputes. And a high percentage of police fatalities result from investigation of such domestic disputes. According to Boudouris (1971), 52% of aggravated assaults committed between 1926 and 1968 in Detroit were between husbands and wives. Violence also appears to be a major complaint of spouses seeking a divorce. Levinger (1974) found that 23% of middle class couples and 40% of working class couples gave "physical abuse" as a major complaint relevant to their desire for a divorce. Violence also appears to be common in the average intact U.S. marriage. Straus (1980) surveyed a representative sample of American couples and found that, during the survey year, 12% of the couples reported some violence between spouses. Such findings probably underestimate the actual extent of violence in marriage because of reticence to admit and/or report violence when it occurs between "loved ones." Nevertheless, the research clearly shows that violence is common, if not typical, in marriage.

What is spouse abuse? One person's "love pat" may be "abuse" for another. People who experience marital violence, as well as theorists and researchers, must face this definitional issue. Spouse abuse is usually defined in terms of violence directed at a spouse. Violence is assumed to be physical, relatively severe, and sometimes repeated over time. Verbal abuse, less severe physical acts, and once-in-a-lifetime occurrences may not be considered to be spouse "abuse." In Straus's (1980) research on a representative sample of intact U.S. marriages, he differentiated spouse "beating" from overall violence. Actions such as throwing something, pushing, grabbing, and shoving were considered violence but not spouse beating. Beating was defined as including slapping, kicking, biting, hitting with fists or something else, threatening with knife or gun, and/or using knife or gun.

What causes spouse abuse? Various causes have been hypothesized and studied, including psychopathology, social class, and sex drives. While violent spouses may appear to be crazy at the time of the violence, spouse abusers, with rare exceptions, are not mentally ill (Straus & Hotaling, 1980). Although there is some evidence (Levinger, 1974) that spouse abuse may be more common among lower class than middle class couples, it is not clear that there is a causal relationship (Steinmetz & Straus, 1974). More violence is reported by or about lower class couples, but this may be true because middle class couples tend to have more resources and more privacy, so that violent acts are less likely to involve the authorities or the public record. The fact remains that spouse abuse occurs among all classes of people. Other causal explanations involving biology, violence and sex connections, or sex drive have been generally discounted (Steinmetz & Straus, 1974). Husbands may be more violent, but both husbands and wives resort to violence and are abused (Straus, 1980). Although not necessarily causal, use of alcohol has been found to be related to spouse abuse (Gelles & Straus, 1979). Abuse often follows drinking. Whether drinking is cause or excuse is yet to be determined.

Straus (1980) proposed a more comprehensive theory of spouse abuse causation. According to this theory, the causes of abuse are to be found "in the structure of American society and its family system" (Straus, 1980, p. 33), and include such factors as a high level of family conflict, high level of violence in society, family socialization to violence (children's experience of physical punishment and observation of parents' violence against each other), cultural norms legitimizing violence, sexual inequality, and coping resources of women.

What keeps spouses in abusive marriages? Wives generally report four factors: economic dependency, presence of young children, fear of living alone, and perceived stigma of divorce (Roy, 1977). Severity and frequency of violence, history of physical punishment in childhood, and relative resources and power also are factors related to wives remaining with abusive husbands (Gelles, 1976).

REFERENCES

Boudouris, J. (1971). Homicide and the family. *Journal of Marriage and the Family, 33,* 667–676.

Gelles, R. (1976). Abused wives: Why do they stay? *Journal of Marriage and the Family, 38,* 659–668.

Gelles, R. J., & Straus, M. A. (1979). Determinants of violence in the family: Toward a theoretical integration. In W. R. Burr, R. Hill, F. I. Nye, & I. L. Reiss (Eds.), *Contemporary theories about the family.* New York: Free Press.

Levinger, G. (1974). Physical abuse among applicants for divorce. In S. K. Steinmetz & M. A. Straus (Eds.), *Violence in the family.* New York: Dodd, Mead.

Roy, M. (1977). A current survey of 150 cases. In M. Roy (Ed.), *Battered women.* New York: Van Nostrand Reinhold.

Steinmetz, S. K., & Strans, M. A. (Eds.). (1974). *Violence in the family.* New York: Dodd, Mead.

Straus, M. A. (1980). Wife-beating: How common and why? In M. A. Straus & G. T. Hotaling (Eds.), *The social causes of husband–wife violence.* Minneapolis, MN: University of Minnesota Press.

Straus, M. A., & Hotaling, G. T. (Eds.). (1980). *The social causes of husband–wife violence.* Minneapolis, MN: University of Minnesota Press.

J. W. ENGEL
University of Hawaii

BATTERED PEOPLE
CHILD ABUSE
CRISIS INTERVENTION
TANTRUMS

SPOUSE SELECTION

The choice of a spouse is the first, and may be the most potent, step in the chain of events that eventually leads to success or failure in marriage. In a society that places high values on individualism (Green, 1941), we are inclined to believe that we choose our spouses on the basis of love-inspired free choice. The average adult has several love affairs before choosing a partner, and love may be secondary to other considerations when the choice is made (Coombs & Kenkel, 1966; Kephart, 1967). Factors such as vocational readiness and the approval of significant others in one's life have great influence upon the decision to marry, and the current companion most closely approximating one's ideal may get the nod as much because of circumstances as for merit (Murstein, 1976).

The question that has interested students of marriage and the family for decades has been: Do opposites attract or do birds of a feather flock together? Review of the data on heterogamy versus homogamy sheds much light on the process and outcome of mate selection.

HETEROGAMY

Winch (1955) has been the most vigorous proponent of the view that courting individuals seek partners whose needs complement rather than duplicate their own. This view is prefigured in the writings of Schopenhauer (1928), who believed that suitors sought mates who had perfections that they lacked, and of Jung (1957), who believed that the masculine *animus* and feminine *anima* dimensions of the personalities of all men and women sought their complements in mates. In this sense, the mating of opposites can be viewed as an implicit contract in which each agrees to interact with the other in ways that compensate for each other's shortcomings to make a more perfect whole (Seyfried & Hendrick, 1973).

While an appealing concept, research has generally failed to support the complementarity hypothesis (Bowerman & Day, 1956; Heiss & Gordon, 1964; Murstein, 1976; Rubin, 1973; Schellenberg & Bee, 1960). Not only have partners been shown to be generally unaware of each other's compensatory strengths (Bolton, 1961), but there has been no support for the notion that complementarities that are serviceable for one sex are equally so for the other (Strauss, 1947) and no formulas have been developed for determining the values that suitors would place on compensatory strengths and weaknesses in any complementarity-determining equation (Rubin, 1973).

HOMOGAMY

While virtually every culture prohibits incest and requires familial exogamy, many subcultural groups prescribe endogamy as a means of preserving the integrity of their social organizations. This may explain the fact that there is a preponderance of evidence showing that suitors are likely to choose partners of their own race, educational level, socioeconomic status, and ethnic subgroup (Udry, 1974). When concessions are made and a party from a higher status group chooses a partner with lower social standing, concessions are usually made in age and beauty, although within strata, men and women typically choose partners with age and appearance characteristics that match their own (Bytheway, 1981; Critelli & Waid, 1980; Murstein, 1972). For example, when higher status men choose lower status wives, their partners are typically younger and more attractive than they are. This is consistent with what

Murstein (1976) has termed an "exchange theory" of mate selection, in which each prospective partner seeks to enhance his or her social and psychological standing by choosing the most outwardly desirable mate possible.

The fact that education and other overt social characteristics do predict mate selection may be explained by the fact that these factors influence the range of potential partners that each suitor will encounter. This "propinquity factor" in mate selection recognizes the fact that residential and occupational segregation strongly determine the field of eligibles one will meet by virtue of time, distance, cost, and opportunity (Morgan, 1981). The fact that religious integration exists at virtually every level of U.S. society may explain the fact that interreligious marriage is fast becoming the norm and, despite its frequent religious consecration, marriage has virtually become a secular institution (Glenn, 1982).

The demographically linked signs of homogamy are fairly easy to distinguish objectively. The less discernible similarity in values, attitudes, and behavior that we tend to seek in friends (Rubin, 1973) have also been shown to be highly valued criteria in the choice of mates (Udry, 1974). The motivation for selecting as intimates those who share one's frame of reference undoubtedly is the resulting ease in achieving consensus on the myriad of decisions that must be made each day, as well as the validation of one's own beliefs and actions. Therefore it is not surprising that literally hundreds of studies have shown that couples appear to display greater consensus as they advance from casual acquaintanceship through marriage (Murstein, 1980). For example, it has been shown that couples share mental health characteristics (Murstein, 1967), such personality characteristics as the intensity of their sensation seeking (Farley & Davis, 1977; Ficher et al., 1981), and a wide variety of personal likes and dislikes (Kerckhoff & Davis, 1962). Unfortunately many of these instances of assumed similarity have been shown to be false for a variety of reasons, and these judgment errors may account in part for high rates of divorce.

Errors in assumed similarity are explained by several factors. First, courtship has been regarded as a time of maximal human deception as each party seeks to gain the other's acceptance by attempting to make the most positive impression possible, often at the price of honesty (Stuart, 1980). Beyond working from faulty data, the processes that courting partners use to organize their impressions of others tend to be more *psychological* than *scientifically* logical, very often leading to false conclusions (Cook, 1979). It has been shown, for example, that observers of others' behavior are likely to draw inferences about enduring traits from isolated events (Monson et al., 1982) and to do so with great confidence (Allen & Potkay, 1981). Inferences are then made that if one trait is present, other presumably related traits must be in evidence as well (Hays, 1958), according to each individual's subjective implicit theory of personality (Wegner & Vallacher, 1977). For example, if Bob breaks a date with Sue on short notice, she is likely to (a) assume that his doing so once means that he will do so often; (b) assume that date breaking is a sign of his characteristic trait of irresponsibility; (c) assume that if he is irresponsible, he is probably also dishonest and careless; and (d) finally conclude that he must be an unworthy suitor. This is clearly an extended chain of inferences and one that is likely to lead to false impressions of similarity or difference on dimensions considered important for each individual's mate-selection efforts.

The choice of partners in marriage has great significance for the stability of societies and their subgroups as well as for the long-term happiness of individuals. Social constraints on opportunities to meet prospective mates and barriers to certain unions considered objectionable are the means through which macrosocial bodies control who will marry whom. Within the pool of eligibles, each person must determine the criteria that he or she will use to select a mate, must gather the data necessary to apply each criterion, and must weigh each datum in an overall go-no-go decision-making matrix. Beyond recognition of the fact that the application of each level of criteria narrows the size of the pool of people considered eligible, little of the precision of decision theory (Hogarth, 1980) has shed light on the precise manner in which decisions are made to marry one person in preference to another at one particular time as opposed to any other time.

REFERENCES

Allen, B. P., & Potkay, C. R. (1981). On the arbitrary distinction between states and traits. *Journal of Personality and Social Psychology, 41,* 916–928.

Bolton, C. D. (1961). Mate selection as the development of a relationship. *Marriage and Family Living, 23,* 234–240.

Bowerman, C. E., & Day, B. R. (1956). A test of the theory of complementarity needs as applied to couples during courtship. *American Sociological Review, 21,* 602–605.

Bytheway, W. R. (1981). The variation with age of age differences in marriage. *Journal of Marriage and Family, 43,* 923–927.

Cook, M. (1979). *Perceiving others: The psychology of interpersonal perception.* London: Methuen.

Coombs, R. H., & Kenkel, W. F. (1966). Sex differences in dating aspirations and satisfaction with computer-selected partners. *Journal of Marriage and the Family, 28,* 62–66.

Critelli, J. W., & Waid, L. R. (1980). Physical attractiveness, romantic love, and equity restoration in dating relationships. *Journal of Personality Assessment, 44,* 624–629.

Farley, F. H., & Davis, S. A. (1977). Arousal, personality, assortative mating in marriage. *Journal of Sex and Marital Therapy, 3,* 122–127.

Ficher, I. V., Zuckerman, M., & Neeb, M. (1981). Marital compatibility in sensation seeking trait as a factor in marital adjustment. *Journal of Sex and Marital Therapy, 7,* 60–69.

Glenn, N. D. (1982). Interreligious marriage in the United States: Patterns and recent trends. *Journal of Marriage and the Family, 44,* 555–556.

Green, A. W. (1941). The 'cult of personality' and sexual relations. *Psychiatry, 4,* 343–348.

Hays, W. L. (1958). An approach to the study of trait implication and trait similarity. In R. Tagiuri & L. Petrullo (Eds.), *Person perception and interpersonal behavior.* Stanford, CA: Stanford University Press.

Heiss, J. S., & Gordon, M. (1964). Need patterns and the mutual satisfaction of dating and engaged couples. *Journal of Marriage and the Family, 26,* 337–339.

Hogarth, R. M. (1980). *Judgment and choice: The psychology of decisions.* New York: Wiley.

Jung, C. G. (1957). *The undiscovered self.* Boston: Little, Brown.

Kephart, W. (1967). Some correlates of romantic love. *Journal of Marriage and the Family, 29,* 470–479.

Kerckhoff, A. C., & Davis, K. E. (1962). Value consensus and need complementarity in mate selection. *American Sociological Review, 27,* 295–303.

Monson, T. C., Keel, R., Stephens, D., & Genung, V. (1982). Trait attributions: Relative validity, covariation with behavior, and the prospect of future interaction. *Journal of Personality and Social Psychology, 42,* 1014–1024.

Morgan, M. (1981). The overjustification effect: A developmental test of self perception interpretations. *Journal of Personality and Social Psychology, 40,* 809–821.

Murstein, B. I. (1967). The relationship of mental health to marital choice and courtship progress: *Journal of Marriage and the Family, 29,* 447–451.

Murstein, B. I. (1972). Physical attractiveness and marital choice. *Journal of Personality and Social Psychology, 22,* 8–12.

Murstein, B. I. (1976). *Who will marry whom? Theories and research in marital choice.* New York: Springer.

Murstein, B. I. (1980). Mate selection in 1970. *Journal of Marriage and the Family, 42,* 777–795.

Rubin, Z. (1973). *Liking and loving.* New York: Holt, Rinehart & Winston.

Schellenberg, J. A., & Bee, L. S. (1960). A re-examination of the theory of complementary needs in mate selection. *Marriage and Family Living, 22,* 227–232.

Schopenhauer, A. (1928). *The philosophy of Schopenhauer* (I. Edman, Ed.), New York: Modern Library.

Seyfried, B. A., & Hendrick, C. (1973). When do opposites attract? When they are opposite in sex and sex-role attitudes. *Journal of Personality and Social Psychology, 23,* 15–20.

Strauss, A. (1947). Personality needs and marital choice. *Social Forces, 23,* 332–335.

Stuart, R. B. (1980). *Helping couples change.* New York: Guilford.

Udry, J. R. (1974). *The social context of marriage* (3rd ed.). Philadelphia, PA: Lippincott.

Wegner, D. M., & Vallacher, R. R. (1977). *Implicit psychology: An introduction to social cognition.* New York: Oxford University Press.

Winch, R. F. (1955). The theory of complementary needs in mate selection: Final results on the test of the general hypothesis. *American Sociological Review, 20,* 552–555.

R. B. STUART
Weight Watchers International

TABOOS

SQUIRE, LARRY R.

Larry Squire received his BA degree from Oberlin College, majoring in psychology. Among his teachers was Celeste McCullough, discoverer of what became known as the McCullough visual aftereffect. He obtained his PhD from the Massachusetts Institute of Technology in the Department of Psychology (now the Department of Brain and Cognitive Science). At MIT he was influenced especially by Hans-Lukas Teuber, department head and founder of a unique program that combined elements of cognitive psychology and systems neuroscience. Squire's graduate research, under the supervision of Peter Schiller, involved studies in rats of the effects of cholinergic drugs on memory.

While doing postdoctoral work with Murray Jarvik at Albert Einstein Medical College, Squire met Samuel Barondes, who was conducting in mice some of the first behavioral studies showing the importance of brain protein synthesis for the formation of long-term memory. Subsequently, when Barondes moved to the new Department of Psychiatry at the University of California School of Medicine, San Diego, Squire joined him to continue work on protein synthesis and memory. During this period, Squire initiated studies of memory in humans, initially with psychiatric patients receiving prescribed electroconovulsive therapy (ECT). This work resulted in the improved instrument for studying retrograde amnesia (for example, a test based on former television programs that had broadcast for a single season). With such methods it was possible to demonstrate that memory loss for premorbid events can be temporally graded across several years, a finding relevant to theories of memory consolidation. This work also led to a number of studies about ECT itself: How severe is the memory impairment associated with ECT? How long does it last? What do patients report about their own memory functions after ECT?

Following these first studies of human memory, Squire established a population of neurological patients with circumscribed and stable memory impairment (amnesia), who could be studied repeatedly. Among other things, this work provided some of the first evidence for the biological reality of multiple memory systems. The major distinction is between declarative, conscious memory, which is impaired in amnesia; and a collection of nonconscious, nondeclarative memory abilities by which performance changes as the result of experience (in this sense deserving the term "memory") but without requiring any conscious memory content or even the experience that memory is being used. Examples of nondeclarative memory include skills, habits, certain aspects of conditioning, and the phenomenon of priming.

In the course of these studies, Squire met Stuart Zola and invited him to join in a collaborative program of primate research for the purpose of obtaining anatomical information about what brain structures and connections were important for memory. This work, some of it in collaboration with David Amaral, led to the establishment of an animal model of human amnesia in the monkey and eventually to the identification of the anatomical components of the medial temporal lobe memory system.

Some anatomical information also came from detailed study of individual amnesic patients. Patient R. B. provided the first strong evidence that the hippocampus itself is a critical component of the medial temporal lobe memory system. This patient, and later patient G. D., proved to have bilateral lesions limited to the CA1 field of the hippocampus. In addition, new protocols for high-resolution magnetic resonance imaging—developed with David Amaral and Gary Press—provided the first direct visualization of hippocampal damage in amnesic patients. An additional program of study using functional magnetic resonance imaging (fMRI) was developed in collaborations with Paul Reber and Craig Stark in order to investigate how the medial temporal lobe contributes to memory. This work showed that the hippocampus is important for elemental forms of declarative memory, such as recognition. To complement their work with monkeys, Squire and Zola subsequently established, in collaboration with Robert Clark, a program of study with rats. This work showed that for the rat, as in humans and monkeys, the hippocampus is essential for recognition memory. The rat is the animal of choice for asking anatomical questions about retrograde amnesia, as well as other questions that are impractical to pursue in the monkey.

In 1989, Squire and four other neuroscientists received an invitation to meet with the Dalai Lama, the secular and spiritual leader of Tibetan Buddhism, on the occasion of the second Mind and Life Conference. The meeting took place in California during a two-day period and happened unexpectedly to coincide with the announcement that the Dalai Lama had been awarded the Nobel Prize for peace. The purpose of the meeting was to explore what had been learned from Western science about the brain and the mind as well as what Buddhist teaching and philosophy might offer. Highlights of the dialogue were subsequently published as *Consciousness at the Crossroads* (1999).

Larry Squire is professor of psychiatry, neurosciences, and psychology at the University of California, San Diego (UCSD), and research career scientist at the adjacent Veterans Affairs Medical Center. He was editor-in-chief of *Behavioral Neuroscience* (1990–1995), editor-in-chief of the *Encyclopedia of Neuroscience,* and a Senior Editor of the textbook *Fundamental Neuroscience.* In addition to more than 300 scientific articles he is author of *Memory and Brain* (1987) and, with Eric Kandel, *Memory: From Mind to Molecules* (1999). From 1988 to 1990, he was secretary of the Society for Neuroscience and served as president from 1993 to 1994. He also served as council delegate for the American Association of Science (AAAS, Section J, Psychology, 1991–1994), founded a section for Neuroscience (Section V) at AAAS, and serves as chair of the section (through 2002). He also served on the AAAS nominating committee (1999). He is a member of the Society for Experimental Psychologists, the National Academy of Sciences, the American Academy of Arts and Sciences, and the American Philosophical Society, and is a William James Fellow of the American Psychological Society. He has received a number of awards, including the Charles Dana Award for Pioneering Achievement in Health (1993), the McGovern Award from AAAS (1993), the Distinguished Scientific Contribution Award from the American Psychological Association (1993), the Karl Lashley Prize from the American Philosophical Society (1994), the New York Metropolitan Life Award (1999), and the UCSD Faculty Research Lecturer Award (2000). Squire has two sons, Ryan and Luke.

STANFORD ACHIEVEMENT TEST

Stanford is a group-administered achievement battery for measuring fundamental learning levels of U.S. primary and secondary school pupils in reading, mathematics, language, science, social studies, and listening skills. The seventh edition (1982) of Stanford is for kindergarten through the 13th grades, and contains 10 levels, with more than 170 subtests and 7,000 items.

First published in 1923, the Stanford was developed by Stanford University professors Lewis M. Terman and Giles M. Ruch (1925/1923). Successive editions of the Stanford chronicle both the changing curricular emphases of U.S. schools and the evolution of the science of educational measurement. In addition to being the first educational achievement test series, the Stanford introduced the "battery" concept (1923 edition)—a collection of several tests designed for the same grade range contained in a single test booklet. The achievement battery innovation facilitated the interpretation of intersubtest strengths and weaknesses. In addition, administration and scoring of the tests were easier. Machine scoring was introduced in the 1940 edition, and various refinements in scaling, norming, and sampling technology have appeared in successive editions (Madden et al., 1975).

Interpretation of the Stanford has typically relied on national norm-referenced derived scores such as grade equivalents, grade-based percentile ranks, and stanines. The seventh edition also offers criterion-referenced test interpretations for test content clusters. The publisher's extensive array of computer-produced scoring service reports permits detailed analyses of individual and group performance.

REFERENCES

Madden, R., Gardner, E. F., Rudman, H. C., Karlsen, B., & Merwin, J. (1975). *Stanford Achievement Test, Manual* (Part V). New York: Harcourt Brace Jovanovich.

Ruch, G. M., & Terman, L. M. (1925/1923). *Stanford Achievement Test, Manual of directions, revised.* Yonkers, NY: World.

G. J. ROBERTSON
Wide Range, Inc. Tampa, Florida

PSYCHOMETRICS
SCHOOL LEARNING

STANFORD–BINET INTELLIGENCE SCALE

More than any other psychological instrument, the Stanford–Binet Intelligence Scale, published by Terman in 1916 in *The Measurement of Intelligence,* has had an impact on U.S. society. While the concept of the intelligence quotient was originated by William Stern, it was Terman who incorporated it into a practical measuring instrument, and made the IQ not only a tool in the hands of educators and psychiatrists, but also a household word. It entered into the thinking of legislators and business people. As its use expanded in the education of bright and dull students and in the treatment of the mentally retarded, controversies developed as to its constancy, the relative contributions of heredity and environment, and its pertinency in theoretical differential psychology and in practical decisions affecting the future of individuals. While research has provided partial answers to these questions, controversy continues.

As a device useful in classifying children for instructional purposes, the intelligence scale was invented by Alfred Binet, a French psychologist, who published his final scale in 1911. He was the first to apply psychological tests to children. As contrasted with earlier testing that emphasized the measurement of sensory and motor functions, Binet was especially interested in developing tests of complex functions, such as finding the similarity between two things, discovering reasons, stating the differences between abstract words, detecting absurdities, and executing commands in sequence. Binet originated the concept of mental age and eventually arranged his tests in age groups.

The 1916 Stanford–Binet was definitely a revision of Binet's scale, with many tests taken from it directly. However, it included a number of new tests, mostly from Terman's own work. Comprehensive, systematic research resulted in better placement of the tests in age groups. The scale as a whole was carefully standardized, using extensive, representative samples of children and adults. The scale was extended to lower and higher ages than Binet had attempted to measure. Directions for administration and scoring were made explicit. The most important innovation, the IQ, was defined as the ratio of mental age to chronological age, with the maximum chronological age at a point where measured mental ability tends to level off.

The wide acceptance of the Stanford–Binet resulted in efforts by its originator, his colleagues, and the publishers to embark on a program of continued improvement. This produced two major revisions.

In 1937, Terman and Merrill published *Measuring Intelligence,* which included two carefully equated scales, Form L and Form M, each containing 129 tests with minimal overlap, as contrasted with the 54 tests in the single form of the 1911 Binet and the 90 in the 1916 Stanford Revision. Changes, based on 10 years of effort, included extension of the range of measurement to lower ages and to higher levels of adult ability, richer sampling of tasks representing intelligent behavior and more rigorous definition of procedures. Tables were provided for the computation of the IQ.

The third revision, *The Stanford–Binet Intelligence Scale,* by Terman and Merrill, appeared in 1960, four years after Terman's death. Based on the analysis of records of scales administered over a five-year period, the two 1937 forms were consolidated into Form L-M, with many items eliminated and some relocated. A major change was the redefinition of the IQ as a standard score with a mean of 100 and standard deviation of 16. This type of "deviation IQ" had been a characteristic of the Wechsler intelligence scales for two decades and avoided some of the difficulties of an IQ obtained by dividing chronological age by mental age, such as variation in variability in different age groups, and inconsistency in the system of computing IQ's of children and adults.

In 1972, revised norms were published, covering the age range from 2 to 18 and taking into account the impact on test performance of recent social and cultural developments.

For years the Stanford–Binet was the only individual verbal scale generally accepted in the United States. While it now shares the spotlight with scales produced by Wechsler, it seems likely to continue to be a useful instrument in schools and psychological clinics as an overall measure of the ability to profit from formal schooling.

REFERENCES

Terman, L. M. (1916). *The measurement of intelligence.* Boston: Houghton Mifflin.

Terman, L. M., & Merrill, M. A. (1960). *Stanford–Binet Intelligence Scale: Manual for the third revision form L-M.* Boston: Houghton Mifflin/Riverside.

Terman, L. M., & Merrill, M. A. (1937). *Measuring intelligence.* Boston: Houghton Mifflin.

P. H. DuBois

INTELLIGENCE MEASURES
WECHSLER INTELLIGENCE TESTS

STATE-DEPENDENT LEARNING

The phenomenon of state-dependent learning relates principally to the use of drugs and their effects on memory or performance. When subjects are trained to perform a particular task followed by an injection of either a drug or saline solution during a test sessions, any impairment caused by the drug cannot necessarily be attributed to the direct effect of the drug on the nervous system (Overton, 1964). Overton demonstrated this with a simple experiment. One-half of the rats received a drug before training, while the other half received saline before training. Each of these groups was subdivided so that one subgroup was tested with the drug and the other subgroup was tested with saline. Rats trained with the drug and tested with saline showed definite impairment, as did rats trained with saline and tested with the drug. Rats that received saline during both sessions or drug during both sessions showed perfect retention. In short, impairment was not caused by the action of the drug on the nervous system but instead was due to the difference in the state of the organism between sessions, which Overton called state-dependent or dissociated learning. The conclusion is that in order to remember it is necessary for the organism to be in essentially the same physiological state as during acquisition.

One explanation of this phenomenon relates to McGeoch's (1942) point that any change in stimulus conditions between acquisition and recall produces poorer retention. This is true for both internal conditions or set (e.g., Irion, 1948) and external context (e.g., Chiszar & Spear, 1969). Presumably, this effect is simply an-

other example of the principle of stimulus generalization decrement, namely that stimuli out on the generalization gradient away from the original stimulus to which the response was learned have a weakened response tendency. That is, the internal state of the organism is a critical component of the total stimulus context for the learned response, and altering it produces forgetting.

An alternative interpretation of state-dependent learning has been called subsystem replacement. The drugs that affect the central nervous system are usually selective with reference to which group of neurons is involved. Under normal conditions a particular population of neurons mediates the learning of a particular task, but other neurons are also capable of doing this. So if the action of the dominant group of neurons is blocked by a drug, the next population in line would mediate the acquisition of the task. Testing for retention with the subject under the influence of the drug should yield good performance; but retention without the drug should be poor, for that part of the nervous system now in control was not involved in the acquisition of this task.

Although there is some experimental evidence in favor of the subsystem replacement interpretation, the notion of generalization decrement is still quite viable. And it is certainly possible that both interpretations can apply, although probably for different situations.

State-dependent learning also occurs with the use of electroconvulsive shock (ECS) and hypothermia, and here it is quite clearly related to stimulus similarity or generalization decrement. It has been demonstrated that ECS-induced retrograde amnesia for a punished response can be alleviated simply by presenting a noncontingent foot shock that makes recall more similar to acquisition conditions (Miller & Springer, 1973). Amnesia for a learned appetitive response was eliminated by the presentation of food but not by foot shock, whereas the reverse was true with amnesia for a punished response (Miller, Ott, Berk, & Springer, 1974).

With hypothermia-induced retrograde amnesia, studies have shown that the subject must reach a critical level of recooling during recall before the learned response occurs. That is, the internal stimulus contexts for acquisition and recall must match well (Mactutus, McCutcheon, & Riccio, 1980).

It also is possible that state dependency can help explain the Kamin (1957) effect. In shuttlebox avoidance learning, performance deteriorates with the passage of time and is poorest after about an hour away from the task (Kamin effect). This sort of forgetting can be eliminated by treatments administered just before testing. These reminders (stressors) are designed to reduce the contextual "mismatch" between acquisition and recall. Thus injections of ACTH, forced swimming, and noncontingent foot shock all improve the rat's performance during testing (Denny, 1958; Klein, 1972; Klein & Spear, 1970).

REFERENCES

Chiszar, D. A., & Spear, N. E. (1969). Stimulus change, reversal learning and retention in the rat. *Journal of Comparative and Physiological Psychology, 69,* 190–195.

Denny, M. R. (1958). The "Kamin effect" in avoidance conditioning [Abstract]. *American Psychologist, 13,* 419.

Irion, A. L. (1948). The relation of "set" to retention. *Psychological Review, 55,* 336–341.

Kamin, L. J. (1957). The retention of an incompletely learned avoidance response. *Journal of Comparative and Physiological Psychology, 50,* 457–460.

Klein, S. B. (1972). Adrenal-pituitary influence in reactivation of avoidance memory in the rat after intermediate intervals. *Journal of Comparative and Physiological Psychology, 79,* 341–349.

Klein, S. B., & Spear, N. E. (1970). Forgetting by the rat after intermediate intervals ("Kamin effect") as retrieval failure. *Journal of Comparative and Physiological Psychology, 71,* 165–170.

Mactutus, C. F., McCutcheon, K., & Riccio, D. C. (1980). Body temperature cues as contextual stimuli: Modulation of hypothermia-induced retrograde amnesia. *Physiology and Behavior, 25,* 875–883.

McGeoch, J. A. (1942). *The psychology of human learning: An introduction.* New York: Van Rees Press.

Miller, R. R., & Springer, A. D. (1973). Amnesia, consolidation, and retrieval. *Psychological Review, 80,* 69–79.

Overton, D. A. (1964). State dependent or "dissociated" learning produced with pentobarbitol. *Journal of Comparative and Physiological Psychology, 57,* 3–12.

M. R. Denny
Michigan State University

AMPHETAMINE EFFECTS
CENTRAL NERVOUS SYSTEM (CNS)

STATISTICAL SIGNIFICANCE

Researchers often employ statistical tests to evaluate the results of their studies. The term "statistical significance" is used in relation to the use of these tests. If a researcher's results or data reflect statistical significance, then an interpretation that the outcomes are not likely due to chance is thought appropriate.

Statistical tests basically evaluate the results of an investigation in light of chance occurrences. These tests permit the researcher to assess the probability that such results might have been due to chance. For example, one might be comparing the recall performance of two groups and find that there were mean correct responses of 25 and 42 for groups A and B respectively. It is important for the researcher to determine how frequently such differences might be expected by chance alone.

The label "statistically significant" is applied to results where the probability of chance is equal to or below an agreed-upon level. Most psychologists accept a 5% (or lower) probability of chance as being statistically significant. This is typically reported as $P < .05$, which means that if the study were replicated 100 times, we would expect to observe these results less than five times due to chance. Another frequently used level of significance is the 1% level, which is generally reported as $P < .01$. In this case we would expect to observe the results by chance only one time out of 100. These significance levels are based on convention and are widely accepted, but

are not derived from mathematical justification. There are some differences among various disciplines regarding what is considered statistically significant.

Statistical significance may be determined for both tests of difference and relationship. For difference questions, one can establish how often such differences would be obtained due to chance. For relationship questions, one can assess how often a given relationship level (correlation coefficient) would be observed due to chance. Statistical significance and the resulting decision regarding the likelihood of an effect due to chance is considerably influenced by the research design employed.

SUGGESTED READING
Aron, A., & Aron, E. N. (1999). *Statistics for psychology* (2nd ed.). Upper Saddle River, NJ: Prentice Hall.

Cortina, J. M., & Dunlap, W. P. (1997). On the logic and purpose of significance testing. *Psychological Methods, 2,* 161–172.

Kurtz, N. R. (1999). *Statistical analysis for the social sciences.* Boston: Allyn & Bacon.

McClelland, G. H. (1997). Optimal design in psychological research. *Psychological Methods, 2,* 3–19.

Thompson, B., & Snyder, P. A. (1998). Statistical significance and reliability analyses in recent Journal of Counseling and Development research articles. *Journal of Counseling and Development, 76,* 436–441.

C. J. Drew
University of Utah

STATISTICS IN PSYCHOLOGY

STATISTICS IN PSYCHOLOGY

This term refers to the application of quantitative measures and techniques to reporting and analyzing the results of psychological studies. The first use of statistics in psychology is often credited to Sir Francis Galton (1822–1911), an Englishman whose work on individual differences led him to develop many basic techniques still used today. The use of statistics is essential to psychology as a science. Observing, recording, and analyzing quantitative data permit meaningful comparisons based on objective standards. Statistics in psychology is commonly divided into two branches—descriptive and inferential.

DESCRIPTIVE STATISTICS

Descriptive statistics are procedures used to organize, summarize, and describe data (McCall, 1970). Some everyday forms of descriptive statistics are grade point average, rate of inflation, and unit pricing. Such indicators describe relatively large bodies of data in quick, efficient ways.

The most commonly used descriptive procedures are frequency distributions, measures of central tendency, and measures of relative standing. Regression and correlation are techniques used to describe relationships between variables.

Frequency Distributions

A frequency distribution shows the tally of how many times each score or value (or interval of scores or values) occurred in a set of data. Relative frequencies, the percent of responses of each value, are also often reported. The frequency distribution provides quick insight into the pattern of results, insight that would be difficult to achieve by working directly with raw data, the actual unsummarized observations. Graphics, including histograms, regular frequency polygons, and cumulative frequency polygons, are often used to provide visual representations of frequency data.

Measures of Central Tendency

Measures of central tendency are summary statistics that describe what is typical of a distribution. The *mode* is the most frequently occurring score. The *median* is the score that divides the distribution in half, so that half the distribution falls above the median and half below. The *mean* is the arithmetic average of all the scores. Whether the mean, median, or mode provides the best description depends upon the shape of the distribution. If the distribution is symmetrical and has one mode (is unimodal), the mean, median, and mode will coincide. Because the mean is based on every score, it is most sensitive to deviations from symmetry. The mean is pulled in the direction of extreme scores, making it the least useful measure of distributions that are badly skewed (asymmetrical).

Other useful descriptions of distributions are provided by measures of variability. Variability is the degree to which scores in a distribution differ. Two distributions may have the same mean, median, and mode, but differ greatly in the degree of variability. (See Figure 1.) Variability is measured by two statistics, the variance and the standard deviation. The variance is computed by calculating the average squared difference between each score and the mean. The standard deviation is the square root of the variance. It is used to transform variability back into the same units (in effect, unsquared units) used to measure raw scores. Although they are

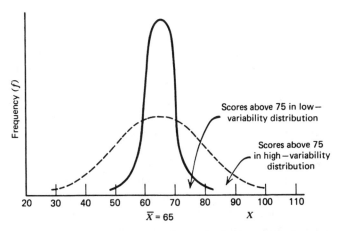

Figure 1.   Frequency polygons of two distributions with the same mean but different variability. From J. Welkowitz, R. B. Ewen, and J. Cohen, *Introductory statistics for the behavioral sciences* (New York: Academic Press, 1971, p. 47).

primarily descriptive measures, the variance and standard deviation also are important to inferential questions.

Measures of Relative Standing

These measures, which include percentiles and standard scores, are used to describe where a particular score falls in relation to the rest of the distribution. In *Introductory Statistics for the Behavioral Sciences,* Joan Welkowitz and colleagues defined a percentile as "a single number that gives the percent of cases in the specific reference group with equal or lower scores" (Welkowitz et al., 1971, p. 28). If your IQ score places you in the 90th percentile of the population, 90% of the population have scores equal to or lower than yours; only 10% of the population score above you. The percentile is thus more precise than reporting simply that a score falls above or below the mean, median, or mode.

Standard scores (commonly called z scores) express the deviation from the mean in standard deviation units. They are obtained by dividing the difference between the score and the mean by the standard deviation of the distribution. Standard scores are useful because they can be interpreted by reference to the *standard normal curve* (z distribution), a symmetrical bell-shaped curve with known properties: a mean of 0 and a standard deviation of 1. Because the z score is signed, it is a quick indicator of whether a score fell above or below the mean. Since it expresses scores in terms of standard deviations, it indicates how unusual each score is—34% of all scores fall in the interval of 1 standard deviation below and 1 standard deviation above the mean ($z = \pm 1$); 16% fall beyond $z = \pm 1$; only 2½% fall beyond $z = \pm 2$.

Relationships Between Variables

Regression and correlation are procedures commonly used to describe relationships among variables. In *Fundamental Statistics for Psychology,* Robert B. McCall explains that *regression* is a term coined by Francis Galton. Galton found that the sons of tall men were also above average in height, but tended to be closer to the mean height of all men than their fathers were. Galton called this phenomenon *regression toward the mean,* a term still in use. McCall notes that "the word regression also became associated with the process of determining the line which best describes the relationship between two variables" (McCall, 1970, p. 95). Two measures obtained on each subject in a sample can be plotted on *xy* coordinates to create a graphic representation of the relationship between the measures. Often this will yield approximately a straight line, reflecting a *linear relationship.* Numerical procedures are used to obtain the *regression line,* the mathematical equation of the line of best fit through the observed data points. Once the regression line has been derived, it is possible to predict the value of one variable when the other is known, and to estimate the accuracy of the prediction. Although the regression line is a descriptive tool, its use as a predictor is an example of inference.

The accuracy of the regression line as a predictor can be deduced only by computing the *standard error of estimate* of the line, a measure of the variability of scores about the line, which indexes the amount of possible error in estimating one score from another. Because the standard error of estimate is computed in the same units as the predicted scores, it is difficult to compare the relative strength of different variables as predictors. For these reasons, researchers often prefer to calculate the *Pearson product moment correlation coefficient* (*r*). The basic correlational procedures devised by Galton were expanded by Karl Pearson, his student.

The correlation coefficient is a quantitative index of the degree of linear relationship between two variables. The computational procedures eliminate the problem of comparison among different units. The values of *r* can vary between –1 and +1. The sign reflects the direction of the relationship. A negative correlation represents an inverse relationship: As one variable increases, the other decreases. A positive correlation represents a direct relationship: As one variable increases, the other also increases. The absolute value of *r* represents the strength of the relationship. Thus ±1 represents perfect relationships. An *r* of 0 indicates no linear relationship. The value of r^2 indicates the percent of variance in one variable that can be accounted for by the other. Psychologists use this value to gauge how useful a particular measure is for prediction. Although correlations in psychology rarely approach ±1.00, even a moderate correlation (for example, $r = 0.34$) may be statistically significant. If a researcher can show that one variable out of hundreds accounts for more than 10% of the variance in another ($0.34^2 = 0.1156$, for example), the finding merits attention. Inferential procedures are also available to determine the exact odds of obtaining a particular correlation, given the characteristics of the distributions of the variables measured.

The Pearson *r* is designed for interval data on dimensions assumed to be normally distributed. A variety of other correlational procedures are available to handle other types of data: point biserial, phi coefficient, and Spearman's rho, for example. Correlations are often used in psychology as sources for experimental research hypotheses. The fact that two measures are related does not prove that one caused the other. However, researchers can use experimentation to test hypotheses about the causal dynamics of relationships established through correlational procedures. Multiple regression, factor analysis, and canonical correlation are more recent relational techniques made practical by advances in computer technology. These procedures permit analysis of relationships among large numbers of variables.

INFERENTIAL STATISTICS

Inferential statistics are procedures for drawing inferences about large groups (in effect, whole populations) on the basis of observations made on smaller subsets called *samples*. Statistical inference serves two main purposes in psychology: to estimate population parameters from sample statistics, and to assess the odds of obtaining a particular pattern of research results, given the characteristics of the data sampled.

The mean is the most commonly estimated population parameter. A large sample drawn at random (so that each member of the population has an equal chance of being selected) can be used to estimate the population mean: Compute the mean of the sample. The probable accuracy of this statistic can be estimated by computing an estimate of the amount of variability likely among different samples drawn from the population. The amount of variability in a sample statistic is called the *standard error* of that

statistic. The larger the estimated standard error of the mean, the greater is the probable difference between the sample mean and the population mean. Because of the way in which the standard error is computed, larger samples will generally yield smaller standard errors, making statistics computed on larger samples somewhat more accurate indicators of population parameters. By working with the standard error of the mean and standardized probability distributions (such as *t* distributions), it is possible to construct confidence intervals, ranges of values with known odds of containing the true population mean.

Evaluating Research Results

Inferential statistics may be used to assess the likelihood that particular samples belong to a known population. The process of statistical inference begins with a statement of the *null hypothesis* (H_0). The null hypothesis states the assumption that the observed statistics were drawn from a particular population. Depending on the research application, the null hypothesis may state that a statistic (such as a sample mean) was drawn from a known population. The null hypothesis is based on the fact that most differences among means, for example, are attributable to the usual variability among samples, rather than true treatment effects. The null hypothesis is retained or rejected on the basis of how likely the observed outcome is. If the observed differences are large relative to the amount of variability in the measures taken, the researcher will reject the null hypothesis and conclude that the observed differences were unlikely to have occurred by chance. The result is then *statistically significant*. Test statistics with known frequency distributions are calculated to express the relationship between observed differences and variability. The odds of obtaining the observed outcome can then be determined from standardized distribution tables. In psychology, researchers customarily reject the null hypothesis if the observed outcome (the computed test statistic) is so extreme that it could have occurred by chance with a probability of less than 5% ($p < 0.05$). The choice of the significance level and the corresponding critical value of the test statistic is arbitrary. In some situations, the researcher may choose a stricter criterion, rejecting the null hypothesis only when the odds of the observed outcome are $p < 0.01$ or $p < 0.001$.

Parametric Statistics

Parametric statistics can be used when two criteria are met: The variable under study is known or can be assumed to be normally distributed (having values that form a symmetrical bell-shaped curve with known characteristics), and the data are interval or ratio.

If the mean and standard deviation of the population are known, or can be hypothesized, the exact odds of obtaining the observed difference between the known population parameter and a sample statistic can be determined. This is done by transforming the observed difference into a standard normal deviate, or *z* score, the ratio of the observed difference to an estimate of the variability among sample means. The *z* score can be evaluated by comparison with the *standard normal curve* (also called the *z* distribution). The standard normal curve is a normal curve standardized to have a mean equal to 0 and a standard deviation equal to 1. The exact shape of the curve is known, as are the areas under the curve. If the computed test statistic (in this case, z) is more extreme than the chosen critical value, the researcher rejects the null hypothesis and concludes that the results are statistically significant.

Because researchers often rely on small samples, and because population parameters are rarely known, standardized Student t distributions are used more often than z. These were developed by W. S. Gosset, who wrote under the pen name Student. The exact shape of the t distribution varies roughly as a function of the number of cases sampled (more precisely, with the *degrees of freedom*, the number of values free to vary in the sample). Thus the critical values change with sample size, making t tests resistant to biases potentially created if the distribution of the population is not truly normal. The family of t distributions can be used to test the null hypothesis, which states that *two* samples were drawn from the same population. This is commonly done in research involving two groups of subjects, typically an experimental and a control group.

When more than two treatment groups are used, the Analysis of Variance (F test) may be applied. Sir Ronald Fisher developed these procedures. The F is an omnibus test that evaluates differences among all the possible pairs of treatment groups at once. The relative amounts of variance within versus between groups are compared. A variety of *post hoc* procedures are available to pinpoint the pairwise source of a significant F test: Duncan's range, Tukey, and Scheffé tests are common examples.

Nonparametric Statistics

When the assumptions of the parametric tests cannot be met, or when ordinal (rank) or nominal (categorical) data are collected, *nonparametric* procedures are used. These techniques parallel parametric techniques in application and purpose. Nonparametric alternatives to the t test include the Mann–Whitney U test, the Wilcoxon (W) test, and the chi square test for nominal data. Nonparametric alternatives to the Analysis of Variance include the Kruskal–Wallis, Friedman, and chi square tests. The logic of each inferential test is the same: The appropriate null hypothesis is rejected if the computed test statistic is more extreme (less likely) than a predetermined critical value.

Since all statistical inferences are based on probability estimates, two incorrect outcomes are possible: type 1 errors in which the null hypothesis is rejected although true, and type 2 errors in which the null hypothesis is retained although invalid. The former results in incorrect confirmation of the research hypothesis, and the latter in the failure to identify a statistically significant result.

REFERENCES

McCall, R. B. (1970). *Fundamental statistics for psychology.* New York: Harcourt.

Welkowitz, J., Ewen, R. B., & Cohen, J. (1971). *Introductory statistics for the behavioral sciences.* New York: Academic.

SUGGESTED READING

Cooley, W. W., & Lohnes, P. R. (1971). *Multivariate data analysis.* New York: Wiley.

Glass, G. V., & Stanley, J. C. (1970). *Statistical methods in education and psychology.* Englewood Cliffs, NJ: Prentice-Hall.

Myers, A. (1980). *Experimental psychology.* New York: Van Nostrand.

Winer, B. J. (1971). *Statistical principles in experimental design* (2nd ed.). New York: McGraw-Hill.

A. MYERS
St. Jerome Convent, Philadelphia, Pennsylvania

ANALYSIS OF COVARIANCE (ANCOVA)
ANALYSIS OF VARIANCE (ANOVA)
CENTRAL TENDENCY MEASURES
CLUSTER ANALYSIS
FACTOR ANALYSIS
MEASUREMENT
PSYCHOMETRICS
RESEARCH METHODOLOGY
SAMPLING

STEREOTYPING

Studies of prejudice directed toward ethnic groups often mention the important role played by stereotypes—those generalized and usually value-laden impressions that members of one social group use in characterizing members of another group. The term *stereotype* was introduced and popularized by the journalist Walter Lippmann (1922), who employed it in reference to attitudinal constructs that are factually incorrect, based on illogical reasoning, and rigidly inflexible. Many behavioral scientists, such as Brigham (1971), have followed Lippmann's lead and have used the term in a pejorative sense.

The difficulty that arises when "stereotype" is given a purely negative meaning is that the social and cognitive mechanisms that underlie stereotyping are misunderstood. As a result, there is a tendency to overlook the fact that stereotyping normally and naturally occurs whenever social groups interact. Any socially identifiable group may be characterized in an almost infinite number of ways. It is impossible for us to know all there is to know about, say, an ethnic group, nor can we keep more than a few variables in mind when interacting with members of that group. We can assume, of course, that all ethnic groups are alike, having identical attitudes, values, aspirations, and perceptual styles, but that would be as naive as assuming that all ethnic groups are completely different from each other. What is inevitably done is to focus on a few variables believed to characterize the group in question and work them into a frame of reference used when observing, interacting with, or making decisions about members of the group. These frames of reference, or *working stereotypes,* enable people to predict, rightly or wrongly, how members of a given group will behave or react in a given situation. When used in this nonjudgmental sense, stereotype refers to any agreed-upon impression that members of one group have about members of other groups.

The fact that people become dependent on stereotypes is a major source of difficulty. Stereotypes may dominate expectations of other group members and ignore or suppress evidence that indicates that the stereotype may be incorrect or inappropriate in a particular instance. Instead of modifying or setting aside the frames of reference, people become defensive and act as though their intelligence or judgment has been questioned. The stimuli that members of other groups present are inescapably ambiguous. When attempts are made to resolve this ambiguity in order to construct a perceptual frame of reference—a stereotype—we often fall into the error of making attributions based not on empirical data, but on personal needs and concerns. There is a danger, in other words, that stereotypes will be shaped by unconscious needs to project.

Campbell (1965) pointed out that the most pernicious fault with stereotypes lies not so much in their fallacious elements, as in the causal explanation we make for an inadequacy on the basis of a stereotype—for example, that X's are "lazy." Thus, if X's are poor employees because they have not been properly trained, one can arrange to train them, but if they are "lazy," nothing can be done.

Another danger inherent in stereotypes lies in the human tendency to use them as "self-fulfilling prophecies." If we believe, stereotypically, that X's are inadequate and lazy, our interactions with them will take the form of "scenarios," "scripted" to entice them into actions that are likely to cause them to fail and that thus will "prove" the validity of our stereotypes. X's, for their part, may come to believe the stereotypes that others hold for them, and will behave accordingly, especially if they are a low-status group. Thus the stereotypes held by the dominant group become self-fulfilling prophecies for X's as well.

Triandis and Vassiliou (1967) studied the stereotypes that ethnic groups have for themselves (autostereotypes) and for other groups (heterostereotypes) and concluded that there is a "kernel of truth" underlying stereotypes based on firsthand knowledge. American stereotypes of Greeks, for example, are fairly similar to the stereotypes that Greeks have of themselves, and Greek stereotypes of Americans are similar to Americans' autostereotypes, when both groups have frequent contact with each other. Lindgren and Tebcherani (1971) constructed a forced-choice test of Arab and American autostereotypes that proved to be useful as a measure of cross-cultural empathy. Results suggested that Americans had less empathy for Arabs than Arabs had for Americans. Similarly, a study by Abate and Berrien showed that Japanese views of Americans were much closer to Americans' self-stereotypes than Americans' views were with respect to Japanese self-stereotypes.

REFERENCES

Brigham, J. C. (1971). Ethnic stereotypes. *Psychological Bulletin, 76,* 15–38.

Lindgren, H. C., & Tebcherani, A. (1971). Arab and American auto and heterostereotypes: A cross-cultural study of empathy. *Journal of Cross-cultural Psychology, 2,* 173–180.

Lippmann, W. (1922). *Public opinion.* New York: Harcourt Brace.

Triandis, H. C., & Vassiliou, V. (1967). Frequency of contact and stereotyping. *Journal of Personality and Social Psychology, 7,* 316–328.

SUGGESTED READING

Cantor, N., & Mischel, W. (1979). Prototypicality and personality: Effects on free recall and personality impressions. *Journal of Research in Personality, 13,* 187–205.

Rothbart, M., Evans, M., & Fulero, S. (1979). Recall for confirming events: Memory processes and the maintenance of social stereotypes. *Journal of Experimental Social Psychology, 15,* 343–355.

H. C. LINDGREN
San Francisco State University

ATTITUDES
CROSS-CULTURAL PSYCHOLOGY: INTRO & OVERVIEW
INTERPERSONAL PERCEPTION

STEVENS, CHARLES F.

Charles F. Stevens graduated with a BA in psychology in 1956 from Harvard University. He obtained the MD degree in 1960 at Yale University School of Medicine, and the PhD degree in 1964 at The Rockefeller University. He joined the faculty of the University of Washington School of Medicine in 1963 as assistant professor in the Department of Physiology and Biophysics, and attained the rank of full professor after 10 years. In 1975 he moved to Yale University as professor of physiology, was appointed Chair of the Section of Molecular Neurobiology in 1983, and became a Howard Hughes Medical Institute Investigator in 1986. In 1990 he moved to the Salk Institute, where he is professor of molecular neurobiology and adjunct professor of pharmacology at the University of California, San Diego.

Stevens's research centers on mechanisms responsible for synaptic transmission. These problems are approached by a combination of molecular biological, electrophysiological, anatomical, and theoretical methods. He studies neurons both in dissociated cell cultures and in brain slices, and investigates the function of individual membrane proteins of importance to synaptic transmission. One current research focus is the various mechanisms used by the central nervous system for the short- and long-term regulation of synaptic strength. A second major project uses a combination of methods to elucidate the molecular basis of neurotransmitter release at synapses.

Stevens has received the Spencer Award from Columbia University and served as the Grass National Lecturer for the Society for Neuroscience. He is a member of the American Academy of Arts and Sciences and of the National Academy of Sciences.

STAFF

STEVENS, STANLEY SMITH (1906–1973)

Stanley Smith Stevens took the PhD degree in 1933 at Harvard University under Edwin Boring. He was a distinguished psychophysicist and early in his career he established the sensory attribute of tonal density. He also developed a method for equating tones on one attribute when they differed on a second attribute. In the field of auditory theory, Stevens accepted a modification of the resonance theory of Herman von Helmholtz, which involved traveling waves throughout the basilar membrane.

Stevens collaborated with Hallowell Davis on *Hearing* (1938), which summarized much of his research, as well as that of others. He also edited the *Handbook of Experimental Psychology* (1951).

Stevens had an abiding interest in problems of measurement and psychological scaling. He developed some new scaling methods and found that physical continua generally conform to a psychophysical power law rather than Gustav Fechner's logarithmic law. Quantitative sensory continua (intensity) were found to obey the power law while qualitative sensory continua such as hue or pitch may follow Fechner's law.

Shortly after the publication of Percy Bridgman's *The Logic of Modern Physics,* Stevens, joined by other Harvard psychologists, began to explore the significance of operational thinking for psychology. He published several papers on operationism and did more than anyone else to bring operationism before the psychological profession and to establish what might be called operational behaviorism. His paper "Psychology and the science of science" exerted a powerful influence in this regard and revealed the close ties between operationism and logical positivism.

Stevens combined experimental ingenuity and expertise with broad methodological and philosophical interests. His interest in measurement led to collaboration with W. H. Sheldon on *The Varieties of Human Physique* and *The Varieties of Temperament,* books that developed a method for classifying individuals into personality types on the basis of body build.

P. E. LICHTENSTEIN

STIMULANTS

The identification and use of central nervous system stimulants in the form of plant preparations has been prevalent in different cultures for many centuries (Angrist & Sudilovsky, 1978). In more recent times, stimulants have not only been used for recreational reasons, but have enjoyed fairly extensive use in therapeutic contexts. In low doses, stimulants result in mood elevation, euphoria, increased alertness, reduced fatigue, appetite suppression, and motor excitation, whereas higher doses may provoke irritability and anxiety. Furthermore, as the initial effects of the drug wane, the heightened arousal may give way to behavioral depression. The more commonly used stimulants, such as cocaine, amphetamines, and methylphenidate, have been found to elicit a number of untoward side effects, and may induce schizophrenic-like symptoms, particularly paranoia. These compounds will induce stereotyped behavior patterns in a wide variety of species, and it appears likely that their behavioral effects are due to the release of dopamine in the central nervous system (Kelly, 1977). Owing to a variety of dispositional factors, these compounds produce great interindividual differences in response to the drugs (Shulgin, 1978).

Clinically, stimulants such as methylphenidate, d-amphetamine, and pemoline have been used in the treatment of hyperactivity in children. It is likely that the "paradoxical" effects of the catecholamine stimulants are the result of the increased attention produced by these compounds, thereby minimizing the restlessness associated with hyperactivity (Lipman et al., 1978).

Stimulants that inhibit the degradation of biogenic amines (monoamine oxidase inhibitors) or block the neuronal uptake of amine (tricyclic antidepressants) have been used extensively in the treatment of affective disorders. Unlike amphetamine and cocaine, the therapeutic effects of these compounds appear to descend from their action on norepinephrine and serotonin concentrations, or by the down regulation of catecholamine receptors (see Murphy et al., 1978; Schildkraut, 1978).

The two most widely used stimulants are caffeine and nicotine. Caffeine is usually obtained from coffee, but is also found in appreciable concentrations in cola drinks and chocolate. Owing to its action on the cerebral cortex, caffeine will produce wakefulness, alertness, and restlessness. In relatively high doses, brain-stem stimulation occurs, and respiration is stimulated. For this reason, caffeine may be used to offset the effects of sedative-hypnotic agents, such as alcohol and barbiturates. Finally caffeine increases cardiac output and provokes constriction of blood vessels in the brain, an effect that has made caffeine useful in the treatment of some forms of migraine (Ritchie, 1970). Nicotine has pronounced effects on the central and peripheral nervous systems. Peripherally, low doses of nicotine will stimulate ganglion cells and the neuromuscular junction. In addition, nicotine has been shown to stimulate salivation, delay gastric emptying, and inhibit stomach contraction. In higher doses, a functional blockade of receptors may occur. In addition, the release of peripheral catecholamines is produced by nicotine, and as a result vasoconstriction, tachycardia, and elevated blood pressure may ensue. Centrally nicotine is thought to influence the activity of neurons in the reticular formation, cortex, and hippocampus, and it excites vagal and spinal afferent neurons. The drug causes a desynchronized electroencephalogram pattern and reduces alpha-wave activity. In sufficiently high doses, the drug may cause tremor and convulsion (Jaffe & Jarvik, 1978; Volle & Koelle, 1970).

REFERENCES

Angrist, B., & Sudilovsky, A. (1978). Central nervous system stimulants: Historical aspects and clinical effects. In L. L. Iversen, S. D. Iversen, & S. H. Snyder (Eds.), *Handbook of psychopharmacology* (Vol. 11). New York: Plenum.

Jaffe, J. H., & Jarvik, M. E. (1978). Tobacco use and tobacco use disorder. In M. A. Lipton, A. Di Mascio, & K. F. Killam (Eds.), *Psychopharmacology: A generation of progress.* New York: Raven Press.

Kelly, P. H. (1977). Drug-induced motor behavior. In L. L. Iversen, S. D. Iversen, & S. H. Snyder (Eds.), *Handbook of psychopharmacology* (Vol. 8). New York: Plenum.

Lipman, R. S., Di Mascio, A., Reatig, N., & Kirson, T. (1978). Psychotropic drugs and mentally retarded children. In M. A.

Lipton, A. Di Mascio & K. F. Killam (Eds.), *Psychopharmacology: A generation of progress*. New York: Raven Press.

Murphy, D. L., Campbell, I., & Costa, J. L. (1978). Current status of the indoleamine hypothesis of the affective disorders. In M. A. Lipton, A. Di Mascio, & K. F. Killam (Eds.), *Psychopharmacology: A generation of progress*. New York: Raven Press.

Ritchie, J. M. (1970). Central nervous system stimulants: The xanthines. In L. S. Goodman & A. Gilman (Eds.), *The pharmacological basis of therapeutics*. Toronto: Collier/Macmillan.

Schildkraut, J. J. (1978). Current status of the catecholamine hypothesis of affective disorders. In M. A. Lipton, A. Di Mascio, & K. F. Killam (Eds.), *Psychopharmacology: A generation of progress*. New York: Raven Press.

Shulgrin, A. T. (1978). Psychotomimetic drugs: Structure-activity relationships. In L. L. Iversen, S. D. Iversen, & S. H. Snyder (Eds.), *Handbook of psychopharmacology* (Vol. 11). New York: Plenum.

Volle, R. L., & Kolle, G. B. (1970). Ganglionic stimulating and blocking agents. In L. S. Goodman & A. Gilman (Eds.), *The pharmacological basis of therapeutics*. Toronto: Collier/Macmillan.

H. ANISMAN
Carleton University, Ottawa, Canada

AMPHETAMINE EFFECTS
ANTIPSYCHOTIC DRUGS
CENTRAL NERVOUS SYSTEM (CNS)
HALLUCINOGENIC DRUGS
NEUROCHEMISTRY
NEUROPSYCHOLOGY
PSYCHOPHYSIOLOGY: OVERVIEW
PSYCHOPHARMACOLOGY
SUBSTANCE ABUSE

STIMULUS GENERALIZATION

Historically, stimulus generalization referred to a tendency to respond to a stimulus similar in character to, and yet discriminably different from, a stimulus to which an animal was originally trained. This phenomenon was first demonstrated in laboratory experiments with dogs by Pavlov and his associates (Pavlov, 1927). After experiencing a succession of pairings of stimuli, such as a tone with food, the dog would eventually come to salivate reliably to the tone. Following this training a test phase was instituted in which the dog experienced tones varying in similarity to the original tone but without the food. The dog responded to tones similar to the original tone but its responding was not the same to all of the tones: Responding declined as the test stimuli became more dissimilar to the training stimulus. This outcome is referred to as an excitatory gradient of generalization.

A generalization gradient reflects the extent to which the original training stimulus controls responding. A flat gradient implies that the original stimulus exercises little control over the response or that there is complete generalization. In contrast, a steep slope implies little or no generalization; responding is largely confined to the training stimulus. Although the demonstration of generalization gradients appears straightforward, their measurement, the variables that affect them, and the roles they play in the discriminative process is complex.

Stimulus similarity is usually measured with reference to some physical dimension of the stimulus such as wavelength, size, or intensity, although occasionally scales expressed in psychophysical units may be used. Similarly, there are different scales expressing the extent to which responding occurs to the different stimuli. One approach is to count the number of responses made to each of the stimuli during the test phase. Expressing the number of responses made to each stimulus results in an *absolute* gradient of generalization. Absolute gradients can be transformed into *relative* gradients by expressing the response to a test stimulus as the proportion of the total number of responses made to all stimuli presented during the test phase or to responses made previously to the training stimulus. Relative gradients correct for conditions where wide variations in responding are found among subjects. Which type of gradient to use depends on whether the scale corrects for the presence of floor or ceiling effects, remains unchanged when a variable that doesn't affect generalization is manipulated, or makes the results consistent with other experiments. Many investigators report both absolute and relative gradients.

Schedules of reinforcement, degree of learning to the training stimulus, and level of motivation influence the extent to which responses generalize to other stimuli. In early studies, reinforcement followed the training stimulus on every occasion. A disadvantage with this procedure was that responding to test stimuli was limited since each test trial was also an extinction trial. To moderate extinction effects, the training stimulus began to be reinforced intermittently; however, it was soon apparent that the reinforcement schedules themselves affected the generalization gradients. Schedules determine the extent to which incidental, contextual cues present during training and the generalization test influence responding. For instance, when the average time interval to reinforcement is lengthened, responding to test stimuli increase; in other words, the gradient is progressively flattened (Haber & Kalish, 1963; Hearst, Koresko, & Poppen, 1964). Presumably, the proprioceptive stimulation occurring during the time elapsing between reinforcements provides additional information about when the reinforcing event will occur and this stimulation is still present during the generalization test as well (Thomas & Swaitalski, 1966).

As a general rule, the more experience the animal has on the training stimulus prior to the generalization test, the less generalization is observed; in other words, more training results in a steeper generalization gradient (Hearst & Kesko, 1968; Razran, 1949). However, if external stimulation is relatively uniform and proprioceptive stimuli are crucial in controlling behavior, then regardless of how much training is given to the original stimulus, the gradients remain flat (Margolius, 1955; Walker & Branch, 1998).

Interest in motivational effects on stimulus control stems from

Hull's (1943) hypothesis that motivation and habit combine multiplicatively to determine performance. This counterintuitive hypothesis predicts that performance improves with higher levels of motivation, implying higher and steeper absolute gradients of generalization as motivation increases. Although some studies reported findings consistent with the Hullian hypothesis (e.g., Newman & Grice, 1965); others contradict it (Broen, Stroms, & Goldberg, 1963). Apparently, the relation between motivation on stimulus generalization depends on whether the training and test stimuli are easy or difficult to discriminate. When discrimination between stimuli is easy, high levels of motivation result in steep slopes; however, with more difficult discriminations, higher levels of motivation produce flatter gradients (Kalish & Haber, 1966).

The slope of an excitatory gradient is an indicator of the extent to which the original stimulus controls responding. The steeper the gradient, the greater the control and, conversely, the less generalization. In a similar vein, stimuli control the tendency not-to-respond and the extent of their control can be measured by an increase in responding as the similarity between the original inhibitory stimulus and the test stimuli decrease (Honig, Boneau, Burstein, & Pennypacker, 1963; Jenkins & Harrison, 1962; Karpicke & Hearst, 1975). In the case of excitatory gradients, responding declines with the greater the dissimilarity between training and test stimuli, while with inhibitory gradients, responding increases as training and test stimuli become more dissimilar.

Psychologists ascribed an important theoretical role to stimulus generalization. It not only facilitated survival—behavior that had been successful in finding food, securing a mate, or avoiding a predator could generalize to new but similar situations—but was also a process that underlies and explains more complex learning phenomena (Hull, 1943; Spence, 1936).

Conditioning-extinction theory is a major representative of this approach (Hull, 1943, 1952; Spence, 1956). It is based on the notion that excitation (a tendency to respond) develops to a stimulus paired with reinforcement and that this excitation generalizes to other similar stimuli. Similarly, inhibition (a tendency not to respond) develops to the stimulus predicting nonreinforcement and the tendency not to respond generalizes to other similar stimuli. If the reinforced and nonreinforced stimuli are situated along the same physical dimension, there may be overlap between the gradients of excitation and inhibition so that many stimuli would arouse contradictory tendencies to respond or not respond. Eventually the animal chooses one stimulus rather than another because the net excitation (excitation minus inhibition) of the selected stimulus exceeds the net excitation of the unselected stimulus. The theory was extended with some success to more complex discrimination phenomena such as the peak shift effect, transposition, and transfer of discrimination (Hanson, 1959; Logan, 1971; Spence, 1942).

Although it is the case that stimuli acquire excitatory and inhibitory properties and these properties generalize to other similar stimuli, the theory is inadequate in providing an account for the selective nature of associations or the formation or utilization of cognitive strategies during learning. In the context of the theory, any detectible stimulus serving as a signal for reinforcement or nonreinforcement will acquire excitatory or inhibitory properties. But this is not the case: The organization of the neural apparatus determines whether associations between conjoint events will be formed (Garcia & Koelling, 1966), thereby determining whether stimuli acquire the capacity to activate tendencies to respond or not to respond. Moreover, the formation of associations depends on the animal's previous learning history. Stimuli that provide no new information about impending events or that are less reliable or valid predictors of reinforcement may not enter into association with significant and consequential events that they precede (Kamin, 1968; Rickert, Lorden, Dawson, Smyly, & Callahan, 1979; Wagner, Logan, Haberlandt & Price, 1968).

Although the scope of associative theory could probably be widened to accommodate the principle of associative selection (see, e.g., Wagner, 1981), cognitive processes may circumvent the influence of elemental associative mechanisms. For example, applying rules to solve discriminations may result in behavior contrary to what an associative model predicts. Learning set reversal problems were early examples (Bessemer & Stollnitz, 1971). These problems demonstrated that animals abandon response tendencies associated with reinforcement and choose a response previously nonreinforced based on information of the outcome from the immediately preceding trial. A full accounting of the importance of generalization as an explanatory device requires specifying its role in the development and use of cognitive structures and the conditions under which it and other more complex processes interact.

REFERENCES

Bessemer, D. W., & Stollnitz, F. (1971). Retention of discriminations and an analysis of learning sets. In A. M. Schrier and F. Stollnitz (Eds.), *Behavior of nonhuman primates* (Vol. 4). New York: Academic Press.

Broen, W. E., Jr., Stroms, L. H., & Goldberg, D. H. (1963). Decreased discrimination as a function of increased drive. *Journal of Abnormal and Social Psychology, 67,* 345–352.

Gracia, J., & Koelling, R. A. (1966). The relation of cue to consequence in avoidance learning. *Psychonomic Science, 4,* 123–124.

Haber, A., & Kakish, H. I. (1963). Prediction of discrimination from generalization after variations in schedules of reinforcement. *Science, 142,* 412–413.

Hanson, H. M. (1959). Effects of discrimination training on stimulus generalization. *Journal of Experimental Psychology, 58,* 321–333.

Hearst, E., & Koresko, M. B. (1968). Stimulus generalization and the amount of prior training on variable-interval reinforcement. *Journal of Comparative and Physiological Psychology, 66,* 133–138.

Hearst, E., Koresko, M. B., & Poppen, R. (1964). Stimulus generalization and the response-reinforcement contingency. *Journal of the Experimental Analysis of Behavior, 7,* 369–380.

Honig, W. K., Boneau, C. A., Burstein, K. R., & Pennypacker, H. S. (1963). Positive and negative generalization gradients obtained under equivalent training conditions. *Journal of Comparative and Physiological Psychology, 56,* 111–116.

Hull, C. L. (1943). *Principles of behavior.* New York: Appleton-Century-Crofts.

Hull, C. L. (1952). *A behavior system.* New Haven, Conn.: Yale University Press.

Jenkins, H. M., & Harrison, R. H. (1960). Effect of discrimination training on auditory generalization. *Journal of Experimental Psychology, 59,* 246–253.

Kamin, L. J. (1968). Predictability, surprise, attention, and conditioning. In B. Campbell and R. Church (Eds.), *Punishment and Aversive Behavior* (pp. 279–296). New York: Appleton-Century-Crofts.

Kalish, H. I., & Haber, A. (1965). The prediction of discrimination from generalization following variations in deprivation level. *Journal of Comparative and Physiological Psychology, 60,* 125–128.

Karpicke, J., & Hearst, E. (1975). Inhibitory control and errorless discrimination learning. *Journal of the Experimental Analysis of Behavior, 23,* 159–166.

Logan, F. A. (1971). Essentials of a theory of discrimination learning. In H. H. Kendler & J. T. Spence (Eds.), *Essays in neobehaviorism: A memorial volume to Kenneth W. Spence* (pp. 265–282). New York: Appleton-Century-Crofts.

Margolius, G. (1955). Stimulus generalization of an instrumental response as a function of the number of reinforced trials. *Journal of Experimental Psychology, 49,* 105–111.

Newman, J. R., & Grice, G. R. (1965). Stimulus generalization as a function of drive level, and the relation between two levels of response strength. *Journal of Experimental Psychology, 69,* 357–365.

Pavlov, I. P. (1927). *Conditioned reflexes.* (G. V. Anrep, Trans.) London: Oxford University Press.

Razran, G. (1971). *Mind in evolution.* Boston: Houghton Mifflin.

Rickert, E. J., Lorden, J. F., Dawson, R., Jr., Smyly, E., & Callhan, M. F. (1979). Stimulus processing and stimulus selection in rats with hippocampal lesions. *Behavioral and Neural Biology, 27,* 454–465.

Spence, K. W. (1936). The nature of discrimination learning in animals. *Psychological Review, 44,* 430–444.

Spence, K. W. (1942). The basis of solution by chimpanzees of the intermediate size problem. *Journal of Experimental Psychology, 31,* 257–271.

Spence, K. W. (1956). *Behavior theory and conditioning.* New Haven, CT.: Yale University Press.

Thomas, D. R., & Switalski, R. W. (1966). Comparison of stimulus generalization following variable-ratio and variable-interval training. *Journal of Experimental Psychology, 71,* 236–240.

Walker, D. J., & Branch, M. N. (1998). Effects of variable-interval value and amount of training on stimulus generalization. *Journal of the Experimental Analysis of Behavior, 70,* 139–163.

Wagner, A. R. (1981). SOP: A model of automatic memory processing in animal Learning. In N. E. Spear & R. R. Miller (Eds.), *Information processing in animals: Memory mechanism.* (pp. 5–47). Hillsdale, NJ: Erlbaum.

Wagner, A. R., Logan, F. A., Haberlandt, K., & Price, T. (1968). Stimulus selection in animal discrimination learning. *Journal of Experimental Psychology, 76,* 171–180.

E. J. RICKERT
University of South Carolina

CLASSICAL CONDITIONING

STRESS

In the most general sense, the term *stress* is used to refer to a situation in which a person is overtaxed in some way. However, within this very general framework, a number of specific definitions have evolved, each emphasizing a different aspect of the *overtaxing* situation, but basically consistent with one another. Each of these definitions also involves some explicit or implicit reference to strain—the negative, or pathological, outcome of stress.

The first type of definition is stated in terms of the organism's response to some situation. In Selye's formulation in *The Stress of Life,* he pointed to stressors as being stimuli, which, because of their great magnitude, lead to the reaction he termed the General Adaptation Syndrome. Conversely, a person who manifests this syndrome is presumed to be in a state of stress. The first part of the syndrome is the alarm reaction, that is, the individual responds to a signal by going into a state of alarm. The next stage is that of resistance, with the body attempting to limit the effects of the stressor. This stage prepares the organism for either fight against or flight from the stressor. If either reaction is unsuccessful, the individual moves into a state of exhaustion, from which tissue breakdown and even death can result. In other words, continued stress can lead to bodily damage. The body manifests the stress reaction by a rise in blood pressure, increased adrenalin, changed heart beat, more red blood cells, slower digestion, and so on. On the other hand, Selye argued, some stress can be a positive experience; too little stress is also negative.

Although Selye's work was seminal, several shortcomings are evident. First, the definition has a degree of circularity: A stressor is whatever causes stress; there is no independent definition of stressor. Second, Selye's approach does not deal with the cognitive aspect of the stressor. Stressors are defined in physical terms, with little concern for the meaning of the situation for the individual. The sheer magnitude of a stimulus, in many instances, may be less important than its significance for the person. Third, Selye's definition tends to underemphasize the influence of stress on mental health and behavior, since he tends to focus on tissue effects, although concern with mental and behavioral effects is not inconsistent with his approach. Fourth, although Selye does theorize that some intermediate level of stress is positive for the person, he does not point to factors that can determine what will make stress positive. He does suggest magnitude of stimuli as a possible determinant, but has no really independent definition of magnitude of stimulus.

In addition to these difficulties, McGrath, in *Social and Psychological Factors in Stress,* and Cox, in *Stress,* have pointed out that Selye's definition and any other response-based definition of stress is deficient in that too great a variety of stimuli come to be defined as stressors; that the boundaries of the definition are vague; that apparent nonstressors can cause some of the same tissue responses as stressors; and that the various stress responses are not always highly correlated.

A second type of definition of stress focuses on the situation, or the stimuli, defined independently of the reaction of the person, even independently of the person's perceptions. Typically, the situations are of such gravity that they obviously tax most people, so that overlooking the variation in the perceptions of the situation by different people is not a serious shortcoming. Such stress situations include unemployment, extremely high or extremely low rates of input of stimuli, natural disasters, combat in war, conflicting and irreconcilable expectations on a job, and the sheer difficulty of meeting the basic needs of living, as in the case of poverty. The variety of such situations tends to defy unambiguous conceptualizations and measurement. Regardless, these stresses have been found to lead to such forms of strain as diseases like ulcers and heart attack; as changes in body chemistry, such as in uric acid level and blood pressure; and as depression, anxiety, alcoholism, and even death.

A third definition focuses on the perceptions that people have of the demands of various situations. Holmes and Rahe (1967) measured individuals' perceptions of various types of events by having them rate the amount of readjustment each one demanded. The individuals were also asked to indicate the recent frequency of occurrence of these events in their own lives. For each individual, the frequency of each event was multiplied by its adjustment rating and the products were summed. These sums, called Social Readjustment Scores, have been found to be correlated with, and in some instances predictive of, such forms of strain as chronic illnesses, including coronary heart disease, diabetes, and ulcers; alcoholism; accidents and injuries; poor academic performance; and professional and competitive failures.

This approach lumps together both desirable and undesirable changes, although there are some indications that even desirable changes produce stress. This approach also ignores the problem of the perceived cause of the event which can vary between individuals causing it to being completely imposed on that individual. People may feel less stressed by events they caused than by events imposed on them.

The fourth approach, the interactive, exemplified in the formulations of McGrath (1970), Lazarus (1966), and French (1973), goes even further in considering the individual's own responses in dealing with a taxing situation. This approach has been formulated in its most general form by French as a poor fit between an individual's resources and the demands of one's environment. One extreme type of poor fit occurs when the demands of a situation may so *undertax* an individual that he or she is in a state of stress because of the discrepancy between these demands and his or her own abilities. This conception of stress appears to be similar to Selye's notion that too low a level of stimulation can also cause stress.

French and his colleagues found that workers whose abilities were underused experienced dissatisfaction.

At the other extreme, the situation may impose demands beyond the individual's capacity to meet them, even given the resources available in the situation. These demands could be for productivity on a job, for resolving issues of great complexity, or for resolution of conflicting expectations. Obviously the degree of stress is a function of the ability of a given individual to meet these demands in the situation. The poor fit between the person and the environment can also occur if the person's motives are not satisfied by relevant supplies in the environment. Poor fits can have their locus either in the individual's perceptions of his or her inability to meet the demands of the situation and to satisfy personal motives, or in the individual's actual inability.

The individual's perception of the ability to meet the demands of the situation (or achieve his or her goals) may reflect in part the person's perception of his or her general, cross-situational level of ability to control the environment or to be a causal agent. Individuals who have *learned to be helpless* appear to generalize from the situation in which they learned to other situations, thus increasing stress in the latter. On the other hand, if an individual has learned to be dependent on others who generally are reliable supports in meeting his or her needs, then that individual is less likely to be stressed when these others are physically or psychologically present.

Furthermore, Lazarus and others have pointed out that some individuals may perceive high demands on them in a positive light, as challenges, as opportunities to advance their esteem of themselves by attaining high goals. Some challenge-minded individuals may generate stress for themselves by setting themselves extraordinarily high goals. Some researchers have classified people as A-type and B-type, with the former striving with great energy and focus on greater and greater achievement. Such persons suffer more strain, including early, fatal heart attacks, than do the more relaxed B types.

The exact process by which stress leads to strain is not well understood. Furthermore, little is understood as to why strain takes such different forms for different people. For some, it might involve specific, transitory, physiological changes, such as changes in blood pressure and in the acids in the blood. Others may develop some illness such as heart disease, cancer, high blood pressure, or ulcers. Still others might have mental problems, such as anxiety attacks, depression, or even psychosis. Behavior problems, such as alcoholism, crime, drug addiction, or suicide, might occur in other lives. The form the strain takes may depend on the type of stress or each individual may have a propensity to show strain in specific ways. The relationships among these various forms of strain are also not well understood.

Several influences in an individual's life have been found to reduce the incidence of strain, although it is not known whether these influences reduce stress, reduce strain, or reduce both. Most prominent among these ameliorative factors is social support from peers, from spouses, or even from supervisors. Another is exercise, or, more generally, physical exertion. In some cases, special types of exercise appear to have beneficial effects in reducing strain. These ameliorative influences have given rise to therapeutic programs for the reduction of strain. Such reductions may have secondary benefits because many forms of strain cause further stress, as when long illness causes poverty.

REFERENCES

Cox, T. (1978). *Stress.* Baltimore, MD: University Park Press.

French, J. R. P. (1973). Person role fit. *Occupational Mental Health, 3,* 15–20.

Holmes, T. H., & Rahe, R. H. (1967). The social readjustment rating scale. *Journal of Psychosomatic Research, 11,* 213–218.

Lazarus, R. S. (1966). *Psychological stress and the coping process.* New York: McGraw-Hill.

McGrath, J. (1970). *Social and psychological factors in stress.* New York: Holt, Rinehart & Winston.

Selye, H. (1956). *The stress of life.* New York: McGraw-Hill.

E. Stotland
University of Washington

A-TYPE PERSONALITY
B-TYPE PERSONALITY
GENERAL ADAPTATION SYNDROME

STRESS RESPONSE

There are three current stress model paradigms: environmental, psychological, and biological. Regardless of its etiology, stress exerts a powerful influence on the physiology of every bodily system via its impact on both the cognitive and physiological processes of the central nervous system (CNS). In a normal and beneficial stress response, the challenge is resolved and/or the individual adapts to it, and functioning returns to an appropriate base level. When these responses do not maintain homeostasis, and resistance fails due to inadequate, inappropriate, or excessive activation of the compensatory systems, the individual is at high risk of physical and psychological damage.

Due to its variety of specialized extero- and interoceptive sensory transducers and its unique integration capacity, the CNS plays a major role in the defense against and the adaptive response to stress. Stress responses begin with cerebral alterations that lead to behavioral changes—in content, emotions, speech—and alterations in central and peripheral neurotransmitters that effect changes in the physiology of other organ systems. The manifold defense mechanisms directed against stressors to which an organism is subjected form a single and highly integrated regulatory system. This system includes: (a) the complex subcortical CNS networks linking the integrative centers of the hypothalamus, the brain stem, and the limbic system; (b) their major nervous outputs through the peripheral nervous system controlling behavioral and neurovegetative adaptive responses through sympathetic and parasympathetic components; (c) the neurohormonal outputs originating in the endocrine neurons of the hypothalamus; and (d) the immune system.

The normal stress response involves synergistic activation of the sympathetic-adrenal-medullary (SAM) and hypothalamic-pituitary-adrenocortical (HPA) systems through their primary CNS effects of norepinephrine and corticotropin releasing hormone/factor (CRH and CRF, respectively). These effectors activate cortical limbic, hypothalamic, and pituitary mechanisms that promote adaptive changes in the face of an acute threat: Aggression; the focus of attention on the threat; arousal; vigilance; and the shutdown of sexual and feeding behaviors result. As the adrenal medulla secretes catecholamines and the adrenal cortex secretes glucocorticoids, blood flow is increased to the CNS and fuel is made available for immediate skeletal muscle activity, in part through gluconeogenesis. Glucocorticoids also cause immunosuppression, theoretically inhibiting the inflammatory response to any injury endured during the threat, postponing it until the organism has escaped to safety. While the latter effect of glucocorticoids is useful during immediate threat, it may provoke or sustain illness through immunosuppression in the setting of persistent, chronic stress. Glucocorticoids also appear to be critical in the shutdown of the stress response. They suppress the effect of CRH and very likely inhibit catecholamine activity in the locus ceruleus in the SAM system.

Of those two systems, the HPA system exerts significant homeostatic control over the stress response. There is clear evidence of HPA activity in the context of overwhelming, chronic threats and distress, including major depression, where hypercortisolism and other findings support HPA activation (Leonard & Song, 1996). The effects of chronic stress differ from the sequelae of acute, limited stress. A state of persistent, uncontained stress is pathological and loss of neurobiological control over the stress response could be a factor in the development of cancer, various psychiatric disorders (e.g., depression, Post Traumatic Stress Disorder [PTSD], alcohol addiction), and other medical conditions (hypertension, asthma, gastrointestinal and reproductive dysfunction; Breier, 1989).

Repeated stress and the resultant hypercortisolism have consequences for brain function, especially for the hippocampus, with its high concentration of glucocorticoid receptors. The hippocampus is essential for learning through its effect on episodic and declarative memory, and is especially important for the memory of context of time and place where events with a strong emotional basis occur. Thus, hippocampal functioning impairment decreases the reliability and accuracy of such memories. This may contribute to the degree to which events may be perceived as stressful when, had context memory functions been normal, the circumstances of those events might have been perceived as nonthreatening. The mechanism for stress-induced hippocampal dysfunction and memory impairment is twofold. First, acute stress elevates adrenal steroids and suppresses neuronal mechanisms that subserve short-term memory involving the hippocampus and temporal lobe. These effects are reversible and relatively short-lived. Second, repeated stress causes atrophy of the dendrites of pyramidal neurons in the CA3 region of the hippocampus, doing so through a mechanism involving both glucocorticoids and excitatory amino acid neurotransmitters released during and in the aftermath of stress. Although this atrophy is reversible as long as the stress is short-lived, stress lasting many months or years appears to, among other things, be capable of killing hippocampal neurons (Sapolsky, 1996). Stress-related disorders such as recurrent depressive illness, PTSD, and Cushing's syndrome are associated with atrophy of the human hippocampus measured by magnetic resonance imaging (Bremner, 1999).

The hippocampus is also a regulator of the stress response and exerts a largely inhibitory effect to promote shut-off of the HPA axis stress response. Recent evidence suggests that the hippocampal influence on the hypothalamic CRF neurons is via the bed nucleus of the stria terminalis and involves the regulation of an inhibitory output to these neurons (Herman & Cullinan, 1997).

Other areas in the limbic system (e.g., cingulate gyrus and amygdala) and frontal brain regions also have higher concentrations of glucocorticoid receptors. While less is known about the impact of glucocorticoids in these regions, the same general picture as in the hippocampus may hold, particularly early in life when these regions are developing rapidly and forming interconnections (Hatalski, Guirguis, & Baram, 1998; Schneider, 1992).

A third stress response component is endogenous opioid release. Hypercortisolism in the HPA system is accompanied by activation of the endogenous opioid (EO) system. Stress-induced analgesia involving endogenous opioid peptides has been demonstrated in animals and humans, both in association with nociceptive stimuli, as well as in response to non–pain cognitive stress. Since the original demonstration of the endogenous opioid receptor by Pert and Snyder in 1973, various opioid peptides such as beta endorphin and enkephalins have been identified. These endogenous opioids are produced in sites including the pituitary and adrenal glands, linking the EO system to the HPA and SAM components of the stress response. Theoretically, release of endogenous opioids modulates emotional response to stressors through calming effects, by reducing pain and perhaps by altering immune function.

There is now clear evidence of reciprocal interactions between the immune system (IS) and CNS (Cacioppo et al., 1998). Most hormones secreted during the stress response have immunologic effects. Anatomical and functional connections have been demonstrated between the IS and CNS; and cytokines, neuropeptides, and neuromediators have been shown to modulate cells of the two systems via receptors on neurons and lymphocytes. It has become apparent that the IS and CNS are tightly interconnected and interdependent, and interact during development and in the induction of CNS pathology (Herbert & Cohen, 1993). It has also been extensively documented that individuals experiencing acute, subacute, and chronic psychological stress are immunodepressed and that stress is linked with higher morbidity.

One of the most challenging issues in the measurement of response to stress is the characterization of the temporal course of stressors, appraisals, and stress responses. In addition, there is wide variation among individuals in how each responds to potentially stressful situations. Thus, a multifaceted biopsychosocial approach is required to gain a comprehensive view of the relationship among stressors, stress responses, and pathological sequelae. In-

ter-person variation depends on three principal factors. The first is how the individual perceives and interprets the situation. If the stimulus is seen as a threat, then behaviors and physiological responses ensue that can have further consequences; otherwise, responses either are not precipitated or differ from stress responses and are also more benign. The second aspect of individual differences concerns the condition of the body itself. For example, metabolic imbalances leading to obesity and diabetes can increase the vulnerability of an individual to stress, and may have a genetic component (Brindley & Rolland, 1989). The ability of individuals to cope with the same stressor may be vastly different. Differences in coping skills depend on a combination of many factors, including genetics, training, religion, environment, education, coping skills, gender, age, past experiences, nationality, family stability, social relationships, and perceived social supports.

The final major factor is the nature of the stressor itself. Stressors can be characterized in a variety of ways: by etiology (e.g., physical, emotional/cognitive, or both); by duration (acute, chronic, or both); by complexity (due to a single event or to multiple factors); by temporal nature (from the past, present, or future); or by intensity (mild, moderate, or severe). The pattern in which stressors are presented also impacts responses. Baum and colleagues (1993) categorized stress duration through the use of a $2 \times 2 \times 2$ matrix that crossed duration of the event, duration of the perceived threat, and duration of the stress response. This matrix suggests a more sensitive approach to understanding the role of stress duration (e.g., the difference between a persistent stressful event that is no longer appraised as stressful or that no longer elicits a stress response, and a stressful event that has terminated but continues to be appraised as a stressful event and to elicit a stress response [e.g., a traumatic experience]).

The idea that cumulative levels of stress may have deleterious effects on health and longevity has long intrigued investigators, dating from the early work on homeostasis and continuing with the work of Cannon (1939), Selye (1956), and others on the pathologic consequences of excessive physiologic activation. However, much of the early work focused on the effects of stress on specific, individual biologic parameters and associated health consequences. Recently, McEwen and Stellar (1993) introduced the concept of allostatic load—a more cumulative, multi-system view of the long-term effects of the physiologic response to stress. McEwen (1998) described four types of allostatic load situations, each with differing potential for short- and long-term effects: (a) frequent stress exposure with appropriate adaptation; (b) lack of adaptation to the same repeated stressor; (c) prolonged response due to delayed or absent shutdown after the stressor is terminated; and (d) inadequate responses to the stressor trigger compensatory increases in others.

Stress is universal; it is found in every person, in every culture, and in every generation. It is a broad-based phenomenon that exists as a continuum. Individuals showing various stress response patterns are likely to be distributed differently across gradients of socioeconomic status but not confined exclusively to one part of the gradient. Thus, it is important to distinguish between the characteristics of groups and the vulnerability of individuals. It is necessary to continue to study the biology-behavior interface to understand the various forms of stress responses and their relation-ships to health and disease in individuals.

REFERENCES

Baum, A., Cohen, L., & Hall, M. (1993). Control and intrusive memories as possible determinants of chronic stress. *Psychosomatic Medicine, 55*(3), 274–286.

Bremner, J. D. (1999). Does stress damage the brain? *Biological Psychiatry, 45*(7), 797–805.

Breier, A. (1989). Experimental approaches to human stress research: Assessment of neurobiological mechanisms of stress in volunteers and psychiatric patients. *Biological Psychiatry, 26*(5), 438–462.

Cacioppo, J. T., Berntson, G. G., Malarkey, W. B., Kiecolt-Glaser, J. K., Sheridan, J. F., Poehlmann, K. M., Burleson, M. H., Ernst, J. M., Hawkley, L. C., & Glaser, R. (1998). Autonomic, neuroendocrine, and immune responses to psychological stress: The reactivity hypothesis. *Annals of the New York Academy of Sciences, 840,* 664–673.

Brindley, D. N., & Rolland, Y. (1989). Possible connections between stress, diabetes, obesity, hypertension and altered lipoprotein metabolism that may result in atherosclerosis. *Clinical Science, 77*(5), 453–461.

Cannon, W. (1939). *The wisdom of the body.* New York City, NY: Norton.

Hatalski, C. G., Guirguis, C., & Baram, T. Z. (1998). Corticotripin releasing factor mRNA expression in the hypothalamic paraventricular nucleus and the central nucleus of the amygdala is modulated by repeated acute stress in the immature rat. *Journal of Neuroendocrinology, 10,* 663–669.

Herbert, T. B., & Cohen, S. (1993). Stress and immunity in humans: A meta-analytic review. *Psychosomatic Medicine, 55*(4), 364–379.

Herman, J. P., & Cullinan, W. E. (1997). Neurocircuitry of stress: Central control of the hypothalamo-pituitary-adrenocortical axis. *Trends in Neurosciences, 20*(2), 78–84.

Leonard, B. E., & Song, C. (1996). Stress and the immune system in the etiology of anxiety and depression. *Pharmacology, Biochemistry & Behavior, 54*(1), 299–303.

McEwen, B. S. (1998). Protective and damaging effects of stress mediators. *New England Journal of Medicine, 338*(3), 171–179.

McEwen, B. S., & Stellar, E. (1993). Stress and the individual. Mechanisms leading to disease. *Archives of Internal Medicine, 153*(18), 2093–2101.

Pert, C. B., & Snyder, S. H. (1973). Opiate receptor: Demonstration in nervous tissue. *Science, 179*(77), 1011–1014.

Sapolsky, R. M. (1996). Why stress is bad for your brain. *Science, 273*(5276), 749–750.

Schneider, M. L. (1992). Prenatal stress exposure alters postnatal behavioral expression under conditions of novelty challenge in rhesus monkey infants. *Developmental Psychobiology, 25*(7), 529–540.

Selye, H. (1956). *The stress of life.* New York City, NY: McGraw-Hill Publishers.

K. L. Peters
University of Alberta

NEUROCHEMISTRY
PSYCHOPHYSIOLOGY
STRESS

STRIATE CORTEX

The striate cortex, also known as the primary visual cortex, area 17, or V1, is involved in conscious visual perception. It is located in the occipital pole of the cerebral cortex, where much of it is deep within the calcarine fissure. There is a precise, retinotopic representation of the contralateral visual field in each hemisphere. The vertical meridian is represented at the border between V1 and V2 (the secondary visual cortex), and the horizontal meridian bisects it midway. The contralateral lower and upper visual fields are represented in the cuneus and lingual gyrus, respectively. The map is skewed because a much larger proportion of the striate cortex is devoted to the processing of the central visual field than is the periphery. The magnification therefore changes from about 4 mm of cortex per degree of visual field to about 0.5 mm/degree as the representation moves from 1° to 25° away from the center of gaze.

The striate cortex is about 1.5 to 2 mm thick and has six cellular layers, numbered I to VI. Layer IV (granular layer) is expanded into IVA, IVB, and IVC (IVCα and IVCβ). IVA and IVCβ receive input from the parvocellular layers of the lateral geniculate nucleus (LGN), while IVCα is the recipient of magnocellular LGN input. Layer IVB is also known as the stripe of Gennari and contains cortico-cortical fibers rather than geniculate projections. The koniocellular (small-celled) LGN layers project to layers II and III puffs (or supragranular blobs; Figure 1). Signals from layer IV are modified and relayed to supragranular and infragranular layers. Supragranular pyramidal cells then project to other cortical areas, while infragranular pyramidal cells primarily project to subcortical visual centers, the superior colliculus, and LGN.

While the receptive fields (RFs) of retinal ganglion cells and lateral geniculate neurons are circular with concentric center-surround antagonism, only the first stage cortical neurons in layer IVC and layers II and III puffs have similar circular RFs. The RFs of most striate cortical neurons are elongated, and they respond best to lines, bars, slits, borders, and edges that have a specific orientation. The elongated RF center has antagonistic flanking zones on one or both sides. The cells typically respond better to a moving or flickering light stimulus than to a stationary line. Layer IVB has direction-selective cells. In their classical experiments, Hubel and Wiesel (1968) described simple and complex units in the striate cortex of cats and monkeys. Simple cells receive input from three or more LGN neurons, and their RFs are subdivided into ON and OFF regions with an elongated border. They respond best to a bar or edge of light that fills mainly or exclusively the ON region of

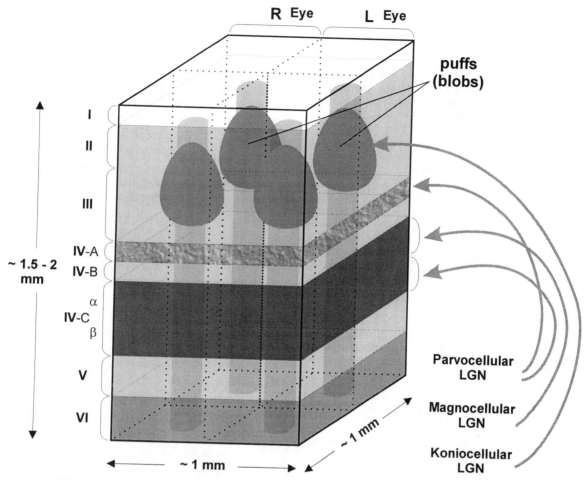

R Eye   L Eye

puffs
(blobs)

I
II
III
IV-A
IV-B
α
IV-C
β
V
VI

~ 1.5 - 2
mm

Parvocellular
LGN

Magnocellular
LGN

Koniocellular
LGN

~1 mm

~ 1 mm

Figure 1.   A schematic diagram of the striate cortex showing cytochrome oxidase-rich (darker) and -poor regions. Layers IVC, IVA, II/III puffs (blobs) and, to a lesser extent, VI receive geniculocortical projections and are moderately to intensely labeled. Each puff is centered on an ocular dominance column (right-eye R or left-eye L), the very center of which also exhibits slightly higher levels of cytochrome oxidase (rod-like shading from layers II to VI). Orientation columns (not shown) are intermingled within each ocular dominance column. A module contains the minimal and necessary sets of orientation columns, ocular dominance columns, and puffs/blobs to analyze a small locus in the visual field.

their RF. The orientation and position of the stimulus are critical. Complex cells respond poorly to stationary spots of light and their RFs do not have discrete ON and OFF regions. An optimally-oriented line placed anywhere in the RF may elicit about the same response. The width of the line is critical, but the length and exact position are not important. Thus, complex cells are specific for orientation but nonspecific for position. They are thought to receive input from a number of simple cells with the same orientation preference. These properties, plus those uncovered by many other investigators, characterize striate cortical neurons according to their preference for color, direction, orientation, high or low spatial frequencies, eye dominance, and contrast sensitivity.

The striate cortex is structurally and functionally laminated but is also organized into vertical domains or columns. Cells within the same functional column (layers I–VI) share similar functions. Ocular dominance columns (ODCs) segregate cells with different eye preference. Within such a column, layer IV cells are strictly monocular, while supra- and infra-granular neurons are binocular but are

dominated by the same eye input as layer IV cells. Orientation columns partition cells by orientation preference (e.g., vertical, horizontal, and oblique at various angles). While ODCs are about 0.5 mm wide in humans, the orientation columns are an order of magnitude smaller, about 50 μm in diameter. These two sets of columns interdigitate within the cortex, together with other functional columns, such as those for color and spatial frequencies.

One of the most striking features of the primate striate cortex is the presence of an extremely regular array of cytochrome oxidase–rich zones in the supragranular layers (II and III; Figure 1). Cytochrome oxidase is a mitochondrial energy-generating enzyme, and these regions are metabolic hot spots. They have been given the name "puffs" or supragranular "blobs" (also known as dots, patches, or spots). Puffs are laid down before birth in the macaque but after birth in the human. Puffs receive direct geniculate input from the konio layers and are centered on ocular dominance columns. Cells within puffs have receptive field properties that are distinctly different from those in the interpuffs.

PUFFS	INTERPUFFS
Cytochrome oxidase–rich	Cytochrome oxidase–poor
Monocular	Binocular
High spontaneous activity	Low spontaneous activity
Receptive field mostly circular; color-opponent center-surround	Receptive field rectangular; ON- or OFF-center with antagonistic flanks
Orientation-nonspecific	Orientation-specific
Respond to low spatial frequency gratings	Respond to high spatial frequency gratings
Greater color-selectivity	Lesser color selectivity
Input: IVCβ and koniocellular LGN layers	Input: IVCβ
Output: thin stripes of V2	Output: interstripes of V2

A piece of visual cortex with a surface area of 1 to 2 mm² probably contains sufficient neural machinery to process visual signals (e.g., size, shape, color, luminance, movement, and depth) from a particular point in the visual space. It would typically include the minimal and necessary sets of ODCs, orientation columns, and puffs (blobs) centered on ODCs. This is known as a cortical module.

The major neurotransmitter of cortical projection neurons is glutamate, the universal excitatory transmitter. GABA is the key transmitter of inhibitory interneurons. Other neurochemicals, such as calbindin, calmodulin, neuropeptide Y, parvalbumin, somatostatin, substance P, and nitric oxide probably serve modulatory roles.

From the geniculocortical pathway, information is channeled to different pathways in over 30 extrastriate cortical areas in the occipital, parietal, and temporal lobes. These multiple streams process different attributes of the visual stimuli: color, contrast, form, and movement. The "what" stream for object recognition is channeled to the inferotemporal cortex, whereas the "where" stream for spatial localization is channeled to the parietal cortex. The "what" or ("ventral") stream is further divided into two parvocellular (P) streams: one for color, form, and movement, the other for color and contrast. The "where" (or "dorsal") stream is also known as the magnocellular (M) stream and is concerned with contrast, movement, and stereopsis. Small cells of the LGN (koniocellular) mediate another less-understood pathway via the cortical puffs. There is, however, much cross-talk among the visual centers, especially at the higher cortical level.

The striate cortex normally has equal representation of both eyes in the binocular part of the visual field. If the signal from one eye is disrupted by infection, patching, strabismus, astigmatism, lesion, or other abnormalities during the critical period of postnatal development, cortical neurons may be irreversibly altered in their functional and structural properties. Cells that receive input from the non-affected eye will become dominant and command more synaptic space at the expense of cells representing the deprived eye. Behaviorally, the individual may suffer from amblyopia, poor depth perception, poor pattern perception, or frank blindness in that eye. Interestingly, binocular deprivation is less detrimental than monocular deprivation, because of the strong binocular competition at the cortical level.

Although mature neurons have long been regarded as being re-fractory to change (unless altered pathologically), recent work has demonstrated that they remain capable of responding to altered functional demands. When impulse activity of one eye is blocked in adult monkeys, cortical neurons deprived of their normal input down-regulate their metabolic enzymes (cytochrome oxidase) as well as other neurotransmitter-related neurochemicals (GABA, glutamate, NMDA receptors, nitric oxide synthase, and others). Synaptic reorganization can also occur in the mature visual cortex when the input from one eye is perturbed. Changes are reversible when there is no denervation in the adult.

In recent years, functional magnetic resonance imaging (fMRI) has been used to study the living visual cortex, and many analogous subdivisions previously mapped in the macaque brain have been uncovered in the human visual cortex.

REFERENCE

Hubel, D. H., & Wiesel, T. N. (1968). Receptive field and functional architecture of monkey striate cortex. *Journal of Physiology, 195,* 215–243.

SUGGESTED READING

DeYoe, E. A., Carman, G., Bandettini, P., Glickman, S., Wieser, J., Cox, R., Miller, D., & Neitz, J. (1996). Mapping striate and extrastriate visual areas in human cerebral cortex. *Proceedings of the National Academy of Sciences, U.S.A., 93*(6), 2382–2386.

Hendry, S. H. C., & Calkins, D. J. (1998). Neuronal chemistry and functional organization in the primate visual system. *Trends in Neuroscience, 21,* 344–349.

Horton, J. C., & Hedley-Whyte, E. T. (1984). Mapping of cytochrome oxidase patches and ocular dominance columns in human visual cortex. *Philosophical Transactions of the Royal Society of London, B, 304,* 255–272.

Kaas, J. H. (1995). Human visual cortex: Progress and puzzles. *Current Biology, 5,* 1126–1128.

Livingstone, M. S., & Hubel, D. H. (1984). Anatomy and physiology of a color system in the primate visual cortex. *Journal of Neuroscience, 4,* 309–356.

Tootell, R. B. H., Silverman, M. S., Hamilton, S. L., Switkes, E., & De Valois, R. L. (1988). Functional anatomy of macaque striate cortex: V. Spatial frequency. *Journal of Neuroscience, 8,* 1610–1624.

Ungerleider, L. G., & Haxby, J. V. (1994). "What" and "where" in the human brain. *Current Opinion in Neurobiology, 4,* 157–165.

Wong-Riley, M. T. T. (1994). Primate visual cortex: Dynamic metabolic organization and plasticity revealed by cytochrome oxidase. In A. Peters & K. Rockland (Eds.), *Cerebral Cortex: Vol. 10. Primary Visual Cortex in Primates* (pp. 141–200). New York: Plenum.

M. T. T. WONG-RILEY
Medical College of Wisconsin

BRODMAN'S AREA

STRICKLAND, BONNIE R. (1936–   )

Bonnie R. Strickland was born in 1936 and grew up in Alabama and Florida. The first of her large, extended family to attend college, Strickland was also a nationally ranked tennis player and supported herself with athletic scholarships and part-time jobs. She graduated from Alabama College with a major in health, physical education, and recreation. Encouraged by the only two psychologists she had ever met—who were on her college faculty—she applied and was accepted into the clinical psychology program at Ohio State University. She left the South to study with such people as Doug Crowne, George Kelly, and Jules Rotter, and she completed both hospital and out-patient internships. Her research in graduate school was primarily related to the construct validation of internal/external control expectancies and need for approval, and she was involved in the early development of the Internal External Locus of Control Scale and the Marlowe-Crowne Social Desirability Scale.

On receiving her PhD in 1962, Strickland returned to the South and became one of the first women to join the faculty at Emory University, where she took on the multiple roles of a clinical psychologist. Not only did she teach, but she also was active in the counseling center, where she saw clients and ran psychotherapy groups. For 3 years she served as Dean of Women and was the youngest to do so at any major university. She was also involved in the Atlanta community, occasionally completing psychological evaluations and testifying in court for civil rights protestors who had been committed to mental hospitals. In her research, she considered the expectancies and beliefs of Black students involved in the civil rights movement in relation to their White counterparts. Her findings demonstrating that internal locus of control beliefs are related to direct social action became a Citation Classic. Strickland's research ranged from the streets to the schools, and from the clinic to the laboratory. She was particularly interested in looking at psychological variables among neglected populations. She was among the first to demonstrate that the mental health status of lesbians (and gay men) were similar to those of their heterosexual counterparts. She was particularly interested in learning more about the effects of discrimination on children's development and conducted several studies on delay of gratification and interpersonal trust among Black and White children. This research led to the need for a more adequate scale to assess internal versus external expectancies in children. With Steve Nowicki, Strickland developed the Nowicki-Strickland Locus of Control Scale for Children, which became one of the most heavily cited and widely used instruments across the world.

In 1973, Strickland joined the faculty at the University of Massachusetts at Amherst. She continued her research on mood regulation and became particularly interested in gender differences in health and illness. As a member of the National Institute of Mental Health's "Depression: Awareness, Recognition, and Treatment" program, Strickland was intrigued as to why women of all countries and across all social strata are 2 to 3 times more likely than men to become depressed. Her students were among the first to consider those biological, psychological, and social factors that might lead to the greater incidence of depression among women.

During this time, Strickland also became active in the American Psychological Association (APA). She has always had a special concern for the education and training of clinical psychologists, and was a participant in most of the major conferences on graduate education in psychology. She served on numerous accrediting committees and evaluation teams and began to write about the history of clinical psychology. Within APA, Strickland was chair of the first Equal Opportunity and Affirmative Action Committee of the Division of Clinical Psychology and eventually became the president of the Division. She was also chair of APA's Policy and Planning Board and was elected president of APA in 1987. At that time, she proposed a task force on women and depression to consider the high rates of depression among women. In 1989, that task force published a report of its findings in what was to become one of APA's most influential books, *Women and Depression: Risk Factors and Treatment Issues*.

In addition to serving APA, Strickland served on a number of national boards and committees, including the Advisory Board of the National Institute of Mental Health (NIMH). She was a founder of the American Psychological Society, and founder and president of the American Association for Applied and Preventive Psychology. Her administrative activities have included being department chair and associate to the chancellor at UMass/Amherst. A distinguished teacher and the author of over 100 articles and book chapters, Strickland has also testified before the U.S. Congress for increased funding for the social and behavioral sciences. In 1999, she received the Award for Distinguished Contributions to the Public Interest from APA; her citation reads, "her impressive, substantial, and innovative contributions to psychology . . . have identified and offered solutions for social problems, exemplified unusual initiative and dedication in meeting community needs, and advanced social justice related to the provision of psychological services and science."

STAFF

STRONG, EDWARD KELLOGG, JR. (1884–1963)

Edward Kellogg Strong, Jr. received the PhD degree under J. McK. Cattell and began his teaching career at the then Carnegie Institute of Technology. His publications included an introductory psychology text and a book on selling and advertising. He also published in the areas of industrial training and job analysis.

While at Carnegie, he participated in a seminar on the measurement of interests conducted by C. S. Yoakum. The Interest Blank developed was a series of items that were answered "like," "dislike," or "?—insufficient information to decide." Several years after moving to Stanford in 1923, he jointly supervised the doctoral dissertation of K. M. Cowdery. This dissertation involved the comparison of interests of doctors, engineers, and lawyers, and used a modification of the Carnegie Interest Blank. Cowdery found distinctive response patterns for each group. The patterns remained consistent on a new sample (cross-validation).

Strong extended Cowdery's work to 18 occupation groups, used larger samples, and in other ways improved the technical quality of the inventory. First published in 1927, the Strong Vocational Interest Blank, or SVIB, quickly became the instrument of choice for the empirically minded. The published instrument had 420 items; slightly more than 40% were retained from Cowdery's version.

Later revisions included separate blanks for men (SVIB-M) and women (SVIB-W). The technically sophisticated 1974 revision by David P. Campbell of Minnesota is called the SCII or Strong–Campbell Interest Inventory. The single form for use by men and women offers 124 occupational scale comparisons as well as other measures. More than 1,500 articles and books have been published concerning the instrument.

Strong spent most of his career in the measurement of vocational interests. His later publications dealt with the variation of interests over time, including a large group studied 18 years after completing college.

C. S. PEYSER
The University of the South

STRONG INTEREST INVENTORY

The Strong Interest Inventory (SII), published in 1995, was the latest in a series of revisions of a test originally developed by E. K. Strong, Jr., in the 1920s. It contains 317 questions that require the test taker to respond with "like," "indifferent," or "dislike" to a variety of occupations, activities, school subjects, and types of people; to indicate preferences between paired options (such as dealing with things vs. dealing with people); and to mark "yes," "no," or "?" to a series of self-descriptive statements.

The SII was developed on the basis of over 60 years of experience with earlier versions of the test and continues the tradition of a counseling instrument that over the years has been used in thousands of research studies and has been given to millions of people. The test must be computer scored, and scores reflect 6 General Occupational Themes, 25 Basic Interests, 211 Occupations (102 occupations separately normed for men and women, plus 7 occupations with single-sex norms), and 4 Personal Styles. Although all people take the same test, separate male and female norms are applied because sex differences in interest patterns frequently occur.

The purpose of the SII is to provide information to the individual and the professional counselor or personnel officer to aid in academic and career decision making. Scores reflect the individual's interests rather than abilities. The occupational scales compare the individual's responses on items known to discriminate between people in the career and men or women in general. For example, the male accountant score is based on items that have been empirically demonstrated to differentiate between male accountants and men in general. People who choose careers that are consistent with their interests have been shown to stay with their career choices longer than do people who enter careers that are inconsistent with their interests.

The SII is widely accepted by academic and career counselors as one of the best and most useful tests available for this purpose. It should be used and interpreted in conjunction with trained counselors.

M. J. ALLEN
California State University, Bakersfield

CAREER COUNSELING
RATING SCALES

THE STROOP EFFECT

The Phenomenon

Since psychology emerged as a distinct discipline, we have known that the time to name objects or their properties is considerably longer than the time to read the corresponding words. Indeed, Cattell (1886) demonstrated this in his dissertation: Saying "horse" to a picture or "blue" to a color patch took more time than did reading the word *horse or blue*. Cattell attributed this empirical difference to the automaticity of word reading developed through extensive practice.

Fifty years later, these two dimensions were combined into a single task by John Ridley Stroop (1935/1992; for a biographical sketch, see MacLeod, 1991b). In his dissertation, Stroop printed words in incongruent colors (e.g., the word RED in blue ink) and asked people to respond selectively to one dimension or the other. He observed a dramatic difference: Asked to read the word and ignore the color, people had little difficulty relative to a control condition where all words appeared in normal black ink. However, asked to name the ink color and ignore the word, people were extraordinarily slow and error-prone relative to a control condition of color patches without words (e.g., a blue patch).

This difficulty in ignoring incongruent words while color naming has come to be called the Stroop effect, or Stroop interference. Following Cattell's lead, the effect is seen as resulting from word reading being so automated that it cannot be prevented even when it disrupts performance. As the "gold standard" measure of attention, this effect is one of the largest and most stable phenomena in cognitive psychology, having served as a fundamental tool in hundreds of investigations (for a review, see MacLeod, 1991a). As evidence of its impact, many other analogous interference situations have emerged over the years; Figure 1 illustrates a few of these.

The Explanations

Several explanations of Stroop interference have been put forward. For many years, the prevalent one was the relative speed of processing account (see Dyer, 1973), in which performance is seen as a kind of "horse race" in which the wrong horse (the word) beats the right one (the color). This view derives from Cattell's data. More recently, theorists have argued that interference results from people having to execute a controlled process (color naming) in the face of

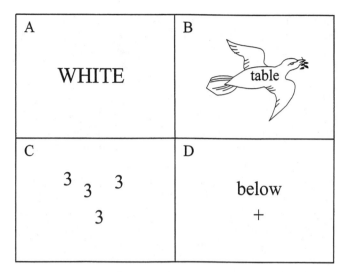

A	B
WHITE	table
C	D
3 3 3 / 3 / 3	below / +

Figure 1.   Variations on the Stroop effect. Panel A is the classic task, in which one must name the print color of the word, ignoring the word itself (i.e., say "black"). Panel B is the most frequently studied variant, in which one must name the picture, ignoring the word printed on it (i.e., say "bird"). In Panel C, the task is to count the number of characters, ignoring their identity (i.e., say "four"); in Panel D, the task is to indicate where the word appears with respect to the fixation cross (i.e., say "above"). All panels represent the case that produces interference relative to a control condition.

an automatic process (word reading). This explanation derives more from Cattell's theory, with automaticity viewed as a continuum that develops with practice (MacLeod & Dunbar, 1988).

Most recently, theories have come to emphasize not speed or automaticity of processing, but rather the strength of the connection between particular stimulus-task ensembles on the one hand and appropriate responses on the other hand. This is most evident in the new connectionist (neural network) models, notably that of Cohen, Dunbar, and McClelland (1990). Here, a layer of stimulus units (the words and colors) is modulated by task demand units (which set the task as color naming or word reading). Learning occurs via changing the strength of connections to a layer of intermediate units, with the results passed forward to a final output layer containing the responses. Such models do quite well at capturing many crucial findings.

Intriguing Aspects of the Stroop Effect

We now know a great deal about the underpinnings of the Stroop effect and the factors that modulate it. Clearly, differential practice on the two dimensions is crucial to the effect. However, this does not mean that differential speed of processing the two dimensions is the mechanism, as shown by studies which have presented the color information well before the word, yet found no "reverse interference" of color on word reading (Glaser & Glaser, 1982). Indeed, the idea of automaticity has not gone unchallenged either, given that undermining the likelihood of reading the word, such as by coloring only a single letter (Besner, Stolz, & Boutilier, 1997), reduces the effect.

The Stroop task is now widely used as a benchmark measure of

attention and automaticity, often appearing on standardized tests and in experiments outside cognitive psychology. Importantly, effects on the color naming of words are not restricted to color words, but can occur for non-color words if they are primed by prior presentation (e.g., Warren, 1972). This has led to numerous priming studies, most notably the recent work on the emotional Stroop effect (for a review, see Williams, Mathews, & MacLeod, 1996). Here, time to name the print colors of non-color words is greater for words related to an individual's anxiety (e.g., WEB for a spider phobic; EXAM for a test anxious person) than for neutral words (e.g., CHAIR), presumably due to "chronic priming." The emotional Stroop effect is now used as a diagnostic tool for the existence of and the successful treatment of anxiety disorders.

In addition, new brain imaging techniques that permit localization of cognitive activity, such as positron emission tomography (PET) and functional magnetic resonance imaging (fMRI), have also been applied to the Stroop effect, with converging results. Like many other attentional tasks, the Stroop effect shows activity in the anterior cingulate cortex, one of the brain centers associated with cognition, and particularly with attention (see Carter, Mintun, & Cohen, 1995).

Overall, then, this seemingly simple demonstration task that has been with us for over sixty years continues to be very fruitful in our exploration of how attention, a fundamental aspect of human cognition, works. We can expect it to be put to continuing creative use in the exploration of cognition.

REFERENCES

Besner, D., Stolz, J. A., & Boutilier, C. (1997). The Stroop effect and the myth of automaticity. *Psychonomic Bulletin & Review, 4,* 221–225.

Cattell, J. M. (1886). The time it takes to see and name objects. *Mind, 11,* 63–65.

Carter, C. S., Mintun, M., & Cohen, J. D. (1995). Interference and facilitation effects during selective attention: An H₂¹⁵O PET study of Stroop task performance. *Neuroimage, 2,* 264–272.

Cohen, J. D., Dunbar, K., & McClelland, J. L. (1990). On the control of automatic processes: A parallel distributed processing account of the Stroop effect. *Psychological Review, 97,* 332–361.

Dyer, F. N. (1973). The Stroop phenomenon and its use in the study of perceptual, cognitive, and response processes. *Memory & Cognition, 1,* 106–120.

Glaser, M. O., & Glaser, W. R. (1982). Time course analysis of the Stroop phenomenon. *Journal of Experimental Psychology: Human Perception and Performance, 8,* 875–894.

MacLeod, C. M. (1991a). Half a century of research on the Stroop effect: An integrative review. *Psychological Bulletin, 109,* 163–203.

MacLeod, C. M. (1991b). John Ridley Stroop: Creator of a landmark cognitive task. *Canadian Psychology, 32,* 521–524.

MacLeod, C. M., & Dunbar, K. (1988). Training and Stroop-like interference: Evidence for a continuum of automaticity. *Journal of Experimental Psychology: Learning, Memory, and Cognition, 14,* 126–135.

Stroop, J. R. (1935). Studies of interference in serial verbal reactions. *Journal of Experimental Psychology, 18,* 643–662. [Reprinted in 1992 as one of the "classic articles" celebrating the centennial of the American Psychological Association, in the *Journal of Experimental Psychology: General, 121,* 15–23.]

Warren, R. E. (1972). Stimulus encoding and memory. *Journal of Experimental Psychology, 94,* 90–100.

Williams, J. M. G., Mathews, A., & MacLeod, C. (1996). The emotional Stroop task and psychopathology. *Psychological Bulletin, 120,* 3–24.

C. M. McLeod
University of Toronto at Scarborough

ATTENTION
AUTOMATICITY
BRAIN IMAGING
COGNITION
CONNECTIONIST MODELING
EMOTION
INTERFERENCE
LEARNING
PRACTICE
PRIMING

STRUCTURAL EQUATION MODELING

Used in an array of topics ranging from the study of scholastic achievement (Miller, Kohn, & Schooler, 1985) to the investigation of mood states (Hertzog & Nesselroade, 1987), structural equation modeling represents the systematic analysis of causal relationships. Alternately referred to as demand analysis, multitrait multimethod analysis, path analysis, linear causal analysis, or simultaneous equations, the expanded use of structural equation modeling is attributable, in large measure, to two features of research in the behavioral sciences (Goldberger, 1973). First, since many behavioral studies are not experimental by design, analysis of nonexperimental data requires the use of statistical procedures as alternatives to experimental manipulation and control. The intent of the statistical procedures inherent in structural equation modeling is to achieve some of the assessment potential of experimental research. Second, the principal focus of many behavioral studies is on hypothetical constructs not directly observable but that decisively impact and order relationships among measured variables. Consequently, models accommodating both the latent aspect of these variables and their empirical relationship to measured variables have been developed.

Informed by theory, structural equation modeling involves the elucidation and analysis of causal relationships among identified variables of interest. The causal relationships modeled can range from recursive bivariate relationships to more complicated reciprocal multivariate relationships. In assessing the magnitude of causal effects, it is important to distinguish between structural equations and regression equations. Regression equations report the degree of empirical association between variables of interest exemplified by a statement of finding such as "as *x* changes so does *y.*" By contrast, structural equations represent a higher level of abstraction in which, given the empirical association among the variables, specific causal linkages are the focus of attention. Notwithstanding this distinction, regression equations can be used to estimate structural equations if certain conditions are met (Dwyer, 1983). First, the causal variables identified in the model must be independent of other unspecified causes or, alternatively, all important causal variables related to the phenomena under study must be specified. Consequently, a high level of conceptual and theoretical exactitude is required in structural equation modeling. Second, the variables of the model are either dichotomous or linearly interrelated. Recognizing that not all substantive domains of study are empirically represented by linear relationships among the variables of interest, linear structural models can nonetheless be used effectively in the investigation of nonlinear relationships if appropriate transformations are performed. Third, either the causal variables are measured without error or explicit procedures for the estimation of measurement error are implemented, as exemplified by the multitrait multimethod approach of multiple indicator models. Fourth, causal direction and order among the variables of interest must be clearly specified. While this may not be particularly problematic in a recursive model, the modeling of reciprocal causality necessitates the deployment of more elaborate and involved analytic procedures (Duncan, 1973). If, in addition to other considerations, these four basic conditions are satisfied, then a causal interpretation of the meaning of the respective structural coefficients can be confidently but nevertheless tentatively proposed.

At the simplest level of analysis, bivariate recursive causal models are illustrated by the following equation: $X \rightarrow Y \leftarrow u$. In this example, the dependent variable (Y) is caused by the joint impact of two distinct influences, X and u. Variable X represents an explicitly defined predictor (or independent) variable. The status of this variable is predicated on a theoretical argument stating X to be a cause of Y. By contrast, u represents all other sources of variation in Y, including other causes not explicitly cited in the model. In representing the combined influence of all non-X sources of variation in the dependent variable, u is referred to as the disturbance term. The disturbance term signifies that no single cause of Y (or finite set of causes) will explain all of the observed variation in the dependent variable. This causal model can be concisely represented by the following equation:

$$Y = b_{YX}X + u.$$

In this equation, the coefficient b refers to the amount of impact the predictor variable (X) has on the dependent variable (Y). Specifically, the coefficient indicates that a unit change in X produces a b unit change in Y. Finally, the disturbance term (u) serves to balance the structural equation by recognizing the impact of sources of variation unspecified in the model. Since the scale of measurement for the disturbance term is the same used in the measurement of the dependent variable, no coefficient is required (Duncan, 1973).

In the behavioral sciences, few phenomena of interest can be adequately described and analyzed in terms of a single cause and effect. Usually behavioral phenomena are imbedded in a network of causal relations (Heise, 1975), requiring more demanding and exacting analytical procedures. Because the linear regression model provides the foundation for virtually all statistical procedures used in the behavioral sciences (Dwyer, 1983), as the level of substantive and theoretical complexity exceeds the limitations of the bivariate recursive model, other linear models can be incorporated in the analysis. If multiple predictor variables are to be recognized in the analysis, then a multiple regression model can be employed. If, in addition, multiple dependent variables are involved, then multivariate regression can be used. Finally, if reciprocal causality among endogenous variables is indicated, then a general linear structural equation model can be deployed.

To illustrate the form of the general linear structural equation model, a nine-variable example will be briefly examined. The relations among these nine hypothetical variables can be diagrammed as follows:

$$
\begin{array}{c}
A \rightarrow D \leftarrow u_D \\
\downarrow \\
B \rightarrow E \leftarrow u_E \\
\uparrow \downarrow \\
C \rightarrow F \leftarrow u_F
\end{array}
$$

These nine variables represent three distinctive categories of variables: endogenous variables, exogenous variables, and disturbance terms. Analogous to the Y variable in the bivariate model cited earlier, endogenous variables are those variables whose values are completely determined by the causal relations specified by the model under consideration. In this illustration, the D, E, and F variables represent endogenous variables. Exogenous variables, represented by the variables A, B, and C, are those variables that are reported to have a theoretically salient impact on the endogenous variables but whose value is determined by processes outside the model currently considered. Disturbance (u) terms associated with each endogenous variable indicate the extent to which variability in the respective endogenous variable is not explained by the other variables in the model. As can be noted in the diagram, several logically possible causal relationships are not specified (e.g., A-E, B-F, and C-D). The reason these relationships are not acknowledged is theoretical. Specifically, for the causal model under consideration, these relationships are not theoretically relevant and, therefore, are not recognized. Moreover, a reciprocal causal relationship between E and F is acknowledged.

The causal model can be translated into the following three structural equations:

$$ D = b_{DA}A + b_{DB}B + u_D $$

$$ E = b_{EB}B + b_{ED}D + b_{EF}F + u_E $$

$$ F = b_{FC}C + b_{FE}E + u_F $$

These three combined equations would thus represent a structural equation model of behavioral and stochastic processes believed to produce a specified set of data.

Even though a series of additional technical issues must be addressed when using structural equation modeling (e.g., model identification and parameter estimation), the role of theory is quite evident. Thus while statistical procedures are inexorably required in the analysis of the proposed causal relationships, the initial impetus as well as guiding focus of structural equation modeling is provided by the interplay of theory and design considerations.

REFERENCES

Duncan, O. D. (1973). *Introduction to structural equation models.* New York: Academic.

Dwyer, J. H. (1983). *Statistical models for the social and behavioral sciences.* New York: Oxford University Press.

Goldberger, A. S. (1973). Structural equation models: An overview. In A. S. Goldberger & O. D. Duncan (Eds.), *Structural equation models in the social sciences.* New York: Seminar.

Heise, D. R. (1975). *Analysis.* New York: Wiley.

Hertzog, C., & Nesselroade, J. R. (1987). Beyond autoregressive models: Some implications of the trait-state distinction for the structural modeling of developmental change. *Child Development, 58,* 93–109.

Miller, K. A., Kohn, M. L., & Schooler, C. (1985). Educational self direction and the cognitive functioning of students. *Social Forces, 63,* 923–944.

D. G. NICKINOVICH
University of Washington

MULTIPLE REGRESSION
SCIENTIFIC METHOD

STRUCTURAL PLASTICITY AND MEMORY

Several structural changes in the basic-wiring diagram of the brain have been related to memory storage. These include alterations in the number and/or pattern of synaptic connections (Moser, 1999), translocation of polyribosomal aggregates to the synaptic spines (Weiler, Hawrylak, & Greenough, 1995), and complex changes in the shape and size of synaptic contact zone (Rusakov et al., 1997). The search for neuronal proteins whose expression correlates with synaptic remodeling has led to the discovery of the growth-associated protein GAP-43, also termed B-50, F1, pp46, and neuromodulin. GAP-43 is a presynaptic membrane phosphoprotein that plays a key role in guiding the growth of axons and modulating the formation of new connections. The GAP-43 gene is highly conserved during evolution and contains two promoters and three exons (Grabzcyk, Federoff, Ng, Pack, & Fishman, 1990). It is localized to chromosome 3 in humans and to chromosome 16 in the mouse (Kosik et al., 1988). Neuroplasticity events such as axonal

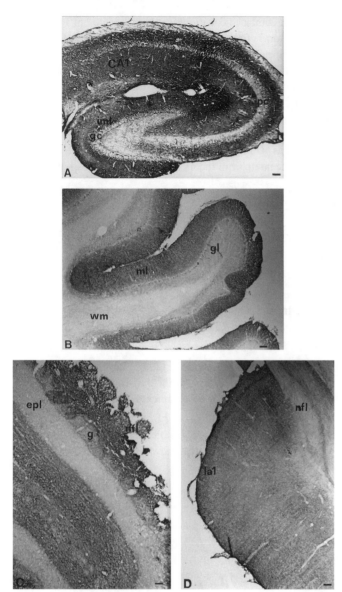

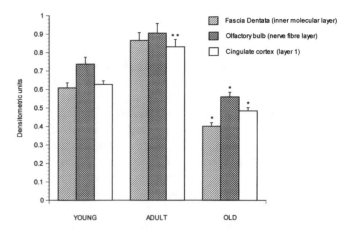

Figure 2. GAP-43 densitometry (mean ±S.E.M.) in the inner molecular layer of dentate gyrus, in the nerve fiber layer of olfactory bulb and in the layer 1 of cingulate cortex for the 3 age groups. *P < 0.01 vs. adult rats. *P < 0.01 vs. young rats, two-way ANOVA, multiple contrasts.

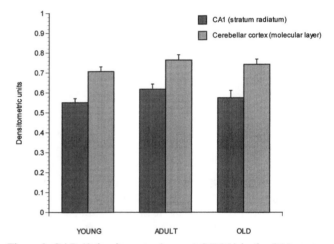

Figure 3. GAP-43 densitometry (mean ± S.E.M.) in the CA1 stratum radiatum and in the molecular layer of cerebellar cortex. No comparisons between the age groups resulted statistically significant.

Figure 1. GAP-43 distribution in different brain regions. A: coronal section of ventral hippocampus; neuronal cell soma within the piramidal (pc) and granular layers (gc) are unlabeled while a moderately dense staining is present in the CA1 stratum radiatum (CA1) and in the inner one-third of the dentate gyrus molecular layer (iml). B: cerebellar cortex; labeling is intense in the molecular layer (ml), lighter in the granule layer (gl) and in the white matter. C: portion of the olfactory bulb; the staining is virtually absent in the external plexiform layer (epl), moderate in the glomeruli(g) and intense in the nerve fiber layer (nfl). D: cingulate cortex. Dense immunolabeling is present in layer 1 (la1). The underlying neuropil layers are lightly stained. Bars: A, B, and D = 100 mm; C = 300mm.

regeneration following nerve injury (Benowitz, Rodriguez, & Neve, 1990) and changes in synaptic efficacy elicited by LTP (long-term potentiation; Meberg, Gall, & Routtenberg, 1993), which is thought to underlie certain forms of learning and memory, determine an increase in GAP-43 expression. Basal values of GAP-43 protein, determined by quantitative immunohistochemistry in selected rat brain regions (Figure 1), are age-dependent. The highest levels of GAP-43 can be found in the adult rat, and considerably lower levels in aged rats (Figures 2 and 3). The decrease of GAP-43 content in 31-month-old rats (aged) as compared to that in 18-month-old rats (adult) was statistically significant in hippocampal dentate gyrus (–54%), cingulate cortex (–42%), and olfactory bulb (–38%, Figure 2). These latter regions of the rat brain exhibit a high degree of plasticity in adulthood, but are severely impaired during aging, while the other regions investigated (viz., CA1 and cerebellar cortex) maintain a constant, though scarce, capacity of sustaining synaptic remodeling throughout life. The age-dependent decrease of the neuron density innervating the regions that showed this marked loss in GAP-43 immunoreactivity is of particular interest in the analysis of these findings. Hilar hippocampal neurons and cortical neurons providing the bulk of innervation to the inner molecular layer of dentate gyrus and to the cingulate cortex, respectively, show a 20 to 30% decrease in aged (as compared to adult) rats (Kosik et al., 1988; Coleman & Flood, 1987). The primary neurons of the olfactory epithelium sending afferents to the nerve fiber layer in the olfactory bulb show a striking decrease in the aged rat, reaching a 48% reduction compared to that in the adult (Hinds & McNelly, 1981). The issues discussed previously indicate that at least two regions showing high levels of GAP-43 in the adult rat brain—namely, the inner molecular layer of the dentate gyrus and layer 1 of the cingulate cortex—significantly decrease their ability to sustain synaptic turnover during aging. The explanation may be that those areas with increased metabolic activity, such as that required for synaptic plasticity, generate free radicals at a higher rate, thus damaging neural tissue. It has been demonstrated that the hippocampus is involved in memory acquisition and consolidation (Shephard, 1988b) while the cingulate cortex is reported to be a center for the expression of emotional behavior (Shephard, 1988a). Both these functions are markedly altered in elderly subjects (Timiras, 1994).

REFERENCES

Benowitz, L. I., Rodriguez, W. R., & Neve, R. L. (1990). The pattern of GAP-43 immunostaining changes in the rat hippocampal formation during reactive synaptogenesis. *Molecular Brain Research, 8,* 17–23.

Coleman, P. D., & Flood, D. G. (1987). Neuron numbers and dendritic extent in normal aging and Alzheimer's disease. *Neurobiology of Aging, 8,* 521–545.

Grabzcyk, E. Z., Federoff, H. J., Ng, S. G., Pack, A., & Fishman, M. C. (1990). Cloning and characterization of the rat gene encoding GAP-43. *European Journal of Neuroscience, 2,* 822–827.

Hinds, J. W., & McNelly, N. (1981). Aging in the rat olfactory system: Correlation of changes in the olfactory epithelium and olfactory bulb. *Journal of Comparative Neurology, 203,* 441–453.

Kosik, K. S., Orecchio, L. D., Bruns, G. A., Benowitz, L. I., MacDonald, G. P., Cox, D. R., & Neve, R. L. (1988). Human GAP-43: Its deduced amino acid sequence and chromosomal localization in mouse and human. *Neuron, 1,* 127–132.

Landfield, P. W., Braun, L. D., Pitler, T. A., Lindsey, J. D., & Lynch, G. (1981). Hippocampal aging in rats: A morphometric study of multiple variables in semithin sections. *Neurobiology of Aging, 2,* 265–275.

Meberg, P. J., Gall, C. M., & Routtenberg, A. (1993). Induction of F1/GAP-43 gene: Expression in hippocampal granule cells after seizures. *Molecular Brain Research, 17,* 295–299.

Moser, M. B. (1999). Making more synapses: A way to store information? *Cellular and Molecular Life Science, 55,* 593–600.

Rusakov, D. A., Davies, H. A., Harrison, E., Diana, G., Richter-Levin, G., Bliss, T. V., & Stewart, M. G. (1997). Ultrastructural synaptic correlates of spatial learning in rat hippocampus. *Neuroscience, 80,* 69–77.

Shephard, G. M. (Ed.). (1988a). *Neurobiology* (2nd ed., pp. 579–580). New York: Oxford University Press.

Shephard, G. M. (Ed.). (1988b). *Neurobiology* (2nd ed., pp. 605–610). New York: Oxford University Press.

Timiras, P. S. (1994). Aging of the nervous system: Functional changes. In P. S. Timiras (Ed.), *Physiological Basis of Aging and Geriatrics* (2nd ed., pp. 103–114). Boca Raton, FL: CRC Press.

Weiler, I. J., Hawrylak, N., & Greenough, W. T. (1985). Morphogenesis in memory formation: Synaptic and cellular mechanisms. *Behavioral Brain Research, 66,* 1–6.

T. CASOLI
I. N. R. C. A., Italy

GENETIC APPROACHES TO MEMORY
MEMORY

STRUCTURALISM

As a school or system of psychology, structuralism had its antecedents in British philosophy of the eighteenth and nineteenth centuries. John Locke had established the empirical tradition stating that all knowledge came from experience and the mind at birth was a *tabula rasa* (blank tablet) on which experiences were imprinted. Locke opposed the continental philosophers such as René Décartes who claimed that some ideas were inborn. The British associationists such as John Stuart Mill, Alexander Bain, and Herbert Spencer had finalized the laws of association but had never put them to the experimental test. In the latter half of the nineteenth century, Gustav Fechner developed the methods of psychophysics whereby changes in various sensory experiences could be quantitatively related to the physical stimuli.

Structuralism began formally with the teachings and writings of Wilhelm Wundt (1832–1920) in the late nineteenth century. Historians of psychology generally agree that Wundt founded the first psychological laboratory in 1879 in Leipzig. We know that he was one of the most important people in the early development of psychology, not only as a discipline separate from philosophy, but also as an experimental science. Many important experiments were performed in Wundt's laboratory: reaction time, color mixing, afterimages, psychophysics, and word associations. Wundt's interpretation of the nature of psychology became the first psychological system or framework within which one could organize the facts and theories of psychology. In his *Outline of Psychology,* Wundt delineated the nature of psychological events, what the psychologist should be studying, and how to handle the results of experimental investigations. Wundt was a popular teacher, a prolific writer, and a careful experimenter.

At the turn of the century, many young pioneers in psychology came to study with Wundt at the University of Leipzig to learn more about the "new" psychology—among them Hall, Cattell, and Titchener. Titchener (1862–1927), an Englishman by birth, took Wundt's psychology to the United States, where he named the system *structuralism.* He modified and enlarged on Wundt's basic tenets and headed the experimental laboratory at Cornell University. (The laboratory at Cornell had been established two years earlier by Frank Angell, who also thought along Wundtian lines.)

Both Wundt and Titchener defined psychology as the study of consciousness or conscious experience. This kind of experience was dependent on the experiencing individual as opposed to experience independent of the individual, which was the subject matter of physics and chemistry. This definition limited the true subject matter of psychology to human experience. Whatever was to be said of lower animals was left to the domain of biology. Throughout the first three decades of the twentieth century, structuralism was a dominant school in American psychology. By the early 1930s, the system was beginning to decline in popularity. Other systems grew up in opposition to it, such as functionalism, behaviorism, and Gestalt psychology.

Wundt and Titchener believed the task of the psychologist was to analyze the contents of consciousness into its elements. For Titchener, there were three classes of elements of experience: sensations, feelings, and images. The elements of sensation came from the various senses: vision, hearing, taste, smell, touch, the muscle sense, and various organic senses. For Wundt, feelings—the inner experience—had three dimensions: pleasantness—unpleasantness, excitement—calm, and strain—relaxation. Titchener considered only the pleasantness-unpleasantness dimension, stating that Wundt's other dimensions could be reduced to actual sensations. Images that constituted the third class of elements were like weak sensations. He described them as separate elements, a distinction Wundt did not make. However, in his book *An Outline of Psychology,* Titchener devoted only one chapter to them. In the same book, he concluded that there were a total of 43,415 different sensory experiences, although most of them came from visual and auditory senses.

Titchener also believed the elements had dimensions or attributes. There was *intensity,* which referred to how strong or weak the sensations were—a loud or soft tone, a bright or dim light, a strong or weak odor or taste. *Quality* referred to the kind of experience, as in a particular pitch of tone; the color of an object (red or green); the sweetness or sourness of something tasted; hot, cold, pain, or tickle in the sense of touch. *Duration* referred to how long the experience lasted. *Clarity* involved the place an experience had in consciousness. Those experiences at the focus of consciousness would be very clear, while those at the fringe would be vague. The element of feelings lacked the dimension of clarity. Finally, Titchener described the attribute of *extensity* or volume, which he believed applied only to visual experience.

Attention referred to the arrangement of conscious elements. It could be voluntary, as when one intentionally directs one's attention to a particular object. Habitual attention developed with repetition, as when a mother attends regularly to the signals from her child. Finally, involuntary attention was exemplified by a sudden flash of lightning or a clap of thunder.

In experience, the elements were combined. The means whereby this combination could occur was association. This was the so-called "glue" that held the elements together. Titchener and Wundt borrowed the laws of association from the tradition of the British empiricists and associationists, who had stated that there were basically two laws of association. Ideas could be associated by contiguity: things happening together in space or time and by similarity.

Both Wundt and Titchener had distinguished the two worlds of experience, the mental (consciousness) and the physical. The relationship between these two worlds had to be explained. The answer to the problem was psychophysical parallelism. That is, the two went hand in hand but never interacted. The experience of a particular color had its parallel in the length of the light wave, or an experience of a certain pitch had its parallel in the frequency of the sound wave.

One aspect of experience that Wundt failed to explain was the meaning of a particular idea or set of experiences. Therefore, Titchener constructed his *context theory of meaning.* Here meaning was divided into *core* and *context.* The core was the raw experience as it came to consciousness: a blue light or a high pitched sound. It was context that gave the experience meaning. Context constituted the various associations conjured up by that core. The blue light might have aroused the associations of a lighthouse off the New England coast where sailors were warned that they were coming near the shore. The high pitch could bring to mind the sound of a train approaching from a distance.

The methodology of structuralism was introspection and experimentation. Introspection was of special importance in analyzing experiences. Titchener maintained that science was dependent on observation and introspection was one of the methods. The person doing the introspective analysis had to be trained in the method. It was no natural gift. In his *An Outline of Psychology,* Titchener laid down certain rules for the introspectionist to follow. (a) One must be unbiased. (b) One must have complete control and not allow one's attention to wander. (c) One's body and mind must be fresh and not fatigued or exhausted. (d) One must feel well, be of good temper, and be interested in the experience being introspected. Titchener warned against the "stimulus error," which constituted a reading into the experience of associations from one's past that would contaminate the raw experience.

Structuralism no longer exists as a systematic position. It died because it had nowhere to go. It very much limited what psychologists could study in their minds and it had no applications. It was a pure "ivory tower" study. In 1933, Edwin Boring, a student of Titchener at Cornell, wrote *The Physical Dimensions of Consciousness,* in which he tried to correlate the attributes of consciousness (intensity, quality, clarity, etc.) with characteristics of impulses going along the sensory nerves to the brain. Intensity supposedly correlated with the rapidity of the impulse and quality with a patterning of the impulses, but this was all purely hypothetical. Marx and Hillix in *Systems and Theories of Psychology* state that Boring's book dealt structuralism its final blow. Boring had tried to hold together what was left of structuralism, but as more objective methods of data analysis emerged, along with a greater emphasis on behavior as opposed to experience, he had to acquiesce to the demise of structuralism.

What is left of structuralism is to be found in various aspects of sensory psychology, but, in a way, structuralism fulfilled its purpose. It set psychology out as a discipline separate from philosophy with a methodology of investigation at least in part experimental. Introspection as a method was subjective and qualitative. It often proved to be very unreliable. As psychology was being directed toward a broader scope to include behavior of both animals and humans, along with applications to the world outside the laboratory, structuralism refused to keep up.

REFERENCES

Boring, E. G. (1933). *The physical dimensions of consciousness.* New York: Century.

Marx, M. H., & Hillix, W. A. (1979/1973/1963). *Systems and theories in psychology* (3rd ed.). New York: McGraw-Hill.

Wundt, W. (1897). *Outline of psychology.* Leipzig: Englemann.

SUGGESTED READING

Boring, E. G. (1957/1950/1929). *A history of experimental psychology* (2nd ed.). New York: Appleton-Century-Crofts.

Lundin, R. W. (1979/1972). *Theories and systems of psychology.* Lexington, MA: Heath.

Titchener, E. B. (1898). The postulates of a structural psychology. *Psychological Review, 7,* 449–465.

Titchener, E. B. (1909). *Lectures on the experimental psychology of the thought process.* New York: Macmillan.

Titchener, E. B. (1923/1916/1910). *A textbook of psychology.* New York: Macmillan.

Wundt, W. (1904/1873–1874). *Principles of physiological psychology.* New York: Macmillan.

R. W. LUNDIN
Wheaton, Illinois

FUNCTIONALISM

STRUCTURED CLINICAL INTERVIEW FOR DIAGNOSIS (SCID)

Since the 1970s, the perception of the low reliability of psychiatric diagnosis and the need for homogeneous research groups have stimulated the improvement of classification systems of psychiatric disorders. This has resulted in classification systems such as the Feighner Criteria, the Research Diagnostic Criteria (RDC), and the *Diagnostic and Statistical Manual of Mental Disorders (DSM).* The establishment of specific diagnostic criteria for each mental disorder, with inclusion criteria, exclusion criteria, and criteria for the evaluation of severity and duration of symptoms, significantly enhanced the reliability of psychiatric diagnosis.

Nevertheless, the refinement of operational diagnostic criteria fails to control other sources of low reliability, such as the interviewer's behavior and expectations and variations in the information obtained from the patient. To overcome these difficulties, structured and semi-structured interview instruments have been developed, based on different classification systems. The development of these instruments is intermingled with the development of the classification systems on which they are based. The instruments began to play an important role not only in research, but also in clinical practice and in the training of mental health professionals.

One of the first structured interviews was the Present State Examination (PSE), which aimed at describing psychopathological phenomena in a reliable and objective way (Wing, 1983). Developed in England in the 1960s, the PSE was published in 1974 after a series of revisions. The PSE consists of 140 items, 107 of them referring to symptoms described by the patient and 33 referring to behavior observed by the interviewer. It includes a glossary with comprehensive and precise definitions of every item, the evaluation of which depends on knowledge of psychopathology, clinical judgment and training with the instrument. The PSE results in a psychological profile that allows clinical diagnoses through the "Catego" computer program. These diagnoses are based on a conceptual framework strongly influenced by classical psychopathology, and they are not comparable to any other diagnostic classification system.

The structured clinical interviews are made of closed-ended questions and may be performed by lay interviewers, after specific training. Rating depends exclusively on the answer given by the person interviewed, and the interview is usually brief. Examples of this kind of interview are the National Institute of Mental Health's (NIMH) Diagnostic Interview Schedule (DIS) and the Composite International Diagnostic Interview (CIDI). The DIS (Robins, Helzer, Croughan, & Ratcliff, 1981) was developed as part of the Epidemiological Catchment Area (ECA) study performed by the NIMH in the United States and is based on three classification systems: *DSM-III,* RDC, and Feighner. Answers to the questions are codified, and the final diagnosis is established from an analysis made by a specific computer program.

The CIDI (Robins et al., 1988) was elaborated as part of a collaborative project between the Division of Mental Health of the World Health Organization (WHO) and the U.S. Alcohol, Drug Abuse and Mental Health Administration (ADAMHA), and was also intended for use in epidemiological studies. The questions of this instrument are modified items from the DIS and PSE.

Interview instruments such as the Schedule for Affective Disorders and Schizophrenia (SADS) and the Structured Clinical Interview for the *DSM-IV* (SCID) can be classified as semi-structured interviews because of their open-ended questions, which allow some flexibility when used. These features of semi-structured interviews require familiarization with the diagnostic criteria of the system on which the interview is based, and on training in the instrument. Since rating is based on clinical judgment and not only on the answer given by the interviewee, only mental health professionals should apply these instruments.

The SADS (Endicott & Spitzer, 1978) was developed during the 1970s; it aimed at the identification of the 25 diagnostic categories included in the RDC. Reliability coefficients obtained with SADS and RDC were significant for the majority of the disorders studied, and were better than for most of the reports available at the time of their publication.

Although the SADS has been well accepted, it is less comprehensive than the *DSM,* because it does not include some Axis I categories, or the disorders of Axis II (Personality Disorders). Also, the instrument gives little attention to Axis IV assessment, and has a separate scale for Axis V evaluation. Due to these shortcomings, the SCID was published in 1985; it had the same outline of SADS, but was based on criteria and diagnostic categories of the *DSM-III-R.* After the publication of *DSM-IV* in 1994, the SCID was adapted to the modified diagnostic criteria.

The SCID (Spitzer, Williams, Gibbon, & First, 1992) can be applied both to patients (SCID-P, patient version) and to individuals not identified as patients (SCID-NP, non-patient version). The instrument better suits adults, but with some changes it may be used with adolescents. For rating, the interviewer is encouraged to use all sources of information available. The scores and diagnostic criteria are integrated into the structure of the interview, and several hypotheses are successively tested. Questions are grouped according to diagnosis or criterion. When an essential diagnostic criterion of a particular disorder is not fulfilled, remaining questions on the disorder may be ignored.

The SCID begins with an overview session, which follows the general process of a non-structured clinical interview. From this overview, the interview is organized in modules that generally refer to the diagnostic classes of the *DSM-IV.* This organization allows the evaluation of only a few modules. Studies of SCID reliability have generally yielded satisfactory results, not only with the original version (Williams et al., 1992), but also with translations and adaptations to other languages (Del-Ben, Rodrigues, & Zuardi, 1996; Skre, Onstad, Torgersen, & Kringlen, 1991). Comparison among reliability studies should be made carefully, because factors unrelated to the features of the instrument can influence the results. One of these factors may be the methodology used. Usually, reliability coefficients are lower in test-retest than in joint interviews. The clinical characteristics of the sample studied may also interfere. Agreement is usually higher in specific diagnostic groups than in heterogeneous samples, and in groups of patients than in groups of community members.

The good reliability indexes obtained with these instruments have allowed studies with more precise information about the clinical picture, evolution, prognosis, and comorbidity of several mental disorders. Nevertheless, the use of structured and semi-structured clinical interviews relies on familiarization with the instrument. For this purpose, adequate training with the instruments is fundamental and should follow the instructions provided by the instruments themselves.

REFERENCES

Del-Ben, C. M., Rodrigues, C. R. C., & Zuardi, A. W. (1996). Reliability of a Portuguese version of the structured clinical interview for DSM-III-R (SCID) in a Brazilian sample of outpatients. *Brazilian Journal of Medical and Biological Research, 29*(12), 1675–1682.

Endicott, J., & Spitzer, R. L. (1978). A diagnostic interview: The Schedule for Affective Disorders and Schizophrenia. *Archives of General Psychiatry, 35,* 837–844.

Robins, L. N., Wing, J., Wittchen, H. U., Helzer, J. E., Babor, T. F., Burke, J., Farmer, A., Jablenski, A., Pickens, R., Regier, D. A., Sartorius, N., & Towle, L. H. (1988). The Composite International Diagnostic Interview: An epidemiologic instrument suitable for use in conjunction with different diagnostic systems and different cultures. *Archives of General Psychiatry, 45,* 1069–1077.

Robins, L. N., Helzer, J. W., Croughan, J., & Ratcliff, K. S. (1981). National Institute of Mental Health diagnostic interview schedule: Its history, characteristics, and validity. *Archives of General Psychiatry, 38,* 381–389.

Skre, I., Onstad, S., Torgersen, S., & Kringlen, E. (1991). High interrater reliability for the Structured Clinical Interview for DSM-III-R Axis I (SCID-I). *Acta Psychiatrica Scandinavica, 84,* 167–173.

Spitzer, R. L., Williams, J. R., Gibbon, M., & First, M. B. (1992). The Structured Clinical Interview for DSM-III-R: I. History, rationale, and description. *Archives of General Psychiatry, 49,* 624–629.

Williams, J. R., Gibbon, M., First, M. B., Spitzer, R. L., Davies, M., Borus, J., Howes, M. J., Kane, J., Pope, H. G., Rounsaville, B., & Wittchen, H. U. (1992). The Structured Clinical Interview for DSM-III-R (SCID): II. Multisite test-retest reliability. *Archives of General Psychiatry, 49,* 630–636.

Wing, J. K. (1983). Use and misuse of the PSE. *British Journal of Psychiatry, 143,* 111–117.

C. M. DEL-BEN
Universidade de São Paulo, Brazil

ASSESSMENT
DIAGNOSTIC INTERVIEW SCHEDULE (DIS)
DIAGNOSTIC & STATISTICAL MANUAL OF MENTAL DISORDERS (DSM)
STRUCTURED AND SEMI-STRUCTURED CLINICAL INTERVIEWS

STRUCTURED AND SEMI-STRUCTURED CLINICAL INTERVIEWS

The past few decades have witnessed a rather striking shift toward the increased use of formal structure in the clinical interview process among clinical psychologists and psychiatrists—especially those engaged in clinical research. In fact, the magnitude of this shift can be discerned from a reading of Harry Stack Sullivan's 1994 seminal textbook on clinical interviewing, which assumes that the interviewer will invariably leave a good portion of the direction of the interview, with respect to both its process and content, to the interviewee. Today, of course, this assumption (a virtual given in Sullivan's day) no longer holds, and it has become commonplace to categorize clinical interviews, on the basis of the degree of intrinsic structure imposed by the interviewer, into one of three distinct subtypes: *structured, semi-structured,* and *unstructured.*

The unstructured interview, as the term has come to be defined, is characterized by the clinician's intentionally refraining from the use of pre-scripted queries or a pre-determined order of content coverage. Instead, emphasis is placed on eliciting more or less spontaneous content from the patient (Shea, 1990; Wiens, 1990). Thus, no two unstructured interviews progress in the same manner, inasmuch as the interviewer allows the patient to direct much of the interview by discussing topics of importance in the order that he or she chooses. In direct contrast, structured interviews are composed of predetermined sets of questions presented in a pre-defined order, with tightly operationalized and standardized criteria used for interview interpretation (Beutler, 1995). Every clinician using a structured interview asks the same questions verbatim, in the same order, with no permitted deviation from the prescribed format; thus, different interviewers may be expected to elicit identical material (or nearly so) from the interviewee. Semistructured interviews, as the name suggests, are something of a hybrid case. Like structured interviews, they consist of predetermined questions that the interviewer must ask in the manner and sequence specified (e.g., "Over the past two weeks, have you lost interest or pleasure in things that you usually enjoy?"); however, after the specified questions have been addressed, the interviewer is free to follow up as he or she deems necessary (e.g., "Could you tell me more about your decision not to go to your friend's party this week?") in order to obtain sufficient information regarding the content area or areas of interest.

The semistructured interview, like its fully structured counterpart, is principally concerned with permitting the clinician to obtain sufficient information to enable him or her to make a reliable and valid rating with respect to some particular content domain (e.g., diagnostic category, symptom severity, level of function, etc.); it differs only to the extent that it allows the clinician a bit more latitude to formulate queries designed to probe those domains to the degree necessary to make such a rating. Thus, in most essential respects, the semistructured interview is best thought of as a mere variation on a theme of the structured interview, and as bearing only a superficial resemblance to the unstructured interview by virtue of the fact that both interview formats involve the clinician in the formulation of novel queries (though in the case of the semistructured interview even such novel queries will typically follow a general formula specified during interview training, for example, "give me an example of a time in which you experienced [blank]"). Accordingly, the present chapter, for the sake of convenience, will subsume both semistructured and fully structured interviews under the "structured interview" rubric.

THE SHIFT FROM UNSTRUCTURED TO STRUCTURED INTERVIEWS

The increasing use of structured interviewing in recent decades may be traced to the confluence of several distinct historical developments. Perhaps no influence was more important in this respect than the growing recognition, during the 1960s and 1970s, that the traditional method of diagnosis (which was based upon information obtained from an unstandardized, unstructured interview) was highly unreliable, and resulted in unacceptably high levels of diagnostic disagreement among different clinicians (see Hersen & Bellack, 1988). In fact, this concern with diagnostic unreliability was a principal catalyst for the publication in 1980 of the third revision of the *Diagnostic and Statistical Manual of Mental Disorders (DSM-III)* (American Psychological Association, 1980). Unlike its predecessors, this revised diagnostic system employed a set of tightly operationalized, mostly objective criteria for the diagnosis of each disorder, thus catalyzing the development of structured interviews (e.g., the Diagnostic Interview Schedule [DIS]; Robins, Helzer, Croughan, & Ratcliff, 1981) with queries organized around each set of diagnostic criterion items. Structured interviews thereby became an invaluable means of assessing each of the *DSM*-specified multi-axial domains (Clinical Symptomatology, Personality Function, Medical/Physical Health, Current Stress Level,

and Global Level of Functioning) in a systematic fashion (Shea, 1990).

Another notable development in this respect has been the recent increase in the influence of managed care organizations (MCOs) regarding the delivery of mental health services. Managed care organizations, by virtue of their concern for cost containment, have provided an impetus for the more widespread use of structured, rather than unstructured, interviewing, because such interviews are more capable of rendering valid diagnoses with minimal prerequisite clinician training and reduced interaction time between clinician and client (Wiens, 1990). Similarly, MCO-driven care has placed a high premium on the use (when available) of short-term, empirically supported interventions for specific clinical disorders (Shea, 1990). The set of reimbursable interventions has thus become increasingly determined by the patient's formal diagnosis; accordingly, the need for accurate and reliable diagnoses has grown, thereby increasing the utility of the structured interview. Of course, structured interviews are now employed for a number of clinical purposes that go beyond the assignment of diagnoses, including the assessment of the patient's mental status, symptom severity, and global functioning, and of the occurrence of stressful life events.

ADVANTAGES AND DISADVANTAGES OF THE STRUCTURED INTERVIEW

As alluded to in the previous section, the structured interview is associated with several advantages over the traditional unstructured interview. One of the more prominent benefits is the fact that, due to their explicit standardization of administration and use of operationalized criteria to aid in interpretation, structured interviews generally facilitate a much higher level of inter-rater reliability than do unstructured interviews (Helzer et al., 1977; Beutler, 1995; Segal, 1997; Segal & Falk, 1998). Standardization in administration decreases the amount of both criterion variance (i.e., differences in criteria employed to rate the presence or absence of a given clinical symptom) and information variance (differences in actual data obtained from the patient during the interview)—two primary sources of reduced diagnostic reliability (Segal, 1997; Segal & Falk, 1998). By controlling for criterion variance, structured interviews attenuate the need for clinical judgment and permit the clinician to rely on operationalized criteria and interpretation based on normative values. In addition, two different interviewers using the same structured interview are less likely to elicit discrepant information due to differences in interviewing technique. And, inasmuch as an instrument's reliability serves as the sine qua non of its validity regarding the target construct(s) assessed, structured interviewing is generally associated with enhanced diagnostic validity (e.g., Hersen & Bellack, 1988).

Due principally to its superior reliability and validity, structured interviewing is now the accepted gold standard of *DSM*-based diagnostic assessment in clinical research. Indeed, it is now quite rare to encounter a published clinical investigation that has utilized any procedure other than a structured interview for the assessment of Axis I or Axis II diagnoses. The most commonly employed structured interviews for the assessment of Axis I and Axis II pathology are listed in Table 1, which also includes a brief de-

Table 1.   Commonly employed structured diagnostic interviews[a]

Name	Purpose/Description	Psychometric Properties	Strengths	Limitations
Structured Clinical Interview for *DSM–IV* (SCID)[a]	Semistructured interview, two versions-targets patients and nonpatients, different modules to assess diagnostic categories based on *DSM–IV*, Assessment of Axis I Disorders	kappa = .72–.84[b]	Can be lengthened or shortened depending on needs; open-ended prompting following close-ended questions; allows skip-outs; computer scored	Rated on a limited Likert scale; moderate level of training required due to higher level of discretion in rephrasing questions
Schedule for Affective Disorders and Schizophrenia (SADS)[c]	Differential diagnosis of affective and psychotic disorders based on Research Diagnostic Criteria (RDC) for Axis I disorders	ICC = .84–1.00[c] kappa = .63–1.00[d]	Assesses past and current psychopathology; questions cluster according to specific disorder; Likert scale ratings; gathers information from many sources	No reliable computer scoring program; strong reliance on clinical judgment; extensive training required
Diagnostic Interview Schedule (DIS)[e]	Investigation of mental illness in general population; assesses prevalence of mental disorders based on *DSM–III* (revisions made for *DSM–IV*), Assessment of Axis I Disorders	kappa = .40–1.0 (most disorders range from .60–.80)[e]	Fully-structured and designed to be used by non-professionals; requires only one hour to administer; computer scored; less extensive training required	Fully-structured (no clarifying or rewording); closed-ended questions and dichotomous scoring with no clarification; inquires only about symptoms
International Personality Disorder Examination (IPDE)[f]	Extensive, semistructured diagnostic interview designed to be administered by experienced clinician; assesses Axis II disorders according to *DSM–IV* and ICD-10	kappa = .51–.87 stability = .52[f]	Begins with open-ended prompts followed by specific questions; uses 5-year rule; administration of sections possible for rule-out diagnoses; requests examples to judge presence or absence of criteria; interview with informants is encouraged	No skip-outs; limited Likert scale; requires extensive training and clinical judgment; administration often requires over 2–3 hours
Structured Clinical Interview for *DSM–IV* (SCID-II)[g]	Semistructured interview for Axis II disorder based on *DSM–IV*; typically administered after the SCID; includes brief, forced, yes/no screening component; pursue only positively	kappa = .48–.98[h]	Screening component to decrease administration time; allows interviewer to follow up with open-ended questions; modules allow clinician to tailor questions to client; complete administration	Questions assessing a particular disorder are grouped together, which increases risk of bias and moving threshold; limited Likert scale; extensive training; requires clinical judgment

Note: Information on instrument strengths and limitations abstracted from Segal & Falk (1998)

[a]First, M. B., Spitzer, R. L., Gibbon, M., & Williams, J. W. B. (1995). *Structured Clinical Interview for Axis I DSM–IV Disorders—Patient Edition (SCID-I/P, Version 2.0)*. New York: New York State Psychiatric Institute.

[b]Williams, J. B. W., Gibbon, M., First, M. B., Spitzer, R. L., Davies, M., Borus, J., Howes, M. J., Kane, J., Pope, H. G., Rounsaville, B., & Wittchen, H. (1992). The Structured Clinical Interview for *DSM–III-R* (SCID): Multisite test-retest reliability. *Archives of General Psychiatry, 49,* 630–636.

Riskind, J. H., Beck, A. T., Berchick, R. J., Brown, G., & Steer, R. A. (1987). Reliability of *DSM–III* diagnosis for Major Depression and Generalized Anxiety Disorder using the Structured Clinical Interview for *DSM–III*. *Archives of General Psychiatry, 44,* 817–820.

[c]Endicott, J., & Spitzer, R. L. (1978). A diagnostic interview: The Schedule for Affective Disorders and Schizophrenia. *Archives of General Psychiatry, 35,* 837–844.

[d]Spitzer, R. L., Endicott, J., & Robins, E. (1978). Research diagnostic criteria. *Archives of General Psychiatry, 35,* 773–782.

[e]Robins, L. N., Helzer, J. E., Croughan, J., & Ratcliff, K. S. (1981). National Institute of Mental Health Diagnostic Interview Schedule. *Archives of General Psychiatry, 38,* 381–389.

[f]Loranger, A. W., Sartorius, N., Andreoli, A., Berger, P., Buchheim, P., Channabasavanna, S. M., Coid, B., Dahl, A., Diekstra, R. F. W., Ferguson, B., Jacobsberg, L. B., Mombour, W., Pull, C., Ono, Y., & Reiger, D. A. (1994). The International Personality Disorder Examination. *Archives of General Psychiatry, 51,* 215–224.

[g]First, M. B., Spitzer, R. L., Gibbon, M., Williams, J. B. W., & Benjamin, L. (1994). *Structured Clinical Interview for DSM–IV Axis II Personality Disorders (SCID-II, Version 2.0)*. New York: New York State Psychiatric Institute.

[h]Maffei, C., Fossati, A., Agostoni, I., Barraco, A., Bagnato, M., Donati, D., Namia, C., Novella, L., & Petrachi, M. (1997). Interrater reliability and internal consistency of the Structured Clinical Interview for *DSM–IV* Axis II Personality Disorders (SCID-II), Version 2.0. *Journal of Personality Disorders, 11,* 279–284.

scription of each measure, a summary of its principal strengths and limitations, and its reported psychometric properties.

Another advantage associated with the use of structured interviews is the fact that their administration and interpretation frequently require less formal clinical training than that requisite for effective unstructured interviewing. Whereas most structured interviews require the clinician to follow a prescribed formula, unstructured interviews often require the interviewer to exercise a more sophisticated degree of clinical judgment and to be more savvy in the data-gathering process, since he or she is allotted considerable discretion in choosing topics to pursue and in formulating the actual wording and sequence of queries. Accordingly, unstructured interviews tend to require a higher level of experience, training, and skill for effective administration (Wiens, 1976; Wiens, 1990). However, structured interviews nonetheless require a considerable amount of specialized training on the part of the interviewer, not only because the initial training in interview administration is often arduous and extensive, but also because periodic retraining is usually required to prevent what one might call interviewer drift (i.e., decrease in adherence to the stated interview protocols for administration and scoring). In this respect, it is notable that structured interviews are still more commonly used in research rather than applied settings (Beutler, 1995).

Although they are commonly regarded as quite rigid assessment instruments, structured interviews are also capable of providing information precisely tailored to the needs of the researcher or the referring clinician. For example, the relevant sections of a lengthy structured diagnostic interview may be abstracted and employed to elicit information designed to address a specific referral question or diagnostic issue at hand, or to provide an assessment of the severity of symptomatology in a given domain. Alternatively, for a more thorough intake assessment, an omnibus diagnostic interview (e.g., the Structured Clinical Interview for Axis I [or II] *DSM-IV* Disorders, or SCID) may be employed to screen a patient for the presence of clinically significant pathology across the entire spectrum of those Axis I and Axis II disorders.

Despite the aforementioned strengths, a few notable limitations are also associated with the use of structured interviews. Clearly, for example, structured interviews constrain the level of freedom interviewers have in rewording questions, introducing new questions, or modifying the order of content coverage in order to suit to the needs of the client (Beutler, 1995; Wiens, 1976; Shea, 1990). Further, the interviewer cannot delay asking particular questions based on his or her clinical judgment that the client is not ready to answer them. In a related vein, the clinician may find that the precise phrasing of queries in a given structured interview is quite different from his or her own preferred phrasing (e.g., "give me an example" versus "can you think of a time when that happened?"); the phrasing may, in fact, feel awkward at times for patient and interviewer alike (Shea, 1990). Although structured interviews are designed to elicit the maximum amount of information in a minimum amount of time, the nature of a structured interview may actually impede this process on occasion. For example, patients may not reveal information unless they are comfortable with the interviewer; thus, questions that are not tailored to the needs of the patient or that do not proceed in a smooth manner may actually result in the patient's revealing less information, or being less truthful (Mackinnon & Michels, 1971; Sullivan, 1954; Scheiber, 1994). Finally, it is to be noted that clinicians who employ structured interviews lack flexibility in exploring their clinical intuitions when interviewing, inasmuch as they are not permitted to diverge from the interview protocol to follow up in greater detail on areas that may be of great clinical importance, but that are not covered by the predetermined interview queries (Beutler, 1995; Wiens, 1990).

CLINICAL CONSIDERATIONS OF THE STRUCTURED INTERVIEW

Despite the limited amount of free time available during a structured interview, the structured interviewer is faced with the need to establish rapport with the client quickly in order to facilitate the process of obtaining accurate and complete information (Beutler, 1995; Scheiber, 1994). How is such rapport to be developed within the confines of the structured interview format? For starters, Beutler (1995) recommends that the clinician "ensure that the desired expectation and mind set are developed by the patient" (p. 99) by interviewing in a quiet, protected area. Interviews given in a quiet and secure area provide reassurance that the interview material will be treated with respect and in a confidential manner (Beutler, 1995; Scheiber, 1994). In other words, the interviewer should ensure that the client perceives a relaxing therapeutic milieu of safety and collaboration. In addition, the clinician can, with the skillful use of nonverbal communication (e.g., body posture, tone of voice, facial expression, eye contact, etc.), convey a sense of empathy and positive regard throughout the structured interview process. Another method of establishing rapport at the outset (prior to the start of the interview itself) requires that the clinician and the patient discuss the patient's chief complaint or major presenting problem (Beutler, 1995). Finally, the interviewer will do well to provide the patient beforehand as much information as possible (e.g., interview format, expected duration, content coverage, etc.) to reassure the patient and to provide him or her with at least some sense of control during the interview process (Beutler, 1995; Mackinnon & Michels, 1971). With such considerations in mind, the clinician will frequently (though not always) be able to employ the structured interview, not only to ascertain the salient clinical information targeted by the interview itself, but also to establish a positive clinical alliance that may prove valuable in the process of implementing subsequent assessment or intervention procedures.

REFERENCES

American Psychological Association. (1980). *Diagnostic and statistical manual of mental disorders* (3rd ed.). Washington, DC: Author.

Beutler, L. E. (1995). The clinical interview. In L. E. Beutler & M. R. Berren (Eds.), *Integrative assessment of adult personality.* New York: Guilford.

Helzer, J. E., Robins, L. N., Taibleson, M., Woodruff, R. A., Reich, T., & Wish, E. D. (1977). Reliability in psychiatric diagnosis. *Archives of General Psychiatry, 34,* 129–133.

Hersen, M., & Bellack, A. S. (1988). *DSM-III* and behavioral assessment. In A. S. Bellack & M. Hersen (Eds.), *Behavioral as-*

sessment: *A practical handbook* (pp. 67–84). New York: Pergamon.

Mackinnon, R. A., & Michels, R. (1971). The psychiatric interview in clinical practice. Philadelphia: W. B. Saunders.

Scheiber, S. C. (1994). The psychiatric interview, psychiatric history, and mental status examination. In R. E. Hales & S. C. Yudofsky (Eds.), *The American Psychiatric Press textbook of psychiatry* (2nd ed.). Washington, DC: American Psychiatric Press.

Segal, D. L. (1997). Structured interviewing and *DSM* classification. In S. M. Turner & M. Hersen (Eds.), *Adult psychopathology and diagnosis.* New York: Wiley.

Segal, D. L., & Falk, S. B. (1998). Structured interviews and rating scales. In A. S. Bellack & M. Hersen (Eds.), *Behavioral assessment: A practical handbook* (4th ed.). Needham Heights, MA: Allyn and Bacon.

Shea, S. C. (1990). Contemporary psychiatric interviewing: Integration of *DSM-III-R*, psychodynamic concerns, and mental status. In G. Goldstein & M. Hersen (Eds.), *Handbook of psychological assessment* (2nd ed.). New York: Pergamon.

Sullivan, H. S. (1954). *The psychiatric interview.* New York: Norton.

Wiens, A. N. (1976). The assessment interview. In I. B. Weiner (Ed.), *Clinical method in psychology.* New York: Wiley.

Wiens, A. N. (1990). Structured clinical interviews for adults. In G. Goldstein & M. Hersen (Eds.), *Handbook of psychological assessment* (2nd ed.). New York: Pergamon.

P. Y. HONG
S. S. ILARDI
University of Kansas

DIAGNOSTIC AND STATISTICAL MANUAL OF MENTAL DISORDERS
CLINICAL ASSESSMENT
STRUCTURED CLINICAL INTERVIEW FOR DIAGNOSIS (SCID)
UNSTRUCTURED CLINICAL INTERVIEW
DIAGNOSTIC INTERVIEW SCHEDULE (DIS)

STRUPP, HANS H.

Hans H. Strupp is currently Distinguished Professor of psychology at Vanderbilt University. He received his PhD from George Washington University in 1954. He is also a graduate of the Washington School of Psychiatry and a diplomate in clinical psychology of the American Board of Professional Psychology. Following two research positions (with the Department of the Air Force and the Department of the Army), he was appointed associate professor in the departments of psychiatry and psychology at the University of North Carolina (UNC) at Chapel Hill and was promoted to full professor in 1962. He also served as director of psychological services in the department of psychiatry at UNC at Chapel Hill. In 1966, he joined the faculty of Vanderbilt University. From 1967 to 1976, Strupp was director of clinical psychology training at Vanderbilt. In 1976, he became Distinguished Professor.

Strupp's publications, which number over 300 articles and several books, have been largely devoted to psychotherapy research, psychoanalytic psychology, the training of psychotherapists and clinical psychologists, and related scientific and professional issues. He began his research career with a series of empirical studies of psychotherapeutic techniques. His attention was soon drawn to analyses of the psychotherapeutic process. He became particularly impressed with complications in patient-therapist transactions resulting from patients' negative attitudes, hostility, and other impediments to progress in therapy. The topic of negative complementarity (therapists' difficulties in dealing effectively with patients' negative attitudes) became the leitmotiv of the Vanderbilt group of researchers who became members of Strupp's research team. In addition to publishing a number of theoretical papers Strupp became interested in the study of negative effects of psychotherapy, a project whose findings were published, in collaboration with Hadley and Gomes-Schwartz, in a book titled *Psychotherapy for Better or Worse* (1977). With Binder, Strupp authored a treatment manual, published in book form as *Psychotherapy in a New Key* (1984). The book became the centerpiece of a five-year project on time-limited dynamic psychotherapy that was designed to study the effects of a specialized training program on process and outcome (the Vanderbilt II project). The project was one of the first empirical investigations on the effects of therapist training and is still in progress.

Strupp is coeditor of the journal *Psychotherapy Research* and advisory editor to numerous professional journals. He is a fellow of APA and has served as president of APA's Division of Clinical Psychology and as president of the Society for Psychotherapy Research. He is the recipient of the Distinguished Professional Achievement Award of the American Board of Professional Psychology, the Distinguished Scientific Contribution Award of the Division of Clinical Psychology, the Distinguished Career Contribution Award of the Society for Psychotherapy Research, and the Distinguished Professional Contributions to Knowledge Award of the American Psychological Association (APA). The University of Ulm (Federal Republic of Germany) conferred on him the honorary degree of Doctor of Medicine. He was a previous contributor, in 1982, to APA's Master Lecture Series.

He continues to be interested in the problem of change in psychotherapy, both long-term and time-limited—how change comes about and factors leading to the maintenance of change or its absence. The focus of his research is the patient-therapist relationship and its vicissitudes.

STAFF

SUBLIMATION

Freudian theory posits that all human beings are motivated by powerful, innate sexual and destructive instincts (drives), including incest and murder. Since society will not tolerate such threats to its existence, it inevitably comes into conflict with the individual. Initially this takes the form of conflict between the child and the first representatives of society whom it encounters, its parents. Subsequently the socializing demands and prohibitions imposed by the parents are internalized by the child, leading to intrapsychic conflicts. To Freud, therefore, mental health consisted of resolving these conflicts by channeling one's drives away from inborn illicit wishes, and into more socially acceptable forms of behavior (*sublimating* them). Thus one may give repressed hostile impulses safe expression by becoming a surgeon or football player, while sublimations of repressed incestuous wishes may take the form of marriage or of painting portraits of the opposite sex. However, these substitute activities are never quite as satisfying as the original ones would be. The individual is left with a residue of unfulfilled desire, which is the price one pays for living in (and enjoying the benefits of) a civilized society.

Psychologists who reject Freud's pessimistic assumption about human nature need not, and do not, regard sublimation as the ideal form of behavior. Thus sublimation has been alternatively defined as the unconscious substitution of one behavior for another that would be more satisfying, but also more threatening. This conception implies that sublimation is not always healthy or advantageous, as it may deprive an individual of the maximum feasible satisfaction when strong (but irrational) anxiety has become associated with a desirable goal that is actually safe and socially accepted.

SUGGESTED READING

Brenner, C. (1974/1973). *An elementary textbook of psychoanalysis* (Rev. ed.). New York: Anchor Books.

Freud, S. (1962/1930). *Civilization and its discontents.* New York: Norton.

Freud, S. (1968/1916). Introductory lectures on psychoanalysis. In *The standard edition of the complete psychological works of Sigmund Freud* (Vols. 15, 16). London: Hogarth Press.

Sullivan, H. S. (1968/1953). *The interpersonal theory of psychiatry.* New York: Norton.

R. B. Ewen
Miami, Florida

COPING
DEFENSE MECHANISMS
PSYCHOANALYSIS

SUBLIMINAL INFLUENCE

Subliminal influence refers to the use of persuasion tactics delivered below the threshold of awareness. Although the term "subliminal perception" is well-defined in the psychological literature (Cheesman & Merikle, 1985; Holender, 1986), the term "subliminal influence" is used to refer to a variety of techniques, ranging from flashing words quickly onto a movie screen to backward phrases in rock music to cleverly hidden images in advertisements (see Pratkanis, 1992 for a history). Scientific research has failed to consistently support claims for the effectiveness of subliminal persuasion. In general, researchers have found that people can minimally process subliminal messages (such as extracting meaning from a single word presented outside of awareness), but cannot process complex subliminal messages (Greenwald, 1992; Pratkanis & Greenwald, 1988).

SENSATIONAL CLAIMS FOR THE POWER OF SUBLIMINAL INFLUENCE

Opinion polls show that most Americans believe in the power of subliminal messages to influence behavior (Haber, 1959; Synodinos, 1988; Zanot, Pincus, & Lamp, 1983). Much of this belief in subliminal persuasion has been stimulated by sensational claims that have appeared in the mass media.

For example, in the late 1950s, Vicary, an advertising expert, circulated a story claiming that he had secretly flashed, at a third of a millisecond, the words "Eat Popcorn" and "Drink Coke" onto a movie screen. As a result, Coke sales supposedly increased 18% and popcorn sales rose almost 58%. In the 1970s, Key (1973, 1976, 1980, & 1989) proclaimed that subliminal implants were routinely placed in print advertisements. In his most notorious examples, Key claimed the word "sex" was printed on Ritz crackers and appeared on the ice cubes in a Gilbey Gin ad. Also in the 1970s, parents and ministers began to evidence concern that rock music contained backward messages, often of a satanic nature. In the late 1980s and early 1990s, manufacturers of subliminal self-help tapes claimed that their tapes improved such things as self-esteem, memory, employee and customer relations, sexual responsiveness, bowling scores, and feelings about being raped. In 1990, the rock band Judas Priest was placed on trial for allegedly putting the subliminal implant "Do it" in one of their songs, which supposedly caused the suicide deaths of two teenage boys.

The public has shown concern over the possible unethical use of subliminal messages, spurring regulatory and legal action. The Federal Communications Commission has declared that the use of subliminal persuasion could result in the loss of a broadcast license. The National Association of Broadcasters prohibited the use of subliminal advertising by its members. Australia and Britain banned subliminal messages. The California State legislature passed a law stating that the distribution of material with backward messages without public notice is an invasion of privacy. A Nevada judge ruled that subliminal messages are not protected as free speech.

DO SUBLIMINAL MESSAGES PERSUADE?

Given the public outrage and civic action, it is useful to ask the question, "How effective are subliminal messages in changing and motivating behavior?" The conclusion from over a hundred years of research is that subliminal messages are generally ineffective at influencing behavior. In a comprehensive review, Moore (1982) concludes, "There is no empirical documentation for stronger subliminal effects, such as inducing particular behaviors or changing motivation. Moreover, such a notion is contradicted by a substantial amount of research and is incompatible with experimentally based conceptions of information processing, learning, and motivation." (For updates see Moore, 1988, 1992). Other reviewers have reached the same conclusion, noting that proclaimed subliminal effects often fail to replicate and that studies claiming to find subliminal influence are methodologically flawed (see Advertising Research Foundation, 1958; Eich & Hyman, 1991; Eriksen, 1956, 1960; McConnell, Cutler, & McNeil, 1958; Pratkanis & Greenwald, 1988).

Consider research after Vicary's claim for increased sales of popcorn and Coke because of subliminal messages. In 1958, the Canadian Broadcast Corporation conducted a replication of the Vicary study by flashing the message "Phone Now" 352 times during a popular Sunday night television show ("Phone Now," 1958). Telephone usage did not go up during the period; nobody called the station. When asked to guess the message, viewers sent close to five hundred letters, but not one contained the correct answer. However, aware of the Vicary study, almost half claimed to be hungry or thirsty during the show. In response to such findings, Vicary admitted to *Advertising Age* that he had handled the affair poorly. He stated, "Worse than the timing, though, was the fact that we hadn't done any research, except what was needed for filing for a patent. I had only a minor interest in the company and a small amount of data—too small to be meaningful." (Danzig, 1962; see also Weir, 1984).

The work of Key has been criticized on methodological grounds (Moore, 1992). For example, Key (1973) reports a study where more than a thousand subjects were shown a Gilbey Gin ad that supposedly contained the word sex embedded in ice cubes. Sixty-two percent of the subjects reported feeling aroused, romantic, and sensuous. However, Key did not include a control group in the study (a group of subjects who saw a similar ad without the implant), and thus we cannot know if these subjects felt aroused, romantic, and sensuous because of the alleged implant, in spite of it, or for some other reason.

Vokey and Read (1985) have conducted an extensive program of research showing that backward messages are ineffective in altering behavior. In their studies, they found that subjects: (a) could not discriminate a backward question from a statement, (b) could not tell if two backward messages had the same or different meaning, (c) could not distinguish nonsense from meaningful backward messages, and (d) could not distinguish between backward nursery rhymes, Christian, satanic, pornographic, or advertising messages. Vokey and Read also found that listening to backward messages did not influence subjects' semantic judgments and that subjects could hear hidden messages in backward messages even when there were no such messages.

Several studies have investigated the efficacy of subliminal self-help audiotapes. For example, Pratkanis, Eskenazi, and Greenwald (1994; Greenwald, Spangenberg, Pratkanis, & Eskenazi, 1991) had subjects listen to subliminal self-help tapes designed to improve either self-esteem or memory. Half the subjects received mislabeled tapes; in other words, some subjects thought they had a memory-improving tape, but really had a self-esteem tape while others thought they had a self-esteem tape, but listened to a mem-

ory tape. After five weeks of listening, the results showed no improvement in self-esteem or memory abilities. However, about half the subjects thought they had improved based on tape label, but not content. Subjects who thought they had listened to a self-esteem tape (regardless of whether they did or not) were more likely to believe that their self-esteem had improved, and those who thought they had listened to a memory tape were more likely to believe that their memory had improved because of listening. In actuality, nobody's self-esteem or memory improved as a result of listening. To date there have been nine independent investigations of subliminal self-help tapes (see Pratkanis, 1992 for a listing). All nine studies have failed to find an effect consistent with the manufacturers' claims.

REFERENCES

Advertising Research Foundation. (1958). *The application of subliminal perception in advertising.* New York, NY: Author.

Cheesman, J., & Merikle, P. M. (1985). Word recognition and consciousness. In D. Besner, T. G. Waller, & G. E. MacKinnon (Eds.), *Reading research: Advances in theory and practice* (Vol. 5, pp. 311–352). New York: Academic.

Danzig, F. (1962, Sept. 17). Subliminal advertising—Today it's just historic flashback for researcher Vicary. *Advertising Age.*

Eich, E., & Hyman, R. (1991). Subliminal self-help. In D. Druckman & R. A. Bjork (Eds.), *In the mind's eye: Enhancing human performance* (pp. 107–119). Washington, D.C.: National Academy Press.

Eriksen, C. W. (1956). Subception: Fact of artifact? *Psychological Review, 63,* 74–80.

Eriksen, C. W. (1960). Discrimination and learning without awareness: A methodological survey and evaluation. *Psychological Review, 67,* 279–300.

Greenwald, A. G. (1992). New look 3: Unconscious cognition reclaimed. *American Psychologist, 47,* 766–779.

Greenwald, A. G., Spangenberg, E. R., Pratkanis, A. R., & Eskenazi, J. (1991). Double-blind tests of subliminal self-help audiotapes. *Psychological Science, 2,* 119–122.

Haber, R. N. (1959). Public attitudes regarding subliminal advertising. *Public Opinion Quarterly, 23,* 291–293.

Holender, D. (1986). Semantic activation without conscious identification in dichotic listening, parafoveal vision, and visual masking: A survey and appraisal. *Behavior and Brain Sciences, 9,* 1–66.

Key, W. B. (1973). *Subliminal seduction.* Englewood Cliffs, NJ: Signet.

Key, W. B. (1976). *Media sexploitation.* Englewood Cliffs, NJ: Signet.

Key, W. B. (1980). *The clam-plate orgy.* Englewood Cliffs, NJ: Signet.

Key, W. B. (1989). *The age of manipulation.* New York: Holt.

McConnell, J. V., Cutler, R. I., & McNeil, E. B. (1958). Subliminal stimulation: An overview. *American Psychologist, 13,* 229–242.

Moore, T. E. (1982). Subliminal advertising: What you see is what you get. *Journal of Marketing, 46,* 38–47.

Moore, T. E. (1988). The case against subliminal manipulation. *Psychology & Marketing, 5,* 297–316.

Moore, T. E. (1992). Subliminal perception: Facts and fallacies. *Skeptical Inquirer, 16,* 273–281.

"Phone now," said CBC subliminally—but nobody did. (1958, February 10). *Advertising Age,* p. 8.

Pratkanis, A. R. (1992). The cargo-cult science of subliminal persuasion. *Skeptical Inquirer, 16,* 260–272.

Pratkanis, A. R., Eskenazi, J., & Greenwald, A. G. (1994). What you expect is what you believe (but not necessarily what you get): A test of the effectiveness of subliminal self-help audiotapes. *Basic and Applied Social Psychology, 15,* 251–276.

Pratkanis, A. R., & Greenwald, A. G. (1988). Recent perspectives on unconscious processing: Still no marketing applications. *Psychology & Marketing, 5,* 339–355.

Synodinos, N. E. (1988). Subliminal stimulation: What does the public think about it? *Current Issues & Research in Advertising, 11,* 157–187.

Vokey, J. R., & Read, J. D. (1985). Subliminal messages: Between the devil and the media. *American Psychologist, 40,* 1231–1239.

Weir, W. (1984, October 15). Another look at subliminal "facts." *Advertising Age,* p. 46.

Zanot, E. J., Pincus, J. D., Lamp, E. J. (1983). Public perceptions of subliminal advertising. *Journal of Advertising, 12,* 37–45.

A. R. PRATKANIS
University of California, Santa Cruz

COMMUNICATION PROCESSES
MOTIVATION

SUBLIMINAL PERCEPTION

Toward the end of the 1950s, a great deal of public concern was expressed when it was claimed that a method existed for presenting advertising messages that could influence behavior at an unconscious level. A typical example used at that time might be at a movie theater, where the message "Buy Popcorn" might be given during the film, and even though viewers were not consciously aware of its presence they might still be motivated to purchase popcorn. The procedures involved quickly flashing messages on the screen at a size, speed, or brightness that was too insignificant to produce conscious awareness. Such stimuli are called *subliminal*—from the Latin for below *(sub)* the threshold for consciousness *(limen)*. Subliminal perception comes about when such stimuli, even though apparently unnoticed, appear to exert an effect on later behavior.

There is still controversy as to whether subliminal stimuli have the ability to persuade in advertising settings. Many researchers note that stimuli which are intended to be subliminal may occa-

sionally make it into our consciousness. It has often been suggested that it is only on those occasions, when the stimulus actually is detected (even if these are statistically rare) that the message can have any effect. To persuade people to any great extent, the message can not be truly subliminal but has to reach consciousness, at least occasionally (e.g., Smith & Rogers, 1994).

The problem with the study of subliminal perception was that it was quickly picked up by the popular media. There were many irresponsible statements made about it, and many of the claims made for subliminal persuasion were extravagant and bizarre. For instance, there were claims that people were being manipulated through subliminal sexual symbolism, which was hidden in television and even magazine advertisements. Strange stories were published in which it was suggested that teenagers were being deliberately exposed to subliminal stimuli in musical recordings which were placed there by revolutionaries and terrorists, who wanted to stir aggressive responses in them. Some fundamentalist groups claimed that these same vehicles (film, television, and musical recordings) were being used by devil worshipers to undermine the morals of the public and to gain new converts. Such suggestions could never be convincingly substantiated; however, they brought the study of subliminal perception into some disrepute for several decades since it seemed to associate it with fringe groups and marginalized (or downright weird) social activities, and a lot of bad science.

Recently, two lines of research have rehabilitated the study of subliminal perception. It began with the publication of Zajonc's (1968) monograph describing what he called the *mere exposure effect.* This effect demonstrates that simple repeated exposure to a stimulus, even if it is not consciously noticed or attended to, can produce positive feelings for that stimulus when it is later encountered. This effect has proven to be a robust, reliable phenomenon, showing that people tend to prefer stimuli that they have seen before, no matter what they are—whether drawings, photographs, nonsense words, or even social behaviors of people. One important aspect of these findings is that the effect seems to be quite primitive. The person does not need to be consciously aware that they have seen the stimulus, nor do they have to be able to remember ever encountering it before. In fact, there have been a number of studies which suggest that the emotional effect associated with mere exposure is even greater if the stimuli are subliminal (e.g., Bornstein & D'Agonstino, 1992).

Clinical psychologists have cited another aspect of how emotional factors play a role in subliminal perception. This is in the case of *perceptual defense.* Typical examples occur in experiments in which observers are briefly shown nonsense syllables or figures and are asked to identify them. If some of the stimuli presented had been previously associated with painful electric shock, they might now be expected to be somewhat anxiety producing. In general, it is found that such negative emotional stimuli are recognized less readily than neutral stimuli—as if the observers are defending themselves from the painful memories evoked by seeing such stimuli. Still, it is possible to show that subliminal perception has taken place. This is done through the use of physiological measures of anxiety, such as the galvanic skin response, which registers the person's negative emotional state for the stimuli, even though the observer cannot consciously identify them. This process, whereby there is an emotional response but no conscious awareness of the stimulus, is sometimes also called *subception*.

The most recent, and probably the most active, lines of research involving subliminal perception have involved cognitive psychologists. They have returned to this process due to their interest in an effect called *priming*. This is where the occurrence of one stimulus may make it easier to perceive a later stimulus which is related to it in some way. For example, a priming study involving word recognition might first present the prime word, which is followed by a target word. Thus, we might briefly present the word "nurse" and follow it with a semantically related word (one that has an associated meaning) such as "doctor" or an unrelated word such as "carrot." Typically, priming is shown when the person responds more quickly to the related word than to the neutral word. It is believed that the prime word has somehow activated cognitive processes associated with the first stimulus, making the stimuli that come later easier to process (see Neely, 1991). The label "priming" comes from the fact that older style water pumps often needed to be primed by first having some water poured into the pump chamber, before they could efficiently draw additional fluid up from the well.

One of the interesting aspects of priming is that the priming stimulus does not have to be conscious, but can be totally unconscious or subliminal (e.g., Klinger & Greenwald, 1995). During the course of such research it has become clear that subliminal perception may actually trigger associations which are necessary for us to read quickly and process written information efficiently. Thus, we subliminally register data from the words that are still ahead of us on the printed page. Our unconscious perception of this material makes it easier for us to recognize those words and ideas when we encounter them later, as our eyes move down the text since these associations have already been subliminally primed (Sereno & Rayner, 1992). This suggests that subliminal perception is not a rare psychological oddity, but that it may be a common and integral component in the way that we process information from our environment.

REFERENCES

Bornstein, R. F., & D'Agonstino, A. (1992). Stimulus recognition and the mere exposure effect. *Journal of Personality and Social Psychology, 63,* 545–552.

Klinger, M. R., & Greenwald, A. G. (1995). Unconscious priming of association judgements. *Journal of Experimental Psychology: Learning, Memory, and Cognition, 21,* 569–581.

Neely, J. H. (1991). Semantic priming effects in visual word recognition: A selective review of current findings and theories. In D. Besner & G. Humphreys (Eds.), *Basic processes in reading: Visual word recognition* (pp. 264–336). Hillsdale, NJ: Erlbaum.

Sereno, S. C., & Rayner, K. (1992). Fast priming during eye fixations in reading. *Journal of Experimental Psychology: Human Perception and Performance, 18,* 173–184.

Smith, K. H., & Rogers, M. (1994). Effectiveness of subliminal messages in television commercials: Two experiments. *Journal of Applied Psychology, 79,* 866–874.

Zajonc, R. B. (1968). Attitudinal effects of mere exposure. *Journal of Personality and Social Psychology Monographs, 9*(2, Pt. 2), 1–27.

S. COREN
University of British Columbia

SELECTIVE ATTENTION

SUBSTANCE ABUSE

Substance abuse has been a controversial issue since ancient times. Debates concerning the use of marijuana, for example, can be traced to Chinese documents dated several centuries B.C. In the United States, concern about the abuse of alcohol and other drugs has existed since the early 19th century.

Substance abuse involves the use of any chemical to modify mood or behavior in a way that differs from socially approved therapeutic or recreational practices. Historically, medical and legal attitudes toward substance abuse have fluctuated.

DIAGNOSIS

The American Psychiatric Association's third edition of the *Diagnostic and Statistical Manual of Mental Disorders* (*Third Edition*) lists three criteria for the diagnosis of substance abuse: a pattern of pathological use; impairment of social or occupational functioning; and duration of the problem for at least one month. Substance dependence can be diagnosed when, in addition to the criteria for abuse, a more severe physiological dependence exists. The dependence may be manifested by tolerance (increased amounts needed to achieve desired effects) or withdrawal (physiological symptoms precipitated by cessation of the substance).

The *DSM-III* presents five classes of substances that can involve both abuse and dependence: alcohol, amphetamines, barbiturates and similarly acting sedatives or hypnotics, cannabis, and opiates. Cocaine, phecyclidine (PCP), and hallucinogens are listed as substances that have been abused, but for which dependence has not been documented. Grinspoon and Bakaler (1980) added solvents to the abuse-only category. Kuehnle and Spitzer (1981) have suggested that eating disorders may be added to the substance abuse classification in future diagnostic manuals.

Many health professionals view caffeine and tobacco as drugs that are abused and cause dependence. Greden (1980) points out that, because of their widespread intake, the problems of these substances were neglected by clinicians and research scientists for many years.

Accurate diagnosis of substance abuse must include attention to the individual's specific cluster of problems. Substance abuse disorders can be continuous, episodic, in remission, or unspecified. In addition, most drugs can cause a variety of organic brain syndromes. Polydrug use is quite common. Alcoholics, for example, tend to smoke tobacco more than do nonalcoholics. Similarly many individuals who abuse barbiturates also abuse amphetamines. Finally, substance abuse problems may coexist with other psychiatric disorders, such as personality or affective disorders.

TREATMENT

Just as substance abuse should be individually assessed, so must it be treated. For example, substance abuse programs are often oriented toward men, as the majority of substance abusers are male. Yet women who have alcohol and other drug problems may have different types of treatment issues. In general, however, several stages of intervention are usually necessary. Immediate attention to emergencies requires treatment of acute medical conditions such as panic reactions or malnutrition. Detoxification necessitates reduction of the substance while monitoring withdrawal symptoms and performing additional laboratory tests and clinical assessment. Individual counseling is usually the next step in treatment.

Support is a critical component of all phases of intervention. Therapeutic communities such as Synanon and self-help groups such as Alcoholics Anonymous can provide group support as well as confrontation, and can serve as long-term programs for treatment and maintenance of drug-free functioning. The involvement of family is also necessary to help the substance abuser, as well as the family members.

PREVENTION

Most substance abuse prevention has been tertiary prevention or treatment of existing cases and prevention of recidivism. Secondary prevention, or early diagnosis and referral, usually have taken place in crisis intervention clinics. Swisher (1979) has emphasized the need for greater primary prevention efforts, or the planning of activities before abuse occurs. Swisher suggests that the most effective primary prevention efforts involve coordination of various community institutions, combinations of informational materials with alternatives to drug use, and the synthesis and integration of existing materials within ongoing community activities.

Given the ubiquitous nature of alcohol and other drug use in our society, most experts recommend greater dialogue and cooperation among health professionals, legislators, law enforcement officials, educators, and, perhaps most important, family members.

REFERENCES

American Psychiatric Association. (1980). *Diagnostic and statistical manual of mental disorders* (3rd ed.). Washington, DC: Author.

Greden, J. (1980). Caffeine and tobacco dependence. In *Comprehensive textbook of psychiatry* (3rd ed., Vol. 2) Baltimore: Williams & Wilkins.

Grinspoon, L., & Bakalar, J. (1980). Drug dependence: Nonnarcotic agents. In H. I. Kaplan, A. M. Freedman, & B. J. Saddock (Eds.), *Comprehensive textbook of psychiatry* (3rd ed., Vol. 2). Baltimore: Williams & Wilkins.

Kuehnle, J., & Spitzer, R. (1981). *DSM-III* classification of substance use disorders. In J. H. Lowinson & P. Ruiz (Eds.), *Substance abuse: Clinical problems and perspectives.* Baltimore: Williams & Wilkins.

Swisher, J. P. (1979). Prevention issues. In R. J. Dupont, A. Goldstein, J. O'Donnell, & B. Brown (Eds.), *Handbook on drug abuse.* Rockville, MD: National Institute on Drug Abuse.

SUGGESTED READING

Dupont, R. J., Goldstein, A., O'Donnelly, J., & Brown, B. (Eds.). (1979). *Handbook on drug abuse.* Rockville, MD: National Institute on Drug Abuse.

Fishbourne, P. M., Abelson, H. I., & Cisin, I. (1979). *National survey on drug abuse: Main findings, 1979.* Rockville, MD: National Institute on Drug Abuse.

Lowinson, J. H., & Ruiz, P. (Eds.). (1981). *Substance abuse: Clinical problems and perspectives.* Baltimore: Williams & Wilkins.

Schucket, M. A. (1979). *Drug and alcohol abuse: A clinical guide to diagnosis and treatment.* New York: Plenum.

C. LANDAU
Brown University Division of Medicine

ADDICTION
ALCOHOLISM TREATMENT
DEPENDENT PERSONALITY

SUCCESSIVE APPROXIMATIONS (SHAPING)

The terms "successive approximation" and "shaping" are shorthand for the phrase "successive reinforcement of closer and closer approximations to the target behavior" (Skinner, 1953). This procedure is distinct from other operant reinforcement methods (e.g., chaining), in that it relies on both reinforcement and extinction applied to a changing set of criteria responses (Galbicka, 1994). The target, or terminal, response is either infrequent or novel to the organism (i.e., it has never been performed), limiting the utility of direct reinforcement of the response. Shaping, as the name implies, involves slow transformations of the organism's behavior over time, much like the process of shaping clay into a fine piece of pottery. Initially, a gross or distal response approximating the terminal behavior is sufficient for the delivery of reinforcement. In time, a more similar and proximal response is required. This process may continue until only the terminal response elicits reinforcement.

Shaping is a powerful tool for expanding the repertoire of organisms, including humans. Shaping may be intentional or unintentional, depending on whether the behavior was produced from planned or accidental reinforcement (i.e., contrived vs. natural consequences).

EXAMPLES

Planned Shaping

Molly would like to teach her 1-year-old daughter, Sally, to call her mommy. Sally currently does not say mommy, but does say "ma" occasionally. Molly begins to pay extra attention (e.g., says, "Great job, Sally," and smiles) when Sally says "ma." Soon Sally says "ma" often. Molly decides it is now time for Sally to say something more similar to "mommy," so she no longer praises her for simply saying "ma." Instead, Molly reinforces Sally for saying "ma" twice in a row, which sounds like "moma." This process continues until "moma" is shaped into "mommy."

Accidental Shaping

Timmy is a 3-year-old boy without a history of tantrums. Timmy is bored with shopping at the store, and begins to whine. His father, Don, tries to console him by picking him up, talking to him, and giving him something with which to play. Don appears to have accidentally reinforced Timmy's whining in similar situations because the next time Timmy is bored while shopping, he begins to whine. However, whining is no longer sufficient to get Don's attention. While Timmy is whining, he erroneously increases his volume, which does catch Don's attention. Now Don tries to console him as he did before. This process continues; each time, Timmy's behavior becomes more and more inappropriate in order to gain his father's attention. Soon Timmy needs to tantrum to gain the attention of his father when they are shopping.

CONSIDERATIONS

Though shaping may be accidental, programmed shaping may be of more use to clinicians, parents, and teachers. To successfully shape behavior, Martin and Pear (1999) indicate four factors to be considered.

Specifying the Final Desired Behavior

The final desired behavior, or terminal behavior, should be well specified. This includes topography (shape or form), intensity, frequency, context, and antecedent conditions. By defining the target behavior with this level of clarity, caretakers and providers will be more likely to apply the shaping procedure consistently.

In the first scenario, Molly wishes for Sally to say "mommy." The topography is well specified—"mommy" is the desired form of response. Intensity of response might refer to volume in this case. Initially, Molly may accept "mommy" at any volume; later, however, Sally will need to say "mommy" at a volume appropriate for the context. Likewise, initially saying "mommy" repeatedly would be acceptable; later, it might be considered annoying. This leaves only the antecedent conditions for comment. Sally might generalize the words "mommy" to many adult females who look more or less like Molly. This is because Sally has not yet learned to discriminate that it is only the presence of Molly for which using the word "mommy" is correct. Over time, Molly will serve as the discriminative stimulus for the response "mommy."

Choosing the Starting Behavior

The starting behavior must occur at a rate likely to receive reinforcement during the training session. This necessity will help select the starting behavior from among the class of possible starting behaviors, even if other behaviors more closely resemble or approximate the target behavior.

Molly might have chosen to begin shaping Sally at an earlier age, when she first began babbling or cooing. Or she may have mistakenly chosen to start with Sally's saying "mommy," a word not yet within her repertoire. Either of these scenarios might not have resulted in success. The starting behavior should be a regularly occurring response.

Choosing the Shaping Steps

Prior to shaping, one should consider the likely permutations between the starting behavior and the terminal behavior. Since complex behavior is composed of multiple chains or patterns of response, the possible permutations may be limitless. Nonetheless, decisions regarding which approximations are sufficient to qualify as progress toward the target behavior must be made. The exact rules for this process are not well specified in the literature.

With the first example, the permutations were fewer; but in the second example, in which Timmy was learning to tantrum, the permutations were many. In this example, it was Timmy's ability to gain attention that pushed the generation of new responses. He only had to become slightly more difficult to ignore on each occasion to gain his father's attention. Outcomes other than tantrums were possible.

Moving Along at the Correct Pace

Shaping protocols are typically flexible; if the organism is failing to display the new approximation response, simpler steps may be created to facilitate learning. Likewise, when progress is more rapid than expected, criteria for reinforcement may be raised (i.e., more advanced steps may be attempted).

As with other forms of operant learning, shaping is highly individualized. This differentiates shaping from nomothetic or group approaches. The pace may be affected by the organism's learning history, the response cost of the behavior, qualitative aspects of the reinforcer, and ratio strain potential. Mathematical models to predict and facilitate this process are relatively rare; Galbicka's work is an exception (1994). Unfortunately, his recommendations for using percentile reinforcement schedules are infrequently followed.

ADDITIONAL CONSIDERATIONS

In addition to the four typical considerations, it is also important to consider selecting reinforcers, tracking progress, and choosing target behaviors.

Selecting Reinforcers

Often overlooked in discussions of shaping, reinforcer selection may be the most important consideration in shaping. Rewards are not the same as reinforcers; reinforcers by definition increase the probability of occurrence of the preceding behavior. Have the person help choose the reinforcer, if possible. Then monitor the shaping process to see if the response frequency is increasing. If it is not, you are not using a reinforcer.

Tracking Progress

Progress is not a given in behavioral psychology. Data need to be collected to evaluate progress—determine reinforcer effectiveness, pacing of steps, and strength of new responses. A graph of the data employing a changing criterion design will help consolidate most aspects of the shaping program into a single, simple form.

Choosing Target Behaviors

Shaping is a highly effective tool for teaching new behavior. Shaping may be used to change behavior even when the organism, or person, is unaware that he or she is being shaped. Careful consideration should be taken when deciding to use shaping, and target behaviors must be appropriate and beneficial for the organism. Take the time to consider the ethics of your decision, and involve the participant in this process if possible.

REFERENCES

Martin, G., & Pear, J. (1966). *Behavior modification: What it is and how to do it* (6th ed.). Englewood Cliffs, NJ: Prentice Hall.

Skinner, B. F. (1953). *Science and human behavior.* New York: Macmillan.

Galbicka, G. (1994). Shaping in the 21st century: Moving percentile schedules into applied settings. *Journal of Applied Behavior Analysis, 27*(4), 739–760.

D. B. HATFIELD
Eastern Washington University

BEHAVIOR MODIFICATION
REINFORCEMENT

SUICIDAL BEHAVIOR AMONG YOUTH

Epidemiology

Suicide rates among youths are alarmingly high (Goldman & Beardslee, 1999). Suicide is the third leading cause of death in adolescents and the fifth leading cause of death in children ages 5 to 14 (Kochanek & Hudson, 1992). In 1994, the suicide rate was .9 per 100,000 for children ages 5 to 14, and 13.8 per 100,000 for youths ages 15 to 24. Firearms are the most common means for suicide completions in youth. The suicide rate for young people has risen steadily since 1950. Explanations for the increase in suicide rates include greater alcohol use and depression, as well as increased availability of firearms (Boyd & Moscicki, 1986). In addition to the available statistics on suicide completions, recent national surveys among randomly selected adolescents reveal that 5% to 6% of youth have tried to commit suicide, 12% to 15% have come close to trying to commit suicide, over 50% report intermittent suicidal ideation, and approximately 60% report that one of their peers had attempted suicide (Gallup, 1994).

As with adults, there are dramatic sex differences in rates of suicidal ideation, attempts, and completions. About four times as many girls as boys report suicidal ideation and about three times as many girls as boys endorse a history of suicide attempts (Joffe, Offord, & Boyle, 1988). However, suicide completions are more common in boys; boys outnumber girls nearly five to one.

There is considerable variability in the rates of suicide across ethnic groups. Historically, the rates of suicide completions have been significantly lower among African American than Caucasian youth. However, during 1980–1995, the gap has narrowed, and the suicide rate for African American youth has increased more than for Caucasian youth (Centers for Disease Control, 1998). In addition, Native American adolescent males exhibit higher suicide rates than any other ethnic group, and this is particularly true for those Native American youth from tribes whose traditional values have diminished most markedly (Berlin, 1987).

There is considerable controversy regarding the relation between sexual orientation and suicidality. The available data suggest that lesbian, gay, and bisexual youth are at greater risk for attempting suicide than their heterosexual counterparts, with marked variability in attempt rates across studies (7% to 38%). There are not adequate data to evaluate whether or not homosexual youth complete suicide more often than heterosexual youth (Hartstein, 1996).

DEVELOPMENTAL PERSPECTIVES

The suicide rate for children and adolescents increases with age throughout adolescence. Suicide attempts and completions are very rare before puberty, although young children do experience suicidal ideation. In preadolescent children, lower suicide rates are attributable to immature cognitive and psychosocial development, decreased ability to plan and execute a completed suicide, lower rates of depression and substance abuse, and decreased access to lethal means (Shaffer & Fisher, 1981). Furthermore, preadolescents cannot conceive of the future as well as adolescents, which diminishes their capability for hopelessness. Finally, as children enter adolescence, the developmental task of autonomy and mastery may result in increased isolation from, and decreased supervision by, adult figures. As a result, by adolescence, there is a marked increase in all forms of suicidal behavior.

RISK FACTORS

A biopsychosocial framework can be used to categorize the risk factors for suicidal behavior in youth. Biological factors include genetics and deficits in serotonin functioning. Psychological factors include psychopathology and deficits in coping and interpersonal functioning. Social factors include stressful life events, family environment, and imitation and contagion.

Genetic and Biological

The role of genetic factors in suicidality among adolescents is supported by twin and adoption studies. Monozygotic twins show higher concordance rates for suicidal behavior than dizygotic twins (Roy, 1992). There is greater suicidal behavior among biological relatives of adoptees who complete suicide than matched adoptees, even controlling for psychiatric illness among biological relatives (Kety, 1986). Most of the research on biological risk factors for suicidal behavior in adults has focused on disturbances in serotonin metabolism (Biegon, Grinspoon, & Blumenfeld, 1990); only recently have investigations begun to examine if suicidal youth have low levels of serotonin.

Psychopathology

A major psychological risk factor for youth suicide is history of a prior suicide attempt. A psychological autopsy study conducted with adolescents who killed themselves found that 20% of the males and 30% of the females had made a previous attempt (Shaffer, Garland, Gould, Fisher, & Trautman, 1988). A number of psychiatric disorders have been found to be risk factors for the continuum of suicidal behavior in youth, including mood, conduct, substance abuse, and personality disorders (Zimmerman & Asnis, 1995).

Coping and interpersonal skills

Suicidal youth tend to evidence impaired social skills, poor interpersonal relationships, and deficient problem-solving skills. Youth with such deficits in coping and interpersonal skills are most vulnerable to engaging in suicidal behavior in response to negative stressors (Yang & Clum, 1994).

Stressful life events

Adolescents who attempt suicide report higher rates of stressful life events 12 months prior to the attempt, as well as over the life span (Paykel, 1989). Specific life stresses identified by suicidal youth include fighting with parents, breaking up with a romantic partner, and loss of a parent due to death or divorce. It is important to note that these life stresses are quite common among youth, and the majority of youth that experience these events do not attempt suicide.

Family

One review of the literature identified several family risk factors for child and adolescent suicidal behavior (Wagner, 1997). The experience of physical or sexual abuse is a risk factor for suicidal behavior; this has been replicated across several empirical studies. Changes in the composition of the family, such as death, parental separation, divorce, or other losses also put adolescents at increased risk for suicidal behavior. Other family risk factors include poor family or parent-child communication, low family cohesiveness, and psychopathology among first-degree relatives.

Imitation and contagion

Direct or indirect exposure to suicide is associated with suicidal behavior among youth (Spirito, Brown, Overholser, & Fritz, 1989). For example, person-to-person contact with another individual that has attempted suicide, particularly a family member or peer, is linked with suicidal behavior. Indirect exposure to suicide, through media coverage of suicide attempts or fictional accounts of suicide, is also linked with suicidal behavior among adolescents. Furthermore, the intensity of media coverage of suicides of well-known celebrities, especially those in entertainment or politics, is positively related to suicidal behavior.

PROTECTIVE FACTORS

The role of protective factors generally is described in models outlining the interrelationship of risk and protective factors. For example, one model focuses on the importance of a supportive and consistent relationship with another individual; protective aspects of such a relationship include providing empathy and structure, as well as meeting the needs of the adolescent (Blumenthal, 1990).

ASSESSMENT

Berman and Jobes (1991) stressed the importance of a multifocused assessment of suicidality, outlining six dimensions: imminent risk, lethality and intent, predisposing conditions and precipitating factors, psychopathology, cooperation with the interviewer, and coping skills and resources. Using these data, the clinician may screen for levels of risk of suicidal behavior. The first level of risk is indicated when one or more risk factors (e.g., depression) is present. The second level of risk is represented by current suicidal ideation along with the presence of one or more risk factors. At the highest level of risk, whether or not an adolescent will act on suicidal ideation depends on a number of situational and characterological factors, such as the present level of stress in the environment, availability of means for self-harm, and impulsiveness of the individual.

Assessment of suicidal behavior is notoriously difficult. One study presented a panel of mental health professionals videotaped interviews of inpatient and outpatient individuals, and asked the panel to evaluate the risk for suicidal behavior over the following week and the likely lethality of the attempt. The intraclass reliability was .57 and .36 for suicide risk and lethality respectively (Kaplan, Kottler, & Frances, 1982).

CRISIS MANAGEMENT AND INTERVENTION

Management of a suicidal youth is singularly focused on the goal of keeping the individual physically safe and alive until the crisis has passed. Management of significant suicidal ideation and behavior is likely to be most effective in the context of a hospital setting, with ready access to such important resources as inpatient hospitalization, medication, safe holding rooms, and colleagues with whom to determine the presence, lethality, and future likelihood of a suicide attempt (Zimmerman & Asnis, 1995). However, most suicidal youth can be managed on an outpatient basis with plans for ongoing monitoring and support.

Several theoretical perspectives address the treatment of suicidal youth, including cognitive-behavioral, family systems, and psychodynamic orientations, among others. Cognitive-behavioral treatment of suicidal behavior generally is highly structured and focuses on building interpersonal, coping, and problem-solving skills. Empirical data suggest that cognitive-behavioral strategies that increase coping skills are useful in decreasing suicidal ideation and suicide attempts (Rudd & Joiner, 1998). A family systems approach targets family functioning as a method for intervening with suicidal youth, including the ability of the family to support the developmental issue of separation-individuation of the adolescent (Zimmerman & Asnis, 1995). Treatment of suicidality from an object-relations perspective emphasizes the importance of building interpersonal skills and social support networks, increasing accessibility to internal representations that are soothing, and decreasing the intensity of self-criticism in the face of perceived abandonment. Recent data reveal that individuals exhibiting suicidal behavior also report poor object relations, suggesting that treatment of suicidal behavior from an object-relational view may be useful (Kaslow et al., 1998).

PREVENTION

Berman and Jobes (1991) outline several approaches to youth suicide prevention, including early detection and referral of at-risk youths, identification of resources, encouragement of help-seeking behavior of at-risk youths, and education of professionals and parents. These researchers advocate both community- and school-based prevention efforts. One recommendation for a community-based approach to prevention is to restrict the availability of lethal means for suicidal behavior, such as limiting prescription dosages of potentially lethal antidepressant medications to a one-week supply. Crisis intervention services, such as crisis hotlines, are another community-based prevention approach. Schools also are popular sites for prevention programs, consisting of three to six sessions in the classroom that utilize a combination of education and discussion.

REFERENCES

Biegon, A., Grinspoon, A., & Blumenfeld, B. (1990). Increased seotonin-2-receptor binding on blood platelets of suicidal men. *Psychopharmacology, 100,* 165–167.

Berlin, I. N. (1987). Suicide among American Indian adolescents: An overview. *Suicide and Life Threatening Behavior, 17,* 218–232.

Berman, A. L., & Jobes, D. A. (1991). *Adolescent suicide assessment and intervention.* Washington, DC: American Psychological Association.

Blumenthal, S. J. (1990). Youth suicide: The physician's role in suicide prevention. *Journal of the American Medical Association, 264,* 3194–3196.

Boyd, J. H., & Moscicki, E. K. (1986). Firearms and youth suicide. *American Journal of Public Health, 76,* 1240–1242.

Centers for Disease Control, (1998). Suicide among black youths – United States, 1980–1995. *MMWR, 47*(10), 193–196.

Gallup Organization. (1994). *Teenage suicide study: Executive summary.* Princeton, NJ: Gallup Organization.

Goldman, S., & Beardslee, W. R. (1999). Suicide in children and adolescents. In D. G. Jacobs (Ed.), *The Harvard Medical School guide to suicide assessment and intervention* (pp. 417–442). San Francisco: Jossey-Bass.

Hartstein, N. B. (1996). Suicide risk in lesbian, gay, and bisexual youth. In R. P. Cabaj & T. S. Stein (Eds.), *Textbook of homosexuality and mental health* (pp. 819–833). Washington, DC: American Psychiatric Press.

Kaplan, R. D., Kottler, D. B., & Frances, A. J. (1982). Reliability and rationality in the prediction of suicidal behavior. *Hospital and Community Psychiatry, 33,* 212–215.

Kaslow, N. J., Reviere, S. L., Chance, S. E., Rogers, J. H., Hatcher, C. A., Wasserman, F., Smith, L., Jessee, S., James, M. E., & Seelig, B. (1998). The psychodynamics of suicide. *Journal of Psychoanalytic Psychology, 46,* 777–796.

Kety, S. (1986). Genetic factors in suicide. In A. Roy (Ed.), *Suicide* (pp. 41–45). Baltimore, MD: Williams & Wilkins.

Kochanek, K. D., & Hudson, B. L. (1992). Advanced report of final mortality statistics. *Monthly Vital Statistics, 43*(6) 1994.

Joffe, R. T., Offord, D., & Boyle, M. H. (1988). Ontario Child Health Study: Suicidal behavior in youths 12–16 years. *American Journal of Psychiatry, 145,* 1420–1423.

Paykel, E. S. (1989). Stress and life events. In L. Davidson & M. Linnoila (Eds.), *Report of the Secretary's Task Force on Youth Suicide: (Vol. 2), Risk factors for youth suicide* (pp. 110–130). DHHS Pub. No. (ADM) 89-1622. Washington, DC: Government Printing Office.

Roy, A. (1992). Genetics, biology, and the family. In R. W. Maris, A. L. Berman, J. T. Maltsberger, & R. I. Yufit (Eds.), *Assessment and prediction of suicide* (pp. 574–588). New York: Guilford.

Rudd, M. D., & Joiner, J. (1998). The assessment, management, and treatment of suicidality: Toward clinically informed and balanced standards of care. *Clinical Psychology: Science and Practice, 5,* 135–150.

Shaffer, D. A., & Fisher, P. (1981). The epidemiology of suicide in children and young adolescents. *Journal of the American Academy of Child and Adolescent Psychiatry, 20,* 545–565.

Spirito, A., Brown, L., Overholser, J. & Fitz, G. (1989). Attempted suicide in adolesence: A review and critique of the literature. *Clinical Psychology Review, 9,* 335–363.

Wagner, B. M. (1997). Family risk factors for child and adolescent suicidal behavior. *Psychological Bulletin, 121,* 246–298.

Yang, B., & Clum, G. A. (1994). Life stress, social support, and problem-solving skills predictive of depressive symptoms, hopelessness, and suicide in an Asian student population: A test of a model. *Suicide and Life-Threatening Behavior, 24,* 127–139.

Zimmerman, J. K., & Asnis, G. M. (1995). *Treatment approaches with suicidal adolescents.* New York: Wiley.

P. ANDERSON
N. KASLOW
Emory University School of Medicine

CHILDHOOD DEPRESSION

SUICIDE

Briefly defined, suicide is the human act of self-inflicted, self-intentioned death. Baechler (1975) has proposed a definition that emphasizes the operational functions the suicidal act is meant to serve: "Suicide denotes any behavior that seeks and finds the solution to an existential problem by making an attempt on the life of the subject." In actuality, the word *suicide* is easily misapplied and has a number of confusing implications (Shneidman, 1973). It can be especially misleading when it is used adjectively, as in suicidal attempt or suicidal threat, because it can obscure many different kinds of intention and degrees of lethality of intention.

Traditionally suicide is one of the four *modes*—as distinguished from the hundreds of *causes*—of death; the other three are natural, accident, and homicide, called acronymically the NASH categories of death. The NASH categories reflect a Cartesian mechanistic attitude toward human beings, omitting entirely the psychological role of an individual in his or her own demise. Common sense tells us that it is obviously possible for one to play some role in actuating one's own natural, "accidental," or homicidal death—by imprudence, daring, risk taking, carelessness, disregard of medical regimen, inattention, heightened emotion, and so on. Shneidman (1963) has proposed a supplementary classification in which all deaths (whatever their NASH label or their cause) are identified as one of three kinds: intentioned; subintentioned (in which the individual has played some partial, latent, covert, or unconscious role in hastening the demise); or unintentioned.

VARIOUS APPROACHES TO SUICIDAL PHENOMENA

A number of different approaches to the assessment, understanding, and treatment of suicidal phenomena are delineated.

Theological

Neither the Old nor New Testament directly forbids suicide. Contemporary Western attitudes are highly colored by Christian doctrine. Historically the martyrdom of the early Christians frightened the church elders sufficiently for them to introduce a serious deterrent; they related suicide to sin. In the fourth century, St. Augustine (345–430) stated that suicide violated the Sixth Commandment (relating to killing) and precluded the possibility of redemption. By 693, the Council of Toledo had proclaimed that an individual who attempted suicide was to be excommunicated. This view was elaborated by St. Thomas Aquinas (1225–1274), who emphasized that suicide was a mortal sin in that it usurped God's power over human life and death. The notion of suicide as sin took firm hold and for hundreds of years played (and continues to play) an important part in the Western view of self-destruction.

Philosophical and Literary

Philosopher Jacques Choron (1972) outlined the position of the major Western philosophers in relation to death and suicide. In general, the "philosophers of suicide" never meant their written speculations to be prescriptions for action, but simply to reflect their own intellectual debates. Among the philosophers who touched upon the topic of suicide are Pythagorus, Plato, Aristotle, Socrates, Epicurus, the Stoics, Seneca, Epictitus, Montaigne, Descartes, Spinoza, Voltaire, Montesquieu, Rousseau, Hume, Kant, Schopenauer, Neitzsche, Kierkegaard, and Camus.

In classical Rome, in the centuries just before the Christian era, life was held rather cheaply and suicide was viewed neutrally, or even positively. The Roman Stoic Seneca said: "Living is not good, but living well. The wise man, therefore, lives as well as he should, not as long as he can. . . . He will always think of life in terms of quality not quantity."

The French philosopher Jean-Jacques Rousseau (1712–1728), by emphasizing the natural state of human beings, transferred the sin (blame) to society, stating that people are generally good and innocent and that society makes them bad. David Hume (1711–1776) was one of the first major Western philosophers to discuss suicide without the concept of sin. His essay "On suicide," published in 1777, a year after his death, was promptly suppressed. It refutes the view that suicide is a crime, and does so by arguing that suicide is not a transgression of our duties to God, to our fellow citizens, or to ourselves: "Prudence and courage should engage us to rid ourselves at once of existence when it becomes a burden."

The existential philosophers of this century—Kierkegaard, Jaspers, Camus, Sartre, Heidigger—have made the meaninglessness of life (and the place of suicide) a central topic. Camus begins *The Myth of Sisyphus* by saying that the topic of suicide is the central problem for philosophy.

A. Alvarez, a successful English poet and critic (and a failed suicide), wrote *The Savage God* (1970) about suicide in literature, in which he discusses "the power that the act of suicide has exerted over the creative literary imagination." Alvarez considers the impact of the idea of suicide on the works of Dante, Donne, Cowper, Chatterton (who committed suicide), Coleridge, Goethe, Dostoevsky, Yeats, Kafka, the Dadaists, Eliot, Pasternak, Mann, Camus, and Beckett.

Demographic

The demographic approach relates to various statistics on suicide. The medieval English coroners (the word *coroner* means the custodian of the Crown's pleas) began to keep "rolls," that is, documents that incorporated death (and birth) records. From the 11th century on, whether or not the property of a deceased individual was to be kept by the heirs or had to be forfeited to the Crown depended on whether or not the death was judged (by the coroner) to be an act of God or a felony. Suicide was the latter, a felony against the self, *felo de se;* thus the way in which a death was certified was of enormous importance to the survivors.

In 1662, John Graunt, a tradesman, published a small book of "observations" on the London bills of mortality—a listing of all deaths—that was to have great social and medical significance. Graunt devised categories of information (sex, locale, type of death) and made mortality tables. He was the first to demonstrate that regularities could be found in mortality phenomena and that these regularities could be used in policy making by the government.

In 1741, the science of statistics, as it is known today, came into existence with the work of a Prussian clergyman, Johann Süssmilch. He called his efforts *political arithmetic* (now called *vital statistics*). From his studies came the "laws of large numbers," which permitted long-range planning (of need for food and supplies based on size of population) in Europe as well as in the American colonies. Cassedy (1969), who wrote about colonial America, says that Süssmilch's "exhaustive analysis of vital data from church registers . . . became the ultimate scientific demonstration of the regularity of God's demographic laws." The traditions about statistics on suicide stem from Graunt and Süssmilch.

Currently, in the United States, the suicide rate is 12.6 per 100,000. Suicide ranks as one of the 10 leading causes of adult deaths. Suicide rates gradually rise during adolescence, increase sharply in early adulthood, and parallel advancing age up to the age bracket 75 to 84, when it reaches a rate of 27.9 suicides per 100,000. Male suicides outnumber female suicides in a ratio of two to one. More whites than nonwhites commit suicide. Suicide is more prevalent among the single, widowed, separated, and divorced.

The suicide rate in young people, 15 to 24, has risen sharply since the 1950s, from 4.2 in 1954 to 10.9 in 1974. The suicide rate for nonwhites has also increased significantly. Data indicate that in the 35 years since 1946, the suicide rate of blacks has doubled, an increase attributed to increased opportunities for mobility and the attendant frustrations, role shifts, and social stress. Since 1960, suicide has increased significantly for women; the ratio of men to women has narrowed from 4:1 to 2:1.

Demographers of suicide in this century include Louis I. Dublin on suicide in the United States (1963) and Peter Sainsbury on suicide in London (1955). International statistics have been given by the World Health Organization (1968).

Sociological

Émile Durkheim's giant book *Le Suicide* (1897) demonstrated the power of the sociological approach. As a result of his analysis of French data on suicide, Durkheim proposed four kinds of suicides, all of them emphasizing the strength or weakness of the person's relationships or ties to society. *Altruistic* suicides are literally required by society. Here the customs or rules of the group "demand" suicide under certain circumstances; harakiri and suttee are examples. *Egoistic* suicide occurs when the individual has too few ties with the community, and is not reached by demands to live. Thus, proportionately, more individuals who are on their own kill themselves than do church or family members. *Anomic* suicides take place when the accustomed relationship between an individual and society is suddenly shattered, such as the shocking, immediate loss of a job, a close friend, or a fortune. *Fatalistic* suicides derive from excessive regulation. Examples would be persons whose futures are piteously blocked, such as slaves.

Today, years after Durkheim, sociologists still have not made major changes in his theory. Henry and Short (1954) added the concept of internal (superego) restraints to that of Durkheim's external restraint and Gibbs and Martin (1964) sought to operationalize Durkheim's concept of social integration.

In a major break with Durkheim, sociologist Jack Douglas (1967) pointed out that the social meanings of suicide vary greatly and that the more socially integrated a group is, the more effective it may be in disguising suicide; further, social reactions to stigmatized behaviors can themselves become a part of the etiology of the very actions the group seeks to control.

Maris (1981) believes that a systematic theory of suicide should be composed of at least four broad categories of variables—those concerning the person, the social context, biological factors, and "temporality," often-times involving "suicidal careers."

Psychodynamic

As Durkheim detailed the sociology of suicide, so Sigmund Freud fathered the psychological explanations of suicide (Friedman, 1967). To him, suicide was essentially within the mind. The principal psychoanalytical position on suicide was that it represented unconscious hostility directed toward the introjected (ambivalently viewed) love object. Psychodynamically, suicide was seen as murder in the 180th degree.

Karl Menninger, in *Man Against Himself* (1938), delineates the psychodynamics of hostility and asserts that the drives in suicide are made up of three skeins: (a) the wish to kill; (b) the wish to be killed; and (c) the wish to die.

Gregory Zilboorg (1937) refined this psychoanalytic hypothesis and stated that every suicidal case contained not only unconscious hostility, but also an unusual lack of capacity to love others. He extended the concern solely from intrapsychic dynamics to include the external world, specifically the role of a broken home, in suicidal proneness.

In an exegesis of Freud's ideas on suicide, Robert E. Litman (1967, 1970) traces the development of Freud's thoughts on the subject from 1881 to 1939. It is evident from Litman's analysis that there is more to the psychodynamics of suicide than hostility. These factors include several emotional states—rage, guilt, anxiety, dependency—as well as a great number of specifically predisposing conditions. Feelings of abandonment, and particularly of helplessness and hopelessness, are important.

A further word about the locus of blame: The early Christians made suicide a personal sin, Rousseau transferred sin from the human being to society, Hume tried to decriminalize suicide entirely, Durkheim focused on societies' inimical effects on people, and Freud—eschewing the notions of both sin and crime—gave suicide back to people but put the locus of action in their unconscious minds.

Psychological

The psychological approach can be distinguished from the psychodynamic approach in that it does not posit a set of dynamics or a universal unconscious scenario but, rather, emphasizes certain general psychologic features that seem to be necessary for a lethal suicide event to occur. Four features have been noted (Shneidman, 1976): acute *perturbation,* that is, an increase in the individual's state of general upsetment; heightened *inimicality,* an increase in self-abnegation, self-hate, shame, guilt, self-blame, and overtly in behaviors that are against one's own best interests; a sharp and almost sudden increase of *constriction* of intellectual focus, a tunneling of thought processes, a narrowing of the mind's content, a truncating of the capacity to see viable options that would ordinarily occur to the mind; and the idea of *cessation,* the insight that it is possible to put an end to suffering by stopping the unbearable flow of consciousness. This last is the igniting element that explodes the mixture of the previous three components. In this context, suicide is understood not as a movement toward death (or cessation), but rather as flight from intolerable emotion.

Constitutional, Biochemical

There is a long historic thread of trying to understand human behavior in terms of inner biological (physiological, biochemical) workings. The ancient Greek physician Hippocrates (130–200 A.D.) posited four humours: sanguine (blood), phlegmatic (phlegm), choleric (yellow bile), and melancholic (black bile). Burton's *Anatomy of Melancholy* (1652) is an explication of melancholy. Early in this century, Ernst Kretchmer (1888–1964) and W. H. Sheldon attempted to link constitutional types to temperament. In our own day, with more sophisticated techniques, there has been a thrust, particularly by physicians, to medicalize different aspects of the human condition, specifically, to reduce suicide to biochemical depression. While there may be some basis for this, it is far from the whole story. Suicide and depression are not synonymous. Nonetheless, the substantial work of current investigators of depression such as George Murphy, Aaron T. Beck, Ari Kiev, and Frederick K. Goodwin merits careful study. The treatment of depression with pharmaceutics enjoys considerable success.

Legal

In the United States, only two states, Alabama and Oklahoma, consider *committing* suicide a crime, but inasmuch as punishments are too repugnant to be enforced, there is no penalty for breaking this law. In several states, suicide attempts are misdemeanors, although these laws are seldom enforced. Thirty states have no laws against suicide or suicide attempts but every state has laws that specify that it is a felony to aid, advise, or encourage another person to commit suicide. Essays and books about the legal aspects of suicide have been written by Silving (1957), Williams (1957), Shaffer (1976), and Battin (1982), among others.

Preventional

Shneidman and colleagues (1970) are generally associated with approaching suicide from a preventive perspective. The Suicide Prevention Center in Los Angeles was established in 1958. They concluded from their research there that the vast majority (about 80%) of suicides have a recognizable presuicidal phase. In reconstructing the events preceding a death by means of a "psychological autopsy" (to help answer "*what* mode of death" and "*why*"), they have concluded that suicidal behavior is often a form of communication, "a cry for help," with clues, "messages of suffering and anguish and pleas for response" (Farberow & Shneidman, 1961).

ATTEMPTED SUICIDE: FORTUITOUS SURVIVALS AND QUASI-SUICIDES

In general, it has been believed that two "populations" (those who commit suicide and those who attempt suicide) are essentially separate (Stengel, 1974). In a sense, the words "attempt suicide" are a contradiction in terms. Strictly speaking, a suicide attempt should refer only to those who sought to commit suicide and fortuitously survived. Over a 10-year period, the overlap of the percentage of individuals who commit suicide with those who previously at-

tempted suicide is 40%, whereas the overlap of those who attempt suicide and those who subsequently commit it is only 5% (Maris, 1981). To attempt suicide with less than total lethality might be called "quasi-suicide," except that this term has the unfortunate connotation that such persons are malingerers or are simply seeking attention, and thus do not merit full professional and sympathetic response. Any event that uses a suicidal modality is a genuine crisis, even though it might not, under strict semantic rules, be called a "suicidal" event.

INDIRECT SUICIDES AND SUBINTENTIONED DEATHS

Karl Menninger's concepts of chronic, focal, and organic suicides (1938) and Shneidman's concept of subintentioned deaths (1973, 1981)—the ways in which individuals can play covert, unconscious, partial roles in hastening their deaths—obviously include what have been called indirect suicides. Farberow (1980) has edited a book that encompasses such topics as drug abuse, addictive behavior, alcohol abuse, obesity, cigarette smoking, drunken driving, and high-risk sports, including scuba diving. Whether or not these activities should be called "suicidal" is a complicated question for which an adequate answer depends on a thorough psychological autopsy of each individual case when a death occurs.

A comprehensive bibliography on suicide from 1897 to 1970 has been compiled by Farberow (1972). A journal, *Suicide and Life-Threatening Behavior*, started publication in 1971.

GLOBAL, POLITICAL, AND SUPERNATIONAL ASPECTS

Henry A. Murray (1954) said: "There will be no freedom for any exuberant form of life without freedom from atomic war. . . . nothing is of single importance today save those thoughts and actions which, in some measure, purpose to contribute to the diagnosis and alleviation of the global neurosis which so affects us."

Contemporary (self-disserving) national neuroses (amounting to an international insanity) may very well lead to the self-induced death of human life as we know it. We live in a death-haunted time. Overwhelmingly, the most important kind of suicide for everyone to know about and to prevent is the *global* suicide that threatens us all and which, by the very presence of that threat, poisons our lives. Lifton (1979) appropriately urges on our consciousness the fact that we are in great danger, even if "The Bombs" do not explode, of breaking our psychological connections to our own sense of continuity, generativity, and fantasized immortality—connections that are necessary to sustain our human relationships.

It may well be that the most important meaning—perhaps the only existential meaning—of the studies of suicidal phenomena and the prevention of individual suicidal deaths is that they serve as paradigms of global human self-destruction, which, if it comes, will render everything except the most primitive impulses meaningless.

REFERENCES

Alvarez, A. (1970). *The savage god.* New York: Random House.

Baechler, J. (1979). *Suicides.* New York: Basic Books. (Original work published 1975)

Battin, M. P. (1982). *Ethical issues in suicide.* Englewood, NJ: Prentice-Hall.

Cassedy, J. H. (1969). *Demography in early America: Beginnings of the statistical mind, 1600–1800.* Cambridge, MA: Harvard University Press.

Choron, J. (1972). *Suicide.* New York: Scribners.

Douglas, J. D. (1967). *The social meanings of suicide.* Princeton, NJ: Princeton University Press.

Dublin, L. I. (1963). *Suicide: A sociological and statistical study.* New York: Ronald Press.

Durkheim, E. (1966/1897). *Suicide: A study in sociology.* Glencoe, IL: Free Press.

Farberow, N. L. (Ed.). (1972/1969). *Bibliography on suicide and suicide prevention, 1897–1970.* Washington, DC: U.S. Department of Health, Education and Welfare (HSM) 72-9080.

Farberow, N. L., & Shneidman, E. S. (Eds.). (1961). *The cry for help.* New York: McGraw-Hill.

Friedman, P. (Ed.). (1967). *On suicide.* New York: International Universities Press.

Gibbs, J. P., & Martin, W. T. (1964). *Status integration and suicide: A sociological study.* Eugene, OR: University of Oregon Press.

Henry, A. F., & Short, J. E., Jr. (1954). *Suicide and homicide.* Glencoe, IL: Free Press.

Lifton, R. J. (1979). *The broken connection.* New York: Simon & Schuster.

Litman, R. E. (1967). Sigmund Freud on suicide. In E. S. Shneidman (Ed.), *Essays in self-destruction.* New York: Science House.

Litman, R. E., & Wold, C. (1976). 1. Beyond crisis intervention. In E. S. Shneidman (Ed.), *Suicidology: Contemporary developments.* New York: Grune & Stratton.

Maris, R. (1981). *Pathways to suicide.* Baltimore: Johns Hopkins University Press.

Menninger, K. (1938). *Man against himself.* New York: Harcourt, Brace.

Murray, H. A. (1981). This I believe (1954). In E. S. Shneidman (Ed.), *Endeavors in psychology: Selections from the personology of Henry A. Murray.* New York: Harper & Row.

Sainsbury, P. (1955). *Suicide in London: An ecological study.* London: Chapman & Hall.

Shaffer, T. L. (1976). Legal views of suicide. In E. S. Shneidman (Ed.), *Suicidology: Contemporary developments.* New York: Grune & Stratton.

Shneidman, E. S. (1963). Orientations toward death: A vital aspect of the study of lives. In R. W. White (Ed.), *The study of lives.* New York: Atherton Press.

Shneidman, E. S. (1973). Suicide. In *Encyclopaedia Britannica* (14th ed.). Chicago: Benton.

Shneidman, E. S. (1976). A psychological theory of suicide. *Psychiatric Annals, 6,* 51–66.

Silving, H. (1957). Suicide and the law. In E. S. Shneidman & N. L. Farberow (Eds.), *Clues to suicide.* New York: McGraw-Hill.

Stengel, E. (1974). *Suicide and attempted suicide.* (Rev. ed.) New York: Aronson (Original work published 1964)

Williams, G. (1957). *The sanctity of life and the criminal law.* New York: Knopf.

Zilboorg, G. (1937). Considerations on suicide. *American Journal of Orthopsychiatry, 7,* 15–31.

E. S. Shneidman
University of California School of Medicine

CRISIS INTERVENTION
DEPRESSION
STRESS
SUICIDE PREVENTION
TELEPHONE COUNSELING
THANATOLOGY

SUICIDE PREVENTION

In general, what is called suicide prevention more accurately could be labeled *suicide intervention.* Primary prevention of suicide involves the radical reduction of national and global economic and social tensions and thoroughgoing beneficent changes in certain governmental and societal patterns.

Provention (a term introduced here) is an aspect of prevention, specifically, the education of the lay and professional public about the subtle and early signs of incipiently or latently suicidal individuals. Provention is the more practical aspect of prevention, in that education is obviously more easily possible than effecting major social changes. Most people, when they talk about suicide prevention, are referring either to health education or to suicide intervention (i.e., response to or treatment of a suicidal person).

On the other hand, *postvention* (Shneidman, 1971) relates to events that can take place after the suicide has occurred. Many suicide prevention centers offer postventive services to survivor victims of suicide (Cain, 1972).

The basic rationale of suicide prevention activities is that overt suicidal behaviors are almost always preceded by certain presuicidal signs, and that suicidal states, once identified, can be mollified (and suicidal acts prevented). Retrospective studies of committed suicide indicate that approximately 90% of cases contain some indications of the decedent's suicidal intentions. These "clues to suicide"—precursors, warning signals, prodromal signs, or premonitory indexes—are either verbal (e.g., "You won't be seeing me around") or behavioral (e.g., giving away prized possessions). Response to presuicidal clues is the pathway to prevention of suicidal deaths.

Two interrelated aspects of suicide prevention centers immediately distinguish their activities from psychotherapy as ordinarily conducted: the use of volunteers and the use of the telephone. Much of the "business" of suicide prevention centers is transacted by nonprofessional personnel who respond to calls over the telephone. The keys to the successful use of volunteers—advocated notably by Dublin (1969) and Varah (1966)—are careful selection, rigorous training, and continual supervision.

TECHNIQUES FOR PREVENTION

Some techniques for suicide prevention of the highly lethal person—which differ from the rules for "ordinary" psychotherapy—can be listed:

1. Take every suicidal incident seriously enough to evaluate its level of perturbation and its potential lethality. Any event that has suicidal overtones is a genuine psychological crisis, no matter how low its lethality.

2. Maintain a continuous assessment of lethality.

3. Recognize that most suicidal persons are ambivalent (wanting to die and to live at the same time) and that a cry for help is a summons to rescue.

4. Appreciate the vital importance of transference, the patient's need to develop a life-sustaining emotionally cemented relationship with the helper. What keeps suicidal people alive are transfusions of hope and succor.

5. Institute active outreach efforts that include a willingness to deal with some of the real-life problems of the patient and a willingness to give, without exhortation.

6. Use community resources, including those relating to employment, law, medical care, Social Security, and veterans' benefits.

7. Maintain a low threshold for seeking consultation, including one's own countertransference, feelings of frustration, helplessness, and even anger.

8. Consider hospitalization. Hospitalizing a person is always a complicating event in treatment, but it should not be eschewed on those grounds alone. Good relationships with the hospital staff and access to one's patient are enormously important.

9. Involve significant others. It is important to meet the spouse, lover, or parents, and to assess each one on a range from being suicidogenic—in which case, some distance between them and the patient should be effected—to being the best possible auxiliary therapist.

10. Be mindful of the possible necessity to modify the usual canons of confidentiality, specifically in relation to collusion in a suicidal plan. One should not become a secret partner in a patient's self-destructive plans.

11. In general, therapy with suicidal persons is a variant or refinement of the rules for effective psychotherapy, whatever its genre (Beck & Rush, 1978; Farberow, 1961; Kiev, 1976; Olin, 1976; Schwartz et al., 1974; Shein & Stone, 1969; Shneidman, 1980; Shneidman et al., 1970; Wekstein, 1979).

SUICIDE PREVENTION CENTERS

Organized suicide prevention efforts are a 20th century development. Noteworthy items include the following: in 1906, in New York City, the National Save-A-Life League, begun by Rev. Harry M. Warren; around 1906, in London, the Anti-Suicide Department, by the Salvation Army; in 1948, in Vienna, the Lebensmüdenfursorgestelle (Suicide Prevention Agency) by psychiatrist Erwin Ringel; in 1953, in London, Samaritans, by Rev. Chad Varah, based on his principle of "befriending"; in 1956, in Berlin, Lebensmüdenbetreuung (Suicide Prevention Service), by Klaus Thomas; in 1958, the Los Angeles Suicide Prevention Center—the first center with systematic research, training, and service components—by Edwin Shneidman, Norman Farberow, and Robert Litman; in 1961, the International Association for Suicide Prevention in Vienna, by Erwin Ringel; in 1966 (to 1972) at the National Institute of Mental Health, Bethesda, MD, the Center for Studies of Suicide Prevention, headed by Shneidman, as a center for research and training support in the United States; in 1968, in Chicago, IL, the American Association of Suicidology (AAS), by Shneidman and others, now headquartered in Denver, CO; in 1970, the quarterly AAS journal, *Suicide and Life-Threatening Behavior.*

As of the early 1980s, there were about 200 suicide prevention centers in the United States, covering almost every major city. The centers are independent of each other. Although many centers now also deal with drug rehabilitation, homicide prevention, response to battered spouses, rape, teenage hot lines, and general crisis intervention (Litman & Wold, 1976), suicide prevention centers have become a vital part of the independently operated mental health services in many countries throughout the world.

REFERENCES

Beck, A. T., & Rush, J. (1978). Cognitive therapy of depression and suicide. *American Journal of Psychotherapy, 32,* 252–269.

Cain, A. C. (Ed.). (1972). *Survivors of suicide.* Springfield, IL: Thomas.

Dublin, L. I. (1969). Suicide prevention. In E. S. Shneidman (Ed.), *On the nature of suicide.* San Francisco: Jossey-Bass.

Farberow, N. L. (Ed.). (1961). Part II—The therapeutic response to the cry for help. In N. L. Farberow & E. S. Shneidman (Eds.), *The cry for help.* New York: McGraw-Hill.

Kiev, A. (1976). Crisis intervention and suicide prevention. In E. S. Shneidman (Ed.), *Suicidology: Contemporary developments.* New York: Grune & Stratton.

Litman, R. E., & Wold, C. (1976). 1. Beyond crisis intervention. In E. S. Shneidman (Ed.), *Suicidology: Contemporary developments.* New York: Grune & Stratton.

Olin, H. (1976). Psychotherapy of the chronically suicidal patient. *American Journal of Psychotherapy, 30,* 570–575.

Schwartz, D., Flinn, D., & Slawson, P. (1974). Treatment of the suicidal character. *American Journal of Psychotherapy, 28,* 194–207.

Shein, H., & Stone, A. (1969). Psychotherapy designed to detect and treat suicidal potential. *American Journal of Psychiatry, 125,* 141–153.

Shneidman, E. S. (1971). Prevention, intervention, and postvention of suicide. *Annals of Internal Medicine, 75,* 453–458.

Shneidman, E. S. (1980). Psychotherapy with suicidal patients. In T. B. Karasu & L. Bellak (Eds.), *Specialized techniques in individual psychotherapy*. New York: Brunner/Mazel.

Shneidman, E. S., Farberow, N., & Litman, R. (1976/1970). *The psychology of suicide*. New York: Aronson.

Varah, C. (1966). *The samaritans*. New York: Macmillan.

Wekstein, L. (1979). *Handbook of suicidology*. New York: Brunner/Mazel.

E. S. SHNEIDMAN
University of California School of Medicine

CRISIS INTERVENTION
HOTLINE SERVICES
SUICIDE

SULLIVAN, HARRY STACK (1892–1949)

Distinguished for his *Interpersonal Theory of Psychiatry,* Harry Stack Sullivan, a lifelong bachelor, defined psychiatry as the "study of interpersonal relations." Psychiatry, for him, was an adjunct of social psychology. A wholesome personality derives from healthy interpersonal relationships. Personality itself is defined in terms of interpersonal relationships.

Sullivan entered Cornell University at the age of 16. Problems arose in his second term, causing him to leave college for the workaday world. By 1915, he had earned sufficient funds to see him through medical school. However, his biographer, A. H. Chapman, writes that, because of his lack of a college education, "he could gain admittance to only a shabby, run-for-profit medical school in Chicago which in later years he described as a 'diploma mill'" (Chapman, 1976, p. 27). In some respects, this lack of a decent undergraduate and professional school education is to his credit, because his accomplishments were in spite of them. Furthermore, it allowed him to enter psychiatry free from preconceived notions regarding mental disorders. Instead he learned psychopathology from first-hand experience, when he began his career at important health centers in Washington, DC, and Baltimore, MD. In Washington at St. Elizabeth's Hospital, Sullivan came under the influence of the distinguished psychiatrist, William Alanson White, and also became familiar with the social psychology and anthropology of Bronislaw Malinowski, Charles Cooley, G. H. Mead, and Edward Sapir. The social psychologist William McDougall and the British psychologist W. H. R. Rivers too had an influence on him.

The social character of psychiatry embedded itself in Sullivan's thinking. Not only is personality couched in interpersonal relations, he believed, but the patient-therapist interpersonal relationship is critical for successful therapy. As a participant observer, the therapist participates in patients' explorations of their problems. Anxiety, basic to virtually all emotional problems, is the incapacitating element that must be displaced with a sense of security, a sense of emotional ease.

As Sullivan's ideas solidified, they were recorded. With the exception of *Conceptions of Modern Psychiatry,* his books appeared posthumously: *The Interpersonal Theory of Psychiatry; The Psychiatric Interview; Schizophrenia as a Human Process; The Fusion of Psychiatry and Social Science;* and *Personal Psychopathology.* Except for *Personal Psychopathology,* a 1921 account of experiences with patients, these later books, the product of lectures and seminars from 1943 to his death in 1949, best represent his thought.

Sullivan was professor of psychiatry and interim director of the Department of Psychiatry at Georgetown University Medical School for several months in 1939, but otherwise never held an academic position. Even his stay from 1923 to 1930 at the Sheppard and Enoch Pratt Hospital in Baltimore was in the capacity of staff psychiatrist. It was in Baltimore at Johns Hopkins that he met Adolf Meyer, a second great influence on his thinking. Sullivan's career came abruptly to a close when he died of a brain hemorrhage in a Paris hotel en route home from an executive meeting of the World Federation of Mental Health.

In addition to the ideas already mentioned, Sullivan is known for a variety of concepts: dynamisms, the self-system, parataxic distortion, the one-genus postulate, and his theory of personality development. Unlike many celebrities, Sullivan gained in fame posthumously.

W. S. SAHAKIAN

SULLIVAN'S INTERPERSONAL THEORY

Interpersonal theory is a theory of interpersonal relations, developed largely in the 1930s and 1940s by Harry Stack Sullivan.

KEY CONCEPTS

Sullivan emphasized the social nature of human nature. He defined psychiatry, personality, and key assessment and treatment concepts in interpersonal terms. He also emphasized the crucial role of anxiety in personality formation and disturbance. Finally, Sullivan emphasized actual interactions or performances in the interpersonal field as the process by which disturbances are formed, revealed, and treated.

The Social Nature of Human Nature

Sullivan defined personality as "the relatively enduring pattern of recurrent interpersonal situations which characterize a human life" (1953, p. 111). Even hermits maintain, through imagery, memory, and fantasy, an interpersonal life. Dynamisms, defined in terms of characteristic patterns of internal or overt social behavior, are the smallest meaningful unit of study of an individual. As ascribed qualities, they may involve thinking, feeling, or acting in relation to other people, who need not be present, or even real.

That behavior often reflects relationships with persons not actually present was a cornerstone of Sullivan's approach. He perceived in the troubled behavior of his patients the distorting effects of such relationships. The inner aspect of this distortion he called personifications, images one holds of self or others, with their attendant feelings, impulses, and ideas. Stereotypes are widely-shared personifications, positive or negative. Personifications built up in one relationship may be triggered in another, with consequent distortions of thinking, feeling, and acting, as when a person perceives and relates to an employer as though to an overly critical and demanding parent.

Anxiety

Anxiety can be the most crucial formative influence in the interpersonal field, and its origins are the origins also of personality and of self. Their common roots lie in the helpless nature of infants, who survive only if nurtured. The distressed infant cries. A caregiver responds. The cry becomes a communication within a relationship and the first tool of need reduction. Over time, such interactions acquire two consequences: satisfaction arising from need reduction, and security arising from the preservation of a necessary relationship.

Threats to biological survival bring fear. Threats to security bring anxiety, which may be devastatingly powerful for a being lacking the maturity and experience to manage or dampen it. Given sufficient experience of anxiety, its subsequent avoidance may become the central goal for the infant or young child. Patterns in the interpersonal field have both inner and outer aspects, and the objectively helpless infant may begin to preserve security subjectively through the dynamism of sleep.

The growing dynamism of self (Sullivan's word for the complex of processes that come increasingly to monitor, evaluate, and regulate activities in the interpersonal field) seeks above all else to preserve security. Behaviors bringing approval from significant others are strengthened; behaviors bringing disapproval are inhibited and may be eliminated.

The processes of awareness and behavior control are increasingly bent on preserving security through conforming to the expectations of others. However, when disapproval attaches to behaviors or events that cannot be managed by the child, then the experience, rather than the event, must be controlled. The young child is in prolonged transition from the experiential world of the very young infant, which is a disconnected jumble of sensory experiences and perceptual impressions, toward a mature mode of rational, logical experience that even adults often fail to maintain. This transitional mode, called the parataxic by Sullivan, is characterized by a primitive associational sense of causality and by developing language use. When a child is confronted by a threat to security, such as parental disapproval of his or her anger, the child may disown the angry feelings through selectively not paying attention to them and by not giving them labels. Thus, while the anger does not cease to exist, the child ceases being aware of it. Sullivan called this process dissociation. Security is preserved by removing awareness from an aspect of personality, which paradoxically places that aspect beyond the corrective effects of experience and may permit it to continue unmodified into adulthood.

Even more common in the preservation of security are parataxic distortions by which significant aspects of self or others are misperceived, mislabeled, and misunderstood in ways that lessen their anxiety-producing properties. This process is facilitated by the child's initially idiosyncratic and personalistic use of language in speech and thought: Without a sense of the external, consensual referents for words, it is no great feat to use them subjectively. Thus the self, central to each person's understanding of his or her own nature, may become isolated from that nature and therefore from all interpersonal relations. For Sullivan, mental health is restored "to the extent that one becomes aware of one's interpersonal relations" (Bullard, 1953, vii–viii).

Performances

Children dominated by the preservation of security grow up to have very distorted understandings of their performances in the interpersonal field. The deceptions they practice upon themselves are often facilitated by persuading others to perceive them as they wish to be seen or, at the least, by preventing others from seeing them as they fear they might really be. All children go through this; it is the way in which cultures preserve their characteristics. Proscribed patterns are inhibited; desired patterns flourish. When children receive the broad, persistent, and intense disapproval of significant others, however, they become more than conforming: They become emotionally disturbed. They not only misperceive their own performances, but also those of others, because of personifications built through disturbing interactions with significant others. They readily perceive the characteristics of these personifications and relate more to them than to the people actually present. Such troubled and isolated adults approach interpersonal situations warily and communicate in guarded, defensive, and sometimes bizarre ways as a result of the myriad distortions they superimpose upon the actual situation.

Sullivan developed numerous strategies for detecting both distortions in interpersonal relations and the often subtle manifestations of anxiety that accompany them, and for relating to disturbed people in such a way that they could begin to experience the truths behind the evasions, thus expanding the self. Central to his methods was the conviction that all the therapist can objectively know is performance in interpersonal situations. All else is inference. Even the patient's effort to describe internal experience becomes a performance in the interpersonal field, and its content is therefore suspect. Sullivan perceived the therapist as a participant in the performances of the patient, and considered that the data of assessment and treatment arise in this process of participant observation. The psychiatric interview is a special kind of interpersonal relation that demands great skill on the part of the therapist. Sullivan's greatest contributions may lie in his sensitivity to the isolation and anxiety of the disturbed persons he treated, in his broad perspective on the processes giving rise to their human misery, and in the richness of his therapeutic strategies on their behalf.

REFERENCES

Bullard, D. M. (1953). Preface to the second edition. In H. S. Sullivan (Ed.), *Conceptions of modern psychiatry.* New York: Norton.

Sullivan, H. S. (1953/1940). *Conceptions of modern psychiatry.* New York: Norton.

SUGGESTED READING

Sullivan, H. S. (1954). *The psychiatric interview.* New York: Norton.

Sullivan, H. S. (1962). *Schizophrenia as a human process.* New York: Norton.

Sullivan, H. S. (1973/1956). *Clinical studies in psychiatry.* New York: Norton.

R. E. ENFIELD
Columbus, GA

HUMANISTIC PSYCHOLOGY
PERSONALITY THEORIES
PSYCHOTHERAPY
SOCIAL INFLUENCE THEORY

SUNDBERG, NORMAN (1922–   )

Norman Sundberg was born in Aurora, Nebraska, on September 15, 1922. After serving 3½ years in the U.S. Field Artillery and finishing as a pilot in Germany in 1946, he obtained his baccalaureate from the University of Nebraska in 1947 and his PhD in psychology at the University of Minnesota in 1952. He married Donna Varner in Paris in 1948, and they have four sons, Charlie, Greg, Scott, and Mark. In the Department of Psychology at the University of Oregon, he founded the University Psychology Clinic during the years 1954 and 1955, and served as director of the doctoral program in clinical psychology from time to time until his retirement in 1988. He also served over the years as a faculty counselor in the university counseling center, as acting dean of the graduate school, and as founding dean of the Lila Acheson Wallace School of Community Service and Public Affairs at the University of Oregon. He was granted two Fulbright awards to India, where he consulted with universities on the development of student services and did research on adolescent interests, time perspectives, values, and family relations. He also has taught and conducted research in Germany, France, Spain, Australia, and Hong Kong and has traveled extensively and lectured in South and Southeast Asia.

Sundberg has received awards from the National Institute of Mental Health and is a fellow of the American Psychological Association, the American Psychological Society, and the Society for Personality Assessment. He has published over a hundred articles on such topics as personality, cross-cultural psychology, counseling, and clinical and community psychology. Among publication topics of special interest are the following: Acceptability of fake test interpretations (1955), the first German translation of the MMPI (1956), conditions for creativity (1959), a survey of psychological testing in the United States (1961), sensitivity to implied meanings (1966), Nepalese Children's Drawings (1968), values of Indian and American adolescents (1970), the community concerns of the university (1970), assessment of personal competence and incompetence (1978), cross-cultural assessment (1981), cross-cultural studies of adolescents' expectations about future events (1983), decade differences in adolescents' views of life possibilities (1984), community assessment methods (1985), boredom proneness (1986), personality in a religious commune (1990), and questions about cross-cultural transfer of prevention programs (1995).

He is the author of *Assessment of Persons* (1977) and primary author of *Clinical Psychology* (1962, 1973, 1983). The fourth edition of this introduction to clinical psychology, co-authored with Allen Winebarger and Julian Taplin, appears in 2001.

STAFF

SUPER, DONALD E. (1910–1994)

Donald E. Super was most often associated with career development theory and its applications. After contributing first to the applications of differential psychology to vocational guidance and personnel selection and classification, he shifted his attention to developmental approaches to vocational choice and development. With students and colleagues such as John Crites, Albert Thompson, and Jean Pierre Jordaan at Teachers College, Columbia University, and colleagues elsewhere, such as Henry Borow and David Tiedeman, he established the terms, and with them the field of vocational or career development, and wrote the first books and monographs using these concepts. Developmental tasks, life stages, and self-concepts have loomed large in his work.

A graduate of Oxford University and the recipient of the PhD degree from Columbia and the DSc degree from Lisbon, he taught at Clark, Harvard, the University of California at Berkeley, the University of Paris (Sorbonne and René Descartes), Virginia Institute of Technology, Lisbon, Cambridge, and the University of Florida (Gainesville), while based primarily at Teachers College, Columbia University, and he maintained active ties with the last six universities. He was international coordinator of the Work Importance Study and professor emeritus of psychology and education at Columbia, where he was for some years chairman of the Department of Psychology and division director.

Super served as president of the Division of Counseling Psychology of the American Psychological Association (APA), the American Personnel and Guidance Association, and the National Vocational Guidance Association, and was president of the International Association for Educational and Vocational Guidance and a member of the board of directors of the International Association for Applied Psychology. A Fellow of APA and of the British Psychological Society, and an Honorary Member of the Spanish Psychological Society, he consulted with a variety of educational and industrial organizations, including IBM, AT&T, General Electric, UNESCO, and OECD.

STAFF

SUPERSTITION

Superstition, from the Latin *superstitio,* may be defined as the acceptance of beliefs or practices that are groundless and inconsistent with the degree of understanding shared by members of a particular group or community. Yet certain ancient beliefs that we now consider superstitions survive. For example, the ancient Northern European fertility rite of decorating a house with greens at Christmas time is still practiced because it is colorful and in keeping with custom.

Some superstitions last primarily for their amusement value, as in fortune telling or the reading of one's horoscope in the morning paper—the latter a carryover from ancient astrology once firmly believed in by many.

The superstitions of primitive people generally involved a belief in the causal effects derived from supernatural powers, since no better naturalistic explanations were known. During the Middle Ages and later, beliefs in demonology and witchcraft abounded in Europe. In this instance, it was believed that the influences came from the powers of darkness reigned over by Satan that could control and direct human behavior in extraordinary ways.

Some superstitions can be traced back to religious writings—for example, the superstition that seating 13 persons at the same dinner table could end in disaster for one. The origin of this belief is to be found in scriptural writings concerning the betrayal and crucifixion of Christ. At the Last Supper, at which Christ prophesied his betrayal, there were 13 men seated around the table—Christ and his 12 disciples.

Early in this century, Sigmund Freud wrote about superstitions in *The Psychopathology of Everyday Life*. He did not believe in supernatural powers, but theorized that such beliefs were the externalization of conflicts and repressions to be found in the unconscious mind.

More recently, B. F. Skinner has interpreted the development of individual superstitious behavior in terms of "accidental" or "chance" contingencies. He demonstrated how this could occur in an animal experiment (Skinner, 1948). Ordinarily in animal experimentation, intended functional relationships are contrived between prior conditions and their consequences. In Skinner's experiment, food was given to pigeons, in separate cages, every 15 seconds regardless of what the birds were doing at the time the food was delivered. At the end of the experimental sessions, in many cases, well-defined superstitious behavior was observed. One pigeon was walking around in a counterclockwise position, two were thrusting their heads into a corner of the cage, and two were moving their heads and bodies in a pendulum-like rhythm. What was conditioned was simply what the birds "happened" to be doing at the time the reinforcements of food were delivered.

This experimental demonstration can be applied to the development of individual human superstitious behavior. A football coach might be wearing a particular pair of socks at a game that his team wins. These become his "lucky" socks, and if he continues to wear them, and his team sometimes wins again (as it probably will), the behavior will be maintained. It is possible that the rain dances of certain American Indian tribes or other "magical" practices originated in the same way. A dance was performed and it happened to rain. In these instances, there was no functional relationships between the two events, but accidental contingencies were established.

REFERENCES

Freud, S. (1968/1901). The psychopathology of everyday life. In *The standard edition of the complete psychological works of Sigmund Freud* (Vol. 6). London: Hogarth Press.

Skinner, B. F. (1948). "Superstition" in the pigeon. *Journal of Experimental Psychology, 38,* 168–172.

SUGGESTED READING

Chandler, C. (1970). *Every man's book of superstition.* Oxford, UK: Maudsay.

Jahoda, G. (1969b). *The psychology of superstition.* London: Lane.

Redford, E., & Redford, M. A. (1949). *Encyclopedia of superstition.* New York: Philosophical Library.

Skinner, B. F. (1953). *Science and human behavior.* New York: Macmillan.

Skinner, B. F., & Morse, W. A. (1957). A second type of superstition in the pigeon. *American Journal of Psychology, 70,* 308–311.

R. W. LUNDIN
Wheaton, Illinois

SURPRISE

Surprise is a highly transient reaction to a sudden and unexpected event. Ongoing activity is momentarily halted. The facial expression is distinctive, with eyes wide, eyebrows raised, brow wrinkled, and mouth opened round. With extreme surprise, and especially with startle, there are eyeblink and postural reactions. It is one of the most easily and universally recognized emotions (Ekman, 1980). Its physiological correlates are, in general, those of increased arousal.

Surprise can be unpleasant, pleasant, or both at once. Darwin (1872) placed surprise among the negative emotions, while Tompkins (1963, forthcoming) classifies it as positive. Tompkins describes surprise as a "resetting" state because, for a fraction of a second, the mind is cleared of thought. The momentary interruption of thought and action is related to the basic adaptive function of facilitating rapid evaluation and response to sudden changes.

Surprise can range from the relatively reflexive to the highly cognitive. On the reflexive side, it is closely related to the startle and orienting reflexes. It is also closely related to cognitive inconsistency—or incongruity, imbalance, or dissonance (see Zajonc, 1960). Specifically it is a reaction to a sudden change in the level of consistency.

SURPRISE—A PRIMARY EMOTION

A number of criteria for distinguishing the primary emotions have been proposed (Izard, 1977; Plutchik, 1962, 1980), including universality of expression and recognition, a neurophysiological substrate, phylogenetic and ontogenetic primacy, an adaptive function, a consistent hedonic tone, and duration over time. If defined so as to include startle, surprise has no difficulty meeting any of these criteria except the last two, which it clearly fails to meet. Most theorists have voted, in effect, to override these two criteria, as surprise appears on virtually every prominant list of primary emotions (e.g., Darwin, 1872; Ekman, 1980; Izard, 1977; Plutchik, 1962, 1980; Tompkins, 1962, 1963, in press). A representative list is that of Plutchik (1980): joy, sadness, acceptance, rejection, fear, anger, anticipation, and surprise.

Startle and the Orienting Response

Pure startle is a complex involuntary reflex to a sudden and intense stimulus (Landis & Hunt, 1939). Unexpectedness can intensify a startle reaction. A high stimulus intensity can increase surprise but is by no means necessary. Suddenness is necessary for startle or surprise.

Surprise is related to the orienting response (OR) (Donchin, 1980; Kimmel et al., 1979; Tompkins, 1962; van Olst, 1971). Called by Ivan Pavlov the "What is it?" reflex, the OR is a reaction to novel stimuli in which the animal or person orients the body and sense organs toward the stimulus. According to the Soviet investigator Sokolov (1963), an OR results from a mismatch between the stimulus and the stimulus representation in the brain. Specialized cell assemblies have been identified in the cat brain that serve as detectors of intensity, motion, time intervals, and novelty (Sokolov, 1975).

LEARNING

Surprise had no formal place in any theory of learning until the late 1960s when a revolution of sorts was touched off in animal learning. Kamin (1969) suggested that a stimulus must be surprising to produce conditioning. In support of this thesis, he provided dramatic demonstrations of blocking, a failure of conditioning in which valid but redundant (and thus unsurprising) cues are ignored. Since then, surprise has "virtually replaced the concept of reinforcement" in this area (Donchin, 1981, p. 33). Counterblocking or "superconditioning" has also been demonstrated (e.g., Fowler, 1978) in which, for example, a good event (food) is made *very* surprising by the expectation of a bad event (shock).

The surprise theory of conditioning was formalized as a simple linear operator model by Rescorla and Wagner (1972). Blocking, counterblocking, and several other diverse and counterintuitive conditioning phenomena have been successfully integrated by this model (Bower & Hilgard, 1981). Wagner (1976, 1978) has extended this model to include both simple habituation and complex information processing in humans. All levels of learning are thus interrelated in this model through the concept of stimulus surprisingness.

COGNITION

One area of research relating surprise to human cognition is that on the P300 component of event-related electroencephalogram potentials (ERPs). The P300 wave is so designated because it is positive and has a minimum latency of about 300 msec. In general, ERP components with short latencies are related to physical stimulus events, while the later ones, including P300, are more closely related to information processing (Pritchard, 1981).

Research by Donchin and collaborators (e.g., Donchin, 1980; Donchin & Isreal, 1979; Donchin et al., 1981; Duncan-Johnson & Donchin, 1977) has demonstrated that surprise can be measured by P300 amplitude. Evidence comes from experiments demonstrating the dependence of P300 amplitude on subjective probability or unexpectedness. In a typical experiment, random sequences of high and low tones are presented, with the relative frequencies varying from one condition to another. The lower the probability of a tone, the more unexpected it is and the greater the P300 amplitude.

From the amplitude of the P300 wave, one learns how much the subject's expectations or schemas are revised; from its latency, one learns how quickly the revision occurs. Comparisons of reaction times with P300 latencies reveal an interesting relationship to quality of decision making. When the reaction time is shorter than the P300 latency, the decision is likely to be wrong. The subject has responded impulsively before fully processing the stimulus information, and in fact the P300 wave, when it comes, may reflect in part the subject's surprise upon realizing that a mistake has been made.

Social Cognition

The literature on social cognition (Nisbett & Ross, 1980), including that specifically on cognitive consistency (Abelson et al., 1968), is not the rich source of research on surprise that might be expected, largely because little attention has been directed to suddenness, a necessary antecedent of surprise. However, the direct correspondence between sudden shifts in consistency level and surprise has been demonstrated (Willis et al., unpublished data). Stimuli were hypothetical interpersonal structures of the *P-O-X* type analyzed by Heider (1958) and used in many experiments on structural balance. From the perspective of person *P*, a *P-O-X* structure is balanced or consistent to the extent that *P*'s feelings toward person *O* match the level of their agreement about *X*. The *P*-to-*O* and *P*-to-*X* feelings are called the attraction and the attitude, respectively, while *P*'s understanding of *O*'s feelings toward *X* is called the perception. Disagreement is defined as the discrepancy between the attitude and the perception.

Values of attraction, attitude, and perception each ranged from "very strongly like" to "very strongly dislike" within the set of 45 stimuli. A quantitative index of imbalance or inconsistency was defined that was of the general form:

$$\text{Inconsistency} = \text{Attraction} \times \text{Disagreement}.$$

Two independent groups of about 60 subjects each rated each stimulus structure. The first group rated complete structures on pleasantness. The second group rated the amounts of surprise that would be experienced if incomplete structures were *suddenly completed* by an announcement by *O* of his previously uncommunicated feelings about *X*.

The findings of interest are the following correlations, all highly significant:

Unpleasantness and inconsistency	0.89
Surprise and inconsistency shift	0.86
Surprise and unpleasantness	0.83

Although the first correlation is noteworthy for showing how accurately pleasantness can be predicted from the level of inconsistency, the second correlation makes the main point. It demonstrates that surprise corresponds very closely to the magnitude of the consistency shifts.

The third correlation shows that here, where all inconsistency shifts are upward, surprise is unpleasant. There is evidence that sudden decreases in inconsistency produce pleasant surprise; the best evidence of this kind is found in the research on humor.

Humor

Freud (1905) distinguished between tendentious or "tendency" humor and "harmless" humor. Corresponding to these two kinds of humor are two families of theories of humor (Berlyne, 1969; Keith-Spiegel, 1972; McGhee, 1979). The foremost motivational theory is the psychoanalytic, which sees humor as based on the indirect expression of taboo sexual and aggressive motives. Clearly it is addressed to accounting for tendency humor in particular. Cognitive theories, addressed primarily toward "harmless" humor, usually take either incongruity (i.e., inconsistency) or surprise as the central construct.

The role of incongruity and surprise in "harmless" or cognitive humor can be easily seen in the joke scenario, which has three parts: (a) the "setup," in which a frame of reference and expectations are established; (b) the "punch line," in which incongruity is suddenly introduced; and (c) the "point" or solution whereby the listener suddenly resolves the incongruity. If insight is delayed, the listener is surprised twice—first by the sudden incongruity of the punch line, and again when the point is seen. The first surprise involves an increase in inconsistency and is unpleasant if not immediately resolved, whereas the second involves a decrease in inconsistency, and is pleasant.

There is much evidence that funniness is directly related to surprisingness for "harmless" or incongruity-based humor (McGhee, 1979). There is also some evidence that tendency jokes are funnier if they are *not* especially surprising (Godkewitsch, 1976; Kenny, 1955), suggesting that the most satisfying tendency humor confirms our expectations or prejudices rather than challenging them. Thus surprise plays contrasting roles in the two kinds of humor.

SUMMARY

As a theoretical concept relevant to many areas of psychology, surprise clearly has considerable integrative power. Surprise signals the possibility that a nonroutine response or decision is required. It generally indicates the need for a shift within the hierarchy of control because the input cannot be processed appropriately at the operative level. The shift may be upward to a level of more elaborate processing, as with cognitive inconsistency that resists routine resolution, or it may be downward to a level of less processing and more immediate output, as with reflexive startle or flight responses. The individual not only must make routine shifts from one kind of activity to another, but also must handle sudden shifts in priorities. Simon (1967) has formulated a model of a general "interrupt system" capable of handling both kinds of changes.

No general treatment of surprise in psychology exists. However, Desai (1939) provides a useful historical survey, and two discussions by Weaver (1948, 1963) are general in their implications.

REFERENCES

Abelson, R. P., Aronson, E., McGuire, W. J., Newcomb, T. M., Rosenberg, M. J., & Tannenbaum, P. H. (Eds.). (1968). *Theories of cognitive consistency: A sourcebook.* Chicago: Rand-McNally.

Berlyne, D. E. (1969). Laughter, humor, and play. In G. Lindzey & E. Aronson (Eds.), *Handbook of social psychology* (Vol. 3). Reading, MA: Addison-Wesley.

Darwin, C. (1965). *The expression of the emotions in man and animals.* Chicago: University of Chicago Press. (Original work published 1872)

Desai, M. M. (1939). *Surprise: A historical and experimental study. The British Journal of Psychology: Monograph Supplements.* Cambridge, England: Cambridge University Press.

Donchin, E. (1981). Surprise! . . . surprise? *Psychophysiology, 18,* 493–513.

Donchin, E., & Isreal, J. B. (1979). Event-related potentials and psychological theory. In H. H. Kornhuber & L. Deeke (Eds.), *Proceedings of the 5th International Symposium on Electrical Potentials Related to Motivation, Motor and Sensory Processes of the Brain.*

Donchin, E., McCarthy, G., Kutas, M., & Ritter, W. (1981). Event-related brain potentials in the study of consciousness. In R. J. Davidson, G. E. Schwartz, & D. Shapiro (Eds.), *Consciousness and self regulation* (Vol. 3). New York: Plenum.

Duncan-Johnson, C. C., & Donchin, E. (1977). On quantifying surprise: The variation of event-related potentials with subjective probability. *Psychophysiology, 14,* 456–467.

Fowler, H. (1978). Cognitive associations as evident in the blocking effects of response-contingent CSs. In S. H. Hulse, H. Fowler, & W. K. Honig (Eds.), *Cognitive processes in animal behavior.* Hillsdale, NJ: Erlbaum.

Freud, S. (1953). Fragment of an analysis of a case of hysteria. In J. Strachey (Ed.), *The standard edition of the complete psychological works of Sigmund Freud* (Vol. 7). London: Hogarth. (Original work published 1905)

Godkewitsch, M. (1976). Thematic and collative properties of written jokes and their contribution to funniness. *Canadian Journal of Behavioral Science, 8,* 88–97.

Heider, F. (1958). *The psychology of interpersonal relations.* New York: Wiley.

Izard, C. E. (1977). *Human emotions.* New York: Plenum.

Kamin, L. J. (1969). Predictability, surprise, attention and conditioning. In B. Campbell & R. Church (Eds.), *Punishment and aversive behavior.* New York: Appleton-Century-Crofts.

Keith-Spiegel, P. (1972). Early conceptions of humor: Varieties and issues. In J. H. Goldstein & P. E. McGhee (Eds.), *The psychology of humor: Theoretical perspectives and empirical issues.* New York: Academic.

Kenny, D. I. (1955). The contingency of humor appreciation on the stimulus-confirmation of joke-ending expectations. *Journal of Abnormal and Social Psychology, 51,* 644–648.

Kimmel, H. D., van Olst, E. H., & Orebeke, J. F. (Eds.). (1979). *The orienting reflex in humans.* Hillsdale, NJ: Erlbaum.

Landis, C., & Hunt, W. A. (1939). *The startle pattern*. New York: Farrar.

McGhee, P. E. (1979). *Humor: Origins and development*. San Francisco: Freeman.

Nisbett, R., & Ross, L. (1980). *Human inference: Strategies and shortcomings of social judgment*. Englewood Cliffs, NJ: Prentice-Hall.

Plutchik, R. (1962). *The emotions: Facts, theories and a new model*. New York: Random House.

Plutchik, R. (1980). *Emotion: A psychoevolutionary synthesis*. New York: Harper & Row.

Rescorla, R. A., & Wagner, A. R. (1972). A theory of Pavlovian conditioning: Variations in the effectiveness of reinforcement and nonreinforcement. In A. H. Black & W. F. Prokasy (Eds.), *Classical conditioning II* (pp. 64–99). New York: Appleton-Century-Crofts.

Simon, H. A. (1967). Motivational and emotional controls of cognition. *Psychological Review, 74*, 29–39.

Sokolov, E. N. (1963). Higher neuron functions: The orienting reflex. *Annual Review of Physiology, 25*, 545–580.

Sokolov, E. N. (1963/1958). *Perception and the conditioned reflex*. New York: Macmillan.

Sokolov, E. N. (1975/1970). The neuronal mechanism of the orienting reflex. In E. N. Sokolov & O. S. Vinogradona (Eds.), *Neutral mechanisms of the orienting reflex*. Hillsdale, NJ: Erlbaum.

Tompkins, S. (1963). Left and right: A basic dimension of ideology and personality. In R. White (Ed.), *The study of lives: Essays on personality in honor of Henry A Murray*. New York: Atherton Press.

Tompkins, S. S. (in press). *Affect, imagery, consciousness* (Vol. 1) New York: Springer. (Vol. 1). *The positive affects*, 1962. (Vol. 2). *The negative affects*, 1963. (Vol. 3).

Van Olst, E. H. (1971). *The orienting reflex*. The Hague: Mouton.

Wagner, A. R. (1976). Priming in STM: An information processing mechanism for self-generated or retrieval-generated depression in performance. In T. J. Tighe & R. N. Leaton (Eds.), *Habituation: Perspectives from child development, animal behavior, and neurophysiology*. Hillsdale, NJ: Erlbaum.

Wagner, A. R. (1978). Expectancies and the priming of STM. In S. H. Hulse, H. Fowler, & W. K. Honig (Eds.), *Cognitive processes in animal behavior*. Hillsdale, NJ: Erlbaum.

Weaver, W. (1948). Probability, rarity, interest and surprise. *Scientific Monthly, 67*, 390–392.

Weaver, W. (1963). *Lady Luck: The theory of probability*. Garden City, NY: Doubleday (Anchor).

R. H. WILLIS
University of Pittsburgh

COGNITIVE COMPLEXITY

CONDITIONING
EMOTIONS
HUMOR
INFORMATION PROCESSING
LEARNING THEORIES

SWITZERLAND, PSYCHOLOGY IN

To understand the evolution of scientific psychology in Switzerland, one must discuss precursors. Jean-Jacques Rousseau (1712–1778) opened the door, as it were, to modern psychology in Switzerland. Many of his works are important to the science. His *Essay on the Origin of Languages* presaged modern linguistics. In *Emile*, he presented and promoted the idea that the educator above all should understand children and should follow the child's natural development. His *Confessions* is a testament of introspection and witness of a vulnerable human being.

Charles Bonnet (1720–1793), author of *Essai Analytique sur les Facultés de L'âme* and *Essai de Psychologie*, was interested in natural psychology: According to him, the human should be studied, "As I have studied insects and plants."

In German-speaking Switzerland during the same period, two authors enhanced the interest in psychology: Lavater and Pestalozzi. Johan Caspar Lavater (1741–1801), a pastor in Zurich, concentrated on physiognomy. Without settling on one particular theory or methodology, he analyzed and described individual character differences in four volumes (1775–1778). These books have been translated into English. Heinrich Pestalozzi (1746–1827) was deeply interested in human misery, especially among children, and spent all his life in education. His experiences led him to the conclusion that education should be based on understanding the natural development of children. His book *Über die Naturgemässheit in der Erziehung* was the result of his pedagogical activities. His best known books, *Lienhard und Gertrud* and *Wie Gertrud ihre Kinder lehrt*, were prepared especially for parents.

These precursors all had strong influences on their times and drew attention to psychological problems. But it was only near the end of the 19th century that scientific psychology in Switzerland took its first step.

THE GENEVA PERIOD

Modern psychology was born in Geneva. Théodore Flournoy (1854–1920), after studying physics, psychology, and philosophy with Wilhelm Wundt in Leipzig, was appointed professor of psychology-physiology of the faculty of science of the University of Geneva. In 1892, Flournoy founded a laboratory of psychology, of which he soon ceded the directorship to his nephew and student, Edouard Claparède (1873–1940). His main publications (1900, 1911) dealt with parapsychology and hypnotism. In 1901, Flournoy, in collaboration with Claparède, founded the *Archives de Psychologie*. In addition to original contributions, this journal, through Claparède's reviews, made known many works by foreign authors.

Claparède became interested in psychology after having studied medicine. Entering the university in the laboratory of psychology, he was appointed professor of experimental psychology. His first important publication, *L'association des Idées,* was a critique of associationism; it stressed the importance of context and, more generally, that all behavior is directed to the achievement of a goal. The next year, Claparède published his biological theory of sleep, in which he announced the idea that sleep has an active function that protects against intoxication. Twenty years later (1928), in referring to research on this subject, Claparède clarified this concept. His experiences concerning the process of thought resulted in one of his most important works, *La Genèse de L'hypothèse.* In discussing theories of intelligence, he pointed out critical problems, emphasizing many experiences in which the method of *réflexion parlée* (thinking aloud) was utilized. In characterizing the steps of the process, he was obliged to state at the end that the formation of hypotheses is independent of consciousness. With regard to child psychology, Claparède found important and profound evidence that enhanced interest in experimental psychology. His book *Psychologie de L'enfant et Pédagogie Expérimentale,* considerably expanded by the sixth edition, was translated into 23 languages. This volume discusses various aspects of development and methods of investigation and of measurement, as well as of interpretation. In *L'education Fonctionnelle,* Claparède not only gave the fundamentals of educational psychology, but also sketched out "the grand laws of conduct" and discussed problems of intelligence, will, and so on.

Claparède founded the J. J. Rousseau Institute in 1911, in collaboration with Pierre Bovet, who was named director. Open to all who wished to apply psychology to general and remedial education, the institute's influence spread to many countries. In 1929, as the Institut des Sciences de l'Education, it joined the Faculté des Lettres of the University of Geneva. Pierre Bovet (1878–1965) was a professor of philosophy at Neuchâtel and of education at Geneva. Among his publications were *Le Sentiment Religieux et la Psychologie de L'enfant* and *L'instinct Combatif.*

Jean Piaget (1896–1980), born in Neuchâtel, succeeded Claparède as a professor of psychology in Geneva, and Bovet as director of the institute. After his studies in the natural sciences, he became interested in psychology. In Paris, he conducted his first experiments with children. After several years at Geneva and four years as professor of philosophy at Neuchâtel, he was appointed professor of the history of science at Geneva, before occupying the chair of psychology vacated with the death of Claparède.

Piaget concentrated on the mental development of children and conducted a great many studies on the acquisition of ideas (causation, number, time, logical classes, etc.). These studies were guided by the idea that mental organization depends on the interaction of external factors with internal structures, especially organic, sensorimotor, and cognitive. Piaget directed his work more and more toward epistemological problems, concerning explanations of scientific knowledge. In 1955, Piaget established Le Centre International D'Epistémologie Génétique. Many volumes appeared in collaboration with people at this center from various scientific disciplines. Some of Piaget's most important works are *La Naissance de L'intélligence Chez L'enfant, La Construction du Réel Chez L'enfant, Biologie et Connaissance, Psychologie et Epistémologie,* and *L'équilibration des Structures Cognitives.* Bärbel Inhelder, as-

sistant and later professor of psychology, collaborated on many works with Piaget. In collaboration with Hermine Sinclair and Magali Bovet, she published *Apprentissage et Structures de la Connaissance,* and with Dasen, Lavalle, and Retschitzki, *Naissance de L'intélligence Chez L'enfant Baoulé de Côte d'Ivoire.*

DEVELOPMENTS AFTER GENEVA

Empirical psychology had difficulty in being accepted at the Swiss–German universities. The presence of Wundt in 1872 and 1873, before he moved to Leipzig, as well as the influence of many German colleagues who were there for a short time, was insufficient to accomplish this. However, the contributions by psychologists whose inspiration was above all philosophical should be mentioned: Paul Häberlin, *Der Gegenstand der Psychologie;* Jules Suter, *Psychologie, Grund und Aufbau;* Wilhelm Keller, *Psychologie und Philosophie des Willens;* and Hans Kunz, *Die anthropologische Bedeutung der Phantasie.*

Modern psychiatry and psychoanalysis have played an important role in Zurich. Eugen Bleuler, who introduced the term *schizophrenia,* from the beginning was interested in the ideas of Sigmund Freud. Carl Jung (1875–1961), of Zurich, who became Freud's most famous disciple, later founded a dissident school. Jung's *Diagnostische Assoziationsstudien* and *Psychologische Typen* are closest to scientific psychology.

Pfister (1913) has given a detailed exposition of Freud's concepts and methods, emphasizing their usefulness for education. Hermann Rorschach developed a diagnostic projective technique, and Ewald Bohm summarized the methods, results, and the theory of the Rorschach test (1951). The use of the Rorschach test for children was discussed by Loosli-Usteri (1938) and Meili-Dworetzki (1956), and a bibliography was published by Lang (1966).

Lipot Szondi developed a different method of psychodiagnosis. His system depended on the idea that hereditary factors determine personality (1972). Lüscher's *Die Psychologie der Farben* and Koch's *Der Baumtest* should also be mentioned as other personality measures.

Intelligence tests were introduced by Claparède. He had edited, in 1925, *Comment Diagnostiquer les Aptitudes des Écoliers,* in which he presented his test methods of measurement and theoretical foundations. In 1936, Richard Meili, also at Geneva, published *Psychologische Diagnostik.* At the request of the J. J. Rousseau Institute, and under the presidency of Claparède, an international conference on psychotherapy already had taken place in 1920, at which time an association with the same name was born. Its ninth congress, the first after World War II, was held in Berne in 1949, and organized by Franziska Baumgarten. From the beginning of the 1920s at Zurich, the training of practical psychologists was assumed by an institute outside the university. Among the more important publications in this area were those by Suter (1922), Walther (1926, 1936), and Baumgarten (1928).

Following on these activities, the *Revue Suisse de Psychologie Pure et Appliquée* (bilingual) appeared in 1942, edited by Piaget, Jung, Morgenthaler, and Forel. The following year, the Swiss Society of Psychology was created under the presidency of Piaget, thus joining psychologists and psychotherapists. As a result of these advances, psychology was accepted as a course of study at various other universities. Berne created a chair of psychology in 1954; Zurich in 1966; Lausanne, Fribourg, and the Federal Polytechnical Institute in Zurich in succeeding years; and finally Bâle in 1981.

EVENTS AFTER 1950

With the establishment of chairs of psychology in all universities, research was extended and diversified. W. R. Hess, a Nobel prize laureate and professor of physiology at Zurich, organized and described all the various aspects of psychology in his book entitled *Psychologie in Biologicher Sicht.* Other works appearing during this period can be divided into different groups according to subject.

Child Psychology

In Geneva, under the influence of Piaget, infant psychology was always a primary consideration. Of special note are the publications of Mounoud (1968), Bullinger (1973), and Rieben (1978). From 1950 on, Meili and his colleagues conducted longitudinal studies as reported by Meili-Dworetzki in *Grundlagen Individueller Persönlichkeitsunterschiede,* and by Pulver (1959), Lang (1967), and others. Meierhofer and Keller studied infant development in institutions (1966), and Meili-Dworetzki compared children's drawings in different cultures (1982).

Individual Differences and Diagnostics

An adaptation of the Children's Apperception Test (CAT) was done by Philippe Muller with Swiss children. Jean-Blaise Dupont, Francis Gendre, Samuel Berthoud, and Jean-Pierre Descombes researched the subject of interests. Cardinet and Rousson (1967, 1968) constructed a series of parallel tests of intelligence. Flammer (1975) published articles on individual differences in learning. Meili began constructing a system of intellectual factors based on Gestalt hypotheses verified by factor analysis. In *Die Strucktur der Intelligenz,* he presented a system of four fundamental factors that exist from 6 to 17 years of age.

Cognitive Psychology

In 1965, Klaus Foppa wrote a book on American studies of learning and memory. In two volumes, Hans Aebli presented a general conception of intellectual processes under the title *Denken: Das Ordnen des Tuns.* A hypothetical-deductive theory was developed by Rudolf Groner in *Hypothesen im Denkprozess* and *Towards a Hypothetical-deductive Theory of Cognitive Activity,* with Marina Groner. Suarez (1980) discussed the validity of the conception of constructivism of Piaget. Steiner (1980) published *Visuelle Vorstellungen Beim Lösen von Elementaren Problemen.*

Psycholinguistics

Sinclair discussed, in *Langage et Opérations,* linguistic themes from the point of view of Piaget's theories. In *Spracherwerb und Interaktion,* Marie-Louise Käsermann studied mother–infant dialogues, analyzing self-corrections by the child. On the same topic, Käsermann and Foppa wrote *Some Determinants of Self Correction, An Interactional Study of Swiss-German.* Also, Hänni and Hunkeler

(1980) wrote *Von der Entwicklung der kindlichen Erzählsprache;* Wettler (1980) discussed modern linguistic theories.

Perception

Important Swiss articles on perception include one by Norbert Bischehof, a professor at Zurich (1966). Among the more recent articles inspired by Piaget's theory are those by Droz (1965) and Munari (1973).

Social Psychology

Von Cranach (1980) discussed, in collaboration with a group of young researchers, a theory of behavior using systematic observations. A method of electronically recording behavior has been presented by Frey and associates (1982). Other works in this area were those by Moser (1965) and Fischer (1962/1971).

Clinical Psychology

The first psychophysiological diagnostics in Switzerland were attributable to André Rey (1906–1965). The results of his activities at the neurological clinic in Geneva were *Psychologie Clinique et Neurologie,* and the two volumes of *Etudes des Insuffisances Psychologiques.* Grawe (1976) insisted on the need to adapt methods of treatment in accordance with different psychic problems and to study the results through controlled studies. In a book by Brauchli (1981), one finds a description of a mathematical method for classifying types of maladjustment, as well as the results obtained through cluster analysis. Moser, von Zeppelin, and Schneider have been progressing in new directions, as indicated by their article "Computer simulation of a model of neurotic defense processes." Of interest to psychologists is *Lehrbuch der Psychopathologie* from a Gestalt point of view by Bash.

Industrial Psychology

Eberhard Ulich, a professor at ETH and at the psychological institute at Berne, has emphasized the organization of work. Major publications in this field include those by Ulich and colleagues (1973); Gubser (1968); Dupont (1954); Orendi (1979); Stoll (1972); and Gendre (1970).

REFERENCES

Aebli, H. (1981/1980). *Denken: Das Ordnen des Tuns (Vol. I): Kognitive Aspekte der Handlungstheorie, Vol. II: Denkprozesse.* Stuttgart, Germany: Klett & Cotta.

Bash, K. W. (1955). *Lehrbuch der Psychopathologie, Grundlagen und Klinik.* Stuttgart, Germany: Thieme.

Baumgarten, F. (1928). *Die Berufseignungprüfungen. Theorie und Praxis.* Munich, Germany: Oldenburg.

Bischehof, N. (1966). Psychophysik der Raumwahrnehmung. In W. Metzger & H. Erkle (Eds.), *Handbuch der Psychologie* (Vol. I/I). Göttingen, Germany.

Bonnet, C. (1781–1783). Essai de psychologie. In *Oeuvres d'histoire naturelle et de philosophie* (Vol. 17).

Bonnet, C. (1970). *Essai analytique sur les faculté de l'âme.* Geneva, Switzerland: Slatkine. (Original work published 1770)

Bovet, P. (1917). *L'instinct combatif.* Neuchâtel, Switzerland: Delachaux et Niestlé.

Bovet, P. (1925). *Le sentiment religieux et la psychologie de l'enfant.* Neuchâtel, Switzerland: Delachaux et Niestlé.

Brauchli, B. (1981). *Zur Nosologie in der Psychiatrie. Methodische Ansätze empirischer Forschung: Theorie und Methodenstudien zur Clusteranalyse.* Stuttgart, Germany: Ferdinand Enke.

Bullinger, A. (1973). Comparison, measure et transitivité [Monographie 1]. *Archives de Psychologie.*

Cardinet, J., & Rousson, M. (1967; 1968). Etude factorielle de tests d'aptitudes scolaires. *Revue Suisse de Psychologie, 26,* 256–270, 362–380; *27,* 40–66.

Claparède, E. (1946). *Psychologie de l'enfant et pédagogie expérimentale.* Neuchâtel, Switzerland: Delachaux & Niestlé. (Original work published 1905)

Claparède, E. (1911). *Experimental pedagogy and the psychology of the child.* London: Longman.

Claparède, E. (1928). Théorie biologique du sommeil et de l'hystérie. Opinions et critiques. *Archives de Psychologie, 21,* 113–174.

Claparède, E. (1934). *La genèse de l'hypothèse.* Bern, Switzerland: Kündig.

Claparède, E. (1940). *Comment diagnostiquer les aptitudes chez les écoliers.* Paris: Flammarion. (Original work published 1925)

Dasen, P., Inbelder, B., Lavallée, M., & Retschitzki, J. J. (1978). *Naissance de l'intelligence chez l'enfant Baoulé de Côte d'Ivoire.* Bern, Switzerland: Huber.

Droz, R. L. (1965). Contribution à l'étude des dévaluations et sousestimations d'existants visuels en présentation tachistoscopique bréve. *Archives de Psychologie.*

Dupont, J. B. (1954). *La sélection des conducteurs de véhicules.* Neuchâtel, Switzerland: Delachaux & Niestlé.

Fischer, H. (1971). *Gruppenstruktur und Gruppenleistung.* Bern, Switzerland: Huber. (Original work published 1962)

Flammer, A. (1975). *Individuelle Unterschiede im Lernen.* Basel, Switzerland: Beltz.

Foppa, K. (1975). *Lernen, Gedächtnis, Verhalten.* Cologne, Germany: Kiepenheuer & Witsch. (Original work published 1965)

Frey, S., Hirsbrunner, H. P., Florin, A., Daw, W., & Crawford, R. (1982). Unified approach to the investigation of nonverbal and verbal behavior in communication research. In S. Moscovici & W. Dois (Eds.), *Current issues in European social psychology.* Cambridge, England: Cambridge University Press.

Gendre, F. (1970). *L'orientation professionnelle à l'ère des ordinateurs.* Neuchâtel, Switzerland: Delachaux & Niestlé.

Grawe, K. (1976). *Differentielle Psychotherapie.* Bern, Switzerland: Huber.

Groner, R. (1978). *Hypothesen im Denkprozess. Grundlagen einer verallgemeinerten Theorie auf der Basis elementarer Informationsverarbeitung.* Bern, Switzerland: Huber.

Groner, R., & Groner, M. (1983). Towards a hypothetico-deductive theory of cognitive activity. In R. Groner & P. Fraisse (Eds.), *Cognition and eye movements.* Berlin, Germany: Deutscher Verlag der Wissenschaften. Amsterdam: North Holland.

Gubser, A. (1968). *Monotonie im Industriebetrieb.* Bern, Switzerland: Huber.

Häberlin, P. (1921). *Der Gegenstand der Psychologie.* Berlin, Germany: Springer.

Hänni, R., & Hunkeler, R. (1980). Von der Entwicklung der kindlichen Erzählsprache. *Schweizerische Zeitschrift für Psychologie, 39,* 16–32.

Inhelder, B., Sinclair, H., & Bovet, M. (1974). *Apprentissage et structures de la connaissance.* Paris: Presses Universitaires de France.

Jung, C. G. (1909/1906). *Diagnostische Assoziationsstudien.* Leipzig, Germany: Barth.

Käsermann, M.-L. (1980). *Spracherwerb und Interaktion.* Bern, Switzerland: Huber.

Käsermann, M.-L., & Foppa, K. (1981). Some determinants of self correction: An interaction study of Swiss-German. In W. Deutsch (Ed.), *The child's construction of language.* New York: Academic.

Keller, W. (1954). *Psychologie und Philosophie des Willens.* Basel, Switzerland: Reinhardt.

Kunz, H. (1946). *Die Anthropologische Bedeutung der Phantasie* (Vols. I & II). Basel, Switzerland: Verlag für Recht Gesellschaft.

Lang, A. (1967). Über Wahrnehmungsverhalten beim 8–10 wöchigen Säugling. *Psychologische Forschung, 30,* 357–399.

Lüscher, M. (1949). *Die Psychologie der Farben.* Basel, Switzerland: Test-Verlag.

Meierhofer, M., & Keller, W. (1966). *Frustration im frühen Kindesalter.* Bern, Switzerland: Huber.

Meili, R. (1936). *Psychologische Diagnostik Eine Einführung Jür Psychologen und Erzieher.* Munich, Germany: Reinhardt.

Meili-Dworetzki, G. (1982). *Spielarten des Menschenbildes. Ein Vergleich der Menschenzeichnungen japanischer und schweizerischer Kinder.* Bern, Switzerland: Huber.

Meili-Dworetzki, G., & Meili, R. (1972). *Grundlagen individueller Persönlichkeitsunterschiede. Ergebnisse eine Längsschnittuntersuchung mit zwei Grup- pen von der Geburt bis zum 8. und 16. Lebensjahr.* Bern, Switzerland: Huber.

Moser, U. (1965). *Psychologie der Partnerwahl.* Bern, Switzerland: Huber.

Mounoud, P. (1968). Construction et utilisation D'instruments chez l'enfant de 4 a 8 ans: Intériorisation des schemes d'action et types de régulation. *Revue Suisse de Psychologie, 27,* 200–208.

Munari, A. (1973). Perception de densités stochastiques. Un essai de généralisation du modèle probabiliste des mécanismes perceptifs proposé par Jean Piaget. *Archives de Psychologie, 72,* 1–205.

Orendi, B. (1979). Die Arbeitssituation von Lokomotivführern. *Schweizerische Zeitschrift für Psychologie, 38,* 228–238.

Pestalozzi, H. (1972). Über die Naturgemässheit in der Erziehung. In E. Dejung (Ed.), *Pestalozzi sämtliche Werke, 23.* Zürich, Germany: Füssli.

Pestalozzi, H. (1978). *Lienhard und Gertrud.* Boston: Heath. (Original work published 1781)

Pfister, O. (1913). *Die psychoanalytische Methode.* Leipzig & Berlin, Germany: Klinkhardt.

Piaget, J. (1954). *The construction of reality in the child.* New York: Basic Books.

Piaget, J. (1967). *Biologie et connaissance.* Paris: Gallimard.

Piaget, J. (1969). *Psychologie et épistémologie.* Paris: Denoël.

Piaget, J. (1975). *L'équilibration des structures cognitives.* Paris: Presses Universitaires de France.

Pulver, U. (1959). *Spannungen und Störungen im Verhalten der Säuglinge.* Bern, Switzerland: Huber.

Rousseau, J. J. (1939). *Les confessions, Genève 1782.* Paris: Bibliothèque de la Pleiade, Nouvelle Revue Francaise.

Rousseau, J. J. (1962). *Emile, or concerning education.* New York: Dutton. (Original work published 1738)

Rousseau, J. J. (1967). *Essai sur l'origine du langage.* Paris: Larousse. (Original work published 1781)

Sinclair, H. (1967). *Langage et opérations.* Paris: Dunod.

Steiner, G. (1980). *Visuelle Vorstellungen beim Lösen von elementaren Problemen.* Stuttgart, Germany: Klett-Cotta.

Stoll, F. (1972). *La construction des échelles d'intérèts professionnels.* Neuchâtel, Switzerland: La Baconnière.

Suarez, A. (1980). Connaissance et action, l'enjeu d' une position épistémologique contemporaine. *Revue Suisse de Psychologie, 39,* 177–199.

Suter, J. (1922). *Intelligenz und Begabungsprüfungen.* Zürich, Switzerland: Rascher.

Suter, J. (1942). *Psychologie, Grund und Aufbau.* Bern, Switzerland: Huber.

Szondi, L. (1972). *Lehrbuch der experimentellen Triebdiagnostik* (3rd ed., Vol. I). Bern, Switzerland: Huber.

Ulich, E., Bruggemann, A., & Groskurth, P. (1973). *Neue Formen der Arbeitsgestaltung* Frankfurt: Europäische Verlagsanstalt.

von Cranach, M., Kalbermatten, U., Indermühle, K., & Gugler, B. (1980). *Zielgerichtetes Handeln.* Bern, Switzerland: Huber.

Walther, L. (1926). *La technopsychologie du travail industriel.* Neuchâtel, Switzerland: Delachaux & Niestlé.

Walther, L. (1936). *Orientation professionnelle et carrières libérales. Etude psychologique.* Paris: Delachaux & Niestlé.

Wettler, M. (1980). *Sprache, Gedächtnis, Verstehen.* Berlin, Germany: De Gruyter.

R. MEILI
University of Bern

SYMPATHETIC NERVOUS SYSTEM

The sympathetic nervous system (SNS) is one division of the autonomic nervous system, which controls the function of organs and glands in the body (the efferent portion) and senses changes in these visceral systems (the afferent portion); the other autonomic division is the parasympathetic nervous system (PNS). The neurons that comprise the efferent SNS arise from the thoracic and lumbar portions of the spinal cord; thus, this system is sometimes referred to as the thoracolumbar division. Sympathetic fibers originating from the thoracic cord innervate organs of the head, neck, chest, and upper abdomen. Sympathetic fibers originating from the lumbar cord innervate the lower gastrointestinal (GI) tract as well as organs of the pelvis.

The anatomy of the efferent autonomic innervation of each organ or gland includes preganglionic neurons, which exit the brain or spinal cord, and postganglionic neurons, which directly innervate the target organ. A ganglion (plural ganglia) is composed of the cell bodies of the postganglionic neurons and is the region where the pre- and postganglionic neurons communicate with one another. In the SNS, the preganglionic fibers that exit the spinal cord are relatively short, and many of them synapse within a chain of ganglia found just outside the vertebral column housing the spinal cord. Other sympathetic preganglionic fibers pass to additional ganglia that do not form part of the sympathetic chain, but that are still some distance from the target organ or gland. Typically, then, the postganglionic fibers of the SNS are relatively long since they extend from a ganglion distant from the target organ.

The neurotransmitter released by the axon terminals of the preganglionic neurons is acetylcholine. Acetylcholine acts on cholinergic receptors of the nicotinic subtype, which are found on the postganglionic neurons. The neurotransmitter released by the postganglionic neurons onto the target organ or gland is typically norepinephrine, except in the sweat glands, where the sympathetic nerves release mostly acetylcholine with only a small contribution by neurons containing norepinephrine. Afferent autonomic fibers reaching the central nervous system run alongside the same nerves carrying efferent autonomic fibers. The visceral afferents comprise a relatively small proportion of the total number of fibers, less than 20% in some sympathetic nerves. Afferent autonomic fibers provide sensory information about the state of an organ, such as distension of the bladder, and also relay signals of pain. It has been hypothesized that the sympathetic afferents relay mostly pain information, and play only a minimal role in visceral sensations needed for bodily regulation (e.g., signals from the GI tract indicating that food is present and needs to be digested).

The organs and glands controlled by the efferent SNS typically receive input from both divisions of the autonomic nervous system, a phenomenon referred to as dual innervation. When organs receive innervation from both autonomic divisions, the activity in the two divisions often produces opposite effects on the organ. For example, the heart rate is controlled by both autonomic divisions. Increased activity of the sympathetic division increases heart rate, whereas decreased activity decreases heart rate. Conversely, increased activity in the parasympathetic division decreases heart rate, and decreased activity increases heart rate. Thus, each of the two divisions are capable of bidirectionally influencing the rate at which the heart beats. A notable exception to the general rule of dual innervation is found in the sweat glands, which are innervated by only the SNS.

When the body is either physically active or is engaged in taxing mental activities, the organs of the body tend to mobilize and use resources, a process called catabolism. Often during such states, activity in the sympathetic system is high relative to periods when the organism is quiescent. During mental distress or when there are high levels of bodily activity, the body has an immediate need for more metabolic energy. For example, increased sympathetic activation enhances blood flow to muscles needed to perform work by increasing heart rate and selectively constricting blood vessels to shunt blood flow from areas of low immediate need, such as the GI tract, to areas of high immediate need, such as the exercising muscles. Once the imminent metabolic need has been met, activation of the sympathetic system tends to decline while activation of the parasympathetic system tends to increase. Even in a person at rest, ongoing sympathetic activity helps to maintain a resting level of tone on the arteries supplying skeletal muscle. In general, humans operate somewhere between the two extremes of inactivity and high energy mobilization; in these cases, sympathetic effects on the organs and glands will be intermediate and tuned to the specific needs of each organ system.

In addition to the tendency for the two autonomic branches to operate in a reciprocal fashion under extremes of activity, the two autonomic divisions can operate non-reciprocally and independently. Thus, although a common pattern of autonomic control consists of the reciprocal activation of one autonomic division accompanied by a decrease in activity in the other division, this is not the only pattern of response that can occur. The two autonomic divisions can have uncoupled effects on a target organ with increased or decreased activity in one autonomic division in the absence of any change in the other division. Alternatively, the two branches can exert coactivational effects such that there are simultaneous increases or decreases in activity in both autonomic divisions. The existence of the nonreciprocal patterns means that one cannot measure function in one autonomic division and, on that basis alone, infer the activation level in the other division.

SUGGESTED READING

Berntson, G. G., Cacioppo, J. T., & Quigley, K. S. (1991). Autonomic determinism: The modes of autonomic control, the doctrine of autonomic space, and the laws of autonomic constraint. *Psychological Review, 98,* 459–487.

Loewy, A. D., & Spyer, K. M. (1990). *Central regulation of autonomic function.* New York: Oxford.

K. S. QUIGLEY
Pennsylvania State University

AUTONOMIC NERVOUS SYSTEM
CENTRAL NERVOUS SYSTEM

SYNAPTIC COMPETITION

Dynamic functional modifications and structural rearrangements of synapses in the developing and mature nervous system allow input-specific adjustments of neural circuit organization. Synaptic competition is a process that allows for selective stabilization and maintenance of a subset of inputs onto a target cell based on the relative activity patterns and strengths of a given input compared with other competing inputs.

SYNAPTIC COMPETITION IN THE DEVELOPING NERVOUS SYSTEM

Synaptic competition plays a vital role during development throughout the nervous system. Initially coarse projection patterns are refined to give rise to functionally specific synaptic connections. In the developing neuromuscular junction, a single muscle fiber is initially innervated by multiple motoneurons, which are subsequently pruned or eliminated in an activity-dependent manner, leaving all but one set of inputs. This process ensures precise innervation of the muscle fiber by a single motoneuron. At the neuromuscular synapse, activity-dependent synaptic competition drives both a decrease in synaptic strength and the subsequent withdrawal and elimination of a motoneuronal input. Heterosynaptic interactions are also important in the elimination of inputs at the neuromuscular junction, indicating a cellular mechanism that somehow compares relative synaptic activation of inputs to the myocyte.

Input pruning and specification of connectivity by synaptic activity also play essential roles in the topological organization of sensory inputs to the cortex in the central nervous system (CNS). Synaptic competition has been particularly well studied in the development of the visual cortex, in which inputs arising from the lateral geniculate nucleus (LGN) segregate within the visual cortex into ocular dominance columns. Early in development, terminals of LGN axons representing each eye overlap within the visual cortex. Segregation of inputs involves elimination of synapses and axonal branches driven by competition between LGN neurons representing each eye. Classical experiments demonstrated that following deprivation of vision in one eye during a critical developmental period, visual cortex neurons receive input from LGN neurons driven largely by the non-deprived eye. Recent evidence suggests that the segregation process depends on correlation-based, activity-dependent modifications in synaptic efficacy and subsequent synaptic cooperation and competition of inputs in the visual cortex.

SYNAPTIC COMPETITION IN THE MATURE NERVOUS SYSTEM

Synaptic competition may also play an important role in the mature nervous system, in which experience-dependent changes in synaptic efficacy or connectivity can alter the stimulus response properties of a postsynaptic neuron. Such changes are well documented for primary sensory areas of the cortex, where topologically organized receptive field maps change in response to alterations of sensory experience. For example, in the somatosensory cortex, deafferentation of an area of the somatotopic map results in an expansion of neighboring receptive zones into this area, increasing the cortical representation of body surface neighboring the denervated area. Similarly, the increased sensory stimulation of an area of the body surface, such as during training of a motor skill involving a fingertip, leads to an expanded representation in the somatotopic map, allowing for a finer topographic grain and detail of that particular sensory information. Analogous sensory experience-evoked changes have been observed in the primary visual and auditory cortical areas.

CELLULAR MECHANISMS UNDERLYING SYNAPTIC COMPETITION

Activity-dependent increases and decreases in synaptic efficacy (long-term potentiation and long-term depression [LTP and LTD, respectively]) provide the necessary cellular cues for stabilization versus elimination of neural connections. The induction of LTP and LTD at glutamatergic synapses in many regions of the CNS involves tight temporal correlation of pre- and postsynaptic activity. The rules for synaptic competition may be based on Hebbian learning rules: Synapses of presynaptic neurons that are highly correlated with activity in the postsynaptic cell are strengthened and stabilized, while those whose activity is temporally uncorrelated with postsynaptic activity are weakened and eliminated. For example, competitive events in input segregation of the ocular dominance columns of the visual cortex are driven primarily by spontaneously generated bursts of action potentials in the retina that spread in waves across restricted domains of each retina. Action-potential bursts of neighboring retinal ganglion cells are temporally correlated, yet those of distant ganglion cells (or ganglion cells in different retinae) are not. Thus, correlated activity may locally promote synaptic cooperation among neurons coming from the same eye, but asynchronous synaptic activity may be the factor that differentiates the competing inputs.

Mechanisms that constrain simple correlation-based rules of synaptic competition serve to conserve the total weight on inputs to a target cell, or the overall activity level of the target cell. Induction of LTP in the hippocampus has been shown to result in heterosynaptic LTD in neighboring synapses, resulting in a balance of synaptic weights onto a postsynaptic neuron. Homeostatic mechanisms regulating the overall activity pattern and excitability of a network have also been demonstrated in vitro.

The development and stabilization of functional synapses involve the localization of pre- and postsynaptic components and extracellular matrix molecules to the site of synaptic contact. Thus, nerve terminals may compete for limited amounts of stabilizing factors on the surface of the target. A surface-constrained stabilizing factor, for example, may be the postsynaptic neurotransmitter receptors, which, when activated by presynaptically released neurotransmitter, diffuse to and cluster at the contact site. Selective localization of receptors may promote cell-cell adhesion while limiting the stability and acceptable number of competing inputs. Modulation of synaptic efficacy can lead to rapid and reversible integration of extrasynaptic neurotransmitter receptors into clusters at postsynaptic densities. Recent evidence for so-called silent glutamatergic synapses supports the possible role of postsynaptic receptors in mediating activity-dependent stabilization of synapses. Silent synapses initially contain N-methyl-d-aspartate (NMDA) receptors but lack α-amino-3-hydroxy-5-methyl-4-isoxazole-propionate receptors; induction of LTP results in incorporation of AMPA receptors at the previously silent synapses. Conversely, at the neuromuscular junction, it has been demonstrated that nicotinic acetylcholine receptors diffuse away from the synaptic site well in advance of withdrawal of a weakened presynaptic terminal.

Synaptic terminals may also compete for limited amounts of factors that are secreted/released in an activity-dependent manner from the target cell. Retrograde signals, including diffusible factors, such as arachidonic acid and nitric oxide, and secreted factors, such as neurotrophins, have been shown to be involved in long-lasting changes in synaptic efficacy. There is evidence suggesting that active presynaptic terminals may be more susceptible to the modulatory actions of retrograde signals, particularly in the case of the neurotrophins. Such a mechanism would confer an activity-dependent advantage of active inputs to receive stabilizing factors available in limited quantities from the target cell. Neurotrophins such as Brain-derived neurotrophic factor (BDNF) and Neurotrophin-3 (NT-3) are good candidates for a signal mediating synaptic competition: Neurotrophins have been shown to regulate morphological changes such as axonal branching and dendritic arborization, can modulate synaptic efficacy by altering neurotransmitter release, and are secreted in an activity-dependent manner. The dependence of both the target-derived secretion and the responsiveness of the presynaptic terminals on activity may serve to sharpen competitive interactions among synapses.

SUGGESTED READING

Buonomano, D. V., & Merzenich, M. M. (1998). Cortical plasticity: From synapses to maps. *Annual Review of Neuroscience, 21,* 149–186.

Colman, H., Nabekura, J., & Lichtman, J. W. (1997). Alterations in synaptic strength preceding axon withdrawal. *Science, 275,* 356–361.

Katz, L. C., & Shatz, C. J. (1996). Synaptic activity and the construction of cortical circuits. *Science, 274,* 1133–1138.

Lichtman, J. W., & Balice-Gordon, R. J. (1990). Understanding synaptic competition in theory and in practice. *Journal of Neurobiology, 21,* 99–106.

Malinow, R. (1998). Silencing the controversy in LTP? *Neuron, 21,* 1226–1227.

McAllister, A. K., Katz, L. C., & Lo, D. C. (1999). Neurotrophins and synaptic plasticity. *Annual Review of Neuroscience, 22,* 295–318.

Miller, K. D. (1996). Synaptic economics: Competition and cooperation in synaptic plasticity. *Neuron, 17,* 371–374.

S. KRUEGER
R. M. FITZSIMONDS
Yale School of Medicine

SZASZ, THOMAS S. (1920–   )

Thomas S. Szasz is best known for his proposition that mental illness is a myth and for his uncompromising opposition to psychiatric coercions and excuses. He received his primary and secondary education in Budapest, migrating to the United States in 1938. He graduated from the College of Medicine at the University of Cincinnati in 1944. Following his medical education, he was trained in psychiatry at the University of Chicago, and in psychoanalysis at the Chicago Institute for Psychoanalysis, where he became a member of the staff.

After a period of private practice in Chicago, Szasz was called to active duty with the United States Naval Reserve and was stationed at the Bethesda Naval Hospital. Following his discharge from the Navy in 1956, he joined the faculty of the State University of New York's Upstate Medical Center in Syracuse, as a professor of psychiatry.

In a series of articles and books, beginning in the mid-1950s, Szasz argued that literal illnesses are bodily illnesses and that so-called mental illnesses are either bodily diseases with mental symptoms (such as organic psychoses) or metaphorical diseases (and hence not diseases at all). Partly on such epistemological grounds, and partly on moral and political grounds, Szasz also opposed the use of psychiatry and psychology in a wide variety of legal situations, from civil commitment to the insanity defense. The two principle themes in his work are thus a philosophical analysis of the medicalization (psychiatrization) of life, creating what he has called the "Therapeutic State," and a libertarian critique of the moral and political consequences of that modern scientistic tendency.

STAFF

T

TABOOS

This word comes from a Polynesian word meaning "forbidden" or "dangerous" (Hawaiian: *kapu*). It may originally have meant "sacred" or "mighty." In Polynesian society taboo referred to anything pertaining to the king and anything which it was dangerous for an ordinary person to touch. Even the king's shadow was dangerous ("potent"). Anything the king touched thus became dangerous ("possessed of power"). But there were other places and things manifesting power that were also taboo—such as specific foods, mountains, or springs.

In Western usage the term has come to represent anything forbidden, as "a tabooed subject." Incest is one such topic. Almost every culture forbids sexual relations between immediate relatives, but the taboo is even stricter concerning the discussion of incestual relations. In the United States, for example, one could not even mention incest publicly until the 1980s. Once the taboo was broken, however, it was found that incest itself is a fairly common phenomenon. The act had apparently been occurring in spite of the taboo, but the taboo against discussion was what had kept the information hidden.

In Victorian England and America all references to sex were forbidden—but this did not prevent illegitimate sexual activity. Not only was prostitution widespread, but there was a substantial "underground" literature dealing with the tabooed subject! In Victorian society one did not refer to the anatomy, except in veiled terms. Women did not have legs, they had limbs; they did not have breasts, they had bosoms. The forbidden words continued to exist, but were not mentioned in polite society.

Reference to the dead is forbidden to some degree in almost all societies, and in some the taboo is so great that any reference at all is forbidden and the language changes very rapidly as a result. In some cases, references to dead persons have to be accompanied by some "insulating act," such as exclaiming "God bless his soul" or crossing oneself. Many other acts exist only to cancel out the forbidden behavior or expression, such as knocking on wood to cancel boastful statements that might be self-defeating.

Taking one's own life is taboo in most societies—although in some (as in Japanese ritual suicide) it is culturally sanctioned under specified conditions. In Western culture, even the discussion of suicide is frowned upon. To Christians, taking one's own life is as abhorrent as taking the life of another. Mental health professionals have been aware of tendencies toward suicide in their patients for many years, but only recently has the taboo been sufficiently broken that these tendencies can be discussed.

Basically what is taboo is that which is forbidden to human beings, and is reserved for the gods or the spirits (or for noble persons who have some of the characteristics of gods). Thus the divine kingship or chieftainship is not vulnerable to the taboo, but that which belongs to the divine king or chieftain is taboo to those who are not divine. It is *dangerous to them*. In some ways *taboo* is related to another Polynesian word, *mana*. Mana means a mysterious power that can harm a person who gets too close to it. Originally, then, something was taboo because it possessed such power that it might be dangerous to any human dealing with it casually.

In modern usage it simply refers to topics or acts that are culturally forbidden. Some such topics (and acts) are absolutely forbidden (as incest), but others are forbidden only in specific contexts (what is forbidden in church may be tolerated at a football game, and conversely).

W. E. GREGORY
University of the Pacific

CROSS-CULTURAL PSYCHOLOGY
RITUAL BEHAVIOR

TABULA RASA

One of the central tenets of the philosophical and psychological position known as Empiricism is that all knowledge derives from experience. This contrasts with the Nativist position, which holds that knowledge derives at least in part from innate ideas or an innate potential for ideas. The *tabula rasa* (a Latin phrase meaning "scraped tablet") is a metaphor used by Empiricists to describe the mind at birth—that is, a blank slate, with no innate ideas. The concept is commonly attributed to the British empiricist John Locke, though Aristotle, in Book III of *De Anima* (*On the soul*), compared the mind to a blank writing tablet, and other philosophers since Aristotle have espoused the principles of Empiricism. However, the presentation or the concept in the works of Locke has had the greatest impact on the development of modern psychology. His *Essay Concerning Human Understanding* is a classic polemic attacking the existence of innate principles and ideas. In Book II of that work, Locke characterized the mind as "white paper, void of all characters, without any ideas. . . ." In the remainder of the *Essay* he demonstrated that all the materials of reason and knowledge could indeed be derived solely from experience.

The concept of the tabula rasa has had a profound effect on the development of Western psychology. The thesis that all knowledge is constructed from ideas that come to us through our senses is at the core of the psychological position known as Associationism. This thesis has led to an emphasis on the study of perception and of the association of ideas that is evident in psychology to this day. And although modern Behaviorists reject the concept of the tabula rasa, as they reject all mental metaphors, the emphasis on the role of experience in shaping the development of organisms is an important principle of Behaviorism.

The concept of the tabula rasa is by no means universally accepted. In Locke's time, the most active critic of this concept was the German Rationalist Gottfried Wilhelm Leibniz, who argued that without some inherent ability to process information, our minds would be unable to receive any ideas from the environment. The position advocated by Leibniz is evident today in the cognitive developmental theories of such writers as Jean Piaget and Noam Chomsky.

Few psychologists today would accept a pure tabula rasa characterization of the human mind. Even Locke admitted the existence of an innate predilection to acquire and combine information. The debate concerns not whether there is structure inherent in the human mind, but the nature and extent of that structure.

REFERENCES

Aristotle. (1941). De anima (On the soul). In R. McKeon (Ed.), *The basic works of Aristotle.* New York: Random House.

Locke, J. (1984). *An essay concerning human understanding.* (A. C. Fraser, Ed.), (2 vols.). London: Oxford University Press.

R. A. SHAW
Brown University

MIND/BODY PROBLEM
PHILOSOPHICAL PSYCHOLOGY

TANTRUMS

A tantrum is a violent outburst, often consisting of kicking, hitting, screaming, crying, destructiveness, and related behaviors. Although most common in children, tantrums also are commonly reported in older, developmentally delayed people. They are usually thought of as a reaction to frustration, and are often very distressing to adults, especially when they occur in public.

Frustration sufficient to precipitate a tantrum may result when children are thwarted from achieving their goal by parents or other adults. Adults often accede to the demands of children to avoid embarrassment, to prevent the child from self-destructive behavior or from damaging property, or otherwise to reduce the immediate effects of the tantrum. Therefore, as Rachel Hare-Mustin (1975) has stated, tantrums often represent a type of power struggle between child and parent. The tantrums are often inadvertently maintained by the parent by meeting the child's wishes on some occasions.

Effective treatments of tantrums have included Hare-Mustin's (1975) approach of having the parents encourage the tantrums; use of a variety of operant conditioning techniques in treatment settings (e.g., time out, response cost, reinforcement of appropriate behavior, extinction), as reported by David Marholin and Elizabeth McInnis (1978); and structured behavior modification techniques imposed by the parents (Coe, 1972).

REFERENCES

Coe, W. C. (1972). A behavioral approach to disrupted family interactions. *Psychotherapy: Theory, Research, and Practice, 9,* 80–85.

Hare-Mustin, R. T. (1975). Treatment of temper tantrums by a paradoxical intervention. *Family Process, 14,* 481–485.

Marholin, D., II, & McInnis, E. T. (1978). Treating children in group settings: Techniques for individualizing behavioral programs. In D. Marholin, II (Ed.), *Child behavior therapy.* New York: Gardner Press.

T. S. BENNETT
Brain Inquiry Recovery Program

CHILD PSYCHOLOGY
TEMPERAMENTS

TARDIVE DYSKINESIA

Tardive dyskinesia (TD) is the most troublesome and feared extrapyramidal side effect (EPS) of long-term conventional antipsychotic drug therapy. Tardive dyskinesia has been defined as an extrapyramidal hyperkinetic movement disorder, characterized by involuntary, repetitive, and irregular abnormal movements, present for a minimum of 4 weeks and occurring after a minimum of 3 months of cumulative classical antipsychotic drug (i.e., neuroleptic [NL]) exposure (Kane et al., 1992).

The presence of TD has been related to poor treatment compliance and, due to its associated stigma, to an important deterioration in quality of life. In spite of the fact that TD is often not severe and may even improve in a significant proportion of cases (Gardos et al., 1994), the severe, disabling, progressive, and irreversible cases (even though a minority) constitute a permanent threat in long-term antipsychotic or NL treatment because it is still not possible to predict who is going to develop TD, nor of what type or severity (Larach, Zamboni, Mancini, & Gallardo, 1997).

EPIDEMIOLOGY OF TARDIVE DYSKINESIA

The prevalence of TD has been reported to range from 3 to 62%, with a mean prevalence of around 20% and a cumulative incidence of 5% for each year of NL exposure. For patients over 50 years of age, cumulative incidence rises to 50% or more after 3 years of NL exposure. The natural history of TD, as suggested on long-term follow-up studies, tends to have a fluctuating course and an overall trend toward amelioration with time, although some researchers have found chronic persistent dyskinesia in more than half of the patients in long-term follow-up studies (Kane, 1995).

RISK FACTORS

The best-identified risk factor is age, with patients under the age of 40 years having about a 10% risk of developing TD; this risk increases five- to seven-fold in elderly patients. Gender differences show that the ratio of women to men developing TD is 1.7:1, and that women tend to have more severe TD and more spontaneous dyskinesias. Vulnerability to drug-induced acute and chronic EPS, secondary to disruption of the nigro-striatal system, is of particular concern in children, who are at special risk because of their immature brains. The presence of schizophrenic negative or deficit symptoms, affective disorders, structural brain abnormalities, diabetes mellitus, and smoking have also been identified as risk factors for TD. Whether the use of either depot neuroleptics or concomitant long-term therapy with such drugs as anticholinergics and lithium presents a special risk still remains controversial. The prolonged use of those NL drugs that are not marketed as NL in the treatment of non-psychotic conditions—drugs that include many antiemetics, various NL-type dyspeptic agents, and some NLs with marked antidepressant effects (e.g., amoxepine)—frequently constitutes the risk of extended NL exposure without the physician's being aware of that risk (Casey, 1995a).

CLINICAL FEATURES OF TARDIVE DYSKINESIA

Clinical features of TD include involuntary, repetitive, and irregular movements affecting different body regions: facial muscles (usually in older adults) involving the lips, jaw, and tongue (bucco-linguo-masticatory dyskinesia), frequently accompanied by involuntary grimacing and spasmodic eye-blinking; and axial musculature and extremities (usually in children and younger patients) involving any type or combination of choreic, athetotic, myoclonic, and dystonic movements. Tardive dyskinesia usually includes other tardive EPS features such as tardive dystonias and tardive akathisia, considered to be tardive because they also appear after prolonged NL exposure. Dystonic features convey a more severe and disabling picture. As with all extrapyramidal syndromes, movements disappear during sleep and worsen with stress.

The severity and complexity of the movements in TD impair motor functions and psychosocial interaction, and produce subjective discomfort symptoms. Motor feature impairment can involve difficulties with speech or swallowing; inability to wear dentures; ulcerations of the mouth mucosae; impairment for daily routines such as walking, sitting, and standing; and significant progressive weight loss that may become a life-threatening condition. These impairments produce different levels of psychological distress that range from no awareness of discomfort to different levels of embarrassment, desperation, and hopelessness, and even to suicidal ideation and behavior (Casey, 1995b).

Early detection of TD may be possible by observing mild and poorly-defined movements such as grimacing or facial tics (especially of the eyes and lips); chewing or other bucal movements; mild and fine vermicular movements of the tongue; and rocking and limb restlessness in the absence of the subjective discomfort of akathisia.

DIFFERENTIAL DIAGNOSIS

The psychotic motor features of schizophrenia, such as stereotypies, mannerisms, and bizarre postures, should first be ruled out. Other hyperkinetic idiopathic syndromes, such as some rarely-spontaneous dyskinesias observed in psychotic patients never exposed to NLs, or others such as senile dyskinesias and Meige's and Tourette's syndromes, should be considered. Secondary dyskinesias caused by systemic diseases such as lupus erythematosus, Sydenham's chorea, Henoch-Schonlein's purpura, chorea gravid-

ium, hyperthyroidism, and hypoparathyroidism, and by hereditary diseases such as Huntington's and Wilson's diseases, should be sorted out. Brain lesions caused by cerebrovascular accidents, tumors, and brain chemical poisoning must also be regarded, as should post-encephalitic dyskinesias. Other drug treatments that may produce reversible and irreversible dyskinesias, such as amphetamines, tricyclic antidepressants, antihistamines, phenytoin, oral contraceptives, and L-dopa (in the treatment of Parkinson's disease) should be considered as causes (Casey, 1995a).

PATHOPHYSIOLOGY

The pathophysiology of TD remains unknown, since there have been no consistent, demonstrable abnormalities found in neurochemical and postmortem receptor studies. The DA nigro-striatal pathways would be functionally abnormal through mechanisms related to the increase in the number of DA receptors secondary to prolonged DA receptor blockade, changes in sensitivity, and poorly understood pre- and postsynaptic DA receptor interactions. High liability for acute EPS seems to be related to increased TD risk. The difficulty with NLs or the so-called typical or classical antipsychotics is that their effective antipsychotic dose range produces more than 70% of D2 receptor blockade in the basal ganglia, an amount very close to the dose needed for the appearance of EPS (around 80% D2 receptor blockade; Farde et al., 1992). The prevailing question in this case is whether the DA role is primary or modulatory. The combination of low D2 and high serotonin (5HT2) receptor blockade activity seems to reduce the risk for EPS symptoms by an (as yet) unclarified mechanism. It appears that serotonin receptor blockade probably modulates DA activity by increasing DA in the substantia nigra as well as in the prefrontal area (Meltzer, 1993). The new generation of antipsychotic drugs—the so-called atypical or novel antipsychotics—have been developed based on these blockade strategies to widen the margin between the dose required for the antipsychotic effect and the dose that causes EPS occurrence.

On the other hand, other, even less confirmed neurochemical theories and substrates have been considered: noradrenergic, cholinergic, and GABAergic; neuropeptide dysfunction (cholecystokinin, substance P, neurotensin, somatostatin); disturbances in mineral metabolism (iron); glucose-insulin-NL interaction; neurotoxicity in the basal ganglia due to high oxidative metabolism caused by increased catecholamine turnover; and so on. Such theories have led the way to miscellaneous pharmacological strategies in the treatment of TD; among them, the more widely used benzodiazepines have helped some patients. Treatment with vitamin E (alpha-tocopherol) at high doses has also been tried, with variable clinical results (Casey, 1995c).

TREATMENT

The treatment of TD remains highly empirical. At present, there is no definite, effective, standard, safe TD treatment, and it is not possible as of the time of this writing to predict the treatment response to a specific agent. Thus, prevention continues to be the best strategy regarding TD (Gardos & Cole, 1995). The use of first-line atypical antipsychotics (e.g., risperidone, olanzapine, and quetiapine) for the long-term maintenance treatment of schizophrenia and for some forms of severe affective disorders represents in varying degrees the most relevant factor in TD prevention, because of the low incidence of EPS associated with these drugs. Clozapine, the best representative agent of the atypical antipsychotics and for which there are virtually no reports of dystonia or definite TD causation, has been reported to be especially effective in ameliorating or resolving roughly 60% of moderate to severe TD with dystonic disabling features (Lieberman et al., 1991; Larach et al., 1997). Its wide and first-line use is limited by the potential of blood dyscrasia and by the necessity of regular blood tests. Treatment of TD with atypical antipsychotics should be maintained long enough to avoid rebound and to assure full therapeutic effect. Ideally, periodic video recording during standard examinations is advisable for long-term follow-up and outcome assessment (Larach et al., 1997). The definite effectiveness of atypical antipsychotics in the treatment of overt TD cases still awaits further testing.

REFERENCES

Casey, D. E. (1995a). Neuroleptic-induced acute extrapyramidal syndromes and tardive dyskinesia. *Psychiatric Clinics of North America,* vol 16(3), 589–610.

Casey, D. E. (1995b). Motor & mental aspects of extrapyramidal syndromes. *International Clinical Psychopharmacology, 10*(Suppl. 3), 105–114.

Casey, D. E. (1995c). Tardive dyskinesia: Pathophysiology. In F. E. Bloom & D. J. Kupfer (Eds.), *Psychopharmacology: The fourth generation of progress* (pp. 1497–1502). New York: Raven.

Farde, L., Nordström, A.-L., Wiesel, F.-A., Paulli, S., Halldin, C., & Sedvall, G. (1992). Positron emission tomographic analysis of central D1 and D2 dopamine receptor occupancy in patients treated with classical neuroleptics and clozapine: Relation to extrapyramidal side effects. *Archives of General Psychiatry, 49,* 538–544.

Gardos, G., & Cole, J. O. (1995). The treatment of tardive dyskinesias. In F. E. Bloom & D. J. Kupfer (Eds.), *Psychopharmacology: The fourth generation of progress* (pp. 1503–1511). New York: Raven.

Gardos, G., Casey, D., Cole, J. O., Perenyi, A., Kocsis, E., Arato, M., Samson, J. A., & Conley, C. (1994). Ten-year outcome of tardive dyskinesia. *American Journal of Psychiatry, 151,* 836–841.

Kane, J. M. (1995). Tardive dyskinesia: Epidemiological and clinical presentation. In F. E. Bloom & D. J. Kupfer (Eds.), *Psychopharamacology: The fourth generation of progress.* New York: Raven.

Kane, J. M., Jeste, D. V., Barnes, J. R. E., et al. (1992). Tardive dyskinesia: A task force report of the American Psychiatric Association. Washington, DC: American Psychiatric Association.

Larach, V., Zamboni, R., Mancini, H., & Gallardo, T. (1997). New strategies for old problems: Tardive dyskinesia (TD) review and report on severe TD cases treated with clozapine with 12, 8 and 5 years of video follow-up. *Schizophrenia Research, 28,* 231–246.

Lieberman, J. A., Saltz, B. L., Johns, C. A., Pollack, S., Borenstein, M., & Kane, J. (1991). The effects of clozapine on tardive dyskinesia. *British Journal of Psychiatry, 158,* 503–510.

Meltzer, H. Y. (1993). Serotonin receptors and antipsychotic drug action. *Psychopharmacology Series, 10,* 70–81.

V. W. LARACH
Universidad de Chile

AKATHISIA

See AKATHISIA

TASK DESIGN

The simplification and standardization of the tasks comprising a job have long been advocated as means of enhancing productivity in organizations (Taylor, 1903). Indeed, these strategies have been shown to lead to simplified production scheduling, lowered training costs, and reduced expenditures for labor through the employment of lower-skilled, more interchangeable, and cheaper workers (cf. Aldag & Brief, 1979). However, simplified and standardized tasks are perceived by job incumbents as monotonous, leading them to feel bored and dissatisfied with their work; in turn, this boredom and dissatisfaction presumably cost employers in terms of increased absenteeism and turnover and reduced production output (Hulin & Blood, 1968).

To counteract these costs, job enlargement (Kilbridge, 1960) and job enrichment (Herzberg, 1968) have been advocated as alternative task-design strategies. Conceptually, however, the two strategies are quite similar and can be thought of as entailing the design of jobs to include a wider variety of tasks and to increase the job incumbent's freedom of pace, responsibility for checking quality, and discretion over method. For the most part, the research addressing the two strategies has taken the form of testimonial evidence; thus, one is unable to assert few, if any, generalizations regarding their efficacy (Aldag & Brief, 1979).

Building on the works of Turner and Lawrence (1965) and Hackman and Lawler (1971), Hackman and Oldham (1975) advanced a model to guide more rigorous research aimed at enhancing both theory and practice. They asserted that through various psychological states, five core dimensions influence job incumbents' affective and behavioral reactions to their jobs. These core dimensions are: (a) skill variety—the degree to which a job requires a variety of different activities; (b) task identity—the degree to which the job requires the completion of a whole and identifiable piece of work; (c) task significance—the degree to which the job has a substantial impact on the lives or work of other people; (d) autonomy—the degree to which the job provides substantial freedom, independence, and discretion to the incumbent in scheduling work and in determining the procedures to be used in carrying it out; and (e) feedback—the degree to which carrying out the work activities required by the job results in the incumbent's obtaining direct and clear information about the effectiveness of his or her performance. Critical reviews of the research generated by the Hackman and Oldham model indicate that the core job dimensions are likely to lead to higher levels of job satisfaction on the part of job incumbents but do not appear to influence their behaviors significantly (Aldag, Barr, & Brief, 1981; Roberts & Glick, 1981).

More recently, knowledge enlargement, which involves adding requirements to the job for understanding procedures or rules relating to the organization's products, has been advanced as an alternative to task enlargement. It has been shown to yield more satisfaction as well as less overload and errors (Campion & McClelland, 1993). Additionally, in response to manufacturing process innovations such as just-in-time inventory control and total quality management, it has been advocated that one consider how worker flexibility and employee learning and development might be encouraged by job design (Parker, Wall, & Jackson, 1997). Thus, greater attention should be focused on the context in which jobs are embedded.

Salancik and Pfeffer's (1978) Social Information Processing Model explicitly considers the importance of social context in the subjective construction of job attitudes. For example, the model posits that in the process of forming job perceptions, job incumbents rely on what their coworkers say. However, evidence in support of the model has not been promising. Critical reviews have suggested that greater attention be paid to factors such as the employee's past experiences and susceptibility to influence by others (Zalesny & Ford, 1990).

The question of how to design tasks to enhance employee motivation, and thus, productivity, remains open. Clearly, personal experiences and intuition lead one to believe that the contents of jobs do vary in terms of their motivational potential. Until that potential is verified empirically and its costs and benefits are compared with those strategies advanced by Taylor's principles of scientific management, a scientific psychology of task design will be more of an aspiration than a reality.

REFERENCES

Aldag, R. J., Barr, S. H., & Brief, A. P. (1981). Measurement of perceived task characteristics. *Psychological Bulletin, 90,* 415–431.

Aldag, R. J., & Brief, A. P. (1979). *Task design and employee motivation.* Glenview, IL: Scott, Foresman and Company.

Campion, M. A., & McClelland, C. L. (1993). Follow-up and extension of the interdisciplinary costs and benefits of enlarged jobs. *Journal of Applied Psychology, 78,* 339–351.

Hackman, J. R., & Lawler, E. E. (1971). Employee reactions to job characteristics. *Journal of Applied Psychology, 55,* 259–286.

Hackman, J. R., & Oldham, G. R. (1975). Development of the Job Diagnostic Survey. *Journal of Applied Psychology, 60,* 159–170.

Herzberg, F. (1968). One more time: How do you motivate employees? *Harvard Business Review, 46,* 53–62.

Hulin, C. L., & Blood, M. R. (1968). Job enlargement, individual differences, and worker responses. *Psychological Bulletin, 69,* 41–55.

Kilbridge, M. D. (1960). Reduced costs through job enrichment: A case. *The Journal of Business, 33,* 357–362.

Parker, S. K., Wall, T. D., & Jackson, P. R. (1997). "That's not my job": Developing flexible employee work orientations. *Academy of Management Journal, 40,* 899–929.

Roberts, K. H., & Glick, W. (1981). The job characteristics approach to task design: A critical review. *Journal of Applied Psychology, 66,* 193–217.

Salancik, G. R., & Pfeffer, J. (1978). A social information processing approach to job attitudes and task design. *Administrative Science Quarterly, 23,* 224–253.

Taylor, F. W. (1903). *Shop management.* New York: Harper.

Turner, A. N., & Lawrence, P. R. (1965). *Industrial jobs and the worker: An investigation of response to task attributes.* Boston: Harvard Graduate School of Business Administration.

Zalesny, M. D., & Ford, J. K. (1990). Extending the social information processing perspective: New links to attitudes, behaviors, and perceptions. *Organizational Behavior and Human Decision Processes, 47,* 205–246.

R. M. Butz
A. P. Brief
Tulane University

APPLIED RESEARCH
JOB ANALYSIS

TASTE PERCEPTION

SENSE OF TASTE
Taste is one of five senses that may be involved in sensory evaluation, each sense being associated with a different type of receptor. The sense of taste is important because of its role in food recognition, selection, and acceptance. The final criteria by which food is judged and wins acceptance relate to sensory properties. How does it look? How does it taste? How does it smell? Individuals use their senses to determine whether a product is edible and whether it pleases them. The first is a judgement, the second a reaction; and the more favourable the reaction the more likely the product is to be acceptable (Woods, 1998).

TASTE RECEPTORS
Taste or gustatory sensations occur with stimulations of chemoreceptors in taste buds on the tongue, soft palate, and throat, the majority being on the tongue. The taste buds are small, oval-shaped protuberances containing two types of cells: supporting cells form capsules that contain gustatory cells, each containing a gustatory hair that projects to the external surface and taste stimulus via a taste pore, which is a small opening in the taste bud.

The rough surface of the tongue is due to the presence of papillae, which vary in size and shape. The largest are the circular circumvallate papillae, which contain taste buds and form an inverted 'V' shape at the back of the tongue. Fungiform papillae, which are mushroom shaped and also contain taste buds, are located on the tip and at the sides of the tongue (Arvidson, 1979). Moderate numbers of taste buds are present in foliate papillae, which occur in the palate and at the back of the throat. Evidence of anatomical influences on the different sensitivities between individuals has been provided by Miller and Bartoshuk (1991) and Bartoshuk, Duffy, and Miller (1994), who correlated counts of papillae and taste buds with taste sensitivity.

STIMULATION OF RECEPTORS

Saliva is an important component of taste function. It acts as a solvent and enables contact between the taste stimulus and the plasma membranes of the gustatory hairs, where a generator potential initiates a nerve impulse. Moistening of the mucous membrane in the mouth by saliva is increased when food is in the mouth.

Chewing stimulates secretion of saliva via receptors in the brain stem known as the superior and inferior salivating nuclei. The stimuli of thought, sight, and smell may lead to anticipation of taste sensation before the food is placed in the mouth, resulting in saliva secretion. These stimuli are based on learned behaviour, memory, and psychological response, and form the basis for the expression "It makes my mouth water."

Saliva secretion results from three types of salivary glands (paratoid, submandibular, and sublingual) and also from the buccal glands, which are located in the mucous membrane lining of the mouth.

Each of the different types of salivary gland contributes different components to the saliva, which is 99.5% water and 0.5% solute. The parotid glands in humans excrete a watery liquid containing the digestive enzyme amylase. The other salivary glands secrete a higher level of mucus and produce less of the enzyme, but chloride, bicarbonate, and phosphate ions are present, which have buffering and temperature control effects important to the eating function (Tortora & Anagnostakos, 1984).

PRIMARY TASTES

It is generally accepted in sensory science that there are four primary tastes, which stimulate taste buds at specific areas of the tongue. Each primary taste is designated as such by the responses of taste buds to different chemical stimulants. Studies on single taste buds have demonstrated that most taste buds can be stimulated by more than one primary taste stimulus (Collings, 1974). As a general rule, however, the specificity theory works well for demonstrating the taste sensation of each of the four primary tastes: sweet, salt, sour, and bitter. Sweet is the sensation recognized predominantly at the tip of the tongue; salt and sour sensations, at the sides, and bitter, at the back. The standards used to demonstrate the primary tastes are based on solutions of sucrose (sweet), sodium chloride (salt), citric acid (sour), and quinine sulphate or caffeine (bitter).

Some substances normally associated with one particular taste sensation may demonstrate other taste sensations over a range of concentrations. Saccharin, which has considerable use as an intense sweetener, can taste bitter as well as sweet. Work by Helgren, Lynch, and Kirchmeyer (1955) demonstrated that some individuals recognize a bitter taste in saccharin at certain concentrations. This bitterness was originally thought to be due to different preparation procedures, but was shown in the study to be inherent in the particular structure of the saccharin molecule to which some individuals demonstrated sensitivity.

Another example of differences in taste sensitivity among individuals is the phenomenon of bitter-taste blindness. This was originally studied using phenylthiourea, originally called phenylthiocarbamide. Fox (1932) and Blakesell (1932) discovered that 20% of the population were unable to detect any bitterness in solutions of the compound. More recent studies into taste blindness have been carried out using the compound 6-n-propothiouracil, which correlates with the phenylthiourea response but is less toxic (Lawless, 1980).

When examining responses to primary tastes, it has been shown that some individuals confuse bitter with sour. This occurs not because of a lack of ability to differentiate, but because the two primary tastes are frequently present together in many products, as in lemons and grapefruit. This confusion can easily be rectified by demonstration using standard solutions.

THRESHOLD LEVELS

Absolute or detection threshold is the lowest perceivable energy level of a physical stimulus, or the lowest perceivable concentration in the case of a chemical stimulus (Lawless & Heymann, 1998). Recognition thresholds are the minimum levels of concentration at which the characteristic taste of a stimulant is evident. As a general rule, the concentration of the recognition threshold is slightly higher than that of the detection threshold. Absolute thresholds vary between individuals, and even with a single individual, as sensitivity may be affected both by emotional and environmental factors and by the substance under investigation.

Difference thresholds relate to the amount by which a stimulus must change before it becomes a just noticeable difference (jnd). Early work on this by Weber and Fischer forms the basis for much of today's sensory methodology (Amerine, Pangborn, & Roessler, 1965).

Measurement of threshold levels has been used extensively in studies of the psychophysics of taste. This concerns the functional relationship between stimulus and response—that is, the physical stimuli are measured and related to psychological sensation (Coon, 1986).

ADAPTATION OF TASTE

Continuous stimulation of the sense of taste, as with the other senses, results in adaptation. This occurs very quickly after contact with the taste stimulant but is slower after 2 to 3 seconds. Complete adaptation to taste can occur in 1 to 5 minutes and involves a psychological adaptation in the central nervous system (Tortora & Anagnostakos, 1989). When food is being tasted, adaptation involves the senses of both taste and smell.

TASTE AND FLAVOR

Flavor is the total sensation realised when a food or beverage is placed in the mouth. The senses of smell and taste involve chemoreceptors, and it is the combination of these with other receptors, such as the mechanoreceptors of touch and electromagnetic receptors of sight, that leads to the overall perception of flavor. When food or drink is consumed, the primary tastes are recognized on the tongue along with textural and other associated sensations in the mouth and on the palate. Identity is conferred as a result of the movement of volatile components of the food from the back of the mouth into the olfactory area, where the smell mechanism operates. Often when a loss of the sense of taste is indicated, it is really a loss of the sense of smell (Murphy & Cain, 1980). This situation arises with people suffering from the common cold or from an allergy and who complain that they cannot taste. In fact, their taste sensations may not be impaired; the olfactory mechanisms are affected because volatile components from foods are prevented from entering the olfactory system by mucus.

TASTE AVERSION

Taste acceptance varies considerably both among and within individuals. Cabanac and Duclaux (1970) demonstrated that hunger influences the degree of acceptability and pleasantness of the sweet taste. Acceptance and preference in relation to food quality depends on a combination of physiological and psychological response (Regor, 1960; Amerine, 1962). Taste aversion is a type of classical conditioning that occurs when illness follows consumption of a particular food; a negative association is developed with that food, which is subsequently avoided (Logue, 1986). Taste aversion can also occur as a result of drug treatment, especially in cancer patients (Bernstein, 1978; Bernstein & Webster, 1980).

UMAMI

The four taste qualities, sweet, sour, salt, and bitter, are adequate for most investigations involving sensory evaluation. UMAMI is the description for the mouthfilling sensation of monosodium glutamate (MSG), 5^1 inosine monophosphate (IMP), and 5^1 guanine monophosphate (GMP) (Kawamura & Kane, 1987). Often described as flavor enhancers, these substances are the subject of ongoing discussions on whether UMAMI can be considered as a separate taste category.

REFERENCES

Amerine, M. A., Pangborn, R. M., & Roessler, E. B. (1965). *Principles of sensory evaluation of food.* New York: Academic.

Arvidson, K. (1979). Location and variation in number of taste buds in human fungiform papillae. *Scandinavian Journal of Dental Research, 87,* 435–442.

Bartoshuk, L. M., Duffy, V. B., & Miller, L. J. (1994). PTC/PROP tasting: Anatomy, psychophysics and sex effects. *Physiology and Behaviour, 56,* 1165–1171.

Bernstein, I. L. (1978). Learned taste aversions in children receiving chemotherapy. *Science, 200,* 1302–1303.

Bernstein, I. L., & Webster, M. M. (1980). Learned taste aversion in humans. *Physiology & Behaviour, 25,* 363–366.

Blakeslee, A. F. (1932). Genetics of sensory thresholds: Taste for phenylthiocarbamide. *Proceedings of the National Academy of Sciences USA, 18,* 120–130.

Cabanac, M., & Duclaux, P. (1970). Obesity: Absence of satiety aversion to sucrose. *Science,* 496–497.

Collings, V. B. (1974). Human taste response as a function of locus on the tongue and soft palate. *Perception and Psychophysics, 16,* 169–174.

Coon, D. (1986). *Introduction to psychology* (4th ed.). St. Paul: West.

Fox, A. L. (1932). The relationship between chemical constitution and taste. *Proceedings of the National Academy of Sciences USA, 18,* 115–120.

Gregson, R. A. M. (1960). Bias in the measurement of food preferences by triangular tests. *Occupational Psychology, 34,* 249–257.

Helgren, F. J., Lynch, M. J., & Kirchmeyer, F. J. (1955). A taste panel study of the saccharin off taste. *Journal of the American Pharmaceutical Association, 14,* 353–355, 442–446.

Kawamura, Y., & Kare, M. R. (1987). *UMAMI: A basic taste.* New York: Dekker.

Lawless, H. T. (1980). A comparison of different methods for assessing sensitivity to the taste of phenylthiocarbamide (PTC). *Chemical Senses, 5,* 247–256.

Lawless, H. T., & Heymann, H. (1998). *Sensory evaluation of food: Principles and practices.* New York: Chapman & Hall.

Logue, A. W. (1986). *The psychology of eating and drinking.* New York: Freeman.

Tortora, G. J., & Anagnostakos, H. P. (1984). *Principles of anatomy and physiology* (4th ed.). New York: Harper and Ross.

Woods, M. P. (1998). Taste and flavour perception. *Proceedings of the Nutrition Society, 57,* 603–607.

M. P. WOODS

PERCEPTION

TELEPHONE COUNSELING

Telephone counseling is a specialized intervention that has its roots in two major developments in public health and mental health. The first was the unfolding of the suicide prevention movement, which began with the opening of the first suicide prevention center in Los Angeles, CA, in the 1950s. The agency adopted the telephone as the primary mode for service delivery because of its ready access to the general public. The second impetus arose from the establishment of poison information centers around the United States aimed at providing immediate counseling regarding antidotes for accidental or intentional ingestion of harmful chemicals. As Lester and Brockopp state in their seminal work *Crisis Intervention by Telephone,* these two types of telephone services provided models for immediate counseling that were later extended in a number of ways.

These authors cite several applications of the models, including the following: hot lines for specific populations such as teenagers, the elderly, and homosexuals; telephone services for specific problems such as drug and alcohol concerns, sex counseling, and child and spouse abuse; and other telephone-related services such as "Dial-a-Prayer," and informational programs in which tape recordings may be listened to by the callers.

Telephone counseling services, then, provide a wide range of services, including information, crisis-oriented counseling, and ongoing therapy for repeat callers. These agencies often employ volunteers to staff the telephone lines and consequently have contributed to the development of the paraprofessional movement in the mental health field.

TELEPHONE COUNSELING VERSUS FACE-TO-FACE COUNSELING

Regardless of the type of telephone service, there is general agreement that interventions by telephone differ from conventional face-to-face counseling in five major ways. First, because of the easy access to telephones, callers often telephone at the moment that their need is most intense. This is unlike conventional counseling where some time may elapse between the onset of a difficulty and actual contact in an office with a counselor. Thus callers are often quite receptive to the telephone counselor's interventions because of the immediacy of the situation. Second, the callers can retain some personal control in whatever difficulty they are encountering. Rather than engaging a social service agency on its terms, the callers keep some power over when, where, and how they contact a counselor on the telephone. This is less true when one is sitting in a counselor's office. Third, the caller can remain anonymous. The obvious advantage here is that greater self-disclosure and openness can occur because of the greater sense of security and lessened threat of ridicule or embarrassment. Fourth, callers can remain in the security of their immediate environments and still make contact with a helper. This is particularly helpful for those individuals whose physical or mental conditions prohibit them from making social contact outside their living situations. Finally, the counselor can remain anonymous. This promotes what can be termed positive transference; that is, the telephone counselor can be whatever the caller wishes him or her to be. The telephone counselor is then likely to be more like the caller's "ideal" than the face-to-face counselor as the caller will have only part of the reality available since visual clues are missing. Such positive transference can aid in the establishment of trust and confidence early in the counseling contact.

While telephone counseling has many advantages, there are certainly some disadvantages as well. For example, the lack of visual clues can be useful from the caller's perspective, but for the counselor it presents a unique challenge since such information is not accessible in assessing counseling goals and strategies. Also, there is an inherent propensity for rapid, succinct counseling since callers frequently make contact on a one-time basis. Sustained, developmentally oriented counseling thus is not always possible to implement.

Nonetheless, telephone counseling has become an established

intervention as a result of the convenience, anonymity, and cost effectiveness it offers to the public.

REFERENCES

Lester, D., & Brockopp, G. W. (Eds.). (1973). *Crisis intervention by telephone.* Springfield, IL: Thomas.

SUGGESTED READING

Barón, A., Jr., Klein, R. L., & Thurman, C. W. (1981). Student use of a university telephone counseling service: A three-year overview. *Crisis Intervention, 11,* 54–59.

Cohen, L. P., Claiborn, W. L., & Specter, G. A. (Eds.). (1982). *Crisis intervention.* New York: Human Sciences Press.

Thurman, C. W., Baron, A., Jr., & Klein, R. L. (1979). Self-help tapes in a telephone counseling service: A three-year analysis. *Journal of College Student Personnel, 20,* 546–550.

A. BARÓN, JR.
University of Texas at Austin

COUNSELING
CRISIS INTERVENTION
HOT LINE SERVICES
SUICIDE PREVENTION

TEMPERAMENTS

Synthesizing ideas from classical Greek medicine and astronomy, a theory of temperaments prevailing well into medieval times held that, for example, a sanguine disposition reflected a particular combination of humors in the body and that, in turn, this combination had been fixed by a certain configuration of the stars at the time of an individual's birth (Neaman, 1973). Indeed, the etymology of the term *temperament* builds on the idea of a mixture of elements in a certain proportion, a regulated or tempered mingling. In more recent times, the German psychiatrist Ernst Kretschmer and, independently, in the United States, Sheldon and Stevens (1942) gathered support for the proposition that temperament is a function at least of inherited body form or physique, if not of the four cardinal humors.

Although it enjoyed a revival beginning in the 1960s, the study of temperament was long in disrepute in contemporary psychology because, given its association with inherited characteristics, it ran counter to the environmental emphasis of behaviorism. In addition, it played only a minor role in psychoanalytic theory. Even Jung (1976/1921), whose theory of personality featured both extensions of psychodynamic concepts and relatively stable or dispositional individual differences, substituted the term *type* for temperament. In his theory a psychological type consisted of a combination of an attitude and a function. With some modification of them, Eysenck (1967) demonstrated a physiological basis for the Jungian attitudes.

While most psychologists emphasize the role of inheritance in the determination of temperament, and some make it definitional (e.g., Buss & Plowin, 1975), more critical features are that temperament refers to a pattern of enduring traits characterizing an individual. As distinguished from personality more generally, temperament consists of the style or manner of behavior, of the expressive rather than the instrumental, of the "how" of behavior rather than its "why." Temperament fits between personality as a whole and a particular discrete trait in terms of breadth of phenomenon.

In a longitudinal study of individual differences in infants, Thomas and Chess (1977) described nine categories of behavioral and physiologic reactivity, such as activity level, rhythmicity, intensity of response, and persistence. They found consistent and stable individual patterns among these, thus constituting individual behavioral styles or temperaments from infancy. Initially a product both of genetics and of perinatal and paranatal environmental factors, a particular temperament affects, and in turn is affected by, the social environment. Far from being a passive respondent to the environment, the child in part provides his or her own temperament and through it affects the tone and responses of the family.

While temperament was found to be a relatively stable aspect of an individual, the recognition that it was a developmental phenomenon continually in interaction with social environment led investigators to raise the question of what constituted an equivalent temperament at different ages (Kagan, 1971). For example, the intensely reactive style of a particular infant may later be expressed through intense anger in response to criticism. The concept of temperament that emerged from its study within a developmental perspective is one broadened beyond strict heritability and immutability over time to a more phenomenological definition, centering on style.

Several convergent developments buttressed this emphasis on individual differences that endure through the life span, operate across different contexts and modes of functioning, and by and large are nonmotivational and noninstrumental—that is, stylistic—aspects of personality. In personality psychology, Witkin (1962) and his associates identified a stable and superordinate individual difference in spatial orientation. Their field-dependence construct measured a temperamental difference among individuals across a broad band of psychological systems—perceptual, cognitive, emotional, and social. In cognitive psychology, beginning with Klein's work (1958), investigators described various cognitive styles, consistencies in individuals across more than one cognitive domain (e.g., reflection–impulsivity and leveling–sharpening). In psychoanalytic ego psychology, Shapiro (1965) located several neurotic styles, each of which consisted of certain modes of perception and action, and a certain experience of self. These styles were held to be direct developments of conflict-free ego energies, independent of id or motivational aspects of personality.

REFERENCES

Buss, A. H., & Plomin, R. (1975). *A temperament theory of personality development.* New York: Wiley.

Eysenck, H. J. (1967). *The biological basis of personality.* Springfield, IL: Thomas.

Jung, C. G. (1976/1921). *Psychological types.* Princeton, NJ: Princeton University Press.

Kagan, J. (1971). *Change and continuity in infancy.* New York: Wiley.

Klein, G. (1958). Cognitive control and motivation. In G. Lindzey (Ed.), *Assessment of human motives.* New York: Rinehart.

Neaman, J. S. (1975/1973). *Suggestion of the devil: The origins of madness.* New York: Doubleday.

Shapiro, D. (1965). *Neurotic styles.* New York: Basic Books.

Sheldon, W. H., & Stevens, S. S. (1942). *Varieties of human temperament: A psychology of constitutional differences.* New York: Harper.

Thomas, A., & Chess, S. (1977). *Temperament and development.* New York: Brunner/Mazel.

Witkin, H. A., Dyk, R. B., Faterson, H. F., Goodenough, D. R., & Karp, S. A. (1974/1962). *Psychological differentiation.* Potomac, MD: Erlbaum.

K. J. SHAPIRO
Psychologist for the Ethical Treatment of Animals

HERITABILITY OF PERSONALITY TRAITS
PERSONALITY TYPES

TERMAN, LEWIS MADISON (1877–1956)

Lewis Madison Terman studied at Clark University, and received his doctorate in 1905 under E. C. Sanford. In 1906, he held a position at Los Angeles State Normal School. From 1910 to 1943, he was at Stanford University; for 20 of those years, he served as head of the Psychology Department there.

Terman's major research contribution to American psychology was his work in intelligence testing and his evaluation of gifted persons. He translated and adapted the French Binet–Simon intelligence to American circumstances. He introduced William Stern's mental quotient to measure intelligence, multiplied it by 100, and called it the intelligence quotient, or IQ. The test became known as the *Stanford–Binet Intelligence Scale* because Terman was at Stanford at this time (1916). The test was revised in 1937 and again in 1960. For a long time, the Stanford–Binet was the most widely used individual intelligence test in the English language.

During World War I, he served with other psychologists in the construction of the first group intelligence test. The Army Alpha and the nonverbal Army Beta were used to assign army recruits to training and duties in the military service.

Terman began a longitudinal study of gifted children in 1921 with a sample of 1,500 California children who had intelligence test quotients of 140 or above. Five volumes were published, at intervals of several years, reporting the findings of this unusual study. The last volume of the *Genetic Studies of Genius* was published after Terman's death, and was entitled *The Gifted Group at Mid-Life*, written with M. H. Oden. Terman dispelled the old belief that gifted persons are eccentric, maladjusted, and sickly; he found instead that they are taller, healthier, and physically better developed than average people, and superior to them in leadership and social adaptability.

N. A. HAYNIE

TERRITORIALITY II

Animals of many species occupy specific portions of their habitats from which they exclude other members of the species. A male stickleback fish in breeding condition will defend an area around a nest against intruding males. This is the essence of territoriality. What is remarkable is that an animal that might lose a contest in a neutral area or in the territory of another individual typically will win while in its own territory.

There is disagreement concerning the best way to define territoriality. Classically, a territory is any defended area (e.g., Noble, 1939). Although most researchers accept such a definition, some problems with it concern others. In some species, individuals dominate critical resources without showing any obvious overt defense. Kaufmann (1983) defines a territory as "a fixed portion of an individual's or group's home range in which it has priority of access to one or more critical resources over others which have priority elsewhere or at another time" (p. 9). There are at least two problems with such a definition. First, the emphasis is on the consequences of behavior rather than on the behavior itself. Second, although it is clear that what territorial defense is control over resources critical to reproductive success, definition in relation to control of resources may be counterproductive. If one is both to define and to explain territoriality in relation to resources, there is a severe risk of circularity. Thus it would appear best to use the term *dominion* in situations in which there is privileged access to resources without overt defense and to reserve *territoriality* for situations with overt defense.

Perhaps the most important fact to remember concerning territories is the diverse nature of different patterns grouped together under this one term. Wilson (1975) lists five types. Type A territories are large, defended areas within which animals can mate, court, and gather most of their food. Various species of fishes, lizards, and birds occupy such all-purpose territories. Type B territories also are relatively large and are used for breeding, but the residents go elsewhere to feed. Nightjays and reed warblers occupy such territories. Type C territories are small, defended areas around a nest, as found in many colonial birds. There is room for little more than breeding. Type D territories are pairing or mating territories; animals go to these territories to mate but, in contrast to the first three types, raise their young elsewhere. Birds such as the sage grouse and ungulates such as the Uganda kob form such "leks." Type E territories are the roosting positions or shelters used by many species of bats, starlings, and domestic pigeons.

Thus territories can be seen to vary along several dimensions. They may or may not be used for feeding, mating, or rearing of the young, depending on the species. The number of residents varies from a single male, a mated male–female pair, or a whole group of animals that defend the territory. Most territories relate to a fixed location. An interesting borderline case can be found with bitterlings, small species of fish that lay eggs in the mantle cavities of certain species of mussels and that defend the area around the mussels, even it they move. It is important when trying to generalize from "territory in animals" to similar phenomena in humans that one remembers the diversity of animal territoriality.

One may ask how big a territory animals should defend. In essence, they should find a size that is economically defensible. Enlarging the size of a territory increases the resources to which the animal gains access. Equally important according to some models, it deprives rivals of such resources. However, enlarging a territory entails a cost, as the animal must expend more time and resources in patrolling and defending it. There would seem to be optimal territory sizes that lead to maximal levels of genetic fitness, the production of viable, fertile offspring. This generally is the case. Often, however, animals appear to defend territories larger than they seem to need to provide all of the resources they require. This is generally because the animals are studied in average or good years. What may affect the evolution of an optimal size for a territory is the amount of space needed in bad years, when resources are scarce.

Territorial defense need not always entail overt fighting; song or odors can serve to mark an area as occupied. In a typical experiment on the function of bird song (e.g., Falls, 1988), some males are removed from their territories and replaced with loudspeakers that do or do not continue to emit the songs. Intrusion by conspecifics is delayed when songs are played. In other experiments, devocalized males have difficulty in keeping out intruders. It seems as though males must sing to keep their space.

Territorial defense generally is conceptualized as occurring within species. Thus a male who may defend the territory against a conspecific intruder will ignore members of other species. There are exceptions, however, such as in the territories of reef fishes (see Myrberg & Thresher, 1974). Resident males typically attack intruders of the same species when they reach some distance from the core of the territory. Members of the same genus but of a different species also will be attacked, but only when they approach closer to the core. Members of other genera that use a similar range of resources also may be attacked. The maximum distance of attack may vary with the season and other variables. Thus it sometimes may be useful to view territory size as a dynamic set of concentric circles of attack, rather than as fixed.

The concept of territory often has been applied to humans in a variety of contexts (e.g., Edney, 1974). Members of a nation may defend a border, members of a gang may defend their turf, and suburban homeowners may defend their property. Indeed, Sebba and Churchman (1983) looked within the homesite to view the dwelling unit as composed of segments of space appropriate for use by different individuals or clusters of individuals. In another experiment (Gustavson, Dawson, & Bonnet, 1987), androstenol was shown to be a human odor that functioned to space males. By treating half of the stalls in a public restroom with the chemical, the experimenters found males to avoid marked "territories." Models of economic defensibility in relation to resources have been applied to human populations by anthropologists (e.g., Dyson-Hudson & Smith, 1978).

REFERENCES

Dyson-Hudson, R., & Smith, E. A. (1978). Human territoriality: An ecological reassessment. *American Anthropologist, 80,* 21–41.

Edney, J. J. (1974). Human territoriality. *Psychological Bulletin, 81,* 959–975.

Falls, J. B. (1988). Does song deter territorial intrusion in white-throated sparrows (*Zonotrichia albicollis*)? *Canadian Journal of Zoology, 66,* 206–211.

Gustavson, A. R., Dawson, M. E., & Bonnet, D. G. (1987). Androstenol, a putative human phermone, affects human (*Homo sapiens*) male choice performance. *Journal of Comparative Psychology, 101,* 210–212.

Kaufmann, J. H. (1983). On the definitions and functions of dominance and territoriality. *Biological Reviews, 58,* 1–20.

Myrberg, A. A., Jr., & Thresher, R. E. (1974). Interspecific aggression and its relevance to the concept of territoriality in reef fishes. *American Zoologist, 14,* 81–96.

Nobel, G. K. (1939). The role of dominance in the life of birds. *Auk, 56,* 263–273.

Sebba, R., & Churchman, A. (1983). Territories and territoriality in the home. *Environment and behavior, 15,* 191–210.

Wilson, E. O. (1975). *Sociobiology: The new synthesis.* Cambridge, MA: Harvard University Press.

SUGGESTED READING

Davies, N. B., & Houston, A. I. (1984). Territory economics. In J. R. Krebs & N. B. Davies (Eds.), *Behavioural ecology: An evolutionary approach* (pp. 148–169). Sunderland, MA: Sinauer.

D. A. DEWSBURY
University of Florida

GENETIC DOMINANCE AND RECESSIVENESS
INSTINCT
NATURALISTIC OBSERVATION

TERTIARY PREVENTION

The concept of tertiary prevention arises from the public health preventive services model (Commission on Chronic Illness, 1957; Last, 1992). In this model, preventive services are categorized into primary, secondary, or tertiary interventions. The goal of primary prevention is to decrease the prevalence of disease via reduction in its rate of occurrence. Primary prevention is therefore directed at eliminating etiologic factors, thereby reducing the incidence of the disease or eradicating it entirely (Greenfield & Shore, 1995). A classic example of primary prevention psychiatric is the use of immunization against measles and rubella to eliminate neonatal neurological impairment caused by these diseases. Secondary prevention works to reduce prevalence (a function of both duration and rate of occurrence of the illness) by decreasing the illness's duration through early intervention and effective treatment. Tertiary prevention refers to interventions that aim to reduce the severity, discomfort, or disability associated with a disorder through rehabilitation or through the reduction of the acute and chronic complications of the disorder (Fletcher, Fletcher, & Wagner, 1988; Mrazek & Haggerty, 1994).

Certain interventions may be considered to be either secondary or tertiary prevention. For example, the use of psychotropic medications and psychotherapies may serve at different times as secondary or tertiary preventive measures. Early intervention and use of these as effective treatments can decrease the duration of the illness and may represent secondary prevention. However, in individuals with a chronic relapsing illness, the use of psychotherapy and psychotropic medications to prevent relapse to a symptomatic stage of the illness would constitute tertiary prevention. For example, maintenance antidepressant medication to prevent relapse to a symptomatic stage of mood disorder can be viewed as tertiary prevention. Another example would be the use of group psychotherapy to prevent relapse in currently abstinent individuals with substance use disorders. Other interventions that diminish social impairment or disability among those with chronic conditions also represent tertiary prevention—for example, vocational rehabilitation or social skills training for those with chronic psychotic disorders. Overall, most tertiary preventive interventions for psychiatric disorders fall into the category of maintenance treatments for chronic conditions. Such maintenance interventions include: (a) interventions that are aimed at increasing compliance with long-term treatment and whose goal is to reduce relapse and recurrence; and (b) aftercare treatments, such as rehabilitation, whose goal is to improve social and occupational function (Mrazek & Haggerty, 1994).

EXAMPLES OF TERTIARY PREVENTION

Most examples of tertiary prevention within mental health are found in the maintenance, treatment, and rehabilitation of individuals with chronic mental disorders. Schizophrenia is a chronic psychotic disorder with onset usually in late adolescence and an overall prevalence in the United States of approximately 1%. The combination of relatively high prevalence and early onset imposes a large burden of personal suffering and need for treatment and rehabilitative services, due to the morbidity and chronic disability the disorder engenders. Tertiary preventive interventions are, therefore, quite important in this population in the form of rehabilitation and prevention of relapse (Preventing schizophrenic relapse, 1995). Medication nonadherence may be responsible for 40% of all exacerbations of schizophrenia that result in hospitalization. In addition, the illness generally interferes with a number of areas of functioning.

A number of tertiary preventive interventions have been designed to improve functioning, increase medication adherence, and reduce relapse, and thereby decrease overall disability due to the illness. Comprehensive psychosocial treatments such as those involving Assertive Continuous Care (Stein, 1990) and behavioral rehabilitation (Anthony & Liberman, 1986; Liberman, Falloon, & Wallace, 1984) can improve patients' medication adherence and help with a number of psychosocial aspects of life, including vocational and recreational activities. For example, behavioral rehabilitation uses a multidisciplinary team to provide services that can help increase adherence to medication and provide support and direction in other areas of the patients' lives, including work, family, and social interactions (Kopelowicz & Liberman, 1995).

Depressive disorders are among the most common psychiatric disorders. For example, the prevalence of Major Depressive Disorder at any one time is estimated to be 2 to 4% in the community, 5 to 10% among primary care outpatients, and 10 to 14% among medical inpatients (Katon & Schulberg, 1992). Depressive illness is generally chronic, relapsing, and can have significant social and economic consequences for the affected individual (Montgomery, Green, Baldwin, & Montgomery, 1989). Tertiary prevention of depressive disorders, therefore, usually focuses on decreasing the likelihood of relapse and recurrence. At least 50% of recurrent episodes of depression are preventable by adequate prophylaxis with antidepressant medication (Montgomery et al., 1989). For major depression, antidepressant treatment for a minimum period of 6 to 9 months following the resolution of symptoms is indicated to decrease the risk of recurrence. In addition, a common tertiary preventive intervention for bipolar disorder is maintenance medication with a mood stabilizer with or without an antidepressant to minimize the risk of another manic or depressive episode (Goodwin & Jamison, 1990).

Tertiary prevention of substance use disorders involves relapse prevention and rehabilitation. Considerable evidence suggests that patient involvement in ongoing treatment is helpful in maintaining abstinence, limiting the total duration of relapses, and improving overall long-term outcome (Greenfield & Shore, 1995; McLellan, Luborsky, Woody, O'Brien, & Druley, 1983; O'Malley, Jaffe, & Chang, 1992; Higgins et al., 1994). Programs that help individuals maintain abstinence from substances or limit the duration of relapse are effective tertiary preventions; they include after-care participation such as training in relapse prevention or coping skills; behavioral treatment; involvement in Alcoholics Anonymous; and methadone maintenance (Galanter, & Kleber, 1999).

REFERENCES

Anthony, W. A., & Liberman, R. P. (1986). The practice of psychiatric rehabilitation. *Schizophrenia Bulletin, 12,* 542–559.

Commission on Chronic Illness. *Chronic illness in the United States* (Vol. 1). (Published for the Commonwealth Fund). Cambridge, MA: Harvard University Press.

Fletcher, R. H., Fletcher, S. W., & Wagner, E. H. (1988). *Clinical epidemiology: The essentials* (2nd ed.). Baltimore: Williams & Wilkins.

Galanter, M., & Kleber, H. D., (Eds.). (1999). *Textbook of substance abuse treatment* (2nd ed.). Washington, DC: American Psychiatric Press.

Goodwin, F. K., & Jamison, K. R. (1990). *Manic-depressive illness.* New York: Oxford University Press.

Greenfield, S. F., & Shore, M. F. (1995). Prevention of psychiatric disorders. *Harvard Review of Psychiatry, 3,* 115–129.

Higgins, S. T., Budney, A. J., Bickel, W. K., Foerg, F. E., Donham, R., & Badger, G. J. (1994). Incentives improve outcome in outpatient behavioral treatment of cocaine dependence. *Archives of General Psychiatry, 51,* 568–576.

Katon, W., & Schulberg, H. (1992). Epidemiology of depression in primary care. *General Hospital Psychiatry, 14,* 237–247.

Kopelowicz, A., & Liberman, R. P. (1995). Biobehavioral treatment and rehabilitation of schizophrenia. *Harvard Review of Psychiatry, 3,* 55–64.

Last, J. M. (1992). Scope and methods of prevention. In J. M. Last & R. B. Wallace (Eds.), *Public health and preventive medicine* (pp. 3–10). Norwalk, CT: Appleton & Lange.

Liberman, R. P., Falloon, I. R. H., & Wallace, C. J. (1984). Drug-psychosocial interactions in the treatment of schizophrenia. In M. Mirabi (Ed.), *The chronically mentally ill: Research and services.* New York: SP Medical and Scientific.

McLellan, A. T., Luborsky, L., Woody, G. E., O'Brien, C. P., & Druley, K. A. (1983). Predicting response to alcohol and drug abuse treatments: Role of psychiatric severity. *Archives of General Psychiatry, 40,* 620–625.

Montgomery, S. A., Green, M., Baldwin, D., & Montgomery, D. (1989). Prophylactic treatment of depression: A public health issue. *Neuropsychobiology, 22,* 214–219.

Mrazek, P. J., & Haggerty, R. J. (Eds.). (1994). Reducing risks for mental disorders: Frontiers for preventive intervention research. Washington, DC: National Academy Press.

O'Malley, S. S., Jaffe, A. J., & Chang, G. (1992). Naltrexone and coping skills therapy for alcohol dependence: A controlled study. *Archives of General Psychiatry, 49,* 881–887.

Preventing schizophrenic relapse [Medical news & perspectives]. (1995). *Journal of the American Medical Association, 273,* 6–8.

Stein, L. I. (1990). Comments by Leonard Stein. *Hospital & Community Psychiatry, 41,* 649–651.

S. F. GREENFIELD
McLean Hospital

ALCOHOLISM TREATMENT
COGNITIVE BEHAVIOR THERAPY
DRUG REHABILITATION
PSYCHOPHARMACOLOGY
SOCIAL SKILLS TRAINING

TEST ANXIETY

Test anxiety refers to the psychological, physiological, and behavioral responses to stimuli an individual associates with the experience of testing or evaluation. It is a special case of general anxiety and is characterized by feelings of heightened self-awareness and perceived helplessness that often result in lowered performance on tests or, more generally, on all types of cognitive and academic tasks. Test-anxious individuals see tasks as difficult or threatening, see themselves as inadequate for handling the task, focus on the undesirable consequences of this perceived inadequacy, have strong self-deprecatory views that interfere with the task activity, and anticipate failure and loss of regard.

Test anxiety is usually conceptualized as having two components—worry and emotionality. The worry component involves self-perceptions: concerns about performance, negative self-evaluations, concerns about the consequences of failure, and comparisons of one's ability with that of others. The emotionality component refers to the affective and physiological concomitants resulting from autonomic arousal: the feelings of tension and distress. A related conception, Jeri Wine's (1971) direction of attention hypothesis, suggests that highly test-anxious persons divide their attention between task-relevant and self-referent variables whereas low-test-anxious persons focus more on the task.

Test-taking anxiety is generally measured by self-report inventories that tap both the worry and emotionality dimensions. Numerous studies (see Sarason, 1980; Tryon, 1980; Wine, 1971) indicate that test anxiety is most prevalent on complex tasks and when the situation is viewed as stressful or evaluative and that highly test-anxious persons are more self-preoccupied and self-deprecatory than low-test-anxious persons and that these tendencies are increased in testing situations. There is also evidence that worry is negatively related to performance but that emotionality is not.

Because test anxiety results in lowered test and academic performance, a variety of treatment programs have been developed. These include systematic desensitization, implosion therapy, cognitive refocusing, relaxation training, modeling and observational learning, simulations, study skills training, and instructional adaptations. Although all these methods have been effective in reducing self-reported anxiety, there is less evidence of their effectiveness in increasing test performance. The most promising results for improving performance involve combining cognitive refocusing and/or study skills training with desensitization and relaxation training.

REFERENCES

Sarason, I. G. (Ed.). (1980). *Test anxiety: Theory, research, and applications.* Hillsdale, NJ: Erlbaum.

Tryon, G. S. (1980). The measurement and treatment of test anxiety. *Review of Educational Research, 50,* 343–372.

Winer, B. J. (1971). *Statistical principles in experimental design.* New York: McGraw-Hill.

SUGGESTED READING

Sarason, I. G. (1980). Introduction to the study of test anxiety. In I. G. Sarason (Ed.), *Test anxiety: Theory, research and applications.* Hillsdale, NJ: Erlbaum.

Sieber, J. E. (1980). Defining test anxiety: Problems and approaches. In I. G. Sarason (Ed.), *Test anxiety: Theory, research, and applications.* Hillsdale, NJ: Erlbaum.

Wine, J. D. (1980). Cognitive-attentional theory of test anxiety. In I. G. Sarason (Ed.), *Test anxiety: Theory, research, and applications.* Hillsdale, NJ: Erlbaum.

F. G. BROWN
Iowa State University

ANXIETY
PERFORMANCE APPRAISAL
PERSONALITY ASSESSMENT
STRESS CONSEQUENCES

TEST STANDARDIZATION

The standardization of a test is the establishment of uniform procedures for the administration and scoring of the instrument. If psychological measurement is defined as the use of rules to assign numbers to relative quantities of psychological constructs associated with persons, then test standardization is the determination and explication of those rules. Without standardization, measurement is only an informal process that varies from examiner to examiner. Historical impetus for the concern with control on the part of examiners arose from the 19th-century experimental psychologists from Leipzig, whose work demonstrated that minor variations in giving instructions and making observations resulted in behavioral differences (Anastasi & Urbina, 1997). The first standardized tests appeared in the early part of the 20th century, when experimental psychologist E. L. Thorndike and others extended the principles learned in a laboratory to psychological measurement. Elaboration of the history of standardized testing may be found in Dubois (1970).

The *Standards for Educational and Psychological Testing* (American Educational Research Association, American Psychological Association, & National Council on Measurement in Education, 1999) provides an outline of procedures that test publishers and test users are urged to follow to insure proper implementation of standardization procedures. Control of test administration procedures is accomplished largely by instructions specified in test manuals. For example, test authors must develop test manuals that clearly describe: (a) those test administration directions under which norming, reliability, and validity data were gathered, and (b) scoring directions so that the possibility of scoring errors is reduced to a minimum. Regarding directions for test administrators, such matters as time limits, procedures for marking answer sheets and scoring tests, and instructions for guessing must be provided in the test manual. Those conditions under which elaboration of typical test instructions may be given should be specified. It is also helpful for test administrators to be informed as to how to deal with questions from test takers. Detailed consideration of these and other aspects of test administration (mostly for tests administered in group settings) are provided by Clemens (1971). Regarding procedures for scoring test responses, the *Standards for Educational and Psychological Testing* specify that it is desirable that detailed instructions for scoring both subjective and objective tests be furnished in the test manual, and, in the case of subjectively graded tests, research as to the extent of agreement among scorers should be enumerated. This research should differentiate the extent of inter-scorer reliability by levels of scorer training, if possible. Standardization should also provide detailed information as to who is qualified to administer and score the test in question. Test users are expected to follow carefully the standardized procedures as described in the manual when administering a test, and, given these procedures, to enable all test takers to perform to their best. An example of this latter point would be keeping favorable environmental conditions for testing, consistent again with standardization procedures. Test users are further charged with meticulously checking all details of test scoring for accuracy.

A final aspect of test standardization is the development of test norms. To establish norms, a test constructor should administer the test under standardized conditions to a large, representative sample (representative in the sense that it resembles the persons for whom the test is intended). The data that result from this experimental testing allow the test constructor to identify the norm or typical behavior (e.g., the 50th percentile) as well as all other percentiles. These values, in conjunction with reliability and validity information, permit psychologists and other professional test users to interpret test scores properly.

Three potential advantages of standardized psychological tests are evident. First, standardized tests are frequently of higher quality than are locally constructed tests. Because these tests may be employed by a large number of client-users, much more expense and professional time can be spent at all stages of the test construction process (e.g., preparing test outlines, editing items, item analysis, test revision, etc.). Second, using standardized examinations may free psychologists and other professionals from spending time on test construction, test administration, and other evaluative activities, and permit them to employ time on more important matters—therapy, instruction, and score interpretation, for example (Nunnally, 1978). Lastly, the use of standardized measures facilitates communication among psychologists. Scores on tests administered under proper conditions are able to communicate information about individuals, groups, and scientific findings quite effectively to other psychologists. One important disadvantage of standardized measures should be noted: Due to their availability, specific standardized tests may be used when they are inappropriate. For example, a standardized selection test for industry might be used in a situation in which it has been neither intended nor validated. Similarly, a local school program with goals unique to that institution could not be effectively evaluated with a nationally-standardized test with its implicitly broad-based orientation.

The term "standardized tests" is sometimes applied to those tests that merely are extensively (e.g., nationally) normed. However, norms generally are useful only when they relate to test scores achieved under uniform conditions. In fact, before the norming of a test can begin, the detailed conditions of standardization must be finalized and described for examiners. Tests that are administered under conditions differing from those for which the test is intended will yield scores that are difficult to interpret.

One special case of interpretation of scores for tests that in many cases must be administered under non-standardized conditions is that for individuals with disabilities. The Americans with Disabilities Act (1990) requires that tests be administered with appropriately accommodated administrations. The fact that such groups of test takers are small makes validation and interpretation somewhat more difficult (Geisinger, 1994; Sandoval et al., 1998), but early validation efforts with nationally-standardized college admissions measures appear promising (Willingham et al., 1988).

REFERENCES

American Educational Research Association, American Psychological Association, & National Council on Measurement in Education. (1999). *Standards for educational and psychological testing.* Washington, DC: American Educational Research Association.

Americans with Disabilities Act of 1990. 42 U.S.C. § 12101 et seq. (1990).

Anastasi, A., & Urbina, S. (1997). *Psychological Testing* (7th ed.). Upper Saddle River, NJ: Prentice Hall.

Clemens, W. C. (1971). Test administration. In R. L. Thorndike (Ed.), *Educational measurement* (2nd ed., pp. 188–201). Washington, DC: American Council on Education.

DuBois, P. H. (1970). *A history of psychological testing.* Boston: Allyn & Bacon.

Geisinger, K. F. (1994). Psychometric issues in testing students with disabilities. *Applied Measurement in Education, 7,* 121–140.

Nunnally, J. C. (1978). *Psychometric theory.* (2nd ed.). New York: McGraw-Hill.

Sandoval, J., Frisby, C. L., Geisinger, K. F., Scheunemann, J. D., & Grenier, J. R. (Eds.). (1998). *Test interpretation and diversity.* Washington, DC: American Psychological Association.

Willingham, W. W., Ragosta, M., Bennett, R. E., Braun, H., Rock, D. A., & Powers, D. E. (1988). *Testing handicapped people.* Boston: Allyn & Bacon.

K. F. GEISINGER
LeMoyne College

MEASUREMENT

TESTING METHODS

Psychological tests have been developed for such a wide variety of purposes that their methods vary greatly from test to test. A number of continua exist along which individual tests can be classified.

Tests can measure maximum performance (the best one can do) or typical performance (how one generally performs). For example, an ability test generally measures maximum performance, while a personality test generally measures typical performance. Maximum performance tests have correct or incorrect answers; typical performance tests tend to assess stylistic differences, without specific answers that are uniformly better than others.

Maximum performance tests can be classified into two broad categories: ability tests and achievement tests. Pure ability tests measure what a person is capable of doing and generally present problems with which the person is unlikely to have had direct experience. Pure achievement tests assess the amount of information the person has learned from previous experiences. For example, an archeology student may be asked to classify a new artifact that is unlike any he or she has seen before (an ability test), or to classify artifacts to which he or she has previously been exposed (an achievement test). The distinction is not always clear, since ability tests generally involve making use of previously learned principles. Much of the controversy concerning test bias in ability tests revolves around the issue of whether all potential test takers have been equally exposed to these prerequisite skills.

Ability and achievement tests can be further classified along a speed versus power continuum. Pure speed tests contain questions that are easy to answer correctly, but that must be completed quickly—for example, a clerical speed test may measure how quickly a set of names can be alphabetized or copied. Power tests contain items, usually graded in difficulty, that assess maximum performance without pressure to work quickly. An untimed course examination generally would be a power test. Most maximum performance tests are neither purely speed nor purely power tests, but contain elements of both. For example, typical tests have items of graded difficulty (like a power test), but are administered with strict time limits (like a speed test). If virtually all subjects are given enough time to attempt to answer all problems they are capable of solving, the test primarily is a power test. However, if subjects do not have time to complete all the items they could have answered correctly, the test has a larger speed component.

Another distinction is between performance and nonperformance tests. Performance tests generally require overt, active responses, such as motor or manual behavior, while nonperformance tests generally involve written verbal responses to questions. A performance test for farming ability might include assessing skills at driving tractors and operating other agricultural equipment, whereas a nonperformance test might ask people to identify pictured tractor parts or give the best dates for planting certain crops.

Personality tests tend to be of two major types: objective and projective. Objective personality tests, such as the Minnesota Multiphasic Personality Inventory (MMPI), generally ask true/false or multiple-choice questions that are objectively scored. These items frequently are grouped into scales that measure different aspects of personality; for example, the Eysenck Personality Inventory measures neuroticism and introversion. Although the scores are objectively obtained, the integration of the pattern of scores to describe the whole person generally requires subjective judgments. Computer profile analyses of some tests, such as the MMPI, involve objective criteria, but such analyses should be assessed subjectively by the trained professional. Projective tests involve ambiguous stimuli that the subject must interpret, presumably by projecting aspects of his or her own personality into the interpretation. Classic projective tests are the Rorschach Inkblot Test and the Thematic Apperception Test (TAT). Administering and scoring projective tests require extensive professional training.

Tests can be designed to be administered to individuals or to groups of people. Individually administered tests, such as the Wechsler intelligence tests, require more use of the administrator's time, and thus are more expensive to use. Group-administered tests, such as the Scholastic Aptitude Test (SAT), are less expensive to administer, but generally do not allow the test administrator to analyze an individual's test-taking attitude or strategy or to query about specific responses to seek additional, clarifying information.

Three major approaches to score interpretation involve norm-referenced, criterion-referenced, and ipsative scoring. Norm-referenced scoring occurs most often and involves comparing a person's score with the scores of a norm group. For example, a student's score on the SAT would be compared with the scores of other students who took the exam to see how well that student preformed relative to how others did. Criterion-referenced scoring relates an individual's performance to absolute standards or criteria. Criterion-referenced testing is most commonly used by educators; for example, specific mathematical skills are defined and a test is used to evaluate whether students have mastered these skills. Ipsative scoring involves comparing an individual's scores with each other. For example, the Edwards Personal Preference Schedule measures 15 needs. Relative scores on the need scales are evaluated; for example, an individual's need to achieve may be higher than his or her need to nurture.

A wide variety of psychological testing methods are available. The professional test user is trained to evaluate which type of test would be most useful for specific purposes.

SUGGESTED READING

Anastasi, A., & Urbina, S. (1997). *Psychological testing* (7th ed.). Upper Saddle River, NJ: Prentice Hall.

Kaplan, R. M., & Saccuzzo, D. P. (1997). *Psychological testing* (4th ed.). Pacific Grove, CA: Brooks/Cole.

M. J. ALLEN
California State University, Bakersfield

CLINICAL ASSESSMENT
PERFORMANCE TESTS
PERSONALITY ASSESSMENT
PSYCHOLOGICAL ASSESSMENT
PSYCHOMETRICS

T-GROUPS

The T-Group or Training Group emerged in the summer of 1946 as the result of a serendipitous event in a workshop for intergroup relations being conducted by the State Interracial Commission and the Research Center for Group Dynamics at the Massachusetts Institute of Technology (M.I.T.). Kurt Lewin headed an action-research team with three trainers, Leland Bradford, Kenneth Benne, and Ronald Lippitt, and four graduate student researchers. The Connecticut cosponsors were Frank Simpson (state director), Frank McGuire, and Seigmar Blamberg. The workshop was organized into three clusters of community teams led by the three trainers, with a research observer in each group. In the evening, Lewin convened the staff to analyze and conceptualize the data from the workshop sessions of that day. On the second evening, three women participants asked if they could sit in on the meeting. In his German-English, Lewin said "Yah, please sit down."

Soon a group event was being reported that had involved one of the women. The trainer and researcher gave their observations and the participant protested that she had seen it quite differently. Lewin was excited about the new data. When the women asked if they could attend the next session, Lewin was enthusiastic in his positive response. Nearly all 50 of the participants were there the next night, and every night for the rest of the workshop. These analyses of the process of the day clearly had a major effect on the work of the next day. The level of communication and collaboration seemed to be greatly improved. At the end of the workshop, in a debriefing session, the four workshop leaders decided that the procedure of using the group process as the agenda for group study of its own development and action taking was an important discovery that needed much more study and development. As a result, the following summer the Adult Education Division of the National Education Association (Bradford was the director) and the Research Center for Group Dynamics at M.I.T. cosponsored an action research laboratory at Gould Academy, Bethel, Maine, to develop the concept systematically. A multiprofessional population of 67 people participated in the three-week event with over 20 researchers who were studying individual and group dynamics and the development of the laboratory culture. The study groups were called BST (basic skill training) groups, later shortened to T-groups. To facilitate the study process, each group, in addition to a leader/trainer, had two observers—a research observer reporting to the research director, and a group feedback observer reporting to the group. The interdisciplinary staff came from social psychology, social work, psychiatry, clinical psychology, sociology, and adult education backgrounds.

The developers made a clear distinction between group therapy with its focus on intrapersonal dynamics and the T-group with its focus on the study of group development, leadership–membership dynamics, and the processes of interpersonal interaction.

During the 1950s, practitioners from several different professional disciplines worked on the staff of the National Training Laboratory at Bethel, and began to make adaptations of the T-group to their own disciplines. Those with a clinical, person-centered focus developed the "encounter group," with special interest in the impact on personal development as a result of involvement in intensive group interaction and interpersonal peer feedback, facilitated by a professional trainer.

Other practitioners were interested in the small face-to-face work groups as a crucial unit in organizational productivity. A variety of experiments attempted to adapt the T-group process to working with intact work groups (as contrasted to the Bethel "stranger groups"). New issues of resistance and credibility emerged that had not been encountered in the "cultural island" of not-playing-for-keeps groups at Bethel. There were some dramatic successes and some painful failures.

During this period, Misumi and several Japanese colleagues spent a period studying group dynamics with Lewin and his team and returned to Japan to start a program of study of group dynamics. These developments, along with the interest in quality control, have merged in the development of quality circle groups in many Japanese companies. Some of the practitioners from social work and community development explored the application of the T-group methodology to the development of citizen action groups where the focus was on the development of group effectiveness in taking action.

During the 1960s and 1970s, the personal growth movement sought adaptations of the T-group for the purpose of self-exploration, of freeing individuals from blockages in personal and interpersonal functioning. These developments departed rather completely from the original T-group focus on the study of group and interpersonal dynamics. In the decade of the 1980s, there is a renewal of interest in Lewin's notion that the small face-to-face group is the critical linkage between the large system and the person. With the increased concern about quality of work life as it relates to both productivity and mental health, there is growing evidence that the face-to-face support group is the basic interface between system and person, and the skills and values facilitated by T-group experience seem to have a new importance.

SUGGESTED READING

Benne, K. D. (1964). History of the T-Group in the laboratory setting. In L. P. Bradford, J. R. Gibb, & K. Benne (Eds.), *T-Group theory and laboratory method.* New York: Wiley.

R. LIPPITT

ASSERTIVENESS TRAINING
GROUP DYNAMICS
GROUP PSYCHOTHERAPY

THANATOLOGY

Throughout human history, the idea of death has posed the eternal mystery at the core of many religious and philosophical systems. Yet, except for a few sporadic forays (e.g., G. S. Hall, W. James), the place of death in psychology was practically *terra incognita,* even an off-limits enterprise, until the mid-twentieth century.

Probably a major reason for psychology's inordinate delay in coming to grips with such a universal concern was its need to raise its flag independently of philosophy and ethics. Scientific respectability meant occupying oneself with measurable stimuli and repeatable and public responses. A consequence was restraint in scrutinizing consciousness and neglect of personality. The assault of World War II and the ensuing press of urgent social problems, however, forced psychology to look beyond its traditional positivism. The view that a vital psychology must be rooted in human beings, not in a mathematical physics model, became more insistent. Reinforcing this development in animating consciousness concerning death was progress in medical technology that refocused attention on the manner of dying.

Psychology's first organized approach to death was the 1959 book *The Meaning of Death,* edited by Herman Feifel. Ensuing years witnessed a burst of books dealing with death, two of which deserve special mention in forwarding the death awareness movement. One is the *Psychology of Death* by Robert Kastenbaum and Ruth Aisenberg (1972), the first endeavor to integrate scientific knowledge in the death field. The second is *On Death and Dying* (1969) by Elisabeth Kübler-Ross, which aroused much concern for the situation of the dying person.

The 1960s saw the introduction of numerous workshops and courses on dying, death, and mourning in various universities and medical schools throughout the United States. A prime mover in this early death education development was Daniel Leviton (1969). The year 1969 also saw the establishment of the first university centers devoted to the study of death, dying, and lethal behavior. One was spearheaded by Robert Kastenbaum at Wayne State University, and another by Robert Fulton at the University of Minnesota. Three major journals also came into existence: *OMEGA—Journal of Death and Dying* (1969), *Death Education: An International Quarterly* (1977), and the *Journal of Thanatology* (1973).

Many scientific and professional associations are devoted specifically to issues of thanatology. Among the more prominent are the International Work Group on Death, Dying, and Bereavement, the Forum for Death Education and Counseling, and the Foundation for Thanatology. Bolstering these groups are various self-help and lay groups, such as, Make Today Count, for the terminally ill and their families, started in 1973 by Orville Kelly, himself a victim of cancer; the Society of Compassionate Friends (1969), for bereaved parents; and widow-to-widow programs sparked by Phyllis Silverman (1969).

EMPIRICAL AND CLINICAL FINDINGS

A major realization is that the psychological influence of death is not restricted to the dying, elderly, suicidal, or combat soldier. Young children distinguish between "being" and "nonbeing." Protecting children by shielding them from the realities of death hinders their emotional growth (Anthony, 1940; Wahl, 1958). At the other end of the chronological continuum, many older persons want to share thoughts and feelings about dying and death but are frequently restrained from doing so by society's general reluctance to examine death. A net result is that many elderly persons turn to regressive and inappropriate patterns of conduct in dealing with death. Although the meaning of death can change with maturation and life experiences, the theme remains a seminal one throughout life (Kalish, 1976; Kastenbaum, 1977).

Death possesses many meanings for people. Fear of death is also far from being a unitary or monolithic variable. Various subcomponents are evident—fear of going to hell, fear of the unknown, loss of identity, and the pain inflicted on survivors. Further, significant discrepancies exist in many persons between their conscious and unconscious fear of death. Limited fear of death on a conscious verbal level appears linked with one of ambivalence at a fantasy or imagery level, and with outright aversion at a nonconscious level. This counterbalance of coexisting avoidance—acceptance of personal death seems to serve powerful adaptational needs. In the face of death, the human mind ostensibly operates simultaneously on various levels of reality or finite provinces of meaning, each of which can be somewhat autonomous (Feifel & Branscomb, 1973). Members of the helping professions consequently need to be circumspect in accepting at face value the degree of fear affirmed by persons on a conscious level. Apprehensiveness and concerns about dying and death themselves can assume dissembling guises and gain expression in such symptoms as insomnia and depressed mood, and in sundry psychosomatic and emotional disturbances (Gillespie, 1963; Searles, 1961).

A host of other variables has been examined as possible correlates and contributors to attitudes about death, for example, age, sex, lifestyle, coping strategies, personality, religiosity, emotional health, indulgence in life-threatening behaviors, need for achievement, creativity, ethnic background, and timely and untimely death (Feifel & Nagy, 1980; Goodman, 1981; Kastenbaum & Costa, 1977; Schulz, 1978). There has also been exploration of such features as the "will to live," voodoo death, out-of-body and near-death experiences, and the learned helplessness syndrome as they bear upon the meaning of death (Cannon, 1942; Kastenbaum & Costa, 1977; Moody, 1975; Richter, 1959; Ring, 1980; Seligman, 1975; Weisman & Hackett, 1961). Knowledge of the specific bonds and interactive contributions of many of these variables to the meaning of death is still not available in organized fashion because of methodological complexities. In fact, the very definition of death itself is being subjected to reinterpretation and revision (Bernat et al., 1982; Schulz, 1978; Towers, 1982).

TREATMENT OF THE DYING PERSON

As a consequence of medical advances, prolongation of the dying process is aggravating the problem of personal dignity and control. Too often, germ orientation and the diseased organ are the center of gravity rather than the person. Both clinical and empirical findings, however, underline that dying is not just a biological process, but a psychosocial process as well. The essential communication of dying patients is for open and honest dialog with caregiver and family, and the need for confirmation of care and concern. When this is responded to, untapped potentials for responsible and effective behavior become conspicuous (Feifel, 1977; Feigenberg, 1980; Kübler-Ross, 1969; Le Shan, 1969).

An influential five "stages of dying" model has been presented by Kübler-Ross: denial and isolation, anger, bargaining, depression, and acceptance. The model has proved helpful as a lead in understanding the dying experience. Incoming data, however, do not support these stages as inevitable hoops through which most dying patients pass. Stages have been found to coexist, be reversed, or even omitted (Kastenbaum & Costa, 1977; Schulz & Aderman, 1974).

A frequent drawback in treatment of the dying person is that many professionals lose interest and transfer their motivation and resources elsewhere when efforts to forestall the dying process fail. A major response to this state of affairs has been the emergence of the hospice movement (a name derived from the Middle Ages institution that welcomed passing pilgrims who were weary, hungry, and sometimes ill). It has focused on the problem of chronic pain, regard for the quality of life, and inclusion of the patient's family in the treatment process (Saunders, 1977). Critics of hospice claim that its continuing separate and autonomous development may add to fragmentation, overspecialization, and discontinuity in medical care.

New alternatives now available as a result of increasing medical expertise (organ transplantation, brain death survival, genetic engineering, hemodialysis) have heightened awareness that economic, legal, and ethical, as well as medical and psychological, aspects are inherent in dealing with the dying experience. This has been accompanied by a surging interest in such issues as living wills, informed consent, and euthanasia (Veatch, 1976).

GRIEF

Expression of grief is not a sign of weakness or self-indulgence. Rather, it reflects a necessary, deep, and human need that normal persons have. The funeral and ritual involved in mourning are important because they underscore the reality of death (acceptance of which is crucial to the grieving process), bring support and the warmth of other human beings when needed, and provide a transitional bridge to the new circumstances brought about by the death of someone close.

It is frequently difficult to distinguish between appropriate normal grief and abnormal bereavement. Abnormal bereavement lacks precise criteria as a clinical entity. Clinicians suggest that it usually reveals itself in a number of ways, such as morbid preoccupation with worthlessness, prolonged and marked functional impairment, delay or arrest of mourning, exaggeration of symptoms, and deviant behavior that violates conventional expectations or jeopardizes the health and safety of self and others (Parkes, 1972; Weisman, 1975).

METHODOLOGICAL CONSIDERATIONS

Inconsistent findings reported in the death literature reflect the use of differing populations, ages, assessment devices, "conditions under which," and failure to appreciate fully the complex and multifaceted nature of attitudes toward death. Some pitfalls, already alluded to, are nonconsideration of the multimeanings that death possesses for people and perception of fear of death as a homogeneous variable. Another shortcoming has been neglect of the discrepancies that exist in individuals between conscious and nonconscious levels of death anxiety. Analysis of these incongruities may prove more instructive than merely noting the presence or degree of death concern (Feifel & Nagy, 1981; Kastenbaum & Costa, 1977; Schulz, 1978).

Experimental manipulation of variables has been sparse. Case-based offerings continue to be informative in identifying phenomena and in suggesting leads for theory and practice. Nevertheless, although intricacies of human response to death-related situations are often well illustrated by clinical observations, these do not, *per se,* provide a robust foundation for empirical generalizations.

At this stage of development, major desiderata for the field are longitudinal studies, cross-validation and reliability analyses of prevailing procedures, more astute incorporation of multilevel aspects, extended examination of functional and behavioral correlates of attitudes toward death, alertness to sociocultural context, and the conversion of major assumptions about death-related cognitions, feelings, and coping styles into operationalized empirical inquiry. Most pertinent, perhaps, is the need to integrate the clinician's esteem for individuality and complexity with the researcher's demand for precise and ample documentation.

PSYCHOLOGICAL MANDATE

Perspectives about death can enlarge understanding of such self-destructive and antisocial behaviors as alcoholism, drug abuse, suicide, and violence, which involve confrontation in one way or another with the threat of possible injury or ultimate death to self and others. Notions about death are additionally contained in such pressing social issues as abortion, capital punishment, and mercy killing. They also weave through our reactions to events of crisis and disaster, and contribute to the absurd and irrational so marked in the moral temper of our times. All of these can be illumined by a more comprehensive theory of death.

Death has many faces and images that vary in differing cultures and eras. It is plainly too intricate to be the special province of any one discipline. Psychology's contributions, nevertheless, have been responsible for enlarging and deepening our understanding of how death can serve life.

REFERENCES

Anthony, S. (1940). *The child's discovery of death: A study in child psychology.* New York: Harcourt, Brace, & World.

Bernat, J. L., Culver, C. M., & Gert, B. (1982). Defining death in theory and practice. *The Hastings Center Report, 12,* 5–9.

Cannon, W. B. (1942). Voodoo death. *American Anthropologist, 44,* 169–181.

Feifel, H. (1977/1959). *New meanings of death.* New York: McGraw-Hill.

Feifel, H., & Nagy, V. T. (1980). Death orientation and life-threatening behavior. *Journal of Abnormal Psychology, 89,* 38–45.

Feifel, H., & Nagy, V. T. (1981). Another look at fear of death. *Journal of Consulting and Clinical Psychology, 49,* 278–286.

Feigenberg, L. (1980). *Terminal care: Friendship contracts with dying cancer patients.* New York: Brunner/Mazel.

Gillespie, W. H. (1963). Some regressive phenomena in old age. *British Journal of Medical Psychology, 3,* 203–209.

Goodman, L. M. (1981). *Death and the creative life: Conversations with prominent artists and scientists.* New York: Springer.

Kalish, R. A. (1976). Death and dying in a social context. In R. H. Binstock & E. Shanas (Eds.), *Handbook of aging and the social sciences.* New York: Van Nostrand Reinhold.

Kastenbaum, R. (1977). Death and development through the life span. In H. Feifel (Ed.), *New meanings of death.* New York: McGraw-Hill.

Kastenbaum, R., & Aisenberg, R. (1972). *The psychology of death.* New York: Springer.

Kastenbaum, R., & Costa, P. T. (1977). Psychological perspectives on death. *Annual Review of Psychology, 28,* 225–249.

Kübler-Ross, E. (1969). *On death and dying.* New York: Macmillan.

Le Shan, L. (1969). Psychotherapy and the dying patient. In L. Pearson (Ed.), *Death and dying: Current issues in the treatment of the dying person.* Cleveland, OH: The Press of Case Western Reserve University.

Leviton, D. (1969). The need for education on death and suicide. *Journal of School Health, 39,* 270–274.

Moody, R. A., Jr. (1975). *Life after life.* Atlanta, GA: Mockingbird Books.

Parkes, C. M. (1972). *Bereavement: Studies of grief in adult life.* New York: International Universities Press.

Richter, C. P. (1959). The phenomenon of unexplained sudden death in animals and man. In H. Feifel (Ed.), *The meaning of death.* New York: McGraw-Hill.

Ring, K. (1980). *Life at death: A scientific investigation of the near-death experience.* New York: Coward, McCann & Geoghegan.

Saunders, C. (1977). Dying they live: St. Christopher's Hospice. In H. Feifel (Ed.), *New meanings of death.* New York: McGraw-Hill.

Schulz, R. (1978). *The psychology of death, dying and bereavement.* Reading, MA: Addison-Wesley.

Schulz, R., & Aderman, D. (1974). Clinical research and the stages of dying. *Omega, 5,* 137–143.

Searies, H. (1961). Schizophrenia and the inevitability of death. *Psychiatric Quarterly, 35,* 634–665.

Seligman, M. E. P. (1975). *Helplessness: On depression, development, and death.* San Francisco: Freeman.

Silverman, P. R. (1969). The widow-to-widow program: An experiment in preventive intervention. *Mental Hygiene, 53,* 333–337.

Towers, B. (1982). Changing concepts of death: Clinical care. *Death Education, 6,* 125–135.

Veatch, R. M. (1976). *Death, dying and the biological revolution: Our last quest for responsibility.* New Haven, CT: Yale University Press.

Wahl, C. W. (1958). The fear of death. *Bulletin of the Menninger Clinic, 22,* 214–223.

Weisman, A. D. (1975). Thanatology. In A. M. Friedman, H. J. Kaplan, & B. J. Sadock (Eds.), *Comprehensive textbook of psychiatry/II* (2nd Ed.). Baltimore: Williams & Wilkins.

Weisman, A. D., & Hackett, T. P. (1961). Predilection to death: Death and dying as a psychiatric problem. *Psychosomatic Medicine, 23,* 232–256.

SUGGESTED READING

Fulton, R. (1977). Death, grief and bereavement: A bibliography, 1845–1975. New York: Arno Press.

Pine, V. R. (1977). A socio-historical portrait of death education. *Death Education, 1,* 57–84.

Simpson, M. A. (1979). *Dying, death, and grief: A critically annotated bibliography and source book of thanatology and terminal care.* New York: Plenum.

H. FEIFEL
Veterans Administration Outpatient Clinic, Los Angeles

SUICIDE

THEMATIC APPERCEPTION TEST (TAT)

The thematic apperception test (TAT), originally designed by Morgan and Murray (1935), was formally published by Murray in 1943. It consists of 30 pictures, most of which depict single individuals or two or more persons in ambiguous social interactions. Different combinations of 20 pictures each (selected for age and sex from the total 30) are recommended for use with men, women, boys, and girls. The instructions stress imaginative fantasy by asking the subject to create dramatic stories about the picture. The subject is asked: (a) What has led up to the situation in the picture? (b) What is happening now? Describe the feelings and thoughts of the characters. (c) What will the outcome be?

The TAT was devised at the Harvard Psychological Clinic as part of a long-term intensive study of 51 men of college age. Along with extensive interviews, autobiographies, and data on childhood memories and sexual development, it was one of many tests used as exploratory procedures to construct working hypotheses about each subject's personality, to be verified by all the other data obtained. To guide this research, Murray (1938) proposed a theory of personality dynamics strongly influenced by psychoanalytic thinking as well as by the theories of William McDougall and Kurt Lewin.

This account of the TAT focuses upon Murray's type of analysis and interpretation based upon the theoretical assumptions of Murray and his students and colleagues at Harvard (e.g., Tomkins, Bellak, Lindzey, Holt, and White).

Murray proposed a descriptive method of content analysis. The stories were analyzed in terms of motivational forces from within the individual (called *need*) and forces from the environment (called *press*). The combining of the press, need, and outcome of the story defined a *thema* (e.g., mother died—son is mourning—he commits suicide). The themas for the significant stories provided the main basis of interpretation.

The following propositions originally described by Murray in 1951 are still accepted by most clinicians:

1. The TAT is a method for revealing to the trained interpreter the dominant drives, emotions, complexes, and conflicts of a personality.

2. The story teller will tend to identify with the principal character (usually a person resembling the subject in sex and age) and will project his or her own perceptions, motives, feelings, and thoughts onto the hero or heroine of the imaginative story. The outcome of the hero or heroine's endeavors is also likely to reveal his or her general competence and adequacy in meeting stress.

3. In describing the other major persons in the pictures and the hero or heroine's interactions with them, the story teller is likely to disclose his or her perceptions and feelings toward significant others (e.g., parental figures, siblings, rivals, loved ones).

4. Since only a fraction of the total material collected reveals significant constituents of the story teller's personality, Murray proposed the following five criteria for determining which thema are really significant enough to be given weight in the final interpretation:

(a) Repetition.

(b) Uniqueness.

(c) Self-involvement.

(d) Symbolic significance.

(e) Interrelatedness (a thema dynamically consistent with thema already judged significant by the criteria listed earlier).

Murray's propositions place heavy demands upon the interpreter of the TAT, who must in addition face the question of what level of the personality is revealed by each significant thema. Does it reveal the unconscious, preconscious, or conscious level? Although Murray believed that all three levels influence the content of a story, his focus of interest was in discovering the latent thema. In the *TAT Manual* he stated that the special value of the TAT resides in its power to expose the underlying inhibited tendencies that the subject "is not willing to admit, or cannot admit because he is unconscious of them."

Allport (1953) disagreed sharply with Murray. He thought that in a TAT situation the normal subject, through conscious control, can outwit the examiner by omitting disturbing material and naked unconscious content. He admitted that the neurotic subject is less able to do so. Murstein (1961) presents research evidence that favors Allport's position, as does the research of Fiester and colleagues (1972). From the evidence, then, the extent to which the TAT reveals latent thema depends upon a number of variables: the type of subject, the type of motive, and the conditions under which the test is administered.

The clinician must also face still another difficult question. Do the TAT thema predict the actual, overt public behavior of the story teller? Murray believed that the fantasy material is more apt to be related by contrast to public conduct because of the defense systems built to guard against the overt expression of unconscious impulses. The extent of the distortion by defenses depends on the degree to which the expression of a motive is restricted by cultural sanctions. As evidence, Murray reports in the *TAT Manual* that for male subjects dominance showed a positive correlation between fantasy and action, sex a negative one, and achievement a zero correlation.

From Murray's theory one would also expect the relation between fantasy and action to vary depending upon whether conflict or congruence exists between different aspects of the personality. This point is supported by Purcell (1956), who found a direct relation between the amount of aggression expressed in TAT stories and overt antisocial behavior only in the case of those subjects who also expressed no conflicting guilt or remorse in their aggressive stories. Thus, in an expression—inhibition conflict, the strength of both forces must be taken into account to predict overt behavior. Olwens (1979) also supports this point. Olwens obtained correlations of +0.55 or –0.50 between aggressive fantasy and overt aggression depending upon the strength of the inhibitory forces.

From a psychometric point of view, the TAT has many weaknesses. First, no standardized method of administration is used since the clinician is encouraged to feel free to modify the instructions to facilitate similar understanding of the task by subjects varying in age and type. Second, few examiners use all 20 of the standard pictures, and some even substitute some favorite pictures of their own choice. Third, no standard objective method of scoring is used although several have been devised by the Harvard group and others. Moreover, since objective norms for determining the uniqueness of a given story are not available for different types of groups, clinicians depend on their own subjective norms based upon experience.

The validity of the TAT has also been questioned. The type of validity most relevant to the TAT is labeled construct validity. Construct validity for the TAT means consistency with data from other sources and predictable psychodynamic congruence of the data from all sources. This is what Murray meant by his criterion of interrelatedness. He predicted an association between TAT thema and other depth material obtained from the case histories, interviews, dreams, and free associations of the story tellers. Examples of this type of validation in the Murray tradition are found in the individual case studies published by White in *Lives in Progress* and Holt in *Assessing Personality*.

Despite its weaknesses, the TAT has had considerable heuristic value. It has stimulated a tremendous amount of clinical and experimental research, especially in the following areas (summarized by Murstein, 1965):

1. Attempts to prove or disprove Murray's original assumptions.

2. Attempts to provide reliable methods for scoring the stories and obtaining norms for the Murray pictures.

3. Reliable quantitative measurement of the strength of particular motives, especially achievement, affiliation, and power by David McClelland and his colleagues, reported in *The Achieving Society* and "Love and power: The psychological signals of war."

4. The creation of other projective offspring based upon the TAT concept such as Bellak's Children's Apperception Test, Thompson's TAT, Symond's Picture-Story Test, and Blum's Blacky Pictures.

5. Cross-cultural research to compare the motivational pattern of diverse cultural groups surveyed by Gardner Lindzey in *Projective Techniques and Cross-Cultural Research.*

The sheer quantity and quality of the research on the TAT, using a wide variety of groups of all ages, colors, and cultures and with a broad variety of applications, mark the TAT as a highly useful contribution to the study of human motivation and personality.

REFERENCES

Allport, G. W. (1953). The trend in motivational theory. *The American Journal of Orthopsychiatry, 23,* 107–119.

Fiester, S., & Süpola, E. (1972). Effects of time pressure on the management of aggression in TAT stories. *Journal of Personality Assessment, 36,* 230–240.

Holt, R. R. (1969). *Assessing personality.* New York: Harcourt Brace Jovanovich, 1971. Also in I. L. Janis, G. F. Mahl, J. Kagan, & R. R. Holt, *Personality: Dynamics, development, and assessment* (Part 4). New York: Harcourt, Brace & World.

Morgan, C. D., & Murray, H. A. (1935). A method for investigating fantasies: The Thematic Apperception Test. *Archives of Neurology and Psychiatry, 34,* 289–306.

Murray, H. A. (1938). *Explorations in personality: A clinical and experimental study of fifty men of college age.* New York: Oxford.

Murray, H. A. (1943). *Thematic Apperception Test manual.* Cambridge, MA: Harvard University Press.

Murray, H. A. (1951). Foreword. In E. S. Shneidman (Ed.), *Thematic test analysis.* New York: Grune & Stratton.

Murray, H. A. (1951). Uses of the Thematic Apperception Test. *The American Journal of Psychiatry, 10,* 577–581.

Murstein, B. I. (1961). Assumptions, adaptation-level and projective techniques. *Perceptual and Motor Skills, 12,* 107–125.

Murstein, B. I. (1965). *Theory and research in projective techniques (Emphasizing the TAT).* New York: Wiley.

Olweus, D. (1979). Stability of aggressive reaction patterns in males: A review. *Psychological Bulletin, 86,* 852–875.

Purcell, K. (1956). The Thematic Apperception Test and antisocial behavior. *Journal of Consulting Psychology, 20,* 449–456.

White, R. W. (1975/1966). *Lives in progress.* New York: Holt.

SUGGESTED READING

Lindzey, G. (1952). Thematic Apperception Test: Interpretative assumptions and related empirical evidence. *Psychological Bulletin, 49,* 1–25.

Varbie, D. L. (1971). Current status of the Thematic Apperception Test. In P. McReynolds (Ed.), *Advances in psychological assessment* (Vol. 2). Palo Alto, CA: Science and Behavior Books.

E. M. SIIPOLA
Smith College

CLINICAL ASSESSMENT
PROJECTIVE TECHNIQUES
RORSCHACH TECHNIQUE

THOMPSON, RICHARD

Richard Thompson is currently Keck Professor of Psychology and Biological Sciences at the University of Southern California, and director of the neuroscience program at USC. He also holds appointments in the Department of Neurology, USC School of Medicine, and the School of Gerontology.

Thompson was born and raised in Portland, Oregon, and attended Grant High School and Reed College. He developed his interest in science early, an interest that was strengthened by an outstanding physics teacher in high school, Mrs. Curie, who as a graduate student had worked on a project to measure the charge on the electron. In her class Thompson made heavy water as an extra project. At Reed he became fascinated with philosophy and was torn between the study of mind and matter, ending up with a major in psychology but with additional course background in physics and mathematics. For his undergraduate thesis (required at Reed) he set out to solve the continuity versus non-continuity controversy in learning, using the Lashley jumping apparatus. He learned a great deal about animal behavior (his rats did everything except what they were supposed to do) but did not solve the controversy.

He was offered graduate fellowships from W. J. (Wulf) Brogden at the University of Wisconsin (Madison) and Kenneth Spence at the University of Iowa. By that time Thompson had developed his deep and continuing interest in the brain substrates of learning and memory, and he joined the psychology graduate program at Wisconsin—Brogden had been a pioneer in this field. The graduate program in psychology at Wisconsin was superb but very Darwinian—of about 35 students who began the program in 1952 only about six eventually received the PhD.

Thompson worked with Brogden in studies of human learning and animal conditioning, and completed a thesis on auditory frequency stimulus generalization (cats, avoidance conditioning). He obtained National Institute of Mental Health (NIMH) postdoctoral fellowship to work in Clinton Woolsey's neurophysiology laboratory at the medical school at the University of Wisconsin, where Thompson completed studies of the role of the auditory cortex in frequency discrimination and mapped cortical auditory areas and the nonspecific association response areas in the cat. During this time he mastered methods of experimental animal neurosurgery (subpial asperation), anatomical reconstruction, electrophysiological recording, and brain stimulation with Woolsey (and Akert and Hind) and experimental design and conditioning with Brogden. These two superb scientists had a profound and continuing influence on him.

Thompson returned to Portland to his first position as assistant professor in the psychiatry department (and later in medical psychology) at the University of Oregon Medical School. There he joined forces with a close friend from undergraduate days at Reed, William Alden Spencer, who had gone on to medical school and postdoctoral research in Wade Marshall's laboratory at National Institutes of Health (NIH), working with Eric Kandel in their classic studies of the hippocampus. Spencer came back to Oregon as an assistant professor in the physiology department. Thompson and Spencer completed their now classic studies on habituation as a model system for the study of non-associative learning. They characterized the behavioral properties of habituation, showed that spinal flexion reflexes exhibited these properties, and used spinal reflexes as a model system to analyze mechanisms of habituation.

During this period (1959–1967) Thompson was promoted to full professor. In 1960 he married Judith Pedersen, a psychiatric nurse at the medical school, and they had their first two children, Kathryn and Elizabeth. In 1967 they moved to southern California where Thompson accepted a position as professor of psychobiology at the University of California, Irvine. He continued his studies of habituation and played a key role in the development of the graduate program, one of the first neuroscience-related programs in the country. Their third daughter, Virginia, was born during the Irvine years.

In 1972–73 Thompson was lured to the psychology department at Harvard, where he held the chair held earlier by Karl Lashley. Meanwhile, at Irvine Thompson had adapted classical conditioning of the eyeblink response in the rabbit as a model system to analyze brain substrates of associative learning and memory. At Harvard, he and his students discovered the critical involvement of the hippocampus in this form of learning—hippocampal neurons became massively engaged, even though hippocampal lesions did not abolish the learned response.

Thompson and his family returned to U.C., Irvine in 1975. In 1980, Thompson, always restless, accepted an appointment as professor of psychology and Bing Professor of Human Biology at Stanford. At Stanford, Thompson and his students discovered the essential role of the cerebellum in classical conditioning of the eyeblink and other discrete responses (cerebellar lesions always abolish the learned response). He views this as his most important discovery, the first and, as yet, the only time a memory trace has been localized to a particular structure/localized region of the mammalian brain.

Finally, in 1987 Thompson accepted his current position as Keck Professor at the University of Southern California and became director of the neuroscience program (termed the Program in Neural, Informational, and Behavioral Sciences, or NIBS), where he continued his work on the cerebellar system as well as work on the role of stress and hormones on long-term potentiation in the hippocampus.

Thompson has received a number of honors and awards for his work, including the Research Scientist Award (NIH, 1967–1977), the American Psychological Association (APA) Distinguished Scientific Contribution Award (1977), the Warren Medal of the Society of Experimental Psychologists (1989), the John P. McGovern Award (AAAS, 1999), and the D. G. Marquis Behavioral Neuroscience Award (1999). Thompson is a past president of Division 6 of APA (1971), Western Psychological Association (1994–1995), and American Psychological Society (APS, 1995–1996). He was councilor for the Society of Neuroscience (1972–1976), Warren medal from the Society of Experimental Psychologists (1973), and chaired the governing board of the Psychonomic Society (1975). Thompson has been a Fellow of the American Association for the Advancement of Science (1977) and William James Fellow of APS (1989). He has been elected to the National Academy of Sciences (1977), the American Academy of Arts and Sciences (1989), and the American Philosophical Society (1999).

Thompson has published nearly 400 research papers and written several books, beginning with the very influential *Foundations of Physiological Psychology* (1967, Harper & Row), considered by many to be the first modern text on the topic. He has edited several journals, including the now-leading journal in the field, *Behavioral Neuroscience,* which he developed from the earlier *Journal of Comparative and Physiological Psychology.* He has been involved in a wide range of national committees and activities (e.g., for NIMH, NSF, NAS, NRC, etc.).

Thompson is one of the leading scientists today in the broad field concerned with mammalian brain substrates of learning and memory. His laboratory has received continuous federal research grant support since 1959 and is currently funded to 2003.

STAFF

THORNDIKE, EDWARD LEE (1874–1949)

Edward Lee Thorndike was an undergraduate at Wesleyan University, and then studied under William James at Harvard University where he began animal research in psychology. He moved to Columbia University and continued his work with dogs, cats, and chicks. He created puzzle boxes with which he studied animal intelligence, and his work was published in a monograph, "Animal intelligence." He received his doctorate in 1898.

Thorndike stayed at Columbia for all of his career; at James M. Cattell's suggestion, he applied animal research techniques to children. During his 50 years at Columbia, he did research and teaching in human learning, education, and mental testing, and published many books and monographs.

Thorndike taught that psychology should study behavior, not mental elements or conscious experience. He described *connectionism*—not associations between ideas, but connections between situations and responses. He said that the stimulus-response units are the elements of behavior, the building blocks from which more complex behaviors are constructed.

In 1898, Thorndike discovered the *law of effect,* which was similar to Pavlov's *law of reinforcement* reported four years later. Pavlov recognized Thorndike's work as preceding his, a simultaneous independent discovery, and complimented Thorndike's classical style of research and presentation for its "bold outlook" and accuracy. The law of effect was defined as the stamping in or out of a response tendency. Response tendencies that lead to success are stamped in after a number of trials—through "trial-and-error" learning. In the 1930s, in a study of the law of effect with humans, Thorndike found that rewarding the response was effective in stamping in or strengthening the behavior, but that punishment did not have a comparable negative effect of stamping out. Rather, prolonged disuse of the response led to a weakening of the behavior. These results were reported in his book *Human Learning.*

Thorndike's research and theories of association or learning catapulted learning theory to its prominent place in American psychology.

N. A. HAYNIE

THORNDIKE'S LAWS OF LEARNING

In the first third of this century, Edward Lee Thorndike (1874–1949) and John B. Watson (1878–1958) were the two most prominent American psychologists. Both were concerned with the learning process but reached fundamentally differing conclusions. Watson's views are mentioned here only in contrast to the principles promoted by Thorndike, who might be regarded as the "father" of American learning psychology.

Thorndike started his long career at Columbia University

where he observed many kinds of animals in what he called "puzzle-box" problems. An animal, say a cat, would be placed in a box from which it could escape in only one way, for example, by pulling a string that raised a door. In such a situation, a cat would initially engage in a variety of behaviors (sniffing, scratching, climbing the walls, etc.) before, in one way or another, getting the string in its claws and pulling away from it with the happy result of door opening. Thorndike chose to call all the responses that the cat emitted "trials" and, because they appeared to be essentially random, he labeled them "chance" operations. The cat with the door open would emerge from the box and find some food (a reward) but showed no apparent appreciation of the relationship between pulling the string and the open door. Upon replacement in the box, the cat would again wander about emitting chance responses until again the string was grasped in some way with the successful result. Over a series of such episodes, the cat would eventually pull the string earlier and earlier in the situation and would show what Thorndike called a gradual improvement in escape time. Examination of the graphs published by Thorndike might leave some doubts about how gradual the drops in escape time actually were, but Thorndike saw in them only a gradual improvement and summarized the findings as reflecting learning as a matter of "trial and error and chance success."

The last part of this phrase should be emphasized as much as the first. Learning was not only a blind affair of trial and error; one of the trials had to be successful, that is, lead to an outcome that could be characterized as rewarding or, in Thorndike's expression, "satisfying." In Thorndike's formulation, a satisfier or "satisfying state of affairs" was "one that the animal did nothing to avoid and frequently strove to attain." This expression was meant to be an objective definition of rewards and did not necessarily have anything to do with pleasurable feelings or subjective experiences.

Thorndike himself was satisfied that his studies had exposed the basic operations in learning that could be described as a gradual strengthening of some stimulus–response "connections" that at first occurred purely by chance and that happened to be "successful." There was no room in Thorndike's theory for anything like "insight" or intelligent or rational analysis. Learning was a matter of dumb luck. Sooner or later, if one tried one thing after another, one would stumble on the correct response. Because the correct response would be "satisfying," the "bond" between the stimulus and the response would be strengthened to some degree and eventually would be strong enough to occur first or early in a test situation. Thorndike was so convinced that he had discovered a basic rule or law of learning in the presumed importance of a satisfying state of affairs following upon a chance response that he formally proposed a summary of his belief in what he called the "law of effect."

THE LAW OF EFFECT

The law of effect was stated in many ways by Thorndike and his followers but it amounts to a statement that a stimulus–response connection or bond is strengthened when the response is followed by a satisfier. The term *satisfier* is commonly described as a reward, but later psychologists (Clark L. Hull and B. F. Skinner) chose to substitute the term *reinforcement* for reward. Originally Thorndike felt

called upon to explain why unsuccessful responses dropped out and he attributed such elimination of incorrect reactions to the occurrence of annoyers or annoying states of affairs. Annoyers, which might be defined as punishment, were, according to Thorndike, anything that "the animal avoids and makes no effort to attain." The two-part law of effect then amounted to the statement that one learned or retained whatever responses were followed by satisfiers and refrained from responses that were followed by annoyers. If this sounds like ancient statements about pleasure and pain, carrots and sticks, or rewards and punishments, it may be considered so, but the law of effect was a more sophisticated restatement of such old and common views.

OTHER LAWS OF LEARNING

Thorndike saw the law of effect as the basic principle governing learning but not quite sufficient to account for all learning that occurred or failed to occur. Two sublaws were regarded as necessary additions: these were the laws of *exercise* and of *readiness*. Thorndike's followers were very prominent in education (Thorndike became the head of Teachers College at Columbia) and would usually cite the laws in sloganlike fashion: *exercise, readiness,* and *effect.*

The Law of Readiness

The law of readiness was essentially a statement of the need to attend if one were to learn anything. A learner would have to be set to respond to specific stimuli of consequence in a situation. Readiness had nothing to do with maturation or age and was more of a situational condition. Thorndike tried to offer a semineurological proposal in suggesting that the nervous system had to be tuned or "ready" for certain connections to be operative. Unlike the law of effect, the law of readiness was not one a teacher could manipulate. Readiness just had to be there.

The Law of Exercise

In many cases, the law of effect, being blind, could not accomplish complete learning in one trial. For some connections, many trials might be needed. Each successful trial added strength to a connection. The law of exercise supported common practices of drill in many learning situations.

Additional Laws

While exercise, readiness, and effect at first seemed to cover the field, Thorndike found it useful to introduce additional laws from time to time. In 1931, for example, he modified the law of effect to drop the negative side. Punishment had been found, he believed, to have no effect on eliminating wrong responses. At best, punishment might create a temporary situation in which a correct response could be rewarded and strengthened. Thorndike also introduced the law of *belongingness.* This law was meant to suggest that some kinds of material were more readily learnable than others; some things seemed to go together more naturally than others. Thus first and last names might be learned better than sets of first or last names. Many Thorndike adherents spent great amounts of time trying to arrange curricula wherein belongingness might be useful, without notable success. Another law, *associative shifting,* was introduced to meet the challenge from followers of Watson who were committed to the notion that all learning amounted to conditioning. The law of associative shifting was meant to incorporate conditioning into the law of effect. It amounted to a statement that stimuli associated with the original S-R bond could come, in time, to participate in the initiation of the response, even in the absence of the original stimulus.

CRITIQUE

All of Thorndike's laws have been criticized or found wanting by one critic or another. Currently the supporters of Skinner still operate on what amounts to the law of effect. The other laws are not thought of as something that should be enforced by educators as new alleged principles (e.g., "discovery") are promoted. Supporters of one-trial learning oppose the exercise law and supporters of conditioning ignore the "satisfying states of affairs" so basic for Thorndike. In the words of Ernest Hilgard (1956), "There are no laws of learning that can be taught with confidence." This statement probably is still a meaningful appraisal.

SUGGESTED READING

Hilgard, E. R., & Bower, G. H. (1975). *Theories of learning* (4th ed.). New York: Appleton-Century-Crofts.

Thorndike, E. L. (1932/1899). *The fundamentals of learning.* New York: Teachers College.

B. R. BUGELSKI
State University of New York, Buffalo

LEARNING THEORIES
OPERANT CONDITIONING
PUNISHMENT
REINFORCEMENT
REWARDS AND INTRINSIC INTEREST

THURSTONE, LOUIS LEON (1887–1955)

Considered the foremost American leader in psychometrics, Louis Leon Thurstone spent his childhood in Sweden, and returned to the United States to earn a degree in electrical engineering at Cornell University in 1912. While still a student, he invented and patented a motion picture projector. It attracted the attention of Thomas A. Edison, who hired him as an assistant. Working in Edison's laboratory, Thurstone became interested in problems of acoustics, sensory psychology, and the objective measurement of sensation. This led him to graduate study in psychology at the University of Chicago, where he received the PhD degree in 1917. After eight years at the Carnegie Institute of Technology, where he became professor and chairman of the Psychology Department, Thurstone returned to the University of Chicago, to serve as professor of psychology for 28 years. The last three years of his life

were spent at the University of North Carolina as the first director of the Psychometric Laboratory, which now bears his name. He was president of the American Psychological Association in 1932; in 1936, he was one of the founders, and first president, of the Psychometric Society.

Thurstone made many contributions to measurement theory and its applications to psychophysics, cognitive abilities, attitudes, social judgment, and personality. Essentially he invented methods for devising interval and ratio scales for the measurement of psychological variables. He was the first to point out the psychometric inadequacies of Binet's concept of mental age (MA) as a scale for mental ability, and of the IQ when calculated as the ratio of MA to chronological age (CA). Mental age has the undesirable property that it can mean two quite different things: the average test score of children of a given age, or the average age of children obtaining a given score. There is no rational basis for choosing between these meanings of MA. Therefore, Thurstone argued that percentile ranks or standard scores should replace MA and IQ, a practice that has been adopted by all modern tests. (Today most IQ's are standard scores with a population mean of 100 and standard deviation of 15 or 16.) Thurstone also invented a ratio scale for the measurement of intelligence. He estimated the absolute zero of intelligence on the measurement scale by extrapolating the variance downward on the scale until it decreased to zero; zero intelligence thus was defined as the level of ability at which individual differences completely vanish.

Thurstone is best known for his contributions to factor analysis. The conceptual limitations and mathematical unwieldiness of Spearman's method of factor analysis when there is more than one factor made Thurstone's development of multiple factor analysis a boon to psychometrics and, at the time, was virtually essential for analyzing large correlation matrices that comprised a number of factors. Thurstone's multiple factor theory has endured, although, with the advent of electronic computers, his centroid method of factor extraction has been replaced by more exact, but computationally more difficult, methods such as principal component analysis and principal factor analysis.

By subjecting the matrix of intercorrelations among more than 50 diverse tests of mental abilities to a multiple factor analysis, Thurstone extracted a number of factors he labeled "primary mental abilities." He devised relatively "factor-pure" tests for each of these factors, such as verbal comprehension, reasoning, word fluency, number, spatial visualization, perceptual speed, and associative memory. Spearman's *g* (general ability) factor seemed to have disappeared in Thurstone's analysis, which for a time was a point of great contention between British and American psychometricians. The conflict was resolved when Thurstone showed that the primary mental abilities were themselves positively intercorrelated and that, when they are factor analyzed, Spearman's *g* is recovered as a second-order or superfactor. It has, in fact, proved impossible to construct factor-pure tests of Thurstone's primary mental abilities that do not also measure Spearman's *g,* and usually each test is more highly loaded on *g* than on the special factor it was specially devised to measure. Hence factor-pure tests, at best, measure *g* plus one primary ability.

Thurstone's most important contribution to factor analysis was the principle of "simple structure," a criterion for the rotation of the factor axes (or principal dimensions of the matrix) that results in a set of factors, each with very high loadings on a few tests and near-zero loadings on the rest—a condition that facilitates psychological interpretation of the factors. The principle of simple structure dominates modern computerized techniques of factor analysis, such as Kaiser's widely used varimax method.

A. R. JENSEN
University of California at Berkeley

THURSTONE SCALING

Thurstone scaling, also known as the method of equal-appearing intervals, is a technique devised by Thurstone for constructing quantitative attitude measurement instruments.

The first step in Thurstone scaling is to gather a large number of statements representing a wide range of opinions about the attitude object (e.g., capital punishment). Statements ranging from extremely negative through neutral to extremely positive are drawn from persons holding varying viewpoints or from the popular literature. These statements are then independently sorted by judges into 11 piles of equal-appearing intervals ranging from least favorable (toward the attitude object, with a score of 1) through neutral (6) to most favorable (11). The median and semi-interquartile range (Q) of the judges' scores for each statement are then calculated, and statements with large Q values are discarded as ambiguous. The remaining statements are item-analyzed for internal consistency, and inconsistent statements are discarded as irrelevant.

What remains from this process is a pool of consistent, unambiguous statements with scale values (median judges' scores) ranging from 1 to 11. The attitude scale itself is then constructed by including two or more statements from each of the 11 intervals on a questionnaire. Respondents check all of the statements with which they agree; the median scale values of the statements endorsed by respondents are their attitude scores. If the item pool is large enough, several parallel scales can be constructed and the reliability of the attitude score can be determined.

Thurstone's technique is time consuming and has been largely supplanted in popularity by newer techniques for developing measures of attitude. However, Thurstone scaling is a major step in the development of behaviorally anchored rating scales, mixed standard rating scales, and weighted checklists for measuring work performance.

SUGGESTED READING

Thurstone, L. L., & Chave, E. J. (1929). *The measurement of attitude.* Chicago: University of Chicago Press.

W. I. SAUSER, JR.
Auburn University

RATING SCALES

TIME-LIMITED PSYCHOTHERAPY

Many experts on the demographics of the mental health field have commented on the gap between the limited number of patients that can be accommodated by the arduous process of classical psychoanalysis and population needs for psychotherapy. Estimates of need have varied from 10 to 15% of the population of the United States in any one year, representing a potential of between 20 and 30 million applicants for psychotherapy, which, if acted on, would clog the service completely.

The juxtaposition between this vast potential need and the limited supply of trained psychotherapists has created a continuous pressure for brief modes of treatment. The experience of those offering services to the population at large is that most applicants for psychotherapy seek and are willing to commit themselves to no more than five or six interviews (Garfield, 1978; Butcher & Koss, 1978).

Marmor (1980) pointed out that psychoanalysis in its early phases tended toward short durations. He called attention to Sigmund Freud's successful treatment of symphony conductor Bruno Walter in six sessions in 1906 and of composer Gustav Mähler in four sessions in 1908. Accompanying the evolution of psychoanalysis complex theoretical superstructure and the increasing ambitiousness of its goals, was the lengthening of analytic treatments into years to the point where their founder became concerned with their "interminability." Over the years there has been an almost continuous effort to evolve methods of treatment designed for the more limited efforts for which most psychotherapy applicants are ready or need.

These developments, have come both within and outside the psychoanalytic framework. Certain classes of interventions, usually designated as crisis or supportive, are directed at helping the individual to recover from the effects of a temporary, often event-related, state. This kind of intervention is almost universally brief and directed toward helping the person to return to a previous level of functioning. Change in that level is not the goal. Brief and time-limited psychotherapies are used here to designate treatments in which the goals are enduring changes in the person's level of effectiveness and style of functioning. The most useful distinction between brief and time-limited psychotherapy is that in the latter there is an explicit setting of a limit in either calendar terms or in the number of sessions. Finally, the number of sessions designated as "brief" has varied, ranging from several to 40 and from several weeks to 12 months. Butcher and Koss (1978) state that most practitioners consider 25 sessions the upper limit of "brief" therapy.

DEVELOPMENTS IN BRIEF PSYCHOTHERAPY

It will be useful to divide the discussion of developments in brief therapy into those evolving within the psychoanalytic framework and those beyond that framework. This discussion will prepare the way for the direct consideration of the time-limited version of psychotherapy, which, while departing from psychoanalysis, is psychodynamically oriented.

Developments Within Psychoanalysis

The first responses to the ever-lengthening process of psychoanalysis took the form of modifications designed to reduce the austerity of the rule of free association and the strictures of the therapist as "blank screen." Ferenczi and Stekel are often cited as experimenters with various kinds of active interventions that ranged from proposing actions, introducing prohibitions, and even hugging, kissing, and nonerotic fondling. This development was so antithetical to Freud's basic assumptions about the need to keep the therapeutic relationship uncontaminated by immediate gratifications that it aroused an outright rejection of these deviations.

These developments during the early decades of the twentieth century, after a quiescent period, were revived by Alexander and French (1946). Their direction was to control the frequency of visits to limit dependence on the therapist and actively to contravene the patient's transference- (based on parental paradigms) distorted perceptions of the therapist. Through this means, Alexander and French contended, it became possible to provide a corrective emotional experience, which in a brief time loosened the hold of earlier based nonfunctional emotional responses. Although these proposals aroused strong opposition within psychoanalytic circles, this time their influences took hold, spawning and expanding the stream of ideas about the usefulness and applicability of psychoanalytic theory to brief psychotherapy. Malin (1976) offers a summary of these developments. He points out that all share an emphasis on active intervention and a limitation in the goals of the treatment. Malin proposed that the focus of attention should fall somewhere between the highly abstract formulation, for example, the oedipal conflict, and the pure pragmatic presenting problem. These formulations, which he labeled psychodynamic hypotheses, are to be stated in simple nontechnical terms. They seek to specify the kind of stress to which the patient is vulnerable, the criterion of recovery, and how this specific stress must be faced without developing new symptoms.

Developments Outside Psychoanalysis

The three decades of the 1950s, 1960s, and 1970s saw an ever-increasing rate of proliferation of psychotherapeutic methods, most of them claiming to represent briefer paths to treatment goals. A great many of these methods gain their legitimacy from the convictions of the practitioners and their patients and clients. These methods have waxed and waned in the mode of fashions. Some of these methods are mainly utilized by atypically trained professionals or semiprofessionals.

Two of the most empirically tested brief treatments are operating under the umbrella of client-centered therapy and the even broader umbrella of the behavior therapies. Carl Rogers (1965/1951) the founder of client-centered therapy, evolved a method designed to keep responsibility in the client within an atmosphere in which he or she felt understood and accepted. While not explicitly designed to be brief, this therapy was seen as avoiding the kind of dependence on the therapist that can lengthen psychotherapy. Moreover, it was geared to whatever goals, limited or extensive, that the client set. In fact, the length of client-centered treatments, though early taking a brief form, has sometimes included lengthy treatments stretching well beyond 40 interviews.

Similarly, the various versions of behavior therapy have tended toward the brief form. The learning theory ideology and the methodology based on it pushed in that direction. Behavior ther-

apy draws its inspiration from academic and research-based theories of learning. The most radical forms, inspired by Skinner, eschewed complex inferential formulations about the individual. Thus attention is concentrated on specific sets of actions as targets of the change process, which, under the circumstances of the voluntary entry in therapy, are represented by the person's complaints. While the spectrum of the behavior therapies includes a range toward somewhat more inferential formulations, falling in the class of self-cognitions and self-instructions, the extremely parsimonious set of the behavior therapist operates as a constraint so that the experiences that the therapist arranges for a client/patient usually fall within a relatively brief effort.

THEORY OF TIME-LIMITED PSYCHOTHERAPY

The foregoing review of practical pressures, theoretical developments, and clinical experimentation provides a context for the consideration of time-limited psychotherapy that is more than brief therapy dictated by the large gap between need and resources. There are two theoretical roots from which Mann's (1974) development of a pattern of 12 interviews can be traced. Receiving his original inspiration from within Freud's Vienna Circle and interacting with Ferenczi, Rank (1945/1929), eventually broke with Freud as he replaced sexual energy by the need to reconcile the simultaneous imperatives of individuation and unity with others. He saw this need to balance a sense of self and uniqueness against the equally strong need for oneness with others as a continual imperative accompanying growth, starting with the biological separation from mother that birth represented. The various stages of physical, social, and psychological maturation create further separation from mother and then from nuclear family, setting up conditions for a new creative synthesis of self and others. The viscissitudes of each of these transitions, starting with birth itself, was seen by Rank as the major sources of guilt and anxiety that could stultify people's lives. His therapy stressed working with the expression of those problems as they arose in the separations between patient and therapist, either temporally (at the end of hours or at termination) or interpersonally (around limits on behavior and boundaries between them). Rank advocated setting a fixed date for the termination of therapy to provide an important base for his will therapy.

Though acknowledging the relevance of Rank's ideas and their applications, Mann took his main inspiration from his analysis of the psychology of time. Pointing to observation of the evolution of the sense of time from the child-based feeling of infinite time to the increasing awareness of finiteness in any individual's life, he designed a pattern of treatment around this feature, geared to what he saw as one important component of psychopathology. Mann evolved a pattern based on 12 interviews, a number first selected somewhat arbitrarily, but later confirmed by a clinical experience as appropriate. This explicitly established limit, when combined with an established focus on a statement of the patient's chronic enduring pain, Mann claimed, can provide an important arena for a more effective straightening out of ways in the individual's resolution of dependence–independence, loneliness–intimacy, and self-alienation–self-engrossment issues.

Psychotherapists have accumulated considerable favorable experience with this method (Mann & Goldmann, 1982), but the empirical base is still very sketchy. Comparisons of time-limited (18) and unlimited (averaging 37 interviews) client-centered and Adlerian treatments found essentially no differences in outcome (Shlien et al., 1962). A similar result was obtained in limited (eight interviews) as compared with unlimited social casework (Wattie, 1973). Both of these investigations compare only the effect of an explicitly imposed time limit, instead of the Mann specifications about working with both the time limit and the focus.

Thus we now have a theory and a delineated pattern for the use of time limits in psychotherapy and evidence that time limits *per se* do not limit the outcome. We do not yet know why certain outcomes can be achieved and whether this particular pattern can be used to achieve certain outcomes better or more efficiently.

REFERENCES

Alexander, F. G., & French, T. M. (1946). *Psychoanalytic therapy.* New York: Ronald Press.

Butcher, J. N., & Koss, M. P. (1978). Research on brief and crisis-oriented therapies. In S. L. Garfield & A. E. Bergin (Eds.), *Handbook of psychotherapy and behavior change: An empirical analysis* (2nd ed., pp. 725–767). New York: Wiley.

Garfield, S. L. (1978). Research on client variables in psychotherapy. In S. L. Garfield & A. E. Bergin (Eds.), *Handbook of psychotherapy and behavior change: An empirical analysis.* New York: Wiley.

Malin, D. H. (1976). *The frontier of brief psychotherapy.* New York: Plenum.

Mann, J. (1974). *Time-limited psychotherapy.* Cambridge, MA: Harvard University Press.

Mann, J., & Goldman, R. (1982). *A casebook in time-limited psychotherapy.* New York: McGraw-Hill.

Marmor, J. (1980). Historical roots. In H. Davenloo (Ed.), *Short-term dynamic psychotherapy* (Vol. 1). New York: Aronson.

Rank, O. (1945/1929). *Will therapy and truth and reality.* New York: Knopf.

Rogers, C. R. (1965/1951). *Client-centered therapy.* Cambridge, MA: Houghton Mifflin.

Shlien, J. M., Mosak, H. H., & Dreikurs, R. (1962). Effects of time limits: A comparison of two psychotherapies. *Journal of Counseling Psychology, 9,* 31–34.

Wattie, B. (1973). Evaluating short term casework in a family agency. *Social casework, 54,* 609–616.

E. S. BORDIN
University of Michigan

COUNSELING
CRISIS INTERVENTION
PSYCHOTHERAPY

TIME-SERIES ANALYSIS

A time-series analysis is the statistical analysis of data that have been collected on a single unit (e.g., a person, a family, or an organization) at equally spaced time intervals (or in a continuous form). Time-series methods are employed to describe the relationship between variables (e.g., biochemical measures in person A and the behavior of person A); to forecast (predict) future behavior; to describe the statistical nature of a process; and to estimate intervention effects. Hence, the applications for time-series analysis have much in common with the applications for conventional data analytic methods.

A major difference between time-series and conventional methods is the nature of the designs to which they are applied. Time-series designs generally involve the collection of a large number of observations across time on a single subject or unit, whereas conventional designs generally involve only one or just a few observations on a reasonably large number of subjects. This difference in design characteristics often leads to a need for analytic methods that are not necessary in the analysis of most conventional designs. Time-series analyses, unlike most conventional analyses, are characterized by: (a) formal evaluations of the assumption of independent errors; (b) analytic strategies to accommodate any existing lack of independence; and (c) models that contain terms to describe how behavior changes across time.

TIME-SERIES DOMAINS

Approaches to time-series modeling generally fall into one of two major categories: time domain models and frequency domain models. Although the two correspond mathematically, they represent different ways of conceptualizing the nature of time-series, and they are designed to focus on different descriptive features of the data.

Time Domain Models

Time domain models contain parameters that are used to relate the behavior of process Y to other variables and/or to the history of process Y. For example, certain time domain models, known as autoregressive moving-average (ARMA) models, relate the current value Y_t of the time-series to earlier values of the series and to values of present and past random errors. A more general modeling approach that allows for the modeling of data that contain random trends is known as ARIMA (autoregressive integrated moving-average). ARIMA models have become popular in the behavioral sciences; software for estimating the parameters of these models is widely available. However, the recommendation that sample size be reasonably large (a minimum of 50–100 is typical) before attempting such modeling has recently led to the development of alternative procedures for small samples. Some of these alternatives are closely related to conventional regression models.

The key issues in the selection of an adequate time-series analysis are the question or questions to be answered, the nature of the process that generates trends (if any), and whether the errors are independent. Some version of ARIMA or a simpler alternative model is usually chosen. Certain versions of time-series regression models are appropriate in some situations in which it was previously thought that ARIMA models were required. In some cases ordinary multiple regression methods using time as one of the predictor variables provide a satisfactory analysis. But because independence of the errors is assumed by conventional regression models, it is necessary to identify and model dependency (if it exists) among the errors.

The errors in a time-series regression model are the difference between the observed and the predicted outcome scores. The predictions are based on variables in the regression equation that model deterministic trends (linear and nonlinear), interventions, and other systematic changes. If the dependency is not modeled, inferential tests on the parameters of the model, confidence intervals, and predictions based on ordinary regression methods will be distorted. Under some conditions the distortion can be severe. Hence, a preliminary step in the application of regression models to time-series data is to determine whether the errors of the model are approximately independent. A test of the hypothesis of independent errors is often carried out for this purpose.

If the errors are not independent the model should be modified by either: (a) identifying and including in the model additional variables responsible for the dependency; or (b) accommodating the dependency by including terms in the model that describe it. The former should always be attempted before the latter. When the latter approach is taken several different types of coefficient are available to describe various types of dependency among the errors. One type is called an autoregressive coefficient. The first-order autoregressive coefficient, for example, provides a measure of the relationship between the error measured at time t and the error measured at time $t - 1$; the value of this coefficient must fall between -1 and 1. A positive value of ϕ_1 indicates that a positive error tends to be followed by another positive error and that a negative error tends to be followed by another negative error. Alternatively, a negative value of ϕ_1 indicates that a positive error tends to be followed by a negative error and a negative error tends to be followed by a positive error. If $\phi_1 = 0$ the error measured at one time point provides no information on whether the subsequent error will be positive or negative. The equation $\varepsilon_t = \phi_1 \varepsilon_{t-1} + u_t$ can be used to show that the error at time t (i.e., ε_t) is equal to a portion of the previous error and a random component u_1. Hence it can be seen that the error at any particular time point t is partly determined by the error at time point $t - 1$; this makes it clear that the errors are not independent unless the value of ϕ_1 is 0.

If the dependency in the errors is adequately described by the first-order autoregressive coefficient, this term is added to the regression model. Sometimes dependency remains after adding the first order autoregressive coefficient to the model; in this case a more complex model containing additional terms may be required. The final model will then contain parameters to describe systematic trends and other deterministic changes such as intervention effects across time as well as parameters to describe patterns among the errors of the model. A practical problem associated with models of this type is that the time-series should contain a minimum of about 50 observations if typical time-series regression methods (often called generalized least-squares) are used to carry out the analysis. Recently-developed computer intensive methods, however, provide adequate estimation with fewer observations.

Frequency Domain Models

Frequency domain models differ from time domain models in terms of the framework used for describing the behavior of the time-series. Whereas a time domain model represents an attempt to explain current behavior of the series using time and other variables (including previous errors) as predictors, frequency domain models focus on breaking down the total series variation into basic frequency components. Frequency is related to the number of cycles of the response measure that occur during a defined period of time; frequency domain methods (called harmonic analysis, periodogram analysis, and spectral analysis) provide a decomposition of the time-series variance into proportions that are explained by different cycles (if any). It turns out, however, that many applications of frequency domain methods are appropriate only after first attempting to model trends in the original data using linear and curvilinear regression (or other methods). Consequently, frequency domain analyses are often applied to the errors of regression models rather than to the original values of the series. In this case the total time-series analysis includes both a time domain regression component applied to the original values of the series and a frequency domain component applied to the errors of the regression model. The outcome of this combined approach is a description of deterministic trends in the original series, a decomposition of the cycles in the errors, and in some cases, a description of how the properties of these cycles change over time.

SUGGESTED READING

Box, G. E. P., Jenkins, G. M., & Reinsel, S. G. (1994). *Time-series analysis, forecasting and control.* San Francisco: Holden-Day.

Huitema, B. E., & McKean, J. W. (2000). Design specification issues in time-series intervention models. *Educational and Psychological Measurement, 60,* 38–58.

McCleary, R., & Welsh, W. N. (1992). Philosophical and statistical foundations of time-series experiments. In T. R. Kratochwill & J. R. Levin (Eds.), *Single-case research design and analysis: New directions for psychology and education* (pp. 41–91). Hillsdale, NY: Erlbaum.

McKnight, S. D., McKean, J. W., & Huitema, B. E. (in press). A double bootstrap method to analyze linear models with autoregressive error terms. *Psychological Methods.*

Warner, R. M. (1998). *Spectral analysis of time-series data.* New York: Guilford.

B. E. Huitema
Western Michigan University

CORRELATION METHODS

TITCHENER, EDWARD BRADFORD (1867–1927)

Edward Bradford Titchener attended Malvern College and then Oxford University, where he studied philosophy, the classics, and physiology. He became interested in Wilhelm Wundt's new psychology and spent two years studying in Leipzig, receiving his degree in 1892. Titchener was a genuine disciple of his mentor Wundt and he kept his German temperament, both personally and professionally, throughout his life.

Titchener transplanted structuralism to U.S. soil from Wundt's laboratory in Leipzig. At the age of 25, he went to Cornell University, where he taught psychology and developed a laboratory of his own. He remained at Cornell for the rest of his life. Through his more than 50 doctoral students, Titchener's ideas were disseminated with systematic attention to research that reflected his thoughts and theories.

Titchener translated the works of Wundt, wrote over 200 articles, and had many books to his credit. The four volumes of *Experimental Psychology,* were widely used as laboratory manuals and sped the growth of research in psychology. Through these volumes, Titchener influenced experimental psychology in the United States, including John B. Watson, the founder of behaviorism. *A Textbook of Psychology* was published in 1909.

The subject matter of structuralism was experience. Consciousness was defined as the sum total of experience at any given moment, and mind as the sum total of experience over a lifetime. Titchener felt that psychology should study the generalized human mind, not individual minds, and certainly not individual differences. Titchener's psychology was a pure science with no application to cures or reforms. The method of introspection was highly developed and formalized; the well-trained observers have been compared to impartial and detached human machines, objectively recording the characteristics of the object being observed.

Titchener taught that there are three elementary states of consciousness—sensations, images, and affective states. Sensations are the basic elements of perception; images are the elements of ideas; affections are the elements of emotion. Research on affection or feeling resulted in the rejection of Wundt's tridimensional theory, with support being found for one dimension only, pleasure-displeasure.

Toward the later years of his life, Titchener began to argue that psychology should not study elements but the dimensional attributes of mental life, which he listed as quality, intensity, protensity (duration), extensity, and attensity (clearness). He came to question the controlled method of introspection and to favor a more open, phenomenological approach.

N. A. HAYNIE

TOILET TRAINING

The practice of toilet training children is the cause of a great deal of anxiety and frustration for parents and has resulted in debates among professionals. Freud, in *The Problem of Anxiety,* suggested that inappropriate toilet training can result in lifetime trauma for the child. Others submit that the process of toilet training reinforces the self-centered nature of the young child. Wenar (1971) states that "toilet training enhances the sense of power in the toddler whose thinking is naturally inclined to be omnipotent."

Whether one harbors anxiety over the prospects of toilet train-

ing one's child or views the process as a natural phenomenon that will, in time, run its course, the question "What approach should parents take in toilet training their children?" remains. Two psychologists who have examined toilet training philosophies and practices and have developed a strategy sensitive to the range of ideas are Azrin and Foxx. In their book, *Toilet Training in Less Than a Day,* Azrin and Foxx have developed a toilet training program that is responsive to "the psychoanalytic emphasis on the possible effect of harsh toilet training on later personality . . . , the medical knowledge about toilet training . . . , and the importance of Pavlovian learning . . . operant learning . . . , imitation and social influence. . . . "

HOW TO AND WHEN TO

Azrin and Foxx suggest that there are four "preliminary considerations" to regard before commencing toilet training: age, bladder control, physical readiness, and instructional readiness. They submit that at age 20 months the child is usually capable of being toilet trained. They further submit that a child is ready for toilet training when the child demonstrates bladder control by strength of urine stream, as well as quantity of urine eliminated. Readiness is also indicated when the child presents good finger and hand coordination, enough to pick up objects, and also is capable of walking independently. Finally, Azrin and Foxx suggest that toilet training readiness is indicated when the child can follow simple directions and/or imitate actions.

Once it is determined that a child is ready for toilet training, specific procedures can be followed that task-analyze the bowel and bladder elimination of the child and the steps necessary for toilet training success (Holmes, 1990).

SPECIAL PROBLEMS

Numerous articles have been written on subjects pertaining to toilet training problems. Ellis (1963) addressed the special needs of disabled individuals. O. H. and W. M. Mowrer (1938) addressed nighttime wetting, and Wagner and Paul (1970) discussed bowel accidents. Whether one adheres to a psychoanalytic, behavioristic, or other viewpoint, there is consensus among theoreticians and practitioners that toilet training is a most important developmental milestone. Well-informed parents with a clearly defined approach will be most helpful to the child navigating the course of toilet training.

REFERENCES

Azrin, N., & Foxx, R. (1974). *Toilet training in less than a day.* New York: Simon & Schuster.

Baumeister, A., & Klosowski, R. (1965). An attempt to group toilet train severely retarded patients, *Mental Retardation, 3,* 24–26.

Ellis, N. R. (1963) Toilet training and the severely defective patient: An S-R reinforcement analysis. *American Journal of Mental Deficiency, 68,* 48–103.

Freud, S. (1936). *The problem of anxiety.* New York: Norton.

Holmes, D. L. (1990). *The Eden Curriculum: Vol. I. Core curriculum.* Princeton, NJ: The Eden Press.

Mowrer, O. H., & Mowrer, W. M. (1938) Enuresis: A method for the study and treatment. *American Journal of Orthopsychiatry, 8,* 426–459.

Sears, R. R., Maccoby, E. E., & Levin, H. (1957). *Patterns of child rearing.* Evanston, IL: Row, Peterson.

Van Wagener, R. K., Meyerson, L., Karr, N.J., & Mahoney, K. (1966). Field trials of a new procedure for toilet training. *Journal of Experimental Child Psychiatry, 3,* 312–314.

Wagner, B. R., & Paul, G. L. (1970). Redirection of incontinence in chronic mental patients: A pilot project. *Journal of Behavior Therapy and Expermental Psychiatry, 1,* 29–38.

Wemar, C. (1971). *Personality Development from Infancy to Adulthood.* Boston: Houghton Mifflin.

D. L. HOLMES
The Eden Institute

BRAIN
PARENT-CHILD RELATIONS
SENSORIMOTOR PROCESSES

TOKEN ECONOMIES

Token economies have been with us since money took the place of barter. The generally acknowledged theoretical source of contemporary token economies is Skinner. Applications with severely disabled people in psychiatric hospitals is associated with the work of Ayllon and Azrin (1968) and Atthowe and Krasner (1968), and the strongest documentation of the value of the procedure is presented by Paul and Lentz (1977). Work with children was fostered by Bijou and his students (Bijou & Orlando, 1961) and in classrooms by Becker and his colleagues (Becker, 1973; O'Leary & Drabman, 1971). Another area of application is with delinquents (Cohen & Filipzak, 1971; Phillips et al., 1971). These examples are within institutions, but the concepts are readily applicable to family settings (Sulzer-Azaroff & Mayer, 1977) and self-control (Krasner & Ullmann, 1973).

All token economies have in common a target set of desirable responses and an explicit payoff for these acts. The targeted responses mirror the behaviors that the society considers appropriate and desirable for people of a given age, sex, and socioeconomic status. Deviation from such responses to situations takes the form of deficits in responses that should be increased and responses that are unexpected, disruptive, and self-defeating that should be decreased. The responses selected are a picture of what any given dominant (i.e., teacher, parent, employer, therapist) group considers "normal." The responses are specified and, if complex, are broken down.

First, the explicit specification of overt behavior helps avoid inference that is both unreliable and likely to stigmatize the subject. Second, explicitly designated overt behaviors facilitate communication. Third, explicit overt behavior permits measurement so that both subject and instructor may ascertain the success of a program and hence decide rationally whether it needs to be changed to permit greater success or, if success at one level has been attained, whether a new and more challenging target should be designated. Above all, when working with children, delinquents, or people called schizophrenic, the token economy makes the person's acts meaningful. A contract is made and both subject and instructor are held to it as responsible humans.

The token economy may start out with simple acts of self-care and self-feeding in the psychiatric hospital or simple academic tasks in the schoolroom. The instructor starts where the subject has a low rate of response but is capable of being successful. This is essentially the concept of shaping.

There is payoff for acts to be increased. Food and drink are primary reinforcers; and while candy may be used, it has a number of drawbacks. Primary reinforcers satiate. Also, after an early age, the majority of meaningful behavior is under control of secondary, acquired, or generalized reinforcers—tokens, such as money, or indicants on the part of significant others of pleasure, such as smiles, praise, and attention. Secondary reinforcers do not satiate; and if they are backed up with meaningful consequences, do not extinguish. Eventually an adult role is one in which the person is under control of acquired reinforcers and self-schedules, self-monitors, and self-reinforcers. With age and socialization, payoffs become more abstract and more delayed. The token economy is a preparation for this role, and all treatment decisions are made with this goal in mind.

Usually a token economy will have a contingency contract known to both subject and instructor. At the start, primary reinforcing stimuli may be used, but as soon as possible, acquired reinforcers, such as tokens or points, bridge the time between the act and the receipt of an explicit value, such as food, privacy, television, toys, or various privileges. As treatment progresses, the time between receipt of tokens and their exchange for the explicit backup reinforcers is increased: from twice a day, to once a day, to every other day, to once a week, and so on. The acts for which there are payoffs are increased in complexity and difficulty—again, a process of shaping. Acts that originally led to payoffs are made necessary parts of or conditions for larger social acts. An example is the act of reading for which a child may receive stars or praise and which is maintained in the adult because it permits perusal of love letters and psychological journals. The token economy may be devised in stages so that what was formerly a privilege becomes a necessary condition for movement upward and functioning at a higher level; for example, being allowed to leave the ward to go by oneself to a hospital industry job. All behavioral procedures, such as shaping, prompting and fading, chaining, modeling, variable ratio schedules, reinforcer sampling, extinction, and time out from reinforcement, may be used in developing and maintaining new behaviors.

An important concept is called the "dead man rule." The targets should not be things a dead person can do: be quiet, be unobtrusive. Rather than "do nots," the instructor in a token economy strives to find activities that are incompatible with the targets to be decreased. For example, rather than aiming to avoid daydreaming, activities should be of such interest and payoff that people will pay attention in an effort to succeed. Attention is a necessary condition for the response and occurs because it is worthwhile. In extreme cases, to avoid injurious behavior or the like, there may be a fine or response cost or a rare use of aversive stimulation. As soon as possible, the incompatible, alternative behavior that is more socially useful is taught as a way to deal with the situation.

Since the goal is independent, socially successful reaction to situations, a person may well receive tokens for his or her own scheduling and evaluation of behavior. The subject is encouraged to make suggestions as to new behaviors to be reinforced or new backup reinforcers. Eventually a successful token economy becomes the expression of all the people within it, not only the instructors. Ultimately the subjects become their own therapists—programming and reinforcing themselves. The ultimate goal is response in the extra-treatment environment, fulfilling because of intrinsic interest and naturally occurring social reinforcement.

While the token economy is a very useful set of applied procedures, it also has a major role in theoretical formulations of "normal" and "abnormal" behavior. For example, the very responsiveness and social attainments of people called schizophrenic to explicit contingencies argue against disease models of schizophrenia. The target behaviors selected by therapists provide insights into their definitions of normality. The token economy may be used to formulate, manipulate, and test a broad spectrum of political, economic, and sociological theories (Krasner, 1980). Treatment *is* social living. The token economy is an illustration.

REFERENCES

Atthowe, J. M., Jr., & Krasner, L. A. (1968). A preliminary report on the application of contingent reinforcement procedures (token economy) on a "chronic" ward. *Journal of Abnormal Psychology, 73,* 37–43.

Ayllon, T., & Azrin, N. H. (1968). *The token economy.* New York: Appleton-Century-Crofts.

Becker, W. C. (1973). Applications of behavioral principles in typical classrooms. In C. E. Thoresen (Ed.), *Behavior modification in education. NSSE 72nd yearbook.* Chicago: University of Chicago Press.

Bijou, S. W., & Orlando, R. (1961). Rapid development of multiple-schedule performances with retarded children. *Journal of Experimental Analysis of Behavior, 4,* 7–16.

Cohen, H. L., & Filipzak, T. (1971). *A new learning environment.* San Francisco: Jossey-Bass.

Krasner, L. (Ed.) (1980). *Environmental design and human behavior: A psychology of the individual in society.* Elmsford, NY: Pergamon.

Krasner, L., & Ullmann, L. P. (1973). *Behavior influence and personality: The social matrix of human action.* New York: Holt, Rinehart & Winston.

O'Leary, K. D., & Drabman, R. (1971). Token reinforcement programs in the classroom: A review. *Psychological Bulletin, 75,* 379–398.

Paul, G. L., & Lentz, R. J. (1977). *Psychosocial treatment of chronic mental patients.* Cambridge, MA: Harvard University Press.

Phillips, E. L., Phillips, E. A., Fixsen, D. L., & Wolf, M. M. (1971). Achievement place: Modification of the behaviors of predelinquent boys within a token economy. *Journal of Applied Behavior Analysis, 4,* 45–59.

Sulzer-Azaroff, B., & Mayer, G. R. (1977). *Applying behavior-analysis procedures with children.* New York: Holt, Rinehart & Winston.

L. P. ULLMANN
Incline Valley, Nevada

BEHAVIOR MODIFICATION
BEHAVIORISM
OPERANT CONDITIONING
SOFT-DETERMINISM

TOLMAN, EDWARD CHASE (1886–1959)

Edward Chase Tolman received his first degree, in engineering, from the Massachusetts Institute of Technology. However, he later changed to psychology, and was awarded the PhD degree by Harvard in 1915. He taught at Northwestern University but spent most of his career at the University of California at Berkeley, where he established a rat laboratory.

In his early years, he was much impressed with John Watson's new behaviorism. However, he departed from the typical S-R (stimulus-response) psychology and began to develop a different concept, which he called "purposive behaviorism." Unlike the more traditional behaviorists, he placed great emphasis on cognition, emphasizing the importance of how individuals perceive the fields they are in.

Tolman is primarily known for his theory of learning. Many psychologists consider this theory a "cognitive field theory," although in his many experiments, primarily with the white rat, he always stressed behavior. He considered the behavioral event to be molar rather than molecular, which means that the event should be identified and described as a whole rather than reduced to a series of reflexes. Furthermore, he considered behavior to be purposive, indicating the importance of goal direction; the direction an organism takes depends on its perception of the goal and the totality of the situation along with expectations developed with regard to the situation.

Learning as such consists of the organism's moving along a path guided by various stimuli, both internal and external. One learns by signs, that is, what leads to what. What is learned is not a series of movements, but meanings. One learns a route to a goal and a "cognitive map" results that enables an organism to go from one point in the environment to another without depending on a set of bodily movements. Learning involves both expectancies and their confirmation. The importance of the goal is not to be thought of as a reward or reinforcement as in the learning theories of Thorndike,

Hull, and Skinner, but merely as a confirmation of the expectancies.

Tolman is usually credited with introducing the concept of the "intervening variable" into psychology. Intervening variables involve inferred or unobservable factors that help in the explanation of the event but are not directly verifiable.

Finally, he believed that learning could occur in the absence of a goal. He identified this as "latent learning." Although not directly observable, learning could take place implicitly, and later, when a goal was introduced, the reality of the latent learning would become evident.

R. W. LUNDIN
Wheaton, Illinois

TOUCH THERAPY RESEARCH

Touch therapy or massage therapy is defined as the manipulation of body tissues by the hands for wellness and the reduction of stress and pain. Its therapeutic effects derive from its impact on the muscular, nervous, and circulatory systems. Massage therapy sessions usually combine several techniques, including Swedish massage (stroking and kneading), Shiatsu (pressure points), and neuromuscular massage (deep pressure). Oils are typically used and aromatic essences are often added for an additional effect. The sessions also feature soft background music, usually classical or new age.

The practice of massage has existed since before recorded time. The word "massage" can be found in many classic texts including the Bible and the Ayur-Veda. Hippocrates, as early as 400 BC, talked about the necessity of physicians' being experienced in the art of rubbing. Ancient records from China and somewhat more recent ones from Japan refer to massage therapy, and it was also widely used by people of other early cultures, including the Arabs, Egyptians, Indians, Greeks, and Romans. During the Renaissance massage spread throughout Europe, and early in the 19th century Swedish massage was developed.

Based on existing research, clients who receive massage therapy are expected to show improved mood state and affect and decreased anxiety and stress hormone levels (salivary cortisol). These changes have been highly significant based on observations of the client, self-reports by the client, and saliva assays for cortisol. In addition, whenever an EEG is performed, changes are shown in the direction of heightened alertness. Longer-term changes also measured in research have typically been evaluated after 4 to 6 weeks of treatment. These changes invariably include a decrease in depression, improved sleep patterns, lower stress (as measured by urinary cortisol, norepinephrine, and epinephrine levels), and enhanced immune function (an increase in natural killer cells). Changes on clinical measures that are specific to different conditions or considered by clinicians to be gold standards for those conditions have also been noted. For example, increases have been noted in pulmonary functions, such as peak air flow for children with asthma, and in blood glucose levels, as for children with diabetes, following a month of massage. Significant increase in weight gain has been noted in premature infants given 10 days of massage. These

changes are unique to each of these conditions and would not be expected to occur generally across medical conditions.

Although the primary indications have been for wellness and for stress and pain reduction, massage therapy is clinically useful in many ways, including the following: (a) pain reduction when used during childbirth and other painful circumstances, and when used prior to debridement for burn patients; (b) pain reduction in chronic conditions such as fibromyalgia, premenstrual syndrome, lower back pain, and migraine headaches; (c) alleviation of depression and anxiety, as with bulimia, anorexia, and chronic fatigue; (d) reduction of stress, including job stress and separation stress; and (e) increasing natural killer cells (the front line of the immune system which also ward off viral and cancer cells) in individuals with such immune and autoimmune disorders as AIDS, diabetes, and asthma.

Some therapists have warned of contraindications for massage, such as contagious skin conditions, high fever, scar tissue, varicose veins, and tumors. However, virtually no research supports these concerns.

Many massage therapists are located in private clinics in the community, or they have treatment rooms in their own homes. They can also be found in spas, workout clubs, hair salons, hotels, airports, and even at car washes in some cities. Finally, they can be hired to come to one's own home with a portable table or chair. Unfortunately, although as recently as the 1950s massage therapy was practiced routinely in hospitals, it is rarely seen in them today. The costs are relatively low ($1 per minute is the going rate), and the therapy has been shown to be cost-effective. For example, if each of the 470,000 infants who are born prematurely each year were given massage therapy, which typically results in an earlier discharge by about 6 days and hospital-cost savings of $10,000 per infant, a total of $4.7 million in medical costs could be saved annually. Similarly, using senior citizen volunteers as massage therapists for infants has been cost effective, resulting in lower amounts of stress hormones for those infants after about one month of massage, as well as fewer trips to the doctor's office. Similar cost-effectiveness figures are likely to emerge for other conditions that may benefit significantly from the stress reduction effects of massage therapy, which lowers amounts of the stress hormone cortisol and subsequently enhances immune function, resulting in less illness and greater wellness.

T. M. FIELD
University of Miami

TOWER OF HANOI PROBLEM

The Tower of Hanoi is a classical puzzle applied in the psychology of problem-solving and cognitive skill learning. In the standard version, it consists of three vertical wooden pegs and a variable number of wooden disks, usually three to six, each with a different diameter (figure 1). The disks have a hole in the middle and are stacked on the left peg in the order of diameter, the largest at the bottom. The task is to transfer the disks to the right peg with a minimum of moves. Disks must be moved from one peg to another.

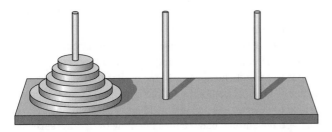

Figure 1.

Any peg may serve as a temporary target for any disk. Only one disk may be moved at a time, and larger disks must not be placed above smaller ones. Performance is measured by either the number of moves or the time required to complete the task, or both. In addition, different types of errors can be classified and assessed. The minimum number of moves is $2^n - 1$, where n is the number of disks (e.g., 31 for the 5-disk version). Approximate mean performances on the first attempt are 22 moves in 2 minutes for the 4-disk version and 64 moves in 10 minutes for the 5-disk version. In aged subjects, mean baseline performance declines.

The problem can be broken down to n similar subgoals (i.e., moving the next-largest disk to the right peg). Before one of these key moves is possible, the corresponding disk is isolated on alternately the left or the middle peg, and all smaller ones are stacked on the remaining peg. Thus goal, subgoal, and lower-order subgoal are self-similar and require equivalent strategies. At any stage, it is crucial for the subject to decide, by counting disks, where to make the first move; otherwise the process of unloading can lead to a blockade of the current target peg. Naive subjects tend to apply less efficient, ad hoc strategies and/or the trial-and-error approach.

The Tower of Hanoi problem requires different visuo-spatial abilities—that is, visual imagery and visuo-spatial working memory for the mental manipulation of disk configurations, and spatial long-term memory for the retention of move sequences. In normal subjects, a measure of spatial ability has, among several cognitive variables, been found to correlate most highly with time required to solve the 4-disk problem. In amnesic patients, performance was highly correlated with residual declarative memory capacity (Schmidtke, Handschu, & Vollmer, 1996). It is furthermore assumed that performance depends on frontal lobe, or executive, function. Patients with prefrontal lesions were reported to require more time and moves to solve the Tower of Hanoi and derived problems. Their deficit has been assigned to deficits of planning and to an inability to resolve goal-subgoal conflicts (Goel & Grafman, 1995; Morris, Miotto, Fiegenbaum, Bullock, & Polkey, 1997). Subnormal performances in other patient groups have been attributed to impairments of spatial memory or strategy formation. Since the Tower of Hanoi problem involves several cognitive capacities, its value as a neuropsychological test is limited. Although sensitive, it is not specific to prefrontal dysfunction.

Repeated execution of the problem leads to improvement of performance. In the 4-disk version, many normal subjects achieve a ceiling level of performance within few attempts; higher numbers of disks require considerably more trials. The rules and basic procedure of moving small stacks of disks from one peg to another are quickly proceduralized. Perfect performance requires explicit knowledge of the strategies mentioned previously. Before this level is achieved, relapses (i.e., markedly worse single performances) occur even at advanced stages of learning. Procedural learning of the Tower of Hanoi problem thus involves both declarative and nondeclarative components, the exact contributions of which are difficult to determine.

The problem has also been employed as a paradigm for the study of procedural learning in cognitively impaired subjects, specifically in patients with amnesia and basal ganglia disease. Amnesic patients, who may not remember having encountered the problem before, usually make considerable progress over trials. However, their learning is slowed in comparison to that of normal subjects, which is likely to be due to the deficient retention of explicit strategies and to deficits of planning and other cognitive capacities that typically go along with amnesia. Word fluency applied as a measure of prefrontal function has been found to correlate with measures of learning of the Tower of Hanoi problem (Schmidtke et al., 1996). Negative effects of age on the rate of learning have not been shown.

Variants of the Tower of Hanoi Problem have been developed to study planning and problem solving in normal subjects, psychiatric patients, and patients with organic brain damage. As an alternative to moving the whole stack of disks to another peg, the defined goal can be a rearrangement of disks from one given configuration to another. Isomorphs of the problem, such as the so-called Monster Problems, involve an analogous problem space and set of rules, but different outer appearance (Kotovsky, Hayes, & Simon, 1985). The Tower of London (Shallice, 1982) has also been applied in a number of versions. It is thought to depend more on planning and less on visuo-spatial abilities. Originally, it involves three beads of different colors and three pegs of different lengths that can carry one, two, and all three beads, respectively. From variable starting positions, the beads must be rearranged in patterns shown on cards, whereby the number of moves needed is indicated. Difficulty varies from one to five moves. Computerized versions use colored balls and touch-sensitive screens. In normal subjects, functional imaging studies of the task showed, among other areas, activation of the dorsolateral prefrontal cortex bilaterally, the lateral parietal cortex bilaterally, and the left anterior cingulate gyrus (Baker et al., 1996).

REFERENCES

Baker, S. C., Rogers, R. D., Owen, A. M., Frith, C. D., Dolan, R. J., Frackowiak, R. S. J., & Robbins, T. W. (1996). Neural systems engaged by planning: A PET study of the Tower of London task. *Neuropsychologia, 34,* 515–526.

Goel, V., & Grafman, J. (1995). Are the frontal lobes implicated in "planning" functions? Interpreting data from the Tower of Hanoi. *Neuropsychologia, 33,* 623–642.

Kotovsky, K., Hayes, J. R., & Simon, H. A. (1985). Why are some problems hard? Evidence from the Tower of Hanoi. *Cognitive Psychology, 17,* 248–294.

Morris, R. G., Miotto, E. C., Feigenbaum, J. D., Bullock, P., & Polkey, C. E. (1997). The effect of goal-subgoal conflict on planning ability after frontal- and temporal-lobe lesions in humans. *Neuropsychologia, 35,* 1147–1157.

Schmidtke, K., Handschu, R., & Vollmer, H. (1996). Cognitive procedural learning in amnesia. *Brain and Cognition, 32,* 44–467.

Shallice, T. (1982). Specific impairments of planning. *Philosophical Transactions of the Royal Society of London, B, 298,* 198–209.

K. SCHMIDTKE
University of Frieberg, Germany

TRANSACTIONAL ANALYSIS (TA)

Transactional analysis (TA) is an interactional therapy grounded in the assumption that people make current decisions based on past premises that at one time might have been appropriate for survival, but frequently are no longer valid. Although TA can be used in individual therapy, it is particularly suitable for groups. The approach emphasizes the cognitive, rational, and behavioral aspects of personality. The basic goal of the therapeutic process is to assist individuals in making new decisions regarding their present behavior and the direction of their lives. As a therapy, TA is geared to helping them gain awareness of how they have restricted their freedom of choice by following early decisions about their life positions, and it provides alternatives to deterministic modes of living.

The originator of TA, Eric Berne, based his personality theory on a framework of three separate ego states: Parent, Adult, and Child. The Parent part of the personality is an introject of parental standards, and as such it contains *shoulds* and *oughts.* This ego state can be the "Nurturing Parent" or the "Critical Parent." The Adult ego state is the processor of information that computes possibilities and makes objective decisions. The Child ego state consists of feelings and impulses; it is the spontaneous part. This can be a "Natural Child" or an "Adapted Child." Clients are expected to learn how to identify the functioning of their ego states, so that they can make conscious choices as to how they will function in a given situation.

Robert Goulding and Mary McClure Goulding, in *Changing Lives Through Redecision Therapy,* describe their redecisional approach to group therapy, which differs from the classical approach of Eric Berne. They have developed a modified version of TA that combines its principles and techniques with those of Gestalt therapy, family therapy, psychodrama, and behavior modification.

Transactional analysis focuses on injunctions, early decisions, strokes, games, rackets, the life script, and redecisions. Children grow up with certain parental messages (or injunctions) given both verbally and nonverbally. The Gouldings have specified a list of what they consider to be the 10 basic injunctions: Don't. Don't be. Don't be close. Don't be important. Don't be a child. Don't grow. Don't succeed. Don't be you. Don't be sane (*or don't be well*). Don't belong. According to the Gouldings, we accept these injunctions and make early decisions based on them.

Early decisions are aimed at receiving parental *strokes* (attention from parents). Transactional analysis pays attention to the manner in which people seek recognition and the kinds of strokes they ask for and receive. *Games,* which are a series of ulterior transactions with a predictable outcome and some type of payoff, develop as a way of supporting one's early decisions. Members of TA groups are taught to make connections between the games they played as children and the games they currently play. The basic goal of a TA group is to provide members with the opportunity to reduce game playing in favor of responding directly and honestly. Along with learning to detect games, group members learn about their *rackets,* which are the chronic bad feelings that flow from one's early decisions, are collected by people playing games, and justify one's basic decisions. Thus a woman who has been brought up on the *don't be close* injunction, and who has made the decision not to trust others, might find a variety of ways to look for and "save up" angry feelings to justify her need for distance. If she collects enough bad feelings, she is likely to prove her basic assumption—that it is not wise to get close, and that people cannot really be trusted.

All of these elements fit into the *life script,* which includes one's expectations of how one's life drama will be played out. Members of TA groups learn how their life scripts influence their feelings, attitudes, and behaviors in the present. These life scripts include injunctions that were incorporated, the games we play to maintain early decisions, the rackets we experience to justify our decisions, and our expectations concerning the way we think our life drama will be played out and will eventually end. The Gouldings' approach to TA rejects the notion that we are passively "scripted" and that we are victims of early conditioning; rather they assert that we make decisions in response to real and imagined parental messages and that we basically "script" ourselves. A major contribution to TA theory and practice is the role of *redecisions.* Once early decisions have been made, through a variety of therapeutic techniques group members can reexperience early childhood scenes, can relive situations in which they made certain self-defeating decisions about themselves and about life, and eventually can make a *new decision* on both an intellectual and emotional level.

A basic part of TA practice consists of the *contract* that sets the focus for therapy and determines the basis for therapeutic relationships. The therapeutic contract contains a specific statement of client goals, as well as ways in which these goals will be met and evaluated. Clients in TA decide those specific beliefs, emotions, and behaviors that they plan to change about themselves in order to reach their self-designated goals. After a redecision, people tend to think, behave, and feel in different ways and to move in the direction of becoming autonomous.

SUGGESTED READING

Berne, E. (1964). *Games people play: The psychology of human relationships.* New York: Grove Press.

Corey, G. (1982/1977). *Theory and practice of counseling and psychotherapy* (2nd ed.). Monterey, CA: Brooks/Cole.

Goulding, M. M., & Goulding, R. L. (1979). *Changing lives through redecision therapy.* New York: Brunner/Mazel.

G. COREY
California State University

PSYCHOTHERAPY

TRANSCENDENTAL MEDITATION TECHNIQUE

In the West, the physical sciences probe the nature of matter; the biological sciences probe the nature of living organisms; and the social sciences probe the nature of human thought and behavior. In the East, systematic meditation techniques have been developed that probe the essential nature of the knower underlying human thought and behavior. The Transcendental Meditation® (TM®) technique[1] has been revived from the vedic tradition of India, and disseminated worldwide by Maharishi Mahesh Yogi. The TM technique is easily learned and practiced 15 to 20 minutes twice daily. It requires no change in lifestyle or belief, and consequently is practiced by over 5 million people of all faiths, from all walks of life, and from all cultures. With this large group of TM subjects, more than 600 studies have been conducted on the TM technique at more than 200 universities and research institutions worldwide.

DESCRIPTION OF TM PRACTICE

TM practice is a dynamic process characterized by: (a) movement of attention from the active, surface level of thinking and perception to the more silent and abstract levels of thought; (b) transcendence of the subtlest thinking level to a state of fully awake self-awareness (called Transcendental Consciousness, or *Atman,* in Sanskrit); and (c) movement of attention back to more active levels (Wallace, 1986). These three phases, which can by physiologically distinguished (Travis & Wallace, 1997), cycle many times in each TM session, and define a state of "restful alertness"—deep rest for the body and increased alertness for the mind. The state of restful alertness releases mental & physical stress.

Transcendental Consciousness is the defining experience of TM practice. Phenomenologically, Transcendental Consciousness is characterized by "silence," "unboundedness," and "the absence of time, space, and body-sense" (Travis & Pearson, 2000). Transcendental Consciousness is described as a state of self-awareness (subjects are awake during this state and can describe its nature afterward) without customary waking processing and contents.

This description of Transcendental Consciousness is admittedly outside of the usual paradigm of waking experiences. Since William James, the prevailing Western view has been that conscious awareness is always mixed with "mental-instances" in consciousness (Ferrari, 1998)—that is, consciousness is never found without its processes or objects of experience. However, the experience of Transcendental Consciousness cannot be disregarded simply because it is outside current paradigms. It is a direct experience—not merely a conceptual reality—with defining physiological characteristics: (a) apneustic breathing (slow prolonged inhalation) for 10 to 40 sec (Kesterson & Clinch, 1989); (b) autonomic orienting at the onset of breath changes (Travis & Wallace, 1997);

(c) increased EEG coherence; and (d) 1.0 Hz increases in the frequency of peak power (Travis & Wallace, 1997).

These unique subjective and objective markers of Transcendental Consciousness support its description as a fourth major state of consciousness (Maharishi, 1963), in addition to the three commonly experienced states of waking, sleeping, and dreaming. Repeated experience of Transcendental Consciousness, followed by daily activity, leads to the integration of this silent alert state with ongoing waking, sleeping, and dreaming processes, forming a sequential unfolding of three higher states of consciousness (Maharishi, 1963). Initial findings suggest unique EEG patterns (Mason et al., 1997) and unique cortical preparatory response patterns (Travis & Tecce, 1998) in subjects reporting the experience of cosmic consciousness, the first of these three higher states.

COMPARISON WITH OTHER PRACTICES

Some researchers have questioned whether effects produced during TM practice are common to all meditation and relaxation techniques (Holmes, 1984). Using objective quantitative methods, five meta-analyses suggest that TM practice is fundamentally different from other techniques. Compared to eyes-closed rest, other meditation techniques, and relaxation responses, these meta-analyses found that TM practice results in: (a) significantly larger reductions in anxiety ($N = 141$ studies) (Eppley, Abrams, & Shear, 1989); (b) significantly lower breath rates, skin conductance levels, and plasma lactate levels ($N = 31$ studies) (Dillbeck & Orme-Johnson, 1987); (c) significantly higher levels of self-actualization ($N = 42$ studies) (Alexander, Rainforth, & Gelderloos, 1991); (d) significantly greater reductions in the use of illegal drugs, alcohol, and cigarettes ($N = 198$ studies) (Alexander, Robinson, & Rainforth, 1994); and (e) significantly greater reductions in systolic and diastolic blood pressure (Barnes, Schneider, Alexander, & Staggers, 1997).

APPLICATION TO INDIVIDUAL AND SOCIETY ISSUES

TM practice has practical benefits for:

1. *Health.* In comparison to matched controls, TM subjects ($N = 2,000$) showed 50% lower inpatient and outpatient medical use over a 5-year period, and lower sickness rates in 17 disease categories, including 87% fewer hospitalizations for heart disease (Orme-Johnson, 1987).

2. *Elderly care.* A randomized study with 73 institutionalized elderly people (81 years of age) indicated that practice of the TM technique reduced blood pressure and cognitive decline (over 3 months) and mortality rate (over 15 years) compared to mental relaxation, mindfulness training, or no treatment (Alexander et al., 1996).

3. *Prison rehabilitation.* California inmates ($N = 259$) who learned the TM technique had a 40% decrease in recidivism rate over a 5-year period compared to controls matched on social history and on use of training programs while in prison (Bleick & Abrams, 1987).

4. *Business.* A 5-month longitudinal study ($N = 800$) conducted by the Japanese National Institute of Health found that em-

[1]®Transcendental Meditation, TM, and TM-Sidhi are service marks registered in the U.S. Patent and Trademark Office, licensed to Maharishi Vedic Education Development Corporation, and used under sublicense.

ployees practicing the TM technique showed significant decreases in physical health complaints, anxiety, insomnia, and smoking compared to controls from the same industrial site (Haratani & Henmi, 1990).

5. *Quality of life.* More than 40 sociological studies indicate that TM practice by a small proportion of a society—or a smaller number practicing the advanced TM-Sidhi program—leads to significant reductions in crime, auto accidents, and political violence, and improvements in the economy (Orme-Johnson, Alexander, Davies, Chandler, & Larimore, 1988). This effect was highlighted in a 2-month planned sociological experiment in Washington, D.C. in 1993, which resulted in significant reductions in violent crime as the group size increased from 1,000 to 3,800 (Hagelin et al., 1999).

CONCLUSION

TM practice, by systematically enlivening the full range of the mind, releasing mental & physical stress, and integrating the essential nature of the knower with ongoing waking processes, may be instrumental in unfolding the full range of human potential, and in understanding the dynamic relation between the individual and society.

REFERENCES

Alexander, C., Barnes, V., Schneider, R., Langer, E., Newman, R., Chandler, H., Davies, J., & Rainforth, M. (1996). Randomized controlled trial of stress reduction on cardiovascular and all-cause mortality in the elderly: Results of 8 year and 15 year follow-ups. *Circulation, 93*(3), 19.

Alexander, C. N., Rainforth, M. V., & Gelderloos, P. (1991). Transcendental Meditation, self actualization and psychological health: A conceptual overview and statistical meta-analysis. *Journal of Social Behavior and Personality, 6,* 189–247.

Alexander, C. N., Robinson, P., & Rainforth, M. (1994). Treating alcohol, nicotine and drug abuse through Transcendental Meditation: A review and statistical meta-analysis. *Alcoholism Treatment Quarterly, 11*(1–2), 11–84.

Barnes, V. A., Schneider, R. H., Alexander, C., & Staggers, F. (1997). Stress, stress reduction and hypertension in African Americans: An updated review. *Journal of the National Medical Association, 89,* 469–476.

Bleick, C. R., & Abrams, A. I. (1987). The Transcendental Meditation program and criminal recidivism in California. *Journal of Criminal Justice, 15*(3), 211–230.

Dillbeck, M. C., & Orme-Johnson, D. W. (1987). Physiological differences between Transcendental Meditation and rest. *American Psychologist, 42,* 879–881.

Eppley, K. R., Abrams, A. I., & Shear, J. (1989). Differential effects of relaxation techniques on trait anxiety: A meta-analysis. *Journal of Clinical Psychology, 45*(6), 957–974.

Ferrari, M. (1998). Being and becoming self-aware. In M. Ferrari & R. J. Sternberg (Eds.), *Self-awareness—Its nature and development* (387–422). New York: Guilford.

Hagelin, J. S., Rainforth, M. V., Orme-Johnson, D. W., Cavanaugh, K. L., Alexander, C. N., Shatkin, S. F., Davies, J. L., Hughes, A. O., & Ross, E. (1999). Effects of group practice of the Transcendental Meditation program on preventing violent crime in Washington, DC: Results of the National Demonstration Project, June–July, 1993. *Social Indicators Research, 47*(2), 62–76.

Haratani, T., & Henmi, T. (1990). Effects of Transcendental Meditation on health behavior of industrial workers. *Japanese Journal of Public Health, 37*(10), 729.

Holmes, D. S. (1984). Meditation and somatic arousal reduction. *American Psychologist, 39,* 1–10.

Kesterson, J., & Clinch, N. (1989). Metabolic rate, respiratory exchange ratio, and apneas during meditation. *American Physiological Society, 89,* R632—R638.

Maharishi Mahesh Yogi. (1963). *The Science of Being and Art of Living.* Livingston Manor, NY: Maharishi International University Press.

Mason, L., Alexander, C. N., Travis, F., Marsh, G., Orme-Johnson, D. W., Gackenbach, J., Mason, D., Rainforth, M., & Walton, K. (1997). Electrophysiological correlates of higher states of consciousness during sleep in long-term practitioners of the Transcendental Meditation program. *Sleep, 20*(2), 102–110.

Orme-Johnson, D. W. (1987). Medical care utilization and the Transcendental Meditation program. *Psychosomatic Medicine, 49,* 493–507.

Orme-Johnson, D. W., Alexander, C. N., Davies, J. L., Chandler, H. M., & Larimore, W. E. (1988). International peace project in the Middle East: The effects of the Maharishi Technology of the Unified Field. *Journal of Conflict Resolution, 32*(4), 776–812.

Travis, F. T., & Pearson, C. (2000). Pure consciousness: Distinct phenomenological and physiological correlates of "consciousness itself." *International Journal of Neuroscience, 100,* 77–89.

Travis, F. T., & Tecce, J. J. (1998). CNV rebound and distraction effects before and after a TM session. *Psychophysiology, 34,* S89.

Travis, F. T., & Wallace, R. K. (1997). Autonomic patterns during respiratory suspensions: Proposed markers of transcendental consciousness. *Psychophysiology, 34,* 39–46.

Wallace, R. K. (1986). *The physiology of consciousness,* Fairfield, IA: Maharishi International University Press.

F. TRAVIS
Maharishi University of Management

MEDITATION
PHILOSOPHY AND PSYCHOLOGY
RELIGION AND PSYCHOLOGY

TRANSPERSONAL PSYCHOLOGY: AN EDITORIAL NOTE

Because of the importance of this topic, which relates to interpenetration of two conceptions and the creation of an emergent between Western and Eastern psychologies, I asked Dr. Norman Sundberg, a psychologist, and Dr. Roger Walsh, a psychiatrist, to write independent entries. They, in turn, took on collaborators, and so the reader is presented with two somewhat overlapping but nevertheless distinctive views of a phenomenon that may have considerable importance not only for psychology, but for humanity as well.

R. J. CORSINI

TRANSPERSONAL PSYCHOLOGY I

Transpersonal psychology has a short history but a long past. As a branch of psychology, it appeared in the late 1960s as an outgrowth of humanistic psychology under the leadership of Maslow, Grof, Sutich, and several others (Vaughan, 1982). The first issue of the *Journal of Transpersonal Psychology* appeared in the spring of 1969 and the Association for Transpersonal Psychology was founded in 1971. However, as an area of human concern, transpersonal psychology goes back to prehistoric times. In 1902, one of the founders of scientific psychology, William James, wrote about transpersonal phenomena in *The Varieties of Religious Experience* (1961). Jung was apparently the first to speak of the "transpersonal unconscious" (*das überpersönliche Unbewusste*), a term he used interchangeably with "collective unconscious" in his essay. "The structure of the unconscious" in 1917. Jung's concepts of archetypes, synchronicity, and the collective unconscious have had major impact on writers in the field (Jung, 1934; Keutzer, 1982). Many transpersonal psychologists see the emerging tradition as an integration of ancient wisdom and modern science and a rapprochement between Eastern mysticism and Western rationalism.

"Transpersonal" literally means across or beyond the individual person or psyche. It refers to an expansion or extension of consciousness beyond the usual ego boundaries and beyond the limitations of time and/or space and is concerned with aspects of psychology related to "ultimate human capabilities and potentialities that have no systematic place in positivistic or behavioristic theory ('first force'), classical psychoanalytic theory ('second force'), or humanistic psychology ('third force')" (Sutich, 1969, pp. 15–16). This emerging "fourth force" covers empirical study, application, and theorization about a wide variety of topics, such as some of those listed in the statement of purpose of the *Journal of Transpersonal Psychology:* values, unitive consciousness, mysticism, the sacredness of everyday life, cosmic awareness, cosmic play, individual and species-wide synergy, the spiritual paths, theories and practices of meditation, compassion, and transpersonal cooperation. In one of the first contemporary reference books, *Transpersonal Psychologies,* Tart (1975) presents excerpts from several Eastern religions (Zen Buddhism, Yoga, Sufism), the Christian mystical literature, and other esoteric traditions. Belief systems are particularly important because they transcend the self and involve identification with the larger values and goals of groups and societies that often motivate a fully developed, unselfish human being (Frank, 1982; Maslow, 1969). One of the premises of the transpersonal perspective is the necessity to examine belief systems. In fact,

the transpersonal perspective is a metaperspective that suggests looking at the relative merits of different belief systems rather than becoming so identified with them that they are imposed on others (Walsh & Vaughan, 1980).

Much of the rationale for transpersonal psychology starts with a questioning of the basis for knowledge in orthodox scientific psychology. Is human knowledge to be confined only to that derived from rational thinking and sensory experiences of the waking state? The transpersonal position is that there are several ways to obtain and prove knowledge (cf. Wilber, 1982) and that there are many states of consciousness, all of which should be of importance for psychology. The altered states of consciousness (as in dreams, trance, ecstasy, awe, or hypnotic conditions, or under the influence of psychotropic drugs) may have special laws different from those of ordinary waking life. Tart (1975, 1976) presents a long list of assumptions or common beliefs of Western science that need to be reconsidered if we are to have a full psychology of human experience and behavior; for instance, the only events that are real are those recorded by physical instruments or the senses that are measurable by physical instruments; altered states of consciousness are inferior or pathologic; death is the end of life; reasoning is the highest skill; or hedonistic desire is the basic motive that keeps life going. If these and other assumptions are not questioned, scientists rule out many phenomena, including such paranormal aspects as extrasensory perception, faith healing, out-of-body experiences, and survival after death. Tart, who equates the transpersonal with the spiritual, insists on the importance of studying these phenomena and others that are mystical, subjective, and ephemeral—phenomena that are readily accepted in many cultures (Tart, 1976). Some psychologists (e.g., Frank, 1982; Hampden-Turner, 1981) note that these phenomena and spiritual beliefs are particularly difficult to describe or study, because they relate to the processing going on in the largely nonverbal, right side of the brain, whereas most science is ultimately communicated linearly in words and numbers. The rational, verbal side of the brain is dominant in the Western scientific world view. This view, based on the notion of physicalism, has built an impressive physical world exploiting natural resources; it has not been successful in the nonphysical realms, to which it has paid little attention.

Even in the natural sciences, transpersonal scientists raise possibilities for explanations of phenomena that differ from the common laws of causality by using such concepts as "formative causation" and "synchronicity" (Keutzer, 1982). Although many eminent scientists have been intrigued by Jung's concept of synchronicity (a meaningful but acausal confluence of events), it was not until quite recently that science could consider such an unconventional phenomenon—an event outside of a space–time cause-and-effect sequence. This was made possible by dramatic findings in modern physics that presented a world view so radical and far-reaching in its implications as to alter the very foundations of science (Walsh & Vaughan, 1980). Quantum mechanics, for example, seems to have demonstrated some synchronicities of its own, most notably the apparent underlying connectedness shown by the "distant correlation" experiments based on Bell's theorem that suggest the possibility that everything in the universe, including human beings, might be invisibly linked rather than unrelated and separate

(Keutzer, 1982). Transpersonal psychologists view the contemporary reformulations in philosophy, psychology, neurophysiology, and physics as a direct challenge to what is typically called "objective reality."

A coherent organization of research and theory in transpersonal psychology is yet to be developed. There are many possibilities for research, for example, Eastern and Western belief systems and their hypotheses about experience and behavior, the correlates of drug-induced altered states of consciousness, study of individual differences in sensitivity to paranormal phenomena, the beliefs and conditions of healing in different cultures, changes in perception in different states of consciousness, types of altered states of consciousness that accompany intuitive mathematical and scientific discoveries, and the conditions and experiences surrounding mystical and religious experience and conversion phenomena. One aspect of Yoga that was once considered mystical and untested has already been moved into the "normal" arena of psychology, namely, control over autonomic body functions, which has spawned much research and application in biofeedback. Another common transpersonal topic that seems to be gaining acceptance is meditation. Obtaining fairly broad appeal in the 1960s, transcendental meditation and other forms of meditation have been shown to have definite physiological effects different from other phenomena and to be useful for people under stress. Walsh (1981, 1982) has reviewed the literature and advocates meditation as an inexpensive, self-regulated, and effective procedure, which may result in the deepest transformation of identity, life-style, and relationship to the world.

In alliance with its predecessor, humanistic psychology, transpersonal psychology takes an antireductionistic stance toward the sources of human experience and focuses on the phenomenology of consciousness—especially those states of consciousness that apparently transcend the impression of personal isolation, centrality, and self-sufficiency. As an interdisciplinary and cross-cultural movement, the transpersonal orientation presents many challenges to conventional psychology: Is there a cosmic meaning of life and death? What are the explanations of unusual and impactful experiences? Are there relationships and interactions among all sentient beings? With strong support from some areas in modern physics, it also presents many challenges to commonly held views of linearity, causality, fixed space—time relationships, and a purely mechanistic view of the universe. Needless to say, the fringes of transpersonal psychology engender much skepticism. As Tart says, "It is a vast area, containing . . . an incredible mixture of the scientific, the spiritual, the pathological, and the nonsensical, with a little touch of just plain fraudulent" (Tart, 1975, p. 151).

REFERENCES

Frank, J. D. (1982). Therapeutic components shared by all psychotherapies. In J. H. Harvey & M. M. Parks (Eds.), *The master lecture series: Vol. 1. Psychotherapy research and behavior change* (pp. 9–37). Washington, DC: American Psychological Association.

Hampden-Turner, C. (1981). *Maps of the mind: Charts and concepts of the mind and its labyrinths.* New York: Macmillan.

James, W. (1914). *The varieties of religious experience: A study in human nature.* New York: Longmans, Green. (Original work published 1902)

Jung, C. G. (1969/1959/1934). *The archetypes and the collective unconscious. The collected works of C. G. Jung* (Vol. 9, Pt. I). Princeton, NJ: Princeton University Press.

Jung, C. G. (1972/1917–1928). *Two essays on analytical psychology.* Princeton, NJ: Princeton University Press.

Keutzer, C. S. (1982). Archetypes, synchronicity, and the theory of formative causation. *Journal of Analytic Psychology, 27,* 255–262.

Maslow, A. H. (1969). The farther reaches of human nature. *Journal of Transpersonal Psychology, 1,* 1–9.

Sutich, A. J. (1969). Some considerations regarding transpersonal psychology. *Journal of Transpersonal Psychology, 1,* 11–20.

Tart, C. T. (1975). *States of consciousness.* New York: Dutton.

Tart, C. T. (1976). The basic nature of altered states of consciousness: A systems approach. *Journal of Transpersonal Psychology, 8,* 45–64.

Vaughan, F. E. (1982). The transpersonal perspective: A personal overview. *Journal of Transpersonal Psychology, 14,* 37–45.

Walsh, R. N. (1981). Meditation. In R. J. Corsini (Ed.), *Handbook of innovative psychotherapies.* New York: Wiley.

Walsh, R. N. (1982). A model for viewing meditation research. *Journal of Transpersonal Psychology, 14,* 69–84.

SUGGESTED READING

Murphy, G., & Murphy, L. B. (Eds.) *Asian psychology.* New York: Basic Books.

Tart, C. T. (Ed.) (1975). *Transpersonal psychologies.* New York: Harper & Row.

Walsh, R. N., & Vaughan, F. E. (Eds.). (1980). *Beyond ego: Transpersonal dimensions in psychology.* Los Angeles: Tarcher.

Wilber, K. (1977). *The spectrum of consciousness.* Wheaton, IL: Theosophical.

N. D. SUNDBERG
C. S. KEUTZER
University of Oregon

ASIAN PSYCHOLOGY
CROSS-CULTURAL PSYCHOLOGY
RELIGION AND PSYCHOLOGY
TRANSPERSONAL PSYCHOLOGY (II)

TRANSPERSONAL PSYCHOLOGY II

Born out of a concern with pathology, Western psychology and psychiatry have recently begun to turn their attention toward psychological health and well-being. This in turn has suggested models of human nature and potential different from those derived from the study of pathology. Evidence from several disciplines suggests that the human potential for psychological growth and well-being may have been underestimated. Much of the new data are inconsistent with traditional models.

Transpersonal psychology attempts to research those experiences in which the sense of identity expands beyond (*trans*) the individual person, personality, or ego to encompass aspects of humankind, life, and the universe. Such experiences have been valued in most cultures at times. Transpersonal psychology aims to explore the nature, varieties, effects, and means of inducing such experiences as well as the philosophies and traditions inspired by them. It attempts to integrate contemporary science and philosophy with the perennial wisdom of East and West. While it investigates what Abraham Maslow called "the farther reaches of human nature," this investigation should be integrated with knowledge from fields such as neuroscience, cognitive science, anthropology, philosophy, and comparative religion and incorporate Eastern as well as Western theory and research (Walsh & Vaughan, 1980, 1993; Wilber, Engler, & Brown, 1986). As such it is a wide-ranging, integrative, and interdisciplinary field. Topics of special interest include consciousness and altered states, cross-cultural studies, meditation, contemplation and yoga, lucid dreaming, mythology, psychedelics, philosophical foundations, values, ethics, relationships, exceptional psychological well-being and capacities, transconventional development, transpersonal emotions such as love and compassion and motives such as altruism and service, transpersonal pathologies, psychotherapies and related clinical concerns, comparative religion, and psychological roots of contemporary global crises.

Transpersonal psychology emerged in the late 1960s largely out of humanistic psychology when pioneers such as Maslow found the humanistic model unable fully to encompass exceptional levels of psychological health, meditative and yogic techniques and experiences, and some altered states of consciousness. Its emergence also was facilitated by a number of movements in psychology and the culture at large. These included a growing interest in the nature of consciousness and its alterations and the advent of psychedelics. These drugs evoked powerful experiences and states of consciousness, some of which lay outside the realm of daily living or of phenomena previously recognized by Western psychology. At the same time, interest in Eastern cultures and disciplines was expanding. Gradually, there emerged the recognition that aspects of certain non-Western psychologies, such as those associated with Buddhism, Hinduism, Sufism, and Taoism, were sophisticated systems especially concerned with well-being and human potential. The accumulation of empirical research in such areas as biofeedback, meditation, lucid dreaming, and various altered states of consciousness gradually lent research support to the emerging transpersonal perspective.

Transpersonal psychology recognizes that all psychologies are essentially models and as such no one model is the truth but rather only a necessarily partial and limited representation of reality. It, therefore, views different psychological models as embodying partially valid data and theories and as potentially complementary rather than necessarily oppositional. The transpersonal model thus is not intended to invalidate earlier ones, but rather to place them within an expanded context of human nature. Of course, the claims it makes about human nature are recognized as hypotheses

that must remain open to testing and modification. The following outline focuses on claims that are uniquely transpersonal and because of space limitations, must state them with less tentativeness and qualification than would be ideal.

THE TRANSPERSONAL MODEL

Consciousness

The transpersonal perspective holds that a large spectrum of states of consciousness exists, that some are potentially useful and functionally specific (i.e., possessing some functions not available in the usual state but lacking in others), and that some are higher states. *Higher* is used here in the sense of possessing the properties and capacities of lower states plus additional ones. Literature from a variety of cultures and disciplines attests to the attainability of these higher states. On the other hand, the traditional Western view holds that a limited range of states exists, for example, waking, dreaming, intoxication, and delirium. Moreover, nearly all altered states are considered detrimental and "normality" is considered optimal (Tart, 1983a, 1983b).

Motivation

Many psychologists have argued about which is the fundamental human motive, such as libido, superiority strivings, or self-esteem. Transpersonal models tend to follow Maslow in seeing motives as hierarchically organized and encompassing higher motives. Analogous models can be found in several Asian psychologies (Wilber, 1980; Wilber et al., 1986).

Following Maslow, motives can be viewed as hierarchically organized according to their potency and primacy. Motives with a clear physiological and survival basis, such as hunger and thirst, are seen as most powerful and prepotent. When these are fulfilled, less powerful needs such as security, social belongingness, and self-esteem are thought to become effective motivators in their turn. As these are satisfied, self-actualization emerges.

Beyond self-actualization lie motives that tend to predominate in exceptionally healthy individuals, recognized only in transpersonal and Eastern psychologies. One is self-transcendence, a drive toward experiences and modes of being that transcend the usual limits of identity. For the few persons who attain these levels, such as the prototypic sage, master, or saint of Taoism, Buddhism, Zen, or Vedanta, individual identity and motivation are said to be transcended. Reports suggest that such people are motivated primarily by altruism and respond spontaneously and compassionately to the needs of others (Walsh & Shapiro, 1983).

In ascending this hierarchy, motives appear to shift in several ways: from clearly physiological to apparently more psychological, from strong to subtle, from prepotent to less potent and more easily disrupted, from deficiency to sufficiency, from egocentric to allocentric, from avoidance to approach, from external to internal reinforcement, from field dependence to field independence, from spontaneous to requiring cultivation, and from frequent to rare in the population.

Identity

One of the ways in which the transpersonal perspective differs most sharply from other Western views is its concept of the sense of identity. Western psychologists usually assume that individuals' normal, natural, and optimal sense of identity or self-sense is what Alan Watts called "the skin encapsulated ego." However, Eastern and transpersonal psychologies suggest that our self-sense may be considerably more plastic than usually recognized and can expand to include aspects of the mind and the world usually regarded as "other" or "not me." One example comes from Carl Jung. He pointed out that in successful psychotherapy and maturation certain personality traits, emotions, and motives that were repressed and projected as the shadow are then recognized and reowned as aspects of the self.

A variety of transpersonal and mystical experiences, either spontaneous or deliberately induced, suggest that expansion of the self-sense can extend further to encompass aspects, or even all, of humanity and the world, thereby transcending the sense of separateness and isolation in recognition of the interrelated unity of existence. For example, a variety of meditative and yogic practices aim at refining awareness and directing it to a careful examination of the self-sense. What has been reported for centuries by yogis and more recently by Westerners is that what was formerly thought to be a solid unchanging sense of self is recognized as a continuously changing flux of thoughts, images, and emotions. The egoic self-sense is thus deconstructed by this precise examination and revealed to be an illusory product of imprecise awareness. With the dissolution of the egoic self-sense, a broader identification with humanity and the world may occur (Goldstein, 1983). In the deepest levels of insight the me—not me, self—other dichotomy is deconstructed, resulting in a loss of egocentricity and a sense of identification with all people and all things. This is the basis of such sayings as "the universe is the body of the saint" and "to study the self is to forget the self and to be one with all things." This unitive experience is regarded in many cultures as the most valued of all experiences.

PSYCHOTHERAPY

With its interest in exceptional degrees of development, the domain of transpersonal psychotherapy may extend beyond traditional therapeutic goals and adjustments. Although it addresses basic ego needs and aspirations, it also is open to considering the experiences and potentials available to individuals who already have achieved a satisfactory level of coping. In acknowledging a greater potential for psychological well-being, it aims to afford those individuals who are ready to do so the opportunity of working at transpersonal levels (Vaughan, 1986).

Transpersonal psychotherapy, therefore, tends to be eclectic. Specific tools and approaches are chosen according to the particular needs of the individual client. Ideally, a transpersonal therapist would have available a broad range of approaches from traditional Western psychotherapies as well as skills such as meditation and yoga. A transpersonal therapist would be expected to be familiar with the potential for inducing transpersonal experiences and able to assist clients with associated difficulties that may emerge (Wilber et al., 1986).

SUPPORTIVE DATA

Schools of psychology and psychotherapy abound; supportive data for their claims are less abundant. What support can be found for the claims of transpersonal psychology? Two types of evidence may be advanced: theoretical and empirical.

The transpersonal model derives support from a convergent network of concepts derived, in turn, from overlapping aspects of several Western psychologies, Eastern psychologies and philosophies, states of consciousness, meditation, biofeedback, and recent theorizing on development. There exists considerable empirical data on meditation (Shapiro & Walsh, 1984); some on altered states of consciousness (Tart, 1983a, 1983b), including lucid dreaming (Gackenbach & Laberge, 1988) and near-death experiences; and a little on exceptionally healthy individuals and transconventional development (Alexander & Langer, 1990; Walsh & Shapiro, 1983).

LIMITATIONS

What factors limit this field? First, more empirical research is essential. If the transpersonal is truly to be an effective synthesis of Eastern wisdom and Western science, extensive testing of its claims and implications is essential. Empirical rigor must be wedded to greater conceptual and philosophical rigor, especially to a far-reaching analysis of the field's philosophical presuppositions.

Because the field draws so extensively on cross-cultural data, it requires better and more extensive cross-cultural studies, adequately informed by contemporary anthropological thought and carried out by transpersonally sensitive investigators. A field of transpersonal anthropology has emerged that draws heavily on its psychological sibling (Laughlin, McManus, & Shearer, 1990). Transpersonal psychology also must be better integrated with other schools of psychology and therapy.

Those who explore transpersonal psychology and experiences in any depth realize that a personal experiential foundation is essential for both intellectual comprehension and skillful therapy. Both therapists and researchers need to be aware of this requirement and to undertake a personal discipline—such as depth psychotherapy, meditation, or yoga—so as to have the personal experiences essential for deep understanding and effective practice in this field.

Transpersonal psychology is also facing the two-edged sword of popularity. Increasing numbers of people are attracted to it, some of whom do not display an adequate rigor of theory and practice.

Transpersonal psychology has made significant contributions to understanding fundamental topics such as human identity, health, consciousness and altered states, motivation, potential, development, and meditation. The extent and rigor of its practitioners' theoretical, experimental, and experiential explorations may well be the major determinants of its fate and contributions.

REFERENCES

Walsh, R. N., & Shapiro, D. H. (Eds.). (1983). *Beyond health and normality: Explorations of exceptional psychological wellbeing.* New York: Van Nostrand Reinhold.

Wilber, K. (1980). *The Atman project.* Wheaton, IL: Quest.

R. WALSH
University of California, College of Medicine

F. VAUGHAN
California Institute of Transpersonal Psychology

TRANSSEXUALISM

The term "transsexual" has existed in the professional literature since the early 1920s (Hirschfeld, 1923). Only from 1949 on was it used in its modern sense: to denote individuals who desire to live (or who actually do live) permanently in the social role of the opposite gender and who want to undergo sex reassignment (Cauldwell, 1949). The desire for sex reassignment originates from an experienced discrepancy between one's sex of assignment on the one hand and one's basic sense of self as a male or female (gender identity) on the other hand.

In the current widely-used psychiatric classification system *Diagnostic and Statistic Manual of Mental Disorders–Fourth Edition (DSM-IV;* American Psychiatric Association), the term "transsexualism" has been abandoned. Instead, the term "Gender Identity Disorder" (GID) is used for individuals who show a strong and persistent cross-gender identification and a persistent discomfort with their anatomical sex or a sense of inappropriateness in the gender role of that sex, as manifested in a preoccupation with getting rid of one's sex characteristics or the belief to be born in the wrong sex. The *International Classification of Diseases and Related Health Problems–10 (ICD–10* of the World Health Organization), the other currently used classification system still lists transsexualism as a diagnosis.

A subdivision in types of transsexualism is often made; the terms "homosexual" (i.e., sexually oriented toward individuals of the same biological sex) and "nonhomosexual" transsexuals, or "primary" and "secondary" transsexuals are often used. The groups have been found to differ in several important ways, such as age at presentation, erotic arousal when cross-dressing, sexual orientation, and showing postoperative regrets. It is assumed that these differences reflect different etiologies.

ATYPICAL GENDER DEVELOPMENT.

Individuals may develop Gender Identity Disorder at the age of 2 or 3 years, but not all children with GID turn out to be adult transsexuals. Prospective studies of GID boys show that childhood GID is more strongly related to later homosexuality than to later transsexualism. It is estimated that only 1% to 5% will appear to be transsexual after puberty (see Zucker & Bradley, 1995 for a review).

Both parental/family factors and biological factors have been proposed to explain atypical gender development. Studies reporting psychopathology in parents of GID children support some parental influence on atypical gender identity development. However, the specific mechanisms that lead to GID instead of to other clinical conditions remain to be clarified. It is also possible that child-related factors evoke specific parental responses, (such as fostering femininity in a son) in an already unstable or vulnerable par-

ent. Indeed, the impression of clinicians that GID boys are very attractive was supported in experimental studies among boys (Zucker, Bradley 1995), whereas the opposite was found for GID girls. Retrospective studies in adult transsexuals have shown differences in recalled child-rearing patterns between parents of transsexuals and parents in normative groups. Male-to-female transsexuals (MFs) characterized their fathers as less emotionally warm, more rejecting and more (over-) controlling. Female-to-male (FMs) transsexuals rated both parents as more rejecting and less emotionally warm, but only their mothers as more (over-) protective than their female control equivalents rated theirs (see Cohen-Kettenis & Gooren 1999 for a review).

Potential biological determinants of transsexualism have been found in two areas: (1) Subjects with an abnormal pre- and perinatal endocrine history (an excess of androgens in females and a lack of androgen action in males) seem to be at higher risk for gender identity disorder (e.g., Meyer-Bahlburg et al., 1996); and (2) In humans, several hypothalamic nuclei are sexually dimorphic with respect to size and/or shape. In MFs it was found that one of these nuclei, the Bed Nucleus of the Stria Terminalis (BSTc), was not only significantly smaller than in non-transsexual males, but was also in the size range of females (Zhou, Hoffman, Gooren, & Swaab, 1995); that is, in this study a female brain structure was observed in genetically male transsexuals. Indirect evidence of atypical prenatal hormone exposure comes from studies showing that transsexuals differed, before hormone treatment, from nontranssexuals in sex-related cognitive functioning and cerebral functional asymmetry (Cohen-Kettenis, van Goozen, Doorn, & Gooren, 1998).

PREVALENCE OF GID AND TRANSSEXUALISM

There are no epidemiological studies providing data on the prevalence of childhood GID. Prevalence estimates of transsexualism among the population age 15 years and older are usually based on the number of transsexuals treated at major centers, or on responses of registered psychiatrists within a particular country or region to surveys concerning their number of transsexual patients. The numbers vary widely across studies. The estimated prevalence now varies between 1 in 10,000 to 40,000 men, and 1 in 30,000 to 100,000 women. As not all persons suffering from Gender Identity Disorder seek medical treatment, no estimation can be made regarding the prevalence of the wider spectrum of Gender Identity Disorder.

SEX REASSIGNMENT

Although individuals with non-transsexual gender problems may profit from psychological treatment modalities, transsexualism is not curable by means of psychotherapy. Therefore, the recommended procedure in the *Standards of Care* of the International Harry Benjamin Gender Dysphoria Association (an international professional organization in the field of transsexualism; Levine et al., 1998) is to approach the decision of whether to have sex reassignment surgery (SRS) in two phases. In the first phase, a diagnosis is made on formal psychiatric (*DSM* or *ICD*) classification criteria. Because diagnosis alone does not provide sufficient information for a decision to start the sex reassignment procedure, the patient must move on to the second phase, the so-called real-life test or real life experience. In this phase the applicant's ability to live in the desired role and the strength of his or her wish for SRS are evaluated, in the face of disappointments while living in the opposite gender role.

Hormonal Therapy

The social-role change during the real-life test usually is supported by hormonal therapy. In MFs, suppression of the original sex characteristics can be obtained by various drugs (e.g. progestational com-pounds or cyproteronacetate). As a result of this part of the hormone treatment, bodily hair growth diminishes drastically, as do penile erections and sexual appetite. Be-cause facial hair growth is very resistant to antiandrogen therapy, additional electric hair removal techniques are necessary for successful de-masculinization. Speech therapy is also needed, because the vocal cords will not shorten by antiandrogenic treatment, and the MF has to learn to use his voice in a female fashion. Surgical techniques to shorten the vocal cord are still considered to be experimental. Transsexuals who have started hormone treatment before adulthood usually do not need facial hair removal and speech therapy. To induce female sex characteristics, such as breasts and a more female-appearing body shape due to a change of body fat around the waist, hips, shoulders, and jaw, estrogens are used. In FMs, androgens are used for the induction of male body features, such as a low voice, facial and body hair growth, and a more masculine body shape.

Surgery

When the real-life test has resulted in a satisfactory social-role change, the applicant is referred for surgery. In MFs, vaginoplasty, and in cases of unresponsiveness of breast tissue to estrogen therapy, breast enlargement, are performed. In FMs, breast reduction takes place in all cases. As phalloplasty is still in an experimental stage, some FMs prefer to have a neoscrotum with a testical prosthesis with or without a metaidoioplasty, which transforms the hypertrophic clitoris into a microphallus.

RESULTS OF SRS

Since the first sex change operations, the therapeutic effectiveness of SRS has been investigated in many studies. Pfäfflin and Junge (1992) extensively reviewed 79 studies between 1961 and 1991. After 1991 several more have appeared (see Cohen-Kettenis & Gooren, 1999, for a review). Early reviews report satisfactory results in 71.4% of the MFs and 89.5% of the FMs. Later numbers are 87% and 97%, respectively. In most respects FMs fare better than their MF counterparts. Negative results, such as severe postoperative regrets to the point of returning to the original gender role, are estimated to be around 1%. From the follow-up studies one may infer that the currently-employed and often extensive diagnostic methods are sufficiently strict. Nonetheless, most of the results make it clear that alleviating the gender problem does not guarantee a trouble-free life, and that some form of psychological guidance may also be necessary after SRS.

REFERENCES

Cauldwell, D. C. (1949). Psychopathia transsexualis. *Sexology, 16,* 274–280.

Cohen-Kettenis, P. T., & Gooren, L. J. G. (1999). Transsexualism: A review of etiology, diagnosis, and treatment. *Journal of Psychosomatic Research, 46,* 315–333.

Cohen-Kettenis, P. T., van Goozen, S. H. M., Doorn, C. D., & Gooren, L. J. G. (1998). Cognitive ability and cerebral lateralisation in transsexuals. *Psychoneuroendocrinology, 23,* 631–641.

Hirschfeld, M. (1923). Die intersexuelle Konstitution [The intersexual state]. *Jahrbuch der sexuellen Zwischenstufen, 23,* 3–27.

Levine, S. B., Brown, G., Coleman, E., Cohen-Kettenis, P. T., Hage, J. J., Van Maasdam, J., Peterson, M., Pfäfflin, F., & Schaefer, L. (1998). *The Standards of Care for gender identity disorders* (5th ed.). Düsseldorf, Germany: Symposion Publishing.

Meyer-Bahlburg, H. F. L., Gruen, R. S., New, M. I., Bell, J. J., Morishima, A., Shimshi, M., Bueno, Y., Vargas, I., & Baker, S. W. (1996). Gender change from female to male in classic CAH. *Hormones and Behavior, 30,* 319–332.

Pfäfflin, F., & Junge, A. (1992). *Geschlechtsumwandlung: Abhandlun-gen zur Transsexualität [Sex change: Treatises on transsexualism].* Stuttgart, Germany: Schattauer.

Zhou, J., Hofman, M. A., Gooren, L. J. G., & Swaab, D. F. (1995). A sex difference in the human brain and its relation to transsexuality. *Nature, 378,* 68–70.

Zucker, K. J., & Bradley, S. J. (1995). *Gender identity disorder and psychosexual problems in children and adolescents.* New York: Guilford.

P. J. COHEN-KETTENIS
Utrecht University, The Netherlands

SEXUALITY: ORIENTATION AND IDENTITY

TRIANDIS, HARRY C. (1926–   )

Harry C. Triandis received an engineering degree from McGill University, and a masters of commerce degree from the University of Toronto. During the latter studies, he became interested in psychology, which led to graduate work at Cornell University (PhD, 1958). He was assistant professor of psychology (1958–1961), associate professor (1961–1966), and full professor (1966) at the University of Illinois at Urbana-Champaign. He was visiting scholar and professor (1968–1969) at the Center for International Studies of Cornell University. He was named University of Illinois scholar in 1987.

His books include *Attitudes and Attitude Change, The Analysis of Subjective Culture, Variations of Black and White Perceptions of the Social Environment, Interpersonal Behavior,* and *Management of R & D Organizations.* He was the general editor of the six-volume *Handbook of Cross-Cultural Psychology.* He has published about

75 chapters in books and about 90 articles and monographs in journals.

He has been president of the Society for the Psychological Study of Social Issues, the Society for Personality and Social Psychology, the International Association of Cross Cultural Psychology, the Interamerican Society of Psychology (whose Award for Major Contributions to the Science and Profession of Psychology he received in 1983), and the International Association of Applied Psychology.

STAFF

TRICYCLIC ANTIDEPRESSANTS

The tricyclic antidepressants were first introduced in the early 1960s and soon became widely used for the treatment of depression. The introduction of the tricyclics, along with the development of the phenothiazine antipsychotics for the treatment of schizophrenia and the use of lithium for treatment of bipolar illness, ushered in the modern era of psychopharmacology. The robust effectiveness of the tricyclics is somewhat offset by their problematic side effects, and though in recent years they have been largely supplanted by the selective-serotonin reuptake inhibitors (SSRIs) as "first-line" treatment, the tricyclics still remain a widely used treatment for depression and other psychiatric syndromes.

CLINICAL PHARMACOLOGY

The tricyclic antidepressants are so named because all of the compounds share a three-ring substructure and differ primarily in the side chain attached to the middle ring (see Figure 1). The most frequently prescribed are imipramine, amitriptyline, desipramine,

TERTIARY

Amitriptyline   **Imipramine**

SECONDARY

Nortriptyline   **Desipramine**

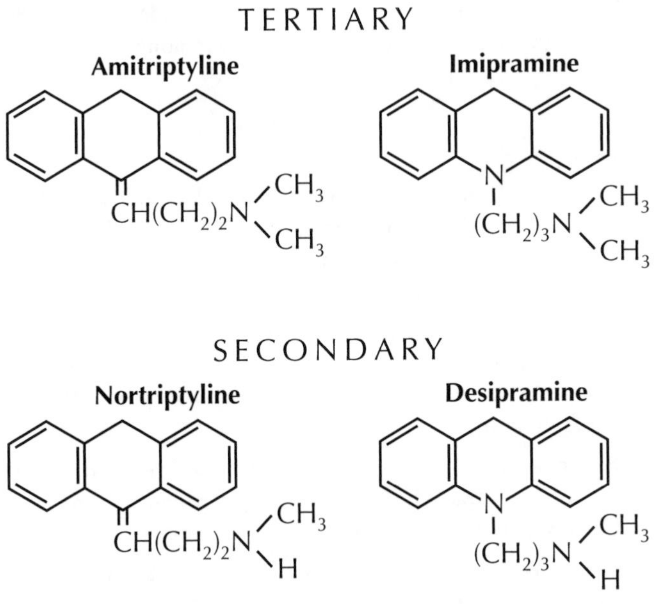

Figure 1: Tricyclic Antidepressants Compounds

and nortriptyline. (Note that desipramine and nortriptyline are simply the demethylated metabolites of imipramine and amitriptyline, respectively).

The tricyclics are lipid-soluble and are given orally; they are well absorbed from the gastrointestinal tract. There is considerable "first pass" effect in the liver, where the drugs are metabolized by transformation of the tricyclic nucleus and alterations of the side chain. The critical step in metabolism is hydroxylation at the 2-position of the ring, thereby creating a water-soluble metabolite which is then secreted from the body.

A critical advance in maximizing the effectiveness of tricyclics has been the documentation of a strong correlation between plasma level of antidepressant and clinical outcome (Glassman et at., 1985). In patients treated with desipramine and imipramine, there is a threshold effect such that maximum response is achieved at plasma levels over 150 nanograms per ml and 200 nanograms per ml, respectively. Patients treated with nortriptyline have a curvilinear response, or "therapeutic window," in which maximum response is achieved when the plasma level is in the range between 50 and 150 nanograms per ml (see Figure 2).

MECHANISM OF ACTION

The major effect of the tricyclic antidepressants is to block the reuptake of neurotransmitters. The secondary amine tricyclics, desipramine and nortriptyline, block the reuptake of norepinephrine more specifically, whereas the tertiary amine tricyclics, imipramine and amitriptyline, to some degree block the reuptake of both norepinephrine and serotonin. Competitive blockade of the serotonin and norepinephrine uptake pumps is believed to potentiate monoaminergic neurotransmission. However, even though blockade of amine uptake occurs within 12 hours, the antidepressant effects of the tricyclics do not occur for several weeks. Therefore, there are critical, though as yet undefined, events that result from uptake blockade and eventually lead to the antidepressant effect.

SIDE EFFECTS

Despite their robust effectiveness, the clinical usefulness of tricyclic antidepressants has been limited by their side effects. The problems range from minimal seriousness with high nuisance value which can markedly reduce patient compliance, to problems of potential lethality in certain patient populations. The most frequent side effects of tricyclics are due to their peripheral anticholinergic (antimuscarinic) effects, which accounts for dry mouth, constipation, tachycardia, and blurred vision (Richelson, 1989). In older patients, the anticholinergic effect can result in urinary retention and acute confusional states. The tricyclics also block histamine receptors which may be related to the significant weight gain that is associated with long-term treatment in some patients.

Another frequent and significant side effect of the tricyclic antidepressants is orthostatic hypotension (Roose & Glassman, 1989). This effect results in part from peripheral alpha-adrenergic receptor blockade and occurs in approximately 10 percent of patients treated with tricyclics. Orthostatic hypotension can result in serious injury and fatalities.

The cardiovascular effects of the tricyclics account for most of

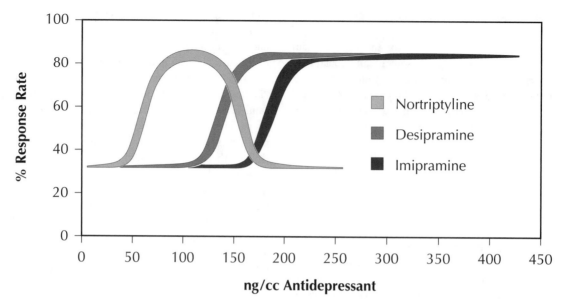

Figure 2: The Relationship Between Blood Levels and Outcome: Comparison of Three Antidepressants

the morbidity and mortality associated with these medications (Roose & Glassman, 1989). The tricyclics are type 1A antiarrhythmic drugs and have a "quinidine-like" action on the heart that results in an antiarrhythmic effect and slowing of cardiac conduction. Consequently, tricyclics can be dangerous in patients with preexisting conduction system disease such as bundle branch block and can increase mortality in patients with ischemic heart disease. When taken in overdose tricyclics are frequently lethal due to heart block and ventricular tachycardia. The extensive cardiovascular effects of the tricyclic antidepressants serve as a reminder that the therapeutic label of a medication (an antidepressant), does not necessarily describe all of the systems that are significantly affected. The clinician must be equally aware of the effects of a medication other than the intended mechanism of action.

CLINICAL INDICATIONS

The tricyclic antidepressants are effective in the treatment of unipolar major depressive disorder (Richelson, 1989). They are also effective in the treatment of a bipolar depressive episode. However, since their use can cause a switch into mania, it is standard practice for a depressed bipolar patient to be treated with both a mood stabilizer and an antidepressant. Studies have also established the effectiveness of the tricyclics in the treatment of dysthymia, a form of chronic mild depression that often presents early in life (Kocsis, 1997).

Despite being labeled antidepressants, the tricyclics also produce significant benefit in the treatment of certain anxiety disorders, notably panic attacks and generalized anxiety (Roy-Byrne & Lydiard, 1989). Tricyclics have been shown to significantly decrease the rate of binges in patients with bulimia, although they have been ineffective in the treatment of anorexia nervosa (Walsh et al., 1997). Tricyclics are also used for the treatment of other conditions which are not considered primarily psychiatric but which often are accompanied by affective or anxiety symptoms. Notable

among these conditions are irritable bowel syndrome and chronic pain.

Though the tricyclic antidepressants have been largely supplanted by the selective-serotonin reuptake inhibitors as the first-line treatment for depressive and anxiety disorders, they remain widely used compounds. Up to 30 percent to 40 percent of depressed patients do not achieve remission when treated with an SSRI alone, and it is common clinical practice to combine an SSRI with a tricyclic as a second treatment strategy. Furthermore, there are some types of depressive disorder that may preferentially respond to the tricyclics compared to the SSRIs (e.g., the melancholic subtype of depression). All of the tricyclics are available as generic compounds and so are significantly less expensive than most other antidepressants. In summary, the tricyclics remain in widespread clinical use, but their problematic side-effect profile means that they are rarely used as a first-line treatment for depression.

REFERENCES

Glassman A. H., Schildkraut J. J., Orsulak P. J., et al. (1985). APA Task Force: Tricyclic antidepressants—Blood level measurements and clinical outcome: An APA Task Force Report. *American Journal of Psychiatry, 142,* 155–162.

Kocsis, J. H. (1997) Chronic depression: The efficacy of pharmacotherapy. In A. H. S. Akiskal, G. B. Cassano (Eds.), *Dysthymia and the spectrum of chronic depressions* (pp. 66–74). New York: Guilford.

Richelson, E. (1989). Antidepressants: Pharmacology and clinical use. In T. B. Karasu (Ed.), *Treatments of psychiatric disorders* (p. 1773). Washington, DC: American Psychiatric Press.

Roose S. P., & Glassman A. H.(1989). Cardiovascular effects of tricyclic antidepressants in depressed patients with and without heart disease. *Journal Clinical Psychiatry, 50*(suppl), 1–18.

Roy-Byrne P. P., & Lydiard R. B. New developments in the psychopharmacologic treatment of anxiety. In P. P. Roy-Byrne (Ed.), *Anxiety: New findings for the clinician* (pp. 151–178). Washington DC: American Psychiatric.

Walsh B. T., Wilson G. T., Loeb K. L., et al. (1997). Medication and psychotherapy in the treatment of bulimia nervosa. *American Journal Psychiatry, 154,* 523–531.

Walsh, B. T., Wilson, G. T., Loeb, K. L., Devlin, M. J., Pike, K. M., Roose, S. P., Fleiss, J. L., & Waternaux, C. (1997). Medication and psychotherapy in the treatment of bulimia nervosa. *American Journal of Psychiatry, 154,* 523–531.

S. P. ROOSE
Columbia University

C. RIZZO
New York State Psychiatric Institute

TRUST

Trust is a concept that has been considered from a variety of perspectives by psychologists and behavioral scientists. Many definitions of trust are similar to one published by Bhattacharya, Devinney, & Pillutla (1998): "Trust is the expectancy of positive outcomes that one can receive based on the expected action of another party in an interaction characterized by uncertainty." However, different psychological models and research studies dealing with trust handle the concept differently. For the psychologist, trust may be considered to be both a long-term dispositional variable (i.e., a personality trait), and a temporary state that is related to a number of situational antecedents and consequences. Both of these perspectives will be explored here.

TRUST AS A DISPOSITIONAL VARIABLE

This first perspective holds trust to be a stable individual difference variable (i.e., that some people are generally more trusting than others). This perspective presupposes that an individual will react in a similar way toward most others with whom he or she interacts. Those who are predisposed to trust are less likely to use deceptive tactics when dealing with others. They are also more willing to give other persons the benefit of the doubt unless they have clear evidence that the other is untrustworthy. Similarly, those who are shown to be predisposed to trust are more likely to see others as trustworthy and to cooperate with other players in prisoner's dilemma and social dilemma experiments (see Parks, Henager, & Scamahorn, 1996 et al., 1983).

The predisposition to *distrust* is also of interest to psychologists. An "inflexible . . . tendency to act in a . . . suspicious manner" is described by Deutsch (1973) as irrational distrust. It is related to so-called sinister attribution errors, in which a distrustful person often believes another person's negative behavior is due to that person's hostile interpersonal motives, whereas more trustful individuals attribute such behavior to other, impersonal factors. Distrust and trust are usually considered opposite poles on the same continuum, although they may also be qualitatively different.

Trust is related to several other personality variables (Ross & LaCroix, 1996). Individuals with a predisposition to trust have lower scores on Machiavellianism. They tend to be not only trusting but also trustworthy in their behaviors; they also have low Authoritarianism scores. However, links between a predisposition to trust and other individual difference variables have not been widely researched.

TRUST AS A TEMPORARY STATE

The Many Faces of Trust

The second perspective holds trust to be a temporary state that may be induced by a variety of stimuli and that may guide action with respect to another person. Most theories and research studies investigating trust from this perspective are characterized by one of three themes (a) Trust follows from a cooperative motivational orientation; (b) Trust in another person follows from the other's predictable pattern of behavior; and (c) Trust is based on the problem-solving perspective of each person in a relationship when conflicts arise.

Trust and Cooperative Motivational Orientation. The first research theme treats cooperation as the behavioral consequence—and therefore, the operationalization—of trust. This implies that trust is both a cognitive and an emotional state caused by a more general cooperative motivational orientation (MO). Motivational orientation is defined as a state in which one's motivation falls along a continuum ranging from competition (i.e., seeking to maximize one's own outcomes relative to those of another) to cooperation (i.e., seeking to maximize both one's own outcomes and those of another). In certain situations (e.g., prisoner dilemma experiments), this may be reasonable. In other situations, however, cooperation is due to other factors or may even be a ploy to secure additional gains.

Motivational orientation can be manipulated experimentally, thus it follows that trust can be manipulated indirectly through instructions and other forms of preparatory sets designed to manipulate MO and subsequent behavior. Research taking this approach demonstrates that self-report measures of trust are indeed related to cooperation, and that distrust often leads to a more contentious relationship. At high levels, distrust leads to refusing to work or deal with the other party.

Finally, this theme also allows trust to be defined as the expectation that the other person will have a cooperative MO. Such expectations are predictive of whether workers will be satisfied with allowing managers to make autocratic decisions—the workers are willing to give up a decision-making role based on the belief that their managers will cooperate by considering their interests.

Trust and Predictability. The second research theme defines trust as predictability. A person who behaves consistently and who keeps his or her word is trustworthy. This theme also suggests that a pattern of repeated, predictable cooperative behavior establishes trust. Note that the focus of this approach is on establishing trust and not on simply operationalizing trust.

Several authors distinguish between trust as goodwill (cooperative MO) and trust as predictability. Predictability allows the other person to infer that there is a high probability that you will keep your word. For example, Butler (1991) reports that behaviors associated with predictability (e.g., consistency, promise fulfillment, and loyalty) can be instrumental in establishing trust among business managers. Clear, predictable behavior by one party increases the other party's belief that the first party is reliable and honest—what Shapiro, Sheppard, and Cheraskin call knowledge-based trust (1992). The latter authors suggest that even if one person is not cooperative, provided he or she is consistent, others may still devise effective strategies for dealing with that person.

If one demonstrates both a cooperative MO and predictability, the other person will be more likely to see one as trustworthy. Osgood's (1962) Graduated and Reciprocated Initiatives in Tension reduction (GRIT) system asks those in conflict to make a series of small, unilateral concessions to their opponents and to announce that these are offered as gestures of goodwill, as a way to demonstrate both predictability and cooperative MO. Research is generally supportive. Thus, the combination of predictability and cooperation can be a potent prescription for establishing mutual trust.

Trust and a Problem-Solving Perspective. The third research theme relates trust to factors that enhance a problem-solving orientation. This perspective is seen in bargaining research, in which trust is defined as "a belief that the other negotiator (a) has a problem-solving orientation, and/or (b) is generally unselfish" (Kimmel, Pruitt, Magenau, Konar-Goldband, & Carnevale, 1980, p. 10). These researchers have given subjects instructions that promote either a problem-solving orientation only (trust condition), or a problem-solving orientation with the warning that the other persons with whom they would deal might not have similar orientations (distrust condition). They report that for parties with high aspirations (goals), high trust leads to the exchange of more information and to more-cooperative behavior. In the distrust condition, subjects share little information about their priorities and instead engage in more competitive behavior.

Kimmel and colleagues (1980) observe that while trust affects bargaining behaviors, it has little effect on negotiated payoffs. Others offer similar findings (see Ross & LaCroix, 1996 for a review). Thus, trust may affect the interpersonal bargaining process far more than it affects the outcome levels of the specific issues under consideration.

In business, trust between a home office and a subsidiary is associated with problem-solving activities. Zand (1972) treats a problem-solving orientation as an important element for establishing trust among group members. He reports that conditions that promote creative, integrative bargaining (e.g., a mutual fate if negotiations fail) also promote trust, and that trust in turn, promotes specific integrative bargaining behaviors, such as the revealing of information among group members. Thus if trust is not present, then the parties are unlikely to successfully conclude integrative problem solving.

Shapiro, Sheppard, and Cheraskin (1992) suggest that trust is greatest when the cooperative MO perspective and the problem-solving perspectives merge into what they call identification-based trust. Here, trust is maximized when each side not only considers but also internalizes the other's interests. The shared sense of interdependence is so great that each side's interests meld to become both sides' shared interests.

In conclusion, when considering the perspective of trust as a temporary state, we see that trust is defined in various ways by behavioral scientists. Among the many definitions of trust are the following: (a) "a confident reliance on the integrity, honesty, or justice of another; faith"; (b) "a confidence in the reliability of persons or things without careful investigation" (both from Landau, 1966); and (c) a belief that another person has a problem-solving orientation. Although similar, each definition is distinct. For example one may trust another person to have one's best interests at heart when making a decision; one may trust a second person to act in a consistent or reliable manner, even though he or she does not consider one's own interests; and one may trust a third person to take a problem-solving perspective so that each side's interests are satisfied. An understanding of trust is important because many decisions and actions result in one party's vulnerability to another, if the one party trusts the other, then the one party may be more willing to become vulnerable; the perceived risk of exploitation may be reduced.

ANTECEDENTS OF TRUST

Surprisingly little has been written about how the presence or absence of objective situational factors leads to the creation of trust between parties (see Zand, 1972). Because trust is rooted in social relationships, most writing dealing with antecedents has focused on social factors. For example, Butler (1991) focuses on how one person's behavior and characteristics (e.g., availability, competence, openness, loyalty, and fairness) elicit trust from others. Osgood's GRIT approach suggests that small, predictable concessions elicit trust. Techniques such as GRIT are particularly likely to elicit trust after a long period of stalemate.

A growing area of interest is that of the way how social situations are interpreted. What exactly is the role of cognitive processes in establishing trust or distrust? Bazerman (1994) identifies several cognitive heuristics—mental shortcuts—that may lead to the creation of trust or distrust. The first is the illusory correlation bias, in which people incorrectly link two behaviors or personality characteristics. This bias is relevant because if one person associates another's particular behavior (e.g., a competitive stance on an issue) with attempted exploitation, that person may react in a distrustful way that only escalates the conflict. Second, the behavior of another may evoke a particular perspective (a cognitive frame) or sequence of behavior (a script) that creates trust or distrust, which affects subsequent behavior. Initially-trusting individuals may approach interactions from a framework of mutual gain, which may promote cooperation; those who are initially distrustful may approach interactions from a perspective of wanting to limit their own losses, and thus may be more competitive. The frame may determine the person's behavior, the behavior, in turn, may provoke a reaction that confirms the initial tendency to trust or distrust, thus, the behavior becomes a self-fulfilling prophecy, further increasing or decreasing the level of trust. Third, the confirmation trap suggests that people tend to seek, store, and recall information that is consistent with their previous beliefs. For example, distrustful persons tend to recall easily information confirming their initial predisposition when describing others. While trust or distrust may be the appropriate response in many situations, Bazerman's work suggests that there are many situations in which cognitive heuristics can lead people to erroneous conclusions.

In addition to mental heuristics, other cognitive processes may play a role in establishing trust or distrust. For example, individuals are quite capable and willing to generate further information when only partial information is available. Certain types of information may be more easily noticed (e.g., evidence of betrayal is often vivid) and stored. Negative outcomes may lead to sinister attributions that another person is responsible for these outcomes, creating distrust. Finally, how information is combined and evaluated may be related to the magnification of trust or distrust. If negative experiences carry inordinate weight when information is combined (e.g., a univalent decision rule), distrust may increase. However, if inconsistent information is weighed appropriately and then combined (e.g., an aggregated decision rule), judgments of a more tentative nature may be made. These mental processes suggest what most lay people know from experience—that it is much easier to create distrust than it is to create trust.

CONSEQUENCES OF TRUST

There are numerous consequences of trust and distrust. Generally, trust leads to a willingness to be vulnerable to another. Pruitt (1981) notes that trust may lead to one's involvement in a variety of risk-taking behaviors when dealing with another. These include a willingness to share information (the experience of information loss) a willingness to make concessions to the other (the experience of position loss), a willingness to risk looking foolish (the experience of image loss), and the loss of opportunities to compete against the other party.

Trust may also lead to an enhanced relationship, which usually provides long-term benefits to all involved parties. The research on communal sharing relationships is relevant here. Communal sharing relationships such as nuclear families, extended kinship groups, fraternal organizations, clubs, and communes provide members with feelings of belonging and unity, the group identity is often as salient as the individual's own identity. Members in these relationships typically have long-term commitments to and high levels of trust in other group members. Research suggests that in many of these groups, interpersonal interactions are characterized by greater empathy, cooperation, information sharing, and mutual concern for each party's well-being and outcomes; the parties are also less likely to use coercive tactics (Lewicki, Saunders, & Minton, 1999). These are positive outcomes for the parties involved.

However, high levels of trust can sometimes prove unwise—with a close friend one may often fail to insure the full consideration of his or her own interests and thus produce objectively poorer solutions to problems, perhaps out of fear that looking after personal interests will damage the friendship. Also, if one party is quite trusting, then he or she is less likely to notice or give full consideration to evidence of betrayal from the other. In the same vein, trust

may also lead to one's using fewer objective standards and verification mechanisms to ensure that each side is behaving appropriately (Ross & LaCroix, 1996). Thus, trust may sometimes cause one to be blind to another's untrustworthy behavior.

In conclusion, trust is seen as both a dispositional trait and a temporary state. Within each perspective, numerous research themes have emerged investigating trust as a cooperative MO, as predictability, and as a problem-solving orientation. While many specific antecedents have been noted, in the end, they serve as reminders that trust is fundamentally a social, affective, and cognitive phenomenon that, if nurtured, may yield lasting benefits to the involved parties.

AUTHOR

TWIN AND ADOPTION STUDIES

With the recent emergence of human gene mapping technologies and data analytical methods, considerable effort is being devoted to the detection of genetic loci underlying normal and psychopathologic behavior. However, before embarking on a search for responsible genes, it is necessary to establish whether and to what extent genetic factors contribute to a behavioral trait or disorder. The fact that a trait shows familial aggregation, or runs in families, does not, in itself, provide definitive evidence of genetic influence. In addition to sharing genes, family members share many environmental factors that could influence trait development. Also, unlike classic Mendelian or monogenic diseases (e.g., cystic fibrosis, Huntington's disease), the inheritance of complex behavioral characteristics (e.g., personality, psychiatric disorder) cannot be attributed to the effects of a single gene. Rather, human behavioral traits derive from a complex interplay of multiple genetic and environmental factors. To disentangle these different sources of variation, researchers have traditionally relied upon the twin and adoption study designs. These experiments of nature are a powerful resource for assessing the relative influences of genes and environment, and their application has yielded remarkable insights into the origins of behavioral development and disorder.

The classical twin approach is based on comparisons between monozygotic (MZ) and dizygotic (DZ) twins. Monozygotic or identical twins derive from a single fertilized ovum (zygote) and therefore are genetically identical. In contrast, DZ or fraternal twins come from two separately fertilized ova and, like normal siblings, have on average only half of their segregating genes in common. If heredity is an influential factor in the development of a particular trait or disorder, MZ twins should be more behaviorally similar than DZ twins. If a trait is attributable solely to genetic influence, MZ twins should be 100% concordant for the trait while DZ twins should be only 50% concordant. Differences between MZ and DZ twins also can be used to derive numerical estimates of genetic and environmental contributions to a trait or disease. The statistical methods that form the basis of this strategy have improved considerably since their inception, and newer model-fitting approaches allow for quantitative dissection of complex behavioral traits into additive and nonadditive gene effects as well as individual-specific and shared environmental factors. Further, if several traits are examined simultaneously, multivariate statistical methods may be employed to determine if the traits are mediated by common and/or specific influences.

The validity of twin studies, however, depends critically on certain underlying assumptions. First, the approach is predicated on what is commonly referred to as the "equal environment assumption"; that is, the notion that MZ and DZ twins are equally similar in terms of their rearing environments. If, for example, MZ twins were treated more similarly than DZ twins, and this differential treatment influenced the expression of the trait of interest, the contribution of genetic influence would be overestimated. The equal environments assumption has been tested in several different ways and appears tenable for at least most traits and disorders. A second issue concerns the accuracy of zygosity determination (i.e., MZ versus DZ). Parents and twins are occasionally misinformed about zygosity, and ascertainment methods that rely solely on self-report questionnaire and/or physical resemblance may lead to misclassification errors. Due to the widespread availability of cost-effective DNA analysis methods, the probability of zygosity misdiagnosis has been lowered considerably. Finally, the twin approach presupposes that twins are representative of the population as a whole, but they may differ systematically in several important ways. Of particular concern are influences related to pregnancy, delivery, and pre- and postnatal development. If unaccounted for, factors uniquely associated with the twinning process may limit the generalizability of results.

The adoption or separation design is an alternative and relatively direct method for investigating genetic and environmental influences on behavior. Adoption produces a situation in which genetically related individuals do not share a common environment. Thus, the degree of trait similarity between biological relatives living apart estimates the contribution of genetic influence. Examples include comparisons between biological parents and their adopted-away offspring, or between twins separated at birth. Conversely, comparisons between genetically unrelated individuals who live together estimate the contribution of shared environmental factors. This includes adopted children and their adoptive parents, and genetically unrelated children reared in the same family environment.

As with the twin method, valid interpretation of adoption data may be limited by certain methodological issues. First, adoption agencies may practice selective placement, in which the biological parents are matched to prospective adoptive parents on certain characteristics. This may overestimate environmental influence since the adopted offspring may be similar to their adoptive parents by virtue of nonrandom placement. Another concern is representativeness. The biological parents of adoptees are often atypical in some way, and therefore results may not be applicable to the general population. Finally, prior to adoption, children live in their prenatal environments with their birth mothers. Thus, resemblance between biological parents and adopted-away offspring may be attributable to prenatal environmental influences. This possibility can be tested, however, in several ways.

In summation, the twin and adoption study paradigms represent powerful and versatile methods for elucidating genetic and environmental components of complex human behavior. However, given their respective limitations, conclusions should be based only on convergence of evidence from several study designs.

Applications of these methods to traits of psychological relevance have demonstrated a role for genetic influences with remarkable consistency across studies. For example, investigations of normal personality variation have suggested that the majority of traits are roughly 50% heritable. Interestingly, for the behavioral dimensions that have been studied, shared environmental factors appear to have only a negligible impact. The interested reader is referred to a series of studies by Bouchard and colleagues (e.g., 1990) on a sample of twins reared apart.

Twin and adoption studies have demonstrated a substantial genetic contribution to the development of various forms of psychopathology. Notably, studies of schizophrenia and bipolar disorder have both yielded heritability estimates as high as 80%. More recently, twin and adoption studies have begun to move beyond the simple documentation of heritable influence to address topics such as changes in genetic effects across the lifespan, gene-environment interaction, and the specification of disease phenotypes. For example, research on schizophrenia has provided evidence that what is inherited is not the disease per se but a neurobiologic susceptibility that manifests phenotypically as subtle neuroanatomical changes, deficits in certain neurocognitive functions, and, potentially, increased vulnerability to central nervous system disturbance following certain environmental exposures such as oxygen deprivation at birth (see Cannon, 1996, for review).

Over the past two decades, striking technological advances in molecular biology have sparked a revival of interest in behavioral and psychiatric genetics and much research is aimed at the localization of specific gene loci that mediate human psychological differences. Twin and adoption study methods will play an integral role in this endeavor for several reasons. First, epidemiological methods inform the selection of appropriate behaviors for DNA analysis by establishing which facets of the trait or disorder are most heritable. For example, twin studies of alcoholism have shown that disease severity is positively correlated with degree of genetic influence. Thus, ascertainment of a patient sample consisting largely of severe alcoholics may enhance the likelihood of identifying relevant genes. By the same token, these approaches may facilitate identification of environmentally induced disease variants by defining which aspects of the environment causally contribute to the trait of interest. Finally, once genes have been detected, twin and adoption studies can incorporate specific genetic markers to characterize their contribution to trait expression or liability.

REFERENCES

Bouchard, T. J., Jr., Lykken, D. T., McGue, M., Segal, N. L., & Tellegen, A. (1990). Sources of human psychological differences: The Minnesota study of twins reared apart. *Science, 250,* 223-228.

Cannon, T. D. (1996). Abnormalities of brain structure and function in schizophrenia: Implications for aetiology and pathophysiology. *Annals of Medicine, 28,* 533-539.

SUGGESTED READING

Plomin, R., DeFries, J. C., McClearn, G. E., & Rutter, M. (1997). *Behavioral genetics*. New York: W. H. Freeman and Company.

T. L. GASPERONI
T. D. CANNON
University of California, Los Angeles

HERITABILITY OF PERSONALITY

TWO-PROCESS LEARNING THEORY

The central premise of two-process learning theory is that the laws of classical and instrumental conditioning are not functionally equivalent. During the first half of the 20th century, the general trend was to treat classical and instrumental conditioning according to a single set of principles (Hull, 1929, 1943; Guthrie, 1935). Nevertheless, even during its formative period, learning theory had expressed an alternative view. As early as 1928, Miller and Konorski had distinguished between two forms of conditioned response: Type I was Pavlov's secretory conditioned response (CR), formed by establishing a positive correlation between the conditioned stimulus (CS) and the unconditioned stimulus (US); Type II differed from the classical CR in that its occurrence was dependent on its consequences. Despite the early work of Konorski and others (Hilgard, 1937; Schlosberg, 1937; Skinner, 1938) regarding the adequacy of uni-process theories of learning, it was not until drive reduction theory encountered theoretical problems accounting for avoidance learning that two-process theory emerged to challenge the prevailing view. For drive reduction theory, the motive for the avoidance response derived from the occurrence of an aversive US and reinforcement of the response from US termination. However, since the avoidance response prevents the US from occurring, the theory cannot account for the learning or maintenance of avoidance behavior (Kimble, 1961).

To resolve this problem, Mowrer (1947, 1950) proposed that avoidance learning was the result of two processes. Fear instigated avoidance behavior; fear reduction maintained the behavior. Classical conditioning established the fear reaction to the CS by pairing a CS with an aversive US. This view contrasted sharply with that of Hull (1929), who had argued that the cessation of an aversive US was reinforcing. By demonstrating that there was no difference in the conditionability of fear when the onset of an aversive US coincided with the CS or when the CS was coincident with both the onset and the offset of the aversive event, Mowrer showed that fear was formed through classical conditioning. On this account, classical conditioning established the association between the CS and fear CR. Once aroused, fear motivated instrumental behavior. The response that was successful in removing the CS was reinforced by reducing the fear. Cast in this form, two-process theory assigned considerable importance to classical conditioning; the processes established by this form of learning functioned as motivators or reinforcers mediating instrumental behavior.

Ironically, Hull (1929, 1931) provided the hypothetical mechanism that served as the basis for extending two-process theory to appetitive behavior. For Hull, components of the consummatory response became anticipatory following repeated elicitation of the US. These fractional anticipatory goal reactions (r_g) were associated with stimuli that antedate (and hence signal) the appetitive US. The r_g mechanism also produced its own sensory aftereffects, which were designated as s_g. Although Hull originally used the r_g-s_g as an associative mechanism to explain disruptive behavior following a change in the quality of a reward, later theorists employed it as a devise that mediated incentive motivation; r_g-s_g somehow selectively energized responses that had previously been successful in enabling the organism to encounter a goal object (Logan, 1960; Seward, 1952; Spence, 1956).

Since fear and r_g-s_g were treated as implicit peripheral CRs, considerable research was devoted to determining their role in mediating instrumental behavior. Classically conditioned responses such as heart rate and salivation were used to index these implicit events and the temporal relationship between them and instrumental responses. After an exhaustive review of the literature, Rescorla and Solomon (1967) concluded that the strategy on indexing these inferred events by overt CRs and mapping their relationship to instrumental activity failed because there was no temporal consistency between the observable Pavlovian CRs and the sequence of instrumental responses. In the course of an experiment, the Pavlovian CR might precede, occur coincident with, or follow the instrumental response (Sheffield, 1965).

Rescorla and Solomon argued that a more promising approach was to view the events established by classical conditioning as central states and to determine their role indirectly with the transfer-of-control paradigm. The transfer-of-control paradigm involves multiple stages of training. Classical or instrumental conditioning is given during the first stage of learning; then, depending on which of the two conditioning procedures was first administered, subjects receive the other conditioning procedure. In the test phase, Pavlovian CSs that presumably evoke central states established by classical conditioning are presented during instrumental responding. Either the enhancement or disruption of instrumental behavior infers the nature of the central state (e.g., Mellgren & Ost, 1969; Shapiro & Miller, 1965).

Trapold and Overmier (1972) have questioned the notion that classical and instrumental training procedures establish distinct Pavlovian and instrumental processes. They suggest instead the adoption of a neutral terminology, namely, response-independent and response-dependent learning. One implication of this usage is a greater reciprocity between the two forms of learning: Response-independent learning is not necessarily a result of classical conditioning, even though the process established by this type of learning may affect instrumental behavior. Moreover, the representation formed during response-dependent learning may interact with stimulus-stimulus associations (Alloy & Ehrman, 1981).

The initial formulation of two-process theory held that the laws governing the formation of associations were different although what was learned (namely, stimulus-response associations) were the same. By contrast, the current view argues that classical and instrumental conditioning obey the same laws. They differ, however, in the sort of associations established by the two training procedures. Classical conditioning promotes the formation of stimulus-

stimulus (S-S) associations, while instrumental conditioning results in the establishment of response-stimulus (R-S) associations (e.g., Dickinson, 1980; Mackintosh, 1974). One problem with this account is that while S-S associations can explain the initiation of behavior by assuming that the CS evokes an internal representation of the US, which, in turn, elicits the CR, R-S learning must rely on the formation of two separate representations: one between the context and the US, and the other between the US and the response. The excitation necessary for response evocation must flow from the US to the response. This conceptualization does not enjoy a substantial empirical base (Mackintosh, 1983).

Dickinson's (1989) expectancy theory of conditioning provides a possible resolution to the conundrum of response selection in instrumental conditioning. It is a two-process theory in the sense that a mechanistic associationistic mode of explanation is retained for classical conditioning, but an intentional, cognitive account is advanced for non-automatic forms of instrumental behavior. The mechanistic account suffices for response elicitation in classical conditioning and assigns a role for Pavlovian processes in mediating some types of instrumental learning, especially those that evidence automaticity. In contrast, voluntary behavior involves the activation of expectancy. On this account, when an animal experiences a contingency between its behavior and an outcome, an expectancy the content of which is the representation of that relationship is formed. The associations arranged by the contingency are mapped into a declarative structure that refers to an actual state of affairs. In other words, the contents of the representation are of the form "this action leads to that reinforcer." If the content of this belief is accompanied by a relevant motivational state that serves the purpose of enhancing the desirability of the reinforcer, then the activated expectancy results in the issuance of a command to execute the response. Thus knowledge and desire form the basis of voluntary behavior through some sort of computational process. The nature of the psychological mechanism, if, indeed, there is one, that captures the intentionality of instrumental conditioning remains, as Dickinson himself points out, open.

REFERENCES

Alloy, L. B., & Ehrman, R. N. (1981). Instrumental to Pavlovian transfer: Learning about response-reinforcer contingencies affects subsequent learning about stimulus-reinforcer contingencies. *Learning and Motivation, 12,* 109–132.

Dickinson, A. (1980). *Contemporary animal learning theory.* Cambridge, UK: Cambridge University Press.

Dickinson, A. (1989). Expectancy theory in animal conditioning. In S. B. Klein & R. R. Mowrer (Eds.), *Contemporary learning theories: Pavlovian conditioning and the status of traditional learning theory* (pp. 279–308). Hillsdale, NJ: Erlbaum.

Guthrie, E. R. (1935). *The psychology of learning.* New York: Harper & Row.

Hilgard, E. R. (1937). The relationship between the conditioned response and conventional learning experiments. *Psychological Bulletin, 34,* 61–102.

Hull, C. L. (1929). A functional interpretation of the conditioned reflex. *Psychological Review, 36,* 498–511.

Hull, C. L. (1943). *Principles of behavior.* New York: Appleton-Century-Crofts.

Kimble, G. A. (1961). *Hilgard and Marquis' conditioning and learning.* New York: Appleton-Century-Crofts.

Logan, F. A. (1960). *Incentive.* New Haven, CT: Yale University Press.

Mackintosh, N. J. (1974). *The psychology of animal learning.* New York: Academic.

Mellgren, R. L., & Ost, J. W. P. (1969). Transfer of Pavlovian differential conditioning to an operant discrimination. *Journal of Comparative and Physiological Psychology, 67,* 323–336.

Miller, S., & Konorski, J. (1928). Sur une forme particuliere des reflexes conditionnels. *Social Biology, 99,* 1155–1157.

Mowrer, O. H. (1947). On the dual nature of learning: A reinterpretation of "conditioning" and "problem-solving." *Harvard Educational Review, 17,* 102–148.

Mowrer, O. H. (1950). *Learning theory and personality dynamics.* New York: Ronald.

Rescorla, R. A., & Solomon, R. L. (1967). Two-process learning theory: Relationships between Pavlovian conditioning and instrumental learning. *Psychological Review, 74,* 151–182.

Schlosberg, H. (1937). The relationship between success and the laws of conditioning. *Psychological Review, 44,* 379–394.

Seward, J. P. (1952). Introduction to a theory of motivation in learning. *Psychological Review, 59,* 405–413.

Shapiro, M. M., & Miller, T. M. (1965). On the relationship between conditioned and discriminative stimuli and between instrumental and consummatory response. In W. K. Prokasy (Ed.), *Classical conditioning: A symposium.* New York: Appleton-Century-Crofts.

Sheffield, F. D. (1965). Relation between classical conditioning and instrumental learning. In W. F. Prokasy (Ed.), *Classical conditioning: A symposium.* New York: Appleton-Century-Crofts.

Skinner, B. F. (1938). *The behavior of organisms: An experimental analysis.* New York: Appleton-Century-Crofts.

Spence, K. W. (1956). *Behavior theory and conditioning.* New Haven, CT: Yale University Press.

Trapold, M. A., & Overmier, J. B. (1972). The second learning process in instrumental learning. In A. A. Black & W. F. Prokasy (Eds.), *Classical conditioning: II. Current research and theory.* New York: Appleton-Century-Crofts.

SUGGESTED READING

Hull, C. L. (1931). Goal attraction and directing ideas conceived as habit phenomena. *Psychological Review, 38,* 487–506.

Mackintosh, N. J. (1983). *Conditioning and associative learning.* Oxford: Oxford University Press.

E. J. RICKERT
University of South Carolina

LEARNING THEORIES

TYLER, LEONA E. (1906–1993)

Leona E. Tyler is best known for her textbooks *The Psychology of Human Differences, The Work of the Counselor,* and *Tests and Measurements,* and for the offices she has held in psychological associations, culminating in the presidency of the American Psychological Association in 1972–1973. She grew up in the Iron Range country of northern Minnesota and received the BA from the University of Minnesota, where she majored in English. The next 13 years were spent teaching, mainly English and mathematics, in junior high schools in Minnesota and Michigan. Her career as a psychologist did not really begin until she returned to the University of Minnesota in 1938 for graduate work in psychology. She was awarded the PhD degree in 1941.

Tyler's thinking was a synthesis of ideas from three major sources. The first was her teaching specialty, individual differences. The second was practical counseling activity, which was an important part of her work for many years. The third was research on interest measurement, in which she was continuously involved from 1937 to the early 1960s. Out of this combination has emerged a philosophical-theoretical point of view expressed most clearly in her book *Individuality: Human Possibilities and Personal Choice in the Psychological Development of Men and Women* and in *The Concept of Multiple Possibilities in Psychology.*

Tyler had been a member of the faculty of the University of Oregon since 1940, teaching a variety of courses and serving for six years as dean of the Graduate School. She retired from active duty in 1971.

STAFF

TYPE A PERSONALITY

As initially described by Friedman and Rosenman (1959), individuals with type A, coronary-prone personality exhibit behaviors characterized as aggressive, hard-driving, and competitive, often with an element of hostility. They were described as alert, restless, and impatient, with increased amplitude of speech and motor movement, and as generally hard-working, goal-directed individuals who often achieved a high level of success in their careers. They were thought to pay a price for their success, however, in that they had an increased risk of coronary heart disease (CHD) over and above the known risks of hypertension, atherosclerosis, smoking, lack of exercise, or a diet high in saturated fats.

A study begun in 1963 followed almost 3,000 men for 8.5 years who showed no initial signs of CHD (Rosenman et al., 1975). At the end of the study, the incidence of CHD was more than twice as great among type A than among type B personalities (who lack type A traits). Other research found that type A individuals tended to work at a continuous maximum rate on a task, regardless of a deadline, perhaps because type A's believe time is passing by more quickly than do type B's (Burnam, Pennebaker, & Glass, 1975). Type A's also seemed better able than type B's to focus attention on

a primary task when confronted with a distracting task (Matthews & Brunson, 1979).

Studies of physiological differences between type A and type B individuals suggested a possible biologic basis for the higher CHD risk among the former in that, when presented with a challenging or competitive task, type A's showed greater increases in heart rate or blood pressure than did type B's. Resting heart rates were equivalent for the two groups (Dembroski, MacDougall, & Lushene, 1979). Apparently a lack of stimulation can also be a stressor for type A's, as evidenced by their higher levels of adrenaline secretion as compared to those of type B's during a boring, no-task situation (Frankenhaeuser, Lundberg & Forsman, 1980).

Despite its promising beginnings, the type A construct did not hold up well in subsequent research. A review by Dimsdale (1988) concluded that the critical link between type A behavior and CHD failed to replicate in several large-scale studies. One possible reason for these mixed results was that personality was originally assessed using a time consuming, face-to-face interview technique (Jenkins, Rosenman, & Friedman, 1967), whereas later studies generally used standardized questionnaires that could be machine scored. One of the latter was the Jenkins Activity Survey (JAS), which contained more than 50 questions such as, "How would your spouse (or your closest friend) rate you?" Four available responses ranged from "Definitely hard-driving and competitive" to "Definitely relaxed and easygoing." Classifications of subjects scoring near or at the extremes of the scale as "incompletely" or "fully" developed type A's or B's were said to agree in 73% of cases with classifications derived from the structured interview (Jenkins et al., 1971). A factor analysis revealed three independent components of the type A score: H (Hard-driving), J (Job-involvement), and S (Speed and impatience). Jenkins and colleagues reported that the H factor was the one that discriminated most clearly between men experiencing CHD and non-coronary controls. Even the JAS was too lengthy for most research purposes, so 21 items having the strongest association with the overall type A score were extracted from the original questionnaire (Glass, 1977), and this became the most widely used instrument for assessing the coronary-prone personality in numerous studies conducted from the 1970s through the 1980s. As an example of this work, Glass (1977) found that the type A person's initial response to feedback that he or she is *not* coping successfully with a problem-solving task is to intensify his or her efforts but also to show a collapse of effective coping—called learned helplessness—when failure feedback is very salient or prolonged. Some studies have supported this description of type A coping strategies (Brunson & Matthews, 1981), whereas others have contradicted it (Lovallo & Pishkin, 1980). Such conflicting results eventually discouraged researchers in this area. Though a few validating studies showed significant correlations among the three techniques for assessing the coronary-prone personality, the relationships were not of sufficient magnitude to demonstrate strong construct validity. According to Dimsdale (1988), most damaging of all to this personality construct were failures to replicate the connection between type A behavior and CHD, even in investigations utilizing the gold standard semi-structured interview.

Research into the type A coronary-prone personality appears to have effectively ended in the early 1990s. The most recent article found in a medline search (Buchman et al., 1991) reported statistically significant but weak negative correlations between type A behavior and physical fitness. Dimsdale (1988) suggested that future work might focus on a more "virulent core" of the coronary-prone personality, such as the H factor identified by Jenkins and colleagues (1971) or a hostility component shown to correlate with the extent of coronary atherosclerosis by MacDougall and colleagues (1985). Instead, the type A construct was abandoned, though the possibility remains that it will eventually be rediscovered, probably in a revised form.

REFERENCES

Brunson, B. I., & Matthews, K. A. (1981). The type A coronary-prone behavior pattern and reactions to uncontrollable stress: An analysis of performance strategies, affect, and attributions during failure. *Journal of Personality and Social Psychology, 40,* 906–918.

Buchman, B. P., Sallis, J. F., Criqui, M. H., Dimsdale, J. E., Kaplan, R. M. (1991). Physical activity, physical fitness, and psychological characteristics of medical students. *Journal of Psychosomatic Research, 35,* 197–208.

Burnam, M. A., Pennebaker, J. W., & Glass, D. C. (1975). Time consciousness, achievement striving and the type A coronary-prone behavior pattern. *Journal of Abnormal Psychology, 84,* 76–79.

Dembroski, T. M., MacDougall, J. M., & Lushene, R. (1979). Interpersonal interaction and cardiovascular response in Type A subjects and coronary patients. *Journal of Human Stress, 5,* 28–36.

Dimsdale, J. E. (1988). A perspective on Type A behavior and coronary disease. *New England Journal of Medicine, 318*(2), 110–112.

Friedman, M., & Rosenman, R. H. (1989). Association of specific overt behavior pattern with blood and cardiovascular findings. *Journal of the American Medical Association, 169,* 1286–1296.

Glass, D. C. (1977). *Behavior patterns, stress, and coronary disease.* Hillsdale, N.J.: Erlbaum.

Jenkins, D., Rosenman, R. H., & Friedman, M. (1967). Development of an objective psychological test for the determination of the coronary-prone behavior pattern in employed men. *Journal of Chronic Diseases, 20,* 371–379.

Jenkins, C. D., Zysanski, S. J., & Rosenman, R. H. (1971). Progress toward validation of a computer-scored test for the Type A coronary-prone behavior pattern. *Psychosomatic Medicine, 33,* 193–202.

Lovallo, W. R., & Pishkin, V. (1980). Performance of type A (coronary-prone) men during and after exposure to uncontrollable noise and task failure. *Journal of Personality and Social Psychology, 38,* 963–971.

MacDougall, J. M., Dembroski, T. M., Dimsdale, J. E., & Hackett, T. P. (1985). Components of type A, hostility, and anger-in: Further relationships to angiographic findings. *Health Psychology, 4,* 137–152.

Matthews, K. A., & Brunson, B. I. (1979). Allocation of attention and the type A coronary-prone behavior pattern. *Journal of Personality and Social Psychology, 37,* 2081–2090.

Rosenman, R. H., Brand, R. J., Jenkins, C. D. (1975). Coronary heart disease in the Western Collaborative Group Study: Final follow-up experience of 8 1/2 years. *Journal of the American Medical Association, 233,* 872–877.

W. SAMUEL
F. SIMJEE MCCLURE
University of California, San Diego

LEARNED HELPLESSNESS
PSYCHOSOMATIC DISORDERS
STRESS
TYPE B PERSONALITY

TYPE B PERSONALITY

During the late 1970s and early 1980s, when interest in the type A, coronary-prone personality was at its peak, people exhibiting the contrasting type B personality served mainly as a control group against which the characteristics of type A individuals were compared. Thus, according to a review by Matthews (1982), type B's described themselves as less aggressive, hard-driving, active, achievement-oriented, loud, and explosive, and as speaking less quickly than did their type A counterparts. Type B's felt more self-controlled and satisfied with their work, social, and marital lives than did type A's. Psychophysiological studies generally found type B participants to be less autonomically responsive than type A's during exposure to a difficult problem-solving task.

A few studies outlined other potentially distinguishing features between these personality types. On tasks demanding patience and deliberation type B's tended to excel, in comparison to type A's (Glass et al., 1974). Type B's were more likely to persist in their problem-solving efforts in the face of highly salient feedback that their efforts were unsuccessful (Brunson & Matthews, 1981). Type B's seemed to have a broader focus of attention in that they outperformed type A's on a task designed to distract attention from a primary task (Matthews & Brunson, 1979).

Despite these intriguing findings, the type B personality was essentially defined as the absence of type A, coronary-prone traits, and so never became an independent focus of research. Consequently, when the relationship between type A and coronary heart disease could not be reliably replicated (see *Type A Personality*) interest in the type B personality waned along with the decline in research on type A. Typical of the difficulties encountered in this area is the observation that even in the original research demonstrating the possible epidemiological consequences of having type A versus type B personality styles, almost one-third of the men who developed coronary heart disease had type B personalities (Rosenman et al., 1975). Thus, type B's were significantly less coronary-prone than type A's but were by no means coronary-immune. Extreme type B's, if they ever were extensively studied, might therefore have been found to possess qualities that could have negative as well as positive relationships with health and effective coping behavior. Certainly someone who is the opposite of type A in terms of being *un*hurried, *non*competitive, *un*motivated, and so forth does not sound like a picture of psychological health. Perhaps some blend of type A and B characteristics would come closer to what in our present cultural milieu might be regarded as an ideal personality type.

REFERENCES

Brunson, B. I., & Matthews, K. A. (1981). The type A coronary-prone behavior pattern and reactions to uncontrollable stress. An analysis of performance strategies, affect, and attributions during failure. *Journal of Personality and Social Psychology, 40,* 906–918.

Glass, D. C., Snyder , M. L., & Hollis, J. (1974). Time urgency and the Type A coronary-prone behavior pattern. *Journal of Applied Social Psychology, 4,* 125–140.

Matthews, K. A., & Brunson, B. I. (1979). Allocation of attention and the type A coronary-prone behavior pattern. *Journal of Personality and Social Psychology, 37,* 2081–2090.

Matthews, K. A. (1982). Psychological perspectives on the type A behavior pattern. *Psychological Bulletin, 91,* 293–323.

Rosenman, R. H., Brand, R. J., Jenkins, C. D. (1975). Coronary heart disease in the Western Collaborative Group Study: Final follow-up experience of 8 ½ years. Journal of the American Medical Association, 233, 872–877.

W. Samuel
F. Simjee McClure
University of California, San Diego

PSYCHOSOMATIC DISORDERS
TYPE A PERSONALITY
TYPOLOGIES

U

ULLMANN, LEONARD P. (1930–   )

Leonard P. Ullmann was born in 1930. He graduated Lafayette College in 1951 and earned his MA (1953) and PhD (1955) at Stanford University. Upon completion of his internship (1952–1956) at the VA Hospital in Palo Alto, he became coordinator of the psychiatric evaluation project at that hospital. At this time he joined Leonard Krasner in studying verbal operant conditioning, and this work led to a direct, rather than indirect, formulation of the development, maintenance, and change of behavior. The research and clinical data were first summarized in *Case Studies in Behavior Modification* (Ullmann & Krasner) and *Research in Behavior Modification* (Krasner & Ullmann; both Holt, Rinehart & Winston, 1965). The direct, educational (rather than the indirect, medical) model led to a focus on individuals' target behaviors that were considered changeworthy by the individuals themselves or by significant others in their environment (Ullmann & Krasner, *A Psychological Approach to Abnormal Behavior,* Prentice Hall, 1969, 1973).

The thread in Ullman's work is that being precedes essence—that the focus of study should be overt behavior, which is observable, rather than personality, which is inferred after the fact. Individuals know themselves by their own responses and by the reactions of both others and themselves to these behaviors. The total situation, including the person's self-generated physiological and verbal cues in reaction to a situation, should be studied rather than traits or reactions in isolation (Krasner & Ullmann, *Behavior Influence and Personality,* Holt, Rinehart & Winston, 1971).

A number of changes from the then-current formulations of professional intervention followed. First, since what is considered changeworthy varies with time, place, and person, the total social situation needs to be taken into account. Second, the gate-keeping, intervening professional becomes responsible as a societal agent rather than as physician who labels and treats a disease within and limited to an individual. Related to this is that the professional person or responsible organization is a necessary object for study (Ullmann, *Institution and Outcome: A Comparative Study of Psychiatric Hospitals,* Pergamon Press, 1967). Third, the focus on the total situation extends naturally to community, environmental, preventive psychology, and the study of public policy (Kasschau, Rehm, & Ullmann, *Psychology Research, Public Policy, and Practice,* Praeger, 1985).

From 1963 to 1986, Ullmann serves on the faculties of the University of Illinois, University of Hawaii, and University of Houston. He has served in various professional organizations, including as president of the Association for the Advancement of Behavior Therapy. Retired from teaching, he continues work on abstractions such as art and research, with the conviction that these labels are human inventions after the fact of human activity, and should be treated as such.

STAFF

THE UNCONSCIOUS

The unconscious is a hypothetical construct used to describe behaviors, phenomena, material, processes, and so on that are out of immediate awareness (English & English, 1958, 1974). Prior to Sigmund Freud, this concept has been used to explain a variety of behaviors such as dissociation, mesmerism, and early trancework. Freud initiated the formal term unconscious (Rychlack, 1981). Later, Erickson and Rossi refined it via Ericksonian hypnotherapy and state-dependent memory learning and behavior systems or the mind-body approaches (Erickson, Rossi, & Rossi, 1976; Rossi, 1993).

There are a variety of definitions and views of the unconscious, depending on one's theoretical background. The concept is difficult to define, and English and English (1958, 1974) found 39 distinct meanings.

HISTORICAL VIEWS

Psychoanalysis

Sigmund Freud was the first modern-day theorist to explore personality in depth. One of his observations involved the unconscious. He divided awareness into three levels: (a) conscious awareness; (b) preconscious awareness; and (c) unconscious awareness. Conscious awareness is considered to include any materials, experiences, learnings, perceptions, feelings, or thoughts in immediate awareness. The preconscious—an intermediate level—consists of any materials that enter conscious awareness. The unconscious comprises all repressed thoughts, feelings, behaviors, memories, experiences, learnings, and so forth, and remains totally outside awareness (Norby & Hall, 1974). Defense mechanisms are considered to be unconscious dynamics that protect the ego by denying and distorting reality. The unconscious also contains repressed sexual impulses, instincts, id impulses, wishes, dreams, and psychological conflicts (Hall & Lindzey, 1978).

Hypnotic, Ericksonian Views

Erickson worked directly and indirectly with various processes of the unconscious (Havens, 1985; Erickson, Rossi, & Rossi, 1976). Erickson's view of the unconscious was developed through trancework. His view of the unconscious was that of a reservoir of past memories, a storehouse of learning patterned from experiences (Beahrs, 1971; McGarty, 1985; Yapko, 1986). The unconscious is considered to be a positive constructive force by Erickson. Through the work of Erickson and others, the trance state has been connected to unconscious or unconscious functioning (Yapko, 1984).

Trance is considered to provide a direct access to or a window into the unconscious process. Specific trance behaviors include age regression (remembering past memories without prior conscious recollection); age progression (experiencing futuristic scenarios before the actual events occur); hidden observer phenomena (imagining watching oneself doing something); dissociation; catalepsy (muscular suspension or immobility and rigidity in the limbs, based on concentration/suggestion); ideodynamic or psychomotor behaviors (involuntary behavioral movements—finger movements, hand movements, etc.—outside ordinary conscious awareness); autohypnosis; anesthesia (by suggestion and concentration); amnesia; automatic writing; imagery; time distortion; eye closure; and relaxation (Carich, 1990a, 1990b; Erickson, Rossi, & Rossi, 1976). Lankton and Lankton (1983) furthered the Ericksonian view of the unconscious by emphasizing a right hemispheric physiological base along with behaviors and processes such as spatial modes, pantomime (nonverbal movement), involuntary movements, imagery, sensory modalities, intuition, artistic-creative tendencies, literalism, psychophysiological functioning, music, symbolic representations/meanings, rhythmic patterning, and spontaneity.

Rossi (1993) took a psychophysiological view of the unconscious along with the previously stated Ericksonian views. He postulated that the key not only to the unconscious processes but also to the issue of causality is the state-dependent memory learning and behavior (SDML & B) system (Rossi, 1993). Rossi (1987) described state-dependent memory, stating that "what is learned and remembered is dependent on one's psychophysiological state at the time of the experience" (p. 372).

The SDML & B system is considered to stem from the limbic-hypothalamic system, which regulates much of human behavior and brain activity through information substances or messenger molecules. These regulatory processes are the substance of the unconscious. Rossi (1993) further contended that behaviors and/or learning consist of encoding perceptions into state-dependent memories at the limbic-hypothalamic level. More specifically, learning, memories, and/or perceptions are transduced into information via molecular processes within the brain, whereas sensory input is transduced through cellular interaction. This, then, is primarily the basis of the unconscious processes. Rossi (1993) also related this with psychophysiological rhythms (circadian and ultradian cycles). Ultradian cycles are the natural rest cycles that facilitate natural rest states (Rossi & Nimmons, 1991). These cycles provide a window into the unconscious. As an example, Rossi (1993) emphasized the similarities between ultradian cycles (20-min natural rest period occurring every 90 to 120 min) and trance states. These 20-min periods are called basic rest activity cycles, in which the mind and body may be rejuvenated.

The conceptual meaning of the unconscious is controversial within the field of psychology. Research into the unconscious and the related concepts of hypnosis and dissociation is continuing. Kihlstrom (1987) cites research suggesting that humans cognitively process information that is not in immediate awareness. Consciousness is best viewed on a continuum, ranging in degrees, or levels, from the storage of information and the processing of that information in immediate awareness to a lack of awareness (unconsciousness).

APPLICATIONS

Among the applications of the concept of the unconscious are the changing of behaviors and the resolving of problems. To accom-

plish these goals, the unconscious must be accessed and used. People are generally self-programmed through a series of choices based on a variety of experiences. Many problems are self-programmed at unconscious levels (unconscious choices or choices made at unconscious levels) and need to be reprogrammed at those unconscious levels. Some methods of accessing and using the unconscious are internal visualization or imagery, fantasy and daydreams, dreams, self-talk, music, art, body rhythms (basic rest activity cycles), relaxation, and hypnotic techniques.

Imagery is the internal visualization of some image or scenario with a theme and goal (Aroaz, 1982, 1985). Imagery enhances fantasies, dreams, and daydreams and adds a reality element to the experience. Similarly, imagination is related to imagery along with fantasy and dreams. By using imagery, fantasy, and daydreams, one gains the experience that something actually happened. When using imagery and/or imagination or fantasy, one should use sensory modes (auditory [hearing], kinesthetic [movement], taste, and smell) (Aroaz, 1982, 1985). To prepare for upcoming events, one should develop a detailed image and/or scenario of the event and rehearse the scenario over and over, imagining successfully completing the task.

Aroaz (1982, 1985) suggested that self-talk is a type of hypnotic suggestion that self-programs one's mind at an unconscious or subconscious level. By monitoring one's self-talk or self-statements and changing them, one can reprogram one's unconscious belief systems.

Another way to access unconscious processes and change dysfunctional behavior is through hypnosis and relaxation techniques that can directly access unconscious processes. Most people drift in and out of trance states all day long. These naturalistic trance states are considered part of the ultradian rest cycles (Rossi & Nimmons, 1991; for more information on hypnotic techniques, see Hammond, 1990; Erickson, Rossi, & Rossi, 1976; Carich, 1990a, 1990b; and Aroaz, 1982, 1985).

Rossi (1987, 1993) emphasized the importance of the body's naturalistic rhythms. Rossi (1992, 1990) broke this into biomolecular exchanges of so-called housekeeping genes (genes that regulate human metabolism). The unconscious can be accessed by taking advantage of these rest cycles (Rossi & Nimmons, 1991).

Music, often a soothing method of relaxation, also can be a motivating and stimulating source of creativity. Both music and art can serve as pathways to the unconscious, if one has learned to be receptive. Literally, most music and art work involve unconscious elements (Lankton & Lankton, 1983).

REFERENCES

Aroaz, D. L. (1982). *Hypnosis and sex therapy.* New York: Brunner/Mazel.

Aroaz, D. L. (1985). *The new hypnosis.* New York: Brunner/Mazel.

Beahrs, J. O. (1971). The hypnotic psychotherapy of Milton H. Erickson. *The American Journal of Clinical Hypnosis, 14*(2), 73–90.

Carich, M. S. (1990a). The basics of hypnosis and trancework. *Individual Psychology, 46*(4), 401–410.

Carich, M. S. (1990b). Hypnotic techniques and Adlerian constructs. *Individual Psychology, 46*(2), 1660–1677.

English, H. B., & English, A. C. (1974). *A comprehensive dictionary of psychological and psychoanalytical terms.* New York: David McKay. (Original work published 1958)

Erickson, M. H., Rossi, E. L., & Rossi, S. I. (1976). *Hypnotic realities: The induction of clinical hypnosis and forms of indirect suggestion.* New York: Irvington.

Hall, C. S., & Lindzey, G. (1978). *Theories of personality.* New York: Wiley.

Hammond, D. L. (Ed.). (1990). *Handbook of hypnotic suggestions & metaphors.* New York: Norton.

Havens, R. (1985). *The wisdom of Milton H. Erickson.* New York: Irvington.

Kihlstrom, J. (1987). The cognitive unconscious. *Science, 237,* 1445–1452.

Lankton, S., & Lankton, C. H. (1983). *The answer within: A clinical framework of Ericksonian hypnotherapy.* New York: Brunner/Mazel.

McGarty, R. (1985). Relevance of Ericksonian psychotherapy to the treatment of chemical dependency. *Journal of Substance Abuse Treatment, 2,* 147–151.

Norby, V., & Hall, C. (1974). *A Guide to psychologists and their concepts.* San Francisco: Freeman.

Rossi, E. L. (1987). Mind/body communication and new language of human facilitation. In J. K. Zeig (Ed.), *The evolution of psychotherapy* (pp. 369–387). New York: Brunner/Mazel.

Rossi, E. L. (1990). From mind to molecule: More than a metaphor. In J. K. Zeig & S. Gilligan (Eds.), *Brief therapy: Myths, methods, and metaphors* (pp. 445–472). New York: Brunner/Mazel.

Rossi, E. L. (1993). *The psychobiology of mind-body healing: New concepts in therapeutic hypnosis.* New York: Norton.

Rossi, E. L., & Nimmons, D. (1991). *The 20 minute break: Using the new science of ultradian rhythms.* Los Angeles: Jeremy Tarcher.

Rychlack, J. F. (1981). *Introduction to personality and psychotherapy* (2nd ed.). Boston: Houghton Mifflin.

Yapko, M. D. (1984). *Trancework: An introduction to clinical hypnosis.* New York: Irvington.

Yapko, M. D. (1986). What is Ericksonian hypnosis? In B. Zilbergeld, M. G. Edelstein, & D. L. Aroaz (Eds.), *Hypnosis: Questions & answers* (pp. 223–231). New York: Norton.

M. S. CARICH
Chicago, Illinois

BLOCKING
ERICKSONIAN VIEWS
FANTASY
FORGETTING
HYPNOSIS
IMAGELESS THOUGHT
MIND-BODY PROCESS
PSYCHOANALYSIS

UNDERWOOD, BENTON J. (1915–1994)

Benton J. Underwood received the BA degree from Cornell College (Iowa) and the PhD degree from the University of Iowa in 1942 where he studied under John A. McGeoch, a specialist in human learning. After serving in the U.S. Navy during World War II, he joined the faculty at Northwestern University, where he remained. He was a member of the National Academy of Science.

His first book, *Experimental Psychology,* has been a widely used undergraduate text in that area. It stresses methodology and design rather than content. His discussions on experimental design are applied to motivation, frustration, and various areas of learning and memory. He published *Psychological Research,* and was coauthor of *Elementary Statistics* with C. P. Duncan and Janet Taylor.

Over the years, his research efforts were devoted to the field of human learning, and he was the author or coauthor (with Duncan, Jack Richardson, and others) of more than 120 articles. Underwood explored many facets of verbal learning processes, including problems of retroactive and proactive inhibition, distributed practice, and the role of meaningfulness in associative learning, as well as a variety of variables that contribute to the degree of remembering and forgetting following verbal learning.

STAFF

THE UNSTRUCTURED CLINICAL INTERVIEW

The clinical interview has long been regarded as a foundational element of psychiatric and clinical psychological practice (Sullivan, 1954; Wiens, 1976). The interview format, of course, affords the clinician the direct opportunity to solicit from the patient salient, first-hand information regarding his or her presenting problems and the exigencies thereof—assessment information that typically proves germane to the ongoing process of case conceptualization (e.g., diagnosis) and the formulation of appropriate intervention strategies (Scheiber, 1994). In addition, under many circumstances the clinical interview involves the interviewer in the process of not only assessment, but also of implementing de facto interventions—that is, acting as an agent of salubrious clinical change during the interview itself.

Despite the existence of literally thousands of assessment instruments—personality inventories, symptom checklists, historical reviews, and so forth—in actual clinical practice the interview is still the most frequently employed assessment procedure (Beutler, 1995). Unlike many other assessment methods, the interview requires no additional expense on the part of therapist or patient; further, it may be tailored to meet the unique needs of each individual patient, may be modified to accommodate implicit or explicit temporal constraints, and may subserve the important function of assisting in the development of rapport and understanding between clinician and patient.

There are three distinctive subtypes of clinical interviewing, most commonly referred to as structured, semi-structured, and unstructured. In a structured clinical interview, the interviewer proceeds in verbatim fashion through a predetermined list of questions, each of which may be answered by the patient with short, factual responses (Pope, 1979). Because the structured interview has considerable potential to be experienced by both clinician and patient as contrived and inflexible, such an approach is rarely employed in routine clinical practice, and even in research settings it is less frequently employed than is a related, but more flexible, format: the semi-structured interview. In the semi-structured format, the clinician employs a scripted set of initial queries (still asked verbatim), but is permitted to compose ad hoc follow-up questions tailored to the task of obtaining all necessary, clinically relevant information. The Structured Clinical Interview for *DSM-IV* (SCID; First, Spitzer, Gibbon, & Williams, 1995), Longitudinal Interval Follow-up Evaluation (LIFE; Keller et al., 1987), and Anxiety Disorders Interview Schedule-IV (ADIS-IV; DiNardo, Brown, & Barlow, 1994) all serve as examples of commonly employed semistructured interviews.

In rather stark contrast, the unstructured interview does not rely upon an a priori set of specified questions; instead, the interview content develops as an emergent result of the clinician-patient interaction. Although the clinician may enter the interview with a set of content domains about which he or she might wish to gather information (e.g., the patient's presenting problem(s), current level of adaptive function, available social support, prominent psychosocial stressors, coping style, characteristic ego defense mechanisms, etc.), the clinician in an unstructured format quite deliberately refrains from directing the interviewee through a predetermined list of queries regarding such content. Rather, the clinician affords the client ample license to initiate and specify much of the interview content and the pace of content coverage. The clinician's role in such an interview format may be defined principally as skillful interaction, as opposed to the structured interviewer's role of skillful direction. It is to be noted, however, that unstructured interviewing, in comparison with more structured interview formats, has received relatively little in the way of research support vis-à-vis the validity and reliability of the clinical inferences derived therefrom (Segal, Hersen, & Van Hasselt, 1994). Nevertheless, the unstructured interview remains the most commonly employed form of interviewing in the clinical setting (Beutler, 1995).

The unstructured interview format, of course, is closely tied historically to psychoanalytic practice. Within a psychoanalytic conceptual framework, the clinician's creation of an unstructured context is considered to be the essential prerequisite for the patient's subsequent communication of unconscious material, in the form of, for example, so-called transference reactions, free associations, and so forth. It is noteworthy, however, that use of the unstructured interview is not limited to psychoanalytic practice. In fact, unstructured interviewing may be employed by clinicians across the theoretical spectrum, although certainly the focus of the interview will vary somewhat according to the clinician's theoretical orientation. For example, a psychodynamic clinician might show keen interest in the discussion of material regarding the patient's childhood history and familial dynamics (Pope, 1979), while a behavior therapist would be more likely to provide subtle reinforcement (e.g., by attending more carefully) for the patient's reporting of specific and detailed information concerning present difficulties, and the environmental antecedents and sequelae of such functional problems (Sarwer & Sayers, 1998). The behavior therapist would also likely play a more active role in the interview, for example, asking more questions, than would his or her psychodynamic counterpart, while still operating within the broad bounds of the unstructured format by virtue of the deliberate avoidance of predetermined queries.

In the view of many practicing clinicians, the unstructured interview is the format of choice for the efficient gathering of useful clinical information, chiefly due to the extraordinary flexibility associated with the unstructured format. As Johnson (1981) has stated, "although haphazard questioning should be avoided, the interview must be loosely enough structured so that the interviewer can pursue avenues of inquiry that present themselves during the course of the interview" (p. 86). Similarly, it has been claimed that, in order for an interview to be optimally effective, it must be organized around the patient, rather than around a specific psychiatric interview format (MacKinnon & Michels, 1971). Likewise, clinicians from the Rogerian tradition hold that the unstructured format, by virtue of its implicit insistence that the clinician attend to the issues and topics raised by the patient (rather than vice versa), may more easily facilitate the establishment of a positive therapeutic alliance (e.g., Rogers, 1951). However, as we will see, despite the possible intuitive appeal of the aforementioned claims, they have received very little in the way of empirical corroboration.

FORMAT VARIABLES

Unstructured interviewing is a difficult skill to acquire. Not surprisingly, therefore, clinical training programs (e.g., master's and doctoral programs of clinical psychology, counseling psychology, social work, and—less so—psychiatric residency programs) typically devote considerable attention to the development of such skills among their students. Interviewing is likely to be taught with an overt emphasis on the cultivation of listening skills (as opposed to questioning skills, per se), perhaps because it is not uncommon for the novice clinician to conduct interviews in an ineffectual manner that might charitably be described as "a barrage of questions." The acquisition of solid unstructured-interviewing skills typically requires considerable practice, in addition to a capacity on the part of the interviewer for critical self-reflection (in order to learn from one's inevitable interviewing missteps), and a recognition of the fact that the interview is based, ultimately, upon a human relationship (Johnson, 1981). In an attempt to facilitate the training of interviewing skills, various clinical theorists have sub-divided the interview into discrete phases, steps, or objectives.

Harry Stack Sullivan, a seminal figure in both the theory and practice of American psychiatry, was one of the first clinicians to give extensive attention to the interview process. In his still-influential book, *The Clinical Interview* (Sullivan, 1954), he described four principal stages characteristic of the unstructured interview (along with the caveat that such stages be recognized as "hypothetical, fictional, abstract, and artificial"). These four stages Sullivan termed the "inception," the "reconnaissance," the "detailed inquiry," and the "termination." The inception includes the clinician's welcoming of the patient and the establishment of what is to be expected from the interview. The reconnaissance stage consists of questions regarding the patient's history, social situation, and therapeutic needs. During the inquiry stage, the clinician begins to test various clinically relevant hypotheses, especially those germane to the patient's presenting set of problems. The fourth stage, termination, refers to the delicate process of ending the interview in mutually satisfactory fashion.

A somewhat related, contemporary description of the unstructured interview process is to be found in Shea's (1988) proposed five-phase structural model. This model suggests a broad interview outline that may prove especially helpful for the beginning interviewer, and that appears applicable to most forms of unstructured interviewing, regardless of the theoretical context within which the interview occurs. Phase one, the introduction, refers to the initial contact between patient and therapist. During this phase, the therapist may attempt to put the patient at ease with conversational small talk, and to educate the patient about the interview process itself. Phase two, the opening, entails the clinician's encouraging the patient to provide a first-person account of presenting problems, elicited by a statement such as "Tell me what brought you to therapy." Phase three is the body of the interview. During this phase, the interviewer works to gather relevant information based upon material presented during the opening. Such information will subsequently be used by the clinician in the process of case conceptualization and treatment planning. During the closing phase, the interviewer begins the simultaneous process of summarizing material covered during the interview and communicating the clinician's own conceptualization of the manner in which the patient's problems may be optimally addressed—a process that often helps foster a sense of hopefulness in the patient (Frank & Frank, 1991). The final phase, termination, describes the formal cessation of the interview and the exiting of the patient. Shea's model nicely illustrates the point that, although the interview format may remain unstructured (inasmuch as the questions and wording thereof are not planned prior to the session), the interviewer typically retains a general idea of the sequence and flow of the interview.

RELATIONSHIP VARIABLES

The interview process, regardless of its degree of structure, provides the clinician with an implicit opportunity to cultivate a therapeutic alliance with the patient. Moreover, the flexibility of the unstructured situation permits the therapist considerable latitude to respond empathically to the stated concerns of the patient, while also providing the patient an opportunity to observe the clinician's distinctive interpersonal style in action. What, though, are the actual strategies to be employed by the interviewer in promoting a positive working alliance? Carl Rogers, on the basis of considerable clinical observation and research evidence, has suggested a set of general principles that may guide the clinician in such an endeavor,

among them: (a) maintaining a nonjudgmental attitude toward the patient and toward the material that he or she relates during the interview; (b) viewing the patient with "unconditional positive regard"; (c) reflecting accurate empathy; and (d) conveying a sense of authenticity and genuineness (Rogers, 1961). In a similar vein, Othmer and Othmer (1994) have identified a set of guiding principles that may be employed by the clinician to help facilitate clinician-patient rapport, notably: putting the patient at ease with the interview situation (e.g., by greeting the patient in a warm, yet professional, manner); determining the source of the patient's suffering and showing appropriate empathy; assessing the patient's own (subjective) understanding of his or her problems and communicating a sense of being on the patient's side; and acting as a credible clinical expert.

RESEARCH

Despite the ubiquity of the unstructured interview in clinical practice, it is noteworthy that there exists a paucity of research concerning its clinical utility. Nevertheless, there are a handful of published investigations that have some bearing on this issue. Following is a brief summary of the relevant literature.

As noted previously, the unstructured interview is employed primarily as a method of clinical assessment—that is, as a means of gathering information pertinent to case conceptualization (e.g., diagnosis) and treatment planning. But how valid and reliable is the information obtained in the unstructured interview format? With respect to the assignment of *DSM*-based diagnoses, the scant available evidence suggests that unstructured interviews may be inferior to structured/semi-structured diagnostic interviews with respect to both the reliability and validity of interview-based diagnoses (Segal, Hersen, & Van Hasselt, 1994; Vitiello, Malone, Buschle, & Delaney, 1990; Widiger, Sanderson, & Warner, 1986; Young, O'Brien, Gutterman, & Cohen, 1987). In fact, it appears that structured interviewing exhibits psychometric properties superior to unstructured interviewing even regarding the assessment of the patient's psychiatric social history (Ferriter, 1993) and treatment expectations (Ruggeri, Dall'Agnola, Agostini, & Bisoffi, 1994). Additional support for the hypothesis of generally poor unstructured-interview psychometric properties comes from a recent meta-analysis of the use of structured versus unstructured interview formats in employment selection decisions (McDaniel, Whetzel, Schmidt, & Maurer, 1994). Finally, there is some evidence that the unstructured interviewer's own beliefs and preconceptions may exert a biasing effect on the interview process itself, affecting what the patient is willing to discuss in the ongoing reciprocal process of selecting pertinent information (Gordon, 1969).

In light of the continued widespread use of unstructured interviewing as a principal source of information upon which clinical diagnoses are assigned, it is rather puzzling that clinical researchers have given so little attention to clarifying the extent to which such a practice may be regarded as reliable and valid. Certainly, on the basis of the scant available evidence, there is some reason to question the psychometric soundness of such a practice, but it is equally clear that more systematic evaluation is necessary before any unequivocal conclusions may be drawn. Similarly, there appear to be no published investigations of the claim that unstructured interviews are superior to structured interviews in the facilitation of the therapeutic alliance. This would appear, therefore, to be another important domain for future clinical investigation.

REFERENCES

Beutler, L. E. (1995). The clinical interview. In L. E. Beutler & M. R. Berren (Eds.), *Integrative assessment of adult personality* (pp. 94–120). New York: Guilford.

DiNardo, P., Brown, T., & Barlow, D. (1994). *Anxiety Disorders Interview Schedule for DSM-IV.* Albany, NY: Greywind.

Ferriter, M. (1993). Computer aided interviewing and the psychiatric social history. *Social Work and Social Sciences Review, 4,* 255–263.

First, M. B., Spitzer, R. L., Gibbon, M., & Williams, J. W. B. (1995). *Structured Clinical Interview for Axis I DSM-IV Disorders—Patient Edition (SCID-I/P, Version 2.0).* New York: New York State Psychiatric Institute.

Frank, J. D., & Frank, J. B. (1991). *Persuasion and healing: A comparative study of psychotherapy.* Baltimore: Johns Hopkins University Press.

Gordon, R. L. (1969). *Interviewing: Strategies, techniques, and tactics.* Homewood, IL: Dorsey.

Johnson, W. R. (1981). Basic interviewing skills. In C. E. Walker (Ed.), *Clinical practice of psychology: A guide for mental health professionals.* Elmsford, NY: Pergamon.

Keller, M. B., Lavori, P. W., Friedman, B., Nielsen, E., Endicott, J., & McDonald-Scott, P. A. (1987). The Longitudinal Interval Follow-up Evaluation: A comprehensive method for assessing outcome in prospective longitudinal studies. *Archives of General Psychiatry, 44,* 540–548.

MacKinnon, R. A., & Michels, R. (1971). *The psychiatric interview in clinical practice.* Philadelphia: W. B. Saunders.

McDaniel, M. A., Whetzel, D. L., Schmidt, F. L., & Maurer, S. D. (1994). The validity of employment interviews: A comprehensive review and meta-analysis. *Journal of Applied Psychology, 79,* 599–616.

Othmer, E., & Othmer, S. C. (1994). *The Clinical Interview Using DSM-IV (Vol. 1: Fundamentals).* Washington, DC: American Psychiatric Press.

Pope, B. (1979). *The mental health interview: Research and application.* Elmsford, NY: Pergamon.

Rogers, C. (1951). *Client-centered therapy.* Boston: Houghton-Mifflin.

Rogers, C. (1961). *On becoming a person.* Boston: Houghton-Mifflin.

Ruggeri, M., Dall'Agnola, R., Agostini, C., & Bisoffi, G. (1994). Acceptability, sensitivity and content validity of the VECS and VSSS in measuring expectations and satisfaction in psychiatric patients and their relatives. *Social Psychiatry and Psychiatric Epidemiology, 29,* 265–276.

Sarwer, D. B., & Sayers, S. L. (1998). Behavioral interviewing. In A. S. Bellack & M. Hersen (Eds.), *Behavioral assessment: A practical handbook (4th ed.).* Boston: Allyn & Bacon.

Scheiber, S. C. (1994). The psychiatric interview, psychiatric history, and mental status examination. In R. E. Hales & S. C. Yudofsky (Eds.), *The American psychiatric Press textbook of psychiatry (2nd Ed.).* Washington, DC: American Psychiatric Press.

Segal, D. L., Hersen, M., & Van Hasselt, V. B. (1994). Reliability of the Structured Clinical Interview for DSM-III-R: An evaluative review. *Comprehensive Psychiatry, 35,* 316–327.

Shea, S. C. (1988). *Psychiatric interviewing: The art of understanding.* Philadelphia: W. B. Saunders.

Sullivan, H. S. (1954). *The psychiatric interview.* New York: Norton.

Vitiello, B., Malone, R., Buschle, P. R., & Delaney, M. A. (1990). Reliability of DSM-III diagnoses of hospitalized children. *Hospital and Community Psychiatry, 41,* 63–67.

Widiger, T. A., Sanderson, C., & Warner, L. (1986). The MMPI, prototypal typology, and borderline personality disorder. *Journal of Personality Assessment, 50,* 540–553.

Wiens, A. N. (1976). The assessment interview. In I. B. Weiner (Ed.), *Clinical method in psychology,* New York: Wiley.

Young, J. G., O'Brien, J. D., Gutterman, E. M., & Cohen, P. (1987). Research on the clinical interview. *Journal of the American Academy of Child and Adolescent Psychiatry, 26,* 613–620.

S. S. ILARDI
A. D. BRANSTETTER
University of Kansas

**CLINICAL ASSESSMENT
STRUCTURED AND SEMI-STRUCTURED CLINICAL INTERVIEWS**

U.S.S.R., NEUROPSYCHOLOGY (IN THE FORMER)

GENERAL TRENDS IN THE DEVELOPMENT OF NEUROPSYCHOLOGY

The development in neuropsychology can be described by the following model (Glozman, 1999a), comprising three overlapping and coexisting phases:

I. BRAIN→MENTAL ACTIVITY
II. MENTAL ACTIVITY→BRAIN
III. (BRAIN) MENTAL ACTIVITY⇔SOCIETY

In the first phase, the emphasis for neuropsychologists was on the brain and its relationship to different behaviors. The main and most valuable attainment of this phase is a revision by Luria of the concepts of localizationism and antilocalizationism, the creation of the theory of the dynamic and systemic cerebral organization of mental processes and description of frontal, parietal, temporal, and other syndromes (Luria, 1966; 1973). Recent development of the functional systems approach follows two main lines: (a) a study of intrahemispheric specialization (asymmetry) and interhemispheric interactions, and (b) research into subcortical brain pathology.

In the second phase, the structure of mental activity or higher mental functions, and secondarily the localization of such processes in the brain, were the focus of attention. Such a focus has produced studies examining the neuropsychology of memory (Luria, 1976a; Luria et al., 1970; Korsakova & Mikadze, 1982); neurolinguistics (Luria, 1976b; Akhutina, 1981; Akhutina & Glozman, 1995; Glozman, 1978); diffuse syndromes after cerebrovascular pathology (Moscovichyute et al., 1982); syndromes of underdevelopment or atypical development; and the neuropsychology of individual differences in normal subjects. At this phase, quantitative and qualitative integration of Lurian procedures was proved necessary (Glozman, 1999b).

The third phase of development in neuropsychology focuses on the interrelationship between patients and their society or environment. The neuropsychological assessment should emphasize patients' strengths, which are important in their rehabilitation program and predict their ultimate integration into society. This principle was first realized in aphasiology as the so-called "sociopsychological aspect of rehabilitation" (Tsvetkova et al., 1979; Tsvetkova, 1985), then later developed in studies of interrelations between communication disorders and personality in different nosological groups (Glozman, 1987) and in developmental neuropsychology.

THE PROBLEM OF INTERHEMISPHERIC SPECIALIZATION AND INTERACTION

Research has revealed interhemispheric specialization for different forms of memory (Korsakova & Mikadze, 1982; Korsakova, Moskovichyute, & Simernitskaya, 1979; Simernitskaya, 1978), as well as greater vulnerability of the right hemisphere to cerebral pathology and lower compensating capabilities (Korsakova et al., 1978; Vasserman & Lassan, 1989). The right hemisphere was proved slower in information processing than the left one (Krotkova, Karaseva, & Moskovichyute, 1982), and less able to regulate and accelerate its own mental activity (Enikolopova, 1998; Homskaya, 1995). It has also been shown that each hemisphere is specific for different types of reasoning, such as empirical or logical reasoning, as well as for intensity and stability of human emotions. Moreover, there are unilaterally and bilaterally realized functions, or a "competence" of each hemisphere (Homskaya & Batova, 1998; Meerson & Dobrovolskaya, 1998; Nikolaenko et al., 1997; Zalzman, 1989). Each mental activity is realized through the interaction of both hemispheres, with each making a specific contribution. New evidence proves that interhemispheric differences exist both on the cortical and subcortical levels. Cognitive defects specific to the left hemisphere are more evident in cortical lesions, while subdominant syndromes appear predominantly after subcortical lesions of the right hemisphere (Moscovichyute, 1998).

SUBCORTICAL BRAIN PATHOLOGY

A good model for studying cognitive disturbances due to subcortical damages is Parkinson's Disease (PD) (Glozman, 1999a; Glozman et al., 1996; Korsakova & Moskovichyute, 1985). The pattern of cognitive disturbances in persons with PD is a specific combination of "natural" brain alterations appearing with age and specific impairments caused by the disease. This pattern is not the sum of both components, but a qualitatively new complex of symptoms.

Dementia should not be considered as an obligatory component of PD, and it is not limited to the symptoms of so-called subcortical dementia. It includes some cortical cognitive disorders, the patterns of which are different from that of Alzheimer's disease (AD).

NEUROPSYCHOLOGY OF OLDER PERSONS

Luria's conception of three functional units of the brain (Luria, 1973) may help to differentiate normal from abnormal aging (Glozman, 1999a; Korsakova, 1998). In normal aging the functioning of the first unit—that of activation—is predominantly disturbed, and this is manifested in general slowness, aspontaneity in all activities, increased inhibition of memorized information by interfering stimuli, and restriction of the volume of mental activities when different programs must be simultaneously retained and realized. This normal aging represents a stage of individual development, necessitating a change in strategies, voluntary selection, and use of new forms of mediating mental activity. In pathological atrophic states, such as AD or senile dementia, not only these symptoms are aggravated, but defects in functioning of the two other cerebral units are also demonstrated. Progression of cognitive disturbances leading to the appearance of vascular dementia is predominantly due to regulatory and operational deficits connected to cortical brain regions. A "corticalization" of the cognitive and executive disturbances thus occurs. The evolution of AD is realized by the consecutive "frontalization" and "subcorticalization" of impairments; that is, by superimposed neurodynamic and regulatory impairments upon operational ones.

DEVELOPMENTAL NEUROPSYCHOLOGY

Studies of cognitive evolution and specific disturbances of mental activity after brain damage in children (Simernitskaya, 1982) revealed interhemispheric and intrahemispheric differentiation, which are also typical for adults. Nevertheless, some symptoms, namely aphasic disturbances, were significantly less frequent and had a different pattern than those found in adults after similar lesions. Another difference consisted of a quick regression or resolution of symptoms after surgery, explained by underdevelopment of inter- and intrahemispheric connections.

The further growth of developmental neuropsychology in Russia follows two main lines: study of individual features during the development of cognitive functions (Akhutina, 1998; Mikadze, 1996) and analysis of interhemispheric interaction and "dysgenetic syndrome" in childhood (Semenovich et al., 1998).

Neuropsychological diagnosis of causes of learning problems proved heterogeneity in the maturation of brain structures, connections in the development of functional systems, and significance of a correspondence between the child's abilities and exigencies of the learning programs. The emphasis of the assessments is a modification from diagnostic evaluation to prognostic and corrective suggestions.

NEUROPSYCHOLOGY OF INDIVIDUAL DIFFERENCES

Neuropsychology of individual differences is an application of neuropsychological concepts and methods to the assessment of healthy subjects, which tries to explain normal functioning by using principles of cerebral organization, particularly characteristics of interhemispheric asymmetry (motor, acoustic, and visual) and interhemispheric interaction. These studies have been conducted by E. D. Homskaya and her Moscow colleagues, Orenburg and Kharkov (Ukraine) (Homskaya, 1996; Homskaya et al., 1997; Homskaya & Batova, 1998; Moskvin & Moskvina, 1998; Privalova, 1998). The authors identified 27 possible profiles of lateral brain organization and identified their correlation with aspects of cognitive, motor, and emotional activity of the normal subjects, as well as their adaptive abilities. Each profile of interhemispheric organization has its own "psychological status" (Homskaya et al., 1997).

To summarize, three main trends can be seen in the development of neuropsychology in the former U.S.S.R.:

1. Extensive further expansion of research and practice embracing numerous new domains and nosological patient groups;

2. Combination of qualitative and quantitative approaches;

3. A social and personality-based orientation.

REFERENCES

Akhutina, T. V. (1981). Lexical organization upon aphasiological data. In A. A. Zalevskaya (Ed.), *Psycholinguistic studies of vocabulary and phonetics.* Kalinin: Kalinin University Press. (in Russian)

Akhutina, T. V. (1998). Neuropsychology of individual differences in children as a basis for the application of neuropsychological methods at school. In E. D. Homskaya & T. V. Akhutina (Eds.), *First international Luria memorial conference proceedings.* Moscow: Russian Psychological Association Press. (in Russian)

Akhutina, T. V. & Glozman, J. M. (1995). The neurolinguistic study of semantics. *Aphasiology, 9,* 143–152.

Enikolopova, E. V. (1998). Dynamic characteristics of mental processes and their role in neuropsychological diagnosis. In E. D. Homskaya & T. V. Akhutina (Eds.), *First international Luria memorial conference proceedings.* Moscow: Russian Psychological Association Press. (in Russian)

Glozman, J. M. (1978). Neurolinguistic study of agrammatism in aphasia. In H. Mierzejaeska (Ed.), *Linguistic research on aphasia.* Wroclaw: Ossolineum. (in Polish and Russian)

Glozman, J. M. (1987). *Communication disorders and personality.* Moscow: Moscow University Press. (in Russian) (English revised edition, New York: Plenum, in press.)

Glozman, J. M. (1999a). Russian neuropsychology after Luria. *Neuropsychology Review, 9*(1), 33–44.

Glozman, J. M. (1999b). Quantitative and qualitative integration of Lurian procedures. *Neuropsychology Review, 9*(1), 23–32.

Glozman, J. M., Artemiev, D. V., Damulin, I. V., & Kovyazina, M. S. (1996). Age related features of neuropsychological disorders in Parkinson's disease. *Journal of Russian and East European Psychology, 34,* 46–59.

Homskaya, E. D. (1995). On asymmetry of brain units. In E. D. Homskaya (Ed.), *Neuropsychology today.* Moscow: Moscow University Press. (in Russian)

Homskaya, E. D. (1996). Neuropsychology of individual differences. *Vestnik Moskovskogo Universiteta, Series 14*(2), 24–32. (in Russian)

Homskaya, E. D. & Batova, N. Ya. (1998). *Brain and emotions.* Moscow: Russian Pedagogical Agency Press. (in Russian)

Homskaya, E. D., Efimova, I. V., Budyka, E. V., & Enikolopova, E. V. (1997). *Neuropsychology of individual differences.* Moscow: Russian Pedagogical Agency Press. (in Russian)

Korsakova, N. K. (1998). Neuropsychogerontology: Development of A. R. Luria's school of ideas. In E. D. Homskaya & T. V. Akhutina (Eds.), *First international Luria memorial conference proceedings.* Moscow: Russian Psychological Association Press. (in Russian)

Korsakova, N. K., & Mikadze, Yu. V. (1982). Neuropsychological studies of memory: Results and perspectives. In E. D. Homskaya, L. S. Tsvetkova, & B. V. Zeigarnik (Eds.), *A. R. Luria and modern psychology.* Moscow: Moscow University Press. (in Russian)

Korsakova, N. K., & Moskovichyute, L. I. (1985). *Subcortical structures and mental processes.* Moscow: Moscow University Press. (in Russian)

Korsakova, N. K., Moskovichyute, L. I., & Simernitskaya, E. G. (1979). On functional interaction of cerebral hemispheres in mnestic processes. In *Memory and information processing.* Puschino (in Russian).

Korsakova, N. K., Moscovichyute, L. I., Simernitskaya, E. G., & Smirnov, N. A. (1978). Lateralization of lesion as a risk factor in genesis of consciousness loss and seizures after cerebral hemorrhages. In *Stroke-risk factors.* Tashkent, Uzbekistan. (in Russian)

Krotkova, O. A., Karaseva, T. A., & Moskovichyute, L. I. (1982). Lateral differences in the time course of higher mental functions in endonasal glutamic acid electrophoresis. *Voprocy Neurohirurgii, 3,* 48–52. (in Russian)

Luria, A. R. (1966). *Higher cortical functions in man.* New York: Basic Books.

Luria, A. R. (1973). *The working brain. An introduction to neuropsychology.* London: Penguin.

Luria, A. R. (1976a). *The neuropsychology of memory.* Washington: Winston.

Luria, A. R. (1976b). *Basic problems of neurolinguistics.* The Hague: Mouton.

Luria, A. R., Konovalov, A. N., & Podgornaya, A. Ya. (1970). *Memory disturbances associated with aneurysms of the anterior communicating artery.* Moscow: Moscow University Press. (in Russian; English translation, New York: Plenum, in press).

Meerson, Ya. A., & Dobrovolskaya, N. V. (1998). Disorders in perception of absolute and relative objects localization in spatial depth (depth agnosia) after focal damage of the right or left cerebral hemisphere. In E. D. Homskaya & T. V. Akhutina (Eds.), *First international Luria memorial conference proceedings.* Moscow: Russian Psychological Association Press. (in Russian)

Mikadze, Yu. V. (1996). Neuropsychological diagnosis of the ability to learn. *Vestnik Moskovskogo Universiteta, series 14,* 2, 46–52. (in Russian)

Moscovichyute, L. I. (1998). Cerebral hemisphere asymmetry on the cortical and subcortical levels. In E. D. Homskaya & T. V. Akhutina (Eds.), *First international Luria memorial conference proceedings.* Moscow: Russian Psychological Association Press. (in Russian)

Moscovichyute, L. I., Serbinenko, F. A., Lysachev, A. G., & Smirnov, N. A. (1982). Neuropsychological studies in endovascular neurosurgery. In E. D. Homskaya, L. S. Tsvetkova & B. V. Zeigarnik (Eds.), *A. R. Luria and modern psychology.* Moscow: Moscow University Press. (in Russian)

Moskvin, V. A., & Moskvina, N. V. (1998). Problems of correlation of lateral and individual features in neuropsychology of individual differences. *First international Luria memorial conference proceedings.* Moscow: Russian Psychological Association Press. (in Russian)

Nikolaenko, N. N., Trachenko, O. P., Egorov, A. Yu., & Gritsyshina, M. A. (1997). Linguistic competence of the right and left hemispheres. *Moskovsky Linguistic Journal, 4,* 46–58. (in Russian)

Semenovich, A. V., Arhipov, B. A., Frolova, T. G., & Isaeva, E. V. (1998). On the ontogenesis of interhemispheric interaction. *First international Luria memorial conference proceedings.* Moscow: Russian Psychological Association Press. (in Russian)

Simernitskaya, E. G. (1978). *Hemispheric dominance.* Moscow: Moscow University Press. (in Russian)

Simernitskaya, E. G. (1982). On subjects and specific features of developmental neuropsychology. In E. D. Homskaya, L. S. Tsvetkova, & B. V. Zeigarnik (Eds.), *A. R. Luria and modern psychology.* Moscow: Moscow University Press. (in Russian)

Tsvetkova, L. S. (1985). *Neuropsychological rehabilitation of patients.* Moscow: Moscow University Press. (in Russian)

Tsvetkova, L. S., Glozman, J. M., Kalita, N. G., Maximenko, M. Yu., & Tsyganok, A. A. (1979). *Sociopsychological aspect of aphasics' rehabilitation.* Moscow: Moscow University Press. (in Russian)

Vasserman, L. I., & Lassan, L. P. (1989). Effect of lateralization of subcortical stereotaxic destruction on post surgery dynamics of mental functions in subjects with epilepsy. In *Clinical aspects of the problem of brain functional asymmetry.* Minsk, Belarus. (in Russian)

Zalzman, A. G. (1989). Method of lateral tachistoscopic presentations in study of hemispheric functional asymmetry. In *New methods of neuropsychological research.* Moscow: Psychology Institute of U.S.S.R. Academy of Science. (in Russian)

J. M. GLOZMAN
Moscow University, Russia

ALEXANDER LURIA
ALZHEIMER'S DISEASE
PARKINSON'S DISEASE

VARIABLES IN RESEARCH

Kerlinger (1973) defines a variable as a "symbol to which numerals or values are assigned" (p. 29). This generic description, albeit applicable to psychological variables in research, denotes a mathematical base. Any variable, x or y, therefore infers one of the four basic measurement scales: nominal, ordinal, interval, or ratio. The nature, type, and number of variables available to the researcher are of numerous types. Their relative contributions in research investigations are not fixed but are related primarily to the experimental design involved in the research study. Hence, it is difficult, if not impossible, to rank the research variables being discussed in this section with respect to importance or frequency of use or, as a matter of fact, with respect to any other categorical designation. The discussion of variables that follows should be viewed in this context.

RESEARCH VARIABLES

Initially, variables are classified into one of two broad categories: those considered to be continuous and those considered to be discrete. Continuous variables can be measured along a continuum on points that are graduated (e.g., from low to high). These variables are those that are ordinarily measured by the interval or ratio scale. Examples in psychological research are scores on standardized tests, grade-point averages, and galvanic skin response. Discrete variables are categorical in nature, ordered or unordered, and measured by the nominal scale. Unlike continuous variables, in which magnitude is involved in the measurement, discrete variables are evaluated simply in terms of either/or. Examples are gender, race, ethnic origin, and religious affiliation. A special note regarding discrete variables is that they may be classified into true dichotomies (e.g., male-female), true polytomies (e.g., eye color: brown, blue, or hazel), arbitrary dichotomies (e.g., pass-fail), or arbitrary polytomies (e.g., yes-no-undecided). Continuous variables are referred to as quantitative variables; discrete ones are qualitative variables.

Another important classification is of independent and dependent variables. The independent variable in a research study is presumed to be the cause of the dependent variable. Like variables in general, these have a mathematical base. In the equation $y = f(x)$, the dependent variable, y, is a function of the independent variable, x. This means that the outcome (y) depends on the manipulation of the x variable. In this context, it may be surmised that other variables exist in research: those that may be manipulated and those that may not. Variables manipulated by the researcher are characteristic of a true experimental design. Those not manipulated are typical in a pseudoexperimental, quasi-experimental, or correlational study in which attention is focused simply on the relationship extant between the independent and dependent variables. Kerlinger (1986) refers to these variables as active and attribute ones, respectively. Both types of variables assume an important and necessary role in research design in that they serve interactively to control extraneous systematic variance and minimize error variance in the experiment. This fact brings up the issue of drawing long-standing erroneous conclusions from faulty experiments. A classic example is the famous (or infamous, depending on the side of the fence on which the critic stands) Hawthorne experiments. The so-called Hawthorne effect—the unexpected impact of non-manipulated variables on manipulated ones—has since 1932 been accepted by researchers as an effect based on correct interpretations. Yet many researchers have been unaware that serious questions began to be raised in the 1940s about faulty designs involving the active and attribute variables in the experiments that may have led to erroneous conclusions. Gillespie (1991) has written an extensive history of the Hawthorne experiments that should serve to clarify issues relating to the proper use of variables in research.

INTERVENING VARIABLES

It is well known within the discipline of psychology, and even beyond, that purely psychological attributes are elusive to the human senses; they are merely inferred concepts or constructs. As such they cannot be directly observed and measured; their latent manifestations in behavior can only be inferred from measurements of observable variables. Such attributes—constructs such as assertiveness and sociability—are rather elusive concepts, because they defy definite description in behavioral terms. However, observable variables relating to them play important roles in psychological research. Such variables are referred to as intervening variables, according to Tolman (1958), who first coined the term. Inferences regarding the presence and/or magnitude of intervening variables are presumed, through the interpretation of such measures as psychological test scores and protocols designed to assess these constructs.

SPECIFIC TYPES OF VARIABLES

As stated earlier, innumerable variables may become involved in research designs. In addition to the more general ones discussed previously are many specific to the design of experiments. Prominent among these are the following:

- *Predictor Variables.* These are variables (usually continuous) that are used in the independent set of regression equations in correlational analyses that are the presumed causes of the dependent or criterion variables. Most commonly, the statistical methods involving such variables are multiple regression, canonical, and discriminant function analyses.

- *Predicted Variables.* These are continuous or discrete variables, depending on the statistical analysis used, that represent one or more dependent variables in the prediction equation. They are often called criterion or endogenous variables.

- *Dummy Variables.* On occasion, a researcher may choose or be obliged, for some legitimate reason, to change a continuous variable to a discrete one (either independent or dependent). It also may occur that the researcher wishes to include a truly discrete variable among a set of continuous variables in a prediction equation. A common example is to include gender as a predictor variable in a regression equation. It may also occur that the dependent variable in the equation may be changed from being measured on an interval scale, as psychological measures usually are, to being measured on the nominal scale. An example of the use of this procedure is to substitute pass-fail or acceptable-marginal-reject for the underlying continuous measure. Such variables are referred to as dummy variables. Researchers who do employ them in their experiments should not lose sight of the true nature of such variables, or of the fact that employing such variables usually entails a loss of statistical power, and take account of this in the interpretation of their results.

- *Between-Subjects Variables.* This term is used primarily in the context of analysis of variance (ANOVA) designs to indicate any independent variable in which different subjects are assigned to the different levels of the variable. The purpose of this procedure is to ensure that each subject serves in only one level of the design of the study.

- *Within-Subjects Variables.* This term is used primarily in the context of repeated measures in ANOVA designs to indicate any independent variable in which each subject receives all levels of the variable. The purpose of this procedure is usually to increase the amount of control of error variance in the design of the study.

- *Mediator Variables.* A mediator variable is usually defined as a variable that accounts for the relationship between an independent variable and a dependent variable.

- *Moderator Variables.* A moderator variable is usually defined as a variable that affects the direction or strength of the relationship between an independent variable and a dependent variable.

There are still other types of specific variables that may be considered in research design. For definitions and descriptions of these the reader is referred to Harrison (1979).

REFERENCES

Gillespie, R. (1991). *Manufacturing knowledge: A history of the Hawthorne experiment.* Cambridge: Cambridge University Press.

Harrison, N. (1979). *Understanding behavioral research.* Belmont, CA: Wadsworth.

Kerlinger, F. N. (1986). *Foundations of behavioral research.* New York: Holt, Rinehart & Winston.

Tolman, E. (1958). *Behavior and psychological man.* Berkeley, CA: University of California Press.

P. F. MERENDA
J. S. ROSSI
University of Rhode Island

VIDEO: MAJOR APPLICATIONS IN BEHAVIORAL SCIENCE

Video is used in psychology and neuroscience to gather and disperse information, to help people change (behavior, feelings, attitudes), and as experimental stimuli. These uses are summarized here under seven headings (cf. Dowrick, 1991).

ANALYZING AND DOCUMENTING

The most extensive use of video in behavioral science is to capture and analyze the actions and interactions of humans and other species. Video has been widely used in the analysis of motor activity, nonverbal communication, and social interaction; for medical diagnosis; and for surveillance. Relatively low-cost, digital video equipment has replaced high-speed cine film in the analysis of complex movements in dance and athletics. Comparative psychologists have used video to study animal behavior from the courtship of the praying mantis to language development in gorillas.

Video analysis of facial expression has evolved greatly, under the leadership of Paul Ekman and others, and this methodology has been extended to the social interactions in families and other groups. Essentially, the video allows any level of analysis within available resources, once a coding system has been operationalized. It is also possible to take video [moving] X rays for diagnostic clarification in such situations as the inability to swallow by children with severe disabilities.

Video can be used in surveillance—for example, in sleep laboratories (using infrared lighting) or from cameras mounted in the motor vehicles of drug influenced drivers. Less literature exists to support the use of video for more general purposes of documentation. Examples include an economical system to track the progress of clients through treatment.

EDUCATIONAL VIDEOS

Videotapes and disks, including CD-ROM and DVD, are often designed for the purposes of instructing and informing. Research into components of this medium has been unsystematic, although some total training packages have been thoroughly evaluated. Most information influencing production (style, length, pace, etc.) comes from the entertainment and public relations industries. Promising applications can be listed under three broad headings.

The first is *classroom education*—for school-age children (e.g., interactive video for learning mathematics), in university settings (e.g., illustrations of attribution theory), and for on-the-job training (e.g., supported employment). Applications in this area are rapidly merging with computer and internet technology. The second area is *clinical treatment preparation,* in which medical and dental patients or their family members are shown previews of intended therapeutic procedures. The third area is *health and safety education,* including such topics as childhood development and the consequences of drug use. A modest amount of use, with considerable promise, exists for special populations (e.g., the deaf or those with physical disabilities).

The most rapidly expanding strategy across all these areas is the use of interactive video. These systems incorporate computer software that uses a student's responses to alter exposure to learning materials and tasks.

PEER MODELING

To support people in changing their behavior, another widespread use of video is to provide a trainee or client with demonstrations of effective behavior by a similar person in a similar situation. The range of training and therapeutic purposes is extensive. Applications in professional training range from divorce mediation to flying an airplane. Other productive areas are parent training and child self-management. In social skills and daily living, children and youth are most often featured. Motor performance (e.g., sport) is another area of extensive application. The potential for appropriately designed modeling videos for diverse populations (e.g., people with cognitive disabilities) is promising but underdeveloped.

Strategies for developing video-based modeling have not extended much beyond the strategies for live demonstrations (e.g., similar, coping, and multiple models). However, there are obvious advantages to the potential for repetitive review (with exact, unvarying information), close-ups, slow motion, and so forth, to the benefit of the learning situation and lower costs.

SELF MODELING

Effective behavior can also be illustrated, for learning purposes, on videotapes by the clients or trainees themselves, through planning and editing in various ways. Self modeling is a procedure in which people see themselves showing only adaptive behavior (Dowrick, 1999). Videos, audiotapes, still photographs, stories in print, and individuals' imaginations have been used for self modeling. Researched interventions exist for a wide variety of applications: disruptive behavior, selective mutism, depression, anxiety, sports, social skills, personal safety, self-control, physically challenging situations, academic skills, the training of service providers, and others.

The most effective form of self modeling uses feedforward, a term coined to refer to images of desired skills not yet achieved, created by editing together components of the skill, usually coached and practiced for the camera. For example, a child cannot read independently, but he can point at the words and repeat a phrase or a sentence at a time; these elements can be videotaped separately and edited together into the image of a novel, complex activity, showing competence in a developmentally manageable way.

A simpler but not as dramatically effective strategy is positive self-review, which refers to watching selectively-compiled best examples of skills infrequently or inconsistently achieved. For ex-

ample, a volleyball player gets to review her best service or overhead slam after a full day of many attempts.

In either form, self modeling tapes are typically 2 to 3 minutes long and are reviewed about once a day, six or more times for maximum effect. Sometimes they are reviewed again after 2 or 3 months if a maintenance booster is desirable.

SELF-CONFRONTATION AND FEEDBACK

The practice of video feedback is frequently used, although its theoretical basis remains in dispute. One positive use involves viewing oneself on video in personally demanding situations to improve self-assessment. Video feedback is thus applied in a wide variety of circumstances: competitive sports, professional skills, interpersonal communication, and so on. It appears to be most effective when the behavior required for correction or improvement is clearly indicated; the behavior must also be attainable, with some other training or support (e.g., coaching, counseling) provided, if there is a need.

Another value of viewing videos of oneself performing naturalistic behavior may come from the motivational or emotional impact. The effect of seeing oneself perform poorly on video, without being able to interact with or change the situation, can range from despair, to anxiety, to heightened sensitivity, to increased engagement and determination to succeed. The rules for these reactions are as yet unclear. Overall it seems that the people most likely to benefit include those with pre-existing high levels of self-esteem (self-efficacy, ego strength, etc.).

SCENE SETTING

The use of video to promote discussions, memories, emotions, or judgments is common but under-studied in practice. The use of interpersonal process recall (reviewing videotapes to re-examine the thought processes and feelings associated with specific actions) has been quite well developed in such applications as interviewing and counseling.

The term "triggers" has been coined to refer to brief videos that provoke discussions as the basis for group learning experiences. These are typically very short, unresolved vignettes, designed to promote discussion on contentious topics (e.g., child abuse or attitudes towards different cultures). Vignettes have been used surprisingly little in therapy, although promising uses have been documented in social skills training, exposure therapy, and sex therapy.

A related use of video, employed more in practice than studied empirically, is the therapeutic and developmental impact on people (e.g., teens with emotional disturbance, criminal offenders) who take part in scripting and producing their own videos, sometimes airing them on public access television.

VIDEO AS EXPERIMENTAL STIMULI

A vast number of research studies mention the use of video vignettes, but the methodological principles are minimally defined. Video content may provide the independent variable (e.g., depressed affect in one vignette but not in another). Or video may be contrasted with another medium (e.g., seeing oneself on closed circuit video vs in a mirror). It is common to use a single vignette but to create different conditions by labelling (e.g., "she has an attention deficit" vs "she is disruptive") or to use subjects of different categories (e.g., experts vs novices).

Video can even be a dependent variable, as when subjects adjust a distorted image to meet some criterion (e.g., assessment of body size in weight disorders).

CONCLUSION

The potential for using video in behavioral science is ready for another expansion. With improving technology and easier editing, with or without computer interface, the potential effective uses of video will increase.

REFERENCES

Dowrick, P. W. (1991). *Practical guide to using video in the behavioral sciences.* New York: Wiley Interscience.

Dowrick, P. W. (1999). A review of self modeling and related interventions. *Applied and Preventive Psychology, 8,* 23–39.

P. W. DOWRICK
University of Hawaii

BEHAVIORAL MODELING
EDUCATIONAL PSYCHOLOGY
JOB ANALYSIS

VINELAND SOCIAL MATURITY SCALE

Originally developed by Edgar A. Doll, the Vineland Social Maturity Scale represented an early attempt to measure social competence. Doll, in his *Measurement of Social Competence,* defined social competence as "a functional composite of human traits which subserves social usefulness as reflected in self-sufficiency and in service to others." This component of human behavior has also been termed "adaptive behavior." It has been incorporated as a major component in the definition of mental retardation and has been the focus of considerable measurement effort over the past few decades.

The Vineland evaluates social competence from a developmental perspective and was normed on males and females from birth to 30 years of age. Assessment using the Vineland typically involves interviewing a person who is familiar with the individual being evaluated (e.g., a parent or sibling). The interview is intended to determine the behaviors customarily performed by the target person. In some circumstances observations or direct interviews with the person being assessed are used.

Multiple revisions of the Vineland have been undertaken. Now entitled the Vineland Adaptive Behavior Scales (VABS), it consists of multiple scales including the Classroom Edition, the Interview Edition–Survey Form, and the Interview Edition–Expanded Form. The VABS covers individuals from birth through early adulthood and older individuals with disabilities. Third parties still represent major sources of information, with the Classroom Edition being completed by teachers and the Interview–Expanded Edition being administered to parents. Several assessment domains are addressed, including communication skills, daily living skills, socialization, motor skills, and maladaptive behavior. The VABS samples numerous behavioral elements, making it useful for a variety of clinical applications. The VABS has also established itself as a useful measurement tool for a broad range of research on developmental status and on intellectual conditions ranging from Alzheimer's disease to the effects of social circumstances such as poverty. Although questions have been raised about its norm group, the sample was reasonably large and drawn nationally. Considerable training is needed to appropriately administer the assessment, and care must be taken in scoring and interpretation.

SUGGESTED READING

Aiken, L. R. (1997). *Psychological testing and assessment* (9th ed.). Boston: Allyn & Bacon.

Coll, C. G., Buckner, J. C., Brooks, M. G., Weinreb, L. F., & Bassuk, E. L. (1998). The developmental status and adaptive behavior of homeless and low-income housed infants and toddlers. *American Journal of Public Health, 88,* 1371–1373.

Crayton, L., Oliver, C., Holland, A., Bradbury, J., & Hall, S. (1998). The neuropsychological assessment of age related cognitive deficits in adults with Down's syndrome. *Journal of Applied Research in Intellectual Disabilities, 11,* 255–272.

Gregory, R. J. (1996). *Psychological testing: History, principles, and applications* (2nd ed.). Boston: Allyn & Bacon.

C. J. DREW
University of Utah

MENTAL RETARDATION

VIOLENCE

The study of violence has been an area filled with controversy. Even brief discussions of violence are laden with interpersonal and political as well as scientific overtones. Great concern is often expressed over the level of violence prevalent in U.S. society. Most debates are reduced to the question of the source of violence and whether it is inherent in human nature or part of the societies that have evolved. Any discussion of violence must first concern itself with the varying available definitions. Part of the controversy alluded to surrounds the issues of alternative definitions of violence. In the extreme case, violence and its definition are obvious. When one thinks about murder, aggravated assault, rape, and so on there seems to be a consensus concerning a definition of violence. However, once one proceeds beyond these common examples, and particularly as the field of psychology has proceeded to study violence, a good deal more controversy arises. For example, many definitions of violence would include only harm caused to persons (e.g., Rubin, 1972). Others would define violence more broadly to include the destruction of property, violent intentions, and specific other behaviors (Monahan, 1981). As one proceeds to study violence and its correlates, different results emerge, depending on the definition adopted.

A second dimension along which definitions of violence vary involves legality. Some would define violence only in terms of illegal behavior. This excludes forms of sanctioned violence such as may occur in war or during social unrest. Others would place emphasis only on the form of the act (a more behavioral definition) and its intent. Our current legal system differentiates between personal or property destruction resulting from intentional violence and that caused by negligence.

Awareness of these differing definitions helps in understanding the alternative explanations of violence that exist. No consensual definition of violent behaviors or violent persons is likely to emerge given the social and cognitive components of contemporary definitions. The psychological study of violence has concerned itself with two primary approaches. The first has been the prediction of violence before its occurrence (e.g., Monahan, 1981; Shah, 1978; Megargee, 1976). The prediction approach involves a before-the-fact judgment from statistical profiles, personality tests, behavior patterns, demographic characteristics, and behavioral histories that an individual or group of individuals is likely to commit violent acts in the future. Monahan (1981) summarizes the following as being the best predictors of violence: lack of support from immediate family members, history of violence among the family, violent behavior patterns among peers, the absence of steady employment, the availability of "willing" victims, the availability of weapons, the availability of alcohol, and the recency and prevalence of violence by the individual. The degree to which predictions concern similar situations and the immediate rather than distant future predictions of violence are reasonably accurate. The extent to which predictions are made over a long time period and across a variety of situations dramatically reduces their accuracy (Blakely & Davidson, 1981).

An area of somewhat greater controversy concerns the control procedures that follow the prediction of violence. Treatment approaches for remediating violence involve the loss of freedom for the individual about whom the violent prediction is being made. Habitual offender statutes that require extended sentences are examples of such approaches. Psychology has played a role in providing data, and occasionally expert testimony concerning the use of extensive control procedures. Such control procedures are often put in place after an individual has committed violent acts repeatedly and further predictions are made concerning a high probability of future violence. A great deal of controversy has arisen concerning the use of such procedures. The debate has not centered around the theoretical accuracy of the predictions but rather on the way such predictions have been used for purposes of long-term incarceration, apparently without justification (Thornberry & Jacoby, 1979). The use of incarceration as a means of controlling violence is typically preceded by expert clinical judgments concerning the future probability of dangerousness. In addition, periodic recertifications of that prediction are often required.

A related and insufficiently studied domain of violence involves that which is prevalent in the corporate world. Our society in particular allows corporate and automotive violence to occur at high rates. More people die annually on the nation's highways than fall victim to the murderer's weapon. Similarly, corporate pollution, unsafe working conditions, and toxic wastes actually claim more victims than do our habitual criminals. In the field of psychology and social science very little is known about such forms of violence. They have been surrounded by political sensitivities and hence have not been the topic of systematic investigation.

In sum, there has been considerable debate about exactly what constitutes violence. Varying definitions have included personal as well as property harm as part of the core ingredients. Considerable knowledge has been accumulated concerning those individuals likely to perform illegal acts. Less is known about violence more broadly.

REFERENCES

Blakely, C., & Davidson, W. S. (1981). Prevention of aggression. In A. P. Goldstein, E. G. Carr, W. S. Davidson & P. Wehr (Eds.), *In response to aggression.* New York: Pergamon.

Megargee, E. (1976). The prediction of dangerous behavior. *Criminal Justice and Behavior, 3,* 3–21.

Monahan, J. (1981). *The clinical prediction of violent behavior* (DHHS Publication No. ADM 81-92). Washington, DC: National Institute of Mental Health.

Rubin, B. (1972). Prediction of dangerousness in mentally ill criminals. *Archives of General Psychiatry, 72,* 397–407.

Shah, H. (1978). Dangerousness and mental illness: Some conceptual prediction and policy dilemmas. In C. Frederick (Ed.), *Dangerousness behavior: A problem in law and mental health* (NIMH DHEW Publication No. ADM 78-563, pp. 153–191). Washington, DC: U.S. Government Printing Office.

Thornberry, T., & Jacoby, J. (1979). *The criminally insane: A community followup of mentally ill offenders.* Chicago: University of Chicago Press.

W. S. DAVIDSON, II
Michigan State University

VIRTUAL REALITY EXPOSURE THERAPY

Virtual reality (VR) offers a new human-computer interaction paradigm in which users are no longer simply external observers of images on a computer screen, but are active participants within a computer-generated three-dimensional virtual world. Virtual environments differ from traditional displays in that computer graphics and various display and input technologies are integrated to give the user a sense of presence or immersion in the virtual environment.

The most common approach to the creation of a virtual environment is to outfit the user with a head-mounted display (HMD). Head-mounted displays consist of separate display screens for each eye, along with some type of display optics and a head-tracking device. The head-tracking device provides head location and orientation information to a computer, which computes visual images on the display screen consistent with the direction in which the user is looking within the virtual environment. This technology integrates real-time computer graphics, body tracking devices, visual displays, and other sensory input devices to immerse a participant in a computer-generated virtual environment that changes in a natural way with head and body motion. For some environments, users may also hold a second position sensor or joystick in their hands, allowing them to manipulate or move around the virtual environment—for example, to use a virtual hand to push an elevator button and ascend.

Exposure therapy is the treatment of choice for many of the anxiety disorders, especially when avoidance is a prominent symptom. Virtual Reality Exposure Therapy (VRE) has been introduced as a new medium of exposure therapy; it is intended to be a component of a comprehensive treatment package and is recommended at the point in therapy at which exposure therapy would be introduced. It has the advantages of conducting time-consuming exposure therapy without leaving the therapist's office, with more control over exposure stimuli, and less exposure of the patient to possible harm or embarrassment. In VRE, the therapist makes appropriate comments and encourages continued exposure until anxiety habituates. The patient is allowed to progress at his or her own pace. The therapist simultaneously views on a video monitor all of the virtual environments with which the patient is interacting and therefore is able to comment appropriately. Therapist's comments are identical to what would be expected for conventional exposure. The therapist is present in the room at all times, although she or he is not visible to the patient wearing the HMD, which covers the eyes. For loud virtual environments such as the Virtual Vietnam, the therapist communicates with the patient via a microphone heard over the earphones. VRE has been applied to several anxiety disorders at this point in time.

VRE was incorporated in the treatment of acrophobia (fear of heights) in the first published controlled study to apply virtual reality to the treatment of a psychological disorder (Rothbaum et al., 1995). Subjects were repeatedly exposed to virtual footbridges of varying heights and stability, outdoor balconies of varying heights, and a glass elevator that ascended 50 floors. VRE was effective in significantly reducing the fear of and improving attitudes toward heights, whereas no change was noted in the waiting list control group. More importantly, 7 of the 10 of those who completed VRE treatment exposed themselves to height situations in real life during treatment, although they had not been instructed to do so.

The efficacy of VRE therapy for the fear of flying was examined in a case study (Rothbaum, Hodges, Watson, Kessler, & Opdyke, 1996). The therapy involved six sessions of graded exposure to flying in a virtual airplane. The specific contributions of anxiety management techniques (AMT) and VRE were examined in a single case design. All self-report measures of the fear and avoidance of flying decreased following AMT and decreased still further following VRE. A planned post-treatment flight was completed with anxiety measures indicating comfortable flight. In preliminary results of a controlled study comparing VRE for the fear of flying to standard exposure therapy and to a waiting list control group, VRE ap-

pears to be as successful as standard exposure therapy in helping patients to fly on an actual airplane at treatment's end. The software and hardware allow the patient/user to be immersed in a computer-generated virtual airplane. The patient/user is seated in an airplane seat and can view most of a typical commercial airline passenger cabin. Looking out of the window, the patient/user can see the various scenes appropriate to different stages of flight, including taxiing, takeoff, flight, and landing. With the earphones in place, the patient/user hears common sounds of a commercial airline flight including the flight attendant's introduction, engine sounds, and outside weather conditions.

VRE has also been adapted for Vietnam combat veterans with Post-Traumatic Stress Disorder (PTSD). During these VRE sessions the patient wears a head-mounted display with stereo earphones that provides visual and audio cues consistent with being in Vietnam. There are two Virtual Vietnam environments: a virtual clearing and a virtual Huey helicopter. The virtual clearing, often referred to as a landing zone, includes several trees and a bunker surrounded by jungle. Audio effects increase in intensity at the therapist's discretion and include recordings of jungle sounds (e.g., crickets), gunfire, helicopters, mortar fire, land mines, and male voices yelling, "Move out! Move out!" Visual effects include muzzle flashes from the jungle to accompany the gunfire, helicopters flying overhead, a helicopter landing and taking off, night, and fog. The virtual Huey helicopter flies over Vietnam terrain. Audio effects include the sound of the rotors (blades), gunfire, bombs, engine sounds, radio chatter, and male voices yelling "Move out! Move out!" Visual effects include the interior of a Huey helicopter in which the backs of the pilot's and copilot's heads with authentic replicas of patches are visible, as well as the instrument control panel and the view out of the side door. This view includes aerial shots of other helicopters flying past, clouds, and the terrain below, which includes rice paddies, jungle, and a river. The idea is for the therapist to assist the patient in imaginal exposure to his most traumatic memories while immersed in Vietnam stimuli. Preliminary evidence suggests this Virtual Vietnam may hold promise (Rothbaum et al., 1999).

Virtual reality was also useful in a case study treating a spider phobic (Carlin, Hoffman, & Weghorst, 1997). Applications are in place or are currently being developed for the fear of driving, fear of thunderstorms, fear of public speaking, and several agoraphobic situations such as shopping malls.

REFERENCES

Carlin, A. S., Hoffman, H. G., & Weghorst, S. (1997). Virtual reality and tactile augmentation in the treatment of spider phobia: A case study. *Behaviour Research and Therapy, 35,* 153–158.

Rothbaum, B. O., Hodges, L., Alarcon, R., Ready, D., Shahar, F., Graap. K., Pair, J., Hebert, P., Goetz, D., Wills, B., & Baltzell, D. (1999). Virtual reality exposure therapy for PTSD Vietnam veterans: A case study. *Journal of Traumatic Stress, 12,* 263–271.

Rothbaum, B. O., Hodges, L. F., Kooper, R., Opdyke, D., Williford, J., & North, M. M. (1995). Effectiveness of virtual reality graded exposure in the treatment of acrophobia. *American Journal of Psychiatry, 152,* 626–628.

Rothbaum, B. O., Hodges, L., Watson, B. A., Kessler, G. D., & Opdyke, D. (1996). Virtual reality exposure therapy in the treatment of fear of flying: A case report. *Behaviour Research and Therapy, 34,* 477–481.

B. O. ROTHBAUM
Emory University

Disclosure Statement: Drs. Rothbaum and Hodges receive research funding and are entitled to sales royalties from *Virtually Better, Inc.,* which is developing products related to the research described in this article. In addition, the investigators serve as consultants to and own equity in *Virtually Better, Inc.* The terms of this arrangement have been reviewed and approved by Emory University and Georgia Institute of Technology in accordance with its conflict of interest policies.

PSYCHOTHERAPY TECHNIQUES

VISUAL ACUITY

Vision is considered to be one of the most important human senses. Objects can be seen only at the end of a very complex process consisting of the following successive stages: refracting and focusing by the cornea and lens (Figure 1), photochemical transduction in the retinal photoreceptors, sorting and transmitting of neural signals in the retina and visual pathways, and higher cortical processing in the brain (Johnson, 1997).

Visual acuity is the spatial-resolving capacity of the visual system and is assessed by testing the ability to distinguish small objects. It is usually assessed in the clinic by various recognition tests that determine the smallest symbols, pictures, numbers, or letters (called optotypes) that can be identified correctly, and it expresses the angular size of the smallest target (or optotype) that can be resolved by the patient. Distance visual acuity is usually measured by Snellen chart at 20 ft (or 6 m) and is expressed as a fraction (e.g., 20/200 or 6/60). The numerator is the test distance, and the denominator represents the distance at which a letter that size would make a visual angle of 5 min (Bailey, 1998). A 20/20- (or 6/6)-size letter has a visual angle of 5 min at 20 ft (or 6 m). A 20/200- (or 6/60)-size letter has a visual angle of 50 min at 20 ft (or 6 m). A patient with 20/200 (6/60) visual acuity can discriminate a size of letter at 20 ft (6 m) that a normal patient with 20/20 (6/6) vision could discriminate at 200 ft (60 m).

The visual acuity test is the single most significant measure of the functional integrity of the eye and should be part of the routine examination of all patients, including children. The first few years of life are crucial for normal development and maturation of the human visual system. Screening eye examinations should be performed periodically on every child, at birth and at ages one, 3, and 5 years, in order to discover and treat sight-threatening disorders such as cataract (lens opacity), retinoblastoma (eye tumor), amblyopia (lazy eye), and so on (Crouch & Kennedy, 1993). Amblyopia is defined as decreased visual acuity (20/30 or worse) in one or both eyes with no organic causes and is reversible if treated early (by the age of approximately 7 years; Von Noorden, 1990). There are three main types of amblyopia: strabismic, refractive, and deprivation (Von Noorden, 1990). Strabismic amblyopia is a decreased visual acuity in one eye associated with squint (strabismus) and is caused by an active cortical inhibition of the visual input originating in the deviated eye. Refractive amblyopia is caused by uncorrected high refractive error, which is a deficiency of the optics of the eye occurring when all light rays entering the eye are not brought to focus on the retina. The three main types of refractive error are hypermetropia, myopia, and astigmatism. Hypermetropia (farsightedness) results from insufficient converging power of the optics of the eye relative to its length and can be corrected by a plus (converging) lens. Myopia (nearsightedness) results from excessive converging power of the optics of the eye relative to its length and can be corrected by a minus (diverging) lens. Astigmatism is a refractive error in which the power of the optics of the eye is different in different meridians (directions) and can be corrected by a cylindrical lens. Bilateral uncorrected hypermetropia of more than +4.0 to +5.0 diopters, or myopia of more than –3.0 diopters, or astigmatism of more than 2.0 diopters can cause bilateral amblyopia (Tongue & Grin, 1993). Moreover, anisometropia, which is a refractive difference of more than 1.5 diopters between the right and the left eye, can also cause amblyopia if uncorrected (Tongue & Grin, 1993). Deprivation amblyopia in infants is due to substantial impairment of the clarity of the image formed on the retina in conditions such as corneal opacities, congenital cataract (lens opacity), and complete ptosis (droopy eyelid), or after prolonged patching of one eye. Amblyopia can be successfully treated by prescribing appropriate spectacles and occluding the unaffected (good) eye with an adhesive patch (Kushner, 1991).

The definition of legal blindness in the United States (validating eligibility for tax deduction) is "best corrected visual acuity of 20/200 (6/60) or less in the better eye, or widest diameter of visual field subtending an angle of no greater than 20 degrees" (Simons, 1997). The prevalence and causes of blindness vary with age, sex, race, geographical factors, and the levels of basic ophthalmic services that are available (Thylefors, Negrel, Pararajasegaram, & Dadzie, 1995). The World Health Organization operates programs for treatment and prevention of blindness (Thylefors, et al., 1995). It is estimated that in 1990, 35 million people in the world were blind (visual acuity less than 3/60 in the better eye; Table 1). Infectious diseases such as trachoma (caused by an organism called

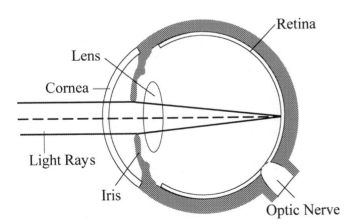

Figure 1.   Schematic diagram of light entering eye.

Table 1.   Prevalence and causes of blindness in the world

Causes of world blindness	Number of people (millions)
Cataract	17.00
Trachoma	5.50
Glaucoma	5.00
Diabetes mellitus	2.50
Vitamin A deficiency (xerophthalmia)	1.00
Onchocerciasis	0.50
Trauma	0.50
Leprosy	0.25
Others	2.75
Total	35.00

chlamydia), onchocerciasis (caused by a roundworm), and leprosy (caused by the bacterium *Mycobacterium leprae*) are preventable causes of blindness (Table 1; Foster, 1997). Cataract (lens opacity that can be cured by surgery), glaucoma (elevated eye pressure associated with progressive damage to optic nerve and visual field), and age-related macular degeneration represent the major causes of blindness after the age of 65 (Table 1; Foster, 1997). Loss of vision is also noted in hysteria (as a conversion reaction; Barris, Kaufman, & Barberio, 1992). The ophthalmologist treating a patient who is suddenly faced with actual or imminent blindness should warmly assist the patient and his or her family with understanding, encouragement, and referral to psychological and rehabilitation services. In this situation it is very important to be alert and treat reactive depression that may occur.

In summary, the visual acuity test is the single most useful clinical test for assessing the function of the visual system. The visual acuity test is also certainly the most frequent measurement that is performed routinely all over the world to detect refractive errors and many other disorders that affect the eye and the visual pathways. Repeated eye examinations during childhood as well as throughout adulthood are highly recommended for earlier detection and more successful treatment results of many sight-threatening conditions.

REFERENCES

Bailey, I. L. (1998). Visual acuity. In W. J. Benjamin (Ed.), *Borish's clinical refraction*. Philadelphia: W. B. Saunders.

Barris, M. C., Kaufman, D. I., & Barberio, D. (1992). Visual impairment in hysteria. *Documenta Ophthalmologica, 82,* 369–382.

Crouch, E. R., & Kennedy, R. A. (1993). Vision screening guidelines. In G. W. Cibis, A. C. Tongue, & M. L. Stass-Isern (Eds.), *Decision making in pediatric ophthalmology.* St. Louis, MO: B. C. Decker.

Foster, A. (1997). Patterns of blindness. In W. Tasman & E. A. Jaeger (Eds.), *Duane's foundations of clinical ophthalmology* (Vol. 5). Philadelphia: Lippincott-Raven.

Johnson, C. A. (1997). Evaluation of visual function. In W. Tasman & E. A. Jaeger (Eds.), *Duane's foundations of clinical ophthalmology* (Vol. 2). Philadelphia: Lippincott-Raven.

Kushner, B. J. (1991). Amblyopia. In L. B. Nelson, J. H. Calhoun, & R. D. Harley (Eds.), *Pediatric ophthalmology.* Philadelphia: W. B. Saunders.

Simons, K. (1997). Visual acuity and the functional definition of blindness. In W. Tasman & E. A. Jaeger (Eds.), *Duane's foundations of clinical ophthalmology* (Vol. 5). Philadelphia: Lippincott-Raven.

Thylefors, B., Negrel, A. D., Pararajasegaram, R., & Dadzie, K. Y. (1995). Available data on blindness (update 1994). *Ophthalmic Epidemiology, 2,* 5–39.

Tongue, A. C., & Grin, T. R. (1993). Refractive errors and glasses for children. In G. W. Cibis, A. C. Tongue, & M. L. Stass-Isern (Eds.), *Decision making in pediatric ophthalmology.* St. Louis, MO: B. C. Decker.

Von Noorden, G. K. (1990). Examination of the patient. In E. A. Klein & K. E. Falk (Eds.), *Binocular vision and ocular motility.* St. Louis, MO: C. V. Mosby.

Y. SHAULY

VISUAL ILLUSIONS

Illusions have fascinated students of vision for over 2,000 years, but the definition of what constitutes an illusion has changed over that period. Almost the whole of visual science is now concerned with illusions—provided they are defined as systematic departures of perceptual measurements of a stimulus from its physical measurements. But what is the physical description of a stick that is partially immersed in water? It is straight if the stick itself is measured, but not if a photograph is taken of it while it is partially immersed. For this reason (among others) a distinction is made between the distal and proximal stimuli (the physical stimulus and its projection onto the retina). If the light striking the retina (the proximal stimulus) has been transformed in some way, it would be remiss not to incorporate that knowledge into the analysis of its perception. Therefore, psychologists would say that an illusion occurs when there is a mismatch between the proximal stimulus and perception.

Visual illusions tend to refer to mismatches in the size and orientation of specific two-dimensional figures. They were called geometrical-optical illusions in the mid-19th century, and they played a role in the emergence of psychology as an independent discipline. Theories of illusions abound and none are widely accepted; a more modest (neuroscience) approach involves relating particular effects to known processes in the visual system.

It is generally held that there is some advance in understanding an illusion when an intermediate measure of stimulus processing is correlated with its perception. For example, the radiating spokes seen in the concentric circles of Figure 1A can be related to the optics of the eye: Dynamic changes in the axis of astigmatism could lead to these effects. The light and dark dots that are visible at the intersections of the lines in Figure 1B have been interpreted in terms of the activity of concentric receptive fields at early stages in

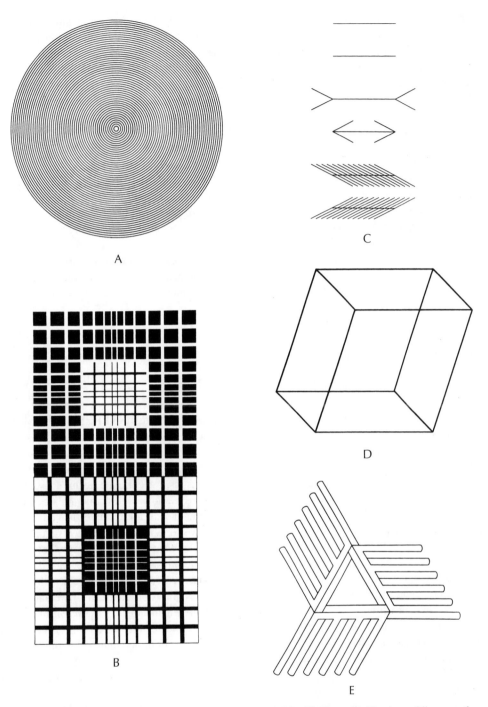

Figure 1.   (A) Purkinje's illusion. (B) Hermann-Hering grids. (C) The paired horizontal lines are the same length and parallel in each of the three cases, but their apparent lengths can be modified by attaching fins to the ends (Müller-Lyer illusion), and the apparent orientation can be changed by the directions of the intersecting lines (Zöllner illusion). The gaps between the cross-hatched lines produce illusory contours. (D) Necker rhomboid. (E) Double impossible figure.

visual processing. It is thus possible to classify illusions according to the level(s) in the visual system to which the distortions are assigned. Many illusions are attributed to processing at higher levels of the visual system, particularly in the visual cortex.

Orientation is a dimension much studied in visual neuroscience. Many single cells in the visual cortex respond to lines or edges in specific orientations. One class of illusions, involving perception of orientation, provides possible matching neural correlates. The horizontal parallel lines in Figure 1C do not appear so when intersected by inclined lines. The perception of orientation must be based on the activity of many orientation selective cells and with interactions between them. The Zöllner illusion could point to bias in the peak of the distribution by the surrounding contours; modification of the receptive field properties of particular cells by their immediate context; or neural inhibition from the cells with similar receptive field orientations. In addition to the simultaneous biasing of perceived orientation, there are tilt aftereffects: Observation of inclined lines for some seconds results in subsequently-viewed vertical lines' appearing tilted in the opposite direction. Such simple manifestations are only correlations and the link between correlation and causation is notoriously tenuous. Increasingly, studies measure both perception and neurophysiology in the same animals so that this link can be strengthened.

The term "visual illusion" is mostly associated with a set of figures produced in the late 19th century, when the likes of Müller-Lyer and Zöllner described their eponymous illusions (Figure 1C). The Müller-Lyer figure provides a compelling illusion of perceived length, and it has been studied experimentally perhaps more than any other, but its basis remains elusive. Visual illusions are generally classified as distortions of orientation or size, and for a long time the former have been taken to provide the better links with neuroscience, but the situation is now changing. In the last decade functional distinctions between dorsal and ventral streams of visual cortical processing have been attributed to defining an object's location and identity, respectively. A current reinterpretation is in terms of perception and action: The dorsal stream is said to be concerned with motor control and the ventral with perceptual representation. The difference between the way size illusions look to us and the way we respond to them is taken to support the latter distinction. While our perception is distorted by these patterns, our motor control is not. If sticks were positioned in place of the horizontal lines in the Müller-Lyer figure, observers would adjust their fingers to the appropriate physical length rather than to their perceived inequality.

Visual neuroscience is generally concerned with neural and/or behavioural responses to contours or colours. For the distal stimulus, contours are usually defined as luminance discontinuities, and these can be enhanced by lateral inhibition at early stages of visual processing. However, one set of stimuli involves seeing discontinuities of brightness where no luminance differences exist. They can be induced by line terminations as in the case of the gaps in the Zöllner figure. Illusory contours behave much like physical ones—they interact with one another and can produce aftereffects. Some single cells in areas V1 and V2 of the macaque monkey respond to aligned gaps or aligned discontinuities of line endings. It is as if the visual system is filling in the incomplete parts of the proximal stimulus.

Pictures provide allusions to objects, and tricks can be played with the transition from three to two dimensions. Indeed, this is grist to the artistic mill: Pictures incorporate ambiguities and impossibilities that are rarely or never present in objects. One such ambiguity is the depth represented in simple line drawings like the Necker rhomboid (Figure 1D): The front face appears to be pointing either down and to the right or up and left. The picture is interpreted as representing a three-dimensional structure, but there is insufficient detail (for occluding contours, perspective convergence, or texture) to define which parts would be near and which far. However, both depth interpretations are not entertained si-

multaneously: The perception flips from one possibility to the other, so that the apparent depth undergoes reversals. Other pictures are far more paradoxical and have been called impossible. A rectangular rod can be depicted by three lines and a quadrilateral, whereas a cylinder can be described by only two lines and an ellipse. The so-called impossible triangle shown in Figure 1E has four rectangular rods extending from each side which are transformed into six cylinders at the extremities of the lines. They are called impossible figures because the solid objects to which they allude could not be constructed.

Pictorial allusions, like ambiguities and impossibilities, are fascinating to figure out, but it is not readily apparent whether there are corresponding links to neuroscience. Indeed, searching for them might point us in the wrong direction because such ambiguities rarely occur with objects. Pictures are complex symbolic stimuli with a relatively recent history in evolutionary terms. Understanding pictures in general and distortions within them will probably require a more cognitive interpretation.

N. J. WADE
University of Dundee, Scotland

VOCATIONAL INTEREST MEASUREMENT

American psychologists have devoted many of their research efforts to the study of what men and women can do and will do in various environments. Developments in the fields of psychometrics, statistics, and computer technology have produced a great variety of psychological tests that address this problem. Ability and achievement tests, for example, deal directly with what people can do or have done. Measures of interests and personality speak to the question of what people will do or want to do. Anastasi's *Psychological Testing* (1982) and the several editions of the *Mental Measurements Yearbook,* originally edited by Buros (1978), are basic references in this broad area of psychology. In the cumulative index of the *Eighth Mental Measurements yearbook* there are over 1,500 citations to various editions of the Strong Vocational Interest Blank, in addition to many citations to other measures of vocational interests.

We shall be concerned here with the measurement of vocational interests, what people want to do in the workplace. The pioneer in this field was Edward K. Strong, Jr. (1884–1963). The first edition of the Strong Vocational Interest Blank appeared in 1927. The most recent derivative, the Strong—Campbell Interest Inventory, was published in 1974; the third edition of its manual was published in 1981 (Campbell & Hansen, 1981.) Thus there is a history of over 50 years of research and refinement for this instrument. It is estimated that as many as 21,300,000 people have taken one or another form of this test. Over the years, its cost per subject has been reduced and its technical structure has been greatly improved and expanded. In the most recent form of the Strong—Campbell Interest Inventory, there are 162 occupational scales representing 85 occupations; for 77 of these occupations there is a male and a female sample of successful workers, for four of them there is only a male scale, and for the remaining four there is only a female scale. Additionally, statistically superior samples of 300 men in general and 300 women in general have been constructed for the establishment of the item statistics under which a particular item receives a weight for a particular occupational scale, for either sex.

There have been three major research centers for this work: the Carnegie Institute of Technology, where Strong served on the faculty from 1919 to 1923; Stanford University, where he served on the faculty from 1923 until his retirement in 1949; and the University of Minnesota, where Strong's friend and colleague, Donald G. Paterson (1892–1961), trained many psychologists whose research was in the field of interest measurement.

In the beginning, interest measurement was concerned with practical problems of vocational choice and vocational planning for individuals; it was highly empiric and with little theoretical foundation. In the first manual for the test, Strong stated the three assumptions that had guided his work: Men will be more effective and happier when they engage in work that they like. Men who have stayed in an occupation for a considerable period of time and who are perceived as successful must like their occupational environment fairly well. The interests of young men are largely responsible for their career choices—if such interests are strong, the individual becomes an artist, a lawyer, or an accountant, almost regardless of environmental factors, but if interests are weak, environmental factors will play a much larger role in determining his occupation. But there was a beginning of theory; the first factor analysis of interest test scores was done by Strong's friend and colleague, Louis L. Thurstone (1931). Using the intercorrelations among 18 occupational keys on the first edition, he derived four general factors: interest in science, interest in language, interest in people, and interest in commercial activities. Strong himself grouped his growing number of occupational keys by their patterns of intercorrelations.

The theory here is simply stated: "Birds of a feather tend to flock together." In the *Dictionary of Occupational Titles* (U.S. Department of Labor, 1977), there are over 20,000 job or payroll titles; many of them can be grouped into a much smaller number of families of occupations. Engineers, mathematicians, and chemists, for example, are more like each other in their interests than are salespeople. Authors, editors, and journalists are more alike in their interests than are accountants, clerical workers, and bookkeepers. As the number of occupational keys increased, both factor analyses and intercorrelational groupings kept pace.

It remained for Holland (1966) to provide the typology that is now incorporated in the current edition of the Strong–Campbell Interest Inventory. He proposed that most persons can be categorized in terms of six broad personality types—realistic, investigative, artistic, social, enterprising, or conventional. An individual can be located in one, or some meaningful combination, of these six. The same six categories can also be used to define occupational environments or work settings. People will search out those environments that will let them use their skills and abilities, that will be consonant with their values and attitudes, that will let them take on satisfying roles and tasks, and that will permit them to avoid responsibilities they find distasteful or incongruent. Job performance, job satisfaction, and job stability will thus be the result of the interaction between the individual's personality structure and the characteristics of the work environment.

Holland recognized that his typology owed much to the factor analytic study by Guilford and colleagues (1954), in which military personnel were used as subjects in the derivation of primary interest dimensions. Notice the implications of these ideas: Occupational interests are determined *before* job experience occurs. Occupational interests are special cases of personality theory and motivational theory. *Within* types of interests, *levels* of performance can be postulated to take account of the different levels of ability required in occupations.

What is the scale or key or score that measures vocational interests? The test consists of a series of stimulus questions to each of which the individual responds with one of three possible response positions; there are lists of occupations, school subjects, activities, characteristics of people, preferences for tasks, and self-descriptors. In the first edition, there were 420 such items; in the 1974 edition, there are 325. Any item will be scored if the responses to it given by a sample of successful men or women in an occupation are significantly different from the responses given by a sample of men or women in general. Thus any single item can appear in several occupational scales if it meets a statistical criterion of significance.

A graphic way to look at an occupation's distance from "men in general" is shown in Figure 1. In drawings *a* and *b* of the figure, the samples of men in occupations I and II are the same, but in *b* the sample of "men in general" is drawn from a lower level of the total "men-in-general" group than in *a*. Two things then happen: Men in occupations I and II are *farther from* the "men-in-general" reference group; men in occupations I and II are *more like each other* in drawing *b* than in drawing *a* (the angular separation marked at the point of origin in "men-in-general" is smaller in *b* than in *a*).

In drawing *c*, men in occupation I are still clearly apart from their "men-in-general" reference group, whereas men in occupation III emerge from the mass of workers less clearly.

In drawing *d*, the samples in the chosen occupations IV and V

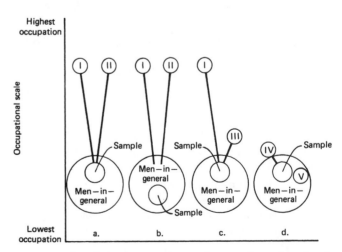

Figure 1.   The relation between the men-in-general sample and various occupational samples. From J. G. Darley & T. Hagenah, *Vocational Interest measurement: Theory and practice* (Minneapolis: University of Minnesota, Press, 1955, p. 24.)

are so close to "men-in-general" that an interest scoring key based on differences in responses cannot be devised unless a drastic lowering occurs in the sample of "men-in-general." Men in occupations IV and V may have no likes or dislikes that truly separate them from "men-in-general."

A comparable figure would display the same information for women in various occupations contrasted with samples of "women-in-general."

An individual's raw score for a particular occupation is the algebraic sum of the score values attached to the significant items in that occupational scale or key. This absolute sum can be converted to a common metric by the use of so-called standard deviation scores (or sigma scores), which are based on raw score distributions with different averages and standard deviations. This conversion permits direct comparison of standard deviation scores in terms of normal curve theory of deviation units above and below the obtained average of a distribution of raw scores. These sigma scores, in turn, can be further divided into broader degrees of similarity or nonsimilarity to the interests of the sample of successful individuals in each occupation for which the test can be scored.

Letter grade scores on the original Strong Vocational Interest Blank were used to represent these broad bands of relative scores derived from the various absolute raw score distributions of the occupational keys. An A score was assigned to the sigma score range of 45 and up; a C score was assigned to the sigma score range of 30 or lower.

Given this brief description of the test, we now turn to several practical questions in its use. First, what are the relations between claimed and measured interests?

In our relatively mobile society, the occupation that an individual ultimately enters may be the hallmark of status in the community; the job title carries both prestige and status. As adults we frequently ask children what they want to be when they "grow up." By the high school years, more pressure is placed on individuals to make occupational choices; education beyond high school is heavily influenced by the individual's choice of a vocation. These we call claimed interests; they emerge under the confluence of many societal pressures and with limited knowledge of the world of work. This leads to a kind of "water faucet" theory of interests and motivation, as if interests could be turned off or on. Parents will often insist that children can do anything they want to if they would "just get interested in it." Unfortunately this is an inaccurate assumption. The relation between claimed and measured interests is significant for groups of individuals, but in individual cases the relation is not high enough to assume that claimed and measured interests are interchangeable.

Table 1 shows the specific claimed interests of 845 University of Minnesota freshman men, grouped into the occupational families listed vertically; the measured interests of these same individuals, classified as related or unrelated to their claimed interests, appear in the body of the table. Out of the seven broad families of interests, these college freshmen tended to choose specific occupations within the biological sciences, physical sciences, business management, and verbal-linguistic families most frequently, but in three of these four families of occupations, their measured interests were more frequently unrelated to these claimed interests. Their least

Table 1. Types of Measured Interests Related and Unrelated to Claimed Interest Types for a Sample of Freshman Men from Three Colleges of the University of Minnesota[a]

| | Measured Interests | | | | | |
| | Related to Claimed Interests | | Unrelated to Claimed Interests | | Total | |
Claimed Interest Type	No.	%	No.	%	No.	%
Biological sciences	34	26	93	74	127	100
Physical sciences	103	32	214	68	317	100
Skilled trades	20	59	14	41	34	100
Social service	12	26	34	74	46	100
Business management	92	64	51	36	143	100
Business contact	18	67	9	33	27	100
Verbal-linguistic	56	37	95	63	151	100
Total:	335		510		845	

[a] $\chi^2 = 69.37$ (significant at the 1% level); $C = 0.28$. Adapted from Table 16, Darley and hagenah (1955, page 67).

frequently claimed interests were found in the skilled trades, social service, or business contact families of occupations; but in two of these three families, skilled trades and business contact, their measured interests were more frequently related to, or congruent with, the claimed interests.

These data can be analyzed in another fashion. If individuals have measured interests in a particular family, what claimed interests will they have? The answer for two families is illustrated in Table 2. In the physical science family of occupations, 103, or 79%, of the 131 freshmen will have claimed interests in the same family, while 21% will not. In the business contact family, 18, or 10%, of the 187 freshmen will have claimed interests in the family, while 90% will not.

How stable are measured interests? The stability, or reliability,

Table 2. Relationships Between Claimed and Measured Interests Within Two Families of Occupations for a Sample of Freshman Men in Three Colleges of the University of Minnesota[a]

| | Claimed Interests | | | | | |
| | Physical Sciences | | Other | | Total | |
Measured Interests	No.	%	No.	%	No.	%
Physical sciences	103	79	28	21	131	100
Other	214	30	500	70	714	100
Total	317		528		845	
	Business contact		Other		Total	
	No.	%	No.	%	No.	%
Business contact	18	10	169	90	187	100
Other	9	1	649	99	658	100
Total	27		818		845	

[a] Adapted from Table 15, Darley and Hagenah (1955, p. 66).

of interest scores among individuals and within an individual can be determined by standard test–retest procedures. Campbell and Hansen (1981) report two-week, 30-day, and three-year test–retest correlations for three different samples of men and women on the 1981 Strong–Campbell Interest Inventory. The median test–retest values for all the occupational scales in these three samples were, respectively, 0.91, 0.89, and 0.87. These are Pearsonian correlations. If an individual's scores for each occupation are ranked from high to low by their standard score values at a test and a retest period, the Spearman rank-order correlation becomes the relevant statistic. Darley and Hagenah report several studies of test–retest reliabilities of earlier editions of the Strong Vocational Interest Blank, using subjects of differing ages at original testing and different intervals between test and retest, and using both Pearsonian and Spearman correlations. Their conclusions are as follows: "These interest test–retest correlations are a little lower than those in the literature for intelligence test–retest scores and somewhat higher than personality or attitude test–retest scores. Thus the behavior we measure with the occupational keys of the Strong Vocational Interest Blank seems to remain fairly stable over time . . ." (Darley & Hagenah, 1955, p. 39).

How well do scores on this test predict ultimate occupational participation for individuals? Four studies may be cited. Strong (1955), in 1949, determined the occupation-engaged-in for 663 Stanford University students who had been tested, on the average, 18 years earlier, while they were in college. He analyzed his data three ways: How well did the students score while in college on the keys for the occupations in which they were actually employed in 1949? How do the original scores of those engaging in an occupation in 1949 compare with the original scores of those not engaging in that occupation in 1949? How do expert judges in 1949 rate the degree of agreement between the original profile of scores and the 1949 occupation? On all three counts, the predictive validity of the Strong Vocational Interest Blank was powerful.

Berdie (1960) reviewed 90 different research studies published during and after 1950. Against the criterion of professional curricular choice, or occupation entered, or final occupational status, the Strong Vocational Interest Blank was a substantial predictor of the individual's future employment. The most recent study of the predictive validity of the earlier forms of the Strong Vocational Interest Blank was completed by Robert Dolliver and his colleagues at the University of Missouri in 1972. They concluded that: "The chances are about 1 to 1 that a man would end up in an occupation for which he received an A score . . . the chances are about 8 to 1 that a person will not end up in an occupation for which he received a C score" (Dolliver et al., 1972, p. 216).

One major study of the validity of the Strong–Campbell Interest Inventory has been produced by Arnold Spokane (1979); over a 3½ year period, excellent predictive validity occurred among 42.5% of 120 female students and among 59.3% of 236 male students at the University of Rochester.

What are the relationships between measured interests and measured ability or academic achievement? Darley and Hagenah, after reviewing several studies of such relations, concluded that: "From all accumulated research literature on the use of the SVIB, a dependable generalization emerges: there is a low relation be-

tween measured interests and measured ability or scholastic achievement" (Darley & Hagenah, 1955, p. 57).

Can an individual "fake" his or her scores on such an instrument? The answer is yes. Campbell (1971) devotes 10 pages to studies of the power of individuals to falsify or distort their scores on these inventories. A summary of these studies would run as follows: When instructed to "fake," respondents can bias their scores substantially, but when individuals respond to the items in ordinary administrations of the test, they usually answer truthfully, even in situations where they might be expected to bias their scores, as in applying for jobs or for admission to professional school programs. The detectable bias is not very many score points, and infrequently changes the broad interpretive band of scores from which similarity or dissimilarity of occupational interests is judged.

Do men and women show different patterns of vocational interests? Before answering this question, some historical considerations must be noted.

In the decades from the 1930s, when Strong published the first women's test, to the 1970s, the role of women in the labor force was changing drastically. More women were in the work force. More women were entering occupations hitherto viewed as "men's work." Allegations of bias in psychological testing, many of which were well-founded, were heard more often. Campbell and Hansen (1981) devoted an entire chapter to the problem. Their conclusions were as follows:

1. Men and women, on the average, respond differently to almost half of the inventory items.

2. The size of the differences is considerable.

3. The differences do not disappear when only men and women who have made the same occupational choice are compared.

4. The differences have not lessened appreciably since 1930.

5. Attempts to develop combined-sex scales appear to be premature, and the validity of these scales varies from occupation to occupation.

6. Empirical scales constructed on the basis of same-sex criterion and reference samples work better (are more valid) than scales based on opposite-sex samples.

Another question: At what age do patterns of vocational interests begin to emerge in individuals? The reading level of the present Strong–Campbell Interest Inventory is at about the junior high school level—about a grade lower than the earlier forms of the Strong Vocational Interest Blank. Studies of the earlier forms of the Strong Vocational Interest Blank indicated that meaningful and relatively stable patterns of interests can be seen in students averaging about the tenth grade level, if they are of average general ability. However, if an interest test is used, it should be repeated, if possible, on an annual retesting, to study patterns of stability and differential development within the individual cases.

There have been many studies of the relations between vocational interests and personality measures. Some of these were reviewed by Darley and Hagenah in their 1955 volume. Strong himself had developed at least three nonoccupational keys for the Strong Vocational Interest Blank: interest, maturity, masculinity–femininity, and occupational level. Each of these presumably tapped a personality dimension related to occupational interests. On the Strong–Campbell Interest Inventory, Campbell and Hansen (1981) have retained two nonoccupational measures: academic comfort and introversion–extroversion. It is to be noted also that Holland's typology is essentially a personality typing within his six themes.

Anne Roe (1951a, 1951b, 1953) has reported three highly significant studies of eminent research scientists in biological, physical, and social science fields. Her subjects were members of the National Academy of Science: 20 in the biological science group, with an average age of 51.2; 22 in the physical science group, average age 44.7; and 22 psychologists and anthropologists in the social science group, with an average age of 47.7. Her studies included detailed life histories, performance of all subjects on projective tests and a special measure of intellectual competence, and a careful assessment of their scientific work. These are classic collections of case histories. Darley and Hagenah (1955, p. 126) summarized these studies as follows:

. . . her groups come from above-average socioeconomic backgrounds; the cultural patterns of the homes stressed and valued learning for its own sake and in its own right; strong needs to achieve and maintain personal independence characterized all her subjects; the psychosocial development of the biological and physical scientists shows a picture of "apartness" and a pattern of general avoidance of intimate personal contacts and a "decided preference for a very limited social life." This pattern of psychosocial development is less characteristic of her social scientists. The biologists and physicists show also considerable independence of parental relations, whereas the social scientists still show some evidence of rebellion and resentment of parental ties. Most of the group are happiest when working, finding strong intrinsic satisfactions in work and placing secondary value on economic returns or prestige factors. The occupational choice point for most of her group fell in the modal age range of the last two years in college and was tied to the discovery of the possibility of doing research as a lifetime task. The high value placed upon independence as a way of life may partly be compensatory for insecurities, mild and variously defined, and may reflect a deep-rooted personal need in a society that otherwise tends toward interdependence. With regard to imagery, or perception, the biologists and experimental physicists depend strongly on visual imagery, whereas the theoretical physicists and social scientists lean more heavily on verbal symbols. The early interests of all her subjects, as they recalled them, were strongly tinged with an intellectual flavor.

As described by Roe, personality factors played a large role in determining vocational direction for these eminent scientists.

Another example was found in the thesis by Segal (1954). He used the Strong Vocational Interest Blank to identify a sample of 15 accountants and a sample of 15 creative writers. Each sample was carefully chosen from among advanced students preparing for the two occupations; both samples were comparable in age, ability, and socioeconomic background. Segal tested three psychoanalytic concepts in his two occupational groups: the process of identification, the development of defense mechanisms, and the concept of sublimation. He then listed hypotheses about behaviors on which his two samples would be expected to differ. For example, he suggested that creative writing students would show greater expressions of hostility than would accounting students, and that ac-

counting students would show a greater acceptance of social norms than would the creative writing students. For the hypotheses he derived from these three concepts, Segal found support in his measures for 17 and no support for 14. Segal concluded that "vocational choice is a resultant of the emotional development of the individual and is in part an expression of the individual's method of adjusting to his environment" (Segal, 1954, p. 22).

The development of vocational interests is affected by sex, age, and personality factors. But however they develop, measured vocational interests represent one of the three major elements to be identified in predicting job performance, job satisfaction, and job stability in our society's complex world of work. Levels of ability and available opportunity are the other two elements.

REFERENCES

Anastasi, A. (1982). *Psychological testing* (5th ed.). New York: Macmillan.

Buros, O. K. (Ed.). (1978). *The eighth mental measurements yearbook.* Highland Park, NJ: Gryphon Press.

Campbell, D. P. (1971). *Handbook for the Strong Vocational Interest Blank.* Stanford, CA: Stanford University Press.

Campbell, D. P., & Hansen, J. C. (1981). *Manual for the SVIB–SCII Strong–Campbell Interest Inventory* (3rd ed.). Stanford, CA: Stanford, University Press.

Darley, J. G., & Hagenah, T. (1955). *Vocational interest measurement.* Minneapolis, MN: University of Minnesota Press.

Dolliver, R. H., Irvin, J. A., & Bigley, S. E. (1972). Twelve-year follow-up of the Strong Vocational Interest Blank. *Journal of Counseling Psychology, 19,* 212–217.

Guilford, J. P., Christensen, P. R., Bond, N. A., Jr., & Sutton, M. A. (1954). A factor analysis study of human interests. *Psychological Monographs, 68*(4, entire no. 375).

Holland, J. L. (1966). *The psychology of vocational choice.* Waltham, MA: Blaisdell.

Roe, A. (1951). A psychological study of eminent physical scientists. *Genetic Psychological Monographs, 43,* 121–239.

Roe, A. (1951). A study of imagery in research scientists. *Journal of Personality, 19,* 459–470.

Roe, A. (1953). A psychological study of eminent psychologists and anthropologists, and a comparison with biological and physical scientists. *Psychological Monographs, 67*(2, entire no. 352).

Segal, S. J. (1954). The role of personality factors in vocational choice: A study of accountants and creative writers (Doctoral thesis, University of Michigan, 1954). *Microfilm Abstracts, 14*(4), 714.

Spokane, A. R. (1979). Occupational preference and the validity of the Strong–Campbell Interest Inventory for college women and men. *Journal of Counseling Psychology, 26,* 312–318.

Strong, E. K. (1955). *Vocational interests 18 years after college.* Minneapolis, MN: University of Minnesota Press.

Thurstone, L. L. (1931). A multiple factor study of vocational interests. *Personnel Journal, 10,* 198–205.

U.S. Department of Labor. (1977/1965). *Dictionary of occupational titles* (3rd ed.). Washington, DC: U.S. Government Printing Office.

J. G. DARLEY
University of Minnesota, Minneapolis

CAREER COUNSELING
EXECUTIVE SELECTION
FACTOR ANALYSIS
INTEREST INVENTORIES
JOB ANALYSIS
JOB SATISFACTION
MULTIDIMENSIONAL SCALING
QUESTIONNAIRES

*The author wishes to thank Jo-Ida Hansen, Janet M. Hively, and Loralie Lawson for their careful reviews of this article.

VOLTAGE-GATED SODIUM AND POTASSIUM CHANNELS

Voltage-gated sodium and potassium channels form the molecular basis for conduction of the neural impulse, and along with calcium channels, are involved in the generation of electrical activity in virtually every excitatory cell type. Like all ion channels, voltage-gated sodium and potassium channels are thought to be aqueous pores. When the pore is open ions can diffuse through it at a rapid rate, similar to their diffusion through water (Hille, 1992). The term "voltage-gated" refers to the control of these channels. Unlike ligand-gated channels, which open or close in response to the binding of an agonist or antagonist, these channels open or close in response to a change in transmembrane potential. Such channels are classified as either sodium or potassium channels depending upon which ionic species is preferentially passed through the open aqueous pore.

VOLTAGE-DEPENDENT PROPERTIES

The Nernst Potential

When ion channels are classified, the first property to be identified is ion selectivity. That is, when the channel is open, what type of ion is preferentially passed through the pore? Sodium channels pass sodium much more readily than they will pass potassium. Under normal physiological conditions, an open sodium channel will pass approximately 10 sodium ions for every potassium ion it allows to diffuse through its aqueous pore. This relative ability of ions to permeate through the open channel is referred to as the permeability ratio; sodium channels generally have a permeability ratio of sodium to potassium of about 10 (Hille, 1992). Potassium channels are often more selective, and have permeability ratios for potassium to sodium permeability that can be > 100 (Hille, 1992).

Thus, ion channels are highly selective for one species of permeant ion.

This ionic selectivity gives rise to the most basic voltage-dependent property of ion channels. This property is the reversal potential, or Nernst potential. Since an open channel is simply an aqueous pore, ions move through it following the laws of diffusion. Since sodium is high in extracellular spaces and low in the intracellular space, sodium tends to diffuse from the outside of the cell in the inward direction. Conversely, potassium, which is high in the cytosol but low in the extracellular space, would tend to diffuse in the outward direction. Sodium and potassium both carry a positive charge and are therefore influenced by the transmembrane voltage. This voltage exerts a force on the channels that can augment or oppose the diffusive process. The voltage at which a membrane potential exactly balances the diffusive forces is called the reversal, or Nernst, potential. For a perfectly selective channel, this voltage can be calculated by the Nernst equation; for sodium channels, the reversal potential is typically around +60 mV, and for the potassium channel, around −100 mV (Hille, 1992). These two potentials define the range of physiologically relevant membrane potentials. Cells typically rest near the potassium reversal potential and during peak membrane potential may approach the sodium reversal potential.

Voltage Clamp Measurements

The functional properties of ion channels are studied by electrical measurements of currents generated by the channels. There are many different variations in exact method used, but all of these measurements can be classified as voltage clamp experiments and are based largely on the formalisms and analysis proposed by Hodgkin and Huxley (1952) to explain electrical activity in the squid axon. In general, an electrical apparatus is used to apply step changes in membrane potential to a cell or a portion of a cell membrane. The resulting current response is then analyzed to determine four key voltage-dependent kinetic properties of the ion channels. These properties are called activation, inactivation, deactivation, and recovery from inactivation. Figure 1 shows a typical current trace that might be recorded during such an experiment. The membrane was stepped from near the resting membrane potential to some positive potential and a current was recorded. In

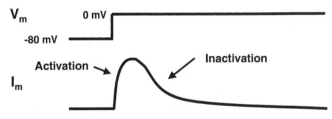

Figure 1. Activation and inactivation of an outward current during voltage clamp. The figure shows a typical current response for an ion channel undergoing activation and inactivation in response to a step change in membrane potential from rest (–80 mV) to a positive potential (0 mV). Activation is usually, but not always, the first and most rapid event which causes the increase in current. Inactivation is usually a slower process which follows.

this case, the channel current rapidly increased in response to the initial depolarization. This increase is called activation, and is defined as the process by which a voltage-gated channel enters a conducting state in response to a depolarization. As depolarization is sustained, the current decreases. This decrease is called inactivation, and is defined as the process by which activated channels become non-conducting in response to a sustained depolarization. Upon switching from a sustained period at depolarized (positive) potentials to the resting membrane potential, activation and inactivation must reverse themselves. Deactivation is defined to be the reversal of activation that occurs on a return to the resting membrane potential; recovery from inactivation is defined to be the reversal of inactivation. It is important to note that these processes are defined functionally and may represent multiple processes on a molecular level.

STRUCTURE AND FUNCTION OF VOLTAGE-GATED SODIUM AND POTASSIUM CHANNELS

Many voltage-gated sodium and potassium channels have been cloned and characterized (Pongs, 1992; Jan & Jan, 1992; Marban, Yamagishi, & Tomaselli, 1998; Plummer & Meisler, 1999; Caterall, 1995; Salkoff & Jegla, 1995). Voltage clamp studies combined with mutagenesis of these cloned channels have provided much information on the physical nature of the functional processes of activation and inactivation. A typical pore-forming, voltage-gated potassium channel α-subunit has a topology as described in Figure 2. The N-terminal and C-terminal domains are located on the cytoplasmic side of the membrane. The channel protein itself spans the membrane several times and contains six relatively lipophilic transmembrane segments, S1 through S6; these segments are thought to have an α-helical structure. A short lipophilic segment lies between S5 and S6 and is referred to as the H5 loop, since this segment is too short to span the membrane and appears to dip into the transmembrane domain from the outside, form a small loop, and return to the extracellular side (Jan & Jan, 1992; Pongs, 1992). This H5 segment is thought to form the selectivity filter for the channel and is important as a locus for extracellularly-acting channel blockers (MacKinnon & Yellon, 1992). This general motif is well conserved across voltage-gated potassium channels.

A functional potassium channel contains a tetramer of α-subunits. Each one of the four subunits contributes equally to the pore structure. One strand of each of the H5 domains contributes a strand to form a β-barrel structure that forms the extracellular portion of the pore and most of the selectivity properties of the channel (Lipkind & Fozzard, 1994; Marban et al., 1998). The voltage-gated sodium channel α-subunit contains all of the gross structural features of the voltage-gated potassium channel, with one exception. Instead of the functional channel's being formed from a tetramer of four independent, six-membrane–spanning domain subunits, the sodium channel α-subunit consists of a single peptide chain containing four repeats of the six-membrane–spanning domain motif as shown in Figure 2. Thus, despite a great difference in molecular weight, voltage-gated sodium and potassium channels are very closely related structurally (Catterall, 1995; Marban et al., 1998).

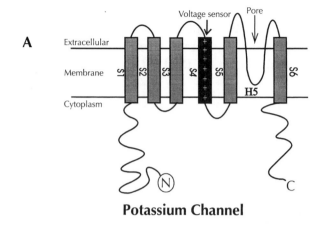

Potassium Channel

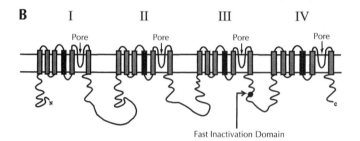

Sodium Channel

Figure 2.   Topology of voltage gated potassium and sodium channel α-subunits. **(A)** Membrane topology of a voltage gated potassium channel α-subunit showing the six hydrophobic membrane spanning domains (S1–S6) and both the amino- and the carboxyl-terminal regions (not drawn to scale) on the cytoplasmic side. Four such subunits are required to form a functional potassium channel. The S4 sequence carries basic residues at every third position, and forms the voltage sensor of the channel. The amino terminal region contains residues that are involved in N-type inactivation, which involve electrostatic and lipophilic interactions between the amino terminus ("inactivation ball") and its receptor. The sequence between the S4 and S5 (the S4–S5 loop) functions as part of the receptor for the fast inactivation gate. Residues at the external mouth of the H5 pore loop have been shown to move during C-type inactivation. **(B)** Membrane topology of the voltage gated sodium channel α-subunit. Instead of being a tetramer of four independent six membrane spanning domain subunits, the sodium channel retains the six membrane spanning domain motif, but repeted four times in the same peptide. In each repeat, the S4 segment remains the primary voltage sensor. Fast inactivation is mediated by a short segment of hydrophobic residues on the loop that connects repeats III and IV.

Molecular Basis of Activation

Activation is a voltage-sensitive event. It opens the channel in response to a change in membrane voltage. Such voltage dependence requires that a net charge be moved some distance in the transmembrane electrical field in order to produce the physical work necessary to move the channel out of its normally stable, closed conformation. As their similar structures would suggest, both sodium and potassium channels share a common voltage-sensing mechanism. The fourth transmembrane-spanning domain (S4) in potassium channels and the analogous domains in sodium channels contain a highly conserved structure. Every third position on S4 is occupied by a lysine or arginine. These residues are important because they contain an amino group that is permanently positively charged in the physiological range of pH. At the resting membrane potential, many of these positive charges are present on the intracellular face of the membrane. When the membrane is depolarized, these residues migrate through the membrane due to the increased electrical driving force and become present on the extracellular face (Mannuzzu, Moronne, & Isacoff, 1996). This transmembrane movement of S4 initiates a host of large-scale conformational changes that allow formation of the open conducting pore (Marban et al., 1998; Catterall, 1995). This opening of the pore is a significant change in protein structure. The entire volume of the pore has been measured to be around 800 to 2000 $Å^3$ for voltage-gated sodium and potassium channels, or approximately the volume of 50 water molecules (Rayner, Starkus, Ruben, & Alicata, 1992; Zimmerberg, Bezanilla, & Parsegian, 1990).

Molecular Basis of Inactivation

Inactivation involves the closing of the permeation pathway following activation of the channel. Unlike activation, there is much more variability in mechanism of inactivation among channel types. The first and most detailed information about inactivation was determined in potassium channels; thus, potassium-channel inactivation will be discussed first. At the time of this writing, there are two main accepted mechanisms of potassium-channel inactivation: N-type and C-type (for review see Rasmusson et al., 1998).

N-type inactivation occurs by a sort of ball-and-chain mechanism (Hoshi, Zagotta, & Aldrich, 1990; Zagotta, Hoshi, & Aldrich, 1990; Armstrong, 1971). The molecular mechanism resides in the binding and unbinding of small group of amino acids in the NH_2 terminus that are lipophilic in nature. The remainder of the cytosolic N-terminal domain is hydrophilic. When the channel is open, the N-terminal domain, or ball, diffuses until it binds to the open mouth of the activated channel and occludes the permeation pathway (Hoshi et al., 1990; Zagotta et al., 1990). Functionally, it is of interest to note that while activation is a voltage-dependent process, N-type inactivation does not directly involve the transmembrane potential. The only voltage dependence associated with inactivation is indirect, when activation opens the intracellular pore and makes the binding site for the N-terminal ball available. This type of indirect voltage dependence is called coupling, and in cases in which activation need not be complete for inactivation to occur, the interaction is called partial coupling.

The lipophilic binding of the N-terminal domain may not be specific. No sequence similarity has been found among the N-termini of the various N-type inactivating *Shaker* K⁺ channels and mammalian Kv1.4 or Kv3.3 channels. Only weak structural similarity for the N-termini of these channels, as determined using NMR spectroscopy (Antz et al., 1997), has been reported. Despite this apparent structural diversity, many channels have been demonstrated to have an N-type inactivation mechanism (Ruppersberg, Frank, Pongs, & Stocker, 1991; Ruppersberg, Stocker, et al., 1991; Tseng-Crank, Yao, Berman, & Tseng, 1993), and for all such channels, N-type inactivation will obscure the most common binding lipophilic binding sites for local anesthetic channel-blocking compounds.

In addition to the N-type mechanism, another type of inactivation, called C-type, was identified in voltage-gated K⁺ channels (see Pongs, 1992, for review). This mechanism is visible in some drosophila *Shaker* potassium-channel splice variants that lack N-type inactivation. It can be revealed in some N-type inactivating channels by deletion of the N-terminus (Hoshi, Zagotta, & Aldrich, 1991). Thus, N- and C-types of inactivation can exist simultaneously in voltage-dependent potassium channels. C-type inactivation occurs via a mechanism by which the external mouth of the channel becomes occluded during sustained depolarization (Busch, Hurst, North, Adelman, & Kavanaugh, 1991) and involves conformational changes that involve cooperativity between the four subunits forming the functional potassium channel (Ogielska et al., 1995; Panyi, Sheng, Tu, & Deutsch, 1995). Despite being potentially a more widespread mechanism of K⁺ channel inactivation than N-type, C-type inactivation is less well understood. It is also possible that C-type inactivation actually covers multiple inactivation mechanisms that are not N-type. P-type and V-type inactivation mechanisms have also been proposed (De Biasi et al., 1993; Jerng, Shahidullah, & Covarrubias, 1999).

Inactivation of sodium channels is thought to involve similar types of mechanisms. Fast inactivation of sodium channels is not mediated by the N-terminal domain. However, like N-type inactivation in potassium channels, it is mediated by a relatively small lipophilic domain that occludes the intracellular mouth of the pore (Catterall, 1995). This lipophilic domain resides on the intracellular loop that connects the third and fourth six-membrane–spanning domain repeats (Figure 2). Fast inactivation in sodium channels, like N-type inactivation, is also partially coupled in the sense that it requires channel activation to occur and has no intrinsic voltage sensitivity. Similarly, it also plays an important role in the ability of local anesthetic drugs to bind a there high affinity binding site. Slow inactivation of sodium channels, like C-type inactivation, is less well understood. Recent evidence suggests that it, too, involves conformational changes at the extracellular mouth of the pore (Balser et al., 1996; Wang & Wang, 1997; Todt, Dudley, Kyle, French, & Fozzard, 1999).

Molecular Diversity and Ancillary Subunits

Expression of the α-subunits of sodium and potassium channels alone is sufficient to produce selective ion channels with most of the gross physiological properties of native channel types (Catterall, 1995; Marban et al., 1998). However, sodium channels are always associated with ancillary β-subunits. There also exist several potassium channel β-subunits, although it is not yet clear the degree to which these assemble in native tissue. For both the sodium and potassium channels, the main consequence of co-expression of these ancillary subunits is modification of activation and inactivation properties. The exact mechanisms by which these ancillary subunits make their modifications on channel gating is a current topic of research interest, although at least some subunits modify function by adding additional N-type inactivation domains to the functional channel (Rettig et al., 1994). Thus, there is not a one-to-one relationship between channel isoform and cellular ionic current. In addition to modification of channel behavior by second messenger systems, the underlying molecular basis of channels can vary considerably based on subunit composition. This is particularly true for potassium channels, which can have more than one type of α-subunit in the core tetramer. The ability to "mix and match" α- and β-subunits is a powerful mechanism for generating the diversity of dynamic currents underlying electrical activity and function in the various cells in the nervous system.

REFERENCES

Antz, C., Geyer, M., Fakler, B., Schott, M. K., Guy, H. R., Frank, R., Ruppersberg, J. P., & Kalbitzer, H. R. (1997). NMR structure of inactivation gates from mammalian voltage-dependent potassium channels. *Nature, 385,* 272–275.

Armstrong, C. M. (1971). Interaction of the tetraethylammonium ion derivatives with the potassium channels of giant axons. *Journal of General Physiology, 58,* 413–437.

Balser, J. R., Nuss, H. B., Chiamvimonvat, N., Perez-Garcia, M. T., Marban, E., & Tomaselli, G. F. (1996). External pore residue mediates slow inactivation in MU-I rat skeletal muscle sodium channels. *Journal of Physiology, 494,* 431–442.

Busch, A. E., Hurst, R. A., North, R. A., Adelman, J. P., & Kavanaugh, M. P. (1991). Current inactivation involves a histidine residue in the pore of the rat lymphocyte channel RGK5. *Biochemistry and Biophysics Research Communications, 179,* 1384–1390.

Catterall, W. A. (1995). Structure and function of voltage-gated ion channels. *Annual Review of Biochemistry, 64,* 493–531.

De Biasi, M., Hartmann, H. A., Drewe, J. A., Taglialatela, M., Brown, A. M., & Kirsch, G. E. (1993). Inactivation determined by a single site in K+ pores. *Pflügers Archives, 422,* 354–363.

Hille, B. (1992). *Ionic channels of excitable membranes* (2nd ed.). Sunderland, MA: Sinauer.

Hodgkin, A. L., & Huxley, A. F. (1952). A quantitative description of membrane current and its application to conduction and excitation in nerve. *Journal of Physiology, 117,* 500–544.

Hoshi, T., Zagotta, W. N., & Aldrich, R. W. (1990). Biophysical and molecular mechanisms of *Shaker* potassium channel inactivation. *Science, 250,* 533–538.

Hoshi, T., Zagotta, W. N., & Aldrich, R. W. (1991). Two types of inactivation in *Shaker* K+ channels: Effects of alterations in the carboxy-terminal region. *Neuron, 7,* 547–556.

Jan, L. Y., & Jan, Y. N. (1992). Structural elements involved in specific K+ channel functions. *Annual Review of Physiology, 54,* 537–555.

Jerng, H. H., Shahidullah, M., & Covarrubias, M. (1999). Inactivation gating of Kv4 potassium channels: Molecular interactions involving the inner vestibule of the pore. *Journal of General Physiology, 113*(5), 641–660.

Lipkind, G. M., & Fozzard, H. A. (1994). A structural model of the tetrodotoxin and saxitoxin binding site of the Na+ channel. *Biophysical Journal, 66*(1), 1–13.

MacKinnon, R., & Yellen, G. (1990). Mutations affecting TEA+ blockade and ion permeation in voltage-activated K+ channels. *Science, 250,* 276–279.

Mannuzzu, L. M., Moronne, M. M., & Isacoff, E. Y. (1996). Direct physical measure of conformational rearrangement underlying potassium channel gating. *Science, 271*(5246), 213–216.

Marban, E., Yamagishi, T., & Tomaselli, G. F. (1998). Structure and function of voltage-gated sodium channels. *Journal of Physiology, 508*(3), 647–657.

Ogielska, E. M., Zagotta, W. N., Hoshi, T., Heinemann, S. H., Haab, S., & Aldrich, R. W. (1995). Cooperative subunit interactions in C-type inactivation of K channels. *Biophysical Journal, 69,* 2449–2457.

Panyi, G., Sheng, Z. F., Tu, L. W., & Deutsch, C. (1995). C-type inactivation of a voltage-gated K+ channel occurs by a cooperative mechanism. *Biophysical Journal, 69,* 896–903.

Plummer, N. W., & Meisler, M. H. (1999). Evolution and diversity of mammalian sodium channel genes. *Genomics, 57*(2), 323–331.

Pongs, O. (1992). Molecular biology of voltage-dependent potassium channels. *Physiology Review, 72*(Suppl.), 69–88.

Rasmusson, R. L., Morales, M. J., Wang, S., Liu, S., Campbell, D. L., & Strauss, H. C. (1998). Inactivation of voltage-gated cardiac K+ channels. *Circular of Research, 82,* 739–750.

Rayner, M. D., Starkus, J. G., Ruben, P. C., & Alicata, D. A. (1992). Voltage-sensitive and solvent-sensitive processes in ion channel gating: Kinetic effects of hyperosmolar media on inactivation and deactivation of sodium channels. *Biophysical Journal, 61,* 96–108.

Rettig, J., Heinemann, S. H., Wunder, F., Lorra, C., Parcej, D. N., Dolly, J. O., & Pongs, O. (1994). Inactivation properties of voltage-gated K+ channels altered by presence of beta-subunit. *Nature, 369,* 289–294.

Ruppersberg, J. P., Frank, R., Pongs, O., & Stocker, M. (1991). Cloned neuronal I_{K(A)} channels reopen on recovery from inactivation. *Nature, 353,* 603–604.

Ruppersberg, J. P., Stocker, M., Pongs, O., Heinemann, S. H., Frank, R., & Koenen, M. (1991). Regulation of fast inactivation of cloned mammalian I_{K(A)} channels by cysteine oxidation. *Nature, 52,* 711–714.

Salkoff, L., & Jegla, T. (1995). Surfing the DNA databases for K+ channels nets yet more diversity. *Neuron, 15*(3), 489–492.

Todt, H., Dudley, S. C., Jr., Kyle, J. W., French, R. J., & Fozzard, H. A. (1999). Ultra-slow inactivation in mu1 Na+ channels is produced by a structural rearrangement the outer vestibule. *Biophysical Journal, 76*(3), 1335–1345.

Tseng-Crank, J., Yao, J.-A., Berman, M. F., & Tseng, G.-N. (1993). Functional role of the NH2-terminal cytoplasmic domain of a mammalian A-type K+ channel. *Journal of General Physiology, 102,* 1057–1083.

Wang, S. Y., & Wang, G. K. (1997). A mutation in segment I-S6 alters slow inactivation of sodium channels. *Biophysical Journal, 72,* 1633–1640.

Zagotta, W. N., Hoshi, T., & Aldrich, R. W. (1990). Restoration of inactivation in mutants of *Shaker* potassium channels by a peptide derived from ShB. *Science, 250,* 568–571.

Zimmerberg, J., Bezanilla, F., & Parsegian, V. A. (1990). Solute inaccessible aqueous volume changes during opening of the potassium channel of the squid giant axon. *Biophysical Journal, 57,* 1049–1064.

R. L. Rasmusson
Allegheny University of the Health Sciences

SODIUM-POTASSIUM PUMP

VYGOTSKY, LEV SEMYONOVICH (1896–1934)

Educated at Moscow State University, Vygotsky was one of the significant postrevolutionary Soviet psychologists. His first entrance into psychology was with a paper in which he made a strong plea for the inclusion of consciousness in the subject matter of psychology. He opposed the reflexology of Bekhterev, arguing that a study of mind was necessary, since it distinguished humans from lower animals. However, he rejected introspection as a method. In this sense, he was closer to behaviorism than to the psychologists who accepted introspection, not only as a legitimate method, but as the main method of psychology. Thus consciousness consisted of a relationship among the psychical functions and should be the major topic of Soviet psychology.

Perhaps Vygotsky is best known for his theory of signs. The genesis of signs was a process of internalizing the means of social communication. According to this theory, during the cultural development of a child, each higher psychical function passes through an external phase, since it originally had a social function. There are three phases in the process of internalization, which can be illustrated in the development of speech. In the first, words express the relationship of the child to objects. In the second, the relationship between words and things is used by the adult as a means of communication with the child. In the third, words become intrinsically meaningful to the child. Hence words as signs become a social tool that help people to control the "lower" mental functions. Finally, the concept of sign was assumed to provide a resolution between a biological and social conflict.

R. W. LUNDIN
Wheaton, Illinois

WALDORF EDUCATION

Also known as Steiner education, this alternative educational system is based on the ideas of Rudolf Steiner (1861–1925), the Austrian scientist, educator, and philosopher. Steiner founded the first Waldorf school in 1919 in Stuttgart, Germany. The movement soon became international; there are now more than 650 Waldorf schools throughout the world.

The uniqueness of the Waldorf curriculum lies in the way the children are taught. In presenting material, first comes the encounter, then encounter becomes experience, and out of experience crystallizes the concept: Perception, feeling, and idea are the three steps in a genuine learning process.

Steiner recognized that children's emotional, intellectual, and physical natures change from year to year. It is fundamental to Waldorf education that the material presented and the ways in which it is presented are appropriate and enriching to the children's nature and needs at every level. Thus, the potential that the child brings to each stage of development is allowed and encouraged to develop to its full capacity.

The curriculum integrates the arts, sciences, and humanities, and teaching is done from an artistic point of view, taking into account that individuals learn at different rates and through different modalities. Assessment is principally through narrative report, supported by more conventional grading in the upper grades. Students create their own books and projects, from the teacher's examples in the early years and later from their own research as well. Primary source material is used whenever possible. The focus of Waldorf education is on the development of the whole human being socially, artistically, physically, and intellectually. The pedagogy is premised on a strong conviction that the human being is spiritual in origin and that his or her life is a journey of unfolding and growth toward goodness, beauty, and truth.

Waldorf schools may begin with a nursery class and go through high school, depending on the particular school. Pedagogical and policy decisions are made by a designated group of faculty members. Teacher training consists of at least two years of postgraduate work at Waldorf institutes.

SUGGESTED READING

Blunt, R. (1995). *Waldorf education: Theory and practice.* (Capetown, South Africa) Novalis Press.

Carlgren, F. (1976). *Education towards freedom.* East Grinstead, England: Lanthorn Press.

Childs, G. (1993). *Steiner education in theory and practice.* Edinburgh: Floris Books.

Healy, J. (1990). *Endangered minds.* New York: Simon and Schuster.

Mattke, H.-J. (Ed.). (1994). *Waldorf education worldwide.* Stuttgart, Germany.

Nobel, A. (1994). *Educating through art, the Steiner school approach.* Edinburgh: Floris Books.

B. D. OZAKI
Honolulu Waldorf School

WALKER, C. EUGENE

C. (Clarence) Eugene Walker was born in Monongahela, PA on January 8, 1939. He graduated from Madison High School in Madison, OH in 1956; attended Cedarville College in Cedarville, OH during 1956–1957; and graduated from Geneva College in Beaver Falls, PA in 1960 with a BS degree in psychology with highest honors and special honors in psychology. He received both his MS (1963) and PhD (1965) from Purdue University, with a major in clinical psychology and minors in experimental psychology and sociology. His psychology internship was completed at West Tenth Street Veteran's Administration Hospital and Riley Children's Hospital, both in Indianapolis.

Walker taught at Westmont College in Santa Barbara, CA from 1964 to 1968, where he was assistant professor and chair of the division of psychology, education, and physical education, as well as the school's athletic director. From 1968 to 1974, he was assistant professor and then associate professor at Baylor University in Waco, TX. From 1974 to 1995 he taught at the University of Oklahoma Medical School in Oklahoma City, OK, where he was promoted from associate to full professor, director of training in pediatric psychology, and cochief of mental health services for Children's Hospital of Oklahoma. Upon retirement, he was named professor emeritus from the Medical School and formed a corporation, Psychological Consultants, Inc., located in Edmond, OK.

Walker published over one hundred articles, reviews, and chapters and more than twenty books on research and clinical practice with children and adults. His early work involved research on psychological testing and measurement, and his later work involved behavioral approaches to psychotherapy and the effects of pornography on behavior. Walker's still later interests included hyperactive behavior in children, child abuse, and juvenile and adolescent sex offenders. He is a leading expert on the treatment of enuresis and encopresis, the treatment of young sex offenders, and behavioral approaches to psychotherapy.

Active on many professional committees of the American Psychological Association, he is on the editorial board of numerous journals and was a member of the founding editorial board of the journal *Professional Psychology* and of the *Journal of Clinical Psychology in Medical Settings.* He was president of the Central Texas Psychological Association (1973), the Section for Continuing Professional Development in the Division of Clinical Psychology of the American Psychological Association (1973), the Southwestern Psychological Association (1977), the Oklahoma Psychological

Association (1983), and the Society of Pediatric Psychology (1986). He was chair of the Corresponding Committee of Fifty for the Division of Clinical Psychology (1970–1973). He is a fellow of the American Psychological Association; he is also listed in *Who's Who in America, Who's Who in the World,* and numerous other reference works.

A very sought-after consultant and lecturer, Walker received the Distinguished Contribution to the Profession of Psychology from the Oklahoma Psychological Association (1986), the Oklahoma Psychological Association Distinguished Psychologist Citation (1996), and the Society of Pediatric Psychology Distinguished Service Award (1996).

In a career that involved teaching at all levels, including undergraduate, graduate, postdoctoral, intern, resident, adult education, and university without walls, Walker received numerous awards, including the Award for Excellence in Classroom Teaching presented by Biological Psychology graduate students at University of Oklahoma Health Sciences Center (1984), the Gordon H. Deckert Award for Sustained Excellence in Departmental Educational Endeavors from the Department of Psychiatry and Behavioral Sciences of the University of Oklahoma Medical School (1988), the Award for Sustained Leadership from Psychology Interns of the University of Oklahoma Health Sciences Center (1992), and the Award of Appreciation from Psychology Interns of the University of Oklahoma Health Sciences Center (1996).

STAFF

WALK-IN CLINICS

Walk-in clinics provide short-term treatment and referral for individuals with psychological problems. These community mental health services are usually open 24 hours a day, do not require an appointment, and often include telephone hot lines.

There are several historical precursors of walk-in clinics, including New York's Parish of All Strangers, a suicide prevention service founded by the Reverend Harry M. Warren in 1905. Almost 60 years later, relying on the works of Gerald Caplan and Erich Lindemann, the Community Mental Health Act, passed by the Congress in 1963, recommended walk-in clinics as one of the essential components of community mental health centers. Two of the earliest such clinics, the Benjamin Rush Center in Los Angeles and the New York Medical College–Metropolitan Hospital Center Walk-In Clinic, were established in 1967.

Most walk-in clinics are operated by community mental health centers or emergency rooms within general hospitals. Specialized services dealing with problems of alcohol, drugs, suicide, and rape also include walk-in clinics. In their *Handbook of Psychiatric Emergencies,* Slaby and colleagues cite a study by Cheryl Taubman, which analyzed all the walk-in psychiatric patients seen in a hospital emergency room in a 70-day period. Results indicated that 25.8% of the patients were schizophrenic, 21.1% were alcoholic, 18.6% were depressed, and 24.7% had other diagnoses.

With the guiding principle of being available when the person needs help, and with the emphasis on short-term treatment, often by paraprofessionals, walk-in clinics are one answer to the great need for expanded mental health services.

SUGGESTED READING

Caplan, G. (1961). *An approach to community mental health.* New York: Grune & Stratton.

Caplan, G. (1974/1964). *Principles of preventative psychiatry.* New York: Basic Books.

Greenstone, J., & Leviton, S. (1981). *Crisis intervention directory.* New York: Facts on File.

Hatton, C. L., Valente, S. M., & Rink, A. (1977). *Suicide: Assessment and intervention.* New York: Appleton-Century-Crofts.

Lindemann, E. (1944). Symptomatology and management of acute grief. *American Journal of Psychiatry, 101,* 141–148.

C. LANDAU
Brown University Division of Medicine

COMMUNITY PSYCHOLOGY
HALFWAY HOUSES

WANG, ZHONG-MING

Zhong-Ming Wang is professor of industrial-organizational psychology and human resource management at the Department of Psychology and School of Management and director of the Center for Human Resources and Strategic Development, Zhejiang University (formerly Hangzhou University), in China. He received an MA in applied psychology from Gothenburg University, Sweden (1985), and a PhD in industrial/organizational psychology from Hangzhou University as part of a joint doctoral program with Gothenburg University (1987). He is the president of the industrial psychology division (Chinese SIOP) of the Chinese Psychology Society and leads China's national key doctoral program of industrial-organizational psychology. He is also vice-president of both the Chinese National Committee of Personnel Assessment and the Chinese Ergonomics Society.

Wang is the coordinator of several international projects, including joint research projects on team decision making; international human resource management; international joint venture management and cross-cultural work adjustment; leadership assessment process; and development of multicultural leadership teams.

Wang is associate editor for the *Chinese Journal of Applied Psychology* and *Journal of Management Development,* and serves on the editorial boards of *Applied Psychology, Journal of Cross-Cultural Psychology, Organizational Behavior and Human Decision Processes, Journal of Managerial Psychology, International Journal of Human Resources Management, Journal of Organizational Behaviour,* and *International Journal of Selection and Assessment.* His main research areas include personnel selection and assessment, competence-performance modeling, team processes, organizational decision making, leadership, organization development, cross-cultural organizational psychology, and human resource management. Wang has published several books and more than 150 articles, including "Psychology in China" (in the *Annual Review of Psychology,* 1993, Vol. 44) and "Culture, economic reform and the role of industrial and organizational psychology in China," in the *Handbook of Industrial and Organizational Psychology* (1994, 2nd ed., Vol. 4), edited by M. D. Dunnette and L. M. Hough.

STAFF

WATSON, JOHN B. (1878–1958)

The founder of American Behaviorism, John B. Watson was the first University of Chicago student to receive a degree in psychology. "With animals I was at home," he said, and so he devoted much of his life to animal psychology. Even his doctoral dissertation in 1903 was on *Animal Education.* So impressed with it was Chicago's Henry Donaldson, that he lent Watson $350 to have it published.

By the 1920s, Watson had developed an interest in human subjects. Not long after his son John was born in 1904, he remarked: "A baby is more fun to the square inch than all the rats and frogs in creation." During this period, his range of friends extended from J. R. Angell and Harvey Carr to J. M. Baldwin and R. M. Yerkes.

Watson left Chicago in 1903 for a professorship at Johns Hopkins. During his Johns Hopkins tenure, behaviorism was born. He found its two tenets (psychology as an objective science, and psychology as the science of behavior) in W. B. Pillsbury's *Essentials of Psychology.* His behaviorist manifesto "Psychology as a behaviorist views it" appeared in 1913, and its book-length elaboration, *Behavior: An Introduction to Comparative Psychology,* the following year.

A career crisis occurred in 1920 with his abrupt dismissal from Johns Hopkins. He married Rosalie Rayner, a graduate student, and together they published two important papers on human conditioning and counterconditioning: "Conditioned emotional reactions" and "Studies in infant behavior." During this period, he wrote chapters for his *Psychology From the Standpoint of a Behaviorist,* and used some of his observations on children for it.

On leaving Johns Hopkins for the world of advertising, Watson's penchant for new ideas waned, despite the publication in the 1920s of *Behaviorism, The Ways of Behaviorism,* and some lesser known works. Chiefly known for his *radical behaviorism,* Watson boldly declared: "Give me a dozen healthy infants . . . and I'll guarantee to take any one at random and train him to become any type of specialist" (*Psychology From the Standpoint of a Behaviorist*). His enthusiasm failed to hold, for a mere four years later, he despairingly remarked: "I used to feel quite hopeful of reconditioning even adult personalities. . . . But . . . the zebra can as easily change his stripes as the adult his personality" (*The Ways of Behaviorism*). Nevertheless, when Watson died in 1958, behaviorism virtually dominated American psychology.

W. S. SAHAKIAN

WEBER'S LAW

Ernst Heinrich Weber (1795–1878) was a professor of anatomy at the University of Leipzig. On the basis of experiments with stimuli of pressure, lifted weights, and visual distance (line lengths)— along with reported observations of others—he concluded that, rather than perceiving simply the difference between stimuli that are being compared, we perceive the ratio of the difference to the magnitude of the stimuli. A similar finding had already been made by the French physicist and mathematician Pierre Bouguer (1698–1758) for visual brightness. Gustav T. Fechner (1801–1887), formerly a student of Weber and later also a professor at the University of Leipzig, translated this conclusion into the familiar mathematical form used today. Thus Weber's law is usually given as either $\Delta I/I = k$ or $\Delta I = kI$ where ΔI is the change required for a just noticeable difference in stimulation (JND), I is the stimulus magnitude, and k is a constant for the particular sense. The value of k is termed the "Weber ratio." This second formulation shows more clearly the proportional change in stimulation required for a JND. If, for example, the stimulus magnitude is doubled, the amount of change required for a JND is also doubled.

Over the years since Weber's formulation, it has been observed that k is not strictly constant over the entire stimulus range, increasing for low and high intensities. It is, however, valid for a large range of intermediate intensities for the various senses.

Representative values of the Weber ratio for intermediate ranges include the following: brightness, 0.02 to 0.05; visual wavelength, 0.002 to 0.006; loudness (intensity measure), 0.1 to 0.2; auditory frequency, 0.0019 to 0.035; taste (salt), 0.15 to 0.25; smell (various substances), 0.2 to 0.4; cutaneous pressure, 0.14 to 0.16; and deep pressure, 0.013 to 0.030.

SUGGESTED READING

Baird, J. C., & Noma, E. (1978). *Fundamentals of scaling and psychophysics.* New York: Wiley.

Boring, E. G. (1942). *Sensation and perception in the history of experimental psychology.* New York: Appleton-Century-Crofts.

Laming, D. (1986). *Sensory analysis.* London: Academic Press.

Weber, E. H. (1978). *The sense of touch* (H. E. Ross & D. J. Murray, Trans.). London: Academic Press. (Original work published 1834 [*De Tactu*] and 1846 [*Der Tastsinn*])

G. H. ROBINSON
University of North Alabama

PSYCHOPHYSICS

WECHSLER, DAVID (1896–1981)

David Wechsler is one of the founders of modern clinical psychology and the author of the most widely used tests for assessing individual intelligence.

When David was 6 years old, his family migrated to New York City, where he completed the AB degree at the City College of New

York in 1916. Clinical psychology as it is known today was not yet launched, let alone envisioned by the approximately 1,000 predominately academic and experimental psychologists who were members of the American Psychological Association that year. Nevertheless a few psychologists had left academia and had ventured to work in child guidance, educational, and even psychiatric clinics. Thus young Wechsler was allowed to carry out a thesis for the MA degree (1917) at Columbia University under Robert S. Woodworth on a topic (retention in Korsakoff's psychosis) in the emerging field of experimental psychopathology.

Wechsler also sought out his own opportunities for other clinical experiences in psychology. For example, in 1917, while awaiting Army induction as the United States prepared to enter World War I, Wechsler gained his first applied experience working under E. G. Boring at an Army camp on Long Island. There Wechsler helped score the performances of several thousand recruits on the Army Alpha, a group-administered offshoot of the Stanford–Binet, which had been produced by a handful of U.S. psychologists. After formal induction a few months later, Wechsler was assigned by the Army to the psychology unit at Fort Logan in Texas. There his duties as a psychology technician consisted largely of testing recruits needing individual assessment. This brief experience involved adult recruits who could not read English or who had had no formal schooling, and others for whom the group-administered Army Alpha and Army Beta tests were less appropriate than was one-on-one assessment in which the examiner utilized both verbal (*Stanford–Binet*) and nonverbal (Yerkes and Army Performance Scales) tests of measured intelligence. The realization that written tests such as the Army Alpha yielded an inaccurate index of measured intelligence for these subgroups of adults who previously had functioned adequately as civilians, and the more realistic index of this sociooccupational adaptiveness provided for them by nonverbal tests, gave Wechsler two invaluable insights: First, the debates between Spearman and Thorndike and other academician-theorists on the nature of intelligence were based on a conception that was too narrow to fit the realities presented to a psychologist who examined people in situations in which real-life decisions based on such assessment were necessary. Second, the Stanford–Binet, while suitable for children, was not satisfactory for adults—the literate, as well as the foreign-born Americans who did not understand English.

Following his transfer to France, Wechsler was assigned, in 1919, as an Army student to the University of London, where he studied with Charles Spearman and Karl Pearson. Both men had a great influence on him—Spearman through his concept of general intelligence, which Wechsler later would find inadequate to encompass the "nonintellective" components of intelligence, and Pearson through his innovative correlational methods.

Soon after his Army discharge in England (August 1919), Wechsler won a fellowship to the University of Paris (1920–1922). There he studied with Henri Pieron and Louis Lapique, and also gathered data on the psychogalvanic response and emotion that became the basis for his 1925 PhD dissertation at Columbia, again under the direction of Woodworth. While completing the PhD degree, Wechsler worked as a psychologist in New York City's newly created Bureau of Child Guidance (1922–1924). Following his doc-

torate, he served as acting secretary of the Psychological Corporation (1925–1927), and then spent the next several years in private clinical practice (1927–1932). Wechsler became chief psychologist at Bellevue Psychiatric Hospital in 1932, with a concurrent faculty appointment at New York University College of Medicine (1933). He held both positions until 1967 and combined research with clinical work.

Beginning in 1934, Wechsler's creative efforts were largely directed to two of his most important contributions to psychology: (a) the development and standardization of the adult (and later preschool and children's) intelligence scales that bear his name; and (b) the substitution for Binet's Mental Age of a Deviation Quotient (so important in evaluating the intelligence level of adults) that related each person's raw intelligence test score to his or her own age group as a reference, rather than to a mental age and an upper age limit of 15 years for adults, as had been done by Binet, Terman, and others. The immediate spur to these two contributions was the need for a suitable instrument for testing the multilingual adult population referred to Wechsler for psychological examination at Bellevue. This effort culminated in a single battery called the *Bellevue-Wechsler Scale* (1939).

Wechsler continued using a comparable multitest battery (of 10 or 11 verbal and performance subtests) in the development of his 1942 *Army Wechsler* (*Bellevue–Wechsler II*), *Wechsler Intelligence Scale for Children, Wechsler Adult Intelligence Scale, Wechsler Preschool and Primary Scale of Intelligence, Wechsler Intelligence Scale for Children,* and *Wechsler Intelligence Scale for Adults.* The development of his ideas about the nature of intelligence, which provided the framework for these Wechsler scales, can be found in the test manuals that accompany each scale, in *Wechsler's Measurement and Appraisal of Adult Intelligence: Fifth Edition* by Joseph D. Matarazzo, and in the volume of his selected papers, with Allen J. Edwards's introduction.

J. D. MATARAZZO
Oregon Health Sciences University

WECHSLER INTELLIGENCE TESTS

Although the mental testing movement had been in evidence for decades, by the late 1930s there still was no successful well-standardized individual adult intelligence test. It was not until the publication, in 1939, of Wechsler's *The Measurement of Adult Intelligence* that such an instrument became widely available.

Terman's 1916 edition of the Stanford–Binet and the later, 1937 edition revised by Terman and Merrill had been the most popular individually administered tests of intelligence. Although primarily standardized on samples of children, they had been employed in the assessment of adult intelligence as well. The continued dissatisfaction with the standardization and structure (mental age levels) of the Stanford–Binet served as a major stimulus for Wechsler in introducing the Wechsler–Bellevue Adult Intelligence Scales in 1939.

Wechsler's test was designed as a "point scale" rather than a mental age scale. It attempted to obviate the criticism leveled at the

Stanford–Binet as being too verbal by including a large proportion of performance items and it used a sizable number of adults in the standardization sample. The standardization population of the Wechsler–Bellevue consisted of 670 children, ages 7 to 16, and 1,080 white adults, 17 to 70 years old, all residents of New York City and vicinity. An attempt was made to control for education and occupational status. The final version of the test was intended for use with ages 10 through 60.

The Wechsler–Bellevue (W–B) scales consist of 10 subtests, with five subtests each in the verbal and performance scales. The verbal subtests include an information test, a general comprehension test, memory for digits (forward and backward), an arithmetic test, and a similarities test. The five performance tests in the battery are picture arrangement, picture completion, block design, object assembly, and a digit symbol test. A vocabulary subtest is also included, designed as a substitute for one of the others.

Some of the general factors that governed the final selection of the tests were the evidence that the particular tests correlated at a reasonable level with other intelligence test batteries, that they were sufficiently varied in their functions to prevent any special effects on examinees with particular abilities and disabilities, and that the characteristics of the tests allowed some diagnostic inferences based on the performance of the subjects examined.

After two revised editions of *The Measurement of Adult Intelligence,* Wechsler introduced a new and revised form of his test in the *Manual of the Wechsler Adult Intelligence Scale* (WAIS), in 1949. This was followed by a more detailed fourth edition of the previous volume, in 1958, entitled *The Measurement and Appraisal of Adult Intelligence.*

The WAIS was standardized on 1,700 subjects (evenly divided between the sexes at the several age levels) between the ages of 16 and 64. In addition, a sample of 475 aged (60 to 75+) subjects was included. All parts of the country were represented in this standardization, urban and rural subjects at each age level, and 10% of "nonwhites." The structure of the WAIS, however, remained the same as the W–B: verbal and performance scales and the same 11 subtests. Most subtests were modified by eliminating some nondiscriminating items and by adding new items, as well as by increasing the number of items.

The procedure of assigning an IQ to a subject involves the conversion of the raw scores of each subtest into scaled scores and by obtaining the corresponding verbal, performance, and total IQs from the conversion tables provided for the various age categories. The specific statistical procedures and rationale underlying this method of obtaining IQs are detailed in several manuals and in the fifth edition of *Wechsler's Measurement and Appraisal of Adult Intelligence,* authored by Matarazzo, and published in 1972.

Wechsler defined intelligence as "an aggregate or global capacity of the individual to act purposefully, to think rationally and to deal effectively with his environment." Considering the breadth of this definition and the great flexibility of the W–B and the WAIS, there is little wonder that a great deal of research on the diagnostic aspects of this test, beyond the mere reporting of IQs, has appeared in the literature. Some of the work involves quantitative research on the correspondence between test patterns and certain psychopathologic diagnostic groupings, while other writings concern the "clinical" and qualitative analyses of the test responses and the processes by means of which the subject arrived at them.

In his original work, Wechsler proposed a "deterioration index" based on the ratio between subtests that "do not hold" and those that "hold" up with age. A variety of "scatter" measures consisting of deviation of subtest scores from the means of the entire scale, and other patterns and profiles of subtest score distribution, have been proposed by a number of investigators as diagnostic of sundry personality states and psychopathological conditions. Rabin, in his first review on "The use of the Wechsler–Bellevue scales with normal and abnormal persons" in 1945, as well as in subsequent reviews with Guertin and associates, generally concluded that group differences were obtainable with a number of patterns. However, the utility of scatter in individual diagnosis was questionable. Matarazzo reiterates this conclusion in his book. Yet some positive findings are obtainable when careful definition of patient samples takes place. Thus it is clear from a number of studies that a markedly higher verbal than performance IQ is present in patients with right cerebral hemisphere lesions, while the reverse is true in patients with left hemisphere lesions. Fairly consistent results have been reported pointing to "performance greater than verbal IQ" in delinquents and adult sociopathic persons. Other findings point to a variety of additional relationships between WAIS patterns and diagnostic subgroups. These and qualitative analyses of the W–B by Rapaport and his associates in their volume on *Diagnostic Psychological Testing* still serve as guidelines for many clinicians concerned with psychodiagnosis.

The *Wechsler Intelligence Scale for Children* (WISC) was published in 1949 as a "downward" extension of the W–B. Actually many items of form II of the W–B served as a foundation for the new scale, which was standardized on 2,200 children. Still another scale, for younger children, the WPPSI (*Wechsler Preschool and Primary Scale of Intelligence*) was standardized on a stratified sample of 1,200 children and published in 1967.

REFERENCES

Matarazzo, J. D. (1972/1939). *Wechsler's measurement and appraisal of adult intelligence* (5th ed.). Baltimore: Williams & Wilkins.

Wechsler, D. (1958/1939). *The measurement and appraisal of adult intelligence* (4th ed.). Baltimore: Williams & Wilkins.

Wechsler, D. (1967). *Wechsler Preschool and Primary Scale of Intelligence.* New York: Psychological Corp.

Wechsler, D. (1974/1949). *Wechsler Intelligence Scale for Children, revised.* New York: Psychological Corp.

A. I. RABIN
Michigan State University

HUMAN INTELLIGENCE
INTELLIGENCE MEASURES
MEASUREMENT
STANFORD–BINET INTELLIGENCE SCALE

WEISSMAN, MYRNA M.

Myrna M. Weissman is a professor of epidemiology in psychiatry in the College of Physicians and Surgeons and the Joseph Mailman School of Public Health at Columbia University, and chief of the department of clinical-genetic epidemiology at New York State Psychiatric Institute. She was formerly a professor at Yale University School of Medicine and director of the Depression Research Unit. She was a visiting senior scholar from 1979 to 1980 at the Institute of Medicine, National Academy of Sciences, Washington, D.C.

In 1974 Weissman received a PhD in chronic disease epidemiology from Yale University. Her current research is concerned with the epidemiology of psychiatric disorders in the community, and the treatment and genetics of affective and anxiety disorders.

Weissman has been a consultant to many private and public agencies, including the World Health Organization, the White House Office of Science and Technology Policy, the John D. and Catherine T. MacArthur Foundation, and the Institute of Medicine, National Academy of Sciences. She is also on the editorial boards of several journals, including *Archives of General Psychiatry*. She has been the author or co-author of more than 400 scientific articles and chapters, and of seven books, including *The Depressed Woman: A Study of Social Relationships* (University of Chicago Press, 1974) with E. S. Paykel; *Comprehensive Guide to Interpersonal Psychotherapy of Depression* (Basic Books, 2000) with John Markowitz and with her late husband, G. L. Klerman.

Weissman's awards include the American Psychiatric Association Foundation's Fund Prize for research on the treatment of affective disorder (1978); the Rema Lapouse Mental Health Epidemiology Award, given by the American Public Health Association for contributions to the scientific understanding of the epidemiology and control of mental disorders (1985); with G. L. Klerman, the Anna Monika Foundation Prize, an international award for the "investigation of the physical substrate and functional disturbances of depressions," in recognition of their collaborative research on "The Place of Drugs and Psychotherapy in the Treatment of Endogenous Depressions" (1986); with G. L. Klerman, the National Depressive and Manic Depressive Association and Research awards for their "contribution to combined pharmacologic and psychotherapeutic treatment of depressive illness" (1989); the Research Award of the American Suicide Foundation (1990); the National Institute of Mental Health (NIMH) 10-year Merit Award for her study of the genetics of panic disorder (1990); the Anna Pollock Lederer Award and the National Alliance for Research in Schizophrenia and Depression (NARSAD) Senior Investigator Award for studies of depression (1991); the Selo Prize from NARSAD for outstanding research achievement in depression (1994); with G. L. Klerman (posthumously), the Rhoda and Bernard Sarnat International Prize in Mental Health, Institute of Medicine, National Academy of Sciences (1994); the Joseph Zubin Award from the Society for Research on Psychopathology (1995); The Joseph Zubin Research Prize from the American Psychopathological Association (1996); and the New York State Office of Mental Health Research Award for Outstanding Contributions to Psychiatric Research (1996). Also in 1996, Weissman was elected to the Institute of Medicine of the National Academy of Sciences. In 1998, she was elected a fellow of the Royal College of Psychiatrists (U.K.); and in 1999, she was selected to be the Emily Mumford lecturer at Columbia University. She is a past president (1998–1999) of the American Psychopathological Association, and is a current member (1999–2000) of the National Advisory Mental Health Council of NIMH. She is also currently serving (1999–2002) on the council of the American College of Neuropsychopharmacology (ACNP).

STAFF

WERNICKE-LICHTHEIM MODEL OF LANGUAGE PROCESSING

The functional-anatomical model of language processing formulated by Wernicke and Lichtheim in the late 19th century has provided a useful introduction to aphasia for generations of clinicians. Thirteen years before Wernicke's famous monograph, Broca had revolutionized the study of aphasia by linking speech production deficits to frontal lobe damage (Broca, 1861). Wernicke brought these observations together with new data from aphasic patients with temporal lobe lesions, providing the first neuroanatomical account of both language comprehension and production (Wernicke, 1874). Lichtheim's expanded version of this model was influential because of the diagrammatic clarity with which it was able to predict aphasia syndromes from isolated lesions in functional centers or pathways linking the centers (Lichtheim, 1885) (Figure 1 and Table 1).

WERNICKE APHASIA

Wernicke's area, marked "A" in the diagram, is the center containing "auditory word forms" (*Wortklangbilder*). These word forms (the "phonological lexicon" in more recent terminology) contain information about the sounds of words, essential for decoding speech sound input and for guiding the production of words. Damage to A thus causes impaired speech comprehension as well as incorrect selection or sequencing of phonemes during speaking (phonemic paraphasia). Repetition, which requires both speech sound decoding and production, is also impaired, typically with severe paraphasia. In the classical version of the model, the sound

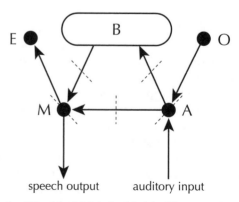

Figure 1.   Wernicke-Lichtheim Model of Language Processing

Table 1.

Syndrome	Lesion Site				
	A Wernicke	M Broca	A-to-M Conduction	A-to-B TC Sensory	B-to-M TC Motor
Spontaneous speech	paraphasic	nonfluent	paraphasic	paraphasic	nonfluent
Spontaneous writing	paragraphic	nonfluent	paragraphic	paragraphic	nonfluent
Naming	impaired	impaired	paraphasic	anomic	anomic
Repetition	paraphasic	nonfluent	paraphasic	nl	nl
Reading aloud	paraphasic	nonfluent	paraphasic	impaired	nl
Auditory comprehension	impaired	nl	nl	impaired	nl
Written comprehension	impaired	nl	nl	impaired	nl

images of words being read must be activated by input from the visual center (center "O" in the diagram) before reading comprehension can occur, and the sound images of words one intends to write are used to guide the motor images used for writing (stored in center "E" in the diagram). Thus, damage to A also causes alexia and paragraphia. The deficits resulting from a lesion in A are collectively called Wernicke aphasia.

Wernicke localized A to the left superior temporal gyrus (STG). Later authors held widely varying views on the location of Wernicke's area, including some for whom the area encompassed middle temporal, angular, and supramarginal gyri as well as STG (Bogen & Bogen, 1976). A strongly localizationist view, originated by Liepmann, Kleist and others and popularized in recent times by Geschwind and his students, places A in the posterior STG, particularly in the planum temporale or posterior dorsal STG (Geschwind, 1971). Lesions restricted to the left planum temporale appear to cause only the paraphasic speech component without comprehension disturbance or alexia (Kleist, 1962; Benson et al., 1973). Patients with Wernicke aphasia, including the patients reported by Wernicke himself, have had large lesions extending well beyond the STG (Wernicke, 1874; Henschen, 1920–1922; Damasio, 1989). Comparative studies in nonhuman primates and functional imaging data from humans strongly implicate the posterior STG in auditory functions (Galaburda & Sanides, 1980; Binder, Frost, Hammeke, Rao, & Cox, 1996); this region is thus no longer considered a center for multimodal language processing but probably participates in the sensory analysis of complex sounds, including speech.

BROCA APHASIA

A second main component of the model is Broca's center for "motor word images" (*Wortbewegungsbilder,* marked "M" in the diagram), which contains motor programs used for movement of the vocal apparatus during speech. Damage to M causes impaired speech production without affecting comprehension. The speaking deficit may be extreme, with complete or nearly complete mutism, or speech may be effortful and nonfluent, with a marked decrease in the length of phrases and the rate of word production. Because M is a final common output node for all speech behaviors, repetition, naming, and reading aloud are all similarly affected. Lichtheim believed that writing movements also depend on input from M; thus, inability to write is often considered a feature of the syndrome. The

deficits resulting from a lesion in M are collectively called Broca aphasia. Broca and other early aphasiologists localized M to the pars opercularis of the left inferior frontal gyrus (Brodmann's area 44), but later authors have variously included pars triangularis (area 45) and ventral premotor cortex (area 6) in the definition of Broca's area. Lesions restricted to the left pars opercularis do not cause the full syndrome, but rather a transient deficit of articulation without writing or naming disturbance (Mohr et al., 1978; Alexander, Benson, & Stuss, 1989). Patients with Broca aphasia, including the patient reported by Broca himself, typically have large lesions extending into insula, sensorimotor cortex, parietal operculum, and middle frontal gyrus (Mohr, 1976).

CONDUCTION APHASIA

Damage to connections between A and M also cause impairment of speech production, a syndrome known as conduction aphasia. Comprehension remains intact because A is spared, and speech remains fluent and well-articulated because M is spared. Although Wernicke predicted that such a lesion would cause difficulty producing whole words (anomia), patients with conduction aphasia show instead a disturbance characterized by phonemic paraphasia (Kohn, 1992). Emphasis is often placed on repetition deficits in conduction aphasia, but the same errors typically occur in all speech output tasks. The concept of conduction aphasia as a disconnection syndrome led to the popular view that the critical lesion is in white matter (external capsule and/or "arcuate fasciculus") connecting superior temporal to inferior frontal cortex. Evidence for such a localization is scant, however, and typical patients with the syndrome have cortical lesions affecting the posterior STG, posterior insula, or parietal operculum (Kleist, 1962; Benson et al., 1973; Damasio & Damasio, 1980).

TRANSCORTICAL APHASIA

A third main component of the model is the "concept field" (*Begriffsfeld*), described as a widely distributed, bihemispheric system containing information about the polysensory properties of objects (center "B" in the diagram). Comprehension is achieved when the auditory word form makes contact with this polysensory information, while speech production requires that the polysensory concepts activate corresponding motor word images. Because of its widely distributed nature, the concept field could not be damaged by a focal lesion. Focal lesions, however, could sever connections between the concept field and more focal language centers, causing the so-called transcortical syndromes. Repetition is normal in such cases because the A-to-M circuit is intact. Lesions between A and B prevent activation of concepts by auditory word images, causing impaired auditory and written word comprehension with intact repetition. This syndrome is known as transcortical sensory aphasia and is usually caused by damage to the posterior ventrolateral left temporal lobe (posterior middle or inferior temporal gyri) or angular gyrus (Alexander, Hiltbrunner, & Fischer, 1989). Lesions between M and B prevent activation of motor speech centers by concepts, causing nonfluent speech with intact repetition. This syndrome is known as transcortical motor aphasia and is caused by damage to the left middle frontal or superior frontal lobe (Alexander, Benson, et al., 1989; Rapcsak & Rubens, 1994). Brain regions in which lesions cause transcortical aphasia have recently been implicated in operations involving verbally encoded semantic knowledge (Démonet et al., 1992; Damasio, Grabowski, Tranel, Hichwa, & Damasio, 1996; Vandenbergh, Price, Wise, Josephs, & Frackowiak, 1996; Binder et al., 1997). The deficits observed in transcortical aphasia may thus be due to direct damage to, rather than disconnection of, these knowledge retrieval systems.

CURRENT STATUS OF THE MODEL

Many advances have been made since the 19th century in our understanding of language processing, and it is not clear that the Wernicke-Lichtheim model in its simple form can accomodate this information. For example, the model has almost nothing to say about syntactic processes or about how spoken or written nonsense words ("brillig," "slithy," "toves") are perceived and pronounced. Empirical observations not accounted for include a variety of context effects in letter and phoneme perception, spared language abilities in auditory or visual modalities, comprehension disturbances in patients with frontal lesions, word frequency effects and short-term memory phenomena in conduction aphasia, spelling regularity and lexicality effects in reading and writing, category-specific naming and comprehension disturbances, and so on. Underlying these difficulties is the fact that the model itself contains little in the way of explicit detail regarding how various transformations—sound to word, print to word, word to concept, concept to word, word to motor sequence—are actually accomplished.

The model has not been entirely abandoned, however, for two reasons. First, the enormous amount of data from modern aphasiology, functional imaging, and cognitive linguistic research has yet to be integrated in a widely-accepted, comprehensive alternative. Second, the range of models employed in the clinical setting may be limited to those that can be readily communicated to students in a diagrammatic or tabular format (Table 1). The Wernicke-Lichtheim model, particularly in its current simplified form, thus continues to serve a useful role as initial common ground for the interested student of aphasiology.

REFERENCES

Alexander, M. P., Benson, D. F., & Stuss, D. T. (1989). Frontal lobes and language. *Brain & Language, 37,* 656–691.

Alexander, M. P., Hiltbrunner, B., & Fischer, R. S. (1989). Distributed anatomy of transcortical sensory aphasia. *Archives of Neurology, 46,* 885–892.

Benson, D. F., Sheremata, W. A., Bouchard, R., Segarra, J. M., Price, D., & Geschwind, N. (1973). Conduction aphasia: A clinicopathological study. *Archives of Neurology, 28,* 339–346.

Binder, J. R., Frost, J. A., Hammeke, T. A., Cox, R. W., Rao, S. M., & Prieto, T. (1997). Human brain language areas identified by functional MRI. *Journal of Neuroscience, 17,* 353–362.

Binder, J. R., Frost, J. A., Hammeke, T. A., Rao, S. M., & Cox, R. W. (1996). Function of the left planum temporale in auditory and linguistic processing. *Brain, 119,* 1239–1247.

Bogen, J. E., & Bogen, G. M. (1976). Wernicke's region—where is it? *Annals of the New York Academy of Sciences, 290,* 834–843.

Broca, P. (1861). Remarques sur le siège de la faculté du langage articulé; suivies d'une observation d'aphemie. *Bulletin de la Société Anatomique de Paris 6,* 330–357.

Damasio, H. (1989). Neuroimaging contributions to the understanding of aphasia. In F. Boller & J. Grafman (Eds.), *Handbook of neuropsychology* (pp. 3–46). Amsterdam: Elsevier.

Damasio, H., & Damasio, A. R. (1980). The anatomical basis of conduction aphasia. *Brain, 103,* 337–350.

Damasio, H., Grabowski, T. J., Tranel, D., Hichwa, R. D., & Damasio, A. R. (1996). A neural basis for lexical retrieval. *Nature, 380,* 499–505.

Démonet, J.-F., Chollet, F., Ramsay, S., Cardebat, D., Nespoulous, J.-L., Wise, R., Rascol, A., & Frackowiak, R. (1992). The anatomy of phonological and semantic processing in normal subjects. *Brain, 115,* 1753–1768.

Galaburda, A., & Sanides, F. (1980). Cytoarchitectonic organization of the human auditory cortex. *Journal of Comparative Neurology, 190,* 597–610.

Geschwind, N. (1971). Aphasia. *New England Journal of Medicine, 284,* 654–656.

Henschen, S. E. (1920–1922). *Klinische und anatomische Beitrage zur Pathologie des Gehirns.* Stockholm: Nordiska Bokhandeln.

Kleist, K. (1962). *Sensory aphasia and amusia.* London: Pergamon.

Kohn, S. E. (Ed.). (1992). *Conduction aphasia.* Hillsdale, NJ: Erlbaum.

Lichtheim, L. (1885). On aphasia. *Brain, 7,* 433–484.

Mohr, J. P. (1976). Broca's area and Broca's aphasia. In H. Whitaker & H. Whitaker (Eds.), *Studies in neurolinguistics* (pp. 201–236). New York: Academic.

Mohr, J. P., Pessin, M. S., Finkelstein, S., Funkenstein, H. H., Duncan, G. W., & Davis, K. R. (1978). Broca aphasia: Pathologic and clinical. *Neurology, 28,* 311–324.

Rapcsak, S. Z., & Rubens, A. B. (1994). Localization of lesions in transcortical aphasia. In A. Kertesz (Ed.), *Localization and neuroimaging in neuropsychology* (pp. 297–329). San Diego: Academic.

Vandenberghe, R., Price, C., Wise, R., Josephs, O., & Frackowiak, R. S. J. (1996). Functional anatomy of a common semantic system for words and pictures. *Nature, 383,* 254–256.

Wernicke, C. (1874). *Der aphasische Symptomenkomplex.* Breslau: Cohn & Weigert.

J. BINDER
Medical College of Wisconsin

BRAIN INJURIES
CONDUCTION APHASIA
SPEECH DISORDERS

WERTHEIMER, MAX (1880–1943)

Max Wertheimer's father Wilhelm directed a private business college for many years; his mother was an accomplished amateur violinist. A competent violinist and pianist himself, Wertheimer was educated at a Catholic school in Prague, and then studied at Charles University in Prague, first law and then philosophy and psychology. He was particularly impressed by the teachings of the philosopher-psychologist Christian von Ehrenfels, who in 1890 had published an important paper on form qualities. In 1902, Wertheimer transferred to the University of Berlin, where he studied primarily philosophy and psychology with a number of notable members of the faculty, especially Carl Stumpf. In 1904, he moved to the University of Würzburg, where he completed the PhD degree in psychology the same year, under Oswald Külpe, with a dissertation on the use of the word-association method for the detection of criminal guilt.

During the next six years, Wertheimer worked at psychological and physiological institutes and clinics in Vienna, Berlin, Würzburg, and Prague, doing further experiments on the word-association technique and applying the methods of experimental psychology to clinical studies of aphasia. In the summer of 1910, while on the train to a vacation destination, he had an insight about the perception of apparent motion, disembarked at Frankfurt, bought a toy stroboscope, and began perceptual experiments in his hotel room. He soon moved his work to Friedrich Schumann's psychological institute at the Frankfurt Academy (later the University of Frankfurt), where Wolfgang Köhler and Kurt Koffka, who served as his subjects in these experiments, joined him in elaborating the principles of what was to become the influential school of Gestalt psychology. All three saw the experiments on the "phi phenomenon" (perception of a particular form of motion in stimuli that are actually stationary) as refuting the then-prevalent theories of this kind of perception; the studies, published in the *Zeitshrift für Psychologie* in 1912, are generally considered to have launched the Gestalt School.

Wertheimer stayed at Frankfurt for some years, worked as a civilian during World War I on a military device for detecting the direction from which a sound is coming, and moved to the University of Berlin in 1922. In 1929, he accepted the chair in psychology at the University of Frankfurt, and early in 1933, wary of the growing Hitler menace, emigrated to Czechoslovakia and then to the United States. He taught at the New School for Social Research in New York from the fall of 1933 until his death in the fall of 1943.

Ehrenfels's form-quality doctrine had challenged the prevailing theories of perception. A whole percept is not just the sum total of its constituent elementary sensations, Ehrenfels argued, but this sum total plus one more element: the form quality (a square, for example, is four equal straight lines plus four right angles, *plus squareness*); the whole is not equal to, but more than, the sum of its parts. Wertheimer's Gestalt theory went much further than Ehrenfels's doctrine. He suggested that the whole is quite *different* from the sum of its parts—not just more, but *prior to* the parts. Most wholes are integrated systems, the subparts of which stand in complex relationships to each other; the parts are what they are *because* of their place, role, and function in the whole of which they are parts. In a genuine systemic whole (a Gestalt), change of one part can cause a major change in the whole and in many other parts.

This radical approach became a major school of psychology during the first half of the 20th century, with Wertheimer, Köhler, and Koffka as its chief proponents. Many Gestalt ideas reappeared during the 1970s and 1980s, in the modern areas of information processing, problem solving, artificial intelligence, and other aspects of cognitive psychology. The approach also stayed viable in the psychology of personality and in social psychology.

Wertheimer's publications were sparse, but they were highly influential. Aside from the 1912 paper on the phenomenon, among the most significant were a fundamental contribution in 1923 that provided a Gestalt analysis of the principles of organization in perception; several papers in the 1930s and 1940s that applied a Gestalt approach to the analysis of the nature of freedom, democracy, and truth; and a posthumous book, *Productive Thinking*. The book's Gestalt analyses of problem solving and of scientific thinking (including how Albert Einstein formulated the theory of relativity) continue to challenge contemporary cognitive psychologists.

M. WERTHEIMER
University of Colorado at Boulder

WERTHEIMER, MICHAEL (1927–   )

A general-experimental psychologist and historian of psychology, Wertheimer authored, co-authored, edited, and co-edited numerous articles and books, and served on various regional and national boards, committees, and other groups. He was born March 20, 1927, in Karlshorst (a district in Berlin, Germany); his family and he moved to Frankfurt in 1929 when his father, Gestalt psychologist Max Wertheimer, accepted the chair in psychology at the University of Frankfurt. The family moved to Czechoslovakia early in 1933 to escape the Nazi menace, and then to the United States in September of that year when his father joined the faculty at the New School for Social Research in New York.

The younger Wertheimer attended public schools in New Rochelle, New York, and Fieldston School in the Bronx. Before he completed his senior year in high school his father Max died.

Max's colleague, Gestalt psychologist Wolfgang Köhler, who was teaching at Swarthmore College got him admitted to Swarthmore. Michael switched majors at Swarthmore from French literature to linguistics, then to philosophy, and finally to psychology. He was elected to Phi Beta Kappa, the national scholarly honor society, and graduated from Swarthmore in 1947 with high honors in psychology. He next attended The Johns Hopkins University, where he was elected to Sigma Xi, the scientific research society, and obtained an MA with Wendell R. Garner in experimental psychology. Thereafter he went to Harvard University, working with, among others, J. G. Beebe-Center, Edwin G. Boring, B. F. Skinner, and S. S. Stevens. He earned his PhD in experimental psychology from Harvard in January, 1952, with a dissertation on psychophysics and psychoacoustics. He interned in clinical psychology with the U.S. Public Health Service at Worcester (MA) State Hospital from 1951 to 1952.

Wertheimer was an instructor of psychology at Wesleyan University in Middletown, Connecticut, from 1952 to 1954, when he was promoted to assistant professor. In 1955 he became assistant professor of psychology at the University of Colorado at Boulder; he was promoted to associate professor in 1957, and became full professor in 1961. Aside from positions as principal research scientist in psychology at Rockland (NY) State Hospital, visiting professor at the University of Hawaii, and Acting Administrative Officer for Educational Affairs of the American Psychological Association (APA) in Washington, D.C. he remained at the University of Colorado, and became professor emeritus there in 1993. At Colorado, he directed doctoral programs in experimental and in sociocultural psychology, was director of the undergraduate psychology honors program for nearly four decades, was president of Alpha of Colorado of Phi Beta Kappa, and served on numerous committees.

A fellow of APA and of the American Psychological Society, Wertheimer served on and chaired many boards and committees of APA (including the Education and Training Board, the Committee on Undergraduate Education, the Committee on Pre-College Psychology, the Publication and Communication Board, the Committee on International Relations in Psychology, and the Membership Committee), and served numerous terms as a member of APA's Council of Representatives. He has been president of four divisions of APA: general psychology (Division 1), teaching of psychology (Division 2), theoretical and philosophical psychology (Division 24, twice), and history of psychology (Division 26). He also was president of the Rocky Mountain Psychological Association (RMPA) and of Psi Chi, the national honor society in psychology. For two decades he was a member, and several times chair, of the Examination Committee of the American Association of State Psychology Boards (now the Association of State and Provincial Psychology Boards), the committee that oversees the Examination for the Professional Practice of Psychology that is used by most U.S. states and Canadian provinces as part of the procedure for access to certification or licensure for the practice of psychology.

Among Wertheimer's honors were an APA award for career contributions to education and training in psychology; an American Psychological Foundation award for distinguished teaching in psychology; distinguished service awards from the University of Colorado, APA's Division 1 (general psychology) and Division 24 (theoretical and philosophical psychology), and from RMPA; and a gender/neutral language award from the University of Colorado's Campus Women's Organization. A frequently invited speaker at regional and national conventions, he has also given numerous colloquia at institutions throughout the United States and abroad (including Canada, Switzerland, Sweden, Austria, Japan, Thailand, and Germany). A member of the editorial boards of technical journals (*Contemporary Psychology, Gestalt Theory, Zeitschrift für Psychologie, Computers in Human Behavior, Philosophical Psychology,* and *Professional Psychology: Research and Practice*), he has also been a consultant to the Long Lane School for Girls in Middletown, Connecticut, several Veterans Administration hospitals, The Martin Company, and Illinois State University. He has served on advisory boards for the Archives of the History of American Psychology, for WGBH/Annenberg, for obituaries in the *American Psychologist,* and for a revision of the Bender-Gestalt Test.

Wertheimer's earliest research was in sensory and perceptual psychology, but his professional publications soon broadened to include projective testing, cognition, individual differences, psycholinguistics, person perception, philosophical psychology, and history of psychology. He has published more than two hundred journal articles, book chapters, and book reviews, dozens of dictionary and encyclopedia entries, and more than two dozen books, several of which were translated into foreign languages. Among his books are *Readings in Perception* (1958, with D. C. Beardslee, Van Nostrand); an enlarged edition of his father's posthumous *Productive Thinking* (1959, Harper and Row; Italian translation, 1965; 1978, Greenwood Press; 1982, University of Chicago Press); *Contemporary Approaches to Creative Thinking* (1962, with H. E. Gruber and G. Terrell, Atherton); *Introduction to Psychological Research* (1962, with W. A. Scott, Wiley; Spanish translation, 1981); *A Psycholinguistic Experiment in Foreign-Language Teaching* (1964, with G. A. C. Scherer, McGraw-Hill); *Confrontation: Psychology and the Problems of Today* (1970, Scott, Foresman); *A Brief History of Psychology* (1970, Holt, Rinehart, and Winston; Japanese translation, 1971; German translation 1971; Portuguese translation, 1972, 1978; Dutch translation, 1977; revised edition 1979, Holt, Rinehart, and Winston; Italian translation, 1983; third edition, 1987, Holt, Rinehart, and Winston; fourth edition, 2000, Harcourt, Brace); *Psychology: A Brief Introduction* (1971, with M. Björkman, I. Lundberg, and D. Magnusson, Scott, Foresman); *Fundamental Issues in Psychology* (1972, Holt, Rinehart, and Winston); *Psychology: An Introduction* (1973, 1977, 1979, with P. Mussen et al., Heath); *Teaching Psychology in Secondary Schools* (1974, with R. A. Kasschau, APA); *Concepts in Psychology* (1974, with P. Mussen et al., Heath); *Introduction to Psychology* (1975, Harper's College Press; 1977, PaperBook Press of Harper and Row; 1978, with W. H. Holtzman et al., Harper and Row); *Psychology and the Problems of Today* (1978, with L. Rappoport, Scott, Foresman); *History of Psychology: A Guide to Information Sources* (1979, with W. Viney and M. L. Wertheimer, Gale Research Co.); *Psychology Teacher's Resource Book: First Course* (1979, with M. Johnson, APA); *Advances in Historiography of Psychology* (1983, with G. Eckardt et al., VEB Deutscher Verlag der Wissenschaften);

History of Psychology in the Rocky Mountain Region (1988, with
N. R. Bartlett and B. Spilka, special issue of *Journal of the History
of the Behavioral Sciences*); *No Small Part: A History of Regional
Associations in American Psychology* (1991, with J. L. Pate, APA);
Portraits of Pioneers in Psychology (Vol. 1, with G. A. Kimble and
C. White, 1991; Vol. 2, with G. A. Kimble and C. A. Boneau, 1996;
Vol. 3, with G. A. Kimble, 1998; Vol. 4, with G. A. Kimble, in
press; Lawrence Erlbaum Associates and APA); and *An Oral History of Psi Chi* (in press, with S. F. Davis, Psi Chi). Later scholarly
efforts have largely been devoted to dictionary and encyclopedia
entries, to historical projects, and to theoretical and biographical
projects associated with his father and with the Gestalt school of
psychology.

STAFF

WIESEL, TORSTEN

Torsten Wiesel is a native of Sweden, where he received a MD degree
from the Karolinska Institute in 1954. In 1955, he joined the Johns
Hopkins Medical School and in 1958 was named assistant professor
in ophthalmic physiology. In 1959, he joined Harvard Medical
School and became chair of the department of neurobiology and was
named the Robert Winthrop Professor in 1973. His pioneering studies of the mammalian visual cortex have significantly shaped current
understanding of brain structure, function, and development.

Wiesel, along with his longtime collaborator, D. Hubel, received
the 1981 Nobel Prize in Medicine and Physiology. In 1983, he joined
the Rockefeller University as head of the Laboratory of Neurobiology and was named the Vincent and Brooke Astor Professor. He became the seventh president of the Rockefeller University in 1992
and president emeritus and director of the Shelby White and Leon
Levy Center for Mind, Brain and Behavior in 1998. Wiesel is a
member of the National Academy of Sciences and the Royal Society. He has received numerous awards and prizes as well as honorary
degrees from universities in the United States and Europe.

STAFF

WILCOX, RICHARD E.

Richard E. Wilcox did his undergraduate work at the University of
Chicago and Butler University. He received a BA in psychology,
magna cum laude, from Butler in 1968. He entered graduate school
in learning psychology in September, 1968, at Southern Illinois
University (SIU), served in the U.S. Army from November, 1968,
until September, 1971 (when he received an honorable discharge),
then returned to SIU to study physiological psychology. Wilcox
credits his change in interests from learning psychology to physiological psychology to his time spent caring for burn patients while
in the army. He received an MA in physiological psychology in
1974 and a PhD in psychopharmacology in 1976, both from SIU,
in the area of opioid receptors and motor functions. He served as
an instructor in neuroscience, anatomy, and physiological psychology at SIU until 1977, when, realizing that brain functions were of

greater interest to him than behavior per se, he accepted a postdoctoral position in neuropharmacology at the University of Texas
College of Pharmacy, and there initiated studies of behavioral sen-
sitization due to dopamine agonist (antiparkinson) drugs. He received a National Research Service Award the National Institute
of Neurological, *Communicative* Disorders and Stroke (NINCDS)
in 1978 to pursue studies of the effects of antiparkinson drugs on
dopamine receptors and behavior. In 1979 he joined the faculty of
the Division of Pharmacology and Toxicology, College of Pharmacy, University of Texas (UT) at Austin, as assistant professor.

Supported by funding from the National Institute of Mental
Health (NIMH), NINCDS (now National Institute of Neurological Disorders and Stroke), and National Science Foundation
(NSF), Wilcox's work has focused on the behavioral and brain-
chemistry changes induced in brain dopamine systems by dosing
with dopamine agonist antiparkinson drugs, psychostimulants,
and endurance training regimens (running). Together, these studies have shown that chronic physiological and pharmacological
stimulation of brain dopamine receptors produces adaptations in
dopamine synthesis, metabolism, release, and dopamine receptor
functions. Furthermore, similar adaptations occur in these parameters in response to a single in vivo drug pretreatment. The pattern
that emerges is a dynamic reduction in the sensitivity of presynaptic mechanisms coupled with a modest reduction in postsynaptic
mechanisms, leading to an enhanced postsynaptic and behavioral
response to subsequent agonist challenge—behavioral sensitiza-
tion. These results led to a need to examine receptor adaptations to
dopamine agonists in more detail than was possible using brain
chemistry approaches. Supported by funding from the National
Center for Research Resources, Wilcox's team measured the affinity and relative intrinsic efficacy of partial agonists at recombinant
D1 and D2 dopamine receptors stably expressed in clonal cell lines.
This work utilized intact cell cAMP accumulation assays and detailed analysis of agonist properties via null pharmacological modeling. To help understand the molecular bases for the differences in
efficacy of partial dopamine agonists, Wilcox turned to the computational chemistry procedure of comparative molecular field
analysis (CoMFA). In a series of papers, he and his colleagues
demonstrated that affinity measurements made using recombinant
receptors are superior to those made in native receptors in brain
tissue for such studies. He also demonstrated that direct comparisons of binding at two receptor subtypes (D1 vs. D2 dopamine receptors) are possible using the same training set of compounds, a
differential QSAR (quantitative structure-activity relationship).
That paper also directly compared the small molecule modeling of
CoMFA with protein homology modeling of agonist actions at the
D2 dopamine receptor. Finally, he and his colleagues used the same
training set of compounds to develop drug-receptor models of wild
type versus three serine-to-alanine point mutations of the D2
dopamine receptor. This combined CoMFA plus protein homology modeling approach allowed evaluation of subtle differences
and similarities in binding to the D2 receptor variants.

Most recently, Wilcox has been funded by the Waggoner
Research Foundation to study the role of the DARPP-32/PP-1
(dopamine and cyclic adenosine monophosphate regulated phosphoprotein of 32 kDa/protein phosphatase 1) in alcoholism. These

studies compared the effects of potential dopaminergic anti-craving drugs and ethanol on expression of DARPP-32 versus that of the NR1 subunit of the NMDA glutamate receptor (a key mediator of the actions of ethanol) in the brain. Wilcox attributes any success that he has had in research to a wonderful group of collaborators and a highly talented set of students.

Currently, Wilcox is Doluisio Fellow and Professor of Pharmacology in the College of Pharmacy and head of the Neuropharmacology Research Program of the Institute for Neuroscience at UT. He has an unusually broad background in basic research because of his direct experience in studies of behavior, brain chemistry, and molecular and computational chemistry aspects of drug action. This has resulted in his being called upon to serve as a member of National Institutes of Health (NIH) Study Sections and as a reviewer for the NSF, Veterans Administration, and various private foundations. Similarly, he has served as a member of the editorial advisory board for the *Journal of Neurotransmission* for a number of years. He has published more than six dozen scientific papers and an equal number of abstracts of his research in these areas, plus textbook chapters in several areas of neuroscience. As a winner of three teaching awards in the College of Pharmacy at UT and a member of the Addiction Science Research and Education Center of the College of Pharmacy, Wilcox is a strong believer in the importance of sharing information about research in the addictive diseases and their treatments. He believes just as strongly in the need to learn about those issues of greatest concern to caregivers of addicted individuals from the caregivers themselves. As winner of a counseling award in the College of Pharmacy at UT, Wilcox tries to facilitate the careers of pharmacy students and graduate students in the pharmaceutical and neurosciences on a daily basis. As an active member of his church, Wilcox is involved in lay education in biomedical science for the community, in facilitating the efforts of local 12-step programs, and in developing the outreach of a local free clinic. Wilcox believes that an academic career is one of the few that provides multiple different opportunities for service each day.

STAFF

WITHDRAWAL SYNDROME

A withdrawal reaction is a group of signs and symptoms that occur either when a drug or substance is ceased or when the amount used is reduced. The signs and symptoms last for a limited time. Withdrawal symptoms are most often associated with substance abuse, but have also been noted with some agents used for therapeutic purposes. The nature of the signs and symptoms depends on the specific substance being used, while the frequency of use and the length of time the substance has been used may also influence the severity of the symptoms. For the most part, withdrawal symptoms are distressing and cause significant impairment of social and occupational functioning. In general, the onset and duration of withdrawal symptoms is short and intense in substances with a short duration of action, and prolonged and mild in substances with a long duration of action.

Inevitably, in a consideration of withdrawal phenomena, the issues of drug abuse, addiction, and dependence are raised. Drug abuse is a pejorative term and refers to the use of a drug in a manner not socially approved. In some societies the use of certain drugs is condoned, whereas the same agents in another society may not be approved or is prohibited by law. Drug dependence refers to the continued use of a drug for its pleasurable effects despite adverse consequences, be they medical or social; the dependent person needs to continue drug use for his or her own well-being. Often the drug dosage must be increased to maintain the desired effect (the phenomenon of tolerance). Frequently, the greater part of an individual's life is consumed with securing a supply of the drug. The term "drug addiction," while often used in lay discussions, has ceased to be meaningful in a medical context. It suggests an individual severely dependent on a drug of abuse.

Epidemiological surveys consistently show that alcohol abuse and dependence significantly exceed the abuse and dependence of all other substances combined. Alcohol withdrawal syndrome is associated with cessation of or a decrease in alcohol consumption in a person who is alcohol dependent. A withdrawal syndrome usually occurs after several days of heavy use, and most of the symptoms observed are due to hyper-irritability of the central nervous system. The onset of symptoms occurs within a few hours of the cessation of alcohol. A mild tremor is noted together with other symptoms such as nausea, vomiting, feeling unwell, tachycardia, hypertension, sweating, anxiety, depressed mood, irritability, restlessness, hallucinations, headache, and insomnia. These symptoms are usually self-limiting in otherwise healthy subjects. A serious complication of delirium or delirium tremens (DTs) occurs in a small percentage of patients withdrawing from alcohol—left untreated, the DTs can be life threatening due to hypothermia, infection, or cardiovascular collapse. Benzodiazepines are often used in the management of alcohol withdrawal syndrome.

Perhaps the best known withdrawal syndrome occurs following the cessation of opioid (heroin, morphine) use. The first onset of withdrawal symptoms is typically seen 6 to 8 hours after the cessation of heroin or morphine and 1 to 3 days after the longer-acting opiate methadone. The signs of withdrawal include piloerection, dilation of the pupils, tremor, elevated vital signs, and flu-like symptoms (muscle aches, general malaise, nausea). Peak withdrawal symptoms occur 2 to 3 days after stopping heroin or morphine and for these short-acting opioids are more severe than for the longer-acting methadone. For otherwise healthy individuals, opioid withdrawal is not usually life threatening but can be uncomfortable.

Cocaine, amphetamines (including ecstasy), hallucinogens (such as lysergic acid diethylamine or LSD), phencyclidine, cannabis, caffeine, and tobacco are all associated with a withdrawal syndrome on cessation of use. The withdrawal of these drugs is associated with either relatively mild symptoms (cannabis, cocaine, amphetamines, caffeine, tobacco smoking) or none at all (hallucinogens). On the other hand, phencyclidine and ketamine may be associated with long-term behavioral changes following withdrawal. The nature of the withdrawal symptoms is related to the effects that the drugs produce when ingested. Cocaine and amphetamines alleviate fatigue and cause anorexia and elevated mood. When these drugs are withdrawn, there is a resultant feeling of fatigue, hyperphagia (increased appetite), and depressed mood.

In the past 10 years the use of therapeutic agents has been associated with the appearance of withdrawal symptoms on cessation of treatment. In particular, drugs used in the treatment of psychiatric disorders are more likely to be implicated. For these classes of drug it is often difficult to distinguish between the emergence of a withdrawal syndrome and a relapse of the psychiatric condition for which the drugs were first prescribed. Barbiturates, benzodiazepines, and other sedative-hypnotic agents (e.g., meprobamate, glutethemide, methaqualone) have marked similarities in their withdrawal syndromes. Increased REM (rapid eye movement) sleep, insomnia, and anxiety are the mildest symptoms observed. In more severe forms additional symptoms of tremor, weakness, and epileptic seizures are present. The severity of the symptoms has been found to depend on the doses of the drug used as well as on the length of time patients used the drug. Higher doses and long treatment periods generally produce more severe symptoms. As with the opioids, the duration of action of the drug also influences the severity of the withdrawal syndrome and the length of time symptoms last after cessation of treatment.

Discontinuation symptoms have been noted after cessation or dose reduction of antidepressant drugs. The distinction is made between a discontinuation and a withdrawal syndrome in that the latter implies the development of tolerance and dependence. Antidepressant discontinuation syndrome is characterized by flu-like symptoms, agitation, nervousness, anxiety, muscle tension, sleep disturbance, and dizziness. Other symptoms may also be present, depending on the particular agent involved. Symptoms usually appear 1 to 3 days after cessation of treatment or lowering the dose and generally resolve within 2 weeks. For most patients symptoms are mild to moderate, and rarely are they severe.

The mechanism by which dependence on a drug occurs is thought to be related to changes in one or more sites in the brain (receptors) on which the drug acts. For example, sedative-hypnotic drugs act on γ-amino-butyric acid (GABA) receptors to facilitate transmission through these sites. Chronic exposure to the drug may be hypothesized to desensitize the receptors. In the absence of the drug, withdrawal symptoms would be postulated to result in a rebound hypersensitivity of receptor function. For different drugs the various symptoms observed during withdrawal may be related to hypersensitivity of one or more central (and peripheral) receptors on which the drug had previously acted.

SUGGESTED READING

Jaffe, J. H. (1985). Drug addiction and drug abuse. In A. G. Gilman, L. S. Goodman, T. W. Rall, & F. Murad (Eds.), *Goodman and Gilman's The pharmacological basis of therapeutics* (7th ed., pp. 532–581). New York: Macmillan.

Kaplan, H. I., Sadock, B. J,. & Grebb, J. A. (1991). *Synopsis of psychiatry* (7th ed.). Baltimore: William & Wilkins.

Leonard, B E. (1992). *Fundamentals of Psychopharmacology.* Chichester: Wiley.

G. D. BURROWS
T. R. NORMAN
University of Melbourne, Australia

PHYSICAL DEPENDENCE
TOLERANCE

WITKIN, HERMAN A. (1916–1979)

Best known for his extensive studies of field dependence-independence, Herman A. Witkin contributed greatly to the conceptualization of the relation between cognitive styles and personality. He was educated in New York City, and received the PhD degree from New York University in 1939. He taught at Brooklyn College from 1940 to 1952, and was a professor in the Department of Psychiatry, Downstate Medical Center, State University of New York, from 1952 to 1971, after which he moved to the Educational Testing Service. At the time of his death, he was a distinguished research scientist at Educational Test Service. His many honors included an honorary doctor of social sciences degree from Tillburg University, presented in 1977 by Queen Juliana of the Netherlands.

Witkin's widely known research on cognitive styles started with his studies in the 1940s of individual differences in the perception of the upright in space. When visual and bodily cues are contradictory, and one has to judge whether an object is upright, some people are more determined by the visual cues (field-dependent people) while others depend more on bodily cues (field-independent people). Pursuing the meaning of such differences was the focus of Witkin's research. In time, he discovered that these differences in perception and cognition were expressions of pervasive aspects of human functioning in the domains of emotion, personality, and neuropsychological processes. People move, in general, from field dependence toward field independence as they mature. However, those who become most field independent are those raised in ways that foster personal autonomy and a secure sense of self. Witkin's research—involving a wide range of empirical and experimental approaches unified within a common theoretical framework—led him and his colleagues into an extraordinary variety of studies, including research on dreaming, cultural differences in socialization, intellectual processes, psychopathology, interpersonal relations (between teachers and students, therapists and patients, and parents and children), brain laterality, and chromosomal aberrations.

Witkin published many research papers and books, including *Personality Through Perception, Psychological Differentiation, Cognitive Styles in Personal and Cultural Adaptation,* and *Cognitive Styles: Essence and Origins.*

S. J. KORCHIN

WITMER, LIGHTNER (1861–1956)

In 1896 Lightner Witmer established the first psychological clinic at the University of Pennsylvania. This event is universally recognized as marking the beginning of the science and profession of clinical psychology—although not yet by that name. In 1907, Witmer founded the journal *The Psychological Clinic,* and in the first issue he called for the establishment of a new helping profession, to be called clinical psychology.

Witmer received the BA from the University of Pennsylvania in 1888, and after teaching briefly at the Rugby Academy in Philadelphia, he enrolled for graduate work at Pennsylvania, where he became an assistant to James McKeen Cattell, the new professor of psychology. In 1891, Cattell moved to Columbia and Witmer left for Leipzig to study with Wilhelm Wundt. After earning the PhD, Witmer returned to head the psychology laboratory at Pennsylvania. For the first few years he immersed himself in experimental research but showed increasing interest in applied work with children, leading to his founding of the clinic. Under Witmer's leadership, the Psychological Clinic grew rapidly and was the model for other early clinics. In conjunction with the University of Pennsylvania's psychology department, which Witmer also headed for many years, it became a major training center for clinical psychologists. In his clinical work, Witmer emphasized direct remedial work and decried overemphasis on tests. Witmer retired in 1937 and died in 1956, after having seen the field he pioneered become a major profession.

P. W. McReynolds
University of Nevada at Reno

WOLMAN, BENJAMIN B. (1908–   )

Originator of the "interactional approach" to psychotherapy, Benjamin B. Wolman received the PhD degree from the University of Warsaw. As clinical professor in psychoanalysis and psychotherapy, he taught a generation of psychiatrists and psychologists. His 40 years in private practice and authorship of over 200 scientific papers and 18 books in psychology and related fields gave birth to the 12-volume *International Encyclopedia of Psychiatry, Psychology, Psychoanalysis, and Neurology.* Many of his publications have been translated into over nine languages. Recipient of the Dartmouth Medal of the American Library Association and the Distinguished Contribution Award of the American Psychological Association, Wolman's experience culminated in the modification of the classic Freudian psychoanalytic technique.

Wolman's interactional psychotherapy "is based on the awareness that all people have problems and experience emotional difficulties. . . . All living organisms have a beginning and end of their life and . . . the only thing which is left between human thinking, dreaming and decision-making is what one can do as long as one is alive" (*Principles of Interactional Psychotherapy*).

As president of the International Organization for the Study of Group Tensions, Wolman organized and chaired the International Scientific Conference on Terror and Terrorism, which brought together governments from all around the world. His varied interests are shown by such diverse works as *Children's Fears; Victims of Success; Call No Man Normal; Psychoanalysis and Catholicism;* and *Handbook of Parapsychology.*

Staff

WOLPE, JOSEPH (1915–1997)

Joseph Wolpe received his medical qualifying degree from the University of Witwatersrand, South Africa, in 1939. After medical and surgical internships, he entered private practice until 1942, when he volunteered for the South African Medical Corps, serving until 1946. Thereafter, he went into psychiatric training and research.

The centerpoint of his research was experimental studies on the production and cure of neuroses in animals that showed these neuroses to be produced by learning and to be reversible by learning. Techniques for treating human neuroses were derived from these findings, and were reported in detail in his book *Psychotherapy by Reciprocal Inhibition,* written during a fellowship at the Center for Advanced Study in Behavioral Sciences at Stanford, CA. Wolpe wrote about 150 papers and three other books, *The Practice of Behavior Therapy; Theme and Variations: A Behavior Therapy Casebook;* and *Our Useless Fears.* He also edited *The Conditioning Therapies,* in collaboration with Andrew Salter and L. J. Reyna, and *Behavior Therapy for Psychiatrists,* in collaboration with Reyna.

Wolpe was professor of psychiatry at the University of Virginia School of Medicine from 1960 to 1965. After 1965, he was professor of psychiatry and director of the Behavior Therapy Unit at Temple University Medical School and a senior research psychiatrist at Eastern Pennsylvania Psychiatric Institute in Philadelphia. In 1979, he received the American Psychological Association's Distinguished Scientific Award for the Applications of Psychology.

Staff

WOMEN, PSYCHOLOGY OF

The psychology of women has emerged as an interdisciplinary effort to understand the behavior of women. The various subdisciplines of psychology have explored the developmental paths that women follow and investigated the inner dynamics of their lives. Biology has provided the physiological underpinnings for understanding some of women's behavior. History, anthropology, and sociology have highlighted the contexts that have shaped women's lives and demonstrated the cultural origins of much of their behavior. Finally, from philosophy has come an understanding of the conceptual frameworks through which the behavior of women has been interpreted.

HISTORY

The "problem" of understanding women has beset men for centuries. Philosophers, clergy, historians, biologists, and more recently psychologists, have expressed opinions on the nature of womankind. Regardless of individual orientation, individuals from a given period of time have generally spoken with one mind, reflecting a cultural attitude of their era. Until recently, however, the opinions did not vary greatly. The general point of view was that women were both inferior and superior to men, that they were lacking in worldly capabilities but excelled in the spiritual spheres.

With the emergence of the psychology of women as an area of

formal investigation in the late 19th century, research attempted to document this point of view with scientific fact. Each new argument enjoyed a moment of popularity before being superseded. First women were considered inferior to men, primarily in mental capabilities, because their brains were smaller (Bain, 1875). When this argument was demolished, scientists turned to specific areas of the brain, and argued that men's frontal lobes—and later parietal lobes—gave them an advantage (Patrick, 1895). As this argument became increasingly suspect, the argument of greater male variability was advanced—that men were both better and worse than women, but overall less mediocre (Ellis, 1894; Cattell, 1903). Finally, in the early 1900s, arguments focused on the "maternal instinct," that women were naturally preoccupied with pregnancy and lactation and had little energy for the development of other capabilities (Spencer, 1891; Thorndike, 1914).

As each of these arguments moved in and out of vogue, few questioned the general assumption that in terms of worldly accomplishment, women were inferior to men. The prevalent attitude was challenged, however, by a small minority of some men and a few women scientists. The dissenting view stated that science was being used "in the cause of supporting a prejudice" (Wooley, 1910), and that scientists were not drawing their conclusions from a clear demonstration of fact. It might as clearly be shown, said the opposition, that such differences as exist between men and women are due to cultural and social experiences as to biology, and are, therefore, a result of male and female experience and not the cause of such experience.

The dissenters in the early 1900s laid the foundation for much of the work on the psychology of women since the 1960s. First, they stated that behavior is not inevitably tied to biology, but is in part a result of the cultural context. Second, they questioned to what degree actual differences in behavior existed between men and women. Third, they laid the foundation for the social activism that is often closely allied with research in the psychology of women, by emphasizing cultural rather than biological causes of behavior.

(If research shows that current conditions produce behavior regarded as "inferior" or unhealthy, then one is compelled to do something to modify those conditions.)

The scientific interest in the behavior of women apparent in the beginning of the century largely disappeared in the following decades. With the advent of behaviorism, arguments that relied on such intangibles as "the maternal instinct" were ignored. Scientific psychologists occupied themselves with observable behavior—and generally ignored sex differences. Results from their research efforts were reported using the generic "he," which was often used in a less generic sense than was proclaimed.

THE PSYCHOANALYTIC INFLUENCE
Popular interest in the psychology of women continued, however. Psychoanalysts drew conclusions about human behavior from their experience with individuals in clinical settings. The psychoanalytic viewpoint strongly influenced popular conceptions of women and has sometimes been credited with originating the psychology of women. It is still one of the dominant viewpoints in the field.

Sigmund Freud's views on feminine psychology have had a powerful impact on modern knowledge of women. Although Freud disclaimed much knowledge of women, he proclaimed that woman was an inferior man. In a 1933 paper (p. 135), he commented that although a "man of about thirty strikes us as a youthful, somewhat unformed individual whom we expect to make powerful use of the possibilities for development, a woman of the same age frightens us by her physical rigidity and unchangeability. . . . There are no paths open to further development; it is as though the whole process had already run its course and remains thenceforward insusceptible to influence—as though, indeed, the difficult development to femininity had exhausted the possibilities of the person concerned. . . ."

Freud's views were strongly opposed by prominent women active in the behavioral and social sciences of the time. The theme elaborated by these women was similar to that from an earlier time: Many of the differences (and inferiorities) were caused by cultural influences and not biological influences and were thus subject to change. One cannot attribute to universal and biological causes what is specific and cultural in origin.

Karen Horney, a neopsychoanalyst, in her own theoretical formulations strongly suggested that many of Freud's views on human beings in general, and women in particular, arose because he drew universalistic conclusions from specific cases. Further, putting forth such conclusions actually tended to justify and increase the behaviors being described. The beliefs, or ideologies, about women thus served several purposes. Horney (1935) wrote: "It is fairly obvious that these ideologies function not only to reconcile women to their subordinate role by presenting it as an unalterable one, but also to plant the belief that it represents a fulfillment they crave, or an ideal for which it is commendable and desirable to strive."

Horney's argument was strengthened by the cross-cultural work of Margaret Mead, published in the same year, which reported no particular behavioral differences between men and women in some other cultures—or reported differences that were the opposite of those in Western society. If male and female behaviors varied from culture to culture, it was easily concluded that male/female differences were unlikely to be either biological in origin or universal: "Many, if not all, of the personality traits which we have called masculine or feminine are as lightly linked to sex as are the clothing, the manners, and the form of headdress that a society at a given period assigns to either sex . . . the evidence is overwhelmingly in favor of the strength of social conditioning" (Mead, 1935/1969, p. 260).

In general, however, the voices of Horney, Mead, and others of their persuasion did not change the popular views toward women. Throughout the decades from the 1920s to the 1960s, scientific psychology continued to ignore the "woman issue" and the general public continued to accept the Freudian and psychoanalytic viewpoint on the nature of women. Women were accepted as inferior to men in worldly and intellectual ways and superior to them in moral and nurturing spheres.

RECENT RESEARCH ON WOMEN
The 1960s, however, saw an increase in empirical studies related to the psychology of women. The new research was spurred on, in

part, by the emergence of the Women's Movement, which challenged psychoanalytic views. Psychologists (and those of other disciplines) set out to determine: (a) what sex differences actually existed; (b) the causes of any such differences; and (c) the key issues in women's lives and how these developed over time.

Research conclusions supported the earlier views of Horney and Mead. Women are not as different from men as had been supposed. Any differences may be explained as easily by cultural as by biological causes. Finally, themes of individual achievement and interpersonal relationships are both important in women's lives and have a different relationship to each other depending on the individual, the time of life, and the historical setting.

SEX DIFFERENCES

Recent research has laid to rest a number of myths about male/female differences and taken a new look at existing differences. Research has found, for example, no support for the contentions that women are biologically weaker or less intelligent than men. There is also no evidence that women are more passive and dependent than men, or that they have lower achievement drives. Finally, women are not asexual but have sexual capacities that match or surpass those of men.

However, in each of these areas, certain previously assumed differences have been shown to exist. Women may not be weaker than men and may be more resilient, but on the average they are generally smaller and have less muscle tissue. Women are not less intelligent and, in fact, are more fluent verbally, but on the average they are less able in mathematical and spatial areas than men. Women may not be more passive than men, but they are less aggressive. They are not less achievement oriented, but focus their desires for achievement less often in public accomplishments. Finally, women have sexual capacities that in some ways surpass those of men, but at the same time they are more intent on interpersonal relationships and more attuned to "love and romance" than are men in general (see Forisha, 1978; Maccoby & Jacklin, 1974; Masters & Johnson, 1966, 1970; O'Leary, 1974).

BIOLOGY VERSUS CULTURE

The causes of sex differences are still a matter of controversy. Some social scientists view them as linked to biology; others argue for social and cultural origins. Arguments on either side can be traced back to the debate on the origins of sex differences in the early years of the century. However, the balance has shifted and the cultural argument generally has the upper hand.

Current biological arguments are more sophisticated but not dissimilar to those from the 1890s and early 1900s. John Money (Money & Ehrhardt, 1972) has proposed that different levels of androgen in prenatal hormones may affect the neural patterns in the brain, thus predisposing individuals to "masculine" or "feminine" mental patterns. Another researcher (Waber, 1976) suggested that since girls mature earlier than boys, the earlier maturation may foreclose certain possibilities for cognitive development, which would occur with later maturation. Still other psychologists have proposed that certain cognitive capacities, particularly spatial ability, are inherited on the X-chromosome, and therefore more likely to be found in males than in females (Stafford, 1961). Finally, some psychologists are interested in determining the influence of hormonal cycles on female behavior, although there is little evidence of a direct and consistent relationship between hormones and behavior for the general population (Parlee, 1973).

Cultural arguments rely on the variability of male and female behavior in different settings and suggest that such variability would not occur if behavior were determined by biological differences between men and women. Even biologically, there is enormous variability; differences in hormone levels between men and women, on the average, are not nearly as great as between men and other men, or women and other women. Further, in many cases, cultural influences have been shown to override biology. For example, Money's work has also shown that sex of rearing takes precedence over chromosomal sex when cases of sex reassignment must be made for some young children. Other examples (such as those described by Mead) show that men and women in other cultures do not show the behavioral differences found in our own society. Finally, many psychologists (e.g., Broverman et al., 1970) have pointed to the distress sometimes caused by men and women who adopt appropriate masculine and feminine behavior. These psychologists argue that if the behavior patterns associated with each sex were indeed "natural," then they would not be as dysfunctional as they often appear to be.

The strong cultural arguments emphasizing the variability of human behavior within sexes and across cultures have made inroads into the acceptance of biological determinism of male/female differences. It is not possible, however, clearly to separate what is biological from what is cultural, unless cultural differences can be eliminated entirely, and the remaining variability measured. Since this is not an immediate possibility, many psychologists are willing to admit to both biological and cultural influences on behavior, but most place greater emphasis on the cultural side (Forisha, 1978).

POWER AND LOVE IN WOMEN'S LIVES

Since the time of Freud, psychologists have stated that individual well-being is signaled by the ability to work productively and to engage in meaningful interpersonal relationships. Others have interpreted this as balancing power and love within human lives, or developing the ability to both get things done and to care for others (e.g., Forisha, 1982). A considerable body of literature stresses the importance of both components in the lives of both women and men. Sandra Bem (1974, 1975) has termed this androgyny.

Much of the literature on women, however, has shown that love outweighs power, and that women are often immersed in interpersonal relationships to the exclusion of individual achievement. Studies of modern marriages have shown that women often place such emphasis on their marital relationships that they are inevitably disappointed and suffer emotional and sometimes physical illness (Bernard, 1972; Gove, 1972). Other surveys have demonstrated that women's depression is most often caused by lack of relationship rather than lack of accomplishment in other spheres (Scarf, 1981). In general, the emphasis on relationships in women's lives is attributed to the cultural injunctions (reinforced by psychoanalytic thought) that urge women to give up personal aspirations and to be a source of support for men.

Women who have entered the world of work, however, and demonstrated the capacity for high levels of achievement, have encountered numerous difficulties, some internal and some external. To the extent that women have internalized the injunctions of their culture, they have difficulty justifying their own achievement drives and retreat when the work environment poses obstacles. On the other hand, external obstacles do exist, often because women are viewed as outsiders within the work force, and the perception of others, generally male, is that they do not belong and need not be afforded the same opportunities offered to male colleagues (Forisha, 1981).

The research on women in relationships and at work has been extensive. Many studies have examined the difficulties that women encounter in meeting the high expectations for their behavior in love and overcoming the low expectations for their behavior at work. Researchers have turned to studies of dual career families to examine the combination of interpersonal relationships and career productivity.

Women who are married, have children, and are pursuing careers appear to many to be "doing it all." Research reports have shown, however, that there are costs. For women who have undertaken career and domestic responsibilities, there is less time for friends and leisure activities (Rapaport & Rapaport, 1972). Stresses are associated with times of overload when conflicts between their varied roles become acute. Further, when crises arise, the wife in the two-career family, more often than the husband, compromises her career objectives to meet domestic needs (Rapaport & Rapaport, 1972; Paloma & Garland, 1971; Bryson et al., 1976). Even for women who are striving for a balance between work and relationships, power and love, the traditional patterns still take precedence in times of difficulty.

The ability of women to find a balance between power and love in their lives also depends on the individual, the time of life, and the historical setting. Numerous studies have reported that women who are able to succeed at work and maintain caring relationships have high energy and intelligence and personal resources to cope with unusual demands (see Forisha & Goldman, 1981). Other work has shown that the balance of power and love may shift during the life cycle as women adjust their career goals around times of childbearing and child rearing (Daniels, 1981; Scarf, 1981). Finally, the opportunities for women to achieve at work and care for others at home depend, in part, on the historical era in which they live. The opportunities for women to blend the two spheres has been greater in the past two decades than at any other time in this century (Forisha, 1978).

Strands of research have contributed to a new understanding of the psychology of women based on empirical results rather than speculation and ideology. The psychology of women has established the areas in which women are similar to and different from men and has begun to establish the key turning points in women's lives. The result is a greater knowledge of the effect of biology and culture on women's lives and on those of people in general.

REFERENCES

Bain, A. (1875). *Mental science.* New York: Appleton.

Bem, S. L. (1974). The measurement of psychological androgyny. *Journal of Consulting and Clinical Psychology, 42,* 155–162.

Bem, S. L. (1975). Sex role adaptability: One consequence of psychological androgyny. *Journal of Personality and Social Psychology, 31,* 634–643.

Bernard, J. (1972). *The future of marriage.* New York: Macmillan.

Broverman, I. K., Broverman, D. M., Clarkson, F. E., Rosenkrantz, P., & Voget, S. R. (1970). Sex-role stereotypes and clinical judgments of mental health. *Journal of Consulting Psychology, 34,* 1–7.

Bryson, R. B., Bryson, J. B., Licht, M. H., & Licht, B. G. (1976). The professional pair: Husband and wife psychologists. *American Psychologist, 31,* 10–16.

Cattell, J. McK. (1903). A statistical study of eminent men. *Popular Science Monthly, 62,* 359–377.

Daniels, P. (1981). Dream vs. drift in women's careers. In B. Forisha & B. H. Goldman (Eds.), *Outsiders on the inside.* Englewood Cliffs, NJ: Prentice-Hall.

Ellis, H. (1894). *Man and woman: A study of human secondary sexual characters.* London: Scott.

Forisha, B. (1978). *Sex roles and personal awareness.* Morristown, NJ: General Learning Press.

Forisha, B. (1981). The inside and the outsider. In B. Forisha & B. Goldman (Eds.), *Outsiders on the inside.* Englewood Cliffs, NJ: Prentice-Hall.

Forisha, B. (1982). *Power of love.* Englewood Cliffs, NJ: Prentice-Hall.

Forisha, B., & Goldman, B. (1981). *Outsiders on the inside.* Englewood Cliffs, NJ: Prentice-Hall.

Freud, S. (1933). The psychology of women. In *New introductory lectures on psychoanalysis.* New York: Norton.

Gove, W. R. (1972, September). Relationships between sex roles, marital status, and mental illness. *Social Forces,* 34–44.

Horney, K. (1935). The problem of feminine masochism. *The Psychoanalytic Review, 22,* 241–257.

Maccoby, E. E., & Jacklin, C. N. (1974). *The psychology of sex differences.* Stanford, CA: Stanford University Press.

Masters, W. H., & Johnson, V. E. (1966). *Human sexual response.* Boston: Little, Brown.

Masters, W. H., & Johnson, V. E. (1970). *Human sexual inadequacy.* Boston: Little, Brown.

Mead, M. (1969/1935). *Sex and temperament in three primitive societies.* New York: Dell.

Money, J., & Ehrhardt, A. (1972). *Man and woman, boy and girl: The differentiation and dimorphism of gender identity from conception to maturity.* Baltimore: Johns Hopkins University Press.

O'Leary, V. E. (1974). Some attitudinal barriers to occupational aspirations in women. *Psychological Bulletin, 81,* 809–826.

Parlee, M. B. (1973). The premenstrual syndrome. *Psychological Bulletin, 83,* 454–465.

Patrick, G. T. W. (1895). The psychology of woman. *Popular Science Monthly, 47,* 209–255.

Rapoport, R., & Rapoport, R. N. (1972). The dual career family: A variant pattern and social change. In C. Safilios-Rothschild (Ed.), *Towards a sociology of women.* Lexington, MA: Xerox.

Scarf, M. (1981). *Unfinished business.* Garden City, NY: Doubleday.

Spencer, H. (1891). *The study of sociology.* New York: Appleton.

Stafford, R. E. (1961). Sex differences in spatial visualization as evidence of sex-linked inheritance. *Perceptual and Motor Skills, 13,* 428.

Thorndike, E. L. (1913–1914/1903). *Educational psychology* (3 vols.). New York: Teachers College, Columbia University.

Waber, D. P. (1976). Sex differences in cognition: A function of maturation rate? *Science, 192,* 572–574.

Woolley, H. T. (1910). Psychological literature: A review of the recent literature on the psychology of sex. *Psychological Bulletin, 7,* 335–342.

B. FORISHA-KOVACH
University of Michigan

ACCULTURATION
ANDROGYNY
BIOLOGICAL RHYTHMS
HUMAN DEVELOPMENT
NATURE-NURTURE CONTROVERSY
SEX DIFFERENCES
SEXUAL DEVELOPMENT
SEX ROLES

WOODWORTH, ROBERT SESSIONS (1869–1962)

An American psychologist, Robert Sessions Woodworth received the AB degree from Amherst College, the MA degree from Harvard University, where he studied under William James, and the PhD degree from Columbia University in 1899. Most of his academic career was spent at Columbia. He was well known for his introductory text *Psychology,* first published in 1921, which went through five editions. His *Experimental Psychology,* first published in 1939, was a major handbook of research in that area. It was later revised in collaboration with Harold Schlosberg in 1954. He presented a systematic position in psychology in his book *Dynamic Psychology,* published in 1918 and later revised as the *Dynamics of Behavior* in 1958.

For Woodworth, the subject matter of psychology was both behavior and consciousness. He felt that the behaviorists of the time such as John Watson, who had rejected any idea of consciousness or mind, had left out part of a legitimate aspect of psychology. Consciousness was very much a part of what the psychologist should study and could be done through introspection. His was not a simple S–R (stimulus–response) psychology. Although psychological events had their causes in the stimulus environment, there was something more to be added, and that was the organism, itself. Therefore, the resulting behavior was a function of both the environmental stimuli and what went on inside the body (organism). Thus the paradigm S–O–R and not simply S–R was appropriate. This idea was later developed in a more sophisticated manner into what Tolman and others called the intervening variable.

Two other basic aspects of Woodworth's psychology were *mechanism* and *drive.* Mechanism referred to how a thing was done and drive referred to why it was done. For example, in the functioning of an automobile, the mechanism referred to those parts that made it run. The drive was the power applied. When these concepts were applied to psychology, an organism might behave in certain ways as when a cat, in its trial-and-error-behavior, attempted to escape from a puzzle box. This was mechanism, but for the activity to occur, the cat had to be hungry. The hunger that motivated the cat to action was the drive.

In the course of the behavioral history of an organism, it was possible for the mechanism to take on the function of drive. What started out as mere mechanism might also involve drive or become drive for other activities. Take, for example, a businessman who worked for a living (mechanism) to fulfill many of his bodily needs (drive) as well as those of his family. After he has acquired a considerable estate with all the money possible to fulfill his needs, he still continued to work for the joy of working or to see his bank account increase. In this instance, the mechanism of working had also taken on the function of its own drive.

R. W. LUNDIN
Wheaton, Illinois

WORK EFFICIENCY

Work efficiency is a behavioral and organizational construct that can be expressed at the individual, group, or organizational levels. Generally, efficiency is the use of minimum input to yield maximum output—that is, doing more with less (Lawson & Shen, 1998). At the organizational or group level, efficiency is bound by the concepts of flexibility and adaptability, such that organizational structures are most efficient when they are open systems that can anticipate, respond, and adapt to changing environments (Organ & Bateman, 1986). For individuals, efficiency is tied to the notions of satisfaction, performance, ability, and motivation (Whetton & Cameron, 1998).

There is evidence that organizations, specifically companies, may realize greater success in business processes (i.e., efficiency) when individual and collective responsibilities are interdependent (Majchrzak & Wang, 1996). Integrating individual and organizational efficiency involves the recognition that the source of efficient work or productivity lies at the macro or systemic level of worker motivation (Lawson & Shen, 1998). For example, although individual accountability for results is often a managerial objective, approximately 80 to 90% of defects in a given product or service may be attributed to the manufacturing system or delivery of service, rather than to a given individual (Lawson & Shen, 1998; Whetton & Cameron, 1998). Thus, work efficiency, motivation, and individual and organizational flexibility, traditionally associated with micro- or individual-level management, have been increasingly focused on systems-level management and service delivery. In these scenarios, the customer or client is seen as the initiator of efficient production.

Possibly the most often-used systemic and client-contextual model of workplace motivation and efficiency is Deming's total quality (TQ) or quality improvement (QI) model (Deming, 1982; Lawson & Shen, 1998). Deming's fundamental difference from previous models is his focus on the client or customer as the first component in motivating workers and streamlining organizational systems. The TQ management doctrine lists five fundamental strategies: (a) Focus on systems rather than on individuals; (b) Use databased problem solving; (c) Be in constant contact with the client; (d) Continuously improve processes, products, and services; and (e) All persons must adopt and model TQ principles. In addition, Deming provides 14 points for implementing and sustaining a TQ plan. A partial list of those points is: Create a constancy of purpose for improving a product or service; break down barriers among department or units; institute a vigorous program of education and retraining; and put everybody in the organization to work to accomplish the transformation (to TQ).

Deming's 5 principles and 14 points are carried out through the use of TQ tools, including schematics and data-analysis tools such as flowcharts, bar charts, and scatter plots. Teamwork is integral to TQ policy implementation. Lawson and Shen (1998) discuss three kinds of TQ teams: quality councils, problem-solving teams, and self-managed teams. The general purpose of these teams is to ensure that the TQ process is implemented and sustained.

Finally, Whetton and Cameron (1998) outline a general model for diagnosing work problems and enhancing worker task-performance and efficiency:

$$\text{Performance} = \text{Ability} \times \text{Motivation}$$

where

$$\text{Ability} = \text{Aptitude} \times \text{Traning} \times \text{Resources}$$

and

$$\text{Motivation} = \text{Desire} \times \text{Commitment}$$

In these equations, Whetton and Cameron describe performance as the product of ability times motivation; ability as a function of aptitude, training, and resources; and motivation as a prod-

uct of desire and commitment. They go on to describe specific strategies for improving ability and enhancing motivation, and provide a six-step motivational program that integrates performance and (employee) satisfaction. The steps include: (a) Establish moderately difficult goals that are understood and accepted; (b) Remove personal and organizational obstacles to performance; (c) Use rewards and discipline appropriately to extinguish unacceptable behavior and reward exceptional performance; (d) Provide salient internal and external incentives; (e) Distribute rewards equitably; and (f) Provide timely rewards and honest feedback on performance.

REFERENCES

Deming, W. E. (1982). *Quality, productivity, and competitive position.* Cambridge, MA: MIT Center for Advanced Engineering Study.

Lawson, R. B., & Shen, Z. (1998). *Organizational psychology.* New York: Oxford University Press.

Majchrzak, A. M., & Wang, Q. (1996). Breaking the functional mind-set in process organizations. In D. Ulrich (Ed.), *Delivering results* (pp. 189–200). Cambridge, MA: President and Fellows of Harvard College.

Organ, D. W., & Bateman, T. (1986). *Organizational behavior.* Plano, TX: Business Publications.

Whetton, D. A., & Cameron, K. S. (1998). *Developing management skills* (4th ed.). New York: Addison-Wesley.

R. M. DAVISON-AVILES
Bradley University

INDUSTRIAL PSYCHOLOGY

WORKING MEMORY

Everyday cognitive tasks, such as language comprehension, reasoning, and decision making, often require one to keep relevant information in mind while processing other information. For example, mental arithmetic requires keeping track of the intermediate results from relevant computations and integrating them to reach the correct answer. A system or a set of processes that supports such maintenance of task-relevant information during the performance of a cognitive task is called working memory. As reflected by the fact that it has been labeled "the hub of cognition" (Haberlandt, 1997, p. 212), working memory is a central construct in cognitive psychology and cognitive neuroscience.

The notion of working memory has evolved from an earlier conception of short-term memory. Like working memory, short-term memory is a system for enabling temporary maintenance of information, but its maintenance functions were considered to be for the sake of memorization (i.e., transferring information to long-term memory) and were far removed from other cognitive processes that support thinking. In contrast, the central idea behind working memory is that its maintenance functions are in the service of complex cognition and that they fundamentally support performance of complex cognitive tasks. In other words, the memory part of working memory is not passive and static, but, rather, active and working, as its name indicates.

A MULTICOMPONENT MODEL OF WORKING MEMORY

There are a number of well-developed models and theories of working memory (for an overview, see Miyake & Shah, 1999), but the best known model is the multicomponent model developed by Alan Baddeley (1986). According to this model, working memory is a system that consists of three major subsystems. Two of the subsystems, called the "phonological (or articulatory) loop" and the "visuospatial sketchpad," are specialized slave systems whose primary functions are the temporary maintenance and processing of speech-based phonological information and visual as well as spatial information, respectively. Each subsystem is considered to consist of two separable components: for the phonological loop, a passive phonological store and an active rehearsal process, and for the visuospatial sketchpad, a visual component (visual cache) and a spatial component (inner scribe). The remaining subsystem is called the "central executive," a general-purpose control structure that regulates the operations of the two slave systems and modulates the flow of information within working memory.

The tripartite structure of Baddeley's (1986) model has been supported by various sources of evidence, particularly with respect to the separability of the two slave systems. For example, a secondary task that taps the phonological loop's functions, such as repeating a familiar phrase over and over (called articulatory suppression), impairs the maintenance of phonological information, but not visuospatial information (Baddeley, 1986), whereas a secondary task that taps the visuospatial sketchpad's functions, such as viewing dynamic visual noise (called the irrelevant picture paradigm), impairs the maintenance of visual information, but not verbal information (Quinn & McConnell, 1996). There are also brain-damaged patients who have demonstrated selective impairments in the phonological loop or the visuospatial sketchpad (Gathercole, 1994). More recently, neuroimaging studies have produced evidence suggesting that different neural circuits mediate the maintenance of phonological and visuospatial information (Smith & Jonides, 1999).

Within the framework of this multicomponent model, the main focus of current research is to specify the organization and functions of the central executive, the least understood subsystem of working memory so far. Although it has been criticized as a homunculus or a theoretical ragbag, interest in understanding this crucial component has been rising (Miyake & Shah, 1999). In particular, researchers have begun to specify the subcomponents or subfunctions of the central executive (Baddeley, 1996) as well as the role of the prefrontal cortex in the executive control of behavior (Smith & Jonides, 1999).

MEASUREMENT OF WORKING MEMORY AND ITS ROLE IN COMPLEX COGNITION

The capacity of short-term memory has traditionally been assessed with a simple span task that requires participants to repeat back a list of digits or words in correct sequence. In contrast to such storage-oriented measures, currently used measures of working memory capacity require participants to perform a dual task, namely the simultaneous processing of some information and remembering of to-be-recalled items. The best known measure of this kind is the reading span test (Daneman & Carpenter, 1980), in which participants read sentences aloud while remembering the final word of each sentence for later recall. Performance on this task has been shown to correlate well with complex cognitive tasks such as reading comprehension. According to a recent meta-analysis (Daneman & Merikle, 1996), the average correlation between the reading span score and global comprehension measures like the Nelson-Denny Reading Test was .41, and was significantly higher than the one between traditional span measures and comprehension measures (.28 for word span and .14 for digit span). Following this success, a number of variants have also been developed, including the operation span, the counting span, and the spatial span tests.

These complex span tasks have served as useful research tools to examine the role of working memory in various complex cognitive tasks. Tasks examined in some depth include language comprehension, language learning, spatial thinking, retrieval from memory, and problem solving and reasoning (see Miyake & Shah, 1999, for some illustrative examples of this line of research). Although the extent to which the capacities measured by the complex span tasks are domain-specific or domain-general is under debate, the proposal that working memory capacity may be the key to (or at least a key component of) general intelligence or g (Kyllonen, 1996) further underscores the importance of working memory in complex cognition.

REFERENCES

Baddeley, A. D. (1986). *Working memory.* New York: Oxford University Press.

Baddeley, A. D. (1996). Exploring the central executive. *Quarterly Journal of Experimental Psychology, 49A,* 5–28.

Daneman, M., & Carpenter, P. A. (1980). Individual differences in working memory and reading. *Journal of Verbal Learning and Verbal Behavior, 19,* 450–466.

Daneman, M., & Merikle, P. M. (1996). Working memory and language comprehension: A meta-analysis. *Psychonomic Bulletin & Review, 3,* 422–433.

Gathercole, S. E. (1994). Neuropsychology and working memory: A review. *Neuropsychology, 8,* 494–505.

Haberlandt, K. (1997). *Cognitive psychology* (2nd ed.). Boston: Allyn & Bacon.

Kyllonen, P. C. (1996). Is working memory capacity Spearman's g? In I. Dennis & P. Tapsfield (Eds.), *Human abilities: Their nature and measurement* (pp. 45–75). Mahwah, NJ: Erlbaum.

Miyake, A., & Shah, P. (Eds.). (1999). *Models of working memory: Mechanisms of active maintenance and executive control.* New York: Cambridge University Press.

Quinn, J. G., & McConnell, J. (1996). Irrelevant pictures in visual working memory. *Quarterly Journal of Experimental Psychology, 49A,* 200–215.

Smith, E. E., & Jonides, J. (1999). Storage and executive processes in the frontal lobes. *Science, 283,* 165–166.

SUGGESTED READINGS

Carpenter, P. A., Miyake, A., & Just, M. A. (1994). Working memory constraints in comprehension: Evidence from individual differences, aphasia, and aging. In M. A. Gernsbacher (Ed.), *Handbook of psycholinguistics* (pp. 1075–1122). San Diego: Academic Press.

Gathercole, S. E., & Baddeley, A. D. (1993). *Working memory and language.* Hove, UK: Erlbaum.

Logie, R. H. (1995). *Visuo-spatial working memory.* Hove, UK: Erlbaum.

Logie, R. H., & Gilhooly, K. J. (Eds.). (1998). *Working memory and thinking.* Hove, UK: Psychology Press.

Miyake, A., & Shah, P. (Eds.). (1999). *Models of working memory: Mechanisms of active maintenance and executive control.* New York: Cambridge University Press.

Richardson, J. T. E., Engle, R. W., Hasher, L., Logie, R. H., Stoltz-fus, E. R., & Zacks, R. T. (1996). (Eds.). *Working memory and human cognition.* New York: Oxford University Press.

Smith, E. E., & Jonides, J. (1997). Working memory: A view from neuroimaging. *Cognitive Psychology, 33,* 5–42.

A. MIYAKE
University of Colorado, Boulder

MEMORY
MNEMONICS
SHORT-TERM MEMORY

WUNDT, WILHELM (1832–1920)

Wilhelm Wundt studied medicine at the University of Tubingen and at Heidelberg, then changed his major to physiology and earned his doctorate from Heidelberg in 1855. He remained there, teaching until 1874, and formulating his ideas about psychology. His books of 1858 and 1862, *Contributions to the Theory of Sensory Perception,* formalized these ideas. He was appointed professor of philosophy in 1875 at Leipzig, where he worked for the next 45 years. Edward B. Titchener was Wundt's student and the proponent of his structural psychology in the United States.

Wundt created and developed the first school of psychological thought, *structuralism,* whose basic building block was sensation. He established a laboratory for experimental research and a journal called *Philosophical Studies,* and he wrote what has been claimed to be the most important book in the history of psychology, *Principles of Physiological Psychology.* His students were carefully instructed in his methodology of introspection or self-observation. Although structuralism is no longer a school of thought in contemporary psychology, Wundt's systematic efforts established psychology as a new and recognized science in Germany in the 19th century.

Using the method of introspection, students and researchers investigated the subject matter of immediate experience through exacting attention to sensations and feelings. The goals of structuralism were to analyze conscious processes into basic elements, to discover how these elements are connected, and to establish the laws of these connections. The elements of immediate experience included sensations that were classified by modality, intensity, and duration, and feelings that were identified in a tridimensional theory of equilibrium between pleasure–displeasure, tension–relaxation, and excitement–depression. Wundt also introduced the idea of apperception, that the creative synthesis of these elements of experience is an active process whereby something new arises. This synthesis has been called the *law of psychic resultants,* and it seems analogous to the Gestalt idea that the whole is more than the sum of its parts.

In the first part of the twentieth century, Wundt concerned himself with the various levels of mental development as expressed in language and myths, art forms, and social customs, including laws and morals. These higher mental processes were recorded in ten volumes of *Folk Psychology,* and were differentiated from the simpler mental processes of sensation and perception. This work served to divide psychology into the experimental, using laboratory methods, and the social, using nonexperimental approaches of sociology and anthropology.

N. A. HAYNIE

Y

YERKES, ROBERT MEARNS (1876–1956)

Robert Mearns Yerkes studied at Harvard University, and received the doctorate in psychology in 1902. He held positions at Harvard and the University of Minnesota before he settled at Yale University in 1924 and remained there for 20 years. Yerkes and E. L. Thorndike were pioneers in the experimental study of animal behavior, following the tradition of C. Lloyd Morgan and George Romanes, the founders of comparative psychology.

Yerkes began his animal studies in 1900 and took charge of comparative psychology at Harvard in 1902. His research included a wide range of animals. He invented an experimental maze to study animal learning and the evolution of intelligence through the animal species. Yerkes is associated with the first primate laboratory at Yale University, where he was the director from 1929 to 1941. The laboratory was later transferred to Orange Park, FL, and is now the Yerkes Regional Primate Center of Emory University in Georgia.

Out of his work in comparative, or animal, behavior, Yerkes formulated methods and techniques to test intelligence, monochromatic light to study color vision, and multiple-choice tests to measure concept formation. From his experiments he formed a theory that is called the Yerkes-Dodson law. It states that there is an optimal level of arousal for tasks, and that moderate levels of motivation facilitate problem solving and change. If stress is too high, the individual may not process relevant cues for learning; if it is too low, irrelevant as well as relevant cues will be processed indiscriminately (Easterbrook, 1959).

Later Yerkes was interested also in human learning and developed a revision of the Stanford–Binet Intelligence Scale called the Point Scale. During World War I, Yerkes was chief of a group of psychologists who developed measures of abilities for assignments of army recruits to military positions and duties. These tests were the Army Alpha and the Army Beta, which were used to classify some 1.75 million men.

N. A. Haynie

YUGOSLAVIA (SERBIA), PSYCHOLOGY IN

The history of psychology in the area that is now Yugoslavia can be divided roughly into four main periods: (a) the Renaissance; (b) the end of the 19th and beginning of the 20th century; (c) between the two world wars; and (d) World War II.

In Yugoslavia, psychology has a tradition that goes back to the Renaissance. During the 15th and 16th centuries, Croatian and Slovenian authors wrote some 10 books on psychology from a philosophical point of view (in Latin), for example: Jurij Dalmatinac, *About Mental Abilities* (*De Animae Potentiis*); Juraj Dragašić, *About the Ruler Mind* (*De Animae Regni Principe*); David Verbec, *A Debate about Temperament* (*Disputatio de Temperamentis*). The most important psychological book in this period was written by Marko Marulić (1450–1520): *Psychology of the Human Soul* (*Psichiologia de Ratione Animae Humanae*). In this work, the word *psychology* was used for the first time. The book itself has been lost, but we know of it from references by Marulić's contemporary, Franjo Božičević Natalis. It is thought that the book was written in 1517 (Brožek, 1973; Krstić, 1964).

In 1859, the first psychological book in a Yugoslav language (Serbo-Croatian) was published in Karlovci—*Empirical Psychology* by Hristifor Ristić. In 1907, the first psychological journal, *Review of Serbian Society for Child Psychology,* was issued in Belgrade (it lasted only three years). Before Yugoslavia was established, about 20 psychological books (not counting manuscripts from the Renaissance) were published. Courses in psychology were taught at some schools—at the Belgrade College Lyceum beginning in 1838, for example. But despite some attempts to build an empirically based psychology (e.g., Pavle Radosavljević), a metaphysical and philosophical approach prevailed (Pečjak, 1981).

At the beginning of the 20th century, many Yugoslav scholars studied with famous European psychologists—Ljubomir Nedić, Branko Petronijević, and Mihajlo Rostohar with Wilhelm Wundt; Pavle Radosavljević and Vićentije Rakić with Meumann; Jelisaveta Branković with Wolfgang Köhler; Ramiro Bujas and Mihajlo Rostohar with Alexius Meinong; Zoran Bujas with Henri Pieron; and Borislav Stevanović with Aveling. Many of them became the pioneers of Yugoslav empirical psychology.

After World War I, the development of psychology was faster and more empirically based. In 1920, Ramiro Bujas founded the first psychological laboratory in Yugoslavia (and in the Balkans) at the University of Zagreb, later called the Institute of Psychology. Its members investigated a broad variety of problems, but the emphasis was on sensory processes, psychogalvanic reactions, abilities and their measurement, and thinking.

In this period, two departments of psychology were founded: in 1928, at the University of Belgrade, and in 1929, at the University of Zagreb. The chairman of the former was Borislav Stevanović, whose main fields were the psychology of thinking and child and educational psychology. The chairman at Zagreb was Ramiro Bujas, whose psychological interests were very broad. He wrote about many topics, including sensations, abilities, tests, psycholinguistics, applied psychology, and parapsychology. In his *Theory of Sensation,* he explained sensations as a result of disturbed equilibrium between processes inside an organism and its environment.

Since 1932, the Institute of Psychology in Zagreb has been publishing its *Acta Psychologica Universitatis Zagrabiensis.* The papers (mostly reports about empirical investigations) are printed in French and/or English.

During this period, about 20 original psychological books were published. They were mostly of a general character (typical titles were *Introduction to Psychology,* and *Basic Psychology*), yet some specialized books were also published, in the field of psychological statistics and psychology in radiotelegraphy, for example. At the same time, many foreign books were translated, including most of Sigmund Freud's and Alfred Adler's works.

Yugoslav applied psychology also began to flourish. Centers for professional guidance were founded in Belgrade (1930), Zagreb (1931), and Ljubljana (1938). The Binet Scale of Intelligence was adapted (Stevanović, 1934) and some original tests were created (e.g., by Ramiro and Zoran Bujas). Professional psychology was the only applied field of Yugoslav psychology in this period.

Psychology in Yugoslavia during the first half of the 20th century was comparable to the state of psychology in major European countries at the end of the 19th century. Institutes and departments were founded, applied psychology started, tests for measuring ability were devised, and some empirical studies were carried out.

Psychology began to grow rapidly only after World War II. Immediately after the war, Yugoslav psychology was, for a time, under the influence of Soviet psychology—until 1951, only Russian psychological books were translated (Brožek, 1972). After this short period, a very accelerated development of relatively independent Yugoslav psychology, yet one that included the main world trends, appeared. Its progress is marked by a positive accelerated curve. As a criterion of this progress, diverse variables can be taken—number of published books and papers, graduated psychologists, conventions and conferences, new departments. For all these variables, the curve has about the same shape. In the past five years, a gradual and slight decline in the growth has been noticeable, which could mean that it is approaching a plateau.

In this period, four psychological reviews were founded: *Psychology* (in Belgrade), *Review of Psychology* and *Applied Psychology* (in Zagreb), and *Anthropos* (in Ljubljana). The following shows the increase in books and papers published from 1921 through 1972 (Stary, 1975).

Period	Number of Books and Papers
1921–1940 (20 years)	136
1941–1950 (war and postwar period)	10
1956–1960	396
1961–1965	880
1966–1970	1,330
1971–1972 (only two years)	546

In 1960, Yugoslav psychologists held their first congress. There since have been congresses every three years. In 1965, the 18th International Congress of Applied Psychology was organized in Ljubljana. The Yugoslav Psychological Association was founded in 1950—it had about 3,000 members in 1982.

In 1950, the Department of Psychology at the University of Ljubljana was established. Its first chairman was Mihajlo Rostohar (who came from Czechoslovakia, where he had founded the first Czech laboratory of psychology). He stimulated empirical research in Slovenia and did many empirical studies (especially in the field of developmental psychology). During the past ten years, departments of psychology also have been founded in Skopje, Niš, Rijeka, Novi Sad, and Zadar. Yugoslav universities now have eight departments and two institutes of psychology (one in Zagreb and one in Belgrade).

During its development, Yugoslav psychology grew out of not only a quantitative, but also a qualitative point of view. It has become more and more heterogeneous and diverse. Today there is almost no academic discipline that is not studied by Yugoslav psychologists. The following, however, are more developed and emphasized: physiological psychology (Zoran Bujas); sensory processes (Zoran Bujas, Predrag Ognjenović); abilities and their measurement (Zoran Bujas, Adela Ostojčić, Ivan Toličić, Vera Smiljanić); psycholinguistics (Ante Fulgosi, Gordana Opačić, Vid Pečjak); social psychology (Rudi Supek, Mladen Zvonarović, Nikola Rot, Josip Obradović, Mišo Jezernik, Marko Peršič); developmental psychology (Ivan Ivić, Ivan Toličič, Vera Smiljanić, Ludvig Horvat); personality (Anton Trstenjak, Janek Musek, Boško Popović, Ante Fulgosi); and mathematical psychology (Ante Fulgosi, Konstantin Momirović).

Much Yugoslav developmental psychology is related to the problems of readiness for school (Toličič and Smiljanić), social factors influencing school success (Toličič and Leon Zorman), and Jean Piaget's work (Ivić). Yugoslav social psychology investigates primarily the problems related to the Yugoslav social and political system, such as self-management by workers (Rot, Nenad Havelka, Obradović, Marjan Šetinc).

In Yugoslavia, all branches of applied psychology (except space psychology) are practiced, although the classical three predominate: clinical psychology, educational psychology (Radivoj Kvaščev, Lidija Vučić, Barica Marentič, Drago Žagar), and industrial psychology (Boris Petz, Ivan Štajnberger, Tomislav Tomeković, Edvard Konrad, Levin Šebek). Clinical psychology (Borut Šali, Josip Berger, Leopold Bregant, Hubert Požarnik) is very diversified and follows different orientations (all techniques, from neoanalytical to humanistic and behavioral, are practiced, as are some newer approaches such as Gestalt therapy). Most applied psychologists are clinical. Among new branches of applied psychology emerging are ecological psychology (Anton Trstenjak, Marko Polič) and economic psychology (Trstenjak).

At present, there are three main centers of Yugoslav psychology. That in Zagreb is the oldest and "hardest"; its dominant fields are experimental, physiological, sensory, mathematical, social, industrial psychology, and psychometrics. In Belgrade, developmental, educational, clinical, personality, and social psychology are stressed most. Psychology in Ljubljana is the most evenly developed, and all main disciplines are about equally represented.

REFERENCES

Brožek, J. (1972). Quantitative explorations in the history of psychology in Yugoslavia: Translations. *Psychological Reports, 31,* 397–398.

Brožek, J. (1973). Marcus Marulus (1450–1524), author of *Psichologia: Early references and the dating.* Proceedings 81st Annual Convention, APA, 21–22.

Krstić, K. Marko Marulić (1964). The author of the term "psychology." *Acta Instituti Psychologic Universitatis Zagrabiensis, 35,* 7–15.

Pečjak, V. (1980). Short history of Yugoslav psychology. *Primenjena psihologija (Applied Psychology), 1,* 205–216.

Stary, D. (1975). Published works of Yugoslav psychologists till 1972. *Revija za psihologiju, 5,* 129–135.

V. PEČJAK

Z

ZEÏGARNIK EFFECT

Work by Bliuma Zeïgarnik (1927) established the fact that subjects ranging widely in age tended to remember interrupted tasks better (and with greater frequency) than they did tasks they had completed.

What amounted to common-sense observations constituted the impetus for a series of germinal experiments by Zeïgarnik. In a typical study, subjects were asked to perform a series of different tasks, ranging from 15 to 22 in number. Some tasks were of a manual manipulatory nature (such as stringing beads); others clearly involved the application of mental ability (such as puzzles). For half of the activities, subjects were allowed to continue until they were finished. In the case of a puzzle, for example, work might proceed until a solution was found. In the remainder of the activities (one-half of the total), the experimenter asked subjects to stop working on a given task, and to move on to something else. Following the activity or task session, the tasks were removed from the subjects' view and each was asked to recall and to jot down some of the activities in which they had been involved. Most subjects were able to recall a number of tasks immediately, but required some deliberation time to recall others. Results of the study confirmed Zeïgarnik's initial hypothesis. The number of *unfinished* or *incompleted* tasks (designated as *I*) that were recalled was significantly higher than was the number of *completed tasks* (designated as *C*). The "*I/C* ratio" constituted the dependent variable of interest in the Zeïgarnik study. In all instances, she reported an *I/C* ratio greater than 1. For a group of adults, the ratio averaged 1.9; for a group of children run under comparable testing conditions, the *I/C* ratio averaged 2.1. By and large, subjects taking part in Zeïgarnik's research were twice as likely to recall incompleted tasks as completed ones.

A number of possible alternative explanations of the Zeïgarnik effect have been advanced that do not emphasize the completion-incompletion variable *per se*. One such explanation is that it is the shock associated with the interruption or the cessation of work on a task that increases the salience of the task in the minds of subjects. This possibility was discounted by Zeïgarnik through a modification of her original design. This time, *all* tasks attempted by subjects were interrupted at some point, with half of them being completed later. Results revealed that the shock of task termination or interruption had little, if anything, to do with the difference in the frequency of recall. Tasks that had been interrupted but were *not* completed later were remembered with almost twice the frequency as the interrupted tasks that *were* completed later (*I/C* ratio = 1.85). A second possible interpretation of Zeïgarnik's original findings was that subjects may have assumed that the interrupted tasks would be completed later on (i.e., that they represented unfinished business). This assumption in itself may have been responsible for the greater recall of such activities, according to this interpretation. In another refinement of her original study, Zeïgarnik addressed and dismissed this alternative. Subjects were given an array of tasks, as before, and asked to perform them. This time, instructions included an explicit reference to the one-shot nature of the experiment. Subjects were told that they would not be returning at a later time. This procedural modification notwithstanding, Zeïgarnik successfully replicated her earlier findings, with an *I/C* ration of 1.80, essentially the same as before.

In the series of Zeïgarnik studies, the recall ratio for tasks interrupted at the middle or toward the end (tasks nearing completion) was higher than for tasks interrupted at or near the beginning of work on them. This finding attested to the increasing involvement of a subject in moving a given task along to completion. The *I/C* ratio was seen to increase as the subject moved nearer and nearer to the goal of a satisfactory task solution.

During the course of her research, Zeïgarnik discovered that persons who could be classified as being ambitious had a higher *I/C* ratio than did persons of average ambitiousness (the latter group tended to display less interest in the tasks at the time of performance). Ambitious (high achiever) subjects forgot completed tasks at a faster rate than did those of average ambitiousness. It may be concluded that the goal for these subjects was not merely task completion, but also some kind of success, thus giving rise to a higher *I/C* ratio. If task interruption were to be interpreted by subjects as signifying that they had failed, generating an ego-threatening situation, the *I/C* ratio would be further increased, with subjects tending to recall incompleted tasks with greater frequency than before.

Other explanations that might account for the Zeïgarnik effect include the following: (a) Task interruption may actively set up a *new* motive involving resentment against the interruption itself or the interrupter and hence a better memory for the cause of the resentment; (b) The interruption may serve as an emphasizer of the interrupted task; (c) In Gestalt terms, the subject may strive for closure; and (d) Subjects' persistence in attending to an unsolved problem may often have been rewarded in the past, hence giving rise to a higher rate of recall for unfinished tasks.

Studies have found that the Zeïgarnik effect is sensitive to a number of factors that may be difficult, if not impossible, to control within the context of a laboratory study: (a) The Zeïgarnik effect is less likely to appear if the subject is, to some extent, ego-involved in the task; (b) The effect is more likely to appear if the interruption of the task does not seem to be part of the experimental game plan; and (c) The effect is most likely to appear if the subject has set a genuine level of aspiration in the interrupted task, that is, has not come to the conclusion that the thing is impossible or beyond his or her capacity.

REFERENCES

Zeïgarnik, B. (1927). Untersuchungen zur Handlungsund Affektpsychologie, Herausgegeben von K. Lewin. 3. Das Behalten erledigter und underledigter Handlungen. *Psychologisches Forschung, 9,* 1–85.

F. L. DENMARK
Pace University, New York

ATTENTION
GESTALT PSYCHOLOGY
INFORMATION PROCESSING
SELECTIVE ATTENTION

ZEITGEBERS

Under natural environmental conditions, many physiological functions such as temperature, blood pressure, blood nutrients, hormones, and sleep/wake cycles fluctuate in a rhythmic pattern over the day. Such fluctuations are called circadian rhythms, meaning "about a day." Having endogenous circadian rhythms allows an organism to anticipate daily environmental fluctuations rather than merely respond to them. The cycle length or period of circadian rhythms when they are measured under constant, aperiodic conditions (such as constant light or constant darkness) typically deviates from a 24-hour period. Under these conditions circadian rhythms are said to be free running. When the young adult circadian system free runs, its periodicity is typically closer to 25 hours than 24 hours. This is due to the fact that certain critical exogenous factors are needed to synchronize or entrain endogenous circadian rhythms into stable period and phase relationships with the external day-night cycle. These exogenous factors are termed "zeitgebers" (time keepers), and include both physical and social factors (Aschoff, Hoffman, Pohl, & Wever, 1975).

HOW ZEITGEBERS ENTRAIN CIRCADIAN RHYTHMS

In many animals, light is the primary zeitgeber that entrains circadian cycles (Aschoff, 1981; Pittendrigh, 1981). The brain pathway by which light entrains circadian rhythms has been clearly elucidated in animal studies (Moore & Eichler, 1972). This neuronal circuit involves ocular mechanisms (Reme, Wirz-Justice, & Terman, 1991) and a projection from the retina directly to a nucleus in the base of the brain called the suprachiasmatic nucleus (SCN; Moore & Lenn, 1972). The suprachiasmatic nucleus has been called the body's biological clock. Evidence that a pathway from the eye to this nucleus (retinohypothalamic tract) is crucial for light/dark (LD) entrainment is provided by experiments demonstrating that only specific lesions of the optic tract, proximal to the retinal hypothalamic pathway, interfere with LD entrainment (Rusak & Zucker, 1979), whereas lesions of other afferent pathways to the SCN do not produce a loss of circadian rhythmicity (for recent reviews see Rusak, 1989; Rusak & Zucker, 1979; Rusak & Haddad, 1993).

PHOTIC AND NON-PHOTIC ZEITGEBERS

It appears that non-photic factors such as social factors or social rhythms may also be important in the setting of circadian rhythms in human subjects (Aschoff, Fatranska, & Giedke, 1971; Wever, 1975, 1979, 1988; Mrosovsky, 1996). As well as acting as direct zeitgebers, social rhythms can indirectly determine when a person is exposed to physical zeitgebers such as daylight and darkness. Moreover, social rhythms also determine when a person goes to bed or gets up and thus set the timing of their sleep-wake cycles. Social entrainment begins soon after birth so that an offspring's eating and sleeping schedules become synchronized with those of their siblings and parents.

In human adults, social rhythms are maintained by a variety of factors such as occupation, marital status, presence or absence of children, and recreational activities. Thus, interruption of these factors has the potential to disrupt normal circadian timing. The mechanism whereby social rhythms participate in entrainment of biological rhythms is unknown. Some authors have suggested, based on animal studies, that social interactions or behavioral activity might cause a non-specific increase in arousal which could then feedback on the pacemaker in the SCN (Mrosovsky, 1988; Turek & Losee-Olsen, 1986; Van Reeth & Turek, 1989). Recently, Moore and Card (1990) proposed that social zeitgebers may entrain the SCN through a specific neuropeptide Y pathway, which involves the intergeniculate leaflet in animals. It has also been suggested that non-photically entrainable oscillators may also exist outside the SCN (Mistlberger, 1992; Mikkelsen, Vrand, & Mrosovsky, 1998).

CONSEQUENCES OF DISRUPTIONS OF ZEITGEBERS

A loss or disruption of a zeitgeber can have important consequences on physiological and psychological functioning. Transmeridian flight has been demonstrated to be a potent source of rhythm disruption (jet lag). When a person takes a transmeridian flight, he or she will be exposed to new physical and social time cues (zeitgebers). Initially this will disrupt the person's rhythmicity. However, these same time cues will eventually help to reset biological rhythms to the new time zone, making jet lag a transient problem for most individuals.

Shift work is another case of rhythm disturbance that can have sustained effects. Shift work can expose the individual to both physical and social factors that may be disruptive. It is perhaps not surprising that in addition to the jet lag–like symptoms of sleep disruption, malaise, and gastrointestinal disorders (Rutenfranz, Colquhoun, Knauth, & Ghata, 1977), shift work has been found to be associated with increases in divorce (Tepas & Monk, 1987; Knutsson, Akerstedt, Jonsson, & Orth-Gomer, 1986). Shift work is also associated with other maladies that may be related to the stress that rhythm disturbance may cause, such as increased risk of heart disease (Knutsson et al., 1986), irritability and difficulty concentrating (Rutenfranz et al., 1977), and heavier use of caffeine and alcohol (Gordon, Cleary, Parlan, & Czeisler, 1986). It appears that a triad of factors—circadian rhythms, sleep, and social/domestic situations—combine to determine a person's ability to cope with shift work (Monk, 1988; Regestein & Monk, 1991).

Like a rotating shift schedule, the presence of newborn baby in the home can lead to considerable sleep disruption, as well as inconsistent bedtimes, wake-up times, exposure to sunlight, and mealtimes. Indeed, the presence of a newborn may thus act as a very potent disruption in zeitgebers and circadian rhythms. Other life events, at least theoretically, may also be envisioned as rhythm disturbers (zeitstörers). For instance, death and divorce could be viewed in certain circumstances to be zeitstörers not unlike transmeridian flight. A couple who live together and share most social rhythms such as eating, sleeping, and work schedules could have those rhythms disrupted by widowhood, divorce, or separation.

ZEITGEBERS AND DEPRESSION

Photic Zeitgebers and Depression

Several recent theories have focused on changes in zeitgebers as an etiology of depression. The effect of physical zeitgebers on the development of depressive symptoms has been stressed by researchers who have studied seasonal affective disorder (SAD; Lewy, Sack, & Singer, 1984; Rosenthal et al., 1984). The classic presentation of SAD is the occurrence of depressive symptoms that begin late in the autumn and resolve in the spring. Typically, SAD is characterized by atypical depressive symptoms such as weight gain, loss of energy, and hypersomnolence. One treatment used for SAD is bright light exposure in early morning and/or late afternoon in order to approximate the daylight levels of a summer day (see Lewy, Wehr, Goodwin, Newsome, & Markey, 1980; Kripke, 1982). Some patients with seasonal affective disorder do obtain relief from depressive symptoms using bright light exposure.

Nonphotic Zeitgebers and Depression

Although many studies suggest that light may play a role in the etiology and treatment of seasonal depressive disorders, studies in nonseasonal depression have not demonstrated any consistent therapeutic effect of bright light. Some theories have stressed the role of social zeitgebers in the onset and course of nonseasonal affective illness. In one model, certain life events and difficulties (Brown, Harris, & Peto, 1973; Brown & Harris, 1986), particularly those that involve separation or loss such as death, divorce, loss of job, moving, are viewed as a loss of social zeitgebers. A loss of social zeitgebers, in turn, is postulated to produce changes in social rhythms, or the rhythmicity of the activities of daily life. Disruption in social rhythms are then thought to lead to changes in biological rhythms. Ultimately it is postulated that chronic disruption of social and biological rhythms can lead to the onset, in vulnerable individuals, of depression. Whether a person actually becomes ill following the loss of a social zeitgeber is thought to depend on certain vulnerability factors such as genetic/familial loading, social supports, past history of affective episodes, and personality variables (Ehlers, Frank, & Kupfer, 1988; Ehlers, Kupfer, Frank, & Monk, 1994). It has also been suggested that therapy for affective disorder should include attention to these social rhythm factors (Frank et al., 1994; Healey & Waterhouse, 1995).

REFERENCES

Aschoff, J. (1981). *Handbook of Behavioral Neurobiology: Vol. 4. Biological Rhythms.* New York: Plenum.

Aschoff, J., Fatranska, M., & Giedke, H. (1971). Human circadian rhythms in continuous darkness: Entrainment by social cues. *Science, 171,* 213–215.

Aschoff, J., Hoffman, K., Pohl, H., & Wever, R. A. (1975). Reentrainment of circadian rhythms after phase-shifts of the Zeitgeber. *Chronobiologia, 2,* 23–78.

Brown, G. W., & Harris, T. (1986). Stressor, vulnerability and depression: A question of replication. *Psychology & Medicine, 16,* 739–744.

Brown, G. W., Harris, T. O., & Peto, J. (1973). Life events and psychiatric disorders. Part II: Nature of causal link. *Psychology & Medicine, 3,* 159–176.

Ehlers, C. L., Frank, E., & Kupfer, D. J. (1988). Social Zeitgebers and biological rhythms: A unified approach to understanding the etiology of depression. *Archives of General Psychiatry, 45,* 948–952.

Ehlers, C. L., Kupfer, D. J., Frank, E., & Monk, T. H. (1994). Biological rhythms and depression: The role of zeitgebers and zeitstörers. *Depression, 1,* 285–293.

Frank, E., Kupfer, D. J., Ehlers, C. L., Monk, T. H., Cornes, C., Carter, S., & Frankel, D. (1994). Interpersonal and social rhythm therapy for bipolar disorder: Integrating interpersonal and behavioral approaches. *The Behavior Therapist, 17,* 143–149.

Gordon, N. P., Cleary, P. D., Parlan, C. E., & Czeisler, C. A. (1986). The prevalence and health impact of shiftwork. *American Journal of Public Health, 76,* 1225–1228.

Healey, D., & Waterhouse, J. M. (1995). The circadian system and the therapeutics of the affective disorders. *Pharmaceutical Therapy, 65,* 241–263.

Knutsson, A., Akerstedt, T., Jonsson, B. G., & Orth-Gomer, K. (1986). Increased risk of schemic heart disease in shift workers. *Lancet, 2,* 89–92.

Kripke, D. F. (1982). Phase-advance theories for affective illness. In T. A. Wehr & F. K. Goodwin (Eds.), *Circadian rhythms in psychiatry* (pp. 41–69). Pacific Grove, CA: The Boxwood Press.

Lewy, A. J., Sack, R. A., & Singer, C. L. (1984). Assessment and treatment of chronobiologic disorders using plasma melatonin levels and bright light exposure: The clockgate model and the phase response curve. *Psychopharmacology Bulletin, 20,* 561–565.

Lewy, A. J., Wehr, T. A., Goodwin, F. K., Newsome, D. A., & Markey, S. P. (1980). Light suppresses melatonin secretion in humans. *Science, 210,* 1267–1269.

Mikkelsen, N., Vrand, N., & Mrosovsky, N. (1998). Expression of Fos in the circadian system following nonphotic stimulation. *Brain Research Bulletin, 47,* 367–376.

Mistlberger, R. E. (1992). Nonphotic entrainment of circadian activity rhythms in suprachiasmatic nuclei-abated hamsters. *Behavioral Neuroscience, 106,* 192–202.

Monk, T. H. (1988). Coping with the stress of shift work. *Work & Stress, 2,* 169–172.

Moore, R. Y., & Card, J. P. (1990). Neuropeptide Y in the circadian timing system. *Annals of the New York Academy of Science, 611,* 247–257.

Moore, R. Y., & Eichler, V. B. (1972). Loss of circadian adrenal corticosterone rhythm following suprachiasmatic lesions in rats. *Brain Research, 42,* 201–206.

Moore, R. Y., & Lenn, N. J. (1972). A retinohypothalamic projection in the rat. *Journal of Comprehensive Neurology, 146,* 1–14.

Mrosovsky, N. (1996). Locomotor activity and non-photic influences on circadian clocks. *Biology Review, 71,* 343–372.

Mrosovsky, N., Reebs, S. G., Honrado, G. I., & Salmon, P. A. (1989). Behavioural entrainment of circadian rhythms. *Experientia, 45,* 696–702.

Pittendrigh, C. S. (1981). Circadian systems: Entrainment. In J. Aschoff (Ed.), *Handbook of behavioral neurobiology: Vol. 4. Biological rhythms* (pp. 95–124). New York: Plenum.

Regestein, Q. R., & Monk, T. H. (1991). Is the poor sleep of shift workers a disorder? *American Journal of Psychiatry, 148,* 1487–1493.

Reme, C. E., Wirz-Justice, A., & Terman, M. (1991). The visual input stage of the mammalian circadian pacemaking system: I. Is there a clock in the mammalian eye? *Journal of Biological Rhythms, 6,* 5–29.

Rosenthal, N. E., Sack, D. A., Gillin, J. C., Lewy, A. J., Davenport, Y., Mueller, P. S., Newsome, D. A., & Wehr, T. A. (1984). Seasonal affective disorder: A description of the syndrome and preliminary findings with light therapy. *Archives of General Psychiatry, 41,* 72–80.

Rusak, B. (1989). The mammalian circadian system: Models and physiology. *Journal of Biological Rhythms, 4,* 121–134.

Rusak, B., & Haddad, G. (1993). Neural mechanisms of the mammalian circadian system. *Journal of Biological Rhythms, 8* (Suppl.), S1–S108.

Rusak, B., & Zucker, I. (1979). Neural regulation of the circadian rhythms. *Physiology Review Annual, 59,* 449–526.

Rutenfranz, J., Colquhoun, W. P., Knauth, P., & Ghata, J. N. (1977). Biomedical and psychosocial aspects of shift work: A review. *Scandinavian Journal of Workplace and Environmental Health, 3,* 165–182.

Tepas, D. I., & Monk, T. H. (1987). Work schedules. In G. Salvendy (Ed.), *Handbook of human factors* (pp. 819–843). New York: Wiley.

Turek, F. W., & Losee-Olson, S. (1986). A benzodiazepine used in the treatment of insomnia phase shifts the mammalian circadian clock. *Nature, 321,* 167–168.

Van Reeth, O., & Turek, F. W. (1989). Stimulated activity mediates phase shifts in the hamster circadian clock induced by dark pulses or benzodiazepines. *Nature, 339,* 49–51.

Wever, R. A. (1975). The circadian multi-oscillator system of man. *International Journal of Chronobiology, 3,* 19–55.

Wever, R. A. (1979). *The circadian system of man: Results of experiments under temporal isolation.* New York: Springer-Verlag.

Wever, R. A. (1988). Order and disorder in human circadian rhythmicity: Possible relations to mental disorders. In D. J. Kupfer, T. H. Monk, & D. J. Barchas (Eds.), *Biological rhythms and mental disorders* (pp. 253–346). New York: Guilford.

C. L. Ehlers
University of California at San Diego

BIOLOGICAL CLOCKS AND SEASONAL BEHAVIOR
CIRCADIAN RHYTHMS
DEPRESSION
HOMEOSTASIS

ZIGLER, EDWARD (1930–   )

Edward Zigler was born in Kansas City, MO on March 1, 1930. He received a BS degree from the University of Missouri at Kansas City and obtained his PhD in clinical psychology from the University of Texas at Austin in 1958. While a graduate student, he began his studies of personality and emotional features of individuals with mental retardation, a line of work he still pursues. In 1957, he did a clinical internship at Worcester, MA, State Hospital; there, in collaboration with L. Phillips, he began work that eventually became the developmental approach to psychopathology. Zigler taught at the University of Missouri at Columbia for one year before coming to Yale University in 1959.

In 1964, Zigler was invited to become a member of the National Planning and Steering Committee of Project Head Start. In 1970, he was named by President R. Nixon to be the first director of the Office of Child Development (OCD; now the Administration on Children, Youth and Families) and chief of the US Children's Bureau. While in Washington, Zigler was responsible for administering the Head Start program. As director of OCD, he led efforts to conceptualize and mount such innovative programs as Education for Parenthood, the Child and Family Resource Program, and the Child Development Associate (which continues to accredit workers in early care and education).

After leaving government, Zigler has continued to assist policymakers. He served on the President's Committee on Mental Retardation and, at President G. Ford's request, chaired the Vietnamese Children's Resettlement Advisory Group. In 1980, Zigler was asked by President J. Carter to chair the Fifteenth Anniversary Head Start Committee, a body charged with plotting the future course of this major intervention. He is the honorary chair and historical mentor of the Head Start 2010 project, a similar group convened for the 45th anniversary. In the 1990s, he was a member of both the Advisory Committee on Head Start Quality and Expansion and the planning committee for the Early Head Start program for families and children ages zero to three.

Zigler played a central role in establishing the Bush Centers in Child Development and Social Policy. The Yale Bush Center, founded in 1978, is one of the original four and is still in operation. The purpose of the Center is to improve the lives of America's children and families through informed social policy. This mission entails analyses of current and proposed government policies, policy-related research, conveying to lawmakers and the public what is known about the developmental needs of children, training researchers to work effectively in the policy arena, and developing innovative solutions to problems encountered by families in today's rapidly changing society.

At Yale, Zigler also directs a distinguished laboratory engaged in a variety of basic and applied studies of child development and family functioning. His scholarly work cuts across the fields of mental retardation, mental health and psychopathology, intervention programs for economically disadvantaged children, preschool education, and out-of-home care for children of working parents. His work in mental retardation is frequently noted in efforts toward more enlightened treatment of individuals with disabilities. He headed a national committee of distinguished Americans charged with examining the possibility of making infant care leaves a reality in America, work that inspired the Family and Medical Leave Act of 1993. He developed the School of the 21st Century, a model that appends elementary schools with child care services for very young children as well as those of school age. In 2000 there were over 600 21C schools in almost 20 states. Some of these schools (CoZi schools) have linked with J. Comer's initiative to enhance parent involvement and participation in their children's education.

Zigler serves as a special consultant to numerous Cabinet rank officers and private foundations. He also appears regularly as an expert witness before many Congressional committees. He is frequently called upon by the media to comment on social policy issues concerning our nation's children and families. Zigler is the author or editor of over 30 books and has written more than 500 scholarly articles. He is a member of the editorial boards of 12 professional journals.

Zigler has received numerous honors, including the 1999 Heinz Award in Public Policy, the Lifetime Achievement Award from the American Association of Applied and Preventive Psychology, the Bronfenbrenner Lifetime Contribution Award from Division 7 of the American Psychological Association, and the Gold Medal Award for Enduring Contribution by a Psychologist in the Public Interest from the American Psychological Foundation. He has also received the Harold W. McGraw, Jr. Prize in Education and awards from the Joseph P. Kennedy, Jr. Foundation, the American Academy of Pediatrics, the National Academy of Sciences, the American Academy of Child and Adolescent Psychiatry, the National Head Start Association, and the American Orthopsychiatric Association, where he was the 1993–94 president.

Zigler is currently Sterling Professor of Psychology at Yale University and director of the Yale Bush Center in Child Development and Social Policy. He is the head of the psychology section of Yale's Child Study Center.

S. J. STYFCO
Yale University

ZORUMSKI, CHARLES F.

Charles F. Zorumski received an undergraduate degree in chemistry and a degree in medicine from St. Louis University in 1974 and 1978, respectively. He subsequently trained in psychiatry and neurobiology at Washington University School of Medicine and joined the faculty at Washington University in 1983.

While a resident in psychiatry, Zorumski began to study mechanisms involved in seizure generation and in the neurodegeneration that accompanies prolonged seizure activity. His early studies were conducted under the guidance of Eric Lothman and David Clifford in the Washington University Department of Neurology. These studies used depth electrode recording and 2-deoxy glucose autoradiography to map seizure activity in two in vivo rodent models: rapid kindling in the hippocampus and seizures induced by the combination of lithium and muscarinic cholinergic agonists. These studies demonstrated the importance of the hippocampus as a site for seizure initiation and as an important structure for studying seizure-related synaptic plasticity. To extend initial observations and to probe factors involved in the neurodegeneration associated with status epilepticus, Zorumski obtained advanced training under John Olney, a pioneer in excitotoxic research and a recognized expert in seizure-related brain damage. Under Olney's guidance, Zorumski used light and electron microscopic methods to demonstrate that much of the brain damage produced by status epilepticus results from activation of glutamate receptors. The brain damage had an ultrastructural pattern involving neuronal cell bodies and dendrites while sparing axons of passage, a pattern that was identical to the damage produced by glutamate. Additionally, the distribution of damage mirrored the distribution of glutamate receptors in the nervous system, and antagonists of the N-methyl-D-aspartate (NMDA) class of glutamate receptors blocked much of the damage. Interestingly, NMDA receptor antagonists blocked neuronal damage in certain regions despite failing to block electrographic seizure activity in the region. This suggested that NMDA receptor antagonists were more effective neuroprotectants than anticonvulsants.

Because of the apparent role of glutamate receptors in seizure-related brain damage and data indicating that excitatory amino acid-mediated neurotoxicity resulted from the flow of ions through glutamate-gated ion channels, Zorumski subsequently trained with Gerald Fischbach in the Washington University Department of Neurobiology. In the Fischbach laboratory, Zorumski used techniques of cell culture and patch clamp recording from whole-cells and isolated membrane patches to examine how glutamate receptors respond to prolonged and repeated activation and whether the process of desensitization is important in regulating the function of these receptors. Studies up to that time using brain slice preparations and current clamp recordings suggested that glutamate receptors did not desensitize and that this was one of the reasons for the severe toxicity associated with their activation. Zorumski and colleagues showed that the two broad classes of glutamate receptors, the NMDA and non-NMDA (AMPA/kainate) receptors, did desensitize but differed markedly in time course and pattern of use-dependent decline. NMDA receptors undergo a slow process of desensitization with a time constant of > 100 ms in physiological solutions. This desensitization is not influenced by glycine but is dependent on the agonist concentration, transmembrane voltage, and presence of extracellular calcium. In contrast, AMPA receptors show extremely rapid desensitization that is dependent on the agonist, being prominent with AMPA, glutamate and quis-qualate but not with kainate or domoate. AMPA receptor desensi-tization is calcium-independent, only weakly dependent on membrane voltage and occurs on a time scale of 10 ms or less in isolated membrane patches.

Since establishing his own laboratory in the Washington University Department of Psychiatry, Zorumski has continued to work on the regulation of glutamate-mediated responses. Early work in his laboratory centered on understanding the desensitization of NMDA and non-NMDA receptors in greater detail. In particular, the Zorumski laboratory examined whether desensitization of glutamate receptors contributes to the regulation of synaptic events mediated by these receptors. To address this question, Zorumski and colleagues used agents that modify desensitization. In the case of AMPA receptors, the group examined a series of lectins that appear to diminish AMPA receptor desensitization by binding to glycosylated residues on or near the receptors. They used the lectins as tools to study single channel correlates of AMPA receptor desensitization and to demonstrate that desensitization may participate in the decay of fast excitatory synaptic currents. In other studies, the group showed that calcium-dependent desensitization of NMDA receptors helps to regulate synaptic responses mediated by these receptors.

In recent years, Zorumski's interests have centered on the modulation of glutamatergic and GABAergic transmission in the hippocampus. His laboratory has focused on studying monosynaptic transmission using microisland hippocampal cultures and examined the role of glutamate transporters, particularly those on glial cells, in regulating the duration of glutamate exposure following synaptic release. Additionally, his laboratory examined how glutamate-mediated synaptic responses change as a function of use, concentrating primarily on paired-pulse forms of synaptic plasticity. Going back to original interests in the kindling model of seizures, the Zorumski lab expanded studies to include longer-term forms of synaptic plasticity in hippocampal slices. These studies examined the role of calcium-dependent second messengers in hippocampal long-term potentiation (LTP), the role of metabotropic glutamate receptors, and the involvement of messengers derived from phospholipase A2. Related to earlier interests in desensitization, the Zorumski laboratory has also examined how low level activation of glutamate receptors modulates synaptic transmission and synaptic plasticity. They demonstrated that untimely activation of NMDA receptors by low concentrations of agonists at NMDA receptors blocks LTP by releasing nitric oxide. This NMDA-mediated LTP inhibition appears to be important in determining the inhibitory effects of brief bouts of anoxia or low glucose exposure on synaptic plasticity.

Presently, the Zorumski laboratory continues to focus on factors that regulate excitatory and inhibitory synaptic transmission and synaptic plasticity. Current goals of their studies are to define more clearly the role of glial-neuronal interactions in synaptic transmission and the actions of neurosteroids in modulating fast synaptic transmission.

Zorumski is a fellow of the American Psychiatric Association and the American Psychopathological Association. He serves on the editorial board of *Neurobiology of Disease*. In 1997, Zorumski was named head of the Department of Psychiatry at Washington University School of Medicine, where he also serves as professor of neurobiology. In 1998, he was named Samuel B. Guze Professor of Psychiatry.

STAFF

Z-SCORE

The letter z denotes a standard score referenced to a normal distribution, i.e., a z-score is a measure of deviation from the mean in terms of the standard deviation as the unit.

If X is a normally distributed variable with mean μ and standard deviation σ, then

$$z = \frac{X - \mu}{\sigma}$$

Any value converted to a z-score is said to be normalized, that is, rescaled to a value within a unit normal distribution with mean 0 and standard deviation 1. The advantage of normalizing disparate distributions is that doing so equates the various distributions to the same scale, thus permitting direct comparison of previously nonhomologous variables.

The area of the normal curve between $z = -1.96$ and $z = +1.96$ contains 95% of all cases, between $z = -2.576$ and $z = +2.576$ contains 99% of all cases, so one of these two sets of z-scores is usually used to define the end points of the critical region for acceptance of the null hypothesis in psychological research.

H. REICH

MEASUREMENT
STATISTICAL SIGNIFICANCE
TEST STANDARDIZATION

Author Index

Frolova, L., 1416
Fromm, E., 432, 440, 705, 751, 1075, 1421, 1469, 1573
Frost, R., 427
Frost, R. O., 1082
Froyd, J. D., 1484
Froyd, J. E., 1484
Fruchter, B., 994–995
Frueh, B. C., 548
Frye, N., 1196
Frye, R. E., 1094
Fryns, J.-P., 593, 594
Fuchs, A. F., 1431
Fuchs, D., 478
Fuchs, L. S., 478
Fudenberg, H. H., 736
Fuendeling, J. M., 143
Fuentes, I., 1033
Fuhrer, R., 1577
Fuhry, L., 1433
Fujina, G., 1402
Fujita, M., 269
Fukunishi, I., 695–697
Fulero, S. M., 1297
Fulford, J. A., 556
Fulker, D. W., 672
Fuller, P., 618
Fuller, R. K., 112
Fullmer, D., 351
Fulmer, R. M., 869
Furmark, T., 234–236
Fuster, J. M., 330
Futuyma, D. J., 1009, 1013
Fuxe, K., 1493

Gabbard, G. O., 934
Gabriel, M., 1038
Gabriel, S., 1568
Gabrielli, J. D. E., 1091, 1250
Gacek, R. R., 153
Gaddum, J. H., 1496
Gade, P. A., 957–959
Gaertner, S. L., 248
Gaeth, G. J., 63
Gaetz, M., 1041
Gage, F. H., 729
Gagliardo, A., 1046
Gagné, R. M., 326, 1452
Gagnon, J., 740, 836
Gagnon, J. H., 571, 923, 1509, 1511, 1512, 1513
Gainotti, G., 1339
Gajdusek, D. C., 75
Galaburda, A. M., 237, 266, 615
Galambos, N. L., 17, 18

Galanter, E., 264
Galbicka, G., 1647, 1648
Galef, B. G., 1600
Galensky, M., 651
Galer, B. S., 1121
Galindo, E., 954
Galis, S. A., 478
Gall, C. M., 1634
Gallagher, R. E., 61
Gallegos, X., 952
Gallimore, R., 758
Gallistel, C. R., 1596
Gallo, D. M., 995
Gallup, G., 1102, 1103
Gallup, G. G., Jr., 1471
Gallup Organization, 1649
Galotti, K. M., 307
Galton, F., 264, 700, 726, 1285, 1501
Gambaro, S., 427
Gan, W., 1414
Ganaway, G., 1436
Gandelman, R., 690
Ganguli, R., 434
Ganschow, L., 128
Gant, N. F., 574, 579
Ganza, W., 1509
Garattini, S., 89
Garb, H. N., 339
Garber, J., 1470
Garcia, J., 161, 333, 341
Garcia-Borreguero, D., 1538
Garcia Cabanes, C., 975
Garcia-Coll, C., 1493
Gard, M. C., 110
Gardell, B., 509
Gardiner, P. C., 913
Gardner, B. T., 104, 334, 785, 786, 852
Gardner, E., 264
Gardner, H., 128, 386, 701, 1292
Gardner, J. E., 478
Gardner, M., 1267, 1338
Gardner, P., 932
Gardner, R. A., 104, 334, 785, 786, 852, 1215, 1216, 1436
Gardner, R. C., 253
Gardner, W. L., 1568
Garfield, S., 695
Garfield, S. L., 473, 1342–1343, 1347, 1348
Garfinkel, P. E., 1319
Garlow, S. J., 1495–1498
Garofalo, P., 729
Garrud, R., 1033

Gartner, J., 1390
Garvey, W. P., 1198
Gaskell, G., 1200–1201, 1520
Gaspar, N. J., 1414
Gastant, H., 1139
Gaston, L., 1347
Gates, A. I., 481
Gathorne-Hardy, J., 835
Gatsonis, C., 468
Gaumond, R. P., 1041
Gautier, T., 1515
Gay, J., 403
Gaynes, B., 794
Gazmararian, J. A., 1152
Gazzaniga, M. A., 1052, 1255
Gazzaniga, M. S., 51, 238, 307, 1606
Gearon, J. S., 1447–1449
Geary, N., 710, 711
Geber, M., 37
Gebhard, P. H., 740, 836, 1161, 1513
Gagnon, J., 740, 836
Gechner, G. T., 137
Geddes, J. F., 1093
Geddes, J. W., 730
Geer, J. H., 908
Geertz, C., 396, 397, 706
Gehringer, W. L., 978
Geiselman, R. E., 557, 558
Geisinger, K. F., 225, 1313–1316, 1362–1364
Geldard, F. A., 321
Gelder, M., 317
Gelemter, C. S., 1570
Gelfand, L. A., 1347
Gelfand, M. M., 571
Geller, B., 213
Geller, D., 225
Geller, J. L., 1519
Gelles, R. J., 1149
Gelles, R., 175, 1608
Gelso, C. J., 379
Gendlin, E. T., 529, 530
Gendre, F., 1665
Genshaft, J., 128
George, C., 144
George, D. T., 1494
George, J. M., 369
George, L., 1390
George, M. S., 884–887
Geracioti, T. D., 711
Geraty, R. D., 934
Gerbaldo, H., 75
Gerbner, G., 968
Gergen, K. J., 328, 674, 741, 744

Gerken, L., 849
Germain, C. B., 1270, 1550
German, P. S., 1152
Gerner, R. H., 214
Gershon, E. S., 213, 1588
Gerson, M., 416
Gerstein, D. R., 464
Gersten, R., 399
Gerstman, L. J., 1055
Geschwind, N., 237, 346
Gesell, A., 54, 471, 665, 750
Geuter, U., 633
Geva, D., 574
Gevins, A., 73
Gewirtz, J., 858
Geyer, J. D., 434
Gheorghiu, S., 1390
Ghiselli, E. E., 790, 820, 821, 1186
Ghobary, B. B., 339
Ghoneim, M. M., 1242
Giannakopoulos, P., 1207
Giargiari, T. D., 1507–1509
Gibb, J. R., 651
Gibbon, J., 765
Gibbon, M., 1223, 1637, 1640
Gibbons, E. F., 1018
Gibbons, P., 1539
Gibbs, J., 971
Gibbs, J. P., 1653
Gibbs, N., 1446
Gibson, B. S., 591, 592
Gibson, C., 942
Gibson, E. J., 735
Gibson, J. J., 977, 1166
Giddens, A., 893
Giel, R., 41
Gietzen, D. W., 1600
Gigerenzer, G., 63, 634, 914
Gigone, D., 1552
Gil, E., 1216
Gil, K. M., 1122–1125
Gilbert, F. J., 1575
Gilbert, R., 702
Gilbertson, S., 40
Giles, D. E., 1588
Gilgin, A. R., 742
Gilgin, C. K., 742
Gilig, P. M., 1543
Gill, F. B., 521
Gill, T. V., 104, 1242
Giller, E. L., Jr., 915, 1223
Gillespie, C., 55
Gillette, C., 550
Gillham, N. W., 1417
Gilliam, F., 434

Gilligan, C., 971, 1148
Gillin, J. C., 434
Gilmour, R., 898
Gilstrap, L. C., III, 574, 579
Gingold, M. K., 169
Ginsberg, L. H., 882
Ginzberg, E., 910
Giorgi, A., 704
Giovannoni, J., 1234
Gitlin, M. J., 212, 213
Gitlin, M., 1094
Gitterman, A., 1270
Giubilato, R. T., 271–272, 1148–1149
Giuffrida, A., 1153
Gjedde, A., 238
Gjerde, P. F., 1360
Gladstein, L., 765
Gladue, B., 571
Glaister, B., 661
Glanzer, M., 1241, 1242
Glaser, M. O., 1631
Glaser, R., 399, 1568
Glaser, W. R., 1631
Glasgow, R. E., 1060
Glass, C. R., 1347, 1570
Glass, D. C., 509
Glass, G. V., 322, 920, 950, 1260, 1261
Glass, T. A., 636–639
Glasser, W., 49, 1374–1375
Glassman, P., 302
Glaze, D. G., 1407, 1409
Glenn, C. M., 1259
Glenn, N. D., 1231, 1609
Glennon, R. A., 663
Gleser, C. C., 1314
Glick, J., 403
Glidewell, J. C., 329
Globus, G. G., 356
Glock, C. Y., 704
Gloor, P., 434
Glosser, G., 61
Glover, G. H., 1091
Glover, J. R., 1416
Gluck, A., 1412
Gluck, J. P., 518
Gluck, M., 1041
Gluck, M. A., 1038, 1039, 1040
Gluckman, M. L., 1078
Gluckman, P., 730
Glueck, E., 1456
Glueck, S., 1456
Godkewitsch, M., 1662
Godley, M., 112

Goetz, C. G., 712
Goff, W. R., 238
Goffman, E., 1423
Gogia, P., 663
Golan, M. J., 910, 912
Golbe, L. I., 1093
Gold, J. R., 323
Gold, L., 1413
Gold, P. E., 730
Gold, R., 549, 550
Goldberg, D. H., 1621
Goldberg, E., 1055
Goldberg, G., 1542
Goldberg, J. F., 212, 213
Goldberg, J. P., 1508
Goldberg, L. R., 582, 913, 1287
Goldberg, P. A., 1489, 1506
Goldberg, T. E., 897
Goldberger, A. S., 1632
Golden, C. J., 264, 265, 901, 902, 1054–1056, 1092
Golden, R. N., 915–917
Goldenberg, H., 566
Goldenberg, I., 566
Goldfried, M., 309, 310
Goldfried, M. R., 48, 322, 473, 1347
Goldgaber, D., 75
Golding, S. L., 336, 1296, 1297, 1298, 1299
Goldin-Meadow, S., 1568
Goldman, J., 1514, 1515
Goldman, M. S., 12
Goldman, R., 530, 531, 1514, 1515
Goldman, S., 1649
Goldman-Rakic, P., 1339
Goldofski, O. B., 540, 542
Goldring, E., 449
Goldschmidt, L., 574
Goldstein, A. J., 167, 549, 551
Goldstein, A. M., 370
Goldstein, A. P., 43–51, 48, 326, 1352, 1575, 1576
Goldstein, D. S., 1073
Goldstein, E., 1436
Goldstein, G., 1054
Goldstein, H., 1270
Goldstein, I., 572
Goldstein, J., 139, 140, 708
Goldstein, J. M., 1447
Goldstein, K., 346, 529, 1421, 1468
Goldstein, M. J., 214
Goldstein, R., 47

Goldstein, S. G., 265
Goleman, D., 935
Golinkoff, R. M., 849
Gollomp, S. M., 1093
Gologor, E., 401
Golper, L. A., 1601
Goltz, F., 239
Gombrich, E. H., 1166
Gomes, D. M., 1152
Gomez, R. S., 233
González, R., 1084
Good, K. P., 1091
Good, M. A., 895
Good, T. L., 1477
Goodale, M. A., 592
Goodall, J., 1016
Goodchilds, J., 708
Goode, E. L., 1091
Goodenough, F. L., 1286
Goodglass, H., 108, 267, 1049
Goodie, J. L., 58–59
Goodman, P., 637
Goodrick, G. K., 308–312, 1079
Goodstein, L. D., 745–748
Goodwin, F. K., 212, 214, 417, 418
Goodwin, J., 1435
Gordon, B., 109
Gordon, B. L., 943
Gordon, L. U., 245
Gordon, M., 1609
Gordon, T. L., 106
Gordon, T. P., 1569
Gore, S., 1577
Goren, C. C., 561
Goringer, H. U., 1416
Gorlitz, D., 1470
Gorman, B. S., 1421–1423
Gorman, C. D., 790
Gorman, J. M., 653, 1125, 1588
Gormezano, I., 875, 1033
Gorning, 22
Gorsuch, R. L., 1353
Goshen, C. E., 944
Gosset, W. S., 950
Gottesman, I. I., 671
Gottfredson, G. D., 668
Gottfried, L. A., 563
Gottlieb, B., 329
Gottlieb, G., 766–767
Gottman, J., 48, 1149
Gottman, J. M., 1231
Gotto, A. M., 1079
Gottschalk, L. A., 1337

Gottschalk, W., 1011
Gottsman, I., 1448
Gough, H. G., 1288, 1503
Gould, C., 1436, 1437
Gould, J. L., 104
Gould, R. L., 30
Gould, S. J., 1009, 1010, 1013
Graber, J. A., 17, 18
Grabowski, T., 266, 615
Grabowski, T. J., 109
Grabzcyk, E. Z., 1633
Grace, A. A., 204
Grace, W. J., 1337
Gracely, R. H., 1248
Gracia, J., 1621
Grafton, S. T., 1527
Graham, B. G., 1093
Graham, C. A., 104
Graham, C. S., 1093
Graham, D. T., 1337
Graham, J. R., 340, 962, 1282, 1288
Graham, M., 978
Graham, S., 1236
Grainger, J., 1042
Granero, M., 1137
Granger, D. A., 934
Granovetter, M., 968
Grant, B. F., 11
Grant, D. L., 790, 1185–1189
Grant, I., 1093
Grant, J. D., 487
Grant, M. Q., 487
Grant, S. G., 627
Grant, S. H., 1409
Grater, M., 1468
Grau, J. W., 767–769
Grawe, K., 530, 1347, 1665
Gray, B., 1525
Gray, C., 204
Gray, E. G., 523
Gray, J. A., 126, 127, 858
Gray, J. A., 1413, 1414
Graziano, W. G., 607
Greaves, G. B., 1436
Greco, C., 776
Greden, J., 1646
Greeley, A. M., 1136
Green, A. W., 1609
Green, D., 826
Green, D. C., 1152
Green, J., 76
Green, J. T., 1527, 1528
Green, P. A., 1090
Green, R., 76, 1415
Green, S. B., 129

Subject Index